Fodor's 95
California

Y0-CBG-301

Fodor's Travel Publications, Inc.
New York • Toronto • London • Sydney • Auckland

Fodor's California

Editor: Daniel Mangin
Contributors: Steven K. Amsterdam, William P. Brown, John Burks, Deke Castleman, Lori Chamberlain, Toni Chapman, Bruce David Colen, Jon and Noonie Corn, Laura Del Rosso, Pamela Faust, Janet Foley, Rosemary Freskos, Sheila Gadsden, Echo Garrett, Claudia Gioseffi, Nicole Harb, Pamela Hegarty, Patrick Hoctel, Mary Jane Horton, Edie Jarolim, Laura M. Kidder, Jacqueline Killeen, Jane E. Lasky, Dawn Lawson, Bevin McLaughlin, Catherine McEver, Ellen Melinkoff, Maribeth Mellin, Emily Miller, Tracy Patruno, Jim Peters, Marcy Pritchard, Mark S. Rosen, Linda K. Schmidt, Mary Ellen Schultz, Kathryn Shevelow, Aaron Shurin, Dan Spitzer, Aaron Sugarman, Robert Taylor, Casey Tefertiller, Nancy van Itallie, Bobbi Zane
Creative Director: Fabrizio La Rocca
Cartographer: David Lindroth
Illustrator: Karl Tanner
Cover Photograph: Ayako Parks/TSW

Design: Vignelli Associates

Special Sales

Contents

Maps

Foreword

Few places in the world combine California's natural and cultural diversity—dramatic coastline from Crescent City to San Diego, the rugged yet magnificent Mojave Desert and Sierra Mountains, Hollywood glitz and Palm Springs glamour, a potpourri of Pacific Rim and Latin American influences. This edition of *Fodor's California* covers more California sights than ever before. There are separate chapters on the Wine Country, Lake Tahoe, and the Far North and expanded treatment of Santa Barbara, Sacramento, and Monterey. There are extended chapters on San Francisco, Los Angeles, and San Diego, with plenty of information for a week's stay, but this book has been written primarily for those travelers who plan to visit several regions of the state. All the writers are local, and they share their best advice on what to see and do up and down the state.

While every care has been taken to ensure the accuracy of the information in this guide, the passage of time will always bring change, and consequently, the publisher cannot accept responsibility for errors that may occur.

All prices and opening times quoted here are based on information supplied to us at press time. Hours and admission fees may change, however, and the prudent traveler will avoid inconvenience by calling ahead.

Fodor's wants to hear about your travel experiences, both pleasant and unpleasant. When a hotel or restaurant fails to live up to its billing, let us know and we will investigate the complaint and revise our entries where the facts warrant it.

Send your letters to the editors of Fodor's Travel Publications, 201 East 50th Street, New York, NY 10022.

Highlights '95 and Fodor's Choice

Highlights '95

San Francisco For residents and visitors alike, the major civic event of the year should be the January 1995 opening of the new, $60 million **San Francisco Museum of Modern Art** across from the Center for the Arts at **Yerba Buena Gardens** on Third Street. For decades, the museum has been housed in rented space on the top floors of the War Memorial Building. The new building, designed by internationally celebrated architect Mario Botta, is as distinctive looking, if not so controversial, as the glittering Marriott Hotel nearby: at its center is a 125-foot-high cylindrical atrium topped by a slanting skylight that's been compared to a gigantic donut. The 225,000-square-foot building will more than double the Museum's exhibition space, and also add to the appeal of the Yerba Buena Gardens development project. The museum bookstore and cafe will open first, in the fall of 1994.

Also in the news will be the **California Palace of the Legion of Honor** art museum in Lincoln Park, overlooking the Golden Gate Bridge. It has been closed for remodeling for two years and is scheduled to reopen in the fall of 1995. New features include six galleries built around a courtyard on the level beneath the museum's entrance colonnade, an expanded restaurant, and a bookshop. The collection of European paintings, sculpture and other artwork that has been scattered elsewhere will be reinstalled. The museum will also have seismic bracing to protect the entire building from the kind of damage that some San Francisco Bay Area structures suffered in the 1989 earthquake.

On the city's eastern waterfront, the primary magnet for visitors, the new attraction will be **Underwater World at Pier 39**. Unlike traditional aquariums, this will take visitors through transparent tunnels on moving walkways, surrounded by marine life, all of which will be indigenous to San Francisco Bay—including the sharks. It is scheduled to open in the fall of 1995, just as a longtime attraction—the city's fabled "Crookedest Street in the World"—closes down for a several-month makeover.

In the early 1980s, San Francisco's transit authority replaced streetcars on Market Street, the city's major thoroughfare, with an underground light-rail system. It was overcrowded almost immediately, so back came the streetcar tracks in a project that has taken years and caused endless traffic congestion. The result, expected to be completed by mid-1995, will offer more than additional transit capacity. The line will carry **historic San Francisco streetcars**—refurbished, shiplike cars from the 1940s and 1950s—between Transbay Terminal downtown and Castro Street to the west. On special occasions, a collection of older restored streetcars from cities around the world will be added to the line. The Castro section of Market Street has also been lined with 37 20-foot-tall Canary Island palm trees.

The city's traditional retail center around **Union Square** changes slowly, but it should be revitalized at several locations this year. In 1994, a posh new branch of **The Gap** brightened the sometimes sleazy cable-car turnaround at Powell and Market streets. By early 1995, a **Disney Store** offering clothing, toys and video entertainment will be open, across from Union Square and the Westin St. Francis Hotel, at Powell and Post streets. At Stockton and Market streets, the former site of a conservative men's clothing store, another franchise of **Planet Hollywood**, the movie memorabilia restaurants, is due to open in late 1994.

Los Angeles   A never-say-die Los Angeles withstood a test of endurance over the past couple of years. In 1992 the city was ravaged by riots. In the summer of 1993, with the local mountains as dry as tinder after a prolonged drought, huge firestorms were set off, destroying hundreds of homes in Malibu, Laguna Beach, and Altadena. Then, in January 1994, came the coup de grâce: the Northridge earthquake. More than 50 lives were lost, some 10,000 buildings were declared unsafe, and huge hunks of freeway collapsed. Thousands were left homeless.

Rebuilding began immediately after the earthquake, however, and despite thousands of aftershocks, businesses planned to reopen as soon as possible. By the time you reach Los Angeles, evidence of this most recent devastation may be limited, except for parts of the San Fernando Valley nearest the epicenter. The most lasting effects, for visitors as well as locals, will probably be the collapsed sections of freeways—the Simi Valley Freeway (Highway 118), the junction of I–5 and the Antelope Valley Freeway (Highway 14), and, most crucial, the missing stretch of I–10, the Santa Monica Freeway, Los Angeles's main thoroughfare between the Westside and downtown.

The collapse of I–10 makes daily commuting a nightmare for thousands of Angelenos, but it's also a hassle for visitors, because it's along the main route from the Los Angeles International Airport (LAX) to downtown. Here are some alternative routes you may choose: **Route A:** On leaving LAX, take Sepulveda Boulevard north approximately 1½ miles to Slauson Avenue, where you turn right. Follow Slauson Avenue a couple of miles to La Brea Avenue. Turn left on La Brea. From here, you can get on to the Santa Monica Freeway going east, bypassing the damaged portion. The Santa Monica will take you into downtown. **Route B:** Leaving LAX, take Century Boulevard north for approximately 5 miles to the Harbor Freeway (Highway 110). Enter the northbound ramp, and go north for about 9 miles. As you reach downtown, you'll spot the Los Angeles Convention Center on your right.

Badly damaged in the quake and its aftershocks, the Los Angeles Memorial Coliseum—home stadium for the Los Angeles Raiders and the University of Southern California Trojans football teams—may not be totally repaired by football season but at press time the two teams still planned to play their home games there.

The **Peterson Automotive Museum** opened in the spring of 1994. Situated across from the Los Angeles County Museum of Art, the new institution offers visitors everything they ever wanted to know about cars. Exhibits include the automobile's role in the L.A. area's growth, "Cars of the Stars," and an extensive look at the history of automotive design and technology. On the first floor are a gas station from the 1920s and a hot-rodder's garage, all decked out in shiny chrome accessories. Muscle cars and exotic European vehicles are also part of this 80,000-square-foot museum.

West Los Angeles awaits the arrival of the **J. Paul Getty Center,** designed by architect Richard Meier and set to occupy some 110 acres atop a hill that allows panoramic views of the Pacific and the Los Angeles basin. It's scheduled to open sometime in 1996. Elsewhere on the Westside, the posh Beverly Hills Hotel has shut down for renovations but will reopen in early 1995.

In downtown Los Angeles, construction continues on the **Walt Disney Concert Hall,** future home of the Los Angeles Philharmonic. Scheduled for completion in 1997, the hall is being designed by local architectural hero Frank Gehry. Word is that this structure will be more conservative than typical Gehry creations.

Meanwhile, in Anaheim, **Disneyland** is considering an expansion, although at press time there were no firm plans. The proposal is that the famous theme park will sprout an addition (akin to Orlando's Epcot and tentatively called Westcot) that will include more hotels, as well as more amusements. The park's newest attraction is Toontown, a three-dimensional cartoon environment that features animated characters' homes and Roger Rabbit's Car Toon Spin. On line for 1995 is Indiana Jones Adventure, a treacherous archaeological expedition by jeep through ancient temple ruins, clouds of smoke, bubbling fire, and active lava pits.

A couple of new hotels are on the horizon for 1995, including the 390-room Halekulani, a downtown version of the highly rated Honolulu property, and the 325-room Hollywood Promenade, to be erected in the heart of Hollywood. Looking ahead to 1996, the 600-room Evergreen Laurel Hotel is set to open in Little Tokyo.

San Diego The downtown San Diego skyline continues to change in subtle and startling ways. Although hotel and office-tower construction seems to have peaked in this newly developed area, growth and refinement of already existing sites are continuing apace.

Designed to tie together the waterfront's many new developments, the landscaped **King Promenade,** a 12-acre park, will run along Harbor Drive from Seaport Village to the Convention Center and north to the Gaslamp Quarter. A section of the promenade near the Convention Center was completed in 1992, and the entire project is expected to be finished by early 1995.

The beginning of 1995 should also see the grand opening of the 150-acre **Arco Training Center** for Olympic athletes. Overlooking Lower Otay Lake, 10 miles east of San Diego Bay, the facility will be a warm-weather counterpart to the U.S. Olympic centers in Lake Placid, NY, and Colorado Springs, CO. Guests can survey the complex and watch athletes training for events, including archery, track, cycling, tennis, and various water-related sports; guided tours will begin at a visitor center, which will house a gift shop, interactive exhibits, and an observation deck.

Home in the past to the **America's Cup** international yacht races, San Diego is once again slated to host this hugely popular event, to be covered live around the world. Foreign and American syndicates began training here in 1994 for the best-of-seven-race series. The Defender (American) and Challenger (foreign) selection events will be held between January and April 1995, with the final, deciding race kicking off in May. A total of 14 challengers from nine nations have laid down the gauntlet for the coveted cup; America's Cup '95 will see South Africa and Russia competing in the event for the first time.

There's always something new at the **San Diego Zoo.** In the summer of 1995 a hippopotamus exhibit will be completed near the Tiger River complex. Visitors will be able to watch the antics of three African river hippos, which can weigh in excess of 3,000 pounds, from both above- and below-water viewing areas.

Public transit is finally coming to **Old Town**—en masse. If all goes as planned, the North County commuter bus line will include Old Town on its downtown route by the end of 1994, and the light rail system will have a trolley stop in place by the end of 1995. (There's also talk of an Amtrak station to follow, but it's as yet unofficial.) The money acquired by selling trolley-stop rights will help the city refurbish the McCoy House, the former residence of one of the area's original settlers; it's slated to become Old Town State Park's new visitor center by late 1995.

The building and transportation boom has spread south to Baja California, where both the Mexican government and private investors are banking on prosperity. Rosarito Beach now boasts exclusive condos and time-share resorts, and new hotels and restaurants are springing up. Ensenada is changing just as quickly, becoming much more than a weekend getaway. A new crop of tour companies specializing in Baja make the trek south hassle-free.

Sacramento   It doesn't have the bay, the ocean, or the weather of the state's other three major cities, but Sacramento, the epicenter of the Gold Rush, has its own special charms. The capital city's historical character has been carefully preserved. Beautiful, old innercity neighborhoods have boulevards lined with examples of early California and Victorian architecture. The **capitol mall area** is a constant bustle of political activity.

Downtown continues to grow according to the Central Business District Urban Design Plan unveiled in 1988. Tacky office buildings are gradually disappearing, but the best of the old is being saved and refurbished. The huge **Downtown Plaza** opened in 1993 amid controversy over its design, which was created by the planners of San Diego's Horton Plaza. Nevertheless, the site has become popular with locals and tourist alike.

Just a short walk away from Downtown Plaza is **Old Sacramento,** a riverfront area complete with paddlewheel boats. The Gold Rush feel comes alive along gaslit cobblestone streets that teem with shops and restaurants. The **Central Pacific Passenger Station** offers weekend rides on historic trains. The depot is next to Old Sacramento's biggest attraction, the 100,000-square-foot **California State Railroad Museum.**

Fodor's Choice

No two people will agree on what makes a perfect vacation, but it's fun—and it can be helpful—to know what others think. Here, then, is a very personal list of Fodor's Choices. We hope you'll have a chance to experience some of them yourself while visiting California. We have tried to offer something for everyone and from every price category. For detailed information about each entry, refer to the appropriate chapters within this guidebook.

Lodging

Four Seasons Clift Hotel, San Francisco, *$$$$*

Hotel Bel-Air, Los Angeles, *$$$$*

Ritz-Carton Hotel, Rancho Mirage, *$$$$*

Ventana Inn, Big Sur, *$$$$*

Petite Auberge, San Francisco, *$$$*

Barnaby's Hotel, Rosecrans, *$$*

Casa Del Zorro, Anza-Borrego, *$$*

San Simeon Pines Motel, Cambria, *$$*

Scenic Drives

17-Mile Drive, Carmel

Highway 49, the Gold Country

I–80, San Francisco to Truckee (for a cross section of the state)

Kings Canyon Highway (Highway 180)

Mulholland Drive, Los Angeles

Historic Buildings

Coit Tower, San Francisco

General Vallejo's House, Sonoma

Hotel del Coronado, San Diego

Larkin House, Monterey

Mann's Chinese Theater, Hollywood

Mission Inn, Riverside

Mission San Carlos Borromeo, Carmel

State Capitol, Sacramento

Lovely Sights

Buena Vista Winery, Sonoma

Carnelian Room, Bank of America, San Francisco

Emerald Bay, Lake Tahoe

Griffith Observatory, Los Angeles

Highlands Inn, Carmel

La Jolla Cove at sunset

Taste Treats

California wines, tasted at the wineries

Chorrizo burrito, burrito stands, Los Angeles

French-fried artichoke hearts, roadside stands, Monterey
Peninsula

Fresh salmon steaks, restaurants along the North Coast

Garlic ice cream, Garlic Festival, Gilroy

Orange freeze, Merlino's, Fulton Avenue, Sacramento

Ripe peaches, especially in the Central Valley

Sourdough bread and sweet butter, San Francisco

State Parks

Anza-Borrego Desert State Park, Borrego Springs

California State Railroad Museum, Sacramento

Columbia State Historic Park, Columbia

Del Norte Coast Redwoods State Park, Crescent City

Empire Mine State Historic Park, Grass Valley

Marshall Gold Discovery State Historic Park, Coloma

Point Lobos State Reserve, Carmel

San Juan Bautista State Historic Park, San Juan Bautista

Restaurants with Fabulous Atmosphere

Ventana Inn, Big Sur, *$$$$*

St. Orres, Gualala, *$$$*

George's at the Cove, La Jolla, *$$–$$$*

Spago, Los Angeles, *$$– $$$*

Greens at Fort Mason, San Francisco, *$$*

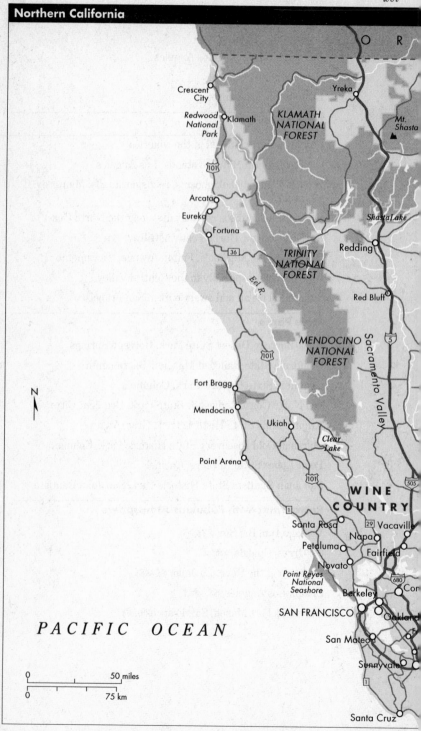

PACIFIC OCEAN

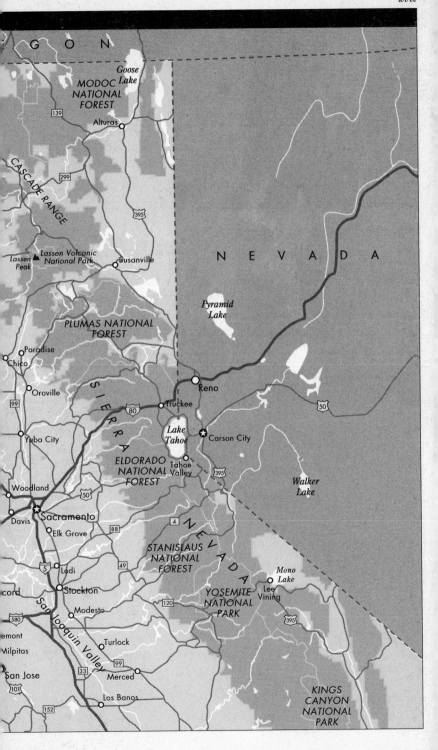

O R E G O N

MODOC NATIONAL FOREST

Goose Lake

139

Alturas

CASCADE RANGE

299

395

Lassen Peak

Lassen Volcanic National Park

Susanville

N E V A D A

PLUMAS NATIONAL FOREST

Pyramid Lake

Paradise

Chico

Oroville

99

SIERRA

80

Truckee

Reno

50

Yuba City

Lake Tahoe

Carson City

ELDORADO NATIONAL FOREST

Tahoe Valley

395

Woodland

50

Davis

Sacramento

Walker Lake

Elk Grove

88

N E V A D A

Lodi

49

STANISLAUS NATIONAL FOREST

4

cord

Stockton

Mono Lake

Modesto

120

Lee Vining

San Joaquin Valley

YOSEMITE NATIONAL PARK

395

580

emont

Milpitas

Turlock

San Jose

99

33

Merced

101

KINGS CANYON NATIONAL PARK

152

Los Banos

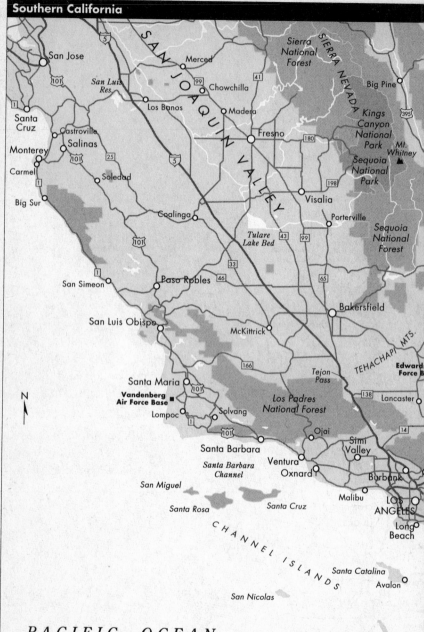

Southern California

San Jose

San Luis Res.

Merced

SAN JOAQUIN VALLEY

Sierra National Forest

SIERRA NEVADA

Big Pine

Chowchilla

Los Banos

Madera

Santa Cruz

Castroville

Salinas

Monterey

Carmel

Soledad

Fresno

Kings Canyon National Park

Mt. Whitney

Sequoia National Park

Visalia

Porterville

Big Sur

Coalinga

Tulare Lake Bed

Sequoia National Forest

San Simeon

Paso Robles

Bakersfield

San Luis Obispo

McKittrick

TEHACHAPI MTS.

Edwards Force B

Santa Maria

Vandenberg Air Force Base

Tejon Pass

Los Padres National Forest

Lancaster

Lompoc

Solvang

Ojai

Simi Valley

Santa Barbara

Ventura

Oxnard

Burbank

Santa Barbara Channel

San Miguel

Malibu

LOS ANGELES

Santa Rosa

Santa Cruz

Long Beach

CHANNEL ISLANDS

Santa Catalina

Avalon

San Nicolas

San Clemente

PACIFIC OCEAN

N

0   50 miles

0   75 km

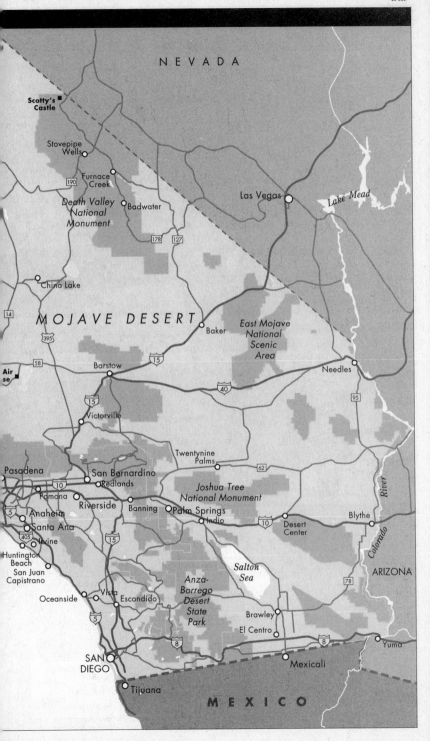

N E V A D A

Scotty's
Castle

Stovepipe
Wells

Furnace
Creek
190

Death Valley
National
Monument

Badwater

Las Vegas

Lake Mead

178 127

China Lake

14

M O J A V E   D E S E R T

395

Baker

East Mojave
National
Scenic
Area

58
Air
se

Barstow

15

Needles

40

95

15

Victorville

Twentynine
Palms

62

Pasadena

San Bernardino

10

Redlands

Joshua Tree
National Monument

Pomona

Riverside

Banning

Palm Springs

5

Anaheim

Santa Ana

15

Indio

10

Desert
Center

Blythe

Colorado   River

405

Irvine

Huntington
Beach
San Juan
Capistrano

Salton
Sea

78

ARIZONA

Oceanside

Vista

Escondido

Anza-
Borrego
Desert
State
Park

Brawley

5

El Centro

8

8

Yuma

SAN
DIEGO

Mexicali

Tijuana

M E X I C O

The United States

CANADA

Vancouver
BRITISH COLUMBIA
Calgary
ALBERTA
SASKATCHEWAN
MANITOB
Regina
Trans-Canada Hwy.
Winnipeg

Seattle
Olympia
WASHINGTON
Spokane
Columbia R.
Great Falls
Missouri R.
MONTANA
Helena
Billings
NORTH DAKOTA
Fargo
Bismarck

Portland
Salem
OREGON
IDAHO
Boise
Snake R.
WYOMING
SOUTH DAKOTA
Pierre
Missouri R.

Carson City
Sacramento
NEVADA
San Francisco
Fresno
Salt Lake City
UTAH
Cheyenne
Denver
NEBRASKA
Lincol

CALIFORNIA
Las Vegas
Colorado R.
Colorado Springs
COLORADO
KANSAS

Santa Barbara
Los Angeles
San Diego
Flagstaff
ARIZONA
Phoenix
Tucson
Santa Fe
Albuquerque
NEW MEXICO
OKLAHOMA
Oklahoma City
Amarillo

PACIFIC OCEAN
BAJA CALIFORNIA
SONORA
El Paso
CHIHUAHUA
Rio Grande
TEXAS
Austin
San Antonio

RUSSIA
ARCTIC OCEAN
Bering Strait
Nome
ALASKA
Fairbanks
Anchorage
CANADA
Bering Sea
MEXICO
COAHUILA
NUEVO LEON

ALEUTIAN ISLANDS
Juneau
PACIFIC OCEAN

0   400 miles
0   400 km
N

Honolulu
Oahu
Maui
HAWAII
Hawaii
PACIFIC OCEAN

World Time Zones

Numbers below vertical bands relate each zone to Greenwich Mean Time (0 hrs.).
Local times frequently differ from these general indications,
as indicated by light-face numbers on map.

Algiers, **29**

Anchorage, **3**

Athens, **41**

Auckland, **1**

Baghdad, **46**

Bangkok, **50**

Beijing, **54**

Berlin, **34**

Bogotá, **19**

Budapest, **37**

Buenos Aires, **24**

Caracas, **22**

Chicago, **9**

Copenhagen, **33**

Dallas, **10**

Delhi, **48**

Denver, **8**

Djakarta, **53**

Dublin, **26**

Edmonton, **7**

Hong Kong, **56**

Honolulu, **2**

Istanbul, **40**

Jerusalem, **42**

Johannesburg, **44**

Lima, **20**

Lisbon, **28**

London (Greenwich), **27**

Los Angeles, **6**

Madrid, **38**

Manila, **57**

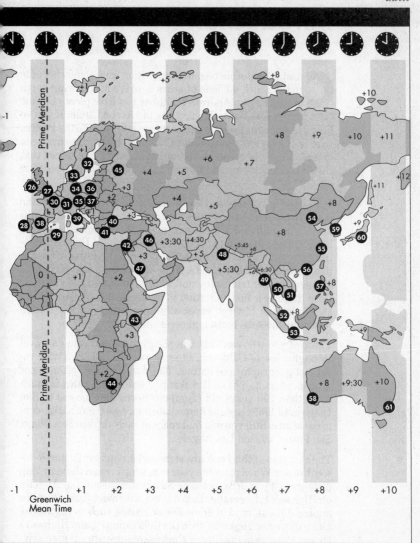

Mecca, **47**	Ottawa, **14**	San Francisco, **5**	Toronto, **13**
Mexico City, **12**	Paris, **30**	Santiago, **21**	Vancouver, **4**
Miami, **18**	Perth, **58**	Seoul, **59**	Vienna, **35**
Montréal, **15**	Reykjavík, **25**	Shanghai, **55**	Warsaw, **36**
Moscow, **45**	Rio de Janeiro, **23**	Singapore, **52**	Washington, D.C., **17**
Nairobi, **43**	Rome, **39**	Stockholm, **32**	Yangon, **49**
New Orleans, **11**	Saigon (Ho Chi Minh	Sydney, **61**	Zürich, **31**
New York City, **16**	City), **51**	Tokyo, **60**	

Introduction

Coastal California began its migration from somewhere far to the south millions of years ago. It's still moving north along the San Andreas fault, but you have plenty of time for a visit before Santa Monica hits the Arctic Circle. If you've heard predictions that some of the state may fall into the Pacific, take the long view and consider that much of the state has been in and out of the ocean all through its history. The forces that raised the mountains and formed the Central Valley are still at work.

For a good introduction to the natural history and geology of the state, there is no better place to start than at the Oakland Museum. An impressive light-and-audio show projected over a large model of the state explains the geography. Exhibits illustrate the state's ecosystems; walking through the exhibit hall is like walking across the state, from the ocean, across the Coast Ranges, the Central Valley, and the Sierra Nevada. On another floor there is a fine collection of artifacts and remains of the state's human history; especially interesting are the Native American baskets, tools, and ceremonial clothing.

Those of you who can't start at the museum but who do travel through a few of California's tourist regions will see a wide variety of geography and nature. The state's history often is not as evident as its physical makeup. None of the cities is much more than 200 years old (Junípero Serra didn't come to San Diego until 1769), and the immediate impression is of a 20th-century culture. Still you will find relics of early days in San Diego, San Francisco, and Los Angeles.

The chapters of this book are arranged in a generally north- to-south order. When planning your trip, keep in mind the very long distances. If you drive between San Francisco and Los Angeles on Highway 1, remember that it is not only more than 400 miles but is a difficult road to drive. Scenic routes, such as Highway 1 along the coast, Highway 49 in the Gold Country, and Highways 50 and 120 across the Sierra Nevada, require attention to driving and enough time for frequent stops.

California's North Coast is a dramatically beautiful region whose main industries are tourism, fishing, and logging. There are no large cities, no large amusement parks, few luxury resorts. There isn't even much swimming, because of a cold current that runs down the coast for most of the state (turning out to sea before it reaches Southern California beaches). And, although the ocean keeps the weather temperate, that doesn't mean there aren't winter storms. August is often the coldest month of the year here (as it can be in San Francisco, too). What you will find along the North Coast are a wonderful scenic drive (Highway 1 and U.S. 101), many small inns (some of them quite luxurious), interesting restaurants serving locally produced fare, some good galleries, and a number of wineries. This is a region for leisurely exploring. It shouldn't be on the itinerary of anyone not interested in the beauties of nature, because the main attractions are tide pools under coastal cliffs, redwood trees, rhododendron, and banana slugs (a large yellow-and-black local oddity) in the lush coastal mountains. The Russians settled this region briefly in the 19th century, and you will find reminders of their presence.

The two main attractions in the Far North are Mt. Shasta, a large volcano that dominates the scenery of the northern part of the state, and Lassen Volcanic National Park. The park is at the southern end of the Cascade Range and is particularly interesting because of the record of past volcanic activity and evidence of current geothermal activity (such as the Sulphur Works). This region also suits those interested in nature, even more than the North Coast, because lodging and dining opportunities are much more limited. Keep in mind also that much of this region can be very hot in summer.

The Wine Country is one of California's most popular tourist regions. There are narrow crowded highways dotted with wineries among the vineyards and valleys of the Coast Ranges north of San Francisco. Many of the wineries are beautiful sites for meals, picnics, or tastings, and there are fine bed-and-breakfasts and restaurants in the area.

San Francisco is a sophisticated city offering world-class hotels and the greatest concentration of excellent restaurants in the state. Because the city is so compact, a visitor can do very well without a car, but this is also a fine base for tours up the coast and to the Wine Country. If you want to drive down to Los Angeles from here, you can do it in a day (7–8 hours) if you take I–5 down the Central Valley, but you should budget at least two days if you want to take the coastal route. A long day's drive down U.S. 101 will get you to Santa Barbara, but you'll bypass Monterey and Big Sur.

The Gold Country, also known as the Mother Lode, is the gold-mining region of the Sierra Nevada foothills. There are many historic sites and small towns to explore, many of them of interest to children. Most impressive are the Empire Mine in Grass Valley, the gold-discovery site at Coloma, and Columbia State Historic Park, a town restored to its Gold Rush condition. As in the Wine Country, there are many B&Bs and small inns, but this is a less expensive, if also less sophisticated, region to visit. In spring there are wildflowers, and in fall the hills are colored by bright-red berries and changing leaves. In summer the hills are golden—and hot. Visitors in that season should probably check weather reports: There are many fine days, but exploring in 90° or hotter weather is not much fun. We've included Sacramento in the Gold Country chapter because it is adjacent and because its history is one with that of the Gold Rush.

Lake Tahoe is famous for its deep blue water and as the largest alpine lake on the continent. It stands up well to its reputation, despite crowded areas around the Nevada casinos. Lake Tahoe is a four-hour drive from San Francisco along I–80; the traffic to the lake on Friday afternoon and to San Francisco on Sunday is horrendous. If you plan to visit in winter, remember to carry chains in your car; they are sometimes required even on the interstate. In summer it's generally cooler here than in the foothills, but still sometimes pretty hot. Luckily, there are lots of beaches where you can swim.

The highlight for many travelers to California is a visit to one of the Sierra Nevada's national parks. Yosemite is the state's most famous park and every bit as sublime as promised. Its Yosemite-type or U-shape valleys were formed by the action of glaciers on the Sierra Nevada during recent ice ages. Other examples are found in Kings Canyon and Sequoia National Parks (which are adjacent to each other and usually visited together). At all three parks there are fine groves of Big Trees (*Sequoiadendron gigantea*), some of the largest living things in the world. The parks are open year-round, but large portions of the higher backcountry are closed in winter. Yosemite Valley is only 4,000 feet high, so winter weather is mild, and the waterfalls are beautiful when hung with ice.

The Monterey Peninsula, a two- or three-hour drive south of San Francisco, offers some of the state's most luxurious resorts and golf courses, interesting historic sites (Monterey was the capital during Spanish and Mexican rule, the state constitution was written here, and Junípero Serra is buried at the Carmel Mission), beautiful coastal scenery (Point Lobos would receive many votes for most treasured state park), and perhaps the most famous scenic drive (the 17-Mile Drive). There are also good restaurants in Monterey and Carmel and plenty of places to shop. The weather is usually mild, but any visitor should be prepared for fog and cool temperatures.

Between Carmel and Santa Barbara is another spectacular stretch of Highway 1, requiring concentration and nerve to drive. This is where you'll find those bridges spanning the cliffs along the Pacific—and Big Sur. Don't expect much in the way of dining, lodging, shopping, or even history until you get to Hearst Castle. Santa Barbara flaunts its Spanish/Mexican heritage. There's a well-restored mission, and almost all of downtown (including some pleasant shopping areas) is done in Spanish-style architecture. The centerpiece is the courthouse, built in the 1920s and displaying some beautiful tile work and murals.

In certain lights Los Angeles displays its own Spanish heritage, but much more evident is its cultural vibrancy as a 20th-century center on the Pacific Rim. Hollywood, the beaches, and Disneyland are all within an hour's drive. Also here are Beverly Hills, noted for its shops and mansions; important examples of 20th-century domestic architecture; and freeways. Dining options are improving, if still not up to the range of San Francisco's choices. Despite the city's reputation for a laid-back lifestyle, a visit here can be fairly overwhelming because of the size and variety of the region. Careful planning will help.

San Diego, at the southwestern edge of the state and the country, is usually the first stop. Junípero Serra founded his first mission in Alta California (as opposed to Baja California, which is still part of Mexico) here in 1769. There are historical sites from Mexican and Victorian times, one of the best zoos in the country, and fine beaches. The weather is agreeable, so this is a year-round destination.

The California deserts are extensive and varied and usually divided into two general areas: the Mojave, or High, Desert and the Colorado, or Low, Desert. Palm Springs and the new cities nearby (including Rancho Mirage) are filling up with expansive new resorts offering elaborate gardens, waterfalls, serpentine sidewalks, and— of course—golf courses. That area doesn't offer much of a desert experience, but it has great weather in winter, and you can use it as an elegant base for exploration. Joshua Tree National Monument is a good day trip (or two trips) from Palm Springs; the northern part is High Desert and the southern part Low Desert, so you can see the difference. Death Valley (*see* Chapter 16) and Anza-Borrego Desert State Park (*see* Excursions from San Diego in Chapter 14) are of interest to those who want to explore the beauties of the desert landscape. Anza-Borrego is far less developed than Palm Springs but has a resort and a fancy golf course.

Running 400 miles down the center of the state from below Mt. Shasta to the Tehachapi Mountains, lying between the Coast Ranges and the Sierra Nevada, is the Central Valley. We haven't written much about the area (*see* Red Bluff and Redding in Chapter 4 and Sacramento in Chapter 7) because this is not much of a tourist region. You may drive across some of it on I–80 or down it on I–5, but there isn't much to stop and see, except in the state capital. This is, however, the most important agricultural region in the state and the fastest growing in terms of population. California is as varied as any state and larger than most and could be the subject of many visits. Don't expect to visit everything the first time. As you travel through the state's regions you will get a sense of its great diversity of cultures, the ongoing pull between preservation and development, and the state's unique place in the landscapes of geography and the imagination.

1 Essential Information

Before You Go

Tourist Information

The **California Division of Tourism** (801 K St., Suite 1600, Sacramento, CA 95814, tel. 916/322–1397 or 916/322–2882, fax 916/322–3402) can answer many questions about travel in the state. You can also order a detailed 146-page book, *Golden California Visitors Guide*, as well as the free publications *Discover the Californias' Accommodations, Ski California, Guide to California Bed & Breakfast Inns, California Special Events,* and *California Escapes*, a guide to California state parks (tel. 800/862–2543). In addition, there are visitors bureaus and chambers of commerce throughout the state; see individual chapters for listings.

Tours and Packages

Should you buy your travel arrangements to California packaged or do it yourself? There are advantages either way. Buying packaged arrangements saves you money, particularly if can find a program that includes exactly the features you want. You also get a pretty good idea of what your trip will cost from the outset. Generally, you have two options: independent packages and fully escorted tours.

Escorted tours are most often via motorcoach, with a tour director in charge. They're ideal if you don't mind having limited free time and traveling with strangers. Your baggage is handled, your time rigorously scheduled, and most meals planned. Escorted tours are therefore the most hassle-free way to see a destination, as well as generally the least expensive. Independent packages allow plenty of flexibility. They generally include airline travel and hotels, with certain options available, such as sightseeing, car rental, and excursions. Independent packages are usually more expensive than escorted tours.

While you can book directly through tour operators, you will pay no more to go through a travel agent, who will be able to tell you about tours and packages from a number of operators. Whatever program you ultimately choose, be sure to find out exactly what is included: taxes, tips, transfers, meals, baggage handling, ground transportation, entertainment, excursions, sports or recreation (and rental equipment if necessary). Ask about the level of hotel used, its location, the size of its rooms, the kind of beds, and its amenities, such as pool, room service, or programs for children, if they're important to you. Find out the operator's cancellation penalties. Nearly everyone charges them, and the only way to avoid them is to buy trip-cancellation insurance (available from your travel agent). Also ask about the single supplement, a surcharge assessed to solo travelers. Some operators do not make you pay it if you agree to be matched up with a roommate of the same sex, even if one is not found by departure time.

Fully Escorted Tours Top operators include **Maupintour** (Box 807, Lawrence, KS 66044, tel. 913/843–1211 or 800/255–4266) and **Tauck Tours** (11 Wilton Rd., Westport, CT 06881, tel. 203/226–6911 or 800/468–2825) in the deluxe category; **Caravan** (401 N. Michigan Ave., Chicago, IL 60611, tel. 312/321–9800 or 800/227–2826), **CIT Tours Corp.** (342 Madison Ave., Suite 207, New York, NY 10173, tel. 212/697–2100 or 800/248–8687, fax 212/697–1394; western part of U.S., tel. 310/670–4269 or

800/248–7245), **Collette Tours** (162 Middle St., Pawtucket, RI 02860, tel. 401/728–3805 or 800/832–4656), **Domenico Tours** (751 Broadway, Bayonne, NJ 07002, tel. 201/823–8687 or 800/554–8687), **Gadabout Tours** (700 E. Tahquitz Way, Palm Springs, CA 92262, tel. 619/325–5556 or 800/952–5068), **Globus** (5301 South Federal Circle, Littleton, CO 80123, tel. 303/797–2800 or 800/221–0090), **Mayflower Tours** (1225 Warren Ave., Box 490, Downers Grove, IL 60515, tel. 708/960–3430 or 800/323–7604), **Parker Tours** (218-14 Northern Blvd., Bayside, NY 11361, tel. 718/428–7800 or 800/833–9600), and **Trieloff Tours** (24301 El Toro Rd., Suite 140, Laguna Hills, CA 92653, tel. 800/248–6877 or 800/432–7125 in CA) in the first-class range; and **Cosmos Tourama** (*see* Globus, *above*) and **Go America Tours** (733 3rd Ave., 7th Floor, New York, NY 10017, tel. 212/370–5080) in the budget category.

Independent Packages Many of the fully escorted operators (*see above*) offer independent tours; in addition, California packages are available from **American Airlines Fly AAway Vacations** (tel. 800/321–2121), **Continental Airlines' Grand Destinations** (tel. 800/634–5555), **Delta Dream Vacations** (tel. 800/872–7786), **TWA Getaway Vacations** (tel. 800/438–2929), **United Airlines' Vacation Planning Center** (tel. 800/328–6877), and **USAir Vacations** (tel. 800/428–4322). Also contact **SuperCities** (139 Main St., Cambridge, MA 02142, tel. 617/621–9988 or 800/333–1234), a specialist in city packages. **Amtrak** (tel. 800/872–7245) also offers a number of packages to various destinations within the state.

Their programs come in a wide range of prices based on levels of luxury and options—in addition to hotel and transportation, sightseeing, car rental, transfers, admission to local attractions, and other extras. Note that when pricing different packages, it sometimes pays to purchase the same arrangements separately, as when a rock-bottom promotional airfare is being offered, for example.

Special-Interest Travel Special-interest programs may be fully escorted or independent. Some require a certain amount of expertise, but most are for the average traveler with an interest and are usually hosted by experts in the subject matter. Because your fellow travelers are apt to be passionate or knowledgeable about the subject, they can prove as enjoyable a part of your travel experience as the destination itself. The price range is wide, but the cost is usually higher—sometimes a lot higher—than for ordinary escorted tours and packages, because of the expert guiding and special activities.

Adventure/ Hiking **REI Adventures** (Box 1938, Sumner, WA 98390–0800, tel. 206/891–2631 or 800/622–2236) inspires naturalists and photographers on its seven-day hike in High Sierra country. **American Wilderness Experience** (Box 1486, Boulder, CO 80306, tel. 303/444–2622 or 800/444–0099) takes you deep into Kings Canyon and Sequoia National Parks. **Outdoor Adventure River Specialists (O.A.R.S.)** (Box 67, Angels Camp, CA 95222, tel. 209/736–4677 or 800/446–2411, fax 209/736–2902) operates white-water rafting trips on the Stanislas, American, Merced, and Tuolumne rivers from late March through early October. **Trek America** (Box 470, Blairstown, NJ 07825, tel. 908/362–9198 or 800/221–0596) includes hiking, camping, and hotels on tours inland and along the Pacific Coast. **Yosemite Mountaineering School** (Yosemite National Park, CA 95389, tel. 209/372–1335) has one- and five-day classes to teach you the basics, as well as guided rock climbing expeditions. **Whitewater Excitement** (Box 5992, Auburn, CA 95603, tel. 916/888–6515 or 800/750–2386) and **Whitewater Voyages** (Box 20400, El Sobrante, CA 94820, tel. 510/222–5994 or 800/488–7238) hurtle you along the state's mighty rivers, and **Kimtu Outdoor Adventures** (Box 938, Willow Creek, CA 95573, tel. 916/629–3843 or 800/562–8475) combines soft adventure with a historical American Indian float tour of the villages and sites of the 2,500-year-old Hoopa reservation.

Ballooning **Napa Valley Balloons** (Box 2860, Yountville, CA 94599, tel. 707/253–2224 or 800/253–2224) and **Sonoma Thunder Wine Country Balloon Safaris** (6984 McKinley St., Sebastopol, CA 95472, tel. 707/538–7359 or 800/759–5638) float over Wine Country valleys toward a champagne brunch. **A Beautiful Morning Balloon Company** (1342 Camino del Mar, Box 2666, Del Mar, CA 92014, tel. 619/481–6225 or 800/255–8807) takes you for a one-hour flight over the San Diego coastal regions of Del Mar. **Fantasy Balloon Flights** (83710 Avenue 54, Thermal, CA 92274, tel. 619/398–6322 or 800/462–2683) floats over San Diego, Palm Springs, and Temecula.

Bicycling **Backroads** (1516 5th St., Suite L101, Berkeley, CA 94710 -1740, tel. 510/527–1555 or 800/245–3874), offers bicycling vacations including inn-to-inn, camping, and Wine Country tours. **Imagine Tours** (917 3rd St., Davis, CA 95616, tel. 800/228–7041) and **Native Cycles** (70-053 Hwy. 111, Rancho Mirage, CA 92262, tel. 800/952–5068) specialize in custom excursions of the southern part of the state's desert.

Food & Wine *See* Chapter 5, The Wine Country, *below.*

Gardens **Coopersmith's England** (6441 Valley View Rd., Oakland, CA 94611, tel. 510/339–2499) explores Southern California.

Gold Prospecting **Gold Prospecting Expeditions** (1817 Main St., Box 974, Jamestown, CA 95327, tel. 209/984–4653) and **Jensens's Pick & Shovel Ranch** (Box 1141, Angels Camp, CA 95222, tel. 209/736–0287), in Northern California's Gold Country, teach you how to pan for the yellow metal.

Golf **Best Golf Tours** (332 Forest Ave., Laguna Beach, CA 92651, tel. 714/752–8881 or 800/227–0212) and **Golf America, Inc.** (7514 Girard Ave., #243, La Jolla, CA 92037, tel. 619/454–2026 or 800/435–5775) have design-your-own golf packages in Palm Springs and Pebble Beach. **Golf Amtrak/Great American Vacations** (1220 Kensington, Oakbrook, IL 60521, tel. 800/872–7245 or 800/321–8684 in Southern California) has several excursions.

Horseback Riding **FITS Equestrian** (685 Lateen Rd., Solvang, CA 93463, tel. 805/688–9494) trips combine nature, riding, elegant inns, and gourmet meals.

Nature & Ecology **Oceanic Society Expeditions** (Fort Mason Center, Bldg. E, San Francisco, CA 94123, tel. 415/441–1106 or 800/326–7491) offers natural history, whale watching, and dolphin research expeditions. **Earthwatch** (680 Mount Auburn St., Watertown, MA 02272, tel. 617/926–8000) recruits volunteers to assist scientists on reserch expeditions. **Lindblad's Special Expeditions** (720 5th Ave., New York, NY 10019, tel. 212/765–7740 or 800/762–0003) sails the historic waterways of the San Francisco Bay, the Sacramento Delta, and Sonoma Valley. **Eco Tour!** (San Diego North County CVB, 720 N. Broadway, Escondido, CA 92025, tel. 619/745–4796 or 800/848–3336) combines vacation with hands-on environmental activities.

Tips for British Travelers

Visitor Information Contact the **United States Travel and Tourism Administration** (Box 1EN, tel. 0171/495–4466).

Passports and Visas British citizens need a valid 10-year passport. A visa is not necessary unless 1) you are planning to stay more than 90 days; 2) your trip is for purposes other than vacation; 3) you have at some time been refused a visa, or refused admission, to the United States, or have been required to leave by the U.S. Immigration and Naturalization Service; or 4) you do not have a return or onward ticket. You will need to fill out the Visa Waiver Form, I-94W, supplied by the airline.

To apply for a visa or for more information, call the **U.S. Embassy's Visa Information Line** (tel. 01891/200–290; calls cost 48p per minute or 36p per minute cheap rate).

Customs British visitors aged 21 or over may import the following into the United States: 200 cigarettes or 50 cigars or 2 kilograms of tobacco; one U.S. liter of alcohol; gifts to the value of $100. Restricted items include meat products, seeds, plants, and fruits. Never carry illegal drugs.

Returning to the U.K. you may import duty-free 200 cigarettes, 100 cigarillos, 50 cigars or 250 grams of tobacco; 1 liter of spirits or 2 liters of fortified or sparkling wine; 2 liters of still table wine; 60 milliliters of perfume; 250 milliliters of toilet water; plus £36 worth of other goods, including gifts and souvenirs.

For further information or a copy of "A Guide for Travellers," which details standard customs procedures as well as what you may bring into the United Kingdom from abroad, contact HM Customs and Excise (New King's Beam House, 22 Upper Ground, London SE1).

Insurance The **Association of British Insurers,** a trade association representing 450 insurance companies, advises extra medical coverage for visitors to the United States.

For advice by phone or a free booklet, "Holiday Insurance," that sets out what to expect from a holiday-insurance policy and gives price guidelines, contact the Association of British Insurers (51 Gresham St., London EC2V 7HQ, tel. 0171/600–3333; 30 Gordon St., Glasgow G1 3PU, tel. 0141/226–3905; Scottish Provincial Bldg., Donegall Sq. W, Belfast BT1 6JE, tel. 01232/249176; call for other locations).

Tour Operators Tour operators offering packages to San Francisco include **British Airways Holidays** (Atlantic House, Hazelwick Ave., Three Bridges, Crawley, West Sussex RH10 1NP, tel. 01293/611611), **Jetsave** (Sussex House, London Rd., East Grinstead, West Sussex RH19 1LD, tel. 01342/312033), **Key to America** (15 Feltham Rd., Ashford, Middlesex TW15 1DQ, tel. 01784/248777), **Kuoni Travel Ltd.** (Kuoni House, Dorking, Surrey RH5 4AZ, tel. 01306/76711), **Premier Holidays** (Premier Travel Center, Westbrook, Milton Rd., Cambridge CB4 1YQ, tel. 01223/355977), and **Trailfinders** (194 Kensington High St., London W8 7RG, tel. 0171/937–5400; 58 Deansgate, Manchester M3 2FF, tel. 0161/839–6969).

Airfares Some travel agents that offer cheap fares to California include **Trailfinders** (42–50 Earl's Court Rd., London W8 6EJ, tel. 0171/937–5400), specialists in Round-the-World fares and independent travel; **Travel Cuts** (295a Regent St., London W1R 7YA, tel. 0171/637–3161), the Canadian Students' travel service; **Flightfile** (49 Tottenham Court Rd., London W1P 9RE, tel. 0171/700–2722), a flight-only agency.

Flying as an on-board courier to California is a possibility. Contact **Courier Travel Services** (346 Fulham Rd., London SW10 9UH, tel. 0171/351–0300) for details.

Car Rental Make the arrangements from home to avoid inconvenience, save money, and guarantee yourself a vehicle. Major firms include **Alamo** (tel. 01800/272–200, **Budget** (tel. 01800/181–181), **EuroDollar** (tel. 01895/233–300), **Europcar** (tel. 0181/950–5050), and **Hertz** (tel. 0181/679–1799).

In the United States you must be 21 to rent a car; rates may be higher for those under 25. Extra costs cover child seats, compulsory for children under 5 (about $3 per day); additional drivers (around $1.50 per day); and the all-but-compulsory Collision Damage Waiver (*see* Car Rentals, *below*). To pick up your reserved car, you will need the reservation voucher, a passport, a United Kingdom driver's license, and a travel insurance policy covering each driver.

When to Go

Any time of the year is the right time to go to California. There won't be skiable snow in the mountains between Easter and Thanksgiving; there will usually be rain in December, January, and February in the lowlands, if that bothers you; it will be much too hot to enjoy Palm Springs or Death Valley in the summer. But San Francisco, Los Angeles, and San Diego are delightful year round; the Wine Country's seasonal variables are enticing; and the coastal areas are almost always cool.

The climate varies amazingly in California, not only over distances of several hundred miles but occasionally within an hour's drive. A foggy, cool August day in San Francisco makes you grateful for a sweater, tweed jacket, or light wool coat. Head north 50 miles to the Napa Valley to check out the Wine Country, and you'll probably wear shirt sleeves and thin cottons.

Daytime and nighttime temperatures may also swing widely apart. Take Sacramento, a city that is at sea level but in California's Central Valley. In the summer, afternoons can be very warm indeed, in the 90s and occasionally over 100°. But the nights cool down, often dropping 40°.

It's hard to generalize much about the weather in this varied state. Rain comes in the winter, with snow at higher elevations. Summers are dry everywhere. As a rule, compared to the coastal areas, which are cool year round, inland regions are warmer in summer and cooler in winter. As you climb into the mountains, there are more distinct variations with the seasons: Winter brings snow, autumn is crisp, spring is variable, and summer is clear and warm.

Climate The following are average daily maximum and minimum temperatures for the major California cities.

Los Angeles									
Jan.	64F	18C	May	69F	21C	Sept.	75F	24C
	44	7		53	12		60	16
Feb.	64F	18C	June	71F	22C	Oct.	73F	23C
	46	8		57	14		55	13
Mar.	66F	19C	July	75F	24C	Nov.	71F	22C
	48	9		60	16		48	9
Apr.	66F	19C	Aug.	75C	24C	Dec.	66F	19C
	51	11		62	17		46	8

San Diego									
Jan.	62F	17C	May	66F	19C	Sept.	73F	23C
	46	8		55	13		62	17
Feb.	62F	17C	June	69F	21C	Oct.	71F	22C
	48	9		59	15		57	14
Mar.	64F	18C	July	73F	23C	Nov.	69F	21C
	50	10		62	17		51	11
Apr.	66F	19C	Aug.	73F	23C	Dec.	64F	18C
	53	12		64	18		48	9

San Francisco

	Jan.	55F	13C		May	66F	19C		Sept.	73F	23C
		41	5			48	9			51	11
	Feb.	59F	15C		June	69F	21C		Oct.	69F	21C
		42	6			51	11			50	10
	Mar.	60F	16C		July	69F	21C		Nov.	64F	18C
		44	7			51	11			44	7
	Apr.	62F	17C		Aug.	69F	21C		Dec.	57F	14C
		46	8			53	12			42	6

Information Sources For current weather conditions and forecasts for cities in the United States and abroad, plus the local time and helpful travel tips, call the **Weather Channel Connection** (tel. 900/932–8437; 95¢ per minute) from a touch-tone phone.

Festivals and Seasonal Events

January Palo Alto's annual **East-West Shrine All-Star Football Classic** (1651 19th Ave., San Francisco 94122, tel. 415/661–0291) is America's oldest all-star sports event. In Pasadena, the 106th annual **Tournament of Roses Parade and Football Game** (391 S. Orange Grove Blvd., Pasadena 91184, tel. 818/449–7673) takes place on New Year's Day 1995, with lavish flower-decked floats, marching bands, and equestrian teams, followed by the Rose Bowl game. From December or January through March, hundreds of gray whales migrate along the California coast, and visitors turn out in force for **whale-watching** (California Division of Tourism, 801 K St., Sacramento 95814, tel. 916/322–2881).

February The legendary **AT&T Pebble Beach National Pro-Am** golf tournament (Box 869, Monterey 93942, tel. 408/649–1533) begins in late January and ends in early February. In San Francisco, home of the largest concentration of Chinese-Americans in the country, **Chinese New Year Celebration** lasts a week, ending with the Golden Dragon Parade (Chinese Chamber of Commerce, 730 Sacramento St., San Francisco 94108, tel. 415/982–3000). This year is the Year of the Boar. Los Angeles also has a Chinese New Year Parade (Chinese Chamber of Commerce, 977 N. Broadway, Suite E, Los Angeles 90012, tel. 213/617–0396). Indio's **National Date Festival and Fair** (46-350 Arabia St., Indio 92201, tel. 619/863–8247) is an exotic county fair with an Arabian Nights theme; it features camel and ostrich races, an Arabian Nights fantasy production, and date exhibits and tastings.

March **Snowfest** in North Lake Tahoe (Box 7590, Tahoe City 96145, tel. 916/583–7625) is the largest winter carnival in the West, with skiing, food, fireworks, parades, and live music. The finest female golfers in the world compete for the richest purse on the LPGA circuit at the **Nabisco Dinah Shore Golf Tournament** in Rancho Mirage (2 Racquet Club Dr., Rancho Mirage 92270, tel. 619/324–4546). The **Mendocino/Fort Bragg Whale Festival** (Fort Bragg–Mendocino Coast Chamber of Commerce, Box 1141, Fort Bragg 95437, tel. 707/961–6300) features whale-watching excursions, marine art exhibits, wine and beer tastings, art exhibits, and a chowder contest.

April A large cast presents the **Ramona Pageant,** a poignant love story based on the novel by Helen Hunt Jackson, on weekends in late April and early May on a mountainside outdoor stage (Ramona Pageant Association, 27400 Ramona Bowl Rd., Hemet 92544, tel. 714/658–3111).

May Inspired by Mark Twain's story "The Notorious Jumping Frog of Calaveras County," the **Jumping Frog Contest** in Angels Camp (39th District Agricultural Association, Box 96, Angels Camp 95222,

tel. 209/736–2561) is for frogs and trainers who take their competition seriously. Sacramento hosts the **Dixieland Jazz Jubilee** (Sacramento Traditional Jazz Society, 2787 Del Monte St., West
Sacramento 95691, tel. 916/372–5277), the world's largest Dixieland
festival, with 125 bands from around the world. In Monterey, the
squirmy squid is the main attraction for the Memorial Day weekend
Great Monterey Squid Festival (2600 Garden Rd., Suite 208, Monterey 93940, tel. 408/649–6547). You'll see squid cleaning and cooking
demonstrations, taste treats, plus the usual festival fare: entertainment, arts and crafts, educational exhibits.

June   A wine event for serious sippers, the **Napa Valley Wine Auction** in
St. Helena features open houses, wine tasting, and the auction. Pre-
registration by April 1 is required (Napa Valley Wine Auction, Box
141, St. Helena 94574, tel. 707/963–5246). Each year on Father's Day
is the **Nevada City Classic Bicycle Race** (Nevada City Chamber of
Commerce, 132 Main St., Nevada City 95959, tel. 916/265–2692 or
800/655–NJOY).

July   During the **Carmel Bach Festival**, the works of Johann Sebastian
Bach are performed for three weeks; events include concerts, recitals, and seminars (Box 575, Carmel 93921, tel. 408/624–1521). During the last weekend in July, Gilroy, the self-styled Garlic Capital of
the World, celebrates its smelly but delicious product with the **Gilroy Garlic Festival** (Box 2311, Gilroy 95021, tel. 408/842–1625), featuring such unusual concoctions as garlic ice cream.

August   The **California State Fair** (Box 15649, Sacramento 95852, tel.
916/263–3000) showcases the state's agricultural side, with high-
tech exhibits, rodeo, horse racing, carnival, big-name entertainment
nightly. It runs 18 days from August to Labor Day in Sacramento.
The **Old Spanish Days' Fiesta** (1122 N. Milpas St., Santa Barbara
93103, tel. 805/962–8101) is the nation's largest all-equestrian parade. The citywide celebration features costumes, several parades,
a carnival, fiesta breakfast, rodeo, dancers, and a Spanish marketplace.

September   In Novato, from Labor Day weekend through mid-October, 3,000
costumed revelers stage an Elizabethan harvest festival, the **Renaissance Pleasure Faire** (Living History Centre, Box B, Novato
94948, tel. 415/892–0937). In Guerneville, jazz fans and musicians
jam at Johnson's Beach for the **Russian River Jazz Festival** (tel.
707/869–3940). The **Los Angeles County Fair** in Pomona (Box 2250,
Pomona 91768, tel. 714/623–3111) is the largest county fair in the
world. It features entertainment, exhibits, livestock, horse racing,
food, and more.

October   San Francisco's **Grand National Rodeo, Horse, and Stock Show** (Cow
Palace, 2600 Geneva Ave., Daly City 94014, tel. 415/469–6057) is a
world-class competition, with 3,000 top livestock and horses. In Carmel, speakers and poets gather for seminars, a banquet, and book
signing at the two-day **Tor House Poetry Festival** (Box 2713, Carmel
93921, tel. 408/624–1813), which honors the poet Robinson Jeffers.
The climax is a walk on the beach, where participants picnic and
read the poet's work aloud.

November   The **Death Valley '49er Encampment,** at Furnace Creek, commemorates the historic crossing of Death Valley in 1849, with fiddlers'
contest and an art show (Death Valley National Monument, Box 579,
Death Valley 92328, tel. 619/786–2331). Pasadena's **Doo Dah Parade,**
a fun-filled spoof of the annual Rose Parade, features the Briefcase
Brigade and kazoo Marching Band (Box 2392, Pasadena 91102, tel.
818/796–2591).

December For the **Christmas Boat Parade of Lights** in Newport Beach (1470 Jamboree Rd., Newport Beach 92660, tel. 714/729–4400), more than 200 festooned boats parade through the harbor nightly December 17–23. In Columbia in early December, the **Miners' Christmas Celebration** includes a Victorian Christmas feast at the City Hotel, lamplight tours, theater, children's piñata, costumed carolers, and Los Posados (Columbia Chamber of Commerce, Box 1824, Columbia 95310, tel. 209/532–4301). San Juan Bautista annually stages the **Shepherd's Play** in the Old Mission (El Teatro Campesino, Box 1240, San Juan Bautista 95045, tel. 408/623–2444); performances are by the internationally acclaimed El Teatro Campesino.

What to Pack

Clothing The most important single rule to bear in mind in packing for a California vacation is to prepare for changes in temperature. An hour's drive can take you up or down many degrees, and the variation from daytime to nighttime in a single location is often marked. Take along sweaters, jackets, and clothes for layering as your best insurance for coping with variations in temperature. Include shorts or cool cottons unless you are packing for a midwinter ski trip. Always tuck in a bathing suit; most lodgings have a pool, spa, and sauna.

While casual dressing is a hallmark of the California lifestyle, in the evening men will need a jacket and tie for many good restaurants, and women will be more comfortable in something dressier than regulation sightseeing garb.

Considerations of formality aside, bear in mind that San Francisco can be chilly at any time of the year, especially in summer, when the fog is apt to descend and stay.

Miscellaneous Although you can buy supplies of film, sunscreen, aspirin, and most other necessities almost anywhere in California, it's a good idea to take along a reasonable supply of the things you know you will be using routinely, to spare yourself the bother of stocking up.

Bring an extra pair of eyeglasses or contact lenses in your carry-on luggage. If you have a health problem that requires a prescription drug, pack enough to last the duration of the trip. Don't pack them in luggage that you plan to check in case your bags go astray. Pack a list of the offices that supply refunds for lost or stolen traveler's checks.

Luggage Regulations Free airline baggage allowances depend on the airline, the route, and the class of your ticket. In general, on domestic flights you are entitled to check two bags—neither exceeding 62 inches, or 158 centimeters (length + width + height), or weighing more than 70 pounds (32 kilograms). A third piece may be brought aboard; its total dimensions are generally limited to less than 45 inches (114 centimeters), so it will fit easily under the seat in front of you or in the overhead compartment. In the United States the Federal Aviation Administration (FAA) gives airlines broad latitude to limit carry-on allowances and tailor them to different aircraft and operational conditions. Charges for excess, oversize, or overweight pieces vary.

Safeguarding Your Luggage Before leaving home, itemize your bags' contents and their worth in case they go astray. To minimize that risk, tag them inside and out with your name, address, and phone number. (If you use your home address, cover it so that potential thieves can't see it.) Put a copy of your itinerary inside each bag, so that you can easily be tracked. At check-in, make sure that the tag attached by baggage handlers bears the correct three-letter code for your destination. If your bags do not arrive with you, or if you detect damage, immediately file a written report with the airline before you leave the airport.

Insurance   In the event of loss, damage, or theft on domestic flights, airlines' liability is $1,250 per passenger, excluding the valuable items such as jewelry, cameras, and more that are listed in the fine print on your ticket. Excess-valuation insurance can be bought directly from the airline at check-in. Your homeowner's policy may fill the gap; or firms such as **The Travelers Companies** (1 Tower Sq., Hartford, CT 06183, tel. 203/277–0111 or 800/243–3174) and **Wallach and Company** (107 W. Federal St., Box 480, Middleburg, VA 22117, tel. 703/687–3166 or 800/237–6615) sell baggage insurance.

Getting Money from Home

Cash Machines   Many automated-teller machines (ATMs) are tied to international networks such as **Cirrus** and **Plus.** You can use your bank card at ATMs to withdraw money from an account and get cash advances on a credit-card account if your card has been programmed with a personal identification number, or PIN. Check in advance on limits on withdrawals and cash advances within specified periods. On cash advances you are charged interest from the day you receive the money from ATMs as well as from tellers. Transaction fees for ATM withdrawals outside your home turf may be higher than for withdrawals at home.

For specific Cirrus locations in the United States and Canada, call 800/424–7787. For U.S. Plus locations, call 800/843–7587 and press the area code and first three digits of the number you're calling from (or of the calling area where you want an ATM).

Wiring Money   You don't have to be a cardholder to send or receive a **MoneyGram from American Express** for up to $10,000. Go to a MoneyGram agent in retail and convenience stores and American Express travel offices, pay up to $1,000 with a credit card and anything over that in cash. You are allowed a free long-distance call to give the transaction code to your intended recipient, who needs only present identification and the reference number to the nearest MoneyGram agent to pick up the cash. MoneyGram agents are in more than 70 countries (call 800/926–9400 for locations). Fees range from 3% to 10%, depending on the amount and how you pay.

You can also use **Western Union.** To wire money, take either cash or a cashier's check to the nearest office or call and use MasterCard or Visa. Money sent from the United States or Canada will be available for pickup at agent locations in 78 countries within minutes. Once the money is in the system it can be picked up at *any* one of 22,000 locations (call 800/325–6000 for the one nearest you).

Traveling with Cameras, Camcorders, and Laptops

About Film and Cameras   If your camera is new or if you haven't used it for a while, shoot and develop a few test rolls of film before you leave home. Store film in a cool, dry place—never in the car's glove compartment or on the shelf under the rear window.

Airport security X-rays generally aren't harmful to film with ISO below 400. To protect your film, carry it with you in a clear plastic bag and ask for a hand inspection. Such requests are honored at

U.S. airports. Don't depend on a lead-lined bag to protect film in checked luggage—the airline may increase the radiation to see what's inside.

About Camcorders   Before your trip, put camcorders through their paces, invest in a skylight filter to protect the lens, and check all the batteries.

About Videotape   Videotape is not damaged by X-rays, but it may be harmed by the magnetic field of a walk-through metal detector, so ask for a hand-check. Airport security personnel may ask you to turn on the camcorder to prove that it's what it appears to be, so make sure the battery is charged.

About Laptops   Security X-rays do not harm hard-disk or floppy-disk storage, but you may request a hand-check, at which point you may be asked to turn on the computer to prove that it is what it appears to be. (Check your battery before departure.) Most airlines allow you to use your laptop aloft except during takeoff and landing (so as not to interfere with navigation equipment).

Car Rentals

Most major car-rental companies are represented in California, including **Alamo** (tel. 800/327–9633); **Avis** (tel. 800/331–1212, 800/879–2847 in Canada); **Budget** (tel. 800/527–0700); **Dollar** (tel. 800/800–4000); **Hertz** (tel. 800/654–3131, 800/263–0600 in Canada); and **National** (tel. 800/227–7368). Unlimited-mileage rates range from $30 per day for an economy car to $48 for a large car; weekly unlimited-mileage rates range from $145 to $192. This does not include tax, which in California is up to 8.5% (plus, in San Francisco, an additional levy of $2 per day up to $16) on car rentals.

Extra Charges   Picking up the car in one city and leaving it in another may entail substantial drop-off charges or one-way service fees. The cost of a collision or loss-damage waiver (*see below*) can be high, also. Some rental agencies will charge you extra if you return the car *before* the time specified on your contract. Ask before making unscheduled drop-offs. Fill the tank when you turn in the vehicle to avoid being charged for refueling at what you'll swear is the most expensive pump in town.

Cutting Costs   Major international companies have programs that discount their standard rates by 15%–30% if you make the reservation before departure (anywhere from 24 hours to 14 days), rent for a minimum number of days (typically three or four), and prepay the rental. More economical rentals may come as part of fly/drive or other packages, even bare-bones deals that only combine the rental and an airline ticket (*see* Tours and Packages, *above*).

Insurance and Collision Damage Waiver   Before you rent a car, find out exactly what coverage, if any, is provided by your personal auto insurer and by the rental company. Don't assume that you are covered. If you do want insurance from the rental company, secondary coverage may be the only type offered. You may already have secondary coverage if you charge the rental to a credit card. Only Diner's Club (tel. 800/234–6377) provides primary coverage in the United States and worldwide.

In general if you have an accident, you are responsible for the automobile. Car-rental companies may offer a collision damage waiver (CDW), which ranges in cost from $4 to $14 a day. You should decline the CDW only if you are certain you are covered through your personal insurer or credit card company. California, New York, and Illinois have outlawed the sale of CDW altogether.

Traveling with Children

In many ways California is made to order for traveling with children: Kids love Disneyland, the San Diego Zoo, the Monterey Aquarium, the San Francisco cable cars, the city-owned gold mine in Placerville, and the caverns at Lake Shasta. The watchword for traveling with children is to plan ahead as much as possible.

Publications
Local Guides
Places to Go with Children in Southern California, by Stephanie Kegan, and *Places to Go with Children in Northern California,* by Elizabeth Pomada (each $9.95 plus $3.50 shipping from Chronicle Books, 275 5th St., San Francisco, CA 94103, tel. 800/722–6657), are good trip-planning guides for families. For more San Francisco ideas, see *San Francisco Family Fun,* by Carole Terwilliger Meyers ($12.95 plus $3 shipping; Carousel Press, Box 6061, Albany, CA 94706, tel. 510/527–5849), and the brochure **"Kidding Around in San Francisco"** (free from the San Francisco Convention & Visitors Bureau, Box 429097, San Francisco 94142, tel. 415/391–2000). For Los Angeles, see the *Parents' Guide 1993,* edited by Karen Mani (Paul Flattery Productions, $22.95), 500 pages of shopping, recreation, and entertainment, and *Kids Connection,* by Elizabeth Topper.

San Francisco/Peninsula Parent (Box 128, Millbrae 94030, tel. 415/342–9203); **Parents Press** (1454 6th St., Berkeley 94710, tel. 510/524–1602); **Parents Monthly** (8611 Folsom Blvd., Suite A, Sacramento 95826, tel. 916/383–7012); **L.A. Parent** (Box 3204, Burbank 91504, tel. 818/846–0400); and **San Diego Family Press** (Box 23960, San Diego 92193, tel. 619/685–6970) are monthly newspapers that list activities for children. The free papers can be found in racks at many libraries and some supermarkets; they are available by mail for a small fee.

Newsletter
Family Travel Times, published 10 times a year by **Travel With Your Children** (TWYCH, 45 W. 18th St., 7th Floor Tower, New York, NY 10011, tel. 212/206–0688; annual subscription $55), covers destinations, types of vacations, and modes of travel. TWYCH also publishes *Cruising with Children* and *Skiing with Children.*

Books
Great Vacations with Your Kids, by Dorothy Jordan and Marjorie Cohen ($13 plus $2 shipping; Penguin USA, 120 Woodbine St., Bergenfield, NJ 07621, tel. 800/253–6476), and *Traveling with Children—And Enjoying It,* by Arlene K. Butler ($11.95 plus $3 shipping per book; Globe Pequot Press, Box 833, 6 Business Park Rd., Old Saybrook, CT 06475, tel. 800/243–0495 or 800/962–0973 in CT) help plan your trip with children, from toddlers to teens. From the same publisher are *Recommended Family Resorts in the United States, Canada, and the Caribbean,* by Jane Wilford with Janet Tice ($12.95), and *Recommended Family Inns of America* ($12.95).

Tour Operators
Grandtravel (6900 Wisconsin Ave., Suite 706, Chevy Chase, MD 20815, tel. 301/986–0790 or 800/247–7651) offers tours for people traveling with their grandchildren. The company's catalogue, as charmingly written and illustrated as a children's book, positively invites armchair traveling with lap-sitters aboard. **Rascals in Paradise** (650 5th St., Suite 505, San Francisco, CA 94107, tel. 415/442–0799 or 800/872–7225) specializes in adventurous, exotic, and fun-filled vacations for families to carefully screened resorts and hotels around the world.

Getting There
Air Fares
On domestic flights, children under two not occupying a seat travel free, and older children currently travel on the "lowest applicable" adult fare.

Baggage The adult baggage allowance applies for children paying half or more of the adult fare.

Safety Seats The FAA recommends the use of safety seats aloft and details approved models in the free leaflet **"Child/Infant Safety Seats Recommended for Use in Aircraft"** (available from the Federal Aviation Administration, APA–200, 800 Independence Ave. SW, Washington, DC 20591, tel. 202/267–3479; Information Hotline, tel. 800/322–7873). Airline policy varies. U.S. carriers allow FAA-approved models bearing a sticker declaring their FAA approval. Because these seats are strapped into regular passenger seats, airlines may require that a ticket be bought for an infant who would otherwise ride free.

Facilities Aloft Some airlines provide other services for children, such as children's meals and freestanding bassinets (only to those with seats at the bulkhead, where there's enough legroom). Make your request when reserving. The annual February/March issue of ***Family Travel Times*** details children's services on dozens of airlines ($10; *see above*). **"Kids and Teens in Flight"** (free from the U.S. Department of Transportation's Office of Consumer Affairs, R-25, Washington, DC 20590, tel. 202/366–2220) offers tips for children flying alone.

Lodging You will have to look carefully to find an inn or bed-and-breakfast that welcomes families (or that you will enjoy with children). Small, charming, and usually old, these places are usually chockablock with antiques and breakables placed down low. If you want to give it a try, get the details when you make your reservation.

Motels and hotels are another story. Often your children can share your room at no extra charge; be sure to ask about the cutoff age. There may be nominal charges for cribs and $5–$10 charged for an extra bed. In addition, major hotels usually have lists of baby-sitters.

Hints for Travelers with Disabilities

California is a national leader in making attractions and facilities accessible to people with disabilities. Since 1982 the state building code has required that all areas for public use be made accessible. State laws more than a decade old provide special privileges, such as license plates allowing special parking spaces, unlimited parking in time-limited spaces, and free parking in metered spaces. Insignia from states other than California are honored.

People with disabilities should plan ahead for travel; check with providers when you make arrangements for transportation, lodging, and special sightseeing and events. Allow plenty of time to meet bus, train, and plane schedules. Be sure your wheelchair is clearly marked if it is carried with other luggage.

Organizations Several organizations provide travel information for people with disabilities, usually for a membership fee, and some publish newsletters and bulletins. Among them are the **Information Center for Individuals with Disabilities** (Fort Point Pl., 27–43 Wormwood St., Boston, MA 02210, tel. 617/727–5540 or 800/462–5015 in MA between 11 and 4, or leave message; TTY 617/345–9743); **Mobility International USA** (Box 10767, Eugene, OR 97440, tel. and TTY 503/343–1284, fax 503/343–6812), the U.S. branch of an international organization based in Britain (*see below*) that has affiliates in 30 countries; **MossRehab Hospital Travel Information Service** (tel. 215/456–9603, TTY 215/456–9602); the **Travel Industry and Disabled Exchange** (TIDE, 5435 Donna Ave., Tarzana, CA 91356, tel.

818/344–3640, fax 818/344–0078); and **Travelin' Talk** (Box 3534, Clarksville, TN 37043, tel. 615/552–6670, fax 615/552–1182).

In the United Kingdom Important information sources include the **Royal Association for Disability and Rehabilitation** (RADAR, 25 Mortimer St., London W1N 8AB, tel. 071/637–5400), which publishes travel information for people with disabilities in Britain, and **Mobility International** (228 Borough High St., London SE1 1JX, tel. 071/403–5688), an international clearinghouse of travel information for people with disabilities.

Tour Operators and Travel Agencies **Flying Wheels Travel** (143 W. Bridge St., Box 382, Owatonna, MN 55060, tel. 507/451–5005 or 800/535–6790) is a travel agency specializing in domestic and worldwide cruises, tours, and independent travel itineraries for people with mobility problems. Adventurers should contact **Wilderness Inquiry** (1313 5th St. SE, Minneapolis, MN 55414, tel. and TTY 612/379–3838 or 800/728–0719), which orchestrates action-packed trips like white-water rafting, sea kayaking, and dog sledding to bring together people who have disabilities with those who don't.

Publications Several free publications are available from the U.S. Consumer Information Center (Pueblo, CO 81009): **"New Horizons for the Air Traveler with a Disability"** (include Dept. 608Y in the address), a U.S. Department of Transportation booklet describing changes resulting from the 1986 Air Carrier Access Act and from the 1990 Americans with Disabilities Act, and the Airport Operators Council's *Access Travel: Airports* (Dept. 5804), which describes facilities and services for people with disabilities at more than 500 airports worldwide.

Travelin' Talk Directory (*see* Organizations, *above*) was published in 1993. This 500-page resource book ($35 check or money order with a money-back guarantee) lists names and addresses of people and organizations who offer help for travelers with disabilities. Twin Peaks Press (Box 129, Vancouver, WA 98666, tel. 206/694–2462 or 800/637–2256) publishes the *Directory of Travel Agencies for the Disabled* ($19.95), listing more than 370 agencies worldwide. Add $2 for shipping. The Sierra Club publishes *Easy Access to National Parks* ($16 plus $3 shipping; 730 Polk St., San Francisco, CA 94109, tel. 415/776–2211). Fodor's publishes *Great American Vacations for Travelers with Disabilities,* detailing services and accessible attractions, restaurants, and hotels in California and other U.S. destinations (available in bookstores, or call 800/533–6478).

Getting There **Greyhound Lines** (tel. 800/752–4841; TDD 800/345–3109) will carry a disabled person and companion for the price of a single fare. **Amtrak** (National Railroad Passenger Corp., 60 Massachusetts Ave. NE, Washington, DC 20002, tel. 800/USA–RAIL) advises that you request red-cap service, special seats, or wheelchair assistance when you make reservations. Also note that not all stations can provide these services. All passengers with disabilities are entitled to 25% off nondiscounted one-way fares, and there are special fares for children with disabilities as well. Contact Amtrak for a free brochure outlining services for the elderly and people with disabilities.

Discounts The **National Park Service** (Box 37127, Washington, DC 20013–7127) provides a Golden Access Passport free to those who are medically blind or have a permanent disability; the passport covers the entry fee for the holder and anyone accompanying the holder in the same private vehicle and a 50% discount on camping and some other user fees. Apply for the passport in person at a national recreation facility that charges an entrance fee; proof of disability is required.

Hints for Older Travelers

Many discounts are available to older travelers: Meals, lodging, entry to various attractions, car rentals, tickets for buses and trains, and campsites are among the prime examples. Some discounts are given solely on the basis of age, without membership requirement; others require membership in an organization. In California, the state park system, which includes more than 200 locations, provides a $2 discount on campsites for anyone 62 or over and others in the same private vehicle; ask for this discount when you make advance reservations.

If you are 50 or older, our advice is to ask about senior discounts even if there is no posted notice. A 10% cut on a bus ticket and $2 off a pizza may not seem like major savings, but they add up.

Organizations The **American Association of Retired Persons** (AARP, 601 E St. NW, Washington, DC 20049, tel. 202/434–2277) provides independent travelers who are members of the AARP (open to those age 50 or older; $8 per person or couple annually) the Purchase Privilege Program, which offers discounts on lodging, car rentals, and sightseeing, and the AARP Motoring Plan, which furnishes domestic trip-routing information and emergency road-service aid for an annual fee of $39.95 per person or couple ($59.95 for a premium version). AARP also arranges group tours, cruises, and apartment living through AARP Travel Experience from American Express (400 Pinnacle Way, Suite 450, Norcross, GA 30071, tel. 800/927–0111 or 800/745–4567).

Two other organizations offer discounts on lodgings, car rentals, and other travel products, along with such nontravel perks as magazines and newsletters: the **National Council of Senior Citizens** (1331 F St. NW, Washington, DC 20004, tel. 202/347–8800; membership $12 annually) and **Mature Outlook** (6001 N. Clark St., Chicago, IL 60660, tel. 800/336–6330; $9.95 annually).

Note: Mention your senior-citizen identification card when booking hotel reservations for reduced rates, not when checking out. At restaurants, show your card before you're seated; discounts may be limited to certain menus, days, or hours. If you are renting a car, ask about promotional rates that might improve on your senior-citizen discount.

Educational Travel The nonprofit **Elderhostel** (75 Federal St., 3rd Floor, Boston, MA 02110, tel. 617/426–7788) has offered inexpensive study programs for people 60 and older since 1975. Held at more than 1,800 educational institutions, courses cover everything from marine science to Greek myths and cowboy poetry. Participants usually attend lectures in the morning and spend the afternoon sightseeing or on field trips; they live in dorms on the host campuses. Fees for programs in the United States and Canada, which usually last one week, run about $300, not including transportation.

Tour Operators The following tour operators specialize in older travelers: If you want to take your grandchildren, look into **Grandtravel** (*see* Traveling with Children, *above*); **Saga International Holidays** (222 Berkeley St., Boston, MA 02116, tel. 800/343–0273) caters to those over age 60 who like to travel in groups. **SeniorTours** (508 Irvington Rd., Drexel Hill, PA 19026, tel. 215/626–1977 or 800/227–1100) arranges motorcoach tours throughout the United States and Nova Scotia, as well as Caribbean cruises.

Publications ***The 50+ Traveler's Guidebook: Where to Go, Where to Stay, What to Do,*** by Anita Williams and Merrimac Dillon ($12.95; St. Martin's Press, 175 5th Ave., New York, NY 10010), is available in bookstores and offers many useful tips. **"The Mature Traveler"** (Box 50820, Reno, NV 89513, tel. 702/786–7419; $29.95), a monthly newsletter, contains many travel deals.

Hints for Gay and Lesbian Travelers

Organizations The **International Gay Travel Association** (Box 4974, Key West, FL 33041, tel. 800/448–8550), which has 700 members, will provide you with names of specialist travel agents and tour operators. The **Gay & Lesbian Visitors Center of New York Inc.** (135 W. 20th St., 3rd Floor, New York, NY 10011, tel. 212/463–9030 or 800/395–2315; $100 annually) mails a monthly newsletter, valuable coupons, and more to its members.

Tour Operators and Travel Agencies The dominant travel agency in the market is **Above and Beyond** (3568 Sacramento St., San Francisco, CA 94118, tel. 415/922–2683 or 800/397–2681). Tour operator **Olympus Vacations** (8424 Santa Monica Blvd., #721, West Hollywood, CA 90069, tel. 310/657–2220) offers all-gay-and-lesbian resort holidays. **Skylink Women's Travel** (746 Ashland Ave., Santa Monica, CA 90405, tel. 310/452–0506 or 800/225–5759) handles individual travel for lesbians all over the world and conducts two international and five domestic group trips annually.

Publications The premiere international travel magazine for gays and lesbians is ***Our World*** (1104 North Nova Rd., Suite 251, Daytona Beach, FL 32117, tel. 904/441–5367; $35 for 10 issues). The monthly **"Out & About"** (tel. 203/789–8518 or 800/929–2268; $49 for 10 issues) is 16 pages on gay-friendly resorts, hotels, and airlines. Many California cities large and small have lesbian and gay publications available in sidewalk racks and at bars and other social spaces. News and events listings can be found in ***San Francisco Bay Times*** (288 7th St., San Francisco 94103, tel. 415/626–8121); ***Mom Guess What Newspaper*** (1725 L St., Sacramento 95814, tel. 916/441–6397); ***Edge*** (6434 Santa Monica Blvd., Los Angeles 90038, tel. 213/962–6994); and ***Gay & Lesbian Times*** (3636 5th Ave., Suite 101, San Diego 92103, tel. 619/299–6397).

Arriving and Departing

From North America by Plane

Flights are either nonstop, direct, or connecting. A **nonstop** flight requires no change of plane and makes no stops. A **direct** flight stops at least once and can involve a change of plane, although the flight number remains the same; if the first leg is late, the second waits. This is not the case with a **connecting** flight, which involves a different plane and a different flight number.

Cutting Costs The Sunday travel section of most newspapers is a good source of deals. When booking, particularly through an unfamiliar company, call the Better Business Bureau and your local or state Consumer Protection Bureau to find out whether any complaints have been registered against the company, pay with a credit card if you can, and consider trip-cancellation and default insurance.

Promotional Airfares Less expensive fares, called promotional or discount fares, are round-trip and involve restrictions, which vary according to the route and season. You must usually buy the ticket—commonly called an APEX (advance purchase excursion) when it's for international travel—in advance (seven, 14, or 21 days are usual), although some of the major airlines have added no-frills, cheap flights to compete with new bargain airlines on certain routes. These new low-cost carriers include **Private Jet** (tel. 800/949–9400), based in Atlanta and serving Miami, Dallas, St. Thomas, St. Croix, Las Vegas, New York's Kennedy, Los Angeles, Chicago, and San Francisco.

With the major airlines the cheaper fares generally require minimum and maximum stays (for instance, over a Saturday night or at least seven and no more than 30 days). Airlines generally allow some return date changes for $25 to $50 fee, but most low-fare tickets are nonrefundable. Only a death in the family would prompt the airline to return any of your money if you cancel a nonrefundable ticket. However, you can apply an unused nonrefundable ticket toward a new ticket, again with a small fee. The lowest fare is subject to availability, and only a small percentage of the plane's total seats will be sold at that price. Contact the U.S. Department of Transportation's Office of Consumer Affairs (I–25, Washington, DC 20590, tel. 202/366–2220) for a copy of "Fly-Rights: A Guide to Air Travel in the U.S." *The Official Frequent Flyer Guidebook*, by Randy Petersen (4715–C Town Center Dr., Colorado Springs, CO 80916, tel. 719/597–8899, 800/487–8893, or 800/485–8893; $14.99 plus $3 shipping and handling), yields valuable hints on getting the most for your air travel dollars.

Consolidators Consolidators or bulk-fare operators—"bucket shops"—buy blocks of seats on scheduled flights that airlines anticipate they won't be able to sell. They pay wholesale prices, add a markup, and resell the seats to travel agents or directly to the public at prices that still undercut the airline's promotional or discount fares (higher than a charter ticket but lower than an APEX ticket, and usually without the advance-purchase restriction). Moreover, some consolidators sometimes give you your money back. Carefully read the fine print detailing penalties for changes and cancellations. If you doubt the reliability of a company, call the airline once you've made your booking and confirm that you do, indeed, have a reservation on the flight.

Discount Travel Clubs Travel clubs offer members unsold space on airplanes, cruise ships, and package tours at as much as 50% below regular prices. Membership may include a regular bulletin or access to a toll-free hot line giving details of available trips departing from three or four days to several months in the future. Most also offer 50% discounts off hotel rack rates, but double check with the hotel to make sure it isn't offering a better promotional rate independent of the club. Clubs include **Discount Travel International** (114 Forrest Ave., Suite 203, Narberth, PA 19072, tel. 215/668–7184; $45 annually, single or family), **Entertainment Travel Editions** (Box 1014, Trumbull, CT 06611, tel. 800/445–4137; price ranges $28–$48), **Great American Traveler** (Box 27965, Salt Lake City, UT 84127, tel. 800/548–2812; $29.95 annually), **Moment's Notice Discount Travel Club** (425 Madison Ave., New York, NY 10017, tel. 212/486–0503; $45 annually, single or family), **Privilege Card** (3391 Peachtree Rd. NE, Suite 110, Atlanta, GA 30326, tel. 404/262–0222 or 800/236–9732; domestic annual membership $49.95, international $74.95), **Travelers Advantage** (CUC Travel Service, 49 Music Sq. W, Nashville, TN 37203, tel. 800/548–1116; $49 annually, single or family), and **Worldwide Discount Travel Club** (1674 Meridian Ave., Miami Beach, FL 33139, tel. 305/534–2082; $50 annually for family, $40 single).

The newsletter **"Travel Smart"** (40 Beechdale Rd., Dobbs Ferry, NY 10522, tel. 800/327–3633; $44 a year) has a wealth of travel deals in each monthly issue.

Enjoying the Flight Because the air aloft is dry, drink plenty of fluids while on board. Drinking alcohol contributes to jet lag, as do heavy meals. Bulkhead seats, in the front row of each cabin—usually reserved for people who have disabilities, are elderly, or are traveling with babies—offer more legroom, but trays attach awkwardly to seat armrests, and all possessions must be stowed overhead.

Smoking Since February 1990, smoking has been banned on all domestic flights of less than six hours' duration; the ban also applies to domestic segments of international flights aboard U.S. and foreign carriers.

Staying in California

Shopping

In California's big cities, opportunities abound to shop for internationally known brands of clothing, jewelry, leather goods, and perfumes, often in shops or boutiques set up by French, Italian, British, or American designers. San Francisco and Los Angeles are centers of clothing manufacture; if you're a bargain hunter, you'll want to explore the factory outlets in both cities.

If you are shopping for something unique to California, look at the output of its many resident artists and craftspeople. You can find their creations from one end of the state to the other in fine city galleries, in small neighborhood shops, in out-of-the-way mountain studios, at roadside stands, and at county fairs. Paintings, drawings, sculpture, wood carvings, pottery, jewelry, handwoven fabrics, handmade baskets—the creativity and the output of California's artisans seem endless.

Another California specialty is wine. You can visit wineries in many parts of the state, not only in the Wine Country north of San Francisco. Wineries and good wine stores will package your purchases for safe travel or shipping.

Participant Sports

Almost any participant sport you can think of is available somewhere in California at some time of the year. Although snow skiing is limited for the most part to the period between Thanksgiving and April, a great many sports, including golf and tennis, go on year round.

Swimming and surfing, scuba diving, and skin diving in the Pacific Ocean are favorite year-round California pleasures in the southern part of the state, although these become seasonal sports on the coast from San Francisco northward.

California has abundant fishing options: deep-sea fishing expeditions, surf fishing from the shore, and freshwater fishing in streams, rivers, lakes, and reservoirs. You'll need a California fishing license. State residents pay $23.25 ($2 for senior citizens and those on limited income), but nonresidents must fork over $62.75 for a one-year license. Both residents and nonresidents can purchase a one-day license for $8.25. For information, contact the **Department of Fish**

and Game (3211 S St., Sacramento 95816, tel. 916/227–2244). The department can also advise you on hunting licenses and regulations.

Hiking, backpacking, bicycling, and sailing are popular throughout the state, and you can readily arrange to rent equipment. River rafting—white-water and otherwise—canoeing, and kayaking are popular, especially in the northern part of the state, where there are many rivers; see individual chapters for detailed information.

Hot-air ballooning is gaining in popularity, although it is not cheap: A ride costs in excess of $100. More and more of the large, colorful balloons drift across the valleys of the Wine Country, where the air drafts are particularly friendly to this sport, as well as in the desert, Temecula, and the Gold Country.

Beaches

With almost 1,000 miles of coastline, California is well supplied with beaches. They are endlessly fascinating: You can walk on them, lie and sun on them, watch seabirds and hunt for shells, dig clams, or spot seals and sea otters at play. From December through March you can watch the migrations of the gray whales.

What you can't always do at these beaches is swim. From San Francisco and northward, the water is simply too cold for any but extremely hardy souls. Even along the southern half of the coast, some beaches are too dangerous for swimming because of undertows. Look for signs and postings and take them seriously. Park rangers patrol beaches and enforce regulations, such as those prohibiting alcohol, dune buggies, fires, and pets (dogs must be on leash at all times).

Access to beaches in California is generally excellent. The state park system includes many fine beaches, and oceanside communities have their own public beaches. In addition, through the work of the California Coastal Commission, many stretches of private property that would otherwise seal off the beach from outsiders have public-access paths and trails. Again, the best advice is to look for signs and obey them.

State and National Parks

State Parks California's state park system includes more than 200 sites; many are recreational and scenic, others historic or scientific. A sampling of the variety of state parks: Angel Island in San Francisco Bay, reached by ferry from San Francisco or Tiburon; Anza-Borrego Desert, 600,000 acres of the Colorado Desert northeast of San Diego; Big Basin Redwoods, California's first state redwood park, with 300-foot trees, near Santa Cruz; Empire Mine, one of the richest mines in the Mother Lode, in Grass Valley; Hearst Castle at San Simeon; Leo Carrillo Beach north of Malibu; Pismo Beach, with surfing, clamming, and nature trails.

Reservations Most state parks are open year round. Parks near major urban areas and on beaches and lakes are often crowded, and campsite reservations are essential. MISTIX (tel. 800/444–7275) handles all state park reservations, which may be made up to eight weeks in advance.

For information on California's state parks, contact the **California State Park System** (Dept. of Parks and Recreation, Box 942896, Sacramento 94296, tel. 916/653–6995).

**National
Parks**
There are five national parks in California: **Lassen, Redwood, Sequoia and Kings Canyon, Yosemite,** and the **Channel Islands.** National monuments include **Cabrillo,** in San Diego; **Death Valley**; **Devil's Postpile,** 7,600 feet up in the eastern Sierra Nevada; **Lava Beds,** in northeastern California; **Muir Woods,** north of San Francisco; **Joshua Tree,** in the desert near Palm Springs; and **Pinnacles,** in western central California.

There are three national recreation areas: **Golden Gate,** with 73,000 acres both north and south of the Golden Gate Bridge in San Francisco; **Santa Monica Mountains,** with 150,000 acres from Griffith Park in Los Angeles to the Ventura County line; and **Whiskeytown-Shasta-Trinity,** with 240,000 acres including four major lakes. **Point Reyes National Seashore** is on a peninsula near San Francisco.

For information on specific parks, see the individual chapters or contact the **National Park Service** (Fort Mason, Bldg. 201, San Francisco, CA 94123, tel. 415/556–0560).

Dining

Over the past decade, California's name has come to signify a certain type of modern, healthful, sophisticated cuisine, using the freshest of local ingredients, creatively combined and served in often stunning presentations. In coastal areas, most restaurants' menus feature at least some seafood, fresh off the boat. California is also a major agricultural state, so local produce is usually excellent. San Francisco and Los Angeles have scores of top-notch restaurants—an expensive meal at one of these gourmet shrines is often the high point of a trip to California. The Wine Country, just north of San Francisco, is also known for superb restaurants. But don't neglect the culinary bounty of California's mixed ethnic population—notably Mexican and Chinese, but also Japanese, Scandinavian, Italian, French, Belgian, English, and German restaurants.

Lodging

Hotels in cities may or may not provide parking facilities, and there is usually a charge. Motels, which are more common along the highways and outside cities, have parking space but may not have some of the amenities that hotels typically have—on-site restaurants, lounges, and room service.

Bed-and-breakfasts and inns have become more numerous in California in recent years. These are not usually economy lodgings—their prices are often at the top of the scale. Most typically, they are large, older homes, renovated and charmingly decorated with antiques, with a half-dozen guest rooms. The price usually includes breakfast, which may be a Continental breakfast—juice, coffee, and some simple pastry—or a four-course feast. Baths may be private or shared. Sometimes the inn is a renovated hotel from the last century with a dozen rooms; occasionally it is a Victorian farmhouse with only three guest rooms.

Few B&Bs allow smoking; virtually none take pets. Antique furniture, delicate fabrics, and the elaborate decorative accessories that are typical of these inns make these restrictions understandable.

Guest ranches and dude ranches are included in lodging listings, as are resorts. Their range of recreation options is greater than the usual, and this is noted.

Home Exchange You can find a house, apartment, or other vacation property to exchange for your own by becoming a member of a home-exchange organization, which then sends you its annual directories listing available exchanges and includes your own listing in at least one of them. Arrangements for the actual exchange are made by the two parties to it, not by the organization. For more information contact the **International Home Exchange Association** (IHEA, 41 Sutter St., Suite 1090, San Francisco, CA 94104, tel. 415/673–0347 or 800/788–2489). **Homelink International** (Box 650, Key West, FL 33041, tel. 800/638–3841), with thousands of foreign and domestic listings, publishes four annual directories plus updates; the $50 membership includes your listing in one book. **Intervac International** (Box 590504, San Francisco, CA 94159, tel. 415/435–3497) has three annual directories; membership is $62, or $72 if you want to receive the directories but remain unlisted. **Loan-a-Home** (2 Park La., Apt. 6E, Mount Vernon, NY 10552, tel. 914/664–7640) specializes in long-term exchanges; there is no charge to list your home, but the directories cost $35 or $45 depending on the number you receive.

Apartment and Villa Rentals If you want a home base that's roomy enough for a family and comes with cooking facilities, a furnished rental may be the solution. It's generally cost-wise, too, although not always—some rentals are luxury properties (economical only when your party is large). Home-exchange directories do list rentals—often second homes owned by prospective house-swappers—and some services search for a house or apartment for you (even a castle if that's your fancy) and handle the paperwork. Some send an illustrated catalogue and others send photographs of specific properties, sometimes at a charge; up-front registration fees may apply.

Among the companies are **Rent-a-Home International** (7200 34th Ave. NW, Seattle, WA 98117, tel. 206/789–9377 or 800/488–7368) and **Vacation Home Rentals Worldwide** (235 Kensington Ave., Norwood, NJ 07648, tel. 201/767–9393 or 800/633–3284). **Hideaways International** (767 Islington St., Box 4433, Portsmouth, NH 03802, tel. 603/430–4433 or 800/843–4433) functions as a travel club. Membership ($99 yearly per person or family at the same address) includes two annual guides plus quarterly newsletters; rentals are arranged directly between members, not by the club staff.

Camping

Camping facilities in the state parks are extensive, though you will need reservations. (*See* State and National Parks, *above*.) Many popular parks have all their spaces reserved several weeks ahead. *California RV Park and Campground Guide* (available for $3, or $7 from overseas, from the **California Travel Parks Association,** Box 5648, Auburn, CA 95604) gives information about nearly 400 private parks and campgrounds throughout the state.

Credit Cards

The following credit-card abbreviations are used: AE, American Express; D, Discover; DC, Diners Club; MC, MasterCard; V, Visa.

2 Portraits of California

Living with the Certainty of a Shaky Future

By John Burks

John Burks is a professor of journalism and humanities at San Francisco State University. He has served as editor-in-chief of two of the city's leading magazines, City and San Francisco Focus, was a Newsweek correspondent and managing editor of Rolling Stone, and currently edits the quarterly American Kite.

There's never been any question *whether* there will be another earthquake in San Francisco. The question is how soon. Even the kids here grow up understanding that it's just a matter of time, and from grade school on, earthquake safety drills become routine. *At the first rumble, duck under your desk or table or stand in a doorway,* they are instructed. *Get away from windows to avoid broken glass. When the shaking stops, walk—don't run—outdoors, as far away from buildings as possible.*

Sure as there are hurricanes along the Gulf of Mexico and blizzards in Maine, San Francisco's earthquakes are inevitable. Nobody here is surprised when the rolling and tumbling begins—it happens all the time. Just in the six months following the jarring 1989 earthquake, for instance, seismologists reported hundreds of aftershocks, ranging from the scarcely perceptible to those strong enough to bring down buildings weakened by October's jolt.

The Bay Area itself was created in upheaval such as this. Eons ago, a restless geology of shifting plates deep in the earth gave birth to the Sierra Mountains and the Pacific Coast Range. Every spring when the snows melted, the runoff rushed down from the mile-high Sierra peaks westward across what would eventually be known as California. Here, the runoff ran up against the coastal range, and a vast inland lake was formed.

The rampaging waters from the yearly thaw eventually crashed through the quake-shattered Coast Range to meet the Pacific Ocean, creating the gap now spanned by the Golden Gate Bridge. This breakthrough created San Francisco Bay, one of the world's great natural harbors, its fertile delta larger than that of the Mississippi River. What a fabulous setting for the city-to-be—surrounded on three sides by water, set off by dramatic mountainscapes to the north and south, and blessed by cool ocean breezes.

All this and gold, too. The twisting and rolling of so-called terra firma exposed rich veins of gold at and near ground level that otherwise would have remained hidden deep underground. The great upheaval pushed the Mother Lode to the surface and set the scene for the Gold Rush. But before the '49 miners came the Europeans. In the late 15th century, the Spanish writer Garci Ordóñez de Montalvo penned a fictional description of a place he called California, a faraway land ruled by Queen Califia, where gold and precious stones were so plentiful the streets were lined with them. Montalvo's vision of wealth without limit helped fuel the voyages of the great 15th- and 16th-century

European explorers in the New World. They never did hit pay dirt here, but the name California stuck nevertheless.

Northern California was eventually settled, and in 1848, the population of San Francisco was 832. The discovery of gold in the California hills brought sudden and unprecedented wealth to this coastal trading outpost and its population exploded; by the turn of the century San Francisco was home to 343,000 people.

En route to its destiny as a premier city of the West, San Francisco was visited by innumerable quakes. Yet while the city's very foundations shook, residents found that each new rattler helped to strengthen San Francisco's self-image of adaptability. Robert Louis Stevenson wrote of the quakes' alarming frequency: "The fear of them grows yearly in a resident; he begins with indifference and ends in sheer panic." The big shaker of 1865 inspired humorist Mark Twain to look at the quakes in a different light by writing an earthquake "almanac" for the following year, which advised:

Oct. 23—Mild, balmy earthquakes.

Oct. 26—About this time expect more earthquakes; but do not look for them . . .

Oct. 27—Universal despondency, indicative of approaching disaster. Abstain from smiling or indulgence in humorous conversation . . .

Oct. 29—Beware!

Oct. 31—Go slow!

Nov. 1—Terrific earthquake. This is the great earthquake month. More stars fall and more worlds are slathered around carelessly and destroyed in November than in any month of the twelve.

Nov. 2—Spasmodic but exhilarating earthquakes, accompanied by occasional showers of rain and churches and things.

Nov. 3—Make your will.

Nov. 4—Sell out.

On the whole, those who settled in San Francisco were more inclined toward Twain's devil-may-care attitude—those who succumbed to Stevenson's panic didn't stick around for long. Certainly the multitude of vices that saturated the metropolis were sufficient to distract many men from their fears; throughout Chinatown and the infamous Barbary Coast opium dens, gin mills, and bordellos operated day and night.

Money flowed. Money tempted. Money corrupted. The city was built on graft, and city hall became synonymous with corruption under the influence of political crooks like Blind Chris Buckley and Boss Ruef. The very building itself was a scandal. Planned for completion in six months at a cost of half a million dollars, the city hall ultimately took 29 years to build at a graft-inflated cost of $8 million, an astronomical sum at the dawning of the 20th century. When the San Andreas Fault set loose the 1906 earthquake, the most devastating ever to hit an American city, city hall was one of the first buildings to come crashing down. Its ruins exposed the shoddiest of building materials, an ironic symbol of the city's crime-ridden past.

The 1906 earthquake and fire has come to define San Francisco both for itself and the outside world. In the immediate aftermath of the catastrophe, San Franciscans wondered whether they ought to believe the preachers and reformers who declared that this terrible devastation had been wrought upon their wicked city by the avenging hand of God. San Franciscans asked themselves whether, somehow, they had earned it.

But the city was quick to prove its character. Fifty years earlier, six separate fires had destroyed most of San Francisco—yet each time it was rebuilt by a citizenry not ready to give up on either the gold or the city that gold had built. Now, in 1906, heroic firefighters dynamited one of the city's main thoroughfares to prevent the inferno from spreading all the way to the Pacific. The mood of San Franciscans was almost eerily calm, their neighborliness both heartwarming and jaunty. "Eat, drink, and be merry," proclaimed signs about town, "for tomorrow we may have to go to Oakland." No sooner had the flames died than rebuilding began—true to San Francisco tradition. Forty thousand construction workers poured into town to assist the proud, amazingly resilient residents.

The 1906 earthquake provided a chance to rethink the hodgepodge, get-rich-quick cityscape that had risen in the heat of Gold Rush frenzy. City fathers imported the revered urban planner Daniel Burnham, architect of the magnificent 1893 Chicago World's Fair, to re-invent San Francisco. "Make no little plans," Burnham intoned. "They have no power to stir men's souls."

The city's new Civic Center, built under Burnham's direction, was raised to celebrate the city's comeback and is regarded as one of America's most stately works of civic architecture. Its city hall stands as a monument to the city's will to prevail—from its colonnaded granite exterior to its exuberant interior, once described by Tom Wolfe as resembling "some Central American opera house. Marble arches, domes, acanthus leaves . . . quirks and galleries and gilt filigrees . . . a veritable angels' choir of gold." The inscription found over the mayor's office seems to sum it all up: "San Francisco, O glorious city of our hearts that has been tried and not found wanting, go thou with like spirit to make the future thine."

In 1915, San Francisco dazzled the world with its Panama–Pacific International Exposition, designed to prove not only that it was back, but that it was back bigger and better and badder than ever before. An architectural wonderland, the Expo was built on 70 acres of marshy landfill, which later became the residential neighborhood called the Marina District. When the October 1989 earthquake struck, this neighborhood was badly damaged, and became a focus as the entire nation tuned in to see how San Francisco and its people would fare this time around.

Like the gold that surfaced in the Mother Lode, the 1989 quake once again brought out the best in this region's people. Out at Candlestick Park, 62,000 fans were waiting for the start of the World Series between the San Francisco Giants and the Oakland A's when everything started shaking. They cut loose with big cheers after the temblor subsided. One San Francisco fan quickly hand-lettered a sign and held it aloft: "That was Nothing—Wait Til the Giants Bat." When it became apparent that there would be no ball played that night, the fans departed from the ballpark, just like in a grade-school earthquake safety drill, quietly and in good order.

This was what millions of TV viewers across the nation first saw of the local response to this major (7.1) earthquake and, by and large, the combination of good humor and relative calm they observed was an accurate reflection of the prevailing mood around the city. San Franciscans were not about to panic. Minutes after the quake struck, a San Francisco couple spread a lace tablecloth over the hood of their BMW and, sitting in the driveway of their splintered home, toasted passersby with champagne. Simultaneously, across San Francisco Bay, courageous volunteers and rescue workers set to work digging through the pancaked rubble of an Oakland freeway in the search for survivors, heedless that they, too, could easily be crushed in an aftershock. Throughout the Bay Area, hundreds volunteered to fight the fires, clear away the mess, assist survivors, and donate food, money, and clothing.

San Francisco's city seal features the image of a phoenix rising from the flames of catastrophe, celebrating the city's fiery past and promising courage in the face of certain future calamity. The 1989 shake possessed only about one fortieth the force of the legendary 1906 quake, and all projections point to the inevitability of another Big One, someday, on at least the scale of '06. Often people from other, more stable, parts of the world have trouble understanding how it is possible to live with such a certainty.

The *San Francisco Bay Guardian,* shortly after the 1989 quake, spoke for many Bay Area residents: "We live in earthquake country. Everybody knows that. It's a choice we've all made, a risk we're all more or less willing to accept as part of our lives. We're gambling against fate, and last week our luck ran out. It was inevitable—as the infamous bumper sticker says, 'Mother Nature bats last.'"

Former San Francisco mayor Dianne Feinstein explained it this way: "Californians seem undaunted. We [know] we'll never be a match for Mother Nature. But the principal thing that seems to arise from the ash and rubble of a quake is the strong resolve to rebuild and get on with life."

There Must Be a There Here Somewhere

"Hollywood is a town that has to be seen to be disbelieved."
—Walter Winchell

By Jane E.
Lasky

While hosting a British broadcaster-friend on his first trip to Los Angeles, I reluctantly took him to the corner of Hollywood and Vine. Driving toward the renowned street-corner, I explained (again) that this part of town isn't the "real" Hollywood. But he wasn't listening. He was on a pilgrimage and too filled with the anticipation of coming upon a sacred place to hear my warning. When we reached the intersection, his reaction was written all over his face: He was, as he later said, "gobsmacked."

As we pulled up to the light, a bedraggled hooker crossed Hollywood Boulevard. Otherwise, nothing was happening. Worse, this looked like someplace where nothing noteworthy or memorable ever had, would, or could happen. The area has been called squalid, but that gives it too much credit for being interesting. All there was to see were a few small and struggling businesses, the hulk of a long-defunct department store, and a couple of unremarkable office buildings.

To rescue the moment from disaster, I went into my standard routine: I pointed out that the northeast corner is where the Brown Derby restaurant once stood. I hoped this would conjure a strong enough image of movie stars dining in a giant hat to blot out the sun-bleached desolation before our eyes. I then recounted historian Richard Alleman's theory about how this unprepossessing street-corner got so famous. Alleman, who wrote *The Movie Lover's Guide to Hollywood*, believes that, because the radio networks, which maintained studios in the vicinity during the 1930s and 1940s, began their broadcasts with the words "brought to you from the corner of Hollywood and Vine . . ." the intersection became glamorous by association—at least to radio listeners who'd never seen it.

Any first-time visitor to Tinseltown is bound for some initial disappointment because, like a matinee idol, the place looks somehow smaller in person. Between the world-famous landmarks and the stars' names embedded in the sidewalks are long stretches of tawdriness that have resisted more than a decade of cleanup and restoration and look all the worse under the vivid glare of the Southern California sun. Even the best of Hollywood looks a little wan and sheepish in broad daylight, as if caught in the act of intruding upon a reality in which it does not belong.

Pressed to show my British friend the "real" Hollywood, I took him on a tour of the more outstanding architecture along Hollywood Boulevard. He was duly captivated by the lunatic exuberance of Hollywood's art-deco movie palaces, exemplified in the zigzaggy Moderne contours of the Pantages, and by the flamboyant absurdity of such thematically designed theaters as Mann's Chinese, the Egyptian, the baroque El Capitan, and other architectural treasures in and around Hollywood that have nothing directly to do with movies, yet are spiritual cousins. Among these are the Tail O' the Pup hotdog stand; the Capitol Records building, looking—deliberately, mind you—like a 14-story stack of 45s; and an assortment of mock Mayan-, Mission-, Moorish-, Moderne-, and made-up-style structures housing video stores, fast-food franchises, and offices.

Yet despite the grand movie houses, the famous names underfoot, and the impressively zany architecture, my friend still felt he'd missed the enchantment, the excitement . . . the movies.

I t's hard to fault the intrepid visitor for expecting a more dynamic, glitzier dream capital. Even seasoned locals, who understand that Hollywood is a state of mind more than a geographical location, can only just manage to intellectualize the concept, and still secretly hunger for evidence that all the magic and glamour come from an appropriately magical and glamorous place. But, except for the occasional gala premiere, you're not likely to see any movie stars in Hollywood. The workaday world of filmmaking and the off-duty hangouts of the movie crowd have largely moved elsewhere. There is only one movie studio—Paramount—still operating within Hollywood's city limits. Universal Studios and the Burbank Studios are both in the San Fernando Valley, across the hills to the north, as are most network-television studios. And, although firmly rooted in the spirit of Hollywood, Disneyland is a world away in Anaheim.

Even a cursory glance at Hollywood's history raises serious doubts that the town was ever as glamorous as we insist it no longer is, and pinning down exactly when its star-studded golden era was is a slippery business. Most people point to the 1930s and 1940s, and the images evoked by those days are irresistible: tan, handsome leading men posed, grinning, with one foot on the running board of a snazzy convertible; heartbreakingly beautiful actresses clad in slinky silk gowns and mink, stepping from long black limousines into the pop of photographers' flash bulbs. Hollywood was an industry—an entire city—whose purpose was to entertain and that further dazzled us with its glittering style of life. The view from ground zero, naturally, was a bit different: long hours; the tedium of the filmmaking process; the rarity of achieving and maintaining a successful career, much less stardom; and, for those who did achieve it, the precarious tightrope walk balancing publicity and privacy. Both sides of the equation are well known and much documented. Indeed, for a place so enamored of its own appeal, Hollywood has never been shy about depicting itself in an unflattering light. Some of the most memorable films ever are rather grim portrayals of the movie business: *A Star is Born, Sunset Boulevard,* and, most recently, *The Player.* That there is a very seamy side to the movie business is very old news and is as much a part of the legend as are fame and fortune. Scandal is a long-running subplot in Hollywood's epic history and has often proved as much a box-office draw as a liability.

The trick to seeing Hollywood is knowing *how* to look at it, as well as where to look for it. The magic of movies is that reality, at least on film, can be made to look any way the filmmakers want it to look. The problem with visiting Hollywood is that your own field of vision isn't as selective as a movie camera's lens, and you're working without a script. It may be helpful to think of Hollywood the town as something of a relic, a symbol of past grandeur (both real and imagined), an open-air museum of artifacts and monuments, but hardly the whole story. Tennessee Williams said, "Ravaged radiance is even better than earnest maintenance," and, as regards Hollywood, I couldn't agree more. It helps a bit to visit in the evening, when the neon, theater marquees, and orchestrated lighting show off the extravagant buildings' shapes to advantage.

It may be that in order to fully experience Hollywood, you have to go outside it.

Only after we'd driven through the canyons, Beverly Hills, and Bel Air and were rounding the last corner of Sunset that leads to the Pacific Coast Highway and out to Malibu did my British visitor feel truly satisfied. "Yes, well," he said finally, "this is really much more like it, then," and seemed almost physically relieved to have found someplace that matched his expectations of luxurious living. And these are physically lovely places, fitting backdrops for a Hollywood lifestyle, and, in fact, where successful movie people live.

The variety of fun and fanciful buildings you'll see throughout Los Angeles reveals, I think, the essence of Hollywood. How else to explain the incongruous jumble of architectural styles sitting side by side in almost any neighborhood? A '50s futuristic house next door to a Queen Anne Victorian, a Craftsman bungalow abutting a French château, a redbrick Georgian across the street from a tile-roof Spanish revival—all on the same block—can be viewed as an extrapolation of a movie-studio back lot, on which a New York street is steps from a Parisian sidewalk café, and both are just a stone's throw from an antebellum plantation house.

If it's celebrity sightings you want, you'll have to take your chances. Many Angelenos live long, happy, and productive lives without ever personally sighting a movie star, but, for the visitor, not seeing one can be a bigger letdown than a rainy week at the beach. Here are a few things you can do to greatly improve the odds of seeing somebody famous: Book a table (weeks in advance) at Spago, Wolfgang Puck's star-studded hot spot off Sunset; dine at Musso & Franks, Hollywood's oldest restaurant and a favorite celebrity hangout for more than 60 years; wander Rodeo Drive on a sunny afternoon, paying close attention to Fred Hayman of Beverly Hills and the Alaia Chez Gallery, known for their high-profile clientele; stroll Melrose Avenue between La

Brea and Fairfax during the dinner hour; stop by Tower Records on Sunset, especially if some blockbuster CD has just been released.

Although it's almost become an amusement-park thrill ride, Universal Studio's tour does give a good in-person approximation of the excitement you get from the movies, and, in the bargain, offers a fun look behind the scenes of filmmaking. Universal Studios aside, the business of Hollywood is making movies and getting people into theaters, not drumming up tourism for the town where it all started. And, besides, there are limits to what even movie magicians can do, especially in broad daylight. Given that the original appeal of Hollywood to moviemakers was the perpetual sunshine that allowed them to shoot outdoors on virtually any day of the year (and thereby make more movies and, therefore, more money) and the ready access to dozens of different landscapes, it is no small irony that over the years the most compelling reason to shoot a movie in Hollywood has become the ready access to soundstages in which the world (this one and others) can be recreated and the weather made to perform on cue. Hollywood has never hesitated to substitute reality with a more convenient or photogenic stand-in. This is an industry whose stock-in-trade is sleight of hand. Along with romance, car chases, and happy endings.

Whatever Hollywood is or isn't, I like the place just the way it is: flawed, scarred, energetic, and full of mysteries and contradictions. Living nearby and seeing it often haven't harmed my love of movies or taken any of the enchantment from the experience of sitting in a darkened theater and giving myself over to the doings on screen. After all, that's where to find the real Hollywood.

Idylling in San Diego

By Edie
Jarolim

Edie Jarolim
is a New
York–born
freelance
writer and
editor who
recently
moved to
Tucson,
which is
within easy
driving
distance of
San Diego.

I've never been to Sea World; performing fish give me the willies. And during the two years I lived within striking distance of Balboa Park, I had to take visiting friends to the San Diego Zoo so many times I began having nightmares about koalas. But if I came to dislike various theme-park aspects of the city, I nevertheless loved San Diego. At first sight.

A typical easterner, I went out to San Diego in the late 1970s expecting to find a smaller version of Los Angeles. The freeways were there, along with a fair share of traffic congestion, but so was an oceanscape of surprisingly pristine beauty. The first drive I took from the University of California, where I was doing graduate research, knocked me for a loop: I rounded a curve on La Jolla Shores Drive to confront a coastline that could match any on the French Riviera.

I was also taken by the distinctiveness of the many shoreline communities. For one thing, the beaches tend to get funkier as you head south from the old-money enclave of La Jolla: Pacific Beach, with its Crystal Pier, looks like an aging Victorian resort taken over by teenagers, while transients and surfers share the turf at Ocean Beach. To the north, Del Mar has a strip of shops that rival those of Rodeo Drive, while Carlsbad and Oceanside show the democratizing influence of nearby Camp Pendleton.

Unlike Los Angeles, San Diego is still strongly defined by its relationship to the ocean—to some degree by default. A building boom in the 1880s was largely based on the assumption that San Diego would become the western terminus of the Santa Fe Railroad line; it hoped in this way to compete with Los Angeles, which was already connected by rail to San Francisco and thus to the national railroad network. The link was completed in 1885 but it proved unsuccessful for a variety of reasons, including the placement of the line through Temecula Canyon, where 30 miles of track were washed out repeatedly in winter rainstorms. The Santa Fe soon moved its West Coast offices to San Bernardino and Los Angeles, and to this day there is no direct rail service from San Diego to the eastern part of the United States.

Instead, San Diego's future was sealed in 1908, when President Theodore Roosevelt's Great White Fleet stopped here on a world tour to demonstrate U.S. naval strength. The Navy, impressed during that visit by the city's excellent harbor and temperate climate, decided to build a destroyer base on San Diego Bay in the 1920s; the newly developing aircraft industry soon followed (Charles Lindbergh's plane *Spirit of St. Louis* was built here). Over the years San Diego's economy became largely dependent on the military and its attendant enterprises, which provided jobs as well as a demand for local goods and services by those stationed here.

San Diego's character—conservative where Los Angeles's is cutting edge—was formed in large part by the presence of its military installations, which now occupy more than 165,000 acres of land in the area. And the city conducts most of its financial business in a single neighborhood, the district fronting San Diego Bay, in this way resembling New York more than its economic rival up the coast. San Diego has set some of its most prestigious scientific facilities on the water—Scripps Institute of Oceanography, naturally, but also Salk Institute. Jonas Salk didn't need the Pacific marine environment for his research, but his regular morning runs along Torrey Pines Beach no doubt cleared his head.

San Diego also has the ocean to thank for its near-perfect weather. A high-pressure system from the north Pacific is responsible for the city's sunshine and dry air; moderating breezes off the sea (caused by the water warming and cooling more slowly than the land) keep the summers relatively cool and the winters warm, and help clear the air of pollution. In the late spring and early summer the difference between the earth and water temperatures generates coastal fogs. This phenomenon was another of San Diego's delightful surprises: I never tired of watching the mist roll in at night, wonderfully romantic, as thick as any I'd ever seen in London and easier to enjoy in the balmy air.

If I loved San Diego from the start, I had a hard time believing in its existence. It was difficult to imagine that a functioning American city could be so attractive, that people lived and worked in such a place every day. Rampant nature conspires in a variety of ways to force you to let your guard down here. In northern East Coast cities, plants are generally orderly and prim: shrubs trimmed, roses demurely draped around railings, tulips in proper rows, the famed cherry blossoms of Washington, DC, profuse in neat columns. In San Diego, the flora, whimsical at best, sometimes border on obscenity. The ubiquitous palms come in comedic pairs: Short, squat trees that look like overgrown pineapples play Mutt to the Jeff of the tall, skinny variety. The aptly named bottle-brush bushes vie for attention with bright red flame trees, beaky orange birds of paradise, and rich purple bougainvillea spilling out over lush green lawns. Only in Hawaii had I previously encountered anthurium, a waxy red plant with a protruding white center that seems to be sticking its tongue out at you. "We're still on the mainland," I felt like telling them all on some days. "Behave yourselves."

Ironically, it was the Victorians who were largely responsible for this indecorous natural profusion. Difficult as it is to imagine now, it's the sparse brown vegetation of San Diego's undeveloped mesas that accurately reflects the climate of the region, technically a semiarid steppe. When Spanish explorer Juan Rodríguez Cabrillo sailed into San Diego Bay in 1542, looking for a shortcut to China, he and his crew encountered a barren, desolate landscape that did not inspire them to settle here, or even stop for very long.

I t wasn't until the late 19th century, when the Mediterranean in general and Italy in particular were all the rage among wealthy residents, that the vegetation now considered characteristic of Southern California was introduced to San Diego. In 1889, money raised by the Ladies Annex to the Chamber of Commerce was used to plant trees in Balboa Park, and between 1892 and 1903 a wide variety of exotic foliage was brought into the city: eucalyptus, cork oak, and rubber trees, to name a few. As homeowners in the area can attest, most of the landscaped local vegetation couldn't survive if it were not watered regularly.

No doubt both the natural setting and the relentlessly fine weather help contribute to the clash of cultures that exists here. The conservative traditionalism of the military presence in town is posed against the liberal hedonism of visiting sunseekers as well as a large local student population. Nude bathing is popular at Black's Beach in La Jolla, a spot that's reasonably private because it's fairly inaccessible: You have to hike down steep cliffs in order to get to the water. Rumor has it that every year a few Navy men are killed when they lose their footing on the cliffs, so intent are they at peering through their binoculars.

Nods to certain So-Cal conventions notwithstanding, San Diego has never come close to approaching the much-touted libertinism of Los Angeles. It has the porno theaters and sleazy clubs you'd expect in a liberty port, but little entertainment of a more sophisticated nature. Celebrities who came down from Hollywood in the 1920s and '30s sought out suites at the La Valencia Hotel and other chic La Jolla locales for the privacy, not the nightlife; the gambling they did at Del Mar racetrack to the north was of the tony, genteel sort. Those who sought thrills—and booze during Prohibition—headed farther south to Mexico. Raymond Chandler, who spent most of his last 13 years in La Jolla and died there in 1959, wrote a friend that the town was "a nice place . . . for old people and their parents."

For all its conservatism, the one thing San Diego didn't conserve was its past—in some cases because there was little to save. When Father Junípero Serra arrived in 1769 to establish the first of the California missions, he did not find the complex dwellings that characterized so many of the Native American settlements he had encountered in Mexico. Nor did his fellow Spaniards improve much upon the site during their stay; the town that the Mexicans took over in 1822 was rudimentary, consisting mostly of rough adobe huts. The mission church had been moved to a new site in 1774 and the original Spanish presidio, abandoned in the 1830s, was in ruins by the next decade; some grass-covered mounds and a giant cross built in 1913 on Presidio Hill, incorporating the tiles of the original structure, are all that's left of it.

Though a romanticized version of the city during the Mexican period (1822–49), today's Old Town district gives a rough idea of San Diego's layout at that time, when somewhat more impressive structures such as Casa Estudillo and the Bandini House were built. San Diego didn't really begin to flourish, however, until 1850, the year that California became a state. At this point the dominant architectural influence came from the East Coast; their enthusiasm for becoming American caused San Diegans to reject their Spanish and Mexican roots as inappropriately "foreign." Thus the first brick structure in the state, the Whaley House (1856), was built in typical New England nautical style. Most of the original Old Town was destroyed by fire in 1872, and a good deal of what was left fell victim to the construction of I–5.

During the Victorian era (1880–1905), the site of the city's development moved south; entrepreneur Alonzo Horton may have miscalculated the success of the rail link to the East Coast but when he bought up a huge lot of land in 1867 for his "Addition," he knew the city's future lay on the harbor. It was in this area, now the city's financial district, that many of the neo-Gothic structures characteristic of the period were built. Perhaps it's perversely fitting that a number of the Victorian relics in downtown San Diego were removed in conjunction with the 15-block Horton Redevelopment Project, of which the huge Horton Plaza shopping complex is the center.

San Diego finally began to reject the East Coast architectural style at the turn of the century, and at the Panama–California Exposition of 1915 the city celebrated its Spanish roots—as well as a Moroccan and Italian past it never had—with a vengeance. The beautiful Spanish-style structures built for the occasion fit right into the Mediterranean landscape that had been cultivated in Balboa Park during the Victorian era; today these buildings house most of the city's museums. San Diego became even more thoroughly Hispanicized during the 1920s and '30s as Spanish Colonial–style homes became popular in new suburbs such as Mission Hills and Kensington, as well as in the beach communities that were developing. Downtown buildings began looking like Italian palaces and Moorish towers.

In some ways, as residents and visitors alike have long feared, San Diego is coming to look more like Los Angeles. Faceless developments are cropping up all over once-deserted canyons and mesas, and the huge, castlelike Mormon temple rising along I–5 north of La Jolla wouldn't look out of place in Disneyland. But in the years since I lived there, San Diego has also become more like a city—that is, what easterners know to be the city in its divinely ordained form.

As recently as 10 years ago, virtually no one went downtown unless required to. It was a desolate place after dark, and people who worked there during the day never stayed around in the evening to play. Gentrification of sorts began in the mid-1970s, as the low rents attracted artists and real-estate speculators. At about the same time the city designated the formerly rough Stingaree neighborhood as the Gaslamp Quarter, but revitalization, in the form of street-level shops and art galleries, didn't really take until Horton Plaza was completed in 1985, and for many years the newly installed gaslights illuminated only the homeless.

The poor and disenfranchised are still here—indeed, many lost their homes to various redevelopment projects—but now the staff at the recently renovated historic U.S. Grant Hotel offers to accompany its guests across the street to Horton Plaza at night so they won't be bothered by vagrants. For the first time there's a concentration of good restaurants, and a serious art and theater scene is developing in the district, too. I like the infusion of life into downtown San Diego, and I even like Horton Plaza, which, with its odd angles and colorful banners, looks like it was designed by Alice in Wonderland's Red Queen. But maybe I miss that spot of unadulterated blight that once helped me to believe in San Diego's reality.

Would I move back to San Diego? In a minute. Like many temporary residents, I left the city vowing to return; unlike many, I've never managed to do more than visit. I used to think that if I had the chance I'd live in Hillcrest, a close-knit inland community with lots of ethnic restaurants and theaters that show foreign films, but I've come to realize that would only be transplanting my East Coast life into the sun. Now I think I'll wait until I'm rich and can afford to move to La Jolla; no doubt I'll be old enough by then to fit in, so I'll fully enjoy that suite in the La Valencia Hotel overlooking the cove.

3 The North Coast

*By Dan
Spitzer*

*Updated by
Emily Miller
and Mark S.
Rosen*

Within the nearly 400 miles of California coastline between the San Francisco Bay and the Oregon border are some of the most beautiful and rugged landscapes in America. Here in the aptly named Redwood Empire are primeval forests of the world's tallest trees, and the nearby shoreline holds a wealth of secluded coves and beaches from which you may well see gray whales migrating, seals sunning, and hawks soaring. The area is also rich in human history, having been the successive domain of Native American Miwoks and Pomos, Russian traders, Hispanic settlers, and more contemporary fishing folk and lumberjacks, all of whom have left legacies that can be seen today. For those in search of untamed natural beauty, great fishing, abundant wildlife, and elegant country inns, the vast panorama of the North Coast is a bit of heaven.

This region is sparsely populated, with only 10 towns of more than 700 inhabitants. Traditionally, residents have made their living from fishing and timber. But today these industries are depressed, and the local economy suffers from the loss of jobs those industries are facing. Tourism, however, is doing well. Some of California's most original restaurants are sprouting up on the North Coast, and locals are lovingly restoring the area's many Victorian mansions to lodge the increasing number of visitors.

Essential Information

Important Addresses and Numbers

An excellent source of information on the North Coast is the **Redwood Empire Association.** Its San Francisco office is filled with brochures, and the staff is knowledgeable. For $3, the association will send you its visitor's guide to the region, or you can pick it up for free at their office and at other stores and tourism offices throughout the North Coast. Write, or stop at the office (785 Market St., 15th Floor, San Francisco, CA 94103, tel. 415/543–8334; open weekdays 9–5).

For **emergency services** on the North Coast, dial 911.

Arriving and Departing

By Plane
United Express (tel. 800/241–6522) offers regular nonstop flights from San Francisco to Eureka Arcata. This is the fastest and most direct way to reach the redwood country. **Hertz** (tel. 800/654–3131) rents cars at the Eureka Arcata airport.

By Car
If Mendocino is your northernmost destination, the most scenic drive from San Francisco is via Route 1, but with its twists and turns, it's slow going, and you should allow at least a full day to get there. Those who wish to explore Point Reyes National Seashore en route might consider an overnight stay at Inverness or another town along the way. You can return directly to San Francisco in about 3½ hours from Mendocino by taking Route 1 south to Route 128, which cuts inland and passes through picturesque farm and forest lands. At Cloverdale, Route 128 intersects with U.S. 101, which continues south to San Francisco.

If Eureka or a point near the Oregon border is your destination, the quickest way from San Francisco is via U.S. 101. This takes a good six to seven hours if you drive straight through. Those with the time and inclination should opt for the more scenic but much slower Route 1, which ultimately intersects with U.S. 101 at Leggett. It would be backbreaking to cover the latter route in less than two days.

Getting Around

By Car Although there are excellent services along Route 1 and U.S. 101, gas stations and mechanics are few and far between on the smaller roads.

Exploring the North Coast

Exploring the Northern California coast is easiest in a car. Route 1 is a beautiful, if sometimes slow and nerve-racking, drive. You'll want to stop frequently to appreciate the views, and there are many portions of the highway along which you won't drive faster than 30–40 mph. You can still have a fine trip even if you don't have much time, but be realistic and don't plan to drive too far in one day (*see* Getting Around, *above*).

We've arranged the exploring section for a trip from San Francisco heading north. The first section follows Route 1 north past Fort Bragg to its intersection with U.S. 101. The second section follows U.S. 101 through the Redwood Empire.

Highlights for First-Time Visitors

Founders Grove, Humboldt Redwoods State Park
Mendocino
Old Town Eureka
Point Reyes National Seashore

The North Coast via Route 1

Numbers in the margin correspond to points of interest on the North Coast maps.

To reach Route 1 heading north from San Francisco, cross the Golden Gate Bridge and proceed north on U.S. 101 to the Stinson Beach/Route 1 exit. Follow Route 1 north, and as it winds uphill, you
❶ will see a turnoff for **Muir Woods.** Muir Woods National Monument and the adjoining Mt. Tamalpais State Park are described (as day
❷ trips) in Chapter 6. Past this turnoff, the town of **Stinson Beach** has the most expansive sands (4,500 feet) in Marin County. On any hot summer weekend, every road to Stinson Beach is jam-packed, so factor this into your plans. Along Bolinas Lagoon, you will find the
❸ **Audubon Canyon Ranch,** a 1,000-acre wildlife sanctuary. In the spring, the public is invited to take to the trails to see great blue heron and great egret tree nestings. There is a small museum with displays on the geology and natural history of the region, a natural history bookstore, and a picnic area. *Tel. 415/868–9244. Donation requested. Open mid-Mar.–mid-July, weekends and holidays 10–4.*

At the northern edge of Bolinas Lagoon, a couple of miles beyond the Audubon Canyon Ranch, take the unmarked road running west from Route 1, which leads to the sleepy town of **Bolinas.** Some residents of Bolinas are so wary of tourism that whenever the state tries to post signs, they tear them down. Birders should head down Mesa
❹ Road to the **Point Reyes Bird Observatory,** a sanctuary and research center within the National Seashore harboring nearly 225 species of bird life. *Tel. 415/868–0655. Admission free. Banding May–Nov.,*

The North Coast (Rockport to Oregon)

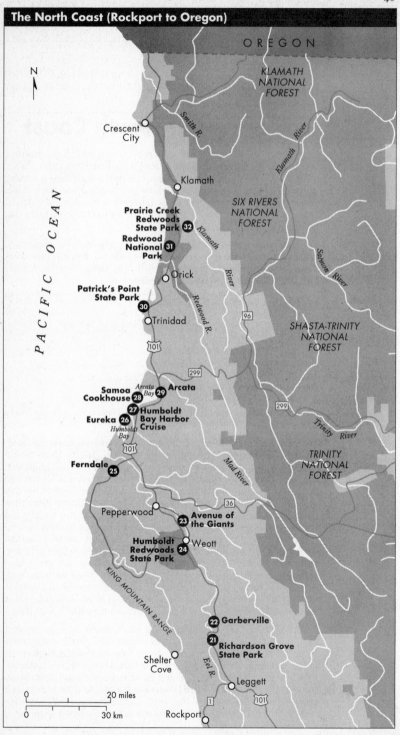

OREGON

KLAMATH
NATIONAL
FOREST

Smith R.

Crescent
City

Klamath

Klamath River

SIX RIVERS
NATIONAL
FOREST

Salmon River

**Prairie Creek
Redwoods
State Park** ③②

Klamath River

**Redwood
National** ③①
Park

Orick

River

**Patrick's Point
State Park**
③⓪

Redwood R.

96

Trinidad

SHASTA-TRINITY
NATIONAL
FOREST

101

299

Samoa Arcata
Cookhouse ②⑧ ②⑨ **Arcata**
Bay
②⑦ **Humboldt**
Eureka ②⑥ **Bay Harbor**
Cruise
Humboldt
Bay

299

Trinity River

101

TRINITY
NATIONAL
FOREST

Ferndale
②⑤

Mad River

36

Pepperwood

②③ **Avenue of
the Giants**

**Humboldt
Redwoods
State Park** ②④ Weott

②② **Garberville**

②① **Richardson Grove
State Park**

KING MOUNTAIN RANGE

Shelter
Cove

Eel R.

Leggett

0   20 miles

0   30 km

1

101

Rockport

PACIFIC OCEAN

N

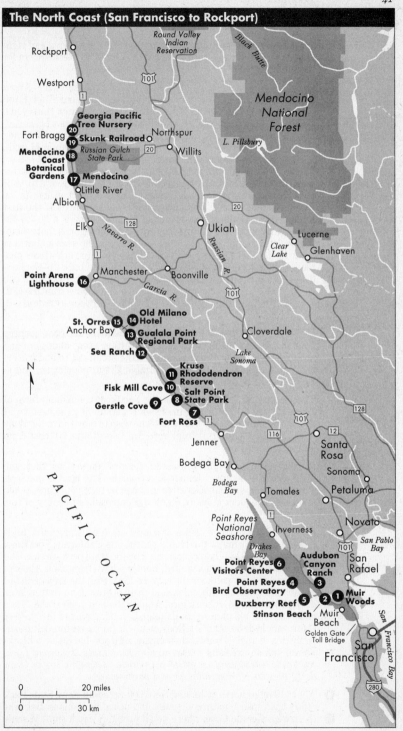

The North Coast (San Francisco to Rockport)

daily; Dec.–Apr., weekends and Wed., weather permitting. Visitor center open daily 8–6.

On the way back to Bolinas, go right on Overlook Drive and right
5 again on Elm Avenue until you come to **Duxberry Reef,** known for
its fine tide pools.

Returning to Route 1, you will pass pastoral horse farms. About
6 ⅓ mile past Olema, look for a sign marking the turnoff for **Point
Reyes National Seashore's Bear Valley Visitors Center.** Here you'll
find exhibits of park wildlife as well as helpful rangers who can advise you about beaches, visits to the lighthouse for whale watching
(the season for gray-whale migration is mid-December–March),
hiking trails, and camping. (Camping, for backpackers only, is free;
reservations should be made through the visitors center.) No matter
what your interests, the beauty of this wilderness is worth your
time. A reconstructed Miwok Indian Village is a short walk from the
visitors center. It provides insight into the daily lives of the first
human inhabitants of this region. The lighthouse is a 30- to 40-
minute drive from the visitors center, across rolling hills that resemble Scottish heath. On busy weekends during the season, parking
near the lighthouse may be difficult. The view alone lures most people to make the effort of walking down–and then back up–the hundreds of steps from the cliff tops to the lighthouse below; but if you
choose to skip the descent, you can still see the whales from the cliff.
*Tel. 415/663–1092. Admission free. Visitors center open weekdays 9–5,
weekends 8–5.*

If you decide to stay overnight in this area, there are good country
inns and decent restaurants (not to mention great hiking) in and
around the towns of **Inverness,** where the architecture and cuisine
reflect the influence of the once-sizable Czech population, and in
Point Reyes Station.

The Russian River empties into the Pacific at the fishing town of
Jenner. If you are lucky, you may spot seals sunning themselves off
the banks of the estuary. Travelers who wish to move on to the Wine
Country (*see* Chapter 5) from here can take Route 116 east from
Jenner.

What is perhaps the most dramatic stretch of North Coast shoreline
is off Route 1 between Jenner and Gualala. The road is one long
series of steep switchbacks after another, so take your time, relax,
and make frequent stops to enjoy the unparalleled beauty of this
wild coast.

About 12 miles north of Jenner is a must-see for history buffs. Built
7 in 1812, Russia's major fur-trading outpost in California, **Fort Ross,**
has been painstakingly reconstructed by the state park service. The
Russians brought Aleut sea-otter hunters down from their Alaskan
bailiwicks to hunt pelts for the czar. In 1841, with the area depleted
of seal and otter, the Russians sold their post to John Sutter, later
of Gold Rush fame. After a local Anglo rebellion against the Mexicans, the land fell under U.S. domain, becoming part of the state of
California in 1850. At Fort Ross, you will find a restored Russian
Orthodox chapel, a redwood stockade, officers' barracks, a block-
house, and an excellent museum. *Fort Ross State Historical Park,
tel. 707/847–3286. Day use fee: $5 per vehicle, $4 senior citizens. Open
daily 10–4:30. No dogs allowed past parking lot.*

8 About 19 miles north of Jenner, the 6,000-acre **Salt Point State Park**
offers a glimpse of nature virtually untouched by humans. Begin at
9 the park's **Gerstle Cove,** where you'll probably catch sight of seals

sunning themselves on the beach's rocks, and deer roaming in the meadowlands. The unusual formations in the sandstone are called "tafoni," and are the product of hundreds of years of erosion. Next

⑩ take the *very* short drive to Salt Point's **Fisk Mill Cove,** where a five-minute walk following the trail uphill brings you to a bench from which there is a dramatic overview of Sentinel Rock and the pounding surf below. Part of the wonder of this spot is that it's all less than a mile off Route 1. *Tel. 707/847–3221. Day use fee: $5 per vehicle, $4 senior citizens. Camping: $14 peak season, $12 off-season, $2 senior-citizen discount. Open daily sunrise–sunset.*

⑪ About 200 yards beyond Fisk Mill Cove, look for the sign to **Kruse Rhododendron Reserve.** If you're around here in May, take this turn-off to see the towering pink flowers in this 317-acre reserve. *Admission free. Open daily.*

⑫ **Sea Ranch** is a development of pricey second homes, on 5,000 acres overlooking the Pacific about 10 miles south of Gualala. There was a great outcry by conservationists when this development was announced, and much controversy ensued. To appease the critics, Sea Ranch built publicly accessible trails down to the beaches. Even some militant environmentalists deem architect Charles Moore's housing reasonably congruent with the surroundings; others find the weathered wood buildings beautiful.

⑬ An excellent whale-watching spot is **Gualala Point Regional Park** (tel. 707/785–2377), where there is also picnicking (day use: $3 per vehicle) and camping ($14 year round). The park is right off Route 1 and is well marked; entry is possible 8–sunset. Just north of the town of Gualala on Route 1 are two inns worth a visit or a stay (*see*

⑭ Dining and Lodging, *below*). The **Old Milano Hotel,** listed in the National Registry of Historic Places, is an elegant 1905 country inn

⑮ overlooking Castle Rock. **St. Orres,** with its Russian-style turrets, is also a unique bed-and-breakfast inn and has one of the best restaurants on the North Coast. All along this stretch north to Mendocino are fine B&Bs and small hotels, perched in and around the coastal cliffs of tiny former lumber ports such as Elk, Albion, and Little River.

For a dramatic view of the surf, take the turnoff north of the fishing

⑯ village of Point Arena to the **Point Arena Lighthouse** (tel. 707/882–2777). First constructed in 1870, the lighthouse was destroyed by the 1906 earthquake that also devastated San Francisco. Rebuilt in 1907, it towers 115 feet from its base, 50 feet above the sea. *Admission: $2.50 adults, 50¢ children under 12. Tours daily 11–2:30, extended hours (to 3:30) in summer and on some holiday weekends.*

⑰ **Mendocino** is the tourism heartbeat on the North Coast and has become a mecca for artists and visitors alike. The appeal is obvious: sweeping ocean views and a stately Victorian flavor, best exemplified by the gingerbreadlike **MacCallum House** (45020 Albion St.) and the **Mendocino Hotel** (45080 Main St.). (For details, *see* Dining and Lodging, *below*.) Water towers dot the town; Mendocino has never had an underground public water system. The town is most easily and best seen on foot, and there are numerous art galleries to stop in while walking around. The **Mendocino Art Center** (45200 Little Lake St., tel. 707/937–5818) has exhibits, art classes, concerts, and a theater. The **Kelley House Museum** (45007 Albion St., tel. 707/937–5791; admission $1; open June–Sept., daily 1–4, Oct.–May, Fri.–Mon. 1–4) is a refurbished 1861 structure displaying historical photographs of Mendocino's logging days, antique cameras, Victorian-era clothing, furniture, and artifacts. Also on Albion Street is

the green and red **Chinese Joss Temple,** dating to 1882. Another restored structure, the **Ford House,** built in 1854, is on Main Street
and serves as the visitors center for Mendocino Headlands State
Park (tel. 707/937–5397, open year round, daily 11–4, with possible
temporary midweek closings in winter; history walks Sat. at 1 PM).
The park itself consists of the cliffs that border the town; access is
free.

⑱ Off Route 1, between Mendocino and Fort Bragg, are the **Mendocino Coast Botanical Gardens.** The gardens were established as a
private preserve in 1962. In 1982 the Mendocino Coast Park District
acquired 17 acres and the Coastal Conservancy added another 30
acres in 1991. Along 2 miles of coastal trails, with ocean views and
observation points for whale-watching, are a splendid array of flowers, with the rhododendron season at its peak from April to June,
and perennials in bloom from May to September. Fuchsias, heather,
and azaleas are resplendent here. This is a fine place to stop for a
picnic. *Tel. 707/964–4352. Admission: $5 adults, $4 senior citizens, $3
children 13–17 and students. Open Mar.–Oct., daily 9–5; Nov.–Feb.,
daily 9–4.*

Fort Bragg is the commercial center of Mendocino County. While
Mendocino boomed with bed-and-breakfasts, art galleries, and
tourists, this loggers' town retained its old-fashioned, workaday
⑲ character. It is also headquarters of the famous and popular **Skunk
Railroad,** on which you can take scenic half- or full-day tours
through redwood forests inaccessible by automobile. A remnant of
the region's logging days, the Skunk Railroad line dates from 1885,
and travels a route from Fort Bragg on the coast to the town of
Willits, 40 miles inland. A fume-spewing, self-propelled train car
that shuttled passengers along the railroad got nicknamed the
Skunk Train, and the entire line has been called that ever since.
Excursions are now given on historic trains and replicas of the
Skunk Train motorcar that are more aromatic than the original. In
summer you have a choice of going part way to Northspur, a three-
hour round-trip, or making the full seven-hour journey to Willits
and back. *California Western Railroad Inc., Fort Bragg, tel. 707/964–
6371. Fort Bragg–Willits: departs daily 9:20. Admission: $23 adults,
$11 children. Fort Bragg–Northspur: departs 2nd Sat. in June–3rd
Sat. in Sept., daily 9:20 and 1:35; Sept. 23–Dec. 4, Dec. 22–31, and Mar.
25–June 7, daily 10 and 2; Dec. 7–21 and Feb. 2–Mar. 17, weekends 10
and 2. Admission: $18.50 adults, $9 children.*

⑳ The **Georgia Pacific Tree Nursery** (Main St. at Cypress St., tel.
707/964–5651) has a visitors center, picnic grounds, and a self-guided
nature trail (open weekdays 8–4). Those who like fishing can charter
boats out of Noyo Harbor, at the southern end of town (*see* Sports,
below).

North on Route 1 from Fort Bragg, past the coastal mill town of
Westport, the road cuts inland around the **King Range,** a stretch of
mountain so rugged that it was impossible to build the intended
major highway through it. Route 1 joins the larger U.S. 101 at the
town of Leggett and continues north into the redwood country of
Humboldt and Del Norte counties.

The Redwood Empire

㉑ **Richardson Grove State Park,** north of Leggett, along U.S. 101,
marks your first encounter with the truly giant redwoods, but there
are even more magnificent stands farther north. A few miles below
㉒ **Garberville,** perched along Eel River, is an elegant Tudor resort, the

Benbow Inn (*see* Dining and Lodging, *below*). Even if you are not staying here, stop in for a drink or meal and a look at the architecture and gardens.

㉓ For an unforgettable treat, take the turnoff for the **Avenue of the Giants** just north of Garberville. Along this stretch of two-lane blacktop you will find yourself enveloped by some of the tallest trees on the planet, the coastal redwoods. This road cuts through part of

㉔ the **Humboldt Redwoods State Park,** 51,222 acres of redwoods and waterways, and follows the south fork of the Eel River. The visitors center near **Weott** (tel. 707/946–2263) is open in the spring and summer, and can provide information on the region's recreational opportunities, and flora and fauna. **Founders Grove** contains some of the tallest trees in the park. The grove's highest tree, at 362 feet, fell in 1991.

㉕ Detour 5 miles west of U.S. 101 from Fortuna to **Ferndale.** This stately town, which is still recovering from an April 1992 earthquake that centered here, maintains some of the most sumptuous Victorian homes in California, many of them built by 19th-century timber barons and Scandinavian dairy farmers. The queen of them all is the **Gingerbread Mansion** (400 Berding St.), once a hospital and now refurbished as a bed-and-breakfast (*see* Dining and Lodging, *below*). A beautiful, sloped **graveyard** sits on Ocean Avenue west of Main Street. Numerous shops carry a local map for self-guided tours of this lovingly preserved town.

The **Ferndale Museum** has a storehouse of antiques from the turn of the century. *515 Shaw Ave., tel. 707/786–4466. Admission: $1 adults, 50¢ children 6–16. Open Oct.–June 1, Wed.–Sat. 11–4, Sun. 1–4; also Tues. 11–4 in summer.*

㉖ With 27,000 inhabitants, **Eureka** ranks as the North Coast's largest city. It has gone through cycles of boom and bust, first with mining and later with timber and fishing. There are nearly 100 elegant Victorian buildings here, many of them well preserved or refurbished. The most splendid is the **Carson Mansion** (at M and 2nd Sts.), built in 1885 by the Newsom brothers for timber baron William Carson. The house is now occupied by a private men's club. Across the street is another Newsom extravaganza popularly known as **The Pink Lady.** For proof that contemporary architects still have the skills to design lovely Victoriana, have a look at the **Carter House** B&B inn (3rd and L Sts., *see* Dining and Lodging, *below*) and keep in mind that it was built in the 1980s, not the 1880s. The **Chamber of Commerce** can provide maps of the town and information on how to join organized tours. *2112 Broadway, tel. 707/442–3738. Open weekdays 9–5.*

Old Town Eureka is one of the most outstanding Victorian-era commercial districts in California, with buildings dating from the 1860s to 1915. The **Clarke Museum** has an extraordinary collection of northwestern California Native-American basketry and contains artifacts from Eureka's Victorian, logging, and maritime heritage. *240 E. St., tel. 707/443–1947. Donations accepted. Open Feb.–Dec., Tues.–Sat. and July 4 noon–4.*

At the south end of Eureka stands **Fort Humboldt,** which guarded settlers against the Indians, and is now a state historic park. Ulysses S. Grant was posted here in 1854. On the fort's grounds are re-creations of the logging industry's early days, including a logging museum, some ancient steam engines, and a logger's cabin. *3431 Fort Ave., tel. 707/445–6567. Open daily 9–4.*

㉗ To explore the waters around Eureka, take a **Humboldt Bay Harbor Cruise.** You can observe some of the region's bird life while sailing past fishing boats, oyster beds, and decaying timber mills. *Pier at C St., tel. 707/445–1910 or 707/444–9440. Fare: $8.50 adults, $7.50 senior citizens and children 12–17, $5.50 children 6–11. Departs May— Sept., daily 1, 2:30, and 4. Cocktail-cruise fare: $5.50. Departs daily 5:30.*

㉘ Across the bridge in Samoa is the **Samoa Cookhouse** (tel. 707/442– 1659), an example from about the 1860s of the cookhouses that once stood in every lumber and mill town. There is a museum displaying antique culinary artifacts, and breakfast, lunch, and dinner are served family style at long wood tables. (*See* Dining and Lodging, *below.*)

㉙ Just north of Eureka is the pleasant college town of **Arcata,** home of Humboldt State University. One of the few California burgs that retains a town square, Arcata also has some restored Victorian buildings. The town square holds a farmer's market on Tuesday evenings and Saturday mornings May through November. For a self-guided tour, pick up a map from the **Chamber of Commerce.** *1062 G St., tel. 707/822–3619. Open weekdays 10–4.*

After taking the turnoff for the town of **Trinidad,** follow the road a mile to one of the most splendid harbors on the West Coast. First visited by a Portuguese expedition in 1595, the waters here are now sailed by fishing boats trolling for salmon. Picturesque Trinidad Bay's harbor cove and rock formations look both raw and tranquil. *Open daily sunrise–sunset.*

㉚ Twenty-five miles north of Eureka is **Patrick's Point State Park.** Set on a forested plateau almost 200 feet above the surf, the park affords good whale- and sea-lion-watching. There are also tide pools and a small museum with natural history exhibits. *Tel. 707/677–3570. Day use fee: $5 per car; $4 senior citizens. Camping: $14 per car, $12 senior citizens ($2 less in winter).*

㉛ Those continuing north will pass through the 113,200 acres of **Redwood National Park.** After 115 years of intensive logging, this vast region of tall trees came under government protection in 1968, marking the California environmentalists' greatest victory over the timber industry. The park encompasses three state parks (Prairie Creek Redwoods, Del Norte Coast Redwoods, and Jedediah Smith Redwoods), and is more than 40 miles long. *Redwood National Park Headquarters, 1111 2nd St., Crescent City, CA 95531, tel. 707/464– 6101.*

For detailed information about the Redwood National Park, stop at the **Redwood Information Center** in Orick (tel. 707/488–3461). There you can also get a free permit to drive up the steep, 17-mile road (the last 6 miles are gravel) to reach the **Tall Trees Grove,** where a 3-mile round-trip hiking trail leads to the world's first-, third- and fifth-tallest redwoods. Whale-watchers will find the deck of the visitors center an excellent observation point, and birders will enjoy the nearby **Freshwater Lagoon,** a popular layover for migrating waterfowl.

Within **Lady Bird Johnson Grove,** just off Bald Hill Road, is a short circular trail to resplendent redwoods. This section of the park was dedicated by, and named for, the former first lady. For additional spectacular scenery, take Davison Road along a stunning seascape to **Fern Canyon.** This gravel road winds through 4 miles of second-

growth redwoods, then hugs a bluff 100 feet above the pounding
Pacific surf for another 4 miles.

32 To reach the entrance to Redwood's **Prairie Creek Redwoods State
Park,** take the Elk Prairie Parkway exit off the Route 101 bypass.
Extra space has been paved alongside the park lands, providing fine
vantage points from which to observe an imposing herd of **Roosevelt
elk** grazing in the adjoining meadow. **Revelation Trail** in Prairie
Creek is fully accessible to the disabled.

The route through the redwoods and sea views will ultimately lead
past the Klamath River, home of the famous king salmon, to Del
Norte County's largest town, **Crescent City.**

Travelers continuing north to the Smith River near the Oregon border will find fine trout and salmon fishing as well as a profusion of
flowers. Ninety percent of America's lily bulbs are grown in this
area.

Shopping

In the charming town of **Inverness,** Shaker Shops West (5 Inverness
Way, tel. 415/669–7256) has an exceptional array of reproduction
Shaker furniture and gift items. There is a turn-of-the-century sen-
sibility to the fine works exhibited here; open Tuesday–Saturday
11–5, Sunday noon–5. In **Point Reyes Station,** Gallery Route One
(11101 Rte. 1, tel. 415/663–1347) is a nonprofit cooperative of 24 area
artists in all media, open Friday through Monday from 11 to 5,
Thursday through Monday in summer.

Mendocino has earned a reputation as the artistic center of the
North Coast. So many fine artists exhibit their wares here, and the
streets of this compact town are so easily walkable, that you're sure
to find a gallery with something that strikes your fancy. You might
start at the Mendocino Art Center (45200 Little Lake St., tel.
707/937–5818), where artists teach courses and display their creations.

The Victorian village of **Ferndale,** in the Redwood Empire, is a magnet for fine painters, potters, and carpenters. Just walk down Main
Street and stop in to browse at any of the stores along its three
principal blocks.

Eureka has several fine art shops and galleries in the district running from C to I streets between 2nd and 3rd streets. One of note
is the Old Town Art Gallery (233 F St., tel. 707/445–2315). Another
recommended gallery is the Humboldt Cultural Center (422 1st St.,
tel. 707/442–2611 or 707/442–0278).

Sports

The following sporting attractions and facilities are listed in a south-
to-north order.

Bicycling   For the hardy rider who wishes to take in the full beauty of the North
Coast by mountain bike, there are a number of rental services in
San Francisco and the major North Coast towns. Some rental shops
on the coast are **Trailhead Rentals** (88 Bear Valley Rd., corner of
Rte. 1, Olema, tel. 415/663–1958) and **Catch-a-Canoe and Bicycles
Too** (Stanford Inn by the Sea, Mendocino, tel. 707/937–0273).

Camping	Campground reservations for all state parks are usually necessary in summer. For reservations, call MISTIX, tel. 800/444–7275.
Canoeing	Among the many canoe liveries of the North Coast are **Catch-a-Canoe and Bicycles Too** (Stanford Inn by the Sea, Mendocino, tel. 707/937–0273) and **Benbow Inn** (Garberville, tel. 707/923–2124).
Fishing	For ocean fishing, there are plenty of outfits from which you can charter a boat with equipment provided. Among them are **Bodega Bay Sportfishing** (tel. 707/875–3344), **Noyo Fishing Center** (Fort Bragg, tel. 707/964–7609), **Lost Coast Landing** (Shelter Cove, tel. 707/986–7624, closed winter), and **Blue Pacific Charters** (Eureka, tel. 707/442–6682). You can fish for salmon and steelhead in the rivers. There's particularly good abalone diving around Jenner, Fort Ross, Point Arena, Westport, Shelter Cove, and Trinidad.
Golf	Among others, there are courses open to the public at **Bodega Harbour** (Bodega Bay, tel. 707/875–3538), **Little River Inn** (nine holes, Little River, tel. 707/937–5667), **Benbow Inn** (nine holes, Garberville, tel. 707/923–2124), and **Eureka Golf Course** (tel. 707/443–4808).
Horseback Riding	Numerous stables and resorts offer guided rides on the North Coast, including **Five Brooks Stables** (Point Reyes, tel. 415/663–1570), **Chanslor Guest Ranch** (Bodega Bay, tel. 707/875–2721), **Benbow Inn** (Garberville, tel. 707/923–2124), and **Lazy L Ranch** (Arcata, tel. 707/822–6736).
River Tours	**Eel River Delta Tours** (Eureka, tel. 707/786–4187) emphasizes wildlife and history in the estuary.
Whale-Watching	From any number of excellent observation points along the coast, you can watch whales during their annual migration season from December through March. Another option is a **whale-watching cruise.** Some cruises run June–November to the Farallon Islands to watch the Blue and Humpback whale migration. Possibilities include: **Oceanic Society Expeditions** (San Francisco, tel. 415/474–3385) and **New Sea Angler and Jaws** (Bodega Bay, tel. 707/875–3495).

Beaches

Although the waters of the Pacific along the North Coast are fine for seals, most humans find the temperatures downright arctic. But when it comes to spectacular cliffs and seascapes, the North Coast beaches are second to none. So pack a picnic and take in the pastoral beauty of the wild coast. Explore tide pools, watch for seals, or dive for abalone. Don't worry about crowds: On many of these beaches you will have the sands largely to yourself. Day use is usually $5 or $6 per car, depending on the area.

The following beaches are particularly recommended and are listed in a south-to-north order:

Muir Beach. Located just off Route 1, 3 miles from Muir Woods. Free.

Duxbury Reef. Tide pools. From Bolinas, take Mesa Road off Olema–Bolinas Road; make a left on Overlook Drive and a right on Elm Avenue to the beach parking lot.

Point Reyes National Seashore. Limantour Beach is one of the most beautiful of Point Reyes sands. Free.

Tomales Bay State Park. Take Sir Francis Drake Boulevard off Route 1 toward Point Reyes National Seashore, then follow Pierce Point Road to the park.

Fort Ross State Park. About 9 miles north of Jenner.

Sea Ranch Public Access Trails and Beaches. Off Route 1 south of Gualala.

Manchester State Beach. About 9 miles north of Point Arena.

Agate Beach. Tide pools. Set within Patrick's Point State Park off U.S. 101 about 25 miles north of Eureka.

Dining and Lodging

Dining
For years, the better dining establishments of the North Coast specialized in fresh salmon and trout. With the growth of the tourist industry, a surprising variety of fare ranging from Japanese to Continental cuisine is now being served at good restaurants charging reasonable prices. Unless otherwise noted, dress is informal. During the winter months, December to mid-March, tourism slackens on the North Coast; consequently, restaurant days and/or hours are often reduced. It is best to call ahead to check the schedule.

Highly recommended restaurants are indicated by a star ★.

Category	Cost*
$$$$	over $35
$$$	$25–$35
$$	$15–$25
$	under $15

per person for a three-course meal, excluding drinks, service, and tax

Lodging
The North Coast offers some of the most attractive lodging in the country, with a price range to accommodate virtually every pocketbook. You will find elaborate Victorian homes, grand old hotels, and modest motels. Many bed-and-breakfasts along the coast are sold out on weekends months in advance, so reserve early. Budget travelers will find youth hostels in Point Reyes National Seashore, Klamath, and Leggett (summer only).

Highly recommended hotels are indicated by a star ★.

Category	Cost*
$$$$	over $100
$$$	$75–$100
$$	$50–$75
$	under $50

All prices are for a double room, excluding tax.

Albion
Dining
Ledford House. This restaurant specializes in new American cuisine, which the manager translates as "doing whatever we want." The menu is divided into hearty bistro dishes—mainly stews and pastas—and equally large-portioned examples of California cuisine: Ahi tuna, grilled meats, and the like. Ledford House is on a bluff with views—and the auditory accompaniment—of the crashing waves. *3000 N. Hwy. 1, tel. 707/937–0282. Reservations advised. AE, MC, V. No lunch. Open summer Tues.–Sun.; winter Wed.–Sun.* $$$

Dining and
Lodging
★

Albion River Inn. Overlooking the sea, this attractive inn is composed of modern, two-room cabins overlooking the dramatic bridge and seascape where the Albion River empties into the Pacific. Rooms are bright and have fireplaces, decks facing the ocean, and either a Jacuzzi or a tub for two. The decor ranges from antique furnishings to wide-back willow chairs. A full breakfast is included. In the glassed-in dining room, which serves grilled dishes and fresh seafood, the views are as spectacular as the food. *3790 N. Rte. 1, Box 100, 95410, tel. 707/937–1919 or 800/479–4944 (from Northern California only), fax 707/937–2604. 20 rooms. Facilities: restaurant (dinner only), horseback riding 15 mi away. AE, MC, V. $$$–$$$$*

Arcata
Dining

Abruzzi. Salads and hefty pasta dishes take up most of the menu at this upscale Italian restaurant just off the town square. Abruzzi serves *panini* (Italian sandwiches) at lunch, and pastas (such as Linguine Pescara, with a spicy seafood-and-tomato sauce) for lunch and dinner. The dining room and large bar are comfortably decorated in dark colors and wood, lit by candles. *791 8th St., at the corner of H St. (entrance on H St.), tel. 707/826–2345. Reservations advised. AE, D, DC, MC, V. No lunch weekends. $$*

Crosswinds. Recently rebuilt after a major fire, the restaurant offers good Continental cuisine in a casual, sunny Victorian. Classical musicians provide the entertainment. *10th and I Sts., tel. 707/826–2133. Reservations advised on weekends. MC, V. No dinner. Closed Mon. $*

Lodging

Hotel Arcata. The rooms of this conveniently located historic landmark overlooking the town square have character, with their flowered bedspreads and clawfoot bathtubs. The hotel is owned by the Yurok tribe, a Native-American nation based north of Arcata. Rates include use of a nearby health club as well as (on weekdays) Continental breakfast. *708 9th St., 95521, tel. 707/826–0217 or 800/344–1221. 32 rooms with bath. Facilities: restaurant. AE, DC, MC, V. $$*

Bodega Bay
Dining and
Lodging

Inn at the Tides. This complex of modern condominium-style buildings offers spacious rooms with high, peaked ceilings and uncluttered decor. All the rooms here have a view of the harbor and some have fireplaces. Continental breakfast is included. The inn's two restaurants serve excellent seafood dishes. *800 Rte. 1, Box 640, 94923, tel. 707/875–2751 or 800/541–7788, fax 707/875–3023. 86 rooms. Facilities: room service, 2 restaurants, cable TV, refrigerator, pool, sauna, Jacuzzi, laundromat. AE, MC, V. $$$–$$$$*

Crescent City
Dining

Harbor View Grotto. This glassed-in dining hall overlooking the Pacific prides itself on fresh fish. *155 Citizen's Dock Rd., tel. 707/464–3815. MC, V. No lunch. $–$$*

Lodging

Curly Redwood Lodge. This lodge was built from a single, huge redwood tree, which produced 57,000 board feet of lumber. The decor in the guest rooms also makes the most of that tree, with paneling, platform beds, and dressers built into the walls. The rooms are a decent size, and there is a fireplace in the lobby. *701 Redwood Hwy. S, 95531, tel. 707/464–2137, fax 707/464–1655. 36 rooms. Facilities: color TV, phone. AE, DC, MC, V. $–$$*

Elk
Dining and
Lodging

Harbor House. Constructed in 1916 by a timber company to entertain its guests, this redwood ranch-style house has a dining room with a view of the Pacific. Five of the six rooms in the main house have fireplaces, and some are furnished with antiques original to the house. There are also four smallish cottages with fireplaces and decks. The path to the inn's private beach takes you through the lovely garden. Breakfast and dinner are included in the cost of the room. The restaurant ($$$$), which serves Continental cuisine, is highly recommended; reservations are required and there's limited seating for nonhotel guests. *5600 S. Rte. 1, 95432, tel. 707/877–3203. 10 rooms. No credit cards. $$$$*

Lodging **Elk Cove Inn.** Private, romantic cottages are perched on a bluff above the pounding surf. One room's shower has a full-length window that shares this magnificent view of the Pacific. Skylights, wood-burning stoves, and hand-embroidered cloths are just some of the amenities. The 1883 Victorian home features four rooms with spacious dormer windows and window seats, a parlor and ocean-view deck. A Victorian-style gazebo is perched on the edge of the bluff. A full gourmet breakfast is included. *6300 S. Rte. 1, Box 367, 95432, tel. 707/877–3321. 4 cabin rooms (2 with wood stoves) and 4 rooms in Victorian building with bath. No credit cards. $$$–$$$$*

Eureka **301.** Mark and Christi Carter, owners of Eureka's fanciest hotels,
Dining also run one of the town's best restaurants. Most of the vegetables
★ and herbs used in the food are grown at the hotel's greenhouse and nearby ranch, to provide the kitchen with the freshest possible ingredients. Try the superbly presented fish or duck, and don't skip the appetizers—especially the warm goat cheese and pâté. *301 L St., tel. 707/444–8062. AE, D, DC, MC, V. No lunch. Open Thurs.–Sun. Reservations advised during summer. $$–$$$*

Cafe Waterfront. A small corner café with checkered tablecloths and a long bar with TV, Cafe Waterfront is snugly located across from the marina. Sandwiches and affordable seafood dishes dominate the menu. *102 F St., tel. 707/443–9190. Reservations advised Thurs.–Sat. MC, V. $$*

Lazio's. Another restaurant with a prow-of-the-ship theme, Lazio's is notable for its hefty classic seafood and steak dinners, complete with soup, salad, and potatoes. Nouvelle cuisine it's not. *327 2nd St. at E St., tel. 707/443–9717. Reservations advised Fri. and Sat. MC, V. $$*

Ramone's. A bakery and café by day, Ramone's is a casual bistro at night, serving some of Eureka's best California cuisine. The menu changes about twice a week, and emphasizes fish, meats, pasta, and seasonal vegetables. *209 E St., tel. 707/445–1642. Reservations advised. MC, V. Closed Mon. and Tues. (bakery closed holidays only). $$*

★ **Samoa Cookhouse.** A local lumberman's watering hole dating back to the early years of the century, this eatery serves three substantial meals family-style at long wooden tables. Meat dishes dominate the menu. *Short drive from Eureka, across Samoa Bridge, off Rte. 101 on Samoa Rd. (via the R St. Bridge), tel. 707/442–1659. AE, D, MC, V. $*

Lodging **Hotel Carter, Carter House, and Cottage.** Between two small inns
★ and one hotel, the Carter family is single-handedly raising property values in downtown Eureka. The Carter House, built in 1982 following the floor plan of a San Francisco mansion, has an antique-laden sitting area and gorgeous rooms with heirloom furniture. The Cottage two doors down, an original Victorian, contains three rooms and a big sitting area decorated in contemporary style, with lots of rustic wood and Southwestern motifs. The hotel, kitty-corner to the Carter House, has an elegant lobby and suites. Handsome brocaded spreads cover the beds; some rooms have fireplaces and whirlpool tubs. A large breakfast, served in the hotel's sunny dining room, is included with a night's stay in any of the three buildings. *Hotel: 301 L St., 95501, tel. and fax 707/444–8062; 23 rooms. Carter House: 1033*

3rd St., tel. 707/445–1390; 5 rooms. Cottage: 3rd St., tel. 707/445–1390; 3 rooms. All three: AE, D, DC, MC, V. $$$–$$$$

An Elegant Victorian Mansion. This dramatically restored Eastlake mansion in a residential neighborhood east of the Old Town, a National Historic Landmark, lives up to its name. Each room is splendidly decked out in period furnishings and wall coverings, down to the carved wood beds, fringed lamp shades, and pull-chain commodes. The innkeepers may even greet you in vintage clothing and surprise you with old-fashioned ice-cream sodas in the afternoon. An original watercolor in the Van Gogh Room is said to be by the master himself, and the owners further lure you into their time warp with silent movies on tape, old records played on the windup Victrola, croquet on the rose-encircled lawn, and guided tours of local Victoriana in their antique automobile. The Victorian flower garden boasts more than 100 rosebushes. Gourmet breakfast is included. *14th and C Sts., 95501, tel. 707/444–3144 or 707/442–5594. 4 rooms share 4 baths. Facilities: laundry service, sauna, massage, bicycles, croquet. MC, V. $$–$$$*

Ferndale
Lodging

The Gingerbread Mansion. The exterior of this classic Victorian bed-and-breakfast has the most playful paint job on the North Coast. The mansion's carved friezes set off its gables, and turrets dazzle the eye. Inside, comfortable parlors and spacious bedrooms are laid out in flowery Victorian splendor. Some rooms have fireplaces, some have views of the mansion's elegant English garden, and one has side-by-side bathtubs. Breakfast is included. Ask about off-season rates. *400 Berding St., off Brown St., Box 40, 95536, tel. 707/786–4000. 9 rooms with bath. Facilities: bicycles. AE, MC, V. $$$$*

Victorian Inn. This hostelry occupies the second floor of a beautifully renovated Victorian building on Ferndale's perfectly preserved Main Street. The rooms, which are very affordable, are decorated in muted colors and have antique armoires, feather comforters, original moldings, and some clawfoot tubs. Downstairs are the Inn's casual bar and restaurant. *400 Ocean Ave. at Main St., tel. 707/725–9686 or 800/576–5949, fax 707/786–4648. 12 rooms. MC, V. $$–$$$*

Fort Bragg
Dining

The Restaurant. The name may be generic, but this place isn't. California cuisine is served in a dining room that doubles as an art gallery and features a jazz brunch on Sunday. *418 N. Main St., tel. 707/964–9800. Reservations advised. MC, V. No lunch Sun.–Tues. Closed Wed. $–$$*

Lodging

Grey Whale Inn. Once a hospital, this comfortable, friendly abode doesn't look or feel anything like one today. Each room is individually decorated with floral spreads or handcrafted quilts. The two penthouse rooms are exceptionally spacious. Three rooms have fireplaces, four have an ocean view, and the deluxe room has a private, two-person whirlpool tub and sun deck. Generous buffet breakfast is included. *615 N. Main St.,95437, tel. 707/964–0640 or 800/382–7244, fax 707/964–4408. 14 rooms. Facilities: phones, billiards room, living room with fireplace. AE, D, MC, V. $$$–$$$$*

Garberville
Dining

Woodrose Cafe. This unpretentious eatery, a local favorite, serves basic breakfast items and healthy lunches. Dishes include chicken, pasta, and vegetarian specials. *911 Redwood Dr., tel. 707/923–3191. No credit cards. No dinner. $*

Dining and Lodging
★

Benbow Inn. Set alongside the Eel River one highway exit south of Garberville, this three-story Tudor-style manor resort is the equal of any in the region. A magnificent fireplace warms the bar/lobby of this National Historic Landmark, and all rooms are furnished with antiques. The most luxurious rooms are under the terrace, with fine views of the Eel River; some have fireplaces. The wood-paneled dining room offers American cuisine with the focus on fresh salmon and trout dishes. *445 Lake Benbow Dr., 95442, tel. 707/923–2124. 55 rooms. Facilities: restaurant ($$–$$$), VCR movies in lounge, 18 rooms with TV and VCR, 250-tape VCR library, swimming off private beach, canoeing, tennis, golf, fishing, horseback riding. MC, V. Closed Jan. 3–Apr. 21. $$$–$$$$*

Gualala
Dining and Lodging

Sea Ranch Lodge. South of Gualala, the lodge is set high on a bluff, affording ocean views. Some rooms have fireplaces, and some have hot tubs. Handcrafted wood furnishings and quilts create an earthy, contemporary look. The restaurant, which overlooks the Pacific, serves good seafood and homemade desserts. Guests receive a complimentary wine and fruit basket upon arrival. It is close to beaches, trails, golf. *60 Sea Walk Dr., Box 44, 95497, tel. 707/785–2371, fax 707/785–2243. 20 rooms. Facilities: restaurant ($$$). AE, MC, V. $$$–$$$$*

Lodging
★

Old Milano Hotel. Overlooking Castle Rock and a spectacular coast just north of Gualala and set amid English gardens, the Old Milano is one of California's premier bed-and-breakfasts. Established in 1905, this elegantly rustic mansion is listed in the National Registry of Historic Places. Rooms are tastefully furnished and appointed with exceptional antiques; five of the upstairs rooms look out over the ocean, and another looks over the gardens. All upstairs rooms share bathrooms. The downstairs master suite has a private sitting room and a picture window framing the sea. Those in search of something different might consider the caboose with a wood-burning stove. A cottage also comes complete with wood stove. Take advantage of the private outdoor hot tub with an unforgettable view of the surf. Breakfast is included, and dinners are offered Wednesday through Sunday (also Tuesday in summer). This hotel may not be appropriate for children. *38300 Rte. 1, 95445, tel. 707/884–3256. 9 rooms. Facilities: hot tub. No smoking. MC, V. $$$–$$$$*

★

St. Orres. Located 2 miles north of Gualala, St. Orres is one of the North Coast's most eye-catching inns. Reflecting the area's Russian influence, St. Orres's main house is crowned by two onion-domed, Kremlinesque towers. The exterior is further accented by balconies, stained-glass windows, and wood-inlaid towers. Two of the rooms overlook the sea, while the other six are set over the garden or forest; all the rooms in the main house share baths. There are also 11 wonderfully rustic cottages behind the main house in tranquil woods; eight have wood stoves or fireplaces. Those traveling with children are placed in the cottages. Breakfast is included with the room rate; for dinner, the inn's restaurant is one of the finest and most imaginative north of San Francisco. It serves dinner only, a fixed-price meal ($$$$) with a choice of five entrées (meat or fish) plus soup and salad. *Rte. 1, Box 523, 95445, tel. 707/884–3303, fax 707/884–3903. 8 rooms, 11 cottages. Facilities: restaurant (closed Wed. in winter), beach, hot tub, sauna. MC, V. $$–$$$$*

Sea Ranch Escape. The Sea Ranch houses, sparsely scattered on a grass meadow fronting a stretch of ocean, are a striking sight from Route 1. The structures inspired a generation of natural wood architecture. Groups or families can rent fully furnished houses for two nights (minimum) or more. Linen, housekeeping, and catering services are available for a fee, or you can stock up on provisions from one of the markets in Gualala and make use of the full kitchens. All houses have TVs and VCRs; some have hot tubs and some take pets. Rates are most expensive next to the surf; prices recede with distance from the beach, although all the houses have views of the surrounding meadows and forest. *60 Sea Walk Dr., Box 238, 95497, tel. 707/785–2426 or 800/732–7262, fax 707/785–2124. 55 houses. MC, V. $$–$$$*

Inverness
Dining
★

Manka's. A series of three intimate, wood-paneled dining rooms, glowing with candlelight and piano music, provide the setting for creative American-regional cuisine. Specialties include caribou, pheasant, and other unusual game grilled in the fireplace, line-caught fish, and homemade desserts. *30 Calendar Way, tel. 415/669–1034. Reservations advised. MC, V. No lunch. Closed Tues. and Wed. $$–$$$*

Grey Whale. If you're driving through the area, this casual place is a good stop for pizza, salad, pastries, and espresso. *Sir Francis Drake Blvd., in center of town, tel. 415/669–1244. MC, V. $*

Lodging

Blackthorne Inn. Rising from the base of a tranquil wooded slope is one of the most unusual North Coast bed-and-breakfasts. The Blackthorne is architecturally striking, with an octagonal wooden tower sitting above a turreted tree house. It includes a glass-enclosed solarium and large fireplace as well as a penthouse, the Eagle's Nest, with a skylight framing the stars. Buffet breakfast is included; tea and snacks are served in the afternoon. *266 Vallejo Ave., Box 712, Inverness Park, 94937, tel. 415/663–8621. 5 rooms, 3 with bath. Facilities: hot tub. MC, V. $$$$*

Ten Inverness Way. In a lovely 1904 shingle-style house, set on a quiet side street, you will find this homey, low-key B&B. The comfortable living room has a classic stone fireplace and player piano, and a weekend-cabin feel. The cozy rooms are highlighted by such home-spun touches as patchwork quilts, lived-in-looking antiques, and sky-lighted dormer ceilings. The inn's proximity to Point Reyes hiking trails and Mt. Vision is a big draw for many guests. Full breakfast is included. *10 Inverness Way, Box 63, 94937, tel. 415/669–1648. 5 rooms. Facilities: hot tub. MC, V. $$$$*

Jenner
Dining

River's End. The Continental/Germanic fare is very good, featuring seafood, venison, and duck dishes. The brunches here are exceptional. *Rte. 1, north end of Jenner, tel. 707/865–2484. MC, V. Off-season hours vary. $$–$$$*

Lodging

Fort Ross Lodge. The lodge, about 1½ miles north of the old Russian fort, is somewhat dated and wind-bitten, but all but four of its rooms have fireplaces and spectacular views of the Sonoma shoreline. *20705 Rte. 1, 95450, tel. 707/847–3333. 22 rooms, some with private hot tub on back patio; 7 hill suites with sauna, in-room hot tub, VCR, fireplace. Facilities: color TV and VCR. AE, MC, V. $$$–$$$$*

Stillwater Cove Ranch. Sixteen miles north of Jenner, overlooking Stillwater Cove, this former boys' school has been transformed into a pleasant, if Spartan, place to lodge. Peacocks stroll the grounds. *22555 Rte. 1, 95450, tel. 707/847–3227. 7 rooms. No credit cards. $–$$*

Klamath
Lodging

Hostelling International—Redwood National Park. The California coast's northernmost hostel, this turn-of-the-century inn (remodeled in 1987) is a stone's throw from the ocean, and is actually located within Redwood National Park, so hiking begins just beyond its doors. The living room is heated by a wood stove. Lodging is dormitory style. *14480 Rte. 101 at Wilson Creek Rd., 95548, tel. and fax 707/482–8265. No credit cards. $*

Little River
Dining

Little River Restaurant. This tiny restaurant across from the Little River Inn is attached to the post office and gas station. Despite its modest appearance, this eatery serves some of the best dinners in the Mendocino area, featuring steaks and the freshest seafood. *Rte.*

1, tel. 707/937–4945. Reservations advised. No credit cards. No lunch.
Closed June–Nov., Wed. and Thurs.; Dec.–May, Tues.–Thur. $$–$$$

Lodging
★
Glendeven. For a touch of tranquillity, stay at this inn at the north end of Little River. The New England–style main house has five rooms, all with private bath, three with fireplace. The converted barn features a two-bedroom suite with kitchen and an art gallery. The 1986 Stevenscroft building has a high-peaked, gabled roof and weathered barnlike siding. The four rooms within all have fireplaces. The owners, both designers, have decorated the guest rooms with antiques, contemporary art, and ceramics. Breakfast is included. *8221 N. Rte. 1, 95456, tel. 707/937–0083. 9 rooms, 1 suite. AE, MC, V. $$$$*

Heritage House. This famous resort, where the movie *Same Time, Next Year* was filmed, has attractive cottages with stunning ocean views. There is a lovely dining room, also with a Pacific panorama, serving breakfast and dinner, which are included with the room rate for guests; others should make reservations in advance, and the meal is prix fixe. Each room's decor is unique, but all are appointed with plush furnishings, and many have private decks, fireplaces, and whirlpool tubs. *Rte. 1, 95456, tel. 707/937–5885, fax 707/937–0318. 72 rooms. Reserve well in advance. Facilities: restaurant ($$$$, jacket advised). MC, V. Closed Dec. and Jan. $$$$*

Mendocino
Dining
★
Cafe Beaujolais. All the rustic charm of peaceful, backwoods Mendocino is here, with great country cooking to boot. Owner Margaret Fox is a marvelous baker, so be sure to take home several packages of her irresistible *panforte*, made with almonds, hazelnuts, or macadamia nuts. This is the best place in town for breakfast or brunch, and the tree house–like second-story deck is a splendid retreat for a leisurely lunch. If you don't order the delicious chicken-apple sausages, you'll never forgive yourself. You can also get pizza and bread to go from the Brickery. *961 Ukiah St., tel. 707/937–5614. Reservations advised. No credit cards. Closed Tues. and Wed. $$–$$$*

Chocolate Moosse. Firelight warms this cozy café, specializing in soups, quiches, decadent desserts, gourmet coffees, and creative blackboard specials. Sunday brunch is memorable. *390 Kasten St., tel. 707/937–4323. No credit cards. Closed Jan. 31–mid-Feb. $$–$$$*

955 Ukiah St. The interior of this smart restaurant beside Cafe Beaujolais is woodsy, and the California cuisine creative. Note the pastas topped with original sauces, and fresh fish, such as Pacific red snapper wrapped in phyllo dough and topped with pesto and lemon sauce. *955 Ukiah St., tel. 707/937–1955. MC, V. No lunch. Closed July–Nov., Mon. and Tues.; Dec.–June, Mon.–Wed. $$–$$$*

Dining and
Lodging
MacCallum House. The most artfully restored Victorian exterior in Mendocino, this splendid 1882 inn, complete with gingerbread trim, transports you back to another era. Its comfortable period furnishings and antiques provide a turn-of- the-century ambience. In addition to the main house, individual cottages and barn suites are set around a garden with a gazebo. Continental breakfast is included (weekends only in winter). The firelit redwood-paneled restaurant offers a Mediterranean-inspired menu focusing on fresh local seafood. *45020 Albion St., Box 206, 95460, tel. 707/937–0289. 20 rooms. Facilities: restaurant ($$$, dinner only; closed Wed.–Thurs. in winter), bar. MC, V. $$$–$$$$*

Mendocino Hotel. From the outside, this fine hotel looks like something out of the Wild West with a period facade and balcony that overhangs the raised sidewalk. Inside, an elegant atmosphere is achieved by stained-glass lamps, Remington paintings, polished wood, and Persian carpets. All but 14 of the rooms have private baths, and the 19th-century decor is appealing. There are also deluxe garden rooms with fireplaces and TVs. The wood-paneled dining room, fronted by a glassed-in solarium, serves fine fish dishes and the best wild-berry cobblers in California. *45080 Main St., Box 587, 95460, tel. 707/937–0511 or 800/548–0513, fax 707/937–0513. 51 rooms. Facilities: restaurant ($$–$$$), bar, room service 8 AM–9 PM. AE, MC, V. $$–$$$*

Lodging
★ **Stanford Inn by the Sea.** This rustic, two-story lodge has comfortable wood-paneled rooms, each with a fireplace and deck from which you can gaze out over the Pacific and the town of Mendocino. The Stanford is adjacent to a llama farm and a terraced organic garden, and is set along the estuary. Complimentary buffet breakfast is served in the sitting room downstairs. *Just south of Mendocino, east on Comptche–Ukiah Rd., Box 487, 95460, tel. 707/937–5615 or 800/331–8884, fax 707/937–0305. 24 rooms. Facilities: canoes, color TV, stereo, VCRs, coffee makers, telephones, refrigerators, mountain bikes, indoor pool, hot tub, sauna. AE, D, DC, MC, V. $$$$*

Brewery Gulch Inn. This 1860s farmhouse bed-and-breakfast, a short drive from town, has retained its old-fashioned rural character, complete with chickens, which supply the eggs for breakfast. Antiques, wood floors, and hand-sewn quilts enhance cozy rooms, two with fireplace. *9350 N. Rte. 1, 94560, tel. 707/937–4752. 5 rooms, 3 with bath. MC, V. $$$–$$$$*

★ **Headlands Inn.** A magnificently restored Victorian building erected in 1868, the inn combines 19th-century charm and contemporary comforts. All rooms have private baths, feather beds, and fireplaces; some overlook a garden and the pounding surf, others offer fine village views. There is also a private cottage on the premises. Gourmet breakfast is served in your room and afternoon tea is served in the charming sitting room upstairs. *Howard and Albion Sts., Box 132, 95460, tel. 707/937–4431. 5 rooms. No credit cards. $$$–$$$$*

Joshua Grindle Inn. The oldest B&B in Mendocino, this Victorian inn has a reputation for friendliness. Some rooms have ocean views, and some have fireplaces; all are decorated in early-American style with chenille bedspreads or handmade quilts. Three rooms are in a water tower and the two rooms in the backyard cottage are warmed by Franklin stoves. Full breakfast is included. *44800 Little Lake Rd., 95460, tel. 707/937–4143. 10 rooms. MC, V. $$$–$$$$*

Mendocino Village Inn. This refurbished 1882 Queen Anne Victorian inn has a potpourri of styles, with one room providing a Southwestern motif, another reminiscent of a whaling captain's quarters, and a third with California mission–style furnishings. There also is a two-story water tower suite. Eight of the rooms have fireplaces or wood stoves, some have ocean views, and others look out on the garden. Breakfast is included. *44860 Main St., Box 626, 95460, tel. 707/937–0246; in CA, 800/882–7029. 13 rooms, 11 with bath. No credit cards. $$–$$$*

Muir Beach
Dining and Lodging
★ **Pelican Inn.** An atmospheric Tudor-style B&B reminiscent of 16th-century England, the Pelican is a five-minute walk from Muir Beach. The rooms, filled with antiques, have half-canopied two- and four-poster beds. On the ground floor, there's an Old English pub complete with dart boards and a selection of British brews. The dining quarter consists of two sections: a romantic, rustic wood hall and a glassed-in solarium, both warmed by fireplaces and both serving sturdy English fare, from fish and chips to prime rib and Yorkshire pudding. Rates include full English breakfast. *10 Pacific Way at Rte. 1, 94965, tel. 415/383–6000. 7 rooms. Facilities: restaurant ($$–$$$, closed Mon.). MC, V. $$$$*

Point Reyes National Seashore
Lodging

Point Reyes Hostel. Located within the national seashore and a mere 2 miles from Limantour Beach, this is the best deal for budget travelers. Lodging is dorm style in an old clapboard ranch house. The family room is limited to families with children five and under and must be reserved well in advance. *Box 247, Pt. Reyes Station, 94956, tel. 415/663–8811. Send $9 per adult per night with reservation request; state your gender. Facilities: shared kitchen. No credit cards.* $

Point Reyes Station
Dining

Station House Cafe. This modest local hangout serves breakfast, lunch, and dinner in a relaxing paneled dining room. Fresh shellfish, grilled meats, and scrumptious chocolate cake highlight the dinner menu. *11180 Rte. 1, tel. 415/663–1515. MC, V. $–$$*

Shelter Cove
Lodging

Beachcomber Inn. There are three good-size rooms in this converted private home. Two of the rooms have kitchenettes and wood-burning stoves, and ocean views. The decor doesn't get much beyond the basics of a brass bed and a wicker chair. The inn is near the marina and it's an easy walk to the beach. Register at the Shelter Cove General Store on Briceland Avenue (Shelter Cove's main street). *Write c/o 7272 Shelter Cove Rd., Shelter Cove 95589, tel. 707/986–7733. Take the Redway exit from Hwy. 101 to Shelter Cove. 3 rooms. MC, V. $–$$*

Stinson Beach
Dining

Sand Dollar. This pleasant pub serves great hamburgers and other sandwiches for lunch and decent seafood for dinner. An added attraction is the outdoor-dining deck. *Rte. 1, tel. 415/868–0434. MC, V. $–$$*

Tomales Bay
Lodging

Tomales Country Inn. Secluded by trees and bordered by gardens, this Victorian house has a relaxed atmosphere. The previous owner, painter Byron Randall, filled the inn with his own turn-of-the-century, European-style paintings and other local art. Expanded Continental breakfast is included. *25 Valley St., Box 376, 94971, tel. and fax 707/878–2041. 5 rooms, 2 with bath. No credit cards. Closed Dec. 20–Dec. 28. $$*

Trinidad
Dining
★

Larrupin Cafe. Larrupin has earned a widespread reputation for its Cajun ribs and fish, served in a bright yellow, two-story house on a quiet country road 2 miles north of Trinidad. *1658 Patrick's Point Dr., tel. 707/677–0230. Reservations required. No credit cards. No lunch. Closed Mon.–Wed. $$–$$$*

Merryman's Dinner House. Fresh fish, naturally, is the main feature at this romantic ocean-front setting, perfect for hungry lovers. *Moonstone Beach, tel. 707/677–3111. No credit cards. Closed Mon.–Thurs. and winter weekdays. $–$$*

Seascape. With its glassed-in main room, and a deck for alfresco dining, this is an ideal place to take in the splendor of Trinidad Bay over a good meal. The breakfasts are great, the lunches substantial, and the dinners feature good seafood. *At pier, tel. 707/677–3762. MC, V. $–$$*

Lodging

Trinidad Bed and Breakfast. Overlooking Trinidad Bay, this Cape Cod–style shingle house, built in 1949, has an unforgettable ocean view. The innkeepers offer a wealth of information about the nearby wilderness, beach, and fishing habitats. The living room is warmed by a crackling fireplace. Upstairs, three comfortably furnished rooms offer fabulous seascapes which you can enjoy from a seat by a dormer window framed with white eyelet curtains. Breakfast is included. *560 Edwards St., Box 849, 95570, tel. 707/677–0840. 2 rooms and 2 suites (1 with fireplace). Reserve well in advance. D, MC, V. $$$$*

Valley Ford **The Inn at Valley Ford.** The rooms and one private cottage at this
Lodging small B&B along Route 1 are named after literary figures—Virginia
Woolf, Somerset Maugham, and others. The authors' titles grace the
bookshelves of their respective, cozy rooms. Rate include gourmet
breakfast, with specialties such as poached pears. *14395 Rte. 1,
94972, tel. 707/876–3182. 4 rooms share 2 baths, 1 cottage suite has a
private bath. DC, MC, V. $$*

Nightlife

If a swinging, raucous, after-dark scene is what you're hankering
for, the North Coast is not the place for you. Nonetheless, there are
some watering holes favored by locals and visitors that should meet
the needs of those not quite ready for a good night's sleep after
exploring the forest and sea.

Bolinas **Smiley's Schooner Saloon.** The *only* nightlife in Bolinas, Smiley's
has a CD sound system and live music three nights a week (Saturday
only in winter). *41 Wharf Rd., tel. 415/868–1311.*

Eureka **Lost Coast Brewery & Café.** This bustling microbrewery is the
best place in town to relax with a pint of strong ale or porter. The
brewery also serves soups, salads, and light meals for lunch and
dinner, all reasonably priced. *617 4th St., tel. 707/445–4480.*

Garberville **Benbow Inn.** In this elegant Tudor mansion, you can hear a pianist
nightly while you are warmed by a romantic fireplace. *445 Lake Ben-
bow Dr., tel. 707/923–2124.*

Mendocino **Caspar Inn.** An eclectic selection of live music, from folk to jazz to
ska, is featured nightly at this popular spot between Mendocino and
Fort Bragg. *Caspar St. at Rte. 1, tel. 707/964–5565.*

Muir Beach **Pelican Inn.** Set just outside Muir Beach, this is an English-style
pub and restaurant, with imported brews on tap, a dart board, a
stone fireplace, a genial host, and friendly regulars. *10 Pacific Way
at Rte. 1, tel. 415/383–6000. Closed Mon.*

Point Reyes **Western Saloon.** If you are in town on the right Friday night, you
Station can dance your jeans off at this favorite local pub. There's live music
on Thursday night. Other nights it's a friendly place to meet West
Marinites. *11201 Rte. 1, tel. 415/663–1661.*

4 The Far North

Updated by Emily Miller and Mark S. Rosen

While the rest of California was booming with high-tech industries and an influx of sun-seeking Easterners and value-conscious developers, the Far North simply hung up its "gone fishin'" sign. You won't find many hot night spots or cultural enclaves here, but you will find some of the best hiking, fishing, and hunting the state has to offer. Some Bay Area families have been returning to this region of the state year after year. Many enjoy the outdoors from their own piece of paradise—a private houseboat. A good number of retirees have chosen to live out their golden years in the area.

The towering, snow-covered Mt. Shasta dominates the land. Visible for 100 miles, it qualifies the otherwise flat and fast trip through the valley along I–5 as a scenic drive. The 14,000-foot dormant volcano is surrounded by national and state parks. The natural and artificially created wonders include the sulfur vents and areas of bubbling mud of Lassen Volcanic National Park and the immense Shasta Dam.

Almost all of the towns in the Far North are small and friendly, made up of third- and fourth-generation descendants of '49ers who never cared to leave. Proud of their Gold Rush history, each town, no matter how small, has a museum filled with an impressive collection of artifacts donated by locals. California's Far North is the kind of place where people say hello to you as you walk down Main Street.

Essential Information

Important Addresses and Numbers

Tourist Information **Mt. Shasta Convention and Visitors Bureau** (300 Pine St., Mt. Shasta 96067, tel. 916/926–4865 or 800/926–4865). **Red Bluff–Tehama County Chamber of Commerce** (100 Main St., Box 850, Red Bluff 96080, tel. 916/527–6220 or 800/655–6225). **Redding Convention and Visitors Bureau** (777 Auditorium Dr., Redding 96001, tel. 916/225–4100 or 800/874–7562). **Shasta Cascade Wonderland Association** (14250 Holiday Rd.; Redding 96003, tel. 916/275–5555 or 800/326–6944). **Siskiyou County Visitors Bureau** (111 S. Oregon St., Suite A, Yreka 96097, tel. 916/842–7857 or 800/446–7475).

Emergencies Dial 911 for police, fire, and medical help.

Arriving and Departing

By Plane Redding Municipal Airport is served by **United Express** (tel. 800/241–6522) and **American Eagle** (tel. 800/433–7300), which flies daily from San Francisco with a connection in San Jose. Major car-rental agencies are located at the airport.

By Train There are **Amtrak** stations in Redding (1620 Yuba St.) and Dunsmuir (5750 Sacramento Ave.). Call 800/872–7245 for information.

By Bus **Greyhound Lines** buses travel I–5, serving Red Bluff, Redding, Dunsmuir, and Mt. Shasta City (tel. 800/231–2222). In Redding, a city bus system, "The Ride" (tel. 916/241–2877), serves the local area daily except Sunday.

By Car I–5, an excellent four-lane divided highway, runs up the center of California through Red Bluff and Redding, and continues north to Oregon. Lassen Park can be reached by Route 36 from Red Bluff or Route 44 from Redding; Route 299 leads from Redding to McArthur-Burney Falls. These are very good two-lane roads that are kept open year round. If you are traveling through this area in winter, however, always carry snow chains in your car.

Exploring the Far North

The Far North covers a vast area, from the valleys east of the Coast Range to the Nevada border, and from the almond and olive orchards north of Sacramento to the Oregon border. The entire state of Ohio would fit into this section of California.

Redding, the urban center of the Far North, offers the greatest selection of restaurants and the largest concentration of hotels and motels. You'll experience the true flavor of this outdoor country at motels in the smaller towns. Many visitors make the outdoors their home for at least part of their stay. Camping, houseboating, and animal-pack trips into the wilderness are very popular.

This exploring section is arranged south-to-north, following the mostly flat and fast I–5 with the addition of two daylong side trips. The valley around Redding is hot, even in winter, but cooler temperatures prevail at the higher elevations to the east and north. Be aware that many restaurants and museums in this region have limited hours and sometimes close for stretches of the off-season.

Highlights for First-Time Visitors

Lake Shasta
Lassen Volcanic National Park
McArthur–Burney Falls Memorial State Park
Shasta Dam

Red Bluff and Lassen Volcanic National Park

Numbers in the margin correspond to points of interest on the Far North map.

1 The turnoff for **Red Bluff** from I–5 will take you past a neon-lit motel row, but persevere and explore the roads to the left of the main drag, where you'll discover gracefully restored Victorian structures, a fine museum, and an Old West–style downtown.

The **Kelly-Griggs House Museum** is a restored 1880s Victorian dwelling with an impressive collection of antique furniture, housewares, and clothing arranged as though a refined Victorian family were still in residence: an engraved silver tea server waits at the end table; a "Self Instructor in Penmanship" teaching the art of graceful, flowing handwriting sits on the desk; and costumed mannequins seem frozen in conversation in the upstairs parlor. The museum's collection also includes finely carved china cabinets and Native American basketry. *Persephone,* the painting over the fireplace, is by Sarah Brown, daughter of abolitionist John Brown, whose family settled in Red Bluff after his execution. The Brown home is part of the self-guided tour of Red Bluff Victoriana; maps are available here. *311 Washington St., tel. 916/527–1129. Donation suggested. Open Thurs.–Sun. 2–4.*

2 North of town on the banks of the Sacramento River is the **William B. Ide Adobe State Historic Park,** which is a memorial to the man who was the first and only president of the short-lived California Republic of 1846. The Bear Flag Party proclaimed California a sovereign nation, no longer under the dominion of Mexico, and the re-

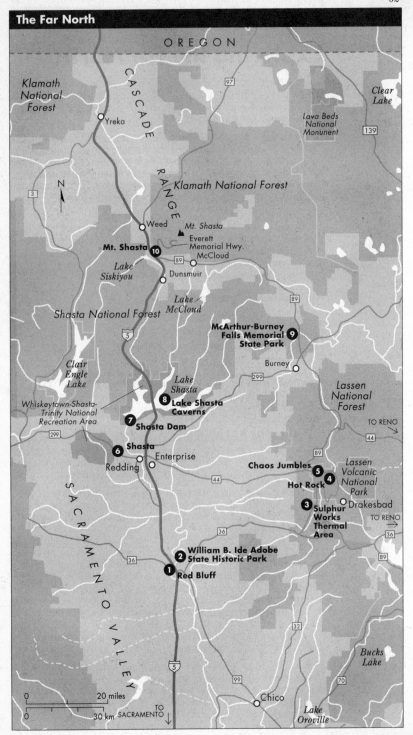

The Far North

OREGON

Klamath National Forest

CASCADE RANGE

Yreka

3

97

Clear Lake

139

Lava Beds National Monunent

Klamath National Forest

N

Weed

Mt. Shasta

Everett Memorial Hwy.

Mt. Shasta 10

McCloud

89

Lake Siskiyou

Dunsmuir

Shasta National Forest

Lake McCloud

5

McArthur-Burney Falls Memorial State Park 9

89

Clair Engle Lake

Lake Shasta

Burney

299

Lassen National Forest

Whiskeytown-Shasta-Trinity National Recreation Area

8 **Lake Shasta Caverns**

299

7

Shasta Dam

TO RENO

44

6 **Shasta**

Enterprise

Chaos Jumbles

89

Lassen Volcanic National Park

Redding

44

5

Hot Rock

4

Drakesbad

3 **Sulphur Works Thermal Area**

TO RENO

36

36

89

2 **William B. Ide Adobe State Historic Park**

1 **Red Bluff**

SACRAMENTO VALLEY

32

Bucks Lake

5

0   20 miles

0   30 km

99

TO SACRAMENTO

Chico

70

Lake Oroville

public existed for 25 days with Ide as chief executive before it was occupied by the United States. The flag concocted for the republic has survived, with only minor refinements, as California's state flag. What is thought to be Ide's adobe home was built in the 1850s, and now displays period furnishings and artifacts of the era. Also on the park grounds are a friendly donkey named Lucy and a living history museum with a blacksmith's workshop. *21659 Adobe Rd., tel. 916/527–5927. Admission: $3 donation requested per vehicle. Home open 11–4 in summer; in winter, look for ranger on park grounds to unlock the house; park and picnic facilities open year-round from 8 AM to sunset.*

Take Route 36 east from Red Bluff to Route 89, which meanders north for 34 miles through **Lassen Volcanic National Park,** offering a look at three sides of the world's largest plug volcano. Except for the ski area, the park is largely inaccessible from late October to early June because of snow. Route 89 through the park is closed to cars in winter but open to intrepid cross-country skiers, conditions permitting.

In 1914 the 10,457-foot Mt. Lassen began a series of 300 eruptions that went on for seven years. Molten rock overflowed the crater, and the mountain emitted clouds of smoke and hailstorms of rocks and volcanic cinders. Proof of the volcano's volatility becomes evident **❸** shortly after you enter the park at the **Sulphur Works Thermal Area.** Boardwalks take you over bubbling mud and hot springs, and through the nauseating sulfur stink of steam vents. Five miles farther along Route 89 you'll find the start of the **Bumpass Hell Trail,** a 3-mile round-trip hike to the park's most interesting thermal-spring area where you'll see hot and boiling springs, steam vents, and mud pots. The trail climbs and descends several hundred feet.

Back on the road, continue through forests and past lakes, looking **❹** out for deer and wildflowers, to **Hot Rock.** This 400-ton boulder tumbled down from the summit during the volcano's active period, and was still hot to the touch when locals found it. Although cool now, **❺** it's still an impressive sight. Five miles on is **Chaos Jumbles,** created 300 years ago when an avalanche from the Chaos Crags lava domes spread hundreds of thousands of rocks 2 to 3 feet in diameter over 2 square miles.

An important word of warning: Stay on trails and boardwalks near the thermal areas. What may appear to be firm ground may be only a thin crust over scalding mud, and serious burns could result if you step through it. Be especially careful with children!

Lassen is a unique, lovely, and relatively uncrowded national park, but services are rather sparse. In the southwest corner of the park, at the winter-sports area, there is a café and a gift shop that's open during the summer and the ski season. At the Manzanita Lake campground another store, open only in summer, offers gas and fast food. *Lassen Volcanic National Park, Box 100, Mineral 96063–0100, tel. 916/595–4444. Admission: $5 per car in summer, free in winter.*

The Shasta Area

A few miles west of Redding on Route 299 are the ruins of the gold-**❻** mining town of **Shasta,** now a **state historic park** with a few restored buildings. A museum located in the old courthouse has an eclectic array of California paintings as well as memorabilia including period newspapers advertising "Gold Dust Bought and Sold," a "Prairie Traveler" guidebook with advice on encounters with Indians, and the 1860 census of this once-prosperous town. Continue down to the basement to see the iron-barred jail cells, and step outside for a look at the scaffold where murderers were hanged. *Tel. 916/243–8194. Admission: $2 adults, $1 children 6–12. Open Mar.–Oct., Thurs.–Mon. 10–5; Nov.–Feb., Fri.–Sun. 10–5.*

❼ Take the Center Valley/Shasta Dam exit west off I–5 about 12 miles north of Redding and follow the signs to **Shasta Dam.** You'll be able to see the mammoth construction from several points; this is the second-largest and the fourth-tallest concrete dam in the United States.

Whether you drive across the dam, or park at the landscaped visitors area and walk across, you'll see three Shastas: the dam, the lake spreading before you, and the mountain presiding over it all. At twilight the sight is magical, with Mt. Shasta gleaming above the not-quite-dark water and deer frolicking on the hillside beside the dam. The dam is lighted after dark, but there is no access from 10 PM to 6 AM. In addition to providing fact sheets, the **Visitor Information Center** (tel. 916/275–4463) offers photographic and historic displays (June–Aug., daily 7:30–5; Sept.–May, weekdays 7:30–4). Daily guided tours of the dam are given hourly in the summer from 9 to 4; in winter, tours are given hourly on weekends from 12 to 3, and on weekdays at 10, 12, and 2:30.

Lake Shasta has 370 miles of shoreline and 21 varieties of fish. You can rent fishing boats, ski boats, sailboats, canoes, paddleboats, Jet Skis, and Windsurfer boards at one of the many marinas and resorts along the shore. But Lake Shasta is known as the houseboat capital of the world, and around here the houseboat is king.

Houseboats come in all sizes except small. The ones that sleep 12 to 14 people are 55 feet by 14 feet; the smallest sleeps six. As a rule these moving homes come with cooking utensils, dishes, and most of the equipment you'll need to set up housekeeping on the water. (You supply food and linens.) Renters are given a short course in how to maneuver the boats before they set out on cruises; it's not difficult.

The houseboats are slow-moving, and life aboard is leisurely. You can fish, swim, sunbathe on the flat roof, or just sit on the deck and watch the world go by. The shoreline of Lake Shasta is beautifully ragged, with countless inlets; exploring it is fun, and it's not hard to find privacy.

Expect to spend a minimum of $170 a day for a craft that sleeps six. There is usually a three-night minimum in peak season. Contact the **Shasta Cascade Wonderland Association** (14250 Holiday Rd., Redding, CA 96003, tel. 916/275–5555 or 800/326–6944) for specifics.

❽ Stalagmites, stalactites, odd flowstone deposits, and crystals entice visitors of all ages to the **Lake Shasta Caverns.** The two-hour tour includes a catamaran ride across the McCloud arm of Lake Shasta and a bus ride up Grey Rock Mountain to the cavern entrance. The caverns are a constant 58°F year round, making them an appealingly cool retreat on a hot summer day. All cavern rooms are well lit, and the crowning jewel is the spectacular cathedral room. The guides are friendly, enthusiastic, and informative. *Take the Shasta Caverns Rd. exit from I–5. Tel. 916/238–2341 or 800/795–2283. Admission: $12 adults, $6 children 4–12. Hourly tours May–Sept., daily 9–4; Oct.–Apr., at 10 AM, noon, and 2 PM.*

Take the Route 299 East exit off I–5 just north of Redding, past the
9 town of Burney, and turn north on Route 89 to get to **McArthur-Burney Falls Memorial State Park.** It's a two-hour round-trip drive from
I–5, so you may want to plan to spend the day here. Just inside the
southern boundary of the park, Burney Creek wells up from the
ground and divides into two cascades that fall over a 129-foot cliff
and into a pool below. The thundering water creates a mist at the
base of the falls, often highlighted by a rainbow. Countless ribbon-
like falls stream from hidden moss-covered crevices creating an
ethereal backdrop to the main cascades. Each day, 100 million gallons of water rush over these falls; Theodore Roosevelt proclaimed
them "the eighth wonder of the world." A self-guided nature trail
descends to the foot of the falls. There is a lake and beach for swimming. A campground, picnic sites, trails, and other facilities are
available. The camp store is open Memorial Day–Labor Day. *24898
Hwy. 89, Burney 96013, tel. 916/335–2777. Day-use admission: $5 per
vehicle; camping: May–Sept., $14 per night; Oct.–Apr., $12 per night.
Campground reservations (necessary in summer) are made through
MISTIX, Box 85705, San Diego, CA 92186–5705, tel. 619/452–0150 or
800/444–7275.*

If you drive up the valley on I–5, past the 130 million-year-old granite outcroppings of Castle Crags towering over the road, through
the quaint old railroad town of Dunsmuir, you'll reach the town of
10 **Mt. Shasta,** nestled at the base of the huge mountain. If you are
interested in hiking on Mt. Shasta, stop at the **Forest Service
Ranger Station** (204 W. Alma St., tel. 916/926–4511) as you come
through town for the latest information on trail conditions, or call
the **Fifth Season Mountaineering Shop** in Mt. Shasta City (tel.
916/926–3606), which also offers a recorded 24-hour climber/skier
report (tel. 916/926–5555). The **Mt. Shasta Convention and Visitors
Bureau** (300 Pine St., tel. 916/926–4865) also has information on hiking and local accommodations.

The central Mt. Shasta exit east leads out of town along the **Everett
Memorial Highway.** This scenic drive climbs to almost 8,000 feet,
and the views of the mountain and the valley below are extraordinary.

If you are wondering where all those eye-catching pictures of Mt.
Shasta reflected in a lake are shot, take the central Mt. Shasta exit
west and follow the signs to **Lake Siskiyou.** This is the only man-
made lake in California created solely for recreational purposes. On
the way, stop at the oldest **trout hatchery** in California. The pools
there literally swarm with more than 100,000 trout.

Off the Beaten Track

The hand-painted sign along Main Street in **McCloud** reads "Population 1,665, Dogs 462." To reach this time-capsule town, take the
Route 89 exit east from I–5 just south of the town of Mt. Shasta.
McCloud began as a lumber-company town in the late 1800s, and
was one of the longest-lived company towns in the country. In 1965,
the U.S. Plywood Corp. acquired the town, its lumber mill, and the
surrounding forest land, and allowed residents to purchase their
homes. The immense mill has been cut back to a computerized operation, but the spirit of the townsfolk has kept McCloud from becoming a ghost town. Picturesque hotels, churches, a lumber
baron's mansion, and simple family dwellings have been renovated,
and the 60,000-pound Corliss steam engine that powered the original mill's machinery stands as a monument behind the town's small

museum. On Main Street, you'll find an enormous old-style dance hall and a classic small-town soda fountain.

Sports

Fishing For licenses, current fishing conditions, guides, or special fishing packages, contact **The Fly Shop** (4140 Churn Creek Rd., Redding 96002, tel. 916/222–3555), **The Fishin' Hole** (3844 Shasta Dam Blvd., Central Valley 96019, tel. 916/275–4123), or **Shasta Cascade Wonderland Association** (14250 Holiday Rd., Redding 96003, tel. 916/275–5555 or 800/326–6944).

Golf **Churn Creek Golf Course** (7335 Churn Creek Rd., Redding, tel. 916/222–6353) is a nine-hole, par-36 course. Carts are available. **Gold Hills Country Club** (1950 Gold Hills Dr., Redding, Oasis Rd. exit from I–5, tel. 916/246–7867) is an 18-hole, par-72 course. Carts, club rentals, driving range, pro shop, and restaurant are available. **Lake Redding Golf Course** (1795 Benton Dr., Redding, in Lake Redding Park, tel. 916/243–5531) is a nine-hole, par-31 course. Pull carts, electric carts, and rentals are available.

Mountain Climbing **Shasta Mountain Guides** (1938 Hill Rd., Mt. Shasta 96067, tel. 916/926–3117) leads hiking and ski-touring groups to the snow-covered, 14,161-foot summit of Mount Shasta.

Raft/Canoe Rentals **Park Marina Watersports** (2515 Park Marina Dr., Redding, tel. 916/246–8388).

Skiing **Mt. Shasta Ski Park.** On the southeast flank of Mt. Shasta are three lifts on 300 skiable acres. The terrain is 20% beginner, 60% intermediate, 20% advanced. Top elevation is 6,600 feet; its base, 5,500 feet; its vertical drop 1,100 feet. The longest run is 1.2 miles. Night skiing goes till 10 PM Wednesday–Saturday. There is a ski school with a beginner's special: lifts, rentals, lessons. The "Powder Pups" program is for ages 4–7. Lodge facilities include food and beverage, ski shop, and rentals. *Rte. 89 exit east from I–5, just south of Mt. Shasta, tel. 916/926–8610. Snow phone 916/926–8686.*

Snowshoe Tours National Park Service rangers conduct snowshoe tours at Mt. Lassen Ski Park. A variety of natural history topics are covered. *Tel. 916/595–4444. No reservations. $1 donation for upkeep of snowshoes. Winter, Sat. at 1:30 PM.*

Dining and Lodging

Dining Cafés and simple, informal restaurants are ample in the Far North. Most of the fast-food restaurants are clustered in Redding, though they are also found along I–5 in some of the larger communities. The restaurants listed here are of special interest because of their food and/or unique atmosphere. Dress is always casual in the Far North; reservations aren't necessary except where noted.

Highly recommended restaurants are indicated by a star ★.

Category	Cost*
$$$$	over $35
$$$	$25–$35

$$	$15–$25
$	under $15

*per person for a three-course meal, excluding drinks, service, and tax

Lodging   Motel chains, such as Best Western and Motel 6, have branches in many of the communities in the Far North, though Redding has the greatest selection by far. Upscale hotels with business facilities are found only in Redding.

Highly recommended establishments are indicated by a star ★.

Category	Cost*
$$$$	over $100
$$$	$75–$100
$$	$50–$75
$	under $50

*All prices are for a double room, excluding tax.

Dunsmuir
Lodging
★
Railroad Park Resort. At this railroad buff's delight, antique cabooses have been converted to cozy, wood-paneled motel rooms in honor of Dunsmuir's railroad legacy. Nine railcars have been transformed into an *Orient Express*–style dining room and a lounge with a karaoke machine. The landscaped grounds feature a huge logging steam engine and restored water tower. *100 Railroad Park Rd., 96025, tel. 916/235–4440 or 800/974–7245, fax 916/235–4470. 24 cabooses with bath, 4 cabins. Facilities: pool, Jacuzzi. AE, D, MC, V. $$*

Lake Shasta
Dining
Tail O' the Whale. Reminiscent of a ship's prow, this restaurant overlooking the lake is distinguished by its nautical decor. Seafood, prime rib, poultry, and Cajun pepper shrimp are the specialties. *10300 Bridge Bay Rd., Bridge Bay exit from I–5, tel. 916/275–3021. Reservations advised for summer Sun. brunch. MC, V. $$*

Lassen Volcanic National Park
Lodging
Drakesbad Guest Ranch. The only lodging inside the park is the 100-year-old guest ranch at Drakesbad, near its southern border on Lake Almanor, and isolated from most of the park. Reservations should be made well in advance. *Booking office: 2150 Main St., Suite 5, Red Bluff 96080, tel. 916/529–1512. Open early June–early Oct.; closed winter. $$$$*

Mt. Shasta
Dining
Lily's. In a sunny, white clapboard house complete with picket fence, Lily's serves pastas (the house specialty is spinach fettuccine with artichoke hearts or scallops), salads (Thai noodle, Caesar), and Mexican, Italian, Asian, and American entrées. *1013 S. Mt. Shasta Blvd., tel. 916/926–3372. MC, V. $–$$*

Michael's Restaurant. Wood paneling, candlelight, and wildlife prints by local artists create an unpretentious setting for such Italian specialties as stuffed calamari, filet mignon scaloppine, and linguine pesto. *313 N. Mt. Shasta Blvd., tel. 916/926–5288. AE, D, MC, V. Closed Sun., Mon.; no lunch Sat. $–$$*

★
Marilyn's. This charming, homespun eatery in the shadow of Mt. Shasta just might be the best small-town diner north of the Bay Area. Local historical memorabilia lines the walls. Neighborly waitresses serve large portions of delicious food in carved wooden booths. Much of the town comes in for breakfast; complete dinners

including soup and salad cost less than $8. *1136 S. Mt. Shasta Blvd., tel. 916/926–2720. MC, V. $*

Lodging   **Tree House Best Western.** The clean, standard rooms at this motel, two blocks from the center of the town of Mt. Shasta, are decorated with natural wood furnishings and a range of colors. *I–5 and Lake St., Box 236, 96067, tel. 916/926–3101 or 800/528–1234, fax 916/926–3542. 95 rooms. Facilities: restaurant, lounge, indoor pool. AE, D, DC, MC, V. $$*

★   **Wagon Creek Inn.** This lodgepole pine log home in a quiet residential neighborhood 2 miles outside town is one of the area's newest and most affordable inns, with crisp, country decor; a living room with fireplace, television, and VCR; and laid-back hospitality. Generous Continental breakfast is included. *1239 Woodland Park Dr., 96067, tel. 916/926–0838 or 800/995–9260. 3 rooms, 1 with bath. MC, V. $$*

Red Bluff   **Hatch Cover.** Offering views of the adjacent Sacramento River, this
Dining   attractive establishment is decorated in dark-wood paneling to resemble a ship's interior. The menu features seafood, but you can also get steaks and combination plates. Check out the exotic after-dinner drinks. *202 Hemsted Dr., tel. 916/223–5606. No lunch weekends. From the Cypress Ave. exit off I–5, turn left, then right on Bechelli La., and left on Hemsted Dr. AE, D, MC, V. $$–$$$*

The Snack Box. This renovated Victorian building is cheerfully decorated in country-French blue and dusty rose. The carved wooden murals, like the omelets, soups, and sandwiches, are homemade by the owner. *257 Main St., 1 block from Kelly-Griggs Museum, tel. 916/529–0227. No credit cards. No dinner. $*

Redding   **Jack's Grill.** Although it looks like a dive from the outside, this steak
Dining   house and bar is immensely popular with residents throughout the territory, who come in for the famous 16-ounce steaks. The place is usually jam-packed and noisy. *1743 California St., tel. 916/241–9705. AE, MC, V. No lunch. Closed Sun. $–$$*

Lodging   **Red Lion Motor Inn.** Nicely landscaped grounds and a large, attractive patio area with outdoor food service are the highlights here. The rooms are spacious and comfortable. Misty's, the lobby's fancy restaurant ($$$), is popular among locals for its steak Diane. *1830 Hilltop Dr., Rte. 44 and 299 exit east from I–5, 96002, tel. 916/221–8700 or 800/547–8010, fax 916/221–0324. 194 rooms with bath. Facilities: restaurant, coffee shop, lounge, pool, wading pool, whirlpool, putting green, room service, movies. Pets allowed; mention when booking room. AE, D, DC, MC, V. $$$–$$$$*

Oxford Suites. This hotel with more than 100 suites (and 24 studios) offers excellent value. All rooms have two televisions, a VCR, and refrigerator. Most have microwave ovens and three have whirlpool tubs. Complimentary cocktails and a full buffet breakfast are included. Advance reservations are recommended. *1967 Hilltop Dr., 96002, tel. 916/221–0100 or 800/762–0133, fax 916/221–8265. 139 rooms. Facilities: lounge, pool, whirlpool, 24-hour snack-and-video shop. AE, D, DC, MC, V. $$–$$$*

La Quinta. The Texas-based La Quinta chain recently bought and remodeled this comfortable Redding motel. The spacious lobby has a cozy sitting area, and the rooms are all tastefully decorated with dark-wood furniture; the spotless, white-tile bathrooms have full-length mirrors. *2180 Hilltop Dr., tel. 916/221–8200 or 800/531–5900. 140 rooms. Facilities: pool, Jacuzzi, cable TV. AE, D, DC, MC, V. $$*

Camping

There are an infinite number of camping possibilities in the Far North's national and state parks, forests, and recreation areas. You'll find every level of rusticity, too, from the well-outfitted campgrounds in McArthur-Burney State Park, which have hot water, showers, and flush toilets, to isolated campsites on Lake Shasta that can be reached only by boat.

There are seven campgrounds within Lassen Volcanic National Park. Reservations are not accepted; it's first come, first served. For campground and other information, contact Lassen Volcanic National Park (Box 100, Mineral 96063–0100, tel. 916/595–4444). For information about camping in the region, contact the **Shasta Cascade Wonderland Association** (14250 Holiday Rd., Redding, CA 96003, tel. 916/275–5555 or 800/326–6944).

Nightlife

Although the larger hotels in Redding usually have weekend dance bands geared to the younger set, there's not much nightlife in this outdoors country where the fish bite early. Country-western fans will enjoy the **Derringer** (2655 Bechelli La., behind the bowling alley, Redding, tel. 916/221–2727), which features live music Wednesday through Saturday and recorded music other nights. There's a $2 cover charge on weekends, $1 weeknights. If C&W isn't your cup of tea, check out the bar at **Jack's Grill** (*see above*), which is almost always jumping.

5 The Wine Country

In 1862, after an extensive tour of the wine-producing areas of Europe, Count Agoston Haraszthy de Mokcsa reported to his adopted California with a promising prognosis: "Of all the countries through which I passed," wrote the father of California's viticulture, "not one possessed the same advantages that are to be found in California. . . . California can produce as noble and generous a wine as any in Europe; more in quantity to the acre, and without repeated failures through frosts, summer rains, hailstorms, or other causes."

The "dormant resources" that Haraszthy saw in the temperate valleys of Sonoma and Napa, with their balmy days and cool nights, are in full fruition today. While the wines produced here are praised and savored by connoisseurs throughout the world, the area continues to be a fermenting vat of experimentation, a proving ground for the latest techniques of grape-growing and wine-making.

In Napa Valley, it seems that every available inch of soil is combed with neat rows of vines; would-be wine-makers with very little acreage can rent the cumbersome, costly machinery needed to stem and press the grapes. Many say making wine is a good way to turn a large fortune into a small one, but that hasn't deterred the doctors, former college professors, publishing tycoons, and airline pilots who come to try their hand at it.

Twenty years ago, Napa Valley had no more than 20 wineries; today there are almost 10 times that number. In Sonoma County, where the web of vineyards is looser, there are more than 100 wineries, and development is now claiming the cool Carneros region at the head of the San Francisco Bay, deemed ideal for growing the currently favored chardonnay grape.

All this has meant some pretty stiff competition, and the wine-makers are constantly honing their skills, aided by the scientific know-how of graduates of the nearby University of California at Davis, as well as by the practical knowledge of the grape-growers. They experiment with planting the vine stock closer together and with "canopy management" of the grape cluster, as well as with "cold" fermentation in stainless steel vats and new methods of fining, or filtering, the wine.

In the past, the emphasis was on creating wines to be cellared, but today "drinkable" wines that can be enjoyed relatively rapidly are in demand. This has led to the celebration of dining as an art in the Wine Country. Many wineries boast first-class restaurants, which showcase excellent California cuisine and their own fine wines.

The stretch of highway from Napa to Calistoga rivals Disneyland as the biggest tourist draw in the state. Two-lane Highway 129 slows to a sluggish crawl on weekends throughout the year, and there are acres of vehicles parked at the picnic places, upscale gift shops, and restaurants in the area.

The pace in Sonoma County is less frenetic. While Napa is upscale and elegant, Sonoma is overalls-and-corduroy, with an air of rustic innocence. But the county's Alexander, Dry Creek, and Russian River valleys are no less productive of award-winning vintages. The Sonoma countryside also offers excellent opportunities for hiking, biking, camping, and fishing.

In addition to state-of-the-art viticulture, the Wine Country also provides a look at California's history. In the town of Sonoma, you'll find remnants of Mexican California and the solid, ivy-covered, brick wineries built by Haraszthy and his disciples. The original attraction here was the water, and the rush to the spas of Calistoga, promoted by the indefatigable gold-rush entrepreneur Samuel Brannan in the late 19th century, left a legacy of fretwork, clapboard, and Gothic architecture. More recent architectural details can be found at the Art Nouveau mansion of the Beringer brothers in St. Helena and the latter-day postmodern extravaganza of Clos Pegase in Calistoga.

The courting of the tourist trade has produced tensions, and some residents wonder whether projects like the Wine Train, running between Napa and St. Helena, brings the theme-park atmosphere a little too close to home. These fears may or may not be realized, but the natural beauty of the landscape will always draw tourists. Whether in the spring, when the vineyards bloom yellow with mustard flowers, or in the fall, when fruit is ripening, this slice of California has a feel reminiscent of the hills of Tuscany or Provence. Haraszthy was right: This is a chosen place.

Essential Information

Important Addresses and Numbers

Tourist Information
Calistoga Chamber of Commerce (1458 Lincoln Ave., Calistoga 94515, tel. 707/942–6333).

Healdsburg Chamber of Commerce (217 Healdsburg Ave., Healdsburg 95448, tel. 707/433–6935 or 800/648–9922 in CA).

Napa Valley Conference and Visitors Bureau (1310 Napa Town Center, Napa 94559, tel. 707/226–7459).

Redwood Empire Association (785 Market St., 15th Floor, San Francisco 94103, tel. 415/543–8334, fax 415/543–8337). The Redwood Empire Visitors' Guide is available free at the office or for $3 by mail.

St. Helena Chamber of Commerce (1080 Main St., Box 124, St. Helena 94574, tel. 707/963–4456 or 800/767–8528, fax 707/963–5396).

Sonoma County Convention and Visitors Bureau (5000 Roberts Lake Rd., Rohnert Park 94928, tel. 707/586–8100 or 800/326–7666, fax 707/586–8111).

Sonoma Valley Visitors Bureau (453 1st St. E, Sonoma 95476, tel. 707/996–1090).

Emergencies
The emergency number for fire, police, ambulance, and paramedics is 911; or dial 0 for operator and ask to be connected with the appropriate agency.

Getting Around

By Plane
The San Francisco and Oakland airports are closest to the Wine Country.

By Bus
Greyhound (tel. 800/231–2222) runs buses from the Transbay Terminal at 1st and Mission streets to and from Sonoma (two each day) and Santa Rosa (two each day). Sonoma County Area Transit (tel. 707/585–7516) and Napa Valley Transit (tel. 707/255–7631) provide local transportation within towns in the Wine Country.

By Car
Although traffic on the two-lane country roads can be heavy, the best way to get around the Wine Country is by private car. Rental cars are available at the airports and in San Francisco, Oakland, Santa Rosa, and Napa.

The Rider's Guide (484 Lake Park Ave., Suite 255, Oakland 94610, tel. 510/653–2553) produces tapes about the history, landmarks, and wineries of the Sonoma and Napa valleys that you can play in your car (maps also provided). The tapes are available at some local bookstores or can be ordered directly from the Rider's Guide for $12.95, plus $2 postage.

Guided Tours

Full-day guided tours of the Wine Country usually include lunch and cost about $50. The guides, some of whom are winery owners themselves, know the area well and may show you some lesser-known cellars.

Gray Line Inc. (425 Mission St., San Francisco 94105, tel. 415/558–9400) has bright-red double-deckers that tour the Wine Country. Reservations are required.

Great Pacific Tour Co. (518 Octavia St., San Francisco 94102, tel. 415/626–4499) offers full-day tours, including a picnic lunch, to Napa and Sonoma, in passenger vans that seat 13.

HMS Tours (707 Fourth St., Santa Rosa 95404, tel. 707/526–2922 or 800/367–5348) offers customized tours of the Wine Country by appointment.

Napa Valley Wine Train (1275 McKinstry St., Napa 94559, tel. 707/253–2111, 800/522–4142, or 800/427–4124 in CA) allows you to enjoy lunch, dinner, or a weekend brunch on one of several restored 1915 Pullman railroad cars that now run between Napa and St. Helena on tracks that were formerly owned by the Southern Pacific Railroad. Round-trip fare is $29; a three-course brunch costs $22, a three-course lunch is $25 and a five-course dinner is $45 (train fare is reduced to $14.50 for dinner parties of two or more). During the winter, service is limited to Thursday–Sunday. There is a special car for families with children on the weekend brunch trips.

Superior Sightseeing (642 Alvarado St., Suite 100, San Francisco 94114, tel. 415/550–1352) limits its full-day excursions to 20 passengers. The company offers personalized itineraries on request and provides free hotel pickup as well as group and senior-citizen rates. Reservations are required.

Wine Country Wagons (Box 1069, Kenwood 95452, tel. 707/833–2724, fax 707/833–1041) offers four-hour horse-drawn wagon tours that take in three wineries and end at a private ranch for a lavish buffet lunch. Tours depart daily at 10 AM, May–October; advance reservations are required.

Exploring the Wine Country

There are three major paths through the Wine Country: U.S. 101 north from Santa Rosa, Highways 12 and 121 through Sonoma County, and Highway 29 north from Napa.

From San Francisco, cross the Golden Gate Bridge and follow U.S. 101 to Santa Rosa and points north. Or cross the Golden Gate, go north on U.S. 101, east on Highway 37, and north on Highway 121 into Sonoma. Yet another route runs over the San Francisco Bay

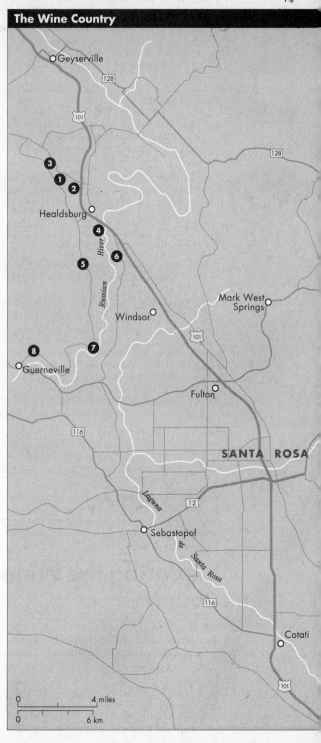

The Wine Country

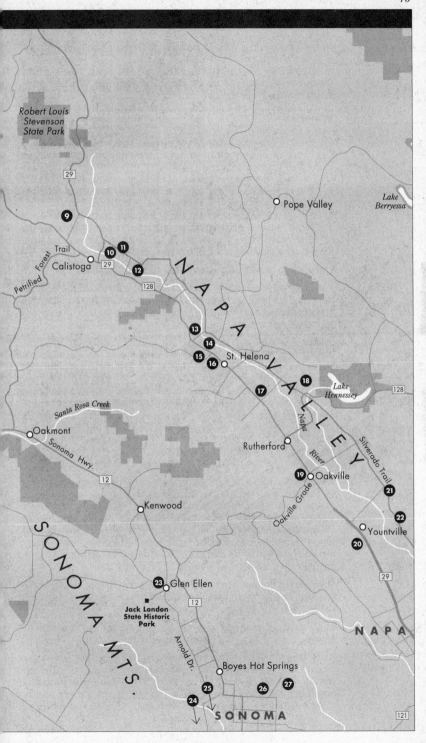

Bridge and along I–80 to Vallejo, where Highway 29 leads north to Napa.

If you approach the Wine Country from the east, you'll travel along I–80 and then turn northwest on Highway 12 for a 10-minute drive through a hilly pass to Highway 29. From the north, take U.S. 101 south to Geyserville, turn southeast on Highway 128, and drive down into the Napa Valley.

Wineries

Choosing which of the 400 or so wineries to visit will be difficult, and the range of opportunities makes it tempting to make multiple stops. Being adventurous will pay off. The wineries along Napa Valley's more frequented arteries tend to charge nominal fees for tasting, but in Sonoma County, where there is less tourist traffic, fees are the exception rather than the rule. In Sonoma, you are more likely to run into a wine-grower who is willing to spend part of an afternoon in convivial conversation than you are along the main drag of Napa Valley, where the waiter serving yards of bar has time to do little more than keep track of the rows of glasses.

Unless otherwise noted, visits to the wineries listed are free.

Highway 29 The town of **Napa** is the gateway into the famous valley, with its unrivaled climate and neat rows of vineyards. The towns in the area are small, and their Victorian Gothic architecture adds to the self-contained and separate feeling that permeates the valley.

A few miles north of Napa is the small town of **Yountville.** Turn west off Highway 29 at the Veterans Home exit and then up California Drive to **Domaine Chandon,** owned by the French champagne producer Moet-Hennessy and Louis Vuitton. You can tour the sleek modern facilities of this beautifully maintained property and sample flutes of the méthode champenoise sparkling wine. Champagne is $3–$4 per glass, the hors d'oeuvres are complimentary, and there is an elegant restaurant. *California Dr., Yountville, tel. 707/944–2280. Tours May–Oct., daily 11–5; Nov.–Apr., Wed.–Sun. 11–5. Closed major holidays. Restaurant closed Mon. and Tues. (Nov.–Apr.), Jan. 1–19; closed for dinner May–Oct., Mon. and Tues.*

Vintage 1870, a 26-acre complex of boutiques, restaurants, and gourmet stores, is on the east side of Highway 29. The vine-covered brick buildings were built in 1870 and originally housed a winery, livery stable, and distillery. The original mansion of the property is now **Compadres Bar and Grill,** and the adjacent **Red Rock Cafe** is housed in the train depot Samuel Brannan built in 1868 for his privately owned Napa Valley Railroad. The remodeled railroad cars now accommodate guests at the Napa Valley Railway Inn.

Washington Square, at the north end of Yountville, is a complex of shops and restaurants; **Pioneer Cemetery,** where the town's founder, George Yount, is buried, is across the street.

Many premier wineries lie along the route from Yountville to St. Helena.

At **Robert Mondavi,** tasters are encouraged to take the 60-minute production tour with complimentary tasting before trying the reserved wines ($1–$5 per glass). In depth, 3- to 4-hour tours and gourmet lunch tours are also popular. There is an art gallery, and in summer there are concerts on the grounds. *7801 St. Helena Hwy.,*

Oakville, tel. 707/963–9611. Open May–Oct., daily 9–5:30; Nov.–Apr., daily 9:30–4:30. Reservations advised in summer. Closed major holidays.

The **Charles Krug Winery** opened in 1861 when Count Haraszthy loaned Krug a small cider press. It is the oldest winery in the Napa Valley, and is run by the Peter Mondavi family. There is also a gift shop. *2800 N. Main St., St. Helena, tel. 707/963–5057. Open May–Oct., Mon.–Thurs. 10–5, Fri.–Sun. 10–6; Nov.–Apr., Mon.–Thurs. 10:30–4:30, Fri.–Sun. 10–5. Closed major holidays.*

The wine made at **V. Sattui** is sold only on the premises; the tactic draws crowds, as does the huge gourmet delicatessen with its exotic cheeses and pâtés. Award-winning wines include dry Johannisberg Rieslings, zinfandels, and Madeiras. *1111 White La., St. Helena, tel. 707/963–7774. Open daily 9–5. Closed Christmas.*

The town of St. Helena boasts many Victorian buildings. Don't overlook the **Silverado Museum,** two blocks east from Main Street on Adams. Its Robert Louis Stevenson memorabilia consist of more than 8,000 artifacts, including first editions, manuscripts, and photographs. *1490 Library La., tel. 707/963–3757. Admission free. Open Tues.–Sun. noon–4. Closed major holidays.*

Beringer Vineyards has been operating continually since 1876. Tastings are held in the Rhine House mansion, where hand-carved oak and walnut and stained glass show Belgian Art Nouveau at its most opulent. The Beringer brothers, Frederick and Jacob, built the mansion in 1883 for the princely sum of $30,000. Tours are given every 30 minutes, and include a visit to the deep limestone tunnels in which the wines mature. *2000 Main St., St. Helena, tel. 707/963–4812. Open daily 9:30–4; summer hours are sometimes extended to 5. Closed major holidays.*

Freemark Abbey Winery was founded in the 1880s by Josephine Tychson, the first woman to establish a winery in California. *3022 St. Helena Hwy. N, St. Helena, tel. 707/963–9694. Open Mar.–Dec., daily 10–4:30; Jan.–Feb., Thurs.–Sun. 10–4:30. One tour daily at 2 PM.*

The **Hurd Beeswax Candle Factory** is next door, with two restaurants and a gift shop that specializes in handcrafted candles made on the premises.

The **Sterling Vineyards** sits on a hilltop to the east near Calistoga. The pristine white Mediterranean-style buildings are reached by an enclosed gondola from the valley floor; the view from the tasting room is superb. *1111 Dunaweal La., Calistoga, tel. 707/942–5151. Tram fee: $6 adults, children under 16 free. Open daily 10:30–4:30. Closed major holidays.*

At **Clos Pegase,** neo-classicism sets the tone. The winery, designed by architect Michael Graves, the exemplar of postmodernism, and commissioned by Jan Schrem, a publisher and art collector, pays homage to art, wine, and mythology. *1060 Dunaweal La., Calistoga, tel. 707/942–4981. Open daily 10:30–5. Closed major holidays.*

Calistoga, at the head of the Napa Valley, is noted for its mineral water, hot mineral springs, mud baths, steam baths, and massages. The Calistoga Hot Springs Resort was founded in 1859 by maverick entrepreneur Sam Brannan, whose ambition was to found "the Saratoga of California." He tripped up the pronunciation of the phrase at a formal banquet—it came out "Calistoga"—and the name stuck. One of his cottages, preserved as the Sharpsteen Museum, has a magnificent diorama of the resort in its heyday. *1311 Washing-*

ton St., tel. 707/942–5911. Donations accepted. Open May–Oct., daily
10–4; Nov.–Apr., daily noon–4.

Chateau Montelena is a vine-covered 1882 building set amid Chinese-inspired gardens, complete with a lake, red pavilions, and arched bridges. It's a romantic spot for a picnic, but you must reserve in advance. *1429 Tubbs La., Calistoga, tel. 707/942–5105 or 800/222–7288. Open daily 10–4. Tours at 11 and 2 by appointment only.*

The **Silverado Trail,** which runs parallel to Highway 29, takes you away from the madding crowd to some distinguished wineries as you travel north from Napa.

Clos du Val. Bernard Portet, the French owner, produces a celebrated cabernet sauvignon at this winery on the Silverado Trail. *5330 Silverado Trail, tel. 707/259–2200. Open daily 10–5.*

Stag's Leap Wine Cellars. In 1993, the winery's 1990 Reserve Chardonnay garnered a platinum award designating it the highest ranked premium Chardonnay in the world by the World Wine Championships. Also in 1993, *Bon Appetit*'s "Best Wines of the Year" featured both the 1990 Chardonnay and the Stag's Leap 1989 Cabernet. *5766 Silverado Trail, tel. 707/944–2020. Tasting fee: $3. Open daily 10–4. Tours by appointment. Closed major holidays.*

Rutherford Hill Winery. The wine here is aged in French oak barrels stacked in more than 30,000 square feet of caves. You can tour the nation's largest such facility and picnic on the grounds. *200 Rutherford Hill Rd., Rutherford, tel. 707/963–7194. Open weekdays 10–4:30, weekends 10–5, summer weekends (Fri.–Sun.) 11–6. Tour times vary seasonally; call ahead for detailed information.*

Cuvaison. This Swiss-owned winery specializes in chardonnay, merlot, and cabernet sauvignon for the export market. There are several picnic areas on the grounds, all with views of Napa Valley. *4550 Silverado Trail, tel. 707/942–6266. Open daily 10–5. Tours by appointment.*

Calistoga Gliders will give you a bird's-eye view of the entire valley, and on a clear day you can also see the San Francisco skyline, snow-capped Sierra peaks, and the Pacific Ocean. *1546 Lincoln Ave., tel. 707/942–5000. Fees: $110–$150 for two passengers, depending on length of ride. Open daily 9 AM–sunset, weather permitting. Closed Thanksgiving and Christmas.*

You don't have to be a registered guest at a spa to experience a mud bath. At **Dr. Wilkinson's Hot Springs** a $45 fee gets you "The Works": mud baths, individual mineral-water showers and a mineral-water whirlpool, followed by time in the steam room and a blanket wrap. For $65, you also get a half-hour massage. *1507 Lincoln Ave., Calistoga, tel. 707/942–4102. Open daily 8–3:30. Reservations are recommended.*

Highway 12 Rustic Sonoma is anchored by its past. It is the site of the last and the northernmost of the 21 missions established by the Franciscan order of Fra Junipero Serra, and its central plaza includes the largest group of old adobes north of Monterey. The **Mission San Francisco Solano,** whose chapel and school labored to bring Christianity to the Indians, is now a museum that displays a collection of 19th-century watercolors. *114 Spain St. E, tel. 707/938–1519. Admission: $2 adults, $1 children 6–12; includes the Sonoma Barracks on the central plaza and General Vallejo's home, Lachryma Montis (see* below*). Open daily 10–5. Closed Thanksgiving, Christmas, New Year's Day.*

Time Out The four-block **Sonoma Plaza** is an inviting array of shops and food stores that overlook the shady park and attract gourmets from miles around. You can pick up the makings for a first-rate picnic here. The **Sonoma French Bakery** (466 1st St. E) is famous for its sourdough bread and cream puffs. The **Sonoma Sausage Co.** (453 1st St. W) produces a mind-boggling selection of bratwurst, bologna, boudin, bangers, and other Old World sausages. There are good cold cuts, too. The **Sonoma Cheese Factory** (2 Spain St.), run by the same family for four generations, makes Sonoma jack cheese and a tangy new creation, Sonoma Teleme. You can peer through the windows at the cheese-making process: great swirling baths of milk and curds and the wheels of cheese being pressed flat to dry.

A few blocks west (and quite a hike) is the tree-lined approach to **Lachryma Montis,** which General Mariano Vallejo, the last Mexican governor of California, built for his large family in 1851. The Victorian Gothic house is secluded in the midst of beautiful gardens; opulent Victorian furnishings, including a white marble fireplace in every room, are particularly noteworthy. The state purchased the home in 1933. *Spain St. W, tel. 707/938–1519. Admission: $2 adults, $1 children 6–12. Open daily 10–5. Closed Thanksgiving, Christmas, New Year's Day.*

The **Sebastiani Vineyards,** originally planted by Franciscans of the Sonoma Mission in 1825, were bought by Samuele Sebastiani in 1904. The Sebastianis are renowned producers of red wines, and Sylvia Sebastiani has recorded her good Italian home cooking in a family recipe book, *Mangiamo,* to complement them. Tours include a look at an unusual collection of impressive carved oak casks. *389 4th St. E, tel. 707/938–5532. Open daily 10–5; last tour at 4:30. Closed major holidays.*

The landmark **Buena Vista Carneros Winery** (follow signs from the plaza), set among towering trees and fountains, is a must-see in Sonoma. It was here, in 1857, that Count Agoston Haraszthy de Mokcsa laid the basis for modern California wine-making, bucking the conventional wisdom that vines should be planted on well-watered ground by instead planting on well-drained hillsides. Chinese laborers dug the cool aging tunnels 100 feet into the hillside, and the limestone they extracted was used to build the main house. Although the wines are produced elsewhere in the Carneros region today, there are tours, a gourmet shop, an art gallery, and great picnic spots. *18000 Old Winery Rd., tel. 707/938–1266. Open daily 10–4:30.*

In the Carneros region of the Sonoma Valley, south of Sonoma, the wines at **Gloria Ferrer Champagne Caves** are aged in a "cava," or cellar, where several feet of earth maintain a constant temperature. *23555 Carneros Hwy. 121, tel. 707/996–7256. Tasting fees vary by the glass and the type of champagne. Open daily 10:30–5:30, tours every hour from 11–4.*

One of the newer wineries in Sonoma Valley is **Viansa,** opened by a son of the famous Sebastiani family, who decided to strike out on his own. Looking like a transplanted Tuscan villa, the winery's ocher-colored building is surrounded by olive trees and overlooks the valley. Inside is an Italian food and gift market. *25200 Arnold Dr., Sonoma, tel. 707/935–4700. Open daily 10–5.*

Continue north on Highway 12 through lush Sonoma Valley, where writer Jack London lived for many years; much around here has been named for him. The drive along Highway 12 takes you through orchards and rows of vineyards, with oak-covered mountain ranges flanking the valley. Some 2 million cases of wine are bottled in this area annually, and the towns of Glen Ellen and Kenwood are rich in history and lore. **Glen Ellen,** with its century-old Jack London Bar, is nestled at the base of the hill leading to Jack London State Park and the Benziger Family Winery. Nearby is Grist Mill Inn, a historic landmark with shops, and Jack London Village, with a charming bookstore filled with London's books and memorabilia. **Kenwood** is home to several important wineries, a historic train depot, and several eateries and shops specializing in locally produced gourmet products.

In the hills above Glen Ellen, known as the Valley of the Moon, is **Jack London State Historic Park.** The House of Happy Walls is a museum of London's effects, including his collection of South Sea artifacts. The ruins of Wolf House, which London designed and which mysteriously burned down just before he was to move in, are nearby, and London is buried on the property. *2400 London Ranch Rd., tel. 707/938–5216. Parking: $5 per car; $4 per car driven by senior citizen. Park open daily 9:30–sunset, museum daily 10–5. Museum closed Thanksgiving, Christmas, New Year's Day.*

The Glen Ellen Winery is now the **Benziger Family Winery,** specializing in premium estate and Sonoma County wines. Their Imagery Series is a low-volume release of unusual red and white wines distributed in bottles with art labels by well-known artists from all over the world. *1883 London Ranch Rd., Glen Ellen, tel. 707/935–3000. Complimentary tasting of Sonoma County wines; fees vary for tasting estate and Imagery wines. Open daily 10–4:30.*

The beautifully rustic grounds of **Kenwood Vineyards** perfectly match the winery's approach to presenting wine, from the tasting room to bottle labels. While they produce all premium varietals, they are best known for their signature Jack London Vineyard reds—pinot noir, zinfandel, cabernet and merlot, and their Artist Series Cabernet. *9592 Sonoma Hwy., Kenwood, tel. 707/833–5891. Tasting available, no tours. Open daily 10–4:30.*

U.S. 101   Santa Rosa is the Wine Country's largest city and your best bet for a moderately priced hotel room, especially if you haven't reserved in advance.

The **Luther Burbank Home and Gardens** commemorate the great botanist, who lived and worked on these grounds for 50 years, single-handedly developing modern techniques of hybridization. Arriving as a young man from New England, he wrote: "I firmly believe... that this is the chosen spot of all the earth, as far as nature is concerned." The Santa Rosa plum, the Shasta daisy, and the lily of the Nile agapanthus are among the 800 or so plants he developed or improved. In the music room of his house, a Webster's Dictionary of 1946 lies open to a page on which the verb "burbank" is defined as "to modify and improve plant life." *Santa Rosa and Sonoma Aves., tel. 707/524–5445. Gardens free and open Nov.–Mar., daily 8–5; Apr.–Oct., daily 8–7. Guided tours: $2, children under 12 free; tours Apr.–Oct., Wed.–Sun. 10–4.*

The wineries of Sonoma County are located along winding roads and are not immediately obvious to the casual visitor; a tour of the vineyards that lie along the Russian River is a leisurely and especially bucolic experience. For a free map of the area, contact Russian River Wine Road (Box 46, Healdsburg 95448, tel. 707/433–6782).

For a historical overview, start at the imposing **Korbel Champagne Cellars,** which displays photographic documents of the North West Railway in a former train stop on its property. *13250 River Rd., Guerneville, tel. 707/887–2294. Open Oct.–Apr., daily 9–4:30; May–Sept., daily 9–5. Tours on the hour 10–3.*

Armstrong Woods State Reserve, just outside of Guerneville, contains 752 acres of virgin redwoods and is the best place in the Wine Country to see California's most famous trees. West of Guerneville along the Russian River Road (Highway 116) that leads to the Pacific Ocean and the rugged Sonoma coast is more redwood country, and a string of small towns. **Duncans Mills** is an old logging and railroad town with a complex of shops and a small museum in an old train depot. At the coast is **Jenner,** where the Russian River meets the Pacific. A colony of harbor seals makes its home here March through June. There are several bed-and-breakfasts here, and restaurants specializing in seafood.

Traveling down the River Road east of Guerneville, turn left down Westside Road and follow it as it winds past a number of award-winning wineries.

Davis Bynum Winery is an up-and-coming label that offers a full line of varietal wines that have done well in recent competitions. *8075 Westside Rd., Healdsburg, tel. 707/433–5852. Open daily 10–5.*

The **Hop Kiln Winery** is in an imposing hops-drying barn, which was built during the early 1900s and used as the backdrop for such films as the 1960 *Lassie* with James Stewart. *6050 Westside Rd., Healdsburg, tel. 707/433–6491. Open daily 10–5.*

Dry Creek Vineyard is one of California's leading producers of white wines and well known for its fumé blanc. Their reds, especially zinfandels and cabernets, have also begun to earn notice. There is a lovely picnic area. *3770 Lambert Bridge Rd., Healdsburg, tel. 707/433–1000. Open daily 10:30–4:30.*

The **Robert Stemmler Winery** draws on German traditions of winemaking and specializes in pinot noir. There are picnic facilities on the grounds. *3805 Lambert Bridge Rd., Healdsburg (Dry Creek Rd. exit from Hwy. 101, northwest 3 mi to Lambert Bridge Rd.), tel. 707/433–6334. Open 10:30–4:30 by appointment only.*

Lytton Springs Winery produces the archetype of the Sonoma Zinfandel, a dark, fruity wine with a high alcohol content. There is still dispute over the origin of this varietal and whether it was transplanted from stock in New England, but the vines themselves are distinctive, gnarled, and stocky, many of them over a century old. *650 Lytton Springs Rd., Healdsburg, tel. 707/433–7721. Open daily 10–4.*

In its new location five miles north of Healdsburg, **Clos du Bois** continues to produce the fine estate chardonnays of the Alexander and Dry Creek Valleys that have been mistaken for great French wines. *19410 Geyserville Ave., Box 940, Geyserville, tel. 707/857–1651 or 800/222–3189. Open daily 10–4:30. Call for tasting appointments.*

South of Healdsburg, off U.S. 101, is **Piper Sonoma,** a state-of-the-art winery that specializes in méthode champenois sparkling wines. *11447 Old Redwood Hwy., Healdsburg, tel. 707/433–8843. Open daily 10–5.*

Time Out   Once you've seen, heard about, and tasted enough wine for one day, head over to **Kozlowski's Raspberry Farm** (5566 Gravenstein, Hwy. 116N), in Forestville, where jams are made from every berry imaginable.

Also in Forestville, **Brother Juniper's** makes a heavenly Struan bread of polenta, malted barley, brown rice, buttermilk, wheat bran, and oats. *6544 Front St., Hwy. 116, tel. 707/887–7908; 463 Sebastopol Ave., Santa Rosa, tel. 707/542–9012. Open Mon.–Sat. 9–3.*

What to See and Do with Children

In the **Bale Grist Mill State Historic Park** there is a partially restored 1846 flour mill powered by a 36-foot overshot water wheel. Short paths lead from the access road to the mill and the old pond site. *3 mi north of St. Helena on Hwy. 29, tel. 707/942–4575. Day use: $2 adults, $1 children 6–17. Open daily 10–5. Water-wheel demonstrations on weekends. Call ahead for special tour arrangements.*

Old Faithful Geyser of California blasts a 60-foot tower of steam and vapor about every 40 minutes; the pattern is disrupted if there's an earthquake in the offing. One of just three regularly erupting geysers in the world, it is fed by an underground river that heats to 350°F. The spout lasts three minutes. Picnic facilities are available. *1299 Tubbs La., 1 mi north of Calistoga, tel. 707/942–6463. Admission: $4.50 adults, $3.50 senior citizens, $2 children 6–11. Open daily 9–6 during daylight saving time, 9–5 in winter.*

In the **Petrified Forest** you can see the result of volcanic eruptions of Mount St. Helena 3.4 million years ago. The force of the explosion uprooted the gigantic redwoods, covered them with volcanic ash, and infiltrated the trees with silicas and minerals, causing petrification. There is a museum, and picnic facilities are available. *4100 Petrified Forest Rd., 5 mi west of Calistoga, tel. 707/942–6667. Admission: $3 adults, $2 senior citizens, $1 children 4–11. Open summer, daily 10–6; winter, daily 10–5.*

The Redwood Empire Ice Arena in Santa Rosa is not just another skating rink. It was built by local resident Charles Schulz, creator of *Peanuts.* The Snoopy Gallery and gift shop, with Snoopy books, clothing, and life-size comic strip characters, is delightful. *1667 W. Steele La., tel. 707/546–7147. Public skating in the afternoons.*

A scale steam train at **Train Town** runs for 20 minutes through a forested park with trestles, bridges, and small animals. *20264 Broadway (Hwy. 12), 1 mi south of Sonoma Plaza, tel. 707/938–3912. Admission: $3.50 adults, $2.50 children under 16 and senior citizens. Open mid-June–Labor Day, daily 10:30–5; Sept.–mid-June, Fri.–Sun. and holidays 10:30–5. Closed Christmas.*

Howarth Memorial Park, in Santa Rosa, has a lake where canoes, rowboats, paddleboats, and small sailboats can be rented for $6 an hour. The children's area has a playground, pony rides, a petting zoo, a merry-go-round, and a miniature train. Fishing, tennis, and hiking trails are also available. *Summerfield Rd. off Montgomery Rd., tel. 707/543–3282. Amusements: 75¢–$1. Park open daily; children's area open summer, Wed.–Sun.; spring and fall, weekends.*

Off the Beaten Track

You'll see breathtaking views of both the Sonoma and Napa valleys along the hairpin turns of the **Oakville Grade,** which twists along the range dividing the two valleys. The surface of the road is good, and if you're comfortable with mountain driving, you'll enjoy this half-hour excursion. Driving the road at night however, can be difficult. Trucks are advised not to take this route at any time.

Robert Louis Stevenson State Park, on Highway 29, 3 miles northeast of Calistoga, encompasses the summit of Mount St. Helena. It was here, in an abandoned bunkhouse of the Silverado Mine, that Stevenson and his bride, Fanny Osbourne, spent their honeymoon in the summer of 1880. The stay inspired Stevenson's "The Silverado Squatters," and Spyglass Hill in *Treasure Island* is thought to be a portrait of Mount St. Helena. The park's 3,000 acres are undeveloped except for a fire trail leading to the site of the cabin, which is marked with a marble tablet, and then on to the summit. Picnicking is permitted, but fires are not.

Shopping

Most wineries will ship purchases. Don't expect bargains at the wineries themselves, where prices are generally as high as at retail outlets. Residents report that the area's supermarkets stock a wide selection of local wines at lower prices. For connoisseurs seeking extraordinary values, the **All Seasons Cafe Wine Shop** in Calistoga (tel. 707/942–6828) is a true find. Gift shops in the larger wineries offer the ultimate in gourmet items—you could easily stock up early on Christmas presents.

Sports and the Outdoors

Ballooning   This sport has fast become part of the scenery in the Wine Country, and many hotels arrange excursions. Most flights take place soon after sunrise, when the calmest, coolest time of day offers maximum lift and soft landings. Prices depend on the duration of the flight, number of passengers, and services (some companies provide pickup at your lodging, champagne brunch after the flight, and so forth). Expect to spend about $165 per person. Companies that provide flights include **Balloons Above the Valley** (Box 3838, Napa 94558, tel. 707/253–2222 or 800/464–6824 in CA), **Napa Valley Balloons** (Box 2860, Yountville 94599, tel. 707/944–0228 or 800/253–2224), **Once in a Lifetime** (Box 795, Calistoga 94515, tel. 707/942–6541 or 800/659–9915), and **Napa's Great Balloon Escape** (Box 795, Calistoga 94515, tel. 707/253–0860 or 800/564–9399), featuring a catered brunch finale at the Silverado Country Club overlooking the golf course.

Bicycling   One of the best ways to experience the countryside is on two wheels, and the Eldorado Bike Trail through the area is considered one of the best. Reasonably priced rentals are available in most towns.

Golf   Although the weather is mild year-round, rain may occasionally prevent your teeing off in the winter months. Call to check on greens fees at **Fountaingrove Country Club** (1525 Fountaingrove Pkwy., Santa Rosa, tel. 707/579–4653), **Oakmont Golf Club** (west course: 7025 Oakmont Dr., Santa Rosa, tel. 707/539–0415; east course: 565 Oak Vista Ct., Santa Rosa, tel. 707/538–2454), **Silverado Country Club** (1600 Atlas Peak Rd., Napa, tel. 707/257–0200), or **The Char-**

donnay Club (2555 Jameson Canyon Rd., Napa, tel. 707/257–8950), a favorite among Bay Area golfers.

Dining

Revised by
Catherine
McEver

A Bay Area
resident for
over 20 years
and a freelance
writer,
Catherine
McEver has
covered every
aspect of the
local food
scene—from
appetizers to
ambience—for
SF Magazine
and the East
Bay Express.

The restaurants in the Wine Country have traditionally reflected the culinary heritage of early settlers from Italy, France, and Mexico. Star chefs from urban areas are the most recent influx of immigrants, bringing creative California cuisine, seafood, and an eclectic range of American-regional and international fare. Food now rivals wine as the prime attraction in the region. A common element in today's Wine Country restaurants is reliance on fresh produce, meats, and prime ingredients from local farms. Those on a budget will find an appealing range of reasonably priced eateries. Gourmet delis offer superb picnic fare, and brunch is a cost-effective strategy at high-end restaurants.

With few exceptions (which are noted), dress is informal. Where reservations are indicated to be essential, you may need to reserve a week or more ahead; during the summer and early fall harvest seasons you may need to book several months ahead.

Category	Cost*
$$$$	over $40
$$$	$25–$40
$$	$16–$25
$	under $16

per person for a three-course meal, excluding drinks, service, and 7¹/4% sales tax

Calistoga
$$

All Seasons Cafe. Bistro cuisine has a California spin in this sun-filled setting with marble tables and a black-and-white checkerboard floor. A seasonal menu featuring organic greens, wild mushrooms, local game birds, house-smoked beef and salmon, and homemade breads, desserts, and ice cream from their on-site ice-cream plant, is coupled with a superb listing of local wines at bargain prices. For lunch there's a tempting selection of pizza, pasta, and sandwiches. *1400 Lincoln Ave., tel. 707/942–9111. Reservations advised on weekends. MC, V. Brunch Fri.–Sun. Closed Tues. dinner and Wed.*

$–$$

Silverado Restaurant & Tavern. In a setting straight out of a spaghetti western, savvy locals and seasoned wine connoisseurs linger over an award-winning wine list with over 700 selections priced just above retail. The eclectic menu includes egg rolls, chicken-salad sandwiches, Caesar salad, and great burgers. *1373 Lincoln Ave., tel. 707/942–6725. Reservations advised. MC, V. Closed Wed.*

$

Boskos Ristorante. Settling nicely into its second decade and its second home—a restored sandstone building that dates back to the 1800s—this popular eatery continues to dish up homemade pasta, pizza, and garden-fresh salads. *Glorioso* (pasta shells with garlic, mushrooms, and red chilies), is a favorite entrée. Leave room for the homemade chocolate cheesecake. *1364 Lincoln Ave., tel. 707/942–9088. No reservations. No credit cards.*

Geyserville
$–$$

Château Souverain Café. Those who mourned the closing of the Château's restaurant now have reason to celebrate. The new café has the same spectacular view of Alexander Valley vineyards and the same outdoor terrace for tranquil summer lunches, but now features radically reduced prices. The low tab makes chef Martin Courtman's seductive menu of French country fare such as braised lamb shanks, Sonoma roast chicken, or grilled buckwheat polenta with gorgonzola cheese irresistible. Check for expanded hours as café matures. *400 Souverain Rd. (Independence La. exit west from Hwy. 101), tel. 707/433–3141. Reservations advised. AE, MC, V. Closed Mon.–Thurs.*

Healdsburg **The Restaurant at Madrona Manor.** A brick oven, smokehouse, or-
$$$$ chard, and kitchen garden on-site, paired with fresh Sonoma produce, lamb raised by local rancher Bruce Campbell, and choice seafood, enable chef Todd Muir to turn out dishes fit for a wine baron: smoked lamb salad, Dungeness crab mousse, acorn squash soup, oven-roasted pork tenderloin, and Grand Marnier crème caramel. The 1881 Victorian mansion surrounded by eight acres of wooded and landscaped grounds provides a storybook setting for a candlelight dinner in one of the formal dining rooms, or brunch on the outdoor deck. A la carte and prix fixe. *1001 Westside Rd. (take central Healdsburg exit from Hwy. 101, turn left on Mill St.), tel. 707/433–4231. Reservations advised. AE, D, DC, MC, V. Dinner only. Sun. brunch.*

$$ **Tre Scalini Ristorante.** Neo-Tuscan decor with mellow golden hues and live classical music Friday and Saturday nights provide the perfect backdrop for chef-owner Fernando Urroz's contemporary take on northern Italian cuisine. The menu changes quarterly to feature dishes such as fresh sea scallops baked in paper with saffron-infused polenta and sweet roasted peppers; wild mushroom fettuccine with crushed chilis, garlic, essence of white peppers and truffle oil; and braised Sonoma rabbit with a sauce of red wine, balsamic vinegar, and sweet onions. *241 Healdsburg Ave. (¼ block south of town plaza), tel. 707/433–1772. Reservations advised. AE, MC, V. Dinner only. Closed Tues.*

$–$$ **Bistro Ralph.** Ralph Tingle, once executive chef of the defunct Fetzer Vineyards Sun Dial Grill in Mendocino, has created a culinary hit with his California homestyle cuisine. The small, frequently changing menu includes Szechuan pepper calamari, braised lamb shanks with mint essence (from Bruce Campbell's ranch), and sea bass braised with ginger and carrot juice. Wine is used liberally in the cooking and the wine list features picks from small local wineries. *109 Plaza St., tel. 707/433–1380. Reservations advised. MC, V. No lunch weekends.*

$–$$ **Samba Java.** This lively café manages to cram a lot of tables, colorful decor, and culinary action into a very small space. The menu covers an eclectic range of California-American cuisine, is based exclusively on Sonoma ingredients, and changes daily. Everything on it is made from scratch: from breads and preserves to a succulent roasted pork loin with a sweet-potato *galette* (razor-thin slices layered with olive oil and herbs) and wilted bitter greens to a coconut *tuille* (delicate cookie cup) filled with chocolate mousse and raspberry sauce. *109A Plaza St., tel. 707/433–5282. Reservations accepted for dinner; lunch reservations for 6 or more only. AE, MC, V. No lunch Mon. No dinner Sun.–Wed. Breakfast served Tues.–Sun.*

Napa **Silverado Country Club.** There are two restaurants and a bar and
$$$ grill at this large, famous resort. Vintner's Court, with California-Continental cuisine, serves dinner only; there is a seafood buffet on Friday night and a champagne brunch on Sunday. Royal Oak serves steak and seafood for dinner nightly. The bar and grill is open for breakfast and lunch year-round; in the summer, lunch offerings in-

clude an outdoor barbecue with chicken and hamburgers. *1600 Atlas Peak Rd. (follow signs to Lake Berryessa), tel. 707/257–0200. Reservations required for two restaurants only. Jackets suggested in Vintner's Court. AE, D, DC, MC, V. Vintner's Court closed Mon. and Tues. No dinner Sun.*

$$–$$$ **La Boucane.** Chef-owner Jacques Mokrani has created a gorgeous little gem of a restaurant in a restored 1885 Victorian decorated with period antiques. Classic French cuisine (rack of lamb, champagne-crisp duck) is delivered with style in a candlelit dining room enhanced by silver, linen, and a red rose on each table. *1778 2nd St. (at Jefferson St. in downtown Napa), tel. 707/253–1177. Reservations advised. MC, V. Dinner only. Closed Sun. and Jan.*

$–$$ **Bistro Don Giovanni.** Rumor has it that Alice Waters' first venture in the Wine Country, Table 29, failed because there weren't enough Napa Valley selections on the wine list. Giovanni and Donna Scala, the culinary couple behind the success of Ristorante Piatti, have created a new hit on this site, dishing up Italian and French fare with a California twist. Ingredients such as pesto, goat cheese, and shrimp top individual pies from the wood-burning pizza oven. The carpaccio is a standout. Don't miss the delectable fruit-crisp dessert, which changes daily. *4110 St. Helena Hwy., tel. 707/224–3300. Reservations advised. AE, DC, MC, V.*

$ **Jonesy's Famous Steak House.** This spacious and informal local favorite has been providing lots of entertainment for aviation buffs, steak lovers, and kids of all ages since 1946. One entire wall has an expanse of windows with a prime view of the landing strip. Inside, prime steaks weighted down with Sacramento River rocks are seared over a dry grill. Broasted chicken, homemade soups, and fresh fish round out the fare. Kids get their own menu. *2044 Airport Rd. (halfway between Napa and Vallejo, off Hwy. 29), tel. 707/255–2003. Reservations advised. AE, D, DC, MC, V. Closed Mon. and a week at Christmas.*

Oakville **Stars Oakville Cafe.** Jeremiah Tower, father of California Cuisine,
$$ and Marc Franz (executive chef of Tower's legendary Stars Restaurant in San Francisco) have transformed an old building next to the Oakville Grocery store into a Mediterranean café with glazed tile floors, white walls, lots of flowers, and picture windows that look into the kitchen. Franz designed the wood-burning ovens to turn out rustic fare such as roasted leg of lamb, roast salmon, and roast pumpkin-filled pasta with white truffle oil, for a menu that changes daily. A stellar wine list complements the cuisine; the desserts (brownie-steamed pudding, pumpkin cheesecake) are sublime. Space heaters on the tented outdoor patio add comfort to alfresco dining, and the adjacent garden with lemon trees, lavender, and an antique aviary is the perfect setting for an after-dinner stroll. *7848 St. Helena Hwy. (corner of Hwy. 29 and Oakville Crossroad), tel. 707/944–8905. Reservations required weekends, advised weekdays. AE, D, DC, MC, V. No lunch Mon. and Tues.*

Rutherford **Auberge du Soleil.** The dining room is a setting of rustic elegance:
$$–$$$$ earth tones, wood beams, and outdoor deck with panoramic views of the valley. The menu changes monthly and features local produce and American Wine Country cuisine with some innovative twists. House specialties include roasted lobster sausage and braised California pheasant. There is a moderately-priced bar menu (Dungeness crab quesadillas, black-bean chili) and a fine list of wines from California, France, and Italy. This place is also a 48-room inn (*see* Lodging, *below*). *180 Rutherford Hill Rd. (off Silverado Trail just north of Rte. 128), tel. 707/963–1211. Reservations advised. AE, D, MC, V. Breakfast daily.*

St. Helena
$$–$$$

The Restaurant at Meadowood. This sprawling resort looks like a scene from an F. Scott Fitzgerald novel, complete with croquet lawns, and provides the perfect setting for weekend brunch. Classic French cuisine is offered at dinner in either a dining room that sports a fireplace, lush greenery, and skylights in a cathedral ceiling or outdoors on a terrace overlooking the golf course. A lighter menu of American and French bistro fare can be had at breakfast and lunch (and early dinners Friday and Saturday) at a second, less formal and less expensive Meadowood restaurant, the Grill. *900 Meadowood La., tel. 707/963–3646. Reservations required. Jacket recommended for The Restaurant. AE, D, DC, MC, V.*

$$–$$$

Terra. The delightful couple that owns this lovely, unpretentious restaurant housed in a century-old stone foundry learned their culinary skills at the side of chef Wolfgang Puck. Hiro Sone was head chef at L.A.'s Spago, and Lissa Doumanie was the pastry chef. The menu has an enticing array of southern French and northern Italian favorites, prepared with Hiro's Japanese-French-Italian finesse. Favorites include pear and goat cheese salad with warm pancetta and sherry vinaigrette, and filet of salmon with Thai red-curry sauce and basmati rice. Save room for Lissa's desserts. *1345 Railroad Ave., tel. 707/963–8931. Reservations advised. MC, V. Dinner only. Closed Tues.*

$$–$$$

Trilogy. Chef-owner Diane Pariseau pairs one of the best and most extensive contemporary wine lists in the valley with superb renditions of California-French cuisine on a prix-fixe menu that changes daily. Pariseau has a deft touch at juxtaposing flavors, textures, and artful presentation in her soups, appetizers, salads, and all-star entrées, such as grilled chicken breast on a nest of sautéed apples and green peppercorns or grilled tuna steak with olive oil and sweet red pepper purée. The atmosphere is that of a gracious home: There are just 10 tables tucked away in semiprivate dining areas on two different levels. *1234 Main St., tel. 707/963–5507. Reservations required. MC, V. No lunch weekends. Closed Mon. and 3 wks in Dec.*

$$

Brava Terrace. Owner Fred Halpert is part of the recent influx of all-star chefs who are creating a culinary renaissance in the Wine Country. American-born, French-trained Halpert has worked with head chef Peter McCaffrey to create a menu featuring pasta, risotto, and a trademark lentil cassoulet. The chocolate-chip crème brûlée provides a grand finale. The restaurant has a comfortably casual ambience, a full bar, a large stone fireplace, an outdoor terrace, and an enclosed, heated deck with views of the valley floor and Howell Mountain. *3010 St. Helena Hwy. (Hwy. 29, 1/2 mi north of St. Helena), tel. 707/963–9300. Reservations advised. AE, D, DC, MC, V. Closed Wed. Nov.–Apr. and Jan. 17–26.*

$$

Tra Vigne. A Napa Valley fieldstone building has been transformed into a striking trattoria with beaded lamps and plush banquettes. Homemade breads, pastries, mozzarella, pastas, sauces, olive oils, and vinegar, and house-cured pancetta and prosciutto contribute to a one-of-a-kind tour of Tuscan cuisine. Seating is hopeless without a reservation, but drop-ins are welcome at the bar. The courtyard offers alfresco dining and Mediterranean ambience, and the Cantinetta delicatessen in the corner of the courtyard offers wine by the glass and gourmet picnic fare. *1050 Charter Oak Ave. (off Hwy. 29), tel. 707/963–4444. Reservations required in dining room. D, DC, MC, V.*

Santa Rosa
$$–$$$

John Ash & Co. The thoroughly regional cuisine here emphasizes beauty, innovation, and the seasonal availability of food products grown in Sonoma County and in the restaurant's organic garden. In spring, local lamb is roasted with hazelnuts and honey; in fall, farm pork is roasted with fresh figs and Gravenstein apples. There are fine desserts and an extensive wine list. The place looks like a Spanish villa amid the vineyards, with patio seating outside and a cozy fireplace indoors. This is a favorite spot for Sunday brunch. *4330 Barnes Rd. (River Rd. exit west from Hwy. 101), tel. 707/527–7687. Reservations advised. Jacket preferred. D, MC, V. Closed Mon.*

$–$$ **Lisa Hemenway's.** A shopping center on the outskirts of town seems an unlikely location for a restaurant find, but Hemenway, who trained under John Ash (*see* John Ash & Co., *above*) has created a light and airy eatery with soft wine-country colors, works by local artists on the walls, and a garden view from the patio. The fare (updated every four months) provides a deliciously eclectic tour through American and international cuisine, from grilled Indonesian chicken served over angel hair pasta to vegetable tamales with ancho-chili sauce, black beans, salsa, and sour cream. The adjacent deli, Tote Cuisine, has a vast selection of tempting take-outs for picnickers. *714 Village Ct. Mall (east on Hwy. 12, north on Farmer's La., right on Sonoma), tel. 707/526–5111. Reservations advised. D, MC, V. Sun. brunch.*

$ **Omelette Express.** As the name implies, some 300 omelet possibilities are offered in this friendly no-frills eatery in historic Railroad Square. *112 4th St., tel. 707/525–1690. No reservations weekends. MC, V. Breakfast and lunch only.*

Sonoma **The Grille at Sonoma Mission Inn & Spa.** There are two restaurants
$$$ at this famed resort (*see* The Cafe, *below*). The Grille offers formal dining in a light, airy setting with original art on the walls, French windows overlooking the pool and gardens, and a patio for alfresco dining. Wine Country cuisine changes seasonally to feature favorites like Sonoma leg of lamb and basil-roasted chicken with garlic mashed potatoes. On weekends there's a prix-fixe menu, pairing each course with the appropriate wine from the restaurant's extensive selection. The special spa menu provides a tempting way to stay in shape. *18140 Hwy. 12 (2 mi north of Sonoma at Boyes Blvd.), tel. 707/938–9000. Reservations strongly advised. AE, DC, MC, V. Sun. brunch.*

$$–$$$ **L'Esperance.** The dining room is small and pretty, with flowered tablecloths, burgundy overcloths, and burgundy chairs. There is a choice of classic French entrées, such as rack of lamb, plus a prix-fixe "menu gastronomique" that includes hot and cold appetizers, salad, entrée, dessert, and coffee. *464 1st St. E (down a walkway off the plaza, behind the French bakery), tel. 707/996–2757. Reservations required weekends. AE, MC, V. Sun. brunch. Closed Mon. and Tues.*

$$ **Eastside Oyster Bar & Grill.** Chef-owner Charles Saunders, renowned for his stint at the Sonoma Mission Inn (*see above*), received rave reviews for his creative culinary flair (and health-conscious approach) when this place opened in the fall of 1992. The California fare incorporates fresh fish, local meat and poultry, and produce from an organic kitchen garden. Hits here include a surprisingly delicate hangtown fry (plump oysters on a bed of greens and beets with a Sonoma mustard vinaigrette); creative renditions of roast chicken or Sonoma lamb; and stellar salads and vegetarian dishes. Inside, the restaurant has a fireplace and an intimate bistro atmosphere; outside there's a wisteria-draped terrace where diners enjoy a picture-window view into the pastry kitchen. *133 E. Napa St. (just off downtown plaza square), tel. 707/939–1266. Reservations advised. AE, DC, MC, V. Sun. brunch.*

$$ **Kenwood Restaurant & Bar.** This place's highest recommendation is the fact that when Napa and Sonoma chefs take their night off, they come here. Both in tastes and looks it will remind you of a sunny

hotel dining room in the south of France. Patrons indulge in country French cuisine such as braised rabbit and warm sweetbread salad in the airy dining room, or head through the French doors to the patio where there's a memorable view of the vineyards. *9900 Hwy. 12, Kenwood, tel. 707/833–6326. Reservations advised. MC, V. Sun. brunch. Closed Mon.*

$$ **Ristorante Piatti.** On the ground floor of the remodeled El Dorado Hotel, a 19th-century landmark building, this is the Sonoma cousin of the Yountville Piatti *(see below)*. Pizza from the wood-burning oven and northern Italian specials (spit-roasted chicken, ravioli with lemon cream) are served in a rustic Italian setting with an open kitchen and bright wall murals, or on the outdoor terrace. *405 First St. W (facing the plaza), tel. 707/996–2351. Reservations advised. AE, MC, V.*

$ **The Cafe.** This is Sonoma Mission Inn's *(see above)* second restaurant, featuring an informal bistro atmosphere, overstuffed booths, ceiling fans, and an open kitchen renowned for its country breakfasts, pizza from the wood-burning oven, and tasty California renditions of northern Italian cuisine. *18140 Sonoma Hwy. (2 mi north of Sonoma on Hwy. 12 at Boyes Blvd.), tel. 707/938–9000. Reservations recommended at dinner; accepted for 6 or more for breakfast and lunch. AE, DC, MC, V. Weekend brunch.*

$ **La Casa.** "Whitewashed stucco, red tile, serapes, and Mexican glass" describes this restaurant just around the corner from Sonoma's plaza. There's bar seating, a patio out back, and an extensive menu of traditional Mexican food: chimichangas and snapper Veracruz for entrée, sangria to drink, and flan for dessert. *121 E. Spain St., tel. 707/996–3406. Reservations advised. AE, DC, MC, V.*

Yountville **Domaine Chandon.** The menu of expertly prepared, artfully pre-
$$$$ sented light French cuisine (featuring seafood, poultry, venison, and lamb) has a California accent and changes daily. The architecturally dramatic dining room has views of vineyards and carefully preserved native oaks. There is also outdoor service on a tree-shaded patio. *California Dr. (Yountville exit off Hwy. 29, toward Veterans' Home), tel. 707/944–2892. Reservations essential. Jacket required at dinner. AE, D, DC, MC, V. No dinner Mon. and Tues. year-round; no lunch Mon. and Tues. Oct.–May.*

$$ **Anesti's Grill and Rotisserie.** Specialties at this spacious, cheerful restaurant include leg of lamb and duckling roasted to perfection on the only French rotisserie in Napa and rack of lamb from the mesquite grill. The open kitchen provides entertainment indoors; a patio offers alfresco dining and vistas of vineyards and hills. *6518 Washington St., tel. 707/944–1500. Reservations advised. AE, DC, MC, V.*

$$ **Mustard's Grill.** Grilled fish, hot smoked meats, fresh local produce, and a good wine list are offered in a boisterous, noisy bistro with a black-and-white marble floor and upbeat artwork. Expect to encounter a crowd. *7399 St. Helena Hwy., Napa Valley (Hwy. 29, 1 mi north of Yountville), tel. 707/944–2424. Reservations advised (2 months in advance). D, DC, MC, V.*

$$ **Ristorante Piatti.** A small, stylish trattoria with a pizza oven and open kitchen, this cheery place is full of good smells and happy people. Its authentic regional Italian cooking—from the antipasti to the grilled chicken to the tiramisu—is the perfect cure for a jaded appetite. The homemade pastas are the best bet. *6480 Washington St., tel. 707/944–2070. Reservations advised. AE, MC, V.*

$ **The Diner.** This is probably the best-known and most-appreciated stop-off in the Napa Valley, especially for breakfast. Be sure to have the local sausages and the house potatoes. At night, you'll find healthful, California-cuisine versions of Mexican and American classics. *6476 Washington St., tel. 707/944–2626. Reservations accepted for 6 or more; expect a wait for seating. No credit cards. Closed Mon.*

Lodging

Make no mistake, staying in the Wine Country is expensive. The inns, hotels, and motels are usually exquisitely appointed, and many are fully booked long in advance of the summer season. Since Santa Rosa is the largest population center in the area, it has the largest selection of rooms, many at moderate rates. Try there if you've failed to reserve in advance or have a limited budget. For those seeking romantic and homey atmospheres, check out the dozens of bed-and-breakfast inns that have been established in the Victorian homes and old hotels of the Wine Country (the tourist bureaus of Sonoma and Napa counties both provide information and brochures on B&Bs). Families should note, however, that small children are often discouraged as guests. Aside from the charm and romance, an advantage of B&Bs (which cost more than the average motel) is the often sumptuous breakfast that is included in the price. In the Wine Country, the morning meal often features local produce and specialties. For all accommodations in the area, rates are lower on weeknights and about 20% less in the winter.

Highly recommended hotels are indicated by a star ★.

Category	Cost*
$$$$	over $100
$$$	$80–$100
$$	$50–$80
$	under $50

*All prices are for a double room, excluding 12% tax.

Calistoga
$$$–$$$$
★
Brannan Cottage Inn. This exquisite Victorian cottage with lacy white fretwork, large windows, and a shady porch is the only one of Sam Brannan's 1860 resort cottages still standing on its original site. The restoration is excellent and includes elegant stenciled friezes of stylized wildflowers. All rooms have private entrances. Full breakfast is included. *109 Wapoo Ave., 94515, tel. 707/942–4200. 6 rooms. MC, V (for room payment; reservations held by mailed check only).*

$$–$$$
Calistoga Spa and Inn. One of the oldest hot springs spa resorts in the area is a longtime favorite of northern Californians and tourists alike. Its rooms are functional but well-maintained. The main lure is the spa itself, where there are separate fees. "The works" includes mud bath, steam room, mineral bath, blanket wrap, and massage. *1006 Washington St., 94515, tel. 707/942–6962. Facilities: 4 mineral pools (83°–106°), exercise equipment, complimentary poolside steam bath. MC, V.*

$$
Comfort Inn Napa Valley North. All the rooms in this motel have one king- or two queen-size beds, and many have vineyard views. Continental breakfast is included. There are rooms for nonsmokers and travelers with disabilities and discounts for senior citizens. *1865 Lincoln Ave., 94515, tel. 707/942–9400 or 800/228–5150, fax 707/942–5262. 54 rooms with bath. Facilities: natural mineral-water pool, spa sauna, steam room. AE, D, DC, MC, V.*

$$ **Mountain Home Ranch.** This rustic ranch, built in 1913, is set on 300 wooded acres, with hiking trails, a creek, and a fishing lake. There is just one TV, in the dining room, and no phones. In summer, the modified American plan (full breakfast and dinner) is used; otherwise, Continental breakfast is included. The seven cabins spread over the grounds are ideal for families; each has a full kitchen and bath, and the majority have wood-burning fireplaces. Special children's rates are available. *3400 Mountain Home Ranch Rd., 94515 (north of town on Hwy. 128, left on Petrified Forest Rd., right on Mountain Home Ranch Rd., to end; 3 mi from Hwy. 128), tel. 707/942–6616. 6 rooms in main lodge; 7 cabins, all with private bath. Facilities: 2 pools, tennis. MC, V. Closed Dec. and Jan.*

Glen Ellen
$$$–$$$$
Beltane Ranch. On a slope of the Mayacamas range on the eastern side of the Sonoma Valley is this 100-year-old house built by a retired San Francisco madam. The inn is part of a working cattle and grape-growing ranch. The inn's location is the big draw; miles of trails wander through the oak-studded hills around the property. The comfortable living room has dozens of books on the area. The rooms all have private baths and antique furniture and open onto the building's wraparound porch. *11775 Sonoma Hwy. (Hwy. 12), 95442, tel. 707/996–6501. 4 rooms. Facilities: tennis. No credit cards, but personal checks accepted.*

$$$–$$$$
Glenelly Inn. Just outside the hamlet of Glen Ellen is this sunny little establishment, built as an inn in 1916. Rooms are cozy and furnished with country antiques. Most bathrooms have claw-foot tubs. Mother and daughter innkeepers Ingrid and Kristi Hallamore serve breakfast in front of the common room's cobblestone fireplace and local delicacies in the afternoons. If the weather is warm, ask to have breakfast outside under one of the shady oak trees; it's a tranquil way to begin your day. The inn's hot tub is enclosed in a small garden. *5131 Warm Springs Rd., 95442, tel. 707/996–6720. 8 rooms. MC, V.*

Healdsburg
$$$$
Madrona Manor. A splendid, three-story, 1881 Gothic mansion, carriage house, and outbuildings sit on eight wooded and landscaped acres. Mansion rooms are recommended: All nine have fireplaces, and five contain the antique furniture of the original owner. The approach to the mansion leads under a stone archway and up a flowered hill; the house overlooks the valley and vineyards. Full breakfast is included, and there's a fine restaurant on the premises that serves dinner. Pets are allowed. *1001 Westside Rd., Box 818, 95448, tel. 707/433–4231 or 800/258–4003, fax 707/433–0703. 21 rooms with bath. Facilities: pool, restaurant. AE, DC, MC, V.*

$$
Best Western Dry Creek Inn. Continental breakfast and a bottle of wine are complimentary at this three-story Spanish Mission-style motel. There is a coffee shop next door. Small pets are allowed. Midweek discounts are available, and direct bus service from San Francisco Airport can be arranged. *198 Dry Creek Rd., 95448, tel. 707/433–0300, 800/528–1234, or 800/222–5784 in CA, fax 707/433–1129. 102 rooms with bath. Facilities: pool, spa, laundry. AE, D, DC, MC, V.*

Napa
$$$$
Sheraton Inn Napa Valley. This modern, comfortable motel was completely renovated in late 1993. A convenient restaurant and lounge are on the premises, with live music in the lounge. Movies and rooms for travelers with disabilities are also available. *3425 Solano Ave., 94558 (1 block west off Hwy. 29; take Redwood-Trancas exit), tel. 707/253–7433 or 800/325–3535, fax 707/258–1320. 191 rooms. Facilities: heated pool, spa, lighted tennis courts. AE, D, DC, MC, V.*

$$$$
Silverado Country Club. This luxurious 1,200-acre resort in the hills east of the town of Napa offers cottages, kitchen apartments, and

one- to three-bedroom efficiencies, many with fireplaces. There are also two dining rooms, a lounge, a sundries store, seven pools, 20 tennis courts, and two championship golf courses designed by Robert Trent Jones. Fees are charged for golf, tennis, and bike rentals. *1600 Atlas Peak Rd., 94558 (6 mi east of Napa via Hwy. 121), tel. 707/257–0200 or 800/532–0500, fax 707/257–5425. 277 condo units. Facilities: 3 restaurants. AE, D, DC, MC, V.*

$$$ **Chateau.** There's a French country-inn atmosphere at this modern motel. Continental breakfast, in-room refrigerators, facilities for travelers with disabilities, and discounts for senior citizens are offered. *4195 Solano Ave., 94558 (west of Hwy. 29; exit at Trower Ave.), tel. 707/253–9300 or 800/253–6272 in CA. 115 rooms. Facilities: outdoor pool and spa. AE, D, DC, MC, V.*

$$–$$$$ **Best Western Inn Napa.** This immaculate modern redwood motel with spacious rooms has a restaurant on the premises and same-day laundry and valet service. There are suites, as well as rooms for nonsmokers and travelers with disabilities. Small pets are allowed. *100 Soscol Ave., 94558 (from the direction of the Golden Gate Bridge, take Imola Ave./Hwy. 121 exit east from Hwy. 29 to junction of Hwy. 121 and Soscol), tel. 707/257–1930 or 800/528–1234. 68 rooms. Facilities: pool, spa. AE, D, DC, MC, V.*

Rutherford **Auberge du Soleil.** As you sit on a wisteria-draped deck sipping a
$$$$ late-afternoon glass of wine, with acres of terraced olive groves and
★ rolling vineyards at your feet, you'll swear you're in Tuscany. *180 Rutherford Hill Rd., 94573, tel. 707/963–1211 or 800/348–5406, fax 707/963–8764. 50 rooms. Facilities: outdoor pool, spa, tennis, masseuse, nature trail, exercise room. AE, MC, V.*

$$$–$$$$ **Rancho Caymus Inn.** California-Spanish in style, this inn has well-maintained gardens and large suites with kitchens and whirlpool baths. Also of note are the home-baked breads, an emphasis on decorative handicrafts, unusual beehive fireplaces, tile murals, stoneware basins, and llama-hair blankets. *1140 Rutherford Rd., 94573 (junction of Hwys. 29 and 128), tel. 707/963–1777 or 800/845–1777, fax 707/963–5387. 26 rooms. Facilities: restaurant. 2-night minimum Apr. 1–Nov. 30. AE, MC, V.*

St. Helena **Harvest Inn.** This English Tudor inn with many fireplaces overlooks
$$$$ a 14-acre vineyard and hills beyond. Although the property is flat and set close to a main highway, the award-winning landscaping creates an illusion of remoteness. The furnishings are antiques, and most rooms have wet bars, refrigerators, and fireplaces. Pets are allowed in certain rooms for a $20 fee. Complimentary breakfast is served in the breakfast room and on the patio overlooking the vineyards. *1 Main St., 94574, tel. 707/963–9463 or 800/950–8466, fax 707/963–4402. 55 rooms. Facilities: 2 pools, 2 whirlpools. AE, D, MC, V.*

$$$$ **Meadowood Resort.** The resort is set on 256 wooded acres, with a golf course, croquet lawns, and hiking trails. The hotel is a rambling country lodge reminiscent of a turn-of-the-century New England seaside cottage, and separate bungalow suites are clustered on the hillside. Half the suites and some rooms have fireplaces. *900 Meadowood La., 94574, tel. 707/963–3646 or 800/458–8080, fax 707/963–3532. 82 rooms. Facilities: 2 restaurants, lounge, room service, 2 pools, saunas, 9-hole and par golf courses, tennis, masseuse, wine school. AE, DC, MC, V.*

$$$$ **The Wine Country Inn.** Surrounded by a pastoral landscape of vineyards and hills dotted with old barns and stone bridges, this New England–style inn feels peaceful. Rural antiques fill all of the rooms, and most face the splendid view with either a balcony, patio, or deck. There are fireplaces in almost every room, and private hot

tubs in a few of the higher-priced rooms. A hearty country breakfast is presented buffet-style in the sun-splashed common room. There is no TV; this is a place for readers and dreamers. *1152 Lodi La., 94574, tel. 707/963–7077 or 800/473–3463, fax 707/963–9018. 24 rooms with bath. Facilities: outdoor pool and Jacuzzi with shower, gift shop, complimentary breakfast, kitchen will pack a picnic lunch. MC, V.*

$$$–$$$$ Hotel St. Helena. The oldest standing wooden structure in St. Helena, this restored 1881 hostelry aims at Old World comfort. It is completely furnished with antiques and decorated in rich, appealing tones of burgundy. Complimentary Continental breakfast is included. Smoking is discouraged—the only evidence of the New World. *1309 Main St., 94574, tel. 707/963–4388, fax 707/963–5402. 14 rooms with bath, 4 rooms with shared bath. AE, DC, MC, V.*

$$–$$$$ Cinnamon Bear Bed and Breakfast. Built in 1904 as a wedding gift, this house is decorated with a period flavor, from the antique quilts and toys to the claw-foot tubs, and there's a cozy fireplace in the parlor. Full breakfast is included. Rooms for nonsmokers are available. *1407 Kearney St., 94574 (from Main St., Hwy. 29, turn west on Adams St., then 2 blocks to Kearney), tel. 707/963–4653. 4 rooms with bath. MC, V.*

$$ El Bonita Motel. Remodeled throughout 1992 and 1993, this roadside motel now boasts 20 additional rooms, most with whirlpool spas, and a new look. Hand-painted grape vines surround the windows, and flower boxes overflow with new colors every season. Although sauna and Jacuzzi facilities are offered all year, the outdoor pool is only available in summer. There are 16 rooms in the main motel and six smartly-furnished garden rooms with kitchenettes. *195 Main St., 94574, tel. 707/963–3216 or 800/541–3284, fax 707/963–8838. 42 rooms. AE, MC, V.*

Santa Rosa

$$$$ Vintner's Inn. Set on 50 acres of vineyards, this attractive inn has large rooms, French-provincial furnishings, and wood-burning fireplaces. The trellised sundeck is delightful. Breakfast is complimentary, and there is an excellent restaurant on the premises. There are rooms for travelers with disabilities. VCRs are available for a small fee. *4350 Barnes Rd., 95403 (River Rd. exit west from U.S. 101), tel. 707/575–7350 or 800/421–2584, fax 707/575–1426. 44 rooms. Facilities: restaurant, spa and outdoor showers, affiliated full-service health club nearby. AE, DC, MC, V.*

$$$ Fountaingrove Inn. This elegant, comfortable inn located in the
★ heart of the Sonoma valley boasts a redwood sculpture, *Equus III*, and a wall of cascading water in the lobby. Rooms have work spaces with modem jacks. Buffet breakfast is included, and there's an exceptional restaurant. Discounts for senior citizens and rooms for nonsmokers and travelers with disabilities are available. *101 Fountaingrove Pkwy. (near U.S. 101), 95403, tel. 707/578–6101 or 800/222–6101, fax 707/544–3126. 85 rooms. Facilities: complimentary health club nearby, golf and tennis available, lap pool, spa, lounge, room service, movies. AE, DC, MC, V.*

$$–$$$ Los Robles Lodge. This pleasant, relaxed motel has comfortable
★ rooms overlooking a pool set into a grassy landscape. Rooms for the handicapped and nonsmokers are available. Pets are allowed, except in executive rooms, which have whirlpools. *925 Edwards Ave., 95401 (Steele La. exit west from Hwy. 101), tel. 707/545–6330 or 800/255–6330, fax 707/575–5826. 105 rooms. Facilities: restaurant, coffee shop, lounge with nightly entertainment, pool, outdoor whirlpool, fitness center nearby, laundry. AE, D, DC, MC, V.*

$ Best Western Hillside Inn. Some rooms at this cozy, nicely landscaped, small motel have balconies or patios. Kitchenettes and suites are available. *2901 4th St., 95409 (at Farmers La., 2 mi east off*

U.S. 101 on Hwy. 12), tel. 707/546–9353 or 800/528–1234. 35 rooms.
Facilities: pool, restaurant, sauna, shuffleboard. AE, DC, MC, V.

Sonoma **Sonoma Mission Inn.** This elegantly restored, nicely landscaped
$$$$ 1920s resort blends Mediterranean and old-California architecture
for a result that's early Hollywood—you half expect Gloria Swanson
to sweep through the lobby. The location is a surprise, off the main
street of tiny, anything-but-posh Boyes Hot Springs. The rooms in
the newer buildings are much larger and more attractive than the
smallish standard rooms in the main building. The hotel is known
for its extensive spa facilities and treatments. *18140 Hwy. 12 (just
north of Sonoma), Box 1447, 95476, tel. 707/938–9000, 800/358–9022,
or 800/862–4945 in CA, fax 707/996–5358. 170 rooms. Facilities: restaurant, coffee shop, 2 bars, lounge, 2 pools, weight room, steam room,
whirlpools, sauna, tennis. AE, DC, MC, V.*

$$$$ **Thistle Dew Inn.** A half-block from Sonoma Plaza is this turn-of-the-
century Victorian home filled with collector-quality Arts-and-
Crafts furnishings. Owners Larry and Norma Barnett live on the
premises, and Larry cooks up creative, sumptuous breakfasts and
serves hors d'oeuvres in the evenings. Upgraded in 1993, four of the
six rooms now have private entrances and decks. There is a hot tub,
and bicycles are provided free to guests. Smoking is not permitted
indoors. *171 W. Spain St., 95476, tel. 707/938–2909 or 800/382–7895 in
CA. 6 rooms. AE, MC, V.*

$$$–$$$$ **Best Western Sonoma Valley Inn.** Just one block from the historical
town plaza, this motel features balconies, hand-crafted furniture,
wood-burning fireplaces, and whirlpool baths. Continental break-
fast and a complimentary split of wine are included. Kitchenettes
and rooms for nonsmokers and travelers with disabilities are avail-
able. *550 2nd St. W, 95476, tel. 707/938–9200 or 800/334–5784, fax
707/938–0935. 72 rooms. Facilities: pool, whirlpool, laundry. AE, D,
DC, MC, V.*

$$$–$$$$ **El Dorado Hotel.** In 1990, Claude Rouas, the owner of Napa's ac-
★ claimed Auberge du Soleil, entered the Sonoma scene with this fine
small hotel and its popular restaurant, Piatti (*see* Dining, *above*).
Rooms reflect Sonoma's mission era, with Mexican-tile floors and
white walls. The best rooms are numbers 3 and 4, which have big
balconies overlooking Sonoma Plaza. Only four of the rooms—the
ones in the courtyard by the pool—have bathtubs; the rest have
showers only. *405 1st St. W (on Sonoma Plaza), tel. 707/996–3030 or
800/289–3031, fax 707/996–3148. 27 rooms. Facilities: restaurant,
heated pool. AE, MC, V.*

$$–$$$ **Vineyard Inn.** Built as a roadside motor court in 1941, this red-tiled-
roof inn has been refurbished to add Mexican village charm to an
otherwise lackluster location at the junction of two main highways.
The inn is in the heart of Sonoma's Carneros region, across from
two vineyards. It is also the closest lodging to Sears Point Raceway.
Rooms have queen-size beds. Continental breakfast is provided.
*23000 Arnold Dr. (at the junction of Hwys. 116 and 121), 95476, tel.
707/938–2350 or 800/359–4667. 9 rooms, 3 suites with wet bar, 1 resi-
dent suite with kitchenette. AE, MC, V.*

Yountville **Vintage Inn.** All the rooms at this luxurious inn have fireplaces,
$$$$ whirlpool baths, refrigerators, private verandas or patios, hand-
painted fabrics, window seats, and shuttered windows. A welcome
bottle of wine, Continental breakfast with champagne, and after-
noon tea are all complimentary. In season, bike rentals and hot-air
ballooning are available. *6541 Washington St., 94599, tel. 707/944–
1112 or 800/351–1133, fax 707/944–1617. 80 rooms with bath. Facili-
ties: lap pool, spa, tennis. AE, D, DC, MC, V.*

$$$–$$$$ **Napa Valley Lodge.** Spacious rooms overlook vineyards and the valley in this hacienda-style lodge with a tile roof, covered walkways, balconies, patios, and colorful gardens. Freshly brewed coffee is provided in rooms, as is Continental breakfast and the morning paper. Some rooms have fireplaces. Rooms with wet bars and rooms for nonsmokers and travelers with disabilities are available. *2230 Madison St. at Hwy. 29, 94599, tel. 707/944–2468 or 800/368–2468, fax 707/944–9362. 55 rooms. Facilities: exercise room, pool, spa, sauna, refrigerators, refreshment bars. AE, D, DC, MC, V.*

The Arts and Nightlife

Galleries throughout the Wine Country display the work of local artists: painters, sculptors, potters, and jewelry makers. The **Luther Burbank Performing Arts Center** in Santa Rosa (50 Mark West Springs Rd., 95403, tel. 707/546–3600; box office open Mon.–Sat. noon–6) offers a full events calendar featuring concerts, plays, and other performances by locally and internationally known artists. Write for the calendar in advance if you're planning a trip. For the symphony, ballet, and other live theater performances throughout the year, call the **Spreckels Performing Arts Center** in Rohnert Park (tel. 707/584–1700 or 707/586–0936; box office open Tues.–Sat. noon–5). The most highly recommended theater groups among the valley's 30 ensembles include: **Cinnebar** in Petaluma (tel. 707/763–8920), **Main Street Theatre** in Sebastopol (tel. 707/823–0177), **SRT** (Summer Repertory Theatre) in Santa Rosa (tel. 707/527–4307) and the **Actors Theatre** also in Santa Rosa (tel. 707/523–4185). In addition to the sounds at local music clubs and the larger hotels, wineries often schedule concerts and music festivals during the summer. Popular music aficionados might also try the **Mystic Theatre** in Petaluma where Chris Isaak plays now and then (tel. 707/765–6665), and movie lovers can take in a foreign or first-run film at the **Raven Theatre** in Healdsburg (tel. 707/433–5448). The **Sebastiani Theatre** on historic Sonoma square (tel. 707/996–2020) features first-run movies and hosts special events during the year.

Many believe that the best way to savor evenings in the Wine Country is to linger over an elegant dinner, preferably on a patio under the stars, at one of the restaurants for which the area is justly famous.

6 San Francisco

Not so many centuries ago the area that was to become San Francisco was a windswept, virtually treeless, and, above all, sandy wasteland. The sand is still there, but—except along the ocean—it's well hidden. City Hall is built on 80 feet of it. The western section of the city seems flat only because sand has filled in the contours of the hills. But the hills that remain are spectacular. They provide vistas all over the city—nothing is more common than to find yourself staring out toward Angel Island or Alcatraz, or across the bay at Berkeley and Oakland.

Historically, San Francisco is a boom town. The boom began in 1848. At the beginning of that year, San Francisco wasn't much more than a pleasant little settlement that had been founded by the Spaniards back in the auspicious year of 1776. The future came abruptly when gold was discovered at John Sutter's sawmill in the Sierra foothills, some 115 miles to the northeast. By 1850, San Francisco's population had zoomed from 500 to 30,000, and a "western Wall Street" sprang up as millions upon millions of dollars' worth of gold was panned and blasted out of the hills. Just as the gold mines began to dry up, prospectors turned up a fabulously rich vein of silver in what is now Nevada and San Francisco—the nearest financial center—prospered again. Nowadays, the city prides itself on its role as a Pacific Rim capital, and overseas investment has become a vital part of its financial life. In terms of both geography and culture, San Francisco is about as close as you can get to Asia in the continental United States.

San Francisco has always been a loose, tolerant—some would say licentious—city. As early as the 1860s, the "Barbary Coast"—a collection of taverns, whorehouses, and gambling joints along Pacific Avenue close to the waterfront—was famous, or infamous. Bohemian communities seem to thrive here. In the 1950s, North Beach, the city's Little Italy, became the home of the Beat Movement. Lawrence Ferlinghetti's City Lights Bookstore still stands on Columbus Avenue as a monument to the era. The Bay Area, particularly Berkeley, was the epicenter of '60s ferment, too. In San Francisco, the Haight-Ashbury district was synonymous with hippiedom and gave rise to such legendary bands as the Jefferson Airplane, Big Brother and the Holding Company (fronted by Janis Joplin), and the Grateful Dead.

The Lesbian and Gay Freedom Day Parade, each June, vies with the Chinese New Year Parade, in February, as the city's most elaborate. They both get competition from Japantown's Cherry Blossom Festival, in April; the Columbus Day and St. Patrick's Day parades; the June Carnaval in the Hispanic Mission District; and the May Day march, a labor celebration in a labor town. The mix of ethnic, economic, social, and sexual groups might confound other towns, but the city's residents—whatever their origin—face it with aplomb and even gratitude. Everybody in San Francisco has an opinion about where to get the best burrito or the hottest Szechuan eggplant or the strongest cappuccino. The most staid citizens have learned how to appreciate good camp. Nearly everyone smiles on the fortunate day they arrived on, or were born on, this windy, foggy patch of peninsula.

Exploring San Francisco *(Boxes Refer to Detail Maps)*

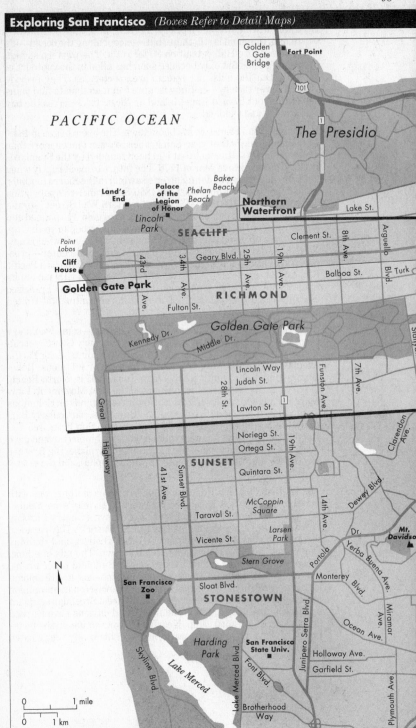

PACIFIC OCEAN

Golden Gate Bridge
Fort Point
101
The Presidio
Land's End
Palace of the Legion of Honor
Phelan Beach
Baker Beach
Northern Waterfront
Lake St.
Lincoln Park
SEACLIFF
Clement St.
8th Ave.
Arguello Blvd.
Point Lobos
Cliff House
Geary Blvd.
43rd Ave.
34th Ave.
25th Ave.
19th Ave.
Balboa St.
Turk
Golden Gate Park
RICHMOND
Fulton St.
Golden Gate Park
Kennedy Dr.
Middle Dr.
Lincoln Way
Judah St.
Lawton St.
28th St.
Funston Ave.
7th Ave.
Stan
Noriega St.
Ortega St.
SUNSET
Quintara St.
41st Ave.
Sunset Blvd.
19th Ave.
Clarendon Ave.
Great Highway
Taraval St.
McCoppin Square
14th Ave.
Dewey Blvd.
Vicente St.
Larsen Park
Dr.
Mt. Davidson
Stern Grove
Portola
Yerba Buena Ave.
Monterey Blvd.
Miramar Ave.
San Francisco Zoo
Sloat Blvd.
STONESTOWN
Ocean Ave.
Harding Park
San Francisco State Univ.
Junipero Serra Blvd.
Font Blvd.
Holloway Ave.
Garfield St.
Plymouth Ave.
Skyline Blvd.
Lake Merced
Lake Merced Blvd.
Brotherhood Way

N

0   1 mile
0   1 km

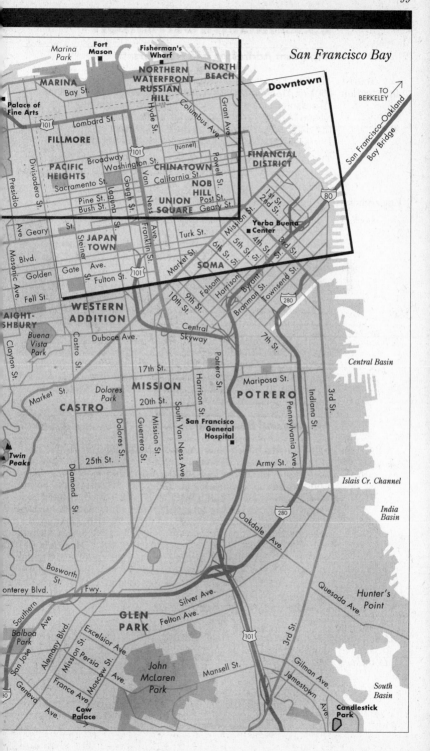

San Francisco Bay

Downtown

TO BERKELEY

Marina Park

Fort Mason

Fisherman's Wharf

NORTHERN WATERFRONT

NORTH BEACH

RUSSIAN HILL

MARINA

Bay St.

Palace of Fine Arts

Lombard St.

FILLMORE

PACIFIC HEIGHTS

Broadway

Washington St.

Sacramento St.

Pine St.

Bush St.

CHINATOWN

Columbus Ave.

Grant Ave.

Hyde St.

[tunnel]

Van Ness Ave.

Powell St.

California St.

NOB HILL

Post St.

Geary St.

UNION SQUARE

FINANCIAL DISTRICT

San Francisco-Oakland Bay Bridge

1st St.

2nd St.

3rd St.

4th St.

5th St.

6th St.

Mission St.

Yerba Buena Center

Presidio

Divisadero St.

Geary

St.

Steiner

JAPAN TOWN

Turk St.

Franklin St.

Gough St.

Laguna St.

Masonic Ave.

Blvd.

Golden Gate Ave.

Fell St.

Fulton St.

Market St.

SOMA

Folsom

Harrison

Bryant

Brannan

Townsend St.

WESTERN ADDITION

9th St.

10th St.

Central Skyway

7th St.

HAIGHT-ASHBURY

Buena Vista Park

Clayton St.

Duboce Ave.

Castro St.

Market St.

17th St.

Dolores Park

MISSION

20th St.

Harrison St.

Potrero St.

Mariposa St.

POTRERO

Indiana St.

Pennsylvania Ave.

Central Basin

CASTRO

Dolores St.

Guerrero St.

Mission St.

South Van Ness Ave.

San Francisco General Hospital

Twin Peaks

25th St.

Diamond St.

Army St.

Islais Cr. Channel

India Basin

Oakdale Ave.

3rd St.

Bosworth St.

Monterey Blvd.

Fwy.

Silver Ave.

Felton Ave.

Hunter's Point

Quesada Ave.

Southern Ave.

Balboa Park

San Jose Ave.

Alemany Blvd.

Excelsior Ave.

Mission St.

Persia Ave.

Moscow St.

France Ave.

Geneva Ave.

GLEN PARK

John McLaren Park

Mansell St.

Gilman Ave.

Jamestown Ave.

Cow Palace

Candlestick Park

South Basin

Essential Information

Important Addresses and Numbers

Tourist
Information

The **San Francisco Convention and Visitors Bureau** (tel. 415/391–2001 or 415/974–6900 for a summary of daily events) maintains a visitor information center on the lower level at Hallidie Plaza (Powell and Market streets), just three blocks from Union Square, near the cable-car turnaround and the Powell Street entrance to BART. It's open weekdays 9–5:30, Saturdays 9–3, and Sundays 10–2.

The **Redwood Empire Association Visitor Information Center** on the 15th floor at 785 Market Street (tel. 415/543–8334) is open weekdays 9 AM–5 PM.

Emergencies

For **police** or **ambulance,** telephone 911.

Doctors

Two hospitals with 24-hour emergency rooms are **San Francisco General Hospital** (1001 Potrero Ave., tel. 415/206–8000) and the **Medical Center at the University of California, San Francisco** (500 Parnassus Ave. at 3rd Ave., near Golden Gate Park, tel. 415/476–1000).

Access Health Care provides drop-in medical care at two San Francisco locations, daily 8–8. No membership is necessary. *Davies Medical Center, Castro St. at Duboce Ave., tel. 415/565–6600; 26 California St. at Drumm St., tel. 415/397–2881.*

Pharmacies

Several **Walgreen Drug Stores** have 24-hour pharmacies, including stores at 500 Geary Street near Union Square (tel. 415/673–8413) and 3201 Divisadero Street at Lombard Street (tel. 415/931–6417). Also try the Walgreen pharmacy at 135 Powell Street near Market Street (tel. 415/391–7222), which is open Monday–Saturday 8 AM–midnight, Sunday 9 AM–9 PM.

Arriving and Departing

By Plane
*Airports and
Airlines*

San Francisco International Airport (tel. 415/761–0800) is just south of the city, off U.S. 101. American carriers serving San Francisco are **Alaska Air** (tel. 800/426–0333), **American** (tel. 800/433–7300), **Continental** (tel. 800/525–0280), **Delta** (tel. 800/221–1212), **Southwest** (tel. 800/435–9792), **TWA** (tel. 800/221–2000), **United** (tel. 800/241–6522), and **USAir** (tel. 800/428–4322). International carriers include **Air Canada** (tel. 800/776–3000), **British Airways** (tel. 800/427–9297), **China Airlines** (tel. 800/227–5118), **Japan Airlines** (tel. 800/525–3663), **Lufthansa** (tel. 800/645–3880), **Mexicana** (tel. 800/531–7921), **Philippine Airlines** (tel. 415/391–0470), and **Qantas** (tel. 800/227–4500). Several domestic airlines serve the Oakland Airport (tel. 415/577–4000), which is across the bay but not much farther away from downtown San Francisco (via I–880 and I–80), although traffic on the Bay Bridge may at times make travel time longer.

*Between the
Airport and
Downtown*

SFO Airporter (tel. 415/495–8404) provides bus service between downtown and the airport, making the round of downtown hotels. Buses run every 20 minutes from 5 AM to 11 PM, from the lower level outside the baggage claim area. The fare is $8 one-way, $14 round-trip.

For $11, **Supershuttle** will take you from the airport to anywhere within the city limits of San Francisco. At the airport, after picking up your luggage, call 415/871–7800 and a van will pick you up, usually within five minutes. To go to the airport, make reservations (tel. 415/558–8500) 24 hours in advance. The Supershuttle stops at the upper level of the terminal, along with several other bus and van transport services.

Taxis to or from downtown take 20–30 minutes and average $30.

By Train **Amtrak** (tel. 800/872–7245) trains (the *Zephyr,* from Chicago via Denver, and the *Coast Starlight,* traveling between Los Angeles and Seattle) stop in Oakland; from there buses will take you across the Bay Bridge to the Ferry Building on the Embarcadero at the foot of Market street in San Francisco.

By Bus **Greyhound** serves San Francisco from the Transbay Terminal at 1st and Mission streets (tel. 415/558–6789 or 800/231–2222).

By Car Route I–80 finishes its westward journey from New York's George Washington Bridge at the Bay Bridge, which links Oakland and San Francisco. U.S. 101, running north–south through the entire state, enters the city across the Golden Gate Bridge and continues south down the peninsula, along the west side of the bay.

Getting Around

Because San Francisco is relatively compact and because it's so difficult to find parking, we recommend that you do your exploring on foot or by bus as much as possible. You may not need a car at all, except perhaps for exploring the Presidio, Golden Gate Park, Lincoln Park, the Western Shoreline, and for making excursions out of town.

How to Get There from Union Square will tell you how to reach approximately 50 points of interest in the city by public transportation. It's free from the Redwood Empire Association Visitor Information Center (*see* Tourist Information in Important Addresses and Numbers, *above*).

By BART **Bay Area Rapid Transit** (tel. 415/992–2278) sends air-conditioned aluminum trains at speeds of up to 80 miles an hour across the bay to Oakland, Berkeley, Concord, Richmond, and Fremont. Trains also travel south from San Francisco as far as Daly City. Wall maps in the stations list destinations and fares (85¢–$3). Trains run Monday–Saturday 6 AM–midnight, Sunday 9 AM–midnight.

A $2.60 excursion ticket buys a three-county tour. You can visit any of the 34 stations for up to four hours as long as you exit and enter at the same station.

By Bus The **San Francisco Municipal Railway System,** or **Muni** (tel. 415/673–6864), includes buses and trolleys, surface streetcars, and below-surface streetcars, as well as cable cars. There is 24-hour service, and the fare is $1 for adults, 35¢ for senior citizens and children 5–17. The exact fare is always required; dollar bills or change are accepted. Transfers are good for two changes in any direction. Eighty-cent tokens can be purchased (in rolls of 10, 20, or 40) for convenience and savings. They can be purchased at Muni's kiosk at the Powell Street cable-car terminus.

A $6 pass good for unlimited travel all day on all routes can be purchased from ticket machines at cable-car terminals and at the Visitor Information Center in Hallidie Plaza (Powell and Market Sts.).

By Cable Car In June 1984 the cable-car system, first introduced in 1873, returned to service after a $58.2-million overhaul. Because the cable cars had been declared a National Historic Landmark in 1964, renovation methods and materials had to preserve the historical and traditional qualities of the system. The rehabilitated moving landmark has been designed to withstand another century of use.

The Powell-Mason line (No. 59) and the Powell-Hyde line (No. 60) begin at Powell and Market streets near Union Square and terminate at Fisherman's Wharf. The California Street line (No. 61) runs east and west from Market Street near the Embarcadero to Van Ness Avenue.

Cable cars are popular, crowded, and an experience to ride: Move toward one quickly as it pauses, wedge yourself into any available space, and hold on! The sensation of moving up and down some of San Francisco's steepest hills in a small, open-air clanging conveyance is not to be missed.

The fare (for one direction) is $2 for adults and children. Exact change is preferred but not required. There are self-service ticket machines (which make change) at a few major stops and at all the terminals. The one exception is the busy cable-car terminus at Powell and Market streets; purchase tickets at the kiosk there. Be wary of street people attempting to "help" you buy a ticket.

By Taxi Rates are high in the city, although most rides are relatively short. It is almost impossible to hail a passing cab, especially on weekends. Either phone or use the nearest hotel taxi stand to grab a cab.

By Car Driving in San Francisco can be a challenge because of the hills, the one-way streets, and the traffic. Take it easy, remember to curb your wheels when parking on hills, and use public transportation whenever possible. This is a great city for walking and not so great for parking. On certain streets, parking is forbidden during rush hours. Look for the warning signs; illegally parked cars are towed. Downtown parking lots are often full and always expensive. Finding a spot in North Beach at night, for instance, may be impossible. The city's 5th and Mission, Ellis–O'Farrell, and Sutter–Stockton garages are your best bets in the downtown–Union Square area.

Guided Tours

Orientation Tours **Golden City Tours** offers 14-passenger vans and small buses for their 6½-hour city tours, which include such landmarks as Twin Peaks, the Cliff House, and Chinatown as well as a drive across the Golden Gate Bridge. Customers are picked up at all major airport hotels. A shorter afternoon tour omits Sausalito. *Tel. 415/692–3044. Tours daily. Make reservations the day before. Cost: $39.50; afternoon tour $29.50.*

Golden Gate Tours uses both vans and buses for its 3½-hour city tour, offered mornings and afternoons. You can combine the tour with a bay cruise. Customers are picked up at hotels and motels. Senior citizen and group rates are available. *Tel. 415/788–5775. Tours daily. Make reservations the day before. Cost: $22.50 adults, $11 children under 12, $20.50 senior citizens. Cruise combo: $30 adults, $15 children under 12, $28 senior citizens.*

Gray Line offers a variety of tours of the city, the Bay Area, and Northern California. The city tour, on buses or double-decker buses, lasts 3½ hours and departs from the Transbay Terminal at 1st and Mission streets five to six times daily. Gray Line also picks up at centrally located hotels. **Gray Line-Cable Car Tours** sends motorized cable cars on a one-hour loop from Union Square to Fisherman's Wharf and two-hour tours including the Presidio, Japantown, and the Golden Gate Bridge. *Tel. 415/558–9400. Tours daily. Make reservations the day before. Cost: $25 adults, $12.50 children. Cable car tours, $12 and $18 adults, $6 and $9 children. No reservations necessary.*

The Great Pacific Tour uses 13-passenger vans for its daily 3½-hour city tour. Bilingual guides may be requested. They pick up at major San Francisco hotels. Tours are available to Monterey, the Wine Country, and Muir Woods. *Tel. 415/626–4499. Tours daily. Make reservations the day before, or, possibly, the same day. Cost: $27 adults, $25 senior citizens, $20 children 5–11.*

Superior Sightseeing Company operates 20-passenger vans and picks up visitors at hotels for 3½-hour tours of the city, ending at Fisherman's Wharf. There is also a full-day excursion to the Wine Country. *Tel. 415/550–1352. Cost: $24–$40 adults, $22–$38 senior citizens, $14–$20 children.*

Special-Interest Tours
Near Escapes plans unusual activities in the city and around the Bay Area. Recent tours and activities included tours of a Hindu temple in the East Bay, the Lawrence Berkeley Laboratory, the aircraft maintenance facility at the San Francisco Airport, and the quicksilver mines south of San Jose. Send $1 and a self-addressed, stamped envelope for a schedule for the month you plan to visit San Francisco.

Walking Tours
Castro District. Trevor Hailey leads a 3½-hour tour focusing on the history and development of the city's gay and lesbian community, including restored Victorian homes, shops and cafés, and the NAMES Project, home of the AIDS memorial quilt. Tours depart at 10 AM Tuesday–Saturday from Castro and Market streets. *Tel. 415/550–8110. Cost: $30, including brunch.*

Chinatown with the "Wok Wiz." Cookbook author Shirley Fong-Torres leads a 3½-hour tour of Chinese markets, other businesses, and a fortune cookie factory. *Tel. 415/355–9657. Cost: $35, including lunch; $25 without lunch. Shorter tours, $15–$22.*

Chinese Cultural Heritage Foundation (tel. 415/986–1822) offers two walking tours of Chinatown. The Heritage Walk leaves Saturday at 2 PM and lasts about two hours. The Culinary Walk, a three-hour stroll through the markets and food shops, plus a dim sum lunch, is held every Wednesday at 10:30 AM. *Heritage Walk: $12 adults, $2 children under 12. Culinary Walk: $25 adults, $10 children under 12.*

Exploring San Francisco

By Toni Chapman

Revised by Daniel Mangin

"You could live in San Francisco a month and ask no greater entertainment than walking through it," waxed Inez Hayes Irwin, the author of *The Californiacs,* an effusive 1921 homage to the state of California and the City by the Bay. Her claim remains as true as ever today, and, as in the '20s, touring on foot is the best way to experience this diverse metropolis.

San Francisco is a relatively small city, with fewer than 750,000 residents nested on a 46.6-square-mile tip of land between San Francisco Bay and the Pacific Ocean. San Franciscans cherish the city's colorful past, and many older buildings have been spared from demolition and nostalgically converted into modern offices and shops. Longtime locals rue the sites that got away—spectacular railroad and mining-boom-era residences lost in the '06 quake, the elegant

Fox Theater, Playland at the Beach. But despite acts of God, the indifference of developers, and the at best mixed record of the city's Planning Commission, much of architectural and historical interest remains. Bernard Maybeck, Julia Morgan, Willis Polk, and Arthur Brown, Jr., are among the noted architects whose designs still grace the city's downtown and neighborhoods.

San Francisco's charms are both great and small. First-time visitors won't want to miss Golden Gate Park, the Palace of Fine Arts, the Golden Gate Bridge, or an exhilarating cable-car ride. A walk down the Filbert Steps or through Macondray Lane, though, or a peaceful hour gazing east from Ina Coolbrith Park, can be equally inspiring.

It's no accident that the San Francisco Bay Area has been a center for the environmental movement. An awareness of geographical setting permeates San Francisco life, with ever-present views of the surrounding mountains, ocean, and bay. Much of the city's neighborhood vitality comes from the distinct borders provided by its hills and valleys, and many areas are so named: Nob Hill, Twin Peaks, Eureka Valley, the East Bay. San Francisco neighborhoods are self-aware, and they retain strong cultural, political, and ethnic identities. Locals know this pluralism is the real life of the city. If you want to experience San Francisco, don't just stay downtown, visit the neighborhoods: the bustling Mission District, gay Castro, freaky Haight Street, serene Pacific Heights, historic Chinatown, still-exotic North Beach.

The famed 40-plus hills can be a problem for drivers who are new to the terrain. Those museums on wheels—the cable cars—or the numerous buses or trolleys can take you to or near many of the area's attractions. In the exploring tours that follow, we have often included information on public transportation.

Highlights for First-Time Visitors

Chinatown
The Cliff House
Coit Tower
Cruise to Alcatraz Island
Golden Gate Bridge
Hyde Street Cable Car
Japanese Tea Garden
Union Square

Union Square

Numbers in the margin correspond to points of interest on the Downtown San Francisco map.

Since 1850 Union Square has been the heart of San Francisco's downtown. Its name derives from a series of violent pro-Union demonstrations staged in this hilly area just prior to the Civil War. This area is where you will find the city's finest department stores and its most elegant boutiques. There are 40 hotels within a three-block walk of the square, and the downtown theater district is nearby.

The square itself is a 2.6-acre oasis planted with palms, boxwood, and seasonal flowers, peopled with a kaleidoscope of characters: office workers sunning and brown-bagging, street musicians and artists, several vocal and determined preachers, and the usual parade of panhandlers. Throughout the year, the square hosts numerous public events: fashion shows, free noontime concerts, ethnic celebrations, and noisy demonstrations. Auto and bus traffic is often gridlocked on the four streets bordering the square. Post, Stockton, and Geary are one-way, while Powell runs in both directions until it crosses Geary, where it then becomes one-way to Market Street. Union Square covers a convenient but costly four-story underground garage. Close to 3,000 cars use it on busy holiday shopping and strolling days.

❶ Any visitor's first stop should be the **San Francisco Visitor Information Center** (tel. 415/391–2000) on the lower level of Hallidie Plaza at Powell and Market streets. It is open daily, and the multilingual staff will answer specific questions as well as provide maps, brochures, and information on daily events. You can pick up coupons for substantial savings on tourist attractions here. If you're in need of a room for the night, most of the downtown area hotels leave pamphlets (and, depending on the season, discount vouchers) here. The office provides 24-hour recorded information (tel. 415/391–2001).

❷ The **cable-car terminus** at Powell and Market streets is the starting point for two of the three operating lines. The Powell-Mason line climbs up Nob Hill, then winds through North Beach to Fisherman's Wharf. The Powell-Hyde car also crosses Nob Hill, but then continues up Russian Hill and down Hyde Street to Victorian Park across from the Buena Vista Cafe and near Ghirardelli Square.

Today there are 39 cars in the three lines, and the network covers just 12 miles. Most of the cars date from the last century, although the cars and lines had a complete $58 million overhaul during the early 1980s. There are seats for about 30 passengers, with usually that number standing or strap-hanging. If possible, plan your cable-car ride for mid-morning or mid-afternoon during the week to avoid crowds. In summertime there are often long lines to board any of the three systems. Buy your ticket ($2, good in one direction) at nearby hotels or at the police/information booth near the turnaround. (*See* Getting Around San Francisco in Essential Information, above.)

❸ If you resist the urge to hop onto San Francisco's moving landmarks, you can head over to a stationary one, the **Old San Francisco Mint,** and get an instant immersion in San Francisco and California history. Walk one block south of the cable-car terminus past the 5th Street side of the San Francisco Shopping Centre. The old mint, at 5th and Mission streets, was built in 1873 and reopened as a museum in 1973. Its priceless collection of gold coins was removed in late 1993 for security reasons, but visitors can view an authentic recreation of a miner's cabin and other historical exhibits, tour the mint's original vaults, and strike their own souvenir medal on an 1869 press. Several photos depict the sturdy building standing virtually alone amid the rubble of the 1906 earthquake and fire. "The Millionaire," a gigantic, old-fashioned calculator, and several Victrolas are among the other curiosities on display. *Tel. 415/744–6830. Admission free. Open weekdays 10–4:15.*

❹ A two-block stroll, heading north of the cable-car terminus along bustling Powell Street, leads to **Union Square** itself. At center stage, the Victory Monument by Robert Ingersoll Aitken commemorates Commodore George Dewey's victory over the Spanish fleet at Manila in 1898. The 97-foot Corinthian column, topped by a bronze figure symbolizing naval conquest, was dedicated by Theodore Roosevelt in 1903 and withstood the 1906 earthquake.

Downtown San Francisco

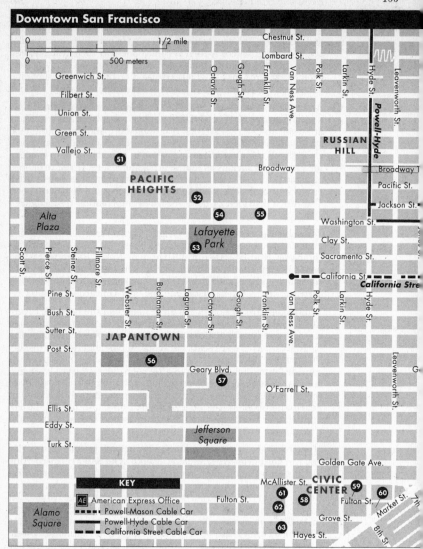

After the earthquake and fire in 1906, the square was dubbed "Little St. Francis" because of the temporary shelter erected for residents of the St. Francis Hotel. Actor John Barrymore was among the guests pressed into volunteering to stack bricks in the square. His uncle, thespian John Drew, remarked, "It took an act of God to get John out of bed and the United States government to get him to work."

⑤ The **Westin St. Francis Hotel,** on the southwest corner of Post and Powell, was built here in 1904 and was gutted by the 1906 disaster. The second-oldest hotel in the city was conceived by Charles Crocker and his associates as an elegant hostelry for their millionaire friends. Swift service and sumptuous surroundings were hallmarks of the property. A sybarite's dream, the hotel's Turkish baths had ocean water piped in. A new, larger, more luxurious residence was opened in 1907 to attract loyal clients from among the world's rich and powerful. The hotel has known its share of notoriety as well. Silent comedian Fatty Arbuckle's career plummeted faster than one of the St. Francis's glass-walled elevators after a wild 1921 party in one of the hotel's suites went awry. In 1975, Sara Jane Moore tried to shoot then-president Gerald Ford in front of the building. As might be imagined, plaques do not commemorate these events in the establishment's lobby. The ever-helpful staff will, however, gladly direct you to the traditional teatime ritual—or, if you prefer, to champagne and caviar—in the dramatic Art Deco Compass Rose lounge. Elaborate Chinese screens, secluded seating alcoves, and soothing background music make it an ideal time-out after frantic shopping or sightseeing.

⑥ Both the Geary and Curran theaters are a few blocks west on Geary Street. The 1,300-seat **Geary** (415 Geary St., tel. 415/749–2228), built in 1910, is home of the American Conservatory Theater, one of North America's leading repertory companies (*see* The Arts in The Arts and Nightlife, *below*). The building's serious neo-classical design is lightened somewhat by the colorful, carved terra-cotta columns, depicting a cornucopia of fruits, that flank the theater's largest windows. The theater was closed as a result of the October 1989 earthquake, and currently productions are being run at the Stage Door theater (420 Mason St.) and elsewhere until repairs are complete, probably in time for the 1995–96 season. Its main box office **⑦** remains open. The **Curran** (445 Geary St., tel. 415/474–3800) is noted for showcasing traveling companies of Broadway shows.

⑧ **TIX Bay Area,** formerly known as STBS, has a booth on the Stockton Street side of Union Square, opposite Maiden Lane. It provides day-of-performance tickets (cash or traveler's checks only) to all types of performing-arts events at half-price, as well as regular full-price box-office services. You can also buy $10 Golden Gate Park Cultural Passes here, which get you into the park's museums at a bargain rate. *Tel. 415/433–7827. Open Tues.–Thurs. 11–6, Fri. and Sat. 11–7.*

⑨ Just a dash up from TIX Bay Area, in front of the Grand Hyatt San Francisco (345 Stockton St.), is sculptor **Ruth Asawa's fantasy fountain** honoring the city's hills, bridges, and unusual architecture plus a wonder world of real and mythical creatures. Children and friends helped the artist shape the hundreds of tiny figures from baker's clay; these were assembled on 41 large panels from which molds were made for the bronze casting. Asawa's distinctive designs decorate many public areas in the city. You can see her famous mermaid fountain at Ghirardelli Square.

⑩ Directly across Stockton Street from TIX Bay Area is **Maiden Lane,** which runs from Stockton to Kearny streets. Known as Morton Street in the raffish Barbary Coast era, this red-light district reported at least one murder a week. But the 1906 fire destroyed the brothels and the street emerged as Maiden Lane. It has since become a chic and costly mall. The two blocks are closed to vehicles from 11 AM until 4 PM.

Note **140 Maiden Lane:** This handsome brick structure is the only Frank Lloyd Wright building in San Francisco. With its circular interior ramp and skylights, it is said to have been a model for his design for the Guggenheim Museum in New York. It now houses the Circle Gallery, a showcase of contemporary artists. Be sure to examine the unique limited-edition art jewelry designed by internationally acclaimed Erté. *Open Mon.–Sat. 10–6, Sun. noon–5.*

At 301 Sutter Street, at the corner of Grant Avenue, is the colorful
⑪ **Hammersmith Building.** The small Beaux-Arts structure was completed in 1907. Its extensive use of glass is noteworthy, as is the playful design. Sutter Street is lined by prestigious art galleries, antiques dealers, smart hotels, and noted designer boutiques. Art Deco aficionados will want to head one block up Sutter Street for a
⑫ peek at the striking medical/dental office building at **450 Sutter Street.** Handsome Mayan-inspired designs are used on both exterior and interior surfaces of the 1930 terra-cotta skyscraper.

South of Market (SoMa) and the Embarcadero

The vast tract of downtown land **South of Market** Street along the waterfront and west to the Mission District is also known by the acronym SoMa (patterned after New York City's south-of-Houston SoHo). In the mid-1960s, the San Francisco Redevelopment Agency grabbed 87 acres of run-down real estate in the center of this district, leveled anything that stood on them, and planned the largest building program in the city's history: **Yerba Buena Center.** After more than two decades, the area has finally taken shape, although a few parts of it are still under construction and still other portions aren't past the blueprint stage.

⑬ **Moscone Convention Center,** on Howard Street between 3rd and 4th streets, was the first major Yerba Buena Center building to be completed. The site of the 1984 Democratic convention, it is distinguished by a contemporary glass-and-girder lobby at street level (most of the exhibit space is underground) and a monolithic, column-free interior. In 1992, the center finished a $150 million expansion project that doubled its size and incorporated a new building across Howard Street with underground exhibit space.

⑭ Above the new exhibit space is the **Yerba Buena Gardens** complex (in the block surrounded by 3rd, Mission, Howard, and 4th streets). A large expanse of green is surrounded by a circular walkway lined with benches and artworks. A waterfall memorial to Martin Luther King, Jr., gushes a few yards off from an overhead walkway that traverses Howard Street to Moscone Center. On the eastern side of
⑮ the block is the **Center for the Arts** (701 Mission St., tel. 415/978–2787), which opened in late 1993. The center includes two theaters, three visual-arts galleries, a film and video screening room, and an outdoor performance esplanade.

⑯ The **San Francisco Museum of Modern Art** (SFMOMA) takes its place as the centerpiece of the SoMa arts scene in January 1995. The striking Modernist structure was designed by Swiss architect

Mario Botta. It features a stepped-back burnt-sienna brick facade and a central tower constructed of alternating bands of black and white stone. Inside, natural light from the tower floods the central atrium and some of the museum's galleries. A grand staircase leads from the atrium up to four floors of galleries. *151 3rd St., tel. 415/357-4000. Admission: $7 adults, $3.50 senior citizens and students over 12; free 1st Tues. of each month. Open daily 11–6, Thurs. until 9 (half-price admission 5–9). Closed major holidays.*

⑰ Just across 4th Street from the Moscone Center is the **Ansel Adams Center.** This gallery showcases historical and contemporary photography, and has an extensive permanent collection of Adams's work. *250 4th St., tel. 415/495-7000. Admission: $4 adults, $3 students, $2 youths 12–17 and senior citizens, free for children under 12 and for all on the 1st Tues. of the month. Open Tues.–Sun. 11–5, 1st Thurs. of the month 11–8.*

One block north of SFMOMA on Third Street, at the traffic island where Third, Market, Kearny, and Geary streets come together, is **Lotta's Fountain.** This quirky monument, which now goes largely unnoticed by local passersby, was a gift to the city from singer Lotta Crabtree, a Madonna prototype. Her "brash music-hall exploits" so enthralled San Francisco's early population of miners that they were known to shower her with gold nuggets and silver dollars after her performances. The buxom Ms. Crabtree is depicted in one of the Anton Refregier murals in Rincon Center (*see below*).

⑱ Heading east on Market Street toward the waterfront, the venerable **Sheraton Palace Hotel** at the corner of New Montgomery St. (tel. 415/392-8600) has a storied past, some of which is recounted in small cases off the main lobby. President Warren Harding died here while still in office in 1923. Late-1980s renovations included the restoration of the glass-domed Garden Court and the installation of original mosaic-tile floors in Oriental-rug designs. Maxfield Parrish's wall-size painting, *The Pied Piper*, graces the wall in the hotel's Pied Piper Room.

Because it bisects the city at an angle, over the years, Market Street has consistently challenged San Francisco's architects. An intriguing response to the problem sits diagonally across Market Street from the Palace. The tower of the **Hobart Building** (582 Market St.) combines a flat facade and oval sides. It is considered to be among architect Willis Polk's best work in the city. Another classic solution is Charles Havens's triangular **Flatiron Building** (540–548 Market St.). At **388 Market** is a sleek, modern variation on the theme, designed by Skidmore, Owings, and Merrill.

⑲ As you approach the waterfront, you'll see the eight buildings, including the **Hyatt Regency Hotel,** that comprise **Embarcadero Center.** The huge complex includes more than 100 shops, 40 restaurants, and two hotels, as well as office and residential space. On the waterfront side of the hotel is **Justin Herman Plaza.** There are arts and crafts shows, street musicians, and mimes here on weekends year-round. Kite flying is popular. A huge concrete sculpture, the **Vaillancourt Fountain,** has had legions of critics since its installation in 1971; most of the time the fountain does not work, and many feel it is an eyesore.

⑳ In one instance, the 1989 Loma Prieta earthquake changed San Francisco for the better: The Embarcadero freeway had to be torn down, making the foot of Market Street clearly visible for the first time in 30 years. The trademark of the port is the quaint **Ferry Building** that stands at the Embarcadero. The clock tower is 230 feet high and was modeled by Arthur Page Brown after the campanile of Seville's cathedral. The four great clock faces on the tower, powered by the swinging action of a 14-foot pendulum, stopped at 5:17 on the morning of April 18, 1906, and stayed that way for 12 months. The 1896 building survived the quake and is now the headquarters of the Port Commission and the World Trade Center.

A waterfront promenade that extends from this point to the San Francisco–Oakland Bay Bridge is great for jogging, in-line skating, watching sailboats on the bay (if the day is not too windy), or enjoying a picnic. Check out the beautiful pedestrian pier adjacent to Pier 1, with its old-fashioned lamps, wrought-iron benches, and awe-inspiring views of the bay. Ferries from behind the Ferry Building sail to Sausalito, Larkspur, and Tiburon.

As you continue down the promenade, notice the curiously styled Audiffred Building at the corner of Mission Street and the Embarcadero. It was built by a homesick gentleman who wanted a reminder of his native France. A few doors down, an old brick YMCA building is now the **Harbor Court Hotel.** Cross the Embarcadero at Howard Street, and turn right on Steuart Street.

㉑ Across Steuart Street from the main entrance to the hotel is the new—and old—**Rincon Center.** Two modern office/apartment towers overlook a small shopping and restaurant mall behind an old post office built in the Streamline Moderne Style. A stunning five-story rain column draws immediate attention in the mall. In the "Historic Lobby" (which formerly housed the post office's walk-up windows) is a mural by Anton Refregier. One of the largest WPA-era art projects, its 27 panels depict California life from the days when Indians were the state's sole inhabitants through World War I.

The Financial District and Jackson Square

The heart of San Francisco's Financial District is Montgomery Street. It was here in 1848 that Sam Brannan proclaimed the historic gold discovery on the American River. At that time, all the streets below Montgomery between California and Broadway were wharves. At least 100 ships were abandoned by frantic crews and passengers all caught up in the '49 gold fever. Many of the wrecks served as warehouses or were used as foundations for new constructions.

The Financial District is roughly bordered by Kearny Street on the west, Washington Street on the north, and Market Street on the southeast. On workdays it is a congested canyon of soaring skyscrapers, gridlock traffic, and bustling pedestrians. In the evenings and on weekends the quiet streets allow walkers to admire the distinctive architecture. Unfortunately, the museums in corporate headquarters are closed then.

㉒ Head down Sutter Street toward the Financial District to see the **Hallidie Building** (130 Sutter St. between Kearny and Montgomery Sts.), named for cable-car inventor Andrew Hallidie. The building, best viewed from across the street, is believed to be the world's first all-glass-curtain-wall structure. Willis Polk's revolutionary design hangs a foot beyond the reinforced-concrete frame.

㉓ The 10-story **Mills Building and Tower** (220 Montgomery St.) was the outstanding prefire building in the Financial District. The original Burnham and Root design of white marble and brick was erected in 1891–92. Damage from the 1906 fire was slight; its walls were somewhat scorched but were easily refurbished. Two compatible additions east on Bush Street were added in 1914 and 1918 by Willis Polk, and in 1931 a 22-story tower completed the design.

㉔ The **Russ Building** (235 Montgomery St.) was called "the skyscraper" when it was built in 1927. The Gothic design was modeled after the Chicago Tribune Tower, and until the 1960s was San Francisco's tallest—at just 31 stories.

㉕ Ralph Stackpole's monumental 1930 granite sculptural groups, *Earth's Fruitfulness* and *Man's Inventive Genius,* flank the **Pacific Stock Exchange** (which dates from 1915) on the south side of Pine Street at Sansome Street. The Stock Exchange Tower around the corner at 155 Sansome Street, a 1930 modern classic by architects Miller and Pfleuger, features an Art Deco gold ceiling and black marble-walled entry. *301 Pine St., 94104, tel. 415/393–4000. Tours by 2-week advance reservation; minimum 8 persons.*

㉖ The granite-and-marble **Bank of America** building dominates the territory bounded by California, Pine, Montgomery, and Kearny streets. The 52-story polished red granite complex is crowned by a chic cocktail lounge and restaurant. In the exterior mall, a massive abstract black granite sculpture designed by the Japanese artist Masayuki has been dubbed the "Banker's Heart" by local wags.

㉗ A quick but interesting stop is the **Wells Fargo Bank History Museum,** which displays samples of nuggets and gold dust from major mines, a mural-size map of the Mother Lode, original art by Western artists Charlie Russell and Maynard Dixon, mementos of the poet bandit Black Bart, and letters of credit and old bank drafts. The showpiece is the red, century-old Concord stagecoach that in the mid-1850s carried 15 passengers from St. Louis to San Francisco in three weeks. *420 Montgomery St., tel. 415/396–2619. Admission free. Open banking days 9–5.*

㉘ The city's most-photographed high rise is the 853-foot **Transamerica Pyramid** at 600 Montgomery Street, between Clay and Washington streets at the end of Columbus Avenue. Designed by William Pereira and Associates in 1972, the controversial $34 million symbol has become more acceptable to local purists over time. There is a public viewing area on the 27th floor (open weekdays 8–4). You can relax in a redwood grove along the east side of the building.

㉙ In the Gay '90s San Francisco earned the title of "the Wickedest City in the World." The saloons, dance halls, cheap hotels, and brothels of its Barbary Coast attracted sailors and gold rushers. Most of this red-light district was destroyed in the 1906 fire; what remains is now part of **Jackson Square.** A stroll through this district recalls some of the romance and rowdiness of early San Francisco.

Directly across Washington Street from the Transamerica redwood grove is Hotaling Place, a tiny alley east of and parallel to Montgomery Street. The alley is named for the head of the **A. P. Hotaling and Company whiskey distillery,** which was located at 451 Jackson. A plaque on the side of the building repeats a famous query about its surviving the quake: "If, as they say, God spanked the town/for being over-frisky,/Why did He burn the churches down/and spare Hotaling's Whisky?" The **Ghirardelli Chocolate Factory** was once housed at 415 Jackson.

Chinatown

San Francisco is home to one of the largest Chinese communities outside Asia. While Chinese culture is visible throughout the city, this area, bordered roughly by Bush, Kearny, Powell, and Broadway, remains the community's spiritual and political center. Recent immigrants from Southeast Asia have added new character and life to the neighborhood.

㉚ Visitors usually enter Chinatown through the green-tiled dragon-crowned **Chinatown Gate** at Bush Street and Grant Avenue. To best savor this district, explore it on foot (it's not far from Union Square), even though you may find the bustling, noisy, colorful stretches of Grant and Stockton streets north of Bush difficult to navigate. Parking is extremely hard to find, and traffic is impossible. As in Hong Kong, most families shop daily for fresh meats, vegetables, and bakery products. This street world shines with much good-luck crimson and gold; giant beribboned floral wreaths mark the opening of new bakeries, bazaars, and banks. Note the dragon-entwined lampposts, the pagoda roofs, and street signs with Chinese calligraphy.

Dragon House Oriental Fine Arts and Antiques (455 Grant Ave.), several doors up from the Chinatown gate, is an excellent place to start your Chinatown visit. Its collection of ivory carvings, ceramics, and jewelry dates back 2,000 years and beyond. The shop's display window is a history lesson in itself.

㉛ The handsome brick **Old St. Mary's Church** at Grant and California streets served as the city's Catholic cathedral until 1891. Diagonally
㉜ across California Street is **St. Mary's Park,** a tranquil setting for local sculptor Beniamino (Benny) Bufano's heroic stainless-steel and rose-colored granite *Sun Yat-sen.* The 12-foot statue of the founder of the Republic of China was installed in 1937 on the site of the Chinese leader's favorite reading spot during his years of exile in San Francisco. Bufano's stainless-steel and mosaic statue of St. Francis welcomes guests at San Francisco International Airport.

㉝ Head down Grant Avenue, turn right Clay Street, continue one block to Kearny Street, and then turn left to reach **Portsmouth Square.** This is where Captain John B. Montgomery raised the American flag in 1846. Note the bronze galleon atop a nine-foot granite shaft. Designed by Bruce Porter, the sculpture was erected in 1919 in memory of Robert Louis Stevenson, who often visited the site during his 1879–80 residence. In the morning, the park is crowded with people performing solemn t'ai chi exercises. By noontime, dozens of men huddle around mah-jongg tables, engaged in not-always-legal competition. Occasionally, undercover police rush in to break things up, but this ritual, though as solemn as the t'ai
㉞ chi, is hardly as productive. From here you can walk to the **Chinese Cultural Center,** which frequently displays the work of Chinese-American artists as well as traveling exhibits of Chinese culture. The center also offers $15 Saturday-afternoon (2 PM) walking tours of historic points in Chinatown. *In the Holiday Inn, 750 Kearny St., tel. 415/986–1822. Admission free. Open Tues.–Sat. 10–4.*

㉟ In an alley parallel to and a half-block south of the side of the Holiday Inn, the **Chinese Historical Society** traces the history of Chinese immigrants and their contributions to the state's rail, mining, and fishing industries. *650 Commercial St., parallel to Clay St. off Kearny, tel. 415/391–1188. Admission free. Open Tues.–Sat. noon–4.*

㊱ The original Chinatown burned down after the 1906 earthquake; the first building to set the style for the new Chinatown is near Portsmouth Square, at 743 Washington Street. The three-tier pagoda called the **Old Chinese Telephone Exchange** (now the Bank of Canton) was built in 1909. The exchange's operators were renowned for their "tenacious memories," about which the San Francisco Chamber of Commerce boasted in 1914: "These girls respond all day with hardly a mistake to calls that are given (in English or one of five Chinese dialects) by the name of the subscriber instead of by his number—a mental feat that would be practically impossible to most high-schooled American misses."

Time Out   Skip that Big Mac you've been craving; opt instead for dim sum, a variety of pastries filled with meat, fish, and vegetables, the Chinese version of a smorgasbord. In most places, stacked food-service carts patrol the premises; customers select from the varied offerings, and the final bill is tabulated by the number of different saucers on the table. A favorite on Pacific Avenue, two blocks north of Washington Street, is **New Asia.** *772 Pacific Ave., tel. 415/391–6666. Open for dim sum 8:30 AM–3 PM.*

③⑦ Waverly Place is noted for ornate painted balconies and Chinese temples. **Tien Hou Temple** was dedicated to the Queen of the Heavens and Goddess of the Seven Seas by Day Ju, one of the first three Chinese to arrive in San Francisco in 1852. As you enter the temple, elderly ladies are often preparing "money" to be burned as offerings to various Buddhist gods. A (real) dollar placed in the donation box on their table will bring a smile. *125 Waverly Pl. Open daily 10 AM–4 PM.*

Throughout Chinatown you will notice herb shops that sell an array of Chinese medicines. The **Great China Herb Co.** (857 Washington St.), around the corner from the Tien Hou Temple, is one of the largest. All day, sellers fill prescriptions from local doctors, measuring exact amounts of tree roots, bark, flowers, and other ingredients with their hand scales, and add up the bill on an abacus (an ancient calculator). The shops also sell "over-the-counter" treatments for the common cold, heartburn, hangovers, and even impotence!

The other main thoroughfare in Chinatown, where locals shop for everyday needs, is Stockton Street, which parallels Grant Avenue. This is the real heart of Chinatown. Housewives jostle one another as they pick apart the sidewalk displays of Chinese vegetables. Double-parked trucks unloading crates of chickens or ducks add to the all-day traffic jams. You'll see excellent examples of Chinese archi-

③⑧ tecture along this street. Most noteworthy is the elaborate **Chinese Six Companies** (843 Stockton St.), with its curved roof tiles and elaborate cornices. Around the corner at 965 Clay St. is the handsome, redbrick **Chinatown YWCA,** designed by architect Julia Morgan, who was also responsible for the famous Hearst Castle at San Simeon, California.

It's an easy 15-minute walk back downtown to Union Square via the
③⑨ **Stockton Street Tunnel,** which runs from Sacramento Street to Sutter Street. Completed in 1914, this was the city's first tunnel to accommodate vehicular and pedestrian traffic.

North Beach and Telegraph Hill

Like neighboring Chinatown, North Beach, centered on Columbus Avenue north of Broadway, is best explored on foot. In the early days there truly was a beach. At the time of the gold rush, the bay extended into the hollow between Telegraph and Russian hills. North Beach, less than a square mile, is the most densely populated district in the city and is truly cosmopolitan. Novelist Herbert Gold, a North Beach resident, calls the area "the longest running, most glorious American bohemian operetta outside Greenwich Village."

Among the first immigrants to Yerba Buena during the early 1840s were young men from the northern provinces of Italy. By 1848, the village, renamed San Francisco, had become an overnight boom-town with the discovery of gold. Thousands more poured into the burgeoning area, seeking the golden dream. For many, the trail ended in San Francisco. The Genoese started the still-active fishing industry, as well as much-needed produce businesses. Later the Sicilians emerged as leaders of the fishing fleets and eventually as proprietors of the seafood restaurants lining Fisherman's Wharf. Meanwhile, their Genoese cousins established banking and manufacturing empires.

40 **Washington Square** may well be the daytime social heart of what was once considered "Little Italy." By mid-morning, groups of conservatively dressed elderly Italian men are sunning and sighing at the state of their immediate world. Nearby, laughing playmates of a half-dozen cultures race through the grass with Frisbees or colorful kites. Denim-clad mothers exchange shopping tips and ethnic recipes. Elderly Chinese matrons stare impassively at the passing parade. Camera-toting tourists focus their lenses on the adjacent **41** Romanesque splendor of **Sts. Peter and Paul,** often called the Italian Cathedral. Completed in 1924, its twin-turreted terra-cotta towers are local landmarks. On the first Sunday of October, the annual Blessing of the Fleet is celebrated with a mass followed by a parade to Fisherman's Wharf.

The 1906 earthquake and fire devastated this area, and the park provided shelter for hundreds of the homeless. **Fior d'Italia,** facing the cathedral, is San Francisco's oldest Italian restaurant. The original opened in 1886 and continued to operate in a tent after the 1906 earthquake until new quarters were ready. Surrounding streets are packed with savory Italian delicatessens, bakeries, Chinese markets, coffeehouses, and ethnic restaurants. Wonderful aromas fill the air; coffee beans roasted at **Graffeo** at 735 Columbus Avenue are shipped to customers all over the United States. Stop by the **Panelli Brothers deli** (1419 Stockton St.) for a memorable, reasonably priced meat-and-cheese sandwich to go. **Florence Ravioli Factory** (1412 Stockton St.) features garlic sausages, prosciutto, and mortadella, as well as 75 tasty cheeses and sandwiches to go. **Victoria** (1362 Stockton St.) has heavenly cream puffs and eclairs. Around the corner on Columbus Avenue is **Molinari's,** noted for the best salami in town and a mouth-watering array of salads—there is usually a wait for service.

South of Washington Square and just off Columbus Avenue is the **42** **St. Francis of Assisi Church** (610 Vallejo St.). This 1860 Victorian Gothic building stands on the site of the frame parish church that served the gold-rush Catholic community.

Over the years, North Beach has attracted creative individualists. The Beat Renaissance of the 1950s was born, grew up, flourished, then faltered in this then-predominantly Italian enclave. The Beat gathering places are gone, and few of the original leaders remain, **43** though poet Lawrence Ferlinghetti still holds court at his **City Lights Bookstore** (261 Columbus Ave.).

44 **Telegraph Hill** rises from the east end of Lombard Street to about 300 feet and is capped with the landmark Coit Tower, dedicated as a monument to the city's volunteer fire fighters. Early during the gold rush, an eight-year-old who would become one of the city's most memorable eccentrics, Lillie Hitchcock Coit, arrived on the scene. Legend relates that at age 17, "Miss Lil" deserted a wedding party and chased down the street after her favorite engine, Knickerbocker No. 5, clad in her bridesmaid finery. She was soon made an honorary member of the Knickerbocker Company, and after that always signed herself "Lillie Coit 5" in honor of her favorite fire engine. Lillie died in 1929 at the age of 86, leaving the city about $100,000 of her million-dollar-plus estate to "expend in an appropriate manner to the beauty of San Francisco."

Telegraph Hill residents command some of the best views in the city, as well as the most difficult ascent to their aeries. The Greenwich stairs lead up to Coit Tower from Filbert Street, and there are steps down to Filbert Street on the opposite side of Telegraph Hill. Views are superb en route, but most visitors should either take a taxi up to the tower or take the Muni bus No. 39-Coit at Washington Square. To catch the bus from Union Square, walk to Stockton and Sutter streets, board the Muni No. 30, and ask for a transfer to use at Washington Square (Columbus Ave. and Union St.) to board the No. 39-Coit. Public parking is very limited at the tower, and on holidays and weekends there are long lines of cars and buses winding up the narrow road.

45 **Coit Tower** stands as a monument not only to Lillie Coit and the city's fire fighters but also to the influence of the political and radical Mexican muralist Diego Rivera. Fresco was Rivera's medium, and it was his style that unified the work of most of the 25 artists who painted the murals in the tower. The murals were commissioned by the U.S. government as a Public Works of Art Project. The artists were paid $38 a week. Some were fresh from art schools; others found no market for art in the dark depression days of the early 1930s. An illustrated brochure for sale in the tiny gift shop explains the various murals dedicated to the workers of California.

Ride the elevator to the top to enjoy the panoramic view of both the Bay Bridge and Golden Gate Bridge; directly offshore is the famous Alcatraz and just behind it, Angel Island, a hikers' and campers' paradise. There are often artists at work in Pioneer Park, at the foot of the tower. Small paintings of the scene are frequently offered for sale at modest prices. *Discoverer of America*, the impressive bronze statue of Christopher Columbus, was a gift of the local Italian community.

Nob Hill

If you don't mind climbing uphill, Nob Hill is within walking distance of Union Square. Once called the Hill of Golden Promise, it became Nob Hill during the 1870s when "the Big Four"—Charles Crocker, Leland Stanford, Mark Hopkins, and Collis Huntington—built their hilltop estates. It is still home to many of the city's elite as well as four of San Francisco's finest hotels.

In 1882 Robert Louis Stevenson called Nob Hill "the hill of palaces." But the 1906 earthquake and fire destroyed all the palatial mansions. The shell of one survived. The Flood brownstone (1000 California St.) was built by the Comstock silver baron in 1886 at a reputed cost of $1.5 million. In 1909 the property was purchased by **46** the prestigious **Pacific Union Club.** The 45-room exclusive club remains the bastion of the wealthy and powerful. Adjacent is a charming small park noted for its frequent art shows.

47 Neighboring **Grace Cathedral** (1051 Taylor St.) is the seat of the Episcopal church in San Francisco. The soaring Gothic structure, built on the site of Charles Crocker's mansion, took 53 years to build. The gilded bronze doors at the east entrance were taken from casts of Ghiberti's Gates of Paradise on the baptistery in Florence. The cathedral's superb rose window is illuminated at night. Architect Lewis Hobart's grand design was finally completed in 1994, when a four-story building was demolished to make way for a sweeping staircase. There are often organ recitals on Sundays at 5 PM, as well as special programs during the holiday seasons.

48 What sets the **Fairmont Hotel** (California and Mason Sts.) apart from other luxury hotels is its legendary history. Its dazzling opening was delayed a year by the 1906 quake, but since then the marble palace has hosted presidents, royalty, and local nabobs. Prices are up a bit, though: on the eve of World War I, you could get a room for as low as $2.50 per night—meals included! Nowadays, prices run as high as $6,000, which will get you a night in the eight-room penthouse suite that was showcased regularly in the TV series "Hotel." The apartment building on the corner of Sacramento Street across from the Fairmont is also a media star. In 1958 it was a major location in Alfred Hitchcock's *Vertigo* and was more recently (1993) featured in the BBC production of Armistead Maupin's homage to San Francisco in the wacky '70s, *Tales of the City.*

49 On the Fairmont's other flank at California and Mason streets is the **Mark Hopkins Inter-Continental Hotel,** which is remembered fondly by thousands of World War II veterans who jammed the Top of the Mark lounge before leaving for overseas duty.

50 The **Cable Car Museum,** at the corner of Washington and Mason streets, exhibits photographs, old cars, and other memorabilia from the system's 115-year history. An overlook allows you to observe the cables that haul the city's cars in action. *1201 Mason St., at Washington St., tel. 415/474–1887. Admission free. Open daily 10–5.*

Pacific Heights

Pacific Heights forms an east–west ridge along the city's northern flank from Van Ness Avenue to the Presidio and from California Street to the bay. Some of the city's most expensive and dramatic real estate, including mansions and town houses priced at $1 million and up, are located here. Grand old Victorians, expensively facelifted, grace tree-lined streets, although here and there glossy, glass-walled high-rise condos obstruct the view.

A good place to begin a tour of the neighborhood is at the corner of Webster Street and Pacific Avenue, deep in the heart of the Heights. You can get here from Union Square by taking Muni Bus 3 from Sutter and Stockton to Jackson and Fillmore streets. Head one block east on Jackson to Webster Street.

North on Webster Street, at 2550, is the massive Georgian brick mansion built in 1896 for William B. Bourn, who had inherited a Mother Lode gold mine. The architect, Willis Polk, was responsible for many of the most traditional and impressive commercial and private homes built from the prequake days until the early 1920s. (Be sure to see his 1917 Hallidie Building, 130 Sutter Street; *see* The Financial District and Jackson Square, *above.*)

Neighbors include a consulate and, on the northwest corner, two **51** classic showplaces. **2222 Broadway** is the three-story Italian Renaissance palace built by Comstock mine heir James Flood. Broadway uptown, unlike its North Beach stretch, is big league socially. The former Flood residence was given to a religious order. Ten years later, the Convent of the Sacred Heart purchased the Baroque brick Grant house (2220 Broadway) and both serve as school quarters today. A second top-drawer school, the Hamlin (2120 Broadway), occupies another Flood property.

Movie buffs may want to make the effort to travel another block west on Broadway to Steiner Street for a gander at the handsome home (at the southeast corner) used in the hit movie *Mrs. Doubtfire*.

52 Return east on Broadway past the Hamlin School and turn right (south) on Buchanan Street, then left on Jackson Street to Laguna Street. The massive red sandstone **Whittier Mansion,** at 2090 Jackson Street, was one of the most elegant 19th-century houses in the state, built so solidly that only a chimney toppled over during the 1906 earthquake.

53 One block south on Laguna, at Washington Street, is **Lafayette Park,** a four-block-square oasis for sunbathers and dog-and-Frisbee teams. During the 1860s, a tenacious squatter, Sam Holladay, built himself a big wooden house in the center of the park. Holladay even instructed city gardeners as if the land were his own, and defied all attempts to remove him. The house was finally torn down in 1936.

54 Walking east on Washington street along the edge of Lafayette Park, the most imposing residence is the formal French **Spreckels Mansion** (2080 Washington St.). Sugar heir Adolph Spreckels's wife, Alma, was so pleased with her house that she commissioned architect George Applegarth to design the city's European museum, the California Palace of the Legion of Honor in Lincoln Park. Alma, one of the city's great iconoclasts, is the model for the bronze figure atop the Victory Monument in Union Square.

55 At 2007 Franklin is the handsome **Haas-Lilienthal Victorian.** Built in 1886, at an original cost of $18,000, this grand Queen Anne survived the 1906 earthquake and fire and is the only fully furnished Victorian open to the public. The carefully kept rooms offer an intriguing glimpse into turn-of-the-century taste and lifestyle. A small display of photographs on the bottom floor proves that this elaborate house was modest compared with some of the giants that fell to the fire. It is operated by the Foundation for San Francisco's Architectural Heritage. Tours of the house are given by docent volunteers two days a week. The volunteers also conduct an informative two-hour tour of the eastern portion of Pacific Heights on Sunday afternoons. *Tel. 415/441–3004. Admission: $4 adults, $2 senior citizens and children under 12. Open Wed. noon–4 (last tour at 3:15), Sun. 11–5 (last tour at 4:15). Pacific Heights tours ($3 adults, $1 senior citizens and children) leave the house Sun. at 12:30 PM.*

The **Coleman House** at 1701 Franklin St. is an impressive, twin-turreted Queen Anne mansion. At 1818 and 1834 California are two stunning **Italianate Victorians.** A block farther at 1990 California is the Victorian-era **Atherton House.** The much-photographed row of Italianate Victorians on the east side of the **1800 block** of Laguna Street (at Pine Street) cost only $2,000–$2,600 when they were built during the 1870s.

Japantown

Japanese-Americans began gravitating to the neighborhood known as the Western Addition prior to the 1906 earthquake. Early immigrants arrived about 1860, and they named San Francisco Soko.

After the 1906 fire had destroyed wooden homes in other parts of the stricken city, many survivors settled in the Western Addition. By the 1930s the pioneers had opened shops, markets, meeting halls, and restaurants and established Shinto and Buddhist temples. Japantown was virtually disbanded during World War II when many of its residents, including second- and third-generation Americans, were "relocated" in camps.

Today **Japantown,** or "Nihonmachi," is centered on the slopes of Pacific Heights, north of Geary Boulevard, between Fillmore and Laguna streets. The Nihonmachi Cherry Blossom Festival is celebrated two weekends every April with a calendar of ethnic events. Walking in Nihonmachi is more than just a shopping and culinary treat; it is a cultural, sensory experience. We recommend visiting Japantown and the Western Addition during the day. From Union Square, take the No. 38-Geary Muni bus or the No. 2, 3, or 4 buses on Sutter Street. Though the hotel, restaurant, and Kabuki movie complex are relatively safe in the evenings, it is often difficult to avoid long waits at isolated bus stops or to find a cruising cab when you want to get back to the hotel. The proximity of the often-hostile street gangs in the Western Addition could cause unpleasant incidents.

The buildings around the traffic-free **Japan Center Mall** between Sutter and Post streets are of the shoji screen school of architecture, and Ruth Asawa's origami fountain sits in the middle. (*See* Union Square, *above,* for more information on Ms. Asawa.) The mall faces the three-block-long, five-acre **Japan Center.** In 1968, the multimillion-dollar development created by noted American architect Minoru Yamasaki opened with a three-day folk festival. The three-block cluster includes an 800-car public garage and shops and showrooms selling Japanese products: electronic products, cameras, tapes and records, porcelains, pearls, and paintings.

The center is dominated by its Peace Plaza and Pagoda located between the Tasamak Plaza and Kintetsu buildings. The five-tier, 100-foot Peace Pagoda overlooks the plaza, where seasonal festivals are held. The pagoda draws on the tradition of miniature round pagodas dedicated to eternal peace by Empress Koken in Nara more than 1,200 years ago. It was designed by the Japanese architect Yoshiro Taniguchi "to convey the friendship and goodwill of the Japanese to the people of the United States." A cultural bridge modeled after Florence's Ponte Vecchio spans Webster Street, connecting the Kintetsu and Kinokuniya buildings.

Time Out   **Isobune** (tel. 415/563–1030), on the second floor of the Kintetsu Building, is unusual. The sushi chef prepares a variety of sushi, placing each portion on a small wooden boat that floats on a "river" of water that circles the counter. The customer then fishes out a sampling. The inexpensive but superb **Mifune** (tel. 415/922–0337), diagonally across from Isobune, serves both hot and cold noodle dishes, either boiled and served in a broth or prepared toss-fried, with bits of greens and meat added for flavor.

Walk back east on Geary Boulevard's north side to Gough Street. Dramatic **St. Mary's Cathedral,** on the south side of Geary, was dedicated in 1971. The impressive Catholic cathedral seats 2,500 people around the central altar. Above the altar is a spectacular cascade made of 7,000 aluminum ribs. Four magnificent stained-glass windows in the dome represent the four elements: the blue north window, water; the light-colored south window, the sun; the red west window, fire; and the green east window, earth.

Civic Center

San Francisco's Civic Center stands as one of the country's great city, state, and federal building complexes with handsome adjoining cultural institutions. It's the realization of the theories of turn-of-the-century proponents of the "City Beautiful."

58 Facing Polk Street, between Grove and McAllister streets, **City Hall** is a French Renaissance Revival masterpiece of granite and marble, modeled after the Capitol in Washington. Its dome is even higher than the Washington version, and it dominates the area. It will be closed three years for seismic upgrading beginning in early 1995. In front of the building are formal gardens with fountains, walkways, and seasonal flower beds. Brooks Exhibit Hall was constructed under this plaza in 1958 to add space for the frequent trade shows and other events based in the Bill Graham Civic Auditorium, recently renamed in honor of the late rock promoter, on Grove Street.

59 Across the plaza from City Hall on Larkin Street is the main branch of the **San Francisco Public Library.** (A new library is being built directly across Fulton Street; when that is completed in early 1996, this site may become the new Asian Art Museum.) History buffs should visit the San Francisco History Room and Archives on the third floor. Historic photographs, maps, and other memorabilia are carefully displayed for the layman or research scholar. *Archives, tel. 415/557–4567. Open Tues., Wed., Fri. 1–6, Thurs. and Sat. 10–noon and 1–6.*

60 Just east of the new library, at the end of Fulton Street set on an angle between Hyde and Market streets, is **United Nations Plaza,** the site of a bustling farmers' market on Wednesday and Sunday.

61 On the west side of City Hall, across Van Ness Avenue, are the Veterans Building, the Opera House, and Davies Symphony Hall. The northernmost of the three is the **Veterans Building** (401 Van Ness Ave.), the third and fourth floors of which formerly housed the San Francisco Museum of Modern Art (as of January 1995 located in Yerba Buena Center, *see* South of Market (SoMa) and the Embarcadero, *above*). Herbst Theatre, on the first floor, remains a popular venue for lectures and readings, classical ensembles, and dance performances. In 1995, celebrations are planned to commemorate the 50th anniversary of the signing of the United Nations Charter in the theater.

62 An ornate horseshoe carriage entrance on its south side separates the Veterans Building from the **War Memorial Opera House** (301 Van Ness Ave.), which opened in 1932. Modeled after European counterparts, the interior has a vaulted and coffered ceiling, a marble foyer, and two balconies. The San Francisco Opera (September–December) and the San Francisco Ballet (February–May, with December *Nutcracker* performances) perform here. (*See* The Arts in The Arts and Nightlife, *below*.)

63 South of Grove Street, still on Van Ness, is the $27.5-million home of the San Francisco Symphony, the modern 3,000-plus-seat **Louise M. Davies Symphony Hall,** made of glass and granite. Tours are available of Davies Hall and the adjacent Performing Arts Center, which encompasses the Opera House and Herbst Theatre; architecture and art-history buffs will find the tours interesting. *201 Van*

Ness Ave., tel. 415/552–8338. Cost: $3 adults, $2 senior citizens and students. Tours of Davies Hall Wed. 1:30 and 2:30, Sat. 12:30 and 1:30. Tours of Davies Hall and the Performing Arts Center every half-hour Mon. 10–2.

The Northern Waterfront

Numbers in the margin correspond to points of interest on the Northern Waterfront map.

For the sight, sound, and smell of the sea, hop the Powell-Hyde cable car from Union Square to the end of the line. From the cable-car turnaround, Aquatic Park, and the National Maritime Museum are immediately to the west; Fort Mason, with its several interesting museums, is just a bit farther west. If you want to explore the more commercial attractions, Ghirardelli Square is behind you and Fisherman's Wharf is to the east. We recommend casual clothes, good walking shoes, and a jacket or sweater for mid-afternoon breezes or foggy mists.

You could begin your day with one of the early-morning boat tours that depart from the Northern Waterfront piers. On a clear day (almost always), the morning light casts a warm glow on the colorful homes on Russian Hill, the weather-aged fishing boats cluttered at Fisherman's Wharf, rosy Ghirardelli Square and its fairy-tale clock tower, and the swelling seas beyond the entrance to the bay.

San Francisco is famous for the arts and crafts that flourish on the streets. Each day more than 200 of the city's innovative jewelers, painters, potters, photographers, and leather workers offer their wares for sale. You'll find them at Fisherman's Wharf, Union Square, Embarcadero Plaza, and Cliff House. Be wary: Some of the items are from foreign factories and may be overpriced. If you can't live without the item, try to bargain.

❶ The **National Maritime Museum** exhibits ship models, photographs, maps, and other artifacts chronicling the development of San Francisco and the West Coast through maritime history. *Aquatic Park, at the foot of Polk St., tel. 415/556–3002 (if no answer call 929–0202). Admission free. Open daily 10–5, until 6 in summer.*

❷ The museum also includes the **Hyde Street Pier** (two blocks east), where historic vessels are moored. The pier, one of the wharf area's best bargains, is always bustling with activity; depending on when you arrive, you might see boatbuilders at work or children manning a boat or ship as though it were still the early 1900s. The highlight of the pier is the *Balclutha,* an 1886 full-rigged, three-mast sailing vessel that sailed around Cape Horn 17 times. The *Eureka,* a side-wheel ferry, and the *C.A. Thayer,* a three-masted schooner, can also be boarded. *Tel. 415/929–0202. Admission: $3 adults, $1 children 12–18; children under 12 and senior citizens free. (Note: Travelers with a National Park Service Golden Eagle Pass enter the pier free.) Open fall–spring, daily 10–5; summer, daily 10–6.*

❸ Spend some time strolling through **Ghirardelli Square,** which is across Beach Street from the National Maritime Museum. This charming complex of 19th-century brick factory buildings has been transformed into specialty shops, cafés, restaurants, and galleries. Until the early 1960s, the Ghirardelli Chocolate Company's aromatic production perfumed the Northern Waterfront. Two unusual shops in the Cocoa Building deserve mention: **Xanadu Gallery** and **Folk Art International** display museum-quality tribal art from Asia, Africa, Oceania, and the Americas. Xanadu's array of antique and

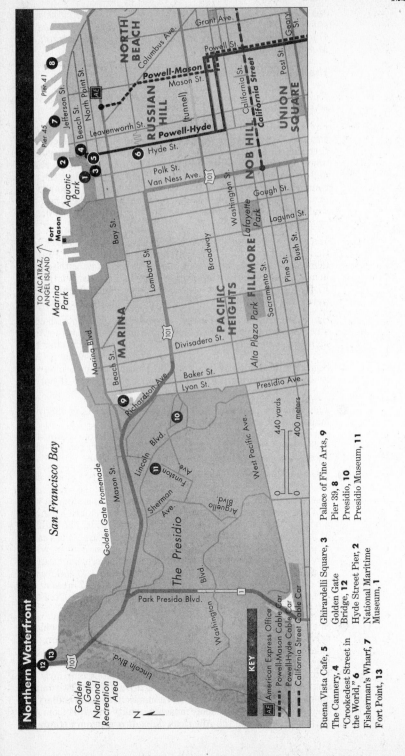

Northern Waterfront

San Francisco Bay

Golden Gate National Recreation Area

TO ALCATRAZ, ANGEL ISLAND

Marina Park

Fort Mason

Aquatic Park

The Presidio

Golden Gate Promenade

Park Presido Blvd.

Lincoln Blvd.

Marina Blvd.

Mason St.

Bay St.

Beach St.

Lombard St.

MARINA

PACIFIC HEIGHTS

Divisadero St.

Baker St.

Lyon St.

Richardson Ave.

Funston Ave.

Sherman Ave.

Arguello Blvd.

West Pacific Ave.

Presidio Ave.

Washington

Lincoln Blvd.

NORTH BEACH

Columbus Ave.

Grant Ave.

Powell St.

Mason St.

North Point St.

Jefferson St.

Beach St.

Leavenworth St.

Hyde St.

Polk St.

Van Ness Ave.

Washington St.

Broadway

RUSSIAN HILL

Powell-Mason

Powell-Hyde (tunnel)

NOB HILL

FILLMORE

Lafayette Park

Alta Plaza Park

Gough St.

Laguna St.

Pine St.

Bush St.

Sacramento St.

California St.

California Street

Post St.

Geary St.

UNION SQUARE

101

440 yards
400 meters

KEY

AE American Express Office
Powell-Mason Cable Car
Powell-Hyde Cable Car
California Street Cable Car

Buena Vista Cafe, **5**
The Cannery, **4**
"Crookedest Street in the World," **6**
Fisherman's Wharf, **7**
Fort Point, **13**

Ghirardelli Square, **3**
Golden Gate Bridge, **12**
Hyde Street Pier, **2**
National Maritime Museum, **1**

Palace of Fine Arts, **9**
Pier 39, **8**
Presidio, **10**
Presidio Museum, **11**

N

ethnic jewelry is peerless. Also of interest, on the Lower Plaza level of the Cocoa Building, is the **Creative Spirit Gallery** (tel. 415/441–1537), a space sponsored and run by the National Institute of Art and Disabilities to showcase works by artists with disabilities. Nearby, in Ghirardelli's Rose court, is the **California Crafts Museum** (tel. 415/771–1919), which honors the state's craft artists.

④ Just east of the Hyde Street Pier, **The Cannery** is a three-story structure built in 1894 to house what became the Del Monte Fruit and Vegetable Cannery. Shops, art galleries, and unusual restaurants ring the courtyard today. The **Museum of the City of San Francisco** (open Wed.–Sun. 10–4, tel. 415/928–0289; $2 donation requested) can be found on the third floor. *2801 Leavenworth St.*

⑤ The mellow **Buena Vista Cafe** (2765 Hyde St., tel. 415/474–5044) claims to be the birthplace of Irish Coffee stateside; the late San Francisco columnist Stan Delaplane is credited with importing the Gaelic concoction. The BV opens at 9 AM weekdays, 8 AM weekends, and serves a great breakfast. It is always crowded, but try for a table overlooking nostalgic Victorian Park with its cable-car turntable.

For an even more sweeping view of the bay, walk five (steep) blocks up Hyde Street to Lombard Street. This puts you at the top of one **⑥** of San Francisco's signature sites, the **"Crookedest Street in the World."** Note: the street will be closed for repairs for a few months during 1995.

⑦ A bit farther west, at Taylor and Jefferson streets, is **Fisherman's Wharf.** Numerous seafood restaurants are located here, as well as sidewalk crab pots and counters that offer take-away shrimp and crab cocktails. Ships creak at their moorings; sea gulls cry out for a handout. By mid-afternoon, the fishing fleet is back to port. T-shirts and sweats, gold chains galore, redwood furniture, and acres of artwork—some original—beckon visitors. Wax museums, fast-food favorites, amusing street artists, and the animated robots at Lazermaze provide diversions for all ages.

The ***Pampanito,*** at Pier 45, is a World War II submarine. An audio tour has been installed. *Tel. 415/929–0202. Admission: $4 adults, $2 senior citizens and students 12–18, $1 children 6–11 and active military. Open fall–spring, daily 9–6; summer, daily 9–9.*

Time Out The swingin'est place on the wharf is the airy **Lou's Pier 47 Restaurant** and bar (300 Jefferson St., tel. 415/771–0377). You won't be able to miss this joint: the sounds of live jazz bands, many of them quite fine, flood the wharf, starting most days at noon. The food at Lou's—standard American fare—is not bad either.

Cruises are an exhilarating way to see the bay. Among the cruises offered by the **Red and White Fleet,** berthed at Pier 41, are frequent 45-minute swings under the Golden Gate Bridge and along the Northern Waterfront. More interesting—and just as scenic—are the tours to Sausalito, Angel Island, Muir Woods, Marine World Africa USA, and the Napa Valley Wine Country. A real treat is the popular tour of **Alcatraz Island.** The boat ride to the island is brief (15 minutes), but affords beautiful views of the city, Marin County, and the East Bay. The audio tour, highly recommended, features observations of guards and prisoners about life in one of America's most notorious penal colonies. Advanced reservations, even in the off-season, are strongly recommended. *Recorded information on all Red and White tours, tel. 415/546–2628. Alcatraz tours (including* *audio guide) are $8.75 adults and children 12–18, $7.75 senior citizens, $4.25 children 5–11; without audio, subtract $3 for adults and senior citizens, $1 for children 5–11. Add $2 per ticket to charge by phone at 415/546–2700.*

The **Blue and Gold Fleet,** berthed at Pier 39, provides its passengers with validated parking across the street. The 1¼-hour tour sails under both the Bay and Golden Gate bridges. Friday and Saturday night dinner-dance cruises run April–mid-December. *Tel. 415/781–7877. Reservations not necessary. Bay Cruise: $15 adults, $7 senior citizens, active military, and children 5–18, under 5 free. Summertime dinner-dance cruise: $35 per person (group rates available). Daily departures.*

8 **Pier 39** is the most popular of San Francisco's waterfront attractions, drawing millions of visitors each year to browse through its dozens of shops. Check out The Disney Store, with more Mickey Mouses than you can shake a stick at; Left Hand World, where left-handers will find all manner of gadgets designed with lefties in mind; and Only in San Francisco, the place for San Francisco memorabilia and the location of the Pier 39 information center. Ongoing free entertainment, accessible validated parking, and nearby public transportation ensure crowds most days. Opening in late 1995 is a new attraction: Underwater World at Pier 39. Moving walkways will transport visitors through a space surrounded on three sides by water. The focus will be on indigenous San Francisco Bay marine life, from fish and plankton to sharks. Above water, don't miss the hundreds of sea lions that bask and play on the docks on the pier's north side. Bring a camera.

The Marina and the Presidio

Numbers in the margin correspond to points of interest on the Northern Waterfront map.

9 San Francisco's rosy and Rococo **Palace of Fine Arts** is at the very end of the Marina, near the intersection of Baker and Beach streets. The palace is the sole survivor of the 32 tinted plaster structures built for the 1915 Panama-Pacific International Exposition. Bernard Maybeck designed the Roman Classic beauty, and in the ensuing 50 years the building fell into disrepair. It was reconstructed in concrete at a cost of $7 million and reopened in 1967, thanks to legions of sentimental citizens and a huge private donation that saved the palace from demolition. The massive columns, great rotunda, and swan-filled lagoon will be familiar from fashion layouts as well as from many recent films.

The interior houses a fascinating hands-on museum, the **Exploratorium,** which has been called the best science museum in the world. The curious of all ages flock here to try to use and understand some of the 600 exhibits. Be sure to include the pitch-black, crawl-through Tactile Dome in your visit. *Tel. 415/561–0360 for general information, 415/561–0362 for required reservations for Tactile Dome. Admission: $8 adults, $6 students over 18 with ID, $4 children 6–17, free 1st Wed. of every month. Open Tues.–Sun. 10–5, Wed. 10–9:30, legal Mon. holidays 10–5.*

If you have a car, now is the time to use it for a drive through the **10** **Presidio.** (If not, Muni bus No. 38 from Union Square will take you to Park Presidio; from there use a free transfer to bus No. 28 into the Presidio.) A military post for more than 200 years, this headquarters of the U.S. Sixth Army is in the process of becoming a public park. De Anza and a band of Spanish settlers claimed the area in 1776. It became a Mexican garrison in 1822 when Mexico gained its independence from Spain. U.S. troops forcibly occupied it in 1846.

The more than 1,500 acres of rolling hills, majestic woods, and attractive redbrick army barracks present an air of serenity in the middle of the city. The **Officers' Club** (Moraga Ave. at Arguello Blvd.), a long, low adobe built around 1776, was the Spanish commandante's headquarters and is the oldest standing building in the

⑪ city. The **Presidio Museum,** housed in a former hospital built in 1857, focuses on the role played by the military in San Francisco's development. Behind the museum are two cabins that housed refugees from the 1906 earthquake and fire. *On the corner of Lincoln Blvd. and Funston Ave., tel. 415/556–0856. Admission free. Open Tues.– Sun. 10–4.*

⑫ Muni bus No. 28 will take you to the **Golden Gate Bridge** toll plaza. Nearly 2 miles long, connecting San Francisco with Marin County, its Art Deco design is powerful, serene, and tough, made to withstand winds of over 100 miles per hour. Though frequently gusty and misty (walkers should wear warm clothing), the bridge offers unparalleled views of the Bay Area. The east walkway offers a glimpse of the San Francisco skyline as well as the islands of the bay. On a sunny day sailboats dot the water, and brave windsurfers test the often treacherous tides beneath the bridge. The view west confronts you with the wild hills of the Marin headlands, the curving coast south to Land's End, and the majestic Pacific Ocean. There's a vista point on the Marin side, where you can contemplate the city and its spectacular setting.

⑬ **Fort Point** was constructed during the years 1853–1861 to protect San Francisco from sea attack during the Civil War. It was designed to mount 126 cannons with a range of up to 2 miles. Standing under the shadow of the Golden Gate Bridge, the national historic site is now a museum filled with military memorabilia. Guided group tours are offered by National Park Rangers, and there are cannon demonstrations. There is a superb view of the bay from the top floor. *Tel. 415/556–1693. Admission free. Open Wed.–Sun. 10–5.*

From here, hardy walkers may elect to stroll about 3½ miles (with bay views) along the Golden Gate Promenade to Aquatic Park and the Hyde Street cable-car terminus.

Golden Gate Park

Numbers in the margin correspond to points of interest on the Golden Gate Park map.

It was a Scotsman, John McLaren, who became manager of Golden Gate Park in 1887 and transformed the brush and sand into the green civilized wilderness we enjoy today. Here you can attend a polo game or a Sunday band concert and rent a bike, boat, or roller skates. On Sunday, some park roads are closed to cars and come alive with joggers, bicyclists, skaters, museum goers, and picnickers. There are tennis courts, baseball diamonds, soccer fields, a buffalo paddock, and miles of trails for horseback riding in this 1,000-acre park.

Because it is so large, the best way for most visitors to see it is by car. Muni buses provide service, though on weekends there may be a long wait. On Market Street, board a westbound No. 5-Fulton or

No. 21-Hayes bus and continue to Arguello and Fulton streets. Walk south about 500 feet to John F. Kennedy Drive.

From May through October, free guided walking tours of the park are offered every weekend by the Friends of Recreation and Parks (tel. 415/221–1311).

❶ The oldest building in the park and perhaps San Francisco's most elaborate Victorian is the **Conservatory** (tel. 415/752–8080), a copy of London's famous Kew Gardens. The ornate greenhouse was originally brought around the Horn for the estate of James Lick in San Jose. The Conservatory was purchased from the Lick estate with public subscription funds and erected in the park. In addition to a tropical garden, there are seasonal displays of flowers and plants and a permanent exhibit of rare orchids. *Admission: $1.50 adults, 75¢ senior citizens and children 6–12, children under 6 and 1st and last half-hour free. Open daily 9–5.*

❷ The eastern section of the park has three museums. Purchase of a $10 Golden Gate Park Cultural Pass gains you one-day admission to all three, plus the Japanese Tea Garden and the Conservatory, a substantial savings (for adults) if you are planning to visit all these attractions. Purchase your pass at any of the museums or at TIX Bay Area in Union Square. The **M. H. de Young Memorial Museum** was completely reorganized in 1989. It now features American art, with collections of paintings, sculpture, textiles, and decorative arts from Colonial times through the 20th century. Fifteen new galleries highlight the work of American masters, including Copley, Eakins, Bingham, and Sargent. Don't miss the room of landscapes, dominated by Frederic Church's moody, almost psychedelic *Rainy Season in the Tropics.* There is a wonderful gallery of American still-life and trompe l'oeil art and a small selection of classic Shaker furniture. The De Young also has a dramatic collection of tribal art from Africa, Oceania, and the Americas, which includes pottery, basketry, sculpture, and ritual clothing and accessories. In addition to its permanent collections, the museum hosts selected traveling shows— often blockbuster events for which there are long lines and additional admission charges. The museum has an outstanding shop with a wide selection of art objects. The **Cafe de Young,** which has outdoor seating in the Oakes Garden, serves a complete menu of light refreshments until 4 PM. *Tel. 415/863–3330 for 24-hr information. Admission: $5 adults, $3 senior citizens, $2 youths 12–17, under 12 free; free 1st Wed. (until 5) and Sat. (10–noon) of the month. Note: One admission charge admits you to the de Young, Asian Art, and Legion of Honor (when it reopens in fall of 1995) museums on the same day. Open Wed.–Sun. 10–5 1st Wed. of the month only, 10–8:45; suggested admission after 5 PM that day is $1.*

❸ The **Asian Art Museum** is located in galleries that adjoin the De Young. This world-famous Avery Brundage collection consists of more than 10,000 sculptures, paintings, and ceramics that illustrate major periods of Asian art. Very special are the Magnin Jade Room and the Leventritt collection of blue and white porcelains. On the second floor are treasures from Iran, Turkey, Syria, India, Tibet, Nepal, Pakistan, Korea, Japan, Afghanistan, and Southeast Asia. Both the De Young and Asian Art museums have daily docent tours. *Tel. 415/668–8921. Admission collected when entering the de Young. Open Wed.–Sun. 10–5, 1st Wed. of the month 10–8:45.*

Time Out   The **Japanese Tea Garden,** next to the Asian Art Museum, is ideal
❹ for resting after museum touring. This charming four-acre village

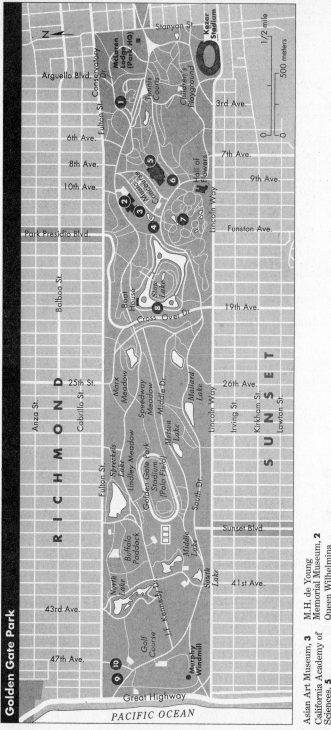

Golden Gate Park

PACIFIC OCEAN

Asian Art Museum, **3**
California Academy of Sciences, **5**
Conservatory, **1**
Dutch Windmill, **9**
Japanese Tea Garden, **4**

M.H. de Young Memorial Museum, **2**
Queen Wilhelmina Tulip Garden, **10**
Shakespeare Garden, **6**
Stow Lake, **8**
Strybing Arboretum, **7**

was created for the 1894 Mid-Winter Exposition. Small ponds, streams, and flowering shrubs create a serene landscape. The cherry blossoms in spring are exquisite. The Tea House (tea, of course, and cookies are served) is popular and busy. *Tel. 415/752–1171. Admission: $2 adults and children 13–17, $1 senior citizens and children 6–12. Open daily 9–6 in the summer, daily 8:30–6 in the winter.*

⑤ The **California Academy of Sciences** is directly opposite the de Young Museum. It is one of the top five natural history museums in the country, and has both an aquarium and a planetarium. Throngs of visitors enjoy its Steinhart Aquarium, with its dramatic 100,000-gallon Fish Roundabout, home to 14,000 creatures, and a living coral reef with colorful fish, giant clams, tropical sharks, and a rainbow of hard and soft corals. The Space and Earth Hall has an "earthquake floor" that enables visitors to experience a simulated California earthquake. The Wattis Hall of Man presents rotating natural history, art, and cultural exhibits. In the Wild California Hall are a 14,000-gallon aquarium tank showing underwater life at the Farallones (islands off the coast of northern California), life-size elephant-seal models, and video information on the wildlife of the state. The innovative Life Through Time Hall tells the story of evolution from the beginnings of life on earth through the age of dinosaurs to the age of mammals. A popular attraction at the Academy is the permanent display of cartoons by Far Side creator Gary Larson. There is an additional charge for Morrison Planetarium shows (depending on the show, up to $2.50 adults, $1.25 senior citizens and students, tel. 415/750–7141 for daily schedule). Laserium (tel. 415/750–7138 for schedule and fees) presents laser-light shows at Morrison Planetarium, accompanied by rock, classical, and other musical forms. Educational shows outline laser technology. A cafeteria is open daily until one hour before the museum closes, and the Academy Store offers a wide selection of books, posters, toys, and cultural artifacts. *Tel. 415/750–7145. Admission: $7 adults, $4 senior citizens and students 12–17, $1.50 children 6–11. $2 discount with Muni transfer. Free 1st Wed. of each month. Open July 4–Labor Day, daily 10–7; Labor Day–July, daily 10–5.*

A short stroll from the Academy of Sciences will take you to the free **⑥** **Shakespeare Garden.** Two hundred flowers mentioned by the Bard, as well as bronze-engraved panels with floral quotations, are set throughout the garden.

⑦ **Strybing Arboretum** specializes in plants from areas with climates similar to that of the Bay Area, such as the west coast of Australia, South Africa, and the Mediterranean. There are many gardens inside the grounds, with 6,000 plants and tree varieties blooming seasonally. *9th Ave. at Lincoln Way, tel. 415/661–0668. Admission free. Open weekdays 8–4:30, weekends and holidays 10–5. Tours leave the bookstore weekdays at 1:30 PM, weekends at 10:30 AM and 1:30 PM.*

The western half of Golden Gate Park offers miles of wooded greenery and open spaces for all types of spectator and participant sports. **⑧** Rent a paddleboat or stroll around **Stow Lake.** The Chinese Pavilion, a gift from the city of Taipei, was shipped in 6,000 pieces and assembled on the shore of Strawberry Hill Island in Stow Lake in 1981. At the very western end of the park, where Kennedy Drive meets **⑨** the Great Highway, is the beautifully restored 1902 **Dutch Windmill ⑩** and the photogenic **Queen Wilhelmina Tulip Garden.**

Lincoln Park and the Western Shoreline

No other American city provides such close-up viewing of the power and fury of the surf attacking the shore. From Land's End in Lincoln Park you can look across the Golden Gate (the name was originally given to the opening of San Francisco Bay long before the bridge was built) to the Marin Headlands. From the Cliff House south to the San Francisco Zoo, the Great Highway and Ocean Beach run along the western edge of the city.

The wind is often strong along the shoreline, summer fog can blanket the ocean beaches, and the water is cold and usually too rough for swimming. Carry a sweater or jacket and bring binoculars.

At the northwest corner of the San Francisco Peninsula is **Lincoln Park**. At one time all the city's cemeteries were here, segregated by nationality. Today there is an 18-hole golf course with large and well-formed Monterey cypresses lining the fairways. There are scenic walks throughout the 275-acre park, with particularly good views from **Land's End** (the parking lot is at the end of El Camino del Mar). The trails out to Land's End, however, are for skilled hikers only: There are frequent landslides, and danger lurks along the steep cliffs.

Also in Lincoln Park is the **California Palace of the Legion of Honor.** The building itself—modeled after the 18th-century Parisian original—is architecturally interesting and spectacularly situated on cliffs overlooking the ocean and the Golden Gate Bridge. The museum closed in 1992 for seismic and other renovations, and is set to reopen in late 1995.

The Cliff House (1066 Point Lobos Ave.), where the road turns south along the western shore, has existed in several incarnations. The original, built in 1863, and several later structures were destroyed by fire. The present building has restaurants, a pub, and a gift shop. The lower dining room overlooks Seal Rocks (the barking marine mammals sunning themselves are actually sea lions).

An adjacent attraction is the **Musée Mécanique,** a collection of antique mechanical contrivances, including peep shows and nickelodeons. The museum carries on the tradition of arcade amusement at the Cliff House. *Tel. 415/386–1170. Admission free. Open weekdays 11–7, weekends 10–8.*

Two flights below the Cliff House is a fine observation deck and the Golden Gate National Recreation Area **Visitors Center.** There are interesting and historic photographs of the Cliff House and the glass-roofed **Sutro Baths.** The baths covered three acres just north of the Cliff House and comprised six enormous baths, 500 dressing rooms, and several restaurants. The baths were closed in 1952 and burned in 1966. You can explore the ruins on your own or take ranger-led walks on weekends. The Visitors Center offers information on these and other trails. *Tel. 415/556–8642. Open daily 10–4:30.*

Because traffic is often heavy in summer and on weekends, you might want to take the Muni system from the Union Square area out to the Cliff House. On weekdays, take the Muni No. 38-Geary Limited to 48th Avenue and Point Lobos and walk down the hill. On weekends and during the evenings, the Muni No. 38 is marked "48th Avenue." Don't take the No. 38 bus marked "Ocean Beach," though, or you'll have to walk an extra 10 minutes to get to the Cliff House.

Time Out   The Cliff House (tel. 415/386–3330) has several restaurants and a busy bar. **The Upstairs Room** features a light menu with a number of omelet suggestions. The lower dining room, the **Seafood & Beverage Co. Restaurant,** has a fabulous view of Seal Rocks. Reservations are recommended, but you may still have to wait for a table, especially at midday on Sunday.

Below the Cliff House are the **Great Highway** and **Ocean Beach.** Stretching for 3 miles along the western (Pacific) side of the city, this is a beautiful beach for walking, running, or lying in the sun—but not for swimming. Although dozens of surfers head to Ocean Beach each day, you'll notice they are dressed head-to-toe in wet suits, as the water here is extremely cold. Across the highway from the beach is a new path, which winds through landscaped sand dunes from Lincoln Avenue to Sloat Boulevard (near the zoo)—an ideal route for walking and bicycling.

At the Great Highway and Sloat Boulevard is the **San Francisco Zoo.** The zoo was begun in 1889 in Golden Gate Park. At its present home there are 1,000 species of birds and animals, more than 130 of which have been designated endangered species. Among the protected are the snow leopard, Sumatran tiger, jaguar, and the Asian elephant. A favorite attraction is the greater one-horned rhino, next to the African elephants.

Gorilla World, a $2-million exhibit, is one of the largest and most natural gorilla habitats in a zoo. The circular outer area is carpeted with natural African Kikuyu grass, while trees and shrubs create communal play areas. With the late-1993 birth of a lowland gorilla named Barney, three generations of the species now inhabit the zoo. The $5-million Primate Discovery Center houses 14 endangered species in atriumlike enclosures. One of the most popular zoo residents is Prince Charles, a rare white tiger and the first of its kind to be exhibited in the West.

There are 46 "storyboxes" throughout the zoo that, when turned on with blue and red keys ($2), recite animal facts and basic zoological concepts in four languages—English, Spanish, Cantonese, and Tagalog.

The children's zoo has a minipopulation of about 300 mammals, birds, and reptiles, plus an insect zoo, a baby-animal nursery, and a beautifully restored 1921 Dentzel Carousel. A ride astride one of the 52 hand-carved menagerie animals costs $1.

Zoo information, tel. 415/753–7083. Admission: $6.50 adults, $3 youths 12–15 and senior citizens, $1 children 6–12, under 5 free when accompanied by an adult; free first Wed. of the month. Open daily 10–5. Children's zoo admission: $1, under 3 free. Open daily 11–4.

Shopping

By Sheila Gadsden

Updated by Daniel Mangin

San Francisco is a shopper's dream—major department stores, fine fashion, discount outlets, art galleries, and crafts stores are among the many offerings. Most accept at least Visa and MasterCard charge cards, and many also accept American Express and Diner's Club. A very few accept cash only. Ask about traveler's checks; policies vary. The *San Francisco Chronicle* and *Examiner* advertise sales; for smaller innovative shops, check the San Francisco *Bay Guardian.* Store hours are slightly different everywhere, but a generally trusted rule is to shop between 10 AM and 5 or 6 PM Monday–Wednesday, Friday, and Saturday; between 10 AM and 8 or 9 PM on

Thursday; and from noon until 5 PM on Sunday. Stores on and around Fisherman's Wharf often have longer summer hours.

Major Shopping Districts

Fisherman's Wharf San Francisco's Fisherman's Wharf is host to a number of shopping and sightseeing attractions: **Pier 39,** the **Anchorage, Ghirardelli Square,** and **The Cannery.** Each offers shops, restaurants, and a festive atmosphere as well as such outdoor entertainment as musicians, mimes, and magicians. Pier 39 includes an amusement area and a double-decked Venetian carousel. One attraction shared by all the centers is the view of the bay and the proximity of the cable car lines, which can take shoppers directly to Union Square.

Union Square Serious shoppers will find the entire Union Square area richly rewarding. Bordering the square itself are leading department and specialty stores. **I. Magnin & Co.,** on the south side of Union Square at Stockton Street, is noted for its designer fashions, magnificent fur salon, and precious jewelry salon. Just across Stockton Street is the checkerboard-faced **Neiman Marcus,** opened in 1982. Philip Johnson's controversial design replaced an old San Francisco favorite, the City of Paris; all that remains is the great glass dome. **Macy's,** with entrances on Geary, Stockton, and O'Farrell streets, has huge selections of clothing, plus extensive furniture and household accessories departments. The men's department—one of the world's largest—occupies its own building across Stockton Street. Opposite is an **FAO Schwarz** children's store, with its extravagant assortment of life-size stuffed animals, animated displays, and steep prices.

A half block down Stockton Street from FAO Schwarz is the new **Virgin Megastore** (scheduled to open in late 1994), four floors of music, entertainment, and software in a building also housing a **Planet Hollywood** restaurant (whose owners include Demi Moore, Danny Glover, Arnold Schwarzenegger, Bruce Willis, and Sylvester Stallone). Also livening up the already lively Union Square area: a huge new **Disney Store** (to open in November 1994), selling memorabilia and other merchandise from the famous movie studio. The Disney space, across Post Street from the St. Francis Hotel, also includes a 45,000-square-foot **Borders Books and Music** store. Across Powell Street from Disney, **Saks Fifth Avenue** still caters to the upscale shopper. Nearby are the pricey international boutiques of Hermès of Paris, Gucci, Celine of Paris, Alfred Dunhill, Louis Vuitton, and Cartier.

Across from the cable car turntable at Powell and Market streets is the **San Francisco Shopping Centre,** with the fashionable **Nordstrom** department store and more than 35 other shops. And underneath a glass dome at Post and Kearny streets is **Crocker Galleria,** a complex of 50 shops and restaurants topped by two rooftop parks.

Embarcadero Center Five modern towers of shops, restaurants, and offices plus the Hyatt Regency Hotel make up the downtown Embarcadero Center at the end of Market Street. The center's 175 stores and services include such nationally known stores as **The Limited, B. Dalton Bookseller,** and **Ann Taylor,** as well as more local or West Coast–based businesses such as the **Nature Company** and **Lotus Designer Earrings.** Each tower occupies one block, and parking garages are available.

Chinatown The intersection of Grant Avenue and Bush Street marks "the Gateway" to Chinatown; here shoppers and tourists are introduced to 24 blocks of shops, restaurants, markets, and temples. There are daily "sales" on gems of all sorts—especially jade and pearls—alongside stalls of bok choy and gingerroot. Chinese silks and toy trinkets are also commonplace in the shops, as are selections of colorful pottery, baskets, and large figures of soapstone, ivory, and jade.

North Beach The once largely Italian enclave of North Beach gets smaller each year as Chinatown spreads northward. It has been called the city's answer to New York City's Greenwich Village, although it's much smaller. Many of the businesses here tend to be small clothing stores, antiques shops, or such eccentric specialty shops as **Quantity Postcard** (1441 Grant Ave.), which has an inventory of 15,000 different postcards. If you get tired of poking around in the bookstores, a number of cafés dot the streets and there are lots of Italian restaurants.

Union Street Out-of-towners sometimes confuse Union Street—a popular stretch of shops and restaurants five blocks south of the Golden Gate National Recreation Area—with downtown's Union Square (*see above*). Nestled at the foot of a hill between Pacific Heights and the Marina District, Union Street shines with contemporary fashion and custom jewelry. Here are some local favorites: **Arte Forma** (1775 Union St.), which sells wild, yet elegant, contemporary art furniture; the magical, mystical **Enchanted Crystal** (1771 Union St.); the **Armani Exchange** (2090 Union St.) clothing boutique; and **Yankee Doodle Dandy** (1974 Union St.), home to a delightful collection of teddy bears and antique American quilts. The main shopping area runs from Laguna Street to Steiner Street, and also north on Fillmore to Lombard Street.

Japantown Unlike Chinatown, North Beach, or the Mission, the 5-acre **Japan Center** (between Laguna and Fillmore Sts., and between Geary Blvd. and Post St.) is contained under one roof. The three-block cluster includes an 800-car public garage and shops and showrooms selling Japanese products: cameras, tapes and records, new and old porcelains, pearls, antique kimonos, beautiful tansu chests, and paintings. The center always feels a little empty, but the good shops here are well worth a visit, as are the adjoining ones on Post and Buchanan streets.

The Haight Haight Street is always an attraction for visitors, if only to see the sign at Haight and Ashbury streets—the geographic center of flower power during the 1960s. These days, in addition to renascent tie-dyed shirts, you'll find good-quality vintage clothing, funky jewelry, art from Mexico, and reproductions of Art Deco accessories. The street also boasts several used-book stores and some of the best used-record stores in the city.

South of Market Dozens of outlet shops, most of them open seven days a week, have sprung up along the streets and alleyways bordered by 2nd, Townsend, Howard, and 10th streets. A good place to start is at the **Six Sixty Center** (660 3rd St.), two floors of shops offering everything from designer fashions to Icelandic sweaters. The **Burlington Coat Factory** (899 Howard St., tel. 415/495–7234) in the Yerba Buena Square Mall carries a full range of clothing, shoes, and toys.

Sports, Fitness, Beaches

Participant Sports

By Casey Tefertiller

Updated by Daniel Mangin

One great attraction of the Bay Area is the abundance of activities. Joggers, bicyclists, and aficionados of virtually all sports can find their favorite pastimes within driving distance, and often within walking distance, from downtown hotels. Golden Gate Park has numerous paths for runners and cyclists. Lake Merced in San Francisco and Lake Merritt in Oakland are among the most popular areas for joggers.

For information on running races, tennis tournaments, bicycle races, and other participant sports, check the monthly issues of *City Sports* magazine, available free at sporting goods stores, tennis centers, and other recreational sites. The most important running event of the year is the *Examiner* Bay-to-Breakers race on the third Sunday in May. For information on this race call 415/512–5000, category 2222.

Bicycling Two bike routes are maintained by the San Francisco Recreation and Park Department (tel. 415/666–7201). One route goes through Golden Gate Park to Lake Merced; the other goes from the south end of the city to the Golden Gate Bridge and beyond. Many shops along Stanyan Street rent bikes.

Boating and Sailing **Stow Lake** (tel. 415/752–0347) in Golden Gate Park has rowboat, pedalboat, and electric boat rentals. The lake is open daily for boating, but call for seasonal hours. San Francisco Bay offers year-round sailing, but tricky currents make the bay hazardous for inexperienced navigators. Boat rentals and charters are available throughout the Bay Area and are listed under "boat rentals" in the Yellow Pages. A selected charter is **A Day on the Bay** (tel. 415/922–0227). **Cass' Marina** (tel. 415/332–6789) in Sausalito has a variety of sailboats that can be rented or hired with a licensed skipper. Local sailing information can be obtained at **The Eagle Cafe** on Pier 39.

Fishing Numerous fishing boats leave from San Francisco, Sausalito, Berkeley, Emeryville, and Point San Pablo. They go for salmon outside the bay or striped bass and giant sturgeon within the bay. Temporary licenses are available on the charters. In San Francisco, lines can be cast from San Francisco Municipal Pier, Fisherman's Wharf, or Aquatic Park. Trout fishing is available at Lake Merced. Licenses can be bought at sporting goods stores. The cost of fishing licenses ranges from $5.50 for one day to $23.25 for a complete state license. For charters, reservations are suggested. Some selected sportfishing charters are listed below. Mailing addresses are given, but you're more likely to get a response if you call.

Capt. Fred Morini (Fisherman's Wharf. Write to 138 Harvard Dr., Larkspur, CA 94939, tel. 415/924–5575).
Muny Sport Fishing (156 Linden Ave., San Bruno, CA 94066, tel. 415/871–4445). Leaves daily from Fisherman's Wharf.
Sea Breeze Sportfishing (Box 713, Mill Valley, CA 94942, tel. 415/474–7748). Departs daily from Fisherman's Wharf.
Wacky Jacky (Fisherman's Wharf. Write Jacky Douglas at 473 Bella Vista Way, San Francisco, CA 94127, tel. 415/586–9800).

Golf San Francisco has four public golf courses; visitors should call for tee times: **Harding Park** (Lake Merced Blvd. and Skyline Blvd., tel. 415/664–4690), an 18-hole, par-72 course; **Lincoln Park** (34th and

Clement Sts., tel. 415/221–9911), 18 holes, par 69; **Golden Gate Park** (47th Ave. at Fulton St., tel. 415/751–8987), a "pitch and putt" 9-holer; **Glen Eagles Golf Course** (2100 Sunnydale Ave., tel. 415/587–2425), a full-size 9-holer in McLaren Park. Another municipal course, the 18-hole, par 72 **Sharp Park** (tel. 415/355–8546), is south of the city in Pacifica.

Tennis The San Francisco Recreation and Park Department maintains 130 free tennis courts throughout the city. The largest set of free courts is at **Dolores Park** (18th and Dolores Sts.), with six courts available on a first-come, first-served basis. There are 21 public courts in **Golden Gate Park**; reservations and fee information can be obtained by calling 415/753–7101.

Spectator Sports

For the sports fan, the Bay Area offers a vast selection of events—from yacht races to rodeo to baseball.

Baseball A local investment group saved the **San Francisco Giants** from a move to Tampa/St. Petersburg in 1993, and San Francisco city officials hope to build a new stadium for the team. In the meantime the Giants will continue to play at chilly Candlestick Park (tel. 415/467–8000). The **Oakland A's** play at the Oakland Coliseum (tel. 510/638–0500). Game-day tickets are usually available at the stadiums. Premium seats, however, often do sell out in advance. City shuttle buses marked "Ballpark Special" run from numerous bus stops. Candlestick Park is often windy and cold, so take along extra layers of clothing. The Oakland Coliseum can be reached by taking BART trains to the Coliseum stop.

Basketball The **Golden State Warriors** play NBA basketball at the Oakland Coliseum Arena from October through April. Tickets are available through BASS (tel. 510/762–2277). Again, BART trains to the Coliseum stop are the easiest method of travel.

Football The **San Francisco 49ers** play at Candlestick Park, but the games are almost always sold out far in advance, so call first (tel. 415/468–2249).

Hockey The Bay Area welcomed the **San Jose Sharks** as its first National Hockey League team in 1991. Their popular home games can be seen at the new arena in downtown San Jose, where they began playing in the 1993–94 season. The team has been a wild success, and though many of their games sell out, try calling BASS (tel. 510/762–2277) for tickets.

Tennis The Civic Auditorium (999 Grove St.) is the site of the **Volvo Tennis/San Francisco tournament** in early February (tel. 415/239–4800). The **Virginia Slims women's tennis tour** visits the Oakland Coliseum Arena in October.

Beaches

San Francisco's beaches are perfect for romantic sunset strolls, but don't make the mistake of expecting to find Waikiki-by-the-Metropolis. The water is cold, and the beach areas are often foggy and usually jammed on sunny days. They can be satisfactory for afternoon sunning, but treacherous currents make most areas dangerous for swimming. During stormy months, beachcombers can stroll along the sand and discover a variety of ocean treasures: glossy agates and jade pebbles, sea-sculptured roots and branches, and—rarely—glass floats.

Baker Beach Baker Beach is not recommended for swimming: Watch for larger-than-usual waves. In recent years, the north end of the beach has become popular with nude sunbathers. This is not legal, but such laws are seldom enforced. The beach is in the southwest corner of the Presidio and begins at the end of Gibson Road, which turns off Bowley Street. Weather is typical for the bay shoreline: summer fog, usually breezy, and occasionally warm. Picnic tables, grills, day-camp areas, and trails are available. The mile-long shoreline is ideal for jogging, fishing, and building sand castles.

China Beach From April through October, China Beach, south of Baker Beach, offers a lifeguard, gentler water, changing rooms, and showers. It is also listed on maps as Phelan Beach.

Ocean Beach South of Cliff House, Ocean Beach stretches along the western (ocean) side of San Francisco. It has a wide beach with scenic views and is perfect for walking, running, or lying in the sun—but not for swimming.

Dining

By Jacqueline Killeen

Jacqueline Killeen has been writing about San Francisco restaurants for over 25 years. She is a restaurant critic for San Francisco Focus *magazine.*

San Francisco probably has more restaurants per capita than any other city in the United States, including New York. Practically every ethnic cuisine is represented. That makes selecting some 90 restaurants to list here from the vast number available a very difficult task indeed. We have chosen several restaurants to represent each popular style of dining in various price ranges, in most cases because of the superiority of the food, but in some instances because of the view or ambience.

Because we have covered those areas of town most frequented by visitors, this meant leaving out some great places in outlying districts such as Sunset and Richmond. The outlying restaurants we *have* recommended were chosen because they offer a type of experience not available elsewhere.

All listed restaurants serve dinner and are open for lunch unless otherwise specified; restaurants are not open for breakfast unless the morning meal is specifically mentioned.

Parking accommodations are mentioned only when a restaurant has made special arrangements; otherwise you're on your own. There is usually a charge for valet parking. Validated parking is not necessarily free and unlimited; often there is a nominal charge and a restriction on the length of time.

Restaurants do change their policies about hours, credit cards, and the like. It is always best to make inquiries in advance.

Highly recommended restaurants are indicated by a star ★.

The price ranges listed below are for an average three-course meal. A significant trend among more expensive restaurants is the bar menu, which provides light snacks—hot dogs, chili, pizza, and appetizers—in the bar for a cost that is often less than $10 for two.

Category	Cost*
$$$$	over $45
$$$	$30–$45

$$	$18–$30
$	under $18

per person for a three-course meal, excluding drinks, service, and 8¹/2% sales tax

American   Before the 1980s, it was hard to find a decent "American" restaurant in the Bay Area. In recent years, however, the offerings have grown and diversified, with fare that includes barbecue, Southwestern, all-American diner food, and that mix of Mediterranean-Asian-Latino known as California cuisine.

Civic Center   **Stars.** This is the culinary temple of Jeremiah Tower, the superchef
★   who claims to have invented California cuisine. Stars is a must on every traveling gourmet's itinerary, but it's also where many of the local movers and shakers hang out, a popular place for post-theater dining, and open till the wee hours. The dining room has a clublike ambience, and the food ranges from grills to ragouts to sautés— some daringly creative and some classical. Dinners here are pricey, but if you're on a budget, you can have a hot dog at the bar or by standing in line for a table at the informal Star's Cafe around the corner at Van Ness Avenue and McAllister Street. *150 Redwood Alley, tel. 415/861–7827. Reservations accepted up to 2 wks in advance, some tables reserved for walk-ins. Dress: casual. AE, DC, MC, V. No lunch weekends. Valet parking at night. $$$*

Embarcadero   **Fog City Diner.** This is where the diner and grazing crazes began
North   in San Francisco, and the popularity of this spot knows no end. The
★   long, narrow dining room emulates a luxurious railroad car with dark wood paneling, huge windows, and comfortable booths. The cooking is innovative, drawing its inspiration from regional cooking throughout the United States. The sharable "small plates" are a fun way to go. *1300 Battery St., tel. 415/982–2000. Reservations advised. Dress: casual. DC, MC, V. $$*

MacArthur Park. Year after year San Franciscans acclaim this as their favorite spot for ribs, but the oakwood smoker and mesquite grill also turn out a wide variety of all-American fare, from steaks, hamburgers, and chili to seafood. *607 Front St., tel. 415/398–5700. Reservations advised. Dress: casual. AE, DC, MC, V. No lunch weekends and major holidays. Valet parking at night. $$*

Embarcadero   **Boulevard.** Chef Nancy Oakes and designer Pat Kuleto, two of San
South   Francisco's top restaurant talents, teamed up in 1993 in one of the city's most magnificent landmark buildings. The setting is the 1889 Audiffred Building, a Parisian look-alike that was one of the few to survive the 1906 earthquake and fire. Oakes's menu is seasonally in flux, but you can be certain to find her signature juxtaposition of aristocratic fare—foie gras is a favorite—with homey comfort foods like pot roast with mashed potatoes. There will be a long wait for a reservation, but you can always drop in for a bite from the bar menu. *1 Mission St., tel. 415/543–6084. Reservations advised 3 wks in advance. Jacket and tie suggested at night. AE, MC, V. No lunch weekends. Valet parking. $$–$$$*

Financial   **Cypress Club.** Fans of John Cunin have flocked here since 1990 when
District   Masa's long-time maître d' opened his own place, which he calls a "San Francisco brasserie." This categorizes the contemporary American cooking somewhat, but the decor defies description. It could be interpreted as anything from a parody of an ancient temple to a futuristic space war. *500 Jackson St., tel. 415/296–8555. Reserva-*

tions advised. Dress: casual. AE, DC, MC, V. No lunch. Valet parking at night. $$$

Nob Hill
★ **Ritz-Carlton Restaurant and Dining Room.** There are two distinctly different places to eat in this neoclassical Nob Hill showplace. The Restaurant, a cheerful, informal spot with a large patio for outdoor dining, serves breakfast, lunch, dinner, and a Sunday jazz brunch. The Dining Room, formal and elegant with a harpist playing, serves only two- to five-course dinners, which are uniquely priced by the course, not by the item. Except for the chef's five-course tasting menu, there's a wide selection of choices at the Dining Room. The culinary master behind both restaurants is chef Gary Danko. *600 Stockton St., tel. 415/296–7465. Reservations advised. Dress: casual in the Restaurant, jacket and tie requested in the Dining Room. AE, DC, MC, V. The Dining Room closed Sun. Valet parking. $$–$$$*

North Beach
Bix. The owners of Fog City Diner have re-created a '40s supper club in a historic building that was an assay office in gold-rush days. The place resembles a theater, with a bustling bar and dining tables downstairs and banquettes on the balcony. Opt for the lower level; the acoustics upstairs are dreadful. The menu offers contemporary renditions of 1940s fare; there's piano music in the evenings. *56 Gold St., tel. 415/433–6300. Reservations advised. Dress: casual. AE, DC, MC, V. No lunch weekends. Valet parking at night. $$*

Union Square
★ **Postrio.** This is the place for those who want to see and be seen; there's always a chance to catch a glimpse of some celebrity, including Postrio's owner, superchef Wolfgang Puck, who periodically commutes from Los Angeles to make an appearance in the restaurant's open kitchen. A stunning three-level bar and dining area is highlighted by palm trees and museum-quality contemporary paintings. The food is Puckish Californian with Mediterranean and Asian overtones, emphasizing pastas, grilled seafood, and house-baked breads. A substantial breakfast and bar menu (with great pizza) are served here, too. *545 Post St., tel. 415/776–7825. Reservations advised. Jacket and tie suggested. AE, DC, MC, V. Valet parking. $$$–$$$$*

★ **Campton Place.** This elegant, ultrasophisticated small hotel put new American cooking on the local culinary map. Chef Todd Humphries carries on the innovative traditions of opening chef Bradley Ogden with great aplomb and has added his own touches, such as embellishing traditional American dishes with ethnic flavors from recent immigrations. Breakfast and brunch are major events. A bar menu offers some samplings of appetizers, plus a caviar extravaganza. *340 Stockton St., tel. 415/955–5555. Reservations suggested, 2 wks in advance on weekends. Jacket required at dinner, tie requested. AE, DC, MC, V. Valet parking. $$$*

Chinese
For nearly a century, Chinese restaurants in San Francisco were confined to Chinatown and the cooking was largely an Americanized version of peasant-style Cantonese. The past few decades, however, have seen an influx of restaurants throughout the city representing the wide spectrum of Chinese cuisine: the subtly seasoned fare of Canton, the hot and spicy cooking of Hunan and Szechuan, the northern style of Peking, where meat and dumplings replace seafood and rice as staples, and, more recently, some more esoteric cooking, such as Hakka and Chao Chow.

Embarcadero North
★ **Harbor Village.** Classic Cantonese cooking, dim sum lunches, and fresh seafood from the restaurant's own tanks are the hallmarks of this 400-seat branch of a Hong Kong establishment, which sent five

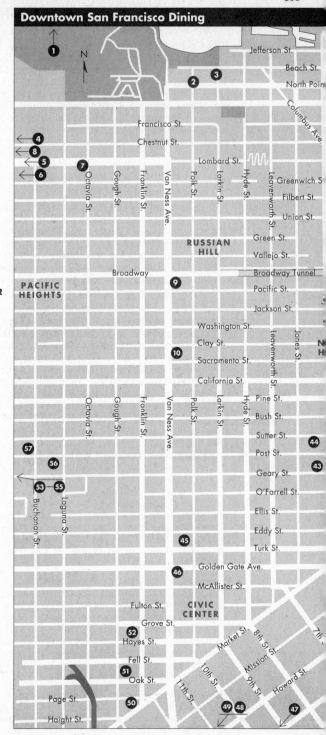

Downtown San Francisco Dining

0   1/2 mile

0   500 meters

The Embarcadero

Bay St.

Francisco St.

Chestnut St.

Lombard St.

NORTH
BEACH

Columbus Ave.

TELEGRAPH
HILL

Front St.

The Embarcadero

Mason St.

Powell St.

Stockton St.

Grant Ave.

Kearny St.

Montgomery St.

Sansome St.

Battery St.

Davis St.

Drumm St.

CHINATOWN

Front St.

Davis St.

Steuart St.

Spear St.

Main St.

Beale St.

Fremont St.

1st St.

UNION
SQUARE

Market St.

New Montgomery St.

Hawthorn St.

2nd St.

3rd St.

4th St.

Mission St.

5th St.

6th St.

Howard St.

Folsom St.

Harrison St.

Bryant St.

Brannan St.

Townsend St.

King St.

KEY

AE American Express Office

of its master chefs to San Francisco to supervise the kitchen. The setting is opulent, with Chinese antiques and teak furnishings. *4 Embarcadero Center; tel. 415/781–8833. Reservations not accepted for lunch on weekends. Dress: casual. AE, DC, MC, V. Validated parking in Embarcadero Center Garage. $$*

Embarcadero South **Wu Kong.** Tucked away in the splashy Art Deco Rincon Center, Wu Kong features the cuisine of Shanghai and Canton. Specialties include dim sum; braised yellow fish; and the incredible vegetarian goose, one of Shanghai's famous mock dishes, created from paper-thin layers of dried bean-curd sheets and mushrooms. *101 Spear St., tel. 415/957–9300. Reservations advised. Dress: casual. AE, DC, MC, V. Validated parking at Rincon Center garage. $$*

Financial District **Yank Sing.** This tea house has grown by leaps and branches with the popularity of dim sum. The Battery Street location seats 300 and the older, smaller Stevenson Street site has recently been rebuilt in high-tech style. *427 Battery St., tel. 415/362–1640; 49 Stevenson St., tel. 415/495–4510. Reservations advised. Dress: casual. AE, MC, V. No dinner. Stevenson site closed weekends. $*

North Beach **Hunan.** Henry Chung's first café on Kearny Street had only six tables, but his Hunanese cooking merited six stars from critics nationwide. He has now opened this larger place on Sansome Street; it's equally plain but has 250 seats. Smoked dishes are a specialty, and Henry guarantees no MSG. *924 Sansome St., tel. 415/956–7727. Reservations advised. Dress: casual. AE, DC, MC, V. $*

Richmond District ★ **Hong Kong Flower Lounge.** Many Chinaphiles swear that this outpost of a famous Asian restaurant chain serves the best Cantonese food in town. The seafood is spectacular, as is the dim sum. *5322 Geary Blvd., tel. 415/668–8998. Reservations advised. Dress: casual. AE, DC, MC, V. $$*

French French cooking has gone in and out of vogue in San Francisco since the extravagant days of the Bonanza Kings. A renaissance of the classic haute cuisine occurred during the 1960s, but recently a number of these restaurants closed. Meanwhile, nouvelle cuisine went in and out of fashion, and the big draw now is the bistro or brasserie.

Civic Center **California Culinary Academy.** This historic theater houses one of the most highly regarded professional cooking schools in the United States. Watch the student chefs at work on the double-tier stage while you dine on classic French cooking. Prix-fixe meals and bountiful buffets are served in the main dining room, and there's an informal grill on the lower level. *625 Polk St., tel. 415/771–3500. Reservations advised (2–4 wks for Fri. night buffet). Jacket and tie requested. AE, DC, MC, V. Closed weekends. $$–$$$*

Financial District **Le Central.** This is the quintessential bistro: noisy and crowded, with nothing subtle about the cooking. But the garlicky pâtés, leeks vinaigrette, cassoulet, and grilled blood sausage with crisp french fries keep the crowds coming. *453 Bush St., tel. 415/ 391–2233. Reservations advised. Dress: casual. AE, DC, MC, V. Closed Sun. $$*

North Beach **Ernie's.** This famous old-timer recently had a face-lift and now conjures up innovative light versions of French classics. Even so, Ernie's is still steeped with the aura of Gay '90s San Francisco and is about the only place in town that offers tableside service. *847 Montgomery St., tel. 415/397–5969. Reservations advised. Jacket required. AE, DC, MC, V. No lunch. Valet parking. $$$$*

Richmond District ★ **Alain Rondelli.** A career beginning at a legendary three-star kitchen in Burgundy (L'Esperance) and leading to a modest block in San Francisco's Richmond District may sound like it's headed down, but for Paris-born chef Alain Rondelli—and his loyal clientele—it's a dream come true. After a three-year stint at Ernie's (*see above*), this enormously talented young Frenchman opened his own beguiling little restaurant in 1993. The cuisine adapts Rondelli's background in classic-yet-contemporary French cooking to the agricultural abundance and Asian and Hispanic influences of his adopted state. *126 Clement St., tel. 415/387–0408. Reservations advised. Dress: casual. MC, V. Closed Mon. $$–$$$*

Union Square ★ **Fleur de Lys.** The creative cooking of chef-partner Hubert Keller is drawing rave reviews for this romantic spot that some consider the best French restaurant in town. The menu changes constantly, but such dishes as lobster soup with lemongrass are a signature. The intimate dining room, like a sheikh's tent, is encased with hundreds of yards of paisley. *777 Sutter St., tel. 415/673–7779. Weekend reservations advised 2 wks in advance. Jacket required. AE, DC, MC, V. No lunch. Closed Sun. Valet parking. $$$$*

★ **Masa's.** Chef Julian Serrano carries on the tradition of the late Masa Kobayashi. In fact, some Masa regulars even say the cooking is better. The artistry of the presentation is as important as the food itself in this pretty, flower-filled dining spot in the Vintage Court Hotel. *648 Bush St., tel. 415/989–7154. Reservations accepted up to 2 mos in advance. Jacket and tie required. AE, DC, MC, V. No lunch. Closed Sun., Mon., and several weeks in late Dec. and early Jan. Valet parking. $$$$*

Liberté. Celebrity chef Elka Gilmore helped design the menu at this smart new restaurant, formerly called Lascaux. On-site chef Bonnie Calabrese prepares innovative French cuisine using American products, with an emphasis on locally produced ingredients. A huge fireplace cheers the romantically lighted subterranean dining room. *248 Sutter St., tel. 415/391–1555. Reservations advised. Dress: casual. AE, DC, MC, V. No lunch weekends. $$*

City of Paris. In this new bistro smack in the middle of theater row, every effort was made to replicate a typical Parisian bistro—jammed-together tables, an open kitchen where plump chickens slowly turn on an ornate cast-iron and brass rotisserie, and such bistro classics as *petit salé* (pork pickled in brine), *gite gite* (skirt steak with frites), and French onion soup. But unlike prices in the City of Lights, the prices here (same at lunch and dinner) are remarkably low. *101 Shannon Alley (off Geary St. between Jones and Taylor), tel. 415/441–4442. Reservations advised. Dress: casual. AE, MC, V. Valet parking. $–$$*

Greek and Middle Eastern The foods of Greece and the Middle East have much in common: a preponderance of lamb and eggplant dishes, a widespread use of phyllo pastry, and an abundance of pilaf.

North Beach **Maykadeh.** Here you'll find authentic Persian cooking in a setting so elegant that the modest check comes as a great surprise. Lamb dishes with rice are the specialties. *470 Green St., tel. 415/362–8286. Reservations advised. Dress: casual. AE, MC, V. Valet parking at night. $–$$*

South of Market **S. Asimakopoulos Cafe.** Terrific Greek food at reasonable prices keeps the crowds waiting for seats at the counter or at bare-topped tables in this storefront café. The menu is large and varied, but lamb dishes are the stars. Convenient to Showplace Square. *288 Connecti-*

cut St., Potrero Hill, tel. 415/552–8789. No reservations. Dress: casual. AE, MC, V. No lunch weekends. $–$$

Indian   The following restaurants serve the cuisine of northern India, which is more subtly seasoned and not as hot as its southern counterparts. They also specialize in succulent meats and crispy breads from the clay-lined tandoori oven.

Northern   **Gaylord's.** A vast selection of mildly spiced northern Indian food is
Waterfront   offered here, along with meats and breads from the tandoori ovens
and   and a wide range of vegetarian dishes. The dining rooms are ele-
Embarcadero   gantly appointed with Indian paintings and gleaming silver service. The Ghirardelli Square location offers bay views. *Ghirardelli Sq., tel. 415/771–8822; Embarcadero 1, tel. 415/397–7775. Reservations advised. Dress: casual. AE, DC, MC, V. No lunch Sun. at Embarcadero. Validated parking at Ghirardelli Sq. garage and Embarcadero Center garage. $$*

Marina   **North India.** Small and cozy, this restaurant has a more limited menu and hotter seasoning than Gaylord's. Both tandoori dishes and curries are served, plus a range of breads and appetizers. Everything is cooked to order. *3131 Webster St., tel. 415/931–1556. Reservations advised. Dress: casual. AE, DC, MC, V. No lunch weekends. Parking behind restaurant. $$*

Italian   Italian food in San Francisco spans the "boot" from the mild cooking of northern Italy to the spicy cuisine of the south. Then there is the style indigenous to San Francisco, known as North Beach Italian—such dishes as *cioppino* (a fisherman's stew) and Joe's special (a mélange of eggs, spinach, and ground beef).

Embarcadero   **Il Fornaio.** An offshoot of the Il Fornaio bakeries, this handsome
North   tile-floored, wood-paneled complex combines a café, bakery, and up-scale trattoria with outdoor seating. The cooking is Tuscan, featuring pizzas from a wood-burning oven, superb house-made pastas and gnocchi, and grilled poultry and seafood. Anticipate a wait for a table, but once seated you won't be disappointed—only surprised by the moderate prices. *Levi's Plaza, 1265 Battery St., tel. 415/986–0100. Reservations advised. Dress: casual. AE, DC, MC, V. Valet parking. $$*

Financial   **Palio d'Asti.** This moderately priced venture of restaurateur Gianni
District   Fassio draws a lively Financial District lunch crowd. Some specialties are Piedmontese, and a good show is provided by the open kitchen and pizza oven, as well as the rolling carts of antipasti. *640 Sacramento St., tel. 415/395–9800. Reservations advised. Dress: casual. AE, DC, MC. No lunch Sat. Closed Sun. $$*

Marina   **Ristorante Parma.** This is a warm, wonderfully honest trattoria with excellent food at modest prices. The antipasti tray, with a dozen unusual items, is one of the best in town, and the pastas and veal are exceptional. Don't pass up the spinach gnocchi when it is offered. *3314 Steiner St., tel. 415/567–0500. Reservations advised. Dress: casual. AE, MC, V. No lunch Sat. Closed Sun. $$*

Midtown   **Acquarello.** This exquisite restaurant is one of the most romantic
★   spots in town. The service and food are exemplary, and the menu covers the full range of Italian cuisine, from northern Italy to the tip of the boot. Desserts are exceptional. *1722 Sacramento St., tel. 415/567–5432. Reservations advised. Dress: casual. AE, DC, MC, V. No lunch. Closed Sun. and Mon. $$–$$$*

North Beach   **Buca Giovanni.** Giovanni Leoni showcases the dishes of his
★   birthplace, the Serchio Valley in Tuscany, and grows many of the

vegetables and herbs used in his recipes at his Mendocino County ranch. Pastas made on the premises are a specialty, and the calamari salad is one of the best around. The subterranean dining room is cozy and romantic. *800 Greenwich St., tel. 415/776-7766. Reservations advised. Dress: casual. AE, DC, MC, V. No lunch. Closed Sun and Mon. $$*

South of Market

Ristorante Ecco. Hidden within a labyrinth of industrial sprawl is South Park, one of the city's most fashionable addresses in the 1850s. Now the tree-filled square is being gentrified with lofts of artists and designers and one of the city's best new Italian cafés— Ecco. The cooking is robust; select from zesty antipasti like deep-fried polenta. The kitchen performs best with hearty main dishes like osso buco and braised rabbit. Ask for a seat in the main dining room, which overlooks the square. *101 South Park, tel. 415/495-3291. Reservations advised. Dress: casual. AE, MC, V. No lunch Sat. Closed Sun. $$*

Union Square

Emporio Armani Express. Designer Giorgio Armani is best known for his clothing, but with little fanfare he has also designed some smart little cafés within his boutiques in London, Costa Mesa, Seoul—and now San Francisco. Here, under the Pantheon-like dome of a former bank building, tables and banquettes are set on a mezzanine overlooking the store's main floor. The food is exquisite northern Italian fare uncluttered by clichés. For antipasti, try the *breseaoloa* (paper-thin slices of air-dried beef) tossed with baby greens and artichoke hearts, or the grilled polenta, crowned with sautéed wild mushrooms. The pastas are also recommended, and the desserts—often the weak spot of an Italian meal—are superb. *1 Grant Ave., tel. 415/677-9010. Reservations advised. Dress: casual. AE, DC, MC, V. Closed Sun. $$*

Japanese

To understand a Japanese menu, you should be familiar with the basic types of cooking: *yaki*, marinated and grilled foods; *tempura*, fish and vegetables deep-fried in a light batter; *udon* and *soba*, noodle dishes; *domburi*, meats and vegetables served over rice; *ramen*, noodles served in broth; and *nabemono*, meals cooked in one pot, often at the table. Sushi bars are extremely popular in San Francisco; most offer a selection of *sushi*, vinegared rice with fish or vegetables, and *sashimi*, raw fish. Western seating refers to conventional tables and chairs; *tatami* seating is on mats at low tables.

Chinatown Financial District ★

Kyo-ya. Rarely replicated outside Japan, the refined experience of dining in a fine Japanese restaurant has been introduced with extraordinary authenticity at this new showplace within the Sheraton Palace Hotel. In Japan, a *kyo-ya* is a nonspecialized restaurant that serves a wide range of food types. And, at this Kyo-ya, the range is spectacular—encompassing tempuras, one-pot dishes, deep-fried and grilled meats, not to mention a choice of some three dozen sushi selections. The lunch menu is more limited than dinner, but does offer a *shokado*, a sampler of four classic dishes encased in a handsome lacquered lunch box. *Sheraton Palace Hotel, 2 New Montgomery St., at Market St., tel. 415/546-5000. Reservations advised. Dress: casual. AE, DC, MC, V. Closed weekends. $$-$$$*

Japantown

Sanppo. This small place has an enormous selection of almost every type of Japanese food: yakis, nabemono dishes, domburi, udon, and soba, not to mention feather-light tempura and interesting side dishes. Western seating only. *1702 Post St., tel. 415/346-3486. No reservations. Dress: casual. MC, V. Closed Mon. Validated parking in Japan Center garage. $*

Richmond **Kabuto Sushi.** For one of the most spectacular acts in town, head
District out Geary Boulevard past Japantown to tiny Kabuto. Here, behind
his black-lacquered counter, master chef Sachio Kojima flashes his
knives with the grace of a samurai warrior to prepare sushi and
sashimi of exceptional quality. Traditional Japanese dinners are also
served in the adjoining dining room with both Western seating and,
in a shoji-screened area, *tatami* seating. *5116 Geary Blvd., tel.
415/752–5652. Reservations advised for dinner. Dress: casual. MC, V.
No lunch. Closed Mon. $$*

Mediter- In its climate and topography, its agriculture and viticulture, and
ranean the orientation of many of its early settlers, northern California re-
sembles the Mediterranean region. But until quite recently no res-
taurant billed itself as "Mediterranean." Those that do so now
primarily offer a mix of southern French and northern Italian food,
but some include accents from Spain, Greece, and more distant
ports of call.

Civic Center **Zuni Cafe Grill.** Zuni's Italian-Mediterranean menu and its unpre-
★ tentious atmosphere pack in the crowds from early morning to late
evening. A balcony dining area overlooks the large bar, where shell-
fish, one of the best oyster selections in town, and drinks are dis-
pensed. A second dining room houses the giant pizza oven and grill.
Even the hamburgers have an Italian accent—they're served on
herbed focaccia buns. *1658 Market St., tel. 415/552–2522. Reserva-
tions advised. Dress: casual. AE, MC, V. Closed Mon. $$–$$$*

Embarcadero **Square One.** Chef Joyce Goldstein introduces an ambitious new
North menu daily, with dishes based on the classic cooking of the Mediter-
★ ranean countries, although she sometimes strays to Asia and Latin
America. The dining room, with its views of the open kitchen and
the Golden Gateway commons, is an understated setting for some
of the finest food in town—and an award-winning wine list. A bar
menu is available. *190 Pacific Ave., tel. 415/788–1110. Reservations
advised. Dress: casual. AE, DC, MC, V. No lunch weekends. Valet
parking in evenings. $$–$$$*
Splendido. Mediterranean cooking is the focus at this handsome new
restaurant. Diners here are transported to the coast of southern
France or northern Italy by the pleasant decor; only the bay view
reminds you that you are in San Francisco. Among the many win-
ners are the shellfish soup and warm goat-cheese and ratatouille
salad. Desserts are truly *splendido.* A bar menu is available. *Em-
barcadero 4, tel. 415/986–3222. Reservations advised. Dress: casual.
AE, DC, MC, V. Validated parking at Embarcadero Center garage. $$*

North Beach **Moose's.** Longtime San Francisco restauranteur Ed Moose's res-
★ taurant was destined to become a top celebrity hangout from the
moment it opened in 1992. Politicians and media types have followed
him from his former digs at Washington Square Bar & Grill just
across the large, tree-shaded plaza. Along with a host of local luminaries, Tom Brokaw, Walter Cronkite, Tom Wolfe, and Senator Dianne Feinstein head for Moose's when they're in town. And the food
impresses as much as the clientele: A Mediterranean-inspired menu
highlights innovative appetizers, pastas, seafood, and grills. There's
live music at night and a fine Sunday brunch. *1652 Stockton St., tel.
415/989–7800. Reservations advised several wks in advance. Dress:
casual. AE, DC, MC, V. Valet parking. $$*

South of **LuLu.** Since opening day in 1993, a seat at this boisterous café has
Market been about the hottest ticket in town. Chef Reed Hearon has
★ brought a touch of the French-Italian Riviera to a spacious and stun-
ningly renovated San Francisco warehouse. Under the high, barrel-

vaulted ceiling, beside a large open kitchen, diners feast on sizzling mussels roasted in an iron skillet, pizza with calamari and aioli, ricotta gnocchi with butternut squash, and wood-roasted Dungeness crab. Sharing dishes family-style is the custom here. For those who like a quieter ambience, Hearon has opened a little bistro, LuLu Bis, just next door, and offers four-course prix-fixe dinners at communal tables. *816 Folsom St., tel. 415/495–5775. Reservations advised. Dress: casual. AE, MC, V. $–$$*

Union Square   **Aioli.** The food and decor of this tiny bistro is a sunny potpourri derived from the exotic locales in chef Sebastien Urbain's background, ranging from his birthplace on the French island of Réunion in the Indian Ocean to cities in Africa, France, and the Middle East in which he served as chef for Méridien hotels. These culinary influences are bound together with a passion for garlic, as the name of the restaurant suggests. The garlicky sauce of Provence embellishes an extraordinary platter of mixed seafood. Sample the oysters baked in their shells with caramelized onions and a pungent puree of garlic. The soups are robust, and the pastas are outstanding. *469 Bush St., tel. 415/249–0900. Reservations advised. Dress: casual. AE, MC, V. $$*

Mexican/ Latin American   In spite of San Francisco's Mexican heritage, until recently most south-of-the-border eateries were locked into the Cal-Mex taco-enchilada-beans syndrome. But now some newer places offer a broader spectrum of Mexican and Latin American cooking.

Marina
★   **Café Marimba.** Chef Reed Hearon struck gold in 1993. First he and partner Louise Clement opened the sensationally popular LuLu (*see above*). Later that year, they launched this casual café as a showplace for their contemporary renditions of regional specialties. The colorful Mexican folk art that adorns the walls was collected during Hearon's numerous trips south of the border—as were the recipes: a silken *mole negro* from Oaxaca that appears in tamales and other dishes, shrimp prepared with roasted onions and tomatoes in the style of Zihuatenejo, chicken with a marinade from Yucatán stuffed into one of the world's greatest tacos. Though he imparts his own imaginative touches, Hearon is fanatic about the authenticity of preparation—onions, tomatoes, and chilies are dry-roasted in the ancient tradition of the *comal*, and the guacamole is made to order in a *molcajete* (the three-legged version of a pestle). *2317 Chestnut St., tel. 415/776–1506. Reservations advised. Dress: casual. MC, V. $$*

Seafood   Like all port cities, San Francisco takes pride in its seafood, even though less than half the fish served here is from local waters. In winter and spring look for the fresh Dungeness crab, best served cracked with mayonnaise. In summer, feast on Pacific salmon, even though imported varieties are available year-round. A recent development is the abundance of unusual oysters from West Coast beds and an outburst of oyster bars.

Civic Center
★   **Hayes Street Grill.** Eight to 15 different kinds of seafood are chalked on the blackboard each night at this extremely popular restaurant. The fish is served simply grilled, with a choice of sauces ranging from tartar to a spicy Szechuan peanut concoction. Appetizers are unusual, and desserts are lavish. *320 Hayes St., tel. 415/863–5545. Reservations should be made precisely 3 wks in advance. Dress: casual. AE, DC, MC, V. No lunch weekends. $$*

Financial District
★   **Aqua.** This quietly elegant and ultrafashionable spot is possibly the city's most important seafood restaurant ever. Chef-owner George Morrone has a supremely original talent for creating contemporary versions of French, Italian, and American classics: Expect mussel,

crab, or lobster soufflés; lobster gnocchi with lobster sauce; shrimp and corn madeleines strewn in a salad; and ultrarare ahi paired with foie gras. Desserts are miniature museum pieces. *252 California St., tel. 415/956–9662. Reservations essential. Dress: casual. AE, DC, MC, V. No lunch Sat. Closed Sun. Valet parking at night.* $$$

Sam's Grill. Sam's and Tadich (*see below*) are two of the city's oldest restaurants and so popular for lunch that you must arrive before noon to get a table. No frills here. The aura is starkly old-fashioned; some booths are enclosed and curtained. Although the menu is extensive and varied, those in the know stick with the fresh local seafood and East Coast shellfish. *374 Bush St., tel. 415/421–0594. Reservations accepted only for parties of 6 or more. Dress: casual. AE, DC, MC, V. Closed weekends.* $$

Tadich Grill. Owners and locations have changed many times since this old-timer opened during the gold-rush era, but the 19th-century atmosphere remains, as does the kitchen's special way with seafood. Simple sautés are the best choices, or the cioppino during crab season. *240 California St., tel. 415/391–2373. No reservations. Dress: casual. MC, V. Closed Sun.* $$

Japantown   **Elka.** One of the most talked-about chefs in town nowadays is Elka Gilmore. Her innovative East-meets-West seafood cuisine has had the critics turning cartwheels since 1992 when she arrived at the Miyako Hotel, which rechristened its handsome multilevel dining room in her honor. For a starter, Elka's "Japanese box filled with small seafood dishes" is a must. It's a small wooden cabinet with nooks and crannies that conceal the changing whims of the chef— perhaps a dab of sturgeon mousse, a scallop garnished with foie gras, or a crab cake with corn relish. For desserts, Elka looks to the West with the likes of apple pie and ice cream. *1611 Post St., tel. 415/922–7788. Reservations advised. Dress: casual. AE, MC, V.* $$– $$$

Northern   **McCormick & Kuleto's.** This seafood emporium in Ghirardelli
Waterfront   Square is a visitor's dream come true: a fabulous view of the bay from every seat in the house; an old San Francisco atmosphere; and some 30 varieties of fish and shellfish prepared in some 70 globe-circling ways, from tacos, pot stickers, and fish cakes to grills, pastas, and stew. The food has its ups and downs, but even on foggy days you can count on the view. *Ghirardelli Sq., tel. 415/929–1730. Reservations advised. Dress: casual. AE, DC, MC, V. Validated parking in Ghirardelli Sq. garage.* $$

Southeast   In recent years San Franciscans have seen tremendous growth in
Asian   the numbers of restaurants specializing in the foods of Thailand, Vietnam, and, most recently, Cambodia. The cuisines of these countries share many features, and one characteristic in particular: The cooking is highly spiced, and often very hot.

Civic Center   **Thepin.** It seems as if there's a Thai restaurant on every block now, but this is the jewel in the crown. The stylish dining room sparkles with linen napery, fresh flowers, Thai artworks, and a wine list that surpasses the Asian norm. Notable are the duck dishes and the curries, each prepared with its own mixture of freshly blended spices. *298 Gough St., tel. 415/863–9335. Reservations advised. Dress: casual. AE, MC, V. No lunch weekends.* $–$$

Marina   **Irrawaddy.** Cambodian cuisine has given way to Burmese at the former Angkor Palace restaurant. At press time (fall 1994), the new operation was just getting up to speed: split-pea fritters, ginger salad, and Burmese beef curry showed promise, though national favorites catfish noodle soup and tea salad were inexplicably omitted from the menu. *1769 Lombard St., tel. 415/931–2830. Dress: casual. MC, V. No lunch. $*

South of Market **Manora.** When this homey Thai café way out on Mission Street first opened, crowds from all over town were lined up for a table to try the extensive selection of carefully prepared dishes. Now there is a more conveniently located Manora, not far from the Performing Arts Center, with the same great food. Good choices are the fish cakes and the exemplary curries. *3226 Mission St., tel. 415/550–0856; 1600 Folsom St., tel. 415/861–6224. Dress: casual. MC, V. No lunch and closed Mon. at Mission St.; no lunch weekends at Folsom St. $*

Steak Houses Although San Francisco traditionally has not been a meat-and-potatoes town, the popularity of steak is on the rise. Following are some of the best steak houses, but you can also get a good piece of beef at most of the better French, Italian, and American restaurants.

Marina **Izzy's Steak & Chop House.** Izzy Gomez was a legendary San Francisco saloonkeeper, and his namesake eatery carries on the tradition with terrific steaks, chops, and seafood, plus all the trimmings— such as cheesy scalloped potatoes and creamed spinach. A collection of Izzy memorabilia and antique advertising art covers almost every inch of wall space. *3345 Steiner St., tel. 415/563–0487. Reservations accepted. Dress: casual. AE, DC, MC, V. No lunch. Validated parking at Lombard Garage. $$*

Midtown **Harris'.** Ann Harris knows her beef. She grew up on a Texas cattle
★ ranch and was married to the late Jack Harris of Harris Ranch fame. In her own elegant restaurant she serves some of the best dry-aged steaks in town, but don't overlook the grilled seafood or poultry. There is also an extensive bar menu. *2100 Van Ness Ave., tel. 415/673–1888. Reservations recommended. Dress: casual. AE, DC, MC, V. No lunch. Valet parking. $$$*

Vegetarian Aside from the restaurant mentioned below, vegetarians should also consider Gaylord's (*see* Indian restaurants, *above*), which offers a wide variety of meatless dishes from the Hindu cuisine.

Marina **Greens at Fort Mason.** This beautiful restaurant with its bay views
★ is a favorite with carnivores as well as vegetarians. Owned and operated by the Tassajara Zen Center of Carmel Valley, the restaurant offers a wide, eclectic, and creative spectrum of meatless cooking, and the bread promises nirvana. Dinners are à la carte on weeknights, but only a five-course prix-fixe dinner is served on Friday and Saturday. *Bldg. A, Fort Mason, tel. 415/771–6222. Reservations advised. Dress: casual. MC, V. No dinner Sun. Closed Mon. Public parking at Fort Mason Center. $$*

Lodging

By Laura Del Rosso and Patrick Hoctel Few cities in the United States can rival San Francisco's variety in lodging. There are plush hotels ranked among the finest in the world, renovated older buildings that have the charm of Europe, bed-and-breakfasts in the city's Victorian "Painted Ladies," and the popular chain hotels found in most cities in the United States.

One of the brightest spots in the lodging picture is the transformation of handsome early 20th-century downtown high rises into small, distinctive hotels that offer personal service and European ambience. Another is the recent addition of ultradeluxe modern hotels such as the Nikko, Pan Pacific, ANA, and Mandarin Oriental, which promote their attentive Asian-style hospitality. On top of those offerings are the dozens of popular chain hotels that continually undergo face-lifts and additions to keep up with the competition.

The **San Francisco Convention and Visitors Bureau** (tel. 415/391–2000) publishes a free lodging guide with a map and listing of all hotels. Send $2 for postage and handling to Box 429097, San Francisco 94142-9097.

Because San Francisco is one of the top destinations in the United States for tourists as well as business travelers and convention goers, reservations are always advised, especially during the May–October peak season.

San Francisco's geography makes it conveniently compact. No matter their location, the hotels listed below are on or close to public transportation lines. Some properties on Lombard Street and in the Civic Center area have free parking, but a car is more a hindrance than an asset in San Francisco.

Although not as high as the rates in New York, San Francisco hotel prices may come as a surprise to travelers from less urban areas. Average rates for double rooms downtown and at the wharf are in the $120 range. Adding to the expense is the city's 12% transient occupancy tax, which can significantly boost the cost of a lengthy stay. The good news is that because of the hotel building boom of the late 1980s, there is now an oversupply of rooms, which has led to much discounting of prices. Check for special rates and packages when making reservations.

If you are looking for truly budget accommodations (under $50), consider the Adelaide Inn (*see* Union Square/Downtown, *below*) and the **YMCA Central Branch.** *220 Golden Gate Ave., 94102, tel. 415/885-0460. 102 rooms, 3 with bath. Facilities: health club, pool, sauna. MC, V.*

An alternative to hotels and motels is staying in private homes and apartments, available through **American Family Inn/Bed & Breakfast San Francisco** (Box 420009, San Francisco 94142, tel. 415/931–3083), **Bed & Breakfast International–San Francisco** (Box 282910, San Francisco 94128-2910, tel. 415/696–1690 or 800/872–4500, fax 415/696–1699), and **American Property Exchange** (170 Page St., San Francisco 94102, tel. 415/863–8484 or 800/747–7784).

Highly recommended hotels are indicated by a star ★.

Category	Cost*
$$$$	over $175
$$$	$120–$175
$$	$80–$120
$	under $80

*All prices are for a double room, excluding 12% tax.

Union Square/ Downtown   The largest variety and greatest concentration of hotels are in the city's downtown hub, Union Square, where hotel guests can find the best shopping, the theater district, and convenient transportation to every spot in San Francisco.

$$$$ ★   **Campton Place Kempinski.** Behind a simple brownstone facade with white awning, quiet reigns. Highly attentive, personal service—

from assistance with unpacking to nightly turndown—begins the moment uniformed doormen greet guests outside the marble-floored lobby. The rooms are done with Asian touches in subtle tones of gold and brown and are relatively small but well appointed, with double-pane windows, Chinese armoires, and good-size writing desks. From the ninth floor up, there are only four rooms to a floor. They overlook an atrium, which lends a cozy, residential feel. The hotel is a 10-minute walk from the Moscone Center and the new Yerba Buena Center complex. The Anjou Restaurant, famed for its French cuisine, is on Campton Place, beside the hotel. *340 Stockton St., 94108, tel. 415/781–5555 or 800/426–3135, fax 415/955–5536. 126 rooms. Facilities: restaurant, bar. AE, DC, MC, V.*

$$$$ **Four Seasons Clift.** The Clift towers over San Francisco's theater
★ district. Its crisp, forest-green awnings and formal door service give hint of the elegance inside. The Clift is noted for its swift personalized service; a phone call will get you everything from an interpreter to a chocolate cake. Color schemes differ from room to room: from dark woods, burgundies, and reds, to lighter palettes. The furniture includes a large writing desk, and plants and flowers are scattered throughout. Be sure to sample a cocktail in the famous Redwood Room lounge; it's an art-deco lover's dream, with chandeliers and a sweeping redwood bar. *495 Geary St., 94102, tel. 415/775–4700 or 800/332–3442, fax 415/441–4621. 329 rooms. Facilities: restaurant, lounge, exercise room, meeting rooms, complimentary morning limousine downtown. AE, DC, MC, V.*

$$$$ **Westin St. Francis.** Host to the likes of Emperor Hirohito, Queen Elizabeth II, and many presidents, the St. Francis, with its imposing, immediately recognizable facade, black marble lobby, and gold-topped columns, looks more like a great public building than a hotel. However, the effect is softened by the columns and exquisite woodwork of the Compass Rose bar and restaurant; since its inception, this has been a retreat from the bustle of Union Square, especially for those in a romantic frame of mind. The guest rooms in the original building are rather small by modern standards and retain some of the 1904, Victorian-style moldings and bathroom tiles. The rooms in the modern tower are larger and have brighter, lacquered furniture. *335 Powell St., 94102, tel. 415/397–7000 or 800/228–3000, fax 415/774–0124. 1,200 rooms. Facilities: 5 restaurants, 5 lounges, fitness center, shopping arcade. AE, DC, MC, V.*

$$$ **Galleria Park.** This hotel a few blocks east of Union Square is close
★ to the Chinatown gate. The staff is remarkably pleasant and helpful. The rooms are done in a simple French-country style, with floral bedspreads and white furniture that includes a writing desk. Guests can often be found sitting around the lobby's inviting fireplace or in the adjacent Bentley's Seafood Grill. *191 Sutter St., 94104, tel. 415/781–3060 or 800/792–9639, fax 415/433–4409. 162 rooms, 15 suites. Facilities: 2 restaurants, rooftop park and jogging track, 3 floors of nonsmoking rooms. AE, DC, MC, V.*

$$$ **Holiday Inn–Union Square.** Given the rather undistinguished, '60s-style facade of this convention-oriented hotel right on the cable-car line, you probably wouldn't expect the recently renovated rooms to be done in charming, 19th-century English decor. Back rooms on upper floors have commanding views of the bay; from the front rooms, you can see west all the way to the Avenues. Every room has a large writing desk and two phones. For an evening of intimacy, try the Sherlock Holmes lounge on the 30th floor—great views, two fireplaces, and the lights are kept low. *480 Sutter St., 94108, tel. 415/398–8900 or 800/465–4329, fax 415/989–8823. 400 rooms. Facilities: restaurant, lounge, health club. AE, DC, MC, V.*

Downtown San Francisco Lodging

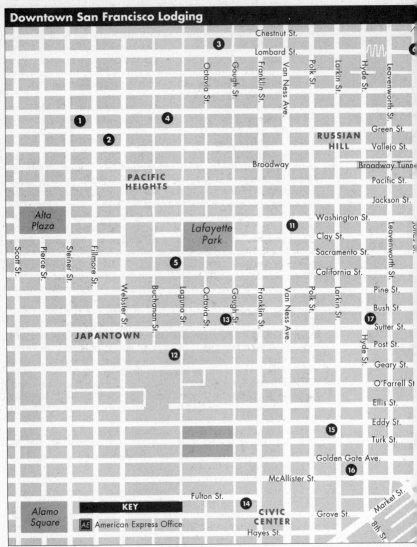

Abigail Hotel, **16**
Adelaide Inn, **18**
Bed and Breakfast Inn, **4**
Campton Place Kempinski, **33**
The Cartwright, **23**
Chancellor Hotel, **30**
Clarion Hotel, **46**
Crown Sterling Suites–Burlingame, **43**
Fairmont Hotel and Tower, **22**
Four Seasons Clift, **26**
Galleria Park, **36**
Grant Plaza, **39**

Harbor Court Hotel, **42**
Holiday Inn–Union Square, **32**
Holiday Lodge and Garden Hotel, **11**
Hotel Diva, **25**
Hotel Sofitel–San Francisco Bay, **44**
Huntington Hotel, **20**
Hyatt-Fisherman's Wharf, **6**
Hyatt Regency, **41**
Inn at the Opera, **14**
Inn at Union Square, **29**
King George, **27**

Majestic Hotel, **13**
Mandarin Oriental, **40**
The Mansion, **5**
Mark Hopkins Inter–Continental, **21**
Miyako Hotel, **12**
Nob Hill Lambourne, **37**
Petite Auberge, **19**
Phoenix Inn, **15**
Prescott Hotel, **24**
Radisson Hotel, **47**
The Raphael, **28**
Ritz–Carlton San Francisco, **38**
San Francisco Airport Hilton, **45**

San Francisco Marriot–Fisherman's Wharf, **7**
San Remo Hotel, **8**
Sheraton Palace, **35**
Sherman House, **2**
Sir Francis Drake, **31**
Town House Motel, **3**
Travelodge at the Wharf, **9**
Tuscan Inn, **10**
Union Street Inn, **1**
Westin St. Francis, **34**
York Hotel, **17**

$$$ **Inn at Union Square.** When you step through the dark-timber double doors of this inn, you may feel like you're stepping into the foyer of someone's home. The tiny but captivating lobby, with trompe l'oeil bookshelves painted on the walls, adds to the illusion. Comfortable, Georgian-style rooms promote indolence with goosedown pillows and four-poster beds; brass lion's-head door knockers are a unique touch. Complimentary Continental breakfast and afternoon tea are served in front of a fireplace in a sitting area on each floor. *440 Post St., 04102, tel. 415/397–3510 or 800/288–4346, fax 415/989–0529. 30 rooms. No smoking. AE, DC, MC, V.*

$$$ **Petite Auberge.** "The Teddy Bears' Picnic" might be an alternate name for this whimsical recreation of a French country inn a couple of blocks uphill from Union Square. The lobby, festooned with teddies of all shapes, sizes, and costumes, sets the tone of this B&B; the country kitchen and side garden create a pastoral atmosphere despite the downtown location. The rooms are rather small, but each has a teddy bear, bright flowered wallpaper, an old-fashioned writing desk, and a much-needed armoire—there's little or no closet space. Some rooms have wood-burning fireplaces. *863 Bush St., 94108, tel. 415/928–6000, fax 415/775–5717. 26 rooms. Facilities: breakfast rooms, parlors. AE, MC, V.*

$$$ **Prescott Hotel.** A gourmet's delight might be the best way to describe this plush hotel, thanks to the presence of Wolfgang Puck's Postrio (*see* Dining, *above*), which consistently hovers near the top of San Francisco's best-restaurant lists. Cuisine-conscious guests can order room service—from Postrio—and avoid trying to make a reservation. The rooms, which vary only in size and shape, are traditional in style, with dark, rich color schemes. Each bed is backed by a partially mirrored wall and has a boldly patterned spread; the bathrooms have marble-top sinks and gold fixtures. The Prescott's personalized service includes complimentary limousine service to the Financial District. *545 Post St., tel. 415/563–0303 or 800/283–7322, fax 415/563–6831. 166 rooms. Facilities: restaurant, lounge, health club next door at Press Club. AE, DC, MC, V.*

$$$ **Sir Francis Drake.** Although Beefeater-costumed doormen and dramatic red theater curtains still grace the front of the Drake, the inside has undergone a profound change. The lobby is still opulent, with wrought-iron lion balustrades, chandeliers, and Italian marble, but guest rooms now have the flavor of a B&B, with California mission-style furnishings and floral-print fabrics. The decor seems designed to appeal to pleasure travelers, but business travelers will appreciate the modem hookups and voice mail. Party-giver extraordinaire Harry Denton will soon run the renowned Starlite Roof supper club here. *450 Powell St., 94102, tel. 415/392–7755 or 800/227–5480, fax 415/677–9341. 417 rooms. Facilities: 2 restaurants, meeting room. AE, DC, MC, V.*

$$ **The Cartwright.** A block or so northwest of Union Square and just off the cable-car line, this family-owned hotel's motto is "It's like being at home." This is only true, however, if your home is filled with authentic European antiques, fresh-cut flowers, and floral-print bedspreads and curtains and serves an English tea from 4 to 6. Guests may choose rooms with old-fashioned carved-wood or brass beds. *524 Sutter St., 94102, tel. and fax 415/421–2865 or 800/227–3844. 114 rooms. Facilities: coffee shop. AE, DC, MC, V.*

$$ **Chancellor Hotel.** This family-owned and -oriented hotel, although not as grand as some of its neighbors, more than lives up to its promise of comfort without extravagance—it's one of the best buys on Union Square. All rooms are of moderate size, have high ceilings, and are done in an Edwardian style with a peach, green, and rose

color scheme. The ceiling fans and deep bathtubs are a treat; connecting rooms are available for couples with children. *433 Powell St., 94102, tel. 415/362–2004 or 800/428–4748, fax 415/362–1403. 140 rooms. Facilities: restaurant, lounge. AE, DC, MC, V.*

$$ **Hotel Diva.** A black awning and beaten-and-burnished silver facade give this hotel a slick, high-tech look that sets it apart from all other hotels in San Francisco. The clientele is mostly theater folk—the Diva is directly across from the landmark Curran—and others of an artistic bent. The black-and-silver color scheme with touches of gray extends to the nightclub-esque lobby and to the rooms, which vary in size and are comfortable but not fussy. *440 Geary St., 94102, tel. 415/885–0200 or 800/553–1900, fax 415/346–6613. 125 rooms. Facilities: restaurant, lounge, small fitness center. AE, DC, MC, V.*

$$ **King George.** Behind the 80-year-old George's white-and-green Victorian facade, the rooms are a bit compact but nicely furnished in classic English style, with walnut furniture and a pastel-and-earth-tone color scheme. British and Japanese tourists and suburban couples seeking a weekend getaway frequent this adult-oriented hotel. *334 Mason St., 94102, tel. 415/781–5050 or 800/288–6005, fax 415/391–6976. 144 rooms. Facilities: tea room. AE, DC, MC, V.*

$$ **The Raphael.** With its own marquee proclaiming it San Francisco's "little elegant hotel," the Raphael has few pretensions to grandeur, preferring to focus its efforts on service: tour bookings, limousine service, same-day laundry, and valet service. The moderate-size rooms are austere, with simple, dark furnishings; each has a unique hand-painted door. *386 Geary St., 94102, tel. 415/986–2000 or 800/821–5343, fax 415/397–2447. 152 rooms. Facilities: restaurant, lounge. AE, DC, MC, V.*

$$ **York Hotel.** This hotel several blocks west of Union Square is probably the most gay-friendly of San Francisco's more elegant hotels; it's also popular with businesspeople and European tourists. The moderate-size rooms are a mix of contemporary and Victorian styles with a dark gray and rose color scheme. The Plush Room cabaret, where you can catch such entertainers as Dixie Carter, Michael Feinstein, and Andrea Marcovicci, is the York's drawing card. *940 Sutter St., 94109, tel. 415/885–6800 or 800/227–3608, fax 415/885–2115. 96 rooms. Facilities: nightclub, fitness center, complimentary chauffeured limousine. AE, DC, MC, V.*

$ **Adelaide Inn.** The bedspreads at this quiet retreat may not match the drapes or carpets, and the floors may creak, but the rooms are clean and cheap ($48–$58 for a double) and get bright sunlight. Tucked away in an alley, this funky European-style pension hosts primarily guests from Germany, France, and Italy. *5 Isadora Duncan Ct. (off Taylor between Geary and Post Sts.), 94102, tel. 415/441–2474 or 415/441–2261, fax 415/441–0161. 18 rooms share baths. Facilities: sitting room, refrigerator for guest use. AE, MC, V.*

$ ★ **Grant Plaza.** Serious Asian-cuisine aficionados take note—this bargain-price hotel in the shadow of the Chinatown gate has small but clean, attractively furnished rooms from $39. The Grant stands midway between the shopping options of Union Square and the Italian cafés and restaurants of North Beach. *465 Grant Ave., 94108, tel. 415/434–3883 or 800/472–6899, fax 415/434–3886. 72 rooms. AE, MC, V.*

Financial District High-rise growth in San Francisco's Financial District has turned it into a mini-Manhattan and a spectacular sight by night.

$$$$ **Hyatt Regency.** The gray concrete, bunkerlike exterior of the Hyatt Regency at the foot of Market Street doesn't prepare the traveler for the spectacular 17-story atrium lobby inside. A favorite convention site, this hotel is a good place to work and play. Embarcadero

Center (with its 125 shops) is right next door. The rooms, some of which have bay-view balconies, come in two slightly different styles. Both styles have cherry-wood furniture, but one strikes a decidedly more masculine tone with a black-and-brown color scheme; the other has soft rose-and-plum combinations. *5 Embarcadero Center, 94111, tel. 415/788–1234 or 800/233–1234, fax 415/398–2567. 803 rooms. Facilities: 2 restaurants, coffee shop, lounge, affiliated health club 1 block away, 24-hr room service, gift shop. AE, DC, MC, V.*

$$$$ **Mandarin Oriental.** The Mandarin comprises the top 11 floors (38–48) of San Francisco's third-tallest building, the California Center, so no matter what room you're in, you'll get some of the most panoramic vistas of the city and beyond. The front and back towers of this Financial District structure are connected by a sky bridge. Rooms in the front tower are reserved most quickly because of their dramatic, sweeping view of the ocean all the way to Angel Island; the Mandarin Rooms in each tower are favorites because their bathtubs are flanked by windows. The extremely appealing rooms are done in California style with Asian touches—a light, creamy yellow with black accents and wood tones. *222 Sansome St., 94104, tel. 415/885–0999 or 800/622–0404, fax 415/433–0289. 154 rooms, 4 suites. Facilities: restaurant, lounge, in-room fitness equipment available. AE, DC, MC, V.*

$$$$ **Sheraton Palace.** One of the city's grand old hotels—with a guest list that has included Enrico Caruso, Woodrow Wilson, and Al Jolson—the Palace has a pool with skylight, a health club, and a business center. The famous Golden Court restaurant has been resurrected, and its leaded-glass, domed ceiling is more breathtaking than ever. With their 14-foot ceilings, the rooms are splendid on a smaller scale. Modern amenities are carefully integrated into the classic decor, from the TV inside the mahogany armoire to the telephone in the marble bathroom. Service is the only element that is not quite up to par. *2 New Montgomery St., 94105, tel. 415/392–8600 or 800/325–3535, fax 415/543–0671. 550 rooms. Facilities: 3 restaurants, 2 lounges, fitness center with sauna and whirlpool, 24-hr room service. AE, DC, MC, V.*

$$$ ★ **Harbor Court Hotel.** Within shouting distance of the Bay Bridge, the hot South of Market area, and new waterfront districts with their plentiful nightclubs and restaurants, this boutique-style hotel, formerly a YMCA, is noted for the exemplary service of its warm, friendly staff. The adult-oriented Harbor Court attracts corporate types (especially on weekdays) as well as the average traveler. Guests have the use of YMCA facilities to one side of the hotel, and Harry Denton's Bar and Grill is on the other side. *165 Steuart St., tel. 415/882–1300 or 800/346–0555, fax 415/882–1313. 131 rooms. Facilities: adjacent health club, business center, complimentary limousine to Financial District. AE, DC, MC, V.*

Nob Hill Synonymous with San Francisco's high society, Nob Hill contains some of the city's best-known luxury hotels. All offer spectacular city and bay views and noted gourmet restaurants. Cable-car lines that cross Nob Hill make transportation a cinch.

$$$$ **Fairmont Hotel and Tower.** Perched atop Nob Hill and queen of all she surveys, the Fairmont has the most awe-inspiring lobby in the city, with a soaring, vaulted ceiling; towering, hand-painted, faux-marble columns; gilt mirrors; red-velvet upholstered chairs; and a memorable staircase. The tower rooms reflect a more modern style than their smaller Victorian counterparts in the older building. Done in a beige scheme, the tower rooms are often preferred because of their city and bay views. *950 Mason St., 94108, tel. 415/772–5000 or 800/527–4727, fax 415/772–5013. 596 rooms. Facilities: 5*

restaurants, 5 lounges, health club and spa, gift shops, 24-hr room service. AE, DC, MC, V.

$$$$ **Huntington Hotel.** Across from Grace Cathedral and the small but
★ captivating Huntington Park, the redbrick, ivy-covered Huntington provides a quiet alternative to the larger, more famous hotels down the street. The crowd here is mostly regulars who return year after year for the attentive personal service that is the hallmark of this hotel; the concierge calls each guest to offer complimentary sherry or formal tea. The management style is impeccably British in preserving the privacy of its celebrated guests. *1075 California St., 94108, tel. 415/474–5400, 800/227–4683, or 800/652–1539 in CA, fax 415/474–6227. 143 rooms. Facilities: restaurant, lounge with entertainment, health club available across street at Fairmont. AE, DC, MC, V.*

$$$$ **Mark Hopkins Inter-Continental.** The circular drive across from the Fairmont leads to a lobby with floor-to-ceiling mirrors and marble floors. The rooms, with dramatic neoclassical furnishings of gray, silver, and khaki and bold leaf-print bedspreads, are lovingly maintained. The bathrooms are lined with Italian marble. Even-number rooms on high floors have views of the Golden Gate Bridge. No visit would be complete without a gander at the panoramic views from the Top of the Mark, *the* rooftop lounge in San Francisco since 1939. *999 California St., 94108, tel. 415/392–3434 or 800/327–0200, fax 415/616–6907. 392 rooms. Facilities: restaurant, 2 lounges, workout room, gift shops. AE, DC, MC, V.*

$$$$ **Ritz-Carlton San Francisco.** Rated one of the top three hotels in the
★ world by *Condé Nast Traveler,* the Ritz-Carlton is a stunning tribute to beauty, grandeur, and warm, attentive service. Beyond the neoclassical facade, crystal chandeliers and museum-quality 18th-century oil paintings grace a fabulous lobby. The rooms are elegant and spacious, and every bath is appointed with double sinks, hair dryers, and vanity tables. There is maid service twice a day, and guests staying on the butler level enjoy the added luxury of their own butler. The hotel's main dining room is a worthy destination in its own right. *600 Stockton St., at California St., 94108, tel. 415/296–7465 or 800/241–3333, fax 415/291–0288. 336 rooms. Facilities: 2 restaurants, 3 lounges, health club with indoor pool, retail stores. AE, DC, MC, V.*

$$$ **Nob Hill Lambourne.** This urban retreat designed with the traveling executive in mind takes pride in taking care of business while offering stress-reducing pleasures. Personal computers, fax machines, personalized voice mail, laser printers, and a fully equipped boardroom help you maintain your edge, and the on-site spa, with massages, body scrubs, herbal wraps, manicures, and pedicures, helps you take it off. Except for the two winged horses joined at the tail on the awning, you might miss this rather squat hotel, dwarfed by taller buildings on either side. The rooms have queen-size beds and contemporary furnishings in Mediterranean colors. A deluxe Continental breakfast is complimentary. *725 Pine St., at Stockton, 94108, tel. 415/433–2287 or 800/274–8466, fax 415/433–0975. 20 rooms. Facilities: kitchenettes in every room. AE, DC, MC, V.*

Fisherman's   Fisherman's Wharf, San Francisco's top tourist attraction, is also
Wharf/   the most popular area for lodging. All accommodations are within a
North Beach   couple of blocks of restaurants, shops, and cable-car lines. Because of city ordinances, none of the hotels exceeds four stories; thus, this is not the area for fantastic views of the city or bay. Reservations are always necessary, sometimes weeks in advance during peak summer months (when hotel rates rise by as much as 30%). Some street-side rooms can be noisy.

$$$$ Hyatt Fisherman's Wharf. Location is the key to this hotel's popularity with business travelers and families: It's within walking distance of Ghirardelli Square, the Cannery, Pier 39, Aquatic Park, and docks for ferries and bay cruises. It's also across the street from the cable-car turnaround and bus stop. The moderate-size guest rooms are done in greens and burgundies with dark woods, brass fixtures, and double-pane windows to keep out the often considerable street noise. Each floor has a laundry room. The Marble Works Restaurant, which still has the original facade of the 1906 Musto Marble Works, has a children's menu. *555 North Point St., 94133, tel. 415/563–1234 or 800/233–1234, fax 415/563–2218. 313 rooms. Facilities: restaurant, sports bar, outdoor pool and whirlpool, small gym and sauna, valet parking. AE, DC, MC, V.*

$$$ San Francisco Marriott–Fisherman's Wharf. Behind an unremarkable sand-color facade, the Marriott strikes a grand note in its lavish, albeit low-ceilinged, lobby with marble floors and English club-style furniture. The recently renovated rooms have dark natural wood, Asian art touches, and a king-size bed or two double beds and follow a turquoise, blue, and white color scheme. *1250 Columbus Ave., 94133, tel. 415/775–7555 or 800/228–9290, fax 415/474–2099. 256 rooms. Facilities: restaurant, lounge, health club, gift shop. AE, DC, MC, V.*

$$$ Tuscan Inn. The major attraction of this beautifully maintained hotel is its friendly, attentive staff. The concierge is particularly helpful—if she doesn't know the answer to your question, she'll find someone who does. The charming if relatively small, Italian-influenced guest rooms are decorated with white-pine furniture and floral bedspreads and curtains. *425 North Point St., 94133, tel. 415/561–1100 or 800/648–4626, fax 415/561–1199. 220 rooms. Facilities: restaurant, valet parking, complimentary limousine to Financial District, meeting rooms, nonsmoking rooms. AE, DC, MC, V.*

$$ Travelodge at the Wharf. Taking up an entire city block, the Travelodge is the only bayfront hotel at Fisherman's Wharf and is known for its reasonable rates. The higher-price rooms (third and fourth floors) have balconies that provide unobstructed views of Alcatraz and overlook a landscaped courtyard and pool. The rooms at this family-oriented hotel have either a king-size bed or two double beds and are simply and brightly furnished. *250 Beach St., 94133, tel. 415/392–6700 or 800/255–3050, fax 415/986–7853. 250 rooms. Facilities: 3 restaurants, heated outdoor pool, free parking. AE, DC, MC, V.*

$ ★ San Remo Hotel. A guest recently described a sojourn at the San Remo as being "like staying at Grandma's house." This three-story, blue-and-white Italianate Victorian just a couple of blocks from Fisherman's Wharf has reasonably priced rooms and a down-home, slightly tatty elegance. The rooms are crowded with furniture: vanities, rag rugs, pedestal sinks, ceiling fans, antique armoires, and brass, iron, or wooden beds. The rooms share six black-and-white tiled shower rooms, one bathtub chamber, and six scrupulously clean toilets with brass pull chains and oak tanks. Daily and weekly rates are available. *2237 Mason St., 94133, tel. 415/776–8688 or 800/352–7366, fax 415/776–2811. 62 rooms, 61 with shared baths. AE, DC, MC, V.*

Lombard Street/ Cow Hollow Lombard Street, a major traffic corridor leading to the Golden Gate Bridge, stretches through San Francisco's poshest neighborhoods: Pacific Heights, Cow Hollow, and the Marina District.

$$$$ ★ Sherman House. This magnificent landmark mansion partway down the northern slope of Pacific Heights is the most luxurious small hotel in San Francisco. Each room is individually decorated with

Biedermeier, English Jacobean, or French Second Empire antiques. Tapestry-like canopies over four-poster beds, wood-burning fireplaces with marble mantels, and black-granite bathrooms with whirlpool baths complete the picture. *2160 Green St., 94123, tel. 415/563–3600 or 800/424–5777, fax 415/563–1882. 14 rooms. Facilities: dining room, sitting rooms, valet parking. AE, DC, MC, V.*

$$$ **Bed and Breakfast Inn.** This ivy-covered Victorian is hidden in an alleyway off Union Street between Buchanan and Laguna. The English country–style rooms are done in florals and pastels— Pierre Deux and Laura Ashley are the inspirations—with antiques, plants, and floral paintings by the owner placed throughout. The Mayfair, a private apartment above the main house, with a living room, kitchen, latticed balcony, and spiral staircase leading to a sleeping loft, is a new addition. *4 Charlton Ct., 94123, tel. 415/921– 9784. 7 rooms with bath, 4 rooms share baths, apartment. Facilities: breakfast room. No credit cards.*

$$ **Union Street Inn.** A retired schoolteacher has transformed this ivy-
★ draped, Edwardian, 1902 home into a delightful B&B filled with antiques and fresh flowers. The popular Wildrose room has a garden view that can be seen from the Jacuzzi. The Carriage House, separated from the main house by an old-fashioned English garden complete with lemon trees, a flagstone path, and a white picket fence, also has a Jacuzzi and lots of privacy. A Continental breakfast is served to guests in the parlor, in the garden, or in their rooms. *2229 Union St., 94123, tel. 415/346–0424. 6 rooms with bath. Facilities: breakfast room. AE, MC, V.*

$ **Holiday Lodge and Garden Hotel.** The decor of this modest hotel has a '50s feel, with white beamed ceilings, beige wood paneling, and floral bedspreads. The rooms either overlook or open onto land-scaped grounds with palm trees and a small, heated swimming pool. The Holiday's low-key atmosphere endears it to older couples, who enjoy its laid-back, West Coast style. *1901 Van Ness Ave., 94109, tel. 415/776–4469 or 800/367–8504, fax 415/474–7046. 77 rooms. Facilities: free parking, kitchenettes in some rooms. AE, MC, V.*

$ **Town House Motel.** What this family-oriented motel lacks in luxury
★ and ambience it makes up for in value: The simply furnished, well-kept rooms are one of the best buys on Lombard Street. The modest, medium-size rooms have a pastel, Southwestern color scheme, lacquered-wood furnishings, and either a king-size bed or two doubles. Continental breakfast is complimentary. *1650 Lombard St., 94123, tel. 415/885–5163 or 800/255–1516, fax 415/771–9889. 24 rooms. Facilities: free parking. AE, DC, MC, V.*

Civic Center/ The governmental heart of San Francisco, flanked by a boulevard
Van Ness of cultural institutions, is enjoying a renaissance that has engendered fine restaurants, fashionable night spots, and well-situated small hotels.

$$$ **Inn at the Opera.** This seven-story hotel a block or so from City Hall,
★ the Performing Arts Center, and Stars Restaurant hosts the likes of Pavarotti and Baryshnikov. Behind the yellow faux-marble front and red carpet are rooms of various sizes, decorated with creamy pastels and dark wood furnishings. Even the smallest singles have queen-size beds. The bureau drawers are lined with sheet music, and every room is outfitted with terry-cloth robes, microwave oven, minibar, fresh flowers, and a basket of apples. Those in the know say the back rooms are preferable because the front ones get street noise. *333 Fulton St., 94102, tel. 415/863–8400, 800/325–2708, or 800/423–9610 in CA, fax 415/861–0821. 48 rooms. Facilities: restaurant, lounge. AE, DC, MC, V.*

$$$ **Majestic Hotel.** The Majestic is one of San Francisco's original grand
★   hotels. The gingerbread and scrollwork on this five-story, yellow-
and-white Edwardian are so ornate that the building bears a strong
resemblance to a wedding cake. Stepping through the portals of the
immaculate, gay-friendly hotel is like stepping into an earlier, more
gracious era. Most rooms contain a fireplace and either a large,
hand-painted, four-poster, canopied bed or two-poster bonnet twin
beds, and most have a mix of French Empire and English antiques
and custom furniture. *1500 Sutter St., 94109, tel. 415/441–1100 or
800/869–8966, fax 415/673–7331. 57 rooms. Facilities: restaurant,
lounge. AE, DC, MC, V.*

$$$ **Miyako Hotel.** Next to the Japantown complex and near Fillmore
Street, this hotel is frequented by Asian travelers and others who
appreciate a taste of the East. The guest rooms are in either the
tower building or the garden wing, which has traditional seasonal
gardens. The rooms are done in Western or Japanese style, the
major difference being that the former have a traditional Western
bed with a mattress, and the latter have futon beds with tatami mats.
Both room styles are strikingly decorated with Japanese touches.
Chocolates set by the bedside on top of a haiku await each guest.
*1625 Post St., at Laguna St., 94115, tel. 415/922–3200 or 800/533–4567,
fax 415/921–0417. 218 rooms. Facilities: restaurant, lounge, Japanese
baths, saunas. AE, DC, MC, V.*

$$ **The Mansion.** This twin-turreted Queen Anne was built in 1887 and
today houses one of the most unusual hotels in the city. Rooms con-
tain an odd collection of furnishings and vary from the tiny Tom
Thumb Room to the opulent Josephine Suite, the favorite of such
celebrities as Barbra Streisand. Owner Bob Pritikin's pig paintings
and other "porkabilia" are everywhere. Full breakfast is included.
*2220 Sacramento St., 94115, tel. 415/929–9444, fax 415/567–9391. 21
rooms. Facilities: dining room, nightly concerts, sculpture and
flower garden. AE, DC, MC, V.*

$$ **Phoenix Inn.** Dubbed the "hippest hotel" in San Francisco by *People*
magazine, this turquoise-and-coral hideaway on the fringes of the
Tenderloin district is a little bit south-of-the-equator and a little bit
Gilligan's Island. The Phoenix bills itself as an urban retreat in a
resortlike environment. Its bungalow-style rooms, decorated with
casual, handmade, bamboo furniture and original art by San Francisco artists, have white beamed ceilings, white wooden walls and
vivid tropical-print bedspreads. An in-house cable channel plays
films made in San Francisco and films about bands on the road. Miss
Pearl's Jam House restaurant and bar is a good place to hear reggae;
the Chef Delicious Jerked Chicken should not be missed. *601 Eddy
St., 94109, tel. 415/776–1380, 415/861–1560, or 800/248–9466. 44 rooms.
Facilities: restaurant, bar, lounge, free parking, heated pool. AE, DC,
MC, V.*

$ **Abigail Hotel.** This hotel, a former B&B, retains its distinctive at-
mosphere with an eclectic mix of faux-stone walls, a faux-marble
front desk, and an old-fashioned telephone booth in the lobby. Hiss-
ing steam radiators, sleigh beds, and antiques set the mood. Room
211–the hotel's only suite—is the most elegant and spacious. *246
McAllister St., 94102, tel. 415/861–9728, 415/861–1560, or 800/243–
6510. 60 rooms. Facilities: restaurant. AE, DC, MC, V.*

The Airport   Because they cater primarily to midweek business travelers, the
airport hotels often cut weekend prices drastically; be sure to inquire. A full complement of services and airport shuttle buses are
provided by all of the following ($$$$) hotels:

Crown Sterling Suites–Burlingame (150 Anza Blvd., Burlingame
94010, tel. 415/342–4600 or 800/433–4600, fax 415/343–8137); **Hotel**

Sofitel–San Francisco Bay (223 Twin Dolphin Dr., Redwood City 94065, tel. 415/598–9000 or 800/763–4835, fax 415/598–0459); **San Francisco Airport Hilton** (San Francisco International Airport, Box 8355, 94128, tel. 415/589–0770 or 800/445–8667, fax 415/589–4696). Two good bargains ($$) are the **Clarion Hotel** (401 E. Millbrae Ave., Millbrae 94030, tel. 415/692–6363 or 800/223–7111, fax 415/697–8735) and the **Radisson Hotel** (1177 Airport Blvd., Burlingame 94010, tel. 415/342–9200 or 800/333–3333, fax 415/342–1655).

The Arts and Nightlife

The Arts

By Robert Taylor

Robert Taylor is a longtime San Francisco arts and entertainment writer.

The best guide to arts and entertainment events in San Francisco is the "Datebook" section, printed on pink paper, in the Sunday *Examiner and Chronicle*. The *Bay Guardian* and *S.F. Weekly,* free and available in racks around the city, list more neighborhood, avant-garde, and budget-priced events. For up-to-date information about cultural and musical events, call the Convention and Visitors Bureau's *Cultural Events Calendar* (tel. 415/391–2001).

Half-price tickets to many local and touring stage shows go on sale (cash only) at 11 AM, Tuesday–Saturday, at the **TIX Bay Area** booth on the Stockton Street side of Union Square, between Geary and Post streets. TIX is also a full-service ticket agency for theater and music events around the Bay Area (open until 6 PM Tuesday–Thursday, 7 PM Friday–Saturday). While the city's major commercial theaters are concentrated downtown, the opera, symphony, and ballet perform in the Civic Center. For recorded information about TIX tickets, call 415/433–7827.

The city's charge-by-phone ticket service is **BASS** (tel. 510/762–2277), with one of its centers in the TIX booth mentioned above and another at **Tower Records** (Bay St. at Columbus Ave.), near Fisherman's Wharf. Other agencies downtown are the **City Box Office,** 153 Kearny Street, Suite 402, (tel. 415/392–4400) and **Downtown Center Box Office** in the parking garage at 320 Mason Street (tel. 415/775–2021). The opera, symphony, the ballet's *Nutcracker,* and touring hit musicals are often sold out in advance; tickets are usually available within a day of performance for other shows.

Theater San Francisco's "theater row" is a single block of Geary Street west of Union Square, but a number of other venues are located within walking distance, along with resident companies that enrich the city's theatrical scene. The three major commercial theaters are operated by the Shorenstein-Nederlander organization, which books touring plays and musicals, some of them before they open on Broadway. The most venerable is the **Curran** (445 Geary St., tel. 415/474–3800). A production of Andrew Lloyd Webber's *The Phantom of the Opera* opened there in December 1993 and was expected to run as long as two years. The **Golden Gate** is a stylishly refurbished movie theater (Golden Gate Ave. at Taylor St., tel. 415/474–3800), now primarily a musical house. The 2,500-seat **Orpheum** (1192 Market St. near the Civic Center, tel. 415/474–3800) is used for the biggest touring shows.

The smaller commercial theaters, offering touring shows and a few that are locally produced, are the **Marines Memorial Theatre** (Sutter and Mason Sts., tel. 415/441–7444) and **Theatre on the Square** (450 Post St., tel. 415/433–9500). For commercial and popular success, nothing beats *Beach Blanket Babylon,* the zany revue that has been running for years at **Club Fugazi** (678 Green St. in North Beach, tel. 415/421–4222). Conceived by imaginative San Francisco director Steve Silver, it is a lively, colorful musical mix of cabaret, show-biz parodies, and tributes to local landmarks. (*See* Cabarets in Nightlife, *below*.)

The city's major theater company is the **American Conservatory Theater (ACT)**, which was founded in the mid-1960s and quickly became one of the nation's leading regional theaters. It presents a season of approximately eight plays in rotating repertory from October through late spring. ACT's ticket office is at 405 Geary Street (tel. 415/749–2228), next door to its **Geary Theater**, closed since the 1989 earthquake. During reconstruction (to be completed by late 1995), ACT is performing at the nearby **Stage Door Theater** (420 Mason St.) and the **Marines Memorial Theatre** (Sutter and Mason Sts.).

The leading producer of new plays is the **Magic Theatre** (Bldg. D, Fort Mason Center, Laguna St. at Marina Blvd., tel. 415/441–8822). The city boasts a wide variety of specialized and ethnic theaters that work with dedicated local actors and some professionals. Among the most interesting are **The Lamplighters**, the delightful Gilbert and Sullivan troupe that often gets better reviews than touring productions of musicals, performing at **Presentation Theater** (2350 Turk St., tel. 415/752–7755); the **Lorraine Hansberry Theatre**, which specializes in plays by black writers (620 Sutter St., tel. 415/474–8800); and two stages that showcase gay and lesbian performers: **Theatre Rhinoceros** (2926 16th St., tel. 415/861–5079) and **Josie's Cabaret & Juice Joint** (3583 16th St., tel. 415/861–7933). The **San Francisco Shakespeare Festival** offers free performances on summer weekends in Golden Gate Park (tel. 415/666–2222).

Avant-garde theater, dance, opera, and "performance art" turn up in a variety of locations, not all of them theaters. The major presenting organization is the **Theater Artaud** (499 Alabama St. in the Mission District, tel. 415/621–7797), which is situated in a huge, converted machine shop. Some contemporary theater events, in addition to dance and music, are scheduled at the theater in the **Center for the Arts at Yerba Buena Gardens** (3rd and Howard Sts., tel. 415/978–2787).

Music   The completion of Davies Symphony Hall at Van Ness Avenue and Grove Street finally gave the San Francisco Symphony a home of its own. It solidified the base of the city's three major performing arts organizations—symphony, opera, and ballet—in the Civic Center. The symphony and other musical groups also perform in the smaller, 928-seat Herbst Theatre in the Opera's "twin" at Van Ness Avenue and McAllister Street, the War Memorial Building. Otherwise the city's musical ensembles can be found all over the map: in churches and museums, in restaurants and parks, and in outreach series in Berkeley and on the peninsula.

San Francisco Symphony (Davies Symphony Hall, Van Ness Ave. at Grove St., tel. 415/431–5400. Tickets, $8–$65, at the box office or through BASS, tel. 510/762–2277). The symphony plays from September through May, with music director Herbert Blomstedt conducting for about two-thirds of the season. Michael Tilson Thomas, who is California-born and relatively young for a conductor of a major orchestra, takes over as music director in September 1995. He is expected to offer innovative programming and more performances of 20th century and American works. Guest conductors often include Edo de Waart and Riccardo Muti. Soloists include artists of the caliber of Andre Watts, Peter Serkin, and Pinchas Zukerman. Special events include a summer festival built around a particular composer, nation, or musical period, and summer Pops Concerts in the nearby Civic Auditorium. Throughout the season, the symphony presents a Great Performers Series of guest soloists and orchestras.

Opera   **San Francisco Opera** (Van Ness Ave. at Grove St., tel. 415/864–3330). Founded in 1923, and the resident company at the War Memorial Opera House in the Civic Center since it was built in 1932, the Opera presents a 13-week repertory season of eight to 10 operas, beginning on the first Friday after Labor Day. The Opera uses "supertitles": Translations are projected above the stage during almost all the operas not sung in English. For many years the Opera has been considered a major international company and the most artistically successful operatic organization in the United States outside New York. International opera stars frequently sing major roles here, and the Opera is well known for presenting the American debuts of singers who have made their names in Europe. Ticket prices range from about $35 to $100. Standing-room tickets (less than $10) are always sold at 10 AM for same-day performances, and patrons often sell extra tickets on the Opera House steps just before curtain time. Note that the Opera House will be closed in 1996 for repairs; performances will probably take place at the Civic Auditorium a block east at Grove and Polk Streets.

Dance   **San Francisco Ballet** (War Memorial Opera House, Van Ness Ave. at Grove St., tel. 415/703–9400). The ballet has regained much of its luster under artistic director Helgi Tomasson, and both classical and contemporary works have won admiring reviews. The company's primary season runs February–May; its repertoire includes such full-length classical ballets and what it likes to call "cutting-edge works that will make you take a second look." The ballet presents the *Nutcracker* in December; its recent production is spectacular.

Nightlife

By Daniel Mangin

A longtime Bay Area resident, Daniel Mangin writes on the arts for several local papers. He is an instructor of film history at City College of San Francisco.

San Francisco provides a tremendous potpourri of evening entertainment ranging from ultrasophisticated cabarets to bawdy bistros that reflect the city's gold-rush past. With the exception of the hotel lounges and discos noted below, the accent is on casual dress—call ahead if you are uncertain.

For information on who is performing where, check the following sources: The Sunday San Francisco *Examiner and Chronicle*'s pink "Datebook" insert lists major events and cultural happenings. The free alternative weeklies, the *Bay Guardian* and *S.F. Weekly*, are good sources for current music clubs and comedy. Another handy reference for San Francisco nightlife is *Key* magazine, offered free in most major hotel lobbies. For a phone update on sports and musical events, call the Convention and Visitor Bureau's *Events Hotline* (tel. 415/391–2001).

Although San Francisco is a compact city with the prevailing influences of some neighborhoods spilling into others, the following generalizations should help you find the kind of entertainment you're looking for. **Nob Hill** is noted for its plush piano bars and panoramic skyline lounges. **North Beach,** infamous for its topless and bottomless bistros, also maintains a sense of its beatnik past and this legacy lives on in atmospheric bars and coffeehouses. **Fisherman's Wharf,** while touristy, is great for people watching and provides plenty of impromptu entertainment from street performers. **Union Street** is home away from home for singles in search of company. South of

Market (**SoMa**, for short) has become a hub of nightlife, with a bevy of highly popular nightclubs, bars, and lounges in renovated warehouses and auto shops. Gay men will find the **Castro** and **Polk Street** scenes of infinite variety.

Rock, Pop, Folk, and Blues

Bottom of the Hill. This great little club "two minutes south of SoMa" in the Potrero Hill District showcases some of the best local alternative rock and blues in the city. *1233 17th St. at Texas St., tel. 415/626–4455. Shows begin 9:30–10 PM. Cover: $3–$7.*

The Fillmore. San Francisco's famous rock music hall, closed for several years, was refurbished and retrofitted in 1994. It serves up a varied menu of national and local acts: rock, reggae, grunge, jazz, comedy, folk, acid house, and more. *1805 Geary Blvd. at Fillmore St., tel. 415/346–6000. Doors open at 8, shows at 9. Tickets: $12.50–$22.50. Credit cards taken for food and beverages, not for tickets. AE, MC, V.*

Freight and Salvage Coffee House. This is one of the finest folk houses in the country; it's worth a trip across the bay. Some of the most talented practitioners of folk, blues, Cajun, and bluegrass perform at the Freight, among them U. Utah Phillips and Rosalie Sorrels. *1111 Addison St., Berkeley, tel. 510/548–1761. Tickets also available through BASS, tel. 510/762–2277. Shows: Sun. and Tues.–Thurs. 8 PM, Fri. and Sat. 8:30. Cover: $6–$12. No credit cards (except through BASS).*

Great American Music Hall. This is one of the great eclectic nightclubs, not only in San Francisco but in the entire country. Here you will find truly top-drawer entertainment, running the gamut from the best in blues, folk, and jazz to rock with a sprinkling of outstanding comedians. This colorful marble-pillared emporium will also accommodate dancing to popular bands. Past headliners here include Carmen McCrae, B.B. King, Billy Bragg, NRBQ, and Doc Watson. *859 O'Farrell St. between Polk and Larkin Sts., tel. 415/885–0750. Shows usually at 8 PM, but this may vary, so call. Cover: $5–$20. No credit cards.*

Jack's Bar. This smoky R&B dive (in every sense of the word) has been serving up hot music since 1932. There's dancing seven nights a week in a soulful atmosphere. The club's Sunday and Monday jam sessions are legendary. It's best to take a cab to and from this place. *1601 Fillmore St., tel. 415/567–3227. Shows begin at 9 PM. Cover: $3 Sun.–Thurs., $5 Fri. and Sat. AE.*

Last Day Saloon. In an attractive setting of wooden tables and potted plants, this club offers some major entertainers and a varied schedule of blues, Cajun, rock, and jazz. Some of the illustrious performers who have appeared here are Taj Mahal, the Zazu Pitts Memorial Orchestra, Maria Muldaur, and Pride and Joy. *406 Clement St., between 5th and 6th Aves. in the Richmond District, tel. 415/387–6343. Shows begin at 9 PM Sun.–Thurs., 9:30 PM Fri. and Sat. Cover: $4–$20. No credit cards.*

The Saloon. Some locals consider the historic Saloon the best spot in San Francisco for the blues. Headliners here include local R&B favorites Johnny Nitro and the Doorslammers. *1232 Grant St., near Columbus Ave. in North Beach, tel. 415/989–7666. Shows begin at 9 or 9:30 PM nightly. Cover: $5–$8 Fri. and Sat. No credit cards.*

Slim's. One of the most popular nightclubs on the SoMa scene, Slim's specializes in what it labels "American roots music"—blues, jazz, classic rock, and the like. The club has expanded its repertoire in recent years with national touring acts playing alternative rock-and-roll and a series of "spoken word" concerts. Co-owner Boz Scaggs helps bring in the crowds and famous headliners. *333 11th St., tel. 415/621–3330. Shows nightly 9 PM. Cover: none–$20, depending on the night and act. AE, MC, V.*

Jazz **Cafe du Nord.** What was once a Basque restaurant now hosts some of the liveliest jam sessions in town. The atmosphere in this basement poolroom/bar is decidedly casual, but the music, provided mostly by local talent, is strictly top-notch. *2170 Market St. at Sanchez St., tel. 415/861–5016. Open daily 4 PM–2 AM (the "tapas-inspired" kitchen serves food 6:30–11 Wed.–Sat.), with live music nightly at 9. Cover: $2, no drink minimum.*

Jazz at Pearl's. This club is one of the few reminders of North Beach's days as a hot spot for cool tunes. Sophisticated and romantic, the club's picture windows overlook City Lights Bookstore across the street. The talent level is remarkably high, especially considering that there is rarely a cover. *256 Columbus Ave., near Broadway, tel. 415/291–8255. Live music Sun.–Thurs. 9 PM–1 AM, Fri.–Sat. 9–1:30. Cover: none, except for special shows, 2-drink minimum every night.*

Kimball's East. This club in a shopping complex in Emeryville, just off Highway 80 near Oakland, hosts jazz greats such as Wynton Marsalis and Hugh Masekela and popular vocalists such as Lou Rawls and Patti Austin. With an elegant interior and fine food, this is one of most luxurious supper clubs in the Bay Area. *5800 Shellmound St., Emeryville, tel. 510/658–2555. Shows Wed.–Sun. at 8 and 10. Cover: $12–$24 with $5 minimum. Advance ticket purchase advised for big-name shows. MC, V.*

Up and Down Club. This hip restaurant and club, whose owners include supermodel Christy Turlington, books up-and-coming jazz artists downstairs Monday through Saturday. There's a bar and dancing to a DJ upstairs Wednesday through Saturday. *1151 Folsom St., tel. 415/626–2388. Downstairs shows begin at 9:30 PM. Cover: $3–$5 (admits you to either bar). AE, MC, V.*

Cabarets **Club Fugazi.** *Beach Blanket Babylon* is a wacky musical revue that has become the longest-running show of its genre in the history of the theater. A send-up of San Francisco moods and mores, *Beach Blanket* has now run for two decades, outstripping the Ziegfeld Follies by years. While the choreography is colorful and the songs witty, the real stars of the show are the exotic costumes—worth the price of admission in themselves. Order tickets as far in advance as possible; the revue has been sold out up to a month in advance. *678 Green St., 94133, tel. 415/421–4222 (for an order form, fax 415/421–4817). Shows Wed. and Thurs. 8 PM, Fri. and Sat. 7 and 10 PM, Sun. 3 and 7 PM. Cover: $17–$40, depending upon date and seating location. Note: those under 21 are admitted only to the Sun. matinee performance. MC, V.*

Finocchio's. The female impersonators at this amiable, world-famous club have been generating confusion for 56 years now. The scene at Finocchio's is decidedly retro, which for the most part only adds to its charm. *506 Broadway, North Beach, tel. 415/982–9388. Note: those under 21 not admitted. Shows Wed.–Sun. at 8:30, 10, and 11:30 (open Thurs.–Sat. in the off-season). Cover: $12, 2-drink minimum. MC, V.*

Comedy **Cobb's Comedy Club.** Bobby Slayton, Paula Poundstone, and Dr. Gonzo are among the super stand-up comics who perform here. *In the Cannery, 2801 Leavenworth St. at the corner of Beach St., tel. 415/928–4320. Shows Mon. 8 PM, Tues.–Thurs. 9 PM, Fri.–Sat. 9 and 11 PM. Cover: $8 weeknights, $10 and 2-drink minimum Fri. and Sat. MC, V.*

The Punch Line. A launching pad for the likes of Jay Leno and Whoopi Goldberg, the Punch Line features some of the top talents around—several of whom are certain to make a national impact.

Note that weekend shows often sell out, and it is best to buy tickets in advance at BASS outlets (tel. 510/762–2277). *444-A Battery St. between Clay and Washington Sts., tel. 415/397–PLSF. Shows Sun.–Thurs. 9 PM, Fri.–Sat. 9 and 11 PM. Cover: $8 Tues.–Thurs., $10 Fri. and Sat.; special $5 showcases Mon. and Sun. 2-drink minimum. MC, V.*

Dancing Emporiums

Bahia Tropical. Here's a truly international club. Dance to Salsa, Caribbean, African, Latin, Brazilian, and reggae music (sometimes in the same night) at this always-jumping joint. Cover includes lambada dance lessons Saturday nights. Some nights are given over to reggae, rap, deep house, and hip hop; live bands perform occasionally. The crowd is young and casual. *1600 Market St., tel. 415/861–8657. Dancing Tues.–Sun. 9:30 PM–1:30 AM. Cover: $3–$10.*

Cesar's Latin Palace. Salsa-style Latin music attracts all kinds of dancers to this popular club in the city's Mission District. Latin dance lessons from 9 to 10 PM are included in the price of admission Friday and Saturday nights. Note: no alcohol is served here. *3140 Mission St., tel. 415/648–6611. Open Sun. and Thurs. 8 PM–2 AM, Fri. and Sat. 9 PM–5 AM. Cover: $5–$7, which includes nearby parking and coat check.*

The Kennel Club. Alternative rock and funk rule in this small, steamy room. Monday, Wednesday, and Friday are live music nights, with bands from Zulu Spear or Sister Double Happiness to esoteric talents from around the world taking the stage. On Sundays DJs spin worldbeat and reggae; the Saturday menu varies from week to week. *628 Divisadero St., tel. 415/931–1914. Open nightly 9 PM–2 AM. Cover: $3–$10.*

Metronome Ballroom. Weekend nights are lively yet mellow at this smoke- and alcohol-free spot for ballroom dancing. Brush up on your steps on your own, or take the beginners' lessons early in the evening. *1830 17th St., tel. 415/252–9000. Open Fri. 9:30–midnight, Sat. 9–midnight, Sun. 7:30–11. Cover: $10 (includes dance lessons, which begin at 7:30 Fri. and Sat., 6:30 on Sun.).*

Oz. Take the St. Francis Hotel's glass elevator way up(scale) to the land of Oz. Surrounded by a splendid panorama of the city, you dance on marble floors and recharge on cushy sofas and bamboo chairs. The fine sound system belts out oldies, disco, Motown, and new wave. *335 Powell St., between Geary and Post Sts. on the top floor of the Westin St. Francis Hotel, tel. 415/397–7000. Open Sun.–Thurs. 9 PM–1:30 AM, Fri. and Sat. 9–2:30. Cover: $8 Sun.–Thurs.; $15 Fri.–Sat.*

Sound Factory. This south of Market club became an instant hit when it opened in 1993. Musical styles change with the night and sometimes the hour. Depending on who's up in the DJ booth, you're likely to hear anything from garage and deep house to '70s disco. Live bands also perform at special events. Some nights the venue becomes an alcohol-free, after-hours club. *525 Harrison St., tel. 415/543–1300. Hours and cover vary; call ahead.*

Up and Down Club (*see* Jazz, *above*).

Piano Bars

Act IV Lounge. A popular spot for a romantic rendezvous, the focal point of this tastefully appointed lounge is a crackling fireplace. *At the Inn at the Opera, 333 Fulton St. near Franklin St., tel. 415/553–8100. Pianist nightly 6–9. No cover.*

Masons. Fine local talents play pop and show standards at this elegant restaurant in the Fairmont Hotel. *California and Mason Sts., tel. 415/392–0113. Piano Tues.–Thurs. and Sun. 7–11, Fri. and Sat. 8–midnight. No cover.*

Ritz-Carlton Hotel. The tastefully appointed Lobby Lounge features a harpist for high tea daily from 2:30 to 5 PM. The lounge shifts to piano (with occasional vocal accompaniment) for cocktails until 11:30 weeknights and 1:30 AM weekends. *600 Stockton St., tel. 415/296–7465. No cover.*

Washington Square Bar and Grill. A favorite of San Francisco politicians and newspaper folk, the "Washbag," as it is affectionately known, hosts pianists performing jazz and popular standards. *On North Beach's Washington Sq., 1707 Powell St., tel. 415/982–8123. Music Sun.–Tues. 6–10, Wed. 7–11, Thurs. 7–11:30, Fri. and Sat. 8:30–12:30. No cover.*

Skyline Bars **Carnelian Room.** At 781 feet above the ground, enjoy dinner or cocktails here on the 52nd floor, where you may drink from the loftiest view of San Francisco's magnificent skyline. Reservations are a must for dinner here. *Top of the Bank of America Building, 555 California St., tel. 415/433–7500. Open Mon.–Thurs. 3–11:30 PM, Fri. 3 PM–12:30 AM, Sat. 4 PM–12:30 AM, Sun. 10 AM–11:30 PM.*

Crown Room. Just ascending to the well-named Crown Room is a drama in itself as you take the Fairmont's glass-enclosed Skylift elevator to the top. Some San Franciscans maintain that this lounge is the most luxurious of the city's skyline bars. Lunch, dinner, and Sunday brunch are also served. *29th floor of the Fairmont Hotel, California and Mason Sts., tel. 415/772–5131. Open daily 11 AM–1 AM.*

Top of the Mark. A famous magazine photograph immortalized this rooftop bar as a hot spot for World War II service people on leave or about to ship out; now folks can dance to the sounds of that era on weekends. There's live music Wednesday through Saturday. *In the Mark Hopkins Hotel, California and Mason Sts., tel. 415/392–3434. Open nightly 4 PM–12:30 AM.*

San Francisco's Favorite Bars **Buena Vista.** Even though the Buena Vista's claim of having introduced Irish coffee to the New World may be dubious, this is the Wharf area's most popular bar. It's usually packed with tourists and has a fine view of the waterfront. *2765 Hyde St., near Fisherman's Wharf, tel. 415/474–5044.*

Edinburgh Castle. Scots all over town went into mourning when this cherished watering hole closed in 1993. After several dark months, the Castle doors reopened, and its jukebox again pours out happy and sometimes baleful Scottish folk tunes the likes of which can be heard nowhere else in town; Fridays feature bagpipe performances. There are plenty of Scottish brews from which to choose. *950 Geary St. near Polk St., tel. 415/885–4074.*

House of Shields. For a taste of an authentic old-time San Francisco saloon, try this bar, which attracts an older, Financial District crowd after work. It closes at 8 PM weekdays, 6 PM Saturday. *39 New Montgomery St., tel. 415/392–7732.*

John's Grill. Located on the fringe of the Tenderloin, this bar was featured in The Maltese Falcon, and mystery fans will revel in its Hammett memorabilia. *63 Ellis St., tel. 415/986–0069.*

Vesuvio Cafe. Near the legendary City Lights Bookstore, this quintessentially North Beach bar is little altered since its heyday as a haven for the Beat poets. *255 Columbus Ave. between Broadway and Pacific Ave., tel. 415/362–3370.*

Gay and Lesbian Nightlife *Lesbian Bars* **The Café.** This bar in the heart of the gay Castro district is always comfortable and often crowded. Chat quietly at one end or cut the rug at the other. *2367 Market St. at 17th St., tel. 415/861–3846. Open noon–2 AM. No cover.*

Girlspot. The best place for a lesbian to be on Saturday night, this hot spot (aka G-Spot) features good dance music, mostly pop (Whitney Houston, etc.,) with a bit of techno-beat. *At the End Up, 6th and*

Harrison Sts., tel. 415/543–7700. Doors open at 9 PM. Sat. only. Cover: $5.

Red Dora's Bearded Lady Café and Cabaret. This neighborhood venue serves a predominantly lesbian and gay clientele. It's also a gallery (mostly women's work) and music outlet for local independent labels. *485 14th St., at Guerrero St., tel. 415/626–2805. Open weekdays 7 AM–7 PM, Sat. and Sun. 9 AM–7 PM. Irregularly scheduled weekend performances begin at 8 PM (cover varies). Call ahead or check gay papers. No alcohol served.*

Gay Male Bars

The Elephant Walk. One of the Castro District's cozier bars, this is among the few where the music level allows for easy conversation. *Castro St., at 18th St., no phone. Open 11 AM–2 AM.*

The Midnight Sun. This is one of the Castro's longest-standing and most popular bars, with giant video screens riotously programmed. Don't expect to hear yourself think. *4067 18th St., tel. 415/861–4186. Open noon–2 AM.*

The Stud. Still going strong after 29 years, the Stud's always-groovin' DJs mix up-to-the-minute music with carefully chosen highlights from the glory days of gay disco. *Harrison and 9th Sts., tel. 415/863–6623. Open daily 5 PM–2 AM. Dancing continues (without alcohol) on weekends as long as the crowd remains frisky. Cover: none–$3.*

Excursion to Sausalito

By Robert Taylor

The San Francisco Convention and Visitors Bureau describes Sausalito's location as "the Mediterranean side of the Golden Gate." With its relatively sheltered site on the bay in Marin County, just 8 miles from San Francisco, it appeals to Bay Area residents and visitors for the same reason: It is so near and yet so far. As a hillside town with superb views, an expansive yacht harbor, the aura of an artist's colony, and ferry service, Sausalito might be a resort within commuting distance of the city. It is certainly the primary excursion for visitors to San Francisco, especially those with limited time to explore the Bay Area. Mild weather encourages strolling and outdoor dining, although afternoon winds and fog can roll over the hills from the ocean, funneling through the central part of town once known as Hurricane Gulch.

There are substantial homes, including Victorian mansions, in Sausalito's heights, but the town has long had a more colorful and raffish reputation. Discovered in 1775 by Spanish explorers and named Saucelito (Little Willow) for the trees growing around its springs, Sausalito was a port for whaling ships during the 19th century. In 1875, the railroad from the north connected with ferryboats to San Francisco and the town became an attraction for the fun-loving. Even the chamber of commerce recalls the time when Sausalito sported 25 saloons, gambling dens, and bordellos. Bootleggers flourished during Prohibition in the 1920s, and shipyard workers swelled the town's population during the 1940s, when tour guides divided the residents into "wharf rats" and "hill snobs."

Ensuing decades brought a bohemian element with the development of an artists' colony and a houseboat community. Sausalito has also become a major yachting center, and restaurants attract visitors for the fresh seafood as well as the spectacular views. Sausalito remains a friendly and casual small town, although summer traffic jams can fray nerves. If possible, visit Sausalito on a weekday—and take the ferry.

Arriving and Departing

By Car Cross the Golden Gate Bridge and go north on U.S. 101 to the Sausalito exit, then go south on Bridgeway to municipal parking near the center of town. The trip takes 30 to 45 minutes one-way. (You will need change for the parking lots' meters.)

By Bus **Golden Gate Transit** (tel. 415/332–6600) travels to Sausalito from 1st and Mission streets and other points in the city.

By Ferry **Golden Gate Ferry** (tel. 415/332–6600) crosses the bay from the Ferry Building at Market Street and the Embarcadero; **Red and White Fleet** (tel. 415/546–2896) leaves from Pier 41 at Fisherman's Wharf. The trip takes 15–30 minutes.

Guided Tours

Most tour companies include Sausalito on excursions north to Muir Woods and the Napa Valley Wine Country. Among them are **Gray Line** (tel. 415/558–9400) and **Great Pacific Tour Co.** (tel. 415/626–4499).

Exploring

Numbers in the margin correspond to points of interest on the Sausalito map.

Bridgeway is Sausalito's main thoroughfare and prime destination, with the bay, yacht harbor, and waterfront restaurants on one side, and more restaurants, shops, hillside homes, and hotels on the other. It is only a few steps from the ferry terminal to the tiny landmark
1 park in the center of town: the **Plaza Vina del Mar,** named for Sausalito's sister city in Chile. The park features a fountain and two 14-foot-tall statues of elephants created for the 1915 Panama-Pacific International Exposition in San Francisco.

2 Across the street to the south is the Spanish-style **Sausalito Hotel,** which has been refurbished and filled with Victorian antiques. Be-
3 tween the hotel and the **Sausalito Yacht Club** is another unusual historic landmark, a drinking fountain with the invitation, "Have a Drink on Sally." It's in remembrance of Sally Stanford, the former San Francisco madam who later ran Sausalito's Valhalla restaurant and became the town's mayor. Actually, the monument is also in re-membrance of her dog. There is a sidewalk-level bowl that suggests, "Have a Drink on Leland." South on Bridgeway, toward San Fran-cisco, there is an esplanade along the water with picture-perfect views. Farther south are a number of restaurants on piers, includ-ing—near the end of Bridgeway at Richardson Street—what was
4 the **Valhalla** and is the oldest restaurant in Sausalito. Built in 1893 as "Walhalla," it was one of the settings for the film *The Lady from Shanghai* in the 1940s, Sally Stanford's place in the 1950s, and most recently a Chart House restaurant.

North on Bridgeway from the ferry terminal are yacht harbors and, parallel to Bridgeway a block to the west, the quieter Caledonia Street, with its own share of cafés and shops. There is a pleasant, grassy park with a children's playground at Caledonia and Litho streets, with a food shop nearby for picnic provisions.

Here and there along the west side of Bridgeway are flights of steps that climb the hill to Sausalito's wooded, sometimes rustic and some-times lavish residential neighborhoods. The stairway just across the

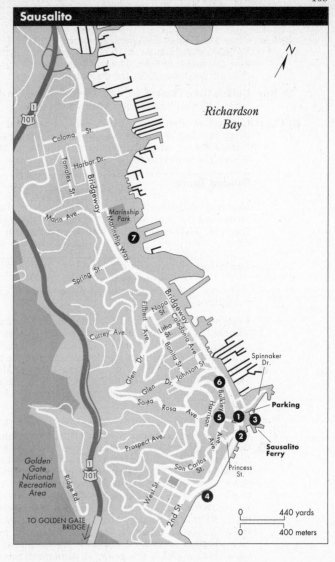

Sausalito

*Richardson
Bay*

Coloma St.

Harbor Dr.

Tomales St.

Bridgeway

Marin Ave.

Marinship
Park

Marinship Way

Spring St.

Filbert Ave.

Currey Ave.

Napa St.

Litho St.

Bonita St.

Caledonia Ave.

Bridgeway

Johnson St.

Glen Dr.

Glen
Dr.

Santa
Rosa Ave.

Bulkley Ave.

Spinnaker
Dr.

Parking

Harrison Ave.

Prospect Ave.

San Carlos St.

Princess
St.

West St.

2nd St.

**Sausalito
Ferry**

*Golden
Gate
National
Recreation
Area*

Ridge Rd.

TO GOLDEN GATE
BRIDGE

0   440 yards

0   400 meters

street from Vina del Mar Park is named Excelsior, and it leads to
the **Alta Mira,** a popular Spanish-style hotel and restaurant with a
spectacular view (*see* Dining, *below*). However, there are vistas of
the bay from all these streets.

Where there isn't a hillside house or a restaurant or a yacht in
Sausalito, there is a shop. Most are along Bridgeway and Princess
Street, and they offer a wide assortment of casual and sophisticated
clothing, posters and paintings, imported and handcrafted gifts, and
the expected variety of T-shirts, ice cream, cookies, and pastries.
The **Village Fair** (777 Bridgeway) is a four-story former warehouse
that has been converted into a warren of clothing, craft, and gift
boutiques. Crafts workers often demonstrate their talents in the

shops, and a winding brick path—Little Lombard Street—connects various levels. The shopping complex is a haven during wet weather.

Sausalito's reputation as an art colony is enhanced by the **Art Festival** held during the three-day Labor Day weekend in September. It attracts more than 35,000 visitors to the waterfront area, and ferry service is extended to the site during the festival. Details are available from the Sausalito Chamber of Commerce (333 Caledonia St., 94965, tel. 415/332–0505).

7 North on Bridgeway, within a few minutes' drive, is the **Bay Model,** a re-creation in miniature of the entire San Francisco Bay and the San Joaquin–Sacramento River delta. It is actually nearly 400 feet square and is used by the U.S. Army Corps of Engineers to reproduce the rise and fall of tides, the flow of currents, and the other physical forces at work on the bay. It is housed in a former World War II shipyard building, and there is a display of shipbuilding history. At the same site is the Wapama, a World War I–era steam freighter being restored by volunteers. *2100 Bridgeway, tel. 415/332–3871. Open Tues.–Fri. 9–4, weekends 10–6. Closed Sun. in winter.*

Along the shore of Richardson Bay, between the Bay Model and U.S. 101, are some of the 400 houseboats that make up Sausalito's "floating homes community." In the shallow tidelands, most of them float only about half the time, but they are always a fanciful collection of the rustic, the eccentric, the flamboyant, and the elegant.

Dining

Updated by Catherine McEver

Restaurants by the bay or perched on Sausalito's hillside feature prime views and fare that covers the waterfront. The town's unique cholesterol-free ordinance means you'll find at least one heart-healthy pick on every menu. Casual dress is acceptable everywhere.

Restaurants are listed according to price category.

Category	Cost*
$$$$	over $30
$$$	$20–$30
$$	$10–$20
$	under $10

per person for a three-course meal, excluding drinks, service, and 7¹/4% sales tax

$$$ **Casa Madrona.** Part of a hotel complex that includes a classic Victorian, a cluster of cottages, and terraced gardens stepping down the hillside, this upscale dining scenario serves up fine American cuisine and all-star views of the bay. The light, airy dining terrace with retractable roof and sliding glass walls is a great spot to splurge on a Sunday brunch buffet. *801 Bridgeway, tel. 415/331–5888. AE, D, DC, MC, V. No lunch Sat.*

$$–$$$ **Alta Mira.** This Sausalito landmark, in a Spanish-style hotel a block above Bridgeway, has spectacular views of the bay from the front terrace and the windowed dining room. It's a favored destination Bay Area–wide for Sunday brunch (try the famed eggs Benedict), an alfresco lunch, or cocktails at sunset. The California-Continental cuisine created here includes succulent rack of lamb, duckling, seafood salad, and a stellar Caesar salad. *125 Bulkley Ave., tel. 415/332–1350. Reservations advised. AE, DC, MC, V.*

$$ **The Spinnaker.** Spectacular bay views, homemade pastas, and sea-food specialties like fresh grilled salmon are the prime attractions in a contemporary building on a point beyond the harbor, near the yacht club. You may see a pelican perched on one of the pilings just outside. *100 Spinnaker Dr., tel. 415/332–1500. Reservations advised. Sunday brunch. AE, DC, MC, V.*

$–$$ **Margaritaville.** Exotic drinks and every Mexican favorite you'd ever crave from fajitas and enchiladas to *camarones ranchero* (fresh Pacific prawns sautéed in a flavorful red sauce) are on the bill of fare in a tropically hip setting with views of the marina and the bay. *1200 Bridgeway, tel. 415/331–3226. Reservations accepted for 8 or more. AE, DC, MC, V.*

$ **Lighthouse Coffee Shop.** This budget-priced coffee shop serves breakfast and lunch (omelets, sandwiches, and burgers) every day starting at dawn. Most find the down-to-earth atmosphere and simple fare a relief from tourist traps and seafood extravaganzas. *1311 Bridgeway, tel. 415/331–3034. No reservations. No credit cards. No alcohol.*

Excursion to Muir Woods

One hundred and fifty million years ago, ancestors of redwood and sequoia trees grew throughout the United States. Today the *Sequoia sempervirens* can be found only in a narrow, cool coastal belt from Monterey to Oregon. (*Sequoiadendron gigantea* grows in the Sierra Nevada.) **Muir Woods National Monument,** 17 miles northwest of San Francisco, is a 550-acre park that contains one of the most majestic redwood groves in the world. Some redwoods in the park are nearly 250 feet tall and 1,000 years old. This grove was saved from destruction in 1908 and named for naturalist John Muir, whose campaigns helped to establish the National Park system. His response: "This is the best tree-lover's monument that could be found in all of the forests of the world. Saving these woods from the axe and saw is in many ways the most notable service to God and man I have heard of since my forest wandering began."

Arriving and Departing

By Car Take U.S. 101 north to the Mill Valley–Muir Woods exit. The trip takes 45 minutes one-way when the roads are clear, but traffic can be heavy on summer weekends, so allow more time. The park staff recommends visiting before 10 AM and after 4 PM to avoid congestion. Note that the narrow, winding entrance road cannot accommodate some larger recreation vehicles.

Guided Tours

Most tour companies include Muir Woods on excursions to the Wine Country, among them **Gray Line** (tel. 415/558–9400) and **Great Pacific** (tel. 415/626–4499).

Exploring

Muir Woods is a park for walking; no cars are allowed in the redwood grove itself. There are 6 miles of easy trails from the park headquarters. The main trail along Redwood Creek is 1 mile long, paved, and wheelchair accessible. The paths cross streams and pass through ferns and azaleas as well as magnificent stands of redwoods such as Bohemian Grove and the circular formation called Cathedral Grove. The trails connect with an extensive network of hiking tails in Mt. Tamalpais State Park. No picnicking or camping is allowed, but snacks are available at the visitor center, along with a wide selection of books and exhibits. The weather is usually cool and often wet, so dress warmly and wear shoes appropriate for damp trails. Pets are not allowed. *Tel. 415/388–2595. Open daily 8 AM–sunset.*

Excursion to Berkeley

By Robert Taylor

Berkeley and the University of California are not synonymous, although the founding campus of the state university system dominates the city's heritage and contemporary life. The city of 100,000 facing San Francisco across the bay has other interesting features for visitors. Berkeley is culturally diverse and politically adventurous, a breeding ground for social trends, a continuing bastion of the counterculture, and an important center for Bay Area writers, artists, and musicians. The city's liberal reputation and determined spirit have led detractors to describe it in recent years as the People's Republic of Berkeley. Wooded groves on the university campus, neighborhoods of shingled bungalows, and landscaped hillside homes temper the environment.

The city was named for George Berkeley, the Irish philosopher and clergyman who crossed the Atlantic to convert the Indians and wrote "Westward, the course of empire takes its way." The city grew with the university, which was created by the state legislature in 1868 and established five years later on a rising plain of oak trees split by Strawberry Canyon. The central campus occupies 178 acres of the scenic 1,282-acre property, with most buildings located from Bancroft Way north to Hearst Street and from Oxford Street east into the Berkeley Hills. The university has more than 30,000 students and a full-time faculty of 1,600. It is considered one of the nation's leading intellectual centers and a major site for scientific research.

Arriving and Departing

By Car Take I–80 east across the Bay Bridge, then the University Avenue exit through downtown Berkeley to the campus, or take the Ashby Avenue exit and turn left on Telegraph Avenue to the traditional campus entrance; there is a parking garage on Channing Way. The trip takes a half-hour one-way (except in rush hour).

By Public Transportation **BART** (tel. 415/992–2278) trains run under the bay to the downtown Berkeley exit; transfer to the Humphrey GoBart shuttle bus to campus. The trip takes from 45 minutes to one hour one-way.

Exploring

Numbers in the margin correspond to points of interest on the Berkeley map.

❶ The Visitors Center (tel. 510/642–5215) in **University Hall** at University Avenue and Oxford Street is open weekdays 8–5. There are maps and brochures for self-guided walks; 1½-hour student-guided tours leave Mondays, Wednesdays, and Fridays at 10 AM and 1 PM.

❷ The throbbing heart of the University of California is **Sproul Plaza,** just inside the campus at Telegraph Avenue and Bancroft Way. It's a lively panorama of political and social activists, musicians, food vendors along Bancroft Way, children, dogs, and students on their way to and from classes at this "university within a park."

The university's suggested tour circles the upper portion of the central campus, past buildings that were sited to take advantage of vistas to the Golden Gate across the bay. The first campus plan was proposed by Frederick Law Olmsted, who designed New York's Central Park, and over the years the university's architects have included Bernard Maybeck and Julia Morgan (who designed Hearst Castle at San Simeon). Beyond Sproul Plaza is the bronze **Sather Gate,** built in 1909, and the former south entrance to the campus; the university expanded a block beyond its traditional boundary in the 1960s. Up a walkway to the right is vine-covered **South Hall,** one of two remaining buildings that greeted the first students in 1873.

Just ahead is **Sather Tower,** popularly known as the Campanile, the campus landmark that can be seen for miles. The 307-foot tower was modeled on St. Mark's tower in Venice and was completed in 1914. The carillon, which was cast in England, is played three times a day. In the lobby of the tower is a photographic display of campus history. An elevator takes visitors 175 feet up to the observation deck. *Open daily except university holidays 10–3:15. Admission: 50¢.*

Opposite the Campanile is **Bancroft Library,** with a rare-book collection and a changing series of exhibits that may include a Shakespeare first folio or a gold-rush diary. On permanent display is a gold nugget purported to be the one that started the rush to California when it was discovered on January 24, 1848. Across University Drive to the north is the **Earth Sciences Building,** with a seismograph for measuring earthquakes. The building also contains the **Paleontology Museum,** which has displays of dinosaur bones and the huge skeleton of a plesiosaur. *Open when the university is in session, weekdays 8–5, weekends 1–5.*

The university's two major museums are on the south side of campus near Bancroft Way. **The Phoebe Apperson Hearst Museum of Anthropology** (formerly the Lowie), in Kroeber Hall, has a collection of more than 4,000 artifacts. Items on display may cover the archaeology of ancient America or the crafts of Pacific Islanders. The museum also houses the collection of artifacts made by Ishi, the lone survivor of a California Indian tribe who was brought to the Bay Area in 1911. *Tel. 510/642–3681. Open Tues.–Fri. 10–4:30, weekends noon–4:30. Nominal admission charge.*

The University Art Museum is a fan-shaped building with a spiral of ramps and balcony galleries. It houses a collection of Asian and Western art, including a major group of Hans Hofmann's abstract paintings, and also displays touring exhibits. On the ground floor is the Pacific Film Archive, which offers daily programs of historic and contemporary films. *2626 Bancroft Way, tel. 510/642–0808; for film-program information, tel. 510/642–1124. Museum open Wed.–Sun. 11–5. Museum admission: $5, $4 senior citizens.*

Many of the university's notable attractions are outdoors. Just south of the Campanile near the rustic Faculty Club is **Faculty Glade** on the south fork of Strawberry Creek, one of the best examples of the university's attempt to preserve a parklike atmosphere. East of the central campus, across Gayley Road, is the **Hearst Greek Theatre,** built in 1903 and seating 7,000. Sarah Bernhardt once performed here; now it is used for major musical events.

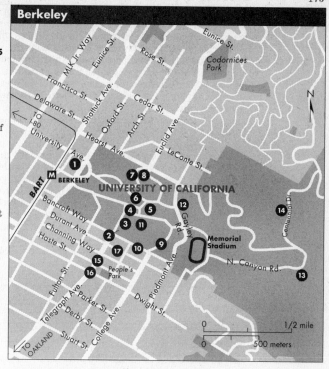

Berkeley

Above the Greek Theatre in Strawberry Canyon is the 30-acre
13 **Botanical Garden,** with a collection of some 25,000 species. It's a
relaxing gathering spot with benches and picnic tables. *Open daily
9–5, except Dec. 25.*

Perched on a hill above the campus on Centennial Drive is the for-
14 tresslike **Lawrence Hall of Science,** which is a laboratory, a science
education center, and—most important to visitors—a dazzling display of scientific knowledge and experiments. Displays are updated
regularly. On weekends there are additional films, lectures, and
demonstrations, especially for children. *Tel. 510/642–5132. Admission: $5 adults, $4 senior citizens and students. Open weekdays 10–
4:30, weekends 10–5.*

Berkeley is a rewarding city to explore beyond the university. Just
south of the campus on **Telegraph Avenue** is the busy student-ori-
ented district, full of cafés, bookstores, poster shops, and street vendors with traditional and trendy crafts items. Shops come and go
with the times, but among the neighborhood landmarks are **Cody's**
15 **Books** (2454 Telegraph Ave.), with its adjacent café; **Moe's** (2476
16 Telegraph Ave.), with a huge selection of used books; and **Leopold**
17 **Records** (2518 Durant Ave.). This district was the center of student
protests during the 1960s, and on the street it sometimes looks as if
that era still lives (it can be unruly at night). People's Park, one of
the centers of protest, is just east of Telegraph between Haste
Street and Dwight Way.

Downtown Berkeley around University and Shattuck avenues is
nondescript. However, there are shops for browsing along College
Avenue near Ashby Avenue south of campus and in the Walnut

Square development at Shattuck and Vine streets northwest of campus. Berkeley's shingled houses can be seen on tree-shaded streets near College and Ashby avenues. Hillside houses with spectacular views can be seen on the winding roads near the intersection of Ashby and Claremont avenues, around the Claremont Hotel. At the opposite side of the city, on Fourth Street north of University Avenue, an industrial area has been converted into a pleasant shopping street with popular eateries such as **Bette's Oceanview Diner** and the **Fourth Street Grill.**

Dining

Berkeley is a food-lover's paradise full of specialty markets, cheese stores, charcuteries, coffee vendors, produce outlets, innovative restaurants, and ethnic eateries. The most popular gourmet ghetto is along Shattuck Avenue, a few blocks north of University Avenue. University Avenue itself has become a corridor of good Indian, Thai, and Cambodian restaurants. You'll find lots of students, interesting coffee houses, and cheap eats on Telegraph, Durant, and Berkeley avenues near the campus. Casual dress is considered politically correct wherever you dine. Restaurants are listed according to price category.

Category	Cost*
$$$$	over $30
$$$	$20–$30
$$	$10–$20
$	under $10

*per person for a three-course meal, excluding drinks, service, and 8¹/4% sales tax

$$$–$$$$ **Chez Panisse Cafe & Restaurant.** President Clinton has joined the ranks of luminaries who have dined at this legendary eatery, but like anyone else without a reservation, he had to settle for a seat in the upstairs café. Alice Waters is still the mastermind behind the culinary wizardry, with Jean-Pierre Moullé supplying hands-on talent as head chef. In the downstairs restaurant, where redwood paneling, a fireplace, and lavish floral arrangements create the ambience of a private home, dinners are prix fixe and pricey, but the cost is lower on weekdays and almost halved on Mondays. The culinary entertainment includes creations like pasta with squid and leeks, grilled sea bream with black olives and anchovies, and roast truffled breast of guinea hen. Upstairs in the café the atmosphere is informal, the crowd livelier, the prices lower, and the flavors come through in dishes like calzone with goat cheese, mozzarella, prosciutto, and garlic. *1517 Shattuck Ave., north of University Avenue. Restaurant (downstairs): tel. 510/548–5525. Reservations required. Dinner only. Café (upstairs): tel. 510/548–5049. Same-day reservations. AE, D, DC, MC, V. Closed Sun.*

$$ **Spenger's Fish Grotto.** This is a rambling, boisterous seafood restaurant serving hearty portions of fairly ordinary food. It's a wildly popular place, though, so expect a wait in their combination oyster/sports bar. *1919 Fourth St., near University Ave. and I–80, tel. 510/845–7771. Reservations for 5 or more. AE, D, DC, MC, V.*

$$ **Venezia Caffe & Ristorante.** This family-friendly eatery was the first to serve fresh pasta in the Bay Area, and it continues to offer a wide

range of tasty pasta selections (pick a dish that includes their house-made chicken sausage). The large dining room looks like a Venetian piazza, with a fountain in the middle, murals on the walls, and laundry hanging overhead. Children get their own menu, free antipasti, and crayons. *1799 University Ave., tel. 510/849–4681. Reservations advised. AE, MC, V. No lunch weekends.*

$–$$ **Pasand Madras Cuisine.** This informal restaurant serves south Indian fare from *masala dhosa* (spiced vegetables in a crispy thin pancake) and savory curries to exotically sticky sweets. There are several large dining rooms decorated with Indian art, and live sitar music is provided most nights. *2286 Shattuck Ave., tel. 510/549–2559. Reservations accepted. AE, MC, V.*

$–$$ **Saul's Delicatessen.** Transplanted New Yorkers agree this is the best Jewish-style deli west of the Rockies. They've got it all from huge corned beef and pastrami sandwiches to chopped liver and chicken soup with table service, a take-out counter, and breakfast served all day. *1475 Shattuck Ave., tel. 510/848–3354. Reservations accepted. MC, V. Closed Yom Kippur.*

Excursion to Oakland

Originally the site of ranches, farms, a grove of redwood trees, and, of course, clusters of oaks, Oakland has long been a warmer and more spacious alternative to San Francisco. By the end of the 19th century, Mediterranean-style homes and gardens had been developed as summer estates. With swifter transportation, Oakland became a bedroom community for San Francisco; then it progressed to California's fastest-growing industrial city. In recent decades, Oakland has struggled to redefine its identity. However, the major attractions remain: the parks and civic buildings around Lake Merritt, which was created from a tidal basin in 1898; the port area, now named Jack London Square, where the author spent much of his time at the turn of the century; and the scenic roads and parks along the crest of the Oakland-Berkeley hills. Also in the hills is the castlelike Claremont Resort Hotel, a landmark since 1915, as well as more sprawling parks with lakes and miles of hiking trails.

Arriving and Departing

By Car Take I–80 across the Bay Bridge, then I–580 to the Grand Avenue exit for Lake Merritt. To reach downtown and the waterfront, take the I–980 exit from I–580. The trip takes 45 minutes.

By Public Transportation Take the BART to Oakland City Center station or to Lake Merritt station for the lake and Oakland Museum. The trip takes 45 minutes one-way.

Exploring

Numbers in the margin correspond to points of interest on the Oakland map.

❶ If there is one reason to visit Oakland, it is to explore the **Oakland Museum,** an inviting series of landscaped buildings that display the state's art, history, and natural science. It is the best possible introduction to a tour of California, and its dramatic and detailed exhibits can help fill the gaps on a brief visit. The natural science department displays a typical stretch of California from the Pacific Ocean to the Nevada border, including plants and wildlife. A breathtaking film, *Fast Flight,* condenses the trip into five minutes. The museum's

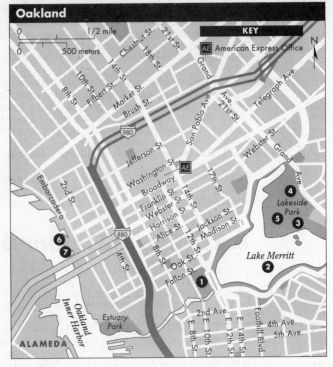

sprawling history section includes everything from Spanish-era artifacts and a gleaming fire engine that battled the flames in San Francisco in 1906 to 1960s souvenirs of the "summer of love." The California Dream exhibit recalls a century of inspirations. The museum's art department includes mystical landscapes painted by the state's pioneers, as well as contemporary visions. There is a pleasant museum café for lunch and outdoor areas for relaxing. *1000 Oak St. at 10th St., tel. 510/834–2413. Admission: $4 adults, $2 children. Open Wed.–Sat. 10–5, Sun. noon–7.*

② Near the museum, **Lake Merritt** is a 155-acre oasis surrounded by parks and paths, with several outdoor attractions on the north side.

③ The **Natural Science Center and Waterfowl Refuge** attracts birds by the hundreds during winter months. *At the foot of Perkins St., tel. 510/238–3739. Open daily 10–5.*

④ **Children's Fairyland** is a low-key amusement park with a puppet theater, small merry-go-round, and settings based on nursery rhymes. *Grand Ave. at Park View Terr., tel. 510/832–3609. Nominal admission charge. Open summer, daily 10–4:30; winter, weekends 10–4:30.*

⑤ The **Lakeside Park Garden Center** includes a Japanese garden and many native flowers and plants. *666 Bellevue Ave., tel. 510/238–3208. Open daily 10–3 or later in summer. Closed Thanksgiving, Dec. 25, and Jan. 1.*

Jack London, although born in San Francisco, spent his early years in Oakland before shipping out for adventures that inspired *The Call of the Wild, The Sea Wolf, Martin Eden,* and *The Cruise of the Snark.*
⑥ He is commemorated with a bronze bust on what is now called **Jack**

London's Waterfront, at the foot of Broadway. A livelier landmark ❼ is **Heinhold's First and Last Chance Saloon,** one of his hangouts. Next door is the reassembled Klondike cabin in which he spent a winter. Restaurants cluster around the plaza, and a Barnes & Noble bookstore offers a wide selection of London's writings. Nearby, Jack London Village has specialty shops and restaurants. The best local collection of the author's letters, manuscripts, and photographs is in the Jack London Room at the Oakland Main Library (125 14th St., tel. 510/273–3134).

Oakland's downtown has been undergoing redevelopment for many years. More stable and pleasant areas for shopping and browsing, with a selection of cafés, can be found on Lake Shore Avenue northeast of Lake Merritt, Piedmont Avenue near the Broadway exit from I–580, and College Avenue west of Broadway in North Oakland. College Avenue is lined with antiques stores, boutiques, and cafés. The neighborhood surrounds BART's Rockridge station. Transferring there to the local No. 51 bus will take visitors to the University of California campus, about 1½ miles away in Berkeley.

The East Bay Regional Park District (tel. 510/562–7275) offers 46 parks in an area covering 60,000 acres to residents and visitors. In the Oakland hills is **Redwood Regional Park,** accessible from Joaquin Miller Road off Highway 13, to which Ashby Avenue will lead you. In the Berkeley hills is the 2,000-acre **Tilden Park,** which includes a lake and children's playground and is accessible from Grizzly Peak Boulevard off Claremont Avenue. There are scenic views of the Bay Area from roads that link the hilltop parks: Redwood Road, Skyline Boulevard, and Grizzly Peak Boulevard. Parks are open daily during daylight hours.

Dining

Oakland's ethnic diversity is reflected in its restaurants and cafés. There is a thriving Chinatown a few blocks northwest of the Oakland Museum, a number of seafood restaurants at Jack London Square, and fare to fit any palate, penchant, or pocketbook on Piedmont and College Avenues. Dress is, as usual, casual. Restaurants are listed according to price category.

Category	Cost*
$$$$	over $30
$$$	$20–$30
$$	$10–$20
$	under $10

per person for a three-course meal, excluding drinks, service, and 8¼% sales tax

$$–$$$ **The Bay Wolf.** A perpetual favorite, in a converted home with a redwood deck out front, elegantly understated dining rooms inside, and a kitchen garden out back. The menu changes frequently to feature fresh seasonal ingredients and innovative California-Mediterranean cuisine in selections like a pork loin salad with stuffed squash, grilled eggplant, peppers, and couscous; or pan-roasted salmon with artichokes, asparagus, spring carrots, and sorrel sauce. *3853 Piedmont Ave., tel. 510/655–6004. Reservations advised. MC, V. No lunch weekends.*

$$ **ZZA's Trattoria.** Pizzas, salads, house-smoked chicken, and home-made pasta, ravioli, and lasagna are served up in a wacko environment on the shore of Lake Merritt. There's a wild neon sign over the open kitchen, butcher-paper table covers and crayons, customers' artwork on the walls, and lines out the door. *552 Grand Ave., tel. 510/839–9124. Same-day reservations for 6 or more. MC, V. No lunch Mon., Tues., and weekends.*

$–$$ **Lantern Restaurant.** Fine Hong Kong cuisine can be had downstairs at the oldest restaurant in Oakland's Chinatown, but the dim sum (steamed dumplings, spring rolls, and assorted exotic delicacies) served in the enormous upstairs dining room is the big deal here. Point to what you want as the carts roll by and pay by the plate. *814 Webster St., tel. 510/451–0627. D, DC, MC, V.*

$–$$ **Oliveto Café & Restaurant.** This is one of the East Bay's prime foodie hangouts, fashioned after a rustic stucco casa in Tuscany and situated on the corner of a bustling gourmet marketplace. Top-notch northern Italian cuisine is served in the formal dining room upstairs, where prices can edge into the $$$ category, but the café at street level is the place to see and be seen sipping wine or espresso and consuming pizzas, tapas, and pastry. *5655 College Ave., tel. 510/547–5356. AE, DC, MC, V. Reservations advised for restaurant. No lunch weekends in restaurant.*

Excursion to the South Bay

San Jose, founded in 1777, was California's first town apart from a Spanish mission or fortification. It was (briefly) the state's first capital during the American occupation, but until the middle of the 20th century it remained primarily an agricultural center. San Jose, 50 miles south of San Francisco, was touted as "the garden city in the valley of heart's delight" when the Santa Clara Valley was filled with orchards. Vineyards and wineries continue to flourish, but the area became "Silicon Valley" with the advent of high-tech industries based on the silicon chip. Santa Clara and nearby Sunnyvale are the high-tech centers, but sprawling San Jose has become the state's third-largest city.

As part of its plans to attract tourists and increase convention business, San Jose has embarked on a massive project to redefine its city center; it has completed a 20-mile light-rail transportation system, a convention center, a 17,000-seat arena for the San Jose Sharks hockey team, and a major addition to the San Jose Museum of Art and has begun to restore the few remaining 19th-century buildings downtown.

Tourist Information

For events information, contact the **Visitor Information Center** (1515 El Camino Real, Box 387, Santa Clara 95050, tel. 408/296–7111). The **San Jose Convention and Visitors Bureau** (333 W. San Carlos St., Suite 1000, San Jose 95110, tel. 408/295–9600) produces an annual events calendar. For schedules for all activities around the clock, call the **San Jose Tourist Bureau's FYI Hotline** (tel. 408/295–2265).

Arriving and Departing

By Car U.S. 101, I–280 (the Junipero Serra Freeway), and I–880 (Highway 17) connect the Valley with the San Francisco Bay Area. The drive south from San Francisco to San Jose on I–280 takes 60 minutes, depending on traffic, which tends to be heavy during rush hours. The drive north from Monterey, on U.S. 101 takes about 90 minutes. Highway 1, which runs along the California coast, takes longer, but is far more scenic.

By Public Transportation The most efficient commuter service available is **CalTrain** (tel. 800/660–4287), which runs from 4th and Townsend streets in San Francisco to San Jose's light-rail system. **Greyhound Lines** (tel. 800/231–2222) also provides public transportation.

By Plane **San Jose International Airport** (tel. 408/277–4759) is just 3 miles from downtown San Jose and is served by the light rail system in addition to airport shuttle services such as **Express Airport Shuttle** (tel. 408/378–6270) and **South & East Bay Airport Shuttle** (tel. 408/559–9477).

Exploring

A good method of exploring is to hop on the light rail that connects San Jose State University on one end with the Center for Performing Arts on the other; its route will give you a good overview of the city, and the convention center stop will drop you in the center of downtown so you can explore on foot.

The **Children's Discovery Museum**, near the convention center, exhibits interactive installations on space, technology, the humanities, and the arts. Children can dress up in period costumes, create jewelry from recycled materials, or play on a real fire truck. *180 Woz Way, at Auzerais St., tel. 408/298–5437. Admission: $6 adults, $5 senior citizens, $4 children 2–18. Open Tues.–Sat. 10–5, Sun. noon–5.*

The **Tech Museum of Innovation**, across from the convention center, presents high-tech information through hands-on lab exhibits that are fun and accessible, allowing visitors to discover and demystify disciplines such as microelectronics, biotechnology, robotics, and space exploration. *145 W. San Carlos St., tel. 408/279–7150. Admission: $6 adults, $4 students and senior citizens. Open Tues.–Sun. 10–5.*

In collaboration with New York's Whitney Museum, the **San Jose Museum of Art** is exploring the development of 20th-century American art with exhibits of pieces from the permanent collections of both. The series will run through the year 2000, and include works by such American artists as Andrew Wyeth, Edward Hopper, and Georgia O'Keeffe. *110 S. Market St., tel. 408/294–2787. Admission: $5 adults, $3 senior citizens, students, and children 6–17. Open Tues.–Sun. 10–5, Thurs. 10–8.*

On the north end of town lies the **Winchester Mystery House.** Convinced that spirits would harm her if construction ever stopped, firearms-heiress Sarah Winchester constantly added to her house. For 38 years beginning in 1884, she kept hundreds of carpenters working around the clock, creating a bizarre, 160-room Victorian labyrinth with stairs going nowhere and doors that open into walls. *525 S. Winchester Blvd. (between Stevens Creek Blvd. and I–280), tel. 408/247–2101. Admission: $12.50 adults, $9.50 senior citizens, $6.50 children 6–12. Open daily 9:30–4; later in summer.*

The **Egyptian Museum and Planetarium** offers some mysteries of its own in the West Coast's largest collection of Egyptian and Babylonian antiquities, including mummies and an underground replica of a pharaoh's tomb. The planetarium offers programs like the popular "Celestial Nile," which describes the significant role astrology played in ancient Egyptian myths and religions. *1600 Park Ave. at Naglee Ave., tel. 408/947–3636. Admission (museum only): $6 adults, $4 senior citizens and students, $3.50 children 7–15. Planetarium admission and show times vary. Open daily 9–5.*

On 176 acres of rolling lawns on the east side of San Jose, off I–280, is **Kelley Park**, which offers a variety of family attractions and shady picnic sites. On the grounds is the creative **Happy Hollow Park & Zoo**, with theme rides, puppet shows, a riverboat replica, and events specially planned for children from 2 to 10 years old. Also in the park is the **Japanese Friendship Garden** (free; open daily), with fish ponds and a teahouse inspired by Japan's Korakuen Garden. Occupying 25 acres of the park is the **San Jose Historical Museum,** which re-creates San Jose in the 1880s with a collection of original and replicate Victorian homes and shops, a firehouse, and a trolley line. The dusty Main Street recalls small-town America without the brightly painted gloss of amusement-park reproductions. *Kelley Park: 1300 Senter Rd. Admission to park free, parking $3 on holidays and in summer. Happy Hollow Park: tel. 408/295–8383, admission: $3.50, $3 seniors, free for visitors under 2 and over 75. Open Mon.–Sat. 10–5, Sun. 11–6 Apr.–Oct; 10–5 Nov.–Mar. Historical Museum: tel. 408/287–2290, admission: $4 adults, $3 senior citizens, $2 children 6–17. Open weekdays 10–4:30, weekends noon–4:30.*

Saratoga, 10 miles west of San Jose, is a quaint, former artists' colony chock-full of antiques shops, upscale jewelry stores, and art galleries. Just south of downtown, nestled on a steep hillside, are the **Hakone Gardens.** This Zen-style retreat was designed in 1918 by a man who had been an imperial gardener in Japan and has been carefully maintained. On the site are *koi* (carp) ponds, sculptured shrubs, and a traditional Japanese teahouse. *21000 Big Basin Way, tel. 408/741–4994. Admission: $3 per car weekends Mar.–Oct., free weekdays and all of Nov.–Feb. Open weekdays 10–5, weekends 11–5.*

Right in the center of the Santa Clara University campus is the **Mission Santa Clara de Assis**, the eighth of 21 California missions founded under the direction of Father Junipero Serra. The mission has a dramatic history. Several early settlements were flooded by the Guadalupe River, the present site was the fifth chosen, and the permanent mission chapel was destroyed by fire in 1926. Roof tiles of the current building, a replica of the original, were salvaged from earlier structures, which dated from the 1790s and 1820s.

Dining

Though the South Bay's billboard-strewn highways lined with motels and fast-food franchises can look like a Nabokov landscape, the Bay Area's reputation as a world-class culinary center remains intact at its southernmost tip. Restaurants are listed according to price category.

Category	Cost*
$$$$	over $30
$$$	$20–$30
$$	$10–$20
$	under $10

*per person for a three-course meal, excluding drinks, service, and 8¼% sales tax

$$$$ **Emile's.** Swiss chef and owner Emile Mooser is well-versed in the
San Jose   classic marriage of food and wine, and will make your wine selection
★   from the restaurant's extensive list for you. House specialties include house-cured gravlax and fresh sturgeon; the menu emphasizes lighter cuisine. Lamps on every table and walls hand-painted with gold leaves create an intimate and elegant backdrop. *545 S. 2nd St., tel. 408/289–1960. Reservations advised. AE, DC, MC, V. Closed Sun. and Mon., lunch Fri. only.*

$$$$ **Le Mouton Noir.** Even President Clinton, who favors a Big Mac
Saratoga   and fries, found his way to Saratoga's most famous restaurant during a visit to Silicon Valley. Anything but the black sheep that its name suggests, the place is filled with aspiring and established foodies and wine connoisseurs, and the kitchen turns out understated dishes that let the full flavor of the ingredients come through. Fine examples are the seafood dishes and the roast rack of lamb with a light, caramelized fennel and raspberry sauce. *14560 Big Basin Way, near Hwy. 9, tel. 408/867–7017. Reservations recommended. AE, DC, MC, V. No lunch Sun. and Mon.*

$$$ **Paolo's Restaurant.** In this spot not far from local cultural centers,
San Jose   grazing is an art, and the the bar menu offers small plates that give you several different tastes in a hurry—great for a snack before or after the theater. Try the eggplant sandwich, antipasto plate, or the mixed salad topped with hearty serving of shrimp. The Italian entrées and the parklike dining room—filled with plants and overlooking a patio, lush greenery, and the Guadalupe River—deserve more leisurely appreciation. *333 W. San Carlos St., tel 408/294–2558. Reservations advised. AE, DC, MC, V. No lunch weekends.*

$$ **Scott's Seafood Grill & Bar.** Young, upwardly mobile types fill the
San Jose   clean-lined, oak-and-brass dining room here. Seafood and shellfish is the specialty; the fresh calamari (dusted with flour and lightly fried in garlic, lemon butter, and wine) and the oyster bar are noted attractions. *185 Park Ave., 6th Floor, tel. 408/971–1700. Reservations accepted. AE, DC, MC, V. No lunch weekends.*

$ **Original Joe's.** Hearty Italian specialties, along with steaks, chops,
San Jose   and hamburgers, are served until 1:30 AM here in a warm cognac-and-green dining room with seating in cozy booths, and at a convivial counter overlooking the open kitchen. This downtown favorite has been in business since 1956. *301 S. 1st St., tel. 408/292–7030. No reservations. AE, D, MC, V.*

$ **Pizzeria Uno.** Some say that eating at one is eating at them all. Still,
Santa Clara   Pizzeria Uno is consistent, reliable, and tasty. You can get the same gourmet deep-dish pizzas here as in the Chicago flagship, classic pies that predate Wolfgang Puck's versions by 45 years. *2570 El Camino Real, tel. 408/241–5152. Reservations for 10 or more. AE, DC, MC, V.*

Lodging

All of the big hotel chains are represented in the valley: Best Western, Howard Johnson, Marriott, Days Inn, Hilton, Holiday Inn, Quality Inn, and Sheraton. Many dot the King's Highway—El Camino Real. If character is more important than luxury, seek out a smaller inn.

Category	Cost*
$$$$	over $175
$$$	$110–$175
$$	$75–$110
$	under $75

All prices are for a double room, excluding 9¹/₂% room tax (10% in San Jose).

$$$$ **Fairmont Hotel.** If you're accustomed to the best, this is the place to stay. Affiliated with the famous San Francisco hotel of the same name, this downtown gem opened in 1987, and offers the utmost in luxury and sophistication. Get lost in the lavish lobby sofas under dazzling chandeliers while waiting for your Louis Vuitton collection to be delivered to your room, or dip your well-traveled feet in the rooftop pool, making rings in the exotic palms mirrored in the water. The rooms have every imaginable comfort, from down pillows and custom-designed comforters to oversize bath towels changed twice a day. The hotel offers complimentary HBO, and has accessible rooms for travelers with disabilities. *170 S. Market St. at Fairmont Pl., San Jose 95113, tel. 408/998–1900 or 800/527–4727, fax 408/280–0394. 500 rooms, 41 suites. Facilities: 5 restaurants, 24-hr room service, lounge, fitness center, business center, nonsmoking floors, currency exchange, valet parking. AE, D, DC, MC, V.*

$$$ **Hotel De Anza.** This lushly appointed French Mediterranean–style hotel, opened in 1931, has an Art Deco facade, hand-painted ceilings, and an enclosed terrace with towering palms and dramatic fountains. You'll also find many business amenities, including computers, cellular phones, and secretarial services. *233 W. Santa Clara St., San Jose 95113, tel. 408/286–1000 or 800/843–3700, fax 408/286–0500. 100 rooms. Facilities: restaurant, jazz club, exercise room, breakfast buffet, complimentary late-night snacks, valet parking. AE, DC, MC, V.*

$$$ **The Inn at Saratoga.** This five-story, European-style inn is actually
★ only 10 minutes from the cultural action of Saratoga, yet it's far in spirit from bustling Silicon Valley, with its aura privacy and calm. All rooms have secluded sitting alcoves overlooking a peaceful creek, and the hotel's sun-dappled patio provides a quiet retreat. Modern business conveniences are available but discreetly hidden. *20645 Fourth St., Saratoga 95070, tel. 408/867–5020, 800/338–5020, or 800/543–5020 in CA, fax 408/741–0981. 46 rooms. Facilities: meeting room; executive services; complimentary breakfast, newspaper, and afternoon tea and wine. AE, DC, MC, V.*

$$ **Sundowner Inn.** Exploiting the Valley's passion for high-tech machinery, this contemporary hotel offers voice mail, computer data ports, and remote-control televisions with ESPN, HBO, CNN, Nintendo, and VCRs, which you can use to play complimentary tapes from the library of 500. There's also a fleet of mountain bikes and a library full of best-sellers you can borrow. The complimentary breakfast buffet is served poolside. *504 Ross Dr., Sunnyvale 94089, tel. 408/734–9900 or 800/223–9901, fax 408/ 747–0580. 105 rooms, 12 suites. Facilities: exercise room, heated outdoor pool, sauna, laundry and valet service, nonsmoking rooms, meeting room. AE, DC, MC, V.*

$ **Motel 6.** Everything the name suggests, Motel 6 is the quintessential highway motel—basic and conveniently located. *3208 El Camino*

Real, Santa Clara, 95051, tel. 408/241–0200 or 800/437–7486. 99 rooms. Facilities: pool, parking, free local calls. AE, DC, MC, V.

Excursion to Marine World Africa USA

This wildlife theme park is one of Northern California's most popular attractions. It has been a phenomenal success since moving in 1986 from a crowded site south of San Francisco to Vallejo, about an hour's drive northeast. The 160-acre park features animals of the land, sea, and air performing in shows, roaming in natural habitats, strolling among park visitors with their trainers. Among the "stars" are killer whales, dolphins, camels, elephants, sea lions, chimpanzees, and a troupe of human water-skiers (April–October). The newest attraction, "Shark Experience," takes visitors on a walk in an acrylic tunnel through a 300,000-gallon coral reef habitat with 15 species of sharks and rays and 100 species of tropical fish.

The park is owned by the Marine World Foundation, a nonprofit organization devoted to educating the public about the world's wildlife. The shows and close-up looks at exotic animals serve that purpose without neglecting entertainment. The park is a family attraction, so it's not just for youngsters. For additional sightseeing, visitors can reach the park on a high-speed ferry from San Francisco, a trip that offers unusual vistas through San Francisco Bay and San Pablo Bay. *Marine World Pkwy., Vallejo, tel. 707/643–6722. Admission: $23.95 adults, $19.95 senior citizens 60 and over, $16.95 children 4–12. Open summer, daily 9:30–6:45; rest of year and some school holidays, Wed.–Sun. 9:30–5.*

Arriving and Departing

By Car Take I–80 east to Marine World Parkway in Vallejo. The trip takes one hour one-way. Parking is $3 at the park.

By Bus **Greyhound Lines** (tel. 800/231–2222) runs buses from downtown San Francisco to Vallejo. You can take the **BART** train (tel. 415/992– BART) to El Cerrito Del Norte Station and transfer to **Vallejo Transit** line (tel. 707/648–4666) to get to the park.

By Ferry **Red and White Fleet's** (tel. 415/546–2896) high-speed ferry departs mornings each day that the park is open, from Pier 41 at Fisherman's Wharf. It arrives in Vallejo an hour later. Round-trip service allows five hours to visit the park. Excursion tickets are $21–$38 and include park admission.

7 The Gold Country

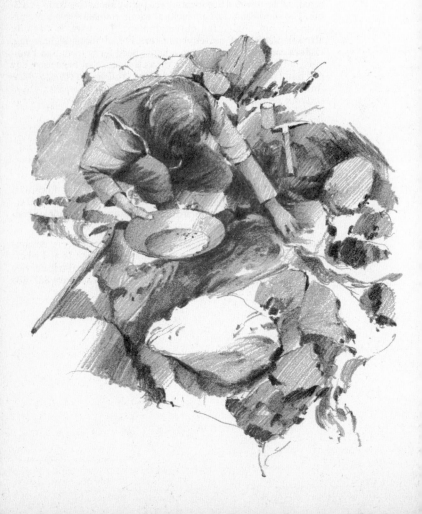

By Rosemary
Freskos

California had its real beginning in Coloma on January 24, 1848, when James Marshall discovered a gold nugget in the tailrace of a sawmill he was building for John Sutter on the South Fork of the American River. The news spread like wildfire when President Polk confirmed the discovery in his State of the Union speech on December 5, 1848. As gold fever seized the nation, California's total population of 15,000 swelled to 265,000 within three years—44,000 newcomers arrived by ship in San Francisco in the first 10 months alone, the majority of them single men under 40. The state would never be the same.

Although the boom towns of the Sierra foothills were virtually abandoned when the gold ran out, today the Gold Country lies waiting to be discovered again, ripe with hidden treasure. You can still join a prospecting expedition and try your hand at panning for the flakes deposited by millennia of trickling streams, but the chief reward here is the chance to walk into the past.

Route 49 winds the 200-mile length of the historic mining area, linking the towns of Nevada City, Grass Valley, Placerville, Sutter Creek, and Sonora, each of which has enough attractions for a weekend of exploring. With populations of generally less than 10,000 souls, these towns have an unspoiled, homey feel to them, which attracts those who are content to live modestly amid the natural beauty of these rolling hills.

Route 49 is only two lanes, however, and it can get clogged with tourists on hot summer weekends; a better time to come here is between March and May, when the weather is mild and the flowering trees are in bloom, or during the autumn harvest. The foothills, with their cool weather, are perfect for growing sweet pears and apples, and vineyards also prosper in this climate. The Shenandoah Valley, near Plymouth, is home to 17 wineries, and El Dorado County around Placerville has 14 wineries. They evoke memories of the quieter era of California's other, now-famous wine regions.

Travelers can experience the region's quiet lifestyle at bed-and-breakfast inns, many in exquisite Victorian buildings that have been taken down to the studs and lovingly restored. Their sumptuous breakfasts and period atmosphere offer a comfortable and romantic base from which to explore tumbledown villages and historic sites that speak of the 19th century.

The Gold Rush's mother lode was a gold-bearing quartz vein 150 miles long, lying between the Sierra ranges and the central valley. It ranged in width from 2 miles to only a few yards. By 1865 more than $750 million in gold had been taken from the stretch between Mariposa and Georgetown. Ironically, Sutter and Marshall never got rich from their discovery, nor did the Mexican government, which had owned the foothills but sold them to the United States about a week after Marshall found the nugget.

The northern California cities of Sacramento, San Francisco, and Stockton grew quickly to meet the needs of the surrounding gold fields. When California became a state, in 1850, Sacramento was made the state capital. Saloon keepers and canny merchants realized that the real gold was to be made from the '49ers' pockets. Potatoes and onions sold for as much as $1 apiece, and entrepreneurs like storekeeper Samuel Brannan became millionaires.

Boom times for the Gold Country ended within 10 years, however. While the rest of the world's economy was stimulated by California's gold, this region became a quiet backwater. The gold-mining companies remained profitable through the 1920s, extracting slate and gravel from the foothills as well as gold, but timber and farming were the main industries. Sacramento, however, remained the state capital, and in the 1950s a freeway (U.S. 50) was built, linking Sacramento to the casinos of Lake Tahoe.

By the 1960s the scars left on the landscape by the mining had largely healed. To promote tourism, townspeople restored vintage structures, including wood sidewalks, and gathered or rebuilt mining relics as museums and recreation areas, bringing to life this extraordinary episode in American history, as vividly described by Mark Twain and Bret Harte. The Gold Country may still be a backwater, but it generously repays leisurely exploration.

Essential Information

Important Addresses and Numbers

Tourist Information
Amador County Chamber of Commerce (30 S. Rte. 49-88, Box 596, Jackson 95642, tel. 209/223–0350). Auburn Area Chamber of Commerce (601 Lincoln Way, Auburn 95603, tel. 916/885–5616). Columbia State Historic Park (Box 151, Columbia 95310, tel. 209/532–4301 or 209/532–0150). El Dorado County Chamber of Commerce (542 Main St., Placerville 95667, tel. 916/621–5885). Golden Chain Council of the Mother Lode (Box 7046, Auburn 95604). Nevada City Chamber of Commerce (132 Main St., Nevada City 95959, tel. 916/265–2692 or 800/655–6569). Nevada County Chamber of Commerce (248 Mill St., Grass Valley 95945, tel. 916/273–4667; in CA, 800/655–4667). Placer County Visitors Information Center (13460 Lincoln Way, Auburn, take Forest Hill Exit off I–80, tel. 916/887–2111; in CA, 800/427–6463). Sacramento Convention and Visitors Bureau (1421 K St., Sacramento 95814, tel. 916/264–7777). Old Sacramento Visitor Information Center (1104 Front St., Old Sacramento, tel. 916/442–7644). Tuolumne County Visitors Bureau (Box 4020, 55 W. Stockton St., Sonora 95370, tel. 209/533–4420 or 800/446–1333).

Emergencies
Dial 911 for police and ambulance in an emergency.

Doctors
These Sacramento hospitals have 24-hour emergency rooms: Mercy Hospital of Sacramento Promptcare (4001 J St., tel. 916/453–4424), Sutter General Hospital (2801 L St., tel. 916/733–3003), and Sutter Memorial Hospital (52nd and F Sts., tel. 916/733–1000).

Arriving and Departing

By Plane
Sacramento Metropolitan Airport, 12 miles northwest of downtown Sacramento on I–5, is served by American (tel. 800/433–7300), Continental (tel. 800/525–0280), Delta (tel. 800/453–9417), Northwest (tel. 800/225–2525), Southwest (tel. 800/531–5601), and United (tel. 800/241–6522). It is an hour's drive from Placerville, and a little closer to Auburn.

San Francisco International Airport (*see* Chapter 6) is about two hours from Sacramento.

By Car
Sacramento lies at the junction of Interstate 5 and Interstate 80, 90 miles northeast of San Francisco. It's about an eight-hour drive north from Los Angeles. I–80 continues northeast through the Gold Country toward Reno, about three hours from Sacramento; Lake Tahoe is two hours east of Sacramento on U.S. 50.

By Train **Amtrak** (tel. 800/872–7245) trains stop in Oakland, where you can connect with frequent train service to Sacramento, a three-hour trip stopping in Berkeley, Richmond, Martinez, and Davis. Three daily shuttle buses connect the Oakland Amtrak station and San Francisco's Ferry Building (30 Embarcadero at the foot of Market St.).

By Bus **Greyhound-Trailways** serves Sacramento, Auburn, and Placerville. It's a two-hour trip from San Francisco to the Sacramento station at 7th and L streets (tel. 800/231–2222 or 916/587–3822).

Getting Around

By Car This is the most convenient way to see the Gold Country, since most of the area's towns are too small to provide a base for public transportation. From Sacramento, three highways fan out toward the east, all intersecting with Route 49: I–80 heads 30 miles northeast to Auburn; U.S. 50 goes east 40 miles to Placerville; and Route 16 angles southeast 45 miles to Plymouth. Route 49 is an excellent two-lane road that winds and climbs through the foothills and valleys, linking the principal Gold Country towns. However, it's about 130 miles from Nevada City down to Sonora—too long to do the whole stretch in one day and still have time for sightseeing.

By Bus **Sacramento Transit Authority** (tel. 916/321–2877) buses and light rail trains transport passengers in Sacramento. Buses run 5 AM–10 PM; trains 4:30 AM–12:30 AM.

Guided Tours

Gold Prospecting Expeditions (18170 Main St., Box 1040, Jamestown 95327, tel. 209/984–4653, fax 209/984–0711) offers one-hour gold-panning excursions, two-week prospecting trips, and a good deal in between. **Outdoor Adventure River Specialists (O.A.R.S.)** (Box 67, Angels Camp 95222, tel. 209/736–4677 or 800/446–2411, fax 209/736–2902) operates a wide range of white-water rafting trips on the Stanislas, American, Merced, and Tuolumne rivers from late March through early October. **River Rat & Co.** (Box 822, Lotus 95651, tel. 916/622–6632) operates one- and two-day rafting trips on the north and middle forks of the American River. For beginners and up, the 21 miles of white water make for an adventurous, full-day trip. **Wells & Associates Tours** (542 Main St., Placerville 95667, tel. 916/621–5885 or 916/626–5117) runs guided tours of the Gold Country, as well as unusual snorkel/scuba-equipped underwater gold prospecting in local rivers. **Capital City Cruises** (1401 Garden Hwy., Suite 125, Sacramento 95833, tel. 916/921–1111) runs two-hour narrated cruises, as well as brunch, dinner-dance, and murder-mystery cruises, on the Sacramento River year-round on the *River City Queen* and the steamer *Elizabeth Louise*. *Spirit of Sacramento* (Channel Star Excursions, 1207 Front St., No. 18, Sacramento 95814, tel. 916/522–2933 or 800/433–0263) is a paddlewheel riverboat, successor to the *Matthew McKinley*, that offers a variety of excursions, including a one-hour narrated cruise, happy hour, dinner, and luncheon cruises, and a champagne brunch.

Exploring the Gold Country

The state capital, Sacramento, is the major city in this part of California, although Route 49 is really the Gold Country's heart. You may want to base yourself in Sacramento and then choose one Gold Country town for a day's excursion; otherwise, stay overnight (preferably in a bed-and-breakfast) in one of the historic towns along Route 49.

If you really want to sightsee in depth, it may be wise to limit yourself to one portion of the road. Grass Valley and Nevada City lie north of I–80. Auburn, Coloma, and Placerville are clustered along the middle section, between I–80 and U.S. 50. South of Route 16 is a string of charming towns from Sutter Creek to Jamestown.

Highlights for First-Time Visitors

California State Railroad Museum, Sacramento
Columbia State Historic Park
Crocker Art Museum, Sacramento
Empire Mine, Grass Valley
Gold Bug Mine, Placerville
Marshall Gold Discovery State Historic Park
Sutter Creek
Sutter's Fort, Sacramento

Sacramento

Numbers in the margin correspond to points of interest on the Sacramento map.

The gateway to the Gold Country, Sacramento has its own slice of Gold Rush history, as the point from which gold prospectors fanned out to seek their fortunes. Sacramento predates the Gold Rush, but came into its own as a center for financial transactions and the shipping of provisions to the gold fields. It ultimately became the western terminus of the Pony Express, the transcontinental railroad, and the telegraph.

Downtown is ideal for walking. Its flat, wide streets are laid out in a grid, so it's easy to locate sights. Along the Sacramento River (take the J St. exit off I–5), **Old Sacramento** is a 28-acre area with more than 100 restored buildings, shops, and restaurants. Wood sidewalks and horse-drawn carriages on cobblestone streets evoke images of the late 19th century, and river cruises and train rides bring Gold Rush history to life. *Call 619/558–3912 for schedule.*

❶ The **Visitor Information Center** (1104 Front St., tel. 916/442–7644) is housed in a former depot for passengers and freight bound down the river to San Francisco by steamship. *Open daily 9–5.*

❷ The **Eagle Theater** (925 Front St.) was built in 1849, and was California's first. A reconstruction was completed in 1976, and the
❸ theater is in regular use today. The building housing the **Sacramento History Museum** was once the nerve center of the town, containing the mayor's offices, council chambers, jail, and policemen's quarters, among other things. It now offers a streamlined, well-presented introduction to the history of Sacramento and its surroundings, complete with gold pans with which you can sift, an Indian thatched hut, memorabilia from the world wars, and a colorful stack of turn-of-the-century cans of local produce. *101 I St., tel. 916/264–7057. Admission: $3 adults, $1.50 children 6–17. Open Wed.–Sun. 10–5.*

❹ Old Sacramento's biggest draw is the **California State Railroad Museum,** once the terminus of the Transcontinental and Sacramento Valley railroads. The 100,000-square-foot museum is the largest of its kind in North America, displaying 21 locomotives and railroad

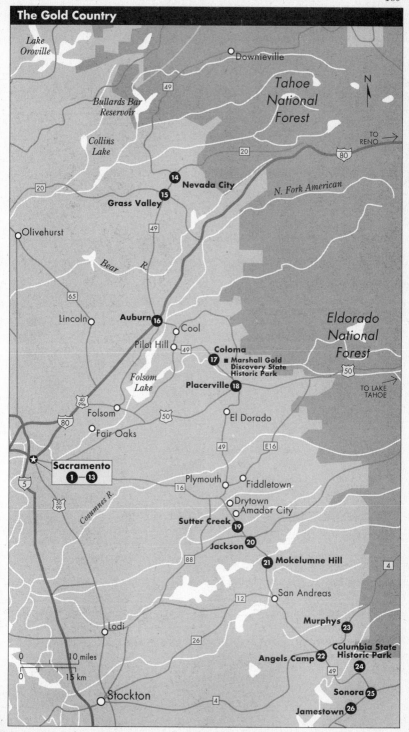

The Gold Country

Lake Oroville

Downieville

Tahoe National Forest

Bullards Bar Reservoir

Collins Lake

49

20

14 **Nevada City**

20

15 **Grass Valley**

49

TO RENO

80

N. Fork American

Olivehurst

Bear R.

65

Lincoln

Auburn 16

Cool

Pilot Hill

49

Coloma

17 ■ Marshall Gold Discovery State Historic Park

Eldorado National Forest

50

TO LAKE TAHOE

Placerville 18

Folsom Lake

Folsom

50

El Dorado

80

40 99e

Fair Oaks

49

E16

Sacramento

1 ― 13

5

50 99

Cosumnes R.

Plymouth

Fiddletown

16

Drytown

Amador City

Sutter Creek 19

Jackson 20

21 Mokelumne Hill

88

4

12

San Andreas

Lodi

26

Murphys 23

Columbia State Historic Park

Angels Camp 22

24

49

Sonora 25

Stockton

4

Jamestown 26

0   10 miles

0   15 km

Sacramento

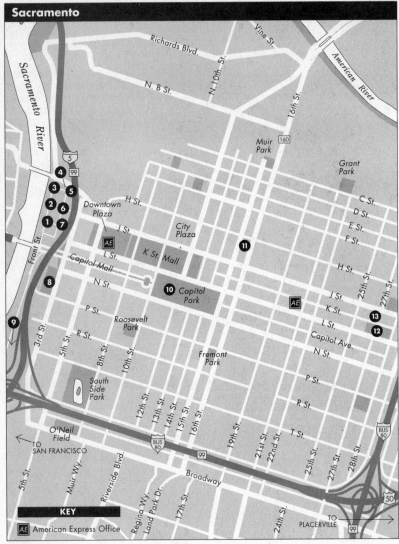

KEY

AE American Express Office

B.F. Hastings
Building, **6**

California Citizen-
Soldier Museum, **7**

California State
Railroad Museum, **4**

Crocker Art
Museum, **8**

Eagle Theater, **2**

Governor's
Mansion, **11**

Huntington, Hopkins
& Co. Store, **5**

Sacramento History
Museum, **3**

State Capitol
building, **10**

State Indian
Museum, **13**

Sutter's Fort, **12**

Towe Ford
Museum, **9**

Visitor's Information
Center, **1**

cars, and 46 exhibits. You can walk through a post-office car and peer into the cubbyholes and canvas bags of mail, or go through a sleeping car that simulates the swaying on the roadbed and the flashing lights of a passing town at night. *125 I St., tel. 916/448–4466. Admission: $5 adults, $2 children 6–12, under 6 free. Open daily 10–5.*

Your ticket to the railroad museum also gets you into the **Central Pacific Passenger Station,** a restored 1813 depot across the street (entrance on Front St.). Rides on a steam-powered excursion train make a 40-minute loop along the riverfront. *Train fare: $4 adults, $2 children. Trains run May–Labor Day, weekends 10–5; Oct.–Apr., 1st weekend of month, noon–3.*

5 The **Huntington, Hopkins & Co. Store** hardware exhibit (111 I St., open daily 11–5) gives a good idea of the kind of store that supplied prospectors during the Gold Rush—it still stocks a variety of mer-
6 chandise typical of the period. The **B. F. Hastings Building** (2nd and J Sts., open daily 10–5) includes the first Sacramento chambers of the California State Supreme Court, built in 1854.

7 The **California Citizen-Soldier Museum** specializes in militia and military history, from pre-statehood to modern times. The documents and memorabilia on display include uniforms and military memorabilia. *1119 2nd St., tel. 916/442–2883. Admission: $2.25 adults, $1.50 senior citizens, $1 children 5–17. Open Tues.–Sun. 10–5.*

8 The **Crocker Art Museum,** a few blocks from old Sacramento, is the oldest art museum in the American West, with a collection of European, Asian, and Californian art, including *Sunday Morning in the Mines,* a large canvas depicting the mining industry of the 1850s. The museum's lobby and magnificent ballroom retain the original 1870s woodwork, plaster moldings, and imported tiles. *216 O St., tel. 916/264–5423. Admission: $3 adults, $1.50 children 7–17. Open Thurs. 10–9, Wed.–Sun. 10–5. Closed Dec.*

9 The **Towe Ford Museum** contains a collection of more than 150 vintage cars, including every year and model manufactured by the Ford company for 50 years, starting from 1903. *2200 Front St., tel. 916/442–6802. Admission: $5 adults, $4.50 senior citizens, $2.50 children 14–18, $1 children 5–13. Open daily 10–6.*

10 The California **state capitol building** was built in 1869 and recently underwent extensive restoration. The lacy plasterwork of the rotunda, 120 feet high, has the complexity and color of a Fabergé Easter egg. There are free guided tours of the building, as well as its 40-acre park with magnificent trees dating from 1870. Plants and shrubs from all over the world are clearly identified. *Capitol Mall and 10th St., tel. 916/324–0333. Admission free. Hourly tours daily 9–4.*

11 The historic **Governor's Mansion,** built in 1877, is a 15-room Victorian house with furnishings that reflect the tastes of previous governors and first ladies. It was home to 13 California governors—until Ronald Reagan turned it down in 1967. It is no longer occupied. *16th and H Sts., tel. 916/323–3047. Admission: $2 adults, $1 children 6–12. Tours on the hour 10–4.*

12 **Sutter's Fort,** Sacramento's earliest settlement, was founded by Swiss immigrant John Augustus Sutter in 1839. Self-guided tours with audio wands explain the exhibits, which include a cooper and blacksmith's shops, bakery, prison, living quarters, and livestock areas. *27th and L Sts., tel. 916/445–4422. Admission: $2 adults, $1 children 6–12. Open daily 10–5.*

13 Directly behind Sutter's Fort, the **State Indian Museum** displays arts and crafts made by California's earliest inhabitants. *2601 K St., tel. 916/324–0971. Admission: $2 adults, $1 children 6–17. Open daily 10–5.*

Route 49

Numbers in the margin correspond to points of interest on the Gold Country map.

14 About 30 miles north of I–80 on Route 49, **Nevada City,** once known as the Queen City of the Northern Mines, is the most complete gold town left in California. It is a thriving, affluent community that fortunately escaped the progress that turned Grass Valley, 4 miles away, into a far-flung suburb of the Bay area. Historic buildings cannot be torn down here, and renovation has only enhanced the town's style. The downtown is filled with antiques shops, galleries, a winery, a microbrewery, and many bed-and-breakfast inns, as well as more fine restaurants than any other Gold Country town. Horse-drawn carriage tours add to the romance of winding streets lit at night by gaslights.

At one point in the the 1850s, Nevada City was as big a place as Sacramento and San Francisco. The **Nevada Theatre** on Broad Street, built in 1865, is California's oldest theater in continuous use, with plenty of cultural events catering to the town's affluent population. Behind the theater is the **Miners Foundry** (325 Spring St.), also built in 1865, a cavernous building that now serves as a cultural center offering plays, concerts, and a wide range of events that include a Victorian Christmas fair, a teddy-bear convention, and antiques shows, as well as themed period parties.

Time Out   For a more palpable reminder of the past, stop at tiny **Cousin Jack Pasties** (239 Commercial St., tel. 619/265–4260), where the specialty is Cornish pasties—meat-filled turnovers that were the mainstay of gold miners who emigrated from the tin and copper mines of Cornwall, England.

15 South along Route 49, **Grass Valley** is worth a full day's browsing. More than half of California's total gold production was extracted from the mines of Nevada County, and some of the area's most interesting exhibits on gold mining are to be found here.

The **Nevada County Chamber of Commerce** (248 Mill St., tel. 916/273–4667) is housed in a reproduction of the home that once stood on this site and was owned by notorious dancer Lola Montez when she moved to Grass Valley in the early 1850s; her bathtub is still here. Built in 1851, the landmark **Holbrooke Hotel** (1212 W. Main St., tel. 916/273–1353) in its day hosted not only Lola Montez but Mark Twain, Ulysses S. Grant, and a stream of U.S. presidents. Its saloon is one of the oldest still operating west of the Mississippi.

The **Empire Mine** was worked from 1850 right up to 1956, and was one of California's richest quartz mines. An estimated 5.8 million ounces of gold were brought up from its 367 miles of underground passages. The mine is now a State Historic Park, and its buildings and grounds are open year round. Tours allow you to peer into the deep recesses of the mine and to view the owner's "cottage," with its exquisite woodwork. The visitors center has films and exhibits on mining and a picnic area. *10791 E. Empire St. (Empire St. exit south from Rte. 49), tel. 916/273–8522. Admission: $2 adults, $1 chil-*

dren 6–12. Open summer, daily 9–6; winter, daily 10–5. Tours and lectures daily in summer on the hour 11–4; weekends only in winter at 1 and 2.

The **North Star Power House and Pelton Wheel Exhibit** boasts a 32-foot-high Pelton wheel, the largest ever built. It was used to power mining operations, and is a forerunner of the modern water turbines that generate hydroelectricity. Period mining equipment and a stamp mill are also on display, as well as the largest operational Cornish pumps in the country, part of the legacy of the tin miners who migrated here from Cornwall in England. There are hands-on displays for children and a picnic area. *Allison Ranch Rd. and Mill St. (Empire St. exit north from Rte. 49), tel. 916/273–4255. Donation requested. Open May–Oct., daily 10–5.*

Time Out A tradition for more than 20 years, **Mrs. Dubblebee's Pasties** (251 S. Auburn St., tel. 916/272–7700) is famous for its Cornish pasties, with flaky, buttery crusts. Besides the traditional beef-filled pasties there are wonderful English scones and sweet pastries.

16 **Auburn,** at the intersection of Route 49 and I–80 (after Rte. 49 crosses under I–80, turn right on Lincoln St. and follow the signs), is a small old town with narrow, climbing streets, cobblestones, wooden sidewalks, and many original buildings. The **Bernhard Museum Complex,** built in 1851 as the Traveler's Hotel, now offers a glimpse of family life in the late-Victorian era, with a carriage house displaying several period conveyances. *291 Auburn-Folsom Rd., tel. 916/889–4156. Admission: $1 adults, 50¢ senior citizens over 65 and children 6–16. Open Tues.–Fri. 11–3, weekends noon–4.*

17 Twenty-five miles farther on is **Coloma,** where the California Gold Rush got started. John Sutter erected a sawmill here on the banks of the American River, and it was in the millrace that one of his employees, a wagon-builder named James Marshall, discovered gold in January 1848. "My eye was caught with the glimpse of something shining in the bottom of the ditch," he recalled later. Unfortunately, Marshall himself never found any more "color," as it came to be called.

Most of Coloma lies within **Marshall Gold Discovery State Historic Park.** Within six months of Marshall's discovery, 2,000 prospectors arrived in the area, and Coloma became the first Gold Rush town. Its population swelled rapidly to 10,000, but when reserves of the precious metal dwindled, the prospectors left as quickly as they had come. A replica of Sutter's mill, based on Marshall's drawings, now stands here, with Marshall's cabin and museum. There are picnic areas, and along the south fork of the American River are campgrounds, good fishing spots, and rafting. *Tel. 916/622–3470. Day use: $5 per car, $4 senior citizens. Park open daily 8 AM–sunset. Museum open summer, daily 10–5; Labor Day–Memorial Day, daily 10:30–4:30.*

18 Follow Route 49 south 10 miles into **Placerville,** one of the largest towns on Route 49, which has plenty of attractions. The town's original name was Hangtown, a graphic allusion to the summary nature of frontier justice. Placerville today has the distinction of being one of the only cities in the world to own a gold mine. The **Gold Bug Mine** has a fully lighted shaft that can be toured. A shaded stream runs through the park, and there are picnic facilities. *⁹/₁₀ mi off Rte. 50, north on Bedford Ave. to Gold Bug Park, tel. 916/642–5232. Admission: $1 adults, 50¢ children 5–16, for self-guided tour of mine. Open*

May–Sept., daily 10–4; late Mar.–Apr. and late Sept.–Oct., weekends 10–4.

If you have the time, take a leisurely drive around **Apple Hill,** an area filled with orchards and 14 vineyards, where roadside stands sell fresh produce, many wineries offer tastings, and picnic areas abound. Drive on U.S. 50 east from Placerville, turning off at the Camino exit (about 5 miles east of Route 49) for a swing into orchard country. Then return to U.S. 50 and go east to Route E–16, which angles southwest to Plymouth. This section of Amador County contains 17 wineries, mostly small family-run operations on scenic backroads. Robust Zinfandels are consistently produced, and these small local vintners have surprised wine experts with a broad new spectrum of wines. Call the **Amador County Chamber of Commerce** (tel. 209/223–0350) for schedules of tours and tastings, which are offered most weekends.

At Plymouth, the Fiddletown Road branches off Route 49. Follow it to visit tiny **Fiddletown,** with its rammed-earth adobe building, one of a few left in the state. There's also a museum here in the **Chew Kee** store, filled with 19th-century relics of the Chinese immigrants who came to the gold fields—complete with intact containers of herbs, drugs, and utensils. *Tel. 209/223–4131. Admission free. Open Apr.–Oct., Sat. 12–4 and by appointment.*

⑲ **Sutter Creek** is a well-kept, charming conglomeration of balconied buildings, Victorian homes, and neo–New England structures. The stores along the highway are worth visiting to hunt for works by the many local artisans and craftsmen. The town's raised wood sidewalks remind you of how muddy unpaved 19th-century roads could be.

⑳ Driving south from Sutter Creek, Route 49 climbs sharply, twists and turns, and then rewards you with a wonderful view of **Jackson,** county seat of Amador county, which once had the world's deepest and richest mines. An old white church sits on a knoll, its small cemetery spread out around it, and from this vantage point the brick buildings below seem to huddle together. The main road through town, Route 49, is lined with ordinary businesses, but the side streets harbor interesting museums, Victorian-era buildings, and a block-long historic district on South Main Street.

㉑ Seven miles south along Route 49 is the town of **Mokelumne Hill,** known as Moke Hill. Unlike busy Jackson, this little village is frozen in an earlier time. Many of the buildings are constructed of light-brown rhyolite tuff, a stone common in much of the Gold Country. Where there are sidewalks, they are wooden, as are the small, frail-looking houses on the hilly side streets.

㉒ Twenty miles farther down the highway is **Angels Camp,** famed chiefly for its jumping-frog contest held each May, based on Mark Twain's "The Jumping Frog of Calaveras County." At the north end of town is a museum with a collection of minerals and early artifacts. *Tel. 209/736–2963. Open Mar.–Labor Day, daily 10–3; Labor Day–Mar., Wed.–Sun. 10–3.*

㉓ East on Route 4, and less than 10 miles up the road, is **Murphys,** a town of white picket fences and Victorian houses. In **Murphys Hotel,** opened in 1856 as the Sperry & Perry and still operating, the guest register records the visits of Horatio Alger and Ulysses S. Grant, who joined the 19th-century swarms visiting the giant sequoias in **Calaveras Big Trees State Park,** about 15 miles farther east on Route 4. *Tel. 209/795–2334. Day use: $5 per car. Open daily.*

Another spectacle of nature, 4 miles out of Murphys, on the Vallecito–Columbia highway, is **Moaning Cavern,** a vast underground chamber with ancient crystalline rock formations. *Tel. 209/736–2708. Admission: $5.75 adults, $2.75 children 6–12. Open summer, daily 9–6; winter, daily 10–5.*

Back on Route 49 driving south, there is a breathtaking ride across the Stanislaus River bridge over the Melones Reservoir. It's a vivid example of the rugged terrain in a part of California where the rivers have dug deep canyons. Horse-drawn wagons must have found it rough going.

㉔ A well-marked turnoff leads to **Columbia State Historic Park,** a pleasingly executed mix of preservation and restoration. The "Gem of the Southern Mines" comes as close to a Gold Rush town in its heyday as you can get. You can ride a stagecoach and pan for gold; street musicians give lively performances in summer; and there is a blacksmith working at his anvil. Restored or reconstructed buildings include a Wells Fargo Express office, Masonic temple, stores, saloons, two elegant hotels, a firehouse, churches, a school, and a newspaper office. All are staffed to simulate a working 1850s town. The Fallon Theater presents plays year round. *Tel. 209/532–4301. Admission free. Exhibits and demonstrations daily 10–6. Museum open 10–5.*

㉕ Route 49 is the main street in **Sonora.** Don't miss the beautiful **St. James Episcopal Church,** built in 1860, the second-oldest frame church in California. In winter, the ski traffic passes through Sonora on the way along Route 108 to Dodge Ridge ski area 30 miles east.

The road turns west for a few miles out of Sonora, and heads to ㉖ **Jamestown,** whose **Railtown 1897 State Historic Park** includes 26 acres of trains, a station, a roundhouse, and facilities for maintaining trains. There are slide presentations, guided tours, and train excursions on the weekends. *Tel. 209/984–3953. Admission: $2 adults, $1.25 children; train excursions $9 adults, $4.50 children. Open daily 10–4.*

The best hotel in town during the Gold Rush was the **National Hotel** (77 Main St., *see* Lodging, *below*), built in 1859 and now a landmarked historic site. The saloon, with its vintage redwood bar, evokes vivid images of Gold Rush glory.

Off the Beaten Track

At the northern end of Route 49, **Downieville** is one of the prettiest of the Gold Rush towns. Stone, brick, and frame buildings seem to cling to the mountainsides or hug the banks of the fast-moving Yuba River. Along the quiet streets, lovely old houses have been well maintained or restored. The spare and elegant **Methodist church,** which dates from 1865, is the oldest Protestant church in continuous use in the state. Drive out Main Street past the last bridge and take a short walk past the Pacific Gas and Electric station to the crystal-clear Yuba River. The river forms pools as it rushes over boulders, and it's a favorite swimming spot.

Shopping

Downtown Sacramento's **K Street Mall** and the new **Downtown Plaza** each have an assortment of shops, restaurants, and galleries to satisfy every whim. Underground parking is reasonably priced or free with purchase. In Sacramento's fashionable Fair Oaks suburb, the upscale **Pavilions Mall** (Fair Oaks Blvd. near Howe Ave.) is a two-level outdoor mall of designer boutiques and trendy restaurants. Be sure to stop by **David Berkeley's** (tel. 916/929–4422), an amalgam of country store and sophisticated European food shop filled with beautiful things to eat and drink—pick up some epicurean takeout, and eat at one of the small tables throughout the mall. The owner, David Berkeley, has been wine consultant to the White House for nearly a decade, and the shop has extensive wine offerings.

Dining and Lodging

Dining Given the small population of the Gold Country, there is a disproportionate number of good restaurants, especially in Nevada City. Many of the menus are ambitious: In addition to standard American, Italian, and Mexican fare, there is Continental, French, and California cuisine, with an emphasis on innovation and the freshest ingredients. The national fast-food chains are few and far between—there just aren't enough people here to support them. It's not difficult, though, to find the makings for a good picnic in most Gold Country towns.

Sacramento has recently enjoyed a period of expansion, and offers a wide range of eating places for its growing population; most restaurants listed are located in Old Sacramento or downtown. Unless otherwise noted, dress is casual.

Highly recommended restaurants are indicated by a star ★.

Category	Cost*
$$$$	over $35
$$$	$25–$35
$$	$15–$25
$	under $15

per person for a three-course meal, excluding drinks, service, and tax

Lodging Among the treasures of the Gold Country today are its inns, many of them beautifully restored buildings dating back to the 1850s and 1860s and furnished with period pieces. If you came here for the history, there's no better way to get a taste of it. In Sacramento, most of the lodgings listed are all in the downtown area, close to Old Sacramento, the capitol, and Sutter's Fort.

Highly recommended hotels are indicated by a star ★.

Category	Cost*
$$$$	over $100
$$$	$75–$100
$$	$50–$75
$	under $50

All prices are for a double room, excluding tax.

Amador City
Dining

Ballads. Contemporary American cuisine is served here—a seasonally changing selection of seafood, poultry, and meat, as well as vegetarian dishes. Tempting appetizers include smoked duck with red-onion marmalade, polenta with wild-mushroom ragout, and spinach salad with scallops and peppers. You'll enjoy the imaginative presentations and interesting wine list. *14220 Rte. 49, tel. 209/267–5403. Reservations advised. AE, MC, V. No lunch. Closed Wed. $$*

Dining and
Lodging

Imperial Hotel. This 1879 hotel has been restored by the present innkeepers, Messrs. Sherrill and Martin, with just the right amounts of flair, pizzazz, comfort, and style. Each of the six rooms is decorated differently; most have custom touches such as furniture painted by a local artist. The modern bathrooms are equipped with heated towel stands and hair dryers. All rooms have views of the quiet, tiny town and the stream below. There's a garden courtyard, restaurant, and bar on the street level (reservations are advised), serving breakfast, dinner, and Sunday brunch. The Continental/American cuisine includes such dishes as fruit-stuffed pork loin with molasses sauce, Cajun prawns with Creole sauce, and mushrooms in pesto sauce over linguine. *Box 195, Rte. 49, 95601, tel. 209/267–9172 or 800/242–5594, fax 209/267–9249. 6 rooms with bath. Facilities: restaurant, bar. 2-night minimum weekends. AE, D, MC, V. $$*

Auburn
Dining

Butterworth's. Housed in a handsome Victorian mansion on a hillside overlooking Old Auburn, this restaurant features California cuisine with a Continental flair, with copious servings and a Sunday brunch. *1522 Lincoln Way, tel. 916/885–0249. Reservations accepted. AE, MC, V. No weekend lunch. $$*

★ **Headquarter House.** This restaurant is set on a hilltop within the Dunipace Angus Ranch, with a lounge on the top floor overlooking pine trees and a nine-hole golf course. The varied menu emphasizes California cuisine, with a good choice of fresh seafood. *14500 Musso Rd., tel. 916/878–1906. Reservations advised. AE, D, DC, MC, V. Closed Mon., Tues. $$*

Cafe Delicias. Located in a picturesque building in Old Auburn, this Mexican restaurant has an extensive menu, and the helpings are generous. One dinner choice is *carne asada a la Tampiqueña*—steak grilled with spices, onions, and bell peppers, served with a cheese enchilada, rice, and beans. *1591 Lincoln Way, tel. 916/885–2050. No reservations. AE, D, MC, V. $*

Lodging

Auburn Inn. This beige and brown multistory inn is exceptionally well maintained. The decor is contemporary, in teal and pastel colors. There are king- and queen-size beds, suites, nonsmoking rooms, and rooms with facilities for the handicapped. *1875 Auburn Ravine Rd., Foresthill exit north from I–80, 95603, tel. 916/885–1800 or 800/272–1444, fax 916/888–6424. 81 rooms. Facilities: pool, spa, laundry. AE, DC, MC, V. $$*

Country Squire Inn. This three-story motel is built around a spacious central area and has modern rooms decorated in browns and blues. Suites are available. There is a restaurant next door. *13480 Lincoln Way, Foresthill exit east from I–80, 95603, tel. 916/885–7025, fax 916/885–9503. 80 rooms. Facilities: pool, spa. Pets allowed. AE, D, DC, MC, V. $–$$*

Coloma
Dining and
Lodging
★

Vineyard House. This 1878 country inn is on the site of a prize-winning winery; the ruins of the wine cellars lie behind flower gardens. Each room is decorated differently, inspired by characters from the 1800s, and furnishings are authentic antiques. The restaurant is a series of small dining rooms with fireplaces or wood-burning stoves, flower-painted chandeliers, and early California memorabilia. Traditional American comfort food is featured—chicken, beef, seafood, and pasta. Specials include pork sausage with polenta, calamari, and braised rabbit. The cozy basement bar with hand-cut granite walls was once an auxiliary jail. *Box 176, Cold Springs Rd., off Rte. 49, 95613, tel. 916/622–2217, fax 209/622–1852. 7 rooms, 6 with shared bath. Facilities: restaurant (dinner only; May–Sept., Wed.–Sun.; Oct.–Dec., Thurs.–Sun.; Jan.–Apr., Fri.–Sun.), bar. No pets. Smoking restricted. AE, MC, V. $$–$$$*

Lodging **Coloma Country Inn.** A restored Victorian bed-and-breakfast built in 1852, this inn is set on 5 acres of state-park land and offers fishing and canoeing on its own pond. The rooms have antique double beds and private sitting areas; the decor features quilts, stenciled friezes, and fresh flowers. Country breakfasts are served. Hot-air ballooning and white-water rafting can be arranged. Reservations recommended. *Box 502, 345 High St., 95613, tel. 916/622–6919. 5 rooms, 2 with shared bath. Advance notice needed for children. No pets. No smoking. No credit cards. $$$*

Columbia **City Hotel.** The rooms in this restored 1856 hostelry are elaborately
Dining and furnished with period antiques. Two rooms have balconies overlook-
Lodging ing Main Street, and the four parlor rooms open onto a second-floor sitting room. Rooms have private half-baths with showers nearby; robes and slippers are provided. Continental breakfast is served in the upstairs parlor; lunch, dinner, and weekend brunch are available in the restaurant, which serves California cuisine, using fresh local produce stylishly prepared. The wine cellar is one of the finest in the state. An adjoining bar, also restored, is called the What Cheer Saloon. *Main St., Columbia State Park, Box 1870, 95310, tel. 209/532–1479, fax 209/532–7027. 10 rooms with ½ bath. Facilities: restaurant ($$$, open Tues.–Sun.), bar, saloon. No pets. AE, MC, V. $$–$$$*

Lodging **Fallon Hotel.** The state of California restored this 1857 hotel to Victorian grandeur. The lobby and rooms are furnished with 1890s antiques. Each accommodation has a private half-bath; there are also men's and women's showers. Continental breakfast is served; if you occupy one of the five balcony rooms, you can sit outside with your coffee and watch the town wake up. One room is equipped for visitors with disabilities. *Washington St., Columbia State Park, next to Fallon House Theater, Box 1870, 95310, tel. 209/532–1470. 14 rooms with ½ bath. No smoking. AE, MC, V. $$–$$$*

Cool **The Nugget.** Started by a German émigré, this unassuming restau-
Dining rant not far from Auburn offers an array of German specialties lovingly prepared, including some delectable goulash, tender Wiener schnitzels, and an excellent pork roast. *Rte. 49, tel. 916/823–1294. Reservations advised on weekends. No credit cards. No Mon. dinner. $*

Downieville **Cirino's at the Forks.** This small, cheerful restaurant on the banks
Dining of the Downie River provides outdoor service in summer on a flagstone patio at the water's edge. The menu features mainly Italian cuisine, with beef, chicken, homemade soup, salads, sandwiches, and 12 varieties of tea. There is a short, very reasonably priced California wine list. *Main St., tel. 916/289–3479 or 800/540–2099. Reservations advised in summer. MC, V. $–$$*

Lodging **Saundra Dyer's Resort and Bed and Breakfast.** The enterprising
★ owner of this small, cheerful, spotlessly clean establishment on the Yuba River gave the place a Victorian makeover. Weekend package deals include dinner at the local eatery, Cirino's at the Forks. Besides the main house there are two cottages and two other houses,

one of which has three bedrooms. Some kitchenettes are available. *9 River St., 1st right from Rte. 49, Box 406, 95936, tel. 916/289–3308; in CA, 800/696–3308. 14 rooms. Facilities: pool. AE, MC, V. $$–$$$*

Grass Valley
Dining

The Stewart House. Dining is casual in this century-old Victorian, whether you eat indoors or in the lovely garden. Generous portions of Continental-style dishes include homemade soups and delectable desserts. Afternoon tea and Sunday brunch are offered. *124 Bank St., tel. 916/477–6368. Reservations advised. AE, MC, V. No dinner Sun. and Mon. $$–$$$*

Lodging
★

Murphy's Inn. An immaculate white house in a leafy setting (there is a giant sequoia in the backyard and some eye-catching topiaries), this outstanding bed-and-breakfast, built in 1866, was once the mansion of a gold mine owner. Some guest rooms have the original wallpaper, four have fireplaces, and many have gas chandeliers. The spacious veranda is festooned with ivy. There are award-winning full breakfasts; Belgian waffles and eggs Benedict are specialties. *318 Neal St., Colfax Rte. Exit 174 from Rte. 49, left on S. Auburn St., 95945, tel. 916/273–6873, fax 209/273–5157. 8 rooms. Facilities: pool, swim spa. No pets (kennel facilities nearby). No smoking. AE, MC, V. $$$*

Holiday Lodge. Conveniently located next to some shops and a restaurant and lounge, this is a basic, well-kept, hospitable motel suited to families and small groups—one special family unit is set up as a bunkhouse. Some rooms are decorated with special themes (such as the Lola Montez Room, gloriously tacky with lots of red velvet); some have king-size beds. Continental breakfast is included in the rate. *1221 E. Main St., 94945, tel. 916/273–4406. 36 rooms. Facilities: outdoor pool, sauna, sundeck. AE, D, MC, V. $$*

Jackson
Dining

Upstairs Restaurant. Chef Layne McCollum, who learned his trade at California's Culinary Institute, takes a creative approach to contemporary American dining in this intimate (12 tables) restaurant. Fresh flowers, white table linens, and soft music accompany gourmet fowl, fresh seafood, and meat, with daily specials. The baked-brie-and-roast-garlic appetizer and homemade soups are specialties. Local wines are featured, and the chef blends and roasts exotic coffees daily. *164 Main St., 95642, tel. 209/223–3342. Reservations advised. AE, D, MC, V. Closed Mon. $–$$*

Rosebud's Cafe. The decor is art deco, black and white with touches of red, and the music is from the '30s and '40s in this casual, homey café. The classic American food includes hot roast beef, turkey, and meatloaf with mashed potatoes smothered in gravy, as well as char-broiled burgers and hot sandwiches. Omelets are a specialty. Freshly baked pies and espresso or gourmet coffees round out the menu, and local wines are served. *26 Main St., 95641, tel. 209/223–1035. No reservations. MC, V. No dinner. $*

Lodging

Court Street Inn. Listed on the National Register of Historic Places, this conveniently situated B&B Victorian has tin ceilings, a redwood staircase, Oriental rugs, and antique furnishings. The cozy first-floor Muldoon Room has a fireplace and king-size bed; Blair Room features a large whirlpool, a Wedgwood stove, and a queen-size brass bed. The Indian House is a two-bedroom guest cottage with a large bathroom. Full breakfast is included, as well as evening refreshments by the grand piano. *215 Court St., 95642, tel. 209/223–0416. 7 rooms. Facilities: TV by request; no in-room phones. AE, MC, V. No smoking indoors. $$–$$$*

Windrose Inn. Set on a 1½-acre hillside lot, this lovely B&B feels as though it's out in the country, although it's within walking distance of downtown Jackson. Rooms are spacious and light. The Sterling

Silver room, with its art-deco furnishings, is the most dramatic; others are decorated in Victorian style. The cottage offers a sleeping loft and a queen-size bed. A full breakfast is served, and there are complimentary afternoon refreshments. *1407 Jackson Gate Rd., 95642, tel. 209/223–3650. 4 rooms. No smoking indoors. MC, V. $$–$$$*

Jamestown
Dining

Bella Union. Newly restored with Victorian-era furnishings, this restaurant serves unusual as well as traditional dishes—wild-game kabobs, buffalo burgers, pizza, seafood salad, and pasta. Entrées are accompanied by gourmet sauces and Yorkshire pudding or wild-mushroom risotto. Desserts and breads are baked daily. Lunch is also served in the comfortable saloon. *18242 Main St., tel. 209/984–2421. Reservations accepted. AE, MC, V. $–$$*

Dining and Lodging

National Hotel. One of California's 10 oldest continously operated hotels, the National has been in business since 1859. Decor is simple—brass beds, patchwork quilts, and lace curtains. Although not all rooms have private baths, those that don't have have antique wash basins. Breakfast is included in the room rate. The saloon, with its original 19th-century redwood bar, is a great place to linger. The highly acclaimed restaurant, tastefully decorated with antiques, offers a good selection of mainly Continental cuisine. *77 Main St., Box 502, 95327, tel. 209/984–3446; in CA, 800/894–3446; fax 209/984–5620. 5 rooms with bath, 6 with shared bath. Facilities: restaurant (reservations required), TV by request; not all rooms have phones. D, MC, V. $$*

Lodging

Railtown Motel. It's a modern, typical motel, but it's good for families. There are standard amenities such as in-room phones and cable TV that you might not get at a B&B. Ground-floor rooms have a double-size spa bath. *Willow St. at Main St., Box 1129, 95327, tel. 209/984–3332. 20 rooms. Facilities: pool, spa. AE, MC, V. $$*

Royal Hotel. Although it dates from the 1920s, this charming small hotel has light, airy Victorian decor. There are 16 rooms in the main building and three cottages—the honeymoon cottage is especially romantic. Guests can enjoy a large private garden area, and breakfast is served on weekends. *18239 Main St., 95327, tel. 209/984–5271. 7 rooms with bath, 9 with shared bath. Facilities: guest laundry, no TV, no in-room phones. AE, MC, V. $$*

Nevada City
Dining

Country Rose Cafe. The exterior of this old brick and stone building, whose original iron shutters date from Gold Rush days, harmonizes well with the antiques inside this French country restaurant. The lengthy menu offers seafood, beef, lamb, chicken, and ratatouille. In the summer, there is outdoor service on a verdant patio. *300 Commercial St., tel. 916/265–6248. Reservations advised. AE, MC, V. No Sun. lunch. $$*

Friar Tuck's. This local gathering spot, which opened in 1974, is one of the area's oldest restaurants. The cozy bar feels like an English pub, with its elaborately carved wood antique back bar, originally in a Liverpool pub. A guitar player sings nightly, and sometimes patrons join in. The dining area is like a catacomb, with cubicles defined by old beams, brick walls, and arches. The menu's hearty offerings include fondue, Iowa beef, Hawaiian fish specials, and Tuck's bouillabaisse. *111 N. Pine St., tel. 916/265–9093. Reservations accepted. MC, V. No dinner. Closed Mon., Tues. $$*

Peter Selaya's California Restaurant. The food is consistently good and very fresh at this sophisticated restaurant with an intimate, elegant Victorian setting. The menu lists a variety of fish, fowl, meat, and pasta dishes, creatively prepared. Appetizers include blue walnut mushrooms and smoked salmon carpaccio. Gnocchi Parisienne are made with Gorgonzola and a garlic, cream, and tomato sauce.

Caesar salads are mixed at your table, and breads and desserts are baked on the premises. *320 Broad St., tel. 916/265–5697. Reservations advised. AE, MC, V. No lunch. Closed Mon. $$*

Cirino's. Fine American-Italian food in an informal bar and grill atmosphere is offered in this popular restaurant, housed in a 19th-century building with a handsome Brunswick back bar from the Gold Rush period. The menu features seafood, pasta, and veal. *309 Broad St., tel. 916/265–2246. Reservations advised. AE, MC, V. $*

Creekside Cafe. The lower level of an ancient building has been turned into a charming restaurant, where a large balcony overhangs a gurgling creek. The American and Continental cuisine features dishes such as lamb rack with kiwi-mint sauce, salmon with lime-dill sauce, pasta *de mer* (with seafood) with Mornay sauce, and pork tenderloin with brandy sauce. Live jazz is performed during dinner, but it's kept quiet enough so diners can still hear each other talk. *101 Broad St., tel. 916/265–3445. Reservations accepted. MC, V. Closed Mon. $*

Posh Nosh. They bake their own bread every day at this restaurant, which offers deli fare and California cuisine. Everything on the lunch menu is available for takeout: sandwiches, salads, and bagel baskets. There's a good wine list, as well as 20 varieties of imported beer and a dozen domestic brands. Dinner features fresh seafood, as well as vegetarian selections. You can dine on the garden patio in nice weather. *318 Broad St., tel. 916/265–6064. Reservations advised for dinner. AE, MC, V. $*

Lodging
★

Deer Creek Inn. This 1887 Victorian mansion sits on a hill overlooking lawns and Deer Creek, and porches and decks on all three floors offer lovely views. Totally renovated with modern conveniences and Queen Anne furnishings, it opened in early 1993. Although each is individually decorated, the light and spacious guest rooms have private baths with marble or claw-foot tubs, and king- or queen-size beds—four-poster or canopy—with down comforters. A hearty breakfast is served in the dining room, and there are two parlors where guests can relax. *116 Nevada St., 95959, tel. 916/265–0363 or 800/655–0363, fax 916/265–0980. 4 rooms. No pets. No smoking indoors. No credit cards. $$$–$$$$*

Flume's End. This unique inn was built at the end of a historic flume that once brought water into the mines. The hillside setting, on 3 wooded acres with an adjacent waterfall, is soothing. The decor is eclectic Victorian, homey and casual, with romantic nooks. A full breakfast is included in the rate, and the large common rooms have a piano and fireplace for guests to gather around. *317 S. Pine St., 95959, tel. 916/265–9665. 6 rooms with bath, 1 cottage. Facilities: Jacuzzi in 2 rooms, kitchenette in cottage. No pets. No smoking indoors. MC, V. $$$–$$$$*

The Red Castle Inn. A state landmark, this 1860 Gothic Revival mansion stands on a hillside overlooking Nevada City. Its brick exterior is trimmed with white icicle woodwork, and its porches and gardens add to the charm. The rooms, some of which look over the town, have antique furnishings and are elaborately decorated. A full buffet breakfast is served. *109 Prospect St., 95959, tel. 916/265–5135. 6 rooms with bath, 2 with shared bath. No pets. MC, V. $$$–$$$$*

Northern Queen. This bright, pleasant, two-story motel has a lovely creekside setting. Accommodations include new and remodeled motel units; eight two-story chalets and eight rustic cottages with efficiency kitchens are located in a secluded, wooded area. Rooms have small refrigerators. Facilities for the disabled are available. *400 Railroad Ave., Sacramento St. exit off Rte. 49, 95959, tel. 916/265–*

5824, fax 916/265–3720. 85 rooms. Facilities: restaurant, heated pool, spa, cable TV. No pets. AE, DC, MC, V. $$–$$$

Placerville
Dining

Zachary Jacques. The location is not easy to find, but call ahead for directions—it's worth the effort. The country French menu changes seasonally and features fresh fish and vegetables. Appetizers may include escargot or mushrooms prepared in several ways, as well as prawns and goat cheese. Traditionally prepared, classic entrées include roast rack of lamb, *daube provençale* (beef stew), scallops and prawns in lime butter, and chateaubriand garni. *1821 Pleasant Valley Rd., tel. 916/626–8045. Reservations advised. AE, MC, V. No lunch. Closed Mon. $$*

Lyons. This is one of a Western chain of family restaurants with reliable, plain food. Dinner choices include prime rib, steaks, chicken, and fried shrimp; for lunch, there are sandwiches, burgers, and salads. Breakfasts are hearty. Open 24 hours a day, it's clean and centrally located. *1160 Broadway, tel. 916/622–2305. No reservations. AE, D, MC, V. $*

★ **Powell Bros. Steamer Co.** This seafood restaurant sports a nautical-theme decor, old brick walls, and dark wood. The menu is primarily shellfish, served in stews, pastas, chowders, cocktails, and sandwiches, and cooked in big steamers—nothing is fried. *425 Main St., tel. 916/626–1091. No reservations. MC, V. Closed Sun. $*

Smith Flat House. Once the last milepost on the Lake Tahoe Wagon Road, this place has been an inn, restaurant, dance hall, Pony Express office, and store, and the restrained decor still suggests the 19th century. Located in the cellar saloon is a mine shaft leading to the heart of the Mother Lode, now filled with water, and occasional ghostly happenings have been reported. The dinner menu is limited, but there is an extensive lunch menu, featuring a build-your-own-sandwich option. On Saturday there's a barbecue lunch. *2021 Smith Flat Rd., tel. 916/621–0667 or 916/621–0471. Reservations advised. AE, DC, MC, V. Closed Mon. $*

Lodging

Chichester-McKee House. This 1892 Victorian is decorated with period furnishings. The queen-size beds have heirloom covers and antique armoires serve as closets. Each room has a half-bath. A large bathroom with antique tub and shower is shared by all. Hillside wildflower and rose gardens overlook the whole city. Innkeeper Doreen Thornhill offers a wealth of knowledge about the history of this area. Full breakfast is served. The parking area is a steep walk from the house. *800 Spring St., 95667, tel. 916/626–1882 or 800/831–4008. 3 rooms. Facilities: air-conditioning. Smoking outside only. No pets. AE, D, MV, V. $$$*

Days Inn. The clean and comfortable rooms here have bright flowered bedspreads and curtains. Continental breakfast is included, and there is a coffee shop next door. *1332 Broadway, U.S. 50 east from Rte. 49, then Schnell School exit south, 95667, tel. 916/622–3124 or 800/325–2525, fax 916/622–2080. 45 rooms. Facilities: cable TV. AE, D, DC, MC, V. $–$$*

Plymouth
Lodging

Shenandoah Inn. Set near the vineyard region of Amador County, about 40 minutes' drive from Sacramento, this modern motel has all the amenities for families, including in-room TVs and phones. Rooms are light-filled and spacious, with floral prints and views of rolling farmlands and vineyards. Beds are king- or queen-size, and the cabinetry was made by local artisans. *17674 Village Dr., 95669, tel. 209/245–4491, fax 209/245–4498. 47 rooms. Facilities: outdoor pool, Jacuzzi, rooms for the disabled, complimentary Continental breakfast. AE, D, MC, V. $$*

Sacramento **Biba's.** Owner Biba Caggiano is an authority on Italian cuisine,
Dining author of several cookbooks, and star of a national TV show on cook-
★ ing. The capitol dining crowd flocks here for her delicate pasta
dishes, baked spinach lasagna, and homemade tortellini. Caggiano
also offers a great osso buco, rabbit tenderloin, and grilled pork loin,
as well as regional specialties. The desserts, including a delectable
tiramisu, are all made on the premises. There is a full bar and extensive wine list. *2801 Capitol Ave., tel. 916/455–2422. Reservations
advised. No smoking. AE, MC, V. No weekend lunch. Closed Sun. $$$*

California Fats. Chef-owner Lina Fat, whose family has two other
restaurants in town (*see below*), expertly orchestrates the atmos-
phere and cuisine at this location and at the adjacent Fat City. The
extensive Pacific Rim–influenced menu is full of different flavors:
There's seared ahi and glazed duck from a wood-fired oven, pizza,
pastas with overtones of ginger and coriander, and venison in
cashew crust, as well as steaks and seafood. The modern decor by
Los Angeles designer Anthony Machado artistically portrays the
history of Chinese immigrants with vibrant colors, railroad ties, a
30-foot-high waterfall, ping-pong-ball wall screens, and bowling-
ball tables. *1015 Front St., tel. 916/441–7966. Reservations accepted.
AE, MC, V. Open daily for lunch and dinner and Sun. for brunch.
$$–$$$*

Frank Fat's. This is the Fat family's first restaurant, which opened
in 1939 and remains the best spot to go for Chinese food in town. A
meeting place for those who work in the nearby Capitol building, it
has been nicknamed "the third House" by the media. The menu of-
fers authentic fare from Canton, Szechuan, Beijing, and Shanghai,
as well as all-American steaks, fish, and chicken. The design is mod-
ern, with a scattering of Chinese antiques. The long bar, busy at
happy hour, serves a large selection of unusual appetizers—chicken
and abalone in lettuce cup, meat-filled dumplings, and others. *806 L
St., tel. 916/442–7092. Reservations suggested. AE, MC, V. $$*

Harlow's. Recently expanded but still crowded most of the time, this
popular spot serves California/Italian cuisine, with extraordinary
seafood specials, tortellini, and wonderful cheesecake. Dining can
be noisy and crowded, but the service is excellent, and people-
watching is fun—the bar here is *the* place in Sacramento for those
who want to be where the action is. *2714 J St., tel. 916/441–4693. Re-
servations advised. AE, D, DC, MC, V. $$*

Fat City Café and Bar. The spectacular stained glass in this bistro
adjacent to California Fats (same owners, same building) gives it
the look of an Art Nouveau, old European café. The bar is 100 years
old. Light fare, sandwiches, and pastas team with grilled entrées
and rich desserts on the menu. *1001 Front St., tel. 916/446–6768. AE,
MC, V. $–$$*

Ernesto's. There's an outdoor feeling to this family-run restaurant,
tastefully decorated in earth tones. Booths line the walls, and picture windows let in the sunshine. Typical Mexican dishes, including
burritos and taco salads, are authentically prepared, not smothered
in cheese and sauce like those at gringo-style eateries. The salsa is
freshly made but not too hot. Try the fajitas—grilled marinated
strips of chicken or beef with sautéed peppers, onions, and mushrooms, accompanied by rice and beans topped with guacamole. This
is a delicious meal for just $6. The bar serves icy margaritas and
Mexican beers as well as cocktails. Weekends, you can stop in for a
hearty breakfast. *Corner of 16th and S Sts., tel. 916/441–5850. No
reservations. AE, MC, V. $*

Lodging **Fountain Suites Hotel.** This newer hotel is conveniently located five
minutes by car from downtown and 10 minutes from the airport.

Discovery Park, two minutes away, offers fishing, bike and horse trails, and a boat launch. The large guest rooms have king-size beds, living area with desk, sofa, and two phones with voicemail. Some have microwaves and refrigerators. The decor is modern, in blues and pastels. The lobby Duck Club with fireplace, giant TV, and cozy bar invites lounging in overstuffed chairs. Free Continental breakfast is offered, weekend packages are available. *321 Bercut Dr., off I–5 at Richards Blvd., 95814, tel. 916/441–1444 or 800/767–1777, fax 916/441–6530. 300 rooms. Facilities: pool, Jacuzzi, free parking, airport/downtown shuttles, 24-hr restaurant. Enterprise car rental in lobby. AE, D, DC, MC, V. $$$$*

Radisson. About seven minutes' drive from downtown, this new hotel—almost a resort, with its lush 18-acre setting—consists of a cluster of low Mission-style buildings facing a small lake with a spectacular fountain. The huge guest rooms are luxuriously appointed. The Palm Court restaurant offers casual dining, lunch buffets, and Sunday brunch; the Cabana Room has a gourmet Californian menu. There are plenty of inviting spots to relax outdoors by the pool or lake. *500 Leisure La., 95815, tel. 916/922–2020 or 800/333–3333, fax 916/649–9463. 314 rooms. Facilities: 2 restaurants, pool, spa, fitness center, bike and paddleboat rentals, conference center. AE, D, DC, MC, V. $$$$*

Amber House Bed & Breakfast Inn. Two elegant, adjacent mansions sit on a quiet street of historic homes just eight blocks from the Capitol. The circa-1913 Artists' Retreat has four large rooms, each done in a light, floral, impressionist motif. Marble-tiled bathrooms have two-person Jacuzzis—the Van Gogh Suite's is heart-shaped and sits in a spacious solarium. The spacious living and dining rooms have light-wood columns and a classic decor. Next door is the Poets' Refuge, a 1905 Craftsman-style home with stained-glass windows, natural-wood accents, and a cozy library. Two smaller rooms have double beds. Three have queen-size beds. The Lord Byron Suite, furnished with antiques and Chinese rugs, has a Jacuzzi for two in a marble-tiled bath. Complimentary beverages include wine, champagne, and sherry. An elaborate breakfast is also included. *1315 22nd St., 95816, tel. 916/444–8085 or 800/755–6526, fax 916/447–1548. 9 rooms, all with baths, TV, phones. AE, D, DC, MC, V. $$$–$$$$*

Aunt Abigail's. This beautifully appointed Colonial Revival mansion near the center of town bills itself as a home away from home. The house was built in 1912, and the decor is appropriately Edwardian. There is a piano, and games are available to play in the elegant living room. A copious breakfast includes home-baked breads and an entrée, and each bedroom has books, flowers, and an old-fashioned radio. *2120 G St., 95816, tel. 916/441–5007 or 800/858–1568, fax 916/441–0621. 6 rooms. D, DC, MC, V. $$$*

Delta King. This grand old riverboat, permanently anchored at Old Sacramento's waterfront, offers 43 mahogany-paneled staterooms, all luxuriously appointed with a queen-size bed, wet bar, bath, and private deck. The restaurant serves sumptuous cuisine, and the lounge and saloon are open for dancing. Conveniently located for Sacramento sightseeing, the Delta King has the romantic charm of a cruise ship. *1000 Front St., 95814, tel. 916/444–5464 or 800/825–5464, fax 916/444–5314. 43 rooms. Facilities: valet parking, conference rooms. AE, D, DC, MC, V. $$$*

Americana Lodge. A no-frills motel, the Americana is conveniently located—four blocks from the state capitol and a block from the convention center. The rooms have king- or queen-size beds and are very clean. *818 15th St., 95814, tel. 916/444–3980, fax 916/922–5283. 40 rooms. Facilities: pool, free parking, airport shuttle. MC, V. $*

Sonora
Dining

Alfredos. Brightly decorated with Mexican accessories, this large restaurant serves the most authentic food around. The owners, who have another Mexican restaurant in Burbank, opened this one recently. The large menu usually includes seafood specialties and steaks, and you'll find traditional combination plates—tacos, enchiladas, burritos, and quesadillas—but they are not smothered in cheese and salsa. The rice is deliciously delicate, as is the garlic soup. *123 S. Washington St., tel. 209/532–8332. Reservations for parties of 6 or more. MC, V. $*

Carmela's Italian Kitchen. On a quiet side street, this modestly furnished Italian restaurant caters to families and casual diners. The menu is limited, but all dishes are cooked to order. Daily specials include homemade ravioli, lasagna, linguine and clam sauce, and homemade gnocchi. Sandwich specials—meatballs, Italian sausage, chicken cutlet, or pepper steak—are served on French rolls. Nothing on the menu costs more than $10, and beer and wine by the glass are $1.50. *221 S. Stewart St., tel. 209/532–8858. No reservations. No credit cards. No Sat. lunch. Closed Sun., Mon. $*

Coyote Creek Cafe & Grill. The friendly, low-key atmosphere of this centrally located restaurant is matched by its fresh Southwestern-style decor. The menu is eclectic—lunch might include pasta Castroville (with artichoke hearts marinara), Zuni black-bean plate, or Szechuan chicken. Dinners can be a selection of Spanish tapas or grilled steak and ethnic specialties. The weekend brunch menu is outstanding. House wines are $1.75 per glass, and there are more than 20 specialty beers, most priced at $2.50. *177 S. Washington St., tel. 209/532–9115. No reservations. D, MC, V. No Sun. dinner. $*

Good Heavens. This pretty café specializes in lunch and Sunday brunch. Homemade soups, unusual quiches, asparagus pasta, steak burgers, a variety of sandwiches and salads—everything is freshly made. Desserts change daily. Beer and wine are available. *49 N. Washington St., tel. 209/532–3663. Reservations accepted. No credit cards. No dinner. Closed Mon. $*

Lodging

Lulu Belle's. Only two blocks from downtown, this lovely B&B is in an 1886 Victorian surrounded by extensive lawns and gardens, complete with gazebo. The Parlor Suite, perfect for honeymooners, is decorated in red velvet with a queen-size brass bed. The Sweet Lorraine Room has two canopy beds, a spacious sitting area, and a balcony overlooking the gardens. There are three rooms in the Carriage House, three steps from the main house. Hearty breakfasts are served in the dining room and can be delivered to your room. *85 Gold St., 95370, tel. and fax 209/533–3455, tel. only in CA 800/538–3455. 5 rooms with bath. AE, DC, MC, V. $$$*

Ryan House Bed and Breakfast Inn. This 1850s farmhouse is steps from town. Furnished with antiques, the guest rooms have queen-size beds. The suite has a parlor with a wood stove, and its large bathroom features a two-person bathtub. Full breakfast is served. *153 S. Shepherd St., 95370, tel. 209/533–3445 or 800/831–4897. 3 rooms with bath. AE, D, MC, V. $$$*

Sonora Inn. This inn stands on the site of the first hotel established by a woman in the Gold Country; its original Victorian facade was plastered over in the 1920s when Spanish Mission architecture came into fashion. The roomy lobby, restaurant, and lounge have tiled floors. Some rooms are in the attached newer motel building. *160 S. Washington St., 95370, tel. 209/532–7468 or 800/321–5261. 61 rooms. Facilities: pool. AE, MC, V. $$*

Sutter Creek
Dining
★

Pelargonium. Kent and Charlene Wilson truly enjoy being chef and hostess of their beautiful restaurant. Charlene is meticulous about the decor, setting out designer china, crystal, and silver and filling the place with bright geraniums. Kent lovingly prepares generous portions with sophisticated sauces and interesting side dishes, which include herb-flavored polenta and imaginative vegetables. His rack of lamb with red wine gravy and spicy plum sauce and his chicken madras on a bed of curry, yogurt, almond, and coconut are not to be missed. The chef can accommodate special diets; there is a good selection of regional wines. *Rte. 49 and Hanford St., tel. 209/267–5008. Reservations advised. No credit cards. No lunch. Closed Sun. $$*

Ron and Nancy's Palace. This popular, unpretentious restaurant offers Continental cuisine, with daily specials such as chicken marsala and veal piccata. The lunch menu is hearty, offering a good sandwich selection and some of the same entrées available for dinner. The cozy bar is conducive to socializing. Senior citizens receive discounts. *76 Main St., tel. 209/267–1355. Reservations advised. AE, D, DC, MC, V. No dinner Tues. and Wed. $$*

Lodging
★

The Foxes Bed & Breakfast. The rooms in this house, built in 1857, are handsome, with high ceilings, antique beds, and lofty armoires topped with floral arrangements. All rooms have queen-size beds; three have wood-burning fireplaces. A menu allows guests to select a full breakfast, cooked to order and brought to each room on a silver service. *Box 159, 77 Main St., 95685, tel. 209/267–5882, fax 209/267–0712. 6 rooms. No pets. No smoking. D, MC, V. $$$*

Hanford House Bed & Breakfast. This modern brick building evokes an earlier period with its California antiques and spacious rooms. The beds are queen-size, and a hearty Continental breakfast is served. One room offers wheelchair access, and there is a rooftop deck. *61 Hanford St., Rte. 49, Box 1450, 95685, tel. 209/267–0747. 9 rooms. No pets. No smoking. D, MC, V. $$$*

Gold Quartz Inn. This inn has all the warmth and romance of a B&B, with the comfort and luxury of an elegant hotel. The spacious rooms are decorated in 19th-century style, with soft pastels, floral wallpaper, ruffled curtains, and period furnishings; yet all rooms have king-size beds, in-room phones, and TVs. The lobby resembles a Victorian parlor. Breakfast is served in the dining room and afternoon tea in the butler's pantry. *15 Bryson Dr., 95685, tel. 209/267–9155; in CA, 800/752–8738, fax 209/267–9170. 24 rooms. Facilities: laundry, 2 rooms for the disabled, VCR in parlor. No smoking indoors. AE, MC, V. $$–$$$*

8 Lake Tahoe

One of California's most beautiful natural attractions, Lake Tahoe lies 6,225 feet above sea level in the Sierra Nevada mountains, straddling the state line between California and Nevada. The border gives this popular resort region a split personality. About half of the visitors here arrive intent on low-key sightseeing, hiking, fishing, camping, and boating. The rest head directly for the Nevada side of the lake, where bargain dining and big-name entertainment draw customers into the glittering casinos, where gambling is legal. Tahoe is also a popular wedding and honeymoon destination, with a number of wedding "chapels" all around the lake where couples can get married with no waiting period or blood tests. On Valentine's Day, four times as many licenses are sold than on other days. Incidentally, the legal marrying age in California and Nevada is 18 years, but one must be 21 to gamble or drink.

Summer's cool temperatures offer respite from the heat in the surrounding deserts and valleys. Although swimming in Lake Tahoe is always brisk—68° is about as warm as it gets—the lake's beaches are generally crowded in summer. Those who prefer solitude can escape to the many state parks, national forests, and protected tracts of wilderness that ring the 22-mile-long, 12-mile-wide lake. From late November through early April, multitudes of skiers and winter-sports enthusiasts are attracted to Tahoe's 15 downhill skiing resorts and 11 cross-country centers—North America's largest concentration of skiing facilities. Ski resorts open at the end of November, sometimes with machine-made snow, and operate through May or even later. Most accommodations, restaurants, and some parks are open year-round, although September and October, when crowds have thinned but the weather is still pleasant, may be the most satisfying time to visit Lake Tahoe.

The first white man to find this spectacular region was Captain John C. Fremont in 1844, guided by famous scout Kit Carson. Not long afterward, silver was discovered in Nevada's Comstock Lode at Virginia City, and as the bonanza hit, the Tahoe Basin's forests were leveled to provide lumber for mine-tunnel supports. By the turn of the century, wealthy Californians were building lakeside estates here, some of which survive. Improved roads brought the less affluent in the 1920s and 1930s, when modest, rustic bungalows began to fill the shoreline, where the woods had grown again. The first casinos opened in the 1940s. Ski resorts brought another development boom as the lake became a year-round destination.

Lake Tahoe's water is 99.7% pure, cleaner than drinking water in most U.S. cities. The water is so clear that you can see as deep as 75 feet into it. Over the last few decades, however, road construction and other building projects washed soil and minerals into the lake, leading to a growth of algae that threatened its fabled clarity. After the environmental movement gained strength in the 1970s, a moratorium on new shoreline construction was declared and a master plan developed for growth.

During some summer weekends it seems that absolutely every tourist—100,000 at peak periods—is in a car on the one main road that circles the 72-mile shoreline, looking for historic sights, uncrowded beaches, parking places, restaurants, or motels. But the crowds and congestion don't exist at a vantage point overlooking Emerald Bay early in the morning, or on a trail in the national forests that ring the basin, or on a sunset cruise on the lake itself. At such moments, one can forget all the nearby glitz and commercial development and just drink in the beauty.

Essential Information

Important Addresses and Numbers

Tourist
Information

Lake Tahoe Visitors Authority (Box 16299, South Lake Tahoe 95706, tel. 916/544–5050 or 800/288–2463) provides information and lodging reservations for the south shore. **Tahoe North Visitors and Convention Bureau** (Box 5578, Tahoe City 96145, tel. 916/583–3494 or 800/824–6348, fax 916/581–4081) provides information and lodging reservations for the California north shore. **Incline Village/Crystal Bay Visitors & Convention Bureau** (969 Tahoe Blvd., Incline Village 89451, tel. 702/831–4440 or 800/GO–TAHOE) stocks information on the Nevada north shore. **Lake Tahoe Hotline** (tel. 916/542–INFO). **Ski Phone** (tel. 415/864–6440) offers around-the-clock ski reports and weather information. **Road Conditions** (tel. 916/445–7623, 702/793–1313, or 415/557–3755).

Emergencies

Dial 911 for **police** or **ambulance** in an emergency, or call the **California Highway Patrol** (tel. 916/587–3510) or the **Nevada Highway Patrol** (tel. 702/687–5300).

Arriving and Departing

By Plane

Reno Cannon International Airport (tel. 702/328–6400), 35 miles northeast of the closest point on the lake, is served by a number of national and regional airlines, including **American** (tel. 800/433–7300), **America West** (tel. 800/247–5692), **Continental** (tel. 800/525–0280), **Delta** (tel. 800/221–1212), **Northwest** (tel. 800/225–2525), **Sky West** (tel. 800/453–9417), **Southwest** (tel. 800/435–9792), **United** (tel. 800/241–6522), and **USAir** (tel. 800/428–4322). **Tahoe Casino Express** (tel. 702/785–2424 or 800/446–6128) has daily scheduled transportation from Reno to South Lake Tahoe, hourly 6:15 AM–3:15 PM, every two hours 3:15 PM–12:30 AM. Cost is $15.

Lake Tahoe Airport (tel. 916/542–6180) on Route 50, 3 miles south of the lake's shore, is served by **Transworld Express** (tel. 800/221–2000), which flies only to Los Angeles.

By Car

Lake Tahoe is 198 miles northeast of San Francisco, a four- to five-hour drive, depending on weather and traffic. Avoid the heavy traffic leaving the San Francisco area for Tahoe on Friday afternoon and returning on Sunday afternoon.

The major route is I–80, which cuts through the Sierra Nevada about 14 miles north of the lake; from there state Routes 89 and 267 reach the north shore. U.S. 50 is the more direct highway to the south shore, taking about 2½ hours from Sacramento. From Reno, you can get to the north shore by heading west on Route 431 off U.S. 395, 8 miles south of town (a total of 35 miles). For the south shore, continue south on U.S. 395 through Carson City, then head west on U.S. 50 (55 miles total).

By Train

There is an **Amtrak** station in Truckee (tel. 800/USA–RAIL).

By Bus

Greyhound Lines (tel. 916/587–3822) stops in Sacramento, Truckee, South Lake Tahoe, and Reno.

Getting Around

By Car

The scenic 72-mile highway around the lake is marked Route 89 on the southwest and west, Route 28 on the north and northeast shores, and U.S. 50 on the southeast. It takes about three hours to drive, but allow plenty of extra time—heavy traffic on busy holiday weekends can prolong the trip, and there are frequent road repairs in summer.

During winter, sections of Route 89 may be closed, making it impossible to complete the circular drive—call 800/427–7623 to check road conditions. I–80, U.S. 50, and U.S. 395 are all-weather highways, but there may be delays as snow is cleared during major storms. Carry tire chains from October to May (car-rental agencies provide them with rental cars).

By Bus **South Tahoe Area Ground Express** (STAGE, tel. 916/573–2080) runs 24 hours along U.S. 50 and through the neighborhoods of South Lake Tahoe. On the lake's west and north shores, **Tahoe Area Regional Transit** (TART, tel. 916/581–6365 or 800/736–6365) runs between Tahoma (from Meeks Bay in summer) and Incline Village daily 6:30–6:30. Free shuttle buses run among the casinos, major ski resorts, and motels of South Lake Tahoe.

By Taxi **Sierra Taxi** (tel. 916/577–8888) serves all of Tahoe Basin. On the south shore, call **Yellow Cab** (tel. 916/542–1234) or **Lake Tahoe Taxi** (tel. 916/546–4444). On the north shore, try **Truckee Town Taxi Service** (tel. 916/582–8294).

Guided Tours

Orientation Tours **Gray Line** (tel. 702/329–1147 or 800/822–6009) runs daily tours to Emerald Bay, South Lake Tahoe, Carson City, and Virginia City. Another tour provider is **Tahoe Limousine Service** (Box 9909, South Lake Tahoe 96158, tel. 916/577–2727 or 800/334–1826).

Adventure Tours **High Mountain Outback Adventures** (2286 Utah Ave., South Lake Tahoe 96150, tel. 916/541–5875) operates a trek skirting the Desolation Wilderness in four-wheel-drive all-terrain vehicles (ATVs), for $79 per half day and $129 per full day (you must be 18, have a driver's license, and be in good health). Those in very good physical shape can take a three-day, two-night Adventure Ride for $595. These rides are available June–October; winter ATV tours are offered in the Pine Nut Mountains, east of the Carson Valley, where Nevada's wild horses roam.

Air Tours **CalVada Seaplanes Inc.** (tel. 916/525–7143) provides rides over the lake for $45–$81 per person, depending on the length of the trip. Soaring rides on gliders over the lake and valley depart from the Douglas County Airport, Gardnerville. Try **High Country Soaring** (tel. 702/782–4944) or **Soar Minden** (tel. 702/782–7627).

Boat Tours The *Tahoe Queen* (tel. 916/541–3364 or 800/23–TAHOE) is a glass-bottom stern-wheeler that makes 2½-hour lake cruises year-round from Ski Run Marina off U.S. 50 in South Lake Tahoe; sunset and dinner cruises are also offered. Fares are $14–$18 adults, $5–$9 children; in winter, the boat shuttles skiers to north-shore ski areas on weekdays for $18 round-trip. The MS *Dixie* (tel. 702/588–3508) sails from Zephyr Cove Marina to Emerald Bay, late April–early November, on breakfast cruises and dinner-dance cruises. Fares run $14–$34 adults, $5–$10 children 4–12, including food and beverages. The *Woodwind* (tel. 702/588–3000) is a glass-bottom trimaran that sails from Zephyr Cove Resort April–October. Fares are $14 adults, $7 children; the evening champagne cruise is $20. The *Sierra Cloud* (tel. 702/831–1111), a larger trimaran with a big trampoline lounging surface, cruises from the Hyatt Regency Hotel in Incline Village April–October.

Exploring Lake Tahoe

The most common way to explore the Lake Tahoe area is to drive the 72-mile road that follows the shore, through wooded flatlands and past beaches, climbing to vistas on the rugged west side of the lake and descending to the busiest commercial developments and casinos. There are plenty of parks, picnic areas, and scenic lookouts to stop at along the way, and many hiking trails are accessible from the shoreline highway.

Although it's easy to do the entire circuit in good weather, we've divided the tour into two sections. If you're arriving on U.S. 50, you'll begin in South Lake Tahoe, on the southern shore; if you drive in on I–80 then Route 89, you'll hit the northern shore of the lake first, at Tahoe City, then swing around the eastern shore, which lies in Nevada.

Highlights for First-Time Visitors

Cave Rock
Ehrman Mansion, Sugar Pine Point State Park
Emerald Bay Lookout
Gatekeeper's Log Cabin Museum, Tahoe City
Heavenly Tram, Heavenly Ski Resort
Ponderosa Ranch
Sand Harbor Beach
Vikingsholm

South Lake Tahoe to Tahoe City

Numbers in the margin correspond to points of interest on the Lake Tahoe map.

U.S. 50 reaches the lake at **South Lake Tahoe,** the largest community on the lake. The road is lined with motels, lodges, and restaurants, but as you head west the lakefront route becomes Route 89, and commercial development gives way to more wooded national-forest lands. You'll notice pleasant bike trails well off the road.

❶ At **Pope-Baldwin Recreation Area,** take in the Tallac Historic Site, where a museum and three magnificently restored estates host cultural events from June to September. The Valhalla Renaissance Festival, recreating the arts, culture, and entertainments of the 15th and 16th centuries, is held at Camp Richardson in June (call the Tahoe Tallac Association at 916/542–4166 for information). Guided tours of the Pope House and a museum at the Baldwin Estate are available in the summer. *Tel. 916/541–5227. Admission free, tour $2. Tours Memorial Day–Labor Day, daily.*

❷ The **Lake Tahoe Visitors Center** on Taylor Creek, operated by the U.S. Forest Service, offers far more than answers to questions. This stretch of lakefront is a microcosm of the area's natural history. You can visit the site of a Washoe Indian settlement; walk self-guided trails through meadow, marsh, and forest; and inspect the Stream Profile Chamber, an underground, underwater display with windows letting visitors look right into Taylor Creek (in the fall you may see spawning salmon digging their nests). For those who are driving a car around the lake, the center offers a free cassette player and a tape that tells about points of interest along the way. *Tel. in season, 916/573–2674; off season, 916/573–2600. Open June–Sept., daily; Oct., weekends.*

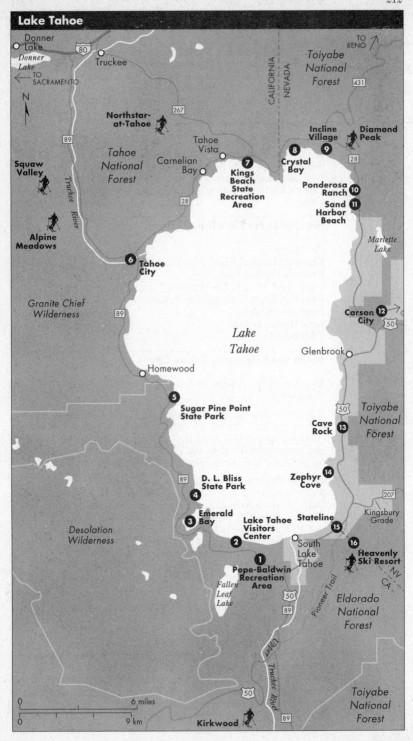

Lake Tahoe

Donner Lake

Donner Lake

TO SACRAMENTO

Truckee

80

TO RENO

Toiyabe National Forest

431

CALIFORNIA
NEVADA

N

89

Northstar-at-Tahoe

267

Squaw Valley

Tahoe National Forest

Tahoe Vista

Carnelian Bay

28

Incline Village

Diamond Peak

7 Kings Beach State Recreation Area

8 Crystal Bay

9

Ponderosa Ranch **10**

Sand Harbor Beach **11**

Alpine Meadows

Truckee River

6 Tahoe City

Granite Chief Wilderness

89

Marlette Lake

Homewood

Lake Tahoe

Carson City **12**

50

Glenbrook

5 Sugar Pine Point State Park

Toiyabe National Forest

Cave Rock **13**

50

4 D. L. Bliss State Park

Zephyr Cove **14**

89

3 Emerald Bay

2 Lake Tahoe Visitors Center

Stateline

15

207

Kingsbury Grade

Desolation Wilderness

1 Pope-Baldwin Recreation Area

South Lake Tahoe

Heavenly Ski Resort **16**

NV
CA

Fallen Leaf Lake

50

89

Pioneer Trail

Eldorado National Forest

Kirkwood

Upper Truckee River

50

89

Toiyabe National Forest

0 _____ 6 miles
0 _____ 9 km

❸ The winding road next takes you to **Emerald Bay,** famed for its
jewel-like shape and colors. The road is high above the lake at this
point; from Emerald Bay Lookout you can survey the whole scene,
which includes Fannette, Tahoe's only island. From the lookout a
steep, mile-long trail leads down to **Vikingsholm,** a 38-room estate
completed in 1929. The owner, Lora Knight, had this precise replica
of a 1,200-year-old Viking castle built out of materials native to the
area, without disturbing the existing trees. She furnished it with
Scandinavian antiques and hired artisans to custom-build period reproductions. The sod roof sprouts wildflowers each spring. There
are picnic tables nearby and a sandy beach for strolling. Be warned:
the hike back up is steep. *Tel. 916/525–7277. Admission: $2 adults,
$1 children under 18. Open Memorial Day–Labor Day, daily 10–4.*

❹ Beyond Emerald Bay is **D. L. Bliss State Park,** which shares 6 miles
of shoreline with the bay. At the north end of the park is **Rubicon
Point,** which overlooks one of the lake's deepest spots. *Tel. 916/525–
7277. Day-use fee: $5 per vehicle. Open spring–fall.*

❺ The main attraction at **Sugar Pine Point State Park** is the **Ehrman
Mansion,** a stately, stone-and-shingle 1903 summer home that displays the rustic aspirations of the era's wealthy residents. It is furnished in period style. *Tel. 916/525–7232 year-round or 916/525–7982
in season. Admission free. State-park day-use fee: $5 per vehicle.
Open Memorial Day–Labor Day, daily 11–4.*

Tahoe City and the Nevada Shore

❻ **Tahoe City** is a nice town to pass time in, with lots of stores and
restaurants. The Truckee River, the lake's only outlet, flows through
town. Before the severe drought of the late 1980s and early 1990s,
you could look down and see the river's giant trout from **Fanny
Bridge,** so called because you can usually see the backsides of rows
of visitors leaning over the railing.

The **Gatekeeper's Log Cabin Museum** provides one of the best records of the area's past, displaying Washoe and Paiute artifacts as
well as late-19th- to early 20th-century settlers' memorabilia. *130
W. Lake Blvd., tel. 916/583–1762. Admission free. Open May 15–Oct.
1, daily 11–5.*

The museum also oversees the nearby **Watson Cabin Living Museum,** a 1909 log cabin built by Robert M. Watson and his son and
filled with turn-of-the-century furnishings. Costumed docents act
out the daily life of a typical pioneer family. *560 N. Lake Blvd., tel.
916/583–8717 or 916/583–1762. Admission free. Open June 15–Labor
Day, daily noon–4.*

At Tahoe City, Route 89 turns north from the lake to Squaw Valley,
Donner Lake, and Truckee (*see* Off the Beaten Track, *below*), while
Route 28 continues northeast around the lake. Traveling 8 miles in
❼ this direction on Route 28 you will reach the 28-acre **Kings Beach
State Recreation Area,** one of the lakeshore parks open year-round.

TimeOut The **Log Cabin Caffe** (8692 N. Lake Blvd., tel. 916/546–7109) is a
good choice for breakfast or lunch, serving health foods, sandwiches, ice cream, and freshly baked pastry.

You don't need a roadside marker to know when you've crossed from
California into Nevada. The lake's water and the pine trees may be
identical, but the flashing lights and elaborate marquees of casinos
announce legal gambling with a bang. Right at the Nevada border,

8 **Crystal Bay** has a cluster of four casinos; one, the **Cal-Neva Hotel/Casino** (*see* Lodging, *below*), is bisected by the state line. The next town
9 is the resort community of **Incline Village,** which has plenty of recreational diversions—hiking and biking trails, the area's greatest concentration of tennis courts, and a **Recreation Center** (980 Incline Way, tel. 702/832–1300) with an eight-lane swimming pool, a cardiovascular-fitness area, and a health-food bar. Route 431 leads north out of Incline Village past the highest ski area in the region, Mt. Rose, and about 30 miles farther, to Reno.

10 South of Incline Village on Route 28 is the **Ponderosa Ranch,** a theme park inspired by the popular 1960s television series "Bonanza." Attractions include the Cartwrights' ranch house, a Western town, and a saloon. There's also a self-guided nature trail, free pony rides for children, and, if you're here from 8 to 9:30 in the morning, a breakfast hayride. *Tel. 702/831–0691. Admission: $7.50 adults, $5.50 children 5–11, hayride $2. Open late Apr.–Oct., daily 9:30–5.*

11 **Sand Harbor Beach** is one of the lake's finest and so popular it's sometimes filled to capacity by 11 AM on summer weekends. A pop-music festival is held here in July and a Shakespeare festival every August. *Festival information: North Tahoe Fine Arts Council, tel. 916/583–9048.*

Spooner Junction, where Route 28 meets U.S. 50, offers several sightseeing options. If you turn east on U.S. 50, away from the lake, in 10 miles you reach U.S. 395, where you turn left and go 1 mile
12 north to **Carson City,** the capital of Nevada. It's one of the nation's smallest capital cities. Most of its historic buildings and other attractions are along U.S. 395, the main street through town. At the south end of town is the **Carson City Visitors Center** (1900 S. Carson St., tel. 702/882–7474). About a half-hour's drive northeast of Carson City (on Rte. 342 off U.S. 50) is the fabled mining town of Virginia City, which has sites and activities of historical interest mixed in with touristy diversions.

If you continue south along the shore (now on U.S. 50 south), you'll
13 pass through **Cave Rock,** 25 yards of solid stone. Tahoe Tessie, Lake Tahoe's version of the Loch Ness monster, is reputed to live in a cavern below Cave Rock. Six miles farther south you'll come to
14 **Zephyr Cove,** a tiny resort with a beach, marina, campground, picnic area, historic log lodge, and nearby riding stables.

A short distance past Zephyr Cove, Kingsbury Grade (Rte. 207) goes off to the east. This was originally a toll road used by wagon trains to get over the Sierras' crest. Now it leads to spectacular views of the Carson Valley. Turn left on Foothill Road (Rte. 206), which leads past **Walley's Hot Springs Resort** (2001 Foothill Rd., tel. 702/782–8155), a small lodge with natural hot-spring pools (admission: $10). Beyond the resort you'll soon come to **Genoa** (population 250), the oldest settlement in Nevada. Along Main Street are some small museums and the state's oldest saloon.

Back on the lakeshore, you'll pass four major (and two minor) casi-
15 nos at **Stateline** before crossing back into California. Traveling southwest along U.S. 50, turn left at Ski Run Boulevard and drive
16 up to the **Heavenly Ski Resort.** Whether you're a skier or not, you'll want to ride 2,000 feet up on the 50-passenger **Heavenly Tram,** which runs part way up the mountain, to 8,200 feet. There you'll find a memorable view of Lake Tahoe and the Nevada desert. *Tel. 702/586–7000. Round-trip tram fare: $12 adults, $5 senior citizens and children under 12. Tram runs June–Sept., daily 10–10; Nov.–May, daily 9–4.*

TimeOut   At the top of the tram, **Monument Peak Cafe** (tel. 702/586–7000, ext. 6347), open daily during tram hours, offers basic American food and cafeteria service. It serves lunch, dinner, and Sunday brunch in summer and breakfast and lunch in winter.

What to See and Do with Children

With its wealth of outdoor recreation, Lake Tahoe is an easy place to keep children and teenagers entertained. All the ski areas offer children's ski programs and most have child-care facilities. Although children are not allowed in the casinos' gambling areas, all these establishments have game arcades and some, like the Hyatt Regency in Incline Village, offer special youth-oriented activities all day. Among the lake's attractions, the **Ponderosa Ranch** (*see* Exploring Lake Tahoe, *above*) is usually a big hit with kids.

Commons Beach in the middle of Tahoe City has a playground for children. The **North Tahoe Beach Center** has a 26-foot hot tub, open year-round; in summer, the heat is turned down until 1 PM for youngsters. The beach has an enclosed swim area and four sand volleyball courts. This popular spot for families has a barbecue and picnic area, a fitness center, windsurfing, boat rental and tours, a snack bar, and a clubhouse with games. *7860 N. Lake Blvd., Kings Beach, tel. 916/546–2566. Daily fee: $6 adults, $3 children.*

Magic Carpet Golf. This miniature golf course, video arcade, and electronic shooting gallery attracts all ages. *5167 Northlake Blvd., Carnelian Bay, tel. 916/546–4279; 2455 Rte. 50, S. Lake Tahoe, tel. 916/541–3787. Fees: 18 holes, $3.50; 28 holes, $4.50. Open Mar.–Nov., daily 10 AM–11 PM.*

In summer the **Lake Tahoe Visitors Center** (*see* Exploring Lake Tahoe, *above*) sets up discovery walks and nighttime campfires, with singing and marshmallow roasts.

Off the Beaten Track

Donner Memorial State Park (off I–80, 2 mi west of Truckee) commemorates the Donner Party, a group of 89 westward-bound pioneers who were trapped here in the winter of 1846–47 in snow 22 feet deep. Only 47 survived, some by cannibalism and others by eating animal hides. The Immigrant Museum offers a slide show hourly about the Donner Party's plight. Other displays relate the history of other settlers and of railroad development through the Sierras. *Tel. 916/582–7892. Admission: $2 adults, $1 children 6–12. Open Dec.– Aug., daily 10–4; Sept.–Nov., daily 10–noon, 1–4.*

Old West facades line the main street of nearby **Truckee,** a favorite stopover for people traveling from the Bay Area to the north shore of Lake Tahoe. Fine-art galleries and upscale boutiques are plentiful, but you will also find low-key diners, discount skiwear, and an old-fashioned five-and-dime store. For a map outlining a walking tour of historic Truckee, stop by the information booth in the Amtrak depot.

On the **Adventure Challenge Course,** set among 40- to 50-foot-high pines with riggings and cables, participants attempt feats of physical derring-do while safely tethered to mountaineering gear. Corporate groups, honeymoon couples, and families—all sorts of people—test their prowess with such stunts as jumping off a tall treetop holding a trapeze line that zips you to the ground and climbing an artificial wall. The course is a great confidence-builder and a whole lot of fun. *Northstar Village Resort, off Rte. 267, Truckee, tel. 916/562–1010 or 916/562–2285 direct; or contact Adventure Associates, 1030 Merced St., Berkeley, CA 94707, tel. 510/525–9391, fax 510/525–4673. Admission: $40 adults, $30 children 10–17. Open June–Sept., daily 11–4:30.*

Shopping

In South Lake Tahoe there's some good shopping south of town at the intersection of Routes 50 and 89, at the **Factory Outlet Stores.** In Tahoe City, try **Boatworks Mall** (780 N. Lake Blvd.), **Cobblestone Mall** (475 N. Lake Blvd.), and the **Roundhouse Mall** (700 N. Lake Blvd.).

Sports and the Outdoors

For most of the popular sports at Lake Tahoe, summer or winter, you won't have to bring much equipment with you, an important factor if you're traveling by air or have limited space. Bicycles and boats are readily available for rent at Lake Tahoe. Golf clubs can be rented at several area courses. All of the major ski resorts have rental shops.

Golf   These courses in the Lake Tahoe area have food facilities, pro shops, cart rentals, and putting greens. **Edgewood Tahoe** (U.S. 50 and Lake Pkwy., behind Horizon Casino, Stateline, tel. 702/588–3566) is an 18-hole, par-72 course with a driving range. Carts are mandatory; the course is open 7–3:30. **Incline Championship** (955 Fairway Blvd., Incline Village, tel. 702/832–1144) is another 18-hole, par-72 course with a driving range. Carts are mandatory. **Incline Executive** (690 Wilson Way, Incline Village, tel. 702/832–1150) has 18 holes but is much easier: Par is 58. Carts are mandatory. **Lake Tahoe Golf Course** (U.S. 50 between South Lake Tahoe Airport and Meyers, tel. 916/577–0788) has 18 holes, par 71, and a driving range. **Northstar-at-Tahoe** (Rte. 267 between Truckee and Kings Beach, tel. 916/562–2490) has 18 holes, par 72, with a driving range. Carts are mandatory before 12:30. **Old Brockway Golf Course** (Rtes. 267 and 28, Kings Beach, tel. 916/546–9909) is a nine-hole, par-35 course. **Resort at Squaw Creek Golf Course** (400 Squaw Creek Rd., Olympic Valley, tel. 916/583–6300) is an 18-hole championship course designed by Robert Trent Jones, Jr. It's open 8–4. **Tahoe City Golf Course** (Rte. 28, Tahoe City, tel. 916/583–1516) is a nine-hole, par-33 course. Golfers use pull carts here. **Tahoe Paradise Golf Course** (Rte. 50 near Meyers, South Lake Tahoe, tel. 916/577–2121) has 18 holes, par 66.

Hiking and   **Desolation Wilderness,** a vast 63,473-acre preserve of granite peaks, Camping   glacial valleys, subalpine forests, the Rubicon River, and more than 50 lakes, offers hiking, fishing, and camping. Trails begin outside the wilderness preserve; Meeks Bay and Echo Lake are two starting points. Permits (free) are required for access and can be obtained from the U.S. Forest Service's **Lake Tahoe Visitors Center** (*see* Exploring Lake Tahoe, *above*), the **Desolation Wilderness** headquarters (870 Emerald Bay Rd., Suite 1, South Lake Tahoe 96150, tel. 916/573–2600 or 916/573–2674), and the **El Dorado National Forest** (tel. 916/644–6048). **D. L. Bliss State Park** (*see* Exploring Lake Tahoe, *above*) has 168 family campsites; the fee is $14 per campsite. There's a $5 day-use fee for entering the park; the park is closed in winter.

Scuba Diving Scuba diving is a surprisingly popular activity at Lake Tahoe. Groups and clubs frequent Sand Harbor, the Rubicon River, and Emerald Bay, which are easily accessible. The water is clear enough to divulge shipwrecks, marine life, and incredible geologic forms. **The Diving Edge** (176 Shady La., Stateline, tel. 702/588–5262), is a full-service PADI dive center offering rentals and instruction.

Skiing The Tahoe Basin ski resorts offer the largest concentration of skiing in the country: 15 downhill ski resorts and 11 cross-country ski centers, with more cross-country skiing available on thousands of acres of public forests and parklands. The major resorts are listed below, but other, smaller places also offer excellent skiing. To save money, look for ski packages offered by lodges and resorts; some include interchangeable lift tickets that allow you to try different slopes. Midweek packages are usually lower in price. **Ski Lake Tahoe Association** (tel. 702/588–8598) furnishes information on skiing in the area. Free shuttle-bus service is available between most ski resorts and hotels and lodges.

Downhill Skiing **Alpine Meadows Ski Area** is a ski cruiser's paradise, with skiing from two peaks—Ward, a great open bowl, and Scott, for tree-lined runs. All main runs are groomed nightly. Alpine has some of Tahoe's most reliable skiing conditions and an excellent snowmaking system; it's usually the first in the area to open each November and the last to close, in May or even June. The base lodge contains rentals, a cafeteria, restaurant-lounge, bar, bakery, sports shop, ski schools for skiers of all skill levels and for skiers with disabilities, and a children's snow school; there's also an area for overnight RV parking. Beginner runs are close to the base lodge. Ski from every lift; there are no "transportation" lifts and snowboarding is prohibited. *6 mi northwest of Tahoe City off Rte. 89, 13 mi south of I–80, Box 5279, Tahoe City, CA 96145, tel. 916/583–4232; snow phone, tel. 916/581–8374; information, tel. 800/441–4423; fax 916/583–0963. 2,000 acres, rated 25% easier, 40% more difficult, 35% most difficult. Longest run 2.5 mi, base 6,835', summit 8,637'. Lifts: 2 high-speed quads, 2 triples, 7 doubles, 1 surface.*

Diamond Peak has a fun, family atmosphere with many special programs and affordable rates. A learn-to-ski package, with rentals, lesson, and lift ticket, is $29; a parent-child ski package is $38, with each additional child's lift ticket $5. There is a half-pipe run just for snowboarding. Snowmaking covers 80% of the mountain, and runs are well-groomed nightly. The ride up mile-long Crystal chair rewards you with the best views of the lake from any ski area. Diamond Peak is less crowded than some of the larger areas, and it offers free shuttles to lodging in nearby Incline Village. There's Nordic skiing here, too (*see* Cross-Country Skiing, *below*). *1210 Ski Way, Incline Village, NV 89450, off Rte. 28 (Country Club Dr. to Ski Way), tel. 702/832–1177 or 800/468–2463, fax 702/832–1281. 655 acres, rated 18% beginner, 49% intermediate, 33% advanced. Longest run 2.5 mi, base 6,700', summit 8,540'. Lifts: 6 doubles, 1 quad.*

Heavenly Ski Resort gives skiers plenty of choices. Go up the Heavenly Tram on the California side (*see* Exploring Lake Tahoe, *above*) to ski the imposing face of Gunbarrel or the gentler runs at the top, or ride the Sky Express high-speed quad chair to the summit and choose wide cruising runs or steep tree skiing. Or drive over the Kingsbury Grade to the Boulder or Stagecoach lodges and stay on the Nevada-side runs, which are usually less crowded. Snowmaking covers both sides, top to bottom, for generally good conditions. The ski school, like everything else at Heavenly, is large and offers a program for everyone, beginner to expert. *Ski Run Blvd., Box 2180, Stateline, NV 89449, tel. 916/541–1330 or 800/243–2836; snow infor-*

mation, tel. 916/541–7544; fax 916/541–2643. 4,800 acres, rated 20% beginner, 45% intermediate, 35% expert. Longest run 5.5 mi, base 6,540', summit 10,040'. Lifts: 25 total, including 2 high-speed quads.

Kirkwood Ski Resort lies 36 miles south of Lake Tahoe in an Alpine-village setting, surrounded by incredible mountain scenery. Most of the runs off the top are rated expert only, but intermediate and beginning skiers have their own vast bowl, where they can ski through trees or wide-open spaces. This is a destination resort, with 120 condominiums, several shops, and restaurants in the base village, overnight RV parking, and a shuttle bus to Lake Tahoe. There's snowboarding on all runs, with lessons, rentals, and sales available. For Nordic skiing, *see* Cross-Country Skiing, *below. Rte. 88, Box 1, Kirkwood, CA 95646, tel. 209/258–6000; lodging information, 209/258–7000; snow information, 209/258–3000; fax 209/258–8899. 2,000 acres, rated 15% beginner, 50% intermediate, 35% advanced. Longest run 2.5 mi, base 7,800', summit 9,800'. Lifts: 10 chairs, 1 surface.*

Northstar-at-Tahoe is the Sierras' most complete destination resort, with lots of activity in summer and winter. The center of action is the picturesque Village Mall, a concentration of restaurants, shops, recreation facilities, and lodging options from hotel rooms to condos and houses. Two northeast-facing, wind-protected bowls offer some of the best powder skiing around, including steep chutes and long cruising runs. Top to bottom snowmaking and intense grooming assure good conditions. There's a half-pipe run for snowboarding, as well as lessons, rentals, and sales. For Nordic skiing, *see* Cross-Country Skiing, *below. Off Rte. 267 between Truckee and North Shore, Box 129, Truckee, CA 96160, lodging reservations, tel. 916/562–1010 or 800/533–6787; snow information, 916/562–1330; fax 916/587–0214. 1,700 acres, rated 25% beginner, 50% intermediate, 25% advanced. Longest run 2.9 mi, base 6,400', summit 8,600'. Lifts: 6-passenger express gondola, 3 doubles, 3 triples, 2 tows, 2 high-speed quads.*

Squaw Valley USA was the site of the 1960 Olympics. The immense resort has changed significantly since then, but the skiing is still first-class, with steep chutes and cornices on six Sierra peaks. Beginners delight in riding the tram to the top, where there is a huge plateau of gentle runs. At the top of the tram, you can find the Bath and Tennis Club in the recently renovated lodge, with impressive views from its restaurants, bars, and outdoor ice-skating pavilion. Base facilities are clustered around the Village Mall, with shops, dining, condos, hotels, and lodges. The valley golf course doubles as a cross-country ski facility. On the other side of the golf course is the new Resort at Squaw Creek, with its own run and quad chair lift that runs to Squaw's ski terrain. *Rte. 89, 5 mi northwest of Tahoe City, Squaw Valley USA, CA 96146, tel. 916/583–6985; reservations, 800/545–4350; snow information, 916/583–6955; fax 916/583–6985. 4,850 acres, rated 25% beginner, 45% intermediate, 30% advanced. Longest run 3 mi, base 6,200', summit 9,050'. Lifts: 6-passenger gondola, cable car, 3 quads, 8 triples, 15 doubles, 5 surface.*

Cross-Country Skiing With 11 areas to choose from on mountaintops and in valleys, this is a Nordic skier's paradise. For the ultimate in groomed conditions, there is America's largest cross-country ski resort, **Royal Gorge** (Box 1100, Soda Springs, CA 95728, tel. 916/426–3871), which offers 317 kilometers of 18-foot-wide track for all abilities, 81 trails on 9,000 acres, two ski schools, and 10 warming huts, as well as four cafés, two hotels, and a hot tub and sauna. **Diamond Peak at Ski Incline** (tel. 702/832–1177) has 15 kilometers of groomed track with skating lanes. The trail system goes from 7,400 feet to 9,100 feet with endless wilderness to explore. The entrance is off Route 431. **Kirkwood Ski Resort** (*see* Downhill Skiing, *above*) has 80 kilometers of groomed-track skiing, with skating lanes, instruction, and rentals. **Northstar-at-Tahoe** (*see* Downhill Skiing, *above*) gives cross-country skiers access to Alpine ski slopes for telemarking and also provides 65 kilometers of groomed, tracked trails with a wide skating lane. There's a ski shop, rentals, and instruction.

Skiers who want to tour the backcountry should check with the **U.S. Forest Service** (tel. 916/587–3558) prior to entering the wilderness.

Sledding and Snowmobiling

There are five public **Sno-Park** areas in the vicinity, some for snow-mobiling and cross-country skiing, as well as sledding. All are maintained by the Department of Parks and Recreation, and to use them you need to obtain a permit in advance. Call the parks department at 916/322–8993 or contact the Lake Tahoe Visitor Center (*see* Exploring Lake Tahoe, *above*).

Several companies in the area offer snowmobile tours. **Snowmobiling Unlimited** (Box 1591, Tahoe City 96145, tel. 916/583–5858), one of the area's oldest operators, offers guided tours and rentals, as well as a track to zoom around on, for $30 per half hour, $40 per hour for a single snowmobile and $60 for a double.

Swimming

There are 36 public beaches on Lake Tahoe. Swimming is permitted at many of them, but since Tahoe is a high mountain lake with fairly rugged winters, only the hardiest will be interested, except in midsummer. Even then the water warms to only 68°F. Lifeguards are on duty at some of the swimming beaches, and yellow buoys mark safe areas where motorboats are not permitted. Opening and closing dates for beaches vary with the climate and available park-service personnel. Parking fees range from $1 to $4.

Gambling

Nevada's major casinos are also full-service hotels and resorts, and they offer discounted lodging packages throughout the year. Five are clustered on a strip of U.S. 50 in Stateline—Caesars, Harrah's, Harvey's, Horizon, and Lakeside. Four others stand on the north shore: the Hyatt Regency, Cal-Neva, Tahoe Biltmore, and Crystal Bay Club. Open 24 hours a day, 365 days a year, these casinos offer more than 150 table games (craps, blackjack, roulette, baccarat, poker, keno, pai gow, bingo, and big six), race and sports books, and thousands of slot machines—1,750, for instance, at Harrah's. Admission is free, and there is no dress code.

Of the north-shore casinos, the Hyatt offers the most amenities. Frank Sinatra was once a part-owner of the Cal-Neva Lodge, one of Tahoe's original casinos. It recently underwent a major renovation. The other two are small, not luxurious properties.

Stateline is where the major Tahoe action takes place. The casinos share an atmosphere of garish neon and noise, but air-conditioning eliminates the smoky pall of the past, and today there are no-smoking areas. Each casino has its own distinctive decor in the lobby and common areas. Caesars is Greco-Roman, with lots of marble, real and simulated. Harrah's uses dark wood, red fabrics, and mirrors to the max. Harvey's has elegant Continental decor that uses soft blues, crystal light fixtures, and period furnishings. The Horizon has a Beaux Arts look, very light (but only on the first level). Lakeside, the smallest, looks Western-rustic, using dark wood and stone. Bill's, a "junior" casino owned by Harrah's (no lodging, but there's a McDonald's restaurant on the premises), appeals to younger and less-experienced players because it tends to have lower stakes.

The hotel-casinos attract visitors with shows, celebrity entertainers, and restaurants and lounges open around the clock. Gamblers are offered complimentary beverages. Valet parking, in enclosed garages, is technically free, but a $1–$2 tip is customary. In addition to the big casinos, in Nevada visitors will find slot machines in every conceivable location, from gas stations to supermarkets.

Dining and Lodging

Dining   Restaurants at Lake Tahoe range from rustic rock-and-wood decor to elegant French, with stops along the way for Swiss chalet and spare modern. The food, too, is varied and may include delicate Continental or nouvelle-Californian sauces, mesquite- and olive-wood-grilled specialties, and wild game in season.

Casinos use their restaurants to attract gaming customers, so their marquees might tout "$5.99 prime rib dinners" or "$2.99 full breakfasts." Some of these specials may not be top quality (meat is rarely "prime," and service is usually from a buffet), but the finer restaurants in casinos generally offer good food, service, and atmosphere at reasonable prices.

In Stateline, thanks to the cluster of hotel-casinos, there are no less than 22 restaurants concentrated in a block or two. Other choices on the south shore are limited to pizza, Mexican food, delis, and fast-food franchises, except for a handful of fine-dining establishments.

Unless otherwise noted, dress is casual for all restaurants. Even the most elegant and expensive Tahoe eating places welcome customers in casual clothes—not surprising in this year-round vacation mecca—but don't expect to be served in a very expensive restaurant if you're barefoot and wearing beach clothes. On weekends and in high season, expect a long wait to be seated in the more popular restaurants. During slow seasons some places may close temporarily or limit their hours, so call ahead to verify.

Highly recommended restaurants are indicated by a star ★.

Category	Cost*
$$$$	over $35
$$$	$25–35
$$	$15–$25
$	under $15

per person for a three-course meal, excluding drinks, service, and tax

Lodging   Quiet inns on the water, motel rooms in the heart of the casino area, rooms at the casinos themselves, lodges close to ski runs—there's a wide range of lodging at Lake Tahoe. Just remember that during summer and ski season the lake is crowded; plan in advance. Spring and fall give you a little more leeway and lower—sometimes significantly lower—rates. Price categories listed below reflect high-season rates. Lake Tahoe has two telephone reservation services:

Tahoe North Visitors and Convention Bureau (tel. 800/824–6348) and, for the south shore, the **Lake Tahoe Visitors Authority** (tel. 800/288–2463).

Highly recommended hotels are indicated by a star ★.

Category	Cost*
$$$$	over $100
$$$	$75–$100
$$	$50–$75
$	under $50

All prices are for a double room, excluding tax.

Carnelian Bay
Dining

Gar Woods Grill and Pier. This elegant but casual lakeside restaurant recalls the lake's past, with wood paneling, a river-rock fireplace, and boating photographs. It specializes in grilled foods, along with pasta and pizza. It also serves Sunday brunch. *5000 N. Lake Blvd., tel. 916/546–3366. Reservations accepted. MC, V. $$*

Crystal Bay
Lodging

Cal-Neva Lodge Resort Hotel/Casino. All of the rooms in this hotel on Route 28 at Crystal Bay have views of Lake Tahoe and the mountains. There is an arcade with video games for children, cabaret entertainment, and, in addition to rooms in the main hotel, 22 cabins with living rooms. *Box 368, 89402, tel. 702/832–4000 or 800/225–6382, fax 702/831–9007. 220 rooms. Facilities: restaurant, coffee shop, pool, sauna, whirlpool, tennis courts, 3 wedding chapels. AE, DC, MC, V. $$–$$$*

Incline Village
Dining

Stanley's Restaurant and Lounge. With its intimate bar and pleasant dining room, this casual local favorite is a good bet any time for straightforward American fare on the hearty side (barbecued pork ribs, beef Stroganoff). Lighter bites, such as seafood Cobb salad, are also available, along with ample breakfasts; try the eggs Benedict or a chili-cheese omelet. There's a deck for outdoor dining in summer and live music on Friday night. *941 Tahoe Blvd., tel. 702/831–9944. No reservations. AE, MC, V. No Tues. dinner in winter. $$*

Azzara's. This typical Italian trattoria with light, inviting decor serves a dozen pasta dishes and a variety of pizzas, as well as chicken, lamb, veal, and shrimp—but no beef. Dinners include soup or salad, vegetable, pasta, and garlic bread. This is a no-smoking restaurant. *930 Tahoe Blvd., Incline Center Mall, tel. 916/831–0346. $*

Dining and Lodging

Hyatt Lake Tahoe Resort Hotel/Casino. Some of the rooms in this luxurious, four-star hotel on the lake have fireplaces. A children's program and rental bicycles are available. The restaurants are Hugo's Rotisserie, Ciao Mein Trattoria (Oriental-Italian), and Sierra Cafe (open 24 hours). *Lakeshore and Country Club Dr., Box 3239, 89450, tel. 702/831–1111 or 800/233–1234, fax 702/831–7508. 460 rooms. Facilities: casino, beach, pool, spa, sauna, tennis, pay movies, health club, laundry, valet parking, entertainment. AE, DC, MC, V. $$$–$$$$*

Olympic Valley
Dining and Lodging

Resort at Squaw Creek. Adjacent to the base of Squaw Valley, this newer resort complex features a main lodge, an outdoor arcade of shops and boutiques, and a 405-room hotel. The decor suggests an opulent Sierra lodge. Nearly half of the guest rooms are suites; some have a fireplace and full kitchen, and all feature original art, custom furnishings, and good views. Outdoors, just a few feet from the hotel entrance, you can get on a triple chair lift to Squaw Valley's slopes. The restaurants include Glissandi, for haute cuisine; the buffet-style Cascades; Montagne, the Italian room; and Sweet Potatoes, a pastry-and-coffee shop. There's also Bullwhackers Pub, a sports bar serving steak and seafood. *400 Squaw Creek Rd., 96146, tel. 916/583–6300, fax 916/581–6632. 405 rooms. Facilities: 4 restaurants, bar, 4 whirlpools, heated pools, ice rink, fitness center, 18-hole golf course, tennis center. AE, MC, V. $$$$*

South Lake Tahoe
Dining

Christiania Inn. Located at the base of Heavenly Ski Resort's tram, this antiques-filled bed-and-breakfast is an old favorite for fine dining. The American-Continental menu emphasizes fresh seafood, prime beef, and veal. There's an extensive wine list. Midday buffets are served on holidays, and appetizers, soups, and salads are available in the lounge daily after 2. *3819 Saddle Rd., tel. 916/544–7337. Reservations advised. MC, V. $$–$$$*

Swiss Chalet. The Swiss decor is carried out with great consistency. The Continental menu features Swiss specialties, charbroiled steaks, veal, fresh seafood, and homemade pastries. *2544 Rte. 50, tel. 916/544–3304. Reservations advised. AE, MC, V. No lunch. Closed Mon., Nov. 23–Dec. 5. $$*

Nepheles. In a quaint old house with stained-glass windows, this restaurant is on the road to the Heavenly Ski Resort. The creative California cuisine emphasizes fresh food freshly prepared. Entrées range from ahi with Asian peanut sauce and Indonesian ketchup to filet mignon with champagne-cognac cream sauce; in between are such standbys as baby back ribs and beef Stroganoff. Appetizers include *Brie en brioche* (Brie in pastry), escargots, and swordfish egg rolls. *1169 Ski Run Blvd., tel. 916/544–8130. Reservations advised. AE, MC, V. No lunch. $–$$*

Red Hut Waffle Shop. A vintage Tahoe diner, all chrome and red plastic, the Red Hut is a tiny place with a dozen counter stools and a few booths. It's a traditional breakfast spot for locals, who are attracted by the huge omelets and other good food. *2749 Rte. 50, tel. 916/541–9024. No reservations. No dinner. No credit cards. $*

Scusa! This intimate Italian restaurant on the road to the Heavenly Ski Resort has smart, modern decor and delectable pasta. Besides the wide range of pasta dishes, there are hearty calzones, exotic pizzas, steak, chicken, and fresh fish entrées. The pan-fried calamari with red peppers and capers are a treat, and don't pass up the rosemary-flavored flat bread, baked fresh daily. A good wine list is presented. This is a no-smoking restaurant. *1142 Ski Run Blvd., tel. 916/542–0100. Reservations advised. MC, V. No lunch. $*

Dining and Lodging
★

Embassy Suites. In this opulent new all-suite hotel, decorated in Sierra-lodge style, fountains and waterwheels splash in the soaring, nine-story atriums, where cooked-to-order buffet breakfasts and complimentary evening cocktails are served daily. Glass elevators rise to guest suites, each with a living room, dining area, and separate bedroom. Restaurants include Pasquale's Pizza, Zachary's (casual Continental dining), and Julie's Deli. Turtles nightclub is on the ground floor. *4130 Lake Tahoe Blvd., 96150, tel. 916/544–5400 or 800/362–2779, fax 916/544–4900. 400 suites. Facilities: 3 restaurants, indoor pool, spa, exercise room, valet parking. AE, MC, V. $$$$*

Lodging
★

Inn by the Lake. This luxury motel across the road from the beach is far from the flashy casinos but connected to them by free shuttle bus. The rooms and bathrooms are spacious and comfortable, furnished in contemporary style (blond oak and pale peach). All rooms have balconies; some have lake views, wet bars, and in-room kitchens. Continental breakfast is served, and a senior-citizen discount is available. *3300 Lake Tahoe Blvd., 96150, tel. 916/542–0330 or 800/877–1466, fax 916/541–6596. 99 rooms. Facilities: heated pool, 2-level spa, sauna, movies, laundry. AE, DC, MC, V. $$$–$$$$*

Tahoe Seasons Resort. This resort, among pine trees on the side of a mountain across from the Heavenly Ski Resort, has outfitted most rooms with a fireplace, and every room with a whirlpool and mini-kitchen. The newly refurbished rooms are done in teal and contemporary decor; all beds are queen-size. *3901 Saddle Rd., 96157, tel. 916/541–6700 or 916/541–6010, fax 916/541–0653. 183 rooms. Facilities: lounge, pool, whirlpool, tennis, indoor parking, valet garage, free Lake Tahoe Airport and casino shuttle. AE, MC, V. $$$–$$$$*

★ **Best Western Station House Inn.** This pleasant inn has won design awards for its exterior and interior. The rooms are nicely appointed, with king- and queen-size beds and double-vanity bathrooms. The location is good, near a private beach yet close to the casinos. American breakfast is complimentary October–May, and a senior-citizen discount is available. *901 Park Ave., 96157, tel. 916/542–1101 or 800/822–5953, fax 916/542–1714. 102 rooms. Facilities: restaurant, lounge, pool, hot tub, shuttle to casinos. AE, D, DC, MC, V. $$$*

Best Western Lake Tahoe Inn. Located near Harrah's Casino on U.S. 50, this large motel is nicely situated on 6 acres, with gardens and the Heavenly Ski Resort directly behind. Rooms are modern and decorated in soothing colors. *4110 Lake Tahoe Blvd., 96150, tel. 916/541–2010 or 800/528–1234, fax 916/542–1428. 400 rooms. Facilities: restaurant, lounge, 2 heated pools, hot tub, valet service. AE, DC, MC, V. $$–$$$*

Forest Inn Suites. The location is excellent—5½ acres bordering a pine forest, a half block from Harrah's and Harvey's, and adjacent to a supermarket, cinema, and shops. Once considered old and staid, this property has changed its image to modern and dynamic with an extensive remodeling in 1993, which included redecorated rooms, and new landscaping and lobby. *1101 Park Ave., Box 4300, 95729, tel. 916/541–6655; in CA, 800/822–5950; fax 916/544–3135. 124 units. Facilities: 2 pools, 2 whirlpools, putting green, health spa. AE, MC, V. $$–$$$*

Lakeland Village Beach and Ski Resort. A town house–condominium complex on 1,000 feet of private beach, Lakeland Village has a wide range of accommodations: studios, suites, and town houses, all with kitchens and fireplaces. *3535 U.S. 50, 96156, tel. 916/544–1685 or 800/822–5969, fax 916/544–0193. 211 units. Facilities: beach, boating and fishing pier, 2 pools, wading pool, whirlpool, saunas, laundry. AE, MC, V. $$–$$$*

Royal Valhalla Motor Lodge. On the lake, at Lakeshore Boulevard and Stateline Avenue, this motel has simple, modern rooms, with queen-size beds and private balconies. There are elevators and some covered parking. It's popular with families because of its two- and three-bedroom suites with complete kitchens. Continental breakfast is complimentary, and a senior-citizen discount is available. *Box GG, 96157, tel. 916/544–2233 or 800/999–4104, fax 916/544–1436. 100 rooms, 33 with kitchenette. Facilities: pool, laundry. AE, DC, MC, V. $$*

★ **Best Tahoe West Inn.** A long-established motel proud of its repeat business, Tahoe West is three blocks from the beach and downtown casinos. The exterior is rustic, rooms are neatly furnished, and beds are queen-size. Coffee and doughnuts are served in the lobby. *4107 Pine Blvd., 96157, tel. 916/544–6455 or 800/522–1021, fax 916/544–0508. 60 rooms, 12 with kitchenette. Facilities: pool, sauna, whirlpool,* *private beach privileges, shuttle to casinos and ski areas. AE, DC, MC, V. $–$$*

Travelodge. There are three members of this national chain of well-run, clean budget lodges in South Lake Tahoe, all of them convenient to casinos, shopping, and recreation. All have some no-smoking rooms, and baby-sitting is available. Free local calls, HBO, and in-room coffee add to the budget appeal. *3489 U.S. 50 at Bijou Center, 96156, tel. 916/544–5266 or 800/982–1466, fax 916/544–6985, 59 rooms; 4011 U.S 50, Stateline, 96156, tel. 916/544–6000 or 800/982–3466, fax 916/544–6869, 50 rooms; 4003 U.S. 50, South Lake Tahoe, 96156, tel. 916/541–5000 or 800/982–2466, fax 916/544–6910, 66 rooms. Facilities: pool at each; Bijou center has restaurant. AE, D, DC, MC, V. $–$$*

Stateline
Dining

The Chart House. It's worth the drive up the steep grade to see the view from here—try to arrive for sunset. The American menu of steak and seafood is complemented by an abundant salad bar. There is a children's menu. *Kingsbury Grade, tel. 702/588–6276. Reservations accepted. AE, D, DC, MC, V. No lunch. $$–$$$*

★ **Llewellyn's Restaurant.** At the top of Harvey's, Llewellyn's deserves special mention. Elegantly decorated in blond wood and pastels, it offers one of the best views of Lake Tahoe from almost all tables. Dinner entrées—seafood, meat, and poultry—are served with unusual accompaniments, such as sturgeon in potato crust with saffron sauce, or veal with polenta, herbs, and pancetta. Lunches are reasonably priced, with gourmet selections as well as hamburgers. The adjacent bar (with the same view) is comfortable. *Harvey's Resort, U.S. 50, tel. 702/588–2411. Reservations accepted. Jacket and tie required. AE, D, DC, MC, V. $$–$$$*

Dining and Lodging

Caesars Tahoe. This luxurious 16-story hotel-casino, built in 1980, underwent a $16 million renovation in 1993, during which most of its 440 rooms and suites were remodeled. Most rooms offer oversize Roman tubs, king-size beds, two televisions, two telephones, and a view of Lake Tahoe or the encircling mountains. There is a lavish 40,000-square-foot casino, and top-name entertainers perform in the 1,600-seat Circus Maximus and Cabaret. Restaurants include Empress Court (Chinese), Cafe Roma (24-hour coffee shop), Pisces (seafood), Primavera (Italian), Broiler Room, and Yogurt Palace. *Box 5800, 89449, tel. 702/588–3515; reservations and show information, 800/648–3353, fax 702/586–2068. 440 rooms. Facilities: 6 restaurants, heated indoor pool, saunas, whirlpool, tennis (fee), health club (fee), movies, valet garage, parking lot. AE, DC, MC, V. $$$$*

Harrah's Tahoe Hotel/Casino. Harrah's is a luxurious 18-story hotel-casino on U.S. 50 in the casino area. All guest rooms have refrigerators (by request), private bars, and two full bathrooms, each with a television and telephone. All rooms have views of the lake and the mountains, but the least-obstructed views are from rooms on higher floors. There is an enclosed children's arcade on the lower level. Top-name entertainment is presented in the South Shore Room and Stateline Cabaret. Among its restaurants, The Summit (reservations advised, jacket and tie required) is a standout, offering romantic dining with spectacular views from the 16th floor. The creative menu includes quail with prune sauce and fritters as an appetizer, as well as artfully presented salads; lamb, venison, or seafood entrées with delicate sauces; and sensuous desserts. Other restaurants include: The Forest (buffet), Cafe Andreotti (Italian bistro), North Beach Deli (New York–style), Asia (Pacific Rim), Friday's Station (steaks and seafood), Sierra Restaurant (open 24 hours), and Bentley's Ice Cream Parlor. *Box 8, 89449, tel. 702/588–6606 or*

800/648–3773, fax 702/788–3274. 534 rooms. Facilities: 8 restaurants, casino, heated indoor pool, hot tubs, health club, valet garage, parking lot, 24-hour room and valet service, kennel. AE, DC, MC, V. $$$$

Harvey's Resort Hotel/Casino. It started as a small cabin in 1944; owner Harvey Gross played an important role in convincing the state to keep U.S. 50 open year-round, making Tahoe accessible in winter. Harvey's is now the largest resort in Tahoe, and any description of the place runs to superlatives, from the 40-foot-tall crystal chandelier in the lobby to the 88,000-square-foot casino. Rooms feature custom furnishings, oversize marble baths, and minibars. The health club, spa, and pool are free to guests, a rarity for this area. Among its restaurants, Llewelyn's (*see* Dining, *above*) is outstanding. The Sage Room Steak House is also excellent, serving prime beef, veal, and seafood, as well as Continental dishes such as pheasant in puff pastry and frog legs. Other restaurants include the Seafood Grotto and more casual options. *Box 128, 89449, tel. 702/588–2411 or 800/648–3361, fax 702/588–0489. 740 rooms. Facilities: 8 restaurants, casino, tennis, lap pool, health club, wedding chapel, valet parking, garage. AE, DC, MC, V. $$$$*

Horizon Casino Resort. Formerly called the High Sierra, this hotel recently underwent a $15 million renovation, sprucing up its lobby and casino and parking garage. Guest rooms reflect an Old West motif, with budget-quality decor, but many have beautiful lake views. The casino has a beaux arts decor, brightened by pale molded wood and mirrors. Entertainment is available at the Grande Lake Theatre, the Golden Cabaret, and the Aspen Lounge. Restaurants include Josh's (steaks, seafood, and pasta), the Four Seasons (open 24 hours), and Le Grande Buffet, with its nightly prime-rib special. *Box C, 89449, tel. 702/588–6211 or 800/322–7723, fax 702/588–1344. 539 rooms. Facilities: 3 restaurants, convention facilities, pool, wading pool, 3 hot tubs. AE, DC, MC, V. $$–$$$*

Lakeside Inn and Casino. The smallest of the Stateline casinos, and not nearly as glitzy as the big four, Lakeside has a rustic look. Guest rooms are in lodges, away from the casino area. *Rte. 50 and Kingsbury Grade, Box 5640, 89449, tel. 702/588–7777 or 800/624–7980, fax 702/588–4092. 123 rooms. Facilities: restaurant, casino. MC, V. $$–$$$*

Tahoe City
Dining
★

Wolfdale's. An intimate dinner house on the lake, Wolfdale's offers Japanese-California cuisine. The menu changes weekly and features a small number of imaginative entrées such as grilled Chinese pheasant with plum sauce and shiitake mushrooms, and baked Norwegian salmon with saffron-scallop sauce. *640 N. Lake Blvd., tel. 916/583–5700. Reservations advised. MC, V. No lunch. Closed Tues. $$$*

Christy Hill. Panoramic lake views and fireside dining distinguish this restaurant, a favorite of locals. The California cuisine features fresh seafood and game, prepared by the owner-chef. *115 Grove St., Lakehouse Mall, tel. 916/583–8551. Reservations advised. MC, V. No lunch. Closed Sun., Mon. $$–$$$*

★ **Sunnyside Restaurant.** Located in the Sunnyside Lodge (*see* Lodging, *below*), this dining room is decoated in a trim, sleek nautical style. The large lounge features rock fireplaces, comfortable sofas, a seafood bar, and snacks. Seafood is a specialty of the Continental menu. *1850 W. Lake Blvd., tel. 916/583–7200. Reservations accepted. AE, MC, V. No lunch in winter. $$–$$$*

★ **Jake's on the Lake.** Continental food is served in spacious, handsome rooms featuring oak and glass, on the water at the Boatworks Mall. There is an extensive seafood bar and a varied menu that includes meat and poultry but emphasizes fresh fish. *780 N. Lake Blvd., tel.*

916/583–0188. Reservations accepted. AE, MC, V. No lunch in winter.
$$

Grazie! Ristorante & Bar. Northern Italian cuisine, emphasizing light sauces, is served here. There are a half-dozen hearty pasta dishes and three pizza choices, but the stars are the antipasti and pasta salads. Leg of lamb and chicken are cooked on a wood-burning rotisserie and a variety of meats and seafood on the grill, served with homemade ketchup and sauces. *Roundhouse Mall, 700 N. Lake Blvd., tel. 916/583–0233. Reservations accepted. AE, D, DC, MC, V. $–$$*

Lodging
★
Chinquapin Resort. This deluxe development on 95 acres of forested lakeside land 3 miles northeast of Tahoe City includes roomy one- to four-bedroom town houses and condos with spectacular views of the lake and the mountains. Every one has a fireplace, a fully equipped kitchen, and laundry facilities. No two units are alike, since there are more than 20 floor plans, and decorating is done by the individual owners. *3600 N. Lake Tahoe Blvd., 96145, tel. 916/583–6991, fax 916/583–0937. 172 town houses and condos. Facilities: pier, beaches, 7 tennis courts, pool, saunas, hiking trails, horseshoe pit; maid service available. 1-wk minimum stay July–Aug. No credit cards. $$$–$$$$*

Sunnyside Lodge. This quaint, sunny mountain lodge has a marina and an expansive lakefront deck with steps down to the beach. Rooms are decorated in a crisp, nautical style with prints of boats hanging on the pinstripe wallcoverings, and sea chests as coffee tables. Each room has its own deck, with lake and mountain views. There's a good restaurant on the premises (*see* Dining, *above*), and Continental breakfast is included in the rate, but this is not a full-service hotel. *1850 W. Lake Blvd., 96145, tel. 916/583–7200; in CA, 800/822–2754, fax 916/583–7224. 23 rooms. MC, V. $$$–$$$$*

Rodeway Inn. Formerly the Pepper Tree Inn, this seven-story lake-view tower is within easy walking distance of the beaches, marina, shops, and restaurants of this quaint town. Rooms are clean and comfortable if not luxurious and offer some of the best lake views. *645 N. Lake Blvd., 96145, tel. 916/583–3711 or 800/228–2000, fax 916/583–6938. 51 rooms. Facilities: pool, whirlpool, laundry. AE, MC, V. $$*

Tahoe Vista
Dining
Captain Jon's. The dining room is small and cozy, with linen cloths and fresh flowers on the tables. On chilly evenings diners are warmed by a fireplace with a raised brick hearth. The lengthy dinner menu is country French, with two dozen daily specials; the emphasis is on fish and hearty salads. The restaurant's lounge, which serves light meals, is in a separate building on the water, with a pier where guests can tie up their boats. *7220 N. Lake Blvd., tel. 916/546–4819. Reservations advised. AE, DC, MC, V. No lunch in winter (usually Nov.–May). Closed Mon. $$$*

AJ's Ristorante. Lakeside views and outdoor dining accompany authentic northern Italian cooking at this restaurant. Pizzas are delicate and varied, cooked quickly in an olive wood–fired brick oven. Other specialties are cooked on a mesquite rotisserie. There's an interesting appetizer menu; Sunday brunch is also served. The decor is elegant rustic, with fine art, sculpture, and white-linen table coverings. *7360 N. Lake Tahoe Blvd., tel. 916/546–3640. Reservations advised. MC, V. No lunch in winter. $$–$$$*

Truckee
Dining and
Lodging
Northstar-at-Tahoe Resort. This 20-year-old resort-village offers a peaceful, scenic getaway year-round. Accommodations range from hotel rooms to condos and private houses, all clustered around the shops and restaurants in the tiny village. Northstar is popular for

meetings, seminars, and families because it offers all facilities, including loads of sports—downhill and cross-country skiing, mountain biking, horseback riding, tennis, and golf. Summer rates are lower than winter rates. *Off Rte. 267 between Truckee and North Shore, Box 129, 96160, tel. 916/562–1010 or 800/533–6787, fax 916/587–0214. 230 units. Facilities: 3 restaurants, deli, 10 tennis courts, 18-hole golf course, skiing, mountain biking, horseback riding, child-care center. AE, D, MC, V. $$$–$$$$*

Nightlife

Major nighttime entertainment is found at the larger casinos. The top venues are the **Circus Maximus** at Caesars Tahoe, the **Emerald Theater** at Harvey's, the **South Shore Room** at Harrah's, and Horizon's **Grand Lake Theatre.** Each theater is as large as a Broadway house. Typical headliners are Jay Leno, David Copperfield, Kenny Rogers, and Johnny Mathis. For Las Vegas–style production shows—fast-paced dancing, singing, and novelty acts—try Harrah's or the Horizon. The big showrooms also occasionally present performances of Broadway musicals by touring Broadway companies or by casts assembled for the casino.

Reservations are almost always required for superstar shows. Depending on the act, cocktail shows usually cost $12–$40, including Nevada's sales and entertainment taxes. Smaller casino cabarets sometimes have a cover charge or drink minimum. There are also lounges with no admission charge, featuring jazz and pop-music soloists and groups. Even these performers don't try to compete all night with gambling; the last set usually ends at 2:30 or 3 AM.

Lounges around the lake offer pop and country-music singers and musicians, and in winter the ski resorts do the same. Summer alternatives are outdoor music events, from chamber quartets to jazz bands and rock performers, at Sand Harbor and the Lake Tahoe Visitors Center amphitheater.

9 The Sierra National Parks

*By Barbara
Elizabeth
Shannon and
Pam Hegarty*

*Updated by
Rosemary
Freskos*

Yosemite, Sequoia, and Kings Canyon national parks are famous throughout the world for their unique sights and experiences. Yosemite, especially, should be on your "don't miss" list. Unfortunately, it's on everyone else's as well, so advance reservations are essential. During extremely busy periods—when snow closes high country roads in late spring or on crowded summer weekends— Yosemite Valley may be closed to all vehicles unless their drivers have overnight reservations, though this rarely happens. Because the parks are accessible year-round, it is possible to avoid these conditions. From mid-April to Memorial Day and from Labor Day to mid-October, the weather is usually hospitable and the parks less bustling. We recommend allowing several days to explore the parks, but if your time is limited, a one-day guided tour will at least allow you a glimpse of the parks' wonders. We also recommend that you make your plans far enough in advance so you can stay in the parks themselves, not in one of the "gateway cities" in the foothills or Central Valley. You'll probably be adjusting to a higher altitude, dealing with traffic, and exercising a fair amount, so save your energy for exploring the park, not driving to and from it.

Yosemite, the most popular of the three parks, hosts about 3.9 million visitors annually. Sequoia and Kings Canyon parks have far fewer attractions and consequently far fewer visitors. All three sites celebrated their centennial as national parks in 1990, and many of the lodgings, restaurants, and exhibits were spiffed up for the occasion.

Yosemite National Park

Yosemite Valley is one of the most famous sights (or collection of sights) in California. The surrounding granite peaks and domes, such as El Capitan and Half Dome, rise more than 3,000 feet above the valley floor; two of the five waterfalls that cascade over the valley's rim are among the world's 10 highest; and the Merced River, placid here, runs through the valley. Such extravagant praise has been written of this valley (by John Muir and others) and so many beautiful photographs taken (by Ansel Adams and others) that you may wonder if the reality can possibly measure up. For almost everyone, it does; Yosemite is a reminder of what "breathtaking" and "marvelous" really mean.

Although Yosemite's 1,170 square miles of national park (about the size of Rhode Island), is 94.5% undeveloped wilderness, accessible only to backpackers and horseback riders, many sites can be explored by the more than 1,000 miles of roads, hiking trails, and bicycle trails. The Valley itself comprises only 7 square miles. Most visitors facilities are located in the Village. Yosemite is so large it functions as five parks: **Yosemite Valley** (open all year), **Hetch Hetchy and Wawona** (open spring to fall), **Mariposa Grove** (open spring to fall) and the high country, **Tuolumne Meadows** (open for summer hiking), and **Badger Pass Ski Area** (winter only). Christmas is a very busy time, with lodging reservations best made up to a year in advance. The western boundary dips as low as 2,000 feet in the chaparral-covered foothills; the eastern boundary rises to 13,000 feet at points along the Sierra crest. Much of this country is accessible only to backpackers and horseback riders (and thus beyond the scope of this guide), but there are many sites to be explored by visitors who do not want to range too far from their cars.

The falls are at their most spectacular in May and June. By the end of the summer, however, some may have dried up, or very nearly so. They begin flowing again in late fall with the first storms, and during the winter, they may be dramatically hung with ice. Yosemite Valley is open year-round. Because the valley floor is only 4,000 feet high, snow does not stay long, and it is possible to camp even in the winter (January highs are in the mid-40s, lows in the mid-20s). Tioga Pass Road is closed in winter (roughly late October–May), so you can't see Tuolumne Meadows then. The road to Glacier Point beyond the turnoff for Badger Pass is also not cleared in winter, but it is groomed for cross-country skiing.

Admission to the park is $5 per car for a week's stay, $3 per person if you don't arrive in a car.

Important Addresses and Numbers

General Information
National Park Service, Information Office (Box 577, Yosemite National Park, CA 95389, tel. 209/372–0265 weekdays 9–5, 209/372–0264 for a 24-hour recording, 209/372–0200 for a 24-hour recording connecting to all recorded information, including road conditions and weather) or **National Park Service, Fort Mason** (Bldg. 201, San Francisco, CA 94123, tel. 415/556–0560). For brochures about the area, contact the **Southern Yosemite Visitors Bureau** (Box 1404, Oakhurst, CA 93644, tel. 209/683–4636).

Reservations
Camping and Recreation Information (tel. 209/372–0200).

Yosemite Company (Central Reservations, 5410 E. Home, Fresno, CA 93727, tel. 209/252–4848).

Arriving and Departing

By Plane
You can fly into one of the large California airports (San Francisco or Los Angeles) and then either rent a car or take public transportation to Yosemite. Fresno is the nearest major airport. It is served by **Delta, American, USAir,** and several regional carriers. **United Express** serves Merced Airport.

By Bus
Yosemite Via (tel. 209/384–1315 or 800/842–5463) runs four daily buses from Merced to Yosemite Valley, connecting with Greyhound and Amtrak. The 2 1/2-hour trip costs $30, which includes admission to the park. **Yosemite/Sequoia Sightseeing** (tel. 209/443–5240 or 800/996–7364 in CA) runs buses from Merced (round-trip fare is $30) and Fresno ($40) to Yosemite Valley, connecting with Amtrak and picking up passengers at selected Fresno and Merced hotels and the Fresno and Merced airports.

By Car
Yosemite is a four- to five-hour drive from San Francisco and a six-hour drive from Los Angeles. From the west, three highways come to Yosemite; all intersect with Route 99, which runs north–south through the Central Valley. Route 120 is the northernmost route—the one that travels farthest and slowest through the foothills. (Note: "Route" and "Highway" are used interchangeably to denote the major state-maintained roads in this region.) The more traveled routes are Route 140 and Route 41. You'll arrive at the park's **Big Oak Flat Entrance,** 88 miles east of Manteca.

Arch Rock Entrance is 75 miles northeast of Merced via Route 140, the least mountainous road. Route 41 through Madera County is the most direct path to Yosemite and offers the most spectacular entrance, via the Wawona Tunnel, into its valley. Sixty-four miles from Fresno (or 60 from Madera on Route 145), Route 41 leaves the San

Joaquin Valley floor to climb through oak-studded hills before descending to the town of Oakhurst, the southern terminus of the historic Gold Chain Highway 49, which links the Gold Country towns for 310 miles to the north. Route 41 continues to the northeast past the Bass Lake turnoff into Fish Camp and on through the park's **South Entrance.** Two miles from this entrance is the **Mariposa Grove** of giant sequoias.

If you are coming from the east, you could cross the Sierra from Lee Vining on Route 120 (Tioga Pass). This route takes you over the Sierra crest, past Tuolumne Meadows, and down the west slope of the range. It's scenic but the mountain driving may be stressful for some, and it's open only in the summer.

Getting Around

Auto traffic in Yosemite National Park is sometimes restricted during peak periods. Check conditions before driving in.

Thanks to the free shuttle bus that runs around Yosemite Valley (7:30 AM–10 PM in the summer, 10–10 the rest of the year), it is possible to visit the park without your own car. From 9 to 5 in the summer, another free shuttle runs from Wawona to Big Trees. Campers are not allowed on this road. You should have tire chains when you drive in these mountains at any time of the year; the eastern entrance to the park at Tioga Pass is at nearly 10,000 feet.

Road Conditions **Yosemite Area Road Conditions** (tel. 209/372–0200).

Northern California Road Conditions (tel. 800/427–7623).

Guided Tours

California Parlor Car Tours (Cathedral Hill Hotel, 1101 Van Ness Ave., San Francisco 94109, tel. 415/474–7500 or 800/227–4250) offers several tours that include Yosemite (along with Monterey or Hearst Castle) and depart from either San Francisco or Los Angeles. Some tours are one-way. Lodging and some meals are included; you can choose to stay in either Yosemite Lodge or the Ahwahnee (there's a difference in price, of course). We recommend that you not consider any tour that leaves you less than one full day in the valley (and that is cutting it very short!).

Yosemite Concession Services (5410 E. Home, Fresno 93727, tel. 209/372–1240) offers daily guided tours. Advance reservations are required. Tickets can also be purchased at Yosemite locations. A two-hour valley-floor tour covers the best sightseeing points. It costs $14.25 for adults, $13.25 for senior citizens, $7.25 children under 12. A six-hour trip to the Mariposa Grove of Big Trees costs $28 adults, $27.50 senior citizens, $13.75 children. The Grand Tour (June 1–Thanksgiving) costs $38.50 adults, $35.25 senior citizens, $19 children. Guided Saddle Trips start from three stables located in the park. Two-hour rides are $30, full-day rides $60. Reservations are recommended.

Yosemite/Sequoia Sightseeing (tel. 209/443–5240 or 800/996–7364 in CA) runs one-day bus tours from Fresno, leaving at 8:30 AM and returning at 6:45 PM. Tours from Merced leave at 10:25 AM and return at 5:45 PM. Cost is $55 adults, $27.50 children 10 and under.

Highlights for First-Time Visitors

Yosemite Falls and Bridalveil Fall
El Capitan and Half Dome
The view from Glacier Point

Exploring Yosemite National Park

Numbers in the margin correspond to points of interest on the Yosemite National Park map.

Although there is more to see in Yosemite National Park than in the valley, this is the primary, if not only, destination for many visitors, especially those who won't be making backpack or pack-animal trips. Because the valley is only 7 miles long and averages less than 1 mile wide, you can visit sites in whatever order you choose and return to your favorites at different times of the day.

At **Yosemite Village,** near the east end of the valley, you'll find the park headquarters, a restaurant, store, and gas station, the Ahwahnee Hotel, Yosemite Lodge, a medical clinic, and a **Visitors Center,** where park rangers provide information and wilderness permits (necessary for overnight backpacking). There are exhibits on natural and human history as well as an adjacent Indian Cultural Museum, and a re-created Ahwahneechee village. *Tel. 209/372–0265. Open daily 9–5, with extended hours in summer.*

Yosemite Falls is the highest waterfall in North America and the fifth-highest in the world. The upper falls (1,430 feet), the middle cascades (675 feet), and the lower falls (320 feet) combine for a total of 2,425 feet and, when viewed from the valley, appear as a single waterfall. From the parking lot there is a 1/4-mile trail to the base of the falls. The Yosemite Falls Trail is a strenuous 3 1/2-mile climb rising 2,700 feet, taking you above the top of the falls. It starts from Sunnyside Campground.

If you arrive in Yosemite via the Wawona Road, your first view of the valley (in John Muir's words "a revelation in landscape affairs that enriches one's life forever") will include **Bridalveil Fall,** a filmy fall of 620 feet that is often diverted as much as 20 feet one way or the other by the breeze. Native Americans called it Pohono ("puffing wind"). There is a very short (1/5-mile) trail from a parking lot on the Wawona Road to the base of the fall.

Across the valley, **Ribbon Fall** (1,612 feet) is the valley's highest single fall, but it is also the first one to dry up in the summer.

Vernal and Nevada falls are on the Merced River at the east end of the valley. **Vernal Fall** (317 feet) is bordered by fern-covered black rocks, and rainbows play in the spray at the base. **Nevada Fall** (594 feet) is the first major fall as the river comes out of the high country. Both falls can be viewed from Glacier Point or visited on foot from Happy Isles nature area, east of Yosemite Village. The roads at this end of the valley are now closed to private cars, but a free shuttle bus runs frequently from the village. From late June through early September, the Happy Isles nature area is open daily 9–5 and features exhibits on ecology.

The hike on a paved trail from Happy Isles to the bridge at the base of Vernal Fall is only moderately strenuous and less than 1 mile long. It's another steep 3/4-mile along the **Mist Trail,** open only in the warmer months, up to the top of the fall, and then an additional 2 miles to the top of Nevada Falls. The top of this trail at Nevada Falls is the beginning of the famous **John Muir Trail,** which leads south for more than 200 miles through the High Sierra to Mt. Whitney, in the southeastern section of Sequoia/Kings Canyon.

Most famous among Yosemite's peaks are El Capitan and Half
❼ Dome. **El Capitan** is the largest exposed granite monolith in the world, almost twice the height of the Rock of Gibraltar. It rises 3,593 feet above the valley, with an apparently vertical front thrust out
❽ from the valley's rim. **Half Dome** is the most distinctive rock in the region: The west side of the dome is fractured vertically and cut away to form a 2,000-foot cliff. Rising 4,733 feet from the valley floor, the top is at an altitude of 8,842 feet above sea level.

❾ **Glacier Point** offers what may be the most spectacular view of the valley and the High Sierra that you can get without hiking. The Glacier Point Road leaves Route 41 about 23 miles southwest of the valley; then it's a 16-mile drive, with fine views into higher country. From the parking area, walk a few hundred yards and you'll be able to see Nevada, Vernal, and Yosemite falls as well as Half Dome and other peaks. This road is closed beyond the turnoff for Badger Pass Ski Area in the winter.

❿ At the **Pioneer Yosemite History Center** in Wawona (on Rte. 41) are local historic buildings moved here from their original sites. A living history program in summer re-creates Yosemite's past, including stagecoach rides. The center is open late June–early September, Wednesday–Sunday 9 AM–1 PM and 2–5 PM.

Farther down the Wawona Road (36 miles from the valley) is the
⓫ **Mariposa Grove of Big Trees.** This fine grove of *Sequoiadendron giganteum* can be visited on foot or on the one-hour tram rides in summer (admission $6 adults, $5.50 for those 62 and older, $3 children 4–12; open May–Oct., daily 9–6). The Grizzly Giant is the oldest tree here; its age is estimated to be 2,700 years; its base diameter is 30.7 feet; its circumference is 96 1/2 feet; and its height 210 feet. The Wawona Tunnel Tree—the granddaddy of Yosemite giants that was the centerpiece of many a vacation photo opportunity featuring family, car, and tree base—fell during the winter of 1968–69 (did anyone hear it?), but two other tunnel trees nearby remain. A museum, which doubles as a bookstore, presents information on the big trees (open Memorial Day–Labor Day, 9:30–4:30).

⓬ **Hetch Hetchy Reservoir** is about 40 miles from Yosemite Valley, via Big Oak Flat Road and Route 120. The reservoir supplies water and power (some of which is sold at a profit) to San Francisco. Some say John Muir died of heartbreak when this beautiful valley was dammed and buried beneath 300 feet of water in 1913.

The Tioga Pass Road (Route 120) crosses the Sierra Nevada and meets U.S. 395 at Lee Vining. This scenic route (open only in sum-
⓭ mer) will take you past **Tuolumne Meadows,** the largest alpine meadow in the Sierra. There are campgrounds, a gas station, store (with very limited and expensive choice of provisions), stables, lodge, and visitors center (open late June–early September, daily 8–7:30). This is the trailhead for many backpack trips into the High Sierra, but there are also shorter day hikes you can take. Remember, though, to give yourself time (a day or two, at least) to get acclimated to the altitude: 8,575 feet. From Yosemite Valley, it's 55 miles to Tuolumne Meadows and 74 miles to Lee Vining.

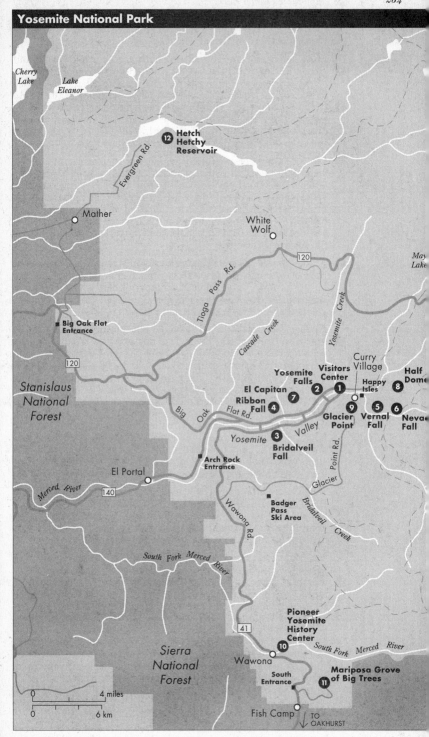

Yosemite National Park

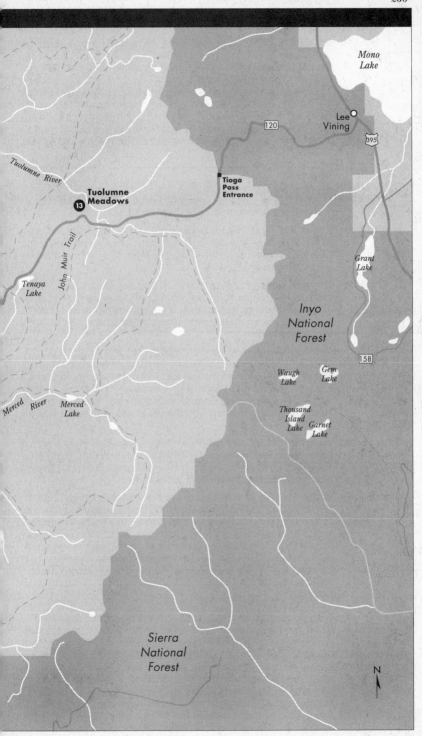

Off the Beaten Track

From early May to late October and during the Christmas holiday week, actor Lee Stetson portrays noted naturalist John Muir, bringing to life Muir's wit, wisdom, and storytelling skill. Stetson's programs—"An Evening with a Tramp" and "The Spirit of John Muir"—are two of the park's best-loved shows. Locations and times are listed in the Yosemite Guide, the newspaper handed to you upon entering the park (and also found at the visitors center and at many local stores). Stetson, as John Muir, also leads free interpretive walks twice a week; the walks start at the visitors center (tel. 209/372–0298).

Sports

Bicycling   Bicycles can be rented at **Yosemite Lodge** or **Curry Village** April–November. The cost is $4.75 per hour or $16 per day.

Fishing   The state Fish and Game Department stocks reservoirs and most roadside streams on public lands with catchable-size rainbow trout. Check with Yosemite Visitor Center or Pines Marina (*see below*) for information on specific locations.

Hiking   Hiking is the primary sport here. If you are hiking up any of the steep trails, remember to stay on the trail. Also consider the effect of the altitude on your endurance. If you plan to backpack overnight, you'll need a wilderness permit (free), available at visitors centers or ranger stations.

Rock Climbing   **Yosemite Mountaineering** (tel. 209/372–1244 Sept.–May or 209/372–1335 June–Aug.) conducts beginner through intermediate rock climbing and backpacking classes. A one-day session includes a hands-on introduction to climbing. Classes are held April–September, weather permitting. In winter, they offer cross-country ski instruction and snow camping trips. They also rent equipment for camping.

Water Sports   **Pines Marina** (tel. 209/642–3565) at Bass Lake Reservoir rents ski boats, house and fishing boats, Jet Skis, and funabouts. Open April 1 through October 31. Lodging facilities range from U.S. Forest Service campgrounds to luxury hotel-chalets.

Winter Sports   **Badger Pass Ski Area,** off the Glacier Point Road (tel. 209/372–1330), has nine runs serviced by one triple and three double chair lifts, and an excellent ski school. Gentle slopes make this an ideal beginners area. The cross-country center has a groomed and tracked 21-mile loop from Badger Pass to Glacier Point where, with reservations, you can overnight in a hut and eat prepared meals. Snowshoeing is also available. There is an outdoor skating rink at **Curry Village.**

Dining

With precious few exceptions, the best meals available in our national parks are probably those cooked on portable grills at the various campgrounds. There is a snack bar in Yosemite Village, as well as coffee shops and a cafeteria at the Ahwahnee and Yosemite Lodge. Even so, if you are just there for a day, you will not want to waste precious time hunting about for food; instead, stop at a grocery store on the way in and fill up your hamper and ice chest with the makings of a picnic to enjoy under the umbrellas of giant fir trees. The price categories in the listings below are based on the cost of a full dinner for one, excluding drinks, tax, and tip.

Highly recommended restaurants are indicated by a star ★.

Category	Cost*
$$$$	over $35
$$$	$25–$35
$$	$15–$25
$	under $15

per person for a three-course meal, excluding drinks, service, and tax

In the Park

$$$ ★ **Ahwahnee Hotel.** With its 34-foot-tall trestle-beamed ceiling, full-length windows, and twinkling chandeliers, this is Yosemite's most impressive and romantic restaurant. Even if it's a splurge, you should dine here at least once during your stay in the Valley. Classic American specialties focus on steak, trout and prime rib, all competently prepared. Generations of Californians have made a ritual of spending Christmas and New Year's here, so make reservations well in advance. *Yosemite Village, tel. 209/372–1489. Reservations advised. Jacket and tie preferred. D, MC, V.*

$$ **Mountain Room Broiler.** The food becomes secondary when you see the spectacular Yosemite Falls through the dining room's window-wall. Best bets are steaks, chops, roast duck, and a fresh herb-basted roast chicken. *Yosemite Lodge, tel. 209/372–1281. Dress: casual. D, MC, V. Dinner only.*

$$ **Wawona Hotel Dining Room.** You can watch deer graze on the meadow from the multipane windows of this romantic, candlelit restaurant dating back to the late 1800s. Vintage, handpainted lamp shades and waitresses in ankle-length skirts set the scene for nostalgia. Classic American dishes focus on chicken, steak, and fish. *Wawona, tel. 209/375–6556. Reservations required for dinner. Dress: casual. D, MC, V.*

$ **Four Seasons Restaurant.** The upscale rustic setting here features high-finish natural wood tables and lots of potted representatives of the local greenery and flora. The breakfast is hearty and all-American; dinner offerings cover the beef, chicken, and fish spectrum, plus vegetarian fare. *Yosemite Lodge, tel. 209/372–1269. Dress: casual. D, MC, V. Closed lunch.*

Outside the Park

$$$$ ★ **Erna's Elderberry House.** As a special treat, stop at this countryside gem, where the owner, Vienna-born Erna Kubin, offers bountiful Continental-California cuisine, along with dishes from whatever country she's visited recently. Prix-fixe, six-course dinners change nightly. *48688 Victoria La., Oakhurst, tel. 209/683–6800. Reservations advised. Jacket advised. MC, V. Sun. brunch. Closed lunch Sat.–Tues., dinner Mon. and Tues., and first 3 wks of Jan.*

$$ **Ducey's on the Lake.** This lodge-style resort overlooking scenic Bass Lake attracts a lively crowd of boaters, locals, and tourists. The high-ceilinged, exposed-beam dining room serves prime rib, steaks, seafood, and pasta. Salmon Wellington prepared with mushrooms and spinach in phyllo dough is a popular dish. Sunday brunch is served from 10 to 2, twilight dinner specials ($9.95) from 4 to 6 daily. Burgers, sandwiches, and salads are the fare at the upstairs Bar & Grill. There is dancing and entertainment Friday and Saturday. Overnight guests can book lakefront suites at the Pines Resort. *54432 Road 432, Box 109, Bass Lake 93604, tel. 209/642–3131. Reser-*

vations advised for dining room, especially for brunch. Dress: casual. AE, D, DC, MC, V.

$ **Coffee Express.** If you're coming into Yosemite via Route 120, this is a cozy, casual, and very inexpensive lunch spot with friendly service. Try their chicken salad with apples and alfalfa sprouts and at least a slice of the irresistible pies. The Iron Door Saloon, across the street, claims to be the oldest operating saloon in California. *Rte. 120, Groveland, tel. 209/962–7393. Dress: casual. No credit cards. Closed dinner.*

Lodging

Most accommodations inside Yosemite National Park can best be described as "no frills." Many have no electricity or plumbing. Other than the elegant Ahwahnee and Wawona hotels, lodging is geared toward those who prefer basic motels, rustic cabins, and campgrounds in natural, forest settings to full service and luxury. Except for the off-peak season, November to March, rates are pricey given the general quality of the lodging because of limited availability. Reservations for park lodging should be made well in advance, especially in summer. Surrounding towns such as Fish Camp, Oakhurst, and Bass Lake offer park visitors additional options. All are within an hour's drive of Yosemite Village. Price categories are based on the cost of a room for two people.

Category	Cost*
$$$$	over $100
$$$	$75–$100
$$	$50–$75
$	under $50

All prices are for a double room, excluding tax.

In the Park All reservations are made through the **Yosemite Company** (Central Reservations, 5410 E. Home Ave., Fresno 93727, tel. 209/252–4848, fax 209/456–0542).

$$$$ **Ahwahnee Hotel.** This grand, 1920s-style mountain lodge is constructed of rocks and sugar-pine logs, with exposed timbers and spectacular views. The decorative style of the Grand Lounge and Solarium is a tribute to the local Miwoks and Paiutes, and the motifs continue in the room decor. The Ahwahnee was renovated for the park's 1990 centennial. *123 rooms. Facilities: restaurant, lounge, pool, tennis. D, MC, V.*

$$–$$$ **Wawona Hotel.** This 1879 National Historic Landmark is in the southern end of Yosemite National Park, near the Mariposa Grove of Big Trees. It's an old-fashioned Victorian estate of whitewashed buildings with wraparound verandas. Guests gather around the fire in the main hotel's parlor, where a pianist sings Cole Porter tunes on weekend evenings. Most rooms are small and half do not have private bath. *105 rooms. Facilities: restaurant, lounge, pool, tennis, stables, golf course adjacent. Closed weekdays. D, MC, V.*

$$–$$$ **Yosemite Lodge.** The rooms in this lodge vary from fairly rustic motel-style units with two double beds and decorated in rust and green, to very rustic cabins with no baths but within walking distance of Yosemite Falls. *495 rooms. Facilities: restaurant, lounge, pool. D, MC, V.*

$–$$ **Curry Village.** These are plain accommodations: cabins with bath and without and tent cabins with rough wood frames and canvas walls and roofs. It's a step up from camping (linens and blankets are provided), but food and cooking are not allowed because of the animals. If you stay in a cabin without bath, showers and toilets are centrally located, as they would be in a campground. *180 cabins, 426 tent cabins, 8 hotel rooms. Facilities: cafeteria, pool, rafting (fee), skating (fee), horseback riding (fee). D, MC, V.*

$ **Housekeeping Camp.** These are also rustic tent cabins, set along the Merced River, but you can cook here on gas stoves rented from the front desk. The cabins are usually rented for several weeks at a time and are difficult to get; reserving at least 366 days in advance is advised. *282 tent cabins with no bath (maximum 4 per cabin). Toilet and shower facilities in central shower house. D, MC, V.*

Outside the Park **Marriott's Tenaya Lodge.** One of the region's newest and largest hotels, this is for people who enjoy hiking in the wilderness but prefer coming home to full-service luxury. A Southwestern motif prevails in the ample rooms, which are decorated in mauve, green, and rust. The hotel is about a one-hour drive from Yosemite Village. *1122 Hwy. 41, Box 159, Fish Camp 93623, tel. 209/683–6555 or 800/635–5807, fax 209/683–8684. 242 rooms. Facilities: 2 restaurants, lounge, conference room, room service, indoor/outdoor pools, health club. AE, D, DC, MC, V.*

$$$$

$$–$$$ **Narrow Gauge Inn.** This is one of several B&Bs close to the park's Fish Camp entrance. It's comfortably furnished, with an old-fashioned decor and railroad memorabilia. The inn's restaurant is one of the best in Fish Camp. *48571 Hwy. 41, Fish Camp 93623, tel. 209/683–7720, fax 209/683–2139. AE, DC, MC, V. Closed Nov.–Mar.*

$$–$$$ Next door to the inn is a major attraction: **Yosemite Mountain-Sugar Pine Railroad.** A 4-mile scenic historic steam train excursion through the forest, this is especially interesting to children. A Saturday evening Moonlight Special excursion includes dinner and old-fashioned entertainment. There's also a small museum at Yosemite Mountain Railroad Station. *56001 Hwy. 41, Fish Camp 93623, tel. 209/683–7273. Trains run Mar.–Oct. and on a limited basis in winter.*

Camping

Reservations for camping are required year-round in Yosemite Valley and from spring through fall at three campgrounds outside the valley. They are strongly recommended at any time. Reservations for all campgrounds in Yosemite are made through **MISTIX** (Box 85705, San Diego, CA 92186-5705, tel. 619/452–0150 or 800/444–7275 U.S. and Canada, TDD 800/284–7275). You can reserve campsites no sooner than eight weeks in advance, and you should indicate the name of the park, the campground, and your first, second, and third choice of arrival dates. Campsites cost $12 per night in the valley, $10 outside the valley. If space is available, you can also make reservations in person at the Campground Reservations Office in Yosemite Valley, but we strongly recommend making them ahead of time. The campgrounds outside the valley that are not on the reservation system are first-come, first-served.

Words of warning: Park regulations mandate that visitors store food properly to prevent bears from getting it. Much property damage is caused when these animals go after food or trash and the physical safety of campers is obviously at risk as well. Canisters may be rented for $3 per day at Yosemite Village. Also, keep an eye peeled for rattlesnakes below 7,000 feet. Though rarely fatal, bites require a doctor's attention. Mineral King marmots, small members of the squirrel family, have particular dining preferences. They enjoy getting under a vehicle and chewing on radiator hoses and car wiring! They aren't afraid of humans, considering their gear a source of food, including boots, backpacks, etc. Always check under the hood before driving away. Finally, don't drink the water directly from streams and lakes as intestinal disorder may result.

Sequoia and Kings Canyon National Parks

The other two Sierra national parks are usually spoken of together. These adjacent parks share their administration and a main highway. Although you may want to concentrate on either Kings Canyon or Sequoia, most people visit both parks in one trip.

Like Yosemite, Sequoia and General Grant national parks were established in 1890. The General Grant National Park was added to over the years to include the Redwood Canyon area and the drainages of the south and middle forks of the Kings River, and eventually renamed Kings Canyon National Park. Both Sequoia and Kings Canyon now extend east to the Sierra crest. The most recent major addition was to Sequoia in 1978, to prevent the development of the Mineral King area as a ski resort.

The major attractions of both parks are the big trees (*Sequoiadendron giganteum*—the most extensive groves and the most impressive specimens are found here) and the spectacular alpine scenery. These trees are the largest living things in the world. They are not as tall as the coast redwoods (*Sequoia sempervirens*), but they are much more massive and older. The exhibits at the visitors centers and the interpretive booklets that you can get there and take with you along the trails will explain the special relationship between these trees and fire (their thick, fibrous bark helps protect them from fire and insects), and how they live so long and grow so big.

The parks encompass land from only 1,200 feet above sea level to more than 14,000 feet. Mt. Whitney, on the eastern side of Sequoia, is the highest mountain (14,495 feet) in the contiguous United States. The greatest portion of both parks is accessible only on foot or with a pack animal. The Generals Highway (46 miles from Rte. 180 in Kings Canyon National Park to the Ash Mountain Entrance in Sequoia National Park) links two major groves in the two parks and is open year-round.

Summer is the most crowded season, but even then it is much less crowded than at Yosemite. Snow may remain on the ground in the sequoia groves into June, but is usually gone by mid-month. The flowers in the Giant Forest meadows hit their peak in July. Fall is an especially good time to visit. The weather is usually warm and calm, and there are no crowds.

The entrance fee is $5 per car, $3 for pedestrians and cyclists, for a week's stay in both parks.

Important Addresses and Numbers

General Information   **Sequoia and Kings Canyon National Parks** (Three Rivers 93271, tel. 209/565–3456 daily 8–4:30 or 209/565–3351 for road and weather conditions) or **National Park Service, Fort Mason** (Bldg. 201, San Francisco 94123, tel. 415/556–0560).

Reservations **Sequoia Guest Services** (Box 789, Three Rivers 93271, tel. 209/561–3314 for both parks).

Arriving and Departing

By Car From the south, enter Sequoia National Park via Route 198, 36 miles from Visalia; from the north, enter Kings Canyon National Park via Route 180, 53 miles east of Fresno. Both highways intersect with Route 99, which runs north–south through the Central Valley. If you are driving up from Los Angeles, take Route 65 north from Bakersfield to Route 198 east of Visalia.

Getting Around

Routes 198 and 180 are connected through the parks by the Generals Highway, a paved two-lane road that is open year-round but may be closed for weeks at a time during heavy snowstorms (carry chains in winter). Drivers of RVs and drivers who are not comfortable on mountain roads should probably avoid the southern stretch between the Ash Mountain Entrance and Giant Forest. These very twisty 16 miles of narrow road rise almost 5,000 feet and are not advised for vehicles over 22 feet long. Few roads up the west slope of the Sierra rise so quickly through the foothills and offer such spectacular views of the high country. The rest of the Generals Highway is a well-graded, two-lane road and a pleasure to drive.

Route 180 beyond Grant Grove to Cedar Grove and the road to Mineral King are open only in summer. Both roads, especially the latter, which is very steep and unpaved in sections, may present a challenge to inexperienced drivers. Large vehicles are discouraged. Campers and RVs more than 30 feet long are not allowed on the Mineral King road. Trailers are not allowed in Mineral King campgrounds.

Guided Tours

Within the park, you can take van tours with **Sequoia Guest Services** (tel. 209/565–3381) of Giant Forest (two hours, $9.50 adults, $8.50 senior citizens, $5 children under 12) or of Kings Canyon (all day, $22 adults, $20 senior citizens, $11 children). You can sign up for either tour at the Giant Forest Lodge. Guest Services also runs a $1 shuttle bus between major points in the park. **Yosemite/Sequoia Sightseeing** runs a day tour from Fresno, lunch included, April through October. The cost is $55 for adults, $27.50 for children under 10.

Highlights for First-Time Visitors

The drive from Grant Grove to Cedar Grove
Redwood Mountain Grove
Lodgepole visitors center
Moro Rock

Exploring Sequoia and Kings Canyon National Parks

Numbers in the margin correspond to points of interest on the Sequoia and Kings Canyon National Parks map.

If you take Route 180 to the parks, you come into Kings Canyon National Park at the Big Stump Entrance, just southwest of Wilsonia (a private community) and **Grant Grove.** This is the grove (or what remained of a larger grove decimated by logging) that was

Sequoia and Kings Canyon National Parks

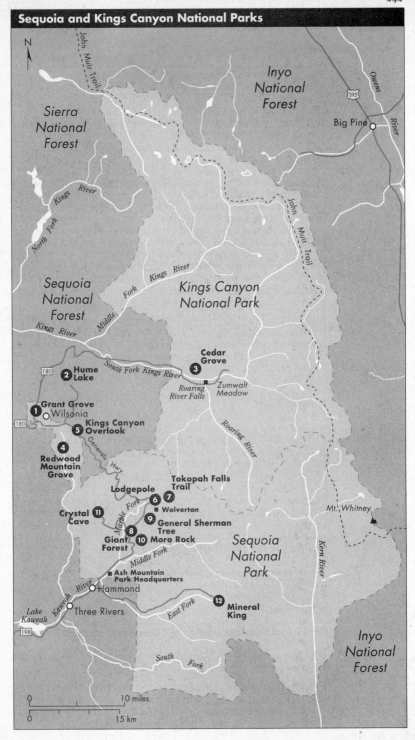

N

Sierra National Forest

Inyo National Forest

John Muir Trail

Owens River

395

Big Pine

Kings River

North Fork

Sequoia National Forest

Middle Fork Kings River

Kings River

Kings Canyon National Park

John Muir Trail

South Fork Kings River

3 Cedar Grove

180

2 Hume Lake

Roaring River Falls

Zumwalt Meadow

1 Grant Grove
Wilsonia

180

5 Kings Canyon Overlook

Roaring River

4 Redwood Mountain Grove

Generals Hwy.

Mt. Whitney ▲

Tokopah Falls Trail

Lodgepole
6 **7**

■ Wolverton

Crystal Cave **11**

Middle Fork

9 General Sherman Tree

8

Giant Forest

10 Moro Rock

Sequoia National Park

Middle Fork

Kern River

■ Ash Mountain Park Headquarters

Kaweah River

Hammond

Three Rivers

Lake Kaweah

East Fork

12 Mineral King

198

South Fork

Inyo National Forest

0 _____ 10 miles

0 _____ 15 km

designated as General Grant National Park in 1890 and is now the most highly developed area of Kings Canyon National Park. A walk along the 1-mile Big Stump Trail, starting near the park entrance, graphically demonstrates the effects of heavy logging on these groves.

At Grant Grove Village, you will find a visitors center, gas station, grocery store, campground, coffee shop, and lodging. The visitors center has exhibits on *Sequoiadendron giganteum* and the area. Trail maps for this and the other major areas of the two parks may be purchased for $1 each here and at all the visitors centers.

A spur road leads west less than 1 mile to the General Grant Grove. An easy ⅓-mile paved trail leads through the grove and is fairly accessible to disabled travelers. The most famous tree here is the **General Grant**. In total mass it is not as large as the General Sherman Tree in Sequoia, but it is nearly as tall and just as wide at its base. The **Gamlin Cabin** is one of several pioneer cabins that can be visited in the parks. A large sequoia was cut for display at the 1876 Philadelphia Exhibition; the **Centennial Stump** still remains.

② **Hume Lake** is a reservoir built early this century by loggers; today it is the site of many Christian camps, as well as a public campground. This is a pretty, small lake with views of high mountains in the distance. It's accessible by side roads off the Generals Highway east of or off Route 180 north of Grant Grove. There are fine views of Kings Canyon from either road, but the route from the Generals Highway is easier to drive.

Beyond the turnoff for Hume Lake, Route 180 (Kings River Hwy.) is closed in winter (usually Nov.–Apr.). In the summer, you can take **③** this road for a spectacular drive to the **Cedar Grove** area, a valley along the south fork of the Kings River. It's a one-hour drive from Grant Grove to the end of the road where you turn around for the ride back. Although it is steep in places, this is not a difficult road to drive. Built by convict labor in the 1930s, the road clings to some dramatic cliffs along the way, and you should watch out for falling rocks. The highway passes the scars where large groves of big trees were logged at the beginning of the century, and it runs along the south fork itself as well as through dry foothills covered with yuccas that bloom in the summer. There are amazing views down into the deepest gorge in the United States, at the confluence of the two forks, and up the canyons to the High Sierra.

Cedar Grove, named for the incense cedars that grow here, has campgrounds and lodging, a small ranger station, snack bar, convenience market, and gas station. Horses are available here, and they are a good way to explore this country. There are also short trails (one around Zumwalt Meadow, one to the base of Roaring River Falls), and Cedar Grove is the trailhead for many backpackers. If you're staying at Grant Grove or Giant Forest, Cedar Grove is a lovely day trip.

The **Generals Highway** begins south of Grant Grove and runs through this smaller portion of Kings Canyon National Park, through a part of Sequoia National Forest, and then through Sequoia National Park to the Giant Forest and on to the southern entrance to these parks at Ash Mountain.

④ The **Redwood Mountain Grove** is the largest grove of big trees in the world. There are several paved turnouts (about 4 miles from the beginning of the highway) from which you can look out over the grove (and into the smog of the Central Valley), but the grove is accessible only on foot or horseback. Less than 2 miles farther, on

5 the north side of the road, a large turnout, **Kings Canyon Overlook,** offers spectacular views into the larger portion of Kings Canyon National Park (the backcountry). You can peer into the deep canyons of the south and middle forks of the Kings River. If you drive east on Route 180 to Cedar Grove along the south fork, you will see these canyons at much closer range.

6 **Lodgepole,** in a U-shaped canyon on the Marble Fork of the Kaweah River, is a developed area with campground, snack bars, grocery store, gas station, and a market complex (open in the summer) that includes a deli, grocery store, gift shop, ice-cream parlor, public showers, public laundry, and post office. Lodgepole pines, rather than sequoias, grow here because the canyon conducts air down from the high country that is too cold for the big trees but is just right for lodgepoles. The **visitors center** (open summer, daily 8–6; winter, daily 9–5) here has the best exhibits in Sequoia or Kings Canyon, a small theater that shows films about the parks, and the Lodgepole Nature Center (open in the summer), which features hands-on exhibits and activities that are geared toward children.

A very short marked nature trail leads from behind the visitors center down to the river. Except when the river is flowing fast (be very cautious), this is a good place to rinse one's feet in cool water, because the trail runs past a "beach" of small rocks along the river.

7 The **Tokopah Falls Trail** is a more strenuous, 2-mile hike up the river from the campground (pick up a map at the visitors center), but it is also the closest you can get to the high country without taking a long hike. This is a lovely trail, but remember to bring insect repellent during the summer, when the mosquitoes can be ferocious.

8 Four miles beyond Lodgepole you will come to the **Giant Forest.** This area presently has the greatest concentration of accommodations, although plans call for moving these to the Wuksachi Village, which is under construction in the Clover Creek area. In the meantime, this is a magical place to stay because of the numerous and varied trails through a series of sequoia groves. There are a year-round grocery store, cafeteria, and two gift shops at Giant Forest Village and a wide range of accommodations at Giant Forest Lodge. The lodge also runs a full-service dining room and a gift shop during the summer.

Whether you are staying here or elsewhere in the parks, get the map of the local trails and start exploring. The well-constructed trails range in length from 1/3 mile to as far as you care to walk. They are not paved, crowded, or lined with barricades, so you quickly get the feeling of being on your own in the woods, surrounded by the most impressive trees you are ever likely to see.

Be sure to visit one of the meadows. They are lovely, especially in July when the flowers are in full bloom, and you can get some of the best views of the big trees. **Round Meadow,** behind Giant Forest Lodge, is the most easily accessible, with its 1/3-mile, wheelchair-accessible "Trail For All People." **Crescent and Log meadows** are accessible by slightly longer trails. Tharp's Log, at Log Meadow, is a small and rustic pioneer cabin built in a fallen sequoia. There is also a log cabin at **Huckleberry Meadow** that children will enjoy exploring.

9 The most famous tree here is the **General Sherman Tree.** If you aren't up for hiking, you can still get to this tree. In summer, there is usually a ranger nearby to answer questions, and there are benches so you can sit and contemplate one of the largest living things in the world. The tree is 274.9 feet tall and 102.6 feet around at its base, but what makes this the biggest tree is the fact that it is so wide for such a long way up: The first major branch is 130 feet up.

The Congress Trail starts here and travels past a series of large trees and younger sequoias. This is probably the most popular trail in the area, and it also has the most detailed booklet, so it is a good way to learn about the ecology of the groves. The booklet costs 50¢ and is available in summer from a vending machine that takes quarters near the General Sherman Tree.

A 2½-mile spur road takes off from the Generals Highway near the village and will lead you to other points of interest in the Giant Forest area as well as to the trails to Crescent and Log meadows. The road actually goes through the Tunnel Log (there is a bypass for RVs that are too tall—7 feet 9 inches and more—to fit). Auto Tree is merely a fallen tree onto which you can drive your car for a photograph (if that seems like a reasonable idea to you).

❿ This is also the road to **Moro Rock,** a granite monolith 6,725 feet high, that rises from the edge of the Giant Forest. During the Depression, the Civilian Conservation Corps built a fabulous staircase to the top. There are 400 steps and, although there is a railing along most of the route, the trail often climbs along narrow ledges over steep drops. The view from the top is spectacular. Southwest you look down the Kaweah River to Three Rivers, Lake Kaweah, and— on clear days—the Central Valley and the Coast Range. Northeast you look up into the High Sierra. Below, you look down thousands of feet to the middle fork of the Kaweah River.

⓫ **Crystal Cave** is the best known of Sequoia's many caves. Its interior was formed of limestone that became stalactites and stalagmites of marble. To reach the cave, drive to the end of the narrow, twisting, 7-mile road west from Generals Highway, south of Giant Forest Village. From the parking area it is a 15-minute hike down a steep path to the cave's entrance. There are 45-minute guided tours daily on the half hour between 10 AM and 3 PM, mid-June to mid-Sept. In the busy season, July to Labor Day, tickets are not sold at the cave; purchase them at park visitor centers. Call 209/565-3758 for prices.

⓬ The **Mineral King** area is a recent addition to the parks. In the 1960s, the U.S. Forest Service planned to have Walt Disney Productions develop a winter-sports resort here, but the opposition of conservation groups led to its incorporation in Sequoia National Park in 1978. It is accessible in summer only by a narrow, twisty, and steep road that takes off from Route 198 at Hammond. The road is only 25 miles long, but budget 90 minutes each way from Route 198. This is a tough but exciting drive to a beautiful high valley. There are two campgrounds and a ranger station; facilities are limited but some supplies are available. Many backpackers use this as a trailhead, and there are a number of fine trails for strenuous day hikes.

Montecito Sequoia Resort (tel. 800/227–9900, fax 209/565–3223), off the Generals Highway between the two parks, offers year-round family-oriented recreation. In winter, there are 21 miles of groomed cross-country ski trails, 120 miles of backcountry trails, ski rentals, and lessons. Rates include all meals, lodging, and trail use ($79 per person, per night, 2-night minimum). In summer, guests stay for six nights in this Club Med atmosphere with access to canoeing, sailing, waterskiing (fee), horseback riding (fee), a preschool program, volleyball, horseshoes, tennis, archery, nature hikes, and a heated pool

($450–$550 per adult, less for children, includes meals, lodging, and all activities and instruction).

Sports

Hiking   As in Yosemite, hiking is the primary sport in these two parks. Talk to the rangers at the visitors centers about which trails they recommend when you are there. Keep in mind that you will have to become acclimated to the altitude (over 6,000 feet at Giant Forest) before you can exert yourself fully.

Horseback Riding   Horseback riding is available at Grant Grove, Cedar Grove, Wolverton Pack Station (between Lodgepole and Giant Forest), and Mineral King. Ask at the visitors centers for specifics.

Swimming   If you get hot and need a swim, try Hume Lake (*see* Exploring, *above*). Don't try to swim in the fast-running Sierra rivers.

Winter Sports   In the winter, there is skiing and snowshoeing. You can ski cross-country at Grant Grove and Giant Forest. Rentals, lessons, and tours are offered by Sequoia Ski Touring Center (tel. 209/565–3435) at Wolverton and Grant Grove.

Rangers lead snowshoe walks through Grant Grove and Giant Forest on winter weekends. You can also use the shoes on the cross-country trails at these two areas. Snowshoes can be rented from Sequoia Ski Touring at Wolverton.

Dining

Dining in Sequoia and Kings Canyon national parks is even less of a gourmet experience than dining in Yosemite, but acceptable food is available. Again, we suggest that you bring food (especially snacks, fresh fruit, and beverages) with you. It will give you more freedom in planning your day. Giant Forest Village has a market. There are places to get a meal inside the parks, and the food is not expensive and will satisfy hunger pangs. All the restaurants within the park are managed by Guest Services (tel. 209/565–3381).

Food should not be left overnight in cars, because bears might be tempted to break in and get it.

$–$$ **Giant Forest Lodge Dining Room.** This is the fanciest restaurant in the two parks, with cloth tablecloths, soft lighting, picture windows overlooking the meadows, and a quiet atmosphere. The cuisine is basic American, featuring prime rib, shrimp, creamy pastas, halibut, vegetarian pastas, and a Sunday buffet brunch. *MC, V. No lunch. Open May–mid-Oct., daily.*

$ **Cedar Grove Restaurant.** This fast-food restaurant serves trout, top sirloin, hamburgers, hot dogs, and sandwiches for lunch and dinner. Breakfast is eggs, bacon, and toast. *No credit cards. Closed Oct.– early May.*

$ **Grant Grove Coffee Shop.** This spacious family-style restaurant, with wood tables and chairs and a long counter, serves American standards for breakfast, lunch, and dinner: eggs, burgers, and steak. There are also chef's salads, fruit platters, and seasonal fish specials. *MC, V.*

$ **Village Cafeteria.** A good selection of entrées, salads, desserts, and vegetables are served in a cafeteria-style setting. Open for breakfast, lunch, and dinner year-round, the cafeteria is where to feed a family on a budget without getting heartburn in the bargain. *No credit cards.*

Lodging

All the park's lodges and cabins are open during the summer months, but in winter only some of those in Giant Forest and Grant Grove remain open. A variety of accommodations is offered, from rustic cabins without baths at Grant Grove to deluxe motels at Giant Forest. From November through April, excluding holiday periods, low-season rates are in effect, resulting in savings of 20%–30%. The town of Three Rivers on Route 198 souithwest of the park has a few more lodges and restaurants from which to choose.

Lodging facilities within the park are operated by **Sequoia Guest Services** (Box 789, Three Rivers 93271, tel. 209/561–3314, fax 209/561–3135; MC, V). Reservations are recommended for visits at any time of the year because it's a long way out if there's no room at these inns.

Category	Cost*
$$$	$75–$100
$$	$40–$75
$	under $50

*All prices are for a double room, excluding tax.

$$$ **Cedar Grove.** At the bottom of Kings Canyon, in one of the prettiest areas of the parks, is Cedar Grove, a good location for those who plan on staying a few days and doing a lot of day hiking. Although accommodations are close to the road and there is quite a bit of traffic through here, Cedar Grove manages to retain a quiet atmosphere. Those who don't want to camp will have to book way in advance—the motel/lodge has only 18 rooms. Each room is air-conditioned and carpeted and has a private shower and two queen-size beds. *Closed Oct.–late May.*

$–$$$ **Giant Forest.** There are seven different types of accommodations in this area, including rustic cabins without bathrooms, family cabins that sleep six, and a deluxe motel. Facilities and decor vary: Some cabins have kerosene lamps and propane heat; motel rooms have carpeted floors and double and queen-size beds. Prices range accordingly. The lower-priced cabins are not available in winter.

$$ **Grant Grove.** The most luxurious accommodations here are the carpeted cabins with private baths, electric wall heaters, and double beds. Other cabins are simpler, with wood stoves providing heat and kerosene lamps providing light. A central rest room and shower facility is nearby.

Camping

Campgrounds are the most economical ($5–$10 per night) accommodations in Sequoia and Kings Canyon, and probably the most fun. Located near each of the major tourist centers, the parks' campgrounds are equipped with tables, grills, drinking water, garbage cans, and either flush or pit toilets. The one campground that takes reservations, and only from Memorial Day through Labor Day, is Lodgepole in Sequoia (contact MISTIX, tel. 800/444–7275). All others assign sites on a first-come, first-served basis, and on weekends in July and August they are often filled by Friday afternoon. Campgrounds permit a maximum of one vehicle and six persons per site.

Potwisha, Grant Grove, Lodgepole, Dorst, and Cedar Grove camp-grounds are the only areas where trailers and RVs are permitted. Sanitary disposal stations are available year-round (snow permitting) in the Potwisha and Azalea campgrounds; from Memorial Day to mid-October in Lodgepole; and from May to mid-October in Sheep Creek. There are no hookups in the parks, and only a limited number of campsites can accommodate larger vehicles. The length limit for RVs is 40 feet, for trailers 35 feet.

Lodgepole, Potwisha, and Azalea campsites stay open all year, but Lodgepole is not plowed and camping is limited to recreational vehicles in plowed parking lots or snow tenting. Other campgrounds open some time from mid-April to Memorial Day or later in September or October. Some campgrounds in Sequoia National Forest (such as Landslide, a very small campground 3 miles from Hume Lake) are just about as convenient as those within the two national parks. Campers should be aware that the nights, and even the days, can be chilly into early June.

Bears can be a problem in every campground. You must use the metal food-storage boxes found at every site. Move all food and coolers from your car to the storage box. Pets must be kept on a leash. Check bulletin boards and ask a ranger for further information. Failure to comply may result in a citation for you and the killing of the offending bear.

10 Monterey Bay

By Maria
Lenhart and
Vicky Elliott

Updated by
Nicole Harb

"The interest is perpetually fresh. On no other coast that I know shall you enjoy, in calm, sunny weather, such a spectacle of ocean's greatness, such beauty of changing color or such degrees of thunder in the sound." What Robert Louis Stevenson wrote of the Monterey Peninsula in 1879 is no less true today—it still provides a spectacle that is as exciting on the first visit as on the 23rd.

A semicircle about 90 miles (144 kilometers) across, Monterey Bay arcs into the coast at almost the exact halfway point between California's northern and southern borders. Santa Cruz sits at the top of the curve, and the Monterey Peninsula, including Monterey, Pacific Grove, and Carmel, occupies the lower end. In between, Route 1 cruises along the coastline, passing windswept beaches piled high with sand dunes. Along the route are fields of artichoke plants, the towns of Watsonville and Castroville, and Fort Ord, which is beginning its transition from army base to civilian mixed-use development.

The bay is blessed by nature. Here are deep green forests of Monterey cypress, oddly gnarled and wind-twisted trees that grow nowhere else. Here also is a vast undersea canyon, larger and deeper than the Grand Canyon, that supports a rich assortment of marine life, from fat, barking sea lions to tiny plant-like anemones.

Carefully preserved adobe houses and missions testify to the Monterey Peninsula's unique place in California history. With the arrival of Father Junípero Serra and Commander Don Gaspar de Portola from Spain in 1770, Monterey became both the military and ecclesiastical capital of Alta California. Portola established the first of California's four Spanish presidios, while Serra founded the second of 21 Franciscan missions, later moving it from Monterey to its current site in Carmel.

When Mexico revolted against Spain in 1822, Monterey remained the capital of California under Mexican rule. The town grew into a lively seaport, drawing Yankee sea traders who added their own cultural and political influence. Then, on July 7, 1846, Commodore John Sloat arrived in Monterey and raised the American flag over the Custom House, claiming California for the United States.

Monterey's political importance in the new territory was short-lived, however. Although the state constitution was framed in Colton Hall, the town was all but forgotten once gold was discovered at Sutter's Mill near Sacramento. After the Gold Rush, the state capital moved from Monterey and the town became a sleepy backwater.

At the turn of the century, however, the Monterey Peninsula began to draw tourists with the opening of the Del Monte Hotel, the most palatial resort the West Coast had ever seen. Writers and artists also discovered the peninsula, adding a rich legacy that remains to this day.

For visitors, the decline of Monterey as California's most important political and population center can be seen as a blessing. The layers of Spanish and Mexican history remain remarkably undisturbed, while the land and sea continue to inspire and delight.

Essential Information

Important Addresses and Numbers

Tourist
Information
The **Monterey Peninsula Chamber of Commerce** (Box 1770, 380 Alvarado St., Monterey 93942, tel. 408/649–1770) and the **Salinas Chamber of Commerce** (119 E. Alisal St., Salinas 93902, tel. 408/424–7611) are both open weekdays 8:30–5. The **Santa Cruz County Conference and Visitors Council** (701 Front St., Santa Cruz 95060, tel. 408/425–1234 or 800/833–3494) is open daily 9–5. Information on the region's 30 or so family-owned wineries can be obtained from **Santa Cruz Winegrowers** (Box 3000, Santa Cruz 95063, tel. 408/479–WINE).

Emergencies
Dial 911 for **police** and **ambulance** in an emergency.

Doctors
The **Monterey County Medical Society** (tel. 408/373–4197) will refer doctors on weekdays 9–5. For referrals at other times, call **Community Hospital of Monterey Peninsula** (23625 Holman Hwy., Monterey, tel. 408/624–5311). The hospital has a 24-hour emergency room.

Pharmacies
Surf 'n' Sand in Carmel at 6th and Junipero streets (tel. 408/624–1543) has a pharmacy open weekdays 9–6:30, Saturday, Sunday, and holidays 9–2.

Arriving and Departing

By Plane
Monterey Peninsula Airport (tel. 408/373–3731) is 3 miles from downtown Monterey and is served by **American Eagle** (tel. 800/433–7300), **United Airlines** and **United Express** (tel. 800/241–6522), and **USAir** (tel. 800/428–4322).

By Car
The drive south from San Francisco to Monterey can be made comfortably in three hours or less. The most scenic way is to follow Route 1 down the coast. Unless the drive is made on sunny weekends when locals are heading for the beach, the two-lane coast highway takes no longer than the freeway.

Of the freeways from San Francisco, a fast but enjoyable route is I–280 south to Route 17, just south of San Jose. Route 17 heads south and connects with Route 1 in Santa Cruz. Another option is to follow U.S. 101 south through San Jose to Salinas, then take Route 68 west to Monterey.

From Los Angeles, the drive to Monterey can be made in less than a day by heading north on U.S. 101 to Salinas and then heading west on Route 68. The spectacular but slow alternative is to take U.S. 101 to San Luis Obispo and then follow the hairpin turns of Route 1 up the coast. Allow at least three extra hours if you do.

By Train
Amtrak (tel. 800/USA–RAIL) runs the *Coast Starlight* train between Los Angeles and Seattle, making a stop in Salinas (11 Station Pl.).

By Bus
From San Francisco, **Greyhound Lines** (tel. 800/231–2222) serves Monterey four times daily on a trip that takes three to five hours.

Getting Around

By Car
Route 1 runs down the coast, past pumpkin and artichoke fields and the seaside communities of Half Moon Bay and Santa Cruz. Route

17 crosses the redwood-filled Santa Cruz mountains between San Jose and Santa Cruz, where it intersects with Route 1.

If your route takes you through San Jose, avoid the rush hour, which starts early and can be horrendous. Note also that parking is especially difficult in Carmel and in the vicinity of the Monterey Bay Aquarium on Cannery Row.

By Bus **Monterey-Salinas Transit** (tel. 408/424–7695) provides frequent service between towns and many major sightseeing spots and shopping areas for $1.25 per ride, with an additional $1.25 for each zone you travel into, or $3.75 for a day pass.

Guided Tours

The "super yacht" *Chardonnay II* (Box 66966, Scotts Valley 95067, tel. 408/423–1213) accommodates 49 passengers for cruises on Monterey Bay, leaving from the yacht harbor in Santa Cruz. **A Seacoast Safari** (tel. 408/372–1288) offers both custom tours and half-day minivan tours of the Monterey Peninsula, which include the 17-Mile Drive, Carmel shopping, Cannery Row, and wine tasting. Motorcoach tours departing from San Francisco that feature the Monterey Peninsula in their Northern California itineraries include **California Parlor Car Tours** (tel. 415/474–7500 or 800/227–4250) and **Gray Line** (tel. 415/558–9400). **The Rider's Guide** (Suite 255, 484 Lake Park Ave., Oakland 94610, tel. 510/653–2553) produces a self-guided audiotape tour about the history, landmarks, and attractions of the Monterey peninsula and Big Sur, for $12.95, or $15.95 in vinyl binder, plus $2 postage.

Exploring Monterey Bay

Despite its compact size, the Monterey Peninsula is packed with diversions—it would take more than a weekend just to get beyond the surface. Although most of the region's communities are situated only a few minutes' drive away from each other, each is remarkably different in flavor.

If you have an interest in California history and historic preservation, the place to start is in Monterey, where you need at least two full days to explore the adobe buildings along the Path of History, a state historic park encompassing much of the downtown area. Fans of Victorian architecture will want to explore the many fine examples in Pacific Grove. In Carmel you can shop till you drop, and when summer and weekend hordes overwhelm the town's boutiques, art galleries, houseware outlets, and gift shops, you can slip off to enjoy the incomparable loveliness of the Carmel coast.

A sweater or windbreaker is nearly always necessary along the coast, where a cool breeze is usually blowing and the fog is on the way in or out. Inland, temperatures in Salinas or Carmel Valley can be a good 15 or 20 degrees warmer than those in Carmel and Monterey.

Highlights for First-Time Visitors

Asilomar State Beach, Pacific Grove
Boardwalk, Santa Cruz
Carmel Mission, Carmel
Monterey Bay Aquarium, Monterey
Monterey State Historic Park, Monterey

Point Piños Light Station, Pacific Grove
San Juan Bautista State Historic Park, San Juan Bautista
Steinbeck Library, Salinas

Santa Cruz

Numbers in the margin correspond to points of interest on the Monterey Bay map.

❶ The beach town of **Santa Cruz** is sheltered by the surrounding mountains from the coastal fog to the north and south, and from the smoggy skies of the San Francisco Bay area. The climate here is mild, and it is usually warmer and sunnier than elsewhere along the coast this far north. Something of a haven for those opting out of the rat race, and a bastion of '60s-style counterculture values, Santa Cruz has been at the forefront of such very Californian trends as health food, recycling, and environmentalism. It is less manicured than its up-market neighbors to the south, but more urban than the agricultural towns between it and the Monterey Peninsula.

The town gets something of its youthful ambience from the nearby **University of California at Santa Cruz.** The school's harmonious redwood buildings are perched on the forested hills above the town, and the campus is tailor-made for the contemplative life, with a juxtaposition of sylvan settings and sweeping vistas over open meadows onto the bay. The humanities faculty offers a major in the "History of Consciousness," and this does seem to be the perfect spot for it.

The earthquake of 1989 laid low much of **Pacific Garden Mall,** in the historic downtown section. The epicenter of the quake was only a few miles away, in the Santa Cruz mountains, and the unreinforced masonry of the town's older buildings proved extremely vulnerable. Rebuilding has been a long process, and there are still gaping lots along Pacific Avenue, in the heart of the downtown area, but the landscapers have been out replanting and widening the sidewalks for the café traffic, and the spirit of the place is alive and well again.

TimeOut — **Caffè Pergolesi** (418 Cedar St., tel. 408/426–1775), a Victorian residence not far from the downtown area, has become a humming coffeehouse with a very European flair. You can read the newspaper and enjoy a pastry at one of the veranda tables, or have a light meal inside, surrounded by local artists' work.

Santa Cruz has been a seaside resort since the mid-19th century, and its **Boardwalk's** 1911 **Merry-Go-Round** and **Giant Dipper** monster roller-coaster are national historic landmarks. Elsewhere along the Boardwalk the **Casino Arcade** has its share of video-game technology, as does **Neptune's Kingdom,** which features a state-of-the-art miniature golf course with robotics and fiber-optics special effects, but this is still primarily a place of good old-fashioned fun. The colonnades of the turn-of-the-century **Cocoanut Grove** (tel. 408/423–2053), now a convention center and banquet hall, host a lavish Sunday brunch beneath the glass dome of its Sun Room. *Boardwalk, tel. 408/423–5590 or 426–7433. Day pass for unlimited rides, $16.95. Open daily Memorial Day–Labor Day, weekends and holidays rest of year; opens at 11 AM, closing times vary between dusk, 9 PM, and 11 PM.*

The **Santa Cruz Municipal Wharf** is lined with restaurants and is enlivened from below by the barking and baying of the sea lions that

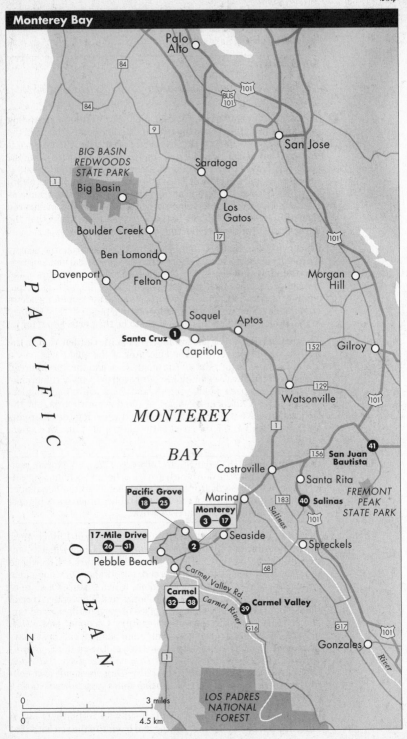

Monterey Bay

lounge in communal heaps under the wharf's pilings and shame-lessly accept any seafood offerings tossed their way.

Down West Cliff Drive along the promontory are **Seal Rock,** another favored pinniped hangout, and the **Lighthouse,** which has a surfing museum (tel. 408/429–3429; open noon–4; closed Tues.–Wed. in winter, Tues. in summer). The road continues on to **Natural Bridges State Park,** famous for its tide pools and a colony of Monarch butterflies. *2531 W. Cliff Dr., tel. 408/423–4609. Open 8 AM–sunset. Visitor Center open 10 AM–4 PM. Parking fee: $6.*

Santa Cruz's temperate climate has attracted some fine wineries, producing chiefly chardonnay, cabernet sauvignon, and Pinot Noir. Among the wineries open on a regular basis for testing are **Bargetto Winery** (3535 N. Main St., Soquel, tel. 408/475–2258; open Mon.–Sat. 10–5, Sun. 11–5), which also has a gift shop and art gallery; **Byington Winery and Vineyard** (21850 Bear Creek Rd., Los Gatos, tel. 408/354–1111; open daily 11–5), headquartered in a handsome château with an ocean view (there's a barbecue area for picnics); and, across the road, **David Bruce Winery** (21439 Bear Creek Rd., Los Gatos, tel. 408/354–4214; open Wed.–Sun. noon–5), home to one of the last winemakers who still stomps his grapes by foot. **Hallcrest Vineyards** (379 Felton Empire Rd., Felton, tel. 408/335–4441; open daily 11–5:30) holds tastings on a big, sunny deck overlooking 52-year-old vines. Many of the area's other wineries are open weekends only; all will arrange tours by appointment.

Monterey and Pacific Grove

2 Follow the curve of the bay's coast south from Santa Cruz along Route 1, and a 45-mile drive will bring you to **Monterey,** California's first capital. A good deal of the city's early history can be gleaned from the well-preserved adobe buildings of **Monterey State Historic Park** (tel. 408/649–7118). Far from being a hermetic period museum, the park facilities are an integral part of the day-to-day business life of the town—some of the buildings still serve as government offices, restaurants, banks, and private residences. A 2-mile self-guided walking tour of the park is outlined in the brochure "Path of History," available at the Chamber of Commerce or at many of the landmark buildings contained in the park. *2–day tour package for multiple sites: $5 adults, $3 for youth 13–18, $2 children 6–12.*

Numbers in the margin correspond to points of interest on the Monterey and Pacific Grove map.

Monterey State Historic Park
3 A logical beginning to the walking tour is at the **Custom House** across from Fisherman's Wharf. Built by the Mexican government in 1827 and considered the oldest government building west of the Rockies, this two-story adobe was the first stop for sea traders whose goods were subject to duty. Its grandest day in Monterey's history came at the beginning of the Mexican-American War in 1846, when Commodore John Sloat raised the American flag over the building and claimed California for the United States. Now the lower floor displays examples of a typical cargo from a 19th-century trading ship. *1 Custom House Plaza, tel. 408/649–2909. Admission free. Open Sept.–May, daily 10–4; June–Aug., daily 10–5.*

4 On the same plaza, the **Monterey Maritime Museum** is devoted to the private collection of maritime artifacts of former Carmel mayor Allen Knight. Among the exhibits of ship models, scrimshaw items, and nautical prints, the highlight is the enormous multifaceted Fresnel Lens from the Point Sur Lighthouse. *5 Custom House Plaza, tel.*

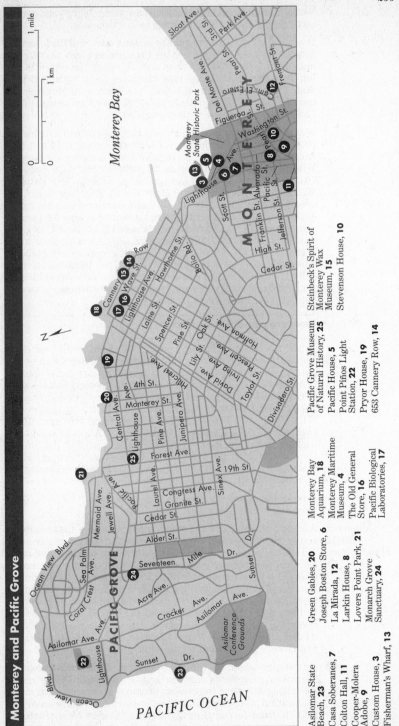

256

Monterey and Pacific Grove

Monterey Bay

PACIFIC OCEAN

MONTEREY

PACIFIC GROVE

Asilomar State Beach, **23**
Casa Soberanes, **7**
Colton Hall, **11**
Cooper-Molera Adobe, **9**
Custom House, **3**
Fisherman's Wharf, **13**

Green Gables, **20**
Joseph Boston Store, **6**
La Mirada, **12**
Larkin House, **8**
Lovers Point Park, **21**
Monarch Grove Sanctuary, **24**

Monterey Bay Aquarium, **18**
Monterey Maritime Museum, **4**
The Old General Store, **16**
Pacific Biological Laboratories, **17**

Pacific Grove Museum of Natural History, **25**
Pacific House, **5**
Point Piños Light Station, **22**
Pryor House, **19**
653 Cannery Row, **14**

Steinbeck's Spirit of Monterey Wax Museum, **15**
Stevenson House, **10**

408/375–2553. Admission: $5 adults, $3 children 12–18, $2 children 6–12. Open daily 10–5.

❺ The next stop along the path is **Pacific House,** a former hotel and saloon, and now a museum of early California life. There are Gold Rush relics, historic photographs of old Monterey, and a costume gallery displaying various period fashions. *10 Custom House Plaza, tel. 408/649–2907. Admission: $2, $1.50 children 12–18, $1 children 6–12. Open Sept.–May, daily 10–4; June–Aug., daily 10–5.*

❻ Monterey's most historic shop is the **Joseph Boston Store,** located in the Casa del Oro adobe. It first opened for business in 1849, and was built from wood from a shipwrecked Portuguese whaler. Now staffed with volunteers from the Monterey History and Art Association, it is stocked with antiques, tea, and a variety of local craft items. *Scott and Oliver Sts., tel. 408/649–3364. Open Sept.–May, Wed.–Sat. 10–4; June–Aug., Wed.–Sat. 10–5, Sun. noon–5.*

❼ The low-ceilinged **Casa Soberanes,** a classic adobe structure, was once a Custom House guard's residence. *336 Pacific St. Admission: $2, $1.50 children 13–18, $1 children 6–12. Closed Tues., Thurs. Tours at 10 and 11, gardens open Sept.–May, 10–4; June–Aug., 10–5.*

❽ Farther along the Path of History is the **Larkin House,** one of the most architecturally significant homes in California. Built in 1835, this two-story adobe with a veranda encircling the second floor reflects the blending of Mexican and New England influences into the Monterey style. The rooms are furnished with period antiques, many of them brought from New Hampshire to Monterey by the Larkin family. *Jefferson St. and Calle Principal. Admission: $2 adults, $1.50 children 13–18, $1 children 6–12. Tours Sept.–May, at 1, 2, and 3; June–Aug., at 2, 3, and 4. Closed Tues., Thurs.*

❾ The largest site along the Path of History is the restored **Cooper-Molera Adobe,** a 2-acre complex that includes an early California house dating from the 1820s, a visitors center, and a large garden enclosed by a high adobe wall. The tile-roofed house is filled with antiques and memorabilia, mostly from the Victorian era, that illustrate the life of a prosperous pioneer family. *Polk and Munras Sts. Admission: $2, $1.50 children 13–18, $1 children 6–12. Open Sept.–May, 10–4, tours at 10 and 11; June–Aug., 10–5, tours at 10, 11, and 12. Closed Mon.*

❿ For literary and history buffs, one of the path's greatest treasures is the **Stevenson House,** named in honor of Robert Louis Stevenson, author of *Treasure Island* and other classics, who boarded there briefly in a tiny upstairs room. In addition to Stevenson's room, which is furnished with items from his family's estate, there is a gallery of the author's memorabilia and several charming period rooms, including a children's nursery stocked with Victorian toys and games. *530 Houston St. Admission: $2 adults, $1.50 children 13–18, $1 children 6–12. Sept.–May, tours at 1, 2, and 3, gardens open 10–4; June–Aug., tours at 2, 3, and 4, gardens open 10–5. Closed Mon.*

⓫ California's equivalent of Independence Hall is **Colton Hall,** where a convention of delegates met in 1849 to draft the first state constitution. Now the historic white building, which has served as a school, courthouse, and county seat, is a museum furnished as it was during the constitutional convention. The extensive grounds outside the hall also include a more notorious building, the Old Monterey Jail, where inmates languished behind thick granite walls. *Pacific St. between Madison and Jefferson Sts., tel. 408/646–5640. Admission free. Open Mar.–Oct., daily 10–noon and 1–5; Nov.–Feb., 10–noon and 1–4.*

Off the Path of History, just across the street from Colton Hall, is the **Monterey Peninsula Museum of Art.** It is especially strong on artists and photographers who have worked in the area, a distinguished lot that includes Ansel Adams and Edward Weston. Another focus is international folk art; the collection ranges from Kentucky hearth brooms to Tibetan prayer wheels. *559 Pacific St., tel. 408/372–7591. $2 donation suggested. Open Tues.–Sat. 10–4, Sun. 1–4.*

⑫ The newest addition to Monterey's art scene is **La Mirada,** a 19th-century adobe house filled with Asian and European antiques. A 10,000-square-foot gallery space, designed by architect Charles Moore, was recently added to house an extensive collection of Asian and Californian regional art. The permanent collection includes works by Armin Carl Hansen, as well as a large netsuke collection. The museum is also home to magnificent rose and rhododendron gardens. *720 La Mirada, at Fremont St., tel. 408/372–3689. Admission: $5 adults, $3 students and active military, free for children under 12 and on the 1st Sun. of every month. Open Thurs.–Sat. 10–4, Sun. 1–4.*

Fisherman's Wharf and Cannery Row Inevitably, visitors are drawn to the waterfront in Monterey, if only because the mournful barking of sea lions that can be heard throughout the town makes its presence impossible to ignore. The whiskered marine mammals are best enjoyed while walking along **⑬** **Fisherman's Wharf,** an aging pier crowded with souvenir shops, fish markets, seafood restaurants, and popcorn stands.

Although tacky and touristy to the utmost, the wharf is a good place to visit, especially with children. For years, an organ grinder with a costumed monkey has entertained crowds at the entrance. Farther down, you can buy a bag of squid to feed the sea lions that beg from the waters below.

From the wharf, a footpath along the shore leads to **Cannery Row,** a street that has undergone several transformations since it was immortalized in John Steinbeck's 1944 novel of the same name. The street that Steinbeck described was crowded with sardine canneries processing, at their peak, nearly 200,000 tons of the smelly silver fish a year. During the mid-1940s, however, the sardines mysteriously disappeared from the bay, causing the canneries to close.

Over the years the old tin-roof canneries have been converted to restaurants, art galleries, and minimalls with shops selling T-shirts, fudge, and plastic otters. Recent tourist development along the row has been more tasteful, however, including several attractive inns and hotels. The Monterey Plaza Hotel (*see* Lodging, *below*) is a good place to relax over a drink and watch for otters.

Although Steinbeck would have trouble recognizing Cannery Row today, there are still some historical and architectural features from **⑭** its colorful past. One building to take note of is **653 Cannery Row,** with its tiled Chinese dragon roof that dates from 1929. On a kitschy note, characters from the novel *Cannery Row* are depicted in wax **⑮** at **Steinbeck's Spirit of Monterey Wax Museum,** which also features a 25-minute description of the history of the area over the past 400 years, with a recorded narration by Steinbeck himself. *700 Cannery Row, tel. 408/375–3770. Admission: $4.95 adults, $3.95 senior citizens and students, $2.95 children 6–12. Open daily 9–9.*

⑯ The building now called the **Old General Store** is the former Wing Chong Market that Steinbeck called Lee Chong's Heavenly Flower Grocery. Across the street, a weathered wooden building at 800 Can-

⑰ nery Row was the **Pacific Biological Laboratories,** where Edward F. Ricketts, the inspiration for Doc in Steinbeck's novel, did much of his marine research.

The most important attraction on Cannery Row is the spectacular
⑱ **Monterey Bay Aquarium,** a $50 million window on the sea. The aquarium is extremely popular—expect long lines and sizable crowds on weekends, especially during the summer. Braving the crowds is worth it, however, especially to see the three-story Kelp Forest exhibit, the only one of its kind in the world, and a re-creation of the sea creatures and vegetation found in Monterey Bay. Among other standout exhibits are a bat-ray petting pool, where the flat velvetlike creatures can be touched as they swim by; a 55,000-gallon sea otter tank; and an enormous outdoor artificial tide pool that supports anemones, crabs, sea stars, and other colorful creatures. *886 Cannery Row, tel. 408/649–6466 or 800/756–3737 for advanced tickets. Admission: $11.25 adults, $8.25 senior citizens and students, $4.75 children 3–12. Open daily 10–6, 9:30–6 on holidays and summer.*

Pacific Grove If not for the dramatic strip of coastline in its backyard, Pacific Grove could easily pass for a typical small town in the heartland. Beginning as a summer retreat for church groups a century ago, the town recalls its prim and proper Victorian heritage in the host of tiny board-and-batten cottages and stately mansions lining its streets.

Even before the church groups migrated here, however, Pacific Grove had been receiving thousands of annual guests in the form of bright orange-and-black monarch butterflies. Known as "Butterfly Town USA," Pacific Grove is the winter home of monarchs that migrate south from Canada and the Pacific Northwest and take residence in the pine and eucalyptus groves between October and March. The site of a mass of butterflies hanging from the branches like a long fluttering veil is unforgettable.

A prime way to enjoy Pacific Grove is to walk or bicycle along its 3 miles of city-owned shoreline, a clifftop area following Ocean View Boulevard that is landscaped with succulents and native plants and has plenty of park benches on which to sit and gaze at the sea. A variety of marine and bird life can be spotted here, including colonies of cormorants are drawn to the massive rocks rising out of the surf.

On the other side of Ocean View Boulevard are a number of imposing turn-of-the-century mansions well worth your attention. One of
⑲ the finest is the **Pryor House** at number 429, a massive shingled structure with a leaded and beveled glass doorway built in 1909 for
⑳ an early mayor. At the corner of 5th Street and Ocean View is **Green Gables,** a romantic Swiss Gothic-style mansion, now a bed-and-breakfast inn, with steeply peaked gables and stained-glass win-
㉑ dows. At **Lovers Point Park,** located midway along the waterfront, there's a pleasant grassy area with a gorgeous coastal view.

Farther out on the promontory stands the oldest continuously op-
㉒ erating lighthouse on the West Coast, the **Point Piños Light Station.** Visitors can learn about the lighting and foghorn operations and wander through a small museum containing historical memorabilia from the U.S. Coast Guard. *Asilomar Ave. between Ocean View Blvd. and Lighthouse Ave., tel. 408/648–3116. Admission free. Open weekends 1–4 PM.*

㉓ Another beautiful coastal area in Pacific Grove is **Asilomar State Beach,** on Sunset Drive between Point Piños and the Del Monte

Forest. The 100 acres of dunes, tide pools, and pocket-size beaches form one of the region's richest areas for marine life. The deep tide pools support 210 species of algae and are alive with sea urchins, crabs, and other creatures.

㉔ Although many of their original nesting grounds have vanished, the **Monarch Grove Sanctuary,** adjacent to the Butterfly Grove Inn (1073 Lighthouse Ave.), is still a good spot for viewing the butterflies.

㉕ If you are in Pacific Grove when the butterflies aren't, an approximation of this annual miracle is on exhibit at the **Pacific Grove Museum of Natural History.** In addition to a finely crafted butterfly-tree exhibit, the museum displays a collection of 400 mounted birds native to Monterey County and screens a film about the monarch butterfly. *165 Forest Ave., tel. 408/648–3116. Admission free. Open Tues.–Sun. 10–5.*

17-Mile Drive

Numbers in the margins correspond to points of interest on the Carmel and 17-Mile Drive map.

㉖ Although some sightseers balk at the $6-per-car fee, most agree that it is well worth the price to explore **17-Mile Drive,** an 8,400-acre microcosm of the Monterey coastal landscape. You can enter off Lighthouse Avenue in Pacific Grove, or, from the other end, off Route 1 and North San Antonio Avenue in Carmel.

Once inside, you see primordial nature preserved in quiet harmony with palatial estates. Among the natural treasures here are many prime examples of the rare Monterey cypress, trees so gnarled and twisted that Robert Louis Stevenson once described them as "ghosts fleeing before the wind." The most photographed of them ㉗ all is the **Lone Cypress,** a weather-sculpted tree growing out of a precipitous, rocky outcropping above the waves. A parking area makes it possible to stop for a view of the Lone Cypress, but walking ㉘ out to it is no longer allowed. Two other landmarks to note are **Bird** ㉙ **Rock** and **Seal Rock,** islands teeming with harbor seals, sea lions, cormorants, and pelicans.

Landscapes created by man are also a big part of the drive's attraction. Perhaps no more famous concentration of celebrated golf ㉚ courses exists anywhere in the world; most notable is the **Pebble Beach Golf Links,** with its famous 18th hole, around which the ocean plays a major role. Even if you're not a golfer, views of impeccable greens can be enjoyed over a drink or lunch at the **Lodge at Pebble Beach** or the **Inn at Spanish Bay,** the two resorts located along the drive.

Among the stately homes, many of which reflect the classic Monterey or Spanish Mission style typical of the region, a standout is ㉛ the **Crocker Marble Palace,** a waterfront estate designed after a Byzantine castle. Located near the Carmel entrance to the drive, this baroque mansion is easily identifiable by its dozens of marble arches. The estate's grounds feature a beach area with water heated by underground pipes.

Carmel

Although the community has grown quickly over the years and its population quadruples with tourists on weekends and during the summer, Carmel retains its identity as a quaint village; buildings

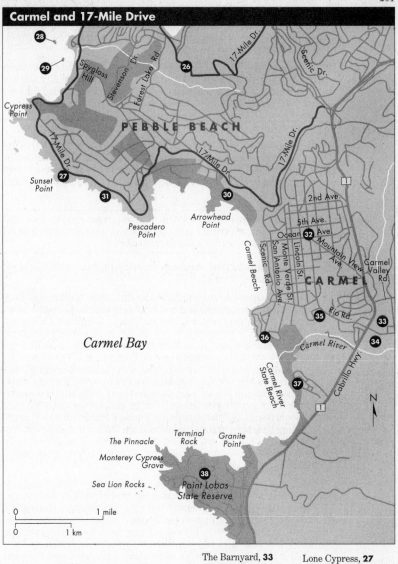

Carmel and 17-Mile Drive

The Barnyard, **33**
Bird Rock, **28**
Carmel Mission, **35**
Carmel Plaza, **32**
Carmel River State Park, **37**
Crocker Marble Palace, **31**
The Crossroads, **34**

Lone Cypress, **27**
Pebble Beach Golf Links, **30**
Point Lobos State Reserve, **38**
Seal Rock, **29**
17-Mile Drive, **26**
Tor House, **36**

still have no street numbers and live music is banned in the local watering holes. You can wander the side streets at your own pace, poking into hidden courtyards and stopping at Hansel-and-Gretel-like cafés for tea and crumpets.

Carmel has its share of hokey gift emporiums, but most of the wares in its hundreds of shops are distinctive and of high quality. Classic sportswear, gourmet cookware, and original art are among the best buys along the main street, **Ocean Avenue,** and its cross streets. Just as notable is the architecture of many of the shops, a charming mish-mash of ersatz English Tudor, Mediterranean, and other styles.

In recent years, the popularity of shopping in Carmel has led to the creation of several attractive, nicely landscaped shopping malls. **②** **Carmel Plaza,** in the east end of the village proper, consists of more than 50 shops, restaurants, and small branches of major department stores.

TimeOut **Patisserie Boissiere** (Mission Ave. between Ocean and 7th Aves., tel. 408/624–5008), a Carmel Plaza café reminiscent of a country French inn, offers light entrées and French pastries.

③③ ④ **The Barnyard** and **the Crossroads** shopping malls are just southeast of the village off Route 1.

Before it became an art colony in the early 20th century and long before it became a shopping and browsing mecca, Carmel was an important religious center in the early days of Spanish California. That heritage is preserved in one of the state's loveliest historic sites, the Mission San Carlos Borromeo del Rio Carmelo, more com- **③** monly known as the **Carmel Mission.** Founded in 1770 and serving as headquarters for the mission system in California under Father Junípero Serra, the Carmel Mission exists today with its stone church and tower dome beautifully restored. Adjoining the church is a tranquil garden planted with California poppies and a series of museum rooms that depict an early kitchen, Father Serra's spartan sleeping quarters, and the oldest college library in California. *Rio Rd. and Lasuen Dr., tel. 408/624–3600. Donations suggested. Open Sept.–May, Mon.–Sat. 9:30–4:30, Sun. 10:30–4:30; June–Aug., Mon.–Sat. 9:30–7:30, Sun. 10:30–7:30.*

Scattered throughout the pines in Carmel are the houses and cot-tages that were built for the steady stream of writers, artists, and photographers who discovered the area decades ago. Among the **③** most impressive dwellings is **Tor House,** a stone cottage built by the poet Robinson Jeffers in 1919 on a craggy knoll overlooking the sea. The low-ceilinged rooms are filled with portraits, books, and un-usual art objects, including a white stone from the Great Pyramid in Egypt. The highlight of the small estate is Hawk Tower, a de-tached edifice set with stones from the Carmel coastline, as well as one taken from the Great Wall of China. Within the tower is a Gothic-style room, which served as a retreat for the poet's wife, Una, an accomplished musician. The docents who lead tours are very well informed about the poet's work and life. Jeffers's home and life pre-sent a fascinating story, even if you are not a fan of his poetry. *26304 Ocean View Ave., tel. 408/624–1813 or 408/624–1840. Admission: $5 adults, $3.50 college students, $1.50 high-school students. No children under 12. Tours by appointment on Fri. and Sat. 10–3.*

Carmel's greatest beauty is the rugged coastline with its pine and cypress forests and countless inlets.

㊲ Carmel River State Park stretches for 106 acres along Carmel Bay. On sunny days the waters appear nearly as turquoise as those of the Caribbean. The park has a sugar-white beach with high dunes and a bird sanctuary that is a nesting ground for pelicans, kingfishers, hawks, and sandpipers. *Off Scenic Rd., south of Carmel Beach, tel. 408/649–2836. Open daily 9 AM–1/2 hour after sunset.*

㊳ The park is overshadowed by **Point Lobos State Reserve,** a 1,250-acre headland just south of Carmel. There are few roads, and the best way to explore is to walk along one of the many hiking trails. The Cypress Grove Trail leads through a forest of rare Monterey cypresses clinging to the rocks above an emerald-green cove, and Sea Lion Point Trail is a good place to observe sea lions, otters, harbor seals, and (during certain times of year) migrating whales. Part of the reserve is an undersea marine park open to qualified scuba divers. *Rte. 1, tel. 408/624–4909, or 800/444–7275 to reserve for scuba diving. Admission: $6 per car, $5 if senior citizen is traveling. Open May–Sept., daily 9–6:30; Oct.–Apr., daily 9–4:30.*

Numbers in the margin correspond to points of interest on the Monterey Bay map.

A world away from the cypress forests and tide pools of the coast are the pastoral ranchlands of Carmel Valley. The rolling meadows studded with oak trees are especially compelling in spring, when the grass is lush, green, and blooming with bright gold California poppies and blue lupines.

Carmel Valley Road, which turns inland at Route 1 just south of Carmel, is the main thoroughfare through this secluded enclave of horse ranchers and other well-heeled residents who prefer the valley's perpetually dry, sunny climate to the fog and wind on the coast. You can spend a pleasant couple of hours rambling up the road and **㊴** back. Stop for a while in tiny **Carmel Valley** village, where there are several crafts shops and art galleries. If you want to stay longer, go to **Garland Ranch Regional Park** (tel. 408/659–4488), 10 miles east of Carmel Valley, which has hiking trails and picnic facilities; or visit tiny Carmel Valley Village, where there are several crafts shops and galleries.

A popular stop along this road, 5 miles off Highway 1, is the tasting room at the beautiful **Château Julien** winery, known for its chardonnay and merlot. Tours are at 10:30 AM and 2:30 PM but must be arranged by calling ahead. *Tel. 408/624–2600. Open weekdays 8–5, weekends 11–5.*

An enjoyable loop drive can be added by turning off Carmel Valley Road about 7 miles out of town onto **Los Laureles Grade,** a 6-mile (10-kilometer) winding road that heads over the mountains to Route 68, ending at a point about halfway between Monterey and Salinas. Located along Route 68 is the award-winning **Ventana Vineyards,** which has a tasting room. *Tel. 408/372–7415. Open daily 11–5.*

Salinas

㊵ While Monterey turns its face toward the sea, **Salinas,** a half-hour inland and a world away in spirit, is deeply rooted as the population center of a rich agricultural valley. This unpretentious town may lack the sophistication and scenic splendors of the coast, but it is of interest to literary and architectural buffs.

The memory and literary legacy of Salinas native John Steinbeck are well honored here. The author's birthplace, a Victorian frame house, has been converted to a lunch-only restaurant called—what else—the **Steinbeck House,** run by the volunteer Valley Guild. The restaurant contains some Steinbeck memorabilia and presents a menu featuring locally grown produce. *132 Central Ave., tel. 408/424–2735. Reservations requested. Open weekdays for 2 sittings at 11:45 AM and 1:15 PM.*

Steinbeck did much of his research for *East of Eden*, a novel partially drawn from his Salinas boyhood, at what is now called the **Steinbeck Library.** The library features tapes of interviews with people who knew Steinbeck and a display of photos, first editions, letters, original manuscripts, and other items pertaining to the novelist. Entrance to the archives, which contain original manuscripts and first editions, is by appointment only. *350 Lincoln Ave., tel. 408/758–7311. Admission free. Open Mon.–Wed. 10–9, Thurs.–Sat. 10–6.*

Salinas's turn-of-the-century architecture has been the focus of an ongoing renovation project, much of which is centered on the original downtown area on South Main Street, with its handsome stone storefronts. One of the finest private residences from this era is the **Harvey-Baker House,** a beautifully preserved redwood house built in 1868 for the city's first mayor. *238 E. Romie La., tel. 408/757–8085. Admission free. Open 1st Sun. of each month 1–4 PM, and weekdays by appointment.*

Of even earlier vintage is the **Jose Eusebio Boronda Adobe,** the last unaltered adobe home from Mexican California open to the public in Monterey County. Located in the meadows above the Alisal Slough, the house, which suffered some damage in the 1989 earthquake, contains furniture and artifacts from the period. *333 Boronda Rd., tel. 408/757–8085. Admission free. Open weekdays 10–2, Sun. 1–4, Sat. by appointment.*

San Juan Bautista

㊶ A sleepy little hamlet tucked off U.S. 101 about 20 miles north of Salinas, **San Juan Bautista** is a nearly unaltered example of a classic California mission village. Protected from development since 1933, when much of it became **San Juan Bautista State Historic Park,** the village is about as close to early 19th-century California as you can get. On the first Saturday of each month, on Living History Day, costumed volunteers entertain visitors with such period events as quilting bees, making tortillas, or churning butter, and refreshments are served in the hotel's bar. *Tel. 408/623–4881. Admission: $2 adults; $1 children 6–17. Open daily 10–4:30.*

The centerpiece for the village is a wide green plaza, ringed by historic buildings that include a restored blacksmith shop, a stable, a pioneer cabin, and jailhouse. Running along one side of the square is **Mission San Bautista,** a long, low colonnaded structure founded by Father Lasuen in 1797. A poignant spot adjoining it is **Mission Cemetery,** where more than 4,300 Native Americans who converted to Christianity are buried in unmarked graves.

After the mission era, San Juan Bautista became an important crossroads for stagecoach travel. The principal stop in town was the **Plaza Hotel,** a collection of adobe buildings with furnishings from the 1860s. Next door, the **Castro-Breen Adobe,** once owned by survivors from the Donner party and furnished with Spanish colonial antiques, presents a view of domestic life in the village.

More contemporary pursuits in San Juan Bautista include poking around in the numerous antiques shops and art galleries lining the side streets. Every August the village holds a popular flea market.

What to See and Do with Children

Dennis the Menace Playground (Fremont St. and Camino El Estero, Monterey), in delightful Lake El Estero Park, is an imaginative playground whose name pays tribute to one of its developers, cartoonist and longtime local resident Hank Ketcham. The play equipment is on a grand scale and made for daredevils; there's a dizzyingly high rotating platform, a clanking suspension bridge, and a real Southern Pacific steam locomotive. Rowboats and paddleboats can be rented on U-shaped Lake El Estero, home to a varied assortment of ducks, mud hens, and geese.

At **Edgewater Packing Co.** (640 Wave St., Monterey, tel. 408/649–1899), a converted sardine cannery and processing plant, kids can sport on an antique carousel with hand-carved animals and mermaids, dating from 1905. A candy store and game arcade are among the other attractions.

Roller skates can be rented from the old-fashioned rink at **Del Monte Gardens** (2020 Del Monte Ave., Monterey, tel. 408/375–3202; closed Mon. and Tues.).

Also in Monterey, children will enjoy the **Monterey Bay Aquarium,** the **Museum of Natural History,** and the **Point Piños Light Station** (*see* Exploring, *above*). **Whale-watching expeditions** are also popular with children (*see* Spectator Sports, *below*).

Off the Beaten Track

A few miles north of Monterey near the tiny harbor town of Moss Landing is one of only two federal research reserves in California, the **Elkhorn Slough** at the National Estuarine Research Reserve. Its 2,500 acres of tidal flats and salt marshes form a complex environment supporting more than 300 species of birds and fish. A 1-mile walk along the meandering waterways and wetlands can reveal swans, pelicans, loons, herons, and egrets, and sharks may be observed in the summer months. You can wander at leisure or, on weekends, take a guided walk (10 AM and 1 PM) to the heron rookery. *1700 Elkhorn Rd., Rte. 1, Watsonville, tel. 408/728–2822. Admission: $2.50 adults over 16. Open Wed.–Sun. 9–5.*

Shopping

Art Galleries   Although few artists can afford the real estate anymore, Carmel's heritage as a thriving art colony lives on in dozens of galleries scattered throughout the town. A wide and eclectic assortment of art—everything from 19th-century watercolors to abstract metal sculpture—is available for browsing and purchase in galleries in Carmel and elsewhere on the peninsula.

The Coast Gallery Pebble Beach (The Lodge at Pebble Beach, 17-Mile Dr., Pebble Beach, tel. 408/624–2002) presents the work of contemporary wildlife and marine artists in forms that range from etchings to bronze sculpture.

The **Masterpiece Gallery** (Dolores St. and 6th Ave., Carmel, tel. 408/624–2163) features early California Impressionists, Bay Area figurative art, and the work of local artist Roger Blum.

Classic impressionism and traditional realism are the focus of the **Cottage Gallery** (Mission St. and 6th Ave., Carmel, tel. 408/624–7888).

The **Dodge/LaRue Gallery** (Dolores St. between 5th and 6th Aves., Carmel, tel. 408/625–5636) has one of the largest collections of contemporary folk art in the West, including gallery co-owner Bill W. Dodge's own turn-of-the-century-style paintings, posters, and prints.

At **The Bighorn Gallery** (26390 Carmel Rancho La., Carmel, tel. 408/625–2288), which showcases the work of nationally recognized artists, the primary themes and styles are western, wildlife, marine, aviation, African, and landscape.

The **Highlands Sculpture Gallery** (Dolores St. between 5th and 6th Aves., Carmel, tel. 408/624–0535) is devoted to indoor and outdoor sculpture, primarily work done in stone, bronze, wood, and metal by West Coast artists.

Photography West Gallery (Ocean Ave. and Dolores St., Carmel, tel. 408/625–1587) exhibits 20th-century photography by such well-known artists as Ansel Adams, who lived and worked in the region for many years.

Gift Ideas In a region known for superb golf courses, you'll find the ultimate in golf equipment and accessories. **John Riley Golf** (601 Wave St., Monterey, tel. 408/373–8855) purveys custom-made golf clubs. **Golf Arts and Imports** (Dolores St. and 6th Ave., Carmel, tel. 408/625–4488) features antique golf prints and clubs, rare golf books, and other golfing memorabilia.

The illustrations of Beatrix Potter are in evidence everywhere at **Peter Rabbit and Friends** (Lincoln Ave. between 7th and Ocean Aves., Carmel, tel. 408/624–6854), which offers toys, nursery bedding, books, music boxes, party supplies, china, and clothing embellished with characters and scenes from Potter's children's tales.

The **Monterey Bay Aquarium Gift Shop** (886 Cannery Row, Monterey, tel. 408/649–6466) offers everything from posters and art prints to silk-screened sweatshirts and lobster-shaped wooden napkin rings—everything with a marine theme.

Sports and the Outdoors

Participant Sports

Bicycling Bicycle paths follow some of the choicest parts of the shoreline, including the 17-Mile Drive and the waterfront of Pacific Grove. Bikes can be rented from **Bay Bikes** (640 Wave St., Monterey, tel. 408/646–9090) **Adventures by the Sea Inc.** (299 Cannery Row, Monterey, tel. 408/372–1807) rents bikes, kayaks, rollerskates, and rollerblades. Mopeds and bikes can be rented from **Monterey Moped Adventures** (1250 Del Monte Ave., tel. 408/373–2696); a driver's license is required.

Fishing Rock cod is a relatively easy catch in Monterey Bay; salmon and albacore tuna are also possible. Several half- and full-day fishing trips leave from Fisherman's Wharf in Monterey, and rates often include equipment rental, bait, fish cleaning, and a one-day license. Try **Monterey Sport Fishing** (96 Fisherman's Wharf, tel. 408/372–2203 or 408/372–1400), **Randy's Fishing Trips** (66 Fisherman's Wharf, tel. 408/372–7440), and **Sam's Fishing Fleet** (84 Fisherman's Wharf, tel. 408/372–0577). In Santa Cruz try **Stagnaro Fishing Trips** (center of the wharf, tel. 408/427–2334).

Golf With 19 golf courses, most of them commanding strips of choice real estate, it is not surprising that the Monterey Peninsula is sometimes called the golf capital of the world. Beginning with the opening of the Del Monte Golf Course in 1897, golf has been an integral part of the social and recreational scene. Japanese golfers—and investors—have recently found the scene irresistible. Greens fees for 18 holes run from $15 to $225, depending on the time and course.

Many hotels will help with golf reservations or offer golf packages; inquire when you make lodging reservations.

Several of the courses are within the exclusive confines of the 17-Mile Drive, where the Del Monte Forest and the surging Pacific help make the game challenging as well as scenic. The most famous of these courses is **Pebble Beach Golf Course** (17-Mile Dr., tel. 408/625–8518), which takes center stage each winter during the AT&T Pro-Am (known for years as the "Crosby"), where show-business celebrities and pros team up for what is perhaps the world's most glamorous golf tournament. Golfers from around the world make this course one of the busiest in the region, despite greens fees of $225 plus $20 for a cart. Individual reservations for nonguests can only be made one day in advance on a space-available basis.

Another famous course in Pebble Beach is **Spyglass Hill** (Spyglass Hill Rd., tel. 408/624–3811), where the holes are long and unforgiving. With the first five holes bordering on the Pacific, and the rest reaching deep into the Del Monte Forest, the views offer some consolation. Greens fees run $175 plus $20 for a cart; reservations are essential and should be made at least one month in advance.

Poppy Hills (17-Mile Dr., tel. 408/625–2035), designed in 1986 by Robert Trent Jones, Jr., was named by *Golf Digest* as one of the world's top 20 courses. Greens fees for the general public are $95, cart $30 additional. Individuals may reserve up to one month in advance, groups up to a year.

The **Spanish Bay Golf Links** (tel. 408/624–3811) opened on the north end of the 17-Mile Drive in 1987. Spanish Bay, which hugs a choice stretch of shoreline, is designed in the rugged manner of a traditional Scottish course with sand dunes and coastal marshes interspersed among the greens. Fees are $135 per player plus $20 cart rental; individuals are advised to make reservations two or more months in advance.

Less experienced golfers and those who want to sharpen their iron shots can try the shortest course in Pebble Beach, the nine-hole "pitch and putt" **Peter Hay** (17-Mile Dr., tel. 408/624–3811). The course fee is $7 per person, no reservations necessary.

Just as challenging as the Pebble Beach courses is the **Old Del Monte Golf Course** (1300 Sylvan Rd., Monterey, tel. 408/373–2436), the oldest course west of the Mississippi. The greens fees—$50 per player plus $15 cart rental, $18 twilight special after 4:30—are the most reasonable in the region.

Another local favorite, with greens fees only a fraction of those in Pebble Beach, is **Pacific Grove Golf Links** (77 Asilomar Blvd., tel.

408/648–3177). Designed by Jack Neville, who also designed the Pebble Beach Golf Links, and updated by H. Chandler Egan, the course features a back nine with spectacular ocean views and ice-plant-covered sand dunes that make keeping on the fairway a must. The course is the only one on the peninsula to offer views of both Monterey Bay and the Pacific. Greens fees range from $24 to $28. Cart rental is $20. Tee times may be reserved up to seven days in advance.

Courses in Carmel Valley lack ocean views, but deer and quail wander across the greens. One of the choicest is **Rancho Cañada Golf Club** (Carmel Valley Rd., tel. 408/624–0111) with 36 holes, some of them overlooking the Carmel River. Fees range from $15 to $65 plus $25 cart rental, depending on course and tee time selected. The club takes reservations up to 30 days in advance.

Up the road a few miles is the **Golf Club at Quail Lodge** (8000 Valley Greens Dr., tel. 408/624–2770), whose course incorporates several lakes. Although private, the course is open to guests at the adjoining Quail Lodge and by reciprocation with other private clubs. The $85 greens fee includes cart rental.

Guests at the nearby Carmel Valley Ranch resort have access to the private Pete Dye–designed **Carmel Valley Ranch Resort** course (1 Old Ranch Rd., tel. 408/626–2510), whose front nine runs along the Carmel River and back nine reaches well up into the mountains for challenging slopes and spectacular views. The $97 greens fee includes cart rental.

Seven miles (11 kilometers) inland from Monterey, off Route 68, is **Laguna Seca Golf Club** (1 York Rd., tel. 408/373–3701), a course with an 18-hole layout designed by Robert Trent Jones, Jr., and open to the public. Greens fees range from $15 to $50, cart rentals from $18 to $25.

Horseback Riding A great way to enjoy the Del Monte Forest, which has 27 miles of bridle trails, is by reserving a horse from the **Pebble Beach Equestrian Center** (Portola Rd. and Alva La., tel. 408/624–2756). You can ride in a group of six to eight people, at 10 AM or 2 PM, on a forest or beach trail, or schedule private rides.

Kayaking Sea kayaking is increasingly popular in Monterey Bay, giving paddlers a chance to come face to face with otters, sea lions, and harbor seals. Kayak rentals, basic instruction, and escorted tours are offered by **Monterey Bay Kayaks** (693 Del Monte Ave., Monterey, tel. 408/373–5357 or 800/649–5357 in CA).

Scuba Diving Although the waters are cold, the marine life and kelp beds attract many scuba divers to Monterey Bay. Diving lessons, rental equipment, and guided dive tours are offered at **Aquarius Dive Shops** (2240 Del Monte Ave., Monterey, tel. 408/375–1933 and 32 Cannery Row, Suite #4, tel. 408/375–6605).

Tennis Public courts are available in Monterey and Pacific Grove; information is available through **Monterey Tennis Center** (tel. 408/372–0172) and **Pacific Grove Municipal Courts** (tel. 408/648–3129). Nonmembers are eligible to play on the courts for a small fee at the **Carmel Valley Inn Swim and Tennis Club** (Carmel Valley Rd. and Los Laureles Grade, Carmel Valley, tel. 408/659–3131).

If tennis is a top vacation priority, you may want to stay at a resort where instruction and facilities are part of the scene. Best bets are the Lodge at Pebble Beach, the Inn at Spanish Bay, Hyatt Regency

Monterey, Quail Lodge, and Carmel Valley Ranch Resort. *See* Lodging, *below,* for details.

Beaches

Surfers in Santa Cruz gather for the spectacular waves and sunsets at **Pleasure Point** (East Cliff Dr. and 41st Ave.) and **New Brighton State Beach** (1500 Park Ave., Capitola), which also has campsites. **Manresa State Beach** (San Andreas Rd., Watsonville, tel. 408/688–3241), farther south, offers premium surfing conditions, and those who surf here tend to be very good—but although there is a lifeguard on duty during most of the summer season, the waters off this beach are notorious for treacherous currents and riptides, and we recommend it only for sunbathing.

Around Monterey, the local waters are generally too cold and turbulent for much swimming. **Monterey Municipal Beach,** east of Wharf No. 2, has shallow waters that are warm and calm enough for wading. Another good beach for kids is **Lovers Point Park** on Ocean View Boulevard in Pacific Grove, a sheltered spot with a children's pool and picnic area. Glass-bottom boat rides, which permit viewing of the plant and sea life below, are available in summer.

Spectator Sports

Car Racing   Four major races take place each year on the 2.2-mile, 11-turn **Laguna Seca Raceway** (SCRAMP, Box 2078, Monterey 93942, tel. 408/648–5100, 800/367–9939 in CA, or 800/327–SECA outside CA). They range from Indianapolis 500–style CART races to a historic car race featuring more than 300 restored race cars from earlier eras.

Rodeo   One of the oldest and most famous rodeos in the West is the annual **California Rodeo** (Box 1648, Salinas 93902, tel. 408/757–2951) in Salinas, which takes place during a week of festivities starting in mid-July.

Whale-Watching   On their annual migration between the Bering Sea and Baja California, 45-foot gray whales can be spotted not far off the Monterey coast. Although they sometimes can be seen with binoculars from shore, a whale-watching cruise is the best way to view these magnificent mammals up close. The migration south takes place between December and March, while the migration north is from March to June. Late January is prime viewing time in Monterey Bay.

Even if no whales are in sight, bay cruises nearly always include some unforgettable marine-life encounter, anything from watching a cluster of sea lions hugging a life buoy to riding the waves alongside a group of 300 leaping porpoises. Whale-watching cruises, which usually last about two hours, are offered by **Monterey Sport Fishing** (96 Fisherman's Wharf, Monterey, tel. 408/372–2203 or 408/372–1400), **Randy's Fishing Trips** (66 Fisherman's Wharf, Monterey, tel. 408/372–7440), and **Sam's Fishing Fleet** (84 Fisherman's Wharf, tel. 408/372–0577). In Santa Cruz, try **Stagnaro Fishing Trips** (center of the wharf, tel. 408/427–2334).

Dining and Lodging

Dining There is little question that the Monterey area is the richest area for dining along the coast between Los Angeles and San Francisco. The surrounding waters abound with fish, there is wild game in the foothills, and the inland valleys are the vegetable basket of California; nearby Castroville prides itself on being the Artichoke Capital of the World. The region also takes pride in producing better and better wines. When it comes to dress, San Francisco's conservatism extends this far south—"casual" tends to mean attractive resort wear.

Highly recommended restaurants are indicated by a star ★.

Category	Cost*
$$$$	over $35
$$$	$25–$35
$$	$15–$25
$	under $15

per person for a three-course meal, excluding drinks, service, and tax

Lodging A recent hotel and resort boom on the Monterey Peninsula has given travelers a far greater choice of accommodations, especially on the most deluxe level, than ever before. The luxury resort scene is flourishing in Carmel Valley and Pebble Beach, whose country-clublike spreads have recently been attracting Japanese investors.

In Monterey, the trend has been toward sophisticated hotels, some with the same range of amenities as the top San Francisco properties. Some of the newer Monterey establishments are a bit impersonal and clearly designed for conventions, but others pamper the individual traveler in grand style.

Pacific Grove has quietly turned itself into the bed-and-breakfast capital of the region. Many of the town's landmark Victorian houses, some more than a century old, have been converted to charming inns with brass beds and breakfast buffets laden with such goodies as cranberry muffins and baked pears.

Rates in the Monterey area are often as high as in a major city, especially between April and October, which is high season, when even modest motels may charge $100 a night for a double.

Highly recommended hotels are indicated by a star ★.

Category	Cost*
$$$$	over $100
$$$	$75–$100
$$	$50–$75
$	under $50

All prices are for a double room, excluding tax.

Capitola
Lodging

The Inn at Depot Hill. This inventively designed hotel in a former rail depot has taken the Orient Express as its theme. Each room, complete with fireplace and feather beds, is inspired by a different European destination—Delft, the Netherlands; Portofino, Italy; Sissinghurst, England; the Côte d'Azur; Paris. One is decorated like a Pullman car for a railroad baron. Most rooms have balconies with private Jacuzzis. Full breakfast is included, as well as wine and hors d'oeuvres. *250 Monterey Ave., Capitola-by-the-Sea, 95010, tel. 408/462–3376, fax 408/462–3697. 8 rooms. AE, MC, V. $$$$*

Carmel
Dining

The Covey at Quail Lodge. Refined European cuisine is served at this elegant restaurant in a romantic lakeside setting. Specialties include rack of lamb, salmon in mango vinaigrette, blackcurrant duck, abalone, and scallop quenelles. *8205 Valley Greens Dr., tel. 408/624–1581. Reservations advised. Jacket required. AE, DC, MC, V. No lunch. $$$$*

French Poodle. The service is attentive in this intimate dining room decorated in warm, raspberry tones and hung with landscapes by local California Impressionists. Specialties on the traditional French menu include duck breast in port and an excellent abalone; for dessert, the "floating island" is delicious. *Junipero and 5th Aves., tel. 408/624–8643. Reservations advised. Jacket recommended. AE, DC, MC, V. No lunch. Closed Sun. and Wed.$$$$*

Pacific's Edge. This restaurant's dramatic views of ancient cypress trees and pounding surf are its strong point. Specialties on the regional California menu include fillet of beef with black pepper raviolis, roquefort, and a red wine shallot sauce, and vegetarian offerings such as a crispy spring roll with local field mushrooms and a winter vegetable fricassee. For dessert, crème brûlée and homemade sherbets are winners. *Rte. 1, Carmel-by-the-Sea, tel. 408/624–0471. Reservations advised. Jacket recommended. AE, D, DC, MC, V. $$$$*

Crème Carmel. This bright and airy small restaurant has a California-French menu that changes according to season. Specialties include breast of duck cooked with tamarind ginger and plum wine, and beef tenderloin prepared with cabernet. *San Carlos St., near 7th Ave., tel. 408/624–0444. Reservations advised. Dress: casual. AE, DC, MC, V. No lunch. $$$*

Raffaello. A sparkling, elegant restaurant in one of the loveliest parts of Carmel, Raffaello offers excellent northern Italian cuisine. The menu includes superb pasta, Monterey Bay prawns with garlic butter, local sole poached in champagne, and the specialty of the house, veal Piemontese. *Mission St. between Ocean and 7th Aves., tel. 408/624–1541. Reservations advised. Dress: casual. AE, DC, MC, V. No lunch. Closed Tues. and 1st week in Jan. $$$*

Anton and Michel. Superb Continental cuisine is served at this elegant restaurant in Carmel's shopping district. The tender lamb dishes are fantastic, and well complemented by the extensive wine list. The real treats, however, are the flaming desserts. Outdoor dining is available in the courtyard. *Ocean and 7th Aves., tel. 408/624–2406. Reservations recommended. Dress: casual. AE, D, DC, MC, V. $$–$$$*

La Bohème. This campy, off-beat restaurant offers a one-selection, fixed-price menu, which includes soup and salad. You may be bumping elbows with your neighbor in the cozy, *faux*-European-village courtyard, but the food is delicious, and the atmosphere is friendly. The cuisine is predominantly French with accents from throughout Europe. Vegetarian meals are available nightly. *Dolores St. and 7th Ave., tel. 408/624–7500. Reservations not accepted. Dress: casual. MC, V, No lunch. $$*

Flaherty's Seafood Grill & Oyster Bar. This is a bright blue-and-white-tiled fish house that serves bowls of steamed mussels, clams, cioppino, and crab chowder. Seafood pastas and daily fresh fish selections are also available. *6th Ave. and San Carlos St., tel. 408/624–0311. Reservations are taken for the grill. Dress: casual. AE, D, MC, V. $$*

Hog's Breath Inn. Former mayor Clint Eastwood's place provides a convivial publike atmosphere and a great outdoor patio in which to enjoy no-nonsense meat and seafood entrées with sautéed vegetables. *San Carlos St. and 5th Ave., tel. 408/625–1044. Dress: casual. AE, DC, MC, V. $$*

Piatti. Here's one more link in this statewide chain of friendly, attractive trattorias that serve authentic, light Italian cuisine. *Junipero and 6th Sts., tel. 408/625–1766. Dress: casual. AE, MC, V. $$*

Pine Inn. An old favorite of locals, this Victorian-style restaurant offers traditional American fare, including venison osso buco, seared duck breast, and broiled swordfish. Outdoor dining is also available at tables set up around the gazebo. *Ocean Ave. and Monte Verde St., tel. 408/624–3851. Reservations advised. Dress: casual. AE, D, DC, MC, V. $$*

★ **Rio Grill.** The best bets in this Santa Fe–style setting are the meat and seafood (such as fresh tuna or salmon) cooked over an oakwood grill. There's also a good California wine list. *101 Crossroads Blvd., Rte. 1 and Rio Rd., tel. 408/625–5436. Reservations required. Dress; casual. AE, MC, V. $$*

The General Store. This Bavarian-influenced restaurant is decorated with artifacts that recall the building's origin as a blacksmith's shop, originating in the 1920s. California cuisine is served in the intimate dining room as well as on the adjacent brick patio and in a more casual saloon. Specialties include fresh seafood, steaks, and one of the best burgers in Carmel. *Junipero St. and 5th Ave., tel. 408/624–2233. Dress: casual. AE, MC, V. $–$$*

Friar Tuck's. This busy, wood-paneled coffee shop serves huge omelets at breakfast, and at lunch offers 16 varieties of hamburgers, including one topped with marinated artichoke hearts. *5th Ave. and Dolores St., tel. 408/624–4274. No reservations. Dress: casual. No credit cards. Dinner July–Aug. only. $*

Thunderbird Bookstore and Restaurant. This well-stocked bookstore is also a good place to enjoy a light lunch or a cappuccino and a pastry and browse among the books. A hearty beef soup, sandwiches, popovers, and cheesecake are the best sellers. *3600 The Barnyard, Rte. 1 at Carmel Valley Rd., tel. 408/624–9414. Dress: casual. MC, V. $*

Lodging **Best Western Carmel Mission Inn.** This modern inn on the edge of Carmel Valley has a lushly landscaped pool and Jacuzzi area and is close to the Barnyard and Crossroads shopping centers. Rooms are large, some with spacious decks. *Rte. 1 and Rio Rd., 3665 Rio Rd., 92923, tel. 408/624–1841 or 800/348–9090, fax 408/624–8684. 165 rooms. Facilities: restaurant, bar, pool, Jacuzzi. AE, D, DC, MC, V. $$$$*

Carriage House Inn. This attractive small inn with a rustic wood-shingled exterior has rooms with open-beam ceilings, fireplaces, down comforters, and sunken baths. Continental breakfast, wine, and hors d'oeuvres are included. *Junipero Ave. between 7th and 8th Aves., Box 1900, 93921, tel. 408/625–2585 or 800/422–4732, fax 408/624–2967. 13 rooms. AE, D, DC, MC, V. $$$$*

★ **Cobblestone Inn.** Recent renovations in this former motel have created an English-style inn with stone fireplaces in the guest rooms and in the sitting-room area. Quilts and country antiques, along with a complimentary gourmet breakfast buffet and afternoon tea (not to mention optional breakfast in bed), contribute to the homey feel. The inn is entirely nonsmoking. *8th and Junipero Aves., Box 3185, 93921, tel. 408/625–5222, fax 408/625–0478. 24 rooms. AE, DC, MC, V. $$$$*

★ **Highlands Inn.** The hotel's unparalleled location on high cliffs above the Pacific just south of Carmel gives it views that stand out even in a region famous for them. Accommodations are in plush condominium-style units with wood-burning fireplaces and ocean-view decks; some have spa tubs and full kitchens. *Rte. 1, Box 1700, 93921, tel. 408/624–3801 or 800/538–9525, 800/682–4811 in CA, fax 408/626–1574. 142 rooms. Facilities: 2 restaurants, lounges, pool, whirlpools, entertainment, florist. AE, D, DC, MC, V. $$$$*

La Playa Hotel. Now a pink, Mediterranean-style villa, the hotel was originally built in 1902 by Norwegian artist Christopher Jorgensen for his bride, a member of the famous Ghirardelli chocolate clan. The Terrace Grill and central garden, riotous with color, provide wonderful views of Carmel's magnificent coastline. All rooms are done in rose, beige, and blue tones, with hand-carved furniture. Some accommodations have ocean views. You can also opt for a cottage; all have full kitchens and a patio or terrace, and some have wood-burning fireplaces. *Camino Real at 8th Ave., Box 900, 93921, tel. 408/624–6476 or 800/582–8900, fax 408/624–7966. 80 rooms. Facilities: restaurant, pool, valet parking. AE, DC, MC, V. $$$$*

Mission Ranch. Former mayor Clint Eastwood rescued this venerable inn, originally built in the 1850s and used as a dairy farm, and brought it back to life in 1992. Set in pastureland next to the ocean where sheep still graze, the main farmhouse has six rooms around a Victorian parlor; other accommodation options include cottages, hayloft, and bunkhouse. The details of rustic comfort include handmade quilts, princess-and-the-pea stuffed mattresses, and carved wooden beds. *26270 Dolores St., 93923, tel. 408/624–6436 or 800/538–8221, fax 408/626–4163. 31 rooms. Facilities: restaurant, piano bar, tennis courts, exercise room, pro shop. AE, MC, V. $$$$*

Tally Ho Inn. This is one of the few inns in Carmel's center that has good views out over the bay. There are suites with kitchenettes and penthouse units with fireplaces and a pretty English garden courtyard. Continental breakfast and after-dinner brandy are included. *Monte Verde St. and 6th Ave., Box 3726, 93921, tel. 408/624–2232 or 800/624–2290, fax 408/644–2661. 14 rooms. AE, MC, V. $$$$*

Tickle Pink Country Inn. Just up the road from the Highlands Inn, this small, secluded inn also features spectacular views. Elegant but casual accommodations include Continental breakfast and wine and cheese, and some rooms are equipped with fireplace and private deck. There is also a cottage on the property that sleeps six people. *155 Highland Dr., 93923, tel. 408/624–1244 or 800/635–4774, fax 408/626–9516. 34 rooms. AE, MC, V. $$$$*

★ **Pine Inn.** This traditional favorite of generations of Carmel visitors features Victorian-style decor complete with grandfather clock, padded fabric panels, antique tapestries, and marble-topped furnishings. Located in the heart of the shopping district and only four blocks from the beach, the inn has its own brick courtyard of specialty shops. *Ocean Ave. and Lincoln St., Box 250, 93921, tel. 408/624–3851 or 800/228–3851, fax 408/624–3030. 49 rooms. Facilities: dining room. AE, D, DC, MC, V. $$$–$$$$*

Lobos Lodge. Pleasant white stucco units set amid oaks and pines on the edge of the business district feature fireplaces and private brick patios. Continental breakfast is included. *Monte Verde St. and Ocean Ave., Box L–1, 93921, tel. 408/624–3874, fax 408/624–0135. 30 rooms. AE, MC, V. $$$*

Carmel Valley
Lodging
★

Carmel Valley Ranch Resort. The resort, situated on 1,700 acres, well off the road on a hill overlooking the Carmel Valley, is a stunning piece of contemporary California architecture. The all-suite resort includes such down-home touches as handmade quilts, wood-burning fireplaces, and watercolors by local artists. Rooms feature cathedral ceilings, oversize decks, and fully stocked wet bars. *1 Old Ranch Rd., 93923, tel. 408/625–9500 or 800/4CARMEL. 100 suites. Facilities: restaurant, pool, golf (fee), tennis club and courts, saunas, Jacuzzis. AE, DC, MC, V. $$$$*

Quail Lodge. One of the area's most highly regarded resorts is beautifully situated on the grounds of a private country club where guests have access to golf and tennis. There are also 853 acres of wildlife preserve, including 11 lakes, frequented by deer and migratory fowl. The rooms, which are clustered in several low-rise buildings, are spacious and modern, with a mixture of Oriental and European decor. *8205 Valley Greens Dr., Carmel 93923, tel. 408/624–1581 or 800/538–9516, fax 408/624–3726. 100 rooms. Facilities: 2 restaurants, 2 lounges, piano bar, 2 pools, Jacuzzi, putting green, golf (fee), tennis. AE, DC, MC, V. $$$$*

Stonepine Estate Resort. The former estate of the Crocker banking family has been converted to an ultradeluxe inn nestled in 330 pastoral acres with riding trails and an equestrian center. The main house, richly paneled and furnished with antiques, offers eight individually decorated suites and a private dining room for guests only. Less formal but still luxurious suites are also available in the ranch-style Paddock House. *150 E. Carmel Valley Rd., Box 1543, 93924, tel. 408/659–2245, fax 408/659–5160. 14 rooms. Facilities: dining room, pool, tennis, weight room, archery, mountain bikes, horseback riding (fee). AE, MC, V. $$$$*

Robles Del Rio Lodge. This pine-paneled charmer in a gorgeous setting of rolling meadows and oak forests dates from 1928. Rooms and cottages feature country-style decor with Laura Ashley prints, and the grounds include a large pool and sunbathing area, and hiking trails. Complimentary breakfast buffet is included. *200 Punta del Monte, 93924, tel. 408/659–3705 or 800/833–0843, fax 408/659–5157. 33 rooms. Facilities: restaurant, lounge, pool, tennis, sauna, hot tub. AE, MC, V. $$$–$$$$*

Valley Lodge. In this small, pleasant inn, there are rooms surrounding a garden patio and separate one- and two-bedroom cottages with fireplaces and full kitchens. Continental breakfast and morning paper are included. *Carmel Valley Rd. at Ford Rd., Box 93, 93924, tel. 408/659–2261 or 800/641–4646, fax 408/659–4558. 31 rooms. Facilities: pool, Jacuzzi, sauna, fitness center. AE, MC, V. $$$–$$$$*

Monterey
Dining
★

Duck Club. This elegant dining room in the Monterey Plaza Hotel (*see* Lodging, *below*) is built over the waterfront on Cannery Row. The continental menu strongly emphasizes duck, but also includes seafood, meat, and pasta. Sunday brunch is served. *400 Cannery Row, tel. 408/646–1700. Reservations advised. Dress: casual. AE, D, DC, MC, V. $$$$*

Fresh Cream. Nine out of ten local residents recommend this outstanding restaurant in Heritage Harbor, with its beautiful views over the bay. The cuisine is French, with light, imaginative California accents. Some favorites on the seasonal menu are the rack of lamb Dijonnaise and the roast boned duck in blackcurrant sauce. *99 Pacific St., Suite 100C, tel. 408/375–9798. Reservations advised. Dress: casual. AE, D, DC, MC, V. Lunch on Fri. only. $$$$*

Sardine Factory. The interior of this old processing plant above Cannery Row has been turned into five attractive, separate dining areas, including a glass-enclosed garden room. The decor is from the gaslight era with lots of Gay Nineties touches. The menu stresses fresh seafood, prepared in an elegant, Italian manner. There's a great wine list. *701 Wave St., tel. 408/373–3775. Reservations advised. Jacket recommended. AE, D, DC, MC, V. $$$*

★ **Whaling Station Inn.** A pleasing mixture of rough-hewn wood and sparkling white linen makes this restaurant a festive yet comfortable place in which to enjoy some of the best mesquite-grilled fish and meats in town. There are excellent artichoke appetizers and fresh salads. *763 Wave St., tel. 408/373–3778. Reservations advised. Dress: casual. AE, D, DC, MC, V. No lunch. $$$*

Abalonetti. From a squid-lover's point of view, this wharfside restaurant is the best place in town, serving all kinds of squid dishes: deep-fried, sautéed with wine and garlic, or baked with eggplant. Abalone is another specialty, and the fresh fish is barbecued and served with beurre blanc or pesto. *57 Fisherman's Wharf, tel. 408/373–1851. Reservations recommended. Dress: casual. AE, D, DC, MC, V. $$*

Bradley's. This restaurant—with possibly the best location on the harbor—offers regional American fare with various ethnic influences. The casual atmosphere recalls a 1920s European bistro. Specialties include avocado pancakes with salsa and rack of lamb with pistachio crust. Finish off your meal with one of the rich, delicious desserts. *32 Cannery Row at the Coast Guard Pier, tel. 408/655–6799. Reservations recommended. Dress: casual. DC, MC, V. Closed Tues. $$*

Cafe Fina. This understated restaurant on the wharf, with fine water views, specializes in Italian seafood dishes. Highlights include mesquite-grilled fish dishes and pasta Fina, a linguine in clam sauce with baby shrimp and tomatoes. The wine list is extensive. *47 Fisherman's Wharf, tel. 408/372–5200. Reservations recommended. Dress: casual. AE, D, DC, MC, V. $$*

Domenico's. Under the same ownership as the Whaling Station Inn and nearby Abalonetti, this restaurant serves Italian seafood preparations, mesquite-grilled meats, and homemade pastas. The blue-and-white nautical decor keeps the place comfortably casual; white drapery lends an air of elegance lacking in most restaurants on the wharf. *50 Fisherman's Wharf, tel. 408/372–3655. Reservations recommended. Dress: casual. AE, D, DC, MC, V. $$*

Ferrante's. Gorgeous rooftop views of both the town and the bay can be seen from this California-Italian restaurant at the top of the 10-story Monterey Marriott (*see* Lodging, *below*). The chicken cashew fettuccine with sun-dried tomatoes is especially good. Brunch is served Sunday. *350 Calle Principal, tel. 408/649–4234. Reservations advised. Dress: casual. AE, D, DC, MC, V. No lunch. $$*

★ **The Fishery.** Popular with locals, this restaurant features a mixture of Asian and Continental influences, in both food and decor. Specialties include calamari, broiled swordfish with macadamia nut butter, and fresh Hawaiian tuna with teriyaki. *21 Soledad Dr., tel. 408/373–6200. Dress: casual. MC, V. No lunch. Closed Sun. and Mon. $$*

Mara's Restaurant. Greek and Armenian dishes such as hummus, shish kebab, moussaka, and a chicken and lemon soup called *avgolemono* are featured at this family restaurant. *570 Lighthouse Ave., tel. 408/375–1919. Reservations advised. Dress: casual. MC, V. Closed Mon. $$*

Casa Gutierrez. Although the basic Mexican dishes here are not extraordinary, the setting, in the low-ceilinged 1841 adobe along the Path of History, definitely is. *590 Calle Principal, tel. 408/375–0095. Dress: casual. AE, D, DC, MC, V. $*

Old Monterey Cafe. Breakfast here, which is served all day, can include fresh-baked muffins and eggs Benedict. This is also a good place to relax with a cappuccino or coffee made from freshly ground beans. *489 Alvarado St., tel. 408/646–1021. No reservations. Dress: casual. DC, MC, V. $*

Lodging   **Best Western Monterey Beach.** This Best Western offers a great waterfront location about 2 miles north of town with panoramic views of the bay and the Monterey skyline. The rooms are nondescript, but the grounds are pleasantly landscaped and feature a large pool with a sunbathing area. *2600 Sand Dunes Dr., 93940, tel. 408/394–3321 or 800/528–1234, fax 408/393–1912. 196 rooms. Facilities: restaurant, lounge, pool, Jacuzzi. AE, D, DC, MC, V. $$$$*

Best Western Victorian Inn. Under the same ownership as the Spindrift Inn, this hotel two blocks above Cannery Row has a more casual feel but also offers such in-room comforts as fireplaces, private balconies or patios, and Continental breakfast. A few rooms have ocean views. Wine and cheese are served in the antiques-filled lobby during the afternoon. *487 Foam St., 93940, tel. 408/373–8000 or 800/232–4141, fax 408/375–4815. 68 rooms. Facilities: garage. AE, D, DC, MC, V. $$$$*

Doubletree Hotel. Adjacent to the downtown conference center, this hotel is geared more toward convention groups and business travelers than toward vacationers seeking local ambience. Rooms, some with good views of Fisherman's Wharf and the bay, are attractively furnished. Resort amenities include a round swimming pool with adjoining Jacuzzi. *2 Portola Plaza, 93940, tel. 408/649–4511 or 800/222–TREE, fax 408/649–4115. 373 rooms. Facilities: 2 restaurants, pool, Jacuzzi, parking (fee). AE, D, DC, MC, V. $$$$*

Hotel Pacific. While other new hotels in downtown Monterey clash with the early California architecture and small-town ambience, the Hotel Pacific is an adobe-style addition that fits right in. All rooms are suites, handsomely appointed with four-poster feather beds, hardwood floors, Indian rugs, fireplaces, honor bars, and balconies or patios. Continental breakfast and afternoon tea are included. *300 Pacific St., 93940, tel. 408/373–5700 or 800/554–5542 in CA, fax 408/649–2566. 105 rooms. Facilities: garage, 2 Jacuzzis. AE, D, DC, MC, V. $$$$*

Hyatt Regency Monterey. Although rooms and atmosphere are less glamorous than at some other resorts in the region, the Hyatt does offer excellent facilities. *1 Old Golf Course Rd., 93940, tel. 408/372–1234, 800/233–1234, or 800/824–2196 in CA, fax 408/375–3960. 575 rooms. Facilities: restaurant, lounge, sports bar, 2 pools, 2 Jacuzzis, golf course, tennis court, fitness room. AE, D, DC, MC, V. $$$$*

Monterey Bay Inn. This hotel, anchoring Cannery Row, is under the same ownership as the Spindrift Inn, and demonstrates the same attention to detail. Spacious rooms, decorated in peach and green tones, offer private balconies, VCR, honor bar, terry-cloth robes, and binoculars for viewing marine life; most rooms have breathtaking bay views. Continental breakfast is included. *242 Cannery Row, 93940, tel. 408/373–6242 or 800/424–6242, fax 408/373–7603. 47 rooms. Facilities: 2 Jacuzzis, fitness room, sauna. AE, D, DC, MC, V. $$$$*

★   **Monterey Plaza.** This sophisticated full-service hotel commands a superb waterfront location on Cannery Row, where frolicking sea otters can be observed from the wide outdoor patio and from many of the room balconies. The architecture and decor blend early California and Oriental styles and retain a little of the old cannery design. *400 Cannery Row, 93940, tel. 408/646–1700, 800/631–1339, or 800/334–3999 in CA, fax 408/646–0285. 285 rooms. Facilities: restaurant, bar, cable TV, garage (fee), fitness center. AE, D, DC, MC, V. $$$$*

★ **Spindrift Inn.** This elegant small hotel on Cannery Row boasts the street's only private beach and a rooftop garden overlooking Monterey Bay. Indoor pleasures include spacious rooms with sitting areas, Oriental rugs, fireplaces, canopied beds, down comforters, and other luxuries. Continental breakfast, brought to the room on a silver tray, and afternoon tea are also included. *652 Cannery Row, 93940, tel. 408/646–8900 or 800/841–1879, fax 408/646–5342. 41 rooms. Facilities: private beach, rooftop garden, valet parking (fee). AE, D, DC, MC, V. $$$$*

Cannery Row Inn. This is a modern small hotel on a street above Cannery Row with bay views from the private balconies of some rooms. Gas fireplaces and complimentary Continental breakfast are among the amenities. *200 Foam St., 93940, tel. 408/649–8580 or 800/876–8580, fax 408/649–2566. 32 rooms. Facilities: Jacuzzi, garage. AE, MC, V. $$$–$$$$*

Monterey Hotel. Originally opened in 1904, this quaint, small, downtown hotel reopened in 1987 after an extensive restoration that left its oak paneling and ornate fireplaces gleaming. Standard rooms are small but well appointed with reproduction antique furniture; master suites have fireplaces and sunken baths. Complimentary Continental breakfast and afternoon tea are included. *406 Alvarado St., 93940, tel. 408/375–3184 or 800/727–0960, fax 408/373–2894. 44 rooms, parking (fee). AE, D, DC, MC, V. $$$–$$$$*

Monterey Marriott. This large convention hotel sticks out like a 10-story sore thumb in the middle of Monterey's quaint downtown. Rooms are small, but many have good views of the town and bay. *350 Calle Principal, 93940, tel. 408/649–4234 or 800/228–9290, fax 408/372–2968. 341 rooms. Facilities: 3 restaurants, lounge, Jacuzzi, pool, health club, garage (fee). AE, D, DC, MC, V. $$$–$$$$*

Otter Inn. This low-rise hotel with a rustic shingle exterior is one block above Cannery Row and has bay views from most of the rooms. Coffee and pastries are provided in rooms, which are spacious, with fireplaces and private hot tubs in some. *571 Wave St., 93940, tel. 408/375–2299, fax 408/375–2352. 31 rooms. AE, MC, V. $$$–$$$$*

Arbor Inn. This stylish motel has a friendly, country-inn atmosphere. Continental breakfast is served in a pine-paneled lobby with a tile fireplace. There is an outdoor Jacuzzi, and rooms are light and airy, some with fireplaces and some with accessibility for visitors with disabilities. *1058 Munras Ave., 93940, tel. 408/372–3381, fax 408/372–4687. 56 rooms. Facilities: hot tub. AE, D, DC, MC, V. $$–$$$*

★ **Monterey Motor Lodge.** A pleasant location on the edge of Monterey's El Estero park gives this motel an edge over its many competitors along Munras Avenue. Indoor plants and a large secluded courtyard with pool are other pluses. *55 Aguajito Rd., 93940, tel. 408/372–8057 or 800/558–1900, fax 408/655–2933. 45 rooms. Facilities: restaurant, pool. AE, D, DC, MC, V. $$–$$$*

Pacific Grove
Dining
★

Old Bath House. A romantic, nostalgic atmosphere permeates this converted bathhouse overlooking the water at Lovers Point. The Continental menu here makes the most of local seafood and produce. When they're available, the salmon and Monterey Bay prawns are particularly worth ordering. *620 Ocean View Blvd., tel. 408/375–5195. Reservations advised. Jacket recommended. AE, D, DC, MC, V. No lunch. $$$$*

Gernot's. The ornate Victorian-era Hart Mansion that now houses this restaurant is a delightful setting in which to dine on seafood and game served with light sauces. Continental specialties include wild boar bourguignonne and roast venison. *649 Lighthouse Ave., tel.*

408/646–1477. Reservations advised. Dress: casual. AE, MC, V. No lunch. Closed Mon. $$$

Melac's. This intimate dining room is complete with white tablecloths and lovely china and crystal. The menu of contemporary French cuisine changes almost weekly according to what's in season; some of the more characteristic dishes include sea bass wrapped in a potato crust and covered in red wine sauce, and roasted duck in balsamic vinegar. *663 Lighthouse Ave., tel. 408/375–1743. Reservations required. Dress: casual. AE, D, DC, MC, V. Lunch Tues.– Fri. Dinner Tues.–Sat. $$$*

Fandango. With its stone walls and country furniture, this restaurant has the earthy feel of a southern European farmhouse. Complementing the ambience are the robust flavors of the cuisine, which ranges from southern France, Italy, Spain, and Greece to North Africa, from couscous and paella to canneloni. *223 17th St., tel. 408/372– 3456. Reservations advised. Dress: casual. AE, D, DC, MC, V. $$*

The Tinnery. The simple, clean lines of this contemporary dining room are framed by picture-window views of Lovers Point. Breakfast, lunch, and dinner are served at this casual, family-oriented restaurant. The eclectic menu includes broiled salmon with fresh Hollandaise sauce, mesquite-grilled meat, and English fish and chips. *Ocean View Blvd. and 17th St., tel. 408/646–1040. No reservations. Dress: casual. AE, D, DC, MC, V. $$*

Peppers. This cheerful white-walled café offers fresh seafood and traditional dishes from Mexico and Latin America. The red and green salsas are excellent. *170 Forest Ave., tel. 408/373–6892. Reservations recommended. Dress: casual. AE, D, DC, MC, V. Closed Tues. Dinner only on Sun. $*

Lodging

★ **Green Gables Inn.** Originally built a century ago by a Pasadena judge to house his mistress, this Swiss Gothic bed-and-breakfast retains an air of Victorian romance. Stained-glass windows framing an ornate fireplace and other details compete with the spectacular bay views. The breakfast buffet is tempting, though breakast in bed is also an option; afternoon hors d'oeuvres are served with wine, sherry, or tea. *104 5th St., 93950, tel. 408/375–2095, fax 408/375–5437. 11 rooms, 7 with bath. AE, MC, V. $$$$*

Martine Inn. While most bed-and-breakfasts in Pacific Grove are Victorian houses, this one is a pink stucco Mediterranean-style villa overlooking the water. The rooms, some of which have ocean views, are individually decorated with such unique items as a mahogany bedroom set featured at the 1969 World's Fair. Full breakfast, wine, and hors d'oeuvres are included. *255 Oceanview Blvd., 93950, tel. 408/373–3388 or 800/284-INNS, fax 408/373–3896. 19 rooms. MC, V. $$$$*

★ **Centrella Hotel.** This handsome century-old Victorian mansion and garden cottages two blocks from Lovers Point Beach has an attractive garden, claw-foot bathtubs, and wicker and brass furnishings. Depending on the time of day, a sideboard in the large parlor is laden with breakfast treats, cookies and fruit, sherry and wine, or hors d'oeuvres. *612 Central Ave., 93950, tel. 408/372–3372 or 800/233-3372, fax 408/372–2036. 26 rooms, 24 with bath. AE, MC, V. $$$–$$$$*

Gosby House Inn. Rooms in this lovely yellow Victorian bed-and-breakfast in the town center are individually decorated, and almost all have private bath (some have fireplaces). Full breakfast and afternoon hors d'oeuvres are served in a sunny parlor or by the fireplace in the living room. *643 Lighthouse Ave., 93950, tel. 408/375–1287 or 800/527–8828, fax 408/655–9621. 22 rooms, 20 with bath. AE, MC, V. $$$–$$$$*

★ **Asilomar Conference Center.** A summer camp–like atmosphere pervades this assortment of 28 rustic but comfortable lodges in the middle of a 100-acre state park across from the beach. Breakfast is included. *800 Asilomar Blvd., Box 537, 93950, tel. 408/372–8016, fax 408/372–7227. 311 rooms. Facilities: cafeteria, pool. No credit cards. $$–$$$*

Pebble Beach
Dining and
Lodging

The Inn at Spanish Bay. Under the same management as the Lodge at Pebble Beach, this 270-room resort sprawls on a breathtaking stretch of shoreline along 17-Mile Drive. The resort has a slightly more casual feel, although the 600-square-foot rooms are no less luxurious. The inn is adjacent to its own tennis courts and golf course, but guests also have privileges at all the Lodge facilities. For dinner, the excellent Bay Club restaurant (reservations advised, jacket requested), decorated in pleasant pastels, overlooks the coastline and the golf links. The haute Italian cuisine includes such offerings as carpaccio with black truffles and shaved Parmesan, veal chop Milanese with oven-roasted vegetables, risotto with seared scallops, and fresh Maine lobster braised with peas and onions. *Box 1589, 2700 17-Mile Dr., 93953, tel. 408/647–7500 or 800/654–9300, fax 408/647–7443. 270 rooms. Facilities: 3 restaurants, tennis, fitness center, pool. AE, DC, MC, V. $$$$*

★ **The Lodge at Pebble Beach.** This renowned resort, built in 1916, features quietly luxurious rooms with fireplaces and wonderful views. The golf course, tennis club, and equestrian center are also highly regarded. Guests of the lodge have privileges at the Inn at Spanish Bay. Overlooking the 18th green, the highly recommended Club XIX restaurant (reservations advised, jacket requested) is an intimate, café-style spot serving classic French preparations of veal, lamb, and duck, as well as foie gras and caviar. *17-Mile Dr., Box 1418, Pebble Beach 93953, tel. 408/624–3811 or 800/654–9300, fax 408/625–8598. 161 rooms. Facilities: 3 restaurants, coffee shop, lounge, pool, sauna, beach club, golf, tennis, riding, weights, massage, bikes for rent. AE, DC, MC, V. $$$$*

Santa Cruz
Dining
★

Chez Renee. This elegant retreat, owned by a husband-and-wife team, serves French-inspired cuisine. Specialties include sweetbreads with two sauces (Madeira and mustard); duck and home-preserved brandied cherries; deep-sea scallops garnished with smoked salmon and dill. Save room for the excellent dessert soufflés. *9051 Soquel Dr., Aptos, tel. 408/688–5566. Reservations suggested. Dress: casual. MC, V. No lunch Sat. $$$$*

The Veranda. In this refurbished Victorian dining room in the Bayview Hotel, the surroundings are attractive and the service cordial. Corn fritters with Smithfield ham and homemade pâtés and terrines stand out among the appetizers. Main-course offerings include cassoulet of local shellfish, baked salmon with a mustard-and-herb sauce, and roast rack of lamb. The best-selling dessert is the white-chocolate macadamia cheesecake. *8041 Soquel Dr., tel. 408/685–1881. Reservations accepted. Dress: casual. AE, D, MC, V. No lunch weekends. $$$*

El Palomar. This spacious restaurant in the Palomar Inn, with vaulted ceilings and wood beams, serves California Mexican cuisine with an emphasis on seafood. Homemade tamales, seviche, and chile verde are among the best dishes. *1336 Pacific Ave., tel. 408/425–7575. Dress: casual. AE, D, MC, V. $$*

O Mei Sichuan Chinese Restaurant. Not your run-of-the-mill chopsuey joint, this sophisticated, attractive place offers some unusual dishes: *gan pung* (boneless chicken crisp-fried and served with a spicy garlic sauce), *gan bian* (dried sautéed beef with hot pepper and ginger on crisp rice noodles), and snapper prepared Taiwan style (fileted and breaded, with chili-vinegar sauce). *2316 Mission, Rte. 1, tel. 408/425–8458. Reservations advised on weekends. Dress: casual. AE, MC, V. No lunch weekends. $–$$*

Lodging
★
Casablanca Motel. Of the many motels along this hurly-burly waterfront, this is perhaps the most interesting. The main building was once the Cerf Mansion, built in 1918 in the Mediterranean style for a federal judge, and every room is individually decorated. There are brass beds, velvet drapes, and fireplaces, and the Luttrell family sets great store on maintaining the tranquillity of the place. Most rooms have views of the ocean. The restaurant here serves innovative cuisine, and has spectacular views. *101 Main at Beach, 95060, tel. 408/423–1570, fax 408/423–0235. 35 rooms. Facilities: restaurant. AE, D, DC, MC, V. $$$–$$$$*

The Darling House Bed and Breakfast by the Sea. This superb 1910 mansion on the promontory overlooking the wharf was built as a summer house for a rich Colorado family by William Weeks, architect of Santa Cruz's Cocoanut Grove. The decor, including antique furnishings and beveled glass, is authentic. Modern plumbing and electricity are among the few concessions made to the 1990s; in all other ways, the house retains an atmosphere of turn-of-the-century elegance. Continental breakfast is offered. No pets; smoking outdoors only. *314 W. Cliff Dr., 95060, tel. 408/458–1958 or 800/458–1958. 8 rooms, 2 with shared bath. Facilities: Jacuzzi. AE, D, DC, MC, V. $$$–$$$$*

The Arts and Nightlife

The Arts

The area's top venue for the performing arts is the **Sunset Community Cultural Center** (San Carlos, between 8th and 10th Aves., tel. 408/624–3996) in Carmel, which presents concerts, film screenings, and headline performers throughout the year. Facilities include the Sunset Theater and the Outdoor Forest Theater, the first open-air amphitheater built in California.

Festivals
Performing-arts festivals have a long tradition in the Monterey area, with the most famous drawing thousands of spectators. Ordering tickets as far in advance as possible is often essential. The **Carmel Bach Festival** (Box 575, Carmel, 93921, tel. 408/624–1521) has presented the work of Johann Sebastian Bach and his contemporaries in concerts and recitals for more than 50 years. The highlight of the three-week event, which starts in mid-July, is a candlelit concert in the chapel of the Carmel Mission Basilica.

Nearly as venerable is the celebrated **Monterey Jazz Festival** (Box JAZZ, Monterey, 93942, tel. 408/373–3366), which attracts jazz and blues greats from around the world to the Monterey Fairgrounds for a weekend of music each September.

Another popular jazz event is **Dixieland Monterey** (177 Webster St., Suite A-206, Monterey, 93940, tel. 408/443–5260), held on the first full weekend of March, which features Dixieland bands performing in cabarets, restaurants, and hotel lounges throughout Monterey, as well as a Saturday-morning jazz parade downtown.

For blues fans, there is the **Monterey Bay Blues Festival** (Box 1400, Seaside 93955, tel. 408/394–2652), which is held in June at the Monterey Fairgrounds, featuring entertainment and a range of food booths.

The Custom House Plaza in downtown Monterey is the setting for free performances outdoors during the **Monterey Bay Theatrefest** (tel. 408/649–6852), which is held on weekend afternoons and evenings during most of the summer.

The **Cabrillo Music Festival** in Santa Cruz (104 Walmut Ave., Suite 206, Santa Cruz 95060, tel. 408/426–6966, or box office 408/429–3444), one of the longest-running new music festivals, showcases contemporary sounds, particularly by American composers, for two weeks in early August.

Concerts   The highly regarded **Monterey County Symphony** (Box 3965, Carmel 93921, tel. 408/624–8511) performs a series of concerts October through May in Salinas and Carmel. Programs range from classical to pop and include guest artists.

The **Chamber Music Society of the Monterey Peninsula** (Box 6283, Carmel 93921, tel. 408/625–2212) presents a series of concerts featuring well-known chamber groups, and holds an annual contest for young musicians. Dance, classical music, and operatic concerts are sponsored by the **Salinas Concert Association** (318 Catharine St., Salinas 93901, tel. 408/758–5027), which presents a series of featured artists between October and May at the Sherwood Hall in Salinas.

Film   Classic films are shown on Thursdays once a month in the community room of the **Monterey Public Library** (625 Pacific St., Monterey, tel. 408/646–3930).

Theater   **California's First Theater** (Scott and Pacific Sts., Monterey, tel. 408/375–4916) is home to the Troupers of the Gold Coast, who perform 19th-century melodramas in the summer in the state's oldest operating little theater, a historic landmark dating from 1846 on Monterey's Path of History.

Specializing in contemporary works, both comedy and drama, is the **GroveMont Theater,** an acclaimed repertory company (320 Hoffman Ave., tel. 408/649–0340 or 408/649–6852). Also part of the Grove-Mont Center is the **Poetic Drama Institute,** which often features solo dramatic performances and poetry readings.

American musicals and comedies, both old and new, are the focus of the **Wharf Theater** (Fisherman's Wharf, Monterey, tel. 408/649–2332), where a local cast is sometimes joined by Broadway actors, directors, and choreographers.

Shakespeare Santa Cruz (Performing Arts Complex, University of California at Santa Cruz, 95064, tel. 408/459–2121) puts on a six-week Shakespeare festival in July and August that also includes 20th-century works.

Nightlife

Cabaret   **Kalisa's** (851 Cannery Row, Monterey, tel. 408/372–3621). This long-established, freewheeling café in a Cannery Row landmark building offers a potpourri of entertainment that can include belly dancing, flamenco, jazz, folk dancing, and magic.

Bars and Nightclubs   **The Club** (Alvarado and Del Monte Sts., Monterey, tel. 408/646–9244). This popular night spot has dancing to Top-40 music Monday through Saturday, plus changing entertainment that includes performances by rock and reggae bands, and male stripteasers.

Doc Ricketts' Lab (95 Prescott St., Monterey, tel. 408/649–4241). Live rock bands perform nightly one block above Cannery Row.

Doubletree Hotel (2 Portola Plaza, Monterey, tel. 408/649–4511). Live music and rock and roll with a DJ is offered nightly except Sundays in the Brasstree Lounge (Thurs., Fri., and Sat. only in winter).

Mark Thomas Outrigger (700 Cannery Row, Monterey, tel. 408/372–8543). Rock 'n' roll and rhythm and blues from the 1960s, '70s, and '80s is played by live bands on Friday and Saturday night.

Monterey Marriott (350 Calle Principal, Monterey, tel. 408/649–4234). Live entertainment is offered nightly, with a DJ on Sunday in Character's Sports Bar and Grill.

Monterey Plaza Hotel (400 Cannery Row, Monterey, tel. 408/646–1700). Automated piano music can be heard in a romantic setting overlooking the bay in the hotel's Duck Club.

Planet Gemini (625 Cannery Row, Monterey, tel. 408/373–1449). Most nights, this club features comedy shows, followed by dancing to live rock music. There is country and western music and dancing Wednesday nights.

Safari Club (1425 Munras Ave., Monterey, tel. 408/649–1020). Karaoke is featured Friday and Saturday nights at this club in the Bay Park Hotel.

Sly McFlys (700 Cannery Row, Monterey, tel. 408/649–8050). This popular local watering hole has a pub atmosphere.

Discos **Virgo's** (2200 N. Fremont St., Monterey, tel. 408/375–6116). This is Monterey's outpost for country and western music.

Piano Bars **Highlands Inn** (Rte. 1, Carmel, tel. 408/624–3801). There is piano music nightly in the Lobos Lounge; dancing on weekends in the Fireside Lounge.

Lodge at Pebble Beach (17-Mile Dr., Pebble Beach, tel. 408/624–3811). You'll find easy listening entertainment in the Cypress Room and Terrace Lounge; there's a jazz band on Friday and Saturday evenings.

11 The Central Coast

The coastline between Carmel and Santa Barbara, a distance of just over 200 miles, is one of the most popular stretches of scenery in California—maybe one of the most popular anywhere. It is what many visitors to the state have come to see, and a drive that many Californians will take, whenever the opportunity presents itself. Except for a few smallish cities—Ventura and Santa Barbara in the south and San Luis Obispo in the north—the area is sparsely populated, with only a few small towns whose inhabitants relish their isolation among the redwoods at the sharp edge of land and sea. Between settlements, the landscape is dotted with grazing cattle and hillsides of wild flowers. Around Big Sur, the Santa Lucia mountains drop down to the Pacific with dizzying grandeur, but as you move south, the shoreline gradually flattens into the long sandy beaches of Santa Barbara and Ventura.

Big Sur has long attracted individualists—novelist Henry Miller comes to mind—drawn by the intractability of the terrain. But even the less precipitous junction of land and sea farther south has pulled in its share, most notably—and visibly—William Randolph Hearst, whose monumental home San Simeon is the biggest single tourist attraction along the coast.

Throughout the region are bed-and-breakfast inns, and pleasant little towns, such as Cambria and Ojai, where resident artists and artisans create and sell their work. In the rolling hills of the Santa Ynez Valley are a growing number of wineries with steadily rising reputations. The Danish town of Solvang is a popular stopover for hearty Scandinavian fare and an architectural change of pace.

Santa Barbara is your introduction to the sand, surf, sun, and unhurried hospitality and easy living of Southern California. Only 90 miles north of Los Angeles, Santa Barbara works hard to maintain its relaxed atmosphere and cozy scale. Wedged as it is between the Pacific and the Santa Ynez Mountains, it's never had much room for expansion. The city's setting, climate, and architecture combine to produce a Mediterranean feel that permeates not only its look but its pace.

Route 1, which runs through most of this region, was the first in the country to be declared a scenic highway, in 1966. Barring fog or rain, the coast is almost always in view from the road. In some sections, the waves break on rocks 11,200 feet below; in other places, the highway is just 20 feet above the surf. The two-lane road is kept in good repair, but it twists, and traffic, especially in summer, can be very slow. Allow plenty of time for this drive, so that you can properly enjoy the breathtaking vistas.

Essential Information

Important Addresses and Numbers

Tourist Information
Free pamphlets on accommodations, dining, sports, and entertainment are available at the **Visitors Information Center** (1 Santa Barbara St. at Cabrillo Blvd., tel. 805/965–3021, open Mon.–Sat. 9–4, Sun. 10–4). Before arriving, contact **Santa Barbara Conference and Visitors Bureau** (510A State St., 93101, tel. 805/966–9222 or 800/927–4688 for mailing of publications).

Information on other towns along the central coast is available from: **Big Sur Chamber of Commerce** (Box 87, 93920, tel. 408/667–2100). **San Luis Obispo Chamber of Commerce** (1039 Chorro St., 93401, tel.

805/781–2777 or 800/756–5056). **Cambria Chamber of Commerce** (767 Main St., 93428, tel. 805/927–3624). **San Simeon Chamber of Commerce** (Box 1, 9190 Hearst St., 93452, tel. 805/927–3500 or 800/342–5613). **Solvang Visitors Bureau** (Box 70, 1511A Mission Dr., 93464, tel. 805/688–6144 or 800/468–6765). **California Dept. of Parks and Recreation** (in Big Sur, tel. 408/667–2315).

Emergencies Dial 911 for **police** and **ambulance** in an emergency.

Doctors Emergency care is available at **St. Francis Hospital** (601 E. Micheltorena St., Santa Barbara, tel. 805/962–7661).

Road Conditions Dial 800/427–7623 for up-to-date information on road conditions throughout the Central Coast area.

Arriving and Departing

By Plane **American** and **American Eagle** (tel. 800/433–7300), **Skywest/ Delta** (tel. 800/453–9417), **United** and **United Express** (tel. 800/241–6522), and **USAir Express** (tel. 800/428–4322) fly into Santa Barbara Municipal Airport (tel. 805/683–4011) 8 miles from downtown at 500 Fowler Road.

Santa Barbara Airbus (tel. 805/964–7374) shuttles travelers between Santa Barbara and Los Angeles Airport. **Aero Airport Limousine** (tel. 805/965–2412) serves Los Angeles Airport (by reservation only). **Metropolitan Transit District** (tel. 805/683–3702) bus No. 11 runs from the airport to the downtown transit center.

By Car The only way to see the most dramatic section of the central coast, the 70 miles between Big Sur and San Simeon, is by car. Heading south on Route 1, you'll be on the ocean side of the road and will get the best views. Don't expect to make good time along here. The road is narrow and twisting with a single lane in each direction, making it difficult to pass slower traffic or the many lumbering RVs. In fog or rain, the drive can be downright nerve-racking. U.S. 101 from San Francisco to San Luis Obispo is the quicker, easier alternative, but it misses the coast entirely. U.S. 101 and Route 1 join north of Santa Barbara. Both, eventually dividing, continue south through Southern California.

By Train **Amtrak** (tel. 800/USA–RAIL) runs the *Coast Starlight* train from Los Angeles and the coast from Santa Barbara to San Luis Obispo. From there it heads inland for the rest of the route to the San Francisco Bay Area and Seattle. Local numbers are, in Santa Barbara, tel. 805/963–1015; in San Luis Obispo, tel. 805/541–0505.

Getting Around

By Car Route 1 and U.S. 101 run more or less parallel, with Route 1 hugging the coast and 101 remaining a few miles inland. Along some stretches the two roads join and run together for a while. Plan on three to four hours' driving time for the 90 miles from Big Sur to Morro Bay on Route 1—this is not a freeway, and you'll probably want to stop at some of the 300 scenic turnouts along this route. Once you start south from Carmel, there is no route off until Route 46 heads inland from Cambria to connect with U.S. 101. At Morro Bay, Route 1 moves inland for 13 miles and connects with U.S. 101 at San Luis Obispo. From here, south to Pismo Beach, the two highways run concurrently, and while you lose the dramatic coastal scenery, the driving is easier. The roads go their separate ways again near Gaviota, just north of Santa Barbara. You can drive between Santa Barbara and Los Angeles in just a couple of hours.

By Bus   From Monterey and Carmel, **Monterey–Salinas Transit** (tel. 408/899–2555) operates daily bus runs to Big Sur May–September. From San Luis Obispo, **Central Coast Transit** (tel. 805/541–2228) runs buses around the town and out to the coast on regular schedules. Local service is also provided by the Santa Barbara Metropolitan Transit District (tel. 805/963–3364).

Guided Tours

California Parlour Car Tours (Cathedral Hill Hotel, 1101 Van Ness Ave., San Francisco 94109, tel. 415/474–7500 or 800/227–4250) offers a number of tours that include the central coast area. Lasting three to 10 days, these are one-way bus trips from San Francisco to Los Angeles (or vice versa) that travel along the coast, visiting Hearst Castle, Santa Barbara, and Monterey, and may also include time in Yosemite or Lake Tahoe. (We recommend that you steer clear of any tour that takes you to Yosemite for less than one full day; readers have been disappointed in the past. Save Yosemite for a trip when you have enough time.)

Santa Barbara Trolley Co (tel. 805/965–0353) has five daily, regularly scheduled runs in Santa Barbara. Motorized San Francisco–style cable cars deliver visitors to major hotels, shopping areas, and attractions. Stop or not, as you wish, and pick up another trolley when you're ready to move on. All depart from and return to Stearns Wharf. The fare is $5 adults, $3 children and senior citizens.

Exploring the Central Coast

Most of the major sights and attractions of the region are right along the coastal route, or just a short detour away. The entire distance from Big Sur to Santa Barbara *could* be tackled in one long day of driving, but that would defeat the purpose of taking the slower, scenic coastal highway. A better option is to plan on taking several days, allowing time to explore Big Sur, Hearst Castle, the beaches, and Santa Barbara, and to savor the changing scenery of the shoreline.

Highlights for First-Time Visitors

The Botanic Gardens, Santa Barbara
Hearst San Simeon State Historical Monument
La Purisma, Lompoc
Mission San Luis Obispo de Tolosa, San Luis Obispo
Morro Rock, Morro Bay
Ojai
Point Sur Light Station
Santa Barbara Mission
Santa Barbara Museum of Art
Solvang

South Along Route 1

Numbers in the margin correspond to points of interest on the Central Coast map.

Just 13 miles south of Carmel is one of the quintessential views of California's coast, the elegant concrete arc of **Bixby Creek Bridge.** This view is a photographer's dream, and there is a small parking area on the north side from which to take a photo or to start a walk across the 550-foot span.

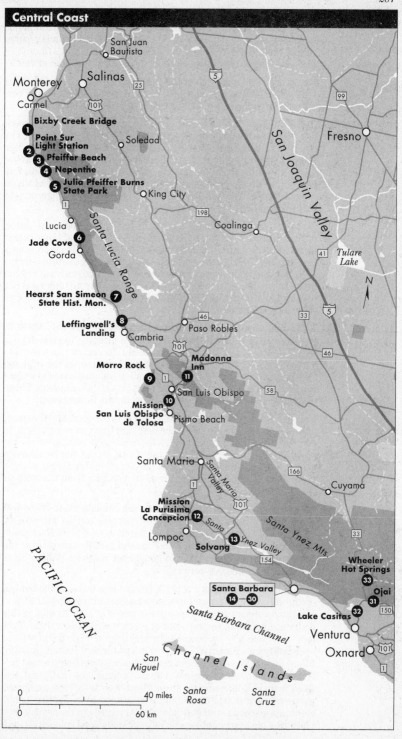

Central Coast

San Juan Bautista

Monterey
Carmel
Salinas
Soledad
Fresno

1 Bixby Creek Bridge
2 Point Sur Light Station
3 Pfeiffer Beach
4 Nepenthe
5 Julia Pfeiffer Burns State Park

King City

Lucia

6 Jade Cove
Gorda

Santa Lucia Range

San Joaquin Valley

Coalinga

Tulare Lake

N

7 Hearst San Simeon State Hist. Mon.

8 Leffingwell's Landing
Cambria

Paso Robles

9 Morro Rock

11 Madonna Inn

10 Mission San Luis Obispo de Tolosa
San Luis Obispo
Pismo Beach

Santa Maria

Santa Maria Valley

Cuyama

12 Mission La Purisima Concepcion

Lompoc

Santa Ynez Valley

Santa Ynez Mts

13 Solvang

33 Wheeler Hot Springs

31 Ojai

14 — **30** Santa Barbara

32 Lake Casitas

Ventura

PACIFIC OCEAN

Santa Barbara Channel

Channel Islands

Oxnard

San Miguel

Santa Rosa

Santa Cruz

0   40 miles
0   60 km

❷ Five miles south is the **Point Sur Light Station,** standing watch from atop a sandstone cliff. The century-old beacon is open to the public on ranger-led tours on Saturday at 9:30 and 1:30, and Sunday mornings at 9:30. *Big Sur State Park District, tel. 408/625–4419 or 667–2315. Admission: $5 adults, $3 children 13–17, $2 children up to 12.*

The small developed area of the Big Sur valley begins a few miles south. Pfeiffer Big Sur State Park, gas, groceries, hotels, and restaurants are all clustered along the next 7 miles of the highway.

❸ One of the few places where you may actually set foot on the coastline you have been viewing from the road is at **Pfeiffer Beach.** The road to the beach turns off Route 1 immediately past the Big Sur Ranger Station; follow it for 2 miles. The picturesque beach is at the foot of the cliffs, and a hole in one of the big sea-washed rocks lets you watch the waves break first on the sea side and then again on the beach side. The water is too cold and the surf too dangerous for swimming much of the year, however.

❹ On the ocean side of Route 1, a towering 800 feet above the water, is **Nepenthe** (*see* Dining, *below*), a favorite hangout of tourists and locals. The restaurant's deck can be an excellent place to take a break from the rather stressful—though very beautiful—drive. Rita Hayworth and Orson Welles spent their honeymoon at the inn here. Downstairs is a craft and gift shop, displaying, among other items, the work of Kaffe Fassett, the famous knitting designer who grew up at Nepenthe.

❺ A few miles south is **Julia Pfeiffer Burns State Park** (tel. 408/667–2315), where a short and popular hike is a nice way to stretch your legs. The trail leads up a small, redwood-filled valley to a waterfall. You can go back the same (easier) way or continue on the trail and take a loop that leads you along the valley wall, with views out into the tops of the redwood trees you were just walking among. There are picnic and camping areas as well as access to the beach.

❻ For the next dozen miles' drive, it is just you, the road, and the coast, and the gas station at Lucia is the first sign that you're returning to civilization. Among the many picnic areas and campgrounds between here and San Simeon is **Jade Cove,** one of the best-known areas on the coast in which to hunt for jade. Rock hunting is allowed on the beach, but you may not remove anything from the walls of the cliffs.

❼ It's another 30 miles to the **Hearst San Simeon State Historical Monument.** One of California's most popular tourist attractions, "Hearst Castle" sits in solitary splendor atop *La Cuesta Encantada* (the Enchanted Hill), and its buildings and gardens spread over the 123 acres that were the heart of newspaper magnate William Randolph Hearst's 250,000-acre ranch.

You'll forget the indignity of being herded into buses at the bottom of the hill once you reach the neoclassical extravaganza above. Hearst devoted nearly 30 years and some $10 million to building this elaborate mansion, commissioning renowned architect Julia Morgan—who was also responsible for buildings at U.C. Berkeley—to erect a "shrine of beauty." The result is a pastiche of Italian, Spanish, Moorish, and French styles; a fitting showcase of Hearst's vast collection of European artwork. The majestic marble halls and art-filled main building, and the three guest "cottages," are connected by terraces and staircases, and surrounded by reflecting pools, elaborate gardens, and statuary at every turn. In its heyday, this place was a playground for Hearst and Hollywood celebrities, and the rich and powerful who were frequent guests here. On the way up or down the hill, you may catch a glimpse of a zebra, one of the last descendants of Hearst's magnificent private zoo.

Although construction began in 1919, the project was never officially completed, and work was halted in 1947 when Hearst had to leave San Simeon due to failing health. The Hearst family presented the property to the state of California in 1958.

There are four tours available, ranging from a half-hour to three hours in length, and all involve covering a considerable distance on foot (the garden tour is offered only from April through October). A new, free visitors center offers an introduction to the life of this master of yellow journalism and inspiration for Orson Welles's film *Citizen Kane*—something about which Hearst was none too pleased. Reservations for the tours are a virtual necessity. *San Simeon State Park, 750 Hearst Castle Rd., tel. 805/927–2020 or 800/444–7275. Admission: $14 adults, $8 children 6–12. Tours daily 8:20 AM–3 PM (later in summer). Reservations may be made up to 8 weeks in advance. AE, D, MC, V.*

Cambria, an artists' colony full of turn-of-the-century homes, is a few minutes south of San Simeon and is becoming a popular weekend getaway spot for people from Los Angeles. The town is divided into the newer West Village and the original East Village, each with its own personality, and full of B&Bs, fine restaurants, art galleries, and shops selling unusual wares. You can still detect traces of the heritage of the Welsh miners who settled here in the 1890s. Moonstone Beach Drive, which runs along the coast, is lined with motels, and **Leffingwell's Landing,** a state picnic ground at its northern end, is a good place for examining tide pools and watching otters as they frolic in the surf.

❽

The coastal ribbon of Route 1 comes to an end at **Morro Bay.** The bay is separated from the ocean by a 4½-mile sandspit and a causeway, built in the 1930s, that leads to the huge monolith of **Morro Rock.** From the town of Morro Bay, it's a quick drive to the rock (actually an extinct volcano); a short walk around the base of the rock will take you to the breakwater, where you can stand with the calm, sheltered harbor (home of a large fishing fleet) on one side and the crashing waves of the Pacific on the other. The breakwater and the area around the oceanside base of Morro Rock are composed of huge boulders piled on top of one another, so walking around here involves stepping carefully and making occasional leaps. Morro Bay is also a wildlife preserve, protecting the nesting areas of endangered peregrine falcons, and you don't have to get too close to see that the rock is alive with birds. The town is dominated by the tall smokestacks of the PG&E plant just behind the waterfront, which can be seen from anywhere in the bay. Also in town is a huge chessboard with human-size pieces.

❾

South from Morro Bay, Route 1 turns inland on its way to **San Luis Obispo,** the halfway point between San Francisco and Los Angeles, and home to two decidedly different institutions: California Polytechnic State University, known as Cal Poly, and the exuberantly goofy, garish Madonna Inn. The town has several restored Victorian-era homes, and the chamber of commerce offers a list of self-guided historic walks. Among the places to see is the **Mission San Luis Obispo de Tolosa** (782 Monterey St., tel. 805/543–6850), one of the chain of missions established along the California coast by 18th-century Spanish missionary priests (*see also* La Purisma and Santa Barbara Mission, *below*). Nearby, several old warehouses along a

❿

stream have been renovated as shops. The **Ah Louis Store** (800 Palm St., tel. 805/543–4332) was established in 1884 to serve the Chinese laborers building the Pacific Coast and Southern Pacific railroads, and is still in business.

⓫ Even if you're not staying at the **Madonna Inn,** drop by the café and shops for a look at the gilt cherubs, pink bar stools, pink trash cans, pink lampposts, and all the other assorted outrageous kitsch that has put this place in a class by itself—a place way beyond any notions of good or bad taste. Begun in 1958 by Alex Madonna, a local highway contractor, and his wife, Phyllis, the inn has more than 100 rooms, each with its own played-to-the-hilt theme. The cave rooms, complete with waterfalls for showers, are among the most popular. *100 Madonna Rd. (take the Madonna Rd. exit from U.S. 101), tel. 805/543–3000.*

Route 1 and U.S. 101 become one road for a short stretch just south of San Luis Obispo. A short detour off this road is **Avila Beach,** a usually quiet beach town that comes alive on weekends when Cal Poly students take over. A bit farther down the highway, 20 miles of wide sandy beaches begin at the town of **Pismo Beach,** where U.S. 101 and Route 1 again go their separate ways. The action at this busy community centers on the shops and arcades near the pier, and there is camping near the beach.

Along the roads in and around **Lompoc** from May through August, you'll see vast fields of brightly colored flowers in bloom, and you will have little trouble in believing the town's boast of being the "Flower-Seed Capital of the World." Lompoc hosts a flower festival each June, and many of the petunias, poppies, marigolds, and other flowers grown here wind up on Rose Parade floats.

⓬ From Lompoc, take Route 246 east to Mission Gate Road, which leads to the **Mission La Purisima Concepcion.** Founded in 1787, this is the most fully restored mission in the state, and its still-remote setting in this stark and serene landscape powerfully evokes the life of the early Spanish settlers in California. Costumed docents demonstrate crafts, and displays illustrate the secular as well as religious life of the mission. A corral near the parking area holds several farm animals, including sheep that are descendants of the original mission stock. *2295 Purisima Rd., Lompoc, tel. 805/733–3713 or 805/733–1303 to schedule a tour. Admission: $5 per vehicle. Park open winter, 9–5; summer, 8–8.*

⓭ Southeast of Lompoc, inland along Route 246 (or U.S. 101 to the turnoff for 246 at Buellton), is the Danish town of **Solvang,** immortalized in William Castle's 1961 film *Homicidal.* You'll know when you've reached Solvang: the architecture suddenly turns to half-timbered buildings, windmills, and flags galore. Although it's aimed squarely at tourists, there is a genuine Danish heritage here—more than two-thirds of the town is of Danish descent. The 300 or so shops selling Danish goods and an array of knickknacks and specialty gift items are all within easy walking distance, many along Copenhagen Drive and Alisal Road. Stop by the narrow and jammed coffee shop attached to the **Solvang Bakery,** on Alisal Road, to try the Danish pastry. It is only one of a half-dozen aroma-filled bakeries in town. At the **Bethania Lutheran Church,** on Atterdag Road at Laurel Avenue, everything but the palm trees outside is traditional; the Danish services are open to the public.

From Buellton, U.S. 101 heads back to the coast, where it joins Route 1 again and runs east to Santa Barbara, about 30 miles away.

Santa Barbara

⑭ The attractions in **Santa Barbara** begin with the ocean: most everything else can be found along Cabrillo Boulevard. In the few miles between the beaches and the hills, you pass the downtown and then reach the old mission and, a little higher up, the botanic gardens. A few miles farther up the coast, but still very much a part of Santa Barbara, is the exclusive residential district of Hope Ranch. To the east is the district called Montecito, where comics Charlie Chaplin, Fatty Arbuckle, and others built the Montecito Inn in 1928. Its first guests included movie stars Norma Shearer, W. R. Hearst mistress Marion Davies, Carole Lombard, and Wallace Beery. Montecito is also where the exclusive San Ysidro Ranch resort is located.

Because the town is on a jog in the coastline, the ocean is to the south, and directions can be confusing. "Up" the coast is west, "down" toward Los Angeles is actually east, and the mountains are north.

Everything in town is so close that the 8-mile drive to the airport seems like a long trip. A car is handy, but not essential, if you're planning on staying pretty much in town. The beaches and downtown are easily explored by bicycle or on foot, and the Santa Barbara Trolley takes visitors to most of the major hotels and sights, which can also be reached on the local buses.

The Visitors Information Center publishes a free guide to a scenic drive that circles the town with a detour into the downtown. It passes the harbor, beaches, Hope Ranch, and the old mission, offers fine views on the way to Montecito, then returns you to the beaches. You can pick up the drive, marked with blue SCENIC DRIVE signs, anywhere along the loop. A free guide to the downtown, the "Red Tile Walking Tour," is also available free from the tourist office. It hits historical spots in a 12-block area.

The town of Goleta, the home of the University of California at Santa Barbara, is located a few miles up the coast via U.S. 101.

Numbers in the margin correspond to points of interest on the Santa Barbara map.

⑮ If you start at the Pacific and move inland, one of the first spots to visit is **Stearns Wharf** on Cabrillo Boulevard at the foot of State Street. You can drive out and park on the pier, then wander through the shops or stop for a meal at one of the wharf's restaurants or at the snack bar. The **Sea Center** (*see* What to See and Do with Children, *below*), a recent addition to the pier, is a branch of the Museum of Natural History that specializes in exhibits of marine life. Originally built in 1872 and reconstructed in 1981 after a fire, the wharf extends the length of three city blocks into the Pacific. The view from here back toward the city gives you a sense of the town's size and general layout.

⑯ The nearby **Santa Barbara Yacht Harbor** is sheltered by a man-made breakwater at the west end of Cabrillo Boulevard. You can take a ½-mile walk along the paved breakwater, check out the tackle and bait shops, or hire a boat from here.

⑰ Planted in 1877, the **Moreton Bay Fig Tree,** at Chapala Street and Route 101, is so huge it reportedly can provide shade for 10,000 people. In recent years, however, the tree has become a gathering place for an increasing number of homeless people.

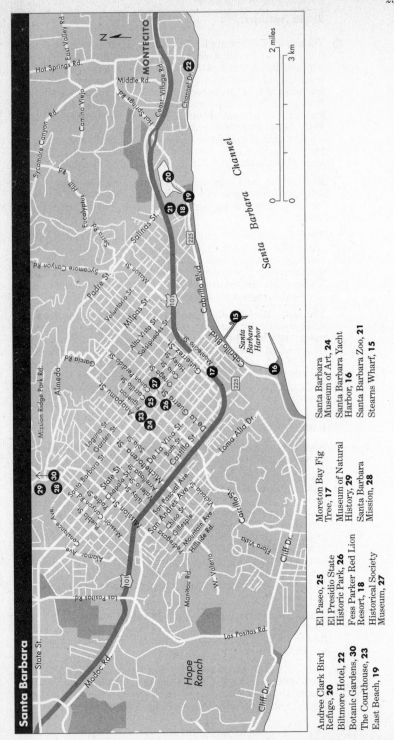

292

Santa Barbara

Andree Clark Bird
Refuge, **20**
Biltmore Hotel, **22**
Botanic Gardens, **30**
The Courthouse, **23**
East Beach, **19**

El Paseo, **25**
El Presidio State
Historic Park, **26**
Fess Parker Red Lion
Resort, **18**
Historical Society
Museum, **27**

Moreton Bay Fig
Tree, **17**
Museum of Natural
History, **29**
Santa Barbara
Mission, **28**

Santa Barbara
Museum of Art, **24**
Santa Barbara Yacht
Harbor, **16**
Santa Barbara Zoo, **21**
Stearns Wharf, **15**

Book Mark

American Express® Cardmembers Know 53 Ideal Places To Relax.

(With Or Without A Good Book.)

There's a lot to see and do in the West. But when it comes time to turn in, American Express® Cardmembers know to turn in at a Red Lion.

Renowned for its oversized rooms, excellent food, free parking and incomparable service, Red Lion is a perfect place to kick back and get spoiled. Without spoiling your travel budget.

And when you make your reservation at a Red Lion Hotel, don't forget to use the American Express Card. With its wide acceptance and 24-hour customer service, the American Express Card is the perfect companion for your travel, dining and shopping needs.

Call your travel agent or 1-800-547-8010 for reservations. As you can see, chances are Red Lion is where you're headed.

RED LION HOTELS & INNS

Don't Leave Home Without I

Back along Cabrillo, sandy beaches stretch for miles. The sprawling
(18) reddish Spanish-style hotel across from the beach is the **Fess Parker
Red Lion Resort.** Parker, the actor who played Davy Crockett and
Daniel Boone on television, owned the oceanfront acreage for many
years and spent several more trying to convince city fathers to allow
him to develop a hotel. He finally did, and the hotel opened in 1987
as the largest in Santa Barbara.

(19) Just beyond the hotel is the area's most popular beach, **East Beach,**
a wide swatch of sand at the east end of Cabrillo. Near by is the
(20) **Andree Clark Bird Refuge,** a peaceful lagoon and gardens. *1400 E.
Cabrillo Blvd. Admission free.*

(21) Adjoining the lagoon is the **Santa Barbara Zoo,** a small, lushly landscaped home to big-game cats, elephants, and exotic birds. *500
Niños Dr., tel. 805/962–6310. Admission: $5 adults, $3 senior citizens
and children 2–12. Open daily in winter 10–5; daily in summer 9–6.*

Where Cabrillo Boulevard ends at the lagoon, Channel Drive picks
(22) up and, a short distance east, passes the **Biltmore Hotel,** now owned
by the Four Seasons chain (*see* Lodging, *below*). For more than 60
years, Santa Barbara's high society and the visiting rich and famous
have come here to indulge in quiet California-style elegance.

To reach the downtown area, return to Cabrillo Boulevard and then
(23) head inland along State Street. **The Courthouse,** in the center of
downtown, has all the grandeur of a Moorish palace. As you wander
the halls, admiring the brilliant hand-painted tiles and spiral staircase, you might just forget that you're in a court house until you
spot a handcuffed group of offenders being marched by. This magnificent building was completed in 1929, as part of the rebuilding of
Santa Barbara made necessary by a 1925 earthquake that destroyed much of downtown. At the time the city was also in the midst
of a cultural awakening, and the trend was toward an architecture
appropriate to the area's climate and history. The result is the harmonious Mediterranean-Spanish look of much of Santa Barbara's
downtown area, especially its municipal buildings. An elevator to
the Courthouse tower takes visitors to a lovely, arched observation
area with a panoramic view of the city, and is a fine spot from which
to take photos. In the supervisors' ceremonial chambers on the
Court house's second floor are murals painted by an artist who did
backdrops for Cecil B. DeMille's silent films. *1100 block of Anacapa
St., tel. 805/962–6464. Open weekdays 8–5, weekends 9–5. Free 1-hr
guided tours Mon.–Sat. 2 PM, Wed. and Fri. 10:30 AM and 2 PM.*

One block down Anapamu Street past the Spanish-style **Public Li-**
(24) **brary** is the **Santa Barbara Museum of Art.** This fine small museum
houses a permanent collection featuring ancient sculpture, Oriental
art, a collection of French Impressionist paintings, and a sampling
of American artists such as Grandma Moses. *1130 State St., tel.
805/963–4364. Admission: $3 adults, $2.50 senior citizens, $1.50 chil-
dren 6–16; admission free Thurs. and first Sun. of each month. Open
Tues.–Sat. 11–5 (until 9 PM Thurs.), Sun. noon–5. Guided tours
Tues.–Sat. 1 PM, Sun. noon and 1 PM.*

(25) Walking south you'll pass **El Paseo,** a shopping arcade built around
an old adobe home. There are several such arcades in this area and
(26) also many small art galleries. A few blocks east is the **El Presidio
State Historic Park.** Built in 1782, the presidio was one of four military strongholds established by the Spanish along the coast of California. The guardhouse, El Cuartel, is one of the two original adobe
buildings that remain of the complex and is the oldest building

owned by the state. *123 E. Cañon Perdido St., tel. 805/966–9719. Admission free. Open daily 10:30–4:30.*

㉗ A block away is the **Historical Society Museum,** with an array of items from the town's past, including a silver-clad riding saddle and a collection of fancy ladies' fans. *136 E. De la Guerra St., tel. 805/966–1601. Admission free. Open Tues.–Sat. 10–5, Sun. noon–5.*

㉘ A short distance from downtown (take State Street north and make a right on Los Olivos) at the base of the hills is the **Santa Barbara Mission,** the gem of the chain of 21 missions established in California by Spanish missionaries in the late 1700s. One of the best preserved of the missions, it is still active as a Catholic church. *2201 Laguna St., tel. 805/682–4713. Admission: $2 adults, children under 16 free. Open daily 9–5.*

㉙
㉚ Continuing north a block you pass the **Museum of Natural History** (2559 Puesta del Sol), and then the **Botanic Gardens,** 1½ miles north of the mission. The 65 acres of native plants are particularly beautiful in the spring. *1212 Mission Canyon Rd., tel. 805/682–4726. Admission: $3 adults, $2 senior citizens, $1 children 5–12. Open 9–5. Guided tours 10:30 AM and 2 PM Thurs., Sat., and Sun.*

Ojai

Numbers in the margin correspond to points of interest on the Central Coast map.

㉛ A half-hour drive east of Santa Barbara over the narrow and winding Route 150 will put you in **Ojai,** a surprisingly rural town reminiscent of earlier days in California when agriculture was the uncontested king. You'll see acres of ripening orange and avocado groves that look like the picture-postcard images of Southern California from decades ago. In recent years the area has seen an influx of show-biz types, and other Angelinos who've opted for a life out of the fast lane. Moviemaker Frank Capra used the Ojai Valley as a backdrop for his 1936 classic, *Lost Horizon.* Be aware that the valley sizzles in the summer when temperatures routinely reach 90 degrees.

The works of local artists can be seen in the Spanish-style shopping arcade along the main street. On Sunday they display their paintings and crafts at the outdoor exhibition in the Security Bank parking lot (205 W. Ojai Ave.). The **Art Center** (113 S. Montgomery, tel. 805/646–0117) features art exhibits, theater, and dance.

A stroll around town should include a stop at **Bart's Books** (302 W. Matilija, tel. 805/646–3755), an outdoor store sheltered by native oaks and overflowing with used books.

㉜ Nearby **Lake Casitas** on Route 150 offers boating, fishing, and camping. It was the venue for the 1984 Summer Olympic rowing events.

㉝ One of the attractions in Ojai is a hot spring that makes use of natural mineral water from the nearby hills. The spa at **Wheeler Hot Springs** emerges like an oasis 7 miles north of town on Route 33. Its tall palms and herb gardens are fed by an adjacent stream, and natural mineral waters fill the four redwood hot tubs and a large pool at the well-kept spa. Massage and skin-care services are also available. A restaurant on site offers dinner and live entertainment Thursday through Sunday, and Saturday and Sunday brunch. *16825 Maricopa Hwy., tel. 805/646–8131 or 800/227–9292. Open Mon.–Thurs. 9–9,*

Fri.–Sun. 9 AM–10 PM. Reservations advised at least a week in advance for weekends, especially for spa.

What to See and Do with Children

Sea Center on Stearns Wharf interests everyone from infants, who are lulled by the sight of fish in water, to teenagers and adults. This educational center is a joint project of the Santa Barbara Museum of Natural History and the Channel Islands National Marine Sanctuary. Exhibits depict marine life from the Santa Barbara coastline to the Channel Islands: aquariums, life-size models of whales and dolphins, undersea dioramas, interactive computer/video displays, and remains of shipwrecks. The Touch Tank lets you handle marine invertebrates, fish, and marine plants collected from nearby waters. *211 Stearns Wharf, tel. 805/962–0885. Admission: $2 adults, $1.50 senior citizens, $1 children 3–17, under 3 free. Open daily 10–5. Touch Tank open Thurs.–Tues. noon–4.*

At the **Santa Barbara Zoo,** youngsters particularly enjoy the scenic railroad and barnyard petting zoo. For children who quickly tire of the beach, there's an elaborate jungle gym play area at Santa Barbara's **East Beach,** next to the Cabrillo Bath House. Outside of Santa Barbara's **Museum of Natural History** is the skeleton of a blue whale, the world's largest creature. Kids are dwarfed by the bones and invited to touch them (they just can't climb on them).

Off the Beaten Track

Channel Islands   Hearty travelers should consider a day visit or overnight camping trip to one of the five Channel Islands that often appear in a haze off the Santa Barbara horizon. The most often visited is Anacapa Island, 11 miles off the coast. The islands' remoteness and unpredictable seas protected them from development, and now provide a nature enthusiast's paradise—both underwater and on land. In 1980 the islands became the nation's 40th national park, and the water a mile around each is protected as a marine sanctuary.

On a good day, you'll be able to view seals, sea lions, and an array of birdlife. From December through March, migrating whales can be seen close up. On land, tide pools alive with sea life are often accessible. Underwater, divers can view fish, giant squid, and coral. Off Anacapa Island, scuba divers can see the remains of a steamship that sank in 1853. Frenchy's Cove, on the west end of the island, has a swimming beach and fine snorkeling.

The waters of the channel are often rough and can make for a rugged trip out to the islands. You can charter a boat and head out on your own, but most visitors head to Ventura Harbor, a 40-minute drive south from Santa Barbara. From here a park-district concessionaire carries small groups to the islands for day hikes, barbecues, and primitive overnight camping.

Island Packers (1867 Spinnaker Dr., Ventura 93001, tel. 805/642–1393) provides day trips to the islands and overnight camping to all five islands. Boats link up with National Park naturalists for hikes and nature programs. A limited number of visitors is allowed on each island and unpredictable weather can limit island landings. Reservations are essential in the summer.

Wineries   Centered in the Solvang area, and spreading north toward San Luis Obispo, is a California wine-making region with much of the variety but none of the glitz or crowds of the Napa Valley in Northern California. Most of the region's 30 wineries are located in the rolling hills in the Santa Maria or Santa Ynez valleys. A leisurely tour of the entire area could take all day, but many wineries are just a short jog off U.S. 101. They tend to be fairly small, and only a few offer guided tours, but most have tasting rooms run by helpful staff, and wine makers will often act as your tour guide. Several of the wineries also have picnic areas on their properties.

Pamphlets with detailed maps and listings of each winery are readily available at motels and tourist centers all along the coast. A map for a self-guided driving tour is available free from the **Santa Barbara County Vintners' Association** (Box 1558, Santa Ynez 93460, tel. 805/688–0881) and from **Paso Robles Wine Country** (1225 Park St., Paso Robles 93446, tel. 805/238–0506).

Shopping

Antiques In Santa Barbara a dozen antiques and gift shops are clustered in restored Victorian buildings on Brinkerhoff Avenue, two blocks west of State Street at West Cota Street.

Arcade In all, 32 shops, art galleries, and studios share the courtyard and gardens of **El Paseo** (Cañon Perdido St., between State and Anacapa Sts., Santa Barbara), a shopping arcade rich in history. Lunch on the outdoor patio is a nice break from a downtown tour.

Beach Wear If you want to go home with the absolutely latest in California beach wear, stop by **Pacific Leisure** (808 State St., Santa Barbara, tel. 805/962–8828), which specializes in volleyball fashions, shorts, tops, and beach towels.

Sports and the Outdoors

Participant Sports

Bicycling In Solvang you'll see people pedaling along on quadricycles, or in four-wheel carriages. Those and other types of bikes are available at **Surrey Cycle Rental** (475 1st St., tel. 805/688–0091) and **Breezy's Carriages** (414 1st St., tel. 686–4633; also at 1564 Copenhagen Dr.).

Santa Barbara's waterfront boasts the level, two-lane Cabrillo Bike Lane. In just over 3 easy miles, you pass the zoo, a bird refuge, beaches, and the harbor. There are restaurants along the way, or you can stop for a picnic along the palm-lined path looking out on the Pacific. Rent bikes from **Beach Rentals** (8 W. Cabrillo Blvd., tel. 805/963–2524; open 8 AM to sunset in winter, and 8 AM–dusk in summer). It also has roller skates for hire. Bikes and quadricycles can be rented from the **Cycles 4 Rent** concession near the pool at Fess Parker's Red Lion Resort (633 E. Cabrillo, tel. 805/564–4333, ext. 444).

Boating **Sailing Center of Santa Barbara** (Santa Barbara Harbor, at the launching ramp, tel. 805/962–2826 or 800/350–9090) offers sailing instruction, rents and charters sailboats, and organizes dinner cruises, sunset champagne cruises, and whale-watching expeditions.

Camping There are many campsites along Route 1, but they can fill up early any time but winter. In **Big Sur**, campsites are at Pfeiffer Big Sur and Julia Pfeiffer Burns state parks. Near **Hearst Castle**, camping is available at several smaller state parks (San Simeon, Atascadero,

Morro Bay, Montana de Oro, Avila Beach, and Pismo Beach). Most of the sites require reservations from MISTIX reservation service (tel. 800/444–7275 or 619/452–1950).

Fishing There is access to freshwater- and surf-fishing spots all along the coast. For deep-sea trips, try **Virg's Sport Fishing** (tel. 805/772–1222) or **Bob's Sportfishing** (tel. 805/772–3340), both in Morro Bay.

At Santa Barbara, surface and deep-sea fishing are possible all year. Fully equipped boats leave the harbor area for full- and half-day trips, dinner cruises, island excursions, and whale-watching from **SEA Landing** (Cabrillo Blvd. at Bath and breakwater, tel. 805/963–3564).

Glider Rides Scenic rides of 15–20 or 35–40 minutes are offered daily, 10–5, through **Windhaven Glider** at the **Santa Ynez Airport** near Solvang.

Golf Play nine or 18 holes at the **Santa Barbara Golf Club** (Las Positas Rd. and McCaw Ave., tel. 805/687–7087). **Sandpiper Golf Course,** 15 miles west (7925 Hollister Ave., Goleta, tel. 805/968–1541), offers a challenging course that used to be a stop on the women's professional tour.

Hiking There are miles of hiking trails in the Ventana Wilderness, with trailheads at state parks and picnic areas on Route 1 from Big Sur to San Simeon. Twelve miles east of Solvang is **Cachuma Lake,** a jewel of an artificial lake offering hiking as well as fishing and boating.

Horseback Riding The **San Ysidro Ranch** hotel (900 San Ysidro La., Montecito, tel. 805/969–5046) offers trail rides for parties of no more than six into the foothills by the hour. Reservations are required.

Tennis Many Santa Barbara hotels have their own courts, but there are also excellent public courts. Day permits, for $3, are available at the courts. **Las Positas Municipal Courts** (1002 Las Positas Rd., Santa Barbara) has six lighted courts. Large complexes are also at the **Municipal Courts** (near Salinas Street and Route 101) and **Pershing Park** (Castillo St. and Cabrillo Blvd.).

Volleyball The east end of Santa Barbara's **East Beach** has more than a dozen sandlots. There are some casual pickup games, but if you get into one, be prepared—these folks play serious volleyball.

Spectator Sports

Polo The public is invited to watch the elegant game at the **Santa Barbara Polo Club,** 7 miles east in Carpinteria. *Take the Santa Claus La. exit from Hwy. 101, turn left under the freeway and then left again onto Via Real. The polo grounds are 1/2 mi farther, surrounded by high hedges. Tel. 805/684–6683. Admission: $6 adults, children under 12 free. Games played Apr.–Oct., Sun.*

Beaches

Santa Barbara's beaches don't have the big surf of the beaches farther south, but they also don't have the crowds. A short walk from the parking lot can usually find you a solitary spot. Be aware that fog often hugs the coast until about noon in May and June.

East Beach, at the east end of Cabrillo Boulevard, is *the* beach in Santa Barbara. There are lifeguards, volleyball courts, a jogging and bike trail, and the Cabrillo Bath House with a gym, showers, and changing rooms open to the public.

Arroyo Burro Beach, a state beach just west of the harbor on Cliff Drive at Las Positas Road, has a small grassy area with picnic tables and sandy beaches below the cliffs. The Brown Pelican Restaurant on the beach serves a delicious breakfast.

Goleta Beach Park, north of Santa Barbara, in Goleta, is a favorite with the college students from the nearby University of California campus. The easy surf makes it perfect for beginning surfers and families with young children.

West of Santa Barbara on Route 1 are **El Capitan, Refugio,** and **Gaviota state beaches,** each with campsites, picnic tables, and fire pits. East of the city is the state beach at **Carpinteria,** a sheltered, sunny, and often crowded beach.

Dining and Lodging

Dining   Although you will find some chain restaurants in the bigger towns, the central coast from Big Sur to Solvang is far enough off the interstate to ensure that each restaurant and café has its own personality—from chic to down-home and funky. You'll find a few burger places, but they won't come with golden arches. In almost all cases, the restaurants will be right off Route 1.

There aren't many restaurants along the coast from Big Sur until you reach Hearst Castle, where there is a large snack bar in the visitors center. From there south, the commercial fishing industry makes it possible for many of the restaurants to serve fresh fish every day. The stretch of Route 1 in and around San Simeon is a popular tour-bus route, and restaurants catering to large groups offer solid, if routine, American fare: generous quantities of prime rib for dinner and bacon and eggs for breakfast. Cambria, true to its British-Welsh flavor, provides a taste of English cooking complete with peas and Yorkshire pudding, but the offerings range far beyond that. In Solvang, where the tone turns to Danish, count on traditional smorgasbord and sausages.

The variety of good food in Santa Barbara is astonishing for a town its size. Menu selections range from classic French to Cajun to fresh seafood, and the dining style from tie-and-jacket and necessary reservations to shorts-and-T-shirt hip. A leisurely brunch or lunch will take the best advantage of the beach and harbor views afforded by many restaurants and cafés. At the Biltmore's acclaimed and expensive Sunday brunch, however, all attention is on the spread of fresh fruits, seafood, and pastries. Served in the hotel's airy glass-roofed courtyard, it is perfect for special occasions.

If it is good, cheap food with an international flavor that you are after, follow the locals to Milpas Avenue on the east edge of Santa Barbara's downtown. A recent count there found three Thai restaurants, Hawaiian, Greek, and New Mexican eateries. Freshly made tortillas are easily found in the markets on Milpas, particularly at La Super Rica, reputedly one of Julia Child's favorites for a quick, authentic Mexican snack.

Highly recommended restaurants are indicated by a star ★. Casual dress is acceptable, unless otherwise noted.

Category	Cost*
$$$$	over $35
$$$	$25–$35
$$	$15–$25
$	under $15

*per person for a three-course meal, excluding drinks, service, and tax

Lodging The choice of places to stay in Big Sur is limited, and there are few hotels or motels between Big Sur and San Simeon. From San Simeon to San Luis Obispo, however, there are many moderately priced hotels and motels—some nicer than others, but mostly just basic lodging. Only the Madonna Inn, the all-pink, one-of-a-kind motel in San Luis Obispo, is worthy of a stay for its own sake. Make your reservations ahead of time, well ahead in the summer, because there very well may not be an alternative just down the road.

Bargain lodging is hard to come by in Santa Barbara, where high-end resorts are the staple. Long patronized by congestion-crazed Los Angeles residents, the resorts promise, and usually deliver, pampering and solitude in romantic settings. The beach area is most frequented and is certainly the most popular locale for lodging. Many places offer discounts in the winter season. Come summer weekends, when 90% of the town's 46,000 motel and hotel rooms are filled, reservations made well in advance are strongly advised.

Highly recommended lodgings are indicated by a star ★.

Category	Cost*
$$$$	over $100
$$$	$75–$100
$$	$50–$75
$	under $50

*All prices are for a double room, excluding tax.

Big Sur
Dining
★

Nepenthe. You'll not find a more spectacular coastal view between Los Angeles and San Francisco than from here. The 800-foot-high cliff site, overlooking lush meadows to the ocean below, was once owned by Orson Welles and Rita Hayworth. The food is adequately average—from roast chicken with sage to sandwiches and hamburgers—so it is the one-of-a-kind location, in magnificent Big Sur, that rates the star. An outdoor café serves breakfast and lunch. *Rte. 1, south end of town, tel. 408/667–2345. Reservations for large parties only. AE, MC, V. $$*

Dining and
Lodging

Ventana Inn. This getaway is essential California chic—restful and hip. Rooms are in buildings that are scattered in clusters on a hillside above the Pacific, done in natural woods with cool tile floors. Activities here are purposely limited to sunning at poolside—there is a clothing-optional deck—and walks in the hills nearby. The hotel's attractive stone and wood dining room is highly recommended for its handling of the light touches of California cuisine; the menu features grilled veal chops, sliced duck, oak-grilled salmon, occasional and unexpected game dishes, and some creative sandwiches. For a real event, come here for weekend brunch on the terrace, with spectacular views over golden hills down to the ocean. *Rte. 1, 93920, tel. 408/667–2331 or 800/628–6500, fax 408/667–2419. 59 rooms. Facilities: restaurant (reservations advised), 2 pools, whirlpool, complimentary Continental breakfast. AE, D, DC, MC, V. Minimum stay 2 nights on weekends, 3 on holidays. $$$$*

Deetjen's Big Sur Inn. Built in bits and pieces in the '20s and '30s, this place has a certain rustic charm, at least for travelers not too attached to creature comforts. There are no locks on the doors (except from the inside), the heating is by wood-burning stove in half of the rooms, and your neighbor can often be heard through the walls. Still, it's a special place, set among redwood trees with each room individually decorated and given a name like "Château Fiasco." The restaurant, which consists of four intimate dining rooms in the main house, serves stylish fare that includes Rock Cornish game hen, filet mignon, and lamb chops for dinner, wonderfully light and flavorful whole-wheat pancakes for breakfast (but no lunch). *Rte. 1, south end of town, 93920, tel. 408/667–2377; restaurant tel. 408/667–2378. 19 rooms, 14 with bath. Facilities: restaurant (reservations required). No credit cards. $$–$$$$*

Lodging ★ **Post Ranch Inn.** This luxurious retreat from the frenzy of urban life opened in 1992, the only commercial development to be approved in the Big Sur for 20 years and the ultimate in environmentally correct architecture. Visitors leave their cars at the gate and are bused up onto the cliff 1,200 feet above the ocean to the redwood guest houses, one butterfly-roofed, some on stilts, some built around trees, and all with dizzyingly splendid views of the Pacific. Each unit has its own spa tub, stereo system, private deck, and massage table, and because there are no televisions, there is every incentive to explore the glorious surrounding hiking country. Continental breakfast is included. *Rte. 1, Box 219, 93920, tel. 408/667–2200 or 800/527–2200, fax 408/667–2824. 30 units. Facilities: restaurant, bar, library, 2 pools, complete spa. AE, D, DC, MC, V. $$$$*

Big Sur Lodge. This hostelry inside Pfeiffer Big Sur State Park is the best place in Big Sur for families. Motel-style cottages are set around a meadow surrounded by redwood and oak trees. Some have fireplaces, some kitchens. All rooms are without TV or phone. *Rte. 1, Box 190, 93920, tel. 408/667–2171 or 800/424–4787, fax 408/667–3110. 61 rooms. Facilities: pool, sauna, restaurant, store. MC, V. $$$–$$$$*

Cambria **Brambles Dinner House.** Although the best-known restaurant in *Dining* Cambria, it can be hit-or-miss. Specialties include fresh salmon cooked over a seasoned oak fire, good Greek food, bouillabaisse, prime rib, and Yorkshire pudding and blackstrap molasses bread. Stop on Sunday for brunch. *4005 Burton Dr., tel. 805/927–4716. Reservations advised. AE, D, DC, MC, V. No lunch. $$*

★ **The Hamlet at Moonstone Gardens.** Set in the middle of a plant nursery, this restaurant has an enchanting patio garden that's perfect for lunch. The upstairs dining room—sleek chrome and lavender with grand piano—looks over the Pacific or the gardens. Service can be slow, but no one seems to mind. Fish of the day comes poached in white wine; other entrées range from hamburgers to rack of lamb. Downstairs is the International Wine Center, where you can taste wines from more than 50 wineries. *East side Rte. 1, tel. 805/927–3535. Reservations accepted. MC, V. Closed Dec. $–$$*

Mustache Pete's. This lively, upbeat restaurant/sports bar with overhead fans and baskets of flowers features Italian food, with seafood, pasta, and poultry selections. *4090 Burton Dr., tel. 805/927–8589. Reservations unnecessary. AE, D, DC, MC, V. $–$$*

Lodging **Fog Catcher Inn.** This hotel, with beautifully landscaped gardens and 10 thatched-roof buildings, has the feel of an English country village. Most rooms have ocean views. All have fireplaces and are done in floral chintz with light wood furniture. Full breakfast is included. *6400 Moonstone Dr., 93428, tel. 805/927–1400 or 800/425–4121. 50 rooms, 10 suites. Facilities: heated pool, Jacuzzi. AE, D, DC, MC, V. $$$–$$$$*

Best Western Fireside Inn. This modern motel has spacious rooms, with sofas and upholstered lounge chairs (plus refrigerators and coffee makers). Some rooms have whirlpools or ocean views, and all have fireplaces. Continental breakfast is served in a room adjacent to the pool. The inn is just across from the beach, with fishing nearby. *6700 Moonstone Beach Dr., 93428, tel. 805/927–8661 or 800/528–1234, fax 805/927–8584. 46 rooms. Facilities: heated pool, whirlpool. AE, D, DC, MC, V. $$$*

★ **Cambria Pines Lodge.** The lodge's buildings, from rustic cabins to fireplace suites, are set among 25 acres of pine trees above the town, with peacocks wandering the grounds. There is a big stone fireplace in the lounge, and all the furnishings—new and old—fit the decor of the 1920s, when the original lodge was established. *2905 Burton Dr., 93428, tel. 805/927–4200 or 800/445–6868, fax 805/927–4016. 120 rooms. Facilities: restaurant, bar, pool, sauna, Jacuzzi, weight room, sand volleyball court. AE, D, MC, V. $$*

San Simeon Pines Resort. Set amid 10 acres of pines and cypresses, this motel-style resort has its own golf course and is directly across from Leffingwell Landing, a state picnic area on the rocky beach. The accommodations include cottages with their own landscaped backyards, and there are areas set aside for adults and families. *7200 Moonstone Beach Dr., Box 117, San Simeon 93452, tel. 805/927–4648. 58 rooms. Facilities: children's playground, 9-hole golf course, pool, shuffleboard. AE, MC, V. $$*

Bluebird Motel. Located between the east and west villages, this older motel was recently fully redecorated, and includes a homey lounge for hanging out. *1880 Main St., 93428, tel. 805/927–4634 or 800/552–5434. 37 rooms. AE, D, DC, MC, V. $–$$$*

Morro Bay **Dorn's.** This very pleasant seafood café overlooks the harbor and
Dining main square. It looks like a Cape Cod cottage, with gray walls, mahogany wainscoting, awnings, and bay windows. Breakfast, lunch, and dinner are served; dinner features excellent fish and native abalone. *801 Market St., tel. 805/772–4415. Weekend reservations advised. MC, V. $$*

★ **Margie's Diner.** This clean and attractive, Mom-and-Pop diner-café serves generous portions of all-American favorites: ham or steak and eggs, three-egg omelets, chili, hot and cold sandwiches, fried chicken steak, deep-dish apple pie—you name it, and don't forget the milk shakes (or the nine kinds of burger). Top quality produce is used and service is excellent. *1698 N. Main St., tel. 805/772–2510. No reservations. No credit cards. $*

Lodging **Sea Air Inn.** Rooms in this modern, well-kept motel, a block from the waterfront, are clean and comfortable, decorated in blues and floral patterns. Some have ocean views, some have refrigerators, and all have coffee makers. Location is the main drawing card. *845 Morro Ave., 93442, tel. 805/772–4437. 25 rooms. AE, D, MC, V. $–$$*

Ojai **Wheeler Hot Springs Restaurant.** The menu, California Mediterra-
Dining nean in spirit, changes weekly but always features herbs and vege-

tables grown in the spa's garden. It's 7 miles north of Ojai on Route 33. The restaurant serves brunch on Saturday and Sunday, and offers packages including brunch and hot tub. *16825 Maricopa Hwy., tel. 805/646–8131. Reservations advised. AE, MC, V. No lunch. Closed Mon. and Tues. $$*

Lodging **Oaks at Ojai.** This is a well-known, comfortable health spa with a
★ solid fitness program that includes lodging, three nutritionally balanced, surprisingly good low-calorie meals, complete use of spa facilities, and 16 optional fitness classes. Weekend rates and packages are offered. *122 E. Ojai Ave., 93023, tel. 805/646–5573 or 800/753–6257, fax 805/640–1504. 88 rooms. Facilities: dining room, whirlpool with pool, Jacuzzis, sauna, weight room. D, MC, V. Minimum stay: 2 days. $$$$*

Ojai Valley Inn and Country Club. Reopened in 1988 after a $40 million renovation, the hotel is set in landscaped grounds lush with flowers. The peaceful setting comes with hillside views in nearly all directions. Some of the nicer rooms are in the original adobe building, which preserve such luxurious features as huge bathrooms and the original tiles. Suites in the cabanas are more expensive than other rooms. The decor is southwestern style, and works by local artists hang throughout the resort. *Country Club Rd., 93023, tel. 805/646–5511 or 800/422–OJAI, fax 805/646–7969. 212 units. Facilities: 2 restaurants, bar, golf course, lighted tennis courts, horseback riding (fee), 2 pools, men's and women's sauna and steam room, bicycles. AE, D, DC, MC, V. $$$$*

Best Western Casa Ojai. On the main street of town, across from the Soule Park Golf Course, is this spacious, modern hotel with a red-tiled roof. The rooms are simple and clean, with pastel bedspreads. Continental breakfast is included. *1302 E. Ojai Ave., 93023, tel. 805/646–8175 or 800/255–8175, fax 805/640–8247. 45 units. Facilities: pool, Jacuzzi. AE, D, DC, MC, V. $$–$$$$*

San Luis **Buona Tavola.** Locals favor this Northern Italian restaurant, next
Obispo door to the Fremont Movie Theater. Specialties include homemade
Dining agnolotti filled with scampi in a creamy saffron sauce and braised lamb shank with grilled polenta. Rotating art displays are featured inside, and outdoor dining is also available on the flower-filled patio. *1037 Monterey St., tel. 805/545–8000. Reservations required. Dress: casual. D, MC, V. $$*

Dining and **Madonna Inn.** A designer's imagination run amok, this place is as
Lodging much a tourist attraction as a place to stay. It is the ultimate in
★ kitsch, from its rococo bathrooms to its pink-on-pink, frou-frou dining areas. Each room is unique, to say the least: "Rock Bottom" is all stone, even the bathroom; the "Safari Room" is decked out in animal skins; "Old Mill" features a water wheel that powers cuckoo-clock-like figurines. Even if you don't stay overnight, try a meal at the restaurant, where the food is perfectly adequate, with decor-matching desserts. There's also a bakery, a gourmet shop, and a couple of gift shops on the premises. *100 Madonna Rd., 93405, tel. 805/543–3000 or 800/543–9666, fax 805/543–1800. 109 rooms. Facilities: dining room (reservations advised), coffee shop. MC, V. $$–$$$$*

Lodging **Apple Farm.** The interior design is the strong point at this country-
★ style hotel, where everything is meant to be soothing to the eye, and no detail has been overlooked. Decorated to the hilt with floral bedspreads and wallpaper, and with watercolors by local artists, each room is individually appointed, some of them with canopy beds and cozy window seats. Complimentary coffee is served in the rooms. The adjoining restaurant serves such hearty country fare as chicken with dumplings and smoked ribs, and the breakfasts are copious.

2015 Monterey St., 93401, tel. 805/544–2040 or 800/255–2040 in CA, fax 805/546–9495. 101 rooms. Facilities: restaurant, bakery, adjacent Mill House. AE, MC, V. $$–$$$$

Adobe Inn. This cozy motel, which bills itself as a bed-and-breakfast inn, is clean and well-run, decorated in a spotless southwestern style, and serves excellent full breakfasts, with fresh muffins and such daily specials as blueberry crepes or waffles topped with strawberries. *1473 Monterey St., 93401, tel. 805/549–0321. 15 rooms. AE, D, MC, V. $*

San Simeon
Dining

Europa. The eclectic menu, which stands out in an area of traditional fare, includes dishes from Germany, Hungary, and Italy—spätzle, egg dumplings and paprika, and homemade pasta. Crisp linen tablecloths brighten the small dining room. Steaks are featured as well as fresh fish specials. *9240 Castillo Dr. (Rte. 1), tel. 805/927–3087. Reservations accepted. MC, V. No lunch. Closed Sun. in winter. $$*

San Simeon Restaurant. This restaurant makes the most of its proximity to Hearst Castle, with a mind-boggling decor of imitation Greek columns, statues, and tapestries. There is a standard American menu; prime rib is the big draw. The dark dining room opens to views of the Pacific across the highway. *East side Rte. 1, tel. 805/927–4604. Reservations advised in summer. AE, D, MC, V. $–$$*

Lodging

San Simeon Lodge. This unpretentious motel is right across from the ocean, and many of its rooms have sea views. And, aside from the location, there's nothing fancy here. Built in 1958, the place has a straightforward stucco facade with wood trim. *9520 Castillo Dr. (Rte. 1), 93452, tel. 805/927–4601, fax 805/927–2374. 63 rooms. Facilities: restaurant, bar, lounge, pool. AE, DC, MC, V. $$*

Motel 6. This is a two-story motel with comfortable, if standard, rooms decorated in blue and rust, opening on an interior corridor. *9070 Castillo Ave. (Rte. 1), 93452, tel. 805/927–8691, fax 805/927–5341. 100 rooms. Facilities: heated pool. AE, D, DC, MC, V. $*

Santa Barbara
Dining

The Stonehouse. The restaurant is in a turn-of-the-century, granite farmhouse, part of the San Ysidro Ranch resort. The classic American regional menu offers such treats as dry-aged New York steak with oyster fritters and crisp whole catfish with fried green tomatoes. The food is good, but the real drawing card is the pastoral setting. Be sure to have lunch— salads, pastas, and sandwiches—on the treehouselike outdoor patio. At night, the candle-lit interior becomes even more romantic and the cuisine more serious, with game, roasts, chicken, steak, and fresh fish entrées. *900 San Ysidro La., tel. 805/969–4100. Reservations required. Jacket recommended. AE, MC, V. $$$–$$$$*

★ **Citronelle.** This offspring of Michel Richard's famed Citrus in Los Angeles has brought Santa Barbara folk some of the best California-French cuisine they've ever had this close to home. The accent is on Riviera-style dishes: light, delicate but loaded with intriguing good tastes. The desserts here are unmatched anywhere in Southern California. There are splendid, sweeping views of the harbor from the dining room's picture windows. *901 East Cabrillo, tel. 805/963–0111. Reservations advised. AE, D, DC, MC, V. $$$*

The Harbor Restaurant. This sparkling spot on the wharf is where locals like to take out-of-town guests. The upstairs, now a bar and grill, offers an extensive menu of fresh seafood, sandwiches, large salads, and a huge variety of appetizers. The spacious room boasts nautical decor and a complete video system. Head downstairs for healthy portions of fresh seafood, prime rib, or steaks, and order one of the house's specialty drinks; every seat has a harbor view. *210*

Stearns Wharf, tel. 805/963–3311. Reservations required. AE, MC, V. $$–$$$

The Palace Café. A stylish and lively restaurant, the Palace has won acclaim for its Cajun and Creole dishes such as blackened redfish and jambalaya with dirty rice. Caribbean fare here includes delicious coconut shrimp. Just in case the dishes aren't spicy enough for you, each table has a bottle of hot sauce. The Palace offers dinner only; be prepared for a wait of up to 45 minutes on weekends. *8 E. Cota St., tel. 805/966–3133. Reservations accepted weekdays, for 5:30 PM and 6 PM seatings on Fri. and 5:30 PM seating on Sat. AE, MC, V. $$–$$$*

Castagnola Bros. Seafood Restaurant. At this unassuming spot just two blocks from the beach, wonderfully good, fresh broiled fish is served on paper plates. The homemade clam chowder is excellent, too. *205 Santa Barbara St., tel. 805/962–8053. No reservations. AE, D, MC, V. Open daily 11–9. $$*

Joe's Café. The vinyl, red-and-white-checked tablecloths and simple round stools at the hefty wooden counter tell the story: nothing fancy, but solid café fare in generous portions. Joe's is a popular hangout and drinking spot, particularly for the younger crowd. *536 State St., tel. 805/966–4638. AE, D, MC, V. No lunch Sun. $$*

Pane & Vino. This tiny trattoria, and its equally small sidewalk dining terrace, is in a tree-shaded, flower-decked shopping center in Montecito, just east of Santa Barbara. The cold antipasto is very good, as are grilled meats and fish, pastas, and salads. *1482 E. Valley Rd., Montecito, tel. 805/969–9274. Reservations advised. No credit cards. Dinner only Sun. $$*

East Beach Grill. Watch the waves break and the action on the sand from a surprisingly pleasant outdoor café right on this busy beach. It's a step above a fast-food joint, with its friendly table service and pleasant shoreline view. You'll find basic breakfast fare served with real plates and cutlery, and hot dogs and burgers for lunch. *At the Cabrillo Bath House, East Beach, tel. 805/965–8805. No reservations. MC, V. Closes daily at 3 PM, at 5 PM during summer. $*

★ **La Super-Rica.** This tiny, tacky foodstand serves the best and hottest Mexican dishes between Los Angeles and San Francisco. Fans drive for miles to fill up on the soft tacos. *622 N. Milpas St. (at Alphonse St.), tel. 805/963–4940. No credit cards. $*

Lodging **Fess Parker's Red Lion Resort.** This is a sprawling resort complex with a slightly Spanish flair. Its two- and three-story stucco buildings are located directly across the street from the beach. A showplace for this chain of hotels, this luxury resort has a huge and lavishly appointed lobby. Guest rooms are spacious, furnished with light-wood furniture, and decorated in pastel colors. All have either private patio or balcony, and many have ocean views. *633 E. Cabrillo Blvd., 93103, tel. 805/564–4333 or 800/879–2929, fax 805/564–4964. 359 rooms. Facilities: 2 restaurants, bar, pool, sauna, tennis courts, exercise room, Jacuzzi, lounge with dance floor, putting green, shuffleboard, basketball court, bikes to rent. AE, D, DC, MC, V. $$$$*

★ **Four Seasons Biltmore.** Santa Barbara's grande dame. The decor of muted pastels and bleached woods gives the cabanas behind the main building a light, airy touch without sacrificing the hotel's reputation for understated elegance. It's a bit more formal than other properties in town and it's surrounded by lush gardens and palm trees galore. *1260 Channel Dr., 93108, tel. 805/969–2261 or 800/332–3442, fax 805/969–4682. 234 rooms. Facilities: 2 restaurants, bar, 2 Olympic pools, whirlpool, croquet, shuffleboard, racquetball, health club, private cabana club, putting green, tennis courts. AE, DC, MC, V. $$$$*

Santa Barbara Inn. This three-story motel, directly across the street from East Beach, has a crisp exterior and a sophisticated interior decor featuring light woods, teal accents, and subdued tones. Many rooms have ocean views, and the lower-priced rooms look toward the mountains (beyond the parking lot). The inn's restaurant, Citronelle, is presided over by French chef Michel Richard, who rustles up California cuisine and has become a favorite of local residents. *901 E. Cabrillo Blvd., 93103, tel. 805/966–2285 or 800/231–0431, fax 805/966–6584. 71 rooms. Facilities: restaurant, pool, whirlpool. AE, D, DC, MC, V. $$$$*

San Ysidro Ranch. At this luxury "ranch" you can feel at home in jeans and cowboy boots, but be prepared to dress for dinner. A hideout for the Hollywood set, this romantic place hosted John and Jackie Kennedy on their honeymoon. Guest cottages, some with down comforters and all with wood-burning stoves or fireplaces, are scattered among 14 acres of orange trees and flower beds. There are 500 acres more left in open space to roam at will on foot or horseback. The hotel welcomes children and pets. *900 San Ysidro La., Montecito, 93108, tel. 805/969–5046 or 800/368–6788, fax 805/565–1995. 44 rooms. Facilities: restaurant, pool, tennis courts, horseback riding, bocce ball, horseshoes. AE, MC, V. Minimum stay: 2 days on weekends, 3 days on holidays. $$$$*

Simpson House Inn. Set on a quiet acre in the heart of town, this lodging complex offers something for almost everyone. Traditional B&B fans will enjoy the beautifully appointed main house. Those put off by Victorian primness and the occasional discomforts of 100-year-old bathrooms may prefer the newest additions to the property: three (very) romantic cottages and a restored 100-year-old barn. Full breakfast is included in room rate. Two-night minimum on weekends. *121 E. Arrellaga St., 93101, tel. 805/963–7067 or 800/676–1280, fax 805/564–4811. 6 rooms with bath, 3 cottages, 4 suites. AE, D, MC, V. $$$$*

The Upham. This beautifully restored Victorian hotel, situated on an acre of gardens in the midst of historic downtown, was established in 1871. Period furnishings and antiques adorn the rooms and cottages, some of which have fireplaces and private patios. Continental breakfast and afternoon wine and cheese are served in the lobby and on the garden veranda. *1404 De La Vina St., 93101, tel. 805/962–0058 or 800/727–0876, fax 805/963–2825. 49 rooms. AE, D, DC, MC, V. $$$$*

Villa Rosa. Inside this 60-year-old hotel, a red-tile roofed Spanish-style house of stucco and wood, the rooms and intimate lobby are decorated in an informal southwestern style. The Villa Rosa is just one block from the beach. Rates include Continental breakfast and wine and cheese in the afternoon. *15 Chapala St., 93101, tel. 805/966–0851, fax 805/962–7159. 18 rooms. Facilities: pool, whirlpool. AE, MC, V. $$–$$$$*

Ambassador by the Sea. The wrought-iron trim and mosaic tiling on this Spanish-style building near the harbor and Stearns Wharf make it seem the quintessential California beach motel. The rooms have verandas, and sundecks overlook the ocean and the bike path. *202 W. Cabrillo Blvd., 93101, tel. 805/965–4577, fax 805/965–9937. 32 units. Facilities: pool, 2 units with kitchenettes. AE, D, DC, MC, V. $$–$$$*

Old Yacht Club Inn. Built in 1912 as a private home in the California Craftsman style, this inn near the beach was one of Santa Barbara's first bed-and-breakfasts. The rooms feature turn-of-the-century furnishings and Oriental rugs. Guests receive complimentary full breakfast and evening wine, along with the use of bikes and beach chairs. No smoking. *431 Corona del Mar Dr., 93103, tel. 805/962–1277 or 800/676–1676, 800/549–1676 in CA, fax 805/962–3989. 9 rooms. Facilities: dining room open Sat. for guests only. AE, D, MC, V. $$–$$$*

Motel 6. The low price and location near the beach are the pluses for this recently redone, no-frills place. Reserve well in advance all year. *443 Corona del Mar Dr., 93103, tel. 805/564–1392. 52 units. Facilities: heated pool. AE, D, DC, MC, V. $*

Solvang **Danish Inn.** The smorgasbord here is popular, but there are also
Dining steaks and an extensive array of Continental-style items—rack of
★ lamb, Wiener schnitzel, and Danish *morbrad* (medallions of pork sautéed with red wine, shallots, and mushrooms), for example. The atmosphere is more formal than in most other Solvang restaurants, but the fireplace and lace curtains keep it cozy. Breakfast is served on the weekends. *1547 Mission Dr., tel. 805/688–4813. Reservations advised. AE, D, DC, MC, V. $$$*

Restaurant Molle-Kroen. A busy upstairs dining room serves smorgasbord and other Danish specialties. It has a cheerful, light setting, with fresh flowers on the tables and booths. The local folks come here when they want a good meal at a good price. *435 Alisal Rd., tel. 805/688–4555. AE, D, DC, MC, V. $$*

★ **Royal Scandia Restaurant.** Despite the size (there are three dining rooms), this restaurant is decorated like a quaint old Danish cottage, with vaulted ceilings, rafters, and lots of brass and frosted glass. There is also dining on an enclosed patio. The menu caters to traditional American tastes, with some Danish offerings, including a smorgasbord every evening. There is also a Sunday champagne brunch. *400 Alisal Rd., tel. 805/688–8000. Reservations advised. AE, D, DC, MC, V. $$*

Lodging **Solvang Royal Scandinavian Inn.** This follows the Danish theme of the town, and its rooms—Scandinavian modern style, of course—have nice touches, like hand-painted furniture. The large, brick-walled, dark-timbered lobby has a fireplace and overstuffed chairs. *400 Alisal Rd., 93464, tel. 805/688–8000 or 800/624–5572, fax 805/688–0761. 133 rooms. Facilities: restaurant, lounge, pool, Jacuzzi. AE, D, DC, MC, V. $$$–$$$$*

Chimney Sweep Inn. All the rooms are pleasant, but it is the cottages in the backyard that are extra special (and expensive) here. Built in a half-timbered style, they were inspired by the C. S. Lewis children's books, *The Chronicles of Narnia.* The cottages have kitchens and fireplaces; some have private Jacuzzis. In the garden are a waterfall and fish pond. Complimentary Continental breakfast includes hot apple cider in cottages. *1554 Copenhagen Dr., 93463, tel. 805/688–2111 or 800/824–6444, fax 805/688–8824. 28 rooms. Facilities: whirlpool, garden. AE, D, MC, V. $$$*

Best Western Kronborg Inn. Three blocks from the center of town, the Kronborg provides comfortable accommodations in keeping with the Danish theme of the town. Rooms, decorated in floral prints, are spacious and some have balconies overlooking the pool and Jacuzzi. Whirlpool baths are also available in some rooms, and Continental breakfast is included. *1440 Mission Dr., 93463, tel. 805/688–2383, fax 805/688–1821. 39 rooms. Facilities: heated pool, Jacuzzi. AE, D, DC, MC, V. $$–$$$$*

The Arts and Nightlife

The Arts Santa Barbara prides itself on being a top-notch cultural center. It supports a professional symphony and chamber orchestra and an impressive art museum. The proximity to the University of California at Santa Barbara assures an endless stream of visiting artists and performers.

The enormous Moorish-style **Arlington Theater** on State Street is home to the Santa Barbara Symphony. The **Lobero,** a state landmark, at the corner of Anacapa and Cañon Perdido streets, shares its stage with community theater groups and touring professionals.

Film The **Santa Barbara International Film Festival** (1216 State St. #710, 93101, tel. 805/963–0023), held each March, pulls in the Hollywood crowd, with premieres and screenings of American and international films.

Music Since 1971, the **San Luis Obispo Mozart Festival** (Box 311, San Luis Obispo, 93406, tel. 805/781–3008) has been held early in August. The settings include the Mission San Luis Obispo de Tolosa and the Cal Poly Theater. There are afternoon and evening concerts and recitals—by professionals and well-known visiting artists—as well as seminars and workshops. Not all the music is Mozart; you'll hear Haydn and other composers. The Festival Fringe offers free concerts outdoors.

Theater Boo and hiss the villains year round at the **Great American Melodrama** (Rte. 1, tel. 805/489–2499) in the small town of Oceano, south of San Luis Obispo.

The **Pacific Conservatory of the Performing Arts** (Box 1700, Santa Maria, 93456, tel. 805/922–8313, or 800/549–7272 in CA) presents a full spectrum of theatrical events, from classical to contemporary, with a few musicals thrown in, in different theaters in Solvang and Santa Maria. The Solvang Festival Theater has open-air performances.

Nightlife Most of the major hotels offer nightly entertainment during the summer season and live weekend entertainment all year. To see what's scheduled at the hotels and many small clubs and restaurants, pick up a copy of the free weekly *Santa Barbara Independent* newspaper for an extensive rundown.

Dancing **Zelo** (630 State St., Santa Barbara, tel. 805/ 966–5792). This high-energy restaurant doubles as a progressive rock and punk dance club featuring offbeat videos and innovative lighting.

12 Los Angeles

You're preparing for your trip to Los Angeles. You're psyching up with Beach Boys CDs, and some Hollywood epics on the laser-disc player. You've pulled out your Hawaiian shirts and tennis shorts. You've studied the menu at Taco Bell. You're even doing a crash regimen at your local tanning salon and aerobics studio so you won't *look* so much like a tourist when you hit the coast.

Well, relax. *Everybody's* a tourist in LaLa Land. Even the stars are starstruck (as evidenced by the celebrities watching the other celebrities at Spago). Los Angeles is a city of ephemerals, of transience, and above all, of illusion. Nothing here is quite real, and that's the reality of it all. That air of anything-can-happen—as it often does—is what motivates thousands to move to and millions to vacation in this promised land each year. Visitors don't just come from the East or Midwest, mind you, but from the Far East, Down Under, Europe, and South America. It's this influx of cultures that's been the life-blood of Los Angeles since its Hispanic beginning.

We cannot predict what *your* Los Angeles will be like. You can laze on a beach or soak up some of the world's greatest art collections. You can tour the movie studios and stars' homes or take the kids to Disneyland, Magic Mountain, or Knott's Berry Farm. You can shop luxurious Beverly Hills' Rodeo Drive or browse for hipper novelties on boutique-lined Melrose Avenue. The possibilities are endless—rent a boat to Catalina Island, watch the floats in Pasadena's Rose Parade, or dine on tacos, sushi, goat-cheese pizza, or just plain hamburgers, hot dogs, and chili.

No matter how fast-forward Los Angeles seems to spin, the heart of the city—or at least its stomach—is still deep in the 1950s. Sure, the lighter, nouvelle-inspired California cuisine has made a big splash (no one here has ever been ridiculed as a "health-food nut" for preferring a healthier diet), but nothing is more quintessentially Californian than Johnny Rockets (a chrome-and-fluorescent burger paradise on Melrose) or Pink's (a beloved greasy spoon of a chili-dog dive on La Brea).

None of this was imagined when Spanish settlers founded their Pueblo de la Reina de Los Angeles in 1781. In fact, no one predicted a golden future for desert-dry southern California until well after San Francisco and northern California had gotten a head start with their own gold rush. The dusty outpost of Los Angeles eventually had oil and oranges, but the golden key to its success came on the silver screen: the movies. Although, if the early pioneers of Holly-wood—religiously conservative fruit farmers—had gotten their way, their town's name would never have become synonymous with cinema and entertainment.

The same sunshine that draws today's visitors and new residents drew Cecil B. DeMille and Jesse Lasky in 1911 while searching for a place to make movies besides New York City. Lesser filmmakers had been shooting reels for the nickelodeons of the day in Holly-wood, but DeMille and Lasky were the first to make a feature-length movie here. It took another 15 years to break through the sound barrier in cinema, but the silent-film era made Hollywood's name synonymous with fantasy, glamour, and, as the first citizens would snicker in disgust, with sin.

Outrageous partying, extravagant homes, eccentric clothing, and money, money, money have been symbols of life in Los Angeles ever since. Even the more conservative oil, aerospace, computer, banking, and import/export industries on the booming Pacific Rim have enjoyed the prosperity that leads inevitably to fun living. But even without piles of bucks, many people have found a kindred spirit in Los Angeles for their colorful lifestyles, be they spiritually, socially, or sexually unusual. Tolerance reigns; live and let live—which explains why you, too, will fit in.

The distance between places in Los Angeles explains why the ethnic enclaves have not merged, regardless of the melting-pot appearance of the city. Especially since the rioting in the spring of 1992, which—among other things—brought to the surface much long-simmering tension between various ethnic groups, it is impossible to gloss over the disparities of race, economics, and social mobility between neighborhoods. Nonetheless, at its best, and most notable for visitors, is the rich cultural and culinary diversity this mix of peoples creates.

Set off from the rest of the continent by mountains and desert, and from the rest of the world by an ocean, this incredible corner of creation has evolved its own identity that conjures envy, fascination, ridicule, and scorn—often all at once. Those from purportedly more sophisticated cities note what Los Angeles lacks. Others from more provincial towns raise an eyebrow at what it has. Yet 12.5 million people visit the city annually, and three-quarters of them come back for more. Indeed, you cannot do Los Angeles in a day or a week or even two. This second largest city in America holds too many choices between its canyons and its coast to be exhausted in one trip; it will exhaust you first.

Essential Information

Important Addresses and Numbers

Tourist Information There is a **Visitor Information Center** at 685 S. Figueroa Street (tel. 213/689–8822). It is open Monday through Saturday 8–5. Or you can stop in at the **Los Angeles Convention and Visitors Bureau** (633 W. 5th St., Suite 6000, tel. 213/624–7300).

Area communities also have information centers, including the **Beverly Hills Visitors Bureau** at 239 South Beverly Drive (tel. 310/271–8174; open weekdays 8:30–5), the **Long Beach Area Convention and Visitors Council** in Suite 300 at 1 World Trade Center (tel. 310/436–3645), the **Santa Monica Visitors Center,** in Palisades Park at 1400 Ocean Avenue (tel. 310/393–7593; open daily 10–4), the **Hollywood Visitors Center** at 6541 Hollywood Boulevard (tel. 213/461–4213; open Mon.–Sat. 9–5), and the **Pasadena Convention and Visitors Bureau** at 171 South Los Robles Avenue (tel. 818/795–9311; open weekdays 9–5, Sat. 10–4).

Information **Surf and Weather Report,** tel. 310/451–8761.

Community Services, tel. 800/339–6993 (24 hours).

Emergencies Dial 911 for **police** and **ambulance** in an emergency.

Doctors The **Los Angeles Medical Association Physicians Referral Service** (tel. 213/483–6122) is open weekdays 8:45–4:45. Most larger hospitals in Los Angeles have 24-hour emergency rooms. A few are: **St. John's Hospital and Health Center** (1328 22nd St., tel. 310/829–5511), **Cedar-Sinai Medical Center** (8700 Beverly Blvd., tel. 310/855–5000), and **Queen of Angels Hollywood Presbyterian Medical Center** (1300 N. Vermont Ave., tel. 213/413–3000).

24-Hour Pharmacies The **Bellflower Pharmacy** (9400 E. Rosecrans Ave., Bellflower, tel. 310/461–4213) is open around the clock. The **Horton and Converse** pharmacies at 6625 Van Nuys Boulevard (Van Nuys, tel. 818/782–6251) and at 11600 Wilshire Boulevard (W. Los Angeles, tel. 310/478–0801) are open until 2 AM.

Arriving and Departing

By Plane **Los Angeles International Airport,** commonly called LAX (tel. 310/646–5252), is the largest airport in the area. Departures are from the upper level and arrivals on the lower level. LAX is serviced by over 85 major airlines, the third largest airport in the world in terms of passenger traffic.

Airlines Among the major carriers that serve LAX are **Air Canada** (tel. 800/776–3000), **America West** (tel. 800/228–7862), **American** (tel. 800/433–7300), **British Airways** (tel. 800/247–9297), **Continental** (tel. 800/525–0280), **Delta** (tel. 800/221–1212), **Japan Air Lines** (tel. 800/525–3663), **Northwest** (tel. 800/225–2525), **Southwest** (tel. 800/435–9792), **TWA** (tel. 800/221–2000), **United** (tel. 800/241–6522), and **USAir** (tel. 800/428–4322).

Between LAX Airport and Hotels A dizzying array of ground transportation is available from LAX to all parts of Los Angeles and its environs. A taxi ride to downtown Los Angeles can take 20 minutes—*if* there is no traffic. But in Los Angeles, that's a big if. Visitors should request the flat fee ($24 at press time) to downtown or choose from the several ground transportation companies that offer set rates. **SuperShuttle** (tel. 310/782–6600) offers direct service between the airport and hotels. The trip to or from downtown hotels runs about $12. The seven-passenger vans operate 24 hours a day. In the airport, phone 310/417–8988 or use the SuperShuttle courtesy phone in the luggage area; the van should arrive within 15 minutes. **Shuttle One** (9100 S. Sepulveda Blvd., No. 128, tel. 310/670–6666) features door-to-door service and low rates ($10 per person from LAX to hotels in the Disneyland/Anaheim area). **Airport Coach** (tel. 714/938–8900 or 800/772–5299) provides regular service between LAX and the Pasadena and Anaheim areas.

The following limo companies charge a flat rate for airport service, ranging from $65 to $75: **Jackson Limousine** (tel. 213/734–9955), **West Coast Limousine** (tel. 213/756–5466), and **Dav-El Livery** (tel. 310/550–0070). Many of the cars have bars, stereos, televisions, and cellular phones.

Flyaway Service (tel. 818/994–5554) offers round-trip transportation between LAX and the central San Fernando Valley for $6. For the western San Fernando Valley and Ventura area, contact the **Great American Stage Lines** (tel. 800/287–8659). They charge $10–$20 one way.

MTA (tel. 800/252–7433) also offers limited airport service to all areas of greater LA; bus lines depart from bus docks directly across the street from airport parking lot C. Prices vary from $1.10 to $3.10; some routes require transfers. The best line to take to downtown is the direct express line 439, which costs $1.50 and takes 45–50 minutes.

If you're driving, leave time for heavy traffic; it really can't be predicted.

Other Airports The greater Los Angeles area is served by several other local airports. **Ontario Airport** (tel. 909/988–2700), located about 35 miles east of Los Angeles, serves the San Bernardino–Riverside area. Domestic flights are offered by **Alaska Airlines, American, America**

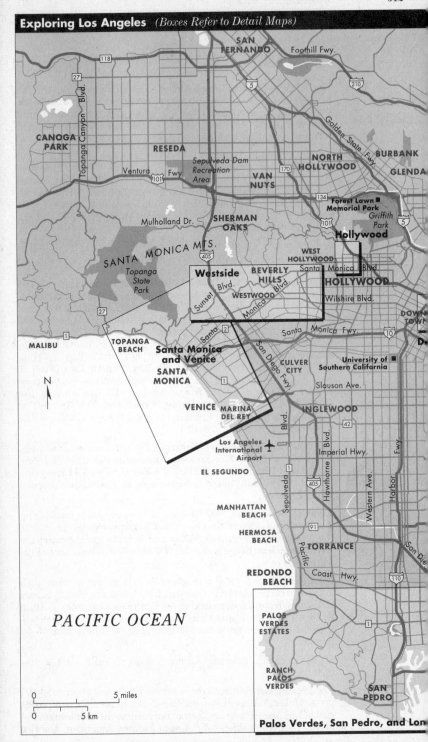

Exploring Los Angeles *(Boxes Refer to Detail Maps)*

SAN FERNANDO

Foothill Fwy.

118

27

CANOGA PARK

RESEDA

Sepulveda Dam Recreation Area

VAN NUYS

NORTH HOLLYWOOD

BURBANK

GLENDA

Topanga Canyon Blvd.

Ventura Fwy.

101

170

Golden State Fwy.

134

Forest Lawn Memorial Park

Griffith Park

5

Mulholland Dr.

SHERMAN OAKS

101

Hollywood

SANTA MONICA MTS.

405

Topanga State Park

Westside

WEST HOLLYWOOD

Santa Monica Blvd.

BEVERLY HILLS

HOLLYWOOD

27

Sunset Blvd.

WESTWOOD

Monica Blvd.

Wilshire Blvd.

DOWN TOWN

Santa Monica Fwy.

10

De

MALIBU

1

TOPANGA BEACH

Santa

2

Santa Monica and Venice

SANTA MONICA

CULVER CITY

San Diego Fwy.

University of Southern California

Slauson Ave.

N

VENICE

1

MARINA DEL REY

INGLEWOOD

42

Los Angeles International Airport

Blvd.

Blvd.

Imperial Hwy.

Hawthorne Blvd.

Western Ave.

Harbor Fwy.

San Die

EL SEGUNDO

MANHATTAN BEACH

Sepulveda

1

405

91

HERMOSA BEACH

TORRANCE

PACIFIC OCEAN

REDONDO BEACH

Pacific

Coast Hwy.

110

PALOS VERDES ESTATES

0 —— 5 miles

0 —— 5 km

RANCH PALOS VERDES

1

SAN PEDRO

Palos Verdes, San Pedro, and Lon

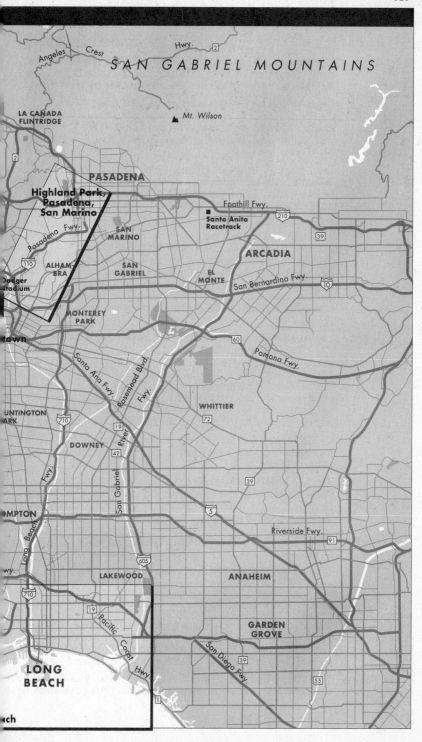

West, Continental, Delta, Northwest, Reno Air (tel. 800/736–6247), **SkyWest** (tel. 800/453–9417), **Southwest, United,** and **United Express.** Ground transportation possibilities include SuperShuttle as well as **Inland Express** (tel. 909/626–6599), **Airport Coach** (tel. 800/772–5299), and **Southern California Coach** (tel. 714/978–6415). **Long Beach Airport** (tel. 310/421–8295), at the southern tip of Los Angeles County, is served by **Alaska, America West, American,** and **Delta.**

Burbank/Pasadena/Glendale Airport (tel. 818/840–8847) serves the San Fernando Valley with commuter, and some longer, flights. **Alaska Airlines, American, America West, Reno Air, SkyWest, Southwest, Transworld Express** (tel. 800/221–2000), and **United** are represented.

John Wayne Airport, in Orange County (tel. 714/252–5006), is served by **Alaska, American, American West, Continental, Delta, Northwest, SkyWest, Southwest, TWA, United,** and **USAir** airlines. **Airport Coach** (tel. 800/772–5299) provides ground transportation.

By Car   Los Angeles is at the western terminus of I–10, a major east-west interstate highway that runs all the way east to Florida. I–15, angling down from Las Vegas, swings through the eastern communities around San Bernardino before heading on down to San Diego. I–5, which runs north-south through California, leads up to San Francisco and down to San Diego. A tangle of freeways converge in the Los Angeles area; *see* Getting Around Los Angeles, *below,* for a freeway map that should help you negotiate around the L.A. sprawl.

By Train   Los Angeles can be reached by **Amtrak** (tel. 800/872–7245). The *Coast Starlight,* a superliner, travels along the spectacular California coast. It offers service from Seattle-Portland and Oakland–San Francisco down to Los Angeles. Amtrak's *San Joaquin* train runs through the Central Valley from Oakland to Bakersfield, where passengers transfer to a bus to Los Angeles. The *Sunset Limited* goes to Los Angeles from New Orleans, the Texas Eagle from San Antonio, and the *Southwest Chief* and the *Desert Wind* from Chicago.

Union Station (800 N. Alameda St.) in Los Angeles is one of the grande dames of railroad stations, and is a remnant of the glory days of the railroads.

By Bus   The Los Angeles **Greyhound Lines** terminal (tel. 800/231–2222) is at 208 East 6th Street, on the corner of Los Angeles Street.

Getting Around

By Bus   A bus ride on the **Metropolitan Transit Authority (MTA)** (tel. 213/626–4455) costs $1.10, with 25¢ for each transfer.

DASH (Downtown Area Short Hop) minibuses travel in a loop around the downtown area, stopping every two blocks or so. You pay 25¢ every time you get on, no matter how far you go. DASH (tel. 213/485–7201) runs weekdays 6:30 AM–6 PM, Saturday 10 AM–5 PM.

By Train   The **Metrorail Blue Line** runs daily, 5 AM–10 PM, from downtown Los Angeles (corner of Flower and 7th streets) to Long Beach (corner of 1st Street and Long Beach Avenue), with 18 stops en route, most of them in Long Beach. The fare is $1.10 one way.

By Subway   The **Metro Red Line,** opened in January 1993, runs 4.4 miles through downtown, from Union Station to MacArthur Park, making five stops. The fare is $1.10. The line will extend to Hollywood by 1998.

By Taxi You probably won't be able to hail a cab on the street in Los Angeles. Instead, you should phone one of the many taxi companies. The metered rate is $1.60 per mile. Two of the more reputable companies are **Independent Cab Co.** (tel. 213/385–8294 or 310/569–8214) and **United Independent Taxi** (tel. 213/653–5050). United accepts MasterCard and Visa.

By Limousine Limousines come equipped with everything from a full bar and telephone to a hot tub and a double bed. Reputable companies include **Dav-El Livery** (tel. 310/550–0070), **First Class** (tel. 310/476–1960), and **Le Monde Limousine** (tel. 310/474–6622 or 818/887–7878).

By Car A car is a must. The freeway map below should help. If you plan to drive extensively, consider buying a Thomas Guide, which contains detailed maps of the entire county. Despite what you've heard, traffic is not always a major problem outside of rush hours (7 AM–9 PM and 3 AM–7 PM). Seat belts must be worn by all passengers at all times.

Guided Tours

Orientation Tours Los Angeles is so spread out and has such a wealth of sightseeing possibilities that an orientation bus tour may prove useful. The cost is about $25. All tours are fully narrated by a driver-guide. Reservations must be made in advance. Many hotels can book them for you.

Gray Line (Box 48030, Los Angeles 90048, tel. 213/933–1475), one of the best-known tour companies in the country, picks passengers up from more than 140 hotels. There are more than 24 tours, taking in Disneyland, Universal Studios, the *Queen Mary,* Catalina Island, and other attractions.

L.A. Tours and Sightseeing (6333 W. 3rd St., at the Farmers' Market, tel. 213/937–3361 or 800/286–8752) covers places of interest in various parts of the city, including downtown, Hollywood, and Beverly Hills. For $36, this tour serves as a good orientation to vast Los Angeles. The company also operates tours to Disneyland and Universal City.

StarLine/Grayline Sightseeing Tours (340 North Camden Dr., Beverly Hills 90210, tel. 213/463–3131 or 310/285–1880) has been showing people around Los Angeles since 1935. Like Gray Line, StarLine uses large tour buses and picks up at most area hotels. There are tours to Knott's Berry Farm, Disneyland, and other "musts"; but the company gets much of its business from its four-hour Stars' Home Tour, which takes visitors to more than 60 estates in Beverly Hills, Holmby Hills, and Bel Air. The tour departs from StarLine's Hollywood terminal at Mann's Chinese Theater hourly in the winter and every half-hour in the summer. Hotel pickup can be arranged.

A more personalized look at the city can be had by planning a tour with **Casablanca Tours** (Roosevelt Hotel, 7000 Hollywood Blvd., Cabana 4, Hollywood 90028, tel. 213/461–0156), which offers an insider's look at Hollywood and Beverly Hills. The four-hour tour, which can be taken in the morning or afternoon, starts in Hollywood or in centrally located hotels. Tours are in minibuses with a maximum of 14 people, and prices are equivalent to the large bus tours—about $29. Guides are college students with a high-spirited view of

Los Angeles Freeways

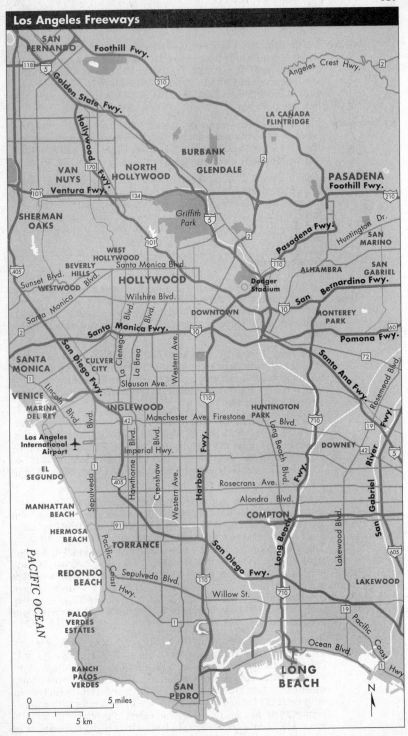

SAN FERNANDO

Foothill Fwy.

118

5

Golden State Fwy.

210

Angeles Crest Hwy.

2

LA CAÑADA FLINTRIDGE

Hollywood Fwy.

170

VAN NUYS

NORTH HOLLYWOOD

BURBANK

GLENDALE

PASADENA

Foothill Fwy.

210

101

Ventura Fwy.

134

2

SHERMAN OAKS

Griffith Park

5

Pasadena Fwy.

Huntington Dr.

SAN MARINO

101

WEST HOLLYWOOD

110

405

BEVERLY HILLS

Sunset Blvd.

WESTWOOD

Santa Monica Blvd.

HOLLYWOOD

Wilshire Blvd.

Dodger Stadium

ALHAMBRA

SAN GABRIEL

San Bernardino Fwy.

Santa Monica

Blvd.

Blvd.

DOWNTOWN

10

MONTEREY PARK

2

Santa Monica Fwy.

10

60

Pomona Fwy.

SANTA MONICA

San Diego Fwy.

CULVER CITY

La Cienega

La Brea

Western Ave.

72

Santa Ana Fwy.

Rosemead Blvd.

1

Slauson Ave.

110

VENICE

Lincoln Blvd.

INGLEWOOD

Manchester Ave.

Firestone

HUNTINGTON PARK

Blvd.

Long Beach Blvd.

710

19

River Fwy.

MARINA DEL REY

42

DOWNEY

Los Angeles International Airport

Hawthorne Blvd.

Crenshaw Blvd.

Western Ave.

Harbor Fwy.

Imperial Hwy.

42

5

EL SEGUNDO

Sepulveda

405

Rosecrans Ave.

San Gabriel

MANHATTAN BEACH

Alondra Blvd.

COMPTON

Lakewood Blvd.

HERMOSA BEACH

91

TORRANCE

Pacific Coast Hwy.

Long Beach Fwy.

LAKEWOOD

605

REDONDO BEACH

Sepulveda Blvd.

110

Willow St.

710

PACIFIC OCEAN

PALOS VERDES ESTATES

1

19

Pacific Coast Hwy.

Ocean Blvd.

1

RANCH PALOS VERDES

SAN PEDRO

LONG BEACH

0   5 miles

0   5 km

N

the city. The tour takes in the usual tourist spots—Hollywood Bowl, Mann's Chinese Theater, the Walk of Fame, and the homes of such stars as Jimmy Stewart and Neil Diamond. It also includes a visit to the posh shops along Rodeo Drive.

Special-Interest Tours
So much of Los Angeles is known to the world through Hollywood, it is fitting that many of the special-interest tours feature Hollywood and its lore.

Grave Line Tours (Box 931694, Hollywood 90093, tel. 213/469–3127 or 213/469–4149) is a clever, off-the-beaten-track tour that digs up the dirt on notorious suicides and visits the scenes of various murders, scandals, and other crimes via a luxuriously renovated hearse. Tours are daily at noon for two hours; cost is $30 per person.

Hollywood Fantasy Tours (6773 Hollywood Blvd., Hollywood 90028, tel. 213/469–8184) has one tour that takes you through Beverly Hills, down Rodeo Drive, around Bel Air, and up and down colorful Sunset Strip, then on to exclusive Holmby Hills, home of *Playboy* magazine's founder Hugh Hefner. If you're only interested in Hollywood, ask about a tour of that area, pointing out television and film studios as well as famous stores such as Frederick's of Hollywood. Cost is $15–$35 per person, depending on the tour.

Visitors who want something dramatically different should check with Marlene Gordon of **The Next Stage** (Box 35269, Los Angeles 90035, tel. 213/939–2688). This innovative tour company takes from four to 46 people, on buses or vans, in search of ethnic L.A., Victorian L.A., Underground L.A. (in which all the places visited are underground), and so on. The Insomniac Tour visits the flower, fish, and produce markets and other places in the wee hours of the morning. Gordon also plans some spectacular tours outside of Los Angeles: a bald eagle tour to Big Bear with a naturalist; a whale-watching and biplane adventure; and a glorious garlic train, which tours Monterey and Carmel and takes in the Gilroy Garlic Fest.

LA Today Custom Tours (14964 Camarosa Dr., Pacific Palisades 90272, tel. 310/454–5730) also has a wide selection of offbeat tours, some of which tie in with seasonal and cultural events, such as theater, museum exhibits, and the Rose Bowl. Groups range from 8 to 50, and prices from $6 to $50. The least expensive is a two-hour walking tour of hotel lobbies in downtown Los Angeles that costs $6.

Guided and self-guided tours of the many architectural landmarks in Los Angeles are becoming increasingly popular. Buildings run the gamut from the Victorian Bradbury Building in the downtown core, to the many fine examples of Frank Lloyd Wright's works—the Ennis-Brown House, Hollyhock House, and Snowden House among them. On the last Sunday of April each year the **Los Angeles County Museum of Art** (tel. 213/857–6500) holds a fund-raising tour of a selection of special houses in the city.

Walking Tours
A very pleasant self-guided walking tour of **Palisades Park** is detailed in a brochure available at the park's Visitors Center (1400 Ocean Blvd., Santa Monica). Many television shows and movies have been filmed on this narrow strip of parkland on a bluff overlooking the Pacific. The 26-acre retreat is always bustling with walkers, skaters, Frisbee throwers, readers, and sunbathers.

The **Los Angeles Conservancy** (tel. 213/623–CITY) offers low-cost walking tours of the downtown area. Each Saturday at 10 AM one of six different tours leaves from the Olive Street entrance of the Biltmore Hotel; reservations are necessary. The Pershing Square Tour includes visits to buildings that span four decades of Los Angeles history, with such stops as the Biltmore Hotel, the Edison Building, and the Subway Terminal Building. The Broadway Theaters Tour takes in splendid movie palaces—the largest concentration of pre–World War II movie houses in America. The Art Deco Tour explores great examples of this modernistic style at such places as the Oviatt Building, the green Sun Realty Building, and the turquoise Eastern Columbia Building.

Personal   **Elegant Tours for the Discriminating** (tel. 310/472–4090) is a per-
Guides   sonalized sightseeing and shopping service for the Beverly Hills area. Joan Mansfield offers her extensive knowledge of Rodeo Drive to one, two, or three people at a time. Lunch is included.

L.A. Nighthawks (Box 10224, Beverly Hills 90213, tel. 310/392–1500) will arrange your nightlife for you. For a rather hefty price, you'll get a limousine, a guide (who insures you're in a safe environment at all times), and immediate entry into L.A.'s hottest night spots. The more in your group, the less you'll pay. Nighthawks proprietor Charles Andrews is a music writer and 20-year entertainment-business veteran.

Exploring Los Angeles

By Ellen   Despite the intensity of the 1994 earthquake and its aftershocks,
Melinkoff   Los Angeles is such a spread-out metropolis that most tourist sights
               are far from the San Fernando Valley epicenter and were spared
Updated and destruction. But because this *is* such a sprawling destination, to see
revised by   the sights—from the Huntington Library in San Marino to the
Jane E. Lasky *Queen Mary* in Long Beach—requires a decidedly organized itinerary. Be prepared to put miles on the car. It's best to view Los Angeles as a collection of destinations, each to be explored separately, and not to jump willy-nilly from place to place. In this guide, we've divided up the major sightseeing areas of Los Angeles into eight major tours: Downtown; Hollywood; Wilshire Boulevard, a major boulevard that slices through a fascinating cross-section of the city; the posh and trendy Westside neighborhoods; the beachside towns of Santa Monica, Venice, Pacific Palisades, and Malibu; the often overlooked coastal towns of Palos Verdes, San Pedro, and Long Beach; the well-to-do northern inland suburbs of Highland Park, Pasadena, and San Marino; and the San Fernando Valley, a world unto itself.

Highlights for First-Time Visitors

Farmer's Market, Wilshire Boulevard
Griffith Park Observatory (*see* Other Places of Interest)
Huntington Library, Art Gallery, and Botanical Gardens, Pasadena
J. Paul Getty Museum, Malibu
Mann's Chinese Theater, Hollywood
Melrose Avenue, the Westside
Olvera Street, Downtown Los Angeles
Queen Mary, Long Beach
Rodeo Drive, Beverly Hills
Santa Monica Pier, Santa Monica
Universal Studios, San Fernando Valley

Downtown Los Angeles

Numbers in the margin correspond to points of interest on the Downtown Los Angeles map.

All those jokes about Los Angeles being a city without a downtown are simply no longer true. They might have had some ring of truth to them a few decades ago when Angelinos ruthlessly turned their backs on the city center and hightailed it to the suburbs. There *had* been a downtown, once, when Los Angeles was very young, and now the city core is enjoying a resurgence of attention from urban planners, real estate developers, and intrepid downtown office workers who have discovered the advantages of living close to the office.

Downtown Los Angeles can be explored on foot (or better yet, on DASH—more about that in a minute). The natives might disagree, but these are the same natives who haven't been downtown since they took out a marriage license at city hall 30 years ago; don't follow their lead. During the day, downtown is relatively safe (though be on your guard when you look around, just as you should be in any major city center). Our tour of downtown cuts through more than a century of history and colorful ethnic neighborhoods.

Getting around to the major sites in downtown Los Angeles is actually quite simple, thanks to DASH (Downtown Area Short Hop). This minibus service travels in a loop past most of the attractions listed here, stopping every two blocks or so. Every ride costs 25¢, so if you hop on and off to see attractions, it'll cost you every time. But the cost is worth it, since you can travel quickly and be assured of finding your way. DASH (tel. 213/689–8822) runs weekdays and Saturday 6:30 AM–10 PM. To follow the tour outlined below, you can get on the DASH at ARCO Plaza (505 S. Flower St., between 5th and 6th Sts.).Hidden directly under the twin ARCO towers, ARCO Plaza is a subterranean shopping mall that's jam-packed with office

❶ workers during the week, nearly deserted on weekends. The **Los Angeles Visitor and Convention Bureau** is nearby. It offers free information about attractions as well as advice on public transportation. *685 S. Figueroa St., between 7th St. and Wilshire Blvd., tel. 213/689–8822. Open weekdays 8–5, Sat. 8:30–5.*

❷ Just north of ARCO, the **Westin Bonaventure Hotel** (404 S. Figueroa St., tel. 213/624–1000) is unique in the L.A. skyline: five shimmering cylinders in the sky, without a 90 degree angle in sight. Designed by John Portman in 1974, the building looks like science-fiction fantasy. Nonguests can use only one elevator, which rises through the roof of the lobby to soar through the air outside to the revolving restaurant and bar on the 35th floor. The food here is expensive; a better bet is to come for a drink (still overpriced) and nurse it for an hour as Los Angeles makes a full circle around you.

In the 19th century, the downtown area called Bunker Hill was the site of many stately mansions. Thanks to bulldozers, there's not much of a hill left, but the area is being redeveloped. Two major sites here showcase visual arts (painting, sculpture, and environmental work) and media and performing arts.

❸ The **Museum of Contemporary Art** houses a permanent collection of international scope, representing art from 1940 to the present. Included are works by Mark Rothko, Franz Kline, and Susan Rothenberg. The red sandstone building was designed by renowned Japanese architect Arata Isozaki, and opened in 1986. Pyramidal skylights add a striking geometry to the seven-level, 98,000-square-

Downtown Los Angeles

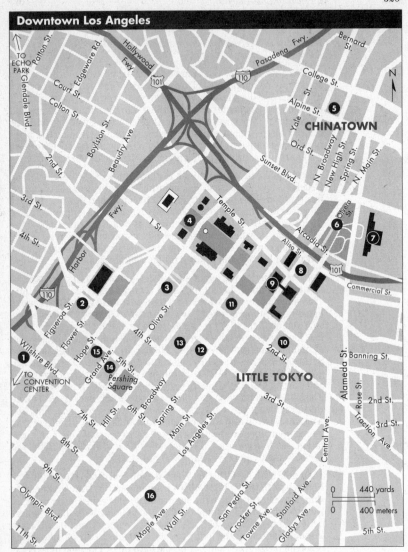

Biltmore Hotel, **14**

Bradbury Building, **12**

Central Library, **15**

Chinatown, **5**

El Pueblo de Los Angeles Historical Monument, **6**

Garment District, **16**

Grand Central Market, **13**

Little Tokyo, **10**

Los Angeles Children's Museum, **8**

Los Angeles City Hall, **9**

Los Angeles *Times* complex, **11**

Los Angeles Visitor and Convention Bureau, **1**

Museum of Contemporary Art, **3**

Music Center, **4**

Union Station, **7**

Westin Bonaventure Hotel, **2**

foot building. Don't miss the gift shop or the lively Milanese-style café. *250 S. Grand Ave., tel. 213/626–6222. Admission: $4 adults, children under 12 free; free to all Thurs. 5–8. Open Tues., Wed., Fri., Sat., and Sun. 11–5, Thurs. 11–8. Closed Mon.*

4 Walk north to the **Music Center,** which has become the cultural center for Los Angeles since it opened in 1969. In spring, it's the site of the Academy Awards presentation: Limousines arrive at the Hope Street drive-through and celebrities are whisked through the crowds to the Dorothy Chandler Pavilion, the largest and grandest of the three theaters. It was named after the widow of the publisher of the *Los Angeles Times,* who was instrumental in fund-raising efforts to build the complex. The round building in the middle, the Mark Taper Forum, is a smaller theater. Most of its offerings are of an experimental nature, many of them on a pre-Broadway run. The Ahmanson, at the north end, is the venue for many musical comedies. The plaza has a fountain and sculpture by Jacques Lipchitz. *1st St. and Grand Ave., tel. 213/972–7211. Free 45-min tours offered Tues.–Sat. 10–1:30. Schedule subject to change; call 213/972–7483 for reservations.*

5 L.A.'s **Chinatown** runs a pale second to San Francisco's Chinatown but still offers visitors an authentic slice of life, beyond the tourist hokum. The neighborhood is bordered by Yale, Bernard, and Ord streets, and Alameda Avenue. The main drag is North Broadway, where, every February, giant dragons snake down the center of the pavement during Chinese New Year celebrations. More than 15,000 Chinese and Southeast Asians (mostly Vietnamese) actually live in the Chinatown area, but many thousands more regularly frequent the markets (filled with exotic foods unfamiliar to most Western eyes) and restaurants (dim sum parlors are currently the most popular).

6 **El Pueblo de Los Angeles Historical Monument** preserves the "birthplace" of Los Angeles (no one knows exactly where the original 1781 settlement was), the oldest downtown buildings, and some of the only remaining pre-1900 buildings in the city. The historical area covers 44 acres, bounded by Alameda, Arcadia, Spring, and Macy streets.

Olvera Street is the heart of the park and one of the most popular tourist sites in Los Angeles. With its tiled walkways, piñatas, mariachis, and authentic Mexican food, Olvera Street should not be dismissed as merely some gringo approximation of the real thing. Mexican–American families come here in droves, especially on weekends and Mexican holidays—to them it feels like the old country.

Begin your walk of the area at the **Plaza,** on Olvera Street between Main and Los Angeles streets, a wonderful Mexican-style park shaded by a huge Moreton Bay fig tree. There are plenty of benches and walkways for strolling. On weekends there are often mariachis and folklorico dance groups here. You can have your photo taken in an oversize velvet sombrero, astride a stuffed donkey (a take-off of the zebra-striped donkeys that are a tradition on the streets of Tijuana). Two annual events are particularly worth seeing here: the Blessing of the Animals, at 2 PM on the Saturday before Easter, when residents bring their pets (not just dogs and cats but horses, pigs, cows, birds, hamsters, and more) to be blessed by a local priest; and Las Posadas, every night December 16–24, when merchants and visitors parade up and down the street, led by children dressed as angels, to commemorate Mary's and Joseph's search for shelter on Christmas Eve.

Head north up Olvera Street proper. Mid-block is the park's **Visitors Center,** housed in Sepulveda House (622 N. Main St., tel. 213/628–1274; open Mon.–Sat. 10–3). The Eastlake Victorian was built in 1887 as a hotel and boardinghouse. **Pelanconi House** (17 Olvera St.), built in 1855, was the first brick building in Los Angeles and has been home to the La Golondrina restaurant for 60 years. During the 1930s, famed Mexican muralist David Alfaro Siquieros was commissioned to paint a mural on the south wall of the **Italian Hall** building (650 N. Main St.). The patrons were not prepared for—and certainly not pleased by—this anti-imperialist mural depicting the oppressed workers of Latin America held in check by a menacing American eagle. It was promptly whitewashed into oblivion, and remains under the paint to this day. While preservationists from the Getty Conservation Trust work on ways of restoring the mural, copies can be seen at the Visitors Center.

Walk down the east side of Olvera Street to mid-block, passing the only remaining sign of Zanja Ditch (mother ditch), which supplied water to the area in the earliest years. **Avila Adobe** (E–10 Olvera St., open Tues.–Sat. 10–3), built in 1818, is generally considered the oldest building still standing in Los Angeles. This graceful, simple adobe is designed with the traditional interior courtyard and is furnished in the style of the 1840s.

On weekends, the restaurants are packed, and there is usually music in the plaza and along the street. Two Mexican holidays, Cinco de Mayo (May 5) and Independence Day (September 16), also draw huge crowds—and long lines for the restaurants. To see Olvera Street at its quietest and perhaps loveliest, visit on a late weekday afternoon. The long shadows heighten the romantic feeling of the street and there are only a few strollers and diners milling about.

South of the plaza is an area that has undergone recent renovation but remains, for the most part, only an ambitious idea. Although these magnificent old buildings remain closed, awaiting some commercial plan (à la Ghirardelli Square in San Francisco) that never seems to come to fruition, docent-led tours explore the area in depth. Tours depart Tuesday–Saturday 10–1, on the hour, from the **Old Firehouse** (south side of plaza, tel. 213/628–1274), an 1884 building that contains early fire-fighting equipment and old photographs. Buildings seen on tours include the Merced Theater, Masonic Temple, Pico House, and the Garnier Block—all ornate examples of the late 19th-century style. Under the Merced, Masonic Temple, and Garnier Block are underground passageways once used by Chinese immigrants.

Time Out   The dining choices on Olvera Street range from fast-food stands to comfortable, sit-down restaurants. The most authentic Mexican food is at **La Luz del Dia** (107 Paseo de la Plaza, tel. 213/628–7495). Here they serve traditional favorites like barbecued goat and pickled cactus, as well as handmade tortillas patted out in a practiced rhythm by the women behind the counter. **La Golondrina** (tel. 213/628–4349) and **El Paseo** (tel. 213/626–1361) restaurants, across from each other in mid-block, have delightful patios and extensive menus.

❼ Union Station (800 N. Alameda St.), directly east of Olvera Street across Alameda, is one of those quintessential Californian buildings that seemed to define Los Angeles to movie goers all over the country in the 1940s. Built in 1939, its Spanish Mission style is a subtle combination of Streamline Moderne and Moorish. The majestic scale of the waiting room alone is worth the walk over.

8 **Los Angeles Children's Museum** was the first of several strictly-for-kids museums now open in the city. All the exhibits here are hands-on, from Sticky City (where kids get to pillow-fight with abandon in a huge pillow-filled room) to a TV studio (where they can put on their own news shows) to The Cave (where hologram dinosaurs lurk, seeming almost real). *310 N. Main St., tel. 213/687–8800. Admission: $5, children under 2 free. Open weekends 10–5.*

9 **Los Angeles City Hall** is another often-photographed building, well-known from its many appearances on "Dragnet," "Superman," and other television shows. Opened in 1928, the 27-story City Hall remained the only building to break the 13-story height limit (earthquakes, you know) until 1957. There is a 45-minute tour and ride to the top-floor observation deck. *200 N. Spring St., tel. 213/485–4423. Tours by reservation only, weekdays at 10 and 11.*

10 **Little Tokyo** is the original ethnic neighborhood for Los Angeles's Japanese community. Most have deserted the downtown center for suburban areas such as Gardena and West Los Angeles, but Little Tokyo remains a cultural focal point. Nisei Week (Nisei is the name for second-generation Japanese) is celebrated here every August with traditional drums, obon dancing, a carnival, and huge parade. Bounded by 1st, San Pedro, 3rd, and Los Angeles streets, Little Tokyo has dozens of sushi bars, tempura restaurants, trinket shops, and even a restaurant that serves nothing but eel. The Japanese American Cultural and Community Center presents such events as kabuki theater straight from Japan.

11 The **Los Angeles *Times* complex** is made up of several, supposedly architecturally harmonious, buildings, and combines several eras and styles, but looks pretty much like a hodgepodge. *202 W. 1st St., tel. 213/237–5000. Two public tours given weekdays: 35-min tour of old plant and 45-min tour of new plant. Tour times vary; reservations required. Free parking at 213 S. Spring St.*

Broadway between 1st and 9th is one of Los Angeles's busiest shopping streets. The shops and sidewalk vendors cater primarily to the Hispanic population with bridal shops, immigration lawyers, and cheap stereo equipment. Be on your guard, as pickpockets and homeless people can approach you on the street, but this can be an exhilarating slice-of-life walk, past the florid old movie theaters like the **Orpheum** (842 S. Broadway) and the Million Dollar (310 S. **12** Broadway) and the perennially classy **Bradbury Building** (304 S. Broadway, tel. 213/626–1893), a marvelous specimen of Victorian-era commercial architecture at the southeast corner of 3rd Street and Broadway. Once the site of turn-of-the-century sweatshops, it now houses somewhat more genteel law offices. The interior courtyard, with its glass skylight and open balconies and elevator, is picture perfect and, naturally, a popular movie locale. The building is only open weekdays 9–5 and Saturday 9–4; its owners prefer that you not wander too far past the lobby.

13 **Grand Central Market** (317 S. Broadway, tel. 213/624–2378) is the most bustling market in the city and a testimony to the city's diversity. It's open Monday–Saturday 9–6, Sunday 10–5. This block-through marketplace of colorful and exotic produce, herbs, and meat draws a faithful clientele from the Latino community, senior citizens on a budget, along with Westside matrons for whom money is no object. Even if you don't plan to buy anything, Grand Central Market is a delightful place in which to browse: The butcher shops display everything from lamb heads and bulls' testicles to pigs' tails; the produce stalls are piled high with locally grown avocados and the ripest, reddest tomatoes; and the herb stalls promise remedies for all your ills.

⑭ The **Biltmore Hotel** (506 S. Grand Ave.), built in 1923, rivals Union Station for sheer architectural majesty in the Spanish-Revival tradition. The public areas have recently been restored, with the magnificent hand-painted wood beams brought back to their former glory.

⑮ Around the corner on 5th Street, the city's **Central Library** reopened in 1993, after a six-year hiatus resulting from major fires. At twice its former size, it's now the third largest public library facility in the nation. The original Goodhue building still stands, completely restored to its 1926 splendor, with shimmering Egyptian-style bas reliefs around its pediment. Go inside, through wooden doors that resemble an old Spanish-era mission, to see Dean Cornwell's murals depicting the history of California. A 1½-acre outdoor garden within the library complex has a restaurant. *630 5th St., tel. 213/228–7000. Admission free. Open Mon. and Thurs.–Sat. 10–5:30; Tues. and Wed. noon–8; Sun. 1–5.*

⑯ The **Garment District** (700–800 blocks of Los Angeles St.) is an enclave of jobbers and wholesalers that sell off the leftovers from Los Angeles's considerable garment industry production. The **Cooper Building** (860 S. Los Angeles St.) is the heart of the district and houses several of what local bargain-hunters consider to be the best pickings.

Hollywood

Numbers in the margin correspond to points of interest on the Hollywood map.

"Hollywood" once meant movie stars and glamour. The big film studios were here; starlets lived in sorority-like buildings in the center of town; and movies premiered beneath the glare of klieg lights at the Chinese and the Pantages theaters.

Those days are long gone. Paramount is the only major studio still physically located in Hollywood; and though some celebrities may live in the Hollywood Hills, there certainly aren't any in the "flats." In short, Hollywood is no longer "Hollywood." These days it is, even to its supporters, little more than a seedy town—though it's finally undergoing a dose of urban renewal (some projects are, in fact, already completed). So why visit? Because the legends of the golden age of the movies are heavy in the air. Because this is where the glamour of Hollywood originated and where those who made it so worked and lived. Judy Garland lived here and so did Marilyn Monroe and Lana Turner. It is a tribute to Hollywood's powerful hold on the imagination that visitors are able to look past the junky shops and the lost souls who walk the streets to get a sense of the town's glittering past. Besides, no visit to Los Angeles is truly complete without a walk down Hollywood Boulevard.

❶ Begin your tour of Hollywood simply by looking to the HOLLYWOOD **sign** in the Hollywood Hills that line the northern border of the town. Even on the smoggiest days, the sign is visible for miles. It is on Mt. Lee, north of Beachwood Canyon, which is approximately 1 mile east of Hollywood and Vine. The 50-foot-tall letters, originally

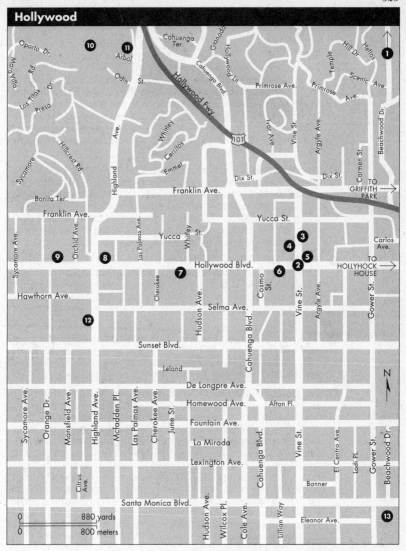

Hollywood

Capitol Records
Building, **3**

Frederick's of
Hollywood, **7**

Hollywood Bowl, **10**

Hollywood High
School, **12**

Hollywood Memorial
Cemetery, **13**

Hollywood sign, **1**

Hollywood Studio
Museum, **11**

Hollywood and Vine, **2**

Hollywood Walk of
Fame, **6**

Hollywood Wax
Museum, **8**

Mann's Chinese
Theater, **9**

The Palace, **4**

Pantages Theater, **5**

spelling out "Hollywoodland," were erected in 1923 as a promotional scheme for a real estate development. The "land" was taken down in 1949.

② Hollywood and Vine was once considered the heart of Hollywood. The mere mention of this intersection still inspires images of a street corner bustling with movie stars, starlets, and moguls passing by, on foot or in snazzy convertibles. But these days, Hollywood and Vine is far from the action, and pedestrian traffic is, well, pedestrian. No stars, no starlets, no moguls. The Brown Derby restaurant that once stood at the northwest corner is long gone, and the intersection these days is little more than a place for visitors to get their bearings.

③ Capitol Records Building (1756 N. Vine St., 1 block north of Hollywood Blvd.) opened in 1956, the very picture of '50s chic. When Capitol decided to build its new headquarters here, two of the record company's big talents of the day (singer Nat King Cole and songwriter Johnny Mercer) suggested that it be done in the shape of a stack of records. It was, and compared to much of what's gone up in L.A. since then, this building doesn't seem so odd.

④ The Palace (1735 N. Vine St., tel. 213/467–4571), just across the street from the Capitol Building, was opened in 1927 as the Hollywood Playhouse. It has played host to many shows over the years, from Ken Murray's *Blackouts* to Ralph Edwards's *This Is Your Life.* It is now the site of popular rock concerts and late-night weekend dancing

⑤ When the Pantages Theater, at 6233 Hollywood Boulevard, just east of Vine, opened in 1930, it was the very pinnacle of movie-theater opulence. From 1949 to 1959, it was the site of the Academy Awards, and today hosts large-scale Broadway musicals.

⑥ The Hollywood Walk of Fame is at every turn along the sidewalks as you make your way through downtown Hollywood. The name of one or other Hollywood legend is embossed in brass, each at the center of a pink-colored star embedded in a dark gray terrazzo circle. The first eight stars were unveiled in 1960 at the northwest corner of Highland Avenue and Hollywood Boulevard: Olive Borden, Ronald Colman, Louise Fazenda, Preston Foster, Burt Lancaster, Edward Sedgwick, Ernest Torrence, and Joanne Woodward (some of these names have stood the test of time better than others!). In the 30 years since, more than 2,300 others have been added. But this kind of immortality doesn't come cheap—the personality in question (or more likely his or her movie studio or record company) must pay $5,000 for the honor. Walk a few blocks and you'll quickly find that not all the names are familiar. To aid in the identification, celebrities are classified by one of five logos: a motion picture camera, a radio microphone, a television set, a record, or theatrical masks. Here's a guide to a few of the more famous stars: Marlon Brando at 1765 Vine, Charlie Chaplin at 6751 Hollywood, W.C. Fields at 7004 Hollywood, Clark Gable at 1608 Vine, Marilyn Monroe at 6774 Hollywood, Rudolph Valentino at 6164 Hollywood, Michael Jackson at 6927 Hollywood, and John Wayne at 1541 Vine.

⑦ After decades of sporting a gaudy lavender paint job, the exterior of Frederick's of Hollywood (6608 Hollywood Blvd., tel. 213/466–8506) has been restored to its original understated Art Deco look, gray with pink awnings. Fear not, however, that the place has suddenly gone tasteful: Inside is all the risqué and trashy lingerie that made this place famous. There is also a bra museum that features the undergarments of living and no-longer-living Hollywood legends.

⑧ Hollywood Wax Museum offers visitors sights that real life no longer can (Mary Pickford, Elvis Presley, and Clark Gable) and a few that even real life never did (Rambo and Conan). Recently added living legends on display include actors Kevin Costner and Patrick Swayze. A short film on Academy Award winners is shown daily. *6767 Hollywood Blvd., tel. 213/462–8860. Admission: $8.95 adults, $7.50 senior citizens, $6.95 children; under 6 free if with adult. Open Sun.–Thurs. 10 AM–midnight, Fri.–Sat. 10 AM–2 AM.*

The **Max Factor Museum** (1666 N. Highland Ave., tel. 213/463–6668) lets civilians in on the beauty secrets of screen idols from flicks from as far back as the turn of the century. Newly opened in the same building is the **Museum of Hollywood History,** displaying memorabilia of favorite films, television shows, and radio programs. *1666 N. Highland Ave. (call Max Factor Museum for information). Admission free. Open Mon.–Sat. 10–4.*

⑨ Angelinos no longer call **Mann's Chinese Theater** (6925 Hollywood Blvd., tel. 213/464–8111) "Grauman's Chinese," and the new owners seem finally to have a firm hold on the place in the public's eye. The architecture is a fantasy of Chinese pagodas and temples as only Hollywood could turn out. Although you'll have to buy a movie ticket to appreciate the interior trappings, the courtyard is open for browsing, where you'll see the famous cement hand- and footprints. The tradition is said to have begun at the theater's opening in 1927, with the premiere of Cecil B. DeMille's *King of Kings,* when actress Norma Talmadge accidentally stepped into the wet cement. Now more than 160 celebrities have added their footprints or handprints, along with a few oddball prints like the one of Jimmy Durante's nose. Space has pretty much run out now, though there's always room to squeeze in another super star, should Hollywood conjure one up.

⑩ Summer evening concerts at the **Hollywood Bowl** have been a tradition since 1922, although the band shell has been replaced several times. The musical fare ranges from pop to jazz to classical; the L. A. Philharmonic has its summer season here. The 17,000-plus seating capacity ranges from boxes (where local society matrons put on incredibly fancy alfresco preconcert meals for their friends) to concrete bleachers in the rear. Some people actually prefer the back rows for their romantic appeal. *2301 N. Highland Ave., tel. 213/850–2000. Grounds open daily sunrise–sunset. Call for program schedule.*

⑪ The **Hollywood Studio Museum** sits in the Hollywood Bowl parking lot, east of Highland Boulevard. The building, recently moved to this site, was once called the Lasky–DeMille Barn; in it Cecil B. DeMille produced the first feature-length film, *The Squaw Man.* In 1927, the barn became Paramount Pictures, with the original company of Jesse Lasky, Cecil B. DeMille, and Samuel Goldwyn. The museum contains a re-creation of DeMille's office, original artifacts, and a screening room showing vintage film footage of Hollywood and its legends. A great gift shop sells such quality vintage memorabilia as autographs, photographs, and books. *2100 N. Highland Ave., tel. 213/874–2276. Admission: $4 adults, $3 children, students, and seniors. Free parking. Open weekends 10–4.*

⑫ Such stars as Carol Burnett, Linda Evans, Rick Nelson, and Lana Turner attended **Hollywood High School** (1521 N. Highland Ave.). Today the student body is as diverse as Los Angeles itself, with every ethnic group represented.

Many of Hollywood's stars, from the silent-screen era on, are buried
⑬ in **Hollywood Memorial Cemetery,** a few blocks from Paramount
Studios. Walk from the entrance to the lake area and you'll find the
crypt of Cecil B. DeMille and the graves of Nelson Eddy and
Douglas Fairbanks, Sr. Inside the Cathedral Mausoleum is Rudolph
Valentino's crypt (where fans, the press, and the famous Lady in
Black turn up every August 23, the anniversary of his death). Other
stars interred in this section are Peter Lorre and Eleanor Powell.
In the Abbey of Palms Mausoleum, Norma Talmadge and Clifton
Webb are buried. *6000 Santa Monica Blvd., tel. 213/469–1181. Open
daily 8–5.*

Wilshire Boulevard

Wilshire Boulevard begins in the heart of downtown Los Angeles
and runs west, through Beverly Hills and Santa Monica, ending at
the cliffs above the Pacific Ocean. In 16 miles it moves through fairly
poor neighborhoods populated by recent immigrants, solidly middle-class enclaves, and through a corridor of the highest priced high-
rise condos in the city. Along the way, and all within a few blocks of
each other, are many of Los Angeles's top architectural sites, museums, and shops.

This linear tour can be started at any point along Wilshire Boulevard, but to really savor the cross-section view of Los Angeles that
this street provides, take the Bullocks-west-to-the-sea approach. If
you have only limited time, it would be better to skip Koreatown and
Larchmont and pare down the museum time than to do only one
stretch. All these sites are on Wilshire or within a few blocks north
or south.

"One" Wilshire, at the precise start of the boulevard in downtown
Los Angeles, is just another anonymous office building. Begin, instead, a few miles westward, past the Harbor Freeway. As Wilshire
Boulevard moves from its downtown genesis, it quickly passes
through neighborhoods now populated by recent immigrants from
Central America. Around the turn of the century, however, this area
was home to many of the city's wealthy citizens, as the faded Victorian houses on the side streets attest.

As the population crept westward, the distance to downtown shops
began to seem insurmountable and the first suburban department
branch store, **I. Magnin Bullocks Wilshire** (3050 Wilshire Blvd.,
tel. 213/382–6161), was opened in 1929. Although it closed for business in March 1993, this giant tribute to early Art Deco is protected
as a historical landmark and will not be torn down. The exterior is
often now used as a background for films. Notice the behind-the-
store parking lot—quite an innovation in 1929 and the first accommodation a large Los Angeles store made to the automobile age. On
the ceiling of the porte cochere, a mural depicts the history of transportation.

Koreatown begins almost at I. Magnin Bullocks Wilshire's back
door. Koreans are one of the latest and largest groups in this ethni-
cally diverse city. Arriving from the old country with generally more
money than most immigrant groups do, Koreans nevertheless face
the trauma of adjusting to a new language, new alphabet, and new
customs. Settling in the area south of Wilshire Boulevard, along
Olympic Boulevard between Vermont and Western avenues, the Korean community has slowly grown into a cohesive neighborhood
with active community groups and newspapers. The area is teeming
with Asian restaurants (not just Korean but also Japanese and Chi-

nese, because Koreans are fond of those cuisines). Many of the signs in this area are in Korean only. For a glimpse of the typical offerings of Korean shops, browse the large enclosed **Koreatown Plaza** mall, on the corner of Western and San Marino avenues.

At the southwest corner of Wilshire and Western Avenue sits the **Wiltern Theater** (3780 Wilshire Blvd.), part of the magnificent Wiltern Center and one of the city's best examples of full-out Art Deco architecture. The 1930s zigzag design was recently restored to its splendid turquoise hue. Inside, the theater is full of opulent detail at every turn. Originally a movie theater, the Wiltern is now a multi-use arts complex.

Continuing west on Wilshire, the real estate values start to make a sharp climb. In the past, the mayor of Los Angeles had his official residence in **Getty House** (605 S. Irving Blvd., one block north of Wilshire), a white-brick, half-timber residence that was donated to the city by the Getty family. This area, known as Hancock Park, is one of the city's most genteel neighborhoods, remaining in vogue since its development in the 1920s. Many of L.A.'s old-money families live here in English Tudor homes with East Coast landscaping schemes that defy the local climate and history.

Drop back down to Wilshire Boulevard again and continue westward. **Miracle Mile,** the strip of Wilshire Boulevard between La Brea and Fairfax avenues, was so dubbed in the 1930s as a promotional gimmick to attract shoppers to the new stores. The area went into something of a decline in the '50s and '60s, but is now enjoying a comeback, as Los Angeles's Art Deco architecture has come to be appreciated, preserved, and restored. Exemplary buildings like the **El Rey Theater** (5519 Wilshire) stand out as examples of period design (in spite of the fact that it now houses a restaurant). In **Callender's Restaurant** (corner of Wilshire and Curson), recent murals and old photographs effectively depict life on the Miracle Mile in its heyday.

Across Curson Avenue is **Hancock Park,** an actual park, not to be confused with Hancock Park, the residential neighborhood. This park is home to the city's world-famous fossil source, the **La Brea Tar Pits.** Despite the fact that *la brea* already means "tar" in Spanish and to say "La Brea Tar Pits" is redundant, the name remains firm in local minds. About 35,000 years ago, deposits of oil rose to the Earth's surface, collected in shallow pools, and coagulated into sticky asphalt. In the early 20th century, geologists discovered that the sticky goo contained the largest collection of Pleistocene fossils ever found at one location: more than 200 varieties of birds, mammals, plants, reptiles, and insects. More than 100 tons of fossil bones have been removed over 70 years of excavations. Statues of mammoths in the big pit near the corner of Wilshire and Curson depict how many of them were entombed: Edging down to a pond of water to drink, animals were caught in the tar and unable to extricate themselves. There are several pits scattered around Hancock Park; construction in the area has often had to accommodate these oozing pits, and in nearby streets and along sidewalks, little bits of tar occasionally ooze up, unstoppable.

The **George C. Page Museum of La Brea Discoveries,** a satellite of the Natural History Museum of Los Angeles County, is situated at the tar pits and set, bunkerlike, half underground. A bas-relief around four sides depicts life in the Pleistocene era, and the museum has over one million Ice Age fossils. Exhibits include reconstructed, life-size skeletons of saber-tooth cats, mammoths, wolves, sloths, eagles, and condors. The glass-enclosed Paleontological Laboratory permits observation of the ongoing cleaning, identification, and cataloguing of fossils excavated from the nearby asphalt deposits. *The La Brea Story* and *A Whopping Small Dinosaur* are short documentary films shown every 15–30 minutes. A hologram magically puts flesh on "La Brea Woman," and an interactive tar mechanism shows visitors just how hard it would be to free oneself from the sticky mess. *5801 Wilshire Blvd., tel. 213/936–2230. Admission: $5 adults, $3.50 students and senior citizens, $2 children; under age 5 free. Open Wed.–Sun. 10–5. Free admission every 2nd Wed. of month.*

The **Los Angeles County Museum of Art,** also in Hancock Park, is the largest museum complex in Los Angeles, comprised of five buildings surrounding a grand central court. The Times Mirror Central Court provides both a visual and symbolic focus for the museum complex. The Ahmanson Building, built around a central atrium, houses the museum's collection of paintings, sculpture, costumes and textiles, and decorative arts from a wide range of cultures and periods. Highlights include a unique assemblage of glass from Roman times to the 19th century; the renowned Gilbert collection of mosaics and monumental silver; one of the nation's largest holdings of costumes and textiles; and an Indian and Southeast Asian art collection considered to be one of the most comprehensive in the world.

The Hammer Building features major special loan exhibitions as well as galleries for prints, drawings, and photographs. The Anderson Building features 20th-century painting and sculpture as well as special exhibitions. The museum's collection of Japanese sculpture, paintings, ceramics, and lacquerware, including the internationally renowned Shin'enkan collection of Japanese paintings and a collection of extraordinary *netsuke*, is on view in the Pavillion for Japanese Art. The Contemporary Sculpture Garden comprises nine large-scale outdoor sculptures. The B. Gerald Cantor Sculpture Garden features bronzes by Auguste Rodin, Emile-Antoine Bourdelle, and George Kolbe. *5905 Wilshire Blvd., tel. 213/857–6000; ticket information, 213/857–6010. Admission: $6 adults, $4 students and senior citizens, $1 children 6–17. Open Wed.–Thurs. 10–5, Fri. 10–9, Sat.–Sun. 11–6.*

The County Museum, Page Museum, and indeed all of Hancock Park itself are brimming with visitors on warm weekends. Although crowded, it can be the most exciting time to visit the area. Mimes and itinerant musicians ply their trades. Street vendors sell fast-food treats and there are impromptu soccer games on the lawns. To really study the art, though, a quieter weekday visit is recommended.

The **Craft and Folk Art Museum,** across Wilshire Boulevard from Hancock Park, was expected to reopen in August 1994 after being closed for a couple of years for extensive renovations. It's worth checking to see if it's open, for the museum offers consistently fascinating exhibits of both contemporary crafts and folk crafts from around the world. The museum's collections include Japanese, Mexican, American, and East Indian folk art, textiles, and masks. Six to eight major exhibitions are planned each year. The International Festival of Masks, one of the more popular, is held annually the last weekend in October across the street in Hancock Park. *5800 Wilshire Blvd., tel. 213/937–5544. Admission: minimal (not set at press time.) Open Tues.–Sat. 10–5, Sun. 11–5.*

Continue west on Wilshire a few blocks to the corner of Fairfax Avenue. On the northeast corner is the former **May Co. department store,** another 1930s landmark with a distinctive curved corner.

Head north on Fairfax a few blocks to the **Farmer's Market,** a favorite L.A. attraction since it opened in 1934. Along with the 120 shops, salons, stores, and produce stalls, there are 30 restaurants (some of which offer alfresco dining under umbrellas), serving an interesting variety of international and domestic fare. Although originally it was exactly what the name implies—a farmer's market—these days you will find not only food and produce, but gifts, clothing, beauty shops, and even a shoe repair. Because it is next door to the CBS Television Studios, you never know whom you will run into, as TV celebrities shop and dine here often. *6333 W. 3rd St., tel. 213/933–9211. Open Mon.–Sat. 9–6:30, Sun. 10–5. Open later during summer.*

Time Out **Kokomo** (on 3rd St. side of market, tel. 213/933–0773) is not only the best eatery inside the Farmer's Market, it's got some of the best new-wave diner food anywhere in L.A. Lively, entertaining service is almost always included in the reasonable prices. For those in a hurry, Kokomo A Go Go, its take-out store, is adjacent.

North of the market, Fairfax is the center of Los Angeles's Jewish life. The shops and stands from Beverly Boulevard north are enlivened with friendly conversations between shopkeepers and regular customers. **Canter's Restaurant, Deli, and Bakery** (419 N. Fairfax, tel. 213/651–2030) is a traditional hangout during the day, and a haven for rockers in the wee hours, after all of L.A.'s bars shut down at 2 AM.

The Westside

Numbers in the margin correspond to points of interest on the Westside map.

The Westside of Los Angeles—which to residents means from La Brea Avenue westward to the ocean—is where the rents are the most expensive, the real estate prices sky-high, the restaurants (and the restaurateurs) the most famous, and the shops the most chic. It's the best of the good life, Southern California style, and to really savor (and understand) the Southland, spend a few leisurely days or half-days exploring this area. Short on such traditional tourist attractions as amusement parks, historic sites, and museums, it more than makes up for those gaps with great shopping districts, exciting walking streets, outdoor cafés, and a lively nightlife.

The Westside can be best enjoyed in at least three separate outings, allowing plenty of time for browsing and dining. Attractions 1 through 4 are in the West Hollywood area; 5 through 8 in Beverly Hills; and 9 through 11 in Westwood. But the Westside is also small enough that you could pick four or five of these sites to visit in a single day, depending on your interests.

West Hollywood Once an almost forgotten parcel of county land surrounded by the city of L.A. and Beverly Hills, West Hollywood became an official city in 1984. The West Hollywood attitude—trendy, stylish, and with plenty of disposable income—spills over beyond the official city borders.

❶ Melrose Avenue provides plenty of fodder for people-watching: post-punk fashion plates, people in spiked hairdos, and just about

Westside

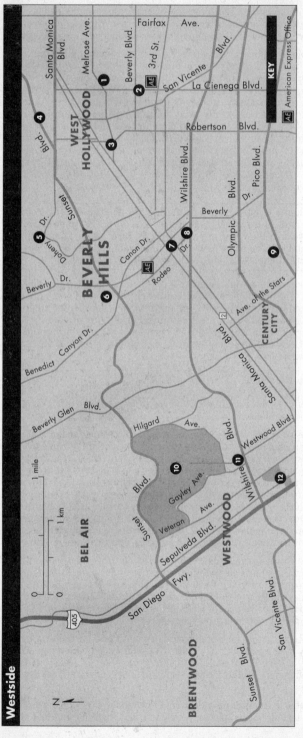

Armand Hammer
Museum of Art and
Cultural Center, **11**
Beverly Center, **2**
Beverly Hills Hotel, **6**
Greystone Mansion, **5**
Melrose Avenue, **1**

The Pacific Design
Center, **3**
Regent Beverly
Wilshire Hotel, **8**
Rodeo Drive, **7**
Sunset Strip, **4**

Tolerance Museum, **9**
University of
California at Los
Angeles, **10**
Westwood Memorial
Park, **12**

the most outlandish ensembles imaginable. It's where panache meets paparazzi, and Beverly Hills chic meets Hollywood hip. The busiest stretch of Melrose is between Fairfax and La Brea avenues. Here you'll find one-of-a-kind boutiques and small, chic restaurants for more than a dozen blocks. Park on a side street (and read the parking signs carefully: Parking regulations around here are vigorously enforced and a rich vein for the city's coffers) and begin walking. On the 7400 block are **Tempest** and **Notorious,** boutiques with the latest of California's trend-setting designers' clothes for women, along with **Mondial,** for men, and **Mark Fox,** which supplies the sought-after Western look. On the next block over, **Maxfield** (8825) provides excellent special occasion designs. In the other direction—in more ways than one—**Wasteland** (7428) is a great find for vintage clothing as well as resale items brought in by locals every day. **Melrose Place Antique Market** (7002 Melrose) is a collection of small items, vintage in nature, high in appeal. (*See* Shopping for more store recommendations.)

Time Out Melrose has no shortage of great eateries, but the ultimate Melrose "joint" is **Johnny Rocket's** (7507 Melrose Ave., tel. 213/651–3361), a remake of a hip '50s-style diner near the corner of Gardner Street. It's just stools at a counter, the best of old-time rock and roll on tape, and great hamburgers, shakes, and fries—and almost always crowded.

2 That hulking monolith dominating the corner of La Cienega and Beverly boulevards is none other than the **Beverly Center** (8500 Beverly Blvd., tel. 310/854–0070). Designed as an all-in-one stop for shopping, dining, and movies, it has been a boon to Westsiders—except for those who live so close as to suffer the consequences of the heavy traffic. Parking is on the second through fifth floors, shops on the sixth, seventh, and eighth, and movies and restaurants on the eighth floors. The street level features a variety of restaurants, the most popular being the **Hard Rock Cafe** (look for the vintage green Cadillac in the roof). In the center proper are two major department stores, **Bullocks** and **The Broadway,** as well as dozens of upscale clothing boutiques, a 14-screen movie theater, and a wide variety of restaurants (California Pizza Kitchen, Panda Express, La Rotisserie, plus Mrs. Field's Cookies and Haagen Daz ice cream outlets). **Sam Goody's,** whose 15,000 square feet make it the world's largest enclosed music store, features a glass-walled, and spectacular, view of Hollywood. The **Warner Bros. Studio Store,** popular with both adults and kids, is crammed with movie and cartoon memorabilia and apparel.

3 West Hollywood is the center of Los Angeles's thriving interior decorating business. The **Pacific Design Center** (8687 Melrose Ave., tel. 310/657–0800) is known to residents as the "Blue Whale." The blue-glass building, designed by Cesar Pelli in 1975, houses to-the-trade-only showrooms filled with the most tempting furnishings, wall coverings, and accessories. In 1988 the center added a second building by Pelli, this one clad in green glass. The building is open to the public (Mon.–Fri. 9–5), who are allowed to browse in many of the more than 200 showrooms or opt for a free tour at 10 AM. Note: Purchases can be made only through design professionals (a referral system is available). The **Murray Feldman Gallery,** featuring various art, design, and cultural exhibitions, sits on the adjacent 2-acre landscaped public plaza (open Tues.–Sat. noon–6).

"Robertson Boulevard," the area that surrounds the Blue Whale, has several more to-the-trade showrooms. These are not confined to the street Robertson Boulevard itself, being well represented also along Beverly Boulevard and Melrose Avenue. This area is exceptionally walkable, and residents often walk their dogs here in the evening (even driving them here to then do their walking) so they can browse the well-lit windows. A few of the showrooms will accommodate an occasional retail buyer, so if you see something to die for, it's worth an inquiry inside.

❹ **Sunset Strip** was famous in the '50s, as in the TV show "77 Sunset Strip," but it was popular as far back as the 1930s, when nightclubs like Ciro's and Mocambo were in their heyday and movie stars frequented the Strip as an after-work gathering spot. This winding, hilly stretch is a visual delight, enjoyed both by car (a convertible would be perfect) or on foot. Drive it once to enjoy the hustle-bustle, the vanity boards (huge billboards touting new movies, new records, new stars), and the dazzling shops. Then pick a section and explore a few blocks on foot. The Sunset Plaza section is especially nice for walking, a stretch of expensive shops and outdoor cafés (including the nouvelle Chinese favorite Chin Chin) that are packed for lunch and on warm evenings. At Horn Street, **Tower Records** (a behemoth of a CD store with two satellite shops across the street), **Book Soup** (L.A.'s literary bookstore), and Wolfgang Puck's famous restaurant **Spago** (a half-block up the hill on Horn) make satisfying browsing, especially in the evening.

Beverly Hills The glitz of Sunset Strip ends abruptly at Doheny Drive, where Sunset Boulevard enters the world-famous and glamorous Beverly Hills. Suddenly the sidewalk street life gives way to expansive, perfectly manicured lawns and palatial homes. Doheny Drive is named ❺ for oilman Edward Doheny, the original owner of the **Greystone Mansion,** built in 1927. This Tudor-style mansion, now owned by the city of Beverly Hills, sits on 18½ landscaped acres and has been used in such films as *The Witches of Eastwick* and *All of Me*. The gardens are open for self-guided tours and peeking (only) through the windows is permitted. Picnics are permitted in specified areas during hours of operation. *905 Loma Vista Dr., tel. 310/550–4796. Admission free. Open daily 10–5.*

❻ West of Sunset Strip a mile or so is the **Beverly Hills Hotel** (9641 Sunset Blvd.), whose Spanish Colonial Revival architecture and soft pastel exterior have earned it the name "the Pink Palace." The venerable hotel is closed for extensive renovations (watch for a re-opening in spring 1995), but you can still look at the outside.

It is on this stretch of Sunset, especially during the daytime, that you'll see hawkers peddling maps to stars' homes. Are the maps reliable? Well, that's a matter of debate. Stars do move around, so it's difficult to keep any map up to date. But the fun is in looking at some of these magnificent homes, regardless of whether or not they're owned by a star at the moment.

Beverly Hills was incorporated as a city early in the century and has been thriving ever since. Within a few square blocks in the center of Beverly Hills are some of the most exotic, to say nothing of high-priced, stores in southern California. Here you can find such items as a $200 pair of socks wrapped in gold leaf, and stores that take customers only by appointment. A fun way to spend an after- ❼ noon is to stroll famed **Rodeo Drive** between Santa Monica and Wilshire boulevards. Some of the Rodeo (pronounced ro-DAY-o) shops may be familiar to you since they supply clothing for major network television shows and their names often appear among the credits. Others, such as Gucci, have a worldwide reputation.

8 The **Regent Beverly Wilshire Hotel** (9500 Wilshire Blvd., tel. 310/275–5200) anchors the south end of Rodeo Drive, at Wilshire. Opened in 1928, and vigorously expanded and renovated since, the hotel is often home to visiting royalty and celebrities; it's where the millionaire businessman played by Richard Gere ensconced himself with the hooker played by Julia Roberts in the movie *Pretty Woman.* The lobby is quite small for a hotel of this size and offers little opportunity to meander; you might stop for a drink or meal in one of the hotel's restaurants.

9 A sobering but moving experience in the midst of all this glamor, the **Museum of Tolerance,** which opened adjacent to the Simon Weisenthal Center in 1993, deserves a thoughtful visit. Using lots of state-of-the-art interactive technology, the museum challenges visitors to confront bigotry and racism. One of the most affecting sections of this museum covers the Holocaust—each visitor is issued a "passport" bearing the name of a child whose life was dramatically changed by the German Nazi rule and by World War II, and ultimately the museum goer learns the fate of that child. Expect to spend at least four hours to see the whole museum. *9786 W. Pico Blvd., tel. 310/553–8403. Admission: $7.50 adults, $5.50 senior citizens, $4.50 teens, $2.50 children 3–12. Open Sun. 11–5, Mon.–Thurs. 10–5, Fri. 10–1 (Apr.–Oct., Fri. 10–3). Advance reservations advised.*

Westwood
10 Westward from Beverly Hills, Sunset continues to wind past palatial estates and passes by the **University of California at Los Angeles.** Nestled in the Westwood section of the city and bound by LeConte Street, Sunset Boulevard, and Hilgard Avenue, the parklike UCLA campus is an inviting place for visitors to stroll. The most spectacular buildings are the original ones, Royce Hall and the library, both in Romanesque style. In the heart of the north campus is the Franklin Murphy Sculpture Garden, with works by Henry Moore and Gaston Lachaise dotting the landscaping. For a gardening buff, UCLA is a treasure of unusual and well-labeled plants. The Mildred Mathias Botanic Garden is located in the southeast section of campus and is accessible from Tiverton Avenue. Sports fans will enjoy the Morgan Center Hall of Fame (west of Campus book store), where memorabilia and trophies of the athletic departments are on display. Maps and information are available at drive-by kiosks at major entrances, even on weekends, and free 90-minute, guided walking tours of the campus are offered on weekdays. The campus has several indoor and outdoor cafés, plus bookstores that sell the very popular UCLA Bruins paraphernalia. *Tours (tel. 310/206–8147) weekdays at 10:30 AM and 1:30 PM. Call for reservations. Meet at 10945 LeConte St., room 1417, on the south edge of the campus, facing Westwood.*

Directly south of the campus is Westwood, once a quiet college town and now one of the busiest places in the city on weekend evenings—so busy that during the summer, many streets are closed to car traffic and visitors must park at the Federal Building (Wilshire Blvd. and Veteran Ave.) and shuttle over.

11 **Armand Hammer Museum of Art and Cultural Center** is one of the city's newest museums. Although small compared to other museums in Los Angeles, the permanent collection here includes thousands of works by Honoré Daumier, and a rare portfolio of Leonardo Da Vinci's technical drawings. The Hammer regularly features special blockbuster displays that cannot be seen elsewhere, such as the 1992 exhibit "Catherine the Great: Treasures of Imperial Russia." *10899 Wilshire Blvd., tel. 310/443–7000. Admission: $4.50 adults,*

*$3 students and senior citizens, children under 17 free. Open Tues.–
Sun. 10–6 (extended hrs during special exhibitions). Parking fee
$2.75.*

The Westwood stretch of Wilshire Boulevard is a corridor of cheek-
by-jowl office buildings whose varying architectural styles can be
jarring, to say the least. Tucked behind one of these behemoths is
② **Westwood Memorial Park** (1218 Glendon Ave.). In this very un-
likely place for a cemetery is one of the most famous graves in the
city. Marilyn Monroe is buried in a simply marked wall crypt. For
25 years after her death, her former husband Joe DiMaggio had six
red roses placed on her crypt three times a week. Also buried here
is Natalie Wood.

Santa Monica, Venice, Pacific Palisades, Malibu

*Numbers in the margin correspond to points of interest on the
Santa Monica and Venice map.*

The towns that hug the coastline of Santa Monica Bay reflect the
wide diversity of Los Angeles, from the rich-as-can-be Malibu to the
yuppie/seedy mix of Venice. The emphasis is on being out in the
sunshine, always within sight of the Pacific. You would do well to
visit the area in two excursions: Santa Monica to Venice in one day
and Pacific Palisades to Malibu in another.

Santa Monica Santa Monica is a tidy little city, about 2 miles square, where expa-
triate Brits tend to settle (there's an English music hall and several
pubs here), attracted perhaps by the cool and foggy climate. The
sense of order is reflected in the economic/geographic stratification:
The most northern section has broad streets lined with superb,
older homes. As you drive south, real estate prices drop $50,000 or
so every block or two. The middle class lives in the middle and the
working class, to the south, along the Venice border.

❶ Begin exploring at **Santa Monica Pier,** located at the foot of Colorado Avenue and easily accessible for beach-goers as well as drive-
around visitors. Cafés, gift shops, a psychic advisor, bumper car
rides, and arcades line the truncated pier, which was severely damaged in a storm a few years ago. The 46-horse carousel, built in 1922,
has seen action in many movie and television shows, most notably
the Paul Newman/Robert Redford film *The Sting. Tel. 310/458–
8900. Rides: 50¢ adults, 25¢ children. Carousel open in summer,
Tues.–Sun. 10–9; in winter, weekends 10–5.*

❷ **Palisades Park** is a ribbon of green that runs along the top of the
cliffs from Colorado Avenue to just north of San Vicente Boulevard.
The flat walkways are usually filled with casual strollers as well as
joggers who like to work out with a spectacular view of the Pacific
as company. It is especially enjoyable at sunset.

The **Santa Monica Visitor Information Center,** located in the
park at Santa Monica Boulevard, offers bus schedules, directions,
and information on Santa Monica–area attractions. *Tel. 310/393–
7593. Open daily 10–4.*

Santa Monica has grown into a major center for the L.A. art com-
❸ munity, and the **Santa Monica Museum of Art** is poised to boost
that reputation. Designed by Frank Gehry, the well-known architect
who's also a local resident, the museum presents the works of performance and video artists and exhibits works of lesser-known
painters and sculptors. *2437 Main St., tel. 310/399–0433. Admis-*

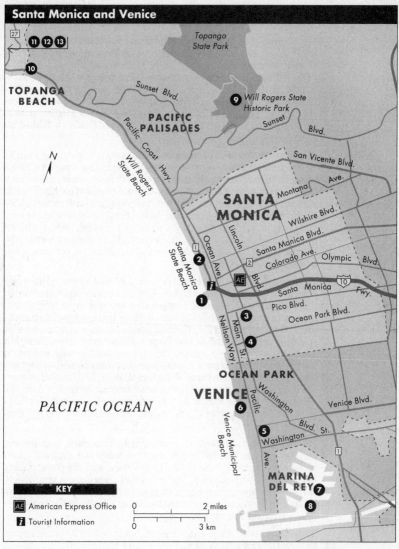

Santa Monica and Venice

Adamson House, **11**
Burton Chase Park, **7**
Canals, **5**
Fisherman's Village, **8**
J. Paul Getty Museum, **10**
Malibu Lagoon State Park, **12**
Palisades Park, **2**

Pepperdine University, **13**
Santa Monica Heritage Museum, **4**
Santa Monica Museum of Art, **3**
Santa Monica Pier, **1**
Venice Boardwalk, **6**
Will Rogers State Historic Park, **9**

sion: suggested donation $4 adults, $1 artists, students, and senior citizens. Open Wed. and Thurs. 11–6, Fri.–Sat. 11–10, Sun. 11–6.

❹ The **Santa Monica Heritage Museum,** housed in an 1894-vintage, late-Victorian home once owned by the founder of the city, was moved to its present site on trendy Main Street in the mid-1980s. Three rooms have been fully restored: the dining room in the style of 1890 to 1910; the living room, 1910–1920; and the kitchen, 1920–1930. The second-floor galleries feature photography and historical exhibits as well as shows by contemporary Santa Monica artists. *2612 Main St., tel. 310/392–8537. Admission: $2. Open Wed.–Sat. 11–4, Sun. noon–4.*

The museum faces a companion home, another Victorian delight moved to the site; it's now occupied by a catering company, **Monica's.** These two dowagers anchor the northwest corner of the funky **Main Street area** of Santa Monica. Several blocks of old brick buildings here have undergone a recent rejuvenation (and considerable rent increases) and now house galleries, bars, cafés, omelet parlors, and boutiques. It's a delightful area to walk around, though with its proximity to the beach, parking can be tight on summer weekends. Best bets are the city pay lots behind the Main Street shops, between Main and Neilsen Way.

Venice Venice was a turn-of-the-century fantasy that never quite came true. Abbot Kinney, a wealthy Los Angeles businessman, envisioned this little piece of real estate, which then seemed so far from downtown, as a romantic replica of Venice, Italy. He developed an incredible 16 miles of canals, floated gondolas on them, and built scaled-down versions of the Doge's Palace and other Venetian landmarks. The name remains but the connection with old-world Venice is as flimsy as ever. Kinney's project was plagued by ongoing engineering problems and disasters and drifted into disrepair. **❺** Three small **canals** and bridges remain and can be viewed from the southeast corner of Pacific Avenue and Venice Boulevard. But long-gone are the amusement park, swank seaside hotels, and the gondoliers.

By the late 1960s, however, actors, artists, musicians, and hippies, and anyone who wanted to live near the beach but couldn't afford to, were attracted by the low rents in Venice, and the place quickly became SoHo-by-the-Sea. Venice's locals today are a grudgingly thrown-together mix of aging hippies, yuppies with the disposable income to spend on inflated rents, senior citizens who have lived here for decades, and the homeless.

Venice has the liveliest waterfront walkway in Los Angeles, known **❻** as both Ocean Front Walk and the **Venice Boardwalk.** It begins at Washington Street and runs north. Save this visit for a weekend. There is plenty of action year-round: bicyclists zip along and bikini-clad roller skaters attract crowds as they put on impromptu demonstrations, vying for attention with the unusual breeds of dogs that locals love to prance along the walkway. A local body-building club works out on the adjacent beach, and it's nearly impossible not to stop to ogle at the pecs as these strong men lift weights.

At the south end of the boardwalk, along Washington Street, near the Venice Pier, in-line skates, roller skates, and bicycles (some with baby seats) are available for rent.

Time Out The boardwalk is lined with fast-food stands, and food can then be carried a few feet to the beach for a picnic. But for a somewhat more relaxing meal, stand in line for a table at **Sidewalk Cafe** (1401 Ocean Front Walk, tel. 310/399–5547). Wait for a patio table, where you can watch the free spirits on parade.

Marina del Rey
Just south of Venice is a quick shift of values. Forget about Venice—Italy or California—Marina del Rey is a modern and more successful, if less romantic, dream. It is the largest man-made boat harbor in the world, with a commercial area catering to the whims of boat owners and boat groupies. The stretch between Admiralty Way and Mindinao Way has some of the area's best restaurants—expensive but worth it. Most of the better hotel chains, such as the Ritz-Carlton, also have properties here.

❼ For boatless visitors, the best place from which to view the marina is **Burton Chase Park,** at the end of Mindinao Way. Situated at the tip of a jetty and surrounded on three sides by water and moored boats, this 6-acre patch of green offers a cool and breezy spot from which to watch boats move in and out of the channel, and it's great for picnicking.

❽ **Fisherman's Village** is a collection of cute Cape Cod clapboards housing shops and restaurants (open daily 8 AM–9 PM). It's not much of a draw unless you stop in for a meal or a snack or take one of the 45-minute marina cruises offered by **Hornblower Dining Outs** that depart from the village dock. *13755 Fiji Way, tel. 310/301–6000. Tickets: $7 adults, $4 senior citizens and children. Cruises leave every hr, weekdays 12–3, weekends 11–5.*

Pacific Palisades
From Santa Monica, head north on Pacific Coast Highway toward Malibu, a pleasant drive in daytime or evening. The narrow-but-expensive beachfront houses were home to movie stars in the 1930s.

❾ Spend a few hours at **Will Rogers State Historic Park** in Pacific Palisades and you may understand what endeared America to this cowboy/humorist in the 1920s and 1930s. The two-story ranch house on Rogers's 187-acre estate is a folksy blend of Navajo rugs and Mission-style furniture. Rogers's only extravagance was raising the roof several feet (he waited till his wife was in Europe to do it) to accommodate his penchant for practicing his lasso technique indoors. The nearby museum features Rogers memorabilia. Short films show his roping technique and his homey words of wisdom. Rogers was a polo enthusiast, and in the 1930s, his front-yard polo field attracted such friends as Douglas Fairbanks for weekend games. The tradition continues, with free games scheduled when the weather's good. The park's broad lawns are excellent for picnicking, and there's hiking on miles of eucalyptus-lined trails. Those who make it to the top will be rewarded with a panoramic view of the mountains and ocean. *1501 Will Rogers State Park Rd., Pacific Palisades, tel. 310/454–8212. Admission free; parking $5. Call for polo schedule.*

Malibu
❿ You'll want to plan in advance to visit the **J. Paul Getty Museum,** which contains one of the country's finest collections of Greek and Roman antiquities. The oil millionaire began collecting art in the 1930s, concentrating on three distinct areas: Greek and Roman antiquities, Baroque and Renaissance paintings, and 18th-century decorative arts. In 1946 he purchased a large Spanish-style home on 65 acres in a canyon just north of Santa Monica to house the collection. By the late 1960s, the museum could no longer accommodate the rapidly expanding collection and Getty decided to build this new building, which was completed in 1974. It's a re-creation of the Villa dei Papiri, a luxurious 1st-century Roman villa that stood on

the slopes of Mount Vesuvius overlooking the Bay of Naples, prior to the volcano's eruption in AD 79. The villa is thought to have once belonged to Lucius Calpurnius Piso, the father-in-law of Julius Caesar. The two-level, 38-gallery building and its extensive gardens (which includes trees, flowers, shrubs, and herbs that might have grown 2,000 years ago at the villa) provide an appropriate and harmonious setting for Getty's classical antiquities.

The main level houses sculpture, mosaics, and vases. Of particular interest are the 4th-century Attic stelae (funerary monuments) and Greek and Roman portraits. The decorative arts collection on the upper level features furniture, carpets, tapestries, clocks, chandeliers, and small decorative items made for the French, German, and Italian nobility, with a wealth of royal French treasures (Louis XIV to Napoleon). Richly colored brocaded walls set off the paintings and furniture to great advantage. All major schools of Western art from the late 13th century to the late 19th century are represented in the painting collection, which emphasizes Renaissance and Baroque art and includes works by Rembrandt, Rubens, de la Tour, Van Dyck, Gainsborough, and Boucher. Recent acquisitions include Old Master drawings, and medieval and Renaissance illuminated manuscripts, works by Picasso, Van Gogh's *Irises*, and a select collection of Impressionist paintings including some by Claude Monet. The only catch in visiting this museum is that parking reservations are necessary—there's no way to visit it without using the parking lot unless you are dropped off or take a tour bus—and they should be made one week in advance by telephoning or writing to the museum's Reservations Office. *17985 Pacific Coast Hwy., tel. 310/458–2003. Admission free. Open Tues.–Sun. 10–5.*

Time Out   One of the best located restaurants in Malibu is **Pierview** (22718 Pacific Coast Highway, tel. 310/456–6962), set right on the ocean just south of the pier. The menu ranges from sandwiches and pizzas to Mexican food, including shark fajitas. Try to get an outdoor seat if the weather's warm.

⓫ **Adamson House** is the former home of the Rindge family, which owned much of the Malibu Rancho in the early part of the 20th century. Malibu was quite isolated then, with all visitors and supplies arriving by boat at the nearby Malibu Pier (and it can still be isolated these days when rock slides close the highway). The Moorish-Spanish home, built in 1928, has been opened to the public and may be the only chance most visitors get to be inside a grand Malibu home. The Rindges led an enviable Malibu lifestyle, decades before it was trendy. The house is right on the beach (high chain-link fences keep out curious beach-goers). The family owned the famous Malibu Tile Company and their home is predictably encrusted with magnificent tile work in rich blues, greens, yellows, and oranges. Even an outside dog shower, near the servants' door, is a tiled delight. Docent-led tours help visitors to envision family life here as well as to learn about the history of Malibu and its real estate (you can't have one without the other). *23200 Pacific Coast Hwy., tel. 310/456–8432. Admission: $2 adults, $1 children. Open Wed.–Sat. 11–3.*

⓬ Adjacent to Adamson House is **Malibu Lagoon State Park** (23200 Pacific Coast Hwy.), a haven for native and migratory birds. Visitors must stay on the boardwalks so that the egrets, blue herons, avocets, and gulls can enjoy the marshy area. The signs that give opening and closing hours refer only to the parking lot; the lagoon itself is open 24 hours and is particularly enjoyable in the early morning and at sunset. Luckily, street-side parking is available then (but not midday).

⓭ Pepperdine University (24255 Pacific Coast Hwy.) looks exactly like a California school should. Designed by William Pereira, this picture-perfect campus is set on a bluff above the Pacific. The school's fine athletic facilities have been used for those televised "Battle of the Network Stars" workouts. On a loftier note: The art center houses an authentic Japanese teahouse where students can learn the correct protocol of the ritual tea ceremony that is so important for those who do business in the Orient.

Palos Verdes, San Pedro, and Long Beach

Numbers in the margin correspond to points of interest on the Palos Verdes, San Pedro, and Long Beach map.

Few local residents take advantage of Long Beach's attractions. If they ever took a day to see the *Queen Mary* when their in-laws visited from back East, they were duly astounded to discover Long Beach's impressive skyline, the string of hotels along Ocean Boulevard, the revitalized downtown area, and the city's close proximity to the rest of L.A. and Orange County. How could this entire city, the fifth largest in the state, have been right here and they never really knew about it?

Palos Verdes Palos Verdes Peninsula is a hilly haven for horse lovers and other gentrified folks, many of them executive transplants from east of the Mississippi. The real estate in these small peninsula towns, ranging from expensive to very expensive, are zoned for stables and you'll often see riders along the streets (they have the right of way).

❶ South Coast Botanic Gardens began life ignominiously—as a garbage dump–cum–landfill. It's hard to believe that as recently as 1960, truckloads of waste (3.5 million tons) were being deposited here. With the intensive ministerings of the experts from the L.A. County Arboreta department, the dump soon boasted lush gardens with plants from every continent except Antarctica, with all the plants eventually organized into color groups. Self-guided walking tours take visitors past flower and herb gardens, rare cacti, and a lake with ducks. Picnicking is limited to a lawn area outside the gates. *26300 S. Crenshaw Blvd., Rancho Palos Verdes, tel. 310/544–6815. Admission: $5 adults, $3 senior citizens and children 5 and older, $1 children under 5. Open daily 9–4:30.*

The drive on Palos Verdes Drive around the water's edge takes you high above the cliffs. An aerial shot of this area was used in the opening of television's "Knots Landing."

❷ Wayfarers Chapel (5755 Palos Verdes Dr. S, Rancho Palos Verdes, tel. 310/377–1650) was designed by architect Lloyd Wright, son of Frank Lloyd Wright, in 1949. He planned this modern glass church to blend in with an encircling redwood forest. The redwoods are gone (they couldn't stand the rigors of urban encroachment), but another forest has taken their place, and the breathtaking combination of ocean, trees, and structure remains. This "natural church" is a popular wedding site.

San Pedro San Pedro shares the peninsula with the Palos Verdes towns, but little else. Here, the cliffs give way to a hospitable harbor. The 1950s-vintage executive homes give way to tidy 1920s-era white clapboards, and horses give way to boats. San Pedro (locals steadfastly ignore the correct Spanish pronunciation—it's "San Peedro" to

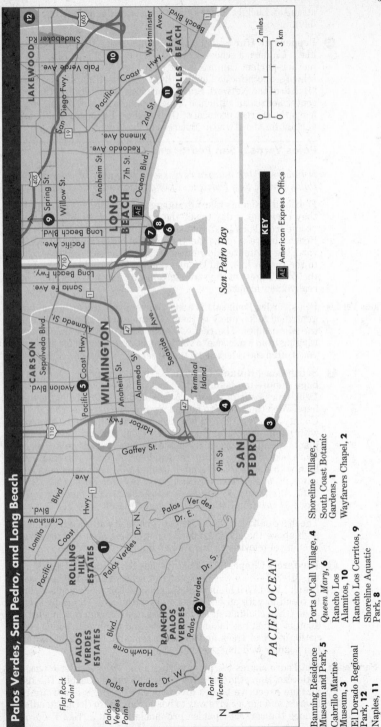

Palos Verdes, San Pedro, and Long Beach

342

KEY

AE American Express Office

Banning Residence Museum and Park, **5**
Cabrillo Marine Museum, **3**
El Dorado Regional Park, **12**
Naples, **11**

Ports O'Call Village, **4**
Queen Mary, **6**
Rancho Los Alamitos, **10**
Rancho Los Cerritos, **9**
Shoreline Aquatic Park, **8**

Shoreline Village, **7**
South Coast Botanic Gardens, **1**
Wayfarers Chapel, **2**

them) is an old seaport community with a strong Mediterranean and Eastern European flavor. There are enticing Greek and Yugoslavian markets and restaurants throughout the town. **Cabrillo Marine Museum** is a gem of a small museum dedicated to the marine life that flourishes off the Southern California coast. Set in a modern Frank Gehry–designed building right on the beach, the museum is popular with school groups because its exhibits are especially instructive as well as fun. The 35 saltwater aquariums include a shark tank, and a see-through tidal tank gives visitors a chance to see the long view of a wave. On the back patio, docents supervise as visitors reach into a shallow tank to touch starfish and sea anemones. *3720 Stephen White Dr., tel. 310/548-7546. Parking $6.60. Admission free. Open Tues.–Fri. noon–5, weekends 10–5.*

If you're lucky enough to visit at low tide, take time to explore the tide pool on nearby Cabrillo Beach (museum staff can direct you).

➍ Ports O' Call Village is a commercial rendition of a New England shipping village, an older version of Fisherman's Village in Marina del Rey, with shops, restaurants, and fast-food windows. Two companies run 1- to 1½-hour harbor cruises ($10 adults, $5 children) and whale-watching cruises, January–April ($15 adults, $5–$8 children). Cruises depart from the village dock; call 310/831–1073 for schedules.

Wilmington In order to preserve transportation and shipping interests for the city of Los Angeles, Wilmington was annexed in the late 19th century. A narrow strip of land, mostly less than a half-mile wide, it **➎** follows the Harbor Freeway from downtown south to the port. **Banning Residence Museum and Park** is a pleasant, low-keyed stop here. General Phineas Banning, an early entrepreneur in Los Angeles, is credited with developing the harbor into a viable economic entity and naming the area Wilmington (he was from Delaware). Part of his estate has been preserved in a 20-acre park that offers excellent picnicking possibilities. A 100-year-old wisteria, near the arbor, blooms in the spring. The interior of the house can be seen on docent-led tours. *401 E. M St., Wilmington, tel. 310/548-7777. Admission to house: $2. House tours Tues.–Thurs. 12:30–2:30, Sat. and Sun. 12:30–3:30, on ½ hr.*

Long Beach Long Beach began as a seaside resort in the 19th century and during the early part of the 20th century was a popular destination for Midwesterners and Dust Bowlers in search of a better life. They built street after street of modest wood homes.

➏ The first glimpse of the ***Queen Mary***—the largest passenger ship ever built, now sitting snugly in Long Beach Harbor—is disarming. What seemed like sure folly when Long Beach officials bought her in 1964 put the city on the proverbial map. The 50,000-ton *Queen Mary* was launched in 1934, a floating treasure of Art Deco splendor. It took a crew of 1,100 to minister to the needs of its 1,900 demanding passengers. Allow a generous half-day to explore this most luxurious of luxury liners, admiring the extensive wood paneling, the gleaming nickel- and silver-plated handrails, and the hand-cut glass. Tours through the ship are available, and guests are invited to browse the 12 decks and witness close-up the bridge, staterooms, officers' quarters, and engine rooms. There are several restaurants and shops on board. *Pier J, tel. 310/435-3511. Admission free. Guided 1-hr tour ($5 adults, $3 children 3–11) daily 10–6.*

➐ **Shoreline Village** is the most successful of the pseudo–New England harbors here. Its setting, between downtown Long Beach and the *Queen Mary*, is reason enough to stroll here, day or evening (when visitors can enjoy the lights of the ship twinkling in the distance). In addition to gift shops and restaurants there's a 1906 carousel with bobbing giraffes, camels, and horses. *Corner of Shoreline Dr. and Pine Ave., tel. 310/590–8427. Rides: 75¢. Carousel open daily 10–10 in summer, 11:30–8 rest of year.*

Time Out   Light and airy by day, romantic with Chinese lanterns by night, **Ciao Chow Express** (245 Pine Ave., tel. 310/495–9022) mixes Italian and Asian cuisine, with dishes such as five-spice duck salad or Fettu China Primavera, all at reasonable prices.

❽ **Shoreline Aquatic Park** (205 Marina Dr.) is literally set in the middle of Long Beach Harbor and is a much-sought-after resting place for RVers. Kite-flyers also love it, because the winds are wonderful here. Casual passersby can enjoy a short walk, where the modern skyline, quaint Shoreline Village, the *Queen Mary,* and the ocean all vie for attention. The park's lagoon is off-limits for swimming, but aquacycles and kayaks can be rented during the summer months. Contact **Long Beach Water Sports** (730 E. 4th St., tel. 310/432–0187) for information on sea kayaking lessons, rentals, and outings.

❾ **Rancho Los Cerritos** is a charming Monterey-style adobe built by the Don Juan Temple family in 1844. Monterey-style homes can be easily recognized by two features: They are always two-storied and have a narrow balcony across the front. It's easy to imagine Zorro, that swashbuckling fictional hero of the rancho era, jumping from the balcony onto a waiting horse and making his escape. The 10 rooms have been furnished in the style of the period and are open for viewing. But don't expect an Old California–style Southwest fantasy, with primitive Mexican furniture and cactus in the garden. The Temple family shared the prevalent taste of the period, in which the American East Coast and Europe still set the style, emphasizing fancy, dark woods and frou-frou Victorian bric-a-brac. The gardens here were designed in the 1930s by well-known landscape architect Ralph Cornell. *4600 Virginia Rd., tel. 310/424–9423. Admission free. Open Wed.–Sun. 1–5. Self-guided tours on weekdays. Free 50-min guided tours on weekends hourly 1–4.*

❿ **Rancho Los Alamitos** is said to be the oldest one-story domestic building still standing in the county. It was built in 1806 when the Spanish flag still flew over California. There's a blacksmith shop in the barn. *6400 E. Bixby Hill Rd., tel. 310/431–3541. Admission free. Open Wed.–Sun. 1–5. 90-min free tours leave every 1/2 hr until 4.*

⓫ The **Naples** section of Long Beach is known for its pleasant and well-maintained canals. Canals in *Naples,* you ask? Yes, this is a misnomer. But better misnamed and successful than aptly named and a bust. The developer who came up with the Naples canal idea learned from the mistakes and bad luck that did in Venice, just up the coast, and built the canals to take full advantage of the tidal flow that would keep them clean. Naples is actually three small islands in man-made Alamitos Bay. It is best experienced on foot—park near Bayshore Drive and 2nd Street and walk across the bridge, where you can begin meandering the quaint streets with very Italian names. This well-restored neighborhood boasts eclectic architecture: vintage Victorians, Craftsman bungalows, and Mission Revivals. You may spy a real gondola or two on the canals. **Gondola Getaway** offers one-hour rides, usually touted for romantic couples, although the gondolas can accommodate up to four people. *5437 E. Ocean Blvd., tel. 310/433–9595. Rides: $50 a couple, $10 for each* *additional person. Reservations essential, at least 1 to 2 wks in advance. Open 4 PM–midnight.*

⑫ El Dorado Regional Park (7550 E. Spring St.) played host to the 1984 Olympic Games archery competition and remains popular with local archery enthusiasts. Most visitors, however, come to this huge, 800-acre park for the broad, shady lawns, walking trails, and the lakes. This is a wonderful picnicking spot. Fishing is permitted in all the lakes (stocked with catfish, carp, and trout), but the northernmost one is favored by local anglers. The Nature Center is a bird and native plant sanctuary.

Highland Park, Pasadena, and San Marino

Numbers in the margin correspond to points of interest on the Highland Park, Pasadena, San Marino map.

The suburbs north of downtown Los Angeles have much of the richest architectural heritage in Southern California as well as several fine museums. To take advantage of the afternoon-only hours of several sites, the Highland part of this tour is best scheduled in the afternoon. Pasadena could take a full day, more if you want to savor the museums' collections.

To reach this area, drive north on the Pasadena Freeway (110), which follows the curves of the arroyo (creek bed) that leads north from downtown. It was the main road north during the early days of Los Angeles, when horses-and-buggies made their way through the chaparral-covered countryside to the small town of Pasadena. In 1942, the road became the Arroyo Seco Parkway, the first freeway in Los Angeles, later renamed the Pasadena Freeway. It remains a pleasant drive in non–rush-hour traffic, with the freeway lined with old sycamores and winding up the arroyo like a New York parkway.

Highland Park Midway between downtown Los Angeles and Pasadena, Highland Park was a genteel suburb in the late 1800s, where the Anglo population tried to keep an Eastern feeling alive in their architecture in spite of the decidedly Southwest landscape. The streets on both sides of the freeway are filled with faded beauties, classic old clapboards that have gone into decline in the past half-century.

❶ Heritage Square is the ambitious attempt by the Los Angeles Cultural Heritage Board to save from the wrecking ball some of the city's architectural gems of the 1865–1914 period. During the past 20 years four residences, a depot, a church, and a carriage barn have been moved to this small park from all over the city. The most breathtaking building here is **Hale House,** built in 1885. The almost-garish colors of both the interior and exterior are not the whim of some aging hippie painter, but rather a faithful re-creation of the palette that was actually in fashion in the late 1800s. The **Palms Depot,** built in 1886, was moved to the site from the Westside of L.A. The night the building was moved, down city streets and up freeways, is documented in photomurals on the depot's walls. *3800 Homer St., off Ave. 43 exit, tel. 818/449–0193. Admission: $5 adults, $3 children 13–17 and senior citizens; $1 children 6–12. Open Sat., Sun., and most holidays noon–4 PM. Tours every 45 min or so.*

❷ El Alisal was the home of eccentric Easterner-turned-Westerner-with-a-vengeance Charles Lummis. This Harvard graduate was captivated by Indian culture (he founded the Southwest Museum), often living the lifestyle of the natives, much to the shock of the staid Angelinos of the time. His home, built from 1898 to 1910, is con-

346

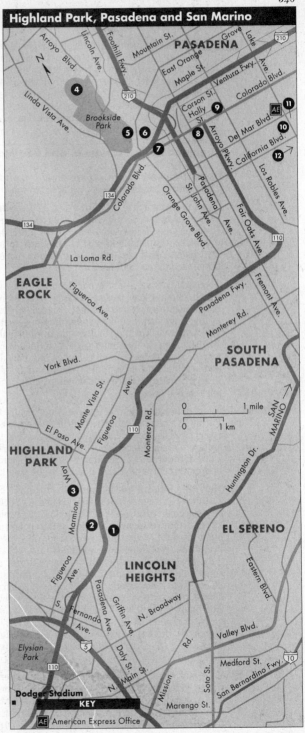

Highland Park, Pasadena and San Marino

structed of boulders from the arroyo itself, a romantic notion until recent earthquakes made the safety of such homes questionable. The Art Nouveau fireplace was designed by Gutzon Borglum, the sculptor of Mount Rushmore. *200 E. Ave. 43 (entrance on Carlota Blvd.), tel. 213/222–0546. Admission free. Open weekends noon–4.*

③ You can spot the **Southwest Museum** from the freeway—it's the huge Mission Revival building standing halfway up Mount Washington. Inside is an extensive collection of Native American art and artifacts, with special emphasis on the people of the Plains, Northwest Coast, Southwest United States, and Northern Mexico. The basket collection is outstanding. *234 Museum Dr., off Ave. 43 exit, tel. 213/221–2163. Admission: $5 adults, $3 senior citizens and students, $2 children 7–18, free to those 6 and under. Open Tues.–Sun. 11–5.*

Time Out Just blocks down the street in either direction from the Southwest Museum you'll discover authentic Mexican food that is downright cheap. The first, **Senior Fish** (5111 Figueroa St., tel. 213/257–2498), looks like a taco stand—but don't pass it up. Its intriguing selections include octopus tostada, scallop burritos, and refreshing ceviche. A few minutes' walk in the other direction, you'll come across **La Abeja** (3700 Figueroa St., tel. 213/221–0474), a Mexican café that's been around for two dozen years. The word inexpensive takes on new meaning at this hangout, known for its salsas and steak picado with chili.

Pasadena Although now fully absorbed into the general Los Angeles sprawl, Pasadena was once a separate and distinctly defined—and refined—city. Its varied architecture, augmented by lush landscaping, is the most spectacular in Southern California. With only a few hours to spend, visitors should consider at least driving past the Gamble House, through Old Town, and then on to the grand old neighborhood of the Huntington Library, spending most of their time there.

④ The **Rose Bowl** (991 Rosemont Ave.) is set at the bottom of a wide area of the arroyo in an older wealthy neighborhood that must endure the periodic onslaught of thousands of cars and party-minded football fans. The stadium is closed except for games and special events such as the monthly Rose Bowl Swap Meet. Held the second Sunday of the month, it is considered the granddaddy of West Coast swap meets.

⑤ **Gamble House,** built by Charles and Henry Greene in 1908, is the most spectacular example of Craftsman-style bungalow architecture. The term "bungalow" can be misleading, since the Gamble House is a huge two-story home. To wealthy Easterners such as the Gambles, this type of vacation home seemed informal compared with their accustomed mansions. What makes visitors swoon here is the incredible amount of hand craftsmanship: the hand-shaped teak interiors, the Greene-designed furniture, the Louis Tiffany glass door. The dark exterior has broad eaves, with many sleeping porches on the second floor. It's on a private road, which is not well marked; take Orange Grove Boulevard to the 300 block to find Westmoreland Place. *4 Westmoreland Pl., tel. 818/793–3334. Admission: $4 adults, $2 students, $3 senior citizens, children 12 and under free. Open Thurs.–Sun. noon–3. 1-hr tours every 15–20 min.*

⑥ The **Pasadena Historical Society** is housed in Fenyes Mansion. The 1905 building still holds the original furniture and paintings on the main and second floors; in the basement, the focus is on Pasadena's history. There are also 4 acres of well-landscaped gardens. *470 W. Walnut St., tel. 818/577–1660. Admission: $4 adults, $3 students and senior citizens, children under 12 free. Open Thurs.–Sun. 1–4.*

7 The **Norton Simon Museum** will be familiar to television viewers of the Rose Parade: The sleek, modern building makes a stunning background for the passing floats. Like the more famous Getty Museum, the Norton Simon is a tribute to the art acumen of an extremely wealthy businessman. In 1974, Simon reorganized the failing Pasadena Museum of Modern Art and assembled one of the world's finest collections, richest in its Rembrandts, Goyas, Degas, and Picassos—and dotted with Rodin sculptures throughout. Rembrandt's development can be traced in three oils—"The Bearded Man in the Wide Brimmed Hat," "Self Portrait," and "Titus." The most dramatic Goyas are two oils—"St. Jerome" and the portrait of "Dona Francisca Vicenta Chollet y Caballero." Down the walnut-and-steel staircase is the Degas gallery. Picasso's renowned "Woman with Book" highlights a comprehensive collection of his paintings, drawings, and sculptures. The museum's collections of Impressionist (van Gogh, Matisse, Cézanne, Monet, Renoir, et al.) and Cubist (Braque, Gris) work is extensive. Older works include Southeast Asian artworks from 100 BC and bronze, stone, and ivory sculptures from India, Cambodia, Thailand, and Nepal. The museum also has a wealth of Early Renaissance, Baroque, and Rococo artworks: Church works by Raphael, Guariento, de Paolo, Filippino Lippi, and Lucas Cranach give way to robust Rubens maidens and Dutch landscapes, still lifes, and portraits by Frans Hals, Jacob van Ruisdael, and Jan Steen, and a magical Tiepolo ceiling highlights the Rococo period. The most recent addition to the collection are seven 19th-century Russian paintings. *411 W. Colorado Blvd., tel. 818/449–6840. Admission: $4 adults, $2 students and senior citizens, children under 12 free. Open Thurs.–Sun. noon–6.*

8 A half-mile east of the museum, **Old Town Pasadena** is an ambitious, ongoing restoration. Having fallen into seedy decay in the past 50 years, the area is being revitalized as a blend of restored brick buildings with a yuppie overlay. Rejuvenated buildings include bistros, elegant restaurants, and boutiques. On Raymond Street, the Hotel Green, now the Castle Apartments, dominates the area. Once a posh resort hotel, the Green is now a faded Moorish fantasy of domes, turrets, and balconies reminiscent of the Alhambra but with, true to its name, a greenish tint. Holly Street, between Fair Oaks and Arroyo, is home to several shops offering an excellent selection of vintage '50s objects, jewelry, and clothes; it's an area that's best explored on foot. Old Town is bisected by Colorado Boulevard, which west of Old Town rises onto the **Colorado Street Bridge,** a raised section of roadway on graceful arches built in 1912 and restored in 1993. On New Year's Day throngs of people line Colorado Boulevard to watch the Rose Parade.

9 The **Pacific Asia Museum** is the gaudiest Chinese-style building in Los Angeles outside of Chinatown. Designed in the style of a Northern Chinese imperial palace with a central courtyard, it is devoted entirely to the arts and crafts of Asia and the Pacific Islands. Most of the objects are on loan from private collections and other museums, and there are usually changing special exhibits that focus on the objects of one country. *46 N. Los Robles Dr., tel. 818/449–2742. Admission: $3 adults, $1.50 students and senior citizens, children free. Open Wed.–Sun. noon–5.*

⑩ **Kidspace** is a children's museum housed in the gymnasium of an elementary school. Here kids can talk to a robot, direct a television or radio station, dress up in the real (and very heavy) uniforms of a fire fighter, an astronaut, a football player, and more. "Critter Caverns" beckons with its large tree house and secret tunnels for exploring insect life up close (don't worry, the bugs are fake). "Illusions" teases one's ability to perceive what is real and what is illusion. *390 S. El Molino Ave., tel. 818/449–9144. Admission: $5 adults and children over 2, $2.50 children 2 and under, $3.50 senior citizens. Open during the school year, Wed. 2–5, weekends 12:30–5; school vacations Mon.–Fri. 1–5; summer Tues.–Fri. 1–5.*

⑪ The **Ritz-Carlton, Huntington Hotel** (1401 S. Oak Knoll Ave., tel. 818/568–3900) is situated in Pasadena's most genteel neighborhood, Oak Knoll, close to San Marino. The hotel, built in 1906, reopened in March of 1991, after five years of renovations necessary to bring it up to earthquake code standards. The original design was scrupulously preserved, including the Japanese and Horseshoe Gardens. Don't miss the historic Picture Bridge with its murals depicting scenes of California along its 20 gables.

San Marino If you only have time for one stop in the Pasadena area, it should be **⑫** the **Huntington Library, Art Gallery, and Botanical Gardens,** the area's most important site. Railroad tycoon Henry E. Huntington built his hilltop home in the early 1900s; since then it has established a reputation as one of the most extraordinary cultural complexes in the world, annually receiving more than a half-million visitors. The library contains 6 million items, including such treasures as a Gutenberg Bible, the earliest known edition of Chaucer's *Canterbury Tales,* George Washington's genealogy in his own handwriting, and first editions by Ben Franklin and Shakespeare. In the library's hallway are five tall hexagonal towers displaying important books and manuscripts. The art gallery, devoted to British art from the 18th and 19th centuries, contains the original "Blue Boy" by Gainsborough, "Pinkie," a companion piece by Lawrence, and the monumental "Sarah Siddons as the Tragic Muse" by Reynolds.

The Huntington's awesome 130-acre garden, formerly the grounds of the estate, now includes a 12-acre Desert Garden featuring the largest group of mature cacti and other succulents in the world, all arranged by continent. The Japanese Garden offers traditional Japanese plants, stone ornaments, a moon bridge, a Japanese house, a bonsai court, and a Zen rock garden. Besides these gardens, there are collections of azaleas and 1,500 varieties of camellias, the world's largest public collection. The 1,000-variety rose garden displays its collection historically so that the development leading to today's strains of roses can be observed. There are also herb, palm, and jungle gardens plus a Shakespeare garden, where plants mentioned in Shakespeare's works are grown.

The Huntington Pavilion, built in 1980, offers visitors unmatched views of the surrounding mountains and valleys and houses a bookstore, displays, and information kiosks as well. Both the east and west wings of the pavilion display paintings on public exhibition for the first time. The Ralph M. Parsons Botanical Center at the pavilion includes a botanical library, a herbarium, and a laboratory for research on plants.

Visitors to this vast property have several options, including: a 12-minute slide show introducing the Huntington; a 1¼-hour guided tour of the gardens; a 45-minute audio tape about the art gallery (which can be rented for a nominal fee); a 15-minute introductory talk about the library; and inexpensive, self-guided tour leaflets. *1151 Oxford Rd., tel. 818/405–2100. Donation requested. Open Tues.–Fri. 1–4:30, weekends 10:30–4:30. Reservations required Sun.*

The San Fernando Valley

The hardest-hit area in the January 1994 earthquake was the San Fernando Valley, a vast sprawl of communities northwest of downtown Los Angeles, past Hollywood and accessible through the Cahuenga Pass (where the Hollywood Freeway now runs). Although there are other valleys in the Los Angeles area, this is the one that people refer to simply as "the Valley." Sometimes there is a note of derision in their tone, since the Valley is still struggling with its stepchild status. City people still see it as a mere collection of bedroom communities, not worth serious thought. But the Valley has come a long way since the early 20th century when it was mainly orange groves and small ranches. It's now home to over one million people (it even has its own monthly magazine), a solidly middle-class area of neat bungalows and ranch-style homes situated on tidy parcels of land, with shopping centers never too far away. It boasts fine restaurants and several major movie and television studios.

The earthquake disrupted the Valley's network of freeways and left widespread property damage. Unless noted otherwise, all of the attractions described here are operating again, though you may have to find an alternate route to get there, and you'll see lots of collapsed buildings along the way. We group the major attractions of the Valley into one Exploring section to give readers a sense of the place, but because the Valley is such a vast area, focus on one or two attractions and make them the destination for a half- or full-day trip. Rush-hour traffic jams on the San Diego and Hollywood freeways used to be brutal even before the earthquake shattered the roadways—until the freeways are repaired, don't even try to drive up here unless it's midday.

Universal City If you drive into the area on the Hollywood Freeway, through the Cahuenga Pass, you'll come first to one of the most recently developed areas of the Valley: Universal City. It is a one-industry town and that industry is Universal Studios. Its history goes back decades as a major film and television studio, but in the past few years it has also become a major tourist attraction. Today this hilly area boasts the Universal Studios Tour, the Universal Amphitheater, a major movie complex, hotels, and restaurants.

Universal Studios Hollywood and CityWalk is the best place in Los Angeles for seeing behind the scenes of the movie industry. The five- to seven-hour Universal tour is an enlightening and amusing (if a bit sensational) day at the world's largest television and movie studio, complete with live shows based on "Miami Vice," *Conan the Barbarian,* and "Star Trek." The complex stretches across more than 420 acres, many of which are traversed during the course of the tour by trams featuring usually witty running commentary by enthusiastic guides. You can experience the parting of the Red Sea, an avalanche, and a flood, meet a 30-foot-tall version of King Kong, live through an encounter with a runaway train, be attacked by the ravenous killer shark of *Jaws* fame, and endure a confrontation by aliens armed with death rays—all without ever leaving the safety of the tram. And now, thanks to the magic of Hollywood, you can also experience the perils of The Big One—an all-too-real simulation of an 8.3 earthquake, complete with collapsing earth, deafening train wrecks, floods, and other life-threatening amusements. There is a New England village, an aged European town, and a replica of an archetypal New York street. The newest exhibits are *Back to the Future,* a $60 million flight simulator disguised as a DeLorean car that shows off state-of-the-art special effects, and *Lucy: A Tribute to Lucille Ball,* a 2,200-square-foot heart-shaped museum containing a re-creation of the set from the "I Love Lucy" television show, plus other artifacts from the hit 1950s program. At the Entertainment Center, the longest and last stop of the day, you can stroll around to enjoy various shows: In one theater animals beguile you with their tricks; in another you can pose for a photo session with the Incredible Hulk; at Castle Dracula you'll confront a variety of terrifying monsters; and at the Star Trek Theater, you can have yourself filmed and inserted as an extra in a scene from a galactic adventure already released. CityWalk opened in 1993, with a slew of quaint shops and restaurants, including Spago, a copy of the star-studded Sunset Strip restaurant. *100 Universal City Pl., tel. 818/508–9600. Box office open daily 9–7. Admission: $29 adults, $23 senior citizens and children 3–11.*

Burbank   Warner Brothers and Columbia Studios share the lot of **Burbank Studios,** where a two-hour guided walking tour is available. Because the tours involve a lot of walking, you should dress comfortably and casually. This tour is somewhat technically oriented and centered more on the actual workings of filmmaking than the one at Universal. It also varies from day to day to take advantage of goings-on on the lot. Most tours see the back-lot sets, prop construction department, and sound complex. *400 Warner Blvd., tel. 818/954–1008. Tours on the hr, weekdays 9–3. Admission: $25. No children under 10 permitted. Reservations essential, 1 wk in advance.*

NBC Television Studios are also in Burbank, as any regular viewer of *The Tonight Show* can't help knowing. For those who wish to be part of a live studio audience, free tickets are still being made available for tapings of the various NBC shows, and studio tours are offered daily. *3000 W. Alameda Ave., Burbank, tel. 818/840–3537. Tours daily 1–3. Admission: $6 adults, $3.75 children, under 5 free.*

San Fernando   San Fernando, in the northeast corner of the valley that bears its name, is one of the few separate cities in the Valley. It has only one important attraction: **Mission San Fernando Rey de España,** one of a chain of 21 missions established by 1823, which extend from San Diego to Sonoma along the coastal route known as El Camino Real. Today U.S. 101 parallels the historic Mission Trail and is one of the state's most popular tour routes. Today, as you walk through the mission's arched corridors, you may experience déjà vu—and you probably have seen it before, in an episode of "Gunsmoke," "Dragnet," or dozens of movies. In 1991, the wacky Steve Martin comedy *L. A. Story* was filmed here. The church's interior is decorated with Indian designs and artifacts of Spanish craftsmanship depicting the mission's 18th-century culture. There is a small museum and gift shop. *15151 San Fernando Mission Blvd., tel. 818/361–0186. Admission: $4 adults, $3 senior citizens and children 7–15. Open daily 9–5.*

Encino   The main attraction at **Los Encinos State Historic Park** is the early California dwelling, which was built in 1849 by Don Vicente de la Osa and is furnished with historically accurate furniture, household goods and tools, and a two-story French-style home, dated 1870. The grounds are serene, especially on weekdays, when there are fewer people around, and you may have the duck pond and shade trees largely to yourself. *16756 Moorpark St., tel. 818/784–4849. Admission to house: $2 adults, $1 children 6–15, under 6 free. Tours available Wed.–Sun. 1–4.*

Calabasas   Calabasas, in the southwest corner of the Valley, was once a stage-coach stop on the way from Ventura to Los Angeles. The name means "pumpkins" in Spanish. The little town has retained some of the flavor of its early days. The **Leonis Adobe** is one of the most charming adobes in the county, due in part to its fairly rural setting and barnyard animals, especially the Spanish red hens. With a little concentration, visitors can imagine life in the early years. The house was originally built as a one-story adobe, but in 1844 Miguel Leonis decided to remodel rather than move and added a second story with a balcony. *Voila!* A Monterey-style home. The furnishings are authentic to the period. Considering its distance, this stop is most highly recommended for history buffs. *23537 Calabasas Rd., tel. 818/222–6511. Admission free. Open Wed.–Sun. 1–4.*

Time Out   **The Sagebrush Cantina** (23527 Calabasas Rd., tel. 818/222–6062), just next door to the Leonis Adobe, is a casual, outdoorsy place, and perfect for families. The specialty here, as the name suggests, is Mexican fare. There's a large bar for the singles set and outdoor tables for leisurely meals. It's busy—and best—on weekends.

Other Places of Interest

Scattered across Los Angeles County are attractions that don't fit neatly into any organized drive or walk. Some, such as Dodger Stadium, are major sites. Others, such as Watts Towers, are quirky places. If Los Angeles is anything, it's a something-for-everybody city.

Dodger Stadium has been home of the Los Angeles Dodgers since 1961, when Chavez Ravine was chosen as the site of the former Brooklyn team's home base. The stadium seats 56,000 and parking is fairly easy. *1000 Elysian Park Ave., tel. 213/224–1400, accessible from the Pasadena Freeway just north of downtown Los Angeles. Open only during games.*

El Mercado lies in East Los Angeles, the heart of the Mexican barrio. While Olvera Street draws both Mexican and gringo customers, this is the real thing: a huge, three-story marketplace that's a close cousin to places like Libertadad in Guadalajara. There are trinkets (piñatas and soft-clay pottery) to buy here, but the real draws are the authentic foods and mariachi music. The mid-level food shops offer hot tortillas, Mexican herbs, sauces, and cheeses. Upstairs is where the action is, especially on weekends when several local mariachi bands stake out corners of the floor and entertain—all at the same time. You'll either love it or hate it. The food on the top floor is only so-so, but the feeling of Old Mexico is palpable. *3425 E. 1st St., Los Angeles, tel. 213/268–3451. Open weekdays 10–8, later on weekends.*

Exposition Park was the site of the 1932 Olympics and the impressive architecture still stands. Adjoining the University of Southern California *(see below)*, Exposition Park is the location of two major museums: the **California Museum of Science and Industry** and the **Natural History Museum**. Also included in the 114-acre park is the **Los Angeles Swimming Stadium** (home of Los Angeles aquatic competitions), which is open to the public in summer, and **Memorial Coliseum**, the site of college football games. There are plenty of picnic areas on the grounds as well as a sunken rose garden. *Figueroa St. at Exposition Blvd., Los Angeles.*

Forest Lawn Memorial Park is more than just a cemetery: It covers 300 formally landscaped acres and features a major collection of marble statuary and art treasures, including a replica of Leonardo da Vinci's "The Last Supper" done entirely in stained glass. In the Hall of the Crucifixion–Resurrection is one of the world's largest oil paintings incorporating a religious theme, "The Crucifixion" by artist Jan Styka. The picturesque grounds are perfect for a leisurely walk. Forest Lawn was the model for the setting of Evelyn Waugh's novel *The Loved One.* Many celebrities are buried here, some more flamboyantly than others. Silent-screen cowboy star Tom Mix is said to be buried in his good-guy clothes: white coat, white pants, and a belt buckle with his name spelled out in diamonds. Markers for Walt Disney and Errol Flynn are near the Freedom Mausoleum. Inside the mausoleum are the wall crypts of Nat King Cole, Clara Bow, Gracie Allen, and Alan Ladd. Clark Gable, Carole Lombard, Theda Bara, and Jean Harlow are among the luminaries buried in the Great Mausoleum. *1712 S. Glendale Ave., Glendale, tel. 213/254–3131. Open daily 8–5.*

Forest Lawn Memorial Park–Hollywood Hills is the 340-acre sister park to Forest Lawn Glendale, situated just west of Griffith Park on the north slope of the Hollywood Hills. Dedicated to the theme of American liberty, it features bronze and marble statuary including Thomas Ball's 60-foot Washington Memorial and a replica of the Liberty Bell. There are also reproductions of Boston's Old North Church and Longfellow's Church of the Hills. The film *The Many Voices of Freedom* is shown daily and Revolutionary War documents are on permanent display. Among the famous people buried here are Buster Keaton, Stan Laurel, Liberace, Charles Laughton, and Freddie Prinze. *6300 Forest Lawn Dr., Hollywood, tel. 213/254–7251. Open daily 8–5.*

Gene Autry Western Heritage Museum celebrates the American West, both the movie and real-life versions, with memorabilia, artifacts, and art in a structure that draws on Spanish Mission and early Western architecture. The collection includes Teddy Roosevelt's Colt revolver, Buffalo Bill Cody's saddle, and Annie Oakley's goldplated Smith and Wesson guns, alongside video screens showing clips from old Westerns. *4700 W. Heritage Way, Los Angeles, tel. 213/667–2000. Admission: $7 adults, $5 senior citizens, $3 children 2–12. Open Tues.–Sun. 10–5.*

Griffith Park Observatory and Planetarium, located on the south side of Mount Hollywood in the heart of Griffith Park, offers dazzling daily shows that duplicate the starry sky. A guide narrates the show and points out constellations. One of the largest telescopes in the world is open to the public for free viewing every clear night. Exhibits display models of the planets with photographs from satellites and spacecraft. A Laserium show is featured nightly, and other special astronomy shows are offered frequently. The outside decks and walkways offer a spectacular view of the city, very popular on warm evenings; you may recognize the location from *Rebel Without a Cause,* the James Dean movie classic. *Griffith Park, tel. 213/664–1191. Enter at the Los Feliz Blvd. and Vermont Ave. entrance. Hall of Science and telescope are free. Planetarium shows: $4 adults, $3 senior citizens, $2 children. Laserium show: $6.50 adults, $5.50 children. Call for schedule. Open Tues.–Fri. 2–10, weekends 12:30–10.*

Hollyhock House was the first of several houses Frank Lloyd Wright designed in the Los Angeles area. Built in 1921 and commissioned by heiress Aline Barnsdall, it exemplifies the pre-Columbian style Wright was fond of at that time. As a unifying theme, he used a stylized hollyhock flower, which appears in a broad band around the exterior of the house and even on the dining room chairs. Now owned by the city, as is Barnsdall Park, where it is located, Hollyhock House has been restored and furnished with original furniture designed by Wright and reproductions. His furniture may not be the comfiest in the world, but it sure looks perfect in his homes. *4800 Hollywood Blvd., Hollywood, tel. 213/662–7272. Admission: $1.50 adults, $1 senior citizens, children free. Tours conducted Tues.–Sun. at noon, 1, 2, and 3.*

Mulholland Drive, one of the most famous thoroughfares in Los Angeles, makes its very winding way from the Hollywood Hills across the spine of the Santa Monica Mountains west almost to the Pacific Ocean. Driving its length is slow, but the reward is sensational views of the city, the San Fernando Valley, and the expensive homes along the way. For a quick shot, take Benedict Canyon north from Sunset Boulevard, just west of the Beverly Hills Hotel, all the way to the top and turn right at the crest, which is Mulholland. There's a turnout within a few feet of the intersection, and at night, the view of the valley side is incredible.

University of Southern California (USC, or simply "SC" to the locals) is the oldest major private university on the West Coast. The pleasant campus, which is home to nearly 30,000 students, is often used as a backdrop for television shows and movies. Two of the more notable of its 191 buildings are the Romanesque **Doheny Memorial Library** and **Widney Hall,** the oldest building on campus, a two-story clapboard dated 1880. The **Mudd Memorial Hall of Philosophy** contains a collection of rare books from the 13th through 15th centuries. *Bounded by Figueroa, Jefferson, Exposition, and Vermont, and adjacent to Exposition Park, tel. 213/740–2300. Free 1-hr campus tours weekdays 10–2, on the hr.*

Watts Towers is the folk-art legacy of an Italian immigrant tile-setter, Simon Rodia, and one of the great folk-art structures in the world. From 1920 until 1945, without helpers, this eccentric and driven man erected three cement towers, using pipes, bed frames, and anything else he could find, and embellished them with bits of colored glass, broken pottery, sea shells, and assorted discards. The tallest tower is 107 feet. Plans are under way to stabilize and protect this unique monument, often compared to the 20th-century architectural wonders created by Barcelona's Antoni Gaudí. Well worth a pilgrimage for art and architecture buffs (or anyone else, for that matter). *1765 E. 107th St., Los Angeles.*

Los Angeles for Free

In Los Angeles, every day is a free event in terms of nature; the sun, sand, and ocean alone can fill a vacation. But there are plenty of other free activities, events, and cultural attractions to keep even those with limited budgets busy.

Cabrillo Marine Museum. *See* Palos Verdes, San Pedro, and Long Beach, *above.*

Christmas Boat Parades at many local marinas celebrate Christmas in a special way. Boat owners decorate their boats with strings of lights and holiday displays and then cruise in a line for dockside visitors to see. Call for specific dates (Marina del Rey, tel. 310/821–0555; Port of Los Angeles, tel. 310/519–3508).

Craft and Folk Art Museum. *See* Wilshire Boulevard, *above.*

El Alisal. *See* Highland Park, Pasadena, and San Marino, *above.*

El Mercado. *See* Other Places of Interest, *above.*

El Pueblo de Los Angeles Historical Monument. *See* Downtown Los Angeles, *above.*

Farmer's Market. *See* Wilshire Boulevard, *above.*

Forest Lawn Memorial Park. *See* Other Places of Interest, *below.*

Grand Central Market. *See* Downtown Los Angeles, *above.*

Greystone Mansion. *See* The Westside, *above.*

Hollywood Memorial Cemetery. *See* Hollywood, *above.*

Huntington Library, Art Gallery, and Botanical Gardens has a policy of admission by voluntary donation, which can be as little as you want. *See* Highland Park, Pasadena, and San Marino, *above.*

J. Paul Getty Museum. *See* Santa Monica, Venice, Pacific Palisades, and Malibu, *above.*

La Brea Tar Pits. *See* Wilshire Boulevard, *above.*

Laurel and Hardy's Piano Stairway. *See* Off the Beaten Track, *below.*

Leonis Adobe. *See* The San Fernando Valley, *above.*

Mulholland Drive. *See* Other Places of Interest, *above.*

Polo Games at Will Rogers State Historic Park. *See* Santa Monica, Venice, Pacific Palisades, and Malibu, *above.*

Rancho Los Alamitos. *See* Palos Verdes, San Pedro, and Long Beach, *above.*

Rancho Los Cerritos. *See* Palos Verdes, San Pedro, and Long Beach, *above.*

Rose Parade, seen from the streets (rather than the bleachers), is as free as it is on television. Arrive before dawn and dress warmly. Thousands of residents prefer to watch on television and then go out to East Pasadena a day or two later to view the floats, which are parked there for a few days for observation. *Corner of Sierra Madre Blvd. and Washington St., Pasadena. Call for viewing hrs, tel. 818/449–ROSE.*

Santa Anita Racetrack Workouts are held during the racing season (December 26–late April). The public is welcome to come out early in the morning to watch the workouts from the grandstands. There is an announcer who'll keep you advised of the horses' names and times. Breakfast is available in the restaurant. *Santa Anita Park, 285 W. Huntington Dr., Arcadia, tel. 818/574–7223. Enter Gate 8 off Baldwin Ave. or Gate 3 off Huntington Dr. Open 7:30 AM–9:30 AM.*

Santa Monica Mountains Nature Walks are led by rangers and docents of the many parks in the Santa Monica Mountains. There's an ambitious schedule of walks for all interests, ages, and levels of exertion. These include wildflower walks, moonlight hikes, tide-pool explorations, and much more. Several outings are held every day. For updated information, call the National Park Service (tel. 818/597–9192).

UCLA. *See* The Westside, *above.*

USC. *See* Other Places of Interest, *above.*

Watts Towers. *See* Other Places of Interest, *above.*

Westwood Memorial Park. *See* The Westside, *above.*

Off the Beaten Track

The Flower Market (just east of downtown, in the 700 block of Wall Street) is a block-long series of stores and stalls that open up in the middle of the night to sell wholesale flowers and house plants to the city's florists, who rush them to their shops to sell that day. Many of the stalls stay open until late morning to sell leftovers to the general public at the same bargain prices. And what glorious leftovers they are: Hawaiian ginger, Dutch tulips, Chilean freesia. The public is welcome after 9 AM and the stock is quickly depleted by 11 AM.

Even if you don't buy, it's a heady experience to be surrounded by so much fragile beauty.

Laurel and Hardy's Piano Stairway (923–927 Vendome St., in the Silverlake section of Los Angeles, a few miles northeast of downtown) was the setting for the famous scene in 1932 film *The Music Box* where Stan Laurel and Oliver Hardy try to get a piano up an outdoor stairway. The stairway remains today much as it was then.

Orcutt Ranch Horticultural Center (23600 Roscoe Blvd., Canoga Park, tel. 818/883–6641, admission free), once owned by William Orcutt, a well-known geologist who was one of the excavators of the La Brea Tar Pits, is a surprisingly lush and varied garden in the west San Fernando Valley. Orcutt is filled with interesting little areas to explore, such as the rose garden, herb garden, and stream banked with shady trees and ferns (a wonderful picnic site). The house, where the Orcutts lived, is open to the public every day, 8–5. Two weekends a year (late June or early July) the extensive orange and grapefruit groves are open for public picking. It's a chance to enjoy the Valley as it was in the years when groves like these covered the landscape for miles. You'll need an A-frame ladder or a special pole for dislodging the fruit up high. Bring along grocery sacks.

Pig Murals (on the corner of Bandini and Soto streets in Vernon) were probably the first public murals in Los Angeles. They were originally painted on the outside walls of the Farmer John Company by Leslie Grimes, who was killed in a fall from the scaffolding while painting. They depict bucolic scenes of farms and contented pigs, rather an odd juxtaposition to what goes on inside the packing plant. Vernon is the heart of Los Angeles's meat-packing industry and to be stuck in traffic on a hot summer afternoon in this part of town is an odorific experience not soon forgotten.

Shopping

By Jane E. Lasky

When asked where they want to shop, visitors to Los Angeles inevitably answer, "Rodeo Drive." But this famous thoroughfare is only one of many enticing shopping streets Los Angeles has to offer. And there's also mall shopping, which in Los Angeles is an experience unto itself—the mall is the modern-day Angelino's equivalent of a main street, town square, back fence, malt shop, and county fair, all rolled into one. Distances between shopping spots can be vast, however, so don't choose too many different stops in one day—if you do, you'll spend more time driving than shopping!

Most Los Angeles shops are open from 10 to 6 although many remain open until 9 or later, particularly at the shopping centers, on Melrose Avenue, and in Westwood Village during the summer. Melrose shops, on the whole, don't get moving until 11 AM but are often open Sunday, too. At most stores around town, credit cards are almost universally accepted and traveler's checks are also often allowed with proper identification. If you're looking for sales, check the *Los Angeles Times*.

Shopping Districts

Downtown Although downtown Los Angeles has many enclaves to explore, we suggest that the bargain hunter head straight for the **Cooper Building** (860 S. Los Angeles St., tel. 213/622–1139). Eight floors of small clothing and shoe shops (mostly for women) offer some of the most fantastic discounts in the city. Grab a free map in the lobby, and seek out as many of the 82 shops as you can handle. Nearby are

American Express offers Travelers Cheques built for two.

Cheques *for Two*™ from American Express are the Travelers Cheques that allow either of you to use them because both of you have signed them. And only one of you needs to be present to purchase them.

Cheques *for Two* are accepted anywhere regular American Express Travelers Cheques are, which is just about everywhere. So stop by your bank, AAA* or any American Express Travel Service Office and ask for Cheques *for Two*.

Travelers Cheques

Pack light.
Take the one number you need for any kind of call, anywhere you travel.

Checking in with your family back home? Calling for a tow truck? When you're on the road, the phone you use might not accept your calling card. Or you might get overcharged by an unknown telephone company. Here's the solution: dial 1 800 CALL ATT.℠ You'll get flawless AT&T service, competitive calling card prices, and the lowest prices for collect calls from any phone, anywhere. Travel light. Just bring along this one simple number: 1 800 CALL ATT.

myriad discount outlets selling everything from shoes to suits to linens.

Near the Hilton Hotel, **Seventh Street Marketplace** (735 S. Figueroa, tel. 213/955–7150) is an indoor/outdoor multilevel shopping center with an extensive courtyard that boasts many busy cafés and lively music. The stores surrounding this courtyard include **G.B. Harb** (tel. 213/624–4785), a fine menswear shop, and **Bullocks** (tel. 213/624–9494), a small version of the big department store, geared to the businessperson.

Melrose Avenue
West Hollywood, especially Melrose Avenue, is where young shoppers should try their luck, as should those who appreciate vintage styles in clothing and furnishings. The 1½ miles of Melrose from La Brea to a few blocks west of Crescent Heights is definitely one of Los Angeles's trendiest shopping areas, with loads of intriguing one-of-a-kind shops and bistros; both east and west of this delineation, Melrose has some other very worthwhile stores, too. A sampling of Melrose stores:

Betsey Johnson (7311 Melrose Ave., tel. 213/931–4490) offers the designer's vivid, hip women's fashions. Watch for twice-yearly sales. **Comme des Fous** (7384 Melrose Ave., tel. 213/653–5330) is an avant-garde (and pricey) clothing shop packed with innovative European designs many women would consider daring to wear. **Cottura** (7215 Melrose Ave., tel. 213/933–1928) offers brightly colored Italian ceramics. **Emphasis** (7361 Melrose Ave., tel. 213/653–7174) offers a pristine collection of fashion-forward clothes for women, including hats, belts, accessories, and a selection of unique lingerie. **Fantasies Come True** (8012 Melrose Ave., tel. 213/655–2636) greets you with "When You Wish upon a Star" playing from a tape deck. The store, needless to say, is packed with Walt Disney memorabilia. **Fred Segal** (8118 Melrose Ave., tel. 213/651–1935) has a collection of shops providing stylish clothing for men and women. Among the designers and manufacturers they carry: Nancy Heller, New Man, Ralph Lauren, Calvin Klein. Children's clothing, accessories, and shoes—an impressive array—are also stocked at the Melrose store. **Harari** (8463 Melrose Ave., tel. 213/463–4413) is, according to this store's hype, "more than just a clothing store." Surprisingly, this is true–the sales staff act as wardrobe consultants, mixing and matching the upscale fashions for a loyal clientele, both locals and out-of-towners. **Kanji** (7320½ Melrose Ave., tel. 213/933–6364) carries an alluring mixture of conservative fashions and clothing with flair. You'll find European-style dresses, pants, and suits.

L.A. Eyeworks (7407 Melrose Ave., tel. 213/653–8255) is a hip boutique run by the world's most successful eye-fashion prognosticators; frame-wise, whatever's next in style around the globe will probably show up first in this leading-edge shop. **Modern Living** (8125 Melrose Ave., tel. 213/655–3898) is a gallery of 20th-century design, representing renowned international furniture designers, including Philippe Starck, Ettore Sottsass, and Massino Iosaghini. **Off the Wall** (7325 Melrose Ave., tel. 213/930–1185) specializes in "antiques and weird stuff": translation—20th-century nostalgia items such as rare Bakelite radios, vintage vending machines, and period furnishings. **Pole** (7378 Melrose Ave., tel. 213/653–3784) offers very progressive women's clothing, with predominantly French labels like Morgan, Tehen, and Kookai. The clientele tends to be body-conscious and fashion-conscious. **Texas Soul** (7515 Melrose Ave., tel. 213/658–5571) is the place for western footwear made in—you guessed it—the Lone Star State. Top-of-the-line boots such as Tony Lama's are big sellers, as are the tooled belts, leather jackets, and spurs that adorn this popular shop. **Time After Time** (7425 Melrose Ave., tel. 213/653–8463), decorated to resemble a Victorian garden, has time-honored garments ranging from turn-of-the-century to the 1960s, especially antique wedding dresses. **Wacko** (7416 Melrose Ave., tel. 213/651–3811) is a wild space crammed with all manner of blow-up toys, cards, and other semi-useless items that make good Los Angeles keepsakes. **Wasteland** (7428 Melrose Ave., tel. 213/653–3028) carries an extensive collection of retro clothing, both used and never-worn, all reasonably priced. It's a fun place to shop for '50s bowling shirts, '40s rayon dresses, funky ties, worn jeans, and leather jackets. **Wild Blue** (7220 Melrose Ave., tel. 213/939–8434) is a fine shop/gallery specializing in functional and wearable art created by exceptional contemporary artists, many of whom hail from the L.A. area. **Wound and Wound** (7374 Melrose Ave., tel. 213/653–6703) has an impressive collection of wind-up toys and music boxes.

Larchmont
One of L.A.'s most picturesque streets is Larchmont Boulevard, adjacent to the expensive residential neighborhood of Hancock Park. Stores that make Larchmont Village worth a detour include **Hollyhock** (214 N. Larchmont Blvd., tel. 213/931–3400), for exceptional new and antique furnishings; **Lavender & Lace** (660 N. Larchmont Blvd., tel. 213/856–4846), specializing in antique textiles, linens, and English pine furniture; **My Favorite Place** (202 N. Larchmont Blvd., tel. 213/461–5713), for comfortable women's clothing—silks and ethnic pieces in particular; and **Robert Grounds** (119 N. Larchmont Blvd., tel. 213/464–8304), for distinctive gifts and antiques.

Westwood
Westwood Village, near the UCLA campus, is a young and lively area for shopping. The atmosphere is invigorating, especially during summer evenings when there's a movie line around every corner, all kinds of people strolling the streets (an unusual phenomenon in L.A., where few folks ever walk anywhere), and cars cruising along to take in the scene. Among the shops worth scouting out in this part of the city:

Aah's (1083 Broxton, tel. 310/824–1688) is good for stationery and fun gift items. **Copelands Sports** (1001 Westwood Blvd., tel. 310/208–6444) offers a cornucopia of sportswear, beachwear, shoes, and shorts, along with a variety of skiing, camping, and other outdoor equipment. **Morgan and Company** (1131 Glendon, tel. 310/208–3377) is recommended for California jewelry. **Shanes Jewelers** (1065 Broxton, tel. 310/208–8404) is a youth-oriented jewelry store specializing in earrings, engagement rings, chains, and watches, at prices that are comparable to wholesale. There is a good repair department. **Sisterhood Book Store** (1351 Westwood Blvd., tel. 310/477–7300) stocks an incredible collection of women's books in all areas—history, health, and psychology among them. **The Wilger Company** (10924 Weyburn, tel. 310/208–4321) offers fine men's clothing with a conservative look, most of it carrying the store's own private label, though other lines like Polo are also stocked.

The Beverly Center and Environs
The **Beverly Center** (tel. 310/854–0070), bound by Beverly Boulevard, La Cienega Boulevard, San Vicente Boulevard, and 3rd Street, covers more than 7 acres and contains some 200 stores. Examples are **By Design** for contemporary home furnishings; **Shauna Stein** and **Ice** for fashionable (and very pricey) women's clothes; **Alexio,** for fashionable men's garments; and two stores called **Traffic** for contemporary clothing for both genders. One of the more innovative and popular stores here is **M.A.C.,** which offers a line of

professional make-up at reasonable prices, sold by knowledgeable staff who help with quick-to-apply beauty hints.

The shopping center is anchored by the **Broadway** department store on one end and **Bullocks** on the other, and it has one of Los Angeles's finest multi-theater complexes, with 14 individual movie theaters. There are also some interesting restaurants, like the **Kisho-an,** a Japanese restaurant known for its fine sushi, and **The Hard Rock Cafe,** known for its bargain cuisine and fascinating decor, including a 1959 Caddy that dives into the roof of the building above the restaurant.

Directly across the street from the Beverly Center, on the east side of La Cienega between Beverly Boulevard and 3rd Street, is another mall, **The Beverly Connection** (tel. 213/651–3611), opened in 1990. Inside, you'll find **Book Star,** a giant warehouse-like store selling every conceivable sort of reading material at low prices; **Sports Chalet,** for all kinds of athletic equipment; **Cost Plus,** a bottom-of-the-line import emporium big on rattan furniture, gourmet food, ethnic jewelry, and simple clothing; and **Rexall Square Drug,** a.k.a. Drugstore of the Stars, where people like Dustin Hoffman and Goldie Hawn have been seen lurking in the amply stocked aisles.

In the immediate neighborhood you'll find some other interesting shops: **Andria's Hole in the Wall** (8236 W. 3rd St., tel. 213/852–4955) is a special store where the talented namesake proprietor pulls together stylish outfits at below wholesale prices. **Charlie's** (8234 W. 3rd. St., tel. 213/653–3657) sells a cornucopia of '40s, '50s, and '60s clothing, along with a few choice furnishings. This place has vintage evening gowns in impeccable condition as well as wild and wonderful hats designed by the namesake owner. **Freehand** (8413 W. 3rd St., tel. 213/655–2607) is a gallery shop featuring contemporary American crafts, clothing, and jewelry, mostly by California artists. **Trashy Lingerie** (402 N. La Cienega, tel. 310/652–4543) is just what the name suggests. This is a place for the daring; models try on the sexy garments to help customers decide what to buy.

Century City **Century City Shopping Center & Marketplace** (tel. 310/277–3898), set among gleaming, tall office buildings on what used to be Twentieth Century Fox Film Studios' back lot, is an open-air mall with an excellent roster of shops. Besides The Broadway and Bullocks, both department stores, you'll find **Pair Wild** for trendy shoes and bags; **Ann Taylor** for stylish but not outlandish clothing and Joan & David shoes; and **The Pottery Barn** for contemporary furnishings at comfortable prices. **Card Fever** is a whimsical boutique with fun and funky messages to send; **Brentano's** is one of the city's largest bookstores; and **Gelson's** is a gourmet food market.

Besides dozens of stores, there are five restaurants on the premises, among them **Houston's,** which gets down with its American fare of grilled fish and steak, and **Stage Deli,** the kind of New York–style deli that previously was hard to find in L.A. Also at Century City is the **AMC Century** 14-screen movie complex.

West Los The **Westside Pavilion** (tel. 310/474–6255) is a pastel-colored post-
Angeles modern mall on Pico and Overland boulevards, a couple minutes' drive from Century City. The three levels of shops and restaurants run the gamut from high-fashion boutiques for men and women to toy stores and houseware shops. Among them are **The Disney Store,** filled with novelties to make all your fantasies come true; **The May Company** and **Nordstrom,** two full-scale department stores; **Mr Gs for Kids,** a good place for children's gifts; **Chanin's,** filled with women's designer clothing; and **Victoria's Secret,** a scented

lingerie boutique. Worth visiting even if you're not here to shop—and a welcome stop, if you are—is **Sisley Italian Kitchen,** which serves California-Italian dishes, pizzas, and terrific salads.

Santa Monica Go west all the way to the ocean to find Santa Monica, an increasingly rewarding area for shopping. It almost feels like a self-contained small town, with a combination of both malls and street shopping.

Santa Monica Place Mall (315 Broadway, tel. 310/394–5451) is a three-story enclosed mall that's nothing special. Some of the stores inside are **Pacific Sunwear,** selling super bathing suits; **The Z Gallery,** for witty home furnishings; **Card Fever,** so you can write the folks back home; **Lechter's,** for stocking up on your favorite gourmet utensils; and **Wherehouse Records,** for the latest tunes. **Robinson's** and **The Broadway** are department stores in this complex.

Next door, **Third Street Promenade** (tel. 310/393–8355) is a pedestrian-only street lined with boutiques, movie theaters, clubs, pubs, and restaurants. It's as busy at night as it is in the day, with wacky street performers to entertain as you mosey along.

Along **Montana Avenue,** a stretch of a dozen or so blocks from 7th to 17th streets showcases boutique after boutique of quality goods, many of them exclusive to this street. Among the more interesting: **A.B.S. Clothing** (1533 Montana Ave., tel. 310/393–8770) sells contemporary sportswear designed in Los Angeles. **Brenda Cain** (1211 Montana Ave., tel. 310/395–1559) features nostalgic clothes and antique jewelry. The hot ticket here is the amazing array of Hawaiian shirts for men and women. **Brenda Himmel** (1126 Montana Ave., tel. 310/395–2437) is known for its fine stationery, but antiques, frames, photo albums and books also enhance this homey boutique. **Lisa Norman Lingerie** (1134 Montana Ave., tel. 310/451–2026) sells high-quality lingerie from Europe and the United States—slips, camisoles, robes, silk stockings, and at-home clothes. **Weathervane II** (1209 Montana, tel. 310/393–5344) is one of the street's larger shops, with a friendly staff who make browsing among the classic and offbeat fashions more fun.

The stretch of **Main Street** leading from Santa Monica to Venice (Pico Blvd. to Rose Ave.) is another of those rare places in Los Angeles where you can indulge in a pleasant walk. While enjoying the ocean breeze, you'll pass some quite good restaurants and unusual shops and galleries.

Farther down the street, where Santa Monica turns into Venice, is an area known as **Abbott Kinney,** a quiet artists' colony amidst what is otherwise the wilder part of town. Among its galleries, cafés, boutiques, and antiques shops, look for **The Psychic Eye Bookstore** (218 Main St., tel. 310/396–0110), a spiritual haven selling wind chimes, incense, and crystal jewelry, as well as books on sorcery and other occult volumes. It's worth a look even for skeptics.

San Fernando and San Gabriel Valleys This is mall country; among the many outlets are **Sherman Oaks Galleria** (tel. 818/783–7100), **The Promenade** in Woodland Hills (tel. 818/884–7090), **Glendale Galleria** (tel. 818/240–9481), and **Encino Town Center** and **Plaza de Oro** in Encino (tel. 818/788–6100). **The Cranberry House** (12318 Ventura Blvd., Studio City, tel. 818/506–8945) is a huge shopping arena covering half a city block, packed with 140 kiosks run by L.A.'s leading antiques dealers. Come here for vintage furniture, clothing, jewelry, and furnishings.

Beverly Hills We've saved the most famous section of town for last. **Rodeo Drive** is often compared to such famous streets as 5th Avenue in New York and the Via Condotti in Rome. Along the couple of blocks between Wilshire and Santa Monica boulevards, you'll find an abundance of big-name retailers—but don't shop Beverly Hills without shopping the streets that surround illustrious Rodeo Drive. There are plenty of treasures to be purchased on those other thoroughfares as well.

Even Beverly Hills has a couple of shopping centers, although owners wouldn't dare call their collection of stores and cafés "malls." The **Rodeo Collection** (tel. 310/276–9600), at 421 North Rodeo Drive between Brighton Way and Santa Monica Boulevard, is nothing less than the epitome of opulence and high fashion. Many famous upscale European designers opened their doors in this piazzalike area of marble and brass. Among them: **Sonia Rykiel,** for country-club clothing for women; **Fila,** for the best in sports gear; **Mondi,** for high-style German fashions; and **Gianni Versace,** for trend-setting Italian designs.

A collection of glossy retail shops called **Two Rodeo Drive** (Rodeo Dr. and Wilshire Blvd.) is housed on a private cobblestone street that somewhat resembles a Hollywood back lot. Amid the Italianate piazza, outdoor cafés, and sculpted fountains of Two Rodeo are some two dozen boutiques, including: **Christian Dior,** for couture fashions known the world over; **Davidoff of Geneva,** for the finest tobacco and accessories; **Gian Franco Ferre,** for quality Italian designs; and **A. Sulka,** a noted men's haberdasher.

The Beverly Hills branch of **Saks Fifth Avenue** (9600 Wilshire Blvd., tel. 310/275–4211) isn't as impressive as the one you'll find next to St. Patrick's in Manhattan. Still, the buyers have good taste.

Some of the many other shops, boutiques, and department stores in Beverly Hills:

Fashions and Home Decor

Emporio Armani Boutique (9533 Brighton Way, tel. 310/271–7790) hangs the lower-priced line of this famous Italian designer, as well as his accessories and perfumes. At the top of the premises is the upscale Italian restaurant **Armani Express** (tel. 310/271–9940). **Oilily** (9520 Brighton Way, tel. 310/859–9145) features fun, colorful clothing and gift items (like stationery and umbrellas) for women, children, and even infants. All are exclusively designed in Holland for this store. **Polo/Ralph Lauren** (444 N. Rodeo Dr., tel. 310/281–7200) serves up a complete presentation of Lauren's all-encompassing lifestyle philosophy. The men's area, reminiscent of a posh British men's club, offers rough wear and active wear. Some 200 antiques are used as a backdrop for the women's area. Upstairs resides the world's most extensive selection of Lauren's home-furnishing designs.

Gifts and Jewelry

Hammacher-Schlemmer (309 N. Rodeo Dr., tel. 310/859–7255) is a fabulous place to unearth those hard-to-find presents for adults who never grew up. **Cartier** (370 N. Rodeo Dr., tel. 310/275–4272) offers all manner of luxury gifts and jewelry. **Tiffany and Company** (210 N. Rodeo Dr., tel. 310/273–8880), the famous name in fine jewelry, silver, and more, packages each purchase in a signature blue Tiffany box. **Van Cleef and Arpels** (300 N. Rodeo Dr., tel. 310/276–1161) sells expensive baubles and fine jewelry.

Men's Fashions

Alfred Dunhill of London (201 N. Rodeo Dr., tel. 310/274–5351) is an elegant shop selling British-made suits, shirts, sweaters, and slacks. Pipes, tobacco, and cigars, however, are this store's claim to fame. **Bernini** (362 N. Rodeo Dr., tel. 310/278–6287) specializes in contemporary Italian designer fashions. Look for fine leather accessories from Giorgio Armani. **Bijan** (420 N. Rodeo Dr., tel.

310/273–6544) is a store where it helps to make an appointment. Bijan claims that many Arabian sheiks and other royalty shop here, along with some of the wealthiest men in the United States. Many designs are created especially by the owner. **Carroll and Co.** (466 N. Rodeo Dr., tel. 310/273–9060) is a conservative men's shop that's been in business for more than a decade. It's known for quality, service, and its professional and celebrity clientele.

Women's Fashions **Alan Austin and Company** (180 N. Canon Dr., tel. 310/275–1162) has traditional clothing in a wide selection of fabrics and colors. The store manufactures its own designs, so clothing can be made to order. **Ann Taylor** (357 N. Camden Dr., tel. 310/858–7840) is the flagship shop of this chain of women's clothing stores, offering the epitome of the young executive look. It also carries a good selection of casual clothing and Joan & David shoes. **Celine** (460 N. Rodeo Dr., tel. 310/273–1243) is for luggage, shoes, and accessories as well as traditionally tailored clothing made of fine fabrics. **Chanel** (400 N. Rodeo Dr., tel 310/278–5500), known for its fashions and cosmetics, now also features fine jewelry, including copies of the original Coco designs popular in the 1920s and '30s. **Fred Hayman** (273 N. Rodeo Dr., tel. 310/271–3000) is an illustrious store where one does not merely shop for glitzy American and European clothing, accessories, and footwear; one also refreshes oneself at the stunning Oak Bar that separates the women's from the men's clothes. **Theodore** (453 N. Rodeo Dr., tel. 310/276–9691) offers trendy items in fabulous fabrics for men and women from Kenzo, Sonia Rykiel, Issey Miyake, and Donna Karan. Everything is done with a real eye for color.

Department Stores **The Broadway** (The Beverly Center, 8500 Beverly Blvd., tel. 310/854–7200) offers merchandise in the moderate price range, from cosmetics to housewares to linens to clothing for men and women. There are stores throughout Los Angeles.

Bullocks (The Beverly Center, 8500 Beverly Blvd., tel. 310/854–6655), which is more upscale than The Broadway, carries an extensive collection of clothing for men and women, as well as housewares and cosmetics. Stores are throughout Southern California.

I. Magnin (9634 Wilshire Blvd., tel. 310/271–2131) is a large store with many designer labels for men and women and a good handbag and luggage department. There are branches throughout Southern California; the flagship store on Wilshire Boulevard, now closed for shopping, is an Art Deco landmark.

The May Company (920 7th St., downtown, tel. 213/683–1144) sells modestly priced clothing and furniture without glitz or glitter in stores throughout Southern California.

Nordstrom (Westside Pavilion, 10830 W. Pico Blvd., West Los Angeles, tel. 310/470–6155) is a Seattle-based department store that has infiltrated Southern California with great enthusiasm. It brings with it a wide selection of clothing for men and women as well as a reputation for fine customer service, a huge shoe department, and the soothing sound of popular music played on the store's grand piano.

Robinson's (9900 Wilshire Blvd., Beverly Hills, tel. 310/275–5464) is a high-end department store that has many women's selections, a few men's selections, a good housewares department, and stores throughout Southern California.

Sports, Fitness, Beaches

Participant Sports

There are almost as many sports in Los Angeles as there are people. The following list is a compilation of the more popular activities. For additional information, two agencies will gladly assist you: **City of Los Angeles Department of Recreation and Parks** (200 N. Main St., Suite 1380, City Hall East, Los Angeles 90012, tel. 213/485–5515); **Los Angeles County Parks and Recreation Department** (433 S. Vermont Ave., 4th Floor, Los Angeles 90020, tel. 213/738–2961).

Bicycling
Perhaps the most famous bike path in the city, and definitely the most beautiful, can be found on the **Pacific Ocean beach,** from Temescal Canyon down to Redondo Beach. **San Vicente Boulevard** in Santa Monica has a nice wide cycling lane next to the sidewalk that runs for about 5 miles. **Balboa Park** in the San Fernando Valley is another haven for two-wheelers. A map of bike trails throughout the county can be obtained from the **L.A. County Parks and Recreation Department** (*see above*). You can pick one up in person or call to have one sent to you.

Billiards and Bowling
The **Hollywood Athletic Club** (6525 W. Sunset Blvd., tel. 213/962–6600) boasts full-size vintage snooker tables, circa 1923, and a tournament room. Open bowling hours vary at **Sports Center Bowl** in the Valley (12655 Ventura Blvd., Studio City, tel. 818/769–7600) and **Hollywood Star Lanes** (5227 Santa Monica Blvd., East Hollywood, tel. 213/665–4111).

Fishing
Shore fishing and surf casting are excellent on many of the beaches (*see* Beaches, *below*). Pier fishing is another popular method of hooking your dinner. The Malibu, Santa Monica, and Redondo Beach piers each offer nearby bait-and-tackle shops, and you can generally pull in a healthy catch. If you want to break away from the piers, however, the **Malibu Pier Sport Fishing Company** (23000 Pacific Coast Hwy., tel. 310/456–8030) offers boat excursions for $20 per half-day. The **Redondo Sport Fishing Company** (233 N. Harbor Dr., tel. 310/372–2111) has half-day and full-day charters. Half-day charters, 7:30 AM–12:30 PM or 1 PM–6 PM, run about $18 per person; a three-quarter day costs $27, and a full day goes for about $65. You can rent a pole for $7. Sea bass, halibut, bonita, yellowtail, and barracuda are the usual catch.

Twenty Second Street Landing (141 W. 22nd St., San Pedro, tel. 310/832–8304) offers an overnight charter. Complete with bunk beds and full galley, these boats leave at 10 PM and 10:30 PM and dock between 5 PM and 9 PM the next night. Per-person price is $60. Day charters are available as well, at $25–$40, with half-day excursions on weekends for $20.

The most popular and unquestionably the most unusual form of fishing in the L.A. area involves no hooks, bait, or poles. The great **grunion runs,** which take place March–August, are a spectacular natural phenomenon in which hundreds of thousands of small silver fish, called grunion, wash up on Southern California beaches to spawn and lay their eggs in the sand. The **Cabrillo Marine Museum** in San Pedro (tel. 310/548–7562, *see* Exploring Los Angeles, *above*) has entertaining and educational programs about grunion during most of the runs. In certain seasons, however, touching grunion is prohibited, so it's advisable to check with the Fish and Game Department (tel. 310/590–5132) before going to see them wash ashore.

Golf The Department of Parks and Recreation lists seven public 18-hole courses in Los Angeles. **Rancho Park Golf Course** (10460 W. Pico Blvd., tel. 310/838–7373) is one of the most heavily played links in the entire country. It's a beautifully designed course but the towering pines will make those who slice or hook regret that they ever took up golf. There's a two-level driving range, a nine-hole pitch 'n' putt (tel. 310/839–4374), a snack bar, and a pro shop where you can rent clubs.

Several good public courses are located in the San Fernando Valley. The **Balboa and Encino Golf Courses** are located right next to each other at 16821 Burbank Boulevard in Encino, tel. 818/995–1170. The **Woodley Lakes Golf Course** (6331 Woodley Ave., Van Nuys, tel. 818/780–6886) is flat as a board and has hardly any trees. During the summer months, however, the temperature in the Valley can get high enough to fry an egg on your putter, so be sure to bring lots of sunscreen and plenty of water. Down the road in Pacoima is the **Hansen Dam Public Golf Course** (10400 Glen Oaks Blvd., tel. 818/899–2200). Perhaps the most concentrated area of golf courses in the city can be found in **Griffith Park.** Here you'll find two splendid 18-hole courses along with a challenging nine-hole course. **Harding Golf Course** and **Wilson Golf Course** (both at 4730 Crystal Springs Dr., tel. 213/663–2555) are located about 1½ miles inside the park entrance at Riverside Drive and Los Feliz Boulevard. The nine-hole **Roosevelt Course** (2650 N. Vermont Ave., tel. 213/665–2011) can be reached through the park's Hillhurst Street entrance.

Yet another course in the Griffith Park vicinity, is the nine-hole **Los Feliz Pitch 'n' Putt** (3207 Los Feliz Blvd., tel. 213/663–7758). Other pitch 'n' putt courses in Los Angeles include **Holmby Hills** (601 Club View Dr., West Los Angeles, tel. 310/276–1604) and **Penmar** (1233 Rose Ave., Venice, tel. 310/396–6228).

Health Clubs There are dozens of health-club chains in the city that offer monthly as well as yearly memberships. **Bally's Nautilus Aerobics Plus** and **Bally's Holiday Spa Health Club and Sports Connection** are the most popular local chains. The Holiday Club located between Hollywood and Sunset boulevards (1628 El Centro, tel. 213/461–0227) is the flagship operation. This place has everything, including racquetball courts, indoor running tracks, pools, men's and women's weight and aerobics rooms, and a juice bar. To find the Bally's nearest you, call 800/695–8111. **Sports Club L.A.** (1835 S. Sepulveda Blvd., West Los Angeles, tel. 310/473–1447) is a hot spot, attracting a diverse group of celebrities such as James Woods and Monaco's Princess Stephanie. Not only does the gym have valet parking, it also contains the newest technology in fitness equipment. **Gold's Gym** (358 Hampton Dr., Venice, tel. 310/392–6004) is where all the incredible hulks turn themselves into modern art for $15 a day or $50 a week. **World Gym** (812 Main St., Venice, tel. 310/399–9888) and **Powerhouse Gym** (formerly Easton's, 8053 Beverly Blvd., West Hollywood, tel. 213/651–3636) are two other well equipped sites.

Hiking **Will Rogers State Park,** off Sunset Boulevard near Pacific Palisades, has a splendid nature trail that climbs from the polo fields to the mountaintop where you can get a spectacular view of the ocean. Other parks in the L.A. area that also have hiking trails include **Brookside Park, Elysian Park,** and **Griffith Park.** For more information on the parks, *see* Exploring Los Angeles.

In the Malibu area, **Leo Carillo State Beach** and the top of **Corral Canyon** offer incredible rock formations and caves to be explored on foot. In the hills east of **Paradise Cove,** a horse trail winds back into the canyons along a stream for several miles, eventually winding up at a beautiful waterfall. *See* Beaches, *below.*

For further information on these or any other hiking locations in Los Angeles, contact the **Sierra Club** (3345 Wilshire Blvd., Suite 508, Los Angeles 90010, tel. 213/387–4287).

Horseback Riding Although horseback riding in Los Angeles is extremely popular, stables that rent horses are becoming an endangered species. Of the survivors, **Bar "S" Stables** (1850 Riverside Dr., Glendale, tel. 818/242–8443) will rent you a horse for $13 an hour (plus a $10 deposit). Riders who come here can take advantage of over 50 miles of beautiful bridle trails in the Griffith Park area. **Sunset River Trails** (Rush St., at end of Peck Rd., El Monte, tel. 818/444–2128) offers riders the nearby banks of the San Gabriel River to explore at $15 an hour. **Los Angeles Equestrian Center** (480 Riverside Dr., Burbank, tel. 818/840–8401) rents pleasure horses—English and Western—for riding along bridle paths throughout the Griffith Park hills. Horses cost $13 per hour. **Sunset Ranch** (3400 Beachwood Dr., Hollywood, tel. 213/469–5450) offers a "dinner cruise" at $30, not including cost of the dinner. At sunset riders take a trail over the hill into Burbank, where they tie up their horses and have a feast at a Mexican restaurant.

Ice Skating Rinks are located all over the city. In the Valley, there's **Ice Capades Chalet Center** (6100 Laurel Canyon Blvd., Laurel Plaza Mall, North Hollywood, tel. 818/985–5555) and the **Pickwick Ice Center** (1001 Riverside Dr., Burbank, tel. 818/846–0032). In Pasadena, try the **Ice Skating Center** (300 E. Green St., tel. 818/578–0800), and in Rolling Hills, try the **Culver City Ice Arena** (4545 Sepulveda Ave., tel. 310/398–5718).

Jogging Just about every local high school and college in the city has a track. Most are public and welcome runners, and the private schools usually don't give a hoot who jogs on their tracks between 5 AM and 8 AM. A popular scenic course can be found at **Exposition Park.** Circling the Coliseum and Sports Arena is a jogging/workout trail with pull-up bars and other simple equipment placed every several hundred yards. **San Vicente Boulevard** in Santa Monica has a wide grassy median that splits the street for several picturesque miles. The **Hollywood Reservoir,** just east of Cahuenga Boulevard in the Hollywood Hills, is encircled by a 3.2-mile asphalt path and has a view of the Hollywood sign. Within hilly **Griffith Park** are thousands of acres' worth of hilly paths and challenging terrain, while Crystal Springs Drive from the main entrance at Los Feliz to the zoo is a relatively flat 5 miles. Circle Drive, around the perimeter of **UCLA** in Westwood, provides a 2.5-mile run through academia, L.A.-style. Of course, the premium spot in Los Angeles for any kind of exercise can be found along any of the beaches.

Racquetball and Handball There are several indoor racquetball facilities throughout the city: **The Racquet Center,** located in the San Fernando Valley (10933 Ventura Blvd., Studio City, tel. 818/760–2303), offers court time for $10–$14, depending on when you play. There's another Racquet Center in South Pasadena (920 Lohman La., tel. 213/258–4178).

Roller-Skating All of the areas mentioned in Bicycling (*see above*) are also excellent for roller skating, though cyclists have the right of way. Venice Beach is the skating capital of the city—and maybe of the world. If you're looking to get off the streets, there are a number of skating rinks in L.A. **Moonlight Rollerway** (5110 San Fernando Rd., Glendale, tel. 818/241–3630) and **Skateland** (18140 Parthenia St., Northridge, tel. 818/885–1491) are two of the more popular rinks in the city.

Tennis Many public parks have courts that require an hourly fee. **Lincoln Park** (Lincoln and Wilshire Blvd., Santa Monica), **Griffith Park** (Riverside Dr. and Los Feliz Blvd.), and **Barrington Park** (Barrington just south of Sunset Blvd. in L.A.), all have well-maintained courts with lights. There are several nice courts on the campus of **USC** (off the Vermont St. entrance), a few on the campus of **Paul Revere Junior High School** (Sunset Blvd. and Mandeville Canyon Rd., Brentwood), and a few more at **Palisades High School** (Temescal Canyon Rd., Pacific Palisades). For a complete list of the public tennis courts in Los Angeles, contact the **L.A. Department of Recreation and Parks** (tel. 213/485–5515) or the **Southern California Tennis Association** (Los Angeles Tennis Center, UCLA Campus, 420 Circle Dr., Los Angeles 90024, tel. 310/208–3838).

Hotel Tennis Courts If you're just in town for a few days and you don't have time to shop around for a court, you may already be staying at a hotel that has facilities. The **Ritz-Carlton Marina del Rey** (4375 Admiralty Way, tel. 310/823–1700) has three lighted courts. Per-person, hourly rates are $20 for hotel guests and $30 for the public.

Water Sports Whether or not the surf's up, the Pacific coast is the preeminent amusement park for water sports. But the ocean isn't the only place to get wet—in Los Angeles you'll have access to everything from crystal mountain-lake fishing to jet skiing in the Pacific.

Boating **Rent-A-Sail** (13719 Fiji Way, Marina del Rey, tel. 310/822–1868) will rent you everything from canoes to power boats or 14–25-foot sailboats for anywhere from $16 to $36 per hour plus a $20 deposit.

Jet Skiing Jet skis are expensive to rent. Two of the more popular places that carry them are **Del Rey Jet Ski** (4144 Lincoln Blvd., Marina del Rey, tel. 310/821–4507), and in the summer, **Malibu Jet Ski** (22718 W. Pacific Coast Hwy., tel. 310/456–2424).

Scuba Diving and Snorkeling Diving and snorkeling off Leo Carillo State Beach, Catalina, and the Channel Islands is considered some of the best on the Pacific coast. Dive shops, such as **New England Divers** (4148 Viking Way, Long Beach, tel. 310/421–8939) and **Dive & Surf** (504 N. Broadway, Redondo Beach, tel. 310/372–8423) will provide you with everything you need for your voyage beneath the waves.

Surfing The signature water sport in L.A. is surfing . . . and rightfully so. Southern California beaches offer a wide variety of surfing venues, along with a number of places to rent boards. For a complete listing of the best surfing areas, *see* Beaches, *below.*

Swimming Pools There are numerous public swimming pools in the L.A. area. The **Los Angeles Swim Stadium** (tel. 213/485–2844), next door to the L.A. Coliseum—not such a safe area, so beware—was built for the 1932 summer Olympic games. Another popular pool is **Pacific Park Pool** (tel. 818/247–1397), affiliated with the Glendale YMCA, in Glendale on the corner of Riverdale Drive and Pacific Avenue. This is a much more woodsy setting than the Olympic pool, and there is a public park right next door. The **Griffith Park** pool (tel. 213/665–4372), at the intersection of Los Feliz Boulevard and Riverside Drive, is another favorite splash point.

Water Parks and Windsurfing **Raging Waters,** off I–210 in San Dimas (tel. 909/592–6453), is a sort of aquatic Disneyland. It's open daily mid-June–mid-September; weekends only, mid-April–mid-June and late September–October. There are a number of places from which to rent equipment for certified windsurfers. **Action Water Sports** (4144 Lincoln Blvd., Marina del Rey, tel. 310/306–9539) rents rigs at $45 per day during the summer. For novices, a three-hour lesson with an instructor runs $70. Farther north, contact **Natural Progression** (22935 Pacific Coast Hwy., Malibu, tel. 310/456–6302). Cost is $40 per day, and the hours are 10–5.

Spectator Sports

Some of the major sports venues in the area are **Anaheim Stadium** (Anaheim, tel. 714/937–7200), **Great Western Forum** (3900 W. Manchester, Inglewood, tel. 310/673–1773), **L.A. Coliseum** (3911 S. Figueroa, downtown, tel. 213/748–6131), and **L.A. Sports Arena** (downtown, next to the Coliseum, tel. 213/748–6131).

Baseball The **Dodgers** take on their National League rivals at Dodger Stadium (1000 Elysian Park Ave., exit off I–110, the Pasadena Fwy.). For ticket information, call 213/224–1400. Down the freeway a bit in Anaheim, the **California Angels** continue their quest for the pennant in the American League West. For Angel ticket information, contact Anaheim Stadium: tel. 714/937–7200.

Basketball The **Los Angeles Lakers'** pro basketball home court is the Forum; for ticket information, call 310/419–3182. L.A.'s "other" team, the **Clippers,** make their home at the L.A. Sports Arena; for ticket information, call 213/748–8000. The **University of Southern California** (for tickets, tel. 213/740–2311) plays at the L.A. Sports Arena, and the Bruins of the **University of California at Los Angeles** (for tickets, tel. 310/825–2101) play at Pauley Pavilion on the UCLA campus.

Boxing and Wrestling Championship competitions take place in both of these sports year-round at the Forum.

Football The **L.A. Raiders** play their National League Football games at the Coliseum, downtown; for tickets, call Ticket Master at 310/322–5901. The N.F.L. **Los Angeles Rams** play at Anaheim Stadium; for ticket information, call 714/937–7200 or 213/625–1123; for team information, call 713/937–6767. The **USC Trojans's** (for tickets, tel. 213/740–2311) home turf is the Coliseum, and the **UCLA Bruins** (for tickets, tel. 310/825–2101) pack 'em in at the Rose Bowl in Pasadena.

Hockey The **L.A. Kings** put their show on ice at the Forum, November–April. Ticket information: tel. 310/673–6003. The **Mighty Ducks** (owned by Disney) push the puck at The Pond in Anaheim, November–April. Ticket information: tel. 714/704–2700.

Horse Racing **Santa Anita Race Track** (Huntington Dr. and Colorado Pl., Arcadia, tel. 818/574–7223) is still the dominant site for exciting Thoroughbred racing. **Hollywood Park** is another favorite venue. The track is next to the Forum in Inglewood, at Century Boulevard and Prairie, tel. 310/419–1500. It's open late April–mid-July. For harness racing, **Los Alamitos** (4961 Katella Ave., Anaheim) has both day and night events. For track information, call 714/236–4400 or 310/431–1361.

Beaches

From downtown, the easiest way to hit the coast is by taking the Santa Monica Freeway (I–10) due west. Once you reach the end of the freeway, I–10 turns into the famous Highway 1, better known as the Pacific Coast Highway, or PCH, and continues up to Oregon. Other basic routes from the downtown area include Pico, Olympic, Santa Monica, Sunset, or Wilshire boulevards. The RTD bus line runs every 20 minutes to and from the beaches along each of these streets.

Los Angeles County beaches (and state beaches operated by the county) have lifeguards. Public parking (for a fee) is available at most. The following beaches are listed in north–south order. Some are excellent for swimming, some for surfing (check with lifeguards for current conditions for either activity), others better for exploring.

Leo Carillo State Beach. This beach along a rough and mountainous stretch of coastline is the most fun at low tide, when a spectacular array of tide pools blossom for all to see. Rock formations on the beach have created some great secret coves for picnickers looking for solitude. There are hiking trails, sea caves, and tunnels, and whales, dolphins, and sea lions are often seen swimming in the offshore kelp beds. The waters here are rocky and best for experienced surfers and scuba divers; fishing is good. Picturesque campgrounds are set back from the beach. Camping fee is $16 per night. *35000 block of PCH, Malibu, tel. 818/880–0350. Facilities: parking, lifeguard, rest rooms, showers, fire pits.*
Zuma Beach County Park. This is Malibu's largest and sandiest beach, and a favorite spot of surfers. *30050 PCH, Malibu, tel. 310/457–9891. Facilities: parking, lifeguard, rest rooms, showers, food, playground, volleyball.*
Westward Beach/Point Dume State Beach. Another favorite spot for surfing, this half-mile-long sandy beach has tide pools and sandstone cliffs. *South end of Westward Beach Rd., Malibu, tel. 310/457–9891. Facilities: parking, lifeguard, rest rooms, food.*
Paradise Cove. With its pier and equipment rentals, this sandy beach is a mecca for sport-fishing boats. Though swimming is allowed, there are lifeguards during the summer only. *28128 PCH, Malibu, tel. 310/457–2511. Facilities: parking, rest rooms, showers, food (concessions open summer only).*
Surfrider Beach/Malibu Lagoon State Beach. The steady 3- to 5-foot waves make this beach, just north of Malibu Pier, a great long-board surfing beach. The International Surfing Contest is held here in September. Water runoff from Malibu Canyon forms a natural lagoon, which is a sanctuary for many birds. There are also nature trails perfect for romantic sunset strolls. *23200 block of PCH, Malibu, tel. 818/880–0350. Facilities: parking, lifeguard, rest rooms, picnicking, visitor center.*
Las Tunas State Beach. Las Tunas is small (1,300 feet long, covering a total of only 2 acres), narrow, and sandy, with some rocky areas, and set beneath a bluff. Surf fishing is the biggest attraction here. There is no lifeguard, and swimming is not encouraged because of steel groins set offshore to prevent erosion. *19400 block of PCH, Malibu, tel. 310/457–9891. Facilities: parking, rest rooms.*
Topanga Canyon State Beach. This rocky beach stretches from the mouth of the Topanga Canyon down to Coastline Drive. Catamarans dance in these waves and skid onto the sands of this popular beach, where dolphins sometimes come close enough to shore to

startle sunbathers. The area near the canyon is a great surfing spot. *18700 block of PCH, Malibu, tel. 310/394–3266. Facilities: parking, lifeguard, rest rooms, food.*

Will Rogers State Beach. This wide, sandy beach is several miles long and has even surf. Parking in the lot here is limited, but there is plenty of beach, volleyball, and body surfing, attracting a predominantly gay crowd. *15800 PCH, Pacific Palisades, tel. 310/394–3266. Facilities: parking, lifeguard, rest rooms.*

Santa Monica Beach. This is one of L.A.'s most popular beaches. In addition to a pier and a promenade, a man-made breakwater just offshore has caused the sand to collect and form the widest stretch of beach on the entire Pacific coast. If you're up for some sightseeing on land, this is one of the more popular gathering places for L.A.'s young, toned, and bronzed. All in all, the 2-mile-long beach is well equipped with bike paths, facilities for the disabled, playgrounds, and volleyball. In summer, free rock and jazz concerts are held at the pier on Thursday nights. *West of PCH, Santa Monica, tel. 310/394–3266. Facilities: parking, lifeguard, rest rooms, showers.*

Venice Municipal Beach. While the surf and sands of Venice are fine, the main attraction here is the boardwalk scene. Venice combines the beefcake of some of L.A.'s most serious bodybuilders with the productions of lively crafts merchants and street musicians. There are roller skaters, comedians, and rappers to entertain you, and cafés to feed you. You can rent bikes at Venice Pier Bike Shop (21 Washington St.) and skates at Skatey's (102 Washington St.). *1531 Ocean Front Walk, Venice, tel. 310/394–3266. Facilities: parking, rest rooms, showers, food, picnicking.*

Playa del Rey. South of Marina del Rey lies one of the more underrated beaches in Southern California. The majority of the crowds that frequent these sands are young. One of the more attractive features of this beach is an area called Del Rey Lagoon, a grassy oasis in the heart of Playa del Rey. A lovely pond is inhabited by dozens of ducks, and barbecue pits and tables are available to picnickers. *6660 Esplanade, Playa del Rey. Facilities: parking, lifeguard, rest rooms, food.*

Manhattan State Beach. Here are 44 acres of sandy beach for swimming, diving, surfing, and fishing. Polliwog Park is a charming, grassy landscape a few yards back from the beach that parents with young children may appreciate. Ducks waddle around a small pond, and picnickers enjoy some convenient facilities like showers and rest rooms. *West of Strand, Manhattan Beach, tel. 310/372–2166. Facilities: volleyball, parking, lifeguard, rest rooms, showers, food.*

Redondo State Beach. The beach is wide, sandy, and usually packed in summer, and parking is limited. Excursion boats, boat launching ramps, and fishing are among the other attractions. There is a series of rock and jazz concerts held at the pier during the summer. *Foot of Torrance Blvd., Redondo Beach, tel. 310/372–2166. Facilities: volleyball, parking, lifeguard, rest rooms, showers, food.*

Dining

By Bruce David Colen

Updated by Jane E. Lasky

In the high-living '80s, Los Angeles emerged as a top gastronomic capital of the world, and it shows no signs of slowing down. Where once the city was known only for its chopped Cobb salad, Green Goddess dressing, drive-in hamburger stands, and outdoor barbecues, today it is home to many of the best French and Italian restaurants in the United States, and so many places featuring international cuisines that listing them would be like roll call at the

United Nations. Despite the recession, many new—and good—dining establishments open every week, and sometimes it seems that there are more chairs, booths, and banquettes than there are bodies to fill them. The result is a fierce competition among upscale restaurateurs that has made L.A. one of the least expensive big cities—here or abroad—in which to eat well.

Locals tend to dine early, between 7:30 and 9 PM, in part a holdover from when this was a "studio" town, and the film-making day started at 6 AM, but these days more to allow for early morning jogging and gym time. Advance reservations are essential at the best restaurants, and at almost all restaurants on weekend evenings.

One caveat: The city recently enforced a no-smoking ordinance that applies to all restaurants. If you do want to smoke, there are ways around this—choose a restaurant with an outdoor area (smoking is allowed outdoors) or one that incorporates a full-scale bar (lounge areas are exempt from the no-smoking rule). Also, some of the incorporated cities like West Hollywood and Beverly Hills make their own rules, so call ahead to see if the place where you want to dine permits smoking.

Highly recommended restaurants are indicated by a star ★.

Category	Cost*
$$$$	over $50
$$$	$30–$50
$$	$20–$30
$	under $20

*per person for a three-course meal, excluding drinks, service, and 8¼% tax

American
Beverly Hills

The Grill on the Alley. This is the closest Los Angeles gets in terms of look and atmosphere to a traditional San Francisco bar and grill, with its dark-wood paneling and brass trim. The Grill is known for great steaks, fresh seafood, chicken pot pies, and crab cakes. Repeat customers like the restaurant's creamy Cobb salad and homemade rice pudding. *9560 Dayton Way, tel. 310/276–0615. Reservations required. Dress: chic casual. AE, DC, MC, V. Closed Sun. Valet parking in evening. $$$*

Ed Debevic's. This is a good place to take the kids, or a good place to go yourself if you're feeling nostalgic. Old Coca-Cola signs, a blaring jukebox, gum-chewing waitresses in bobby sox, and meat loaf and mashed potatoes will take you back to the diners of the '50s. *134 N. La Cienega, tel. 310/659–1952. Reservations for large parties only. Dress: casual. AE, D, DC, MC, V. Valet parking. $*

RJ'S the Rib Joint. The large barrel of free peanuts at the door and the sawdust on the floor set a folksy atmosphere. An outstanding salad bar has dozens of fresh choices and return privileges, and there are gigantic portions of everything—from ribs, chili, and barbecued chicken, to mile-high layer cakes—all at very reasonable prices. *252 N. Beverly Dr., tel. 310/274–RIBS. Reservations advised. Dress: casual. AE, DC, MC, V. Valet parking in evening. $*

Downtown

Pacific Dining Car. This 70-year-old restaurant, one of L.A.'s oldest, is open around the clock. Best known for well-aged steaks, rack of lamb, and an extensive California wine list at fair prices, it's a favorite haunt of politicians and lawyers around City Hall and of

Downtown Los Angeles Dining and Lodging

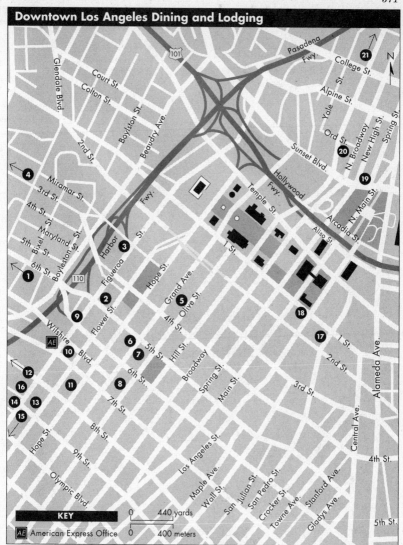

Dining

Mon Kee Seafood Restaurant, **19**

Nicola, **9**

Ocean Seafood Restaurant, **20**

Pacific Dining Car, **1**

Restaurant Horikawa, **17**

Rex Il Ristorante, **8**

Yujean Kang's Gourmet Chinese Cuisine, **21**

Lodging

Best Western Inntowne, **16**

Biltmore Hotel, **7**

Checkers Hotel Kempinski, **6**

Comfort Inn, **4**

Holiday Inn L.A. Downtown, **12**

Hotel Figueroa , **14**

Hotel Inter-Continental Los Angeles, **5**

Hyatt Regency Los Angeles, **11**

The Inn at 657, **15**

Los Angeles Hilton Hotel and Towers, **10**

New Otani Hotel and Garden, **18**

Orchid Hotel, **13**

Sheraton Grande Hotel, **3**

Westin Bonaventure, **2**

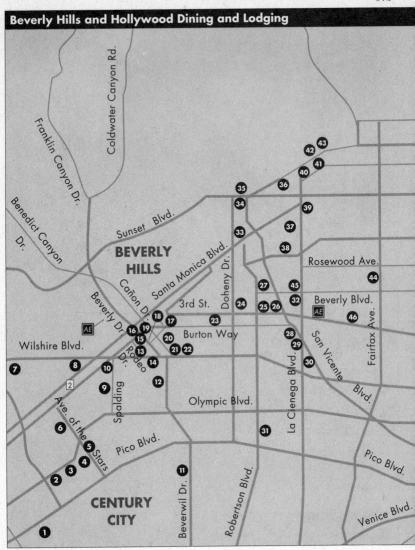

Beverly Hills and Hollywood Dining and Lodging

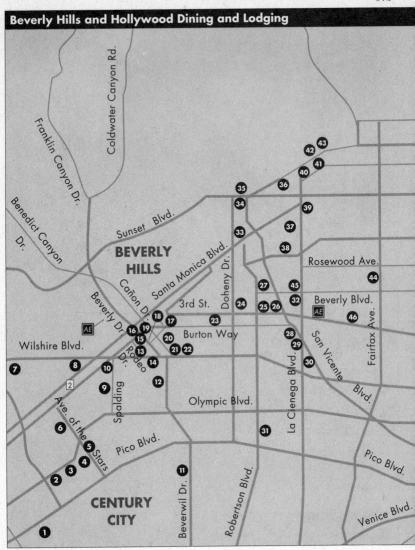

Dining

Antonio's Restaurant, **48**

Arnie Morton's of Chicago, **28**

The Bistro Garden, **21**

Ca'Brea, **47**

California Pizza Kitchen, **12**

Canter's, **44**

Carnegie Deli, **19**

Cava, **26**

Cha Cha Cha, **57**

Chan Dara, **51**

Chasen's, **27**

Chopstix, **50**

Citrus, **52**

Columbia Bar & Grill, **55**

The Dining Room, **14**

Ed Debevic's, **30**

El Cholo, **58**

The Grill on the Alley, **13**

Hard Rock Cafe, **32**

Harry's Bar & American Grill, **5**

Il Fornaio Cucina Italiana, **18**

Jimmy's, **9**

Le Dome, **36**

L'Escoffier, **10**

Locanda Veneta, **25**

L'Orangerie, **37**

The Mandarin, **15**

Nate 'n Al's, **17**

The Palm, **33**

Primi, **1**

Restaurant Katsu, **56**

RJ'S the Rib Joint, **20**

Rustica, **16**

Sofi, **46**

Spago, **35**

Tommy Tang's, **49**

Trader Vic's, **10**

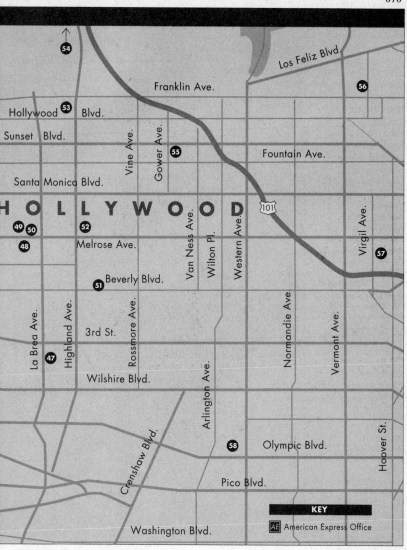

Franklin Ave.

Los Feliz Blvd.

Hollywood 53 Blvd.

Sunset Blvd.

Fountain Ave.

Santa Monica Blvd.

H O L L Y W O O D

Melrose Ave.

Beverly Blvd.

3rd St.

Wilshire Blvd.

Olympic Blvd.

Pico Blvd.

KEY

AE American Express Office

Washington Blvd.

Vine Ave.
Gower Ave.
Van Ness Ave.
Wilton Pl.
Western Ave.
Virgil Ave.
Normandie Ave.
Vermont Ave.
La Brea Ave.
Highland Ave.
Rossmore Ave.
Arlington Ave.
Crenshaw Blvd.
Hoover St.

Lodging

Banana Bungalow Hotel and International Hostel, **54**

Bel Age Hotel, **34**

Beverly Hills Ritz Hotel, **7**

Beverly Hilton, **10**

Beverly Pavilion Hotel, **22**

Beverly Prescott Hotel, **11**

Carlyle Inn, **31**

Century City Courtyard by Marriott, **3**

Century City Inn, **2**

Century Plaza Hotel and Tower, **6**

Château Marmont Hotel, **43**

Four Seasons Los Angeles, **24**

Hollywood Holiday Inn, **53**

Hotel Nikko, **29**

Hotel Sofitel Ma Maison, **45**

Hyatt on Sunset, **42**

J.W. Marriott Hotel at Century City, **4**

Le Parc Hotel, **38**

L'Ermitage Hotel, **23**

Mondrian Hotel, **40**

The Peninsula Beverly Hills, **8**

Regent Beverly Wilshire Hotel, **14**

Saint James's Club/ Los Angeles, **41**

Summerfield Suites Hotel, **39**

Dining

Border Grill, **7**
Broadway Deli, **9**
Chinois on Main, **13**
Dynasty Room, **35**
Gilliland's, **14**
Gladstone's 4 Fish, **1**
Granita, **3**
Hotel Bel-Air, **37**
Orleans, **15**
Remi, **10**
Tra di Noi, **2**
Valentino, **31**
Warszawa, **5**
West Beach Cafe, **16**

Lodging

Airport Marina
Hotel, **23**
Barnaby's Hotel, **30**
Best Western Royal
Palace Hotel, **32**
Carmel Hotel, **4**
Century Wilshire, **34**
Doubletree Marina
del Rey L.A., **21**
Holiday Inn
Crowne Plaza, **29**
Holiday Inn-LAX, **26**
Holiday Inn Santa
Monica Beach, **12**
Hotel Bel-Air, **37**
Hyatt Hotel-LAX, **24**
Loews Santa Monica
Beach Hotel, **8**
Marina del Rey
Hotel, **20**
Marina del Rey
Marriott Inn, **22**
Marina International
Hotel, **18**
Marina Pacific Hotel &
Suites, **17**
Miramar Sheraton, **6**
Palm Motel, **11**
Radisson Bel-Air, **36**
Red Lion Inn, **28**
The Ritz-Carlton,
Marina del Rey, **19**
Sheraton Los Angeles
Airport Hotel, **25**
Westin Hotel LAX, **27**
Westwood Marquis
Hotel and Gardens, **35**

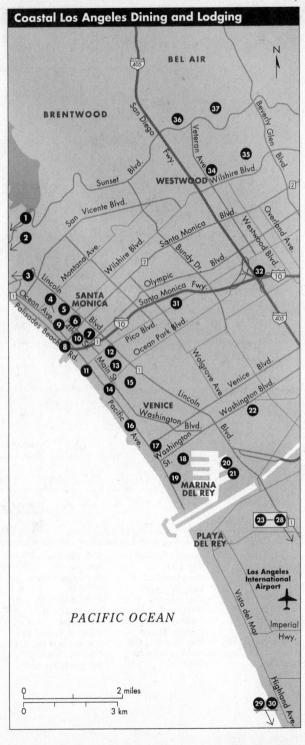

Coastal Los Angeles Dining and Lodging

sports fans after Dodger games. High tea is served every day from 3–5:30 PM. *1310 W. 6th St., tel. 213/483–6000. Reservations advised. Dress: casual. AE, DC, MC, V. Valet parking. $$$*

Nicola. Renowned local architect Michael Rotondi created the contemporary backdrop for this restaurant—celebrity chef Larry Nicola's latest venture. The two-room restaurant provides a contrast in moods, one an intimate dining arena, the other more open and airy. Although the menu is largely American, ethnic touches abound with entrées such as pan-fried monkfish with Chinese pepper sauce and roasted leg of pork with tomatillo gravy. The wine list is very impressive. *601 S. Figueroa St., tel. 213/485–0927. Reservations advised. Dress: casual or business attire. AE, DC, MC, V. No Sat. lunch, closed Sun. Valet parking. $$–$$$*

Hollywood **Columbia Bar & Grill.** Located front and center in the heart of Tinsel Town, this comfortably contemporary restaurant, with Jasper Johns and David Hockneys on the walls, is the daytime mecca for people from the surrounding television and film studios. That's the restaurant's main draw—the food is not always up to par. To be safe, order the crab cakes; Caesar salad; or the fish, fowl, and meats grilled over a variety of flavor-filled woods. *1448 N. Gower St., tel. 213/461–8800. Reservations required. Dress: casual. AE, DC, MC, V. Closed Sun. lunch. Valet parking. $$–$$$*

San Fernando Valley **Paty's.** Located near NBC, Warner Brothers, and the Disney Studio, Paty's is a good place for stargazing without having to mortgage your home to pay for the meal. This is an all-American–style upgraded coffee shop with a comfortable, eclectic decor. Breakfasts are charming; the omelets are plump, and the biscuits are homemade and served with high-quality jam. Lunches and dinners include Swiss steak and a hearty beef stew that is served in a hollowed-out loaf of home-baked bread. Roast turkey is served with dressing and a moist, sweet loaf of home-baked nut or raisin bread. All desserts are worth saving room for: New Orleans bread pudding with a hot brandy sauce is popular, and the Danishes are gigantic. *10001 Riverside Dr., Toluca Lake, tel. 818/760–9164. No reservations. Dress: casual. No credit cards. $*

West Hollywood ★ **Arnie Morton's of Chicago.** The West Coast addition to this ever-expanding national chain brought joy and cholesterol to the hearts of Los Angeles meat lovers, many of whom claim that Morton's serves the best steaks in town. In addition to a 24-ounce porterhouse, a New York strip, and a double-cut filet mignon, there are giant veal and lamb chops, thick cuts of prime rib, and Maine lobsters at market prices. Although the prices are steep, the produce is prime, as is the service and private clublike atmosphere. You can save a few dollars by going elsewhere, but you won't be as happy. *435 S. La Cienega Blvd., tel. 310/246–1501. Reservations advised. Jacket required. AE, D, DC, MC, V. No lunch. $$$–$$$$*

Chasen's. It may no longer be Hollywood's "in" spot (and it hasn't been for a very long time), but the clublike rooms are full of nostalgia and have a quaintly formal charm, two qualities that are making a come-back in the low-profile '90s. The dishes that Alfred Hitchcock, Gary Cooper, and Henry Fonda loved—and George Burns still does—are as good as ever: hobo steak, double-rib lamb chops, boiled beef with matzo dumplings, and the late Dave Chasen's famous chili. Or, you can settle for a hamburger if you don't mind paying the absurd price of $19.95. For the finale, try the sensational banana shortcake or crêpes suzette. This is a place for special celebrations and great old-time service. *9039 Beverly Blvd., tel. 310/271–2168.*

Weekend reservations advised. Jacket and tie required. AE, DC, MC, V. Closed Mon. No weekend lunch. Valet parking. $$$

The Palm. A West-Coast replay of the famous Manhattan steak house—down to the New York–style waiters rushing you through your Bronx cheesecake—this is where you'll find the biggest and best Nova Scotia lobster, good steaks and chops, great french-fried onion rings, and paper-thin potato slices. Have the corned beef hash for lunch, and you can skip dinner. A three-person-deep bar adds to the noise. *9001 Santa Monica Blvd., tel. 310/550–8811. Reservations advised. Dress: casual. AE, DC, MC, V. No weekend lunch. Valet parking. $$$*

Hard Rock Cafe. Big burgers, rich milk shakes, banana splits, BLTs, and other pre-nouvelle food delights, along with loud music and rock 'n' roll memorabilia, have made this '50s-era barn of a cafe the favorite of local teenagers. *8600 Beverly Blvd., tel. 310/276–7605. No reservations. Dress: casual. AE, DC, MC, V. Valet parking in the Beverly Center next door. $$*

Westside (Coastal Los Angeles Dining map) ★

West Beach Cafe. This upscale eatery was Bruce Marder's first big success–he also owns Rebecca's across the street and his most recent hit, the Broadway Deli in Santa Monica (*see below*). Best bets at the West Beach are: Caesar salad, rack of lamb, ravioli with port and radicchio, fisherman's soup, and what many consider the best hamburger and fries in all of Los Angeles. *60 N. Venice Blvd., tel. 310/823–5396. Reservations advised. Dress: casual. AE, DC, MC, V. Valet parking. $$–$$$*

Gilliland's. Gerri Gilliland was teaching cooking in her native Ireland, took a vacation in Southern California, and never went back. Instead, she stayed and created this charming restaurant, which offers the best of both culinary worlds and showcases her fascination with Mediterranean dishes. The soda bread, Irish stew, and corned beef and cabbage are wonderful. All desserts are made on the premises; especially good is the lemon curd tart. The place is warm and friendly, just like its owner. *2424 Main St., Santa Monica, tel. 310/392–3901. Reservations advised. Dress: casual. AE, MC, V. $$*

Broadway Deli. The name is misleading, so don't come here expecting hot corned beef and pastrami sandwiches. This joint venture of Michel Richard (who also owns Citrus, *see below*) and Bruce Marder (of West Beach Cafe and Rebecca's, *see above*) is a cross between a European brasserie and an upscale diner. Whatever you feel like eating, you will probably find it on the menu, from a platter of assorted smoked fish or Caesar salad to chicken pot pie, carpaccio, steak, and broiled salmon with cream spinach. There are also excellent desserts and freshly baked breads. The retail counter is the place to fill a picnic basket with the best European and domestic delicacies. *1457 3rd St. Promenade, Santa Monica, tel. 310/451–0616. No reservations. Dress: casual. AE, MC, V. Valet parking weekends and evening. $–$$*

Gladstone's 4 Fish. This is undoubtedly the most popular restaurant along the Southern California coast, serving well over a million beach goers a year; it has spawned a sister restaurant in Universal Studios' CityWalk, also worth a visit. Perhaps the food is not the greatest in the world, but familiar seashore fare is prepared adequately and in large portions, and the prices are certainly right. Best bets: crab chowder, steamed clams, three-egg omelets, hamburgers, barbecued ribs, and chili. *17300 Pacific Coast Hwy. (at Sunset Blvd.), Pacific Palisades, tel. 310/ GL4–FISH. Reservations advised. Dress: casual. AE, DC, MC, V. Valet parking. $*

Cajun
Westside
(Coastal Los
Angeles
Dining map)

Orleans. The jambalaya and gumbo dishes are hot—in more ways than one—at this spacious eatery, where the cuisine was created with the help of New Orleans celebrity-chef Paul Prudhomme. The blackened salmon is probably the best catch on the menu. Most menu items are available in low-sodium, low-fat versions; just ask. *11705 National Blvd., W. Los Angeles, tel. 310/479–4187. Reservations advised. Dress: casual. AE, DC, MC, V. Valet parking. $$–$$$*

California
Beverly Hills

The Bistro Garden. The flower-banked outdoor dining terrace makes this the quintessential Southern California "ladies who lunch" experience. It's chic and lively without being overly pretentious or too "Hollywood." There's excellent smoked salmon, fresh cracked crab, steak tartare, calves' liver with bacon, and a unique apple pancake. *176 N. Canon Dr., tel. 310/550–3900. Reservations required. Jacket and tie required at dinner. AE, DC, MC, V. Closed Sun. Valet parking. $$$*

★ **The Dining Room.** Located in the Regent Beverly Wilshire, this elegant, European-looking salon is the best thing to happen to L.A. hotel dining in decades. It offers wonderful California cuisine (try the Norwegian salmon coated with Chinese mustard or the mesquite grilled Long Island duck), plus splendid service, at prices that aren't too unreasonable. A three-course fixed price menu costs $33. Adjoining The Dining Room is an equally attractive, sophisticated cocktail lounge, with romantic lighting and a pianist playing show tunes. *9500 Wilshire Blvd., tel. 310/275–5200. Reservations advised. Jacket and tie required. AE, DC, MC, V. Valet parking. $$$*

California Pizza Kitchen. This member of the popular West Coast chain is *the* place to go for a good wood-fired pizza at a fair price, without the usual pizza-parlor surroundings. There's an immaculate, pleasingly modern dining room, plus counter service by the open kitchen, and a wide, rather esoteric choice of pizza toppings. The pastas are equally interesting and carefully prepared. The few sidewalk tables are in great demand. *207 S. Beverly Dr., tel. 310/275–1101. No reservations. Dress: casual. AE, DC, MC, V. $*

West
Hollywood
★

L'Escoffier. Opened in 1955 to celebrate the completion of Conrad Hilton's flagship hotel, this elegant penthouse restaurant introduced L.A. to the high-calorie delights of haute cuisine. With the Beverly Hilton now owned by Merv Griffin, the room and the menu have been updated for the '90s. Chef Michel Blanchet, a brilliant exponent of light French/California cuisine, produces the sort of dishes you can't say no to: smoked salmon and dill pancakes, penne pasta with asparagus and lobster au gratin, baked tournedos of chicken in curry and coconut sauce, and, for dessert, apple tart and cinnamon ice cream. *9876 Wilshire Blvd., tel. 310/274–7777. Reservations required. Jacket and tie advised. AE, D, DC, MC, V. No lunch. Valet parking. $$$–$$$$*

★ **Citrus.** One of L.A.'s most prominent chefs, Michel Richard creates superb dishes by blending French and American cuisines. You can't miss with the delectable tuna burger, the impossibly thin angel-hair pasta, or the deep-fried potatoes, sautéed foie gras, rare duck, or sweetbread salads. Get your doctor's permission before even looking at Richard's irresistible desserts. *6703 Melrose Ave., tel. 213/857–0034. Reservations advised. Jacket required. AE, DC, MC, V. Closed Sun. Valet parking. $$–$$$*

★ **Spago.** This is the restaurant that propelled owner/chef Wolfgang Puck into the international culinary spotlight. He deserves every accolade for raising California cuisine to a totally tantalizing gastronomic experience, using only the finest West Coast produce. The proof is in the tasting: roasted cumin lamb on lentil salad with fresh coriander and yogurt chutney, fresh oysters with green chili and black pepper mignonette, grilled free-range chickens, and grilled Alaskan baby salmon. The biggest seller is not on the menu, so ask: It's known as the Jewish pizza, with cream cheese and smoked salmon as toppings. As for Puck's incredible desserts, he's on Weight Watchers' Most Wanted List. This is the place to see *People* magazine live, but you'll have to put up with the noise in exchange. Be safe: Make reservations at least two weeks in advance. *1114 Horn Ave., tel. 310/652–4025. Reservations required. Jacket required. AE, DC, MC, V. No lunch. Valet parking. $$–$$$*

Westside
(Coastal Los
Angeles
Dining map)

Hotel Bel-Air. You couldn't ask for a lovelier setting, in a romantic country garden, and the menu matches—the California-Continental cooking is very good indeed, be it for breakfast, lunch, or dinner. Seasonal cartes use fresh fare in a fanciful way, like grilled swordfish medallions in a light curry sauce with squid ink pasta in a sauté of shiitakes, snap peas, baby corn, and peppers. A meal at the Bel-Air is a not-to-be-missed experience. *701 Stone Canyon Rd., Bel Air, tel. 310/472–1211. Reservations advised. Jacket and tie advised at dinner. AE, DC, MC, V. Valet parking. $$$*

Granita. Wolfgang Puck's Granita has such stunning interior details as handmade tiles embedded with seashells, blown-glass lighting fixtures, and etched-glass panels with wavy edges. It's as close as you'll come to the beach without getting sand in your shoes. Even the blasé Malibu film colony is impressed. While Puck's menu here favors seafood items such as grilled John Dory with sweet potato puree, a lobster club sandwich on pecan sourdough, and grilled Atlantic salmon in roasted eggplant broth with seared carrots, the menu also features some of his standard favorites: spicy shrimp pizza, roasted quail stuffed with prosciutto on spinach fettuccine, lamb salad with grilled eggplant and sun-dried tomato vinaigrette, and wild mushroom risotto. *23725 W. Malibu Rd., Malibu, tel. 310/456–0488. Reservations required as far ahead as possible, especially for weekends. Dress: chic casual. DC, MC, V. No lunch Mon. and Tues. $$–$$$*

Caribbean
Hollywood

Cha Cha Cha. Off the beaten path, this small shack of a Caribbean restaurant attracts a discerning, eclectic crowd—the place is hip, yet not pretentious or overly trendy. Sit indoors in a cozy room, or in the enclosed patio, very tropical in its decor, à la Carmen Miranda. There's Jamaican jerk chicken, spicy swordfish, fried plantain chips, and assorted flans. If you're in the mood for pizza, try Cha Cha Cha's Caribbean versions. A "Valley" branch (17499 Ventura Blvd., Encino, tel. 818/789–3600) exists in much more stylish quarters. *656 N. Virgil Ave., tel. 310/664–7723. Reservations recommended. Dress: casual. AE, MC, V. Valet parking available (and recommended). $–$$*

Chinese
Beverly Hills
★

The Mandarin. Who said you only find great Chinese food in hole-in-the-wall places with oilcloth tabletops? Here is a good-looking restaurant with the best crystal and linens, serving an equally bright mixture of Szechuan and Chinese country-cooking dishes. Minced chicken in lettuce-leaf tacos, Peking duck, a superb beggars chicken, scallion pancakes, and any of the noodle dishes are recommended. The no-frills, under-$10 luncheon is a great deal. *430 N. Camden Dr., tel. 310/859–0926. Reservations required. Dress: chic casual. AE, DC, MC, V. No weekend lunch. Valet parking evening only. $–$$*

Downtown

Ocean Seafood Restaurant. This is a great place to try garlic crab and catfish, and most customers—including the Chinese—consider its dim sum menu the best in town. This noisy, vast Great Banquet

Hall of a place becomes far more intimate when the staff drops by your table with dozens of tasty little Cantonese treats. The perfect place for a Sunday breakfast or lunch. *750 N. Hill St., tel. 213/687–3088. Reservations accepted. Dress: casual. DC, MC, V. $$*

★ **Mon Kee Seafood Restaurant.** The name pretty much tells you what to expect—except it doesn't convey how good the cooking is and how morning-fresh the fish are. The garlic crab is addictive; the steamed catfish is a masterpiece of gentle flavors. In fact, almost everything on the menu is excellent. Despite its wonderful cuisine, this is a crowded, messy place; be prepared to wait for a table. *679 N. Spring St., tel. 213/628–6717. No reservations. Dress: casual. AE, DC, MC, V. Pay parking lot. $–$$*

Pasadena **Yujean Kang's Gourmet Chinese Cuisine.** Despite its length, this
★ name doesn't say it all. Mr. Kang, formerly of San Francisco, is one of the finest nouvelle-Chinese chefs in the nation. Forget any and all preconceived notions of what Chinese food should look and taste like. Start with the tender slices of veal on a bed of enoki and black mushrooms, topped with a tangle of quick-fried shoestring yams, or the catfish with kumquats and a passion fruit sauce, and finish with poached plums, or watermelon ice under a mantle of white chocolate, and you will appreciate that this is no chop suey joint. No MSG is used in any dish. *67 N. Raymond Ave., tel. 818/585–0855. AE, MC, V. Reservations advised. Dress: casual. $$–$$$*

West **Chopstix.** Never underestimate the ability of Californians to
Hollywood adopt—and adapt—an ethnic-food vogue: in this case, dim sum, subtly doctored for non-Asian tastes. The result is MSG-free, nouvelle Asian fast food served in a mod setting, at high-stool tables or at a diner-like counter. The dishes are interesting (spicy black bean beef, Thai tacos, Bangkok noodles), but don't expect a native Chinese to agree. Nonetheless, branches are appearing around the Southland faster than you can say "I'd like one of those . . ." *7229 Melrose Ave., tel. 213/937–1111. No reservations. Dress: casual. AE, DC, MC, V. $*

Continental **Rustica.** Popular during a sunny day (out back there's a retractable
Beverly Hills roof that allows you to dine alfresco when weather warrants), this contemporary bistro serves a mixture of California and Italian cuisine. It's one of Beverly Hills' most romantic spots, especially the cozy, dimly lit front room, and the service is ace. All entrées are under $25, too, which is very good for this part of town. Try the seared halibut with wilted greens; tricolor mushroom ravioli with sun-dried tomatoes, pesto, and Parmesan; and the blackened goat cheese salad with roasted walnut vinaigrette. More than 200 wines make up the top-notch wine list. *435 N. Beverly Dr., Beverly Hills, tel. 310/247–9331. Reservations recommended. Dress: chic casual. AE, DC, MC, V. Valet parking. No weekend lunch. $$–$$$*

Century City **Jimmy's.** When Beverly Hills CEOs are not dining at home they
(Beverly Hills often head here. Owner Jimmy Murphy provides the warmth in this
and expensive, decorator-elegant restaurant. The best dishes on the
Hollywood broad menu include peppered salmon, veal medallions with orange
Dining map) coffee-bean sauce, roast duckling, and chateaubriand. There's a fine steak or salmon tartare at lunch. *201 Moreno Dr., tel. 310/552–2394. Reservations required. Jacket and tie requested. AE, DC, MC, V. Valet parking. $$$–$$$$*

San **Europa.** The menu here roams the world: great goulash, terrific
Fernando teriyaki—even the occasional matzo ball soup. The dining room is
Valley tiny, charming, and casual; reservations are a must, as this is a community favorite. *14929 Magnolia Blvd., Sherman Oaks, tel.*

818/501–9175. Reservations advised. Dress: casual. MC, V. Closed Mon. No lunch. $–$$

L'Express. At this cheerful bistro, people from Hollywood's soundstages meet, mingle, and relax. Giant murals and soft lighting lend plenty of atmosphere to the jazzy setting. Popular entrées are pastas, salads, croque monsieur, and pizzas of all types; the desserts are very rich. Don't go just for lunch or dinner—it's also a great place for late-night snacks, and there is a full bar. *14190 Ventura Blvd., Sherman Oaks, tel. 818/990–8683. No reservations. Dress: casual. AE, MC, V. $–$$*

Santa Monica **Warszawa.** At this Polish restaurant, the food is hearty and heartwarming. Regional Polish sausage with mashed potatoes and cabbage is a house favorite, as are the potato pancakes sprinkled with cinnamon and garnished with dried plums, sour cream, and apples. And, of course, there are all sorts of variations on goulash and dumplings. On a diet? Stick with the fresh rainbow trout, steamed with leeks and dill. *1414 Lincoln Blvd., tel. 310/393–8831. Reservations advised. Dress: casual. AE, D, DC, MC, V. No lunch. $$*

Westwood (Coastal Los Angeles Dining map) **Dynasty Room.** This peaceful, elegant dining room in the Westwood Marquis Hotel has a European flair and tables set far enough apart for privacy. The well-handled Continental fare includes seafood mixed grill with lobster, halibut, scallops, and mussels. Best of all is the especially lavish, excellent Sunday brunch. *930 Hilgard Ave., tel. 310/208–8765. Reservations required. Dress: chic casual. AE, DC, MC, V. No lunch. Valet parking. $$$*

Deli **Carnegie Deli.** Oil millionaire Marvin Davis got tired of jetting
Beverly Hills cheesecake, pastrami, and lox back from the parent Carnegie in New York City, so he financed a Beverly Hills taste-alike to challenge the preeminence of Nate 'n Al's (*see below*). His big guns are corned beef and pastrami sandwiches that are 4¹/₂ inches high, cheese blintzes under a snowcap of sour cream, and wonderfully creamy cole slaw. *300 N. Beverly Dr., tel. 310/275–3354. No reservations. Dress: casual. AE, MC, V. $*

Nate 'n Al's. A famous gathering place for Hollywood comedians, gag writers, and their agents, Nate 'n Al's serves first-rate matzoh ball soup, lox and scrambled eggs, cheese blintzes, potato pancakes, and the best deli sandwiches west of Manhattan. *414 N. Beverly Dr., tel. 310/274–0101. No reservations. Dress: casual. AE, MC, V. Free parking. $*

San Fernando Valley ★ **Art's Delicatessen.** One of the best Jewish-style delicatessens in the city, Art's serves breakfast, lunch, and dinner daily. The sandwiches, named after celebrities, are mammoth and are made from some of the best corned beef, pastrami, and other cold cuts around. Matzoh ball soup and sweet-and-sour cabbage soup are specialties, and there is good chopped chicken liver. *12224 Ventura Blvd., Studio City, tel. 818/762–1221. No reservations. Dress: casual. AE, D, DC, MC, V. $*

West Hollywood **Canter's.** Ex–New Yorkers claim that this granddaddy of delicatessens (it opened in 1928) is the closest thing in atmosphere, smell, and menu to a Big Apple corned-beef and pastrami hangout. The elderly waitresses even speak with a New York accent. It's open 24 hours a day (attracting an eclectic late-night crowd) and has a yummy in-house bakery. *419 N. Fairfax Ave., tel. 213/651–2030. Reservations accepted. Dress: casual. MC, V. Valet parking. $*

French
San Fernando
Valley
★

Pinot Bistro. Joachim Spliechel, owner-chef of top-rated Patina, opened this perfectly designed synthesis of Parisian bistros. One can smell the fumes of perfectly seasoned escargot and the aroma of perfectly brewed espressos. Dishes are authentic: an array of fresh oysters, country pâtés, bouillabaisse, braised tongue and spinach, pot-au-feu, and steak with pommes frites. The pastry chef specializes in chocolate desserts. There is an extensive wine list. *12969 Ventura Blvd., tel. 818/990–0500. Reservations advised. Dress: chic casual. AE, DC, MC, V. Valet parking. No weekend lunch. $$–$$$*

Barzac Brasserie. Just north of Universal Studios, show business types and other locals seeking French comfort food satiate themselves on chef Didier Poirier's Gallic menu. Start with roasted potato shells with golden and black caviar, or sautéed baby escargot with shiitake mushrooms in a puffed pastry. Popular entrées are grilled baby coho salmon over couscous and curry sauce, and rack of lamb roasted with Dijon mustard and served with red Swiss chard. Don't skip dessert: The crème brûlée is superb. *4212 Lankersheim Blvd., Universal City, tel. 818/760–7081. Reservations recommended. Dress: casual. AE, DC, MC, V. No weekend lunch. Valet parking. $$*

West
Hollywood
★

L'Orangerie. For sheer elegance and classic good taste, it would be hard to find a lovelier restaurant in this country. And the cuisine, albeit nouvelle-light, is as French as the l'Orangerie at Versailles. Specialties include coddled eggs served in the shell and topped with caviar, squab with foie gras, pot-au-feu, rack of lamb for two, and an unbeatable apple tart served with a jug of double cream. *903 N. La Cienega Blvd., tel. 310/652–9770. Reservations required. Jacket and tie required. AE, DC, MC, V. Closed Mon., no weekend lunch. Valet parking. $$$–$$$$*

Le Dome. For some reason, local food critics have never given this brasserie the attention it deserves. Perhaps they are intimidated by the hordes of show- and music-biz celebrities that keep the place humming. By and large the food is honest, down-to-earth French: cockles in white wine and shallots; veal ragout; veal tortellini with prosciutto, sun-dried tomatoes, peas, and Parmesan sauce; and a genuine, stick-to-the-ribs cassoulet. *8720 Sunset Blvd., tel. 310/659–6919. Reservations required. Dress: casual. AE, DC, MC, V. Closed Sun., no Sat. lunch. Valet parking. $$$*

Westside
(Coastal Los
Angeles
Dining map)
★

Chinois on Main. The second of the Wolfgang Puck pack of restaurants, this one is designed in tongue-in-cheek kitsch by his wife, Barbara Lazaroff. Both the look of the place and Puck's merging of Asian and French cuisines are great fun. A few of the least resistible dishes on an irresistible menu include Mongolian lamb with eggplant, poach-curried oysters, whole catfish garnished with ginger and green onions, and rare duck with a wondrous plum sauce. The best desserts are three differently flavored crèmes brûlées. This is one of L.A.'s most crowded spots—and one of the noisiest. *2709 Main St., Santa Monica, tel. 310/392–9025. Dinner reservations required. Dress: chic casual. AE, DC, MC, V. No lunch Sat.–Tues. Valet parking. $$–$$$*

Greek
Mid-Wilshire
(Beverly Hills
and
Hollywood
Dining map)

Sofi. Hidden down a narrow passageway is this friendly little taverna that makes you feel like you've been transported straight to Mykonos. Enjoy your meal in the stone-walled dining room or under a vine-shaded patio. The food is authentic Greek cuisine: *dolmades* (stuffed grape leaves), lamb gyros, a sampling of traditional salads, filo pies, *spanakopita* (spinach pie), and souvlaki. *8030³/4 W. 3rd St, tel. 213/651–0346. Reservation advised. Dress: casual. AE, DC, MC, V. No Sun. lunch. $*

Health Food **Clearwater Cafe.** Not only for the health conscious but also for the
Pasadena   environmentally correct diner, this spiffy restaurant in Pasadena's
Old Town district prints its menu with vegetable-based inks and
serves food with reusable containers. Dishes cater to low-fat, low-
sodium palates, but that doesn't mean a loss in taste—the pecan
catfish with green apple tomatillo salsa has a certain bite and the
mixed vegetable grill with creamy polenta satisfies even the most
discerning vegetarian. Sit in the courtyard patio of this two-level
restaurant if the sun is shining. *168 W. Colorado Blvd., tel. 818/356–
0959. Reservations accepted. Dress: casual. AE, D, MC, V. Valet
parking. $–$$*

Italian   **Primi.** A younger, less expensive brother to Valentino (*see below*),
Beverly Hills   Primi has a menu that features a wide variety of Northern Italian
treats, including pasta and salad selections. This is a cheerful, con-
temporary setting, with a pleasant outside terrace. *10543 W. Pico
Blvd., tel. 310/475–9235. Reservations advised. Dress: chic casual.
AE, DC, MC, V. Closed Sun. Valet parking. $$–$$$*

★ **Il Fornaio Cucina Italiana.** What was once a bakery-café has been
transformed into one of the best-looking contemporary trattorias
in California, and the food is more than worthy of the setting. From
the huge brass-and-stainless-steel rotisserie come crispy roasted
duck, herb-basted chickens, and juicy rabbit. Nearby, cooks paddle
a tasty variety of pizzas and calzones in and out of the oakwood-
burning oven. Also emerging from the latter is a *bomba*, a plate-size,
dome-shape foccacia shell draped with strips of smoked prosciutto.
The thick Porterhouse steak alla Florentina at $17.95 is clearly the
best beef buy around; another top choice is pasta stuffed with lobster, ricotta, and leeks, served with a lemon cream sauce. The wines
come from vineyards Il Fornaio owns in Italy. *301 N. Beverly Dr.,
tel. 310/550–8330. Reservations accepted. Dress: casual. AE, DC,
MC, V. Valet parking. $–$$*

Century City   **Harry's Bar & American Grill.** The decor and selection of dishes
(Beverly Hills   are acknowledged copies of Harry's Bar in Florence. But you'll find
and   that for first-rate food—paper-thin carpaccio, grilled fish and
Hollywood   steaks, and excellent pastas like ravioli filled with artichokes or
Dining map)   tortellini with Maine lobster and shiitake sauce—the check will be
far lower than it would be in Italy. *2020 Ave. of the Stars, tel. 310/277–
2333. Reservations required. Dress: chic casual. AE, DC, MC, V. No
Sun. lunch. Valet parking. $$–$$$*

Downtown   **Rex Il Ristorante.** Owner Mauro Vincenti may know more about
★   Italian cuisine than any other restaurateur in this country. The Rex
is the ideal showcase for his talents: Two ground floors of a historic
Art Deco building were remodeled to resemble the main dining
salon of the circa-1930 Italian luxury liner *Rex*. The cuisine, the
lightest of *nuova cucina*, is equally special. Be prepared for small
and costly. *617 S. Olive St., tel. 213/627–2300. Reservations required.
Jacket and tie required. AE, DC, MC, V. Closed Sun. No lunch Sat.–
Wed. Valet parking. $$$$*

San   **Posto.** Thanks to Piero Selvaggio, Valley residents no longer have
Fernando   to drive to the Westside for good modern Italian cuisine. His chef
Valley   makes a tissue-thin pizza topped with flavorful ingredients, and the
chicken, duck, and veal sausages are made each morning, as are the
different herb breads, fried polenta, and wonderful risotto with porcini mushrooms. *14928 Ventura Blvd., Sherman Oaks, tel. 818/784–
4400. Dress: casual. AE, DC, MC, V. Closed Mon. No weekend lunch.
$$*

West Hollywood ★ **Ca'Brea.** Signoris de Mori and Tomassi were so successful with Locanda Veneta (*see below*) that they took a gamble and opened a much larger and lower-price place only 20 blocks away. Ca'Brea has turned into the Italian-restaurant smash hit of the penny-pinching '90s, and there isn't a pizza on the menu. You won't care, either, what with the osso buco, the linguini and baby clams, baby back ribs, shrimp and crab cakes, risotto with porcini mushrooms, Italian beans and sage, and homemade mozzarella salads. Daily specials include soup, salad, pasta, and fish. *348 S. La Brea Ave., tel. 213/938–2863. Reservations advised. Dress: casual. Closed Sun. No weekend lunch. AE, DC, MC, V. $$*

★ **Locanda Veneta.** The food may be more finely wrought at one or two other spots, but the combination of a splendid Venetian chef, Antonio Tomassi, and a simpatico co-owner, Jean Louis de Mori, have re-created the atmospheric equivalent of a genuine Italian trattoria, at reasonable prices. Specialties include risotto with crabmeat, veal chop, potato dumplings with tomatoes and shrimp, linguini with clams, lobster ravioli with saffron sauce, and a delectable apple tart. *8638 W. 3rd St., tel. 310/274–1893. Reservations required. Dress: chic casual. AE, DC, MC, V. Closed Sun. No Sat. lunch. Valet parking. $$*

Westside (Coastal Los Angeles Dining map) ★ **Valentino.** Rated among the best Italian restaurants in the nation, Valentino is generally considered to have the best wine list outside Italy. Owner Piero Selvaggio is the man who introduced Los Angeles to the best and lightest of modern-day Italian cuisine. There's superb prosciutto, bresola, fried calamari, lobster canneloni, fresh broiled porcini mushrooms, and osso buco. *3115 Pico Blvd., Santa Monica, tel. 310/829–4313. Reservations required. Dress: chic casual. AE, DC, MC, V. Closed Sun. No lunch Sat.–Thurs. Valet parking. $$$–$$$$*

Remi. It's not easy to find authentic Venetian cuisine in Southern California, but there's a top-rate source tucked away in Santa Monica's Third Street Promenade. Order the grilled quail wrapped in bacon and served with radicchio and grilled polenta; or the whole wheat crêpes with ricotta and spinach, topped with a tomato, carrot, and celery sauce; or the roasted pork chop stuffed with smoked mozzarella and prosciutto. *1451 Third Street Promenade, Santa Monica, tel. 310/393–6545. Reservations required. Dress: chic casual. AE, DC, MC, V. Parking in nearby multi-story mall car parks. $$*

Tra di Noi. The name means "between us," and Malibu natives are trying to keep this charming, simple *ristorante* just that—a local secret. It's run by a mama (who does the cooking), son, and daughter-in-law. Regular customers, film celebrities and non–show-biz folk alike, love the unpretentious atmosphere and bring their kids. Nothing fancy or *nuovo* on the menu, just great lasagna, freshly made pasta, mushroom and veal dishes, and crisp fresh salads. *3835 Cross Creek Rd., tel. 310/456–0169. Reservations advised. Dress: casual. AE. Closed Sun. lunch. $–$$*

Japanese Downtown **Restaurant Horikawa.** A department store of Japanese cuisines includes sushi, teppan steak tables, tempura, sashimi, shabu-shabu, teriyaki, and a $75–$90-per-person three-course (kaiseki) dinner. All are good or excellent, but the sushi bar is the best. The decor is traditional Japanese, with private dining rooms, where guests sit on tatami floor mats, for 2 to 24. *111 S. San Pedro St., tel. 213/680–9355. Reservations advised. Dress: casual or business attire. AE, DC, MC, V. Closed Sun. No Sat. lunch. Valet parking. $$–$$$*

Los Feliz
(Beverly Hills
and
Hollywood
Dining map)
★

Restaurant Katsu. A stark, simple, perfectly designed sushi bar with a small table area serves some of the most exquisite and delicious delicacies east of Japan. This is probably the most authentic Japanese restaurant in the city and definitely a treat for both the eye and the palate. *1972 N. Hillhurst Ave., tel. 213/665–1891. Reservations advised. Dress: chic casual. AE, DC, MC, V. No weekend lunch. Valet parking. $$$*

Mexican
Hollywood

El Cholo. The progenitor of this upscale chain, this place has been packing them in since the '20s. It serves good-size margaritas, a zesty assortment of tacos, make-your-own tortillas, and, from June through October, green-corn tamales. It's friendly and fun, with large portions for only a few pesos. *1121 S. Western Ave., tel. 213/734–2773. Reservations advised. Dress: casual. AE, DC, MC, V. Valet parking and parking meters. $*

Santa Monica

Border Grill. This very trendy, very loud eating hall is owned by two talented female chefs with the most eclectic tastes in town. The menu ranges from Yucatán seafood tacos to vinegar-and-pepper-grilled turkey to spicy baby back ribs. It's worth dropping by for the fun of it, if you don't mind the noise. *1445 4th St., tel. 310/451–1655. Reservations advised. Dress: casual. AE, D, DC, MC, V. No lunch. $–$$*

West
Hollywood

Antonio's Restaurant. Don't let the strolling mariachis keep you from hearing the daily specials: authentic (though mediocre) Mexico City dishes that still put this unpretentious favorite a couple of notches above the ubiquitous taco-enchilada cantinas. Be adventurous and try the chayote (squash) stuffed with ground beef; ricotta in a spicy tomato sauce; pork ribs in a sauce of pickled chipotle peppers; veal shank with garlic, cumin, and red pepper; or chicken stuffed with apples, bananas, and raisins. Have the flan for dessert. *7472 Melrose Ave., tel. 213/655–0480. Dinner reservations advised. Dress: casual. AE, MC, V. Closed Mon. Valet parking evenings. $–$$*

Polynesian
Beverly Hills

Trader Vic's. Sure, it's corny, but this Trader Vic's, located inside the Beverly Hilton, is the most restrained and elegant of the late Victor Bergeron's South Sea extravaganzas. Besides, who says corn can't be fun—and tasty, too. The crab Rangoon, grilled cheese wafers, skewered shrimp, grilled pork ribs, and the steaks, chops, and peanut-butter–coated lamb cooked in the huge clay ovens, are just fine. As for the array of exotic rum drinks, watch your sips. *9876 Wilshire Blvd., tel. 310/274–7777. Reservations required. Jacket and tie requested. AE, DC, MC, V. No lunch. Valet parking. $$–$$$*

Spanish
Mid-Wilshire
(Beverly Hills
and
Hollywood
Dining map)

Cava. Not far from the Farmer's Market, this trendy two-level tapas bar and restaurant inside the Beverly Plaza Hotel opened in 1993. The decor is artsy (larger-than-life roses are painted on the walls), the atmosphere a bit noisy but lots of fun, and the cuisine alluring. You can graze on tapas—tiny snacks such as baked artichoke topped with bread crumbs and tomato or a fluffy potato omelette served with créme frâiche—or feast on bigger entrées: The paella is a must, but you may also want to try fillet of sea bass with toasted almonds, garlic, and thyme. *8384 W. 3rd St., tel. 213/658–8898. Reservations advised. Dress: casual. AE, DC, MC, V. Valet parking. $$–$$$*

Thai
Hollywood

Chan Dara. Here you'll find excellent Thai food in a bright and shiny Swiss chalet! Try any of the noodle dishes, especially those with crab and shrimp. Also tops on the extensive menu are satay (appetizers on skewers) and barbecued chicken and catfish. *310 N. Larchmont Blvd., tel. 213/467–1052. Reservations advised for parties of more than 4. Dress: casual. AE, MC, V. $–$$*

West
Hollywood

Tommy Tang's. At this grazing ground for yuppies and celebs, a lot of people-watching goes on. Although portions are on the small side, they are decidedly innovative. The kitchen features crisp duck marinated in ginger and plum sauce, blackened sea scallops, and a spinach salad tossed with grilled chicken. *7473 Melrose Ave., tel. 213/651–1810. Reservations advised. Dress: casual. AE, DC, MC, V. Valet parking. $$*

Lodging

By Jane E.
Lasky

Because Los Angeles is so spread out—it's actually a series of suburbs connected by freeways—it's good to select a hotel room not only for its ambience, amenities, and price but also for a location that is convenient to where you plan to spend most of your time.

West Hollywood and Beverly Hills are at the heart of the city, equidistant from the beaches and downtown. These are also the primary shopping districts of Los Angeles, with Rodeo Drive the central axis of Beverly Hills, and Melrose Avenue the playground for trendier purchases. The more recently developed Century City, located between Westwood and Beverly Hills, offers top-notch hotels, a terrific mall, movie and legitimate theaters, and quick access to Rodeo Drive shopping. It's also an important Los Angeles business center. Hollywood, unfortunately, has lost much of its legendary glamour, so don't book a room there expecting to be in the lap of luxury— parts of Hollywood are downright seedy.

Downtown is attractive if you are interested in Los Angeles's cultural offerings, since this is where the Music Center and the Museum of Contemporary Art are. It is also the heartland for Los Angeles's conventions.

For closest proximity to Pacific Ocean beaches, check in in Santa Monica, Marina del Rey, or Malibu. The San Fernando Valley is a good place to stay if you're looking for a suburban setting and quarters close to the movie and television studios on that side of the hills.

It's best to plan ahead and reserve a room; many hotels offer tickets to amusement parks or plays as well as special prices for weekend visits. A travel agent can help in making your arrangements.

Highly recommended accommodations are indicated by a star ★. Hotels listed below are organized according to their location, then by price category, following this scale.

Category	Cost*
$$$$	over $160
$$$	$100–$160
$$	$65–$100
$	under $65

All prices are for a double room, excluding tax.

Downtown
$$$$

Biltmore Hotel. Since its 1923 opening, the Biltmore has hosted such notables as Mary Pickford, J. Paul Getty, Eleanor Roosevelt, Princess Margaret, and several U.S. presidents. The guest rooms in this historic landmark have been updated, with pastel color schemes and traditional French furniture and armoires. The lobby ceiling was painted by Italian artist Giovanni Smeraldi; imported

Italian marble and plum-color velvet grace the Grand Avenue Bar, which features excellent jazz nightly. Bernard's is an acclaimed Continental restaurant. The swank health club has a Roman bath motif. The 11th floor is designated as the Executive Floor, with desks specially equipped for business travelers. The 10th floor, the Club floor, comes complete with a concierge and a lounge that offers afternoon tea, Continental breakfast, board games, a fax machine, and big-screen TV. *506 S. Grand Ave., 90071, tel. 213/624–1011 or 800/245–8673, fax 213/612–1545. 685 rooms. Facilities: 3 restaurants, lounge, entertainment, health club, 24-hr room service, no-smoking floors. AE, DC, MC, V.*

$$$$ **Checkers Hotel Kempinski.** Set in one of this neighborhood's few remaining historical buildings—it opened as the Mayflower Hotel in 1927—this hotel offers much the same sophistication and luxury as the Biltmore across the street, but on a smaller scale. Guest rooms are furnished with oversize beds, upholstered easy chairs, writing tables, and minibars. A library is available for small meetings or tea. *535 S. Grand Ave., 90071, tel. 213/624–0000 or 800/426–3135, fax 213/626–9906. 188 rooms. Facilities: restaurant, rooftop spa and lap pool, exercise studio, no-smoking floors, valet parking (fee). AE, DC, MC, V.*

$$$$ **Hotel Inter-Continental Los Angeles.** This imposing 17-story structure was introduced to the downtown skyline at the end of 1992, the first hotel to be built in this section of town in the past decade. Part of California Plaza (where the Museum of Contemporary Art is) and within walking distance of the Music Center, the sleek Inter-Continental boasts floor-to-ceiling views. Guest rooms are decorated in contemporary style, with glass-topped tables and desks, in color schemes of either ivory and peach or celadon and brown. The sculpture *Yellow Fin,* by Richard Serra, dominates the large lobby, and other artwork is on view throughout, on loan from the Museum of Contemporary Art. The Angel's Flight restaurant and lounge serves California cuisine; coffee-shop fare is available at The Cafe. *251 S. Olive St., 90012, tel. 213/617–3300 or 800/442–5251, fax 213/617–3399. 429 rooms. Facilities: 2 restaurants, lounge, business center, club floors, health club, outdoor lap pool, 24-hr room service, no-smoking floors. AE, D, DC, MC, V.*

$$$$ **Hyatt Regency Los Angeles.** The Hyatt is located in the heart of the "new" downtown financial district, minutes away from the Convention Center, Dodger Stadium, and the Music Center. Each room has a wall of windows with city views. The Regency Club has a private lounge. The hotel is part of the Broadway Plaza, comprising 35 shops. Tennis is available nearby at an extra cost. *711 S. Hope St., 90017, tel. 213/683–1234 or 800/233–1234, fax 213/629–3230. 485 rooms, 41 suites. Facilities: restaurant, coffee shop, lounge, entertainment, no-smoking floors, health club. AE, DC, MC, V.*

$$$$ **Los Angeles Hilton Hotel and Towers.** Located right on Wilshire Boulevard, the Hilton is convenient to Dodger Stadium, museums, Chinatown, and the Music Center. The spare-looking contemporary decor of the guest rooms is in beige, blue, and green. Among the hotel's restaurants, the standout is a fine Italian eatery, Cardini. Parking is expensive. *930 Wilshire Blvd., 90017, tel. 213/629–4321 or 800/HILTONS, fax 213/612–3977. 900 rooms. Facilities: 4 restaurants, lounge, coffee shop, pool, gym with Nautilus equipment, parking (fee). AE, DC, MC, V.*

$$$$ ★ **Sheraton Grande Hotel.** This 14-story hotel with its reflecting glass facade is near Dodger Stadium, the Music Center, and downtown's Bunker Hill District. Guest rooms are oversize, with wall-to-wall windows and awesome city views. The decor features dark wood furniture, sofas, and minibars; colors are mauve, peach, and

gray; baths are marble. There's butler service with every room. Stay in the penthouse suite if you can afford it. A limousine is available for Beverly Hills shopping. There are privileges at a local, state-of-the-art YMCA, as well as an on-premises pool that's the best hotel pool downtown. *333 S. Figueroa St., 90071, tel. 213/617–1133 or 800/325–3535, fax 213/613–0291. 469 rooms. Facilities: 3 restaurants, bar, outdoor pool, 4 movie theaters, 24-hr room service. AE, DC, MC, V.*

$$$$ **Westin Bonaventure.** This is architect John Portman's striking contribution to downtown Los Angeles: a 35-story, circular-towered, mirrored-glass high-rise in the center of downtown. Rooms— a number of which are on the small side—have a wall of glass, streamlined pale furnishings, and comfortable appointments. The outside elevators provide stunning city views; there are also 5 acres of ponds and waterfalls in the lobby. At the top of the hotel are the Bona Vista revolving lounge and Top of Five restaurant. A popular Sunday brunch is served in the five-story atrium lobby. Parking is expensive. *404 S. Figueroa St., 90071, tel. 213/624–1000 or 800/228–3000, fax 213/612–4894. 1,368 rooms. Facilities: 2 restaurants, lounge, entertainment, pool, executive floor, 5-level shopping arcade, no-smoking floor, parking (fee). AE, DC, MC, V.*

$$$–$$$$ **New Otani Hotel and Garden.** For a quintessential Japanese hotel experience, visit this 21-story, ultramodern hotel, with its ½-acre rooftop Japanese-style garden. The decor is a serene blend of Westernized luxury and Eastern simplicity. Each room has a phone in the bathroom, a refrigerator, an alarm clock, and a color TV; most rooms have a *yukata* (robe). If you're so inclined, book a Japanese suite, where you'll sleep on a futon on the floor. The hotel's concrete exterior walls reduce noise from the street. A Thousand Cranes offers classic Japanese cuisine; the Azalea Restaurant serves Continental cuisine; and there's a Tokyo-style dining room. *120 S. Los Angeles St., 90012, tel. 213/629–1200, 800/421–8795, or 800/273–2294 in CA; fax 213/622–0989. 435 rooms. Facilities: 3 restaurants, 3 lounges, sauna and massage (fee), parking (fee). 24-hr room service. AE, DC, MC, V.*

$$ **Best Western Inntowne.** This three-story hotel has large beige-and-white rooms. It's 1½ blocks from the convention center and just down the street from the 24-hour Pantry restaurant, a favorite place for breakfast. The swimming pool is surrounded by palm trees and a small garden. *925 S. Figueroa St., 90015, tel. 213/628–2222 or 800/457–8520, fax 213/687–0566. 170 rooms. Facilities: coffee shop, lounge, pool, free parking. AE, DC, MC, V.*

$$ **Hotel Figueroa.** This 12-story, 25-year-old hotel has managed to keep its charming Spanish style intact. Terra-cotta-colored rooms carry out the Spanish look, with hand-painted furniture and, in many rooms, ceiling fans. *939 S. Figueroa St., 90015, tel. 213/627–8971, 800/421–9092, fax 213/689–0305. 285 rooms. Facilities: 3 restaurants, coffee shop, lounge, pool, free parking. AE, DC, MC, V.*

$$ **Holiday Inn L.A. Downtown.** This six-floor hotel offers Holiday Inn's usual professional staff and services, and standard no-frills room decor. The hotel is convenient, close to the Museum of Contemporary Art, convention center, and Los Angeles Sports Arena. *750 Garland Ave., 90017, tel. 213/628–5242 or 800/628–5240, fax 213/628–1201. 205 rooms. Facilities: restaurant, lounge, pool, health club, no-smoking floors, in-room coffeemakers, pets allowed, free parking. AE, DC, MC, V.*

$ **Comfort Inn.** With its central location between downtown and Hollywood, near the Wilshire commercial district, this very plain, two-story hotel in four separate buildings is convenient for businesspeople. The guest rooms—modern, not overly large—are decorated in pastel colors with wood trimmings, and have color TVs and VCRs. If you belong to AAA, ask for a discount. *3400 3rd St., 90020, tel. 213/385–0061. 120 rooms. Facilities: coffee shop, pool, Continental breakfast, parking (free). AE, DC, MC, V.*

$ **The Inn at 657.** This unassuming bed-and-breakfast operates like a small apartment building, with stocked kitchens containing coffee, tea, and soft drinks, all included in the price. The rate also includes breakfast, local telephone calls, gratuities, taxes and parking. It's close to the convention center and the University of Southern California campus. *657 W. 23rd St., 90027, tel. 213/741–2200 or 800/347–7512. 6 suites. Facilities: outdoor hot tub, no-smoking rooms. No credit cards.*

$ **Orchid Hotel.** One of the smaller downtown hotels, this 1920s-vintage property is very reasonably priced. There are no frills, but the standard rooms are clean, with modern decor in pastel tones. Note that there is no parking at the hotel, but public lots are close by. If you're staying at least a week, ask about lower weekly rates. *819 S. Flower St., 90017, tel. 213/624–5855, fax 213/624–8740. 64 rooms. Facilities: coin-operated laundry. AE, DC, MC, V.*

Mid-Wilshire
$$$–$$$$

Radisson Wilshire Plaza. The rooms have views of either Hollywood or downtown and have contemporary decor in light beige or gray. Corporate clients often use the large banquet and meeting rooms. *3515 Wilshire Blvd., 90010, tel. 213/381–7411 or 800/333–3333, fax 213/386–7379. 393 rooms. Facilities: 2 restaurants, lounge, pool, health club, no-smoking floor, parking (fee). AE, D, DC, MC, V.*

Hollywood and West Hollywood
$$$$
★

Bel Age Hotel. This elegant, European-style, all-suite hotel just off the Sunset Strip has a soothing, residential feel. The understated country-French decor is in dark woods and rose and mauve color schemes; the suites are spacious, with large living rooms. South-facing rooms have private terraces that look out over the Los Angeles skyline as far as the Pacific. Some touches are downright extravagant, such as three telephones with five lines in each suite, voice mail, original art, private terraces, and a daily newspaper. The hotel has a distinctive restaurant that serves fine Russian meals with a French flair. *1020 N. San Vicente Blvd., West Hollywood 90069, tel. 310/854–1111 or 800/424–4443, fax 310/854–0926. 188 suites. Facilities: 3 restaurants, lounge, business center, health club, pool, 24-hr room service, valet parking (fee), concierge. AE, MC, V.*

$$$$

Mondrian Hotel. This giant structure is a monument to the Dutch artist from whom the hotel takes its name. The exterior of the 12-story hotel is actually a giant surrealistic mural; inside there's fine artwork. Accommodations are spacious, with pale-wood furniture and curved sofas in the seating area. Ask for south-corner suites; they tend to be quieter than the rest. A chauffeured limousine is placed at each guest's disposal for a fee. Progressive California cuisine is served at Cafe Mondrian. The hotel is convenient to major recording, film, and TV studios. *8440 Sunset Blvd., West Hollywood 90069, tel. 213/650–8999 or 800/525–8029, fax 213/650–5215. 224 suites. Facilities: restaurant, pool, health club, 24-hr room service, parking (fee). AE, DC, MC, V.*

$$$$

Saint James's Club & Hotel. Located on the Sunset Strip, this early Art Deco building has been around since the 1930s. All its current furnishings are exact replicas of Art Deco masterpieces, the originals of which are in New York's Metropolitan Museum of Art. Ask for a city or mountain view. Both are great (although the rooms are a bit small by Los Angeles standards), but the cityside accommodations are more expensive. The hotel also features a 1930s-style supper club (California cuisine) with piano entertainment, a club bar, and a lounge. *8358 Sunset Blvd., West Hollywood 90069, tel. 213/654–7100 or 800/225–2637, fax 213/654–9287. 63 rooms. Facilities: restaurant, health center, sauna, pool, secretarial services, small meeting facilities. AE, DC, MC, V.*

$$$$ **Summerfield Suites Hotel.** This four-story luxury hotel features all suites, decorated in a modern style in shades of blue, pink, and salmon. All have private balconies. Great for business travelers, it's near "Restaurant Row on La Cienega," yet not as expensive as other hotels in this price category. *1000 Westmont Dr., West Hollywood 90069, tel. 310/657–7400, 800/833–4353, fax 310/854–6744. 109 suites. Facilities: bar, pool, health club, sun deck, parking (fee). AE, DC, MC, V.*

$$$ **Chateau Marmont Hotel.** Although planted on the Sunset Strip amid giant billboards and much sun-bleached Hollywood glitz, this castle of Old World charm and French Normandy design still promises its guests a secluded hideaway close to Hollywood's hot spots. A haunt for many reclusive show-biz personalities and discriminating world travelers since it opened in 1929, this is the ultimate in privacy. All kinds of accommodations are available, including fully equipped cottages, bungalows, and a penthouse. Small pets are allowed. *8221 Sunset Blvd., Hollywood 90046, tel. 213/656–1010 or 800/CHATEAU, fax 213/655–5311. 63 rooms. Facilities: dining room, pool, fitness room, 24-hr room service, 24-hr concierge, free parking. AE, MC, V.*

$$$ **Hyatt on Sunset.** In the heart of the Sunset Strip, this Hyatt is a favorite of music-biz execs and rock stars who appreciate the two-line phones and voice mail available here. There are penthouse suites, some rooms with private patios, and a rooftop pool. The rooms are decorated in peach colors and modern furniture; some have aquariums. The Silver Screen sports bar is a fun spot. *8401 W. Sunset Blvd., West Hollywood 90069, tel. 213/656–1234 or 800/233–1234, fax 213/650–7024. 262 rooms. Facilities: 2 restaurants, lounge, entertainment, pool, no-smoking floors, parking (fee). AE, DC, MC, V.*

$$ **Hollywood Holiday Inn.** You can't miss this hotel, one of the tallest buildings in Hollywood. It's 23 stories high, topped by Windows, a revolving restaurant-lounge (the Sunday brunch served here is a local favorite). The rooms are decorated in light gray and rose in standard-issue Holiday Inn fashion. There is a safekeeping box in each room. The hotel is only minutes from the Hollywood Bowl, Universal Studios, and Mann's Chinese Theater, and it's a Gray Line Tour stop. *1755 N. Highland Ave., Hollywood 90028, tel. 213/462–7181 or 800/465–4329, fax 213/466–9072. 470 rooms. Facilities: restaurant, coffee shop, pool, coin-operated laundry, parking (fee). AE, DC, MC, V.*

$ **Banana Bungalow Hotel and International Hostel.** You'll get the most for your money at this friendly miniresort in the Hollywood Hills, about ½ mile from the Hollywood Bowl. It's popular with backpackers and college students—don't expect a palace. It offers mostly hostel-style rooms, with three to six beds in each; you'll be sharing a room with people you don't know, unless you book one of the 12 double-occupancy rooms—be sure to specify what you want when booking. The decor is white and gray, with light wood furniture and plants. Checkout is early, by 10:30 AM. *2775 Cahuenga Blvd., West Hollywood 90068, tel. 213/851–1129 or 800/446–7835. 56 rooms. Facilities: Continental breakfast, movie theater, pool, weight room, pool room, games arcade, free parking, free shuttle to attractions, airports, and train and bus terminals. MC, V.*

Beverly Hills   **Beverly Hilton.** This large, contemporary-design hotel complex
$$$$ has a wide selection of restaurants and shops. Most rooms have balconies overlooking Beverly Hills or downtown. The on-premises
Trader Vic's and L'Escoffier are two of the city's better restaurants.
Of special interest to business travelers are a fax machine in the
lobby and cellular phone rentals. *9876 Wilshire Blvd., 90210, tel.
310/274–7777 or 800/445–8667, fax 310/285–1313. 581 rooms. Facilities: 3 restaurants, pool, wading pool, exercise room, refrigerators,
parking (fee). AE, DC, MC, V.*

$$$$ **Four Seasons Los Angeles.** Some say this property resembles a
★   French château with the refinement of a European manor house.
All suites have French doors and a balcony. There is an outstanding
restaurant on the premises serving California cuisine with French
influences, and there's great shopping only five minutes away on
Rodeo Drive and Melrose Avenue. *300 S. Doheny Dr., Los Angeles
90048, tel. 310/273–2222 or 800/332–3442, fax 310/859–3824. 285
rooms. Facilities: restaurant, lounge, pool, exercise equipment, 24-
hr room service, free self-parking and valet parking (fee). AE, DC,
MC, V.*

$$$$ **Hotel Nikko.** Distinctive Japanese accents distinguish this contemporary hotel located near Restaurant Row. Large guest rooms cater
to business travelers: There are oversize desks and work areas with
computer and fax hook-up capabilities. Traditional Japanese soak-
ing tubs dominate luxurious bathrooms, and a bedside remote-control conveniently operates in-room lighting, temperature, TV,
VCRs, and CD players. Pangaea, the hotel restaurant, serves
Pacific Rim cuisine. *465 S. La Cienega Blvd., Los Angeles 90035, tel.
310/247–0400, 800/NIKKO–US, or 800/NIKKO–BH; fax 310/247–
0315. 304 rooms. Facilities: restaurant, lounge, pool, Japanese garden, fitness center, business center, 24-hr room service, free
self-parking and valet parking (fee). AE, DC, MC, V.*

$$$$ **Hotel Sofitel Ma Maison.** Under the command of affable general
manager Richard Schilling, who hails from a long line of French
hoteliers, this hotel offers first-class service and the sort of intimacy
you usually expect in small European-style hotels. The country-
French guest rooms are done in terra-cotta and blues, with small
prints. The hotel is across the street from two giant malls and a
number of restaurants and movie theaters. The back of the property
faces a large brick wall, so insist on a southern view. *8555 Beverly
Blvd., Los Angeles 90048, tel. 310/278–5444 or 800/521–7772, fax
310/657–2816. 311 rooms. Facilities: 2 restaurants, pool, sauna, fitness center, parking (fee). AE, DC, MC, V.*

$$$$ **Le Parc Hotel.** A boutique hotel housed in a modern low-rise building, the four-story Le Parc is in a lovely residential area. Suites are
decorated in earth tones and shades of wine and rust with balconies,
fireplaces, VCRs, and kitchenettes. The hotel is near Farmer's Market, CBS Television City, and the Los Angeles County Museum of
Art. Cafe Le Parc is a private dining room for hotel guests only. *733
N.W. Knoll, West Hollywood 90069, tel. 310/855–8888 or 800/578–
4837, fax 310/659–5230. 154 suites. Facilities: lighted tennis courts,
heated pool, health club, valet and self parking (fee). AE, DC, MC,
V.*

$$$$ **The Peninsula Beverly Hills.** This luxury hotel was the first new
property to open in this prestigious Los Angeles enclave in more
than two decades when it made its debut in 1991. Surrounded by
flowered hedges, poplar trees, and elephant ears, a circular motor-
court greets guests in rare style. The hotel's appearance is classic,
done in French Renaissance architecture with contemporary overtones. Rooms are decorated like luxury homes, with antiques, rich
fabrics, and marble floors. Minibars and refrigerators can be found

behind French doors in all rooms, and all suites are equipped with compact disc players, fax machines, and individual security systems. *9882 Little Santa Monica Blvd., 90212, tel. 310/551–2888 or 800/462–7899, fax 310/788–2319. 195 rooms. Facilities: 2 restaurants, bar, business center, lap pool, health club, poolside cabanas, 24-hour valet parking, 24-hr concierge, voice mail. AE, DC, MC, V.*

$$$$ **Regent Beverly Wilshire.** This famous hotel at the foot of Rodeo Drive combines Italian Renaissance–style architecture with a French neoclassic influence. The guest rooms have appropriate period furnishings and glorious marble bathrooms. The multilingual staff offers personal service (like private butlers) and many other extras, such as the fresh raspberries and cream and designer water that are delivered to your room upon arrival. The hotel's restaurants include The Dining Room, with its Franco-California menu, and the Lobby Lounge Cafe, which serves California cuisine. *9500 Wilshire Blvd., 90212, tel. 310/275–5200 or 800/421–4354; in CA, 800/427–4354; fax 310/274–2851. 301 rooms. Facilities: 3 restaurants, pool, health spas, business center, concierge, no-smoking floors, valet parking (fee). AE, D, DC, MC, V.*

$$$ **Beverly Hills Ritz Hotel.** There's a very family-style European feel at this low-rise hotel; the friendly staff will get to know you by name, given half the chance. The cozy black-and-white lobby has overstuffed sofas and lots of plants. All the suites are off the pool. Furnishings are smart and contemporary; all feature kitchen/living room, one bedroom, and bath. *10300 Wilshire Blvd., 90024, tel. 310/275–5575 or 800/800–1234. 116 rooms. Facilities: restaurant, pool, small gym, Jacuzzi, garage. AE, DC, MC, V.*

$$$ **Beverly Pavilion Hotel.** Located near movie theaters and fashionable shopping, this hotel is popular with commercial travelers, and features the well-known restaurant Colette, with French cuisine and cocktail lounge. The average-size rooms and executive suites have balconies and are decorated in contemporary styles, mostly in beige, blue, and mauve. *9360 Wilshire Blvd., 90212, tel. 310/273–1400, 800/421–0545, or 800/441–5050 in CA. 110 rooms. Facilities: restaurant, lounge, pool, valet. AE, DC, MC, V.*

$$$ **Beverly Prescott Hotel.** This small, 12-story luxury hotel perched on a hill overlooking Beverly Hills, Century City, and the mighty Pacific, opened in May 1993. The open-air architecture is enhanced by soothing rooms decorated in warm salmon and caramel tones. Furnishings are stylish, and the rooms are spacious, with private balconies. *1224 S. Beverwil Dr., 90035, tel. 310/277–2800 or 800/421–3212, fax 310/203–9537. 140 rooms. Facilities: restaurant, pool, health club, business suites with computers and fax machines, 24-hr room service, valet parking (fee). AE, DC, MC, V.*

$$$ **Carlyle Inn.** Service is the byword of this intimate, small hostelry in the city's design district. The four-story, contemporary property offers guests several extras: a buffet breakfast; high tea in the afternoon; and wine by the glass in the evening. Rooms are decorated in peach with light pine furniture and black accents. *1119 S. Robertson Blvd., 90035, tel. 310/275–4445 or 800/3–CARLYLE, fax 310/859–0496. 32 rooms. Facilities: restaurant, free parking, Jacuzzi, in-room computer hookups, free shuttle service within 5-mi radius. AE, D, DC, MC, V.*

Century City
$$$$
★ **Century Plaza Hotel and Tower.** This 20-story hotel (on 10 acres of tropical plants and reflecting pools) features a 30-story tower, which is lavishly decorated with signature art and antiques, and is furnished like a mansion, with a mix of classic and contemporary appointments. Each room has a refrigerator and balcony with an ocean or a city view. There are three excellent restaurants here: the

award-winning La Chaumiere for California/French cuisine, the Terrace for Mediterranean/Italian, and the Cafe Plaza, a French-style café that serves American fare. *2025 Ave. of the Stars, 90067, tel. 310/277–2000 or 800/228–3000, fax 310/551–3395. 1,072 rooms. Facilities: 3 restaurants, 2 pools, whirlpools, poolside fitness centers, parking. AE, DC, MC, V.*

$$$$ ★ **J. W. Marriott Hotel at Century City.** This hotel is the West Coast flagship for the multifaceted Marriott chain. Its elegant, modern rooms are decorated in soft pastels and equipped with minibars, lavish marble baths, and facilities for travelers with disabilities. Ask for accommodations that overlook Twentieth Century Fox's back lot. The hotel offers complimentary limo service to Beverly Hills and provides excellent service. *2151 Ave. of the Stars, 90067, tel. 310/277–2777 or 800/228–9290, fax 310/785–9240. 367 rooms. Facilities: restaurant, indoor and outdoor pools, whirlpools, fitness center. AE, DC, MC, V.*

$$$ **Century City Courtyard by Marriott.** This more-than-comfortable hotel near the Century City business complex mixes California architecture with traditional fabrics and furnishings in soft hues. The entrance is bold, though: a red welcome carpet and a red London phone booth are your first impressions of the place. *10320 W. Olympic Blvd., Los Angeles 90067, tel. 310/556–2777 or 800/947–8521. 133 rooms. Facilities: restaurant, exercise salon, whirlpool, shuttle service to surrounding area, indoor parking (free). AE, DC, MC, V.*

$$ **Century City Inn.** This hotel is small but designed for comfort. Rooms have a refrigerator, microwave oven, remote-control TV and VCR, as well as a 10-cup coffee unit with fresh gourmet-blend coffee and tea. Baths have whirlpool tubs and a phone. Complimentary Continental breakfast is served. *10330 W. Olympic Blvd., Los Angeles 90064, tel. 310/553–1000 or 800/553–1005, fax 310/277–1633. 46 rooms. Facilities: video library, parking (fee). AE, DC, MC, V.*

Bel Air, Westwood, and West Los Angeles
$$$$ **Hotel Bel-Air.** This charming, secluded hotel—a celebrity mecca—is one of Los Angeles's best. Extensive exotic gardens and a creek complete with swans give it the ambience of a top-rated resort. The lovely rooms and suites are impeccably decorated in peach and earth tones. All are villa/bungalow style with Mediterranean decor offering the feel of fine homes. For their quietest accommodation, ask for a room near the former stable area. *701 Stone Canyon Rd., Bel Air 90077, tel. 310/472–1211 or 800/648–4097. 92 rooms. Facilities: 2 restaurants, lounge, pool, parking (fee). AE, DC, MC, V.*

$$$$ **Westwood Marquis Hotel and Gardens.** This hotel near UCLA is a favorite of corporate and entertainment types. Each individualized suite in its 15 stories has a view of Bel Air, the Pacific Ocean, or Century City. South-facing suites overlooking the pool also offer expansive views of the city and sea. Breakfast and lunch are served in the Garden Terrace, which also has a popular Sunday brunch. The award-winning Dynasty Room restaurant features Continental cuisine. European teas are served in the afternoon in the Westwood Lounge. *930 Hilgard Ave., Los Angeles 90024, tel. 310/208–8765 or 800/421–2317, fax 310/824–0355. 258 suites. Facilities: 2 restaurants, lounge, 2 pools, health club, 24-hr room service, no-smoking floor, valet parking (fee). AE, DC, MC, V.*

$$$ **Radisson Bel-Air.** In its lovely garden setting, this two-story hotel feels very southern Californian, with patios and terraces overlooking the lush tropical greenery. Guest rooms are decorated in muted tones of cream and gray, with furniture in sleek, modern shapes and art deco–style fixtures. *11461 Sunset Blvd., Los Angeles 90049, tel. 310/476–6571 or 800/333–3333. 162 rooms. Facilities: restaurant,*

lounge, business center, Continental breakfast, evening hors d'oeuvres, pool, health club, tennis courts, concierge, local shuttle service, no-smoking rooms, parking (fee). AE, DC, MC, V.

$$–$$$ **Century Wilshire.** Most units in this three-story European-style hotel are suites with kitchenettes. There are tiled baths and a homey English-style pastel decor. Within walking distance of UCLA and Westwood Village, this simple hotel has views of Wilshire and the courtyard. The clientele here is mostly European. *10776 Wilshire Blvd., West Los Angeles 90024, tel. 310/474–4506 or 800/421–7223 (outside CA), fax 310/474–2535. 99 rooms. Facilities: Continental breakfast, pool, free parking. AE, DC, MC, V.*

$ **Best Western Royal Palace Hotel.** This small hotel located just off I–405 (San Diego Freeway) is decorated with modern touches, lots of wood, and mirrors. In-room morning coffee and tea are complimentary, as is parking to hotel guests. All the rooms are suites with a kitchenette and a queen sofa sleeper in addition to a king or double bed. A new wing—with about 30 more rooms—is scheduled to open in mid-1995. *2528 S. Sepulveda Blvd., West Los Angeles 90064, tel. 310/477–9066 or 800/528–1234, fax 310/478–4133. 42 suites. Facilities: Continental breakfast, pool, Jacuzzi, exercise room and billiard room, laundry facilities, free parking. AE, DC, MC, V.*

Santa Monica **Loews Santa Monica Beach Hotel.** Set on the most precious of
$$$$ Los Angeles real estate—beachfront—this hotel is two blocks south of the landmark Santa Monica Pier. The property's centerpiece is a five-story glass atrium with views of the Pacific. Rooms are California casual with bleached rattan and wicker furniture. Most have ocean views and private balconies, and all guests have direct access to the beach. *1700 Ocean Ave., 90401, tel. 310/458–6700, fax 310/458–6761. 350 rooms, 31 suites. Facilities: restaurant, café, fitness center, indoor-outdoor pool, business center, no-smoking floors, concierge, self and valet parking (fee). AE, DC, MC, V.*

$$$$ **Miramar Sheraton.** This hotel, "where Wilshire meets the sea," is close to all area beaches, across the street from Pacific Palisades Park, and near deluxe shopping areas and many quaint eateries. The landscape is dominated by a gigantic rubber tree. Many rooms have balconies overlooking the ocean. The decor in some rooms is up-to-the-minute contemporary, with bleached wood, marble, granite, glass, and brick. *101 Wilshire Blvd., 90403, tel. 310/576–7777 or 800/325–3535. 301 rooms. Facilities: restaurant, lounge, health club, heated pool, valet and self parking (fee). AE, DC, MC, V.*

$$ **Holiday Inn Santa Monica Beach.** Close to many restaurants, major shopping centers, the beach, and Santa Monica Pier, this inn has standard Holiday Inn rooms and amenities. *120 Colorado Ave., 90401, tel. 310/451–0676 or 800/947–9175, fax 310/393–7145. 132 rooms. Facilities: restaurant, lounge, pool, laundry facilities, valet parking (fee). AE, DC, MC, V.*

$ **Carmel Hotel.** This charming hotel built in the 1920s is one block from the beach and Santa Monica Place, as well as from movie theaters and many fine restaurants. Electric ceiling fans add to the simple room decor done in wine, hunter green, and beige tones. *201 Broadway, 90401, tel. 310/451–2469 or 800/445–8695, fax 310/393–4180. 102 rooms, 8 suites. Facilities: restaurant, valet or self parking (fee). AE, DC, MC, V.*

$ **Palm Motel.** This quiet, unceremonious motel has old-fashioned rooms, in which the decorative highlight is the color TV. But the Palm does offer complimentary coffee, tea, and cookies at breakfast, and it's only a short drive away from several good restaurants. *2020 14th St., 90405, tel. 310/452–3822. 25 rooms. Facilities: self-service laundry, free parking. MC, V.*

Marina del Rey

$$$$ ★ **Doubletree Marina del Rey L.A.** This luxurious, nine-story, high-rise property has a high-tech design softened by a pastel-toned decor accented in brass and marble. Ask for upper-floor rooms that face the marina. There are lovely touches in this Mediterranean-style hotel, such as a gazebo in the patio and rooms with water views. The restaurant Stones is known for its fresh seafood. *4100 Admiralty Way, 90292, tel. 310/301–3000 or 800/528–0444, fax 310/301–6890. 375 rooms. Facilities: restaurant, lounges, business center, pool, 24-hr airport shuttle, valet and self parking (fee). AE, DC, MC, V.*

$$$$ **Marina del Rey Hotel.** Completely surrounded by water, this deluxe waterfront hotel is on the marina's main channel, making cruises and charters easily accessible. Guest rooms (contemporary with a nautical touch) have balconies and patios, and many have harbor views. The hotel is within walking distance of shopping and only a bike ride away from Fisherman's Village. There are meeting rooms and a beautiful gazebo area for parties. *13534 Bali Way, 90292, tel. 310/301–1000, 800/882–4000, or 800/8–MARINA in CA; fax 310/301–8167. 158 rooms. Facilities: 2 restaurants, lounge, pool, putting green, airport transportation, free parking. AE, DC, MC, V.*

$$$–$$$$ **Marina del Rey Marriott Inn.** Located in a lively area—a shopping center near Fox Hills Mall and across the street from a movie theater—the hotel was built in 1977. The Old World–style rooms are decorated in light blue, rust, or light green. Tropical trees and foliage enhance the pool area; Sunday brunch is served by the water and a goldfish pond. *13480 Maxella Ave., 90292, tel. 310/822–8555 or 800/228–9290, fax 310/823–2996. 283 rooms. Facilities: restaurant, lounge, pool, health club, parking (fee). AE, DC, MC, V.*

$$$–$$$$ **Marina International Hotel.** Across from a sandy beach within the marina, this hotel's village-style decor is done in earth tones with California-style furniture. Each of the very private rooms offers a balcony or patio that faces the garden or the courtyard. Ask for one of the bungalows—they're huge. The Crystal Fountain restaurant has Continental cuisine. Boat charters are available for up to 200 people. *4200 Admiralty Way, 90292, tel. 310/301–2000, 800/8–MARINA, or 800/882–4000; fax 310/301–6687. 110 rooms, 25 bungalows. Facilities: restaurant, lounge, pool, health club, airport transportation, free parking. AE, DC, MC, V.*

$$$–$$$$ **The Ritz-Carlton, Marina del Rey.** This sumptuous property sits on some prime real estate at the northern end of a basin, offering a panoramic view of the Pacific. The well-appointed contemporary rooms have French doors, marble baths, honor bars, and plenty of amenities—from maid service twice a day to plush terry robes. *4375 Admiralty Way, 90292, tel. 310/823–1700, fax 310/823–7318. 306 rooms. Facilities: 2 restaurants, pool, fitness center, business center, tennis courts, valet parking (fee). AE, DC, MC, V.*

$$ **Marina Pacific Hotel & Suites.** This hotel faces the Pacific and one of the world's most vibrant boardwalks; it's nestled among Venice's art galleries, shops, and elegant, offbeat restaurants. The marina is just a stroll away. Comfortable accommodations include suites, conference facilities, full-service amenities, and a delightful sidewalk café. For active travelers, there are ocean swimming, roller skating along the strand, racquetball, and tennis nearby. *1697 Pacific Ave., Venice 90291, tel. 310/399–7770 or 800/421–8151, fax 310/452–5479. 57 rooms, 35 suites; 1-bedroom apartments available. Facilities: restaurant, laundry, free parking. AE, DC, MC, V.*

South Bay
Beach Cities
$$$–$$$$

Holiday Inn Crowne Plaza. Across the street from the Redondo Beach Pier, this swank five-story hotel overlooks the Pacific. There are plenty of amenities, including indoor and outdoor dining and a nightclub. The rooms are decorated in a seaside theme with light woods and soft colors. *300 N. Harbor Dr., Redondo Beach 90277, tel. 310/318–8888 or 800/368–9760, fax 310/376–1930. 339 rooms. Facilities: 2 restaurants, lounge, entertainment, business center, pool, exercise room, game room, sauna, whirlpool, tennis, parking (fee). AE, DC, MC, V.*

$$
★

Barnaby's Hotel. Modeled after a 19th-century English inn, with four-poster beds, lace curtains, and antique decorations, Barnaby's also has an enclosed greenhouse pool. The London Pub resembles a cozy English hang-out, with live entertainment; Barnaby's Restaurant serves Continental cuisine and has private, curtained booths. Complimentary English buffet breakfast is served. *3501 Sepulveda Blvd. (at Rosecrans), Manhattan Beach 90266, tel. 310/545–8466 or 800/552–5285, fax 310/552–5285. 126 rooms. Facilities: 2 restaurants, lounge, pool, health-club privileges, no-smoking floor, free valet parking. AE, DC, MC, V.*

Airport
$$$–$$$$

Sheraton Los Angeles Airport Hotel. This luxurious 15-story hotel is in the perfect setting for business and leisure travelers alike. The contemporary rooms are decorated in muted shades of mauve, brown, green, and purple. There are two restaurants: Plaza Brasserie, a coffee shop, and Landry's, for California cuisine. Forty-eight of the rooms were designed especially for people with disabilities. *6101 W. Century Blvd., Los Angeles 90045, tel. 310/642–1111 or 800/325–3535, fax 310/410–1267. 807 rooms. Facilities: 2 restaurants, lounges, exercise room, voice mail, complimentary in-room coffee, multilingual concierge, currency exchange. AE, DC, MC, V.*

$$$

Hyatt Hotel–LAX. Rich brown marble in the lobby entrance and dark wood columns delineate the neoclassical decor of this contemporary 12-story building close to LAX, Hollywood Park, the Forum, and Marina del Rey. The Hyatt keeps business travelers in mind, offering in-room fax machines, computer hookups, and voice mail, plus large meeting rooms with ample banquet space. The hotel's staff is multilingual. Try T. J. Peppercorn's for California cuisine, and Mrs. Candy's, a '50s-style soda fountain. *6225 W. Century Blvd., Los Angeles 90045, tel. 310/337–1234 or 800/233–1234, fax 310/216–9334. 594 rooms. Facilities: 2 restaurants, lounge, entertainment, pool, health club, no-smoking floors, self and valet parking (fee). AE, DC, MC, V.*

$$$
★

Westin Hotel LAX. This three-wing hotel is a good place to stay if you want to be pampered but also need to be at the airport. Rooms and suites are decorated in muted earth tones to complement the contemporary decor; many suites have private outdoor spas. The expansive, luxurious lobby is decorated in marble and brass. The Trattoria Grande restaurant features pasta and seafood specialties. *5400 W. Century Blvd., Los Angeles 90045, tel. 310/216–5858 or 800/228–3000, fax 310/645–8053. 729 rooms. Facilities: 2 restaurants, lounge, entertainment, pool, sauna, fitness center, business center, parking (fee). AE, DC, MC, V.*

$$

Airport Marina Hotel. Located in a quiet, residential area, perfect for jogging, tennis, and golf, this contemporary hotel consists of four separate wings and several buildings, the main one a 12-story high-rise. The large marbled lobby boasts writing tables, plants, and comfortable sofas. The rooms are warm, with plenty of wood; all have either pool, ocean, or airport views. A shuttle service goes to LAX, Marina del Rey, and Fox Hills Mall. *8601 Lincoln Blvd., Los Angeles 90045, tel. 310/670–8111 or 800/225–8126, fax 310/337–1883. 770* *rooms. Facilities: restaurant, pool, airport transportation. AE, DC, MC, V.*

$ **Holiday Inn–LAX.** This international-style hotel appeals to families as well as business types, with standard Holiday Inn rooms decorated in earth tones—beige, burgundy, orange, and green. Amenities include a California-cuisine restaurant and cocktail lounge, multilingual telephone operators, and tour information. *9901 La Cienega Blvd., Los Angeles 90045, tel. 310/649–5151 or 800/238–8000, fax 310/670–3619. 403 rooms. Facilities: restaurant, pool, parking (fee), LAX shuttle. AE, DC, MC, V.*

$ **Red Lion Inn.** Just three miles north of LAX and a few minutes from Marina del Rey, this deluxe hotel is convenient for business types. There is both elegant and casual dining. The Culver's Club Lounge has lively entertainment and dancing. The oversize guest rooms on twelve floors have a '90s version of art deco–style decor. Extra special is the California Suite, with beautiful decorations and its own Jacuzzi. *6161 Centinela Ave., Culver City 90230, tel. 310/649–1776, fax 310/649–4411. 368 rooms. Facilities: 2 restaurants, lounge, entertainment, pool, sauna, health club, no-smoking floors, free parking. AE, DC, MC, V.*

San Fernando Valley
$$$$

Sheraton Universal. You're apt to see movie and TV stars in this 21-story hotel. It's on the grounds of Universal Studios, and within walking distance of the Universal Amphitheater, Universal Studios Tour, and CityWalk. The rooms are decorated in natural tones, with floor-to-ceiling windows that actually open, should you care to get some fresh air. *333 Universal Terrace Pkwy., Universal City 91608, tel. 818/980–1212. 444 rooms. Facilities: 2 restaurants, sports bar, pool, health club, business center, no-smoking floors, self and valet parking (fee). AE, DC, MC, V.*

$$$ **Burbank Airport Hilton.** Across the street from the Hollywood-Burbank Airport and close to Universal Studios, this hotel is geared to business meetings—there's a state-of-the-art convention center on the premises. The rooms have standard-issue hotel decor and no particularly nice views. *2500 Hollywood Way, Burbank 91505, tel. 818/843–6000, fax 818/842–9720. 500 rooms. Facilities: restaurant, pool, whirlpool spa, in-room color TV and VCR, parking (fee). AE, DC, MC, V.*

$$ **Sportsman's Lodge Hotel.** An English country–style building with a resort atmosphere, this hotel features beautiful grounds with waterfalls, a swan-filled lagoon, and a bright white gazebo. Guest rooms are large, and are decorated in soft colors like mauve and blue. Studio suites with private patios are available, and there's an Olympic-size swimming pool and a restaurant that serves American and Continental cuisine. The hotel is close to the Universal Studios Tour and Universal Amphitheater. *12825 Ventura Blvd., North Hollywood 91604, tel. 818/769–4700 or 800/821–8511, fax 213/877–3898. 193 rooms. Facilities: 3 restaurants, pool, health club, free parking. AE, DC, MC, V.*

$ **Safari Inn.** Often used for location filming, this motel-like property near Warner Brothers Studios, encompassing two buildings, has a homey, neighborhood feel. The decor, in antique white and gold, has a modern flair, as for example in the rooms with sleek rattan-and-bamboo furniture. Suites with bars are available. There's a fine Italian restaurant called Jane's Cucina on the premises. *1911 W. Olive, Burbank 91506, tel. 818/845–8586 or 800/STA–HERE, fax 818/845–0054. 110 rooms. Facilities: restaurant, lounge, pool, Jacuzzi, refrigerators, free parking. AE, DC, MC, V.*

Pasadena
$$$–$$$$

Ritz-Carlton Huntington Hotel. This landmark hotel, built in 1906, was closed in 1986 for five years and virtually rebuilt to conform to earthquake-code standards. Reopened in 1991, it justifies the enormous effort. The main building, a Mediterranean-style structure in warm-colored stucco, fits perfectly with the lavish houses of the surrounding Oak Knoll neighborhood, Pasadena's best. Walk through the intimate lobby into the central courtyard, dotted with tiny ponds and lush plantings, to the wood-paneled grand lounge, where you can have afternoon tea while enjoying a sweeping view of Los Angeles in the distance. Guest rooms are traditionally furnished and handsome, although a bit small for the price; the large marble-fitted bathrooms also look old-fashioned. The landscaped grounds are lovely, with their Japanese and horseshoe gardens and the historic Picture Bridge, which has murals depicting scenes of California along its 20 gables. The food is excellent and the service attentive. *1401 S. Oak Knoll Ave., Pasadena 91106, tel. 818/568–3900, fax 818/568–3700. 383 rooms. Facilities: 2 restaurants, tennis courts, pool, health club, no-smoking floors, valet parking (fee). AE, D, DC, MC, V.*

The Arts and Nightlife

For the most complete listing of weekly events, get the current issue of *Los Angeles* magazine. The Calendar section of the *Los Angeles Times* also offers a wide survey of Los Angeles arts events, as do the more irreverent free publications the *L.A. Weekly* and the *L.A. Reader.* For a telephone report on current music, theater, dance, film, and special events, call tel. 213/688–ARTS.

Most tickets can be purchased by phone (with a credit card) from **Ticketmaster** (tel. 213/365–3500), **TeleCharge** (tel. 800/762–7666), **Good Time Tickets** (tel. 213/464–7383), or **Murray's Tickets** (tel. 213/234–0123).

The Arts

Theater   Los Angeles isn't quite the "Broadway of the West" as some have claimed—the scope of theater here really doesn't compare to that in New York. Still, there are plenty of offerings worth any visitor's time in this entertainment-oriented city.

The theater scene's growth has been astounding. In 1978 only about 370 professional productions were brought to stages in Los Angeles; now well over 1,000 are scheduled each year. Small theaters are blossoming all over town, and the larger houses, despite price hikes to $35 for a single ticket, are usually full.

Even small productions might boast big names from "the Business" (the Los Angeles entertainment empire). Many film and television actors love to work on the stage between "big" projects or while on hiatus from a TV series as a way to refresh their talents or regenerate their creativity in this demanding medium. Doing theater is also an excellent way to be seen by those who matter in the glitzier end of show biz. Hence there is a need for both large houses—which usually mount productions that are road-company imports of Broadway hits or, on occasion, where Broadway-bound material gets a tryout—and a host of small, intimate theaters to showcase the talent that abounds in this city.

Major **The Music Center** (135 N. Grand Ave., tel. 213/972–7211). This big *Theaters* downtown complex includes three theaters: the 3,200-seat **Dorothy Chandler Pavilion,** which offers a smattering of plays in between performances of the L.A. Philharmonic, L.A. Master Chorale, and

L.A. Opera; the 2,071-seat **Ahmanson Theater,** presenting both classics and new plays (closed for renovation until some time in 1995; check local newspaper listings when you hit town to find out if it's open); and the 760-seat **Mark Taper Forum,** under the direction of Gordon Davidson, which presents new works that often go on to Broadway, such as *Angels in America* and *Jelly's Last Jam.*

James A. Doolittle Theater (1615 N. Vine St., Hollywood, tel. 213/972–0700, or call Ticketmaster, tel. 213/365–3500). Located in the heart of Hollywood, this house offers an intimate feeling despite its 1,038-seat capacity. New plays, dramas, comedies, and musicals are presented here year-round.

John Anson Ford Theater (2580 Cahuenga Blvd., Hollywood, tel. 213/744–3466). This 1,300-seat outdoor house in the Hollywood Hills is best known for its Shakespeare and free summer jazz, dance, and cabaret concerts.

Pantages (6233 Hollywood Blvd., Hollywood, tel. 213/468–1770, or call Ticketmaster, tel. 213/365–3500). Once the home of the Academy Awards telecast and Hollywood premieres, this house is massive (2,600 seats) and a splendid example of high-style Hollywood Art Deco, although the acoustics could use some updating. Large-scale musicals from Broadway are usually presented here.

Westwood Playhouse (10886 Le Conte Ave., Westwood, tel. 310/208–6500 or 310/208–5454). An acoustically superior theater with great sight lines, the 498-seat playhouse showcases new plays in the summer, primarily musicals and comedies. Many of the productions here are on their way to or from Broadway. This is also where Jason Robards and Nick Nolte got their starts.

Wilshire Theater (8440 Wilshire Blvd., Beverly Hills, tel. 213/468–1716, or call Ticketmaster, tel. 213/365–3500). The interior of this 1,900-seat house is Art Deco-style; musicals from Broadway are the usual fare.

Smaller Theaters **Cast Theater** (804 N. El Centro, Hollywood, tel. 213/462–0265). Musicals, revivals, and avant-garde improv pieces are done here.

The Coast Playhouse (8325 Santa Monica Blvd., West Hollywood, tel. 213/650–8507). This 99-seat house specializes in excellent original musicals and new dramas.

Fountain Theater (5060 Fountain Ave., Hollywood, tel. 213/663–1525). Seating 80, this theater presents original American dramas and stages Flamenco dance concerts. Marian Mercer and Rob Reiner got their starts here.

Japan America Theater (244 S. San Pedro St., downtown, tel. 213/680–3700). This community-oriented 880-seat theater at the Japan Cultural Arts Center is home to local theater, dance troupes, and the L.A. Chamber Orchestra, plus numerous children's theater groups.

Santa Monica Playhouse (1211 4th St., Santa Monica, tel. 310/394–9779). This 99-seat house is worth visiting for its cozy, librarylike atmosphere; the good comedies and dramas presented here are further incentive.

Skylight Theater (1816½ N. Vermont Ave., Los Feliz, tel. 213/666–2202). With 99 seats, this theater has hosted many highly inventive productions.

Theatre/Theater (1713 Cahuenga Blvd., Hollywood, tel. 213/871–0210). Angelinos crowd into this 70-seat house to view original works by local authors as well as international playwrights.

Concerts Los Angeles is not only the focus of America's pop/rock music recording scene, but now, after years of being denigrated as a cultural invalid, is also a center for classical music and opera.

Major
Concert Halls

The Ambassador Auditorium (300 W. Green St., Pasadena, tel. 818/304–6161). World-renowned soloists and ensembles perform in this elegant and acoustically impressive hall from September through June.

Dorothy Chandler Pavilion (135 N. Grand Ave., tel. 213/972–7211). Part of the Los Angeles Music Center and—with the Hollywood Bowl—the center of L.A.'s classical music scene, the 3,200-seat Pavilion is the home of the Los Angeles Philharmonic. The L.A. Opera presents classics from September through June.

The Greek Theater (2700 N. Vermont Ave., tel. 213/665–1927). This open-air auditorium near Griffith Park offers some classical performances in its mainly pop/rock/jazz schedule from June through October. Its Doric columns evoke the amphitheaters of ancient Greece.

The Hollywood Bowl (2301 Highland Ave., tel. 213/850–2000). Open since 1920, the Bowl is one of the world's largest outdoor amphitheaters, and located in a park surrounded by mountains, trees, and gardens. The Bowl's season runs early July–mid-September; the L.A. Philharmonic spends its summer season here. There are performances daily except Mondays (and some Sundays); the program ranges from jazz to pop to classical. Concert goers usually arrive early, bringing or buying picnic suppers. There are plenty of picnic tables, and box-seat subscribers can reserve a table right in their own box. Restaurant dining is available on the grounds (reservations recommended, tel. 213/851–3588). The seats are wood, so you might bring or rent a cushion—and bring a sweater; it gets chilly here in the evening. A convenient way to enjoy the Hollywood Bowl experience without the hassle of parking is to take one of the Park-and-Ride buses, which leave from various locations around town; call the Bowl for information.

Royce Hall (405 N. Hilgard Ave., tel. 310/825–2101). Internationally acclaimed performers are featured in this 1,800-seat auditorium at UCLA. The university's **Schoenberg Hall,** smaller but with wonderful acoustics, also hosts a variety of concerts.

The Shrine Auditorium (665 W. Jefferson Blvd., tel. 213/749–5123). Built in 1926 by the Al Malaikah Temple, the auditorium's decor could be called Baghdad and Beyond. Touring companies from all over the world, along with assorted gospel and choral groups, appear in this one-of-a-kind, 6,200-seat theater.

The Wilshire Ebell Theater (4401 W. 8th St., tel. 213/939–1128). The Los Angeles Opera Theatre comes to this Spanish-style building, erected in 1924, as do a broad spectrum of other musical performers.

Wiltern Theater (Wilshire Blvd. and Western Ave., tel. 213/380–5005 or 213/388–1400). Reopened in 1985 as a venue for the Los Angeles Opera Theater, the building was constructed in 1930, is listed in the National Register of Historic Places, and is a magnificent example of Art Deco in its green terra-cotta glory.

Dance

Due to lack of Music Center funding, Los Angeles lost the Joffrey Ballet in 1991, and Angelinos have since turned to local dance companies. You can find talented companies dancing around town at various performance spaces. Check the *L.A. Weekly* free newspaper under "dance" to see who is dancing where, or call **The Dance Resource Center** (tel. 213/622–0815).

L.A. still has one resident company, the **Bella Lewistsky Dance Co.** (tel. 213/580–6338), which performs around town.

Visiting companies such as Martha Graham, Paul Taylor, and Hubbard Street Dance Company perform in UCLA Dance Company's home space at **UCLA Center for the Arts** (405 N. Hilgard Ave., tel. 310/825–2101).

Larger companies such as the Kirov, the Bolshoi, and the American Ballet Theater (ABT) perform at various times during the year at the **Shrine Auditorium** (665 W. Jefferson Blvd. tel. 213/749–5123). Also, two prominent dance events occur annually: The Dance Fair in March and Dance Kaleidoscope in July. Both events take place at **Cal State L.A.'s Dance Department** (5151 State University Dr., tel. 213/343–5124).

Movie Palaces   **Mann's Chinese Theater** (6925 Hollywood Blvd., Hollywood, tel. 213/464–8111). Formerly owned by Sid Grauman, this Chinese pagoda-style structure is perhaps the world's best-known movie theater. It still carries on one of the oldest of Hollywood traditions: its famous hand- and footprinting ceremony, which supposedly began after actress Norma Talmadge accidentally stepped into wet cement at the theater's opening in 1927 (the film shown that night was Cecil B. DeMille's *King of Kings*). Today the Chinese houses three movie screens, and it still hosts many gala premieres.

Pacific Cinerama Dome (6360 Sunset Blvd., Hollywood, tel. 213/466–3401). This futuristic, geodesic structure was the first theater designed specifically for Cinerama in the United States. The gigantic screen and multitrack sound system create an unparalleled cinematic experience.

Pacific's El Capitan (6838 Hollywood Blvd., Hollywood, tel. 213/467–7674). Restored to its original Art Deco splendor, this classic movie palace reopened across the street from Mann's Chinese in 1991. First-run movies are on the bill. The Academy Award-winning Disney movie *The Little Mermaid* made its debut here in 1991.

Silent Movie (611 N. Fairfax Ave., tel. 213/653–2389). Though not a movie palace itself, this theater revives classics like Charlie Chaplin's *The Gold Rush* and the portfolio of Buster Keaton films. Open Wednesday, Friday, and Saturday evenings, it's known as the only silent movie house in the world, complete with a vintage organ.

Vista Theater (4473 Sunset Dr., Los Feliz, tel. 213/660–6639). At the intersection of Hollywood and Sunset boulevards, this 70-year-old cinema was once Bard's Hollywood Theater, where both moving pictures and vaudeville played. A Spanish-style facade leads to an ornate Egyptian interior. D. W. Griffith's silent classic *Intolerance* was filmed on this site.

Television   **Audiences Unlimited** (100 Universal City Plaza, Building 153, Universal City 91608, tel. 818/506–0043) is a nifty organization that helps fill seats for television programs (and sometimes theater events, as well). There's no charge, but the tickets are on a first-come, first-served basis. Tickets can be picked up at Fox Television Center (5746 Sunset Blvd., Van Ness Ave. entrance, weekdays 8:30–6, weekends 11–6) or at the Glendale Galleria Information Desk between 10 and 9 daily. Note: You must be 16 or older to attend a television taping. For a schedule, send a self-addressed envelope a couple of weeks prior to your visit to the address above.

Nightlife

Despite the high energy level of the nightlife crowd, Los Angeles nightclubs aren't known for keeping their doors open until the wee hours. This is still an early-to-bed city, and it's safe to say that by 2 AM, most jazz, rock, and disco clubs have closed for the night. Perhaps it's the temperate climate and the daytime sports orientation of the city: Most Angelinos want to be on the tennis court or out jogging first thing in the morning, making a late-night social life out of the question. Others hang out quietly at various coffee houses found around town.

The accent in this city is on trendy rock clubs, smooth country-and-western establishments, intimate jazz spots, and comedy clubs. Consult *Los Angeles* magazine for current listings. The Sunday *Los Angeles Times* Calendar section and the free *L.A. Weekly* and *L.A. Reader* also provide listings.

The Sunset Strip, which runs from West Hollywood to Beverly Hills, offers a wide assortment of nighttime diversions. Comedy stores, restaurants with piano bars, cocktail lounges, and hard-rock clubs proliferate. Westwood, home of UCLA, is a college town, and this section of Los Angeles comes alive at night with rock and new-wave clubs playing canned and live music. It's one of the few areas in the city with a true neighborhood spirit. For years, downtown Los Angeles hasn't offered much in the way of nighttime entertainment (with the exception of the Music Center for concerts and theater), but that has gradually changed over the last year, with the openings of more theaters and trendy clubs. Some of Los Angeles's best jazz clubs, discos, and comedy clubs are scattered throughout the San Fernando and San Gabriel valleys.

Dress codes vary depending on the place you visit. Jackets are expected at cabarets and hotels. Discos are generally casual, although some will turn away the denim-clad. The rule of thumb is to phone ahead and check the dress code, but on the whole, Los Angeles is oriented toward casual wear.

Jazz
Atlas Bar & Grill (3760 Wilshire Blvd., tel. 213/380–8400). The eclectic entertainment at this snazzy supper club includes torch singers as well as a jazz band.

The Baked Potato (3787 Cahuenga Blvd. W, North Hollywood, tel. 818/980–1615). In this tiny club they pack you in like sardines to hear a powerhouse of jazz. The featured item on the menu is, of course, baked potatoes; they're jumbo and stuffed with everything from steak to vegetables.

Birdland West (105 W. Broadway, Long Beach, tel. 310/436–9341). This is the place to come for contemporary jazz, Art Deco decor, and great happy hours.

Jax (339 N. Brand Blvd., Glendale, tel. 818/500–1604). This intimate club serves a wide variety of food, from sandwiches to steak and seafood; live music is an added draw.

The Jazz Bakery (3221 Hutchison, Culver City, tel. 310/271–9039). On weekends Jim Britt opens his photography studio, adjacent to the Helms Bakery Building, to serve coffee, desserts, and a nice selection of world-class jazz, enhanced by great acoustics and a smoke-free environment. The $15 admission (no credit cards) includes refreshments.

The Lighthouse (30 Pier Ave., Hermosa Beach, tel. 310/372–6911 or 213/376–9833). Once one of Los Angeles's finest jazz venues, this club now offers a broad spectrum of music, from blues to reggae—though not much jazz anymore, except at Sunday brunch. The decor is wood, brass, and brick, with a lot of plants. Dine on pizza or burgers while listening to the sounds.

Marla's Memory Lane (2323 W. Martin Luther King Jr. Blvd., Los Angeles, tel. 213/294–8430). Owned by comedy star Marla Gibbs of "The Jeffersons" and "227," the room pops with blues, jazz, and easy listening. James Ingram plays here from time to time. The appetizer menu boasts Cajun tidbits.

Vine Street Bar and Grill (1610 N. Vine St., Hollywood, tel. 213/463–4375). This elegant club in the heart of Hollywood (across the street from the James Doolittle Theater) features two shows nightly. Past performers have included Eartha Kitt, Cab Calloway, and Carmen McRae. Italian food is served.

Folk, Pop, and Rock
Blue Saloon (4657 Lankershim Blvd., North Hollywood, tel. 818/766–4644). For rock 'n' roll, this is the place to go. (You'll also catch a smattering of country and blues at times.) If your seat gets tired while listening to the music, rustle up a game of billiards or darts. This is the friendliest club around.

Club Lingerie (6507 Sunset Blvd., Hollywood, tel. 213/466–8557). One local describes this place as "clean enough for the timid, yet seasoned quite nicely for the tenured scenester." Best of all is its mix of really hot bands.

Ghengis Cohen Cantina (740 N. Fairfax Ave., West Hollywood, tel. 213/653–0640). At this long-time music industry hangout, you can hear up-and-coming talent, usually in a refreshingly mellow format like MTV's *Unplugged* performances. A plus is the restaurant's Chinese cuisine.

Kingston 12 (814 Broadway, Santa Monica, tel. 310/451–4423). This Santa Monica club features Daddy Freddie, the world's fastest rapper. Reggae music is also on tap, as is a menu of fine Jamaican food.

McCabe's Guitar Shop (3101 Pico Blvd., Santa Monica, tel. 310/828–4497; concert information, 310/828–4403). Folk, acoustic-rock, bluegrass, and soul concerts are featured in this guitar store on weekend nights.

The Palace (1735 N. Vine St., Hollywood, tel. 213/462–3000). The "in" spot for the upwardly mobile, this plush Art Deco palace boasts live entertainment, a fabulous sound system, full bar, and dining upstairs. The patrons here dress to kill.

Pier 52 (52 Pier Ave., Hermosa Beach, tel. 310/376–1629). From Wednesday through Sunday there are live dance bands here playing pure rock and roll.

The Roxy (9009 Sunset Blvd., West Hollywood, tel. 310/276–2222). The premier Los Angeles rock club, classy and comfortable, offers performance art as well as theatrical productions.

The Strand (1700 S. Pacific Coast Hwy., Redondo Beach, tel. 310/316–1700). This major concert venue covers a lot of ground, hosting hot new acts or such old favorites as Asleep at the Wheel, blues man Albert King, rock vet Robin Trower, and Billy Vera, all in the same week. Who says you can't have it all?

The Troubador (9081 Santa Monica Blvd., West Hollywood, tel. 310/276–6168). One of the hottest 70's clubs is now rolling again, this time with up-and-coming talent. The adjoining bar is a great place in which to see and be seen.

The Viper Room (8852 Sunset Blvd., West Hollywood, tel. 310/358–1880). This musicians' hangout, part-owned by actor Johnny Depp, devotes itself to live music in the pop, rock, blues, and jazz/fusion genres. Celebrities tend to be attracted to the place.

Whiskey A Go Go (8901 Sunset Blvd., West Hollywood, tel. 310/652–4202). This, the most famous rock 'n' roll club on the Sunset Strip, has hosted everyone from Otis Redding to AC/DC and now presents up-and-coming heavy metal and very hard rock bands.

Cabaret
L.A. Cabaret (17271 Ventura Blvd., Encino, tel. 818/501–3737). This two-room club features a variety of comedy acts as well as karaoke. Famous entertainers often make surprise appearances.

Luna Park (665 Robertson Blvd., West Hollywood, tel. 310/652–0611). A self-described "club in progress," this New York–style cabaret features an eclectic mix of music, with three stages and two bars. Locally (in)famous drag queens strut their stuff here.

Maldonado's (1202 East Green St., Pasadena, tel. 818/796–1126 or 213/681–9462). Complete with velvet upholstered furniture and a garish chandelier, this supper club showcases Broadway music as well as operatic performances. Dressy attire is requested.

The Queen Mary (12449 Ventura Blvd., Sherman Oaks, tel. 818/506–5619). Female impersonators vamp it up as Diana Ross, Barbra Streisand, and Bette Midler in this small club where every seat is a good one. Drinks are the only refreshment served, so eat first. Plenty of cross-dressers parade among the colorful clientele, which is never boring. Open Wednesday–Sunday.

Discos and Dancing

Bar One (9229 Sunset Blvd., Beverly Hills, tel. 310/271–8355). Celebrities such as Warren Beatty and Charlie Sheen have been known to frequent this restaurant and bar. A hot, hip place for dancing, it's L.A.'s club of the moment. There's also a pool table and comfortable lounging areas.

Circus Disco and Arena (6655 Santa Monica Blvd., Hollywood, tel. 213/462–1291 or 213/462–1742). A gay and mixed crowd flocks to these two huge side-by-side discos, which feature techno and rock music.

Coconut Teaszer (8117 Sunset Blvd., Los Angeles, tel. 213/654–4773). Dancing to live music, a great barbecue menu, and killer drinks make for lively fun.

Crush Bar Continental Club (1743 Cahuenga Ave., Hollywood, tel. 213/463–SOUL). If the 1960s is a decade that appeals to you, stop by this happening dance club, open Thursday–Saturday. After all, there's nothing like some golden Motown to get you moving.

Florentine Gardens (5951 Hollywood Blvd., Hollywood, tel. 213/464–0706). One of Los Angeles's largest dance areas, with spectacular lighting to match, it's open Friday and Saturday.

Glam Slam (333 S. Boylston, Los Angeles, tel. 213/482–6626). A New York–style club, this hot spot has a restricted entrance policy—there's a large celebrity clientele, and everybody's dressed to kill. The premises offers a large dance floor, live bands, balcony bar, and restaurant. It's open Friday and Saturday until 4 AM, which is unusually late for this city. This club is in a terrible neighborhood, so be prepared to shell out for valet parking.

Moonlight Tango Cafe (13730 Ventura Blvd., Sherman Oaks, tel. 818/788–2000). This high-energy club-restaurant, big on the swing era, really gets moving in the wee hours, when a conga line inevitably takes shape on the dance floor. Keep an eye on your waiter—he may just burst into song, as all staffers are hired to entertain as well as serve food.

Tatou (233 N. Beverly Dr., Beverly Hills, tel. 310/274–9955). Like a 1990s version of Rick's Place (remember *Casablanca*?), this downstairs club/restaurant attracts a world-weary older crowd who often wander upstairs to mingle with the younger set on the spacious dance floor. Don't expect to hear "As Time Goes By," though—this place is strictly dedicated to contemporary sounds.

Country

In Cahoots (223 N. Glendale Ave., Glendale, tel. 818/500–1665). At this raucous dance hall, á la Nashville, you can learn how to two-step if you don't already know how. All week long there's live music by local country artists like Rosie Flores.

The Palomino (6907 Lankershim Blvd., North Hollywood, tel. 818/764–4010). There's occasionally a wild crowd at this premier country showcase, where good old boys and urban cowboys meet and everybody has a good time.

Comedy and Magic

Comedy Act Theater (3339 W. 43rd St., near Crenshaw, tel. 310/677–4101). This club features comedy by and for the black community, Thursday through Saturday nights. Past performers have been *Hollywood Shuffle*'s Robert Townsend and "Night Court's" Marcia Warfield.

Comedy and Magic Club (1018 Hermosa Ave., Hermosa Beach, tel. 310/372–1193). This beachfront club features many magicians and comedians seen on TV and in Las Vegas. The Unknown Comic, Elayne Boosler, Pat Paulsen, Jay Leno, and Harry Anderson have all played here.

Comedy Store (8433 Sunset Blvd., Hollywood, tel. 213/656–6225). Los Angeles's premier comedy showcase has been going strong for over a decade. Many famous comedians, including Robin Williams and Steve Martin, occasionally make unannounced appearances here.

Groundlings Theater (7307 Melrose Ave., Hollywood, tel. 213/934–9700). The entertainment here consists of original skits, music, and improv, with each player contributing his/her own flavor to the usually hilarious performance.

The Ice House Comedy Showroom (24 N. Mentor Ave., Pasadena, tel. 818/577–1894). Three-act shows here feature comedians, celebrity impressionists, and magicians from Las Vegas, as well as from television shows.

Igby's Comedy Cabaret (11637 Pico Blvd., Los Angeles, tel. 310/477–3553). You'll see familiar television faces as well as up-and-coming comedians Tuesday through Saturday. Cabaret fare includes cocktails and dining in a friendly ambience. Reservations are necessary.

The Improvisation (8162 Melrose Ave., West Hollywood, tel. 213/651–2583 and 321 Santa Monica Blvd., Santa Monica, tel. 310/394–8664). The Improv is a transplanted New York establishment showcasing comedians and some vocalists. This place was the proving ground for Liza Minnelli and Richard Pryor, among others. Reservations are recommended.

Excursion to Big Bear/Lake Arrowhead

Local legend has it that in 1845, Don Benito Wilson—General George Patton's grandfather—and his men charged up along the San Bernardino River in pursuit of a troublesome band of Indians. As Wilson entered a clearing, he discovered a meadow teeming with bears. The rest, of course, is history: Wilson later became mayor of Los Angeles, and the area he'd stumbled into was developed into a delightful mountain playground, centered around the man-made lakes of Arrowhead and Big Bear.

Visitors come in winter for downhill and cross-country skiing, and in summer to breathe cool mountain air, hike in the woods, sniff the daffodils, and play in the water. Along the edge of the San Bernardino Mountains, which connect Lake Arrowhead and Big Bear Lake, is a truly great scenic drive: the Rim of the World Scenic Byway. The alpine equivalent of the Pacific Coast Highway, it reaches elevations of 8,000 feet, offering views of sprawling San Bernardino and east toward Palm Springs.

Arriving and Departing

By Car Take I–10 east from Los Angeles to Highway 330, which connects with Highway 18—the Rim of the World Scenic Byway—at Running Springs. This is approximately the midpoint of the scenic drive, which hugs the mountainside from Big Bear Lake to Cajon Pass. The trip should take about 90 minutes to Lake Arrowhead, and two hours to Big Bear. Highway 38, the back way into Big Bear, is actually longer, but it can be faster when the traffic on the more direct route is heavy.

Exploring

As you wind your way along the Rim of the World near it's intersection with Highway 138, there are several places to park, sip cool water from spring-fed fountains, and enjoy the view. At the village of Crestline, a brief detour off Highway 18 leads you to **Lake Gregory.** The newest of the high mountain lakes, Lake Gregory was formed by a dam constructed in 1938. Because the water temperature in summer is seldom extremely cold—as it can be in the other lakes at this altitude—this is the best swimming lake in the mountains, but it's open in summer only, and there's a $3 charge to swim. You can rent rowboats at Lake Gregory Village.

Continuing east on Highway 18, you will pass the **Baylis Park Picnic Ground,** where you can have a barbecue in a wooded setting. A little farther along, just past the town of Rim Forest, is the **Strawberry Peak** fire lookout tower. Visitors who brave the steep stairway to the tower are treated to a magnificent view and a lesson on fire-spotting by the lookout staff.

Heading north on Highway 173 will lead you to **Lake Arrowhead Village** and the lake itself. Arrowhead Village draws mixed reviews: For some, it is a quaint alpine community with shops and eateries; for others, it has all the ambience of a rustic-theme shopping mall. The lake, on the other hand, is decidedly a gem, although it can become crowded with speedboats and water-skiers in summer. The *Arrowhead Queen,* operated by LeRoy Sports (tel. 909/336–6992, reservations needed in summer) provides 50-minute cruises around the lake, leaving from the waterfront marina. The **Lake Arrowhead Children's Museum** (lower level of the village, tel. 909/336–1332, admission $3.50) has plenty to entertain pint-sized explorers: hands-on exhibits, a climbing maze, and a puppet stage. Call the Arrowhead Chamber of Commerce (tel. 909/337–3715) for information on events, camping, and lodging.

If you are traveling with children, you may also want to stop at nearby **Santa's Village.** The petting zoo, rides, riding stables, and a bakery filled with goodies make this place a favorite of kids. *Located on Hwy. 18, Box 638, Skyforest 92385, tel. 909/337–2484. Admission: $9.50, children under 2 free. Hours change from season to season, so call ahead for information.*

Farther along the Rim drive, 5 miles east of Running Springs, is **Snow Valley** (tel. 909/867–5151), one of the major ski areas in the San Bernardinos, with snowmaking capabilities and a dozen lifts. Summer visitors will find hiking trails, horseback riding, and fishing here, too.

Beyond Snow Valley, the road climbs to **Lakeview Point,** where a spectacular view of the deep Bear Creek Canyon unfolds; Big Bear Lake is usually visible in the distance. A 15.5-mile drive will take you completely around the lake, and **Big Bear Lake Village** is on the lake's south shore. The town is a pleasant combination of alpine and Western-mountain style, with the occasional chalet-like building. The paddle wheeler *Big Bear Queen* (tel. 909/866–3218) departs daily from Big Bear Marina for 90-minute scenic tours of the lake. Fishing-boat and equipment rentals are available from several lakeside marinas, including Pine Knot Landing (tel. 909/866–BOAT), adjacent to Big Bear Village. For general information and lodging reservations, contact the Big Bear Tourist Authority (tel. 909/866–7000).

Snow Summit (tel. 909/866–4627) and **Bear Mountain Ski Resort** (tel. 909/585–2519) are both just to the southeast of the Village. Snow Summit, which has a 8,200-foot peak, is equipped with a high-speed quad chair, 11 chairlifts, and 18 miles of runs at all levels. Bear Mountain has 11 chairlifts and 25 trails, from beginner to expert. On busy winter weekends and holidays, your best bet is to reserve your tickets before you head for the mountain.

Dining

A three-course meal for one person, excluding drinks, service, and tax, costs between $15 and $25 at the following restaurants.

Big Bear **Blue Ox Bar and Grill.** This rustic, casual restaurant, complete with peanut shells on the floor, serves oversize steaks, ribs, burgers, and chicken—all cooked simply but well. *441 W. Big Bear Blvd., Big Bear City, tel. 909/585–7886. AE, MC, V.*

Lake Arrowhead **Cliffhanger.** Moussaka and lamb are the best dishes here. Despite the name, the cliffside locale is part of the charm. *25187 Hwy. 18, Lake Arrowhead, tel. 909/338–3806. MC, V.*

Lodging

Rates for Big Bear lodgings fluctuate widely, depending upon the season. When winter snow brings droves of Angelenos to the mountain for skiing, expect to pay sky-high prices for any kind of room. **Big Bear Central Reservations** (tel. 909/866–7000) can answer any questions you have and make arrangements for you.

Category	Cost*
$$$$	over $100
$$$	$75–$100

*All prices are for a double room, excluding tax.

Big Bear **Big Bear Inn.** This chateau-like inn's rooms are furnished with brass beds and antiques. Developer Paul Rizos's family has three luxury hotels on the Greek island of Corfu, and the inn shows its lineage—right down to the giant Greek statues in front of the property. *Box 1814, Big Bear Lake 92315, tel. 909/866–3471 or 800/BEAR–INN. 75 rooms, 3 suites. Facilities: 1 restaurant (open weekends only), lounge, pool, Jacuzzi. AE, MC, V. $$$$*
Robinhood Inn and Lodge. Near Snow Summit, this well-located hostelry has reasonably priced rooms (with or without kitchen) and condos. Each room (some with fireplaces) is individually decorated with simple modern furniture and bright colors. *Box 3706, Big Bear Lake 92315, tel. 909/866–4643. 20 rooms. Facilities: restaurant, spa. AE, MC, V. $$$–$$$$*

Lake **Arrowhead Hilton Lodge.** The design and Old World graciousness
Arrowhead of the lodge are reminiscent of the Alps. In addition to the lakeside
luxury, guests receive membership privileges at the Village Bay
Club and Spa. *Box 1699, 92352, tel. 909/336–1511. 261 rooms. Facili-*
ties: restaurant, coffee shop, lounge, beach, pool, whirlpools, health
club, tennis (fee). AE, MC, V. $$$$

Carriage House Bed and Breakfast. Within walking distance of
the lake and village, this New England–style country home offers
lake views from most guest rooms. Breakfast and afternoon refreshments are included in the rates. *Box 982, 92352, tel. 909/336–1400.*
3 rooms. D, MC, V. $$$–$$$$

Excursion to Catalina Island

When you approach Catalina Island through the typical early morn-
ing ocean fog, it's easy to wonder if perhaps there has been some
mistake. What is a Mediterranean island doing 22 miles off the coast
of California? Don't worry, you haven't left the Pacific—you've ar-
rived at one of the Los Angeles area's most popular resorts.

Though lacking the sophistication of some European pleasure is-
lands, Catalina does offer virtually unspoiled mountains, canyons,
coves, and beaches. In fine weather, it draws thousands of southern
California boaters, who tie up their vessels at moorings spotted in
coves along the coast. The exceptionally clear water surrounding
the island lures divers and snorkelers. Although there's not much
sandy beach, sunbathing and water sports are also popular. The
main town, Avalon, is a charming, old-fashioned beach community,
where palm trees rim the main street and yachts bob in the cres-
cent-shape bay.

Until recently, Catalina had become a rather seedy, overpriced tour-
ist destination. But now that cruise ships sail into Avalon twice a
week, there's been a lot of sprucing up—smarter merchandise in
the stores, wider choices in restaurants and lodgings. The Catalina
Island Company, which has a near monopoly on sightseeing tours
on the island beyond Avalon, has improved its service, too.

Discovered by Juan Rodriguez Cabrillo in 1542, the island has shel-
tered many dubious characters, from Russian fur trappers (seeking
sea-otter skins), slave traders, pirates, and gold miners, to bootleg-
gers, filmmakers, and movie stars. In 1919, William Wrigley, Jr., the
chewing-gum magnate, purchased controlling interest in the com-
pany developing the island. Wrigley had the island's most famous
landmark, the Casino, built in 1929, and he made Catalina the site
of spring training for his Chicago Cubs baseball team. In 1975 the
Santa Catalina Island Conservancy, a nonprofit foundation, ac-
quired about 86% of the island to help preserve the natural re-
sources here.

Although Catalina can certainly be seen in a day, there are several
inviting hotels that make it worth extending your stay for one or
more nights. Between Memorial Day and Labor Day, be sure to
make reservations *before* heading here. After Labor Day, rooms are
much easier to find on shorter notice, rates drop dramatically, and
a number of hotels offer packages that include transportation from
the mainland and/or sightseeing tours.

Arriving and Departing

By Boat **Catalina Express** (tel. 310/519–1212) makes the hour-long run from Long Beach or San Pedro to Avalon and Two Harbors; round-trip fare from Long Beach is $35.50 for adults, $26.50 for children 2–11; from San Pedro, $34.50 for adults and $25.50 for children. Also available is a 2½–hour trip from San Pedro to Two Harbors; round-trip fare is $34.50 for adults and $25.50 for children. **Catalina Cruises** (tel. 800/888–5939), also leaving from Long Beach, takes two hours and charges $28.50 for adults, $24.50 for seniors, $18.50 for children 2–11, $2 for children under 2. Service is also available from Newport Beach through **Catalina Passenger Service** (tel. 714/673–5245), which leaves from Balboa Pavilion at 9 AM, takes 75 minutes to reach the island, and costs $32.50 round-trip for adults, $16.50 for children 12 and under. The return boat leaves Catalina at 4:30 PM.

By Plane **Island Express** (tel. 310/491–5550) flies hourly from San Pedro and Long Beach. The trip takes about 15 minutes and costs $66 one-way, $121 round-trip.

Guided Tours

Santa Catalina Island Company (tel. 310/510–2000 or 800/428–2566) tours include: coastal cruise to Seal Rocks (summer only), the *Flying Fish* boat trip (evenings, summer only) inland motor tour, the Skyline Drive, the Casino tour, the Avalon scenic tour, dinner tours, and the glass-bottom boat tour. Reservations are highly recommended for the inland tours; the others are offered several times daily. Costs range from $6.75 to $36.50 (adults); discounts are available for children under 12, senior citizens over 55, and for two or more tours booked in combination.

The Catalina Conservancy (tel. 310/510–1421) offers walks led by area docents.

Exploring

Everybody walks in Avalon, where private autos are restricted and there are no rental cars. But taxis, trams, and shuttles can take you to hotels, attractions, and restaurants. If you are determined to have a set of wheels, you can rent a bicycle (about $5 an hour) or a golf cart ($30 an hour, cash only) along Crescent Avenue as you walk in from the dock. To hike into the interior of the island you will need a permit, available free from Doug Bombard Enterprises (Island Plaza, Avalon, tel. 310/510–7265).

The **Chamber of Commerce Visitors Bureau,** on Green Pier, is a good place to get your bearings, check into special events, and plan your itinerary. The **Catalina Island Company Visitors Center** (tel. 310/510–1520) is on the corner of Crescent and Catalina avenues, across from Green Pier.

On the northwest point of Crescent Bay is the **Casino,** Avalon's most prominent landmark. The circular structure, considered one of the finest examples of Art Deco architecture anywhere, has lots of Spanish-influenced details. Its floors and murals show off brilliant blue and green Catalina tiles. "Casino" is the Italian word for "gathering place," and has nothing to do with gambling here. Instead, you can visit the **Catalina Island Museum** (lower level of Casino, admission $1), which displays the history of the island; in the evening, you can see a first-run movie at the **Avalon Theater** (tel.

310/510–0179), which has a classic 1929 theater pipe organ; or on holiday weekends you can go to big-band dances similar to those that made the Casino famous in the 1930s and '40s.

The Wrigley Memorial and Botanical Garden is 2 miles south of Avalon via Avalon Canyon Road. The garden displays only plants native to southern California, including several that grow only on Catalina Island: Catalina ironwood, wild tomato, and rare Catalina mahogany. The Wrigley family commissioned the garden as well as the monument, which has a grand staircase and a Spanish mauso-leum that's decorated with colorful Catalina tile. Tram service be-tween the memorial and Avalon is available daily between 8 AM and 5 PM. There is a nominal entry fee of $1. If modern architecture interests you, be sure to stop by the **Wolfe House** (124 Chimes Rd.). Built in Avalon in 1928 by noted architect Rudolph Schindler, its terraced frame is carefully set into a steep site, affording extraor-dinary views. The house is a private residence, rarely open for public tours, but you can get a good view of it from the path below it and from the street.

El Rancho Escondido is a ranch in Catalina's interior, home to some of the country's finest Arabian horses. Horse shows are pre-sented for passengers on the inland motor tour (*see* Guided Tours, *above*).

Snorkelers and divers can explore the crystal-clear waters of **Un-derwater Marine Park at Casino Point,** where moray eels, bat rays, spiny lobsters, halibut, and other sea animals cruise around kelp forests and along the sandy bottom.

Dining

Avalon restaurants cater to summer crowds; at other times of year, days and hours of operation are sporadic, depending upon the num-ber of visitors in town.

Category	Cost*
$$$	$25–$35
$$	$15–$25
$	under $15

per person for a three-course meal, excluding drinks, service, and tax

Cafe Prego. This waterfront restaurant specializes in pasta, sea-food and steak. *603 Crescent Ave., tel. 310/510–1218. AE, D, DC, MC, V. $$–$$$*

Pirrone's. Located on the second floor of the Vista del Mar hotel, Pirrone's has a bird's-eye view of the bay. The menu includes local seafood, prime rib, steaks, and pasta. *417 Crescent Ave., tel. 310/510–0333. AE, D, DC, MC, V. $$–$$$*

Antonio's Pizzeria. Here you'll find a spirited atmosphere, decent pizza, and appropriately messy Italian sandwiches. *2 locations: 230 Crescent Ave., tel. 310/510–0008, and 114 Sumner Ave., tel. 310/510–0060. MC, V. $–$$*

The Sand Trap. Basically an expanded taco stand on the way to the Wrigley Memorial, the Sand Trap specializes in omelets, burritos, *tortas* (layered tortilla casseroles), and quesadillas. *Falls Canyon, tel. 310/510–1349. Closed for dinner. No credit cards. $*

Lodging

Category	Cost*
$$$$	over $100
$$$	$75–$100

*All prices are for a double room, excluding tax.

Hotel Metropole and Marketplace. This romantic hotel has a French Quarter ambience: it overlooks a flower-decked courtyard of restaurants and shops. Some guest rooms have balconies, ocean views, fireplaces, and Jacuzzis. Continental breakfast is served in the lounge. *225 Crescent Ave., Avalon 90704, tel. 310/510–1884, 47 rooms. AE, MC, V. $$$$*

Inn on Mt. Ada. Occupying the former Wrigley Mansion, the island's most exclusive hotel offers the comforts of a millionaire's mansion—and at millionaire's prices, beginning at more than $300 a night. The six bedrooms are elegantly decorated, some with canopy beds, traditional furniture, and overstuffed chairs. The views across the water to the mainland are spectacular, and the service is discreet. All meals, beverages, snacks, and the use of a golf cart are complimentary. *Box 2560, Avalon 90704, tel. 310/510–2030. 6 rooms. MC, V. $$$$*

Hotel Vista del Mar. This friendly, freshly decorated hotel offers surprisingly bright rooms, most of which open onto a skylighted atrium. There are fireplaces, Jacuzzis, wet bars, contemporary rattan decor, and abundant greenery. Two suites have ocean views. Rates include Continental breakfast. *417 Crescent Ave., Avalon 90704, tel. 310/510–1452. 15 rooms. AE, D, MC, V. $$$–$$$$*

13 Orange County

Updated by
Bobbie Zane

Orange County is one of the top tourist destinations in California, and once you've arrived here it doesn't take long to see why. The county has made tourism its number-one industry, attracting nearly 40 million visitors annually. Two theme parks, Disneyland and Knott's Berry Farm, attract millions on their own. Orange County also offers year-round pro sports action, with the California Angels baseball team, Los Angeles Rams football team, and the Mighty Ducks of Anaheim hockey team. The Anaheim Convention Center is an enormous facility that's constantly booked with conferences and trade shows. There are plenty of places to stay, and they're generally of high quality.

People actually live in Orange County, too—many of them in high-priced pink, Mediterranean-style homes that are strung along the 24 miles of coastline. Orange County residents shop in the classy malls that lure visitors as well. Like visitors, locals can be found at the beach sunning themselves or waiting for the big wave. Locals even dine and stay at the luxurious oceanfront resorts that perch on the edge of the Pacific. Indeed, Orange County people believe that they've discovered the perfect place to live. They're anxious to share the pleasures of life in the Big Orange with visitors.

Served by convenient airports and only an hour's drive from Los Angeles, Orange County is both a destination on its own and a very popular excursion from Los Angeles.

Essential Information

Important Addresses and Numbers

Tourist Information

The main source of tourist information is the **Anaheim Area Convention and Visitors Bureau,** located at the Anaheim Convention Center (800 W. Katella Ave., 92802, tel. 714/999–8999). The **Visitor Information Hot Line** (tel. 714/635–8900) offers recorded information on entertainment, special events, attractions, and amusement parks; information about special events may be outdated.

Other area chambers of commerce and visitors bureaus are generally open weekdays 9–5 and will help with information. These include:
Buena Park Visitors Bureau (6280 Manchester Blvd., 90261, tel. 714/562–3560). **Dana Point Chamber of Commerce** (24681 La Plaza, Suite 120, 92629, tel. 714/496–1555). **Huntington Beach Conference and Visitors Bureau** (2100 Main St., Suite 190, 92648, tel. 800/729–6232). **Laguna Beach Hospitality** (252 Broadway, 92651, tel. 714/494–1018). **Newport Beach Conference and Visitors Bureau** (366 San Miguel Dr., Suite 200, 92660, tel. 800/942–6278). **San Clemente Tourism Bureau** (1100 N. El Camino Real, 92672, tel. 714/492–1131). **San Juan Capistrano Chamber of Commerce and Visitors Center** (26832 Ortega Hwy., 92675, tel. 714/493–4700).

Emergencies

Dial 911 for police and ambulance in an emergency.

Doctors

Orange County is so spread out and comprises so many communities that it is best to ask at your hotel for the closest emergency room. Here are a few: **Anaheim Memorial Hospital** (1111 W. La Palma, tel. 714/774–1450), **Western Medical Center** (1025 S. Anaheim Blvd., Anaheim, tel. 714/533–6220), **Hoag Memorial Hospital** (301 Newport Blvd., Newport Beach, tel. 714/645–8600), **South Coast Medical Center** (31872 Coast Hwy., South Laguna, tel. 714/499–1311).

Arriving and Departing

By Plane Several airports are accessible to Orange County. **John Wayne Orange County Airport** (tel. 714/252–5006), in Santa Ana, is centrally located, and the county's main facility. It is serviced by **Alaska** (tel. 800/426–0333), **America West** (tel. 800/235–9292), **American** (tel. 800/433–7300), **Continental** (tel. 800/525–0280), **Delta** (tel. 800/221–1212), **Northwest** (tel. 800/225–2525), **Southwest** (tel. 800/435–9792), **TWA** (tel. 800/221–2000), **United** (tel. 800/241–6522), and several commuter airlines.

Los Angeles International Airport is only 35 miles west of Anaheim; **Ontario Airport,** just northwest of Riverside, is 30 miles north of Anaheim; and **Long Beach Airport** is about 20 minutes by bus from Anaheim. (*See* Los Angeles, Arriving and Departing, for details on all three airports.)

Between the Airports and Hotels **Airport Coach** (tel. 800/772–5299), a shuttle service, carries passengers from John Wayne Airport and LAX to Anaheim, Buena Park, and Newport Beach. Fare from John Wayne to Anaheim is $10, from LAX to Anaheim $16.

Prime Time Airport Shuttle (tel. 800/262–7433) offers door-to-door service to LAX and John Wayne airports, hotels near John Wayne, and the San Pedro cruise terminal. The fare is $11 from Anaheim hotels to John Wayne and $12 from Anaheim hotels to LAX. Children under 2 ride free.

SuperShuttle (tel. 714/517–6600) provides 24-hour door-to-door service from all the airports to all points in Orange County. Fare to the Disneyland area is $10 a person from John Wayne, $34 from Ontario, $13 from LAX. Phone for other fares and reservations.

By Car Two major freeways, I–405 (San Diego Freeway) and I–5 (Santa Ana Freeway), run north and south through Orange County. South of Laguna they merge into I–5. Avoid these during rush hours (6–9 AM and 3:30–6 PM), when they can slow to a crawl and back up for miles.

By Train **Amtrak** (tel. 800/872–7245) makes several stops in Orange County: Fullerton, Anaheim, Santa Ana, San Juan Capistrano, and San Clemente. There are 11 departures daily, nine on weekends.

By Bus The **Los Angeles RTD** has limited service to Orange County. You can get the No. 460 to Anaheim; it goes to Knott's Berry Farm and Disneyland. **Greyhound** (tel. 714/999–1256 or 800/231–2222) has scheduled bus service to Orange County.

Getting Around

By Car Highways 22, 55, and 91 go west to the ocean and east to the mountains: Take Highway 91 or Highway 22 to inland points (Buena Park, Anaheim) and take Highway 55 to Newport Beach. Caution: Orange County freeways are undergoing major construction; expect delays at odd times.

Pacific Coast Highway (Highway 1; also known locally as PCH or Coast Highway) allows easy access to beach communities, and is the most scenic route. It follows the entire Orange County coast, from Huntington Beach to San Clemente.

By Bus The **Orange County Transportation Authority** (OCTA, tel. 714/636–7433) will take you virtually anywhere in the county, but it will take time; OCTA buses go from Knott's Berry Farm and Disneyland to Huntington and Newport beaches. Bus 1 travels along the coast.

Scenic Drives Winding along the seaside edge of Orange County on the **Pacific Coast Highway** is an eye-opening experience. Here, surely, are the contradictions of southern California revealed—the powerful, healing ocean vistas and the scars of commercial exploitation; the appealingly laid-back, simple beach life and the tacky bric-a-brac of the tourist trail. Oil rigs line the road from Long Beach south to Huntington Beach, and then suddenly give way to pristine stretches of water and dramatic hillsides. Prototypical beach towns like Laguna Beach, Dana Point, and Corona del Mar serve as casual stopping points along the route.

For a scenic mountain drive, try **Santiago Canyon Road,** which winds through the Cleveland National Forest in the Santa Ana Mountains. Tucked away in these mountains are Modjeska Canyon, Irvine Lake, and Silverado Canyon, of silver-mining lore.

Guided Tours

**General-
Interest Tours** **Pacific Coast Sightseeing Tours** (tel. 714/978–8855) provides guided tours from Orange County hotels to Disneyland, Knott's Berry Farm, Universal Studios Hollywood, and the San Diego Zoo.

Boat Tours At the Cannery in **Newport Beach,** you can take a weekend brunch cruise around the harbor. Cruises last two hours and depart at 10 AM and 1:30 PM. Champagne brunches cost $30 per person. For more information call 714/675–5777.

Catalina Passenger Service (tel. 714/673–5245) at the Balboa Pavilion offers a full selection of sightseeing tours and fishing excursions to Catalina and around Newport Harbor. The 45-minute narrated tour of Newport Harbor, at $6, is the least expensive. Whale-watching cruises (Dec.–Mar.) are especially enjoyable.

Hornblower Yachts (tel. 714/646–0155) offers Saturday dinner cruises with dancing for $49 or $54; Sunday brunch cruises are $36. Reservations are required.

Exploring Orange County

Before visiting Orange County, select a primary attraction and then plan visits to other sights. If Disneyland is the highlight, you'll probably want to organize your activities around the tourist attractions that fill the central county and take excursions to selected coastal spots. If you're planning to hang out on the beach, select a coastal headquarters and make forays to the Magic Kingdom.

If you're traveling with children, you could easily devote several days to the theme parks: a day or two for Disneyland, a day for Knott's Berry Farm, and perhaps a day driving to some of the area's lesser-known attractions. To rent sailboards or other water-sports paraphernalia, you'll have to head for the beach towns. Beach days can be a mix of sunning, studying surf culture, and browsing the small shops native to the beach communities.

Highlights for First-Time Visitors

Balboa Pavilion, Balboa Peninsula
Bolca Chica Ecological Reserve
Disneyland, Anaheim
Knott's Berry Farm, Buena Park
Mission San Juan Capistrano

Laguna Beach
Newport Harbor
Richard Nixon Presidential Library and Birthplace, Yorba Linda
South Coast Plaza, Costa Mesa

Inland Orange County

Numbers in the margin correspond to points of interest on the Orange County map.

With Disneyland as its centerpiece, Anaheim is indisputably the West's capital of family entertainment. Now at the center of a vast tourism complex that also includes the Anaheim Convention Center, Anaheim Stadium, and the Pond in Anaheim, Disneyland still dominates the city. The Anaheim Convention Center lures almost as many conventioneers as Disneyland attracts children, and for many visitors, a trip to the Magic Kingdom may be the bonus of an Anaheim meeting.

❶ Perhaps more than any other place in the world, **Disneyland,** the first Disney theme park, and the enduring physical evidence of Walt Disney's dream, is a symbol of the eternal child in all of us. It's a place of delight and enchantment; an exceptionally clean and imaginatively developed wonder.

When Disney carved the park out of the orange groves in 1955, it consisted of four lands and fewer than 20 major attractions radiating from his idealized American Main Street. Much has changed in the intervening years, including the massive expansion of the park to include four more lands and some 40 more attractions. But Main Street retains its turn-of-the-century charm, and in ever sharper contrast with the world just outside the gates of the park. Disney's vision of the Magic Kingdom was one of a never-ending fantasy. Thus designers and engineers continue to devise new ways to tantalize and treat guests, the latest being the Indiana Jones Adventure, scheduled to open in 1995.

Disneyland is big, and, during the busy summer season, crowded. Planning a strategy for your visit, as the locals do, will help you get the most out of it. If you can, pick a rainy midweek day; surprisingly, most Disney attractions are indoors. Arrive early; the box office opens a half-hour before the park's scheduled opening time. Go immediately to the most popular attractions: Space Mountain, Star Tours, Pirates of the Caribbean, Haunted Mansion, It's a Small World, and Splash Mountain. Mickey's Toontown tends to be most crowded in the mornings. Lines for rides will also be shorter during the evening Fantasmic! show, parades, and fireworks display (usually around 9:30), as well as near opening or closing times. Just the same, even on a slow day expect to wait in line for 15 minutes or so. As with the rides, strategize your eating as well. Restaurants are less crowded toward the beginning and end of meal periods. Also, fast-food spots abound, and you can now get healthy fare such as fruit, pasta, and frozen yogurt at various locations throughout the park. Whatever you wind up eating, food prices are higher than on the outside. When shopping, remember that there are lockers just off Main Street in which you can store purchases, and thereby avoid lugging bundles around all day or shopping just before the park's closing time when stores are crowded. If your feet get tired, you can move from one area of the park to another on the train or monorail, or even in a horse-drawn carriage.

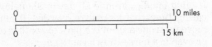

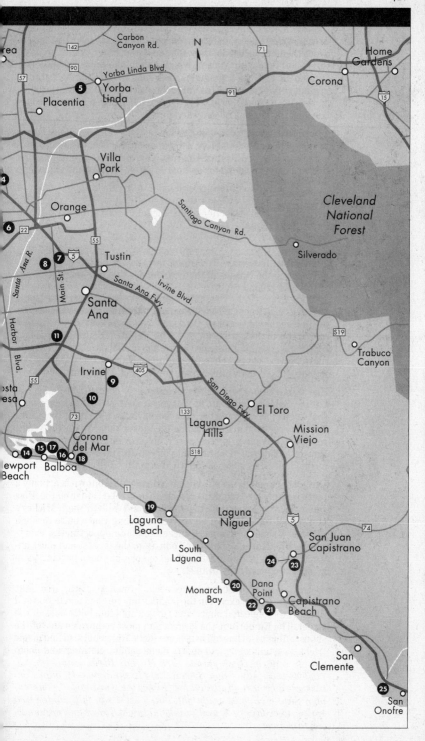

Each of Disney's lands has its own theme rides. Stepping through the doors of Sleeping Beauty's castle into **Fantasyland** can be a dream come true for children. Mickey Mouse may even be there to greet them. Once inside, they can join **Peter Pan's Flight;** go down the rabbit hole with **Alice in Wonderland;** take an aerial spin with **Dumbo the Flying Elephant;** take **Mr. Toad's Wild Ride;** spin around in giant cups at the **Mad Tea Party;** swoosh through the **Matterhorn;** or visit **It's a Small World,** where figures of children from 100 countries worldwide sing of unity and peace.

In **Frontierland** you can take a cruise on the **steamboat** *Mark Twain* or the **sailing ship** *Columbia* and experience the sights and sounds of the spectacular **Rivers of America.** Kids of every age enjoy rafting to **Tom Sawyer's Island** for an hour or so of climbing and exploring.

Some visitors to **Adventureland** have taken the **Jungle Cruise** so many times that they know the patter offered up by the operators by heart. Other attractions here include shops with African and South Seas wares.

TimeOut	**Blue Bayou,** featuring Creole food, is a great place to eat. It is in the entrance to the Pirates of the Caribbean—you can hear the antics in the background.

The twisting streets of **New Orleans Square** offer interesting browsing and shopping, strolling Dixieland musicians, and the ever-popular **Pirates of the Caribbean** ride. The **Haunted Mansion,** populated by 999 holographic ghosts, is nearby. Theme shops purvey hats, perfume, Mardi Gras merchandise, and gourmet items. The **Disney Gallery** here has trendy (and expensive) original Disney art.

The animated bears in **Critter Country** may charm kids of all ages, but it's **Splash Mountain,** the steepest, wettest Disney adventure, that keeps them coming back for more. Disney's vision of the future in **Tomorrowland** has undergone the most changes over the years, reflecting advances in technology. You can still take a **Submarine Voyage** or ride the monorail, but you can also take **Star Tours,** or be hurled into outer space on **Space Mountain.**

Designed to delight small children, **Mickey's Toontown** is actually a pint-sized playground. Kids can climb up a rope ladder on the *Miss Daisy,* Donald's boat, talk to a mailbox, and walk through **Mickey's House** and **meet Mickey,** all the while feeling that you're inside a cartoon. Bring your camera; there are photo opportunities everywhere. The **Roger Rabbit Car Toon Spin,** the largest and most unusual black-light ride in Disneyland history, has been packing them in since it opened here in 1994.

A stroll along **Main Street** evokes a small-town America, circa 1900, that never existed except in the popular imagination and fiction and films. Interconnected shops and restaurants line both sides of the street. **The Emporium,** the largest and most comprehensive of the shops, offers a full line of Disney products. But you'll also find magic tricks, crystal, hobby and sports memorabilia, clothing, and photo supplies here. *Disneyland: 1313 Harbor Blvd., Anaheim, tel. 714/999-4565. Admission: $30 adults, $24 children 3–11; allows entrance to all rides and attractions. Guided tours available. Open summer, Sun.–Fri. 9 AM–midnight, Sat. 9 AM–1 AM; fall, winter, and spring, weekdays 10–6, weekends 9–midnight. Hours and prices subject to change.*

② If Disneyland specializes in a high-tech brand of fantasy, **Knott's Berry Farm**, in nearby Buena Park, offers a dose of reality. The farm has been rooted in the community since 1934, when Cordelia Knott began serving chicken dinners on her wedding china to supplement the family's meager income. The dinners and the boysenberry pies proved more profitable than husband Walter's berry farm, so the family moved first into the restaurant business, and then into the entertainment business. The park, with its Old West theme, is now a 150-acre complex with 100-plus rides and attractions, 60 eating places, and 60 shops, including several that have been here for decades.

Like Disneyland, the park has theme areas. **Ghost Town** offers a delightful human-scale visit to the Old West. Many of the buildings were relocated here from their original mining-town sites. You can stroll down the street, stop and chat with the blacksmith, pan for gold, crack open a geode, ride in an authentic 1880s passenger train, or take the **Gold Mine** ride and descend into a replica of a working gold mine. A real treasure here is the antique **Dentzel carousel** with a menagerie of animals. **Camp Snoopy** is a kid-sized High Sierra wonderland where Snoopy and his Peanuts-gang friends hang out. Tall trees frame **Wild Water Wilderness,** where you can ride white water in an inner tube in **Big Foot Rapids** and commune with the native peoples of the Northwest coast in the spooky new **Mystery Lodge.** Themes aside, thrill rides are placed throughout the park. Teenagers, especially, love the the **Boomerang** roller coaster; **X-K-1,** a living version of a video game; **Kingdom of the Dinosaurs;** and **Montezooma's Revenge,** a roller coaster that goes from 0 to 55 mph in less than 5 seconds. Costumed interpreters offer insight into the natural and human history of the attractions; visitors are encouraged to ask questions.

Knott's also offers entertainment throughout the day with shows scheduled in Ghost Town, the Bird Cage Theater, and the Good Time Theater; occasionally stars appear here. *8039 Beach Blvd., Buena Park, tel. 714/220–5200. Admission: $26.95 adults, $15.95 children 3–11, $17.95 senior citizens. Open in summer from 9 AM; in winter from 10 AM. Closing times vary. Park closes during inclement weather. Times and prices subject to change.*

TimeOut Don't forget what made Knott's famous: Mrs. Knott's fried chicken dinners and boysenberry pies at **Mrs. Knott's Chicken Dinner Restaurant.** It's just outside the park gates in Knott's California MarketPlace, a collection of 32 shops and restaurants.

③ Visitors will find 70 years of movie magic immortalized at **Movieland Wax Museum** in 250 wax sculptures of Hollywood's greatest stars including John Wayne, Marilyn Monroe, and George Burns. Figures are displayed in a maze of realistic sets from movies such as *Gone with the Wind, Star Trek, The Wizard of Oz,* and *Home Alone.* The Chamber of Horrors is designed to scare the daylights out of you. You can buy a combination ticket ($16.50 adults, $9.50 children) that also allows you admission to Ripley's Believe It or Not across the street. *7711 Beach Blvd., 1 block north of Knott's, tel. 714/522–1155. Admission: $12.95 adults, $6.95 children. Open Sun.–Thurs. 9–7, Fri.–Sat. 9–8.*

④ The **Anaheim Museum,** housed in a 1908 Carnegie Library building, illustrates the history of Anaheim including the original wine-producing colony. Changing exhibits include art collections, women's history, and hobbies. *241 S. Anaheim Blvd., tel. 714/778–3301. Sug-*

gested admission: $1.50; children free. Open Wed.–Fri. 10–4, Sat. noon–4.

5 About 7 miles north of Anaheim, off Highway 57 (Yorba Linda Blvd. exit), the **Richard Nixon Library and Birthplace** is more museum than library. Displays illustrate the checkered career of the 37th president, the only one to resign from office. Interactive exhibits give visitors a chance to interview Nixon, press-conference style, and receive prerecorded replies on 300 topics. Displays include impressive life-size sculptures of world leaders, gifts the late president received from international heads of state, and a large graffiti-covered section of the Berlin Wall. Visitors can listen to Nixon's Checkers speech or to the so-called smoking-gun tape from the Watergate days, among other recorded material. After seeing all the high-tech exhibits, visit Pat Nixon's tranquil rose garden, the couple's graves, and the small farmhouse where Richard Nixon was born in 1913. The farmhouse contains original furnishings such as a cast-iron stove, a piano, a Bible, and family photos. Within the main building is a small but interesting gift shop that contains presidential souvenir items. *18001 Yorba Linda Blvd., Yorba Linda, tel. 714/993–3393. Admission: $4.95 adults, $2.95 senior citizens 62 and over, children under 7 free. Open Mon.–Sat. 10–5, Sun. 11–5.*

6 Garden Grove, a community just south of Anaheim and Buena Park, is the home of one of the most impressive churches in the country, the **Crystal Cathedral.** The domain of television evangelist Robert Schuller, this sparkling glass structure resembles a four-pointed star with more than 10,000 panes of glass covering a weblike steel truss to form translucent walls. The feeling as you enter is nothing less than mystical. In addition to tours of the cathedral, two pageants are offered yearly—"The Glory of Christmas" and "The Glory of Easter"—featuring live animals, flying angels, and other special effects. *12141 Lewis St., Garden Grove, tel. 714/971–4013. Donation requested. Guided tours Mon.–Sat. 9–3:30. Call for schedule. For reservations for Easter and Christmas productions, call 714/544–5679.*

7 The **Bowers Museum of Cultural Art,** once a quaint cultural-arts gallery, is now the largest museum in Orange County, having tripled in size after a $12 million expansion and restoration of its original 1936 Spanish-style buildings. The museum houses a first-rate, 85,000-piece collection of artwork by indigenous peoples from around the world. Permanent galleries illustrate sculpture, costumes, and artifacts from Oceania; sculpture from west and central Africa; Pacific Northwest wood carvings; dazzling beadwork of the Plains cultures; and California basketry. The museum's trendy Topaz Cafe offers an ethnically eclectic menu. *2002 N. Main St., Santa Ana, tel. 714/567–3600. Admission: $4.50 adults, $3 students and senior citizens, $1.50 children. Open Tues.–Sun. 10–4, Thur. 10–9.*

8 Santa Ana, the county seat, is undergoing a dramatic restoration in its downtown area. Gleaming new government buildings meld with turn-of-the-century structures to give a sense of where the county came from and where it is going. The **Fiesta Marketplace** along Fourth Street downtown offers a glimpse into contemporary Hispanic culture. The best time to visit is on a Sunday, when the place takes on a lively fiesta atmosphere. You'll find bargain Western wear, imports from Mexico and Guatemala, and authentic tacos and quesadillas. Just a block away is the **Old Orange County Courthouse,** which has been a backdrop for more than 30 movies and TV shows since 1915; it is now a county museum and historical center (400 W. Santa Ana Blvd.; admission free; open weekdays 9–5).

⑨ To glimpse the pristine California landscape as it was before development brought houses and freeways to hillsides, visit the newly opened **Irvine Museum.** Located on the 12th floor of a circular marble-and-glass office building, the museum displays a collection of California impressionist landscape paintings dated 1890 to 1930. The collection was assembled by Joan Irvine Smith, granddaughter of James Irvine, who once owned one-quarter of what is now Orange County. *18881 Von Karman Ave., Irvine, tel. 714/476–2565. Admission free. Open Tues.–Sat. 11–5.*

⑩ Known for its forward-looking concept of community planning, Irvine is also a center for higher education. The **University of California** at Irvine was established on 1,000 acres of rolling ranch land donated by the Irvine family in the mid-1950s. The **Bren Events Center Fine Art Gallery** (tel. 714/856–6610; admission free; open Tues.–Sat. noon–5) on campus sponsors exhibitions of 20th-century art. Tree lovers will be enthralled by the campus; it's an arboretum with more than 11,000 trees from all over the world. *San Diego Fwy. (I–405) to Jamboree Rd., west to Campus Dr. S.*

⑪ It is no small irony that the Costa Mesa/South Coast metro area is known first for its posh shopping mall and second for its performing arts center. A mega-shopping complex, **South Coast Plaza** (3333 S. Bristol St., Costa Mesa) along with its annexes, the Crystal Court and South Coast Village, attracts more than 20 million visitors per year, making it the busiest mall in southern California. It's so big that a shuttle bus transports shoppers between the three complexes. This is Adventureland for the Gold Card set, built around boutiques with names like Polo/Ralph Lauren, Charles Jourdan, Tiffany, Chanel, and Courrèges. The adjacent theater/arts complex contains the acclaimed avant-garde **South Coast Repertory Theater** (655 Town Center Dr., tel. 714/957–4033) and **Orange County Performing Arts Center** (600 Town Center Dr., tel. 714/556–2787). This dramatic 3,000-seat facility for opera, ballet, and symphony hosts such notables as the Los Angeles Philharmonic, the Pacific Symphony, and the New York City Opera. **The California Scenario,** a 1.6-acre sculpture garden designed by Isamu Noguchi, surrounds the theater complex, which also houses restaurants and the South Coast Plaza Hotel.

TimeOut Take a spin around Arnold Schwarzenegger, Sly Stallone, and Bruce Willis's **Planet Hollywood** (1641 W. Sunflower St., across from South Coast Plaza, tel. 714/434–7827), a restaurant that recalls the 1930s and '40s with changing displays of movie memorabilia, giant TV screens showing clips of old movies, and loud rock music. The fare here has a '50s diner flair, with hamburgers topping the menu.

The Coast

Coastal Orange County, dotted with charming beach towns and punctuated with world-class resorts, offers the quintessential laid-back southern California experience. You can catch a monster wave with the bronzed local kids, get a glimpse of some rich and famous lifestyles, and take a walk through the shoreline's natural treasures. Sites and stops on this tour are strung out along some 42 miles of the PCH, and we'll take this route north to south. Although there is bus service along the coast road, it's best to explore it by car.

⑫ If you're interested in wildlife, a walk through **Bolsa Chica Ecological Reserve** (tel. 714/897–7003) will reward you with a chance to see an amazingly restored 300-acre salt marsh, which is home to 315 species of birds, plus other animals and plants. You can see many of them along the 1.5-mile loop trail that meanders through the reserve. The walk is especially delightful in winter, when you're likely to see great blue heron, snowy and great egrets, common loons, and other migrating birds. The salt marsh, which is off PCH between Warner Avenue and Golden West Street, can be visited at any time, but a local support group, Amigos de Bolsa Chica, offers free guided tours from 9 to 10:30 AM on the first Saturday of the month, September through April.

⓭ **Huntington Beach,** with its 9 miles of white sand and sometimes towering waves, offers one of the hippest surf scenes in southern California. Each year it hosts the Pro Surfing Championships competition. This beach is a favorite of Orange County residents and has ample parking, food concessions, fire pits, and lifeguards. For years, the town itself was little more than a string of small, tacky buildings across PCH from the beach, containing surf shops, T-shirt emporiums, and hot-dog stands. In the early '90s, however, work began on a face-lift aimed at transforming the funky surf town into a shining resort area, with the newly reconstructed 1,800-foot-long **Huntington Pier** as its centerpiece. The **Pierside Pavilion,** across PCH from the pier, contains shops, a restaurant, a nightclub, and a theater complex. The **International Museum of Surfing** (411 Olive St., tel. 714/960–3483; call for schedule) has an extensive collection of surfing memorabilia.

Newport Beach has a dual personality: It's best known as the quintessential (upscale) beach town, with its island-dotted yacht harbor and a history of such illustrious residents as John Wayne, author Joseph Wambaugh, and Watergate scandal figure Bob Haldeman. And then there's inland Newport Beach, just southwest of John Wayne Airport, a business and commercial hub with a major shopping center and a clutch of high-rise office buildings and hotels.

Even if you don't own a yacht and don't qualify as seaside high society, you can explore the charming avenues and alleys surrounding ⓮ the famed **Newport Harbor,** which shelters nearly 10,000 small boats. To see it from the water, take a one-hour gondola cruise around the harbor (Gondola Company of Newport, 3404 Via Oporto, tel. 714/675–1212). If you're here during the Christmas holidays, don't miss the Christmas boat parade—one of the best on the West Coast—with hundreds of brightly lighted and decorated yachts cruising through the channels. You can watch the parade from various restaurants overlooking the marina, but reserve a table early.

The waterside portion of Newport Beach consists of a U-shaped ⓯ harbor with the mainland along one leg and the **Balboa Peninsula** along the other leg, separating the marina from the ocean. Set within the harbor are eight small islands, including Balboa and Lido, both well-known for their famous residents. The homes lining the shore may seem modest, but remember that this is some of the most expensive real estate in the world.

You can reach the peninsula from PCH at Newport Boulevard, which will take you to Balboa Boulevard. Begin your exploration of the peninsula at the **Newport Pier,** which juts out into the ocean near 20th Street. Street parking is difficult here, so grab the first space you find and be prepared to walk. A stroll along Ocean Front reveals much of the character of this place. On weekday mornings head for the beach near the pier, where you're likely to encounter the dory fishermen hawking their predawn catches, as they've done for generations. On weekends the walk is alive with kids (of all ages) on skates, roller blades, skateboards, and bikes weaving among the strolling pedestrians and whizzing past fast-food joints, swimsuit shops, and seedy bars.

Continue your drive along Balboa Boulevard nearly to the end of the peninsula, where the charm is of quite a different character. On the bay side is the historic Victorian **Balboa Pavilion,** perched on the water's edge. Built in 1905 as a bath- and boathouse, it hosted big-band dances in the 1940s. Today it houses a restaurant and shops and is a departure point for harbor and whale-watching cruises. Adjacent to the pavilion is the three-car ferry, which connects the peninsula to Balboa Island. Several blocks surrounding the pavilion support restaurants, shops (all a little nicer than those at Newport Pier) and a small Fun Zone—a local hangout with a Ferris wheel, video games, rides, and arcades. On the ocean side of the peninsula the Balboa Pier juts into the surf, backed by a long, wide beach that seems to stretch forever.

The attractions of inland Newport Beach are in striking contrast to the beach scene. **Fashion Island** is a trendy shopping mall centered in a circle of office and hotel buildings and anchored by department stores such as Robinsons–May and Broadway. Atrium Court, an enclosed Mediterranean-style section is popular with upscale shoppers and has shops such as Splash and Flash, with trendy swimwear; and Posh, a men's store. *Newport Center Dr. between Jamboree and MacArthur Blvds., off PCH.*

TimeOut   **Farmer's Market at Atrium Court** (tel. 714/760–0403) is a grocery store and more, selling a vast array of exotic foods, prime meats, and glorious fresh produce arranged in color-coordinated patterns. Also on the ground floor of the Atrium Court is a gourmet food fair, with a salsa bar, a Johnny Rockets hamburger stand, and stands that offer sushi, exotic coffees, and the usual deli selections.

The **Newport Harbor Art Museum** is internationally known for its impressive collection of abstract expressionist works and cutting-edge contemporary works by California artists. Snacks are available in the Sculpture Garden Cafe. *850 San Clemente Dr., tel. 714/759–1122. Admission: $4 adults, $2 students and senior citizens, children free. Open Tues.–Sun. 10–5.*

Just south of Newport Beach, **Corona del Mar** is a small jewel of a town with an exceptional beach. You can walk clear out onto the bay on a rough-and-tumble rock jetty. Much of the beach around here is backed by short cliffs that resemble scaled-down versions of the northern California coastline. The town itself stretches only a few blocks along the PCH, but some of the fanciest stores in the county are here. **Sherman Library and Gardens,** a lush botanical garden and library specializing in Southwest flora and fauna, offers diversion from sun and sand. You can wander among cactus gardens, rose gardens, a wheelchair-height touch-and-smell garden, and a tropical conservatory. *2647 E. Coast Hwy., Corona del Mar, tel. 714/673–2261. Admission: $2; free Mon. Gardens open daily 10:30–4.*

The drive south to Laguna Beach passes some of southern California's most beautiful oceanfront; **Crystal Cove State Beach** stretches from Corona del Mar to Laguna, and its undersea park lures swimmers and divers. Each curve in the highway along here turns up a sparkling vista of crashing surf to one side and, to the other, gently rolling golden brown hills sweeping inland.

Laguna Beach has been called SoHo by the Sea, which is at least partly right. It is an artists' colony that, during the 1950s and '60s, attracted the beat, hip, and far-out, but it is also a colony of conservative wealth. The two camps coexist in relative harmony, with Art prevailing in the congested village, and Wealth entrenched in the canyons and on the hillsides surrounding the town. The November 1993 fire, which destroyed more than 300 homes in the hillsides surrounding Laguna Beach, miraculously left the village untouched.

Walk along Pacific Coast Highway in town or along side streets such as Forest or Ocean, and you'll pass gallery after gallery filled with art ranging from billowy seascapes to neon sculpture and kinetic structures. In addition, you'll find a wide selection of crafts, high fashion, beachwear, and jewelry shops.

⑲ The **Laguna Beach Museum of Art,** near Heisler Park, has exhibits of historical and contemporary California art. *307 Cliff Dr., tel. 714/494–6531. Admission: $3. Open Tues.–Sun. 11–5.*

TimeOut The patio at **Las Brisas** (tel. 714/497–5434), a restaurant next door to the museum, offers one of the loveliest views of the coastline available in Laguna Beach. Stop here for a snack, and drink in the scene.

In front of the Pottery Shack on Pacific Coast Highway is a bit of local nostalgia—a life-size **statue of Eiler Larsen,** the town greeter, who for years stood at the edge of town saying hello and goodbye to visitors. In recent years Number One Archer has assumed the role of greeter, waving to tourists from a spot at the corner of Pacific Coast Highway and Forest Avenue.

Laguna's many arts festivals bring visitors here from all over the world. During July and August, the Sawdust Festival and Art-a-Fair, the Laguna Festival of the Arts, and the Pageant of the Masters take place. The **Pageant of the Masters** (tel. 714/494–1147) is Laguna's most impressive event, a blending of life and art. Live models and carefully orchestrated backgrounds are arranged in striking mimicry of famous paintings. Participants must hold a perfectly still pose for the length of their stay on stage. It is an impressive effort, requiring hours of training and rehearsal by the 400 or so residents who volunteer each year.

Going to Laguna without exploring its beaches would be a shame. To get away from the hubbub of Main Beach, go north to **Woods Cove,** off Pacific Coast Highway at Diamond Street; it's especially quiet during the week. Big rock formations hide lurking crabs. As you climb the steps to leave, you'll see a stunning English-style mansion that was once the home of Bette Davis. At the end of almost every street in Laguna, there is a little cove with its own beach.

⑳ The **Ritz-Carlton Laguna Niguel** is the classiest hotel along the coast; it draws guests from around the world with its sweeping oceanside views, gleaming marble, and stunning antiques. Even if you're not a registered guest, you can enjoy the view and the elegant service by taking English tea, which is served each afternoon in the library. *33533 Ritz-Carlton Dr., Dana Point, tel. 714/240–2000.*

㉑ **Dana Point** is Orange County's newest aquatic playground, a small-boat marina tucked into a dramatic natural harbor surrounded by high bluffs. The harbor was first described more than 100 years ago by its namesake Richard Henry Dana in his book *Two Years Before the Mast.* The marina has docks for small boats and marine-oriented shops and restaurants. Recent development includes a hillside park with bike and walking trails, hotels, small shopping centers, and a collection of eateries. A monument to Dana stands in a gazebo at the top of the bluffs in front of the Blue Lantern Inn. There's a pleasant sheltered beach and park at the west end of the marina. Boating is the big thing here. **Dana Wharf Sportfishing** (tel. 714/496–5794) has charters year-round and runs whale-watching excursions in winter, and the community sponsors an annual whale festival in late February.

A real treasure in Dana Point is the **Nautical Heritage Museum,** a collection of ship models, paintings, 18th- and 19th-century seafaring documents, and navigation instruments. *24532 Del Prado Ave., Dana Point, tel. 714/661–1001. Admission: free. Open weekdays 10–4.*

㉒ The **Orange County Marine Institute** offers a number of programs and excursions designed to entertain and educate about the ocean. Three tanks containing touchable sea creatures are available on weekends. Anchored near the institute is *The Pilgrim,* a full-size replica of the square-rigged vessel on which Richard Henry Dana sailed. Tours of *The Pilgrim* are offered Sunday from 11 to 2:30. A gallery and gift shop are open daily. *24200 Dana Point Harbor Dr., tel. 714/496–2274. Open daily 10–3:30.*

San Juan Capistrano is best known for its mission, and, of course, for the swallows that migrate here each year from their winter haven in Argentina. The arrival of the birds on St. Joseph's Day, March 19, launches a week of festivities. After summering in the arches of the old stone church, the swallows head home on St. John's Day, October 23.

㉓ Founded in 1776 by Father Junipero Serra, **Mission San Juan Capistrano** was the major Roman Catholic outpost between Los Angeles and San Diego. Scaffolding supports the original Great Stone Church, the victim of an 1812 earthquake, which is undergoing a preservation project. Many of the mission's adobe buildings have been restored to illustrate mission life, with exhibits of an olive millstone, tallow ovens, tanning vats, metalworking furnaces, and padres' living quarters. The bougainvillea-covered Serra Chapel is believed to be the oldest building still in use in California. The knowledgeable staff in the mission's visitor center can help you with a self-guided tour, or you can schedule your visit to coincide with the free walking tours offered every Sunday at 1. *Camino Capistrano and Ortega Hwy., tel. 714/248–2048. Admission: $4 adults, $3 children 12 and under. Open daily 8:30–5.*

㉔ Near the mission is the postmodern **San Juan Capistrano Library,** built in 1983. Architect Michael Graves mixed classical design with the style of the mission to striking effect. Its courtyard has secluded places for reading, as well as a running water fountain. *31495 El Camino Real, tel. 714/493–3984. Open Mon.–Thur. 10–9, Fri.–Sat. 10–5.*

The **Decorative Arts Study Center,** just up the street from the mission, presents exhibits and lectures on gardens and interior design, plus an annual antiques show and storytelling festival in October. *31431 Camino Capistrano, tel. 714/496–2132. Open Tues.–Sat. 10–3.*

Galleria Capistrano, occupying the historic Egan House, is one of Southern California's leading galleries devoted to the art of Native Americans. Exhibits include first-rate paintings, prints, jewelry, and sculpture from Southwest and Northwest artists. *31892 Camino Capistrano, tel. 714/661–1781. Open Tues.–Sun. 11–6.*

TimeOut The 1894 Spanish Revival **Capistrano Depot** (26701 Verdugo St., tel. 714/496–8181) is not only the local Amtrak train station but also a restaurant. The eclectic menu runs from rack of lamb to Southwestern fare to pasta. There's entertainment nightly and Dixieland jazz on Sunday. It's a perfect way to see San Juan if you are based in Los Angeles—a train ride, a meal, and then a little sightseeing.

The southernmost city in Orange County, **San Clemente,** is probably best remembered as the site of Richard Nixon's Western White House. Casa Pacifica was often in the news during Nixon's presidency. Situated on a massive 25-acre estate, the house, now a private residence, is visible from the beach; just look up to the cliffs. Nowadays, visitors are more likely to be looking for the San Clemente Pier, a sort of cliché for California: great ocean view, palm-tree-lined beach, and the **Fisherman's Restaurant and Bar** (tel. 714/498–6390), where you can sip blush wine, watch the sunset, and load up on shrimp cocktail.

㉕ A bit farther south is the **San Onofre Nuclear Power Plant,** a collection of space-age domes lending an eerie feeling to the nearby beach, where surfers ride the waves undaunted. The plant is scheduled to be shut down in the near future, but information on its operation is available at the San Onofre Nuclear Information Center, off PCH.

San Onofre State Beach, just south of the nuclear plant, boasts some of the best surfing in California. Below the bluffs here are 3.5 miles of sandy beach, where you can also swim, fish, and watch wildlife.

For avid bicyclists, the next 20 miles south of San Clemente are prime terrain. **Camp Pendleton,** the country's largest Marine Corps base, welcomes cyclists to use some of its roads—just don't be surprised to see a troop helicopter taking off right beside you. Training involves offshore landings; overland treks are also conducted on the installation's three mountain ranges, five lakes, and 250 miles of roads.

Off the Beaten Track

Lido Isle, an island in Newport Harbor, the location of many elegant homes, provides some insight into the upper-crust Orange County mind-set. A number of grassy areas offer great harbor views; each is marked "Private Community Park." *Hwy. 55 to PCH in Newport Beach. Turn left at signal on Via Lido and follow onto island.*

Old Towne Orange contains at least 1,200 buildings documented as historically relevant. A walking tour explores some of the most interesting of these, including the Ainsworth House, a museum dedicated to the city's early lifestyle; the 1901 Finley Home, location of the 1945 film *Fallen Angels;* and O'Hara's Irish Pub, a hangout for local reporters. A brochure describing all the stops is available. *City of Orange, 300 E. Chapman Ave., Room 12, Orange, tel. 714/744–7220.*

Little Saigon, an area of the city of Westminster between Ward Street on the east and Magnolia on the west, is home to 115,000 or so Vietnamese residents, the largest Vietnamese community outside Vietnam. Check out the jewelry and gift shops, Asian herbalists, and restaurants in colorful Little Saigon Plaza (Bolsa and Buishard streets), where Song Phung Restaurant offers an extensive menu of authentic dishes. The Dynasty Seafood Restaurant, in the Asian Garden Mall (Bolsa between Magnolia and Bushard streets), is considered the best place in Orange County for Chinese dim sum.

Shopping

Shopping is Orange County's favorite indoor sport, and it's got the shopping malls to prove it. Indeed, Orange County is home to some of the biggest, most varied, and classiest malls in the world. Even if the merchandise offered by Tiffany, Chanel, and Brooks Brothers is beyond your budget, you can always window-shop. The following is just a small selection of the shopping possibilities in the county.

South Coast Plaza (Bristol and Sunflower Sts., Costa Mesa), the most amazing of all the malls and the largest in Orange County, is actually two enclosed shopping centers, complete with greenery and tumbling waterfalls bisecting the wide aisles, plus a collection of boutiques and restaurants across the street. A free tram makes frequent runs between the three sections. The older section is anchored by Nordstrom, Sears, and Bullocks; the newer Crystal Court across the street has the Broadway department store as its centerpiece. It's the variety of stores, however, that makes this mall special. You'll find Gucci, Burberry's, Armani, FAO Schwarz, Saks Fifth Avenue, and Mark Cross just up the aisle from Sears. Kids will want to browse through the Disney and Sesame Street stores. There's even an outpost of the Metropolitan Museum of Art just a few steps from McDonald's and Eddie Bauer. For literary buffs, there is a branch of the famous Rizzoli's International Bookstore. The mall is particularly festive during the holidays, when Santa's village fills the Carousel Court and a five-story Christmas tree soars to the top of the Crystal Court.

Fashion Island on Newport Center Drive in Newport Beach sits on a hilltop, where shoppers can enjoy the ocean breeze. It is an open-air, single-level mall of more than 200 stores. Major department stores here include Neiman Marcus, Bullocks, and Broadway. The enclosed **Atrium Court** is a Mediterranean-style plaza with three floors of boutiques and stores such as Sharper Image, Benetton, and Caswell-Massey.

Main Place, just off I–5 in Santa Ana, has Robinsons-May, Bullocks, and Nordstrom as its anchors. Although many of the 190 shops are upscale, the mall resembles a warehouse. It's busy and noisy, and local teenagers tend to hang out here.

If you can look past the inflatable palm trees, unimaginative T-shirts, and other tourist novelties, there is some good browsing to be done in **Laguna Beach.** There are dozens of art galleries, antiques shops, one-of-a-kind craft boutiques, and custom jewelry stores. Some of the best can be found along arty Forest Avenue, just a few steps off PCH. Thee Foxes Trot, at 264 Forest Avenue, features a delightful selection of handcrafted items from around the world; Georgeo's Art Glass and Jewelry, at 269 Forest Avenue, contains a large selection of etched and blown-glass bowls, vases, glassware, and jewelry; Rosovsky Gallery, at 263 Forest Avenue, showcases the work of three Russian artists; and Pacific Gallery, at 228 Forest Avenue, specializes in whimsical and lighthearted work by about 60 local artists.

Sports, Fitness, Beaches

Orange County has some of the best unplanned, casual spectator sports; besides the surfers, you are bound to catch a vigorous volleyball or basketball game at any beach on any given weekend. For professional sports, *see* Spectator Sports in the Los Angeles chapter.

Participant Sports

Bicycling   Bicycles and roller skates are some of the most popular means of transportation along the beaches. A bike path spans the distance from Marina del Rey all the way to San Diego, with only some minor breaks. Most beaches have rental stands. In Laguna, try **Rainbow Bicycles** (tel. 714/494–5806) or, in Huntington Beach, **Team Bicycle Rentals** (tel. 714/969–5480).

Golf   Golf is one of the most popular sports in Orange County, and owing to the climate, almost 365 days out of the year are perfect golf days. Here is a selection of golf courses:

Anaheim Hills Public Country Club (tel. 714/748–8900); **Costa Mesa Public Golf and Country Club** (tel. 714/540–7500); **H.G. Dad Miller** (Anaheim, tel. 714/774–8055); **Imperial Golf Course** (Brea, tel. 714/529–3923); **Mile Square Golf Course** (Fountain Valley, tel. 714/968–4556); **Newport Beach Golf Course** (tel. 714/852–8681); **San Clemente Municipal Golf Course** (tel. 714/492–3943); **San Juan Hills Country Club** (San Juan Capistrano, tel. 714/837–0361); **Aliso Creek Golf Course** (South Laguna, tel. 714/499–1919).

Running   The **Santa Ana Riverbed Trail** hugs the Santa Ana River for 20.6 miles between Huntington State Beach and Imperial Highway in Yorba Linda; there are entrances, as well as rest rooms and drinking fountains, at all crossings. The **Beach Trail** runs along the beach from Huntington Beach to Newport. Paths throughout **Newport Back Bay** wrap around a marshy area inhabited by lizards, squirrels, rabbits, and waterfowl.

Snorkeling   The fact that **Corona del Mar**—along with its two colorful reefs—is off-limits to boats makes it a great place for snorkeling. **Laguna Beach** is also a good spot for snorkeling and diving; the whole beach area of the city is a marine preserve.

Surfing   There are 50 surf breaks along the Orange County coastline, with wave action ranging from beginner to expert. If you are not an expert, you can get a sense of the action on a boogie board at one of the beginners' beaches. Surfing is permitted at most beaches year-round, except at **Huntington State Beach, Salt Creek Beach Park, Aliso County Beach, Capistrano Beach, Sunset Beach,** and **Newport Beach,** where it is permitted only in summer. "The Wedge" at **Newport Beach,** one of the most famous surfing spots in the world, is known for its steep, punishing shore break. Don't miss the spectacle of surfers, who appear tiny in the midst of the waves, flying through this treacherous place. San Clemente surfers usually take a primo spot right across from the San Onofre Nuclear Reactor. Rental stands are found at all beaches.

Tennis   Most of the larger hotels have tennis courts. Here are some other choices; try the local Yellow Pages for additional listings.

Anaheim   Anaheim has 50 public tennis courts; phone Parks and Recreation (tel. 714/254–5191) for information. **Tennisland Racquet Club** (1330

S. Walnut St., tel. 714/535–4851) has 10 courts, a teaching pro, and a practice court.

Huntington Beach **Edison Community Center** (21377 Magnolia St., tel. 714/960–8870) has four courts available on a first-come, first-served basis in the daytime. The **Murdy Community Center** (7000 Norma Dr., tel. 714/960–8895) has four courts, also first-come, first-served during the day. Both facilities accept reservations for play after 5 PM; both charge $2 an hour.

Laguna Beach Six metered courts can be found at **Laguna Beach High School,** on Park Avenue. Two courts are available at the **Irvine Bowl,** on Laguna Canyon Road, and six new courts are available at **Alta Laguna Park,** at the end of Alta Laguna Boulevard, off Park Avenue, on a first-come, first-served basis. For more information, call the City of Laguna Beach Recreation Department at 714/497–0716.

Newport Beach Call the recreation department at 714/644–3151 for information about court use at **Corona del Mar High School** (2101 E. Bluff Dr.). There are eight public courts.

Newport Beach Marriott Hotel and Tennis Club (900 Newport Center Dr., tel. 714/640–4000) has eight courts.

San Clemente There are four courts at **San Luis Rey Park,** on Avenue San Luis Rey. They are offered on a first-come, first-served basis. Call the recreation department at 714/361–8200 for further information.

Water Sports Rental stands for surfboards, windsurfers, small power boats, and sailboats can be found near most of the piers. **Hobie Sports** has three locations for surfboard and boogie-board rentals—two in Dana Point (tel. 714/496–2366) and one in Laguna (tel. 714/497–3304).

In the biggest boating town of all, Newport Beach, you can rent sailboats and small motorboats at **Electric Boat Co.** in the harbor (tel. 714/673–7200; open Fri.–Sun. 10–4). Sailboats cost $25 an hour, and motorboats cost $50 an hour, half price for each subsequent hour. You must have a driver's license, and some knowledge of boating is helpful; rented boats are not allowed out of the bay.

Parasailing is also becoming a popular water sport. At **Davey's Locker** in the Balboa Pavilion (tel. 714/673–1434; open summer, daily 9–5:30), you can parasail for 8 to 12 minutes during a 90-minute boat ride. The cost is $45 per person, with as many as six people per boat. The last excursion leaves at 4.

In Dana Point, powerboats and sailboats can be rented at **Embarcadero Marina** (tel. 714/496–6177, open weekdays 8–5, weekends 7–5:30), near the launching ramp at Dana Point Harbor. Boat sizes vary—sailboats range from $15 to $30 an hour, motorboats are $20 an hour. Only cash is accepted. In spring and summer, **Dana Wharf Sports Fishing** (tel. 714/496–5794) offers parasailing. Call for hours and prices.

Beaches

All of the state, county, and city beaches in Orange County allow swimming. Make sure there is a staffed lifeguard stand nearby, and you will be pretty safe. Also keep on the lookout for posted signs about undertow: It can be mighty nasty around here. Most public beaches have fire rings, tidal pools, volleyball courts, showers, and rest rooms. Recently beaches have begun closing at night. Moving from north to south along the coast, here are some of the best beaches:

Huntington Beach State Beach (tel. 714/536–1454) runs for 9 miles along Pacific Coast Highway (Beach Blvd. [Hwy. 39] from inland). There are changing rooms, concessions, barbecue pits, and vigilant lifeguards on the premises, and there is parking. **Bolsa Chica State Beach** (tel. 714/846–3460), just north of Huntington and across from the Bolsa Chica Ecological Reserve, has barbecue pits and is usually less crowded than its neighbor.

Lower Newport Bay provides an enclave sheltered from the ocean. This area, off Pacific Coast Highway on Jamboree Boulevard, is a 740-acre preserve for ducks and geese. Nearby **Newport Dunes Resort** (tel. 714/729–3863) offers RV spaces, picnic facilities, changing rooms, water-sports equipment rentals, and a place to launch boats.

Just south of Newport Beach, **Corona del Mar Beach** (tel. 714/644–3044) has a tidal pool and caves to explore. It also sports one of the best walks in the county—a beautiful rock pier that juts into the ocean. Facilities include barbecue pits, volleyball courts, food, rest rooms, and parking.

Crystal Cove State Park (tel. 714/494–3539, admission $6 per car), midway between Corona del Mar and Laguna, is a hidden treasure: 3.5 miles of unspoiled beach with some of the best tidepooling in southern California. Here you can see starfish, crabs, and lobster on the rocks, and rangers conduct nature walks on Saturday morning.

Located at the end of Broadway at Pacific Coast Highway, Laguna Beach's **Main Beach Park** has sand volleyball, two half-basketball courts, children's play equipment, picnic areas, rest rooms, showers, and road parking.

The county's best spot for scuba diving is in the **Marine Life Refuge** (tel. 714/494–6571), which runs from Seal Rock to Diver's Cove in Laguna. Farther south, in South Laguna, **Aliso County Park** (tel. 714/661–7013) is a recreation area with a pier for fishing, barbecue pits, parking, food, and rest rooms. Swim Beach, inside **Dana Point Harbor,** also has a fishing pier, barbecues, food, parking, and rest rooms, as well as a shower.

Doheny State Park (tel. 714/496–6171), at the south end of Dana Point, one of the best surfing spots in southern California, has an interpretive center devoted to the wildlife of the Doheny Marine Refuge, and there are food stands and shops nearby. Camping is permitted here, and there are picnic facilities and a pier for fishing. **San Clemente State Beach** (tel. 714/492–3156) is a favorite sunbathing and surfing spot. It has ample camping facilities, RV hookups, and food stands.

Dining and Lodging

Dining   In Orange County, restaurant choices used to be limited to fast food, fried chicken, and steak. You can still find fast food, but now there's also fancy French, inspired Italian, zesty Mexican, and savory seafood. Familiar chain restaurants pop up in mini-malls on main streets throughout Orange County—north of Disneyland, for example, the corner of Orangethorpe and Harbor Boulevard supports more than two dozen such spots.

Central Orange County in particular boasts a number of ethnic restaurants, the result of an influx of people from all over the world. Some of these include **Sitar Indian Restaurant** (2632 W. La Palma

Ave., Anaheim, tel. 714/821–8333); **Mandarin Deli** for northern Chinese cuisine (820 N. Euclid St., Anaheim, tel. 714/535–3450); **Lotus Court** for Hong Kong–style Chinese cuisine (181 E. Commonwealth Ave., Fullerton, tel. 714/738–3838); **Phoenix Club,** a German restaurant (1340 Sanderson Ave., Anaheim, tel. 714/563–4164); **Rose and Crown British Pub** (20 S. Anaheim Blvd., Anaheim, tel. 714/778–5606); **Sushi Seiha,** a Japanese restaurant (214 S. State College Blvd., Anaheim, tel. 714/991–8980); **Anita's** New Mexican–style food (600 S. Harbor Blvd., Fullerton, tel. 714/525–0977); and **Song Long,** a Vietnamese/French restaurant (9361 Bolsa Ave., Westminster, tel. 714/775–3724).

Highly recommended restaurants are indicated by a star ★.

Category	Cost*
$$$$	over $35
$$$	$25–$35
$$	$15–$25
$	under $15

per person for a three-course meal, excluding drinks, service, and 7³/₄% tax

Lodging   Lodging to suit every budget and taste is available in Orange County; offerings range from the very expensive four-star Ritz-Carlton on the coast to the comfortable-but-plain chain motels around Disneyland. Those who haven't been to Orange County for a while will be pleasantly surprised to see that many hotels near Disneyland have recently undergone renovation and now have a bright new look. In addition to the choices listed here for the Anaheim area, there are a number of motels; but visitors should be careful to pick only familiar chain names. Central Orange County also supports a number of lodgings that normally cater to business travelers, but offer substantial discounts on weekends.

Prices listed here are based on summer rates. Winter rates, especially near Disneyland, tend to be somewhat less. It pays to shop around for promotional and weekend rates.

Highly recommended lodgings are indicated by a star ★.

Category	Cost*
$$$$	over $100
$$$	$75–$100
$$	$50–$75
$	under $50

All prices are for a double room, excluding 13% tax.

Anaheim   **JW's.** This is an elegant French surprise in the heart of convention-
Dining   busy Anaheim. A quiet place where you can talk serious business or romance, the restaurant is a series of interconnected rooms. The decor is country French with fireplaces, books, subdued lighting, and original art on the walls. While French is the theme, the menu changes frequently to spotlight fresh seafood, game, and produce. The extensive wine list is fairly priced. *Marriott Hotel, 700 W. Con-*

vention Way, tel. 714/750–8000. Reservations suggested. Jacket suggested. AE, D, DC, MC, V. Valet parking. No lunch. Closed Sun. $$$$

The White House. This 80-year-old mansion, which bears a striking resemblance to its namesake, is popular with conventioneers. There are several small dining rooms with crisp linens, candles, flowers, and some fireplaces. The basically Italian menu features a good selection from pasta to scaloppine, with a heavy emphasis on seafood. Vegetarian entrées are available. A four-course prix-fixe menu is available until 6:30 for $25 per person. *887 S. Anaheim Blvd., tel. 714/772–1381. Reservations suggested. Jacket suggested. AE, DC, MC, V. No lunch Sat. and Sun. $$$–$$$$*

The Catch. This very reliable restaurant across the street from Anaheim Stadium is popular with baseball and football fans, who enjoy its sports-bar atmosphere and friendly service. Dining rooms have a comfortable denlike ambience. The menu features hearty portions of steak, seafood, and salads. *1929 S. State College Blvd., Anaheim, tel. 714/634–1829. Reservations advised. Jacket suggested. AE, DC, MC, V. No lunch Fri., Sat., Sun. $$–$$$*

Lodging **Anaheim Hilton and Towers.** This hotel is one of several choices convenient to the Anaheim Convention Center, which in fact is just a few steps from the front door. It is virtually a self-contained city—complete with its own post office. The lobby is dominated by a bright, airy atrium, and guest rooms are decorated in pinks and greens with light wood furniture. Because it caters to conventioneers, it can be busy and noisy, with long lines at restaurants. *777 Convention Way, 92802, tel. 714/750–4321 or 800/222–9923, fax 714/740–4252. 1,600 rooms. Facilities: 4 restaurants, lounges, shops, duty-free shopping, outdoor pool, Jacuzzis, fitness center ($10 charge), sun deck, concierge, summer Vacation Station for kids. AE, D, DC, MC, V. $$$$*

Anaheim Marriott. This contemporary hotel, which consists of two towers of 16 and 18 floors, is another headquarters for Convention Center attendees. The busy lobby's huge windows allow sunlight to stream in, highlighting the gleaming marble and brass. The rooms are compact, but they have balconies and are well equipped for business travelers, with desks, two phones, and modem hookups. A concierge floor was added in 1994. Rooms on the north side have good views of Disneyland's summer fireworks shows. Discounted weekend and Disneyland packages are available. *700 W. Convention Way, 92802, tel. 714/750–8000, fax 714/750–9100. 979 rooms, 54 suites. Facilities: 3 restaurants, 2 lounges, 2 heated pools, Jacuzzi, entertainment, fitness center, video games, concierge. AE, D, DC, MC, V. $$$$*

★ **Disneyland Hotel.** This hotel, which is connected to the Magic Kingdom by monorail, carries the Disney theme in the lobby, restaurants, entertainment, shops, and spacious guest rooms. Consisting of three towers surrounding lakes, streams, tumbling waterfalls, and lush landscaping, the once-tired hotel was recently renovated and now gleams with brass and marble. In Goofy's Kitchen, kids can breakfast with Donald, Mickey, or Chip and Dale. There are marina and park views, and rooms in the Bonita tower overlook the Fantasy Waters, a nighttime Disney-theme lighted fountain and music display. *1150 W. Cerritos Ave., 92802, tel. 714/778–6600, fax 714/778–5946. 1,131 rooms. Facilities: 6 restaurants, 5 lounges, 3 pools, spa, whitesand beach, concierge floor, 10 tennis courts, fitness center, business center, entertainment. AE, DC, MC, V. $$$$*

Sheraton–Anaheim Motor Hotel. This Tudor-style hotel has a contemporary, bright look, though it keeps its castle theme in large tapestries, faux stone walls, and frescoes in the public areas. The large guest rooms open onto interior gardens. A Disneyland shuttle and multi-language services are available. *1015 W. Ball Rd., 92802, tel. 714/778–1700 or 800/325–3535, fax 714/535–3889. 500 rooms. Facilities: dining room, deli, bar, heated pool, suites, game room, wheelchair accessible units. AE, D, DC, MC, V. $$$$*

Holiday Inn Anaheim Center. A big pink Mediterranean-style building, set at the edge of Disneyland at the Santa Ana Freeway, this Holiday Inn was designed for families visiting the Magic Kingdom. It has pleasant, if functional, rooms including some with separate sitting areas. Shuttle service is available to nearby attractions including Knott's Berry Farm, Movieland Wax Museum, and Medieval Times. Children stay free with parents. *1221 S. Harbor Blvd., 92805, tel. 714/758–0900 or 800/545–7275, fax 714/533–1804. 252 rooms, 2 housekeeping suites. Facilities: restaurant, lounge, pool, spa, sauna, video games, disabled access. AE, D, DC, MC, V. $$$*

Holiday Inn Maingate Anaheim. Large glass chandeliers in the lobby set the tone at this establishment one block south of Disneyland. *1850 S. Harbor Blvd., 92802, tel. 714/750–2801 or 800/624–6855, fax 714/971–4754. 312 rooms, including 3 suites. Facilities: dining room, lounge, heated pool, video games. AE, D, DC, MC, V. $$$*

Inn at the Park. This venerable hotel, a longtime favorite of conventioneers, has the spacious rooms of an earlier era. All rooms have balconies, and those in the tower offer good views of Disneyland's summer fireworks shows. The hotel also has one of the most spacious and attractive pool areas around. But despite recent redecoration, rooms and corridors show signs of wear, and the lobby is downright stark. *1855 S. Harbor Blvd., 92802, tel. 714/750–1811, fax 714/971–3626. 497 rooms. Facilities: restaurant, coffee shop, lounge, heated pool, spa, exercise room, video games. AE, D, DC, MC, V. $$$*

Quality Hotel/Maingate. A large, open, red-tile lobby is filled with mirrors, plants, and flowers; guest rooms are decorated in greens and yellows. The hotel is close to Disneyland and the convention center. *616 Convention Way, 92802, tel. 714/750–3131 or 800/231–6215, fax 714/750–9027. 284 rooms, including 12 suites. Facilities: 2 restaurants, lounge, heated pool, game room. AE, DC, MC, V. $$*

Ramada Maingate/Anaheim. Clean and reliable, this chain hotel has recently upgraded guest rooms, added new landscaping, and opened a sports bar. The hotel is across the street from Disneyland and offers free shuttle service to the park. *1460 S. Harbor Blvd., 92802, tel. 714/772–6777 or 800/447–4048, fax 714/999–1727. 465 rooms. Facilities: restaurant, pool, Jacuzzi, game room. AE, MC, V. $$*

Desert Palm Inn and Suites. This budget hotel has many things going for it: it's midway between Disneyland and the Convention Center, it has large suites (some with balconies) that can accommodate as many as eight people, and every room has a microwave and a refrigerator. The decor is attractive, though functional, and the staff is friendly. Book well in advance, especially when large conventions are in town. *631 W. Katella Ave., 92802, tel. 714/535–1133, 800/635–5423, fax 714/491–7409. 102 rooms and suites. Facilities: pool, indoor Jacuzzi, sun deck, exercise room, guest laundry, Continental breakfast. MC, V. $–$$*

Stovall's Inn. Very well-kept, this motel stacks up well against area hotels in a similar price range. Nice touches include the topiary gardens, room decor in soft desert colors, and a friendly staff. Ask about discounts if you're staying several nights. *1110 W. Katella Ave., 92802, tel. 714/778–1880, 800/854–8175, fax 714/778–3805. 290 rooms. Facilities: restaurant, lounge, 2 pools, 2 whirlpool spas, rooms with facilities for the hearing impaired. MC, V. $–$$*

Dining

Angelo's & Vinci's Cafe Ristorante, **1**
Antoine, **31**
Bangkok IV, **26**
The Beach House, **52**
The Cannery, **43**
The Catch, **20**
The Cellar, **2**
Chanteclair, **37**
Crab Cooker, **42**
Delaney's Restaurant, **59**
The Dining Room, **58**
El Adobe, **64**
El Torito Grill, **40**
Emporio Armani, **27**
Etienne's, **66**
Five Feet, **55**
Hard Rock Cafe Newport Beach, **49**
JW's, **12**
Kachina, **54**
La Brasserie, **22**
La Vie En Rose, **4**
Le Biarritz, **44**
L'Hirondelle, **65**
Luciana's, **61**
Mandarin Gourmet, **39**
Marrakesh, **41**
Mulberry Street Ristorante, **3**
Nostrum Mare, **21**
Pascal, **45**
Pavilion, **33**
Prego, **36**
Randall's, **25**
The Ritz, **46**
Texas Loosey's Chili Parlor & Saloon, **23**
Tortilla Flats, **57**
Watercolors, **63**
The White House, **18**
Wolfgang Puck Cafe, **28**

Lodging

Airporter Garden Hotel, **30**
Anaheim Hilton and Towers, **11**
Anaheim Marriott, **12**
Best Western Marina Inn, **62**
Blue Lantern Inn, **60**
Buena Park Hotel, **5**
Casa Clemente Resort, **68**
Country Side Inn and Suites, **38**
Dana Point Resort, **63**

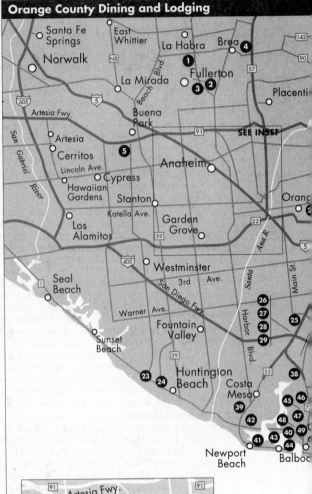

Orange County Dining and Lodging

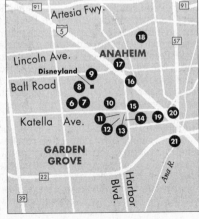

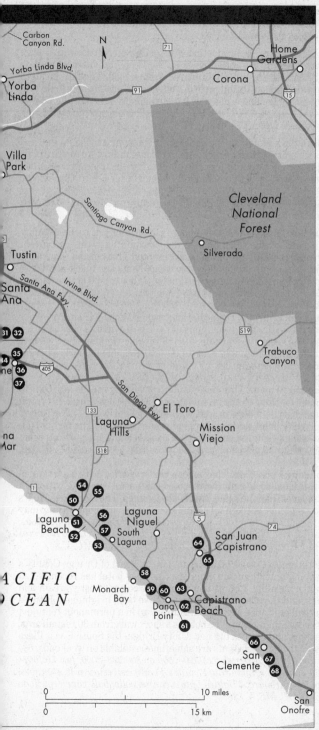

Desert Palm Inn and Suites, **10**

Disneyland Hotel, **8**

Doubletree Hotel Orange County, **21**

Eiler's Inn, **56**

Four Seasons Hotel, **47**

Hampton Inn, **19**

Holiday Inn Anaheim Center, **17**

Holiday Inn Maingate Anaheim, **15**

Hotel Laguna, **51**

Hyatt Regency Irvine, **35**

Inn at Laguna, **50**

Inn at the Park, **13**

Irvine Marriott, **34**

Le Meridien Newport Beach, **31**

Magic Carpet Motel, **7**

Newport Beach Marriott Hotel and Tennis Club, **48**

Quality Hotel/Maingate, **14**

Ramada Maingate/Anaheim, **16**

Ritz-Carlton Laguna Niguel, **58**

San Clemente Inn, **70**

Sheraton-Anaheim Motor Hotel, **9**

Sheraton Newport Beach, **32**

Stovall's Inn, **6**

Surf and Sand Hotel, **53**

Waterfront Hilton, **24**

Westin South Coast Plaza, **29**

Hampton Inn. Basic lodging at a basic price. *300 E. Katella Way, 92802, tel. 714/772–8713. 136 rooms. Facilities: pool, complimentary breakfast. AE, DC, MC, V. $*

Brea
Dining

La Vie en Rose. A reproduction of a Norman farmhouse with a large turret, this restaurant adjacent to the Brea Mall attracts visitors and locals for its artfully prepared French food. The fare includes seafood, lamb, veal, and melt-in-your-mouth pastries. With several cozy dining rooms, it has a warm atmosphere. *240 S. State College Blvd., 91621, tel. 714/529–8333. Reservations suggested. Jacket suggested. AE, DC, MC, V. $$$$*

Buena Park
Lodging

Buena Park Hotel. At the center of a lobby of marble, brass, and glass, a spiral staircase winds up to the mezzanine. Rooms are done in green and peach tones. The hotel, which is adjacent to Knott's Berry Farm, offers complimentary shuttle service to Disneyland. *7675 Crescent Ave., 90620, tel. 714/995–1111 or 800/854–8792, fax 714/828–8590. 350 rooms. Facilities: restaurant, lounge, nightclub, coffee shop, heated pool, Jacuzzi. AE, DC, MC, V. $$–$$$*

Costa Mesa
Dining

Bangkok IV. Despite its shopping-mall location—it occupies an indoor patio on the third floor of the Crystal Court–this restaurant serves artistically prepared and presented Thai cuisine. The decor is dramatic, with stylish flower arrangements and black-and-white appointments. Menu items designated as hot can be prepared with milder spices upon request. *3333 Bear St., tel. 714/540–7661. Reservations required. Dress: casual. AE, DC, MC, V. $$–$$$*

Mandarin Gourmet. Dollar for bite, owner Michael Chang provides what the critics and locals consider the best Chinese cuisine in the area. His specialties include: a crisp-yet-juicy Peking duck, cashew chicken, and, seemingly everyone's favorite, mu-shu pork. There is also a very good wine list. *1500 Adams Ave., tel. 714/540–1937. Reservations accepted. Dress: casual. AE, DC, MC, V. $$*

Emporio Armani. This classy storefront restaurant is adjacent to Armani fashions on the ground floor of South Coast Plaza. In typical Armani style, it's decorated with lots of light wood and accented with white linen, and fashion photos line the walls. The fare is Italian—salads, single-portion pizzas, pasta—and some portions seem a bit small. *3333 Bristol St., tel. 714/754–0300. Dress: casual. AE, DC, MC, V. $*

Wolfgang Puck Cafe. The famous chef has tried here to create an institutional-style café (read school cafeteria), complete with high noise level. Just the same, it's always jammed. The menu lists Wolf's famous pizzas, chicken salad, and pastas; the most popular item may be the half chicken with huge portions of garlic mashed potatoes. *South Coast Plaza, 3333 Bristol Ave., tel. 714/546–WOLF. Reservations for parties of five or more only. Dress: casual. MC, V. $*

Lodging

Westin South Coast Plaza. Located in the heart of Orange County's shopping/entertainment complex, this busy hotel has recently had a major face-lift. Rooms now sport soft colors, mostly cream and beige, and the pleasant public areas have been brightened. Fitness fans will enjoy the new health club set up in a permanent tent next to the swimming pool. The hotel is a short walk from 60 restaurants, theaters, and (across the new Unity Bridge) the South Coast Plaza shopping mall. Discounts are sometimes available on weekends. *686 Anton Blvd., 92626, tel. 714/540–2500 or 800/228–3000, fax 714/662–6695. 390 rooms, including 17 suites. Facilities: restaurant, 2 lounges, pool, shuffleboard, 2 lighted tennis courts, volleyball, concierge floor. AE, D, DC, MC, V. $$$$*

Dana Point **The Dining Room.** The fine-dining restaurant at the Ritz-Carlton
Dining Laguna Niguel gets high marks for its French cuisine and impecca-
ble service within a showcase of fine art and European antiques.
Don't expect to watch the sun setting over the Pacific from The Din-
ing Room; it has no windows. *33533 Ritz-Carlton Dr., Laguna
Niguel, tel. 714/240–2000. Reservations required. Jacket required.
AE, D, DC, MC, V. Dinner only, closed Sun., Mon. $$$$*

Watercolors. This light, cheerful dining room provides a cliff-top
view of the harbor and an equally enjoyable Continental/California
menu, along with low-calorie choices. Try the baked breast of pheasant, roast rabbit, grilled swordfish, and either the Caesar or
poached spinach salad. *Dana Point Resort, tel. 714/661–5000. Reservations advised. Dress: casual but neat. AE, D, DC, MC, V. Valet parking. $$–$$$*

Delaney's Restaurant. Fresh seafood from nearby San Diego's fishing fleet is what this place is all about. Your choice is prepared as
simply as possible. If you have to wait for a table, pass the time at
the clam and oyster bar. *25001 Dana Dr., tel. 714/496–6195. Reserva-
tions advised. Dress: casual. AE, D, DC, MC, V. $$*

Luciana's. This small, intimate Italian restaurant is a real find, es-
pecially for couples seeking a romantic evening. Dining rooms are
small, dressed with crisp white linens and warmed by fireplaces.
The well-prepared food is served with care. *24312 Del Prado Ave.,
tel. 714/661–6500. Reservations advised. AE, DC, MC, V. No lunch. $$*

Lodging **Blue Lantern Inn.** Perched atop the bluffs, this Cape Cod–style bed-
and-breakfast has stunning harbor and ocean views. Rooms are individually decorated with period furnishings, fireplaces, stocked
refrigerators, and private Jacuzzis. Breakfast and afternoon refreshments are included in the price. *34343 St. of the Blue Lantern,
92629, tel. 714/661–1304. 29 rooms. Facilities: library, concierge, fitness facilities. AE, MC, V. $$$$*

★ **Dana Point Resort.** This Cape Cod–style hillside resort is decorated
in shades of sea-foam green and peach. The lobby is filled with large
palm trees and original artwork, and most rooms have ocean views.
The ambience is casual yet elegant. In summer, the Capistrano Valley Symphony performs on the resort's attractively landscaped
grounds. *25135 Park Lantern, 92629, tel. 714/661–5000 or 800/533–
9748, fax 714/661–5000. 350 rooms. Facilities: restaurant, jazz lounge,
3 pools, 3 spas, health club, concierge level, croquet, volleyball, basketball. AE, D, DC, MC, V. $$$$*

★ **Ritz-Carlton Laguna Niguel.** This acclaimed hotel has earned world-
class status for its gorgeous setting right on the edge of the Pacific,
its sumptuous Mediterranean architecture and decor, and its reputation for flawless service. With colorful landscaping outside and an
imposing marble-columned entry, it feels like an Italian country
villa. Every possible amenity, and then some, is available to guests.
Recently redecorated rooms still feature traditional furnishings,
sumptuous fabrics, marble bathrooms, and private balconies with
ocean or garden views. Reduced-rate packages are sometimes available. *33533 Ritz-Carlton Dr., 92677, tel. 714/240–2000 or 800/241–3333,
fax 714/240–0829. 393 rooms. Facilities: 3 restaurants, 3 lounges, club
with entertainment, 2 pools, Jacuzzis, beach access, health club,
beauty salon, 4 tennis courts, concierge, use of nearby 18-hole golf
course. AE, D, DC, MC, V. $$$$*

Best Western Marina Inn. Set right in the marina, this fairly basic
motel is convenient to docks, restaurants, and shops. Rooms vary
in size from basic to family units with kitchens and fireplaces. Many
rooms in this three-level motel have balconies and harbor views.
24800 Dana Point Harbor Dr., 92629, tel. 714/496–1203 or 800/255–

6843. 136 rooms. Facilities: pool, fitness facilities. AE, D, DC, MC, V. $$

Fullerton
Dining

The Cellar. The name tells the story here: an intimate subterranean dining room with beamed ceiling and stone walls, wine racks, and casks. Appropriately, the list of wines from Europe and California is among the best in the West. The bill of fare is classic French cuisine that has been lightened for the California palate. *305 N. Harbor Blvd., tel. 714/525–5682. Reservations required. Jacket and tie advised. AE, DC, MC, V. No lunch. Closed Sun., Mon. $$$$*

Mulberry Street Ristorante. The movers and shakers in north Orange County gather regularly at this friendly, noisy, watering hole, designed to resemble a turn-of-the-century New York eatery. The kitchen serves up prodigious, highly seasoned portions of pasta, seafood, chicken, and veal. Desserts are made on the premises. *114 W. Wilshire Ave., tel. 714/525–1056. Reservations advised. Dress: casual. AE, DC, MC, V. No lunch Sun. $$*

Angelo's & Vinci's Cafe Ristorante. The show's the thing at this funky Italian eatery created by actor/choreographer Steven Peck. Entertaining surroundings include giant knights in shining armor, tableaux of Italian street scenes, an altar with old family photos and cherubs from Sicily, and a pair of aerialist puppets and a tightrope walker overhead. Locally popular for huge portions of Sicilian-style pasta and pizza, this is a busy, noisy place. *550 N. Harbor Blvd., tel. 714/879–4022. Dress: casual. MC, V. $*

Huntington Beach
Dining

Texas Loosey's Chili Parlor & Saloon. This place serves Tex-Mex cooking with the fixin's to make it even hotter, plus steaks, ribs, and burgers. Country-and-western music is played in the evenings. *14160 Beach Blvd., tel. 714/898–9797. Reservations accepted for parties of 6 or more. Dress: casual. AE, D, MC, V. $*

Lodging

Waterfront Hilton. This new oceanfront hotel rises 12 stories above the surf. The Mediterranean-style resort is decorated in soft mauves, beiges, and greens, and offers a panoramic ocean view from many guest rooms. Ocean-view suites have balconies and wet bars. *21100 PCH, 92648, tel. 714/960–7873 or 800/822–7873. 293 rooms. Facilities: 2 restaurants, lounge, 2 lighted tennis courts, pool, Jacuzzi, fitness center, concierge level, bike and beach-equipment rentals. AE, DC, MC, V. $$$$*

Irvine
Dining

Chanteclair. This Franco–Italian country house is a lovely, tasteful retreat amid an island of modern high-rise office buildings. French Riviera–type cuisine is served, and the chateaubriand for two and rack of lamb are recommended. *18912 MacArthur Blvd., tel. 714/752–8001. Reservations advised. Jacket required. AE, D, DC, MC, V. No Sat. lunch. $$$*

Pavilion. Excellent Chinese food is offered in what resembles a formal eating hall in Taiwan. Specialties include steamed whole fish, ginger duck, and Hunan lamb. *14110 Culver Dr., 714/551–1688. Reservations advised. Dress: casual. AE, DC, MC, V. $$*

Prego. A much larger version of the Beverly Hills Prego, this one is located in an attractive approximation of a Tuscan villa and has an outdoor patio. It's a favorite of Orange County yuppies, who rave about the watch-the-cooks-at-work open kitchen and the oak-burning pizza oven. Try the spit-roasted meats and chicken or the charcoal-grilled fresh fish. Also try one of the reasonably priced California or Italian wines. *18420 Von Karman Ave., tel. 714/553–1333. Reservations advised. Dress: casual. AE, DC, MC, V. Valet parking. No weekend lunch. $$*

Lodging **Hyatt Regency Irvine.** Offering all the amenities of a first-class resort, this hotel is elegantly decorated in soft contemporary tones, and the marble lobby is flanked by glass-enclosed elevators. Special golf packages at nearby Tustin Ranch are available. The lower weekend rates are a great deal. *17900 Jamboree Rd., 92714, tel. 714/975–1234, fax 714/852–1574. 526 rooms, 10 suites. Facilities: 2 restaurants, 2 lounges, pool, Jacuzzi, 4 tennis courts, fitness facilities, entertainment, concierge, bike rentals, wheelchair accessible. AE, D, DC, MC, V. $$$$*

Airporter Garden Hotel. This hotel, across the street from John Wayne Airport and convenient to most area offices, caters primarily to business travelers; the newly decorated rooms have large work areas and two phones. One suite has a private swimming pool outside the bedroom door. Special rates are available for weekend guests. *18700 MacArthur Blvd., 92715, tel. 714/833–2770 or 800/854–3012. 195 rooms, 17 suites. Facilities: restaurant, café, 2 lounges, heated pool, fitness center, free shuttle bus, entertainment. AE, D, DC, MC, V. $$$*

Irvine Marriott. This contemporary-looking hotel towers over Koll Business Center, making it a convenient spot for business travelers. Despite its size, the hotel has an intimate feel about it, due in part to the cozy lobby, the friendly staff, and the repeat guests. Rooms, slated for renovation in 1995, carry an Oriental look; they're equipped with small balconies, coffeemakers, and ironing boards. Weekend discounts and packages are usually available. *1800 Von Karman Ave., 92715, tel. 714/553–0100, fax 714/261–7059. 489 rooms, 24 suites. Facilities: 2 restaurants, sports bar, entertainment, indoor-outdoor pool, 4 lighted tennis courts, health club, spa and massage services, concierge floors, business-service center. AE, D, DC, MC, V. $$$*

Laguna **Five Feet.** The first of a number of Chinese/European restaurants
Beach in Orange County, Five Feet continues to delight diners with its
Dining innovative culinary approaches. You'll find delicate pot stickers, wontons stuffed with goat cheese, and a salad featuring sashimi, plus steak and fresh fish. The decor showcases the work of local artists. *328 Gleneyre St., Laguna Beach, tel. 714/497–4955. Reservations advised. Dress: casual. AE, MC, V. Lunch Fri. only. $$$–$$$$*

The Beach House. A Laguna tradition, the Beach House has a water view from every table. Fresh fish, lobster, and steamed clams are the drawing cards. *619 Sleepy Hollow La., tel. 714/494–9707. Reservations advised. Dress: casual. AE, MC, V. $$*

Kachina. The creation of Orange County star chef David Wilhelm, this tiny restaurant housed beneath an art gallery draws locals and visitors with contemporary Southwestern–style cuisine and a boisterous atmosphere. Even hearty eaters can make a meal by selecting several items from the appetizer portion of the menu. *222 Forest Ave., tel. 714/497–5546. Reservations advised. Dress: casual. AE, MC, V. $$*

Tortilla Flats. This hacienda-style restaurant specializes in first-rate chile rellenos, carne Tampiquena, soft-shell tacos, and beef or chicken fajitas. There's also a wide selection of Mexican tequilas and beers. Sunday brunch is served. *1740 S. Coast Hwy., tel. 714/494–6588. Dinner reservations advised. Dress: casual. AE, MC, V. $*

Lodging **Surf and Sand Hotel.** This is the largest hotel in Laguna and is right on the beach. The rooms are decorated in soft sand colors and have wooden shutters and private balconies. Weekend packages are available. *1555 S. Coast Hwy., 92651, tel. 714/497–4477 or 800/524–*

8621. 157 rooms, including 5 suites. Facilities: 2 restaurants, lounge, private beach, pool, concierge. AE, DC, MC, V. $$$$

★ **Inn at Laguna.** This new Southwest-style inn has one of the best locations in town. It's close to Main Beach and Las Brisas restaurant and bar, one of Laguna's most popular watering holes, yet far enough away to be secluded. Set on a bluff overlooking the ocean, the inn has luxurious amenities and many rooms with views. *211 N. Coast Hwy., 92651, tel. 714/497–9722. 70 rooms. Facilities: VCRs in rooms, heated pool, Jacuzzi, Continental breakfast in rooms, free parking. AE, DC, MC, V. $$$–$$$$*

Eiler's Inn. A light-filled courtyard is the focal point of this European-style B&B. Rooms are on the small side, but each is unique and decorated with antiques. Breakfast is served outdoors, and in the afternoon there's wine and cheese, often to the accompaniment of live music. A sundeck in back has an ocean view. *741 S. Coast Hwy., 92651, tel. 714/494–3004. 12 rooms. AE, MC, V. $$$*

Hotel Laguna. This downtown landmark, the oldest hotel in Laguna, has recently been redone, with four rooms now featuring canopy beds and reproduction Victorian furnishings. Lobby windows look out onto manicured gardens, and a patio restaurant overlooks the ocean. *425 S. Coast Hwy., 92651, tel. 714/494–1151. 60 rooms. Facilities: restaurant, lounge, entertainment. AE, D, DC, MC, V. $$$*

Newport Beach Dining

★ **Antoine.** This lovely, candlelighted dining room is made for romance and quiet conversation. It serves the best French cuisine of any hotel in southern California; the fare is nouvelle, but is neither skimpy nor gimmicky. *4500 MacArthur Blvd., tel. 714/476–2001. Reservations advised. Jacket and tie required. AE, DC, MC, V. Dinner only. Closed Sun., Mon. $$$$*

★ **Pascal.** Although it's in a shopping center, you'll think that you're in St-Tropez once you step inside this bright and cheerful bistro. And, after one taste of Pascal Olhat's light Provençale cuisine, the best in Orange County, you'll swear you're in the south of France. Try the sea bass with thyme, the rack of lamb, and the lemon tart. *1000 Bristol St., tel. 714/752–0107. Reservations advised. Jacket advised. AE, DC, MC, V. $$$$*

★ **The Ritz.** This is one of the most comfortable southern California restaurants—the bar area has red leather booths, etched-glass mirrors, and polished brass trim. Don't pass up the smorgasbord appetizer, the roast Bavarian duck, or the rack of lamb from the spit. This is one of those rare places that seems to please everyone. *880 Newport Center Dr., tel. 714/720–1800. Reservations advised. Jacket suggested. AE, DC, MC, V. No lunch Sat., Sun. $$$$*

Le Biarritz. Newport Beach natives have a deep affection for this restaurant, with its country French decor, hanging greenery, and skylighted garden room. There's food to match the mood: a veal-and-pheasant pâté, seafood crepes, boned duckling and wild rice, sautéed pheasant with raspberries, and warm apple tart for dessert. *414 N. Old Newport Blvd., tel. 714/645–6700. Reservations advised. Dress: casual. AE, D, DC, MC, V. No Sat. lunch. Closed Sun. $$*

The Cannery. The building once was a cannery, and it has wonderful wharf-side views. The seafood entrées are good, and the sandwiches at lunch are satisfying, but the location and lazy atmosphere are the real draw. *3010 Lafayette Ave., tel. 714/675–5777. Reservations advised. Dress: casual. AE, D, DC, MC, V. $$*

Marrakesh. In a casbah setting straight out of a Hope-and-Crosby road movie, diners become part of the scene—you eat with your fingers while sitting on the floor or lolling on a hassock. Chicken b'stilla, rabbit couscous, and skewered pieces of marinated lamb are the best of the Moroccan dishes. It's fun. *1100 PCH, tel. 714/645–*

8384. Reservations advised. Dress: casual. AE, DC, MC, V. No lunch. $$

Crab Cooker. If you don't mind waiting in line, this shanty of a place serves fresh fish grilled over mesquite at low, low prices. The clam chowder and coleslaw are quite good, too. *2200 Newport Blvd., tel. 714/673–0100. No reservations. Dress: casual. No credit cards. $*

Hard Rock Cafe Newport Beach. You can pick up your official Hard Rock Cafe T-shirt here while munching a hamburger or a sandwich. Like the other Hard Rocks, this one features an array of rock-star memorabilia and platinum records. *451 Newport Center Dr., tel. 714/640–8844. Dress: casual. AE, MC, V. $*

★ **El Torito Grill.** Southwestern cooking incorporating south-of-the-border specialties is the attraction here. The just-baked tortillas with a green-pepper salsa, the turkey molé enchilada, and the blue-corn duck tamalitos are good choices. The bar serves hand-shaken margaritas and 20 brands of tequila. *951 Newport Center Dr., tel. 714/640–2875. Reservations advised. Dress: casual. AE, D, DC, MC, V. $*

Lodging **Four Seasons Hotel.** This hotel lives up to its chain's reputation.
★ Marble and antiques fill the airy lobby; all rooms—decorated with beiges, peaches, and Southwestern tones—have spectacular views, private bars, original art on walls. Weekend golf packages are available in conjunction with the nearby Pelican Hill golf course, as well as fitness weekend packages. *690 Newport Center Dr., 92660, tel. 714/759–0808 or 800/332–3442, fax 714/760–8073. 285 rooms. Facilities: 2 restaurants, lounge, pool, whirlpool, sauna, 2 lighted tennis courts, health club with steam room and massage service, complimentary mountain bikes, concierge, business center, wheelchair accessible. AE, D, DC, MC, V. $$$$*

Le Meridien Newport Beach. The eye-catching cantilevered design is the trademark of this ultramodern hotel in Koll Center. The decor is southern Californian, with striking pastel accents. Luxuriously appointed rooms have minibars and built-in hair dryers. This is also the home of Antoine (*see above*), one of the best restaurants in Orange County. Special weekend theater and Pageant of the Masters packages are available. *4500 MacArthur Blvd., 92660, tel. 714/476–2001. 435 rooms. Facilities: 2 restaurants, lounge, pool, 2 lighted tennis courts, health club with Jacuzzi, complimentary bicycles, concierge. AE, D, DC, MC, V. $$$$*

Newport Beach Marriott Hotel and Tennis Club. Arriving guests' first view of the hotel's interior is the distinctive fountain surrounded by a high, plant-filled atrium. Rooms in two towers have balconies or patios, overlooking lush gardens; many have a stunning Pacific view. The hotel is across the street from Fashion Island shopping center. *900 Newport Center Dr., 92660, tel. 714/640–4000 or 800/228–9290, fax 714/640–5055. 560 rooms, 15 suites. Facilities: 2 restaurants, 2 lounges, 2 pools, 2 outdoor Jacuzzis, health club, sauna, 8 lighted tennis courts, Jacuzzi, adjacent golf course, business center, concierge. AE, D, DC, MC, V. $$$*

Sheraton Newport Beach. Bamboo trees and palms decorate the lobby in this Southern California beach-style hotel. Vibrant teals, mauves, and peaches make up the color scheme. Complimentary morning paper, buffet breakfast, and cocktail parties are offered daily. *4545 MacArthur Blvd., 92660, tel. 714/833–0570, fax 714/833–3927. 338 rooms. Facilities: 3 restaurants, lounge, entertainment, pool, Jacuzzi, 2 tennis courts. AE, D, DC, MC, V. $$$*

Orange **La Brasserie.** It doesn't *look* like a typical brasserie, but the varied
Dining French cuisine befits the name over the door. One dining room in

the multilevel house is done as an attractive, cozy library. There's also an inviting bar-lounge. *202 S. Main St., tel. 714/978–6161. Reservations advised. Dress: casual. AE, MC, V. No Sat. lunch. Closed Sun. $$*

Nostrum Mare. Located in the Doubletree Hotel, this restaurant specializes in Mediterranean flavors—all of them, it seems, judging from the large menu, which includes Moroccan-style grilled shrimp, Italian carpaccio, Turkish soup, and Spanish paella. This dramatic two-story room has floor-to-ceiling windows, which reveal a garden and pond beyond. Service is welcoming. *100 The City Dr., tel. 714/634–4500. Dress: casual. No Sat., Sun. lunch. AE, MC, V. $–$$*

Lodging **Doubletree Hotel Orange County.** This hotel has a dramatic lobby of marble and granite with waterfalls cascading down the walls. Guest rooms are large and come equipped with a small conference table. The hotel is near the shopping center called The City, UCI Medical Center, and Anaheim Stadium. Discount rates are available for summer weekends. *100 The City Dr., 92668, tel. 714/634–4500 or 800/222–8733, fax 714/978–3839. 435 rooms, 19 suites. Facilities: 2 restaurants, lounge, pool, spa, 2 tennis courts, concierge floor, wheelchair accessible. AE, D, DC, MC, V. $$$–$$$$*

San Clemente **Etienne's.** Smack-dab in the center of town, this restaurant is
Dining housed in a white stucco historic landmark. There is outdoor seating on a terra-cotta patio with fountains. Indoors, the decor is French château. Only the freshest fish is served; chateaubriand, frogs' legs, and other French favorites are on the menu, along with flaming desserts. *215 S. El Camino Real, tel. 714/492–7263. Reservations advised. Jacket advised. AE, D, DC, MC, V. No lunch. Closed Sun. $$$*

Lodging **San Clemente Inn.** This time-share condo resort is in the secluded southern part of San Clemente, adjacent to Calafia State Beach. Studio and one-bedroom units (accommodating as many as six) are equipped with minikitchens and Murphy beds. Limited space is available in summer. *2600 Avenida del Presidente, 92672, tel. 714/492–6103. 95 units. Facilities: pool, Jacuzzi, sauna, tennis, exercise equipment, recreation room, playground, barbecue pits. AE, D, DC, MC, V. $$$*

Casa Clemente Resort. This Mission-style hotel, formerly a Ramada Inn, is beautifully set on a lush hillside. The lobby has a dramatic vaulted ceiling. Rooms have private balconies or patios; many also have refrigerators. *35 Calle de Industrias, 92672, tel. 714/498–8800. 110 rooms. Facilities: restaurant, lounge, pool, wheelchair accessible. AE, D, DC, MC, V. $$*

San Juan **El Adobe.** President Nixon's frequent visits continue to be remem-
Capistrano bered in this Early California–style eatery serving Mexican food.
Dining You can even ask for his favorite table. Mariachi bands play Friday and Saturday nights and for Sunday brunch. *31891 Camino Capistrano, tel. 714/830–8620. Weekend reservations advised. Dress: casual. AE, D, MC, V. $$*

L'Hirondelle. There are only 12 tables at this charming French inn. Duckling is the specialty, and it is prepared three different ways. *31631 Camino Capistrano, tel. 714/661–0425. Reservations required. AE, MC, V. No lunch. Closed Mon. $$*

Santa Ana **Randall's.** Located on the ground floor of an office building with
Dining lakeside views, this restaurant specializes in light Louisiana cuisine. Jazz is presented nightly. *3 Hutton Centre Dr., Santa Ana, tel. 714/556–7700. Reservations advised. Dress: chic casual. AE, MC, V. No lunch Sat., Sun. $$$*

The Arts and Nightlife

The Arts

The **Orange County Performing Arts Center** (600 Town Center Dr., Costa Mesa, tel. 714/556–2787) is the hub of the arts circle, hosting a variety of touring companies year-round. Groups that regularly schedule performances here include the New York City Opera, the American Ballet Theater, and the Los Angeles Philharmonic Orchestra, as well as touring companies of popular musicals such as *Les Misérables.* Information about current offerings can be found in the calendar section of the *Los Angeles Times.*

Concerts The **Irvine Meadows Amphitheater** (8808 Irvine Center Dr., Irvine, tel. 714/855–4515) is a 15,000-seat open-air venue offering a variety of musical events from May through October.
The **Pacific Amphitheater** (Orange County Fairgrounds, Costa Mesa, tel. 714/740–2000) offers musical entertainment from April through October.

Theater **South Coast Repertory Theater** (655 Town Center Dr., Costa Mesa, tel. 714/957–4033), near the Orange County Performing Arts Center, is an acclaimed regional theater complex with two stages that present both traditional and new works. A resident group of actors forms the nucleus of this facility's innovative productions.
La Mirada Theater for the Performing Arts (14900 La Mirada Blvd., La Mirada, tel. 714/994–6310) presents a wide selection of Broadway shows, concerts, and film series.

Nightlife

Bars **Metropolis** (4255 Campus Dr., Irvine, tel. 714/725–0300) is the hottest nightclub ticket in Orange County, with iron-and-gilt decor, pool tables, a sushi bar, and nightly entertainment; admission is $5. **The Cannery** (3010 Layfayette Ave., tel. 714/675–5757) is a crowded Newport Beach bar that offers live entertainment. The **Studio Cafe** (100 Main St., Balboa Peninsula, tel. 714/675–7760) presents jazz musicians every night. In Santa Ana, a young crowd gathers at **Roxbury** (2 Hutton Centre Dr., tel. 714/662–0880) for entertainment and dancing Wednesday through Saturday. The **Fullerton Hofbrau** (323 N. State College Blvd., tel. 714/870–7400), a microbrewery, has live music nightly.

In Laguna Beach, the **Sandpiper** (1183 S. PCH, tel. 714/494–4694) is a tiny dancing joint that attracts an eclectic crowd. And Laguna's **White House** (340 S. PCH, tel. 714/494–8088) has nightly entertainment that runs the gamut from rock to Motown, reggae to pop.

Comedy **Irvine Improv** (4255 Campus Dr., Irvine, tel. 714/854–5455) and **Brea Improv** (945 Birch St., Brea, tel. 714/529–7878) present up-and-coming and well-known comedians nightly.

Country Music **Cowboy Boogie Co.** (1721 S. Manchester, Anaheim, tel. 714/956–1410) offers live country music Tuesday through Sunday night. The complex comprises three dance floors and four bars.

Dinner Theaters Several night spots in Orange County serve up entertainment with dinner.

Tibbie's Music Hall (4647 McArthur Blvd., Newport Beach, tel. 714/252–0834) offers comedy shows along with prime rib, fish, or chicken Thursday through Sunday. **Elizabeth Howard's Curtain**

Call Theater (690 El Camino Real, Tustin, tel. 714/838–1540) presents a regular schedule of Broadway musicals. **Medieval Times Dinner and Tournament** (7662 Beach Blvd., Buena Park, tel. 714/521–4740 or 800/899–6600) takes guests back to the days of knights and ladies. Knights on horseback compete in medieval games, sword fighting, and jousting. Dinner, all of which is eaten with your hands, includes appetizers, whole roasted chicken or spareribs, soup, pastry, and beverages such as mead. **Wild Bill's Wild West Extravaganza** (7600 Beach Blvd., Buena Park, tel. 714/522–6414) is a two-hour action-packed Old West show featuring foot-stomping musical numbers, cowboys, Indians, can-can dancers, trick-rope artists, knife throwers, and audience participation in sing-alongs.

Nightclubs   **Coach House** (33157 Camino Capistrano, San Juan Capistrano, tel. 714/496–8930) draws big local crowds for jazz and rock headliners.

14 San Diego

Each year, San Diego absorbs thousands of visitors who are drawn by the climate: sunny, dry, and warm nearly year-round. They swim, surf, and sunbathe on long beaches facing the turquoise Pacific, where whales, seals, and dolphins swim offshore. They tour oases of tropical palms, sheltered bays fringed by golden pampas grass, and far-ranging parklands blossoming with brilliant bougainvillea, jasmine, ice plant, and birds of paradise. They run and bike and walk down wide streets and paths planned for recreation among the natives, who thrive on San Diego's varied health, fitness, and sports scenes.

San Diego County is the nation's sixth largest—larger than nearly a dozen U.S. states—with a population of more than 2.5 million. It sprawls east from the Pacific Ocean through dense urban neighborhoods to outlying suburban communities that seem to sprout on canyons and cliffs overnight. The city of San Diego is the state's second largest, after Los Angeles. It serves as a base for the U.S. Navy's 11th Naval District and a port for ships from many nations. A considerable number of its residents were stationed here in the service and decided to stay put. Others either passed through on vacation or saw the city in movies and TV shows and became enamored of the city and its reputation as a prosperous Sunbelt playground. From its founding San Diego has attracted a steady stream of prospectors, drawn to the nation's farthest southwest frontier.

Tourism is San Diego's third-largest industry, after manufacturing and the military. San Diego's politicians, business leaders, and developers have set the city's course toward a steadily increasing influx of visitors—which gives residents pleasant attractions as well as not-so-enjoyable distractions. With growth comes congestion, even in San Diego's vast expanse.

Essential Information

Important Addresses and Numbers

Tourist Information
Stop in at the **International Visitor Information Center** (11 Horton Plaza, at 1st Ave. and F St., tel. 619/236–1212; open Mon.–Sat., 8:30–5 year-round, Sun. 11–5 June–Aug.) at the **Balboa Park Visitors Center** (1549 El Prado, in Balboa Park, tel. 619/239–0512; open daily 9–4), or at the **Mission Bay Visitor Information Center** (2688 E. Mission Bay Dr., off I–5 at the Mission Bay Dr. exit, tel. 619/276–8200; open Mon.–Sat. 9–5, Sun. 9:30–4:30 winter, open later in summer).

San Diego City Beach and Weather Conditions Information Line (tel. 619/221–8884).

Weather Forecast (tel. 619/289–1212).

Emergencies
Police, ambulance, and **fire** departments can all be reached by dialing 911. For the **Poison Control Center,** call 619/543–6000 or 800/876–4766.

Doctor
Hospital emergency rooms, with physicians on duty, are open 24 hours. Major hospitals are **Mercy Hospital and Medical Center** (4077 5th Ave., tel. 619/294–8111), **Scripps Memorial Hospital** (9888 Genesee Ave., La Jolla, tel. 619/457–4123), **Veterans Administration Hospital** (3350 La Jolla Village Dr., La Jolla, tel. 619/552–8585), and **UCSD Medical Center** (200 W. Arbor Dr., Hillcrest, tel. 619/543–6222).

Doctors on Call (tel. 619/275–2663) offers 24-hour medical service to San Diego hotels.

Dentist The **San Diego County Dental Society** (tel. 619/275–0244) can provide referrals to those with dental emergencies.

Arriving and Departing

By Plane **Lindbergh Field** (tel. 619/231–2100), just 3 miles northwest of downtown, has regular service to and from many U.S. and Mexican cities via most major and regional carriers, including **Aeromexico** (tel. 800/237–6639), **Alaska Airlines** (tel. 800/426–0333), **America West** (tel. 800/247–5692), **American** (tel. 800/433–7300), **Arizona Airways** (tel. 800/274–0662), **Continental** (tel. 800/525–0280), **Delta** (tel. 800/221–1212), **Mark Air** (tel. 800/627–5247), **Midwest Express** (tel. 800/452–2022), **Northwest** (tel. 800/225–2525), **Reno Air** (tel. 800/736–6247), **Sky West** (tel. 800/453–9417), **Southwest** (tel. 800/435–9792), **Trans World Airlines** (tel. 800/221–2000), **United** (tel. 800/241–6522), and **USAir** (tel. 800/428–4322).

By Car Interstate 5 stretches from Canada to the Mexican border and bisects San Diego. Interstate 8 provides access from Yuma, Arizona, and points east. Drivers coming from Nevada and the mountain regions beyond can reach San Diego on I–15. Avoid rush-hour periods, when the traffic can be jammed for miles.

By Train **Amtrak** trains (tel. 800/872–7245) from Los Angeles arrive at Santa Fe Depot (1050 Kettner Blvd., corner of Broadway, near the heart of downtown, tel. 619/239–9021). There are additional stations in Del Mar (tel. 619/481–0114) and Oceanside (tel. 619/722–4622), both in north San Diego County. Eight trains operate daily in either direction.

By Bus **Greyhound** (tel. 619/239–8082 or 800/231–2222) operates more than 20 buses a day between the downtown terminal at 120 West Broadway and Los Angeles, connecting with buses to all major U.S. cities. Many buses are express or nonstop; others make stops at coastal towns en route.

Getting Around

Many attractions, such as the Gaslamp Quarter, Balboa Park, and La Jolla, are best seen on foot. A variety of public transportation will bring travelers to any major tourist and shopping area, but it is best to have a car for exploring more remote coastal and inland regions. The International Visitor Information Center (*see above*) provides maps of the city.

By Bus Fares on **San Diego Transit** buses are $1.50, $1.75 on express buses; senior citizens pay 75¢ on all buses. A free transfer is included in the fare, but you must request it when you board. Buses to most major attractions leave from 4th Avenue or 5th Avenue and Broadway. The **San Diego Transit Information Line** (tel. 619/233–3004, TTY/TDD 619/234–5005; open daily 5:30 AM–8:30 PM) can provide details on getting to and from any location. The **Day Tripper Transit Pass** is good for unlimited trips on the same day on buses and on the trolley and the ferry for $4; there's also a four-day pass for $12. Passes are available at the **Transit Store** (449 Broadway, tel. 619/234–1060) as well as at the ferry landing and the downtown Amtrak station.

By Taxi Taxi fares are regulated at the airport—all companies charge the same rate (generally $2 for the first mile, $1.40 for each additional mile). Fares vary among companies on other routes, however, including the ride back to the airport. Cab companies that serve most areas of the city are **Coast Shuttle** (tel. 619/477–3333), **Co-op Silver Cabs** (tel. 619/280–5555), **Coronado Cab** (tel. 619/435–6211), **La Jolla Cab** (tel. 619/453–4222), **Orange Cab** (tel. 619/291–3333), and **Yellow Cab** (tel. 619/234–6161).

By Trolley The **San Diego Trolley** (tel. 619/233–3004) travels from downtown to within 100 feet of the U.S.–Mexican border, stopping at 21 suburban stations en route. The basic fare is $1.75 one way. The trolley also travels from downtown to Encanto, Lemon Grove, La Mesa, and El Cajon in East County. Tickets must be purchased before boarding. Ticket-vending machines, located at each station, require exact change. Trolleys operate daily, approximately every 15 minutes, 5 AM–9 PM, the every 30 minutes until 1 AM. The Bayside line serves the Convention Center and Seaport Village; lines to Old Town, Mission Valley, and North County are under construction.

By Train **Amtrak** (tel. 800/872–7245) makes nine trips daily, in each direction, between San Diego, Del Mar, and Oceanside. The round-trip fare from San Diego to Del Mar or Oceanside is $10 ($6 one way). Seats are nonreserved, but tickets should be purchased before boarding.

By Ferry The **San Diego-Coronado** Ferry (tel. 619/234–4111) leaves from the Broadway Pier daily, every hour on the hour, 9 AM–9:30 PM Sunday–Thursday, until 10:30 PM Friday and Saturday. The fare is $2 each way. The **Harbor Hopper** (tel. 619/488–5022, 619/488–2720, or 800/300–7447) is a water-taxi service that shuttles passengers around Mission Bay. The fare is $4 each way, $6 round-trip. Hours and days of operation change with the season; call ahead for information.

By Limousine Limousine companies offer airport shuttles and customized tours. Rates vary and are per hour, per mile, or both, with some minimums established. Companies that offer a range of services include **Advantage Limousine Service** (tel. 619/563–1651), **La Jolla Limousines** (tel. 619/459–5891), **Limousines by Linda** (tel. 619/234–9145), and **Olde English Livery** (tel. 619/232–6533).

By Horse-Drawn Carriage **Cinderella Carriage Co.** (tel. 619/239–8080) will take parties of two to four people through the Gaslamp Quarter, the waterfront, and downtown. The cost is $75 for one hour, $40 for a half-hour ride, and $55 for 45 minutes.

Guided Tours

Orientation Tours **Gray Line Tours** (tel. 619/491–0011 or 800/331–5077) and **San Diego Mini Tours** (tel. 619/477–8687) offer two daily sightseeing excursions for about $25.

Old Town Trolley (tel. 619/298–8687) travels to almost every attraction and shopping area on open-air trackless trolleys. Drivers double as tour guides. You can take the full two-hour, narrated city tour or get on and off as you please at any of the nine stops. An all-day pass costs $16 for adults, $7 for children 6–12. The trolley, which leaves every 30 minutes, operates daily 9–5:30 in the summer, 9–4:30 in winter.

Free two-hour trolley tours of the downtown redevelopment area, including the Gaslamp Quarter, are hosted by **Centre City Development Corporation's Downtown Information Center** (tel. 619/235–2222). Groups of 35 passengers leave from 255 G Street, downtown, the first and third Saturday of each month at 10 AM. Reservations are necessary. The tour may be canceled if there aren't enough passengers.

Special-Interest Tours

Civic Helicopters (tel. 619/438–8424 or 800/438–HELI) has helicopter tours starting at $69 per person per half-hour.

San Diego Harbor Excursion (tel. 619/234–4111) and **Hornblower Invader Cruises** (tel. 619/234–8687) sail on narrated cruises of San Diego Harbor, departing from Broadway Pier. Both companies offer one-hour cruises ($10), departing several times daily, and a two-hour tour ($15) each day at 2 PM (additional tours in summer). No reservations are necessary, and both vessels have snack bars on board. **Mariposa Sailing Cruises** (tel. 619/224–0800) has morning and afternoon tours of the harbor and San Diego Bay for $40 per person.

Balloon Tours

Six-passenger hot-air balloons lift off from San Diego's North Country. Most flights are at sunrise or sunset and are followed by a traditional champagne celebration. Companies that offer daily service, weather permitting, are **Air Affaire** (tel. 619/560–6373 or 800/331–1979), **Pacific Horizon** (tel. 619/756–1790 or 800/244–1790), and **Skysurfer** (tel. 619/481–6800 or 800/660–6809 in CA). Balloon flights average $145 per person for early morning or late afternoon.

Whale-Watching Tours

Gray whales migrate south to Mexico and back north from mid-December to mid-March. As many as 200 whales pass the San Diego coast each day, coming within yards of tour boats. During whale-watching season, *The Apollo* (tel. 619/221–8500), a luxury motor yacht, offers narrated tours twice a day. **Mariposa Sailing Cruises** (tel. 619/224–0800) tailors whale-watching expeditions for up to six people. **H&M Landing** (tel. 619/222–1144) and **Seaforth Sportfishing** (tel. 619/224–3383) have daily whale-watching trips in large party boats.

Walking Tours

The Gaslamp Quarter Foundation (410 Island Ave., tel. 619/233–5227) leads 1½-hour architectural tours of the restored downtown historic district on Saturday at 11 AM ($5 adults, $3 senior citizens and students). Self-guided tour brochures are available at the office, weekdays 10–4:30.

On weekends, the State Park Department (tel. 619/220–5422) gives free walking tours of **Old Town.** Groups leave from 4002 Wallace Street at 2 PM daily, weather permitting.

Walkabout (tel. 619/231–7463) offers several different free walking tours throughout the city each week.

Exploring San Diego

By Maribeth Mellin

Revised by Edie Jarolim

Exploring San Diego is an endless adventure, limited only by time and transportation constraints, which, if you don't have a car, can be considerable. San Diego is more a chain of separate communities than a cohesive city. Many of the major attractions are at least 5 miles away from one another. The streets are fun for getting an up-close look at how San Diegans live, but true southern Californians use the freeways, which crisscross the county in a sensible fashion. Interstate 5 runs a direct north–south route through the county's coastal communities to the Mexican border. Interstates 805 and 15 do much the same inland, with I–8 as the main east–west route. Highways 163, 52, and 94 act as connectors.

If you are going to drive around San Diego, study your maps before you hit the road. The freeways are convenient and fast most of the time, but if you miss your turnoff or get caught in commuter traffic, you'll experience a none-too-pleasurable hallmark of southern California living—freeway madness. Drivers here rush around on a complex freeway system with the same fervor they use for jogging scores of marathons each year. They particularly enjoy speeding up at interchanges and entrance and exit ramps. Be sure you know where you're going before you join the freeway chase. Better yet, use public transportation or tour buses from your hotel and save your energy for walking in the sun.

If you stick with public transportation, plan on taking your time. San Diego's bus system covers almost all the county, but it does so slowly. Since many of the city's major attractions are clustered along the coast, you'll be best off staying there or in the Hotel Circle/Mission Valley hotel zone. Downtown and Fashion Valley Shopping Center in Mission Valley are the two major transfer points.

Highlights for First-Time Visitors

Cabrillo National Monument
Horton Plaza
Hotel Del Coronado
La Jolla Cove
Old Town State Historic Park
Reuben H. Fleet Space Theater and Science Center
San Diego Zoo
Sea World
Seaport Village

Downtown and the Embarcadero

Numbers in the margin correspond to points of interest on the Central San Diego map.

Downtown San Diego, just 3 miles south of the international airport, is changing and growing rapidly, gaining status as a cultural and recreational center for the county's residents and visitors alike.

Downtown's natural attributes were easily evident to its original booster, Alonzo Horton, who arrived in San Diego in 1867. Horton looked at the bay and the acres of flatland surrounded by hills and canyons and knew he had found San Diego's center. Though Old Town, under the Spanish fort at the Presidio, had been settled for years, Horton understood that it was too far away from the water to take hold as the commercial center of San Diego. He bought 960 acres along the bay at 27½¢ per acre and literally gave away the land to those who would develop it or build houses. Within months, he had sold or given away 226 city blocks of land; settlers camped on their land in tents as their houses and businesses rose.

The transcontinental train arrived in 1885, and the land boom was on. Although the railroad's status as a cross-country route was short-lived, the population soared from 5,000 to 35,000 in less than a decade—a foreshadowing of San Diego's future. In 1887, the Santa Fe Depot was constructed at the foot of Broadway, two blocks from the water. Freighters chugged in and out of the harbor, and by the early 1900s, the navy had moved in.

As downtown grew into San Diego's transportation and commercial hub, residential neighborhoods blossomed along the beaches and inland valleys. The business district gradually moved farther away from the original heart of downtown, at 5th Avenue and Market Street, past Broadway, up toward the park. Downtown's waterfront fell into bad times during World War I, when sailors, gamblers, and prostitutes were drawn to one another and the waterfront bars.

But Alonzo Horton's modern-day followers, city leaders intent on prospering while preserving San Diego's natural beauty, have reclaimed the downtown area. Replacing old shipyards and canneries are hotel towers and waterfront parks; the Martin Luther King, Jr., Promenade project is slated to put 12 acres of greenery along Harbor Drive from Seaport Village to the convention center by the end of 1995. Nineteen ninety-two saw the completion of the part of the park near the $160 million, 760,000-square-foot San Diego Convention Center, which hosted its first events in early 1990. And a few blocks inland, the hugely successful Horton Plaza shopping center, opened in 1985, led the way for the hotels, restaurants, shopping centers, and housing developments that are now rising on every square inch of available space in downtown San Diego.

Your first view of downtown, regardless of your mode of transportation, will probably include the **Embarcadero,** a waterfront walkway on Harbor Drive lined with restaurants, sea vessels of every variety—cruise ships, ferries, tour boats, houseboats, and naval destroyers—and a fair share of seals and sea gulls. Many boats along the Embarcadero have been converted into floating gift shops, and others are awaiting restoration. If you plan to spend a good portion of your day in the area, either strolling or taking a harbor excursion, it's a good idea to park at the huge municipal lot ($4 per day) along the south side of the B Street Pier building; much of the parking along Harbor Drive is limited to two-hour meters.

To get some historical perspective on your Embarcadero visit, begin your tour two blocks north of the parking lot at the foot of Ash Street, where the *Berkeley,* an 1898 riverboat, is moored. It's headquarters for the **Maritime Museum,** a collection of three restored ships that may be toured for one admission price. The *Berkeley,* which served the Southern Pacific Railroad at San Francisco Bay until 1953, had its most important days during the great earthquake of 1906, when it carried thousands of passengers across San Francisco Bay to Oakland. Its carved wood paneling, stained-glass windows, and plate-glass mirrors have been restored, and its main deck serves as a floating museum, with exhibits on oceanography and naval history. Anchored next to the Berkeley, the small Scottish steam yacht *Medea,* launched in 1904, may be boarded but has no interpretive displays.

The most interesting of the three ships is the *Star of India,* a beautiful windjammer built in 1863 and docked at the foot of Grape Street. The ship's high wooden masts and white sails flapping in the wind have been a harbor landmark since 1926. Built at Ramsey on the Isle of Man, the *Star of India* made 21 trips around the world in the late 1800s, when she traveled the East Indian trade route, shuttled immigrants from England to Australia, and served the Alaskan salmon trade. The ship languished after she was retired to San Diego Harbor, virtually ignored until 1959. Then a group of volunteers, organized by the Maritime Museum, stripped the wooden decks, polished the figurehead, and mended the sails. On July 4, 1976, the *Star of India* commemorated the bicentennial by setting sail in the harbor. The oldest iron sailing ship afloat in the world, she has made short excursions five times since then, but for the most part stays moored at the pier and open to visitors. *1306 N. Harbor Dr., tel. 619/234–9153. Admission: $6 adults, $4 senior citizens and students 13–17, $2 children 6–12, $12 families. Ships open daily 9–8.*

Exploring San Diego *(Boxes Refer to Detail Maps)*

N

Torrey Pines
State Beach

Mira Mesa Blvd.

N. Torrey Pines Rd.

S21

Genesee Ave.

805

Miramar

MIRAM

Rd.

MIRAMAR
NAVAL AIR
STATION

La Jolla

Torrey Pines

Pines Rd.

Gilman Dr.

Ardath Rd.

52

Clairemont

Mesa

Blvd

163

San Diego Fwy.

La Jolla Blvd.

5

Clairemont Dr.

Balboa Ave.

Genesee Ave.

Aero Dr.

PACIFIC
BEACH

Grand Ave.

Mission
Bay

Mission
Bay

LINDA
VISTA

Cabrillo Fwy.

805

MISSION
BEACH

Mission Blvd.

Ingraham St.

Mission Bay Dr.

Sea World

Linda Vista Rd.

Friars Rd.

San Diego R.

Rd.

Adams A

OCEAN
BEACH

Nimitz Blvd.

Sunset Cliffs Blvd.

Catalina Blvd.

Rosecrans

Old Town

8

163

Universi

Balboa
Park

POINT
LOMA

209

Harbor Dr.

Pacific Hwy.

DOWNTOWN

Impe

Cabrillo Memorial Dr.

North Island
U.S. NAVAL
AIR STATION

Coronado
Beach

Harbor Dr.

75

San Diego Ba

Central San Diego

Silver

Strand Blvd.

PACIFIC OCEAN

Silver Strand
State Beach

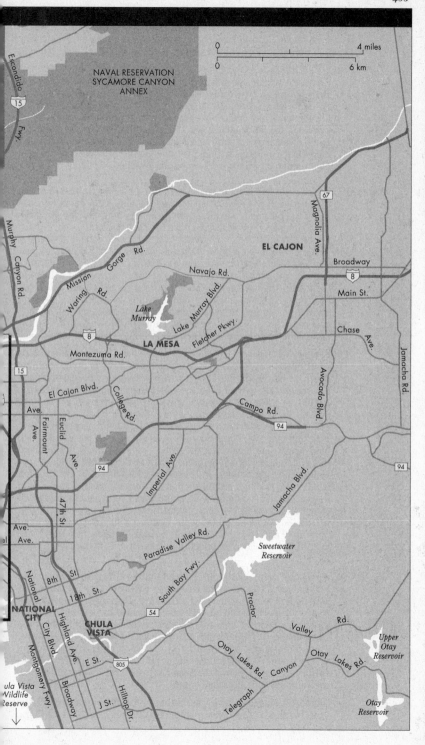

NAVAL RESERVATION
SYCAMORE CANYON
ANNEX

0   4 miles
0   6 km

Escondido Fwy.
15

Murphy Canyon Rd.

Gorge Rd.
Mission Rd.
Waring Rd.

EL CAJON

Magnolia Ave.
67

Broadway
8
Main St.

Navajo Rd.
Lake Murray Blvd.
Lake Murray
Lake Murray Blvd.
Fletcher Pkwy.

Chase Ave.

Jamacha Rd.

8
LA MESA
Montezuma Rd.

15

El Cajon Blvd.
Fairmount Ave.
Ave.
Euclid Ave.
College Rd.

Campo Rd.
94

Avocado Blvd.

94

94

Imperial Ave.

Jamacha Blvd.

47th St.

Ave.
Ave.

Paradise Valley Rd.

Sweetwater
Reservoir

National City Blvd.
8th St.
18th St.
Highland Ave.

South Bay Fwy.
54

Proctor

Valley Rd.

Upper
Otay
Reservoir

NATIONAL
CITY

CHULA
VISTA

E St.
805

Otay Lakes Rd.
Canyon

Otay Lakes Rd.

ula Vista
Wildlife
Reserve
↓

Montgomery Fwy.
Broadway
J St.
Hilltop Dr.

Telegraph

Otay
Reservoir

3 A cement pathway runs south from the *Star of India* along the waterfront to the pastel **B Street Pier,** used by ships from major cruise lines as both a port of call and a departure point. The cavernous pier building has a cruise-information center and a small, cool bar and gift shop.

Another two blocks south on Harbor Drive brings you to the foot of Broadway and **Broadway Pier,** a gathering spot for day-trippers ready to set sail. A cluster of storefront windows sell tickets for the harbor tours and whale-watching trips that leave from the dock in January and February, when the gray whales migrate from the Pacific Northwest to southern Baja. One of the most traditional, and delightful, boat trips to take from the pier is the **Bay Ferry** to Coronado Island (*see* Coronado, *below,* for details).

TimeOut Those waiting for their boats can grab a beer or ice cream at the diner-style **Bay Cafe** and sit on the upstairs patio or on benches along the busy pathway; it's a good vantage point for watching the sailboats, paddle wheelers, and yachts vie for space.

The navy's Eleventh Naval District has control of the next few waterfront blocks to the south, and a series of destroyers, submarines, and carriers cruise in and out, some staying for weeks at a time. On weekends, the navy usually offers tours of these floating cities (call 619/532–1431 for information on hours and types of ships). A steady stream of joggers, bicyclists, and serious walkers on the Embarcadero pathway picks up speed at **Tuna Harbor,** the hub of San Diego's commercial tuna fishing, one of the city's earliest industries.

4 **Seaport Village** (tel. 619/235–4013 for recorded events information or 619/235–4014) is the next attraction you'll reach if you continue south on Harbor Drive. It was a wise developer who saw the good fortune in this prime stretch of waterfront that now connects the harbor with the hotel towers and convention center. Spread out across 14 acres are three connected shopping plazas, designed to reflect the architectural styles of early California, especially New England clapboard and Spanish Mission. A quarter-mile wooden boardwalk that runs along the bay, as well as 4 miles of simulated dirt-road and cobblestone paths, leads to a bustling array of specialty shops, snack bars, and restaurants—more than 75 in all. You can browse through a shell shop, a rubber-stamp shop, and a shop devoted to left-handed people and nosh to your heart's delight on everything from fast Greek, Mexican, and French fare to seafood in nautical-style indoor restaurants. Seaport Village's shops are open daily 10–9 (10–10 in summer); a few eateries open early for breakfast, and many have extended nighttime hours, especially in summer.

Almost as many adults as children enjoy riding the hand-carved, hand-painted steeds on the **Broadway Flying Horses Carousel,** created by I.D. Looff in Coney Island in 1890. The ride was moved from its next home, Salisbury Beach in Massachusetts, and faithfully restored for Seaport Village, where it began operating in the West Plaza on the July 4 weekend of 1980; tickets are $1. Strolling clowns, mimes, musicians, and magicians are also on hand throughout the village to entertain kids; those not impressed by such pretechnological displays can duck into the Sega family entertainment center near the carousel and play video games.

Seaport Village's center reaches out onto **Embarcadero Marine Park North,** an 8-acre grassy point into the harbor where kite-fliers, roller-skaters, and picnickers hang out in the sun. Seasonal celebrations with live music and fireworks are held here throughout the year.

The mirrored towers of the San Diego Marriott Hotel and Marina mark the end of Seaport Village, but the waterfront walkway continues past the hotel's marina, where hotel guests moor their enormous, extravagant yachts. Just beyond the Marriott is the striking **⑤ San Diego Convention Center,** designed by Arthur Erickson; its nautical lines are complemented by the backdrop of blue sky and sea. The center often holds trade shows that are open to the public, and tours of the building are available.

Just south of the convention center, at the **Embarcadero Marina Park South,** the San Diego Symphony (tel. 619/699–4205) presents its annual Summer Pops concert series, complete with fireworks finales that light up the bay. These musical extravaganzas, increasingly popular in recent years, have gone upscale, offering cabaret seating as well as food and bar service.

⑥ One way to reach the heart of downtown is to walk up Market Street from Seaport Village. The **Olde Cracker Factory,** at Market and State streets, houses antiques and collectibles shops. Continue two blocks to Front Street and turn south one block to Island to reach the new facility of the **Children's Museum of San Diego.** *200 W. Island St., tel. 619/233–5437. Admission: $4 adults and children over 2, $2 senior citizens. Open Tues.–Sat. 10–4:30, Sun. noon–4:30.*

Another way to approach the central business district is to walk up Broadway from the Broadway Pier. Two blocks to the west of Harbor Drive, at Kettner Boulevard, you'll come to the Mission Revival-**⑦** style **Santa Fe Depot,** built in 1915 on the site of the original 1887 station. The terminal for north- and southbound Amtrak passengers, the graceful, tile-domed depot hosts an unattended tourist information booth with bus schedules, maps, and brochures. Formerly an easily spotted area landmark, the depot is now overshadowed by **1 America Plaza** next door. At the base of this massive 34-story office tower, designed by architect Helmut Jahn, is a transit center that links the train, trolley, and city bus systems. (The Greyhound bus station is just a few blocks away at 120 West Broadway.) The building's signature crescent-shaped glass-and-steel canopy arching out over the trolley tracks calls attention to the new Sculpture Plaza that fronts the downtown branch of the **San Diego Museum of Contemporary Art,** opened in early 1993. The two-story building adjoining the transit center, with four small galleries, is the main locus for contemporary art exhibits in San Diego while the original facility in La Jolla undergoes expansion. *1001 Kettner Blvd., tel. 619/234–1001. Admission: $2 adults, $1 students, senior citizens, children under 13; free Thurs. 5–9 PM. Open Tues., Wed, and Fri.–Sun. 11 AM–6 PM, Thurs. 11 AM–9 PM.*

Six blocks farther east, at the corner of 1st Avenue and Broadway, **⑧** downtown begins to come alive. Here you'll pass the **Spreckels Theater,** a grand old stage that presents pop concerts and touring **⑨** plays these days. Another block down and across the street, the **U.S. Grant Hotel,** built in 1910, is far more formal than most other San Diego lodgings; the massive marble lobby, gleaming chandeliers, and white-gloved doormen hearken back to the more gracious time when it was built.

The theme of shopping in adventureland carries over from Seaport **⑩** Village to downtown San Diego's centerpiece, **Horton Plaza** (tel. 619/238–1596). Completed in 1985, this shopping, dining, and enter-

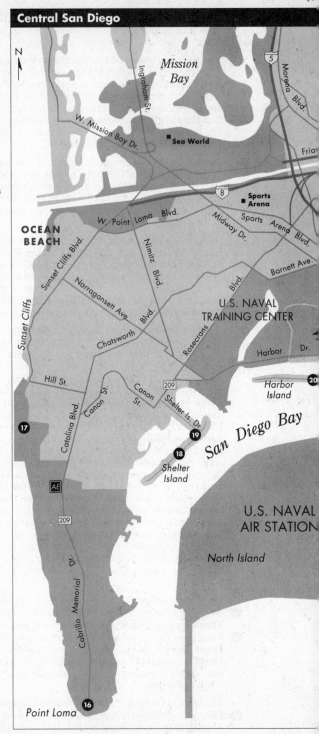

Central San Diego

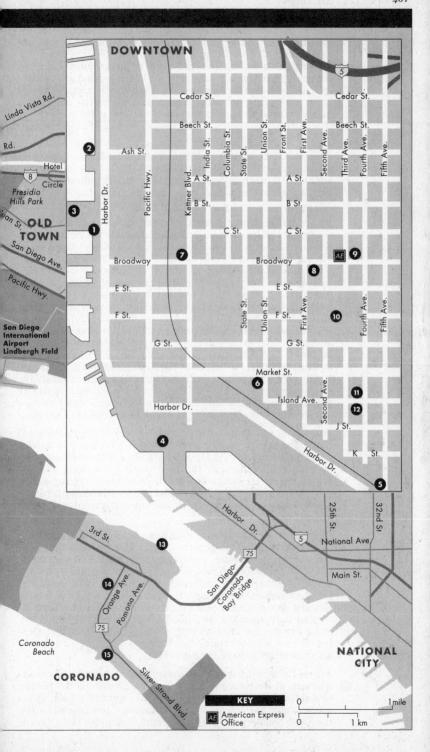

DOWNTOWN

Cedar St.   Cedar St.

Beech St.   Beech St.

Ash St.

A St.   A St.

B St.   B St.

C St.   C St.

Broadway   Broadway

E St.   E St.

F St.   F St.

G St.

Market St.

Island Ave.

J St.

K St.

Harbor Dr.

Linda Vista Rd.

Rd.

Hotel Circle

Presidio Hills Park

OLD TOWN

San Diego Ave.

Pacific Hwy.

San Diego International Airport Lindbergh Field

Harbor Dr.

Pacific Hwy.

Kettner Blvd.

India St.

Columbia St.

State St.

Union St.

Front St.

First Ave.

Second Ave.

Third Ave.

Fourth Ave.

Fifth Ave.

State St.

Union St.

First Ave.

Fourth Ave.

Fifth Ave.

Second Ave.

Harbor Dr.

National Ave.

Main St.

25th St.

32nd St.

3rd St.

San Diego-Coronado Bay Bridge

Orange Ave.

Pomona Ave.

NATIONAL CITY

Coronado Beach

Silver Strand Blvd.

CORONADO

KEY

AE American Express Office

0   1 mile

0   1 km

tainment mall fronts Broadway and G Street from 1st to 4th avenues and covers more than six city blocks. The **International Visitor Information Center,** operated in the complex by the San Diego Convention and Visitors Bureau, is the traveler's best resource for information on the city. The staff members and volunteers who run the center speak an amazing array of languages and are well acquainted with the myriad needs and requests of tourists. They dispense information on hotels, restaurants, and tourist attractions, including Tijuana. *11 Horton Plaza, street level at the corner of 1st Ave. and F St., tel. 619/236–1212. Open year-round, Mon.–Sat. 8:30–5; June–Aug., also open Sun. 11–5.*

Opened in 1992 across from Horton Plaza on 1st Avenue between G and F streets, **The Paladion** (tel. 619/232–1627) is the most recent addition to the thriving downtown retail scene. This ultrahaute complex features a collection of toney boutiques such as Cartier, Tiffany, and Gucci.

Before Horton Plaza became the bright star on downtown's redevelopment horizon, the nearby **Gaslamp Quarter** was gaining attention and respect. A 16-block National Historic District, centered on 5th and 4th avenues from Broadway to Market Street, the quarter contains most of San Diego's Victorian-style commercial buildings from the late 1800s, when Market Street was the center of early downtown. At the farthest end of the redeveloped quarter, the **⓫ Gaslamp Quarter Association** is headquartered in the William Heath Davis House (410 Island Ave., tel. 619/233–5227), one of the first residences in town. Davis was a San Franciscan whose ill-fated attempt to develop the waterfront area preceded the more successful one of Alonzo Horton. In 1850, Davis had this prefab saltbox-style house shipped around Cape Horn and assembled in San Diego. Walking tours of the historic district leave from here on Saturdays at 11; they cost $5 for adults, $3 for senior citizens and students. If you can't make the tour, stop by the house between 10 and 4:30 Monday through Friday and pick up a self-guiding brochure and map.

In the latter part of the 19th century, businesses thrived in this area, but at the turn of the century, downtown's commercial district moved farther west toward Broadway, and many of San Diego's first buildings fell into disrepair. During the early 1900s, the quarter became known as the Stingaree district. Prostitutes picked up sailors in lively area taverns, and dance halls and crime flourished here; the blocks between Market Street and the waterfront were best avoided.

As the move for downtown redevelopment emerged, there was talk of destroying the buildings in the quarter, literally bulldozing them and starting from scratch. In 1974, history buffs, developers, architects, and artists formed the Gaslamp Quarter Council. Bent on preserving the district, they gathered funds from the government and private benefactors and began the painstaking, expensive task of cleaning up the quarter, restoring the finest old buildings, and attracting businesses and the public back to the heart of New Town. Some two decades later, their efforts have paid off. Former flophouses have become choice office buildings, and the area is dotted with characterful shops and restaurants.

⓬ Across the street from the Gaslamp Quarter Association's headquarters, at the corner of Island and 3rd avenues, is the **Horton Grand Hotel.** In the mid-1980s, this ornate, quintessentially Victorian hostelry was created by joining together two historic hotels, the Kahle Saddlery and the Grand Hotel, built in the boom days of the 1880s; Wyatt Earp stayed at the Kahle Saddlery (then called the Brooklyn Hotel) while he was in town speculating on real estate ventures and opening gambling halls. Doomed to demolition and purchased from the city for $1 each, the two hotels were dismantled and painstakingly reconstructed on a new site, about four blocks from their original locations. A small Chinese Museum serves as a tribute to the surrounding Chinatown district, a collection of modest homes that once housed Chinese laborers and their families.

Many of the quarter's landmark buildings are located on 4th and 5th avenues, between Island Avenue and Broadway. Among the nicest are the Backesto Building, the Louis Bank of Commerce, and the Mercantile Building, all on 5th Avenue, and the Keating Building on F Street. Johnny M's 801, at the corner of 4th Avenue and F Street, is a magnificently restored turn-of-the-century tavern with a 12-foot mahogany bar and a spectacular stained-glass domed ceiling.

As more and more artists—and art entrepreneurs—move to the area, the section of G Street between 6th and 9th avenues has become a haven for galleries; stop in at any one of them to pick up a map of the downtown arts district. The three-story brick Pannikin Building, at the corner of 7th Avenue and G Street, houses Ariba, an international folk-art boutique, and a coffee importer and roasting plant.

TimeOut Fifth Avenue between F and G streets is lined with restaurants, a number of them offering outdoor patios; **Trattoria La Strada** (702 5th Ave.) is a good place to sit out on a fine afternoon with a glass of wine and an antipasto. Many hip coffeehouses have also sprung up in the Gaslamp Quarter; you can nurse a double espresso at **Lulu's** (419 F St.) for hours.

Coronado

Coronado Island, an incorporated city unto itself, is a charming, peaceful community. The Spaniards called the island Los Coronados, or "the Crowned Ones," in the late 1500s and the name stuck. Today's residents, many of whom live in grand Victorian homes handed down for generations, tend to consider their island to be a sort of royal encampment, safe from the hassles and hustle of San Diego proper.

North Island Naval Air Station was established in 1911 on the island's north end, across from Point Loma, and was the site of Charles Lindbergh's departure on his flight around the world. Today high-tech air- and seacraft arrive and depart continually from North Island, providing a real-life education in military armament. Coronado's long relationship with the navy has made it an enclave of sorts for retired military personnel.

The streets of the island are wide, quiet, and friendly, with lots of neighborhood parks where young families mingle with the island's many senior citizens. Grand old homes face the waterfront and the Coronado Municipal Golf Course, with its lovely setting under the bridge, at the north end of Glorietta Bay; it's the site of the annual Fourth of July fireworks. Community celebrations and live-band concerts take place in Spreckels' Park on Orange Avenue.

Coronado is visible from downtown and Point Loma and accessible via the arching blue 2.2-mile-long San Diego–Coronado Bridge, a landmark just beyond downtown's skyline. There is a $1 toll for crossing the bridge into Coronado, but cars carrying two or more passengers may enter through the free car-pool lane. The bridge handles more than 20,000 cars each day, and rush hour tends to be slow, which is fine, since the view of the harbor, downtown, and the island is breathtaking, day and night. Until the bridge was completed in 1969, visitors and residents relied on the Coronado Ferry, which ran across the harbor from downtown. When the bridge was opened, the ferry closed down, much to the chagrin of those who were fond of traveling at a leisurely pace. In 1987, the ferry returned, and with it came the island's most ambitious development in decades. Coronado's residents and commuting workers have quickly adapted to this traditional mode of transportation, and the ferry has become quite popular with bicyclists, who shuttle their bikes across the harbor and ride the island's wide, flat boulevards for hours.

You can board the Bay Ferry (tel. 619/234–4111) at downtown San Diego's Embarcadero from the Broadway Pier, at Broadway and Harbor Drive. Boats depart hourly from 9 AM to 9:30 PM Sunday through Thursday, until 10:30 PM Friday and Saturday; the fare is **13** $2 each way. In Coronado, you will disembark at the **Old Ferry Landing**, which is actually a new development on an old site. Its buildings resemble the gingerbread domes of the Hotel del Coronado, long the island's main attraction. The Old Ferry Landing is similar to Seaport Village, with small shops and restaurants and lots of benches facing the water. Nearby, the elegant Le Meridien Hotel accommodates many wedding receptions and gala banquets.

14 A trackless trolley runs from the landing down **Orange Avenue,** the island's version of a downtown. It's easy to imagine you're on a street in Cape Cod when you stroll along this thoroughfare: The clapboard houses, small restaurants, and boutiques—many of them selling nautical paraphernalia—are in some ways more characteristic of New England than they are of California. But the East Coast illusion tends to dissipate as quickly as a winter fog here when you catch sight of one of the avenue's many citrus trees—or realize it's February and the sun is warming your face.

15 At the end of Orange Avenue, the **Hotel Del Coronado** is the island's most prominent landmark. Selected as a National Historic Site in 1977, the Del (as natives say) celebrated its 100th anniversary in 1988. Celebrities, royalty, and politicians marked the anniversary with a weekend-long party that highlighted the hotel's colorful history, integrally connected with that of the island itself.

The Del was the brainchild of wealthy financiers Elisha Spurr Babcock, Jr., and H.L. Story, who, in 1884, saw the potential of the island's virgin beaches and its view of San Diego's emerging harbor. The next year, they purchased a 4,100-acre parcel of land for $110,000 and threw a lavish Fourth of July bash for prospective investors in their hunting and fishing resort. By the end of the year, they had roused public interest—and had an ample return on their investment. The hotel was completed in 1888, and Thomas Edison himself threw the switch as the Del became the world's first electrically lighted hotel. It has been a dazzler ever since.

The Del's ornate Victorian gingerbread architecture is recognized all over the world because the hotel has served as a set for many movies, political meetings, and extravagant social happenings. It is said that the Duke of Windsor first met Wallis Simpson here. Eight presidents have been guests of the Del, and the film *Some Like It*

Hot, starring Marilyn Monroe, was filmed at the hotel. Today, lower-level corridors are lined with historic photos from the Del's early days.

A red carpet leads up the front stairs to the main lobby, with its grand oak pillars and ceiling, and out to the central courtyard and gazebo. To the right is the Crown Room, a cavernous room with an arched ceiling made of notched sugar pine and constructed without nails. Enormous chandeliers sparkle overhead.

The Grand Ballroom overlooks the ocean and the hotel's long white beach. The patio surrounding the sky-blue swimming pool is a great place for just sitting back and imagining what the bathers looked like during the '20s, when the hotel rocked with good times. *1500 Orange Ave., tel. 619/435–6611. Guided tours ($10) leave from the lobby Thurs.–Sat. 10 and 11 AM.*

Coronado's other main attraction is its 86 historic homes—many of them turn-of-the-century mansions—and sites. The **Glorietta Bay Inn,** across the street from the Del, was the residence of John Spreckels, the original owner of North Island and the property on which the Hotel Del Coronado now stands. On Tuesday, Thursday, and Saturday morning at 11, the inn is the departure point for a walking tour of the area's historical homes. Sponsored by the Coronado Historical Association, the tour includes some spectacular mansions along with the Meade House, where L. Frank Baum wrote *The Wizard of Oz.* The cost is $5; call 619/435–5892 or 619/435–5444 for more information.

Point Loma, Shelter Island, and Harbor Island

Point Loma curves around the San Diego Bay west of downtown and the airport, protecting the center city from the Pacific's tides and waves. Although a number of military installations are based here and some main streets are cluttered with motels and fast-food shacks, Point Loma is an old and wealthy enclave of stately family homes for military officers, successful Portuguese fishermen, and political and professional leaders. Its bayside shores front huge estates, with sailboats and yachts packed tightly in private marinas.

16 Take Catalina Drive all the way down to the tip of Point Loma to reach **Cabrillo National Monument,** named after the Portuguese explorer Juan Rodríguez Cabrillo. Cabrillo, who had earlier gone on voyages with Cortés, was the first European to come to San Diego, which he called San Miguel, in 1542. In 1913, government grounds were set aside to commemorate his discovery. Today his monument, a 144-acre preserve of rugged cliffs and shores and outstanding overlooks, is one of the most frequently visited of all National Park Service sites.

Begin your tour at the visitor center, where films and lectures about Cabrillo's voyage, the sea-level tidal pools, and the gray whales migrating offshore are presented frequently. The center has an excellent shop with an interesting selection of books about nature, San Diego, and the sea; maps of the region, posters of whales, flowers, shells, and the requisite postcards, slides, and film are also on sale. Visitors who are unable to do much hiking around the site should inquire here about the park shuttle service. Rest rooms and water fountains are plentiful along the paths that climb to the monument's various viewpoints, but, except for a few vending machines at the Visitor Center, there are no food facilities. Exploring the grounds consumes time and calories; bring a picnic and rest on a bench overlooking the sailboats headed to sea.

Signs along the walkways that edge the cliffs explain the views, with posters depicting the various navy, fishing, and pleasure craft that sail into and fly over the bay. Directly south across the bay from the visitor center is the North Island Naval Air Station on the west end of Coronado Island. Directly left on the shores of Point Loma is the Naval Ocean Systems Center and Ballast Point; nuclear-powered submarines are now docked where Cabrillo's small ships anchored in 1542.

A statue of Cabrillo overlooks downtown from the next windy promontory, where visitors gather to admire the stunning panorama over the bay, from the snowcapped San Bernardino Mountains, some 200 miles northeast, to the hills surrounding Tijuana. The stone figure standing on the bluff looks rugged and dashing, but he is a creation of an artist's imagination—no portraits of Cabrillo are known to exist.

The oil lamp of the **Old Point Loma Lighthouse** was first lit in 1855. The light, sitting in a brass-and-iron housing above a painstakingly refurbished white wooden house, shone through a state-of-the-art lens from France and was visible from the sea for 25 miles. Unfortunately, it was too high above the cliffs to guide navigators trapped in southern California's thick offshore fog and low clouds. In 1891, a new lighthouse was built on the small shore under the slowly eroding 400-foot cliffs. The old lighthouse is open to visitors, and the coast guard still uses the newer lighthouse and a mighty foghorn to guide boaters through the narrow channel leading into the bay.

Continue north on Catalina Boulevard to Hill Street and turn left ⑰ to reach **Sunset Cliffs Park,** at the western side of Point Loma near Ocean Beach. The cliffs are aptly named, since their main attraction is their vantage point as a fine sunset-watching spot. The dramatic coastline here seems to have been carved out of ancient rock. Certainly the waves make their impact, and each year more sections of the cliffs sport caution signs. Don't ignore these warnings: It's easy to lose your footing and slip in the crumbling sandstone, and the surf can get very rough. Small coves and beaches dot the coastline and are popular with surfers drawn to the pounding waves and locals from the neighborhood who name and claim their special spots. The homes along Sunset Cliffs Boulevard are lovely examples of southern California luxury, with pink stucco mansions beside shingle Cape Cod–style cottages.

⑱ **Shelter Island** is actually a peninsula that sits in the narrow channel between Point Loma's eastern shore and the west coast of Coronado. In 1950, the port director thought there should be some use for the soil dredged to deepen the ship channel. Why not build an island?

His hunch paid off. Shelter Island's shores now support towering mature palms, a cluster of mid-range resorts, restaurants, and side-by-side marinas. It is the center of San Diego's yacht-building industry, and boats in every stage of construction are visible in the yacht yards. A long sidewalk runs from the landscaped lawns of the ⑲ **San Diego Yacht Club** (tucked down Anchorage Street off Shelter Island Drive), past boat brokerages to the hotels and marinas, which line the inner shore, facing Point Loma. On the bay side, fishermen launch their boats or simply stand on shore and cast. Families relax at picnic tables along the grass, where there are fire rings and permanent barbecue grills, while strollers wander to the huge Friendship Bell, given to San Diegans by the people of Yokohama in 1960.

㉒ Go back up Shelter Island Drive, turn right on Rosecrans Street, and make another right on North Harbor Drive to reach **Harbor Island,** a peninsula adjacent to the airport that was created out of 3.5 million tons of rock and soil from the San Diego Bay. Again, hotels and restaurants line the inner shores, but here, the buildings are many stories high, and the views from the bayside rooms are spectacular. The bay shore has pathways, gardens, and picnic spots for sightseeing or working off the calories from the island restaurants' fine meals. On the west point, Tom Ham's Lighthouse restaurant has a coast guard–approved beacon shining from its tower.

Balboa Park

Numbers in the margin correspond to points of interest on the Balboa Park map.

Straddling two mesas overlooking downtown and the Pacific Ocean, Balboa Park is set on 1,400 beautifully landscaped acres. Hosting the majority of San Diego's museums and a world-famous zoo, the park serves as the cultural center of the city, as well as a recreational paradise for animal lovers and folks who want to spend a day picnicking or strolling in a lush green space.

Many of the park's ornate Spanish-Moorish buildings were intended to be temporary structures housing exhibits for the Panama–California International Exposition of 1915. Fortunately, city leaders realized the buildings' value and incorporated them in their plans for Balboa Park's acreage, which had been set aside by the city founders in 1868. The Spanish theme first instituted in the early 1900s was carried through in new buildings designed for the California Pacific International Exposition of 1935–36.

The Laurel Street Bridge, also known as Cabrillo Bridge, is the park's official gateway; it leads over a vast canyon, filled with downtown commuter traffic on Highway 163, to El Prado, which, beyond the art museum, becomes the park's central pedestrian mall. At Christmas the bridge is lined with colored lights; bright pink blossoms on rows of peach trees herald the coming of spring. The 100-bell carillon in the California Tower tolls the hour. Figures of California's historic personages decorate the base of the 200-foot spire, and a magnificent blue-tiled dome shines in the sun. If you're driving in via the Laurel Street Bridge, the first parking area you'll come to is off the Prado to the left, going toward Pan American Plaza. Don't despair if there are no spaces here; you'll see more lots as you continue down along the same road.

❶ A good place to begin a visit is at the **Balboa Park Visitors Center.** Maps and pamphlets—as well as the friendly volunteers who run the center—can help you decide what you'd like to see. The office sells the Passport to Balboa Park, which has reduced-price coupons to the museums—worthwhile if you want to visit a number of them and aren't entitled to the other discounts that many give to children, senior citizens, and military personnel. On Tuesdays, the museums offer free admission on a rotating basis; inquire here about the schedule. Also available at the office is a schedule and route map for the free trams that operate around the park, giving you an alternative way to get back to your car or bus if all that culture has tired you. From April through September, trams run 9:30–5:30, approximately every 8–12 minutes; the rest of the year, service is 11–5 and

Balboa Park

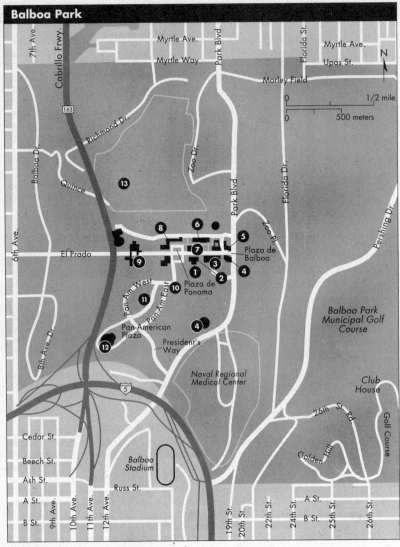

Balboa Park Visitors Center, **1**

Botanical Building, **6**

House of Pacific Relations, **11**

The Museum of Man, **9**

Museum of Photographic Arts, **3**

Reuben H. Fleet Space Theater and Science Center, **4**

San Diego Aerospace Museum and International Aerospace Hall of Fame, **12**

San Diego Museum of Art, **8**

San Diego Natural History Museum, **5**

San Diego Sports Museum Hall of Champions, **2**

San Diego Zoo, **13**

Spreckels Organ Pavilion, **10**

Timken Art Gallery, **7**

frequency is 12–24 minutes. *In the House of Hospitality, on the Prado just past its junction with Pan American Plaza Rd., tel. 619/239–0512. Open daily 9–4.*

Next door to the House of Hospitality, the **Casa de Balboa** houses four museums: the San Diego Hall of Champions Sports Museum, the Museum of Photographic Arts, the San Diego Historical Society–Museum of San Diego History, and the San Diego Model Railroad Museum. Starting from the left as you enter, the **Museum of San Diego History** features rotating exhibits on local urban history after 1850, when California became part of the United States. The society's research library is in the building's basement. *Tel. 619/232–6203. Admission: $3 adults. Open Wed.–Sun. 10–4:30.*

2 Down the hall, the **San Diego Sports Museum Hall of Champions** celebrates local heroes with a vast collection of memorabilia, uniforms, paintings, photographs, and computer and video displays. An amusing bloopers film is screened at the Sports Theater. *Tel. 619/234–2544. Admission: $3 adults, $1 children 6–17. Open daily 10–4:30.*

3 The **Museum of Photographic Arts,** one of the few in the country dedicated solely to photography, celebrated its 10th anniversary in 1993. World-renowned classic photographers, such as Ansel Adams, Imogen Cunningham, Henri Cartier-Bresson, and Edward Weston, are represented by the museum, along with relatively obscure contemporary artists. Volunteers lead tours through the exhibits, which change every six weeks. Gallery talks are given on weekends. *Tel. 619/239–5262. Admission: $3. Open daily 10–5.*

Below MOPA, in the basement of the Casa de Balboa, is the **San Diego Model Railroad Museum.** The room is filled with the sounds of chugging engines, screeching brakes, and shrill whistles when the six model-train exhibits are in operation. *Tel. 619/696–0199. Admission: $3 adults. Open Wed.–Fri. 11–4, weekends 11–5.*

If you continue walking down El Prado, you'll come to the Plaza de Balboa and a large central fountain. Just past the fountain, El Prado ends in a bridge that crosses over Park Boulevard to a perfectly tended rose garden and a seemingly wild cactus grove. From here, you can see across the canyon to even more parkland, with picnic groves, sports facilities, and acres of ranging chaparral.

4 To the right of the Plaza de Balboa fountain, on the same side of the road as the Casa de Balboa, the **Reuben H. Fleet Space Theater and Science Center** features clever interactive exhibits that teach children and adults about scientific principles. On a huge, domed overhead screen at the Omnimax Theater, informative and exhilarating films about nature and space (shown regularly throughout the day) seem to lift the viewer right into the action. The center's gift shop is akin to a museum, with toys and gadgets that inspire the imagination. At night, the Laserium presents laser shows set to rock music. *Tel. 619/238–1233. Science Center admission: $2.25 adults, $1 children 5–15 or included with price of theater ticket. Space Theater tickets: $5.50 adults, $4 senior citizens, $3 children 5–15; laser shows: $7.50 adults, $5 children 5–15. Open Sun.–Tues. 9:30 AM–6 PM, Wed. and Thurs. 9:30 AM–9:30 PM, Fri. and Sat. 9:30 AM–10:30 PM.*

5 Across the Plaza de Balboa fountain from the Reuben H. Fleet Space Theater and Science Center, a short flight of steps will take you up to the **San Diego Natural History Museum,** which features displays on the plants and animals of southern California and Mexico. Children seem particularly impressed by the dinosaur bones and the live-insect zoo. The Hall of Mineralogy hosts an impressive collection of gems. Near the museum entrance, the 185-pound brass Foucault Pendulum, suspended on a 43-foot cable, demonstrates the earth's rotation. The museum frequently schedules nature walks, films, and lectures. *Tel. 619/232–3821. Admission: $6 adults, $5 senior citizens, $2 children 6–17. Open daily 9:30–4:30.*

The action gets lively in the next section of El Prado, where mimes, jugglers, and musicians perform on long lawns beside the Lily Pond in front of the graceful **Botanical Building.** Built for the 1915 exposition, the latticed, open-air nursery houses more than 500 types of tropical and subtropical plants. The orchid collection is stunning, and there are benches beside cool, miniature waterfalls for resting in the shade. The Lily Pond, filled with giant koi fish and blooming water lilies, is popular with photographers. *Admission free. Open Tues.–Sun. 10–4.*

On the other side of the Lily Pond is the only privately owned building in the park, operated by the Putnam Foundation. The small **Timken Art Gallery** houses a selection of minor works by major European and American artists, as well as a fine collection of Russian icons. *Tel. 619/239–5548. Admission free. Open Oct.–Aug., Tues.–Sat. 10–4:30, Sun. 1:30–4:30. Closed Sept.*

Just behind the Timken Gallery on the Plaza de Panama, the **San Diego Museum of Art** is known primarily for its Spanish Baroque and Renaissance paintings, including works by El Greco, Goya, Rubens, and Van Ruisdale. The museum also has strong holdings of Southeast Asian art and Indian miniatures, and its Baldwin M. Baldwin wing displays more than 100 pieces by Toulouse-Lautrec. The museum's latest acquisition is a large collection of contemporary California art. An outdoor Sculpture Garden exhibits both traditional and modernistic pieces in a striking natural setting. *Tel. 619/232–7931. Admission: $5 adults, $4 senior citizens, $2 students with current ID and children 6–17. Open Tues.–Sun. 10–4:30.*

If you get back on El Prado and continue east, you'll come to the **Museum of Man,** located under the California Tower. One of the finest anthropological museums in the country, it houses an extensive collection first assembled for the 1915 exposition and amplified over the years. Exhibits focus on Southwestern, Mexican, and South American cultures; the latest acquisition, in 1993, was a collection of ancient Egyptian artifacts. In the "Lifestyles and Ceremonies" section, high-tech gadgetry is employed in displays on biology, reproduction, and culture, offering a fascinating look at the costumes and rituals of San Diego's many ethnic communities. Weddings are sometimes held at the Chapel of St. Francis, a model of a typical early California hacienda chapel viewed by appointment only. *Tel. 619/239–2001. Admission: $4 adults, $2 children 13–18, $1 children 6–12. Open daily 10–4:30.*

The **Simon Edison Centre for the Performing Arts** (tel. 619/239-2255), including the Cassius Carter Centre Stage, the Lowell Davies Festival Theatre, and the Old Globe, sits beside the Museum of Man under the California Tower. Originally devoted to Shakespearean theater, the Globe now also holds first-rate productions by other playwrights, too. All three theaters are small and intimate, and evening performances on the outdoor stages are particularly enjoyable during the summer.

Across the Prado and back toward the Museum of Art, the **House of Charm** is the permanent home of the San Diego Art Institute. Currently closed for renovations, it's scheduled to reopen sometime in 1995. In the interim, the Art Institute is holding its shows in Mission Valley Center (1640 Camino del Rio N, Suite 1368, tel. 619/220–4800 for information on hours).

At the Plaza de Panama parking lot, west of the Art Institute, another road heads south from El Prado. It's divided by a long island
(10) of flowers as it curves around the **Spreckels Organ Pavilion** and the 5,000-pipe Spreckels Organ, believed to be the largest outdoor pipe organ in the world. You can hear this impressive instrument at one of the concerts offered at 2 PM on Sunday afternoons year-round. On summer evenings, local military bands, gospel groups, and barbershop quartets hold concerts, and at Christmas, the park's massive Christmas tree and life-size nativity display turn the pavilion into a seasonal wonderland. *Tel. 619/226–0819. Admission free. Open Fri.–Sun. 10–4.*

Northeast of the Organ Pavilion, the first phase of a new Japanese Friendship Garden includes an exhibit house, a traditional sand-and-stone garden, and a picnic area with a view of the canyon below. There are also a snack bar and a small gift shop. *Tel. 619/232–2780. Admission: $2 adults, $1 senior citizens, military, disabled visitors, children over 7; free Tues. Open Fri.–Sun. and Tues. 10–4.*

To the right of the organ pavilion, on Pan American West road, the
(11) **House of Pacific Relations** is really a cluster of stucco cottages representing more than 30 foreign countries. The buildings are open on Sunday, and individual cottages often present celebrations on their country's holidays.

Farther west, in the building used as the Palace of Transportation for the 1935–36 exposition, the **San Diego Automotive Museum** maintains a large collection of vintage cars and has an ongoing automobile restoration program. *Tel. 619/231–2886. Admission: $4 adults, $3 senior citizens, $2 children 6–17. Open daily 10–4:30.*

(12) The southern road ends at the Pan American Plaza and the **San Diego Aerospace Museum and International Aerospace Hall of Fame.** Looking unlike any other structure in the park, the sleek, streamlined edifice was commissioned by the Ford Motor Company for the 1935–36 exposition; at night, with a line of blue neon outlining it, the round building looks like a landlocked UFO. Exhibits about aviation and aerospace pioneers line the rotunda, and a collection of real and replicated aircraft fills the center. *Tel. 619/234–8291. Admission: $4 adults, $1 children 6–17. Open daily 10–4:30.*

Next to the aerospace center, the **Starlight Bowl** (tel. 619/544–7800 or 619/544–STAR) presents live musicals during the summer on its outdoor stage; actors freeze in their places when planes roar overhead on their way to Lindbergh Field.

Fronting Park Boulevard is Balboa Park's most famous attraction,
(13) the 100-acre **San Diego Zoo.** More than 3,200 animals of 777 species roam in expertly crafted habitats that spread down into, around, and above the natural canyons. Equal attention has been paid to the flora and the fauna, and the zoo is an enormous botanical garden with one of the world's largest collections of subtropical plants.

From the moment you walk through the entrance and face the swarm of bright pink flamingos and blue peacocks, you know you've entered a rare pocket of natural harmony. Exploring the zoo fully requires the stamina of a healthy hiker, but open-air trams that run throughout the day allow visitors to see 80% of the exhibits on their 3-mile tour. The animals are attuned to the buses and many like to show off; the bears are particularly fine performers, waving and bowing to their admirers. The Skyfari ride, which soars 170 feet above ground, gives a good overview of the zoo's layout and a marvelous panorama of the park, downtown San Diego, the bay, and the ocean, far past the Coronado Bridge.

Still, the zoo is at its best when you can wander the paths that climb through the huge enclosed Scripps Aviary, where brightly colored tropical birds swoop between branches just inches from your face. The Gorilla Tropics exhibit, beside the aviary, is the zoo's latest venture into bioclimatic zone exhibits, where animals live in enclosed environments modeled on their native habitats. Throughout the zoo, walkways wind over bridges and past waterfalls ringed with tropical ferns; giant elephants in a sandy plateau roam so close you're tempted to pet them. The San Diego Zoo houses the only koalas outside Australia and three rare golden monkeys number among its impressive collection of endangered species; a small two-headed snake named Thelma and Louise holds court in the reptile house.

The Children's Zoo is worth a visit, no matter what your age. Goats and sheep beg to be petted and are particularly adept at snatching bag lunches, while bunnies and guinea pigs seem willing to be fondled endlessly. In the nursery windows, you can see baby lemurs and spider monkeys playing with Cabbage Patch kids, looking much like the human babies peering from strollers through the glass. The exhibits are designed in size and style for four-year-olds, but that doesn't deter children of all ages from having fun. Even the rest rooms are child-size. The hardest part of being in the Children's Zoo will be getting your family to move on.

The Wedgeforth Bowl, a 3,000-seat amphitheater, holds various animal shows throughout the day, occasionally hosted by the zoo's ambassador of goodwill, Joan Embery, called "the most widely known inhabitant of the zoo." Embery's frequent appearances on Johnny Carson's *Tonight* show, usually with some charming critter to entertain the host, made the San Diego Zoo a household name among late-night viewers.

The zoo's simulated Asian rain forest, Tiger River, brings together 10 exhibits with more than 35 species of animals. As spectacular as the tigers, pythons, and water dragons are, they seem almost inconsequential among the $500,000 collection of exotic trees and plants. The mist-shrouded trails winding down a canyon into Tiger River pass by fragrant jasmine, ginger lilies, and orchids, giving the visitor the feeling of descending into a South American jungle. In Sun Bear Forest, playful cubs constantly claw apart the trees and shrubs that serve as a natural playground for climbing, jumping, and general rowdiness. Throughout the zoo, plans are under way to remodel exhibit areas into closer facsimiles of the animals' natural habitats.

In many ways also a self-sustaining habitat for humans, the zoo rents strollers, wheelchairs, and cameras; it also has a first-aid office, a lost-and-found, and an ATM. It's best to avert your eyes from the zoo's two main gift shops until the end of your visit; you can spend a half-day just poking through the wonderful animal-related posters, crafts, dishes, clothing, and toys. *Tel. 619/234-3153. Admission (including unlimited access to the Skyfari ride and the Children's Zoo): $12 adults, $4 children 3–11; tram ride: $3 adults, $2.50 children; children 11 and under enter free during the month of October. D, MC, V. Gates open fall–spring, daily 9–4 (visitors may remain until 5); summer, daily 9–5 (visitors may remain until 6).*

Old Town

Numbers in the margin correspond to points of interest on the Old Town San Diego map.

San Diego's Spanish and Mexican history and heritage are most evident in Old Town, just north of downtown at Juan Street, near the intersection of I–5 and I–8. It wasn't until 1968 that Old Town became a state historic park. Fortunately, private efforts kept the area's history alive until then, and a number of San Diego's oldest structures remain in good shape.

Although Old Town is often credited as being the first European settlement in southern California, the true beginnings took place overlooking Old Town from atop Presidio Park (*see below*). There, Father Junipero Serra established the first of California's missions, San Diego de Alcalá, in 1769. Some of San Diego's Native Americans, called the San Diegueños by the Spaniards, were forced to abandon their seminomadic lifestyle and live at the mission. They were expected to follow Spanish customs and adopt Christianity as their religion, but they resisted these impositions fiercely; of all the California missions, San Diego de Alcalá was the least successful in carrying out conversions. For security reasons, the mission was built on a hill, but it didn't have an adequate water supply, and food became scarce as the number of Native Americans and Spanish soldiers occupying the site increased.

In 1774, the hilltop was declared a Royal Presidio, or fortress, and the mission was moved to its current location along the San Diego River, 6 miles east of the original site. Losing more of their traditional grounds and ranches as the mission grew along the riverbed, the Native Americans attacked and burned it in 1775, destroying religious objects and killing Franciscan Padre Luis Jayme. Their later attack on the presidio was less successful, and their revolt was short-lived. By 1800, about 1,500 Native Americans were living on the mission's grounds, receiving religious instruction and adapting to Spanish ways.

The pioneers living within the presidio's walls were mostly Spanish soldiers, poor Mexicans, and mestizos of Spanish and Native American ancestry, many of whom were unaccustomed to farming San Diego's arid land. They existed marginally until 1821, when Mexico gained independence from Spain, claimed its lands in California, and flew the Mexican flag over the presidio. The Mexican government, centered some 2,000 miles away in Monterrey, stripped the missions of their landholdings, and an aristocracy of landholders began to emerge. At the same time, settlers were beginning to move down from the presidio to what is now called Old Town.

A rectangular plaza was laid out along today's San Diego Avenue to serve as the settlement's center. In 1846, during the war between Mexico and the United States, a detachment of marines raised the U.S. flag over the plaza on a pole said to have been a mainmast. The flag was torn down once or twice, but by early 1848, Mexico had surrendered California, and the U.S. flag remained. In 1850, San Diego became an incorporated city, with Old Town as its center.

Old Town's historic buildings are clustered around **Old Town Plaza,** bounded by Wallace Street on the west, Calhoun Street on the north, Mason Street on the east, and San Diego Avenue on the south; you can see the presidio from behind the cannon by the flagpole. These days, the plaza is a pleasant place for resting and regrouping as you

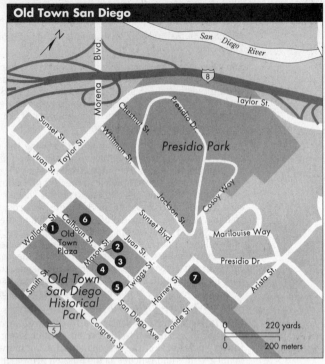

Old Town San Diego

plan your tour of Old Town and watch other visitors stroll by; art shows often fill the lawns around the plaza. San Diego Avenue is closed to traffic here, and the cars are diverted to Juan and Congress streets, both of which are lined with shops and restaurants. There are a number of free parking lots on the outskirts of Old Town, but they fill quickly. By the end of 1995, the San Diego trolley should stop here; in the meantime, if you plan to visit on the weekend, come early to find a spot.

A new visitor center is scheduled to open in Old Town in late 1995, but the **Old Town State Historic Park** office is currently in the **Robinson-Rose House,** on the west (Wallace Street) side of the plaza. This was the original commercial center of old San Diego, housing railroad offices, law offices, and the first newspaper press; one room has been restored and outfitted with period furnishings. Park rangers now show films and distribute information from the living room. An excellent free walking tour of the park leaves from here daily at 2 PM, weather permitting. From 10 to 1 every Wednesday and the first Saturday of the month, park staff and volunteers in period costume give cooking and crafts demonstrations at the Machado y Stewart adobe; adjacent to the Bandini House near Juan Street, you can watch a blacksmith hammering away at his anvil from 10 to 2 every Wednesday and Saturday. *4002 Wallace St., tel. 619/220–5422. Open daily 10–5. Closed Thanksgiving, Christmas, and New Year's.*

Many of Old Town's buildings were destroyed in a huge fire in 1872, but after the site became a state historic park in 1968, efforts were begun to reconstruct or restore the structures that remained. Eight of the original adobes are still intact. The tour map available at the Robinson-Rose House gives details on all of the historic houses on the plaza and in its vicinity; a few of the more interesting ones are noted below. Most of the houses are open to visitors daily 10–4 and most do not charge admission.

2 On Mason Street, at the corner of Calhoun Street, **La Casa de Bandini** is one of the loveliest haciendas in San Diego. Built in 1829 by a Peruvian, Juan Bandini, the house served as Old Town's social center during Mexican rule. Albert Seeley, a stagecoach entrepreneur, purchased the home in 1869, built a second story, and turned it into the Cosmopolitan Hotel, a comfortable way station for travelers on the day-long trip south from Los Angeles. These days, Casa Bandini's colorful gardens and main-floor dining rooms house a popular Mexican restaurant.

3 Next door on Calhoun Street, the **Seeley Stables** became San Diego's stagecoach stop in 1867 and were the transportation hub of Old Town until near the turn of the century, when the Southern Pacific Railroad became the favored mode of travel. The stables now house a collection of horse-drawn vehicles, Western memorabilia, and Native American artifacts. *Admission: $2 adults, $1 children 6–17.*

4 This fee also covers admittance to **La Casa de Estudillo,** built on Mason Street in 1827 by the commander of the San Diego Presidio, Jose Maria Estudillo. The largest and most elaborate of the original adobe homes, it was occupied by members of the Estudillo family until 1887. After being left to deteriorate for some time, it was purchased and restored in 1910 by sugar magnate and developer John D. Spreckels, who advertised it in bold lettering on the side as "Ramona's Marriage Place"; the small chapel in the house was believed to be the setting for the wedding in Helen Hunt Jackson's popular novel.

5 On Twigg Street and San Diego Avenue, the **San Diego Union Newspaper Historical Museum** is in the Casa de Altamirano, a New England–style wood-frame house prefabricated in Maine and shipped around Cape Horn in 1851. The building has been restored to replicate the newspaper's offices of 1868, when the first edition of the *San Diego Union* was printed.

Also worth exploring in the plaza area are the **Dental Museum, Mason Street School, Wells Fargo Museum,** and the **San Diego Courthouse.** Ask at the visitor center for locations.

Northwest of the plaza lies the unofficial center of Old Town, the

6 **Bazaar del Mundo,** a shopping and dining enclave built to represent a colonial Mexican square. The central courtyard is always in blossom, with magenta bougainvillea, scarlet hibiscus, and irises, poppies, and petunias in season. Ballet Folklorico and flamenco dancers perform in the outdoor gazebo on weekend afternoons, and the bazaar frequently holds arts-and-crafts exhibits and Mexican festivals in the courtyard. Colorful shops specializing in Latin American crafts and unusual gift items border the square, beyond a shield of thick bushes and huge bird cages with cawing macaws and toucans. Although many of the shops here have high-quality wares, prices can be considerably higher than those at shops on the other side of Old Town plaza; it's a good idea to do some comparative shopping before you make any purchases.

Old Town's boundaries and reputation as a historic attraction and shopping-dining center have spread in the past few years. Opened in late 1992 on San Diego Avenue beside the state park headquarters, **Dodson's Corner** is a modern retailer in a mid-19th-century setting; two of the shops in the complex, which sells everything from quilts and Western clothing to pottery and jewelry, are reconstructions of homes that stood on the spot in 1848. Farther away from the plaza, art galleries and expensive gift shops are interspersed with curio shops, restaurants, and open-air stands selling inexpensive Mexican pottery, jewelry, and blankets. San Diego Avenue continues as Old Town's main drag, with an ever-changing array of shopping plazas constructed in mock Mexican-plaza style. The best of these is the **Old Town Esplanade,** between Harney and Conde streets. Several shops display Mexican and South American folk art.

❼ Heritage Park, up the Juan Street hill near Harney Street, is the site of several grand Victorian homes and the town's first synagogue, all moved by the Save Our Heritage Organization (SOHO) from other parts of San Diego and restored. Some of the ornate houses may seem surprisingly colorful, but they are accurate representations of the bright tones of the era. The homes are now used for offices, shops, restaurants, and, in one case, a bed-and-breakfast inn. The climb up to the park is a bit steep, but the view of the harbor is great.

Mission Bay and Sea World

Numbers in the margin correspond to points of interest on the Mission Bay Area map.

San Diego's monument to sports and fitness, Mission Bay is a 4,600-acre aquatic park dedicated to action and leisure. Admission to its 27 miles of bayfront beaches and 17 miles of ocean frontage is free. All you need for a perfect day is a bathing suit, shorts, and the right selection of playthings. Above the lawns facing I–5, the sky is flooded with the bright colors of huge, intricately made kites.

When explorer Juan Rodríguez Cabrillo first spotted the bay in 1542, he called it Baja Falso (False Bay) because the ocean-facing inlet led to acres of swampland inhospitable to boats and inhabitants. In the 1960s the city planners decided to dredge the swamp and build a bay with acres of beaches and lawns for play. Only 25% of the land was permitted to be commercially developed, and, as a result, only a handful of resort hotels break up the striking natural landscape.

❶ The **Visitor Information Center,** at the East Mission Bay Drive exit from I–5, is an excellent tourist resource for the bay and all San Diego. The free *Mission Bay Guide* lists everything from places to rent bikes, boats, and diving equipment to local locksmiths and insurance companies; it also includes a good map of the area that notes where swimming, waterskiing, sailing, and other sports are permissible. The center is a gathering spot for the runners, walkers, and exercisers who take part in group activities. From the low hill outside the building, you can easily appreciate the bay's charms. *2688 E. Mission Bay Dr., tel. 619/276–8200. Open Mon.–Sat. 9–5 (until 6 or 7 in summer), Sun. 9:30–4:30 (until 5:30 in summer).*

A 5-mile-long pathway runs through this section of the bay from the trailer park and miniature golf course, south past the high-rise Hilton Hotel to Sea World Drive. Playgrounds and picnic areas abound on the beach and low grassy hills of the park. Group gatherings, company picnics, and birthday parties are common along this stretch, where huge parking lots seem to expand to serve the swelling crowds on sunny days. On weekday evenings, a steady stream of joggers, bikers, and skaters releasing the stress from a day at the office line the path. In the daytime, swimmers, water-skiers, fishers, and boaters—some in single-person kayaks, others in crowded pow-

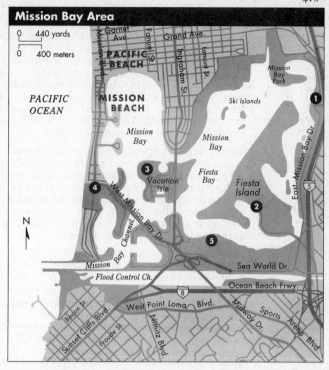

erboats—vie for space in the water. The San Diego Crew Classic, which takes place in April, fills this section of the bay with teams from all over the country and college reunions, complete with flying school colors and keg beer. Swimmers should note signs warning about water pollution; certain areas of the bay are chronically polluted, and bathing is strongly discouraged.

② **Fiesta Island,** off East Mission Bay Drive and Sea World Drive, is a smaller, man-made playground popular with jet- and water-skiers. In July, the annual Over-the-Line Tournament, a competition involving a local variety of softball, attracts thousands of players and oglers, drawn by the teams' raunchy names and outrageous behavior.

Ingraham Street is another main drag through the bay, from the shores of Pacific Beach to Sea World Drive. The focal point of this **③** part of the bay is **Vacation Isle.** You don't have to stay at the island's lavish Princess Resort to visit its lushly landscaped grounds, model yacht pond, and bayfront restaurants. Ducks are as common as tourists here, and Vacation Isle's village is a great family playground. Powerboats take off from Ski Beach, across Ingraham Street, which is also the site of the Taxaco Star Mart Cup hydroplane races, held in September. The noise from these boats is deafening, and the beach is packed from dawn till dark.

West Mission Bay Drive runs from the ocean beyond Mission Boulevard to Sea World Drive. The pathways along the Mission Beach side of the bay are lined with vacation homes, many of which can be rented by the month. Those who are fortunate enough to live here year-round have the bay as their front yards, with wide sandy

beaches, volleyball courts, and—less of an advantage—an endless
❹ stream of sightseers on the sidewalk. **Belmont Park,** once an abandoned amusement park at the corner of Mission Boulevard and West
Mission Bay Drive, is now a shopping, dining, and recreation area
between the bay and the Mission Beach boardwalk. Twinkling lights
outline the refurbished old Belmont Park roller coaster on which
screaming thrill-seekers ride. Nearby, younger riders enjoy the antique carousel, as well as the fresh cotton candy sold at the stand
just next to it. The Plunge, an indoor freshwater swimming pool,
has also been renovated and is open to the public, making Belmont
Park a focal point for the ocean beach area.

Spread over 100 tropically landscaped bayfront acres, where a cool
❺ breeze always seems to rise from the water, **Sea World** is one of the
world's largest marine-life amusement parks. A hospitality center
to the right of the entrance reminds visitors that this popular attraction is owned by Anheuser-Busch: Adults can get two small free
cups of beer in the building, which also houses a deli restaurant.
Next door are stables for the huge Clydesdale horses that are
hitched daily near the Penguin Encounter (*see below*).

The traditional favorite exhibit at Sea World is the Shamu show, with
giant killer whales entertaining the crowds in a recently constructed
stadium, but performing dolphins, sea lions, and otters at other
shows also delight audiences with their antics. At another popular
exhibit, the Penguin Encounter, a moving sidewalk passes through
a glass-enclosed arctic environment, in which hundreds of emperor
penguins slide over glaciers into icy waters (the penguins like it cold,
so you may consider bringing a light sweater along for this one).
Imaginative youngsters are especially fond of the Shark Encounter,
which features a variety of species of the fierce-looking predators.
The hands-on California Tide Pool exhibit gives visitors a chance to
explore San Diego's indigenous marine life with a guide well versed
in the habits of these creatures. At Forbidden Reef, you can feed bat
rays and come nose to nose with creepy moray eels. The newest
exhibit, Rocky Point Preserve, allows visitors to interact with bot-
tlenose dolphins and houses Alaskan sea otters that were treated
after the 1989 *Exxon-Valdez* oil spill.

Not all the exhibits are water oriented. Children are entranced by
Cap'n Kids' World, an enclosed playground with trampolines,
swinging wood bridges, towers for climbing, and giant tubs filled
with plastic balls. The Wings of the World show features a large
assemblage of free-flying exotic birds. Those who want to head aloft
themselves may consider the park's Sky Tower, a glass elevator that
ascends 265 feet; the views of San Diego County from the ocean to
the mountains are especially pleasing in early morning and late evening. A six-minute sky-tram ride that leaves from the same spot
travels between Sea World and the Atlantis Hotel across Mission
Bay. Admission for the Sky Tower and the tram is $2 apiece, or $3
for both.

Sea World is filled with souvenir shops and refreshment stands; it's
difficult to come away from here without spending a lot of money on
top of the rather hefty entrance fee. Many hotels, especially those
in the Mission Bay area, offer Sea World specials; some include price
reductions, while others allow two days of entry for a single admission price—a good way to spread out what can otherwise be a very
full day of activities. *Sea World Dr., at the west end of I–8, tel. 619/226–
3901 for recorded information or 619/226–3815. Admission: $27.95
adults, $19.95 children 3–11; parking $5. 90-minute behind-the-
scenes walking tours: $5 adults, $4 children 3–11. D, MC, V. Gates*

open 10–dusk; extended hours during summer. Call ahead to inquire about park hours for the day you intend to visit.

La Jolla

Numbers in the margin correspond to points of interest on the La Jolla map.

La Jollans have long considered their village to be the Monte Carlo of California, and with good cause. Its coastline curves into natural coves backed by verdant hillsides and covered with lavish homes worth millions. Though La Jolla is considered part of San Diego, it has its own postal zone and a coveted sense of class; old-monied residents mingle here with visiting film stars and royalty who frequent established hotels and private clubs. If development and construction have radically altered the once-serene and private character of the village, it has gained a cosmopolitan air that makes it a popular vacation resort for the international set.

The Native Americans called the site La Hoya, meaning "the cave," referring to the grottos dotting the shoreline. The Spaniards changed the name to La Jolla, meaning "the jewel," and its residents have cherished the name and its allusions ever since.

To reach La Jolla from I–5, take the Ardath Road exit if you're traveling north and drive slowly down Prospect Street so you can appreciate the breathtaking view. If you're heading south, get off at the La Jolla Village Drive exit, which will lead into Torrey Pines Road. For those who enjoy meandering, the best way to approach La Jolla from the south is to drive through Mission and Pacific beaches on Mission Boulevard, past the crowds of roller skaters, bicyclists, and sunbathers. The clutter and congestion ease up as the street becomes La Jolla Boulevard, where quiet neighborhoods with winding streets lead down to some of the best surfing beaches in San Diego. The boulevard here is lined with expensive restaurants and cafes, as well as a few take-out spots.

❶ The town's cultural center, the **San Diego Museum of Contemporary Art** (700 Prospect St.), lies on the less trafficked southern end of Prospect. Housed in a remodeled Irving Gill home, the museum has a fine permanent collection of post-1950 art. The facility is currently undergoing expansion and renovation by architect Robert Venturi; it is not slated to reopen until early 1996. In the meantime, those interested in contemporary art must be content with visiting the much smaller downtown annex, opened in 1993 in the America Plaza complex (*see* Downtown and the Embarcadero, *above*).

❷ Continue north on Prospect and turn west onto Coast Boulevard to reach La Jolla's great natural coastal attraction, **Ellen Browning Scripps Park** at the **La Jolla Cove.** Towering palms line the sidewalk along Coast Boulevard, where strollers in evening dress are as common as Frisbee-throwers. The **Children's Pool,** at the south end of the park, is aptly named for its curving beach and shallow waters protected by a seawall from strong currents and waves. Each September the La Jolla Rough Water Swim takes place here, with hundreds of hardy swimmers plunging into the chilly waters and swimming a mile into the sea.

❸ Just past the far northern point of the cove, in front of the La Jolla Cave and Shell Shop, a trail leads down to **La Jolla Caves;** it's some 133 steps down to the largest one, Sunny Jim Cave. For claustrophobic types, there are photos of the watery grottoes in the shop, along with a good selection of shells and coral jewelry. *1325 Coast*

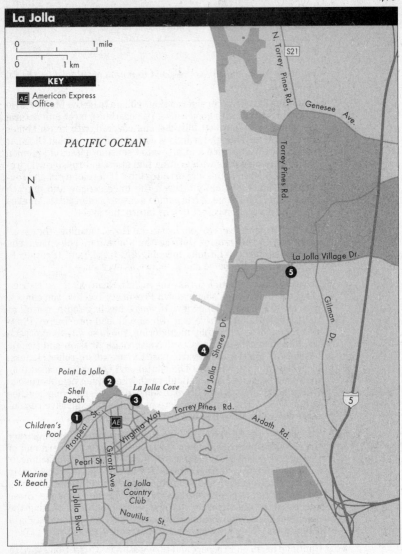

La Jolla

Blvd., tel. 619/454–6080. Admission to caves: $1.25 adults, 50¢ children 3–11. Open Mon.–Sat. 10–5, Sun. 11–5, sometimes open later in summer.

Like Prospect Street, Girard Avenue is lined with expensive shops and office buildings; it also hosts La Jolla's only movie house, which tends to show nonmainstream films. The shopping and dining district has spread to Pearl and other side streets, where a steady parade of amblers and sightseers stroll about, chatting in many languages. Wall Street, a quiet tree-lined boulevard, was once the financial heart of La Jolla, but banks and investment houses can now be found throughout town. The La Jolla nightlife scene is an active one, with jazz clubs, piano bars, and watering holes for the elite younger set coming and going with the trends.

❹ If you continue north of the cove on La Jolla Shores Drive, you'll come to the La Jolla Beach and Tennis Club, host of many tennis tournaments. **La Jolla Shores'** beaches are some of the finest in San Diego, with long stretches allotted to surfers or swimmers. Just beyond the beaches is the campus of the Scripps Institute of Oceanography, formerly the site of the marine institute's aquarium.

❺ The largest oceanographic exhibit in the United States, Scripps' **Stephen Birch Aquarium–Museum** reopened in late 1992 about 1½ miles northwest of its original site, on a signed drive leading off North Torrey Pines Road just south of La Jolla Village Drive. To those familiar with the old facility, the new $1 million marine museum may be a bit of a disappointment. It's considerably more expensive but not very much larger than the former facility, and a single artificial tidal pool at the back of the building is a poor substitute for the many natural seaside tidal pools outside the old aquarium. That said, there's a lot to enjoy here. More than 30 huge tanks are filled with colorful saltwater fish, and a spectacular 70,000-gallon tank simulates a La Jolla kelp forest. Next to the fish themselves, the most interesting attraction is the 12-minute simulated submarine ride (children under 3 not admitted); the ocean noises and marine-life visuals are realistic almost to the point of inducing seasickness. *2300 Expedition Way, tel. 619/534–3474. Admission: $6.50 adults; $5.50 senior citizens 60 and older; $4.50 children 13–17, military, and students with current ID; $3.50 children 4–12; parking $2.50. Open daily 9–5. Closed Thanksgiving and Christmas.*

San Diego for Free

San Diego's main attractions are its climate and natural beauty, which are accessible to all, free of charge. The 70 miles of beaches are free—no boardwalks with admission fees, no high-priced parking lots. You can easily while away a week or two just visiting a different beach community each day. (*See* Beaches, *below, for more details.*) Nearly all San Diego's major attractions in our Exploring section are situated amid huge parks, gardens, and waterfronts, with plenty of natural wonders to keep you amused.

Balboa Park's museums offer free admission on Tuesdays on a rotating basis; call 619/239–0512 for a schedule. Free organ concerts take place in the Spreckels Organ Pavilion on Sunday afternoons, and a variety of choral groups and bands appear there on summer evenings, also for free. There is no charge to wander through the Botanical Building, an enclosed tropical paradise.

Seaport Village hosts a variety of free seasonal events throughout the year, often with fireworks displays. Both the **Embarcadero**

Marina Park South and **Sea World** have fireworks on summer evenings that are visible from downtown, Mission Bay, and Ocean Beach.

Off the Beaten Track

Don't think you've finished seeing San Diego once you've hit all the main attractions. The real character of the place doesn't shine through until you've visited a few neighborhoods and mingled with the natives. Then you can say you've seen San Diego.

Mission Hills is an older neighborhood near downtown that has the charm and wealth of La Jolla and Point Loma without the crowds. The prettiest streets are above Presidio Park and Old Town, where huge mansions with rolling lawns resemble eastern estates; to see them, head up Fort Stockton Drive from the Presidio or Juan Street past Heritage Park in Old Town to Sunset Boulevard. Washington Street runs up a steep hill from I-8 through the center of Mission Hills. Palmier Bistro, at the corner of Washington Street and Goldfinch Street, has wonderful pâtés, pastries, and wines to enjoy there or take away. On Goldfinch, visit the Gathering, a neighborhood restaurant with great breakfasts and outdoor tables for reading the Sunday paper in the sun.

Hillcrest, farther up Washington Street beginning at 1st Avenue, is San Diego's Castro Street, the center for the gay community and artists of all types. University, 4th, and 5th avenues are filled with cafés, boutiques, and excellent bookstores. The Guild Theater and Hillcrest Cinemas, both on 5th Avenue, show first-run foreign films. The Blue Door, next to the Guild, is one of San Diego's best small bookstores. The '50s retro-style Corvette Diner, on 4th Avenue between University Avenue and Washington Street, features burgers and shakes and campy waitresses. Quel Fromage, a coffeehouse on University Avenue between 5th and 6th avenues, has long been the place to go to discuss philosophical or romantic matters over espresso.

Like most of San Diego, Hillcrest has been undergoing massive redevelopment. The largest project is the **Uptown District,** on University Avenue at 8th Avenue. This self-contained residential-commercial center was built to resemble an inner-city neighborhood, with shops and restaurants within easy walking distance of high-price town houses. Restaurants include Cane's, a trendy pasta cafe, and La Salsa, part of a chain of excellent Mexican take-out stands.

Washington Street eventually becomes Adams Avenue, San Diego's Antiques Row, with shops displaying an odd array of antiques and collectibles. Adams Avenue leads into **Kensington** and **Talmadge,** two lovely old neighborhoods overlooking Mission Valley. The Ken Cinema (4061 Adams Ave.) shows older cult movies and current art films.

Shopping

By Marael Johnson

Most San Diego shops are open daily 10–6; department stores and shops within the larger malls stay open until 9 PM on weekdays. Sales are advertised in the daily *San Diego Union–Tribune* and in the *Reader,* a free weekly that comes out on Thursday.

Shopping Districts

San Diego's shopping areas are a mélange of self-contained mega-malls, historic districts, quaint villages, funky neighborhoods, and chic suburbs.

Coronado Across the bay, Coronado is accessible by car or ferry. **Orange Avenue,** in the center of town, has six blocks of ritzy boutiques and galleries. The elegant Hotel del Coronado, also on Orange Avenue, houses exclusive (and costly) specialty shops. **Old Ferry Landing,** where the San Diego ferry lands, is a waterfront center similar to Seaport Village.

Downtown **Horton Plaza,** in the heart of center city, is a shopper's Disneyland—visually exciting, multilevel department stores; one-of-a-kind shops; fast-food counters; classy restaurants; a farmers' market; live theater; and cinemas. Surrounding Horton Plaza is the 16-block Gaslamp Quarter, a redevelopment area that features art galleries, antiques, and specialty shops housed in Victorian buildings and renovated warehouses.

The Paladion, just across 1st Avenue from Horton Plaza, is San Diego's answer to Rodeo Drive. This posh complex, opened in 1992, houses a collection of upscale boutiques—including Cartier, Tiffany, Gucci, Alfred Dunhill, Gianni Versace, and Salvatore Ferragamo.

Hotel Circle The Hotel Circle area, northeast of downtown near I–8 and Freeway 163, has two major shopping centers. **Fashion Valley** and **Mission Valley Center** contain hundreds of shops, as well as restaurants, cinemas, and branches of almost every San Diego department store.

Kensington/ Hillcrest These are two of San Diego's older, established neighborhoods, situated several miles north and east of downtown. **Adams Avenue,** in Kensington, is Antiques Row. More than 20 dealers sell everything from postcards and kitchen utensils to cut glass and porcelain. **Park Boulevard,** in Hillcrest, is the city's center for nostalgia. Small shops, on either side of University Avenue, stock clothing, accessories, furnishings, and bric-a-brac of the 1920s–60s. **Uptown District,** a shopping center on University Avenue, has the neighborhood's massive Ralph's grocery store, as well as several specialty shops.

La Jolla/ Golden Triangle La Jolla, about 15 miles northwest of downtown on the coast, is an ultra-chic, ultra-exclusive resort community. High-end and trendy boutiques line Girard Avenue and Prospect Street. Coast Walk, nestled along the cliffside of Prospect Street, offers several levels of sophisticated shops, galleries, and restaurants, as well as a spectacular ocean view. The Golden Triangle area, several miles east of coastal La Jolla, is served by **University Towne Centre,** between I–5 and Highway 805. This megamall features the usual range of department stores, specialty shops, sportswear chains, restaurants, and cinemas. Nearby **Costa Verde Centre,** on the corner of Genessee and La Jolla Village Drive, is an enormous strip mall of convenience stores and inexpensive eateries.

North County This rapidly expanding area boasts an array of high-range shopping districts. One of the most attractive retail centers in the area, **Del Mar Plaza** (15th St. and Camino Del Mar) boasts a spectacular view of the Pacific and many excellent restaurants, boutiques, and specialty stores. Farther north in Encinitas is the **Lumberyard** (1st St. and Old Hwy. 1), an upscale strip mall where one can find everything from yogurt shops and stationary to sportswear and sushi. Inland from Del Mar in Escondido, one of the area's newest enclosed malls,

North County Fair (Via Rancho Parkway, east of Hwy. 15), is anchored by Nordstrom, Robinson-May, and the Broadway.

Old Town   North of downtown, off I–5, this popular historic district is reminiscent of a colorful Mexican marketplace. Adobe architecture, flower-filled plazas, fountains, and courtyards highlight the shopping areas of **Bazaar del Mundo, La Esplanade,** and **Old Town Mercado,** where you will find international goods, toys, souvenirs, and arts and crafts.

Seaport Village   On the waterfront, a few minutes from downtown, **Seaport Village** offers quaint theme shops, restaurants, arts-and-crafts galleries, and commanding views of Coronado, the bridge, and passing ships.

Sports, Fitness, Beaches

Participant Sports

By Kevin Brass   At least one stereotype of San Diego is true—it is an active, outdoors-oriented community. People recreate more than spectate. It's hard not to, with such a wide variety of choices available.

Bicycling   On any given summer day, Old Highway 101, from La Jolla to Oceanside, looks like a freeway for cyclists. Never straying more than a quarter-mile from the beach, it is easily the most popular and scenic bike route around. Although the roads are narrow and winding, experienced cyclists like to follow Lomas Santa Fe Drive in Solana Beach east into beautiful Rancho Santa Fe, perhaps even continuing east on Del Dios Highway, past Lake Hodges, to Escondido. For more leisurely rides, Mission Bay, San Diego Harbor, and the Mission Beach boardwalk are all flat and scenic. For those who like to race on a track, San Diego even has a velodrome in Balboa Park. Call the Velodrome Office (tel. 619/296–3345) for more information. San Diego County also offers challenging mountain-bike trails. Local bookstores and camping stores sell trail guides.

Bikes can be rented at any number of places, including **Bicycle Barn** in Pacific Beach (746 Emerald St., tel. 619/581–3665) and **Hamel's Action Sports Center** in Mission Beach (704 Ventura Pl, tel. 619/488–5050). **Performance Bicycle Shop** (3619 Midway Dr., tel. 619/223–5415), known for its catalogue business, has an impressive supply of bicycles and bicycling accessories at its San Diego location. A free comprehensive map of all county bike paths is available from the local office of the **California Department of Transportation** (tel. 619/688–6699).

Diving   Enthusiasts from all over the world flock to San Diego to skin-dive and scuba-dive in the areas off La Jolla and Point Loma that are rich in ocean creatures and flora. At La Jolla Cove, you'll find the **San Diego–La Jolla Underwater Park,** an ecological preserve. Farther north, off the south end of Black's Beach, the rim of **Scripps Canyon** lies in about 60 feet of water. The canyon plummets to more than 900 feet in some sections. Another popular diving spot is Sunset Cliffs in Point Loma, where a wide variety of sea life is relatively close to shore. Strong rip currents make it an area best enjoyed by experienced divers.

Diving equipment and boat trips can be arranged through **San Diego Divers** (tel. 619/224–3439), **Ocean Enterprises** (tel. 619/565–6054), **Del Mar Ocean Sports** (tel. 619/792–1903), or at the several **Diving Locker** locations throughout the area. It is illegal to take any wildlife from the ecological preserves in La Jolla or near Cabrillo Point.

Spearfishing requires a license (available at most dive stores), and it is illegal to take out-of-season lobster and game fish out of the water. For general diving information, contact the **San Diego City Lifeguards' Office** (tel. 619/221–8884).

Fishing Variety is the key. The Pacific Ocean is full of corbina, croaker, and halibut just itching to be your dinner. No license is required to fish from a public pier, such as the Ocean Beach pier. A fishing license from the state Department of Fish and Game (tel. 619/525–4215), available at most bait-and-tackle stores, is required for fishing from the shoreline, although children under 15 won't need one.

Several companies offer half-day, day, or multiday fishing expeditions in search of marlin, tuna, albacore, and other deep-water fish. **Fisherman's Landing** (tel. 619/221–8500), **H & M Landing** (tel. 619/222–1144), and **Seaforth Boat Rentals** (tel. 619/223–7584) are among the companies operating from San Diego. **Helgren's Sportfishing** (tel. 619/722–2133) offers trips from Oceanside Harbor.

Golf Most public courses in the area offer an inexpensive current list of fees and charges for all San Diego courses. The **Southern California Golf Association** (tel. 818/980–3630 or 213/877–0901) publishes an annual directory with detailed and valuable information on all member clubs. The following is not intended to be a comprehensive list but offers suggestions on some of the best places to play in the area.

Coronado Golf Course (2000 Visalia Row, Coronado, tel. 619/435–3121): 18 holes, driving range, equipment rentals, clubhouse. Views of San Diego Bay and the Coronado Bridge from the back nine holes on this good walking course make it very popular—and rather difficult to get on.

Mission Bay Golf Course (2702 N. Mission Bay Dr., San Diego, tel. 619/490–3370): 18 holes, driving range, equipment rentals. A not-very-challenging executive (par 3 and 4) course, Mission Bay is lit for night play.

Rancho San Diego Golf Course (3121 Willow Glen Rd., El Cajon, tel. 619/442–9891): 36 holes, driving range, equipment rentals. A good walking course, Rancho San Diego has nice putting greens and lots of cottonwood trees.

Redhawk Golf Course (45100 Redhawk Pkwy., Temecula, tel. 909/695–1424 or 800/451–HAWK in CA): 18 holes, driving range, golf shop, snack bar. The extremely difficult design of this course will prove frustrating to those who are not experienced golfers, but experts should enjoy Redhawk.

Singing Hills Country Club (3007 Dehesa Rd., El Cajon, tel. 619/442–3425): 54 holes, driving range, equipment rentals. Set in a canyon surrounded by small mountains, this lush, green course has lots of water hazards. One of *Golf Digest*'s favorites, Singing Hills comes very highly recommended by everyone who's played it. Hackers will love the executive par-3 course; seasoned golfers can play the championship courses.

Torrey Pines Municipal Golf Course (11480 N. Torrey Pines Rd., La Jolla, tel. 619/452–3226): 36 holes, driving range, equipment rentals. One of the best public golf courses in the United States, Torrey Pines offers stunning views of the Pacific from every hole and is sufficiently challenging to host the Buick Invitational in February. It's not easy to get a good tee time at this justly popular course, but every golfer visiting the area should try to play it at least once.

Whispering Palms Country Club (5690 Concah del Golf, Rancho Santa Fe, tel. 619/756–2471): 27 holes, driving range, equipment rental, pro shop. The well-maintained Whispering Palms, a nice walking course in a pretty area near polo grounds and stables, is one of the more popular places to play in the San Diego area.

Health Clubs Several hotels offer full health clubs, at least with weight machines, stationary bicycles, and spas, including, in the downtown area, the **Doubletree San Diego** (910 Broadway Circle, tel. 619/239–2200) and the **Pan Pacific** (402 W. Broadway, tel. 619/239–4500).

Horseback Riding Expensive insurance has severely cut the number of stables that offer horses for rent in San Diego County. The businesses that remain have a wide variety of organized excursions. **Holidays on Horseback** (tel. 619/445–3997), in the East County town of Descanso, leads rides ranging from a few hours to a few days in the Cuyamaca Mountains. It rents special, easy-to-ride fox trotters to beginners. **Bright Valley Farm** (11990 Campo Rd., Spring Valley, tel. 619/670–1861) is a wonderful place to ride. South of Imperial Beach, near the Mexican border, **Sandi's Rental Stables** (tel. 619/424–3124) leads rides through Border Field State Park.

Jogging There is no truth to the rumor that San Diego was created to be one big jogging track, but it often seems that way. From downtown, the most popular run is along the Embarcadero, which stretches around the bay. There are nice, uncongested sidewalks through most of the area. The alternative for downtown visitors is to head east to Balboa Park, where a labyrinth of trails snake through the canyons. Mission Bay, renowned for its wide sidewalks and basically flat landscape, may be the most popular jogging spot in San Diego. Trails head west around Fiesta Island from Mission Bay, providing distance as well as a scenic route. Del Mar has the finest running trails along the bluff; park your car near 15th Street and run south along the cliffs for a gorgeous view of the ocean. There are organized runs almost every weekend. For more information, call *Competitor* magazine (tel. 619/793–2711) or the **San Diego Track Club** (tel. 619/452–7382). **The Tinley Store** (1229 Camino Del Mar, tel. 619/755–8015) has all the supplies and information you'll need for running in San Diego. Some tips: Don't run in bike lanes, and check the local newspaper's tide charts before heading to the beach.

Surfing In San Diego, surfing is a year-round sport (thanks to wet suits in the winter) for people of all ages. Beginners should paddle out at Mission, Pacific, Tourmaline, La Jolla Shores, Del Mar, or Oceanside beaches. Experienced surfers should hit Sunset Cliffs, the La Jolla reef breaks, Black's Beach, or Swami's (Sea Cliff Roadside Park) in Encinitas (*see* Beaches, *below*, for directions). Most public beaches have separate areas for surfers. Many local surf shops rent boards, including **Star Surfing Company** (tel. 619/273–7827) in Pacific Beach and **La Jolla Surf Systems** (tel. 619/456–2777) and **Hansen's** (tel. 619/753–6595) in Encinitas.

Swimming The most spectacular pool in town is the **Mission Beach Plunge** (3115 Ocean Front Walk, tel. 619/488–3110), in Belmont Park, where the public can swim weekdays 6–8 AM, noon–1, and 3:30–8, weekends 8–4. Admission is $2.25. The **Copley Family YMCA** (3901 Landis St., tel. 619/283–2251) and the **Downtown YMCA** (500 W. Broadway Ave., tel. 619/232–7451) are both centrally located.

Tennis Most of the more than 1,300 courts spread around the county are in private clubs, but there are a few public facilities. **Morley Field** (tel. 619/295–9278), in Balboa Park, has 25 courts, 19 of which are lighted. Nonmembers can make reservations after paying a nominal fee for the use of the courts; if you're lucky, a court may be available when you come in to pay the fee. The **La Jolla Recreation Center** (tel. 619/552–1658) offers nine free public courts near downtown La Jolla, five of them lighted. There are 12 lighted courts at **Robb Field** (tel. 619/531–1563) in Ocean Beach, with a small day-use fee.

The list of hotel complexes with tennis facilities includes the **Bahia Resort Hotel** (tel. 619/488–0551); **Hilton San Diego** (tel. 619/276–4010); the **Hotel del Coronado** (tel. 619/435–6611); the **Kona Kai Beach and Tennis Resort** (tel. 619/222–1191); the **LaCosta Resort and Spa** (tel. 619/438–9111); and the **Rancho Bernardo Inn and Country Club** (tel. 619/487–1611). Intense tennis instruction is available at **Rancho Bernardo Inn Tennis College** (tel. 619/487–2413) in Rancho Bernardo.

Waterskiing Mission Bay is one of the most popular waterskiing areas in Southern California. It is best to get out early when the water is smooth and the crowds are thin. Boats and equipment can be rented from **Seaforth Boat Rentals** (1641 Quivira Rd., near Mission Bay, tel. 619/223–1681). The private **San Diego and Mission Bay Boat and Ski Club** (2606 N. Mission Bay Dr., tel. 619/276–0830) operates a slalom course and ski jump in Mission Bay's Hidden Anchorage. Permission from the club or the Mission Bay Harbor Patrol (tel. 619/291–3900) must be obtained to use the course and jump.

Spectator Sports

For information on tickets to any event, contact **Teleseat** (tel. 619/452–7328). **San Diego Jack Murphy Stadium** is at the intersection of I–8 and I–805.

Baseball From April through September, the **San Diego Padres** (tel. 619/283–4494) slug it out for bragging rights in the National League West. Matches with such rivals as the hated Los Angeles Dodgers and San Francisco Giants are usually the highlights of the home season at San Diego Jack Murphy Stadium. Tickets range from $5 to $11 and are usually readily available, unless the Padres are in the thick of the pennant race.

Football After almost a decade of less-than-stellar seasons, the **San Diego Chargers** (tel. 619/280–2111) have enjoyed a spectacular resurgence. The Chargers were one of the original AFL franchises. They fill San Diego Jack Murphy Stadium August through December. Games with AFC West rivals Los Angeles Raiders and Denver Broncos are always particularly intense.

Horse Racing Begun in the 1930s by Bing Crosby, Pat O'Brien, and their Hollywood cronies, the annual summer meeting of the **Del Mar Thoroughbred Club** (tel. 619/755–1141) on the Del Mar Fairgrounds—"Where the Turf Meets the Surf"—attracts hordes of Beautiful People, along with the best horses and jockeys in the country. The meeting begins in July and continues through early September, every day except Tuesday. But that isn't the end of horse-racing action in Del Mar. The Del Mar Fairgrounds also serves as a satellite-wagering facility (tel. 619/755–1167) with TV coverage of betting on races from tracks throughout California. Take I–5 north to the Via de la Valle Road exit.

Ice Hockey The **San Diego Gulls** (tel. 619/688–1800), competing in and dominating the International Hockey League, bring an exciting game of hockey to this area. Games are played October–April at the San Diego Sports Arena (tel. 619/224–4171), with ticket prices ranging from $6 to $15.50.

Beaches

San Diego's beaches are one of its greatest natural attractions. In some places, the shorefront is wide and sandy; in others, it's narrow and rocky or backed by impressive sandstone cliffs. You'll find beaches teeming with activities and deserted spots for romantic sunset walks. San Diego is a prime destination for surfers; the variety of breaks and their exposure to ocean swells make the surf off this portion of the Pacific coast remarkably consistent and fun. For a surf and weather report, call 619/221–8884.

Overnight camping is not allowed on any San Diego city beaches, but there are campgrounds at some state beaches throughout the county; call 800/444–7275 for state beach camping reservations. Lifeguards are stationed at city beaches (from Sunset Cliffs to Black's Beach) in the summertime, but coverage in winter is provided by roving patrols only. Dogs are not permitted at most beaches in San Diego, and tickets for breaking the law can be very expensive. However, it is rarely a problem to bring your pet to isolated beaches during the winter.

Pay attention to all signs listing illegal activities; undercover police often patrol the beaches, carrying their ticket books in coolers. Glass is prohibited on all beaches, and fires are allowed only in fire rings or barbecues. Alcoholic beverages—including beer—are completely banned on some city beaches; others allow you to partake between 8 AM and 8 PM only. Check out the signs posted at the parking lots and lifeguard towers before you hit the shore with a six pack or some wine coolers. Imbibing in beach parking lots, on boardwalks, and in landscaped areas is always illegal; where drinking is permitted, stay on the sand. For more information on the beach-booze ban, call Pacific Beach Community Relations (tel. 619/581–9920) or Ocean Beach Community Relations (tel. 619/531–1540). For a general beach and weather report, phone 619/289–1212.

Beaches are listed from south to north. For information on Mission Bay, *see* Mission Bay and Sea World in Exploring San Diego, *above.*

South Bay   **Border Field State Beach.** The southernmost San Diego beach is different from the majority of California beaches. Located just north of the Mexican border, it is a marshy area with wide chaparrals and wildflowers, a favorite among horse riders and hikers. However, frequent sewage contamination from Tijuana makes the water dangerous for swimming. For this reason, the beach is often closed. There is ample parking, and there are rest rooms and fire rings. *Exit I–5 at Dairy Mart Rd. and head west along Monument Rd.*

South Beach. One of the few beaches where dogs are free to romp, this is a good spot for long, isolated walks. The often-contaminated water and rocky beach tend to discourage crowds. The downside: There are few facilities, such as rest rooms, and sewage contamination from Tijuana can create a health hazard at times. *Located at the end of Seacoast Dr. Take I–5 to Coronado Ave. and head west on Imperial Beach Ave. Turn left onto Seacoast Dr.*

Imperial Beach. This classic southern California beach, where surfers and swimmers congregate to enjoy the water and waves, provides a pleasant backdrop for the Frisbee games of the predominantly young crowd. There are lifeguards on duty during the summer, parking lots, food vendors nearby, and rest rooms. Note: Although the surf here can be excellent, this is another spot at which

WATCH WHERE YOU'RE GOING!

Get in gear and explore the wild world of sports adventure. Fodor's® *Interactive Sports and Adventure Vacations*™ is a jam-packed multimedia CD-ROM devoted solely to adventure sports, travel and leisure.

There's mountain biking, kayaking, skiing, 4-wheel drive tours, cattle drives, sports fantasy camps - the kinds of vacations families and solo adventurists will remember forever. *Action footage, interactive maps, photos, information,* and *direct contacts* are included, plus a *travel planner* that recommends trips based on your personal preferences.

For a far-from-ordinary vacation, grab the phone and call
1-800-262-7668.

A Multimedia CD-ROM product from

CREATIVE MULTIMEDIA

All the Best Trips Start with Fodor's

COMPASS AMERICAN GUIDES
Titles in the series: Arizona, Canada, Chicago, Colorado, Hawai'i, Hollywood, Las Vegas, Maine, Manhattan, New Mexico, New Orleans, Oregon, San Francisco, South Carolina, South Dakota, Utah, Virginia, Wisconsin, Wyoming.

"A literary, historical, and near-sensory excursion."—*Denver Post*

"Tackles the 'why' of travel...as well as the nitty-gritty details."—*Travel Weekly*

FODOR'S BED & BREAKFASTS AND COUNTRY INN GUIDES
Titles in the series: California, Canada, England & Wales, Mid-Atlantic, New England, The Pacific Northwest, The South, The Upper Great Lakes Region.

"In addition to information on each establishment, the books add notes on things to see and do in the vicinity."
— *San Diego Union-Tribune*

THE BERKELEY GUIDES
Titles in the series: California, Central America, Eastern Europe, Europe, France, Germany, Great Britain & Ireland, Italy, London, Mexico, The Pacific Northwest & Alaska, Paris, San Francisco.

The best choice for budget travelers, from the Associated Students at the University of California at Berkeley.

"Berkeley's scribes put the funk back in travel." — *Time*

"Fresh, funny and funky as well as useful." — *The Boston Globe*

EXPLORING GUIDES
Titles in the series: Australia, Britain, California, Caribbean, Florida, France, Germany, Ireland, Italy, London, New York City, Paris, Rome, Singapore & Malaysia, Spain, Thailand.

"Authoritatively written and superbly presented, they make worthy reading before, during or after a trip. "
— *The Philadelphia Inquirer*

"A handsome new series of guides, complete with lots of color photos, geared to the independent traveler."
— *The Boston Globe*

Visit your local bookstore, or call 24 hours a day 1-800-533-6478
Fodor's The name that means smart travel.

to be careful of sewage contamination. *Take Palm Ave. west from I–5 until it hits water.*

Coronado **Silver Strand State Beach.** Farther north on the isthmus of Coronado (commonly mislabeled an island), Silver Strand was set aside as a state beach in 1932. The name is derived from the tiny silver seashells found in abundance near the water. The water is relatively calm, making this beach ideal for families. Four parking lots provide room for more than 1,500 cars. Parking is free from Labor Day through February; the rest of the year the cost is $4 per car. There is also an RV campground (cost: $14 per night) and a wide array of facilities but no hook-ups; spots are available on a first-come, first-served basis. *Tel. 619/435–5184. Take the Palm Ave. exit from I–5 west to Hwy. 75; turn right and follow the signs.*

Coronado Beach. With the famous Hotel Del Coronado as a backdrop, this wide stretch of sandy beach is one of the largest and most picturesque in the county. It is surprisingly uncrowded on most days, since the locals go to the less touristy areas in the south or north. It's perfect for sunbathing or games of Frisbee and Smash Ball (played with paddles and a small ball). Parking can be a little difficult on the busiest days, but there are plenty of rest rooms and service facilities, as well as fire rings. The view (even for a brief moment) as you drive over the Coronado Bridge makes it a worthwhile excursion. *From the bridge, turn left on Orange Ave. and follow the signs.*

Point Loma **Sunset Cliffs.** Beneath the jagged cliffs on the west side of the Point Loma peninsula is one of the more secluded beaches in the area, popular primarily with surfers and locals. The tide goes out each day to reveal tidal pools teeming with life at the south end of the peninsula, near Cabrillo Point. Farther north, the often-large waves attract surfers and the lonely coves attract sunbathers. Stairs are available at the foot of Bermuda and Santa Cruz avenues, but much of the access is limited to treacherous cliff trails. There are no facilities. Your visit here will be much more enjoyable at low tide; check the local newspaper for tide schedules. *Take I–8 west to Sunset Cliffs Blvd. and head south.*

San Diego **Ocean Beach.** The north end of this beach, past the second jetty, is known as Dog Beach because it's the only one within the San Diego city limits that allows canines to romp around without a leash. The south end of Ocean Beach, near the pier, is a hangout for surfers and transients. Much of the area, though, is a haven for local volleyball players, sunbathers, and swimmers. You'll find food vendors and fire rings here; limited parking is available. *Take I–8 west to Sunset Cliffs Blvd. and head south. Turn right on Voltaire St., West Point Loma Blvd., or Newport Ave.*

Mission Beach. The boardwalk stretching along Mission Beach is popular with strollers, roller skaters, and bicyclists. Surfers, swimmers, and volleyball players congregate at the south end, which tends to get extremely crowded, especially on hot summer days. Toward the north end, near the Belmont Park roller coaster, the beach narrows and the water grows rougher—and the crowd gets even thicker. The refurbished Belmont Park is now a shopping and dining complex. Parking can be a challenge, but there are plenty of rest rooms and restaurants in the area. *Exit I–5 at Garnet Ave. and head west to Mission Blvd. Turn south and look for parking.*

Pacific Beach. The boardwalk turns into a sidewalk here, but there are still bike paths and picnic tables running along the beachfront. The beach is a favorite for families, teens, and surfers alike. Parking can be a problem, although there is a small lot at the foot of Ventura Place. *Exit I–5 at Garnet Ave. and head west to Mission Blvd. Turn north and look for parking.*

La Jolla   **Tourmaline Surfing Park** and **Windansea Beach.** These La Jolla beaches are two of the top surfing spots in the area. Tourmaline has the better parking area of the two and is more hospitable to tourists. The surf at Windansea is world-class, but the local crowd can be "gnarly." *Take Mission Blvd. north (it turns into La Jolla Blvd.) and turn west on Tourmaline St. (for the surfing park) or Nautilus St. (for Windansea Beach).*

Marine Street Beach. This is a classic stretch of sand for sunbathing and Frisbee games. *Accessible from Marine St. off La Jolla Blvd.*

Children's Pool. For the tykes, a shallow lagoon with small waves and no riptide provides a safe, if crowded, haven. *Follow La Jolla Blvd. north. When it forks, take the left, Coast Blvd.*

Shell Beach. Just north of the Children's Pool is a small cove, accessible by stairs, with a relatively secluded and beautiful beach. The exposed rocks just off the coast here have been designated a protected habitat for seals; you can watch them sun themselves and frolic in the water. *Continue along Coast Blvd. north from the Children's Pool.*

La Jolla Cove. Just north of Shell Beach is La Jolla Cove, one of the prettiest spots in the world. A beautiful, palm-tree-lined park sits on top of cliffs formed by the incessant pounding of the waves. At low tide the tidal pools and cliff caves provide an exciting destination for explorers. Divers explore the underwater delights of the San Diego–La Jolla Underwater Park, an ecological reserve. The cove is also a favorite of rough-water swimmers, for whom buoys mark distances. The beach below the cove is beautiful and great for kids over 8 years old. *Follow Coast Blvd. north to the signs, or take the La Jolla Village Dr. exit from I–5, head west to Torrey Pines Rd., turn left and drive down the hill to Girard Ave. Turn right and follow the signs.*

La Jolla Shores. This is one of the most popular and overcrowded beaches in the county. On holidays, such as Memorial Day, all access routes are usually closed. The lures are a wide sandy beach; fun surf for boogie-boarders, body-surfers, and regular surfers alike; and a concrete boardwalk paralleling the beach. There is also a wide variety of facilities, from posh restaurants to snack shops, within walking distance. Go early to get a parking spot. *From I–5 take La Jolla Village Dr. west and turn left onto La Jolla Shores Dr. Head west to Camino del Oro or Vallecitos St. Turn right and look for parking.*

Black's Beach. At one time, this was the only legal nude beach in the country. But the late 1970s prohibition against public nudity doesn't stop people from braving the treacherous cliff trails for a chance to take off their clothes. Above the beach, hang-gliders and sail-plane enthusiasts launch from the Torrey Pines Glider Port. Because of the difficult access, the beach is always relatively uncrowded. The waves here are excellent for surfers, but the shorebreak can be powerful. Only experienced swimmers should take the plunge. *Take Genessee Ave. west from I–5 and follow the signs to the glider port; easier access, via a paved path, is available on La Jolla Farms Rd., but parking there is limited to 2 hrs.*

Dining

By Kathryn Shevelow

In spite of its ranking as the second-largest city in California, San Diego was, until recently, a rather slow-paced, provincial place. The fine weather and splendid beaches that contribute so much to the city's beauty also fostered an open-air, daytime-oriented culture that did little to encourage a sophisticated nightlife. San Diegans seemed to prefer suburban quietude to urban activity; after dark, downtown was given over to sailors, bars, and sex shops.

The restaurant scene was dominated by fast food, overcooked fish, and upper-class stodge. "Good food," with few exceptions, was the quasi-Continental fare served at the kind of indeterminate Chamber of Commerce restaurant humorist Calvin Trillin calls "La Maison de la Casa House." If the one bright light was always the abundance of authentic Mexican restaurants, even these did not often venture far beyond the standard fare of tacos, beans, and burritos.

But all that has begun to change in the past few years. Redevelopment of the downtown area has created a substantial nightlife scene, with a proliferation of clubs and good restaurants—especially on 4th and 5th avenues—that is nothing short of astonishing. Other areas have shared in the new sense of energy. It wasn't long ago that the streets of sleepy La Jolla turned in for the night at sunset (especially in the winter) and the uptown area (Hillcrest, Mission Hills, Normal Heights) was a semi-urban landscape of dreary streets punctuated by an occasional bar. Now night crawlers can party hearty in both sections of town after dark.

All this bodes well for residents and visitors who like to eat. True, for all the efforts it may make in that direction, San Diego is not Los Angeles or San Francisco, and perhaps will never be: There has not yet developed among San Diegans the kind of exacting culinary standards one finds in the demanding and vociferous residents of a truly great food city. Still, one can eat very well these days in San Diego.

Adding to the current proliferation of good restaurants specializing in California cuisine and European (especially Italian) cooking, various immigrant groups have recently arrived in San Diego, bringing their culinary traditions with them. The city now boasts a rich selection of Latin American, Middle Eastern, and Asian cuisines. The many Vietnamese restaurants throughout the city are especially noteworthy. Influenced by Chinese and French cooking styles, Vietnamese food retains its own character: Typically it is inexpensive, fresh, healthy, and very tasty. Particularly recommended are the noodle soups called "pho," the beef grilled in grape leaves, and the many dishes served to be wrapped at the table in lettuce and rice paper. Excellent Vietnamese restaurants, along with their equally good Chinese, Korean, and Japanese counterparts, can be found along Convoy Street and Linda Vista Road in Kearny Mesa; **My Ca'nh** (3904 Convoy St., tel. 619/268–4584) and **Phuong Trang** (4170 Convoy St., tel. 619/ 565–6750) are outstanding among them.

San Diego is an informal city. The advised attire at most of the restaurants listed below falls into three categories: "really casual," "casual," and "dressy casual." "Really casual" means you can come in directly from the beach and eat here if you throw on a shirt and flip flops. "Casual" indicates shorts are not a very good idea (except at lunch), and it's best if your jeans are clean and all in one piece. To the "casual" outfit add a sports jacket, stylish shirt, makeup, or some jewelry (or any combination thereof, depending on your inclination), and voilá—"dressy casual," appropriate for the majority of even the most expensive restaurants at dinnertime. Only one of the restaurants listed below requires men to wear ties.

Restaurants are grouped first by type of cuisine and then by location. Highly recommended restaurants are indicated by a star ★.

Category	Cost*
$$$$	over $50
$$$	$30–$50
$$	$20–$30
$	under $20

per person for a three-course meal, excluding drinks, service, and 7 ¾% tax

American
Downtown
★

Rainwater's. Located directly above the Pacifica Grill, this tony restaurant is as well known around town for the size of its portions as for the high quality of its cuisine. The menu includes a number of meat and fish dishes, but this is really the place to come if you crave a perfectly done, thick and tender steak. All the entrées are accompanied by such tasty side dishes as shoestring potatoes, onion rings, and creamed corn. The food is pricey, but the satisfaction level is high. *1202 Kettner Blvd. (second floor), tel. 619/233–5757. Reservations advised. Dress: dressy casual to jacket and tie. AE, DC, MC, V. No lunch weekends. $$$*

California Café. On the top level of Horton Plaza, this stylish dining room with lots of windows and potted palms serves stylish California cuisine to match. The imaginative menu, which changes daily, may include smoked duck ravioli with basil and goat cheese, soba noodle salad with lemon wasabi dressing and wild mushrooms, or New Mexican chili fettuccine with shrimp and smoked corn. The crusty Italian bread is baked daily on the premises. *Upper Level, Horton Plaza, tel. 619/238–5440. Reservations suggested. Dress: casual to dressy casual. AE, D, DC, MC, V. $$*

Pacifica Grill and Rotisserie. The local chain of Pacifica restaurants has been a mainstay of San Diego's dining renaissance. The downtown link, housed in a creatively refurbished former warehouse and featuring fresh, innovative, and reasonably priced cuisine, has developed a large group of loyal patrons. The crab cakes and the green-lip mussels appetizers are wonderful, and you can't go wrong with any of the fish dishes—say, the seared ahi with shiitake mushrooms—or the meats and poultry prepared on the rotisserie. If possible, save room for the justifiably famous crème brûlée. The selection of California wines is excellent. *1202 Kettner Blvd., tel. 619/696–9226. Reservations advised. Dress: dressy casual. AE, D, DC, MC, V. No lunch weekends. $$*

Croce's. A tribute to the late singer-songwriter Jim Croce run by his widow, Ingrid, the popular Croce's used to be known more for its nightly jazz and pleasant, clublike ambience than for its cuisine. But with a new chef in the kitchen, Croce's now complements its high-quality music with high-quality food. The menu offers good salads and a range of appealing entrées; try the swordfish in grape leaves or the chicken cakes. Even those who are not jazz aficionados will find this restaurant a good bet for late-night dining, since Croce's kitchen doesn't close until midnight. *802 5th Ave., tel.*

619/233–4355. *Reservations accepted. Dress: casual. AE, D, DC, MC, V. $*

Uptown   **Hob Nob Hill.** The type of place where regulars arrive on the same day of the week at the same time and order the same meal they've been having for the past 20 years, this comforting restaurant is still under the same ownership and management as it was when it started in 1944; with its dark wood booths and patterned carpets, Hob Nob Hill seems suspended in the 1950s. But you don't need to be a nostalgia buff to appreciate the bargain-priced American home cooking—dishes such as pot roast, fried chicken, and corned beef like your mother never really made. Reservations are particularly suggested on Sundays, when everyone comes for the copious breakfasts. *2271 1st Ave., tel. 619/239–8176. Reservations accepted. Dress: casual. AE, D, MC, V. $*

La Jolla   **Choices.** Off the beaten path and rather low on atmosphere—it's in the Sports and Health Center at the north end of the Scripps Clinic complex—this small cafeteria offers indoor and outdoor tables with an ocean view, and very tasty, low-fat, low-cholesterol food. There's an excellent all-you-can-eat salad bar and a daily selection of healthy sandwiches and entrées. Choices is open for breakfast and lunch during the week but closes at 7 PM Monday–Thursday; it shuts down at 3 PM on Friday but reopens at 6 PM for dinner and folk music. *10820 N. Torrey Pines Rd., tel. 619/554–3663. No reservations. Dress: casual. AE, MC, V. Closed weekends. $*
Hard Rock Cafe. If you've been to Hard Rock Cafes in other cities, you'll know what to expect here. This high-energy shrine to rock-and-roll and American food cranks its music up to ear-shattering decibels and hangs rock memorabilia on every available inch of wall space. This is not a place to come for intimate—or audible—conversation, but the burgers are fine and you can bring home a T-shirt to commemorate the occasion. You don't have to be accompanied by a teenager, although it helps. *909 Prospect St., tel. 619/454–5101. No reservations. Dress: casual. AE, D, MC, V. $*
Pannikin Brockton Villa. Connected with the local chain of trendy coffeehouses, this informal restaurant in a restored beach house overlooks La Jolla Cove and the ocean. Come here for good coffee, decent muffins and pastries, and stunning views. You'll have to fight the crowds on sunny weekends. The Pannikin opens for breakfast; call ahead for dinner hours (summer only). *1235 Coast Blvd., tel. 619/454–7393. No reservations. Dress: casual. AE, MC, V. Breakfast and lunch only Sept.–May. $*

Belgian   **Belgian Lion.** The lace curtains at the windows of a rather forbid-
Beaches   ding white building, partially enclosed by a high wall, are the only hints of the cozy dining room within, where hearty Belgian dishes have been served to discerning diners for years. Among the signature dishes is the cassoulet, a wonderful rich stew of white beans, lamb, pork, sausage, and duck that makes you feel protected from the elements (even in San Diego, where there aren't many elements to be protected from). Lighter meals include sea scallops with braised Belgian endive or steamed salmon with leeks. An impressive wine list was carefully designed to complement the food. *2265 Bacon St., Ocean Beach, tel. 619/223–2700. Reservations strongly advised. Dress: dressy casual. AE, D, DC, MC, V. Open Thurs.–Sat. only, dinner only. $$–$$$*

Cajun and   **Bayou Bar and Grill.** The ceiling fans revolving lazily over this at-
Creole   tractive room, with dark-green wainscoting and light-pink walls,
Downtown   help create a New Orleans atmosphere for the spicy Cajun and Cre-
★   ole specialties served here. You may start with a bowl of superb

Dining

Anthony's Star of the Sea Room, **74**

Athens Market, **75**

Bayou Bar and Grill, **76**

The Belgian Lion, **37**

Bella Luna, **80**

Berta's Latin American Restaurant, **47**

Cafe Japengo, **20**

Cafe Pacifica, **26**

California Café, **77**

California Cuisine, **55**

Calliope's Greek Cuisine, **78**

Canes California Bistro, **56**

Choices, **16**

Croce's, **68**

Dobson's, **69**

El Indio Shop, **73**

Fio's, **70**

The Fish Market, **71**

George's at the Cove, **1**

Hard Rock Café, **9**

Hob Nob Hill, **79**

Karinya Thai, **29**

Old Town Mexican Café, **46**

Pacifica Grill and Rotisserie, **63**

Palenque, **24**

Panda Inn, **64**

Panevino, **50**

Pannikin Brockton Villa, **5**

Rainwater's, **65**

Ristorante Piatti, **14**

SamSon's, **19**

Star of India, **10**

Thai Chada, **66**

Thai Saffron, **67**

Top O' the Cove, **7**

Tosca's, **27**

Trattoria la Strada, **83**

Triangles, **22**

Lodging

Bahia Resort Hotel, **32**

Balboa Park Inn, **57**

Bay Club Hotel & Marina, **42**

The Bed & Breakfast Inn at La Jolla, **8**

Best Western Hacienda Hotel Old Town, **45**

Best Western Inn by the Sea, **12**

Best Western Posada Inn, **43**

Catamaran Resort Hotel, **25**

Colonial Inn, **2**

Crystal Pier Motel, **23**

Dana Inn & Marina, **35**

Days Inn Hotel Circle, **52**

San Diego Dining and Lodging

La Jolla

Torrey Pines Rd.

Ardath Rd.

Gilman Dr.

Genesee

Soledad

Regents Rd.

Clairemont Dr.

San Diego Fwy.

La Jolla Blvd.

Mission Blvd.

Garnet Ave.

Grand Ave.

Ingraham St.

PACIFIC BEACH

MISSION BEACH

Mission Bay

Fiesta Island

Sea World

W. Mission Bay Dr.

OCEAN BEACH

Cliffs Blvd.

Nimitz Blvd.

Rosecrans Blvd.

Harbor Dr.

Harbor Island

Sunset Blvd.

Catalina Blvd.

Shelter Island

North Island

U.S. NAVAL AIR STATION

Memorial Dr.

Coronado Island

Cabrillo

Cabrillo National Monument

Point Loma

N

0 1 mile
0 1 km

KEY

American Express Office

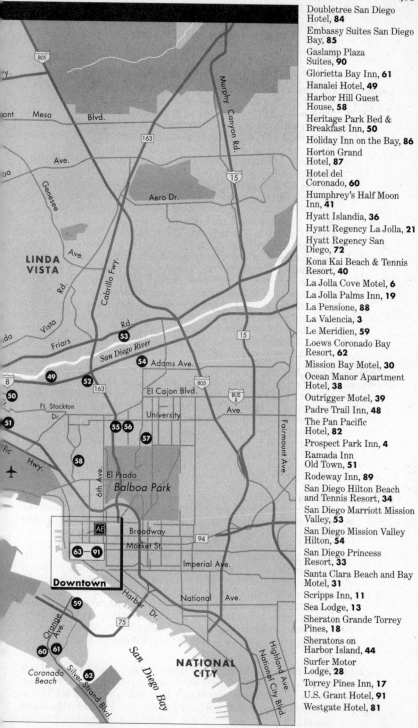

Doubletree San Diego Hotel, **84**

Embassy Suites San Diego Bay, **85**

Gaslamp Plaza Suites, **90**

Glorietta Bay Inn, **61**

Hanalei Hotel, **49**

Harbor Hill Guest House, **58**

Heritage Park Bed & Breakfast Inn, **50**

Holiday Inn on the Bay, **86**

Horton Grand Hotel, **87**

Hotel del Coronado, **60**

Humphrey's Half Moon Inn, **41**

Hyatt Islandia, **36**

Hyatt Regency La Jolla, **21**

Hyatt Regency San Diego, **72**

Kona Kai Beach & Tennis Resort, **40**

La Jolla Cove Motel, **6**

La Jolla Palms Inn, **19**

La Pensione, **88**

La Valencia, **3**

Le Meridien, **59**

Loews Coronado Bay Resort, **62**

Mission Bay Motel, **30**

Ocean Manor Apartment Hotel, **38**

Outrigger Motel, **39**

Padre Trail Inn, **48**

The Pan Pacific Hotel, **82**

Prospect Park Inn, **4**

Ramada Inn Old Town, **51**

Rodeway Inn, **89**

San Diego Hilton Beach and Tennis Resort, **34**

San Diego Marriott Mission Valley, **53**

San Diego Mission Valley Hilton, **54**

San Diego Princess Resort, **33**

Santa Clara Beach and Bay Motel, **31**

Scripps Inn, **11**

Sea Lodge, **13**

Sheraton Grande Torrey Pines, **18**

Sheratons on Harbor Island, **44**

Surfer Motor Lodge, **28**

Torrey Pines Inn, **17**

U.S. Grant Hotel, **91**

Westgate Hotel, **81**

seafood gumbo and then move on to the sausage, red beans, and rice, the duck esplanade, or any of the fresh Louisiana Gulf seafood dishes. A tempting selection of rich Louisiana desserts includes bread pudding, praline cheesecake, and Creole pecan pie. *329 Market St., tel. 619/696–8747. Dinner reservations suggested. Dress: casual. AE, D, DC, MC, V. Dinner only. $–$$*

California
Uptown
★

California Cuisine. Across the street from the Uptown district, this minimalist chic dining room—gray carpet, stark white walls, and black-and-white photographs of urban landscapes—offers a suitably innovative menu. Daily selections may include grilled fresh venison served with wild mushrooms and mashed potatoes; the tasty warm chicken salad entrée is a regular feature. You can count on whatever you order to be carefully prepared and elegantly presented. Service is knowledgeable and attentive, the wine list is good, and the desserts are seriously tempting. Heat lamps make the back patio a romantic year-round option. *1027 University Ave., tel. 619/543–0790. Reservations advised. Dress: dressy casual. AE, D, DC, MC, V. No lunch weekends; closed Mon. $$*

Canes California Bistro. A light-filled neighborhood bistro, whose walls are decked, appropriately enough, with canes of all kinds, Canes attracts a diverse group of diners, from senior citizens to families to Uptown trendies. They come for food that is similarly diverse—everything from meat loaf and mashed potatoes to hamburgers with sun-dried tomato *aioli* (garlic mayonnaise) to pastas with roasted garlic and gorgonzola—and consistently good. The weekend buffet brunch features excellent breakfast breads, French beef stew, and yellow corn pancakes with sour cream and golden caviar. *Vermont St. (at University), tel. 619/299–3551. Reservations advised. Dress: casual. AE, D, DC, MC, V. $–$$*

Chinese
Downtown
★

Panda Inn. Even if you're allergic to shopping, the Panda Inn is reason enough to come to Horton Plaza. Arguably the best Chinese restaurant in town, this dining room at the top of the Plaza serves subtly seasoned and attractively presented Mandarin and Szechuan dishes in an elegant setting that feels far removed from the rush of commerce below. The fresh seafood dishes are noteworthy, as are the Peking duck, spicy Szechuan green beans, and "burnt" pork. Indeed, it's hard to find anything on this menu that's not outstanding. *506 Horton Plaza, tel. 619/233–7800. Reservations advised. Dress: casual. AE, D, DC, MC, V. $–$$*

Continental
Downtown
★

Dobson's. At lunchtime, local politicos and media types rub elbows at the long, polished bar of this highly regarded restaurant; the show biz contingent arrives in the evening in stretch limos. Although the small two-tier building is suggestive of an earlier era—the lower level looks like a men's club and the upper level sports a wrought-iron balcony, elegant woodwork, and gilt cornices—there's nothing outdated about the cuisine. Among the range of carefully prepared entrées, which change daily, you may find roasted quail with fig sauce or chicken risotto. The tasty house salad is laced with fennel and goat cheese, and Dobson's signature dish, a superb mussel bisque, comes topped with a crown of puff pastry. The wine list is excellent. *956 Broadway Circle, tel 619/231–6771. Reservations advised. Dress: dressy casual. AE, DC, MC, V. No lunch Sat.; closed Sun. $$$*

La Jolla

Top O' the Cove. Although the reliable but rather stolid menu of this La Jolla institution has been surpassed by glitzier newcomers, year after year San Diego diners give high marks for romance to this cozy, intimate spot with a beautiful ocean view. The filet mignon and roasted rack of lamb are reliable choices; calorie-counters may opt for the boneless chicken breast sautéed with shrimp and shellfish or sliced duck breast with black-currant sauce. The service is attentive but not overbearing, and the award-winning wine list is enormous. *1216 Prospect St., tel. 619/454–7779. Reservations advised. Jacket and tie suggested. AE, DC, MC, V. $$$*

Triangles. In an attractive if slightly stiff setting—clubby dark wood booths in a contemporary high-rise bank building—this bar and grill in the Golden Triangle area strives for variety. The menu, which changes daily, may include sautéed sweetbreads, potato knishes, ravioli stuffed with porcini mushrooms, or shrimp cassoulet. Along with rich dishes, you'll also find many lighter and vegetarian preparations—nice for the health-conscious diner or the overstuffed vacationer. A small patio, surrounded by lush landscaping, is pleasant at lunch. *4370 La Jolla Village Dr., in the Northern Trust Bldg., tel. 619/453–6650. Reservations advised. Dress: dressy casual to jacket and tie. AE, D, MC, V. No lunch Sat.; closed Sun. $$–$$$*

Deli
La Jolla

SamSon's. As close as you'll come to a real Jewish deli in San Diego, SamSon's has dill pickles set out on the tables; the menu and portions are enormous. If you're having trouble deciding, go for one of the daily soup-and-sandwich specials, especially the whitefish when it's available. And you can't go wrong with a lox plate for breakfast (SamSon's opens at 7 AM) or a corned beef sandwich for lunch. The two ample dining rooms are decorated in corny show-biz style, with movie stills covering the walls. *8861 Villa La Jolla Dr., tel. 619/455–1462. Reservations accepted. Dress: really casual. AE, D, DC, MC, V. $*

Greek
Downtown

Athens Market. This cheerful eatery, decorated with Aegaean island scenes, bustles with downtown office workers and members of San Diego's small but active Greek community. As in many Greek restaurants, the appetizers here—such as *taramasalata* (fish roe dip) and stuffed grape leaves—can be superior to the somewhat heavy traditional beef and lamb entrées. Greek music, folk dancing, and belly dancers add to the festive atmosphere on weekend evenings. The adjacent Victorian-style coffeehouse, under the same ownership, keeps late hours for night owls in search of a caffeine fix. *109 W. F St., tel. 619/234–1955. Reservations suggested. Dress: casual. AE, D, DC, MC, V. $*

Uptown

Calliope's Greek Cuisine. One of the best Greek restaurants in town, Calliope moves beyond the standard Hellenic fare to offer tasty variations on traditional dishes. Included on the menu, along with a good moussaka and lamb souvlaki, are fettuccine Aegean, topped with shrimp, fresh fish, and mushrooms in a tomato wine sauce, and artichokes Athenian, served over linguine in a tomato-herb sauce. Fans of Greek wines will see not only the usual retsinas, but also a selection of harder-to-find regional bottles. The white-walled dining room is light and airy. *3958 5th Ave., tel. 619/291–5588. Dress: casual. Reservations suggested. AE, D, DC, MC, V. No lunch weekends. $–$$*

Indian
La Jolla

Star of India. Rather higher priced than most other local Indian restaurants, the Star of India offers the best Indian food in town in a soothing setting of bamboo and quiet pastels. Particularly recommended are the chicken *tikka masala*, prepared tandoori style in a cream and tomato curry, and *saag gosht*, lamb in a spinach curry. Seafood dishes are generally the least successful. The excellent nan bread, baked in the tandoor oven, comes either plain or stuffed with a variety of fillings. An all-you-can-eat buffet lunch, available daily, is a good way to satisfy your curiosity about a variety of different dishes. *1000 Prospect St., tel. 619/459–3355; 423 F St., tel. 554–9891;*

927 1st St., tel. 619/632–1113. Reservations suggested, especially on weekends. Dress: casual to dressy casual. AE, D, DC, MC, V. \$\$

Italian
Downtown

Bella Luna. A recent, welcome addition to the "Italianization" of 5th Avenue, this small, stylish restaurant, whose owner hails from the island of Capri, more than holds its own against its longer-established neighbors. Paintings of "beautiful moons" in many shapes and sizes adorn the walls, and the service is gracious and attentive. The menu features dishes from all over Italy: Try the stuffed mozzarella appetizer or the calamari in tomato sauce. Pastas are particularly recommended, especially the linguine *alle vongole verace* (with clams in their shells), the fettuccini with salmon, and the black squid-ink linguine served with a spicy seafood sauce; if you still have room for an entrée, consider the rack of lamb. *748 5th Ave., tel. 619/239–3222. Dress: dressy casual. Reservations advised. AE, MC, V. No lunch Sun. \$\$–\$\$\$*

★ **Trattoria La Strada.** La Strada specializes in Tuscan cuisine prepared so well that your taste buds will be convinced they've died and gone to Italy. Try the *antipasto di mare*, with tender shrimp and shellfish, or the salad La Strada, with wild mushrooms, walnuts, and delectable shaved parmesan. The pastas, particularly the *pappardelle all'anitra* (wide noodles with a duck sauce), are excellent. The noise level can be high in the two high-ceilinged dining rooms; if you don't feel like raising your voice, you can always check out the fashions worn by the stylish young diners. *702 5th Ave., tel. 619/239–3400. Reservations advised. Dress: dressy casual. AE, D, DC, MC, V. No lunch weekends. \$\$–\$\$\$*

Fio's. Glitzy young singles mingle with staid business-suit types in this lively, popular place, one of the earliest of the trendy Italian restaurants now proliferating in the Gaslamp District. Contemporary variations on traditional Italian cuisine are served in a high-ceilinged, brick-and-wood dining room overlooking the 5th Avenue street scene. The menu includes a range of imaginative pizzas baked in the wood-fired oven and the occasional hard-to-find classic Italian dish, such as the Emilian *ravioli di zucca*, ravioli stuffed with pumpkin and amaretto cookie crumbs, or the Tuscan *anitra in pignatto*, a casserole of preserved duck, sausage, and white beans. *801 5th Ave., tel. 619/234–3467. Reservations advised. Dress: dressy casual. AE, D, DC, MC, V. No lunch weekends. \$\$*

Panevino. This brick-walled Italian café is often crowded with diners who prefer its casual bistro atmosphere to the more trendy tone of neighboring restaurants. But the menu here is as *au courant* as any other in San Diego. Particularly recommended are the imaginative selection of pizzas and pastas: The spinach ravioli is always a good bet. You could easily make a meal of one of the excellent stuffed foccaccias and a salad or a plate of grilled vegetables, although a range of tasty and sometimes ambitious entrées is also offered; if it's available, try the quail cooked in balsamic vinegar. Panevino is one of the few good downtown restaurants outside of Horton Plaza that's open for lunch on weekends. *722 5th Ave., tel. 619/595–7959. Dress: casual to dressy casual. Reservations advised. AE, D, DC, MC, V. \$\$*

Beaches

Tosca's. This popular Pacific Beach eatery is in some ways typical of pizza restaurants everywhere, with its fluorescent lighting and red-checkered vinyl tablecloths. But you are, after all, in California, which means you can opt for wheat or semolina crusts for your individually sized pizzas or calzones; choose toppings or fillings from an array of exotic ingredients, including artichokes, pesto, and feta cheese; and wash it all down with a microbrew from Sierra Nevada (on tap, yet). The young servers are cheerful and helpful. *3780 Ingraham St., tel. 619/274–2408. Dress: casual. AE, D, DC, MC, V. $*

La Jolla **Ristorante Piatti.** On weekends, this trattoria-style restaurant is filled to overflowing with a lively mix of trendy singles and local families, who keep returning for the excellent country- style Italian food. A wood-burning oven turns out excellent breads and pizzas, and imaginative pastas include the *pappardelle fantasia* (wide saffron noodles with shrimp, fresh tomatoes, and arugula) and a wonderfully garlicky spaghetti *alle vongole* (served with clams in the shell). Among the *secondi* are good versions of roast chicken and Italian sausage with polenta. A fountain splashes softly on the tree-shaded patio, where heat lamps allow diners to sit out even on chilly evenings. *2182 Av. de la Playa, tel. 619/454–1589. Reservations strongly advised. Dress: dressy casual. AE, MC, V. $$*

Latin American **Berta's Latin American Restaurant.** A San Diego rarity—and particularly surprising in a section of town where the food often leans **Old Town** toward the safe and touristy—Berta's features a wide selection of Latin American regional dishes and a nice list of Latin American wines. While the wines are largely Chilean, the food, which manages to be wonderfully tasty and health-conscious at the same time, ranges all over the map. Try the Brazilian seafood *vatapa,* shrimp, scallops, and fish served in a sauce flavored with ginger, coconut, and chilis, or the Peruvian *pollo a la huancaina,* chicken with chilis and a feta cheese sauce. Service is friendly and helpful. The simple dining room is small, but there's also a patio. *3928 Twiggs St., tel. 619/295–2343. Reservations suggested on weekends. Dress: casual. AE, MC, V.*

Mexican **El Indio Shop.** El Indio has been serving some of the city's best **Uptown** Mexican fast food since 1940. The menu is extensive; try the large burritos, the *tacquitos* (fried rolled tacos) with guacamole, or the giant quesadillas. You can eat at one of the indoor tables or on the patio across the street; El Indio is also perfect for beach-bound take-out. *3695 India St., tel. 619/299–0333; 4120 Mission Blvd., tel. 619/272–8226; 409 F St., tel. 619/239–8151; 115 W. Olive Dr., San Ysidro, tel. 619/690–1122. Dress: really casual. D, MC, V. F. St. and San Ysidro shops closed Sun. $*

Old Town **Old Town Mexican Café.** Singles congregate at the bar and families crowd into the wooden booths of this boisterous San Diego favorite, decked out with plants and colorful piñatas; an enclosed patio takes the overflow from both groups. You'll find all the Mexican standards here, as well as specialties, such as *carnitas,* chunks of roast pork served with fresh tortillas and condiments. The enchiladas with spicy ranchero or green chili sauce are nice variations on an old theme. You can watch the corn tortillas being handmade on the premises and pick up a dozen to take home with you. *2489 San Diego Ave., tel. 619/297–4330. Reservations accepted for parties of 10 or more. Dress: casual. AE, D, MC, V. $*

Beaches **Palenque.** A welcome alternative to the standard Sonoran-style ★ café, this family-run restaurant in Pacific Beach serves a wonderful selection of regional Mexican dishes. Recommendations include the chicken with mole, served in the regular chocolate-based or green chili version and the mouth-watering *camarones en chipotle,* large shrimp cooked in a chili and tequila cream sauce (an old family recipe of the proprietor). Piñatas and paper birds dangle from the thatched ceiling, and seating is in comfortable round-backed leather chairs; a small deck in front is nice for warm-weather dining. Palenque is a bit hard to spot from the street and service is often slow, but the food is worth your vigilance and patience. *1653 Garnet Ave., Pacific Beach, tel. 619/272–7816. Reservations advised. Dress: casual. AE, D, DC, MC, V. $–$$*

Pacific Rim
La Jolla

Cafe Japengo. In one of the most stylish dining rooms in town, framed by elegant marbled walls, accented with leafy bamboo trees, and dotted with unusual black-iron sculptures, Cafe Japengo serves excellent Pacific Rim cuisine. The inspiration for this eclectic and imaginative menu is largely Asian, with many North and South American touches. There's a selection of grilled, wood-roasted, and wok-fried entrées for dinner; try the ten-ingredient fried rice, the shrimp and scallops with dragon noodles, or the grilled swordfish with wild mushrooms. The curry fried calamari and the Japengo potstickers appetizers are guaranteed to stimulate your taste buds. You can also order fine sushi from your table or from a seat at the sushi bar. Although it is located in the very trendy, postmodern Aventine center, Cafe Japengo largely escapes the frenzied, noisy singles scene characteristic of the other restaurants in the complex. Unfortunately, the quality of the service doesn't match that of the food. *8960 University Center La., tel. 619/450–3355. Reservations advised. Dress: dressy casual. AE, D, DC, MC, V. No lunch weekends. $$$*

Seafood
Downtown

Anthony's Star of the Sea Room. The Anthony's chain of local seafood restaurants, one of the oldest in San Diego, has long been serving up adequately prepared seafood dishes to tourists and residents alike. The flagship of the Anthony's fleet, the Star of the Sea Room, is much more formal and expensive than the others. The menu offers an enormous selection of fresh fish from around the world, and if the recipes are less exciting than those at other seafood restaurants, the magnificent harbor views go far in the way of compensation. Many of the dishes are prepared at the table. *1360 N. Harbor Dr., tel. 619/232–7408. Reservations strongly advised. Jacket and tie required. AE, D, DC, MC, V. Dinner only. $$$*

The Fish Market. This bustling, informal restaurant offers diners a choice from a large variety of extremely fresh fish, mesquite grilled and served with lemon and tartar sauce. Also good are shellfish dishes, such as steamed clams or mussels. Most of what is served here has lived in the water, but even dedicated fish-avoiders may think it worth their while to trade selection for the stunning view: Enormous plate-glass windows look directly out onto the harbor, and if you're lucky enough to get a windowside table, you can practically taste the salt spray. This is one of the rare places where families with young children can feel comfortable without sacrificing their taste buds. A more formal and expensive upstairs restaurant, The Top of the Market, offers a good Sunday brunch. *750 N. Harbor Dr., tel. 619/232–3474 for the Fish Market or 619/234–4867 for the Top of the Market; also in Del Mar, at 640 Via de la Valle, tel. 619/755–2277. Reservations accepted upstairs and for 8 or more downstairs, and at Del Mar. Dress: casual downstairs and at Del Mar, dressy casual upstairs. AE, D, DC, MC, V. $–$$$*

Old Town

Cafe Pacifica. Like its sister restaurant, Pacifica Grill and Rotisserie, Cafe Pacifica offers a menu that changes daily and features an impressive array of imaginative appetizers, salads, pastas, and entrées; it also does a crème brûlée worth blowing any diet for. The emphasis here is on seafood, however, and this restaurant serves some of the best in town. You can't go wrong with any of the fresh fish preparations grilled over mesquite and served with an herb-butter sauce, a Mexican-inspired salsa, or a fruit chutney. Other good bets include the tasty pan-fried catfish; yummy, greaseless fish tacos; and superb crab cakes. *2414 San Diego Ave., tel. 619/291–6666. Reservations advised. Dress: dressy casual. AE, D, DC, MC, V. $$–$$$*

La Jolla
★

George's at the Cove. At most restaurants you get either good food or good views; at George's, you don't have to choose. The elegant main dining room, with a wall-length window overlooking La Jolla Cove, is renowned for its daily fresh seafood specials; the menu also offers several good chicken and meat dishes. The delectable three-mushroom soup, accented with sherry and rosemary, or the salmon-and-shrimp sausage make fine starters. The charbroiled apple-smoked salmon entrée is highly recommended, as are any of the shellfish pastas. Desserts are uniformly excellent. For more informal dining, try the Cafe on the second floor. The outdoor Terrace, on the top floor, affords a sweeping view of the coast; wonderful for breakfast, lunch, or brunch on a fine day, the Terrace (like the Cafe) does not take reservations, so you may have a wait. *1250 Prospect St., tel. 619/454–4244. Reservations advised for the main dining room. Dress: Main room, dressy casual to jacket and tie; Cafe and Terrace, casual. AE, D, DC, MC, V. Main room, $$$; Cafe and Terrace, $$*

Thai
Uptown
★

Thai Chada. Don't be put off by appearances. Although it's housed in a corner building that looks like a hamburger joint, this is one of the best Thai restaurants in town; the large windows and comfortable booths provide a low-key setting for consistently excellent food. Try any of the noodle dishes, especially the *pad thai*, rice noodles fried with fresh shrimp, egg, bean sprouts, scallions, and ground peanuts; the Tom Ka Kai chicken soup, with coconut milk, lemon grass, lime juice, and scallions; or the roast duck curry. A sister restaurant, Thai Chada 2, has recently opened in Pacific Beach. *142 University Ave., tel. 619/297–9548; Thai Chada 2, 1749 Garnet Ave., tel. 619/270–1888. Reservations advised. Dress: casual. AE, D, DC, MC, V. Sat. lunch at Thai Chada 2 only; both restaurants closed Sun. lunch. $–$$*

Thai Saffron. In recent years, San Diego has seen an upsurge in the growth of take-out restaurants offering tasty, health-conscious food. Saffron is one of the earliest and best of the eateries that specialize in chicken spit-roasted over a wood fire, accompanied by an appealing selection of side dishes. The chicken is wonderfully moist and comes with a choice of sauces: Try the peanut or chili. Among the accompaniments, the Cambodian salad is particularly fresh and crunchy. There's limited outdoor seating, but this is an ideal place to pick up lunch or dinner to take to Mission Bay or the beach. *3731B India St., tel. 619/574–0177. No reservations. Dress: casual. MC, V. $*

Beaches

Karinya Thai. This popular restaurant in Pacific Beach serves excellent Thai cuisine in a relaxed but pretty setting; in one room, diners recline on colorful floor cushions at low tables. It's hard to go wrong with any of the dishes on the extensive menu. You could concoct a meal from appetizers alone: The stuffed chicken wings and spicy fish cakes are particularly recommended. Among the entrées, the scallops in three sauces, beef strips with broccoli, and pad thai noodles are all worth a try. *4475 Mission Blvd., tel. 619/270–5050. Reservations suggested. Dress: casual. No lunch Sat.–Mon. MC, V. $–$$*

Lodging

*By Sharon K.
Gillenwater*

*Revised by
Edie Jarolim*

There are accommodations in San Diego to satisfy every taste, ranging from grand luxury high rises to funky beach cottages. Because new hotels are continually under construction, the city has a surplus of rooms—which means lower prices for those who shop around. The older properties in Hotel Circle frequently offer special rates and free tickets to local attractions, while many luxury hotels promote lower-priced weekend packages to fill rooms after the week's convention and business customers have departed. When you call to make reservations, find out if the place you're interested in is running any specials. It's always a good idea to book well in advance, especially during the busy summer season.

San Diego is very spread out, so the first thing to consider when selecting lodgings here is location. The various neighborhoods are rather diverse: You can choose to stay in the middle of a bustling metropolitan center or to kick back in a serene beach getaway. If you select one of the many hotels with a waterfront location and extensive outdoor sports facilities, you need never leave the premises. If you plan to do a lot of sightseeing, however, you may take into account a hotel's proximity to the attractions you most want to visit. In general, price need not be a major factor in your decision: Even the most expensive areas offer some reasonably priced—albeit rather modest—rooms.

If you are planning an extended stay or if you need lodgings for four or more people, you may consider an apartment rental. **Oakwood Apartments** (Oakwood Mission Bay West, 3866 Ingraham St., 92109; Oakwood Mission Bay E, 3883 Ingraham St., 92109, tel. 619/490–2100 booking for both) offers comfortable, furnished apartments in the Mission Bay area with maid service and linens; there's a minimum 30-day stay. At **San Diego Vacation Rentals** (1565 Hotel Circle S, Suite 390, 92108, tel. 619/296–1000), you can rent a coastal home or condo at competitive weekly and monthly rates; brochures of rentals are available on request.

Those wishing to find bed-and-breakfast accommodations in town can contact the **Bed & Breakfast Guild of San Diego** (tel. 619/523–1300), which currently lists eight high-quality member inns.

Highly recommended hotels are indicated by a star ★.

Category	Cost*
$$$$	over $165
$$$	$110–$165
$$	$70–$110
$	under $70

All prices are for a double room in high (summer) season, excluding 9% room tax.

Coronado

Although Coronado doesn't have as many lodging facilities as some areas, it has a number of outstanding properties, and staying here is a unique experience: This quiet, out-of-the-way place feels as though it exists in an earlier, more gracious era. The peninsula, home to many wealthy retirees and naval personnel from the North Island Naval Air station, is connected to the mainland by the Silver Strand isthmus, but most tourists come here via the Coronado Bay Bridge or the ferry that leaves from San Diego's Embarcadero.

Boutiques and restaurants line Orange Avenue, the main street, and the beaches are fine, but if you plan to see many of San Diego's attractions, you'll probably spend a lot of time commuting across the bridge or riding the ferry.

$$$$
★
Le Meridien. Flamingos greet you at the entrance of this French-owned resort, and other exotic wildlife roam the 16 acres of lushly landscaped grounds. This is a modern, $90 million complex, but it doesn't shout "I'm new and expensive": Instead, the low-slung, Cape Cod–style buildings perfectly capture Coronado's understated old-money ambience. The large rooms and suites are done in a cheerful California–country French fashion, with rattan chairs, blue-and-white-striped cushions, and lots of colorful Impressionist art; all rooms have separate showers and tubs. The glamorous spa facilities are excellent—sauna; steam; and facials, massages, and wraps—and the fitness schedule includes yoga and power walks, along with aerobics and step classes. *2000 2nd St., 92118, tel. 619/435–3000 or 800/543–4300, fax 619/435–3032. 300 rooms. Facilities: 2 restaurants, 3 pools, 2 whirlpools, spa, exercise room, aerobics, 6 lighted tennis courts, marina, shops. AE, D, DC, MC, V.*

$$$$
Loews Coronado Bay Resort. You can park your boat at the 80-slip marina of this resort, set on a 15-acre private peninsula on the Silver Strand. Didn't bring it along this time? Never mind. You can rent one here. Rooms are somewhat formally but tastefully decorated, with pale yellows, pinks, and greens, and flowered bedspreads; all have furnished balconies with views of water—either bay, ocean, or marina. The Commodore Kids Club offers a nice variety of programs for children ages 4–12, and there's nightly entertainment in the hotel lounge. *4000 Coronado Bay Rd., 92118, tel. 619/424–4000, fax 619/424–4400. 450 rooms, 31 suites. Facilities: 3 restaurants, deli, fitness center, marina, 5 lighted tennis courts, 3 pools, 2 spas, bicycle rentals, boat, Windsurfer and Jet-Ski rentals, shops. AE, D, DC, MC, V.*

$$$–$$$$
Hotel del Coronado. Built in 1888, "the Del" is a historic and social landmark (*see* Exploring San Diego, *above*, for details). The rooms and suites in the original ornate Victorian building are charmingly quirky. Some have sleeping areas that seem smaller than the baths, while others are downright palatial; two are even said to come with a resident ghost. The public areas are grand, if perhaps a bit dark for modern tastes; a lower-level shopping arcade lined with historic photographs is fascinating, but tear yourself away to stroll around the hotel's lovely manicured grounds. More standardized accommodations are available in the newer high rise. *1500 Orange Ave., 92118, tel. 619/435–6611 or 800/468–3533, fax 619/522–8238. 691 rooms. Facilities: 3 restaurants, deli, pool, Jacuzzi, steamroom, sauna, croquet, bicycles, 6 lighted tennis courts, beach, shopping arcade. AE, D, DC, MC, V.*

$$–$$$
Glorietta Bay Inn. The main building of this property—located across the street from the Hotel Del, adjacent to the Coronado harbor, and near many restaurants and shops—was built in 1908. Rooms here and in the newer motel-style buildings are attractively furnished and all have refrigerators. Tours of the island's historical buildings depart from the inn's lobby three mornings a week (cost: $5). *1630 Glorietta Blvd., 92118, tel. 619/435–3101 or 800/283–9383, fax 619/435–6182. 98 rooms. Facilities: pool, bicycle rentals. AE, D, DC, MC, V.*

Downtown
Downtown San Diego is still reaping the benefits of a redevelopment effort that began in the early 1980s and attracted many new hotels to the area. There is much to see within walking distance of downtown accommodations—Seaport Village, the Embarcadero, the his-

toric Gaslamp Quarter, a variety of theaters and night spots, and the spectacular Horton Plaza shopping center. The zoo and Balboa Park are also nearby. In addition, a number of good restaurants have opened in this part of town in the past few years. For nonstop shopping, nightlife, and entertainment, downtown can't be beat. Visitors should be aware, however, that the neighborhood is still rather transitional; many streets are rather deserted at night, and street hustlers and homeless people mingle with the crowds of tourists and office workers during the daytime.

$$$$ **Doubletree San Diego Hotel.** Although it is fronted by a startling lighted blue obelisk, this 1987 high rise is all understated marble, brass, and glass inside. The rooms are similarly elegant and low-key, with muted sea-green and coral color schemes. The lobby lounge is packed every night with local financiers and weary shoppers from the adjacent Horton Plaza; a piano player tinkles the ivories there on weekends. *910 Broadway Circle, 92101, tel. 619/239–2200 or 800/528–0444, fax 619/239–0509. 450 rooms. Facilities: restaurant, lobby lounge, sports bar, 2 lighted tennis courts, sauna, spa, pool, health club. AE, D, DC, MC, V.*

$$$$ **Hyatt Regency San Diego.** Opened in late 1992 adjacent to Seaport Village, this high rise successfully combines Old World opulence with California airiness and space. Palm trees pose next to ornate tapestry couches in the high-ceiling, light-filled lobby, and all of the masculine, British Regency–style guest rooms have views of the water. Although its proximity to the convention center attracts a large business trade, this hotel also offers well-heeled leisure travelers an excellent location and fine facilities. *One Market Place, tel. 619/232–1234 or 800/233–1234, fax 619/233–6464. 875 rooms. Facilities: 2 restaurants, health club with weight room, steam, sauna, classes, spa, massage, 4 tennis courts, marina, piano lounge, shops. AE, D, DC, MC, V.*

$$$$ **The Pan Pacific Hotel.** The excellent office and conference facilities at this striking pink hotel, built in 1991, draw business travelers, but the Pan Pacific is also fine for vacationers who want to be near all the downtown sights and restaurants; many of the upper-floor accommodations offer panoramic views of the city. This hotel has a very good health club and such extras as a complimentary airport shuttle. *400 W. Broadway, 92101, tel. 619/239–4500 or 800/626–3988, fax 619/239–3274. 436 rooms. Facilities: 2 restaurants; lounge; heated pool; spa; sun deck; fitness club with lap pool, massage, tanning, sauna, steam room, weight room, and classes; business center; shops. AE, D, DC, MC, V.*

$$$–$$$$ ★ **Westgate Hotel.** A nondescript modern high rise hides what must be the most opulent hotel in town: The lobby, modeled after the anteroom at Versailles, has hand-cut Baccarat chandeliers; rooms are furnished with antiques and Italian marble counters; and bath fixtures have 14-karat-gold overlays. There are breathtaking views of the harbor and the city from the ninth floor up, and afternoon high tea is served in the lobby to the accompaniment of harp music. All this doesn't come cheap, but rates are lower than such luxury would seem to warrant. For a change of venue, the trolley can take you to Tijuana right from the hotel, and complimentary transportation is available within the downtown area. *1055 2nd Ave., 92101, tel. 619/238–1818 or 800/221–3802; in CA, 800/522–1564; fax 619/557–3737. 223 rooms. Facilities: 3 restaurants, lounge, exercise room, beauty salon, barber. AE, D, DC, MC, V.*

$$$ **Embassy Suites San Diego Bay.** It's a short walk to the convention center, the Embarcadero, and Seaport Village from one of downtown's most popular hotels. The front door of each spacious suite

opens out onto the hotel's 12-story atrium. The contemporary-style decor is pleasant, and the views from rooms facing the harbor are spectacular. Business travelers will find it easy to set up shop here, and families can make good use of the in-room refrigerators, microwaves, and separate sleeping areas. A cooked-to-order breakfast and afternoon cocktails are complimentary, as are airport transfers. *601 Pacific Hwy., 92101, tel. 619/239–2400 or 800/362–2779, fax 619/239–1520. 337 suites. Facilities: restaurant, sports bar, pool, Jacuzzi, sauna, exercise room, gift shop. AE, D, DC, MC, V.*

$$$ **Holiday Inn on the Bay.** On the Embarcadero and overlooking San Diego Bay, this high-rise hotel is convenient for vacationers as well as business travelers. Rooms are unsurprising but new and comfortable, and views from the balconies are hard to beat. *1355 N. Harbor Dr., 92101, tel. 619/232–3861 or 800/465–4329, fax 619/232–4914. 600 rooms, 17 suites. Facilities: restaurant, lounge, lobby bar, heated pool, Jacuzzi, laundry facilities, complimentary airport and Amtrak shuttle. AE, D, DC, MC, V.*

$$$ **Horton Grand Hotel.** A delightful Victorian confection opened in 1986 in the heart of the historic Gaslamp District, the Horton Grand comprises two 1880s hotels moved brick by brick from nearby locations. It features delightfully retro rooms, individually furnished with period antiques, ceiling fans, and gas-burning fireplaces. The choicest rooms are those overlooking a garden courtyard, which twinkles with miniature lights each night. There's high tea in the afternoon and jazz in the evening. The place is a charmer, but service can be a bit erratic. *311 Island Ave., 92101, tel. 619/544–1886, 800/542–1886, or 800/HERITAGE; fax 619/239–3823. 132 rooms. Facilities: restaurant, lounge, Chinatown museum. AE, D, DC, MC, V.*

$$$ **U.S. Grant Hotel.** Built in 1910 and reopened in 1985, this San Diego classic is just across the street from Horton Plaza. Crystal chandeliers and marble floors in the lobby and Queen Anne–style mahogany furnishings in the rooms hark back to a more gracious era when such dignitaries as Charles Lindbergh and Franklin D. Roosevelt stayed here (this was also an era when rooms were somewhat small). These days, high-power business types still gather at the hotel's Grant Grill. In early 1994, the hotel was bought by the same company that owns the Horton Grand; renovations of the public areas are in the works. *326 Broadway, 92101, tel. 619/232–3121, 800/237–5029, or 800/HERITAGE; fax 619/232–3626. 280 rooms. Facilities: restaurant, piano lounge, exercise room, dress shop. AE, D, DC, MC, V.*

$$–$$$ **Balboa Park Inn.** Directly across the street from Balboa Park, this charming European-style bed-and-breakfast inn was built in 1915 and restored in 1982. Prices are reasonable for the one- and two-bedroom suites with kitchenettes, which can accommodate two to four people; they're housed in four two-story buildings connected by courtyards. Each suite has a different flavor—Italian, French, Spanish, or early Californian; some have fireplaces, wet bars, or whirlpool tubs. Continental breakfast and a newspaper are delivered to guests every morning. *3402 Park Blvd., 92103, tel. 619/298–0823 or 800/938–8181, fax 619/294–8070. 26 suites with baths. Facilities: sun terrace, deck, outdoor bar. AE, D, DC, MC, V.*

$$ **Harbor Hill Guest House.** This B&B offers quaint, comfortable rooms in a three-story home, with an entryway and kitchenette on each level; a carriage house connected to the main house provides a romantic getaway. Continental breakfast is included, and families are welcome. *2330 Albatross St., 92101, tel. 619/233–0638. 5 rooms with bath. MC, V.*

$–$$ **Gaslamp Plaza Suites.** Built in 1913 as San Diego's first "sky-
★ scraper," this 11-story structure in the Gaslamp district is only a

block from Horton Plaza. It's listed on the National Register of Historic Places; elegant public areas boast lovely old marble, brass, and mosaic. Accommodations—either petite- or one-bedroom suites— are done in shades of burgundy and pink in attractive European style, with contemporary dark wood furniture. Guests can enjoy the view and a complimentary Continental breakfast and newspaper on the rooftop terrace. Many of the rooms rent as time shares; book ahead if you're visiting in high season. *520 E St., 92101, tel. 619/232-9500 or 800/443-8012, fax 619/238-9945. 63 suites. Facilities: restaurant, complimentary airport and Amtrak shuttle. AE, MC, D, DC, V.*

$–$$ ★ **Rodeway Inn.** Situated on one of the better streets downtown, this property is clean, comfortable, and nicely decorated. *833 Ash St., 92101, tel. 619/239-2285, 800/228-2000, or 800/522-1528 in CA, fax 619/235-6951. 45 rooms. Facilities: spa, sauna. AE, D, DC, MC, V.*

$ ★ **La Pensione.** At long last, a decent budget hotel downtown, with daily, weekly, and monthly rates; it's convenient to the restaurants and cafés of the city's version of Little Italy. Rooms are modern, clean, and well designed, with good working areas and kitchenettes. Another location, with 106 units, has a pretty central courtyard and harbor views from some of the rooms. *1700 India St., 92101, tel. 619/236-8000, fax 619/263-8088. 86 rooms. 1546 2nd Ave., 92101, tel. 619/236-9292, fax 619/236-9988. 106 rooms. Reservations tel. 800/232-HOTEL for both. 86 rooms. Facilities: kitchenettes, laundry facilities. AE, MC, V.*

$ ★ **Super 8 Bayview.** There's nothing fancy about this motel, but the location is less noisy than those of other low-cost establishments. The accommodations are nondescript but clean. *1835 Columbia St., 92101, tel. 619/544-0164 or 800/537-9902, fax 619/237-9940. 101 rooms. Facilities: complimentary Continental breakfast, airport and Amtrak courtesy van, car rental agency, laundry facilities, free parking. AE, DC, MC, V.*

Harbor Island/Shelter Island/Point Loma Two man-made peninsulas between downtown and the lovely community of Point Loma, Harbor Island and Shelter Island are both bordered by grassy parks, tree-lined paths, lavish hotels, and good restaurants. Harbor Island is closest to the downtown area and less than five minutes from the airport, while narrower Shelter Island is nearer to Point Loma. Both locations command breathtaking views of the bay and the downtown skyline. Not all the lodgings listed here are on the islands themselves, but all are in their vicinity.

$$$$ **Sheratons on Harbor Island.** Converted in 1992 into a single complex connected by a shuttle bus, former neighbors Sheraton Grand (now called the West Tower) and Sheraton Harbor Island East (the East Tower) are now legally married, but they retain their own personalities. The West Tower, which attracts business travelers, is the more luxurious of the two: Well-appointed rooms have large tables for paperwork and a separate area for entertaining. The East Tower, upgraded and expanded in a $32 million 1994 renovation, is more vacation oriented, with excellent sports facilities. Rooms in both towers afford sweeping views from the upper floors. *1380 Harbor Island Dr., 92101, tel. 619/291-2900 or 800/325-3535, fax 619/291-4847 (West), 619/543-0643 (East). 1,050 rooms. Facilities: 2 restaurants, bakery-deli, 2 lounges, 4 lighted tennis courts, sauna, spa, 3 pools, health club with fitness classes and massage, jogging trails, boat rentals, complimentary airport transfers. AE, D, DC, MC, V.*

$$$ **Bay Club Hotel & Marina.** Rooms in this appealing low-rise Shelter Island property are large, light, and attractively furnished with rattan tables and chairs and Polynesian tapestries; all have refrigerators and offer views of either the bay or the marina from outside

terraces. A buffet breakfast and limo service to the airport or Amtrak are included in the room rate. *2131 Shelter Island Dr., 92106, tel. 619/224–8888 or 800/672–0800, 800/833–6565 in CA, fax 619/225–1604. 105 rooms. Facilities: restaurant, pool, spa, exercise room, gift shop, free underground parking. AE, D, DC, MC, V.*

$$–$$$ **Humphrey's Half Moon Inn.** This sprawling South Seas–style resort
★ has many grassy open areas with palm trees and tiki torches. The rooms are attractive, with rattan furnishings and nautical-style lamps; some have harbor or marina views. Locals throng to Humphrey's, the on-premises seafood restaurant, and to the jazz lounge; the hotel also hosts outdoor jazz concerts June–October. *2303 Shelter Island Dr., 92106, tel. 619/224–3411 or 800/542–7400 (Mon.–Fri. 8–5), 800/345–9995 (reservations), fax 619/224–3478. 182 rooms. Facilities: restaurant, lounge, putting green, pool, spa, bicycles, pingpong, croquet, marina, gift shop, complimentary newspapers and airport/Amtrak transfers. AE, D, DC, MC, V.*

$$ **Best Western Posada Inn.** One of the more upscale members of the Best Western chain, the Posada Inn is not on Harbor Island but is located on one of the neighboring thoroughfares adjacent to Point Loma. Many of the rooms, which are clean, comfortable, and nicely furnished, have wonderful views of the harbor. A number of excellent seafood restaurants are within walking distance. *5005 N. Harbor Dr., 92106, tel. 619/224–3254 or 800/528–1234, fax 619/224–2186. 112 rooms. Facilities: restaurant, pool, spa, exercise room, lounge, complimentary airport transfers. AE, D, DC, MC, V.*

$$ **Kona Kai Beach and Tennis Resort.** Looking like a Polynesian ski lodge—thatched on the outside, with a fireplace and soaring roof indoors—the Kona Kai completed a needed sprucing up of its rooms and public areas in 1994. The hotel, which doubles as a members-only club for locals, has good sports facilities. *1551 Shelter Island Dr., 92106, tel. 619/222–1191, 800/KONA–KAI, fax 619/222–9738. 153 rooms. Facilities: 2 restaurants, lounge, health club, 2 lighted tennis courts, volleyball and racquetball, 2 pools, spa, private beach. AE, D, DC, MC, V.*

$ **Outrigger Motel.** A good bet for those traveling as a family, this
★ motel, adjacent to the two resort peninsulas, is less expensive than its offshore counterparts and offers large rooms with eat-in kitchens. Across the street from the Outrigger are fishing docks and the famous Point Loma Seafoods Market and Restaurant. It's a short, scenic walk along the bay from here to Harbor Island. *1370 Scott St., 92106, tel. 619/223–7105. 37 rooms with kitchens. Facilities: pool, laundry facilities. AE, D, DC, MC, V.*

Hotel Circle/ Lining both sides of the stretch of I–8 that lies between Old Town
Mission and Mission Valley are a number of moderately priced accommoda-
Valley/Old tions that constitute the so-called Hotel Circle. A car is an absolute
Town necessity here, since the only nearby road is the busiest freeway in San Diego. Although not particularly scenic or serene, this location is convenient to Balboa Park, the zoo, downtown, the beaches, the shops of Mission Valley, and Old Town. Old Town itself has a few picturesque lodgings and is developing a crop of modestly priced chain hotels along nearby I–5; when you're making reservations, request a room that doesn't face the freeway.

$$$–$$$$ **San Diego Marriott Mission Valley.** This high rise sits in the middle
★ of the San Diego River valley, where the dry riverbed has been graded and transformed over the years into a commercial zone with sleek office towers and sprawling shopping malls. It has lots of facilities for business travelers but also caters to vacationers, with comfortable rooms, a friendly staff, a piano lounge, a disco, and free transportation to the malls. *8757 Rio San Diego Dr., 92108, tel.*

619/692–3800 or 800/228–9290, fax 619/692–0769. 350 rooms. Facilities: restaurant, lounge, pool, tennis court, exercise room, sauna, whirlpool, disco, gift shop, free parking. AE, D, DC, MC, V.

$$$–$$$$
★

San Diego Mission Valley Hilton. Directly fronting I–8, this property has soundproofed rooms decorated in contemporary southwestern style. When you're indoors, the attractive modern accommodations, along with the stylish public areas and lush greenery in the back, make you forget this business-oriented hotel's proximity to the freeway. Children stay free, and small pets are accepted. 901 Camino del Rio S, 92108, tel. 619/543–9000, 800/733–2332, or 800/HILTONS, fax 619/296–9561. 350 rooms. Facilities: restaurant, sports bar–lounge, spa, pool, fitness center, complimentary parking and airport and shopping transfers. AE, D, DC, MC, V.

$$$

Best Western Hacienda Hotel Old Town. This pretty white hotel, with balconies and Spanish tile roofs, is in a quiet part of Old Town, away from the freeway and the main retail bustle. The layout of this former shopping complex is a bit confusing, and accommodations are not really large enough to earn the "suite" label the hotel gives them, but they're decorated in tasteful southwestern style and equipped with microwaves, coffee makers, minifridges, clock radios, and VCRs. 4041 Harney St., 92110, tel. and fax 619/298–4707 or 800/888–1991. 150 suites. Facilities: restaurant, pool, free indoor parking. AE, D, DC, MC, V.

$$$

Hanalei Hotel. As its name suggests, the theme of this friendly Hotel Circle property is Hawaiian: Palm trees, waterfalls, koi ponds, and tiki torches abound here. A two-story complex offers poolside rooms, and a high-rise building surrounds a lovely Hawaiian-style garden. The rooms were refurbished in 1993–94 with tropical prints in rich colors; some have tile floors, and others have wall-to-wall carpeting. Guests have access to an adjacent golf course. 2270 Hotel Circle N, 92108, tel. 619/297–1101 or 800/882–0858, fax 619/297–6049. 412 rooms. Facilities: 2 restaurants, lounge, pool, spa, free parking and transport to Mission Valley. AE, D, DC, MC, V.

$$–$$$

Heritage Park Bed & Breakfast Inn. One of the restored mansions of Heritage Park in Old Town, this romantic 1889 Queen Anne has eight quaint guest rooms and a suite decorated with period antiques. Breakfast and afternoon refreshments are included in the room rate. This appealing lodging has gone through a number of owners in the past few years. 2470 Heritage Park Row, 92110, tel. 619/295–7088 or 800/995–2470. 6 rooms with bath, 2 rooms with shared bath, 1 2-bedroom suite. AE, MC, V.

$

Days Inn Hotel Circle. Rooms in this large complex are generally par for the chain-motel course but have the perk of a small refrigerator; some units also have stoves. 543 Hotel Circle S, 92108, tel. 619/297–8800 or 800/227–4743 (weekdays only), 800/325–2525 (reservations), fax 619/298–6029. 280 rooms. Facilities: restaurant, pool, spa, laundry, hair salon. AE, D, DC, MC, V.

$

Padre Trail Inn. This standard, family-style motel is located slightly southwest of Mission Valley. Old Town, shopping, and dining are all within walking distance. 4200 Taylor St., 92110, tel. 619/297–3291 or 800/255–9988, fax 619/692–2080. 100 rooms. Facilities: restaurant, lounge, pool. AE, D, DC, MC, V.

La Jolla Million-dollar homes line the beaches and hillsides of La Jolla, one of the world's most beautiful, prestigious communities. The village—the heart of La Jolla—is chock-a-block with expensive boutiques, galleries, and restaurants. Don't despair, however, if you're not old money or even nouveau riche; this popular vacation spot has sufficient lodging choices for every pocket, even those on a budget.

$$$$ **Hyatt Regency La Jolla.** Designed by Michael Graves (who counts New York's Whitney Museum among his projects), the Hyatt is the cornerstone of the Aventine complex in La Jolla's Golden Triangle, about 10 minutes from the beach and the village. The postmodern mix of design elements of the striking lobby is carried out into the spacious, comfortable rooms, where warm cherry wood furnishings contrast with austere gray closets (their stainless-steel handles make them look rather like large wall safes). The hotel's four trendy restaurants include the excellent Cafe Japengo (*see* Dining, *above*); you can work off some of the calories at one of the best health clubs in the city. Rates are lower on the weekends at this business-oriented hotel. *3777 La Jolla Village Dr., 92122, tel. 619/552–1234 or 800/233–1234, fax 619/552–6066. 400 rooms and suites. Facilities: 4 restaurants, lounge, outdoor pool and spa, 2 lighted tennis courts, health club with track and basketball court. AE, D,DC, MC, V.*

$$$–$$$$ **La Valencia.** A La Jolla landmark, this pink Art Deco confection
★ drew film stars down from Hollywood in the 1930s and '40s for its lovely setting and views of La Jolla Cove. The clientele is a bit older and more staid these days, but the hotel is still in prime condition. Many of the individually decorated rooms have a genteel European look, with antique pieces and plush, richly colored rugs. The restaurants are excellent, the Whaling Bar is a popular gathering spot, and the hotel is ideally located near the shops and restaurants of La Jolla village and what is arguably the prettiest beach in San Diego. Prices are quite reasonable if you're willing to look out on the village, but on a clear, sunny day, the ocean views may be worth every extra penny. *1132 Prospect St., 92037, tel. 619/454–0771 or 800/451–0772, fax 619/456–3921. 100 rooms. Facilities: 3 restaurants, lounge, whirlpool, pool, exercise room, library. AE, MC, V.*

$$$–$$$$ **Sea Lodge.** This low-lying compound, on the excellent La Jolla Shores beach, has a definite Spanish flavor to it, with its palm trees, fountains, red-tiled roofs, and Mexican tile work. The attractive rooms feature rattan furniture, nautical-design bedspreads, and terra-cotta lattice-board walls; all have hair dryers, coffee makers, and refrigerators, as well as wooden balconies that overlook lush landscaping and the sea. Early reservations are a must; families will find plenty of room and distractions for both kids and parents. *8110 Camino del Oro, 92037, tel. 619/459–8271 or 800/237–5211, fax 619/456–9346. 128 rooms, 19 with kitchenettes. Facilities: restaurant, lounge, heated pool, hot tub, sauna, beach, 2 tennis courts, pitch-and-putt golf course, ping-pong. AE, D, DC, MC, V.*

$$$–$$$$ **Sheraton Grande Torrey Pines.** The view of the Pacific from this low-
★ rise, high-class property atop the Torrey Pines cliffs is superb. The hotel blends into the clifftop, looking rather insignificant until you step inside the luxurious lounge and look out at the sea and the 18th hole of the lush green Torrey Pines golf course. Amenities include 24-hour concierge service, butler service, limousine service, a health club, a business center, and an excellent restaurant. The oversized rooms, decorated in off-white and pale pastels, are simple but elegant; all have balconies. *10950 N. Torrey Pines Rd., 92037, tel. 619/558–1500 or 800/325–3535, fax 619/450–4584. 400 rooms. Facilities: restaurant, lounge, pool, health club, 3 tennis courts, in-room safes, complimentary transportation within 5 miles. AE, D, DC, MC, V.*

$$$ **Colonial Inn.** A tastefully restored Victorian-era building, this is the oldest hotel in La Jolla, offering turn-of-the-century elegance in its public spaces; in keeping with the period, rooms are a bit formal and staid. Ocean views cost more than village views. On one of La Jolla's main thoroughfares but not in the thick of its busiest people traffic, the Colonial Inn is near boutiques, restaurants, and the cove. *910*

Prospect St., 92037, tel. 619/454–2181, 800/832–5525, or 800/826–1278 in CA; fax 619/454–5679. 75 rooms. Facilities: restaurant, lounge, pool, complimentary Continental breakfast, morning newspaper, and valet parking. AE, DC, MC, V.

$$$ **La Jolla Cove Motel.** Offering studios and suites, some with spacious oceanfront balconies, this motel overlooks the famous La Jolla Cove beach. If it doesn't have the charm of some of the older properties of this exclusive area, this motel gives its guests the same first-class views at much lower rates. The free underground lot is also a bonus in a section of town where a parking spot is a prime commodity. *1155 S. Coast Blvd., 92037, tel. 619/459–2621 or 800/248–2683. 110 rooms. Facilities: solarium, sun deck, putting green, freshwater pool, spa, kitchenettes available, laundry room, complimentary Continental breakfast. AE, D, DC, MC, V.*

$$$ **Scripps Inn.** You'd be wise to make reservations well in advance for this small, quiet inn tucked away on Coast Boulevard. Available kitchen facilities and lower weekly and monthly rates (not available in the summer season) make it particularly attractive to long-term guests. All the rooms are individually decorated; many offer ocean views and some have fireplaces or terraces. A lovely Continental breakfast is served in the lobby each morning. *555 Coast Blvd. S, tel. 619/454–3391, fax 619/459–6758. 13 rooms. Facilities: kitchenettes. AE, D, MC, V.*

$$–$$$$ **The Bed & Breakfast Inn at La Jolla.** Built in 1913 by Irving Gill, this B&B is located in a quiet section of La Jolla just down the street from the Museum of Contemporary Art. The individually decorated rooms cover a wide range of sizes and styles—some are done in Laura Ashley prints, others feature wicker or rattan furnishings—but all are pretty and well tended and come with fresh fruit, sherry, and terry robes. The lovely gardens in the back were planned by Kate Sessions, who was instrumental in landscaping Balboa Park. *7753 Draper Ave., 92037, tel. 619/456–2066. 16 rooms, 15 with private baths. Facilities: gardens, sun deck, library, refrigerators and hair dryers in some rooms. MC, V.*

$$–$$$ **Best Western Inn by the Sea.** In a quiet section of La Jolla Village, within five blocks of the beach, the five-story Inn by the Sea has all the modern amenities at reasonable rates for La Jolla. Rooms are done in cheerful pastel tones and have private balconies with views of either the sea or the village. Continental breakfast and newspaper are included in the room rate. *7830 Fay Ave., 92037, tel. 619/459–4461 or 800/462–9732. 132 rooms. Facilities: pool, Jacuzzi, exercise room, car rental desk, free parking. AE, D, DC, MC, V.*

$$ ★ **Prospect Park Inn.** This European-style inn rents a wide variety of appealing rooms, many with sweeping ocean views from their balconies. Located in a prime spot in La Jolla village, it's near some of the best shops and restaurants in town and one block away from the beach. Continental breakfast is included in the very reasonable room rate, and parking is free. There is no smoking on the premises. *1110 Prospect St., 92037, tel. 619/454–0133 or 800/433–1609, fax 619/454–2056. 23 rooms. Facilities: kitchenettes, lounge. AE, D, DC, MC, V.*

$$ ★ **Torrey Pines Inn.** Located on a bluff between La Jolla and Del Mar, this hotel commands a view of miles and miles of coastline. It's adjacent to the public Torrey Pines Golf Course, one of the best in the county, and very close to scenic Torrey Pines State Beach and nature reserve; the village of La Jolla is a 10-minute drive away. Most of the rooms have been renovated with dark wood furnishings and Oriental fabrics; they're more attractive than the older, rather generic accommodations. This off-the-beaten-path inn is a very good value, especially for golfers. *11480 N. Torrey Pines Rd., 92037, tel. 619/453–*

4420, 800/995–4507, or 800/777–1700 for reservations, fax 619/453–0691. 74 rooms. Facilities: restaurant, coffee shop, 2 bars, pool, adjacent golf course. AE, D, DC, MC, V.

$-$$ ★ **La Jolla Palms Inn.** In the southern section of La Jolla, near some excellent beaches, this modest motel is also near a wide variety of shops and restaurants. Many of the rooms are remarkably large, with huge closets; some have kitchenettes, and three suites offer separate eat-in kitchens. The rooms—done in pastel tones—are nothing to write home about, but this is an excellent value for families who want to stay in this tony area and still have a few dollars left over for shopping. *6705 La Jolla Blvd., 92037, tel. 619/454–7101 or 800/451–0358, fax 619/454–6957. 59 rooms. Facilities: heated pool, spa, pool table, guest laundry, complimentary Continental breakfast. AE, D, DC, MC, V.*

Mission Bay and Beaches Staying near the water is a priority for most people who visit San Diego. Mission and Pacific beaches have the highest concentration of small hotels and motels. Mission Bay Park, with its beaches, bike trails, boat-launching ramps, golf course, and grassy parks, is also a hotel haven. You can't go wrong with any of these locations, as long as the frenzy of hundreds at play doesn't bother you.

$$$–$$$$ ★ **Catamaran Resort Hotel.** If you check in at the right time, parrots will herald your arrival at this appealing hotel, set between Mission Bay and Pacific Beach; the two resident birds are often poised on a perch in the lushly landscaped lobby, replete with a koi fish pond. The grounds are similarly tropical, and tiki torches light the way for guests staying at one of the six two-story buildings or the 14-story high rise (the view from the upper floors of the latter is spectacular). The popular Cannibal Bar hosts Top 40s and rock-and-roll groups, while a classical or jazz pianist tickles the ivories at the Moray Bar; Catamaran guests can also take advantage of the entertainment facilities at the sister Bahia Hotel. Children 18 or under stay free. *3999 Mission Blvd., 92109, tel. 619/488–1101, 800/288–0770, or 800/233–8172 in Canada, fax 619/490–3328. 312 rooms. Facilities: restaurant, coffee shop, nightclub, piano bar-lounge, pool, spa, exercise room, water-sports rentals, evening bay cruises, gift shop; full kitchens available. AE, D, DC, MC, V.*

$$$–$$$$ **San Diego Hilton Beach and Tennis Resort.** Spread out on the picturesque grounds of this deluxe resort, low-level bungalows are surrounded by trees, Japanese bridges, and ponds; a high-rise building offers accommodations with lovely views of Mission Bay Park. Rooms in all the buildings are done in attractive contemporary style and have all the expected amenities. The Kids Club Program offers complimentary day care for children over age 5, and the sports facilities on the property are excellent. *1775 E. Mission Bay Dr., 92109, tel. 619/276–4010 or 800/445–8667, fax 619/275–7991. 354 rooms. Facilities: restaurant, coffee shop, lounge, pool, 4 whirlpools, putting greens, 5 lighted tennis courts, exercise room, playground, hotel yacht, shops. AE, D, DC, MC, V.*

$$$ **Bahia Resort Hotel.** This huge complex, on a 14-acre peninsula in Mission Bay Park, offers tastefully furnished studios and suites with kitchens; many have wood-beamed ceilings and attractive tropical decor. The hotel's *Bahia Belle* cruises Mission Bay at sunset, and guests can return for yuks at the on-premises Comedy Isle club. Rates are reasonable for a place so well located—within walking distance of the ocean—and offering so many amenities, including use of the facilities at the Catamaran Hotel. *998 W. Mission Bay Dr., 92109, tel. 619/488–0551, 800/288–0770, or 800/233–8172 in Canada, fax 619/490–3328. 313 rooms. Facilities: restaurant; 2 lighted tennis*

courts; water-sports, bicycle, and roller-blade rentals; spa, pool, evening bay cruises, comedy club. AE, D, DC, MC, V.

$$$ **Crystal Pier Motel.** You can drive your car onto the Crystal Pier and park in front of one of this classic motel's blue and white cottages, equipped with kitchenettes and patios overlooking the sea. You'll be lulled to sleep by the gentle lapping of waves against wooden pilings; the cries of sea gulls provide a pleasant wake-up call. A landmark since the 1930s, this place is no longer the bargain it once was, nor does it have the amenities of the other properties in its price category; you're paying for character and a unique proximity to the ocean. But it retains a loyal following nevertheless; call four to six weeks in advance for reservations. Weekly rates are available in winter. *4500 Ocean Blvd., tel. 619/483–6983 or 800/748–5894, fax 619/483–6811. 26 cottages. Facilities: kitchens, parking. 3-night minimum stay June 15–Sept. 15. D, MC, V.*

$$$ **San Diego Princess Resort.** You'll feel as though you're staying in a
★ self-sufficient village if you book one of the cottages in this 44-acre resort, so beautifully landscaped that it's been the setting for a number of movies. The wide range of amenities includes access to a marina and beaches. All the accommodations have refrigerators and private patios, and a number have bay views. With something for everyone, this hotel is favored by upscale families, particularly during the summer. The hotel underwent a major renovation in 1993–94. *1404 W. Vacation Rd., 92109, tel. 619/274–4630 or 800/344–2626, fax 619/581–5929. 462 cottages. Facilities: 3 restaurants, 6 tennis courts, 5 pools, bicycle and boat rentals, croquet, 18-hole putting golf course, shuffleboard, volleyball courts, jogging path. AE, D, DC, MC, V.*

$$–$$$ **Hyatt Islandia.** Located in Mission Bay Park, one of San Diego's most appealing seashore areas, the Islandia has rooms in several low-level, lanai-style units, as well as marina suites and rooms in a high-rise building. Many of the tastefully modern accommodations overlook the hotel's gardens and fish pond; others have dramatic views of the bay area. This hotel is famous for its lavish Sunday champagne brunch. In winter, whale-watching expeditions depart from the Islandia's marina. *1441 Quivira Rd., 92109, tel. 619/224–1234 or 800/233–1234, fax 619/224–0348. 423 rooms. Facilities: 2 restaurants, pool, spa, marina with sailboat or sportfishing rentals. AE, D, DC, MC, V.*

$$ **Dana Inn & Marina.** This hotel, which has an adjoining marina, is a bargain in the Mission Bay area. If accommodations are not as grand as those in the nearby hotels, they're more than adequate. There are many on-premises sports facilities, and the Dana Inn is within walking distance of Sea World. *1710 W. Mission Bay Dr., 92109, tel. 619/222–6440 or 800/345–9995, fax 619/222–5916. 196 rooms. Facilities: restaurant, pool, spa, marina, boat rentals, 2 lighted tennis courts, shuffleboard, ping-pong. AE, D, DC, MC, V.*

$$ **Surfer Motor Lodge.** This high rise is right on the beach and directly behind a shopping center with many restaurants and boutiques. Rooms are plain, but those on the upper floors have excellent views. *711 Pacific Beach Dr., 92109, tel. 619/483–7070 or 800/787–3373, fax 619/274–1670. 52 rooms. Facilities: restaurant, cocktail lounge, pool. AE, DC, MC, V.*

$–$$ **Ocean Manor Apartment Hotel.** Some folks have been returning for
★ 20 years to this well-priced Ocean Beach hotel, which rents units by the day (three-day minimum for those with kitchens), week, or month in winter; you'll need to reserve months in advance. Ocean Manor offers lovely views; the beach below has long since washed away, but other beaches are within walking distance and Point Loma is a 10-minute drive away. The comfortable studios and one- and two-bedroom suites are furnished plainly in the style of the 1950s—

which is when the amiable owners took over the place. There is no maid service, but fresh towels are always provided. *1370 Sunset Cliffs Blvd., 92107, tel. 619/222–7901 or 619/224–1379. 22 units. Facilities: pool, shuffleboard, ping-pong, garages. MC, V.*

$ **Mission Bay Motel.** Located a half-block from the beach, this motel offers centrally located, modest units, some with refrigerators. Great restaurants and nightlife are within walking distance, but you may find the area a bit noisy. *4221 Mission Blvd., 92109, tel. 619/483–6440. 50 rooms. Facilities: pool. MC, V.*

$ **Santa Clara Beach and Bay Motel.** This small, no-frills motel is a block from the ocean and right in the middle of restaurant, nightlife, and shopping activity in Mission Beach. All the units have refrigerators. Weekly rates are available. *839 Santa Clara Pl., 92109, tel. 619/488–1193. 17 rooms. AE, MC, V.*

The Arts and Nightlife

The Arts

By Marael Johnson

Revised by Lori Chamberlain

Top national touring companies perform regularly at the Civic Theatre, Golden Hall, Symphony Hall, and East County Performing Arts Center. San Diego State University, the University of California at San Diego, private universities, and community colleges present a wide variety of performing arts programs, from appearances by well-known artists to student recitals. The daily *San Diego Union* lists current attractions and complete movie schedules. The *Reader,* a free weekly that comes out each Thursday, devotes an entire section to upcoming cultural events, as well as current theater and film reviews. *San Diego* magazine publishes a monthly "What's Doing" column that lists arts events throughout the county and reviews of current films, plays, and concerts.

It is best to book tickets well in advance, preferably at the same time you make hotel reservations. There are various outlets for last-minute tickets, though you risk either paying top rates or getting less-than-choice seats—or both.

Half-price tickets to most theater, music, and dance events can be bought on the day of performance at the **TIMES ARTS TIX Ticket Center** (Horton Plaza, tel. 619/238–3810). Only cash is accepted. Advance full-price tickets may also be purchased through ARTS TIX.

Visa and MasterCard holders may buy tickets for many scheduled performances through **Ticketmaster** (tel. 619/278–8497). Service charges vary according to the event, and most tickets are nonrefundable.

Theater
Coronado Playhouse (1775 Strand Way, Coronado, tel. 619/435–4856). This cabaret-type theater, near the Hotel del Coronado, stages regular dramatic and musical performances. Dinner packages are offered on Friday and Saturday.

La Jolla Playhouse (Mandell Weiss Center for the Performing Arts, University of California at San Diego, tel. 619/550–1010). From May to November, look for exciting and innovative presentations, under the artistic direction of Michael Greif. Many Broadway productions, such as *A Walk in the Woods, Big River,* and works by Neil Simon, have previewed here before heading for the East Coast.

Lawrence Welk Resort Theatre (8860 Lawrence Welk Dr., Escondido, tel. 619/749–3448 or 800/932–9355). About a 45-minute drive from downtown, this famed dinner theater puts on polished Broadway-style productions with a professional cast.

Old Globe Theatre (Simon Edison Centre for the Performing Arts, Balboa Park, tel. 619/239–2255). The oldest professional theater in California performs classics, contemporary dramas, experimental works, and puts on the famous summer Shakespeare Festival at the Old Globe and its sister theaters, the Cassius Carter Centre Stage and the Lowell Davies Festival Theatre.

San Diego Comic Opera (Casa del Prado Theatre, Balboa Park, tel. 619/231–5714). Four different productions of Gilbert and Sullivan and similar works are given October–July.

Sledgehammer Theatre (1620 6th Ave., tel. 619/544–1484). One of the cutting-edge theaters in San Diego, Sledgehammer stages avant-garde pieces in St. Cecilia's church.

Sushi Performance and Visual Art (633 9th Ave., tel. 619/235–8466). This nationally acclaimed group provides an opportunity for well-known performance artists to do their thing.

Concerts   **Copley Symphony Hall** (1245 7th Ave., tel. 619/699–4200). The San Diego Symphony is the only California symphony that has its own concert hall. The performance season runs October–May, with a series of outdoor pop concerts held near Seaport Village during the summer.

Open-Air Theatre (San Diego State University, tel. 619/594–6884). Top-name rock, reggae, and popular artists pack in the crowds for summer concerts under the stars.

Organ Pavilion (Balboa Park, tel. 619/226–0819). Robert Plimpton performs on the giant 1914 pipe organ at 2 PM on most Sunday afternoons and on most Monday evenings in summer. All concerts are free.

Sherwood Auditorium (700 Prospect St., La Jolla, tel. 619/454–2594). Many classical and jazz events are held in the 550-seat auditorium in the San Diego Museum of Contemporary Art. August–May, La Jolla Chamber Music Society presents internationally acclaimed chamber ensembles, orchestras, and soloists. San Diego Chamber Orchestra, a 35-member ensemble, performs once a month, October–April.

Sports Arena (2500 Sports Arena Blvd., tel. 619/224–4176). Big-name rock concerts play to more than 14,000 fans, using an end-stage configuration, so all seats face in one direction.

Spreckels Theatre (121 Broadway, tel. 619/235–9500). This beautiful downtown theater, built more than 80 years ago and designated a landmark in 1972, hosts a wide range of musical events—everything from Mostly Mozart to small rock concerts. Ballets and theatrical productions are also held here. Its good acoustics, as well as its historical interest, make this an appealing place to come for a show of any kind.

Opera   **Civic Theatre** (202 C St., tel. 619/236–6510). The San Diego Opera draws international artists and has developed an impeccable reputation. The season of five operas runs January–April in the 3,000-seat, state-of-the-art auditorium. English translations of works sung in their original languages are projected on a large screen above the stage.

Dance   **California Ballet** (tel. 619/560–5676). Four high-quality contemporary and traditional works, from story ballets to Balanchine, are performed September–May. The *Nutcracker* is staged annually at the Civic Theatre; other ballets take place at Poway Center for the Performing Arts (15500 Espola Rd., Poway, tel. 619/748–0505), the Lyceum, and Nautilus Bowl at Sea World.

Issacs McCaleb & Dancers (tel. 619/296–9523). Interpretative dance presentations, incorporating live music, are staged at major theaters and concert halls around San Diego County.

Nightlife

By Dan Janeck

Revised by Jon and Noonie Corn

The unbeatable variety of sun-and-surf recreational activities is the prime reason tourists come to San Diego, but most visitors are surprised and delighted by the new momentum the city gains after dark. The highly mercurial nightlife scene is constantly growing— the flavor of the month may be Top 40 or contemporary, reggae, pop-jazz, or strictly rock-and-roll. Live pop and fusion jazz have become especially popular—some say they are the ideal music for San Diego's typically laid-back lifestyle—and they can easily be found at a dozen or so venues throughout the county. Music at local rock clubs and nightclubs ranges from danceable contemporary Top 40 to original rock and new wave by San Diego's finest up-and-coming groups. Discotheques and bars in the Gaslamp Quarter and at Pacific and Mission beaches tend to be the most crowded spots in the county on the weekends, but don't let that discourage you from visiting these quintessential San Diego hangouts. Authentic country-western music is also an option for those willing to go a bit farther afield. And should your tastes run to softer music, there are plenty of piano bars in which to unfrazzle and unwind. Check the free weekly *Reader* for band information or *San Diego* magazine's "Restaurant & Nightlife Guide" for the full range of nightlife possibilities.

California law prohibits the sale of alcoholic beverages after 2 AM. Bars and nightclubs usually stop serving at about 1:40 AM. You must be 21 to purchase and consume alcohol, and most places will insist on current identification. Be aware that California also has some of the most stringent drunk-driving laws in the United States; sobriety checkpoints are not an uncommon sight.

Bars and Nightclubs

Club Fifth Avenue. One of the Gaslamp Quarter's newer night spots, this place is fast becoming one of the more popular destinations for San Diego's young professionals. There's a dress code (no jeans, T-shirts, or tennis shoes) on Friday and Saturday night. Entertainment varies nightly, and there is a nominal cover charge. *835 5th Ave., downtown, tel. 619/238–7191. Open Tues.–Sun. 8 PM–2 AM. AE, D, DC, MC, V.*

Diego's. This remodeled Mexican restaurant features a party patio and volleyball court and attracts a festive, sophisticated beach crowd as well as students from nearby San Diego State. *860 Garnet Ave., Pacific Beach, tel. 619/272–1241. Open nightly 9 PM–2 AM. AE, D, MC, V.*

The Green Circle. One of the newer spots in town, this place defies easy classification. But you'll enjoy yourself if you like modern rock played by up-and-coming bands and colorful DJs. *827 F St., Gaslamp Quarter, tel. 619/232–8080. Open Tues.–Sun. 7:30 PM–2 AM. MC, V.*

Megalopolis. This funky little club isn't nearly as large or as flashy as the name may suggest, but an eclectic roster of blues, rock, and folk bands is reason enough to visit. *4321 Fairmount Ave., Kensington, tel. 619/584–7900. Open Tues.–Sat. 8 PM–2 AM. No credit cards.*

Patrick's II. This downtown pub with definite Irish tendencies is a prime place to hear live New Orleans–style jazz, blues, and rock. *428 F St., downtown, tel. 619/233–3077. Entertainment nightly 9 PM–2 AM. No credit cards.*

Jazz Clubs

Elario's. This club, on the top floor of the Summer House Inn, has an ocean view and an incomparable lineup of internationally acclaimed jazz musicians every month. *7955 La Jolla Shores Dr., La Jolla, tel. 619/459–0541. Nightly shows at 8:20, 9:45, and 11 PM. AE, DC, MC, V.*

Humphrey's. This is the premier promoter of the city's best jazz, folk, and light-rock summer concert series held out on the grass. The rest of the year the music moves indoors for some first-rate jazz Sunday and Monday. *2241 Shelter Island Dr., tel. 619/523–1010 for taped concert information. Entertainment 8 PM–midnight. AE, D, DC, MC, V.*

The Marine Room. Waves literally crash against the windows here while jazz groups play. *2000 Spindrift Dr., La Jolla, tel. 619/459–7222. Entertainment nightly 6 PM–12:30 AM. AE, D, DC, MC, V.*

Pal Joey's. This comfortable neighborhood bar features jazz and urban blues Friday and Saturday nights. *5147 Waring Rd., Allied Gardens, near San Diego State University, tel. 619/286–7873. Entertainment 9 PM–1:30 AM. MC, V.*

Rock Clubs

Belly Up Tavern. Located in converted Quonset huts, this eclectic live-concert venue hosts critically acclaimed artists who play everything from reggae, rock, new wave, Motown, and folk to—well, you name it. Always a fun choice, the Belly Up attracts people of all ages. Sunday nights are usually free and feature local R&B artists. *143 S. Cedros Ave., Solana Beach, tel. 619/481–9022. Open daily 11 AM–1:30 AM. Entertainment 9:30 PM–1:30 AM. MC, V.*

Bodie's. This Gaslamp Quarter bar hosts the best rock and blues bands in San Diego, as well as up-and-coming bands from out of town. *528 F St., tel. 619/236–8988. Open daily 6 AM–2 AM. No credit cards.*

Casbah. This small club showcases rock, reggae, funk, and every other kind of band—except Top 40—every night of the week. *2812 Kettner Blvd., near the airport, tel. 619/294–9033. Live bands at 9:30 nightly. No credit cards.*

Old Bonita Store & Bonita Beach Club. This South Bay hangout attracts singles 25–35 and features locally produced rock acts. *4014 Bonita Rd., Bonita, tel. 619/479–3537. Entertainment nightly 8:30 PM–1:30 AM. AE, MC, V.*

Spirit. This original-music club emphasizes the top local alternative and experimental-rock groups. *1130 Buenos Ave., Bay Park, near Mission Bay, tel. 619/276–3993. Open nightly 8 PM–1 AM. No credit cards.*

Country-Western Clubs

Big Stone Lodge. The rustic dance hall, formerly a Pony Express station in the last century, now showcases the two-steppin' tunes of the house band, consisting of the owners. If you don't know country-western dances, don't fret; free lessons are given on some nights. *12237 Old Pomerado Rd., Poway, tel. 619/748–1135. Entertainment Tues.–Thurs. 8 PM–12:30 AM, Fri. and Sat. 9 PM–1:30 AM, Sun. 5:30 PM–9:30 PM. DC, MC, V.*

In Cahootz. A great sound system, live bands, and a large dance floor make this lively spot a choice destination for cowgirls and -boys and city slickers alike. Free dance lessons (Sun., Mon., Tues., and Thurs. nights), free dinners, and military and ladies nights are among the many incentives this bar provides for you to stop by. *5373 Mission Center Rd., Mission Valley, tel. 619/291–8635. Open weeknights 5 PM–2 AM, weekends 5:30 PM–2 AM. AE, MC, V.*

Leo's Little Bit O' Country. This is the largest country-western dance floor in the county—bar none. Leo's is another fun place to come for free dance lessons. *680 W. San Marcos Blvd., San Marcos,*

tel. 619/744–4120. Open Tues.–Sat. 4 PM–1 AM, Sun. 5 PM–1 AM. Entertainment 8:30 PM–1 AM, Sun. 6:30 PM–midnight. Closed Mon. MC, V.

Wrangler's Roost. This is a country-western haunt that appeals to
both the longtime cowboy customer and the first-timer. Free dance
lessons start at 8 PM. 6608 Mission Gorge Rd., tel. 619/280–6263. Entertainment 9 PM–2 AM. MC, V.

Comedy Clubs	**Comedy Isle.** Located in the Bahia Resort Hotel, this club offers the latest in local and national talent. 998 W. Mission Bay Dr., Mission Bay, tel. 619/488–6872. Shows Wed., Thurs., and Sun. 8:30, Fri. and Sat. 8:30 and 10:30. Reservations accepted. AE, DC, MC, V.

The Comedy Store. In the same tradition as the Comedy Store in
West Hollywood, San Diego's version hosts some of the best national
touring and local talent. 916 Pearl St., La Jolla, tel. 619/454–9176. One
show Tues.–Thurs. at 8 PM, 2 shows Fri. and Sat. at 8 PM and 10:30
PM. Closed Sun. AE, MC, V.

The Improv. This is a superb Art Deco–style club with a distinct East
Coast feel, where some of the big names in comedy present their
routines. 832 Garnet Ave., Pacific Beach, tel. 619/483–4520. One show
Sun.–Thurs. at 8 PM, 2 shows Fri. and Sat. at 8 PM and 10:30 PM.
Sunday is no-smoking night. AE, MC, V.

Discos   **Club Diego's.** This flashy discotheque and singles scene by the beach
has excellent, nonstop dance music and friendly young (25–35) danc-
ers. 860 Garnet Ave., Pacific Beach, tel. 619/272–1241. Open Tues.–
Sun. 9 PM–1:30 AM. AE, MC, V.

Club Emerald City. Alternative dance music and an uninhibited clientele keep this beach-town spot unpredictable—which is just fine
with everyone. 945 Garnet Ave., Pacific Beach, tel. 619/483–9920.
Open Mon.–Sat. 8:30 PM–2 AM. Closed Sun. No credit cards.

Johnny M's. You'll work up a sweat with lawyers and surfers alike
at this huge disco. A blues room is open from 10 PM to 1:30 AM, and
the DJ plays from 8 PM until 1:30 AM. 801 4th St., Gaslamp Quarter,
tel. 619/233–1131. Open Sun.–Thurs. 11 AM–midnight, Fri. and Sat.
until 2 AM. AE, D, MC, V.

Piano Bars   **Hotel del Coronado.** The fairy-tale hostelry that has hosted royalty
and former presidents features beautiful piano music in its Crown
Room and Palm Court, with dance-oriented standards in the Ocean
Terrace Lounge. 1500 Orange Ave., Coronado, tel. 619/435–6611.
Open daily 10:30 AM–1:30 AM. AE, D, DC, MC, V.

Top O' the Cove. Show tunes and standards from the '40s to the '80s
are the typical piano fare at this magnificent Continental restaurant
in La Jolla. 1216 Prospect St., tel. 619/454–7779. Entertainment Wed.–
Sun. 8 PM–11 PM. AE, MC, V.

Westgate Hotel. One of the most elegant settings in San Diego offers
piano music in the Plaza Bar. 1055 2nd Ave., downtown, tel. 619/238–
1818. Open daily 11 AM–2 AM. Entertainment 8:30 PM–closing. AE, D,
DC, MC, V.

Excursion to the San Diego North Coast

By Kevin Brass

Revised by Edie Jarolim

To say the north coast area of San Diego County is different from
the city of San Diego is a vast understatement. From the northern
tip of La Jolla to Oceanside, a half-dozen small communities each
developed separately from urban San Diego—and from one another. The rich and famous were drawn early on to Del Mar, for
example, because of its wide beaches and thoroughbred horse-rac-

ing facility. Just a couple of miles away, agriculture, not paparazzi, played a major role in the development of Solana Beach and Encinitas. Up the coast, Carlsbad still reveals elements of roots directly tied to the old Mexican rancheros and the entrepreneurial instinct of John Frazier, who told people the area's water could cure common ailments. In the late 19th century, not far from the current site of the posh La Costa Hotel and Spa, Frazier attempted to turn the area into a massive replica of a German mineral springs resort.

Today, the north coast is a booming population center. An explosion of development throughout the 1980s turned the area into a northern extension of San Diego. The freeways started to take on the typically cluttered characteristics of most southern California freeways.

Beyond the freeways, though, the communities have maintained their charm. Some of the finest restaurants, beaches, and attractions in San Diego County can be found in the area, a true slice of southern California heritage. From the plush estates and rolling hills of Rancho Santa Fe and the beachfront restaurants of Cardiff to Mission San Luis Rey, a well-preserved remnant of California's first European settlers in Oceanside, the north coast is a distinctly different place.

Important Addresses and Numbers

Carlsbad Convention and Visitors Bureau (Box 1246, Carlsbad 92008, tel. 619/434–6093). **Del Mar Chamber of Commerce** (1401 Camino del Mar, Suite 101, Del Mar 92014, tel. 619/793–5292). **Oceanside Chamber of Commerce** (928 North Hill St., Oceanside 92051, tel. 619/722–1534).

Arriving and Departing

By Car Interstate 5, the main freeway artery connecting San Diego to Los Angeles, follows the coastline. To the west, running parallel to it, is Old Highway 101, which never strays more than a quarter-mile from the ocean. Beginning north of La Jolla, where it is known as Torrey Pines Road, Old Highway 101 is a designated scenic route, providing access to the beauty of the coastline.

By Train **Amtrak** (tel. 619/481–0114 in Del Mar, 619/722–4622 in Oceanside, or 800/872–7245) operates trains daily between Los Angeles, Orange County, and San Diego, with stops in Del Mar and Oceanside. The last train leaves San Diego at approximately 9 PM each night; the last arrival is at approximately midnight.

By Bus **The San Diego Transit District** covers the city of San Diego up to Del Mar, where the **North County Transit District** (tel. 619/722–6283) takes over, blanketing the area with efficient, on-time bus service.

    Greyhound (tel. 619/722–1587 in Oceanside, or 800/231–2222) has regular routes connecting San Diego to points north, with stops in Del Mar, Solana Beach, Encinitas, and Oceanside.

By Taxi Several companies are based in North County, including **Amigo Cab** (tel. 619/436–8294) and **Bill's Cab Co.** (tel. 619/755–6737).

By Plane **Palomar Airport** (tel. 619/431–4646), located in Carlsbad 2 miles east of I–5 on 2198 Palomar Airport Road, is a general aviation airport run by the county of San Diego and open to the public. Commuter airlines sometimes have flights from Palomar to Orange County and Los Angeles.

Guided Tours

Civic Helicopters (2192 Palomar Airport Rd., tel. 619/438–8424) offers whirlybird tours of the area. The tours run about $70 per person per half-hour and go along the beaches to the Del Mar racetrack.

Exploring

Numbers in the margin correspond to points of interest on the San Diego North Coast map.

Any journey around the north coast area naturally starts at the beach, and this one begins at **Torrey Pines State Beach,** just south of Del Mar. At the south end of the wide beach, perched on top of ❶ the cliffs, is the **Torrey Pines State Reserve,** one of only two places (the other place is Santa Rosa Island off the coast of northern California) where the Torrey pine tree grows naturally (*see* La Jolla, in Exploring San Diego, *above,* for details). *Tel. 619/755–2063. Admission: $4 per car. Open daily 9–sunset.*

❷ To the east of the state beach is **Los Penasquitos Lagoon,** one of the many natural estuaries that flow inland between Del Mar and Oceanside. Following Old Highway 101, the road leads into the small village of **Del Mar,** best known for its chic shopping strip, celebrity visitors, and wide beaches. Years of spats between developers and ❸ residents have resulted in the **Del Mar Plaza,** hidden by boulder walls and clever landscaping at the corner of Old Highway 101 and 15th Street. The upper level has a large deck and a view out to the ocean, and the restaurants and shops are excellent barometers of the latest in southern California style. A left turn at 15th Street leads to Seagrove Park, a small stretch of grass overlooking the ocean, where concerts are performed on summer evenings. A right turn on Coast Boulevard provides access to Del Mar's beautiful beaches, particularly popular with Frisbee and volleyball players.

❹ Less than a half-mile north, Coast Boulevard merges with Old Highway 101. Across the road are the **Del Mar Fairgrounds,** home to more than 100 different events a year, ranging from a cat show to an auto race. *Via de la Valle Rd. exit west from I–5, tel. 619/259–1355 for recorded events line.*

The fairgrounds also host the annual summer meeting of the **Del Mar Thoroughbred Club** (aka "Where the Turf Meets the Surf"). The track brings the top horses and jockeys to Del Mar, along with a cross section of the rich and famous, eager to bet on the ponies. Crooner Bing Crosby and his Hollywood buddies, Pat O'Brien, Gary Cooper, and Oliver Hardy, among others, organized the track in the '30s, primarily because Crosby thought it would be fun to have a track near his Rancho Santa Fe home. Del Mar soon developed into a regular stop for the stars of stage and screen.

During the off-season, horse players can still gamble at the fairgrounds, thanks to a satellite wagering facility. Races from other California tracks are televised, and people can bet as if the races were being run right there. Times vary, depending on which tracks in the state are operating. *Tel. 619/755–1167. Racing season: July–Sept., Wed.–Mon. Post time 2 PM.*

Next to the fairgrounds, on Jimmy Durante Boulevard, is a small exotic bird-training facility, **Freeflight,** which is open to the public.

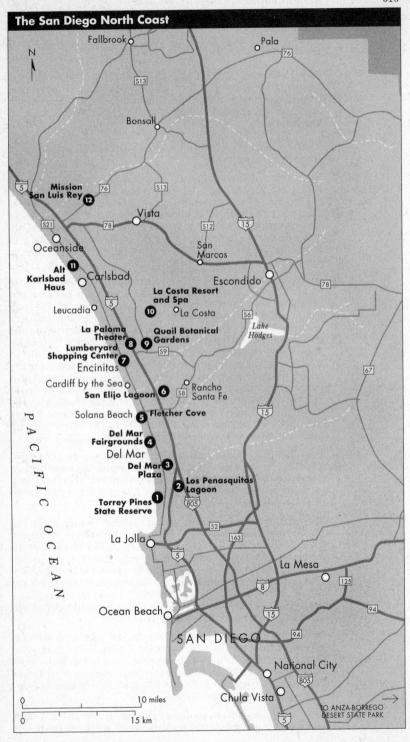

The San Diego North Coast

Fallbrook

Pala

76

N

S13

Bonsall

5

Mission
San Luis Rey 12

76

S13

15

Vista

S21

78

S12

Oceanside

San
Marcos

Alt
Karlsbad 11
Haus

Carlsbad

Escondido

78

La Costa Resort
and Spa

5

10

La Costa

S6

Lake
Hodges

67

Leucadia

Quail Botanical
Gardens

La Paloma
Theater

8 9

Lumberyard
Shopping Center 7

S9

Encinitas

Cardiff by the Sea

San Elijo Lagoon 6

Rancho
Santa Fe

S8

Solana Beach 5 Fletcher Cove

15

Del Mar
Fairgrounds 4

Del Mar

Del Mar 3
Plaza

2 Los Penasquitos
Lagoon

1

Torrey Pines
State Reserve

805

52

PACIFIC OCEAN

163

La Jolla

5

La Mesa

125

8

Ocean Beach

15

SAN DIEGO

94

94

National City

805

0   10 miles

0   15 km

Chula Vista

5

TO ANZA-BORREGO
DESERT STATE PARK

Visitors are allowed to handle the birds—a guaranteed child pleaser. *2132 Jimmy Durante Blvd., tel. 619/481–3148. Admission: $1. Open daily 10–4.*

Following Via de la Valle Road east from I–5 will take you to the exclusive community of **Rancho Santa Fe,** one of the richest areas in the United States. Groves of huge, drooping eucalyptus trees, first imported to the area by a railroad company in search of trees to grow for railroad ties, cover the hills and valleys, hiding the posh estates. The little village of Rancho has some elegant and quaint— and overpriced—shops and restaurants. But it is no accident that there is little else to see or do in Rancho; the residents guard their privacy religiously. Even the challenging Rancho Santa Fe Golf Course, the original site of the Bing Crosby Pro-Am and considered one of the best courses in southern California, is still open only to members of the Rancho Santa Fe community.

Back along the coast, along Old Highway 101 north of Del Mar, is the quiet little oceanside community of **Solana Beach.** A highlight ⑤ of Solana Beach is **Fletcher Cove,** located at the west end of Lomas Santa Fe Drive. Early Solana settlers used dynamite to blast the cove out of the overhanging cliffs. Called Pill Box by the locals because of a bunkerlike lifeguard station that overlooks it, the Fletcher Cove beach is easy to reach and features a large parking lot replete with a small basketball court, a favorite of local pickup game players.

⑥ To the north, separating Solana Beach from Cardiff, is the **San Elijo Lagoon,** home to many migrating birds. Trails wind around the entire area. As you continue along Old Highway 101, past the cluster of hillside homes that make up Cardiff and beyond the campgrounds of the San Elijo State Beach, the palm trees of Sea Cliff Roadside Park (Swami's to the locals) and the golden domes of the Self-Realization Fellowship mark the entrance to downtown **Encinitas.** The Self-Realization Fellowship was built at the turn of the century and is a retreat and place of worship for the followers of a Native American religious sect. Its beautiful gardens are open to the public.

A recent landmark of Encinitas (which was incorporated as a city in 1986, including the communities of Cardiff, Leucadia, and Olivenhain) is the **Lumberyard Shopping Center,** a collection of small ⑦ stores and restaurants that anchors the downtown shopping area. There is a huge selection of shopping centers inland at the intersection of Encinitas Boulevard and El Camino Real.

⑧ An older landmark of Encinitas is the **La Paloma Theater** (471 1st St., near the corner of Encinitas Blvd., tel. 619/436–7469), at the north end of town. Built in the 1920s as a stop for traveling vaudeville troupes, it has served as a concert hall, movie theater, and meeting place for the area ever since. Plays are still being rehearsed and performed here.

Encinitas is best known as the Flower Capital of the World, and although the flower industry is not as prevalent as it once was, the city is still home to Paul Ecke Poinsettias, the largest producer of the popular Christmas blossom. A sampling of the area's dedication ⑨ to horticulture can be found at the **Quail Botanical Gardens,** home to thousands of different varieties of plants, especially drought-tolerant species. Horticultural lectures are given here, and there are often plant sales. *230 Quail Gardens Dr. (take Encinitas Blvd. east from I–5 and turn left on Quail Gardens Dr.), tel. 619/436–3036. Parking: $1. Open daily 8–5; closed first Mon. of every month.*

Old Highway 101 continues north through **Leucadia** (named after a famous Greek promontory), a small community best known for its small art galleries and stores. At the north end of Leucadia, La Costa Avenue meets Old Highway 101. Following La Costa Avenue

❿ east, past the Batiquitos Lagoon, you'll come to **La Costa Resort and Spa** (*see* Lodging, *below*), once famous for its high-profile guests and reputed mafia ties and now noted for its excellent golf and tennis facilities.

La Costa is technically part of the city of **Carlsbad,** which is centered farther north, west of the Tamarack Avenue and Elm Avenue exits of I–5. In Carlsbad, Old Highway 101 is called Carlsbad Boulevard. Large rancheros owned by wealthy Mexicans were the first settlements inland; the coastal area was developed by an entrepreneur, John Frazier, who lured people to the area with talk of the healing powers of mineral water bubbling from a coastal well. The water was found to have the same properties as water from the German mineral wells of Karlsbad—hence the name of the new community. Remnants from the era, including the original well, are found at the

⓫ **Alt Karlsbad Haus,** a small museum–gift shop carrying northern European wares. *2802A Carlsbad Blvd., tel. 619/729–6912. Open Mon.–Sat. 10–5, Sun. noon–5.*

North of Carlsbad is **Oceanside,** home of Camp Pendleton, the country's largest marine base, as well as a beautiful natural harbor teeming with activity. **Oceanside Harbor** (tel. 619/966–4570) is the north-coast center for fishing, sailing, and all ocean-water sports. Salty fisherman types tend to congregate at Oceanside Pier.

Another highlight of a visit to Oceanside is **The California Surf Museum,** which charts the history of surfing from balsa-wood boards up through the present Fiberglas state-of-the-art. Exhibits change regularly. *308 N. Pacific St., tel. 619/721–6876. Admission free, donations appreciated. Open Thurs.–Mon. noon–4, closed. Tues. and Wed., expanded hours in summer.*

⓬ Oceanside is also home to **Mission San Luis Rey,** built by Franciscan friars in 1798 to help educate and convert local Native Americans. One of the best-preserved missions in the area, San Luis Rey was the 18th and largest of the California missions. Retreats are still held here, but a picnic area, gift shop, and museum are also on the grounds today. Self-guided tours are available. *4050 Mission Ave. (take Mission Ave. east from I–5), tel. 619/757–3651. Admission: $3 adults, $1 children. Open Mon.–Sat. 10–4:30, Sun. noon–4:30.*

Dining

Given the north coast's reputation as a suburban area, there is a surprisingly large selection of top-quality restaurants here. In fact, San Diegans often take the drive north to enjoy the variety of cuisines offered in the North County.

Highly recommended restaurants are indicated by a star ★.

Category	Cost*
$$$	over $30
$$	$20–$30
$	under $20

per person for a three-course meal, excluding drinks, service, and tax

$$$
Del Mar
Tourlas. The restaurant at Del Mar's posh L'Auberge resort has undergone a sea change, with a new name and chef and a shift in cooking style from French to contemporary California. The menu is small but impressive: Such appetizers as corn meal–covered crab cakes might be followed by rack of lamb on couscous or halibut coated in pine nuts. The setting is lovely, and the service is attentive. *1540 Camino del Mar, tel. 619/259–1515. Reservations advised. Jacket advised. AE, D, DC, MC, V.*

$$$
Rancho
Santa Fe
★
Mille Fleurs. This gem of a French auberge brightens a tiny village surrounded by country estates. Within a mile of Chino's, the county's most famous vegetable farm, where the chef shops daily, this is a most romantic hideaway, with tempting cuisine to enhance the mood. *6009 Paseo Delicias, tel. 619/756–3085. Reservations strongly advised. Jacket advised. AE, D, DC, MC, V. No lunch weekends.*

$$$
Solana Beach
Frederick's. This husband-and-wife-owned, friendly, relaxed bistro serves traditional French dishes with California-fresh overtones. Leave room for the freshly baked bread and one of the lush desserts. The prix-fixe menu changes weekly. *128 S. Acacia St., tel. 619/755–2432. Reservations strongly advised. Dress: dressy casual. DC, MC, V. Dinner only, closed Sun. and Mon.*

$$
Cardiff
The Chart House. The beach and the sunset above the Pacific are the chief attractions of this surfside dining spot. Entrées include fresh fish, seafood, and beef dishes; there's also a good salad bar. *2588 Rte. 101S, tel. 619/436–4044. Reservations advised. Dress: casual. AE, D, DC, MC, V. Dinner only; Sunday brunch.*

$$
Del Mar
Cilantro's. For a taste of gourmet Mexican and southwestern-style food—creative dishes full of subtle spices—Cilantro's in Del Mar offers a wide variety of unusual creations, including shark fajitas and spit-roasted chicken with a mild chili sauce. The inexpensive tapas menu, with such delicacies as crab tostadas and three-cheese quesadillas, is a little easier on the wallet. *3702 Via de la Valle, tel. 619/259–8777. Reservations advised. Dress: casual. AE, MC, V.*

$$
Del Mar
Il Fornaio. Located within the Del Mar Plaza, this talk-of-the-town ristorante features northern Italian cuisine, such as fresh seafood, homemade pastas, and crispy pizzas. The outdoor piazza affords a splendid ocean view. *1555 Camino del Mar, tel. 619/755–8876. Reservations advised. Dress: casual. AE, DC, MC, V.*

$$
Del Mar
Pacifica Del Mar. Yet another fine Del Mar Plaza restaurant boasting a stunning view, Pacifica Del Mar emphasizes an imaginative California cuisine of fresh ingredients prepared with southwestern, Cajun, Italian, and Pacific Rim touches. Start with the scrumptious smoked corn, chicken, and black-bean chowder, and then go on to the grilled prawn salad, blackened catfish, or one of the free-range chicken dishes. Desserts are tasty, and the wine list is excellent. *1555 Camino del Mar, tel. 619/792–0476. Reservations advised. Dress: casual to dressy casual. AE, D, DC, MC, V.*

$
Encinitas
Vigilucci's. This Italian trattoria has a cozy, bistrolike atmosphere, knowledgeable Italian waiters, and a stylish menu. The pastas are particularly good: Try the *spaghetti al funghetto*, with a fresh mush-

room sauce, or the *tagliatelle alla bolognese*, with ground duck, chicken, and veal in a tomato sauce. *505 1st St. (Hwy. 101), tel. 619/942–7332. Reservations advised. Dress: casual. AE, D, DC, MC, V. No lunch weekends.*

$ **Johnny Rockets.** This '50s-style malt-and-burger joint, on the Del
Del Mar   Mar Plaza's lower level, dishes up juicy burgers, thick malts, and fries to die for. Booth and counter seating come complete with nickel-a-tune jukeboxes. *1555 Camino del Mar, tel. 619/755–1954. Dress: casual. MC, V.*

$ **Rico's Taco Shop.** Short on frills but long on great food, this Mexican
Encinitas   fast-food café is a local favorite. Come here for excellent chicken taquitos, carne asada burritos, and the best fish burritos and tacos in town. The owners are friendly and health conscious, too: No lard is used in the recipes. Rico's is open daily for breakfast, lunch, and dinner. *165-L S. El Camino Real, in the Target Shopping Center, tel. 619/944–7689. Dress: very casual. No credit cards.*

$ **California Pizza Kitchen.** Bright, noisy, and cheerful, this popular
Solana Beach   restaurant in Solana Beach's attractive new Boardwalk shopping center produces a selection of designer pizzas ranging from the conventional to the outlandish. If Caribbean-shrimp, tuna-melt, or mooshu-chicken pizzas are too exotic for you, try the duck sausage (particularly recommended), the mixed grill vegetarian, or the five-cheese and tomato pizzas. *437 S. Hwy. 101, tel. 619/793–0999. No reservations. Dress: casual. AE, D, DC, MC, V.*

$ **Chung King Loh.** One of the better Chinese restaurants along the
Solana Beach   coast, Chung King Loh offers an excellent variety of Mandarin and Szechuan dishes. *552 Stevens Ave., tel. 619/481–0184. Reservations advised. Dress: casual. AE, D, DC, MC, V. No lunch Sun.*

$ **Fidel's.** Rich in North County tradition, both Fidel's restaurants
Solana Beach   serve a wide variety of well-prepared Mexican dishes in a low-key, pleasant atmosphere. The original restaurant in Solana Beach, a two-story building with an outdoor patio area, is particularly nice and draws a lively crowd. *607 Valley Ave., tel. 619/755–5292; 3003 Carlsbad Blvd., Carlsbad, tel. 619/729–0903. Reservations accepted for parties of 8 or more only. Dress: casual. MC, V.*

Lodging

Category	Cost*
$$$$	over $160
$$$	$100–$160
$$	$60–$100
$	under $60

All prices are for a double room, excluding tax.

$$$$ **La Costa Hotel and Spa.** Don't expect glitz and glamour at this fa-
Carlsbad   mous resort; it's surprisingly low-key, with low-slung buildings and vaguely southwestern contemporary–style rooms decorated in neutral tones. The sports facilities, especially golf and tennis, are excellent, and La Costa includes such other amenities as supervised children's activities and a movie theater. A variety of nutrition and stress-reduction classes are available. *2100 Costa del Mar Rd., Carlsbad 92009, tel. 619/438–9111 or 800/854–5000, fax 619/438–9007. 480 rooms. Facilities: 5 restaurants, pool, exercise room, golf, 23 lighted tennis courts, beauty spa, massage, hair salon, theater, shops. AE, D, DC, MC, V.*

$$$$ **L'Auberge Del Mar Resort and Spa.** Across the street from the Del
Del Mar Mar Plaza and one block from the ocean, L'Auberge is modeled on
the Tudor-style Hotel Del Mar, playground for Hollywood's elite in
the early 1900s and the original occupant of this site. The inn is filled
with dark-wood antiques, fireplaces, and lavish floral arrangements. Spacious rooms and suites are tastefully if not memorably
decorated, with beige dominating the color scheme. The grounds
are attractively landscaped, with stone paths leading to gazebos and
pools; the spa specializes in European herbal wraps and treatments.
*1540 Camino del Mar, Del Mar 92014, tel. 619/259–1515 or 800/553–
1336, fax 619/755–4940. 123 rooms. Facilities: restaurant, bar, café, 2
tennis courts, 2 pools, whirlpool, beauty spa, exercise machines, yoga,
water aerobics. AE, D, DC, MC, V.*

$$$$ **Rancho Valencia.** The sister hotel to La Jolla's La Valencia, this re-
Rancho sort is so luxurious that several high-style magazines have chosen
Santa Fe it for fashion backdrops and have named it the most romantic hideaway in the United States. The suites are in red-tile-roofed casitas
with fireplaces and private terraces. Tennis is the other draw here,
with 18 courts and a resident pro; rates include unlimited use of the
courts. *5921 Valencia Circle, 92067, tel. 619/756–1123 or 800/548–3664,
fax 619/756–0165. 43 suites. Facilities: restaurant, 18 tennis courts,
pool, 2 whirlpools, sauna, croquet. AE, DC, MC, V.*

$$$ **Carlsbad Inn Beach Resort.** The palm trees seem a bit out of place
Carlsbad on the manicured lawn of this sprawling European-style inn, with
its gabled roofs and stone supports, but this is Carlsbad after all,
where *alte* Germany meets southern California. The public areas
and rooms are decorated in appealing Old World style; all the ac-
commodations have VCRs, many offer kitchenettes, and some have
fireplaces and private spas. *3075 Carlsbad Blvd., 92008, tel. 619/434–
7020 or 800/235–3939, fax 619/729–4853. 60 rooms. Facilities: pool,
health club, Jacuzzi, sauna. AE, D, DC, MC, V.*

$$ **Best Western Beach View Lodge.** Reservations are essential at this
Carlsbad reasonably priced hotel near the beach. A Mediterranean-style low-
rise building hosts a variety of attractively decorated rooms with
light-wood or whitewashed furnishings; all have refrigerators, and
kitchens, private balconies, and fireplaces are also available. Families tend to settle in for a week or more. *3180 Carlsbad Blvd., 92008,
tel. 619/729–1151, 800/535–5588 or 800/BEACHVU in CA, fax
619/729–1151. 41 rooms. Facilities: whirlpool, sauna, pool, laundry
facilities, in-room safes, complimentary Continental breakfast. AE,
D, DC, MC, V.*

$$ **Stratford Inn.** The inn offers a pleasant atmosphere just outside the
Del Mar center of town and three blocks from the ocean. Rooms are large,
with ample closet space and dressing areas; some have ocean views.
Suites with kitchenettes are available. Continental breakfast is com-
plimentary. *710 Camino del Mar, 92014, tel. 619/755–1501 or 800/446–
7229, fax 619/755–4704. 98 rooms. Facilities: 2 pools, whirlpool,
refrigerators in all rooms. AE, D, DC, MC, V.*

$$ **Moonlight Beach Hotel.** This folksy, laid-back motel is the closest to
Encinitas the beach at Encinitas. Rooms are basic but spacious and clean; all
have kitchenettes. Weekly rates are available. *233 2nd St., 92024, tel.
619/753–0623 or 800/323–1259. 24 rooms. AE, MC, V.*

$$ **Radisson Inn Encinitas.** This attractively designed low-rise blends
Encinitas nicely into an Encinitas hillside just east of Old Highway 101. Rooms
have plush, richly colored rugs and comfy upholstered chairs; some
have kitchenettes and/or ocean views. *85 Encinitas Blvd., 92024, tel.
619/942–7455 or 800/333–3333, fax 619/632–9481. 91 rooms. Facilities:
pool, whirlpool, restaurant, lounge, complimentary Continental
breakfast. AE, D, DC, MC, V.*

<table>
<tr><td>$
Encinitas</td><td>**Budget Motels of America.** Shag carpeting and kitschy murals decorate the rooms at this motel, but the place is clean, low-priced, and convenient to the beach and the freeway. No-smoking rooms are available, and Continental breakfast is included in the room rate. *133 Encinitas Blvd., 92024, tel. 619/944–0260 or 800/795–6044, fax 619/944–2803. 124 rooms. AE, DC, MC, V.*</td></tr>
<tr><td>$
Leucadia</td><td>**Pacific Surf.** This motel is clean, comfortable, and near all the shops and restaurants of Encinitas. All rooms have kitchens, and there are discounts for extended stays. *1076 Rte. 101N, 92024, tel. 619/436–8763 or 800/795–1466. 30 rooms. Facilities: laundry. AE, D, DC, MC, V.*</td></tr>
<tr><td>$
Oceanside</td><td>**Oceanside TraveLodge.** It's near the beach and centrally located. *1401 N. Hill St., 92054, tel. 619/722–1244 or 800/255–3050, fax 619/722–3228. 28 rooms. Facilities: laundry. AE, D, DC, MC, V.*</td></tr>
</table>

Excursion to Anza-Borrego Desert State Park

Every spring, the stark desert landscape east of the Cuyamaca Mountains explodes with color. It's the blooming of the wildflowers in the Anza-Borrego Desert State Park, less than a two-hour drive from central San Diego. The beauty of this annual spectacle, as well as the natural quiet and blazing climate, lures tourists and natives to the area.

The area features a desert and not much more, but it is one of the favorite parks of those Californians who travel widely in their state. People seeking bright lights and glitter should look elsewhere. The excitement in this area stems from watching a coyote scamper across a barren ridge or a brightly colored bird resting on a nearby cactus or from a waitress delivering another cocktail to a poolside chaise longue. For hundreds of years, the only humans to linger in the area were Native Americans from the San Dieguito, Kamia, and Cahuilla tribes, but the extreme temperature eventually forced the tribes to leave, too. It wasn't until 1774, when Mexican explorer Captain Juan Bautista de Anza first blazed a trail through the area as a shortcut from Sonora to San Francisco, that modern civilization had its first glimpse of the oddly beautiful wasteland.

Today, more than 600,000 acres of desert are included in the Anza-Borrego Desert State Park, making it the largest state park in the contiguous 48 states. It is also one of the few parks in the country where people can camp anywhere. No campsite is necessary; just follow the trails and pitch a tent wherever you like.

Five hundred miles of road traverse the park, and visitors are required to stay on them so as not to disturb the ecological balance of the park. However, 28,000 acres have been set aside in the eastern part of the desert near Ocotillo Wells for off-road enthusiasts. General George S. Patton conducted field training in the Ocotillo area to prepare for the World War II invasion of North Africa, and the area hasn't been the same since.

The little town of Borrego Springs acts as an oasis in this natural playground. Not exactly like Palm Springs—it lacks the wild crowds and preponderance of insanely wealthy residents—Borrego is basically a small retirement community, with the average age of residents about 50. For visitors who are uninterested in communing with the desert without a shower and pool nearby, Borrego provides several pleasant hotels and restaurants.

We recommend visiting this desert between October and May to avoid the extreme summer temperatures. Winter temperatures are comfortable, but nights (and sometimes days) are cold, so bring a warm jacket.

Important Addresses and Numbers

For general information about the Borrego and desert areas, contact the **Borrego Springs Chamber of Commerce** (622 Palm Canyon Dr., Box 66, Borrego Springs 92004, tel. 619/767–5555). For details on the state park, phone or write the Visitor Center, **Anza-Borrego Desert State Park** (Box 299, Borrego Springs 92004, tel. 619/767–5311). During the spring blooming season, a special **wildflower hotline** (tel. 619/767–4684) gives 24-hour recorded information on what is flowering at the time of your call and what is expected to bloom shortly. For campsite reservations, call **MISTIX** (tel. 800/444–7275).

Arriving and Departing

By Car Take I–8 east to Route 79 north. Turn east on Route 78.

By Bus The **Northeast Rural Bus System** (NERBS, tel. 619/765–0145) connects Julian, Borrego Springs, Oak Grove, Ocotillo Wells, Agua Caliente, Ramona, and many of the other small communities with El Cajon, 15 miles east of downtown San Diego, and the East County line of the San Diego trolley, with stops at Grossmont shopping center and North County Fair. Service is by reservation, and buses do not run on Sundays or on some holidays.

Exploring

The **Anza-Borrego Desert State Park** is too vast even to consider exploring in its entirety. Most people stay in the hills surrounding Borrego Springs. An excellent underground **Visitor Information Center** (tel. 619/767–5311) and museum are reachable by taking the Palm Canyon Drive spur west from the traffic circle in the center of town. The rangers are helpful and always willing to suggest areas for camping or hiking. A short slide show about the desert is shown throughout the day. For a listing of the interpretive programs scheduled for the year, pick up a copy of the free park newspaper.

One of the most popular camping and hiking areas is **Palm Canyon,** just a few minutes west of the Visitor Information Center. A 1½-mile trail leads to a small oasis with a waterfall and palm trees. If you find palm trees lining city streets in San Diego and Los Angeles amusing, seeing this grove of native palms around a pool in a narrow desert valley may give you a new vision of the dignity of this tree. The Borrego Palm Canyon campground (on the desert floor, a mile or so below the palm oasis) is one of only two developed campgrounds with flush toilets and showers in the park. (The other is Tamarisk Grove Campground at the intersection of Route 78 and Yaqui Pass Road.)

Other points of interest include **Split Mountain** (take Split Mountain Road south from Route 78 at Ocotillo Wells), a narrow gorge with 600-foot perpendicular walls. You can drive the mile from the end of the paved road to the gorge in a passenger car if you are careful (don't get stuck in the sand). Don't attempt the drive in bad weather, when the gorge can quickly fill with a torrent of water; even if the sky is clear when you arrive, check ahead at the visitor center to find out if current road condition allow for a safe trip.

On the way to Split Mountain (while you are still on the paved road), you'll pass a grove of the park's unusual **elephant trees** (10 feet tall, with swollen branches and small leaves). There is a self-guided nature trail; pick up a brochure at the parking lot.

You can get a good view of the Borrego Badlands from **Font's Point,** off Borrego–Salton Seaway (S22). The badlands are a maze of steep ravines that are almost devoid of vegetation and are best navigated by a four-wheel-drive vehicle.

In **Borrego Springs** itself, there is little to do besides lie or recreate in the sun. The challenging 18-hole Rams Hill Country Club course is open to the public (tel. 619/767–5000), as is the more modest course at the Borrego Roadrunner Club (tel. 619/767–5374). Borrego Resorts International Tennis (tel. 619/767–9748) has courts that are open to the public, as does La Casa del Zorro (tel. 619/767–5323). One of the best and most appreciated deals in town is the Borrego Springs High School pool (tel. 619/767–5337), at the intersection of Saddle and Cahuilla roads and open to the public during the summer.

Most people prefer to explore the desert in a motorized vehicle. While it is illegal to drive off the established trails in the state park, the **Ocotillo Wells State Vehicular Recreation Area** (tel. 619/767–5391), reached by following Route 78 east from Borrego, is a popular haven for off-road enthusiasts and those who drive vehicles that are not street legal. The sand dunes and rock formations are challenging as well as fun. Camping is permitted throughout the area, but water is not available. The only facilities are in the small town (really no more than a corner) of Ocotillo Wells.

To the east of Anza-Borrego is the Salton Sink, a basin that (although not as low as Death Valley) consists of more dry land below sea level than anywhere else in this hemisphere. The Salton Sea is the most recent of a series of lakes here, divided from the Gulf of California by the delta of the Colorado River. The current lake was created in 1905–7, when the Colorado flooded north through canals meant to irrigate the Imperial Valley. The water is extremely salty, even saltier than the Pacific Ocean, and it is primarily a draw for fishermen seeking corbina, croaker, and tilapia. Some boaters and swimmers also use the lake. The state runs a pleasant park, with sites for day camping, recreational vehicles, and primitive camping. *Take Rte. 78E to Rte. 111N, tel. 619/393–3059.*

Bird-watchers will love the **Salton Sea National Wildlife Refuge.** A hiking trail and observation tower make it easy to spot the dozens of varieties of migratory birds stopping at Salton Sea. *At the south end of Salton Sea, off Rte. 111, tel. 619/348–5278.*

Dining

Quality, not quantity, is the operable truism of dining in the Borrego area. Restaurants are scarce and hard to find, and many close on holidays during the summer, but the best are high quality.

Category	Cost*
$$	$10–$20
$	under $10

per person for a three-course meal, excluding drinks, service, and tax

$$ **Chinese Panda Restaurant.** The only business in a Quonset hut in Borrego Springs, this friendly Chinese restaurant serves tasty versions of Mandarin and Szechuan dishes. *818 Palm Canyon Dr., tel. 619/767–3182. Reservations accepted. Dress: casual. MC, V. Closed Mon. and Aug.*

$$ **Rams Hill Country Club.** This top-notch Continental restaurant offers a copious Sunday brunch. *1881 Rams Hill Rd., tel. 619/767–5006. Reservations accepted. Dress: casual; jacket required on Sat. AE, MC, V. Closed for dinner Mon.–Wed., July–Oct. 1.*

$ **Mi Tenampa Cafe.** It may seem odd to find good Mexican seafood in the desert, but no stranger, perhaps, than this low-key restaurant's location—just off Christmas Circle. *747 Palm Canyon Dr., no phone. No reservations. Dress: casual. No credit cards. Closed Mon. and Tues.*

Lodging

If camping isn't your thing, there are two very nice resorts near Borrego Springs that offer fine amenities minus the overdevelopment of Palm Springs. In the summer months, rates drop by as much as 50%.

Category	Cost*
$$$$	$370–$500
$$$	$130–$370
$$	$75–$130

*All prices are for a double room, excluding tax.

$$$$ **Ram's Hill Country Club.** Those who want a vacation dedicated to golf can rent fully furnished one-, two-, or three-bedroom homes adjacent to a posh country club. A two-night minimum stay is required. *1881 Rams Hill Rd., Box 664, Borrego Springs 92004, tel. 619/767–5028 or 800/423–0947, fax 619/767–4418. 60 units. Facilities: restaurant, snack bar, golf course, 7 tennis courts, pool, Jacuzzi. AE, MC, V.*

$$–$$$$ **La Casa del Zorro.** This is a small, low-key resort complex in the heart of the desert. You need walk only a few hundred yards to be alone under the sky, and you may well see roadrunners crossing the highway. There are 17 different types of accommodations, set in comfortable one- to three-bedroom ranch-style houses complete with living rooms and kitchens; some three-bedroom suites have private pools, while other suites come with baby grand pianos. The elegant Continental restaurant puts on a good Sunday brunch. *3845 Yaqui Pass Rd., 92004, tel. 619/767–5323 or 800/824–1884, fax 619/767–5963. 77 suites, 94 rooms, 19 casitas. Facilities: restaurant, 6 lighted tennis courts, 3 pools, whirlpool, bicycles. AE, D, DC, MC, V.*

$$ **Palm Canyon Resort.** This is one of the largest properties in the area, with a hotel, an RV park, a restaurant, and recreational facilities. *221 Palm Canyon Dr., 92004, tel. 619/767–5342 or 800/242–0044 in CA only, fax 619/767–4073. 44 rooms. Facilities: restaurant, RV spaces, 2 pools, 2 whirlpools, general store, laundromat. AE, D, DC, MC, V.*

15 Palm Springs

Updated by
Bobbi Zane

What do you get when you start with dramatic scenery, add endless sunshine, mix in deluxe resorts, and spice things up with a liberal dash of celebrities? Palm Springs desert resorts, a magnet for socialites, sun worshipers, and stargazers.

The fashionable community, once limited to the village of Palm Springs, has expanded into other Coachella Valley towns in recent years. Now you'll find resorts stretching all the way from the foot of 10,831-foot Mt. San Jacinto in the north to once-sleepy Indio in the south. Streets are named for the celebrities who live here in unmarked gated estates—Frank Sinatra, Betty Ford, Bob Hope. Although the social, sports, shopping, and entertainment scenes now center around Palm Desert, you'll also find resorts and attractions in Indian Wells, Rancho Mirage, Desert Hot Springs, La Quinta, Cathedral City, and Indio.

During the "season" (January–April) resident celebrities and wealthy winter visitors present a nearly nightly round of parties and balls in conjunction with an endless round of world-class golf and tennis tournaments to support their favorite charities. They play during the day, too. There are more than 85 golf courses in a 20-mile radius, more than 600 tennis courts, 35 miles of bicycle trails, horseback riding, 10,000 or so swimming pools, and even cross-country skiing atop Mt. San Jacinto. Shopping is a serious pursuit here with clutches of chic boutiques to be found along main streets and fashionable department stores such as Saks Fifth Avenue and I. Magnin in enclosed malls. The McCallum Theater in Palm Desert even presents top-name entertainment.

This is the place for stargazing. Bob Hope, Frank Sinatra, Gerald and Betty Ford, and other luminaries can be spotted at charity events and restaurants and on the golf course. Carrie Fisher and Bette Midler have done stints at the Palms spa, and Donna Mills, Goldie Hawn, and Kurt Russell have been seen poolside at the Ingleside Inn. Michael Jackson and Sylvester Stallone escape the crowds at La Quinta resort.

The desert became a Hollywood hideout in the 1920s, when La Quinta Hotel opened the Coachella Valley's first golf course. But it took a pair of tennis-player actors to put Palm Springs on the map in the 1930s; Charlie Farrell and Ralph Bellamy bought 200 acres of land for $30 an acre and opened the Palm Springs Racquet Club, which soon listed Ginger Rogers, Humphrey Bogart, and Clark Gable among its members. Today you can take a tour that points out the homes of celebrities of yesterday and today.

Developers have been careful not to overshadow the stunning beauty of the desert setting: City buildings are restricted to a height of 30 feet; flashing, moving, and neon signs are restricted, preserving an intimate village feeling; and 50% of the land consists of open spaces with palm trees and desert vegetation.

This beauty is particularly evident in the canyons surrounding Palm Springs. Lush Tahquitz Canyon, one of the five canyons that line the San Jacinto Mountains, was the setting for Shangri-La in an early movie version of *Lost Horizon.* The Agua Caliente Band of Cahuilla Indians settled this area about 1,000 years ago. They considered the mineral springs to be sacred, with great curative and restorative powers. The springs became a tourist attraction in 1871 when the tribe built a bathhouse on the site to serve passengers on a pioneer stage route. The Agua Caliente still own about 32,000 acres of Palm Springs desert, 6,700 of which lie within the city limits of Palm Springs. The Indians, while dedicated to preserving their historic homeland, will doubtless account for the next "boom" in the desert. Following the lead of nearby tribes, which operate profitable bingo parlors in Indio and Cabazon, the Agua Caliente have contracted with Caesars World to build a California-style casino near the Spa Hotel in downtown Palm Springs. It's scheduled to open sometime in 1995.

One brief comment on the weather: Although daytime temperatures average a pleasantly warm 88°F, you are still in the desert. And that means during the middle of the day in the summer it is going to be very hot—sometimes uncomfortably so. You'll be told that "it is a dry heat." And it is. But it is still desert hot: Plan activities in the morning and late afternoon, and wear a hat and plenty of sunscreen if you're out for a midday stroll. Anytime of the year be sure to drink plenty of water to prevent dehydration.

Essential Information

Important Addresses and Numbers

Tourist Information Palm Springs Desert Resorts Convention and Visitors Bureau (tel. 619/770–9000 or 800/417–3529) is at 69-930 Highway 111, Suite 201, Rancho Mirage, 92270. The bureau's **Activities Hotline** number is 619/770–1992. **Palm Springs Visitor Information Center** (2781 N. Palm Canyon Dr., Palm Springs, 92262, tel. 800/347–7746) provides tourist information.

Emergencies Dial 911 for police, fire, and ambulance in an emergency.

Doctors **Desert Hospital** (tel. 619/323–6511).

Dentists Dental emergency service is available from **R. Turnage, D.D.S.** (tel. 619/327–8448) 24 hours each day.

Arriving and Departing

By Plane Major airlines serving **Palm Springs Regional Airport** include **Alaska** (tel. 800/426–0333), **American** and **American Eagle** (tel. 800/433–7300), **America West** (tel. 800/235–9292, **Continental** (tel. 800/525–0280), **Delta** (tel. 800/221–1212), **SkyWest/Delta Connection** (tel. 800/453–9417), **United** and **United Express** (tel. 800/241–6522), and **USAir Express** (tel. 800/428–4322). The airport is about 2 miles east of the city's main downtown intersection; most hotels provide service to and from the airport.

By Train **Amtrak** (tel. 800/USA–RAIL) passenger trains serve the Indio area, 20 miles east of Palm Springs. From Indio, Greyhound Lines bus service is available to Palm Springs.

By Bus **Greyhound Lines** stop in Palm Springs (311 N. Indian Canyon Dr., tel. 619/325–2053 or 800/231–2222).

By Car Palm Springs is about a two-hour drive east of Los Angeles and a three-hour drive northeast of San Diego. Highway 111 brings you right onto Palm Canyon Drive, the main thoroughfare in Palm Springs and connecting route to other desert communities. From Los Angeles take the San Bernardino Freeway (I–10E) to Highway 111. From San Diego, I–15N connects with the Pomona Freeway (I–60E), leading to the San Bernardino Freeway (I–10E). If you're coming from the Riverside area, you might want to try the scenic Palms-to-Pines Highway (Hwy. 74). This 130-mile route begins in

Hemet and connects directly with Highway 111; the trek from snow-capped peaks to open desert valley is breathtaking.

Getting Around

By Car The desert resort communities occupy about a 20-mile stretch between I–10 in the east and Palm Canyon Drive in the west. Although some areas such as Palm Canyon Drive in Palm Springs and El Paseo are walkable, having a car is the best way to get around.

By Bus **SunBus** serves the entire Coachella Valley from Desert Hot Springs to Coachella with regular routes. Call 619/343–3451 for route and schedule information. **Palm Desert/Indian Wells Resort Express Shuttle** (tel. 619/346–6111) has regular free service between major hotels and shopping centers Tuesday–Saturday.

By Taxi **Desert Cab** (tel. 619/325–2868) and **Valley Cab Co.** (tel. 619/340–5845) serve the area.

Guided Tours

Orientation Tours **Gray Line Tours** (tel. 619/325–0974) offers several good general bus tours, from the hour-long Palm Springs Special highlight tour to the tour through Palm Springs, Cathedral City, Rancho Mirage, and Palm Desert. Prices are $12 for adults, $9 for children. Most departures are in the morning; call for reservations.

Special-Interest Tours In Palm Springs, special-interest tours mean one thing: celebrity homes. **Gray Line** and **Palm Springs Celebrity Tours** (tel. 619/325–2682) both cover this turf well. Prices range from $10 to $14 for adults. **Desert Adventures** (tel. 619/864–6530) takes to the wilds with jeep tours of Indian canyons, off-road in the Santa Rosa Mountains and into a mystery canyon. For a different perspective of the desert, try floating over the valley in a balloon. Trip lengths and prices vary; call **Fantasy Balloon Flights** (tel. 619/398–6322), or **Sunrise Balloons** (tel. 800/548–9912) for information. Customized helicopter tours are also available from Sunrise Balloons. **Covered Wagon Tours** (tel. 619/347–2161) will take you on an old-time two-hour exploration of the desert with a cookout at the end of the journey. **Golden Eagle Tours** (tel. 800/428–1833) conducts visits to windmill turbine fields that cover the desert hillsides.

Exploring Palm Springs

Highlights for First-Time Visitors

Joshua Tree
Living Desert Reserve
Palm Springs Village Fest (Thursday Nights)
View from Palm Springs Aerial Tramway

Numbers in the margin correspond to points of interest on the Palm Springs map.

Physically, Palm Springs proper is easy to understand. Palm Canyon Drive runs north–south through the heart of downtown; the intersection with Tahquitz Canyon Way is pretty much the center of the main drag. Heading south, Palm Canyon Drive splits: South Palm Canyon Drive leads you to the Indian Canyons and East Palm Canyon becomes Highway 11, taking you east through the resort areas of Cathedral City, Rancho Mirage, Palm Desert, La Quinta, and Indio. The Aerial Tramway is at the northern limits of Palm Springs. Joshua Tree National Monument is about an hour's drive north.

Most Palm Springs desert resort attractions can be seen in anywhere from an hour or two to an entire day, depending upon your interests. Do you want to take the tram up Mt. San Jacinto, see the view, and come right back down, or spend the day hiking? Would you rather linger for a picnic lunch in one of the Indian Canyons, or double back for a snack and people-watching at a sidewalk café along El Paseo? Your best bet is to think of the list of sights and activities as if it were an à la carte menu and pick and choose according to your appetite. To help you organize your outings, we will start in the north and work our way south and southeast. A separate tour of Joshua Tree follows.

Palm Springs and Environs

1 Take the **Palm Springs Aerial Tramway** to get a stunning overview of the desert. The 2½-mile ascent brings you to an elevation of 8,516 feet in less than 20 minutes. On clear days, which are common, the view stretches some 75 miles from the peak of Mt. San Gorgonio to the north and the Salton Sea in the southeast. At the top you'll find several diversions. Mountain Station has an Alpine buffet restaurant, cocktail lounge, apparel and gift shops, and picnic facilities. Mt. San Jacinto State Park offers 54 miles of hiking trails and camping and picnic areas; during winter the Nordic Ski Center has cross-country ski equipment for rent. *Call 619/325–1391 for information; 619/325–4227 for ski and weather conditions. Tram cars depart at least every 30 min from 10 AM weekdays and 8 AM weekends. Cost: $15.95 adults, $9.95 children 3–12. Closed in Aug. for maintenance.*

Once one of the most fashionable shopping streets in Southern California, **Palm Canyon Drive** is not quite as posh these days, but it's undergoing a renaissance into an entertainment and dining center. This is a lively and interesting place to take a stroll. You can take the Palm Springs Starwalk, stars imbedded in the sidewalk (à la the Hollywood Walk of Fame) honoring celebrities; pop into a coffee house for a cup of espresso; or cruise through the tiny but illuminating Showbiz Museum, adjacent to the historic Plaza Theater. Palm Canyon Drive is particularly lively on Thursday nights when the **Village Fest** street fair (*see* Palm Springs for Free, *below*) fills a three-block section of the drive.

Downtown Palm Springs is not without hidden historical treasures.
2 The **Village Green Heritage Center** illustrates pioneer life in Palm Springs in three museums. McCallum Adobe, dating back to 1885, displays the collections of the Palm Springs Historical Society and McCallum family memorabilia. Miss Cornelia White's House, dating back to 1894, exhibits this pioneer family's memorabilia including an extensive collection of bibles, clothing, tools, books, paintings, even the first telephone in Palm Springs. Roddy's General Store Museum dates from a later pioneer era, the 1930s and 1940s, and displays signs, packages, and products of the period. *221 and 223 S. Palm Canyon Dr., tel. 619/323–8297. Nominal admission. House open Wed. and Sun. noon–3, Thurs.–Sat. 10–4; store open Thurs.–Sun. 10–4; summer hrs flexible.*

If further evidence is needed to prove that the desert is no barren
3 wasteland, there is the dramatic **Palm Springs Desert Museum.** This surprisingly large facility contains galleries devoted to western and

Indian art, changing exhibitions, sculpture gardens, plus natural science and history exhibits. It also houses the Annenberg Theater. *101 Museum Dr., just north of Tahquitz Way, on south side of Desert Fashion Plaza, tel. 619/325–7186. Admission: $5 adults, $2 children under 17; free 1st Fri. of month. Open late Sept.–May, Tues.–Fri. 10–4, weekends 10–5.*

A short drive or distinctly long walk farther south on Palm Canyon
❹ is the **Moorten Botanical Garden.** More than 2,000 plant varieties cover the 4-acre site in settings that simulate the plants' original environments. Indian artifacts and rock, crystal, and wood forms are exhibited. *1701 S. Palm Canyon Dr., tel. 619/327–6555. Admission: $2 adults, 50¢ children. Open Mon.–Sat. 9–4:30, Sun. 10–4.*

❺ The **Indian Canyons,** 5 miles south of downtown Palm Springs, are the ancestral home of the Agua Caliente Band of Indians. The Indians selected these canyons for their lush oases, abundant water, and wildlife. Even now visitors can see remnants of this life: rock art, house pits and foundations, irrigation ditches, bedrock mortars, pictographs, and stone houses and shelters built atop high cliff walls. Four canyons are open to visitors: Palm Canyon, noted for its lush stand of Washingtonia palms, the largest such stand in the world; Tahquitz, noted for waterfalls and pools; Murray, home of Peninsula big horn sheep and a herd of wild ponies; and Andreas, where a stand of fan palms contrasts with sharp rock formations. A Trading Post in Palm Canyon has hiking maps, refreshments, Indian art, jewelry, and weavings. *End of S. Palm Canyon Dr., tel. 619/325–5673. Admission: $3.50 adults, $1 children. Open Sept.–June, daily 8–5.*

Elegant resorts, fine dining, world-class golf and tennis tourna-
❻ ments, and celebrity residents come together in **Rancho Mirage.** The city is home to the famed Eisenhower Medical Center and Betty Ford Center, as well as to such celebrities as Walter Annenberg, Gerald and Betty Ford, and Frank Sinatra. Near the Eisenhower Medical Center is the new **Heartland California Museum of the Heart.** Walk through the huge heart-valve portal and experience interactive exhibits such as the 14-foot-tall "Plaque Attack" walk-in replica of a coronary artery, or grab a healthful bite at the Heart Rock Café. *39-600 Bob Hope Dr., tel. 619/324–3278. Suggested donation: $2.50 adults, $2 senior citizens 62 and older, 50¢ children 6–17, students, or military with ID. Open Mon.–Fri. 7–7 (also Sat. 8–noon Sept.–May).*

Some of the best desert people-watching, shopping, and dining can
❼ be found along trendy **El Paseo,** a 2-mile avenue just west of Highway 111 in Palm Desert. The flower-decked avenue is lined with apparel shops, specialty stores, art galleries, and restaurants.

❽ One of the most unique zoological gardens in the country, the **Living Desert Reserve** offers eyeball-to-eyeball views of coyotes, mountain lions, bighorn sheep, golden eagles, and owls. A number of easy to challenging trails go through desert gardens populated with plants of the Mojave, Colorado, and Sonoran deserts. One exhibit pinpoints the famed San Andreas earthquake fault across the valley. Shuttle service, interpretive tours, strollers, and wheelchairs are avialable. *47-900 Portola Ave., less than 2 mi south of Hwy. 111, tel. 619/346–5694. Admission: $7 adults, $3.50 children 3–15. Open daily 9–5, closed mid-June–Aug.*

Time Out   Pamper yourself with the Spa Experience, a sampling of the services available at the newly opened **Spa Hotel Resort and Mineral Springs.** Sink into a tub filled with naturally hot mineral water from

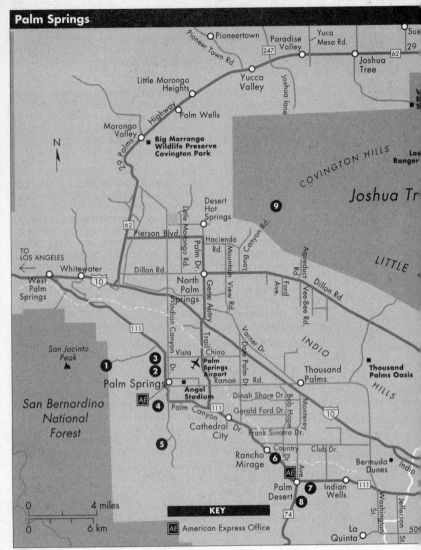

Palm Springs

El Paseo, **7**

Indian Canyons, **5**

Joshua Tree National
Monument, **9**

Living Desert
Reserve, **8**

Moorten Botanical
Garden, **4**

Palm Springs Aerial
Tramway, **1**

Palm Springs Desert
Museum, **3**

Rancho Mirage, **6**

Village Green
Heritage Center, **2**

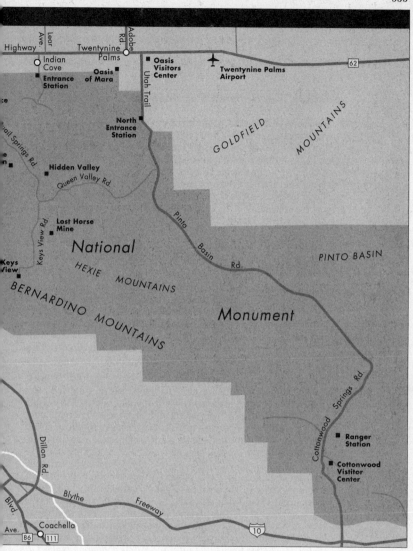

the original Agua Caliente spring, rest in the cool white relaxation room, swim in the outdoor mineral pool, or let the sauna warm your spirits. Massages, skin care, and beauty and body therapies are also available. *100 N. Indian Canyon Dr., Palm Springs, tel. 619/325–1461. Spa Experience $17.25 (includes gratuity), massages $35–$75. Open Sun.–Thurs. 9–6, Fri. and Sat. 9–9.*

Joshua Tree National Monument

9 **Joshua Tree National Monument** is about a one-hour drive from Palm Springs, whether you take I–10 north to Highway 62, which swings east to the Oasis Visitor Center on the park's northern edge, or I–10 south to the Cottonwood Visitor Center. The northern part of the park is in the Mojave (or high) Desert and has the Joshua trees. The southern part is Colorado (or low) Desert; in spring this is one of the desert's best wildflower viewing areas, covered with carpets of white, yellow, purple, and red flowers stretching as far as the eye can see on the hillsides east of I–10. It's possible to take a loop drive in a single long day; enter by way of the Oasis Visitor Center or at Cottonwood and follow the road from either across the park to the other entrance. Pack a picnic and water, as facilities are limited in the area.

On the northern route, you may want to consider stopping at the **Big Morongo Wildlife Preserve Covington Park.** Once an Indian village, then a cattle ranch, and now a regional park, the reserve is a serene natural oasis supporting a wide variety of plants, birds, and animals. There is a shaded meadow for picnics and choice hiking trails. *From I–10 or Indian Canyon Dr., take Hwy. 62 east to East Dr., tel. 619/363–7190. Admission free. Open Wed.–Sun. 7:30–sunset.*

Joshua Tree is immense, complex, and ruggedly beautiful. Its mountains of jagged rock, lush oases shaded by tall, elegant fan palms, and natural cactus gardens mark the meeting place of the Mojave and Colorado deserts. This is prime hiking, rock climbing, and exploring country, where you can expect to see such wildlife as coyotes and desert pack rats, and exotic plants such as the red-tipped ocotillo, sharp barbed cholla cactus, smoke trees, and creamy white yucca. Extensive stands of Joshua trees give the park its name. The trees were named by early white settlers who felt their unusual forms resembled the biblical Joshua raising his arms toward heaven. The **Oasis Visitor Center** (tel. 619/367–7511) is probably the best place to start. The center has an excellent selection of free and low-cost brochures, books, posters, and maps as well as several educational exhibits. Rangers are on hand to answer questions and offer advice. *Hwy. 62 to town of Twentynine Palms, follow signs short distance south to Visitor Center. Admission: $5 per car.*

Near the Visitor Center is the **Oasis of Mara.** Inhabited first by Indians and later by prospectors and homesteaders, the oasis now provides a home for birds, small mammals, and other wildlife. Once inside the park, you will find nine campgrounds with tables, fireplaces, and primitive rest rooms and several picnic areas for day use. Sights range from the **Hidden Valley,** a legendary cattle rustlers' hideout reached by a trail winding through massive boulders; and the **Lost Horse Mine,** a remnant of the gold-mining days; to **Keys View,** an outstanding scenic point commanding a superb sweep of valley, mountain, and desert. Sunrise and sunset are magic times to be here, when the light throws rocks and trees into high relief before (or after) bathing the hills in brilliant shades of red, orange, and gold.

Palm Springs for Free

Big Morongo Wildlife Preserve Covington Park (*see above*) has walking trails and picnic areas.

Several date gardens are open to the public for touring. **Shields Date Gardens** (80225 Hwy. 111, Indio, tel. 619/347–0996) presents a continuous slide program on the history of the date.

Several communities hold **street fairs** on a regular basis with vendors offering everything from antiques and contemporary crafts to clothing, jewelry, and produce. College of the Desert Alumni Association sponsors one of the biggest of these Saturday and Sunday mornings at its campus at Fred Waring Drive and Monterey Ave. in Palm Desert. The **Palm Springs Village Fest,** held Thursday evenings on Palm Canyon Drive, is an ever-changing scene with a different theme each week. There are street musicians, food stalls, handcrafted gifts at low prices, antiques, sculpture, and paintings, and a farmers market.

Off the Beaten Track

The **Eldorado Polo Club** (50-950 Madison St., Indio, tel. 619/342–2223), known as the "Winter Polo Capital of the West," is home of world-class polo events. You can pack a picnic and watch practice matches free during the week; there's a $6 per person charge on weekends.

Hadley's Fruit Orchards (48980 Seminole Dr., Cabazon, tel. 909/849–5255, open daily 7 AM to 9 PM) contains a vast selection of dried California fruit, plus nuts, date shakes, and wines. Taste samples before you buy.

Shopping

The Palm Springs area is full of toney boutiques and lively art galleries. The resort community also has several large air-conditioned indoor malls with major department stores and chic shops. El Paseo in nearby Palm Desert is the desert's fanciest shopping mecca, with its own collection of upscale and elegant galleries and shops. Most stores are open Monday–Saturday 10–5 or 6, and a fair number are open Sunday, typically noon–5.

Shopping Districts **Palm Canyon Drive** is Palm Springs's main shopping destination, although many of the major stores have moved to Palm Desert. What began as a dusty two-way dirt road is now a one-way, three-lane thoroughfare with parking on both sides. Its shopping core extends from Alejo Road on the north to Ramon Road on the south. Anchoring the center of the drive is the **Desert Fashion Plaza,** now a more functional than fashionable mall, which features **Saks Fifth Avenue, Gucci,** and **Sabina Children's Fashions.**

El Paseo is the trendiest shopping spot in the desert. French and Italian fashion boutiques, shoe salons, jewelry designers, children's boutiques, nearly 30 galleries, and restaurants are clustered around fountains and courtyards along this 2-mile Mediterranean-style avenue. Specialty shops include **Polo/Ralph Lauren** (73-111 El Paseo, tel. 619/340–1414), featuring Lauren's classic fashions and accessories for men and women, and **Cabale Cachet** (73-151 El Paseo, tel. 619/346–5805), a collection of European haute couture.

The **Palm Desert Town Center** (Hwy. 111 at Monterey Ave., tel. 619/346–2121) is an enclosed mall anchored by major department stores that include **Bullocks, I. Magnin, J. C. Penney,** and **Robinson's-May.** There are 150 specialty shops ranging from **The Gap** and **Contempo Casuals** to upmarket **Cache** and **Miller Stockman,** as well as 10 movie theaters, five restaurants, fast food, day-care service, and an **Ice Capades Chalet** skating rink.

The Atrium (69-930 Hwy. 111, Rancho Mirage) is a fantasyland for interior designers, containing an array of enterprises selling custom accessories, art objects, and furnishings.

Specialty Shops Although Palm Springs is known for glamour and high prices, the city does offer bargains if you know where to look. Several outlets

Discount can be found in the **Loehmann's Plaza** (2500 N. Palm Canyon Dr.), including **Mikasa Factory Store** (tel. 619/778–1080), **Dansk** (tel. 619/320–3304), and **Loehmann's** (tel. 619/322–0388). **Desert Hills Factory Stores** (48650 Seminole Rd., Cabazon, tel. 619/849–6641) is an outlet center with about 50 name-brand fashion shops selling at a discount.

Golf Equipment **Lady Golf** (42412 Bob Hope Dr., Rancho Mirage, tel. 619/773–4949) features a large selection of apparel and accessories, custom golf-club fitting, and a practice and teaching facility.
Nevada Bob's Discount Golf & Tennis (4721 E. Palm Canyon Dr., Palm Springs, tel. 619/324–0196) offers a large selection of golf and tennis equipment, clothing, and accessories.

Sports and the Outdoors

Participant Sports

The "Desert Guide" from *Palm Springs Life* magazine, available at most hotels and visitor information centers, contains a listing called "Courts and Courses." A complete listing of desert golf courses, including information about public availability and greens fees, is contained in the *Vacation Planner* published by Palm Springs Desert Resorts Convention and Visitors Bureau; it's available at most hotels. A listing of public golf courses also appears in the front of the GTE phone book.

Bicycling There are more than 35 miles of bike trails, with six mapped-out city tours. Trail maps are available at the **Palm Springs Recreation Department** (401 S. Pavilion, tel. 619/323–8272) and bike-rental shops. You can rent a bike at **Palm Springs Cyclery** (611 S. Palm Canyon Dr., Palm Springs, tel. 619/325–9319) and at **Mac's Bicycle Rental** (70053 Hwy. 111, Rancho Mirage, tel. 619/321–9444, which will deliver mountain, three-speed, and tandem bikes to area hotels.

Golf Palm Springs is known as the "Winter Golf Capital of the World," and a number of the courses are open to the public. Among these are the **Palm Springs Municipal Golf Course** (1885 Golf Club Dr., tel. 619/328–1005) and **Fairchilds Bel-Aire Greens Country Club** (1001 S. El Cielo Rd., Palm Springs, tel. 619/327–0332). **Mission Hills Resort Golf Club** (71-501 Dinah Shore Dr., Rancho Mirage, tel. 619/328–3198), a challenging Pete Dye–designed course, is also home to major tournaments. Don't be surprised to spot well-known politicians and Hollywood stars on the greens.

Hiking Nature trails abound in the **Indian Canyons, Mt. San Jacinto State Park and Wilderness,** and **Living Desert Reserve** (*see* Exploring, *above*). The Palm Springs Recreation Department (*see above*) has trail maps for $2.

Physical Fitness In a resort town featuring the "most beautiful bodies money can buy," you'll find a wide selection of fitness facilities. Among the hotels that have health clubs, **Marriott's Desert Springs Resort and Spa** is the most luxurious. Exercise facilities include a 22-station gym, Lifecycles, fitness classes, personal training, and sauna and steam rooms. *Tel. 619/341–1856. Daily membership: $20. Open from 6:30.*

Tennis Of the 600 or so tennis courts in the area, the following are open to the public: the **Palm Springs Tennis Center** (1300 Baristo Rd., tel. 619/320–0020), with nine lighted courts; **Ruth Hardy Park** (Tamarisk and Caballeros, no phone), with eight lighted courts and no court fee; and **Demuth Park** (4375 Mesquite Ave., tel. 619/325–8265), with four lighted courts.

Spectator Sports

Golf More than 100 golf tournaments are presented in Palm Springs; the two most popular are the **Bob Hope Desert Classic** (Jan.–Feb.) and the **Dinah Shore LPGA Championship** (Mar. or Apr.). Call the **Palm Springs Desert Resorts Convention and Visitors Bureau** (tel. 800/417–3529) for exact dates and places.

Tennis The *Newsweek* **Champions Cup tournament** (Feb. or Mar.), held at Hyatt Grand Champions Resort in Indian Wells, attracts the likes of Boris Becker and Yannick Noah. For tickets, tel. 619/341–2757.

Dining and Lodging

Dining Palm Springs area resorts have become weekend and winter homes to so many big-city types that it's not surprising to see the names of familiar restaurants—Scoma's of San Francisco, Morton's, Ruth's Chris Steak House. While there are many expensive, trendy eateries in the desert, diligent diners can also get a good meal quite inexpensively at storefront restaurants, diners, and chains that cater to local clientele. Those who are careful about fat and cholesterol will find that most desert restaurant menus contain a selection of heart-healthy items. Dining is generally casual at desert restaurants; a dress code may mean only that men must wear collared shirts. Most of the restaurants listed here are on or near Highway 111 between Palm Springs and La Quinta.

Highly recommended restaurants are indicated by a star ★.

Category	Cost*
$$$$	over $50
$$$	$30–$50
$$	$20–$30
$	under $20

per person for a three-course meal, excluding drinks, service, and 7 ³/₄% tax

Lodging One of the reasons the Palm Springs desert resorts attract so many celebrities, entertainment-industry honchos, and other notables is its stock of luxurious hotels. There is a full array of resorts, inns, clubs, spas, lodges, and condos, from small and private to big and bustling. Room rates cover an enormous range—from $40 to $1,600 a night—and also vary widely from summer to winter season. It is not unusual for a hotel to drop its rates from 50% to 60% during the summer (June through early Sept.). For a growing number of off-season travelers, the chance to stay in a $180 room for $60 is an offer they just can't refuse. If you're seeking budget or moderate accommodations, you're more likely to find them in Palm Springs than in the newer resort areas. Also discounts are sometimes given for extended stays.

Don't even think of visiting here during winter and spring holiday seasons without advance reservations. The **Palm Springs Chamber of Commerce** (tel. 619/325–1577) and **Palm Springs Tourism** (tel. 800/347–7746) can help you with hotel reservations and information. The *Vacation Planner,* available from the Convention and Visitors Bureau (tel. 800/417–3529), lists major hotels, motels, and resorts, including seasonal rates.

Highly recommended lodgings are indicated by a star ★.

Category	Cost*
$$$$	over $100
$$$	$75–$100
$$	$50–$75
$	under $50

*All prices are for a double room, excluding tax.

Rentals Condos, apartments, and even individual houses may be rented by the day, week, month, or for longer periods. Rates start at about $850 a week for a one-bedroom condo, $1,600 for two bedrooms, and $3,500 for three-bedroom house for a month. Contact **The Rental Connection** (Box 8567, Palm Springs 92263, tel. 619/320–7336 or 800/462–7256).

Cathedral City
Dining **The Wilde Goose.** The award-winning restaurant is popular with celebrities for its beef and lamb Wellington, and five varieties of duck. A specialty of the house is duck with apricot and triple sec sauce. The food and the service here are dependable. *67-938 Hwy. 111, tel. 619/328–5775. Reservations advised. Dress: casual. AE, D, DC, MC, V. No lunch. $$*

Red Bird Diner. Hosts Art and Gayla Morris offer comfort food along with a hearty laugh for guests at their '50s-style diner that even has counter service. This is a cute place with life-size murals of the decade's icons: James Dean, Ed Sullivan, and a bright red T-Bird. The specialty here is lamb, but Art also cooks country-fried steak, liver and onions, and chicken and dumplings. *Mission Plaza Center, 35-955 Date Palm Dr., tel. 619/324–7707. Dress: no jackets required after 4 PM. AE, D, DC, MC, V. $*

Lodging **Doubletree Resort at Desert Princess.** This 345-acre luxury golf resort has attractively decorated rooms and condo units with balconies or terraces, and refrigerators; some rooms have views. *67-967 Vista Chino, 92234, tel. 619/322–7000, fax 619/322–6853. 276 rooms, 13 suites and condos. Facilities: 2 restaurants, lounge with entertainment, golf course, pool, Jacuzzi, 10 tennis courts, health club, and racquetball courts. AE, DC, MC, V. $$$$*

Desert Hot Springs
Lodging

Two Bunch Palms. Reputedly built by Al Capone as an escape from the pressures of gangsterdom in 1920s Chicago, this collection of white-walled villas on 250 acres is still something of a secret hideaway for Hollywood celebrities, who come for its laid-back privacy and state-of-the-art spa. There are one- and two-bedroom villas, plus some condo units with kitchens, living rooms, and private hot tubs. *67-425 Two Bunch Palms Trail, 92240, tel. 619/329–8791 or 800/472–4334, fax 619/329–1317. 44 villas. Facilities: restaurant, pool, 2 tennis courts, jogging and hiking trails, natural rock grotto with mineral hot-water pools, mud baths, spa, Continental breakfast included in price. AE, MC, V. $$$$*

Indian Wells
Dining

Sirocco. This restaurant in the Stouffer Esmeralda Hotel features dishes of the Mediterranean shores: a splendid Spanish paella, roast lamb encrusted with herbs and peppercorns, seafood pastas. This is probably the best hotel restaurant in Palm Springs, both for its food and its gracious, impeccable service. *44400 Indian Wells La., tel. 619/773–4444. Reservations advised in winter. Jacket advised. AE, D, DC, MC, V. No lunch. $$$*

Lodging

Hyatt Grand Champions Resort. This stark white resort on 34 acres of natural desert is home to the *Newsweek* Champions Cup tennis tournament, which is played in the largest stadium in the West. Nicely appointed rooms are suite-style and are either split-level, one- or two-bedroom garden villas, or penthouses. All have balconies or terraces, living areas, and minibars. Some have fireplaces and private butler service. *44-600 Indian Wells La., 92210, tel. 619/341–1000 or 800/233–1234, fax 619/568–2236. 336 units. Facilities: 3 restaurants, lounge, 4 pools, Jacuzzis, 12 tennis courts, 2 golf courses, putting green, driving range, pro shop, health club with sauna, Camp Hyatt. AE, DC, MC, V. $$$$*

Stouffer Esmeralda Resort. The centerpiece of this luxurious Mediterranean-style resort is an eight-story atrium lobby with controlled fountain, surrounded by a dual grand staircase, which flows through a rivulet in the lobby floor to cascading pools and outside to lakes surrounding the property. Spacious, well-appointed guest rooms are decorated in light wood with green and blue accents; they have sitting areas, balconies, refreshment centers, two TV sets, and travertine-marble vanities in bathrooms. One pool has a sandy beach. Golf and tennis instruction are available. *44-400 Indian Wells La., 92210-9971, tel. 619/773–4444 or 800/552–4386, fax 619/773–9250. 560 rooms, 44 suites. Facilities: 3 restaurants, lounge with entertainment, 3 pools, 2 outdoor Jacuzzis, 2 golf courses, 7 tennis courts, health club, gallery. AE, DC, MC, V. $$$$*

La Quinta
Dining
★

Dolly Cunard's. This restaurant in a converted French-style villa features a Franco-Italian menu. The warm atmosphere and inventive cuisine, such as charred chili with four cheeses, grilled duck breast with mangoes and raspberries, and fresh peach in ravioli in a lemon and shallot sauce, have made it the area's biggest hit. *73-045 Calle Cadiz, tel. 619/564–4443. Reservations advised. Jacket and tie required. AE, MC, V. No lunch. Closed June–Sept. $$$*

La Quinta Cliffhouse. This popular "concept" restaurant perched halfway up a hillside offers sweeping mountain views at sunset, the early-California ambience of a western movie set, and an eclectic international menu that includes grilled shrimp Provençal, Caesar salad with chicken, ahi Szechuan style, and tiramisu. *78250 Hwy. 111, tel. 619/360–5991. Reservations advised. Dress: casual. AE, MC, V. No lunch. $–$$*

Lodging
★

La Quinta Hotel Golf and Tennis Resort. Opened in 1926, this lush green oasis with red-roofed, blue-trimmed casitas is the oldest resort in the desert. Rooms are in historic adobe casitas separated by broad expanses of lawn and in newer, two-story units surrounding individual swimming pools and brilliant gardens. Furnishings are simple; there are fireplaces, robes, stocked refrigerators, and fruit-laden orange trees right outside the door. The atmosphere is discreet and sparely luxurious, and a premium is placed on privacy, which accounts for La Quinta's continuing lure for the brightest Hollywood stars. Frank Capra, for example, lived here for many years, and it's said that Greta Garbo roamed the grounds bumming cigarettes from guests. Contemporary stars such as Michael Jackson, Clint Eastwood, and Natalie Cole still seek tranquillity here. Now managed jointly with PGA West, La Quinta arranges access to some of the most celebrated golf courses in the area: Jack Nicklaus Resort Course, PGA West TPC Stadium Course (home of the Skins Game), and the Mountain Course. Golf packages include accommodations, breakfast daily, and rounds of golf. *49-499 Eisenhower Dr., 92253, tel. 619/564–4111 or 800/854–1271, fax 619/564–7656. 640 rooms, including 22 suites. Facilities: 5 restaurants, lounge with entertainment, wine-tasting bar, 25 swimming pools, 35 outdoor Jacuzzis, 30 tennis courts, golf, beauty salon, children's program, holiday events. AE, D, DC, MC, V. $$$$*

Palm Desert
Dining

Mama Gina's. Among the best Italian restaurants in the Palm Springs area, this attractive, simply furnished trattoria was opened by the son of the original Mama Gina in Florence, Italy. There is an open kitchen where you can watch the chef from Tuscany prepare such specialties as deep-fried artichokes, fettuccine with porcini mushrooms, and prawns with artichoke and zucchini. The soups are robust. *73-705 El Paseo, tel. 619/568–9898. Reservations required. Dress: casual. AE, DC, MC, V. $$$*

Palomino Euro Bistro. One of the hot spots in the desert, this restaurant specializes in grilled and roasted entrées: spit-roasted garlic chicken, oak-fired thin-crust pizza, oven-roasted prawns. It's an interesting if noisy setting, with huge reproductions of famous French Impressionist paintings filling the walls. *73-101 Hwy. 111, tel. 619/773–9091. Reservations suggested. Dress: casual. AE, MC, V. No Sat. lunch. $$*

Café des Artistes. The desert version of a sidewalk café, this recently opened bistro has good garlicky French food and a trendy ambience, particularly at lunchtime, when the place is very busy. *73-640 El Paseo, tel. 619/346–0669. Dress: casual. AE, MC, V. No dinner Tues. $–$$*

Daily Grill. The smell of cookies baking might make you more hungry than you thought you were. Good thing, because portions are huge at this bustling deli-coffee shop. A dinner plate–size chicken pot pie is but one fine example. Best buys are the blue-plate specials, which include soup or salad, along with turkey meat loaf, beef-dip sandwiches, turkey steak, and unlimited thirst-quenching lemonade. *73-061 El Paseo, tel. 619/779–9911. Lunch reservations advised. Dress: casual. AE, MC, V. $*

Lodging

Marriott's Desert Springs Resort and Spa. This sprawling hotel is the most spectacular-looking resort in the desert. It's a U-shaped building with arms wrapped around the largest private lake in the desert, with 3 miles of shoreline. The centerpiece is an indoor, stair-stepped waterfall that flows right into the lake. From the base of the fall, guests and visitors can board boats for a worthwhile 10-minute tour of the grounds or a cruise to one of the hotel's restaurants. Nicely appointed rooms have lake or mountain views, balconies, oversize bathrooms, and minibars. There are long walks from lobby to rooms; if driving, request one close to the parking lot.

Because the resort hosts business groups and conventions, guests will find it busier and dressier than most desert hotels, with group activities often occupying pool and lawn areas. *74855 Country Club Dr., 92260, tel. 619/341–2211, fax 619/341–1730. 891 rooms, 51 suites. Facilities: 5 restaurants, 2 lounges, entertainment, 3 pools, Jacuzzis, 21 tennis courts, 2 golf courses, putting green, croquet, lawn bowling, badminton, volleyball, jogging trails, barbecue grills. AE, DC, MC, V. $$$$*

Palm Springs
Dining

Bono Restaurant and Racquet Club. Owned by Palm Springs's former mayor Sonny Bono, this restaurant serves southern Italian dishes like those his mother used to make. It's a favorite feeding station for show-biz folk and the curious, and a good place for pasta, chicken, veal, and scampi dishes. Outdoor dining is available. *1700 N. Indian Canyon Dr., tel. 619/322–6200. Reservations advised. Dress: casual. Valet parking. AE, D, DC, MC, V. No lunch. $$$*

Melvyn's Restaurant. "Lifestyles of the Rich and Famous" calls this Old World–style spot "one of the 10 best." It isn't, but it has a consistent local following. Snugly nestled in the gardens of the Ingleside Inn, it serves a weekend brunch that's a Palm Springs tradition. There is also a piano bar. *200 W. Ramon Rd., tel. 619/325–2323. Reservations advised. Jacket required. MC, V. $$$*

Lyon's English Grille. When was the last time you had real honest-to-goodness roast beef and Yorkshire pudding as only the Brits can make it? Lyon's has it, and other old-country favorites. Good value and good food make this a popular stop for the locals. *233 E. Palm Canyon Dr., tel. 619/327–1551. Reservations advised. Dress: casual. AE, DC, MC, V. No lunch. $$–$$$*

Brussels Cafe. The best spot in town for people-watching is this sidewalk café in the heart of Palm Canyon Drive. Try the Belgian waffles or homemade pâté. Beers from around the world are featured, and there's entertainment nightly. *109 S. Palm Canyon Dr., tel. 619/320–4177. Reservations required. Dress: casual. AE, D, MC, V. $$*

Cafe St. James. From the plant-filled balcony you can watch the passing parade below, and dine on Mediterranean-Italian cuisine, Indian curries, or vegetarian dishes. *254 N. Palm Canyon Dr., tel. 619/320–8041. Reservations advised. Dress: casual. AE, MC, V. No lunch. Closed Mon. $$*

Flower Drum. Related to the highly popular Flower Drum in New York, this health-conscious Chinese restaurant features Hunan, Peking, Shanghai, Canton, and Szechuan cuisines in a setting meant to resemble a Chinese village. *424 S. Indian Canyon Dr., tel. 619/323–3020. Reservations advised. Dress: casual. AE, MC, V. $$*

Las Casuelas Original. A longtime favorite among residents and visitors alike, this restaurant offers great (in size and taste) margaritas and average Mexican dishes: crab enchilada, carne asada, lobster Ensenada. It gets very, very crowded during the winter months. *368 N. Palm Canyon Dr., tel. 619/325–3213. Reservations advised. Dress: casual. AE, MC, V. $$*

Elmer's Pancake and Steak House. Forget about Aunt Jemima—Elmer's offers 25 varieties of pancakes and waffles. There are steaks, chicken, and seafood on the dinner menu. A children's menu is also available. *1030 E. Palm Canyon Dr., tel. 619/327–8419. No reservations. Dress: casual. AE, D, DC, MC, V. $*

Louise's Pantry. A local landmark, in the center of downtown Palm Springs for almost 40 years, the 1940s-style Louise's features downhome cooking such as chicken and dumplings and short ribs of beef. You can get soup, salad, entrée, beverage, and dessert for under $15. There's usually a line to get in. *124 S. Palm Canyon Dr., tel. 619/325–5124. No reservations. Dress: casual. MC, V. $*

Lodging **Autry Resort Hotel.** This venerable resort has recently undergone a complete renovation. Rooms are in two buildings and bungalows on 13 landscaped acres. The place is decked out for a number of activities, including tennis instruction at the Reed Anderson Tennis School, and dining and entertainment are offered nightly. *4200 E. Palm Canyon Dr., 92262, tel. 619/328–1171 or 800/443–6328, fax 619/324–6104. 187 units. Facilities: restaurant, 3 pools, Jacuzzis, 6 lighted tennis courts, fitness center with sauna and massage. AE, DC, MC, V. $$$$*

Hyatt Regency Suites. Located adjacent to the downtown Desert Fashion Plaza, this hotel's striking six-story asymmetrical lobby houses two restaurants. There are one-, two-, and three-bedroom suites with city or golf course/mountain views. *285 N. Palm Canyon Dr., 92262, tel. 619/322–9000 or 800/233–1234, fax 619/322–4027. 194 suites. Facilities: 2 restaurants, lounge, pool, golf privileges at Rancho Mirage Country Club. AE, DC, MC, V. $$$$*

★ **La Mancha Private Pool Villas and Court Club.** Only four blocks from downtown Palm Springs, this Spanish-Moroccan Hollywood-style retreat blocks out the rest of the world with plenty of panache. Opulently appointed villas, surrounded by lushly landscaped gardens, have kitchens, fireplaces, and private pools; four have private tennis courts. *444 N. Avenida Caballeros, 92262, tel. 619/323–1773, fax 619/323–5928. 54 villas. Facilities: restaurant, 7 tennis courts, paddle-tennis court, pool, putting greens, health club with sauna, bicycles, croquet lawns, convertibles available for local transportation. AE, DC, MC, V. $$$$*

Palm Springs Hilton Resort and Racquet Club. The cool, white marble elegance of this plant-filled resort hotel, just off Palm Canyon Drive, and its two superb restaurants make it a popular choice for visitors to the city. Rooms have private balconies and refrigerators. *400 E. Tahquitz Way, 92262, tel. 619/320–6868 or 800/522–6900, fax 619/323–2755. 189 rooms, 71 suites. Facilities: 2 restaurants, pool, 6 tennis courts, pro shop, health club, Jacuzzi. AE, DC, MC, V. $$$$*

Sundance Villas. Beautifully decorated, spacious time-share villas include fireplace, wet bar, kitchen, and private patio for dining or sunning. Each villa has a private pool and Jacuzzi. This is not a place for the weak of pocketbook. *303 Cabrillo Rd., 92262, tel. 619/325–3888, fax 619/323–3029. 19 villas. Facilities: pool, tennis, Jacuzzi, sauna, golf. AE, MC, V. $$$$*

Casa Cody. This very clean, Western-style bed-and-breakfast is just a few steps from the Palm Springs Desert Museum. Simply furnished spacious studios and one- and two-bedroom suites are individually decorated. Service is personal and gracious. *175 S. Cahuilla Rd., 92262, tel. 619/320–9346, fax 619/325–8610. 17 units. Facilities: 2 pools, kitchens, gardens, complimentary Continental breakfast. AE, MC, V. $$$*

Ingleside Inn. Like many desert lodgings, this hacienda-style inn attracts its share of Hollywood personalities, who appreciate good service and relative seclusion. Rooms are individually decorated, many with antiques. Those in the main building are dark and cool, even in summer. The adjacent Melvyn's Restaurant is locally popular. *200 W. Ramon Rd., 92262, tel. 619/325–0046, fax 619/325–0710. 29 rooms. Facilities: pool, Jacuzzi, sauna, tennis. AE, MC, V. $$$*

Korakia Pensione. This bed-and-breakfast is one of several that have opened here recently. A historic Moorish-style home that was built in the 1920s by Scottish artist Gordon Coutts, it was once a center of the arts community. The current owner has refurbished the rooms with antiques, fireplaces, handmade furniture, and Oriental rugs. *257 S. Patencio Rd., tel. 619/864–6411. 12 rooms. Facilities: pool, kitchens in some rooms. No credit cards. $$–$$$$*

Spa Hotel and Mineral Springs. With its brilliant pink facade, you can't miss the Spa as you drive through the Springs. This hotel has had its ups and downs since it was built in 1963 over the original Agua Caliente springs. Now owned by the Agua Caliente tribe, it underwent extensive renovation in 1993, with rooms decorated in soft desert pinks and blues and light-wood furniture. Not trendy or splashy, the Spa seems to appeal to an older crowd that appreciates its soothing waters and downtown location. *100 N. Indian Canyon Dr., 92262, tel. 619/778–1507 or 800/854–1279, fax 619/325–3344. 230 rooms, 20 suites. Facilities: restaurant, 2 lounges, swimming pool, outdoor Jacuzzis, fitness center, spa, beauty salon. AE, D, DC, MC, V. $$–$$$$*

Inn at the Racquet Club. This represents a new name and a new outlook on the legendary Racquet Club. Built originally by actors Charlie Farrell and Ralph Bellamy in the 1930s, the club brought the movie stars to the Springs. Once a private club, notable for Hollywood hijinks, partying, and the "discovery" of Marilyn Monroe, it was later opened to the public to mixed reviews. New owners have reduced the scale and renovated 24 of the original red-roofed cottages used by the stars; most have fireplaces and private patios. *2743 N. Indian Canyon Dr., 92262, tel. 619/325–1281, fax 619/325–3429. 86 units. Facilities: restaurant, lounge, 3 pools, Jacuzzi, sauna, fitness center, 10 tennis courts, volleyball and basketball courts, bicycle rentals. AE, DC, MC, V. $$–$$$*

Courtyard by Marriott. This property represents part of the Marriott chain's effort to expand into comfortable, smaller hotels offering a good value. The concept works nicely. *1300 Tahquitz Canyon Way, 92262, tel. 619/322–6100. 149 rooms. Facilities: restaurant, pool, fitness center, Jacuzzi, tennis. AE, DC, MC, V. $$*

Villa Royale. In this charming bed-and-breakfast, each room is individually decorated with a European theme. Some rooms have private Jacuzzis, fireplaces, kitchens. The grounds feature lush gardens. *1620 Indian Trail, 92264, tel. 619/327–2314, fax 619/322–3794. 34 rooms. Facilities: restaurant, lounge, 2 pools, Jacuzzi. AE, MC, V. $–$$$$*

Mira Loma Hotel. The small scale and friendly atmosphere make this hotel popular with Europeans. Rooms and suites have eclectic decor, some Oriental, some 1940s Hollywood; all have refrigerators, patios, and fireplaces. Marilyn Monroe slept here. Really. *1420 N. Indian Canyon Dr., 92262, tel. 619/320–1178, fax 619/320–5308. 12 rooms. Facilities: pool. AE, MC, V. $*

Villa Rosa Inn. This is a cute pink-and-white inn with rooms surrounding a small flower-filled courtyard. There is no air-conditioning. *1577 S. Indian Trail, 92264, tel. 619/327–5915. 6 units. Facilities: pool, kitchens in rooms. AE, MC, V. $*

Westward Ho Hotel. This typical motel-style property is popular with tour groups. *701 E. Palm Canyon Dr., 92262, tel. 619/320–2700, fax 619/322–5354. 210 rooms. Facilities: coffee shop, lounge, pool, therapy pool. AE, MC, V. $*

Rancho Mirage
Dining

Dominick's. An old favorite of Frank Sinatra's and what's left of his "rat pack," the steaks, pasta, and veal dishes here are the order of the day. *70-030 Hwy. 111, tel. 619/324–1711. Reservations advised. Dress: casual. AE, DC, MC, V. No lunch. $$$*

Wally's Desert Turtle. If price is no object, and you like plush, gilded decor, then this is where to come. You'll be surrounded by the golden names of Palm Springs and Hollywood society, and served old-fashioned French cooking: rack of lamb, imported Dover sole, braised sea bass, veal Oscar, chicken Normande, and dessert soufflés. *71-775 Hwy. 111, tel. 619/568–9321. Reservations required. Jacket required. Valet parking. AE, MC, V. No lunch Sat.–Thurs. $$$*

Bangkok V. Dedicated spicy-food fans gather here at lunch or early evening to savor beautifully prepared and artistically presented Thai cuisine. When you order be sure to tell them how hot you want your food. It's a lovely place, whether you eat in the bright dining rooms or outside at an umbrella-shaded table. *72-930 Hwy. 111, tel. 619/770–9508. Reservations suggested. Dress: casual. AE, DC, MC, V. No lunch Sat., Sun. $$*

Zorba's. This festive spot, tucked away in a shopping center, is a bit hard to locate. But it's worth finding for the tasty Greek food and entertainment. A smallish spot with celebrity photos plastered on the walls, it features kabobs, Greek salad, and dolmas, along with live music, dancing, and singing waiters. *42434 Bob Hope Dr., tel. 619/340–3066. Reservations advised. Dress: casual. AE, MC, V. $$*

Lodging **Ritz-Carlton Rancho Mirage.** This hotel is tucked into a hillside in the Santa Rosa Mountains with sweeping views of the valley below. Sheep from the surrounding bighorn preserve frequently visit the hotel grounds. The surroundings are elegant, with gleaming marble and brass, original artwork, deep plush carpeting, and remarkable comfort. All rooms are enormous and meticulously appointed with antiques, fabric wallcoverings, marble bathrooms, and often two phones and two TVs. Service is impeccable, anticipating your every need. *68-900 Frank Sinatra Dr., 92270, tel. 619/321–8282 or 800/241–3333, fax 619/321–6928. 221 rooms, 19 suites. Facilities: 3 restaurants, lounge with entertainment, pool, outdoor Jacuzzi, 10 tennis courts, croquet, spa, business services center, 9-hole pitch-and-putt golf, basketball, volleyball, children's programs. AE, DC, MC, V. $$$$*

Westin Mission Hills Resort. This sprawling Moroccan-style resort on 360 acres, adjacent to the annual Nabisco Dinah Shore LPGA Classic, is surrounded by fairways and putting greens. Rooms are in two-story buildings enveloping patios and fountains scattered throughout the property. Nicely furnished, the rooms have soft desert colors, terra-cotta tile floors, shuttered windows, and private patios or balconies; amenities include double sinks, in-room coffee makers, and refrigerators. Paths and creeks meander through the complex, encircling a lagoon-style swimming pool with a 60-foot water slide. *71333 Dinah Shore Dr., 92270, tel. 619/328–5955 or 800/228–3000, fax 619/321–2955. 512 rooms. Facilities: 7 restaurants, lounge with entertainment, 3 pools, outdoor Jacuzzis, 7 tennis courts, 2 18-hole golf courses, health club, children's programs. AE, DC, MC, V. $$$$*

The Arts and Nightlife

For complete listings of upcoming events, pick up a copy of *Palm Springs Life* magazine or *Palm Springs Life*'s "Desert Guide," a free monthly publication found in any hotel.

The Arts

The **McCallum Theatre** (73-000 Fred Waring Dr., Palm Desert, tel. 619/340–2787), site of the **Palm Springs International Film Festival** in January, is the principal cultural venue in the desert, offering a number of arts series November through May. Programs include film, classical music, opera, ballet, popular music, and theater.

The **Annenberg Theatre** (Palm Springs Desert Museum, 101 Museum Dr., north of Tahquitz Way, tel. 619/325–7186 or 619/325–4490) is the other film-festival venue. The 450-seat theater hosts film series, Sunday-afternoon chamber concerts, lectures, Broadway shows, and opera.

Of the many arts festivals held in the desert, **La Quinta Arts Festival** (tel. 619/564–1244), normally the third weekend in March, displays the best work and has the classiest entertainment, food, and celebrities.

Concerts **Palm Springs Desert Museum** (*see* Exploring, *above*) presents a regular schedule of classical music concerts on Sunday afternoons.

Theater The **Fabulous Palm Springs Follies,** the hottest show in the desert, presents 10 sellout performances each week. A vaudeville-style revue, starring extravagantly costumed retired (but very much in shape) showgirls, singers, and dancers, is presented afternoons and evenings at the Plaza Theater (128 S. Palm Canyon Dr., tel. 916/327–0225, admission $24.50–$37, call for schedule).

Valley Players Guild, a well-established community theater, performs at the Garden Amphitheater and Actors Showcase Theater, both located at the Desert Fashion Plaza (123 N. Palm Canyon Dr., tel. 619/320–9898).

Nightlife

Two good sources for finding current nightlife attractions are the *Desert Sun* (the local newspaper) and *Guide* magazine, a monthly publication distributed free at most downtown merchants' counters.

Live entertainment, ranging from soft dinner music to song-and-dance numbers, is frequently found in the city's hotels and restaurants. The piano bar at **Melvyn's Ingleside Inn** is popular.

Comedy Clubs **The Comedy Haven.** Stand-up comics and improv groups dished up with American/Italian fare. *Desert Fashion Plaza (enter parking lot from Tahquitz Way), tel. 619/320–7855.*

Dancing Between the flashing lights of its top-40 disco and the retro-memorabilia in its new '50s–'60s room, **Cecil's on Sunrise** (1775 E. Palm Canyon Dr., tel. 619/320–4202) is bound to keep you dancing. There's dancing to live country music at the **Cactus Corral** (67–501 E. Palm Canyon Dr., Cathedral City, tel. 619/321–8558). **Costas** (Marriott's Desert Springs, 74-855 Country Club Dr., Palm Desert, tel. 619/341–1795) has live bands for dancing in a lakeside setting. **Zelda's** (169 N. Indian Canyon Dr., Palm Springs, tel. 619/325–2375) is another active spot featuring talent and fashion shows, hot-body competitions, and limbo contests.

Jazz **Peabody's Jazz Studio and Coffee Bar** (134 S. Palm Canyon Dr., Palm Springs, tel. 619/333–1877) presents jazz in a warm atmosphere. **Lincoln View Coffee House** (278-C N. Palm Canyon Dr., Palm Springs, tel. 619/327–6365) presents jams on Sunday afternoon and live jazz Friday and Saturday nights.

16 The Mojave Desert and Death Valley

By Aaron
Sugarman

When most people put together their "must-see" list of California attractions, the desert isn't often among the top contenders. What with the heat and the vast, seemingly empty tracts of land, the desert is certainly no Disneyland. But then, that's precisely why it deserves a closer look. The desert is one of the last frontiers. It offers an overwhelming richness of natural beauty: rolling waves of sand dunes, black cinder cones thrusting up hundreds of feet into the air from a blistered desert floor, riotous sheets of wildflowers, the bizarre shape of the Joshua tree basking in an orange glow at sunset, and an abundant silence that is both dramatic and startling.

What is probably most surprising about the desert is its accessibility. A large portion of the desert can be seen from the comfort of an air-conditioned car. And don't despair if you are without air-conditioning—just avoid the middle of the day and the middle of the summer, good advice for all desert travel. Believe everything you've ever heard about desert heat; it can be brutal. A temperature of 134° was once recorded at Furnace Creek in Death Valley, the hottest place on the planet. But during mornings and evenings, particularly in the spring and fall, the temperature ranges from cool and crisp to pleasantly warm and dry: perfect for hiking and driving.

The Mojave Desert begins just north of the San Bernardino mountains, along the northern edge of Los Angeles, and extends north 150 miles into the Eureka Valley and east 200 miles to the Colorado River. Death Valley lies north and east of the Mojave, jutting into Nevada near Beatty. Mojave, with elevations ranging from 3,000 to 5,000 feet above sea level, is known as the High Desert; Death Valley, with points at almost 300 feet below sea level, is the lowest spot in the United States.

Because of the vast size of California's deserts, an area about as big as Ohio, and the frequently extreme weather, careful planning is essential for an enjoyable desert adventure. Conveniences, facilities, trails, gas stations, and supermarkets do not lurk just around the corner from many desert sights. Different pieces of the desert can be easily handled in day trips, but more extensive exploring will require overnight stays. Reliable maps are a must, as signage is limited, and, in some places, nonexistent. Other important accessories include a compass, extra food and water (three gallons per person per day is recommended), sunglasses, extra clothes (for wind or cool nights), a hat (if you're going to do any walking around in the sun), and plenty of sunscreen. Other than that, a pair of binoculars can come in handy, and don't forget your camera: You're likely to see things you've never seen before.

Essential Information

Important Addresses and Numbers

Tourist
Information

Bureau of Land Management (BLM) (California Desert District Office, 6221 Box Springs Blvd., Riverside 92507, tel. 909/697–5200 or 800/446–6743) provides information about BLM campgrounds and other recreational activities in the desert areas. Three other resources for brochures, books, or information are **California Desert Information Center** (831 Barstow Rd., Barstow 92311, tel. 619/256–8313); **Death Valley Chamber of Commerce** (Box 157, Shoshone 92384, tel. 619/852–4524); and **Interagency Visitor Center** (Junction, Hwy. 136 and U.S. 395, Drawer R, Lone Pine 93545, tel. 619/876–6222).

Emergencies **BLM Rangers** (tel. 714/383–5652). **Police:** San Bernardino County Sheriff (tel. 619/256–1796). **Hospital:** Community Hospital (Barstow, tel. 619/256–1761).

Getting Around

By Car The Mojave is shaped like a giant *L*, with one leg north and the other east. To travel north through the Mojave, take I–10 east out of Los Angeles to I–15 north. Just through the Cajon Pass, pick up U.S. 395, which runs north through Victor Valley, Boron, the Rand Mining District, and China Lake. To travel east, continue on I–15 to Barstow. From Barstow there are two routes: I–40, which passes through the mountainous areas of San Bernardino County, whisks by the Providence mountains and enters Arizona at Needles; or the more northerly I–15, which passes south of Calico, near Devil's Playground and the Kelso Sand Dunes, and then veers northeast toward Las Vegas.

Some travelers may wish to avoid Cajon Pass, elevation 4,250 feet. To do this, take I–210 north of Los Angeles to Route 14 north. Head east 67 miles on Route 58 to the town of Barstow and pick up I–15 there. Continue east on I–15 to Highway 127, a very scenic route north through the Mojave to Death Valley.

Death Valley can be entered from the southeast or the west. Exit U.S. 395 at either Highway 190 or 178 to enter from the west. From the southeast: Take Highway 127 north from I–15 and then link up with either Highway 178, which travels west into the valley and then cuts north past Funeral Peak, Badwater, Dante's View, and Zabriskie Point before meeting up with Highway 190 at Furnace Creek, or continue on Highway 127 north for 28 miles and then take Highway 190 west straight into the middle of Death Valley.

Guided Tours

The following organizations regularly sponsor hikes, tours, and outings in the California deserts. Call or write them for more information.
Audubon Society (Western Regional Office, 555 Audubon Pl., Sacramento, CA 95825, tel. 916/481–5332). **California Native Plant Society** (1722 J St., #15, Sacramento, CA 95814, tel. 916/447–CNPS). **Fred Harvey** (tel. 619/786–2345) conducts daily bus tours to Death Valley attractions, including Scotty's Castle, Dante's View, and Amaragosa Opera. **Nature Conservancy** (785 Market St., San Francisco, CA 94103, tel. 415/777–0487). **Sierra Club** (730 Polk St., San Francisco, CA 94109, tel. 415/776–2211).

Highlights for First-Time Visitors

Calico Early Man Archeological Site
Dante's View
Petroglyph Canyons

Exploring the Mojave Desert and Death Valley

The Mojave Desert

Numbers in the margin correspond to points of interest on the Mojave Desert map.

Although the Mojave Desert is a sprawling space, many of its visitable attractions are conveniently situated on a north–south axis along U.S. 395 and Highway 178 and an east–west axis that runs between I–15 and I–40. We'll describe tours stretching roughly 120 miles along each axis, and a third tour that winds its way through Death Valley, which is between the two routes. If you plan to stop overnight en route to Death Valley, both Lone Pine and Ridgecrest on U.S. 395 offer tourist services and accommodations, as do Barstow and Baker on I–15.

The Western Mojave

❶ On I–15, just before you reach U.S. 395 on the northbound tour, you cross Cajon Pass, riding over the infamous **San Andreas Fault**—an apocalyptic way to start a desert trip.

❷ About 70 miles farther on U.S. 395, you enter the **Rand Mining District,** consisting of the towns of Randsburg, Red Mountain, and Johannesburg. Randsburg is one of the few authentic gold-mining communities that hasn't become a ghost town. The town first boomed with the discovery of gold in the Rand Mountains in 1895 and, along with the neighboring settlements, grew to support the successful Yellow Aster Mine. Rich tungsten ore was discovered during World War I, and silver was found in 1919. All told, the money brought in by these precious metals is estimated at more than $35 million. Randsburg still sports its authentic Old West heritage. The picturesque town has some original Gold Rush buildings, plus a few antiques shops, a general store, and the city jail.

❸ Just to the northwest of the Rand Mining District is **Red Rock Canyon State Park.** The canyon is a feast for the eyes with its layers of pink, white, red, rust, and brown rocks. Entering the park from the south, you pass through a steep-walled gorge and enter a wide bowl tinted pink by what was once hot volcanic ash. The human history of this area goes back some 20,000 years to the canyon dwellers known only as the Old People. Mojave Indians roamed the land for several hundred years until Gold Rush fever hit the region in the mid- to late 1800s; remains of mining operations dot the countryside. The canyon was later invaded by filmmakers and has starred in westerns. The state park can be found on either side of Highway 14, about 10 miles south of where it meets U.S. 395. The ranger station is northwest on Abbott Drive from Highway 14.

❹ Heading northwest, you will find **Short Canyon** about a half-mile from the intersection of Highway 14 and U.S. 395. Sierra snows and natural springs feed the stream that flows down the rocky canyon, spills over a falls, and then sinks into the sand. In good years, there are large beds of wildflowers, and, even in very dry years, there are still some splashes of color. In the spring, a half-mile hike along the stream brings you to a 20-foot waterfall. Head west on the canyon road you'll find just south of Brady's Cafe on U.S. 395, but only after checking on current road conditions with the BLM (tel. 619/375-7125).

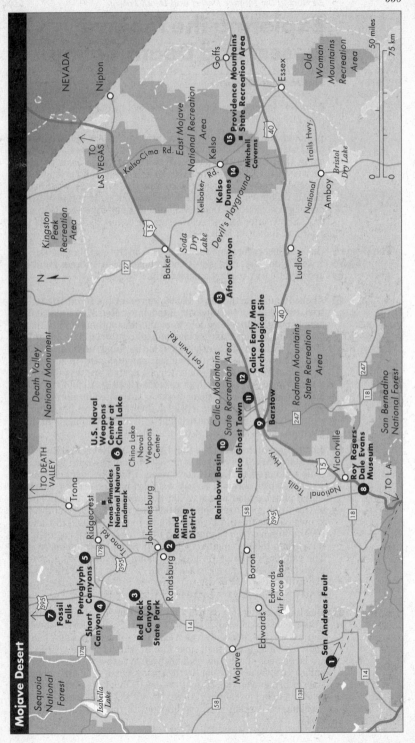

Mojave Desert

550

NEVADA

TO LAS VEGAS

TO DEATH VALLEY

TO LA

Death Valley National Monument

Kingston Peak Recreation Area

Sequoia National Forest

Isabella Lake

Nipton

Goffs

Essex

Old Woman Mountains Recreation Area

East Mojave National Recreation Area

15 Providence Mountains State Recreation Area

Kelso-Cima Rd.

Kelso

Kelso Dunes **14** Mitchell Caverns

Kelbaker Rd.

Devil's Playground

Baker

Soda Dry Lake

13 Afford Canyon
Afton Canyon

Ludlow

Amboy

Bristol Dry Lake

Trails Hwy.

National Trails Hwy.

12 Calico Early Man Archeological Site

Fort Irwin Rd.

Calico Mountains State Recreation Area

11

9 Barstow

Rodman Mountains State Recreation Area

San Bernardino National Forest

TO DEATH VALLEY

Trona

Ridgecrest

Trona Pinnacles National Natural Landmark

U.S. Naval Weapons Center at China Lake
6 China Lake Naval Weapons Center

Trona Rd.

Johannesburg

Rand Mining District 2

Randsburg

Rainbow Basin 10

Calico Ghost Town

Victorville

Roy Rogers-Dale Evans Museum 8

Petroglyph Canyons 5

Short Canyon 4

Red Rock Canyon State Park 3

Fossil Falls 7

Mojave

Edwards

Edwards Air Force Base

Boron

San Andreas Fault 1

N

0   50 miles
0   75 km

⑤ The nearby **Petroglyph Canyons** (from Short Canyon, take U.S. 395 east to Hwy. 178 and continue east) provide one of the desert's most amazing spectacles. The two canyons, commonly called Big and Little Petroglyph, contain what is probably the greatest concentration of rock art in the country. Scratched or pecked into the shiny desert varnish (oxidized minerals) that coats the canyon's dark basaltic rocks are thousands of images. Some are figures of animals and people, some seemingly abstract—maybe just the doodles of ancient man—and all are exceptionally preserved and protected. The feel-

⑥ ing of living history is incredible. The canyons are in the **U.S. Naval Weapons Center at China Lake,** and access is limited. Full-day weekend tours must be arranged well in advance through the **Maturango Museum** (China Lake Blvd. and Las Flores Ave., Ridgecrest, tel. 619/375–6900), which will also provide you with background on what you will see. *Tour admission: $15, children under 6 not admitted.*

⑦ **Fossil Falls** is 20 miles up U.S. 395 from Highway 14 then 1/2 mile east on Cinder Cone Road. On the way, you'll pass Little Lake, a good place to see migrating waterfowl in the spring and fall, including several varieties of ducks and geese and probably pelicans as well. The area just north of the lake is often covered with wildflowers. As you pass the lake, Red Hill comes into view ahead of you. The hill is a small volcano that was active about 20,000 years ago. Approaching the falls you cross a large volcanic field; the falls themselves drop an impressive distance along the channel cut by the Owens River through the hardened lava flows.

The Eastern Mojave We'll start the eastward tour in **Victorville,** less than 20 miles from Cajon Pass. The bit of water flowing along the eastern side of I–15, near **Mojave Narrows Regional Park**, is one of the few places where the Mojave River runs aboveground. For the most part, the 150-mile-long river flows from the San Bernardino mountains north and east underneath the desert floor. The park itself offers boat rentals,

⑧ an equestrian center, fishing, and camping. Then there is the **Roy Rogers–Dale Evans Museum,** which exhibits the personal and professional memorabilia of the famous stars. Yes, Roy's faithful horse, Trigger, is here. *Mojave Narrows Park, 18000 Yates Rd., tel. 619/245–2226. Admission: $4 per vehicle entry fee; camping $9 a night, or $10 with two fishing passes. Open daily 7 AM–dusk. Roy Rogers-Dale Evans Museum, 15650 Seneca Rd., tel. 619/243–4547. Admission: $4 adults, $3 children ages 13–16 and senior citizens, $2 children ages 6–12. Open daily 9–5; closed Thanksgiving and Christmas.*

⑨ Continue north on I–15 to **Barstow,** established in 1886 when a subsidiary of the Atchison, Topeka and Santa Fe Railroad began construction of a depot and hotel at this junction of its tracks and the 35th-parallel transcontinental lines. The **Desert Information Center** (831 Barstow Rd., tel. 619/256–8313) contains exhibits about desert ecology, wildflowers, wildlife, and other features of the desert environment. Travelers information is provided at 1610 AM on the radio dial.

⑩ **Rainbow Basin,** 8 miles north of Barstow, looks as if it could be on Mars, perhaps because so many sci-fi movies depicting the red planet have been filmed here. There is a tremendous sense of upheaval; huge slabs of red, orange, white, and green stone tilt at crazy angles like ships about to capsize. At points along the spectacularly scenic 6-mile drive it is easy to imagine you are alone in the world, hidden among the colorful badlands that give the basin its name. Hike the many washes and you are likely to see the fossilized remains of creatures that roamed the basin 12 million to 16 million years ago: mastodons, large and small camels, rhinos, dog-bears, birds, and insects. Leave any fossils you find where they are—they are protected by Federal law. *Take Fort Irwin Rd. about 5 mi north to Fossil Bed Rd., a graded dirt road, and head west 3 mi. Call the Desert Information Center in Barstow (tel. 619/256–8313) for more information.*

⓫ After a 10-mile drive northeast from Barstow, you can slip into the more recent past at **Calico Ghost Town.** Calico became a wild—and rich—mining town after a rich deposit of silver was found around 1881. In 1886, after more than $85 million worth of silver, gold, and other precious metals were harvested from the multicolored "calico" hills, the price of silver fell and the town slipped into decline. "Borax" Smith helped revive the town in 1889 when he started mining the unglamorous but profitable mineral borax, but that boom busted by the turn of the century. The effort to restore the ghost town was started by Walter Knott of Knott's Berry Farm fame in 1960. Knott handed the land over to San Bernardino County in 1966, and it became a regional park. Today, the 1880s come back to life as you stroll the wooden sidewalks of Main Street, browse through several western shops, roam the tunnels of Maggie's Mine, and take a ride on the Calico–Odessa Railroad. Special festivals in March, May, October, and November add to Calico's Old West flavor. *Ghost Town Rd., 3 mi north of I–15, tel. 619/254–2122. Admission: $6 per vehicle. Open daily 9–5.*

⓬ If you're at all curious about life 200,000 years ago, the **Calico Early Man Archeological Site** is a must-see. Nearly 12,000 tools—scrapers, cutting tools, choppers, hand picks, stone saws, and the like—have been excavated from the site since 1964. Prior to finding the site, many archaeologists believed the first humans came to North America "only" 10,000 to 20,000 years ago. Dr. Louis Leakey, the noted archaeologist, was so impressed with the findings that he became the Calico Project director from 1963 to his death in 1972; his old camp is now a visitor center and museum. The Calico excavations provide a rare opportunity to see artifacts, buried in the walls and floors of the excavated pits, fashioned by the earliest known Americans. Trail maps are available for self-guided tours. *15 mi northeast of Barstow via I–15; take Minneola Rd. north for 3 mi, tel. 619/256–3591. Open Wed.–Sun. 8–4:30. Guided tours of the dig are offered Thurs.–Sun. at 9:30, 11:30, 1:30, and 3:30.*

⓭ Because of its colorful, steep walls, **Afton Canyon** is often called the Grand Canyon of the Mojave. The canyon was carved out over many thousands of years by the rushing waters of the Mojave River, which makes another of its rare aboveground appearances here. And where you find water in the desert, you'll find trees, grasses, and wildlife. The canyon has been popular for a long time; Indians and later white settlers following the Mojave Trail from the Colorado River to the Pacific coast often set up camp here, near the welcome presence of water. *About 38 mi from Barstow on I–15; take the Afton turnoff and follow a good dirt road about 3 mi southwest.*

Although there is a broad range of terrain that qualifies, nothing says "desert" quite like graceful, wind-blown sand dunes. And the ⓮ white-sand **Kelso Dunes,** about 40 miles southeast of Baker, are perfect, pristine desert dunes. They cover 70 square miles, often at heights of 500–600 feet, and can be reached in an easy half-mile walk from where you have to leave your car. When you reach the top of one of the dunes, kick a little bit of sand down the lee side and find out why they say the sand "sings." In Kelso, there is a Mission Revival depot dating from 1925, one of the very few of its kind still standing. *I–15 to Baker, then take Kelbaker Rd. south 35 mi to town of Kelso; dunes are 7 mi ahead.*

⑮ Our last stops in the Eastern Mojave are the **Providence Mountains State Recreation Area** and the **Mitchell Caverns Natural Preserve.** The recreation area's visitor center, at an elevation of 4,300 feet, offers spectacular views of mountain peaks, dunes, buttes, rocky crags, and desert valleys. The caves, known as El Pakiva and Tecopa, offer a rare opportunity to see all three types of cave formations—dripstone, flowstone, and erratics—in one place. The year-round 65° temperature is also a nice break from the heat. *Take I–40 east from Barstow 100 mi to Essex Rd., then head northwest for 16 mi to state recreation area, tel. 619/389–2281. Admission: $4 adults, $2 children. Guided tours of caves offered Sept.–June, weekdays at 1:30 PM, weekends and holidays at 1:30 and 3; July and Aug., weekends only. Tours gather at visitor center.*

Death Valley

Numbers in the margin correspond to points of interest on the Death Valley map.

Distances are deceiving in this large park, which is half again as big as the state of Delaware. It's a good idea to plan excursions carefully; the trip to Scotty's Castle, for example, can take a half-day. Fees of $5 per vehicle, collected at entrance stations and at the visitor center, are valid for seven days.

The topography of Death Valley is a minilesson in geology. Two hundred million years ago, seas covered the area, depositing layers of sediment and fossils. Between 5 million and 35 million years ago, faults in the earth's crust and volcanic activity pushed and folded the ground, causing mountain ranges to rise and the valley floor to drop. The valley was then filled periodically by lakes, which eroded the surrounding rocks into fantastic formations and deposited the salts that now cover the floor of the basin. Today, the area has 14 square miles of sand dunes, 200 square miles of crusty salt flats, 11,000-foot mountains, hills and canyons of many colors. There are more than 1,000 species of plants and trees—21 of which are unique to the valley, like the yellow Panamint Daisy, and the blue-flowered Death Valley Sage.

❶ Starting from the northernmost point, **Scotty's Castle** is an odd apparition rising out of a canyon. This $2.5-million Moorish mansion, begun in 1924 and never completed, takes its name from Walter Scott, better known as Death Valley Scotty. An ex-cowboy, prospector, and performer in Buffalo Bill's Wild West Show, Scotty always told people the castle was his, financed by gold from a secret mine. That secret mine was, in fact, a Chicago millionaire named Albert Johnson, who was advised by doctors to spend time in a warm, dry climate. The house sports works of art, imported carpets, handmade European furniture, and a tremendous pipe organ. Guided tours feature costumed rangers portraying life at the castle in 1939. Tours are conducted frequently, but waits up to two hours can be expected during busy seasons. *Located on Hwy. 190N, tel. 619/786–2392. Admission: $6 adults, $3 children 6–11. Grounds open daily 7 AM–6 PM; tours 9–5.*

❷ Following Highway 190 south, you'll come to the remains of the famed **Harmony Borax Works,** from which the renowned 20-mule teams hauled borax to the railroad town of Mojave. Those teams were a sight to behold: 20 mules hitched up to a single massive

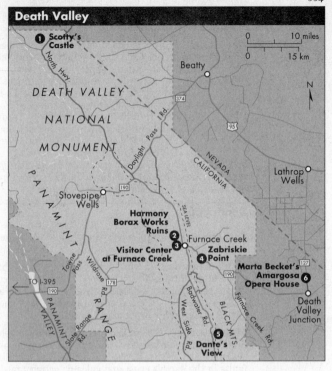

Death Valley

1 Scotty's Castle

Beatty

DEATH VALLEY

NATIONAL

MONUMENT

Lathrop Wells

Stovepipe Wells

Harmony Borax Works Ruins

2

3 Furnace Creek

Visitor Center at Furnace Creek

Zabriskie

4 Point

Marta Becket's Amargosa Opera House 6

Death Valley Junction

5 Dante's View

TO I-395

0   10 miles
0   15 km

N

NEVADA
CALIFORNIA

PANAMINT
RANGE

PANAMINT VALLEY

BLACK MTS.

wagon, carrying a load of 10 tons of borax to a town 165 miles away through burning desert. The teams plied the route between 1884 and 1907, when the railroad finally arrived in Zabriskie. You can visit the ruins of the Harmony Borax Works. The Borax Museum, 2 miles farther south, houses original mining machinery and historical displays in a building that used to serve as a boardinghouse for miners; the adjacent structure is the original mule-team barn. *Look for Harmony Borax Works Rd. on Hwy. 190, about 50 mi south of Scotty's Castle; take road west a short distance to ruins.*

3 Between the ruins and the museum you will see a sign for the **Visitor Center at Furnace Creek.** The center provides guided walks, exhibits, publications, and helpful rangers. The center is open 8–8. Call the National Park Service in Death Valley (tel. 619/786–2331) for more information on visitor-center services.

4 **Zabriskie Point,** about 4 miles south of the visitor center, is one of the park's most scenic spots. Not particularly high—only about 710 feet—it overlooks a striking badlands panorama with wrinkled, cinnamon-color hills. You may recognize it—or at least its name—from the film *Zabriskie Point* by the Italian director Michaelangelo Antonioni. Where Highway 178 splits off from Highway 190, follow it

5 south about 13 miles to **Dante's View.** This viewpoint is more than 5,000 feet up in the Black Mountains. In the dry desert air, you can see most of the 110 miles the valley is stretched across. The oasis of Furnace Creek is a green spot to the north. The view up and down is equally astounding: The tiny blackish patch far below you is Badwater, the lowest point in the country at 280 feet below sea level; on the western horizon is Mt. Whitney, the highest spot in the continental United States at 14,495 feet. Those of you in great shape may

want to try the 14-mile hike up to Telescope Peak. The view, not surprisingly, is breathtaking—as is the 3,000-foot elevation gain of the hike. The best time to visit any of these viewpoints is early morning or late afternoon when the colors and shapes of the surrounding desert are highlighted.

❻ Just outside the park, at Death Valley Junction, is an unexpected pleasure to rival Scotty's Castle—**Marta Becket's Amargosa Opera House.** Marta Becket is an artist and dancer from New York who first saw the town of Amargosa while on tour in 1964. Three years later she came back, had a flat tire in the same place, and on impulse decided to buy a boarded-up theater amid a complex of run-down Spanish colonial buildings. Today, the population of the town is still two people and about a dozen cats, but three nights a week, cars, motor homes, and buses roll in to catch the show she has been presenting for more than 20 years. To compensate for the sparse crowds her show attracted in the early days, Becket painted herself an audience, making the theater a masterpiece of trompe l'oeil painting. Now she often performs her blend of classical ballet, mime, and 19th-century melodrama to sell-out crowds. After the show, you can meet her in the adjacent art gallery, where she sells her paintings and autographs her posters and books. *Amargosa Opera House, Box 8, Death Valley Junction, CA 92328, tel. 619/852–4316. Call ahead for reservations. Admission: $8 adults, $5 children. Performances Nov.–Apr., Fri., Sat., and Mon. at 8:15 PM; May and Dec., shows Sat. only.*

What to See and Do with Children

Many of the desert's attractions should delight children. The following are of particular interest; for more information, *see* Exploring, *above.*

Rand Mining District
Roy Rogers–Dale Evans Museum, Victorville
Calico Ghost Town
Mitchell Caverns
Marta Becket's Amargosa Opera House

Off the Beaten Track

The desert is not a particularly well-beaten track to begin with, but some spots are a bit farther out of the way, or more difficult to reach. **Trona Pinnacles National Natural Landmark,** just 20 miles east of Ridgecrest and 10 miles south of the town of Trona, is not easy to reach—the best road to the area changes with the weather and can be impassable after a rain. But it's worth the effort, especially to sci-fi buffs, who will recognize the pinnacles as *Star Trek's* Final Frontier. These fantasy formations of calcium carbonate, known as tufa, were formed underwater along cracks in the lakebed—first as hollow tubes, then mounds, and finally as the spires visible today. A 1/2-mile trail winds around this surreal landscape. Wear sturdy shoes—tufa cuts like coral! For information about the region, contact the **Ridgecrest Resource Area Office** (300 S. Richmond Rd., Ridgecrest 93555, tel. 619/375–7125). *From the Trona—Red Mountain Rd., take Hwy. 178 east for 7.7 mi. Or, from its junction with U.S. 395, take Hwy. 178 for 29 mi to dirt intersection; turn southeast and go 1/2 mi to a fork. Continue south via right fork, cross railroad tracks, and continue about 5 mi to pinnacles.*

The Bureau of Land Management has developed special desert access areas for off-highway-vehicle (OHV) recreational activities. One popular route is the 130-mile Mohave Road, also known as Old Government Road, an 1860s wagon trail once traveled by mountain men Kit Carson and Jedediah Smith. The road runs parallel to and between I–40 and I–15 from Needles to just east of Barstow. The BLM's Needles office (tel. 619/326–3896) oversees this and other access areas, including the 660-mile East Mohave Heritage Trail (actually a series of trails), which begins and ends off I–40 in Needles.

Dining and Lodging

Plan to eat as carefully as you plan the rest of your desert trip. Dining choices in this section of the desert are limited to the Fred Harvey–operated restaurants in Death Valley, which range from a cafeteria to an upscale nouveau-Italian restaurant, and to fast-food and chain establishments in Victorville and Barstow. Restaurants in other towns tend to be chancy at best, downright unappetizing at worst. Experienced desert travelers carry an ice chest well stocked with food and beverages.

Category	Cost*
$$$$	over $100
$$$	$75–$100
$$	$50–$75
$	under $50

All prices are for a double room, excluding tax.

Barstow
$$

Best Western Desert Villa. This is a slightly above-average AAA-approved motel with a pool and whirlpool. *1984 E. Main St., tel. 619/256–1781, fax 619/256–9265. 79 units. AE, DC, MC, V.*

Death Valley
$$$$

Furnace Creek Inn. This historic rambling stone structure tumbling down the side of a hill is something of a desert oasis; the creek meanders through its beautifully landscaped gardens. There are pleasantly cool dining rooms, a naturally warm spring-fed pool, tennis courts, golf, horseback riding, and a cocktail lounge with entertainment. The attractively decorated rooms have views. *Box 1, Death Valley 92328, tel. 619/786–2345, fax 619/786–2514. 67 rooms and suites. Jackets required evenings in dining room. AE, DC, MC, V. Closed mid-May–mid-Oct.*

$$$–$$$$

Furnace Creek Ranch. An annex of the inn, about a mile away on the valley floor, this was originally crew headquarters for a borax company. A newer section consisting of four two-story buildings adjacent to the golf course has motel-type rooms. The ranch also features a swimming pool, tennis courts, guided carriage rides and hay rides, stables, a coffee shop, steak house, cocktail lounge, and a general store. *Box 1, Death Valley 92328, tel. 619/786–2345, fax 619/786–2514. 225 rooms. AE, DC, MC, V.*

$$

Stove Pipe Wells Village. A landing strip for light aircraft is an unusual touch for a motel, as is a heated mineral pool, but the rest is pretty basic. The property includes a dining room, grocery store, pool, and cocktail lounge. *Hwy. 190, tel. 619/786–2387, fax 619/786–2389. 82 rooms. MC, V.*

Camping

The Mojave Desert and Death Valley have about two dozen campgrounds in a variety of desert settings. Listed below is a sampling of what is available. For further information the following booklets are useful: *High Desert Recreation Resource Guide,* from the Mojave Chamber of Commerce (15836 Sierra Hwy., Mojave, CA 93591); *San Bernardino County Regional Parks,* from the Regional Parks Department (825 E. 3rd St., San Bernardino, CA 92415); and *California Desert Camping,* from the Bureau of Land Management (California Desert District Office, 6221 Box Springs Blvd., Riverside, CA 92507).

Death Valley Most campgrounds have no telephone number—simply show up when you arrive and hope there's a space open.

Furnace Creek (adjacent to the Furnace Creek Visitors Center). One hundred thirty-five RV and tent sites (some shaded), tables, fireplaces, flush and pit toilets, water, dump station. Pay showers, laundry, and swimming pool at Furnace Creek Ranch. Fee: $8. Reservations from Mystix, tel. 800/365–CAMP. Open year-round.

Mahogany Flat (east of Hwy. 178). Ten well-shaded tent spaces in a forest of juniper and piñon pine. Tables, pit toilets; no water. Free. Open Mar.–Nov.

Mesquite Springs (Hwy. 190 near Scotty's Castle). Sixty tent or RV spaces, some shaded, with stoves or fireplaces, tables, flush toilets, water. Fee: $5.

Wildrose (west of Hwy. 178). Thirty-nine tent or RV sites, some shaded, in a canyon. Stoves or fireplaces, tables, pit toilets. No water in winter. Free. Open year-round.

Mojave Desert **Afton Canyon Campground** (38 mi east of Barstow via I–15, 3 mi south on Afton Canyon Rd., tel. 619/256–3591). Twenty-two sites, 1,408 feet up in a wildlife area where the Mojave River surfaces. Surrounded by high desert scenic cliffs and a mesquite thicket. Fee: $4. Open year-round.

Mid-Hills Campground (123 mi east of Barstow via I–40). Hiking, horseback riding, in a wooded setting. Thirty campsites, pit toilets, water. Fee: $4. Open year-round.

Mojave Narrows (I–15). Eighty-seven camping units, hot showers. Secluded picnic areas and two lakes surrounded by cottonwoods and cattails. Fishing, rowboat rentals, bait shop, specially designed trail for visitors with disabilities.

Owl Canyon Campground (12 mi north of Barstow and 1 mi east of Rainbow Basin). Thirty-one camping units, cooking grills, pit toilets, water, hiking trails. Fee: $4. Open year-round.

Index

Personal Itinerary

Departure *Date*

Time

Transportation

Arrival *Date*   *Time*

Departure *Date*   *Time*

Transportation

Accommodations

Arrival *Date*   *Time*

Departure *Date*   *Time*

Transportation

Accommodations

Arrival *Date*   *Time*

Departure *Date*   *Time*

Transportation

Accommodations

Personal Itinerary

Arrival *Date*   *Time*

Departure *Date*   *Time*

Transportation

_____

_____

_____

Accommodations

_____

_____

_____

Arrival *Date*   *Time*

Departure *Date*   *Time*

Transportation

_____

_____

_____

Accommodations

_____

_____

_____

Arrival *Date*   *Time*

Departure *Date*   *Time*

Transportation

_____

_____

_____

Accommodations

_____

_____

_____

Arrival *Date*   *Time*

Departure *Date*   *Time*

Transportation

_____

_____

_____

Accommodations

_____

_____

_____

Personal Itinerary

Arrival   *Date*   *Time*

Departure   *Date*   *Time*

Transportation

Accommodations

Arrival   *Date*   *Time*

Departure   *Date*   *Time*

Transportation

Accommodations

Arrival   *Date*   *Time*

Departure   *Date*   *Time*

Transportation

Accommodations

Arrival   *Date*   *Time*

Departure   *Date*   *Time*

Transportation

Accommodations

Personal Itinerary

Arrival	*Date*	*Time*
Departure	*Date*	*Time*
Transportation		
Accommodations		

Arrival	*Date*	*Time*
Departure	*Date*	*Time*
Transportation		
Accommodations		

Arrival	*Date*	*Time*
Departure	*Date*	*Time*
Transportation		
Accommodations		

Arrival	*Date*	*Time*
Departure	*Date*	*Time*
Transportation		
Accommodations		

Addresses

Name

Address

Telephone

Name

Address

Telephone

Name

Address

Telephone

Name

Address

Telephone

Name

Address

Telephone

Name

Address

Telephone

Name

Address

Telephone

Name

Address

Telephone

Name

Address

Telephone

Name

Address

Telephone

Name

Address

Telephone

Name

Address

Telephone

Name

Address

Telephone

Name

Address

Telephone

Name

Address

Telephone

Name

Address

Telephone

Escape to ancient cities and exotic

islands  *with CNN Travel Guide, a*

wealth of valuable advice. Host Valerie Voss will take you

to all of your favorite destinations,

including those off the beaten path.

Tune into your passport to the world.

CNN TRAVEL GUIDE
SATURDAY 10:00 PMpt   SUNDAY 8:30 AMet

The only guide to explore a
Disney World® you've never seen before:

The one for grown-ups.

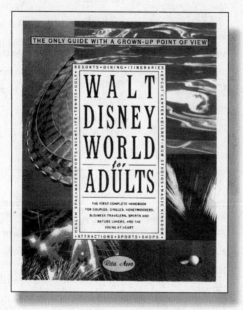

THE ONLY GUIDE WITH A GROWN-UP POINT OF VIEW

RESORTS • DINING • ITINERARIES

HEALTH SPAS • WATERSPORTS • NIGHTLIFE • TENNIS • GOLF

EPCOT CENTER • DISNEY-MGM STUDIOS • MAGIC KINGDOM

WALT DISNEY WORLD *for* ADULTS

THE FIRST COMPLETE HANDBOOK
FOR COUPLES, SINGLES, HONEYMOONERS,
BUSINESS TRAVELERS, SPORTS AND
NATURE LOVERS, AND THE
YOUNG AT HEART

• ATTRACTIONS • SPORTS • SHOPS •

Rita Aero

0-679-02490-5 $14.00 ($18.50 Can)

This is the only guide written specifically for the millions of adults who visit Walt Disney World® each year <u>without</u> kids. Upscale, sophisticated, packed full of facts and maps, *Walt Disney World® for Adults* provides up-to-date information on hotels, restaurants, sports facilities, and health clubs, as well as unique itineraries for adults. With *Walt Disney World® for Adults* in hand, you'll get the most out of one of the world's most fascinating, most complex playgrounds.

At bookstores everywhere, or call **1-800-533-6478**.

Fodor's Travel Guides

Available at bookstores everywhere, or call 1–800–533–6478, 24 hours a day.

U.S. Guides

Alaska

Arizona

Boston

California

Cape Cod, Martha's Vineyard, Nantucket

The Carolinas & the Georgia Coast

Chicago

Colorado

Florida

Hawaii

Las Vegas, Reno, Tahoe

Los Angeles

Maine, Vermont, New Hampshire

Maui

Miami & the Keys

New England

New Orleans

New York City

Pacific North Coast

Philadelphia & the Pennsylvania Dutch Country

The Rockies

San Diego

San Francisco

Santa Fe, Taos, Albuquerque

Seattle & Vancouver

The South

The U.S. & British Virgin Islands

USA

The Upper Great Lakes Region

Virginia & Maryland

Waikiki

Walt Disney World and the Orlando Area

Washington, D.C.

Foreign Guides

Acapulco, Ixtapa, Zihuatanejo

Australia & New Zealand

Austria

The Bahamas

Baja & Mexico's Pacific Coast Resorts

Barbados

Berlin

Bermuda

Brittany & Normandy

Budapest

Canada

Cancún, Cozumel, Yucatán Peninsula

Caribbean

China

Costa Rica, Belize, Guatemala

The Czech Republic & Slovakia

Eastern Europe

Egypt

Euro Disney

Europe

Florence, Tuscany & Umbria

France

Germany

Great Britain

Greece

Hong Kong

India

Ireland

Israel

Italy

Japan

Kenya & Tanzania

Korea

London

Madrid & Barcelona

Mexico

Montréal & Québec City

Morocco

Moscow & St. Petersburg

The Netherlands, Belgium & Luxembourg

New Zealand

Norway

Nova Scotia, Prince Edward Island & New Brunswick

Paris

Portugal

Provence & the Riviera

Rome

Russia & the Baltic Countries

Scandinavia

Scotland

Singapore

South America

Southeast Asia

Spain

Sweden

Switzerland

Thailand

Tokyo

Toronto

Turkey

Vienna & the Danube Valley

Special Series

Fodor's Affordables

Caribbean

Europe

Florida

France

Germany

Great Britain

Italy

London

Paris

**Fodor's Bed &
Breakfast and
Country Inns Guides**

America's Best B&Bs

California

Canada's Great
Country Inns

Cottages, B&Bs and
Country Inns of
England and Wales

Mid-Atlantic Region

New England

The Pacific
Northwest

The South

The Southwest

The Upper Great
Lakes Region

The Berkeley Guides

California

Central America

Eastern Europe

Europe

France

Germany & Austria

Great Britain &
Ireland

Italy

London

Mexico

Pacific Northwest &
Alaska

Paris

San Francisco

**Fodor's Exploring
Guides**

Australia

Boston &
New England

Britain

California

The Caribbean

Florence & Tuscany

Florida

France

Germany

Ireland

Italy

London

Mexico

New York City

Paris

Prague

Rome

Scotland

Singapore & Malaysia

Spain

Thailand

Turkey

Fodor's Flashmaps

Boston

New York

Washington, D.C.

Fodor's Pocket Guides

Acapulco

Bahamas

Barbados

Jamaica

London

New York City

Paris

Puerto Rico

San Francisco

Washington, D.C.

Fodor's Sports

Cycling

Golf Digest's Best
Places to Play

Hiking

The Insider's Guide
to the Best Canadian
Skiing

Running

Sailing

Skiing in the USA &
Canada

USA Today's Complete
Four Sports Stadium
Guide

**Fodor's Three-In-Ones
(guidebook, language
cassette, and phrase
book)**

France

Germany

Italy

Mexico

Spain

**Fodor's
Special-Interest
Guides**

Complete Guide to
America's National
Parks

Condé Nast Traveler
Caribbean Resort and
Cruise Ship Finder

Cruises and Ports
of Call

Euro Disney

France by Train

Halliday's New
England Food
Explorer

Healthy Escapes

Italy by Train

London Companion

Shadow Traffic's New
York Shortcuts and
Traffic Tips

Sunday in New York

Sunday in San
Francisco

Touring Europe

Touring USA:
Eastern Edition

Walt Disney World and
the Orlando Area

Walt Disney World
for Adults

**Fodor's Vacation
Planners**

Great American
Learning Vacations

Great American
Sports & Adventure
Vacations

Great American
Vacations

Great American
Vacations for Travelers
with Disabilities

National Parks and
Seashores of the East

National Parks
of the West

**The Wall Street
Journal Guides to
Business Travel**

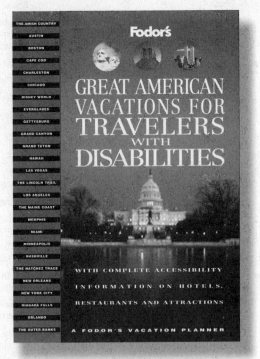

AT LAST

YOUR OWN PERSONALIZED LIST
OF WHAT'S GOING ON IN THE
CITIES YOU'RE VISITING.

KEYED TO THE DAYS WHEN
YOU'LL BE THERE, CUSTOMIZED
FOR YOUR INTERESTS,
AND SENT TO YOU BEFORE YOU
LEAVE HOME.

GET THE INSIDER'S
PERSPECTIVE. . .

UP-TO-THE-MINUTE
ACCURATE
EASY TO ORDER
DELIVERED WHEN YOU NEED IT

Fodor's WORLDVIEW
TRAVEL UPDATE

Now there is a revolutionary way to get customized, time-sensitive travel information just before your trip.

Now you can obtain detailed information about what's going on in each city you'll be visiting <u>before</u> you leave home—up-to-the-minute, objective information about the events and activities that interest you most.

Your Itinerary:
Customized reports available for 160 destinations

Travel Updates contain the kind of time-sensitive insider information you can get only from local contacts – or from city magazines and newspapers once you arrive. But now you can have the same information before you leave for your trip.

The choice is yours: current art exhibits, theater, music festivals and special concerts, sporting events, antiques and flower shows, shopping, fitness, and more.

The information comes from hundreds of correspondents and thousands of sources worldwide. Updated continuously, it's like having your own personal concierge or friend in the city.

You specify the cities and when you'll be there. We'll do the rest — personalizing the information for you the way no guidebook can.

It's the perfect extension to your Fodor's guide and the best way to make the most of your valuable travel time.

Use Order Form on back or call 1-800-799-9609

9
Rege
The
in this
domain
tion as Jo
worthwhile.
the perfoma
Tickets are ust
venue. Alterna
mances are cance
given. For more in
Open-Air Theatre, In
NW1 4NP Open Air
Tel: 935-5756. Ends: 9-1,
International Air Tattoo
Held biennially, the world'
military air display in
d e m o s t r a -
tions, milit
bands

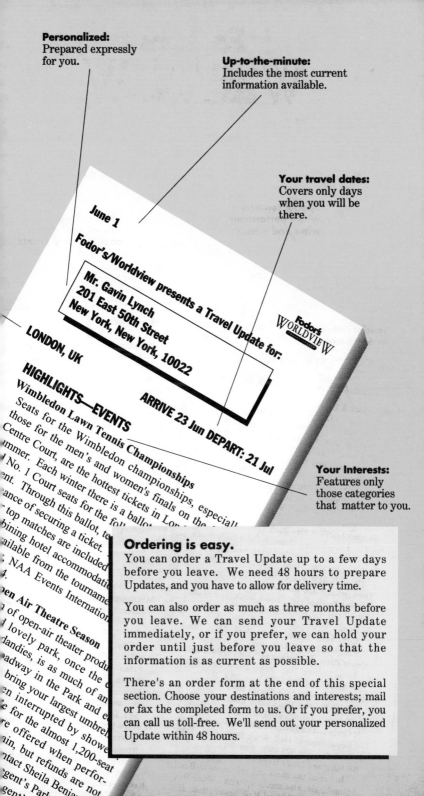

Personalized:
Prepared expressly
for you.

Up-to-the-minute:
Includes the most current
information available.

Your travel dates:
Covers only days
when you will be
there.

June 1

Fodor's/Worldview presents a Travel Update for:

Mr. Gavin Lynch
201 East 50th Street
New York, New York, 10022

Fodor's
WORLDVIEW

LONDON, UK

ARRIVE 23 Jun DEPART: 21 Jul

Your Interests:
Features only
those categories
that matter to you.

HIGHLIGHTS—EVENTS

Wimbledon Lawn Tennis Championships
Seats for the Wimbledon championships, especiall
those for the men's and women's finals in Lon
Centre Court, are the hottest tickets in
mmer. Each winter there is a ballo
No. 1 Court seats for the foll
ent. Through this ballot, t
ance of securing a ticket.
top matches are included
bining hotel accommodati
ailable from the tourname
; NAA Events Internation
4.

en Air Theatre Season
of open-air theater produ
lovely park, once the e
dandies, is as much of an
adway in the Park and e
bring your largest umbre
en interrupted by showe
e for the almost 1,200-seat
re offered when perfor-
ain, but refunds are not
ntact Sheila Benjam
gent's Park
gent's

Ordering is easy.
You can order a Travel Update up to a few days
before you leave. We need 48 hours to prepare
Updates, and you have to allow for delivery time.

You can also order as much as three months before
you leave. We can send your Travel Update
immediately, or if you prefer, we can hold your
order until just before you leave so that the
information is as current as possible.

There's an order form at the end of this special
section. Choose your destinations and interests; mail
or fax the completed form to us. Or if you prefer, you
can call us toll-free. We'll send out your personalized
Update within 48 hours.

Fodor's
WORLDVIEW
TRAVEL UPDATE

**Special concerts—
who's performing
what and where**

**One-of-a-kind,
one-time-only events**

**Special interest,
in-depth listings**

Children — Events

Angel Canal Festival
The festivities include a children's funf
entertainers, a boat rally and displays on
water. Regent's Canal. Islington. N1. Tu
Angel. Tel: 267 9100. 11:30am-5:30pm. 7/

Blackheath Summer Kite Festival
Stunt kite displays with parachuting ted
bears and trade stands. Free admission. S
BR: Blackheath. 10am. 6/27.

Megabugs
Children will delight in this infestation
giant robotic insects, including a prayi
mantis 60 times life size. Mon-Sat 10a
6pm; Sun 11am-6pm. Admission 4.
pounds. Natural History Museum, Cromw
Road. SW7. Tube: South Kensington. Te
938 9123. Ends 10/01.

Childminders
This establishment employs only wome
providing nurses and qualified nannies to

Music — Jazz & Blues

Tito Puente's Golden Men of Latin Jazz
The father of mambo and Cuban rumba king
comes to town. Royal Festival Hall. South Bank.
SE1. Tube: Waterloo. Tel: 928 8800. 8pm. 7/15.

Georgie Fame and The New York Band
Riding a popular tide with his latest album, the
smoky-voiced Fame and his keyboard are on a
tour yet again. The Grand. Clapham Junction.
SW11. BR: Clapham Junction. Tel: 738 9000
7:30pm. 7/07.

Jacques Loussier Play Bach Trio
The French jazz classicist and colleagues.
Kenwood Lakeside. Hampstead Lane.
Kenwood. NW3. Tube: Golders Green, then bus
210. Tel: 413 1443. 7pm. 7/10.

Tony Bennett and Ronnie Scott
Royal Festival Hall. South Bank. SE1. Tube:
Waterloo. Tel: 928 8800. 8pm. 7/11.

Santana
Royal Festival Hall. South Bank. SE1. Tube:
Waterloo. Tel: 928 8800. 8pm. 7/12.

Count Basie Orchestra and Nancy Wilson Trio
Royal Festival Hall. South Bank. SE1. Tube
Waterloo. Tel: 928 8800. 8pm. 7/14.

King Pleasure and the Biscuit Boys
Royal Festival Hall. South Bank. SE1. Tube
Waterloo. Tel: 928 8800. 6:30 and 9pm. 7/16.

Al Green and the London Community Gospel Choir
Royal Festival Hall. South Bank. SE1. Tube
Waterloo. Tel: 928 8800. 8pm. 7/13.

BB King and Linda Hopkins
Mother of the blues and successor to Bessi
Smith, Hopkins meets up with "Blues Boy
King. Royal Festival Hall. South Bank. SE
6:30 and 9pm

Music — Classical

Marylebone Sinfonia
Kenneth Gowen conducts music by
and Rossini. Queen Elizabeth Hall
Bank. SE1. Tube: Waterloo. Tel: 92
7:45pm. 7/16.

London Philharmonic
Franz Welser-Moest and George B
conduct selections by Alexander
Messiaen, and some of Benjamin's o
positions. Queen Elizabeth Hall. Sou
SE1. Tube: Waterloo. Tel: 928 8800.

London Pro Arte Orchestra and Fore
Murray Stewart conducts selec
Rossini, Haydn and Jonathan Willco
Queen Elizabeth Hall. South Ba
Tube: Waterloo. Tel: 928 8800. 7:45

Kensington Symphony Orchestra
Russell Keable conducts Dvorak'

Here's what you get . . .

Detailed information about what's going on — precisely when you'll be there.

Show openings during your visit

Handy pocket-size booklet

Reviews by local critics

Exhibitions & Shows—Antique & Flower

Westminster Antiques Fair

Over 50 stands with pre-1830 furniture and other Victorian and earlier items. Thu-Fri 11am-8pm; Sat-Sun 11am-6pm. Admission 4 pounds, children free. Old Royal Horticultural Hall. Vincent Square. SW1. Tel: 0444/48 25 14. 6-24 thru 6/27.

Royal Horticultural Society Flower Show

The show includes displays of carnations, summer fruit and vegetables. Tue 11am-7pm; Wed 10am-5pm. Admission Tue 4 pounds, Wed 2 pounds. Royal Horticultural Halls. Greycoat Street and Vincent Square. SW1. Tube: Victoria. 7/20 thru 7/21.

Hampton Court Palace International Flower Show

Major international garden and flower show taking place in conjunction with

eater — Musical

Sunset Boulevard

In June, the four Andrew Lloyd Webber musicals which dominated London's stages in the 1980s (Cats, Starlight Express, Phantom of the Opera and Aspects of Love) are joined by the composer's latest work, a show rumored to have his best music to date. The 1950 Billy Wilder film about a helpless young writer who is drawn into the world of a possessive, aging silent screen star offers rich opportunities for Webber's evolving style. Soaring, aching melodies, lush technical effects and psychological thrills are all expected. Patti Lupone stars. Mon-Sat at 8pm; matinee Thu-Sat at 3pm. In-person sales only at the box office; credit card bookings, Tel: 344 0055. Admission 15-32.50 pounds. Adelphi Theatre. The Strand. WC2. Tube: Charing Cross. Tel: 836 7611. Starts: 6/21.

Leonardo A Portrait of Love

A new musical about the great Renaissance artist and inventor comes in for a London pre-... tested by a brief run at Oxford's Old ... The work explores ...

Spectator Sports — Other Sports

Greyhound Racing: Wembley Stadium

This dog track offers good views of greyhound racing held on Mon, Wed and Fri. No credit cards. Stadium Way. Wembley. HA9. Tube: Wembley Park. Tel: 902 8833.

Benson & Hedges Cricket Cup Final

Lord's Cricket Ground. St. John's Wood Road. NW8. Tube: St. John's Wood. Tel: 289 1611. 11am. 7/10.

siness-Fax & Overnight Mail

Post Office, Trafalgar Square Branch

Offers a network of fax services, the Intelpost system, throughout the country and abroad. Mon-Sat 8am-8pm, Sun 9am-5pm. William IV Street. WC2. Tube: Charing Cross. Tel: 930 0580.

Fodor's WORLDVIEW
TRAVEL UPDATE

London, England
Arriving: June 23
Departing: July 21

Interest Categories

For <u>your</u> personalized Travel Update, choose the categories you're most interested in from this list. Every Travel Update automatically provides you with *Event Highlights* - the best of what's happening during the dates of your trip.

1.	**Business Services**	Fax & Overnight Mail, Computer Rentals, Photocopying, Protocol, Secretarial, Messenger, Translation Services

Dining

2.	**All Day Dining**	Breakfast & Brunch, Cafes & Tea Rooms, Late-Night Dining
3.	**Local Cuisine**	In Every Price Range—from Budget Restaurants to the Special Splurge
4.	**European Cuisine**	Continental, French, Italian
5.	**Asian Cuisine**	Chinese, Far Eastern, Japanese, Other
6.	**Americas Cuisine**	American, Mexican & Latin
7.	**Nightlife**	Bars, Dance Clubs, Casinos, Comedy Clubs, Ethnic, Pubs & Beer Halls
8.	**Entertainment**	Theater—Comedy, Drama, English Language, Musicals, Dance, Ticket Agencies
9.	**Music**	Country/Western/Folk, Classical, Traditional & Ethnic, Opera, Jazz & Blues, Pop, Rock
10.	**Children's Activities**	Events, Attractions
11.	**Tours**	Local Tours, Day Trips, Overnight Excursions, Cruises
12.	**Exhibitions, Festivals & Shows**	Antiques & Flower, History & Cultural, Art Exhibitions, Fairs & Craft Shows, Music & Art Festivals
13.	**Shopping**	Districts & Malls, Markets, Regional Specialities
14.	**Fitness**	Bicycling, Health Clubs, Hiking, Jogging
15.	**Recreational Sports**	Boating/Sailing, Fishing, Golf, Ice Skating, Skiing, Snorkeling/Scuba, Swimming, Tennis & Racquet
16.	**Spectator Sports**	Auto Racing, Baseball, Basketball, Boating & Sailing, Football, Golf, Horse Racing, Ice Hockey, Rugby, Soccer, Tennis, Track & Field, Other Sports

Please note that interest category content will vary by season, destination, and length of stay.

Destinations

The Fodor's/Worldview Travel Update covers more than 160 destinations worldwide. Choose the destinations that match your itinerary from this list. (Choose bulleted destinations only.)

Europe
- Amsterdam
- Athens
- Barcelona
- Berlin
- Brussels
- Budapest
- Copenhagen
- Dublin
- Edinburgh
- Florence
- Frankfurt
- French Riviera
- Geneva
- Glasgow
- Istanbul
- Lausanne
- Lisbon
- London
- Madrid
- Milan
- Moscow
- Munich
- Oslo
- Paris
- Prague
- Provence
- Rome
- Salzburg
* Seville
- St. Petersburg
- Stockholm
- Venice
- Vienna
- Zurich

United States (Mainland)
- Albuquerque
- Atlanta
- Atlantic City
- Baltimore
- Boston
* Branson, MO
* Charleston, SC
- Chicago
- Cincinnati
- Cleveland
- Dallas/Ft. Worth
- Denver
- Detroit
- Houston
* Indianapolis
- Kansas City
- Las Vegas
- Los Angeles
- Memphis
- Miami
- Milwaukee
- Minneapolis/ St. Paul
* Nashville
- New Orleans
- New York City
- Orlando
- Palm Springs
- Philadelphia
- Phoenix
- Pittsburgh
- Portland
* Reno/ Lake Tahoe
- St. Louis
- Salt Lake City
- San Antonio
- San Diego
- San Francisco
* Santa Fe
- Seattle
- Tampa
- Washington, DC

Alaska
- Alaskan Destinations

Hawaii
- Honolulu
- Island of Hawaii
- Kauai
- Maui

Canada
- Quebec City
- Montreal
- Ottawa
- Toronto
- Vancouver

Bahamas
- Abaco
- Eleuthera/ Harbour Island
- Exuma
- Freeport
- Nassau & Paradise Island

Bermuda
- Bermuda Countryside
- Hamilton

British Leeward Islands
- Anguilla
- Antigua & Barbuda
- St. Kitts & Nevis

British Virgin Islands
- Tortola & Virgin Gorda

British Windward Islands
- Barbados
- Dominica
- Grenada
- St. Lucia
- St. Vincent
- Trinidad & Tobago

Cayman Islands
- The Caymans

Dominican Republic
- Santo Domingo

Dutch Leeward Islands
- Aruba
- Bonaire
- Curacao

Dutch Windward Island
- St. Maarten/ St. Martin

French West Indies
- Guadeloupe
- Martinique
- St. Barthelemy

Jamaica
- Kingston
- Montego Bay
- Negril
- Ocho Rios

Puerto Rico
- Ponce
- San Juan

Turks & Caicos
- Grand Turk/ Providenciales

U.S. Virgin Islands
- St. Croix
- St. John
- St. Thomas

Mexico
- Acapulco
- Cancun & Isla Mujeres
- Cozumel
- Guadalajara
- Ixtapa & Zihuatanejo
- Los Cabos
- Mazatlan
- Mexico City
- Monterrey
- Oaxaca
- Puerto Vallarta

South/Central America
* Buenos Aires
* Caracas
* Rio de Janeiro
* San Jose, Costa Rica
* Sao Paulo

Middle East
* Jerusalem

Australia & New Zealand
- Auckland
- Melbourne
* South Island
- Sydney

China
- Beijing
- Guangzhou
- Shanghai

Japan
- Kyoto
- Nagoya
- Osaka
- Tokyo
- Yokohama

Pacific Rim/Other
* Bali
- Bangkok
- Hong Kong & Macau
- Manila
- Seoul
- Singapore
- Taipei

* Destinations available by 1/1/95

Fodor's WORLDVIEW TRAVEL UPDATE Order Form

THIS TRAVEL UPDATE IS FOR (Please print):

Name

Address

City	State	Country	ZIP

Tel # (   )   -   Fax # (   )   -

Title of this Fodor's guide:

Store and location where guide was purchased:

INDICATE YOUR DESTINATIONS/DATES: You can order up to three (3) destinations from the previous page. Fill in your arrival and departure dates for each destination. **Your Travel Update itinerary (all destinations selected) cannot exceed 30 days from beginning to end.**

			Month	Day		Month	Day
(Sample)	LONDON	From:	6 /	21	To:	6 /	30
1		From:	/		To:	/	
2		From:	/		To:	/	
3		From:	/		To:	/	

CHOOSE YOUR INTERESTS: Select up to eight (8) categories from the list of interest categories shown on the previous page and circle the numbers below:

1   2   3   4   5   6   7   8   9   10   11   12   13   14   15   16

CHOOSE WHEN YOU WANT YOUR TRAVEL UPDATE DELIVERED (Check one):

❑ Please send my Travel Update immediately.
❑ Please hold my order until a few weeks before my trip to include the most up-to-date information.
Completed orders will be sent within 48 hours. Allow 7-10 days for U.S. mail delivery.

ADD UP YOUR ORDER HERE. *SPECIAL OFFER FOR FODOR'S PURCHASERS ONLY!*

	Suggested Retail Price	Your Price	This Order
First destination ordered	$ 9.95	$ 7.95	$ 7.95
Second destination (if applicable)	$ 6.95	$ 4.95	+
Third destination (if applicable)	$ 6.95	$ 4.95	+

DELIVERY CHARGE (Check one and enter amount below)

	Within U.S. & Canada	Outside U.S. & Canada
First Class Mail	❑ $2.50	❑ $5.00
FAX	❑ $5.00	❑ $10.00
Priority Delivery	❑ $15.00	❑ $27.00

ENTER DELIVERY CHARGE FROM ABOVE: +

TOTAL: $

METHOD OF PAYMENT IN U.S. FUNDS ONLY (Check one):

❑ AmEx   ❑ MC   ❑ Visa   ❑ Discover   ❑ Personal Check (U. S. & Canada only)
❑ Money Order/ International Money Order
Make check or money order payable to: Fodor's Worldview Travel Update

Credit Card —/—/—/—/—/—/—/—/—/—/—/—/—/—/—/— Expiration Date:___/___

Authorized Signature

SEND THIS COMPLETED FORM WITH PAYMENT TO:
Fodor's Worldview Travel Update, 114 Sansome Street, Suite 700, San Francisco, CA 94104

OR CALL OR FAX US 24-HOURS A DAY
Telephone **1-800-799-9609** • Fax **1-800-799-9619** (From within the U.S. & Canada)
(Outside the U.S. & Canada: Telephone 415-616-9988 • Fax 415-616-9989)

(Please have this guide in front of you when you call so we can verify purchase.)
Code: FTG   Offer valid until 12/31/95.